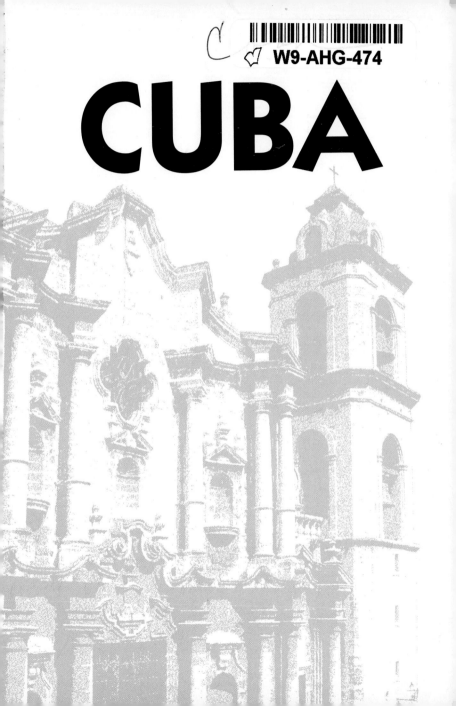

CUBA

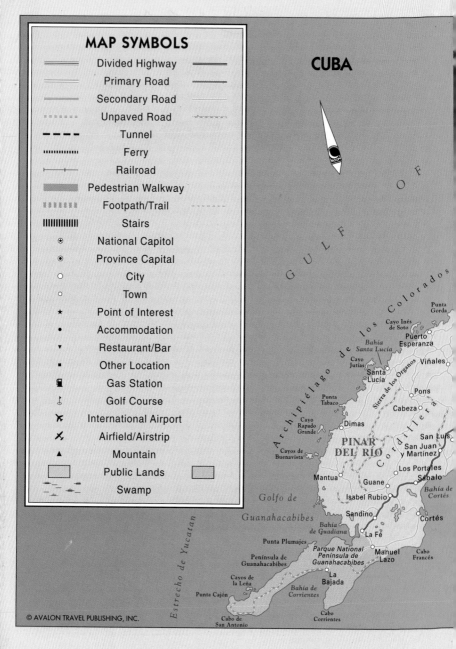

MAP SYMBOLS

═══════	Divided Highway
───────	Primary Road
───────	Secondary Road
┄┄┄┄┄	Unpaved Road
▬ ▬ ▬ ▬	Tunnel
▪▪▪▪▪▪▪▪▪▪	Ferry
├──┼──┤	Railroad
▬▬▬▬	Pedestrian Walkway
▮▮▮▮▮▮▮	Footpath/Trail
▥▥▥▥▥▥▥	Stairs
⊛	National Capitol
◉	Province Capital
○	City
○	Town
★	Point of Interest
•	Accommodation
▼	Restaurant/Bar
▪	Other Location
⛽	Gas Station
⚑	Golf Course
✕	International Airport
✗	Airfield/Airstrip
▲	Mountain
▭	Public Lands
~	Swamp

CUBA

GULF OF

Archipiélago de los Colorados

Sierra de los Órganos

Cordillera

Punta Gorda
Cayo Inés de Soto
Puerto Esperanza
Bahía Santa Lucía
Cayo Jutías
Santa Lucía
Viñales
Pons
Punta Tabaco
Cabeza
Cayo Rapado Grande
Dimas
San Luis
PINAR DEL RÍO
San Juan y Martínez
Cayos de Buenavista
Los Portales
Mantua
Sábalo
Guane
Bahía de Cortés
Golfo de
Isabel Rubio
Guanahacabibes
Sandino
Cortés
Bahía de Guadiana
La Fé
Punta Plumajes
Parque Nacional Península de Guanahacabibes
Manuel Lazo
Cabo Francés
Península de Guanahacabibes
Cayos de la Leña
La Bajada
Estrecho de Yucatán
Punta Cajón
Bahía de Corrientes
Cabo de San Antonio
Cabo Corrientes

© AVALON TRAVEL PUBLISHING, INC.

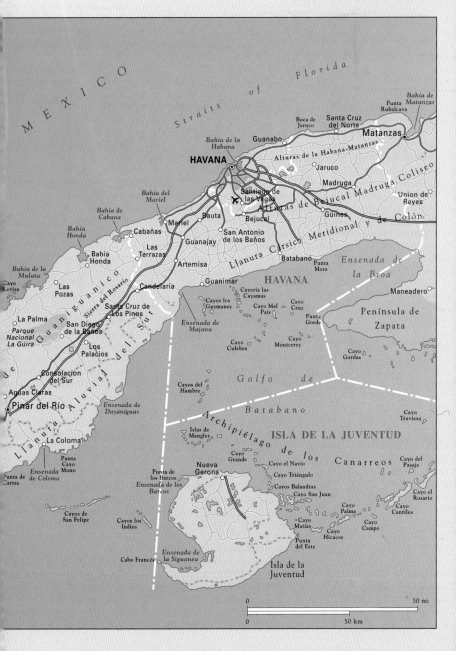

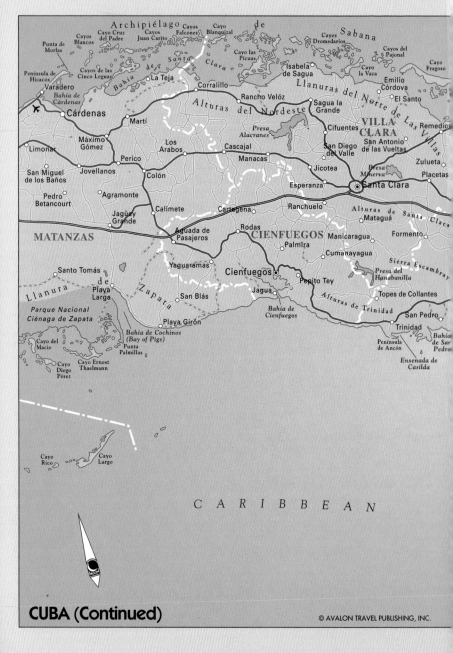

CUBA (Continued)

© AVALON TRAVEL PUBLISHING, INC.

CUBA (Continued)

O C E A N

*Bahía
Río Seco*

Punta de Mulas

Banes *Bahía de
Banes* El
Ramón *Bahía de
Levisa* *Bahía Sagua
de Tánamo* Cayo Moa
Grande Punta
Guarico

Carbonera Cayo Mambí Moa Punta
Gorda *Bahía de
Miel* Punta del
Fraile

*Bahía
de
Nipe* Nícaro *Cuchillas de Moa* Mesa Abajo Maisí

Levisa Sagua de
Tánamo *Cuchillas de Toa* Baracoa Jamal Punta de
Quemado

Guaro Mayarí *Sierra de Cristal* Bernardo *Cuchillas de Baracoa* La Maquina

Mayarí Arriba **GUANTÁNAMO** *Sierra de Purial* Punta Caleta

Altiplanicie de Nipe Bayate Puriales de
Caujeri Cajobabo

**SANTIAGO
DE CUBA** El Salvador Honduras Manuel Tames San Antonio Del Sur

Mella La
Prueba Los
Reynaldos Costa
Rica Héctor Infante

Palmarito de Cauto La Maya Guantánamo

Chile Alto Songo Niceto
Pérez Cainamera Boquerón

San
Luis Dos
Caminos Punta
Barlovento U.S. NAVAL
STATION

Santiago
de Cuba El Caney *Bahía de
Guantánamo*

El
Cobre Siboney Baconao

*Bahía de
Santiago de Cuba*

paso de los Vientos

0 50 mi

0 50 km

MOON

MOON HANDBOOKS

CUBA

SECOND EDITION

CHRISTOPHER P. BAKER

AVALON
TRAVEL
publishing

MOON HANDBOOKS: CUBA
SECOND EDITION

Christopher P. Baker

Published by
Avalon Travel Publishing
5855 Beaudry St.
Emeryville, CA 94608, USA

Please send all comments,
corrections, additions,
amendments, and critiques to:

**MOON HANDBOOKS: CUBA
AVALON TRAVEL PUBLISHING
5855 BEAUDRY ST.
EMERYVILLE, CA 94608, USA
e-mail: info@travelmatters.com
www.moon.com**

Printing History
   1st edition—1997
2nd edition—November 2000
            5 4 3 2 1

ISBN: 1-56691-209-1
ISSN: 153-4170

Editors: Jeannie Trizzino, Erin Van Rheenen
Copyeditor: Carolyn Perkins
Index: Sondra Nation
Illustrations: Bob Race
Graphics Coordinator: Erika Howsare
Production: Karen McKinley, David Hurst
Map Editor: Mike Ferguson
Maps: Chris Alvarez, Doug Beckner, Chris Folks, Mike Morgenfeld

Front cover photo: © 1999 Greg Johnston

All photos by Christopher P. Baker unless otherwise noted.
All illustrations by Bob Race unless otherwise noted.

Distributed in the United States and Canada by Publishers Group West

Printed in the United States by Publishers Press

To Jorge, Marisol, Jessica,
and the indomitable Cuban people

CONTENTS

MAPS

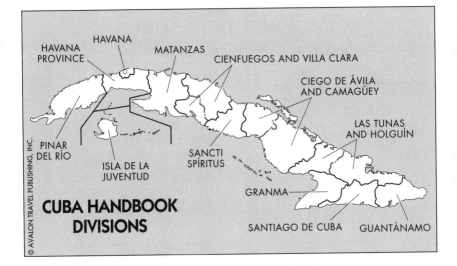

HAVANA
PROVINCE

HAVANA

MATANZAS

CIENFUEGOS AND VILLA CLARA

CIEGO DE ÁVILA
AND CAMAGÜEY

LAS TUNAS
AND HOLGUÍN

PINAR
DEL RÍO

ISLA DE LA
JUVENTUD

SANCTI
SPÍRITUS

GRANMA

**CUBA HANDBOOK
DIVISIONS**

SANTIAGO DE CUBA

GUANTÁNAMO

ACCOMMODATIONS RATINGS

Hotels in this book are classified as:

Budget	less than US$35
Inexpensive	US$35-60
Moderate	US$60-85
Expensive	US$85-110
Very Expensive	US$110-150
Luxury	US$150 and above

Prices at many hotels vary for low and high season. Usually low season is May-June and Sept.-Nov.; high season is Dec.-April and June-Aug. Peak-season rates (Christmas and New Year) sell at a premium. However, this varies. Some hotels have four rates according to peak high season and low low season. Cuba imposes no room tax or service charge to guests' bills (this may change, however).

LET US HEAR FROM YOU

Inevitably, a book of this size and scope is a long time in the making. While every effort has been made to keep abreast of the rapid pace of change and development in Cuba, some information may already be out of date by the time you read this book. A few inaccuracies are also inevitable. You—the reader—are a valuable resource in ensuring that future editions contain the most up-to-date and accurate information. Please let us know about any price changes, new accommodations or restaurants, map errors, travel tips, etc.

To assist future travelers, feel free to photocopy maps in this book: while sightseeing, mark the exact locations of new hotels and other travel facilities and cross off those that may have closed. Mail your revised map, along with any information you wish to provide (including, if possible, a business card, brochure, and rate card for hotels) to:

Moon Handbooks: Cuba
c/o Avalon Travel Publishing
5855 Beaudry Street
Emeryville, CA 94608
USA
e-mail: info@travelmatters.com

ACKNOWLEDGMENTS

Heartfelt thanks are due to many individuals who assisted in the research of this book.

First, thanks go to Juan Carlos Aguilar Caballo, of the Tropicana; Alicia Pérez Casanova, of Horizontes; Alicia Frainas Martínez, Octavio González, and Manuel Estefania, of Gran Caribe; Michael Douglas, of Cuba Travel; Michael Larrow, of Bahatours, Nassau; Stephane Pidobrywnys, of La Giraldilla; Fernando Silva, of Tropicana, Santiago; and Abe Moore, Sue McManus, Christine Foreshaw, and the various managers of SuperClubs.

I also wish to express appreciation to a number of area specialists from whose writings I have drawn heavily, notably Tom Miller (*Trading with the Enemy: A Yankee Travels through Castro's Cuba*), Tad Szulc (*Fidel: A Critical Portrait*), and fellow journalists such as Ann Louise Bardach; and to the many people who otherwise assisted in production of the first edition, including Medea Benjamin and Pamela Montaro at Global Exchange, and Sandra Levinson of the Center for Cuban Studies. Thanks, too, go to all my friends and acquaintances who kindly forwarded clips on Cuba, and especially to those readers who took the trouble to write with recommendations, warnings, and general comments.

The following friends—Cubaphiles one and all—were supportive resources: Tom Miller; Nancy Stout, author of *Havana and Habanos: The Story of the Havana Cigar*; Adolf Hungry Wolf, author of *Letters from Cuba*; my much-loved friend and bon vivant, Ralph Martell, author of *Gardenias and Stars*; and in Cuba, my friends Damaris Bencomo Nay, Lourdes Mulén Duharte, Dulce María, Yamilka García, Laura Marlen (Miss Cuba 1995), and Yanet Morales Martínez. Especially large hugs and gracias amigos! go to Jorge Coalla Potts and his wife Marisol and daughter Jessica, and to my beautiful and cherished friend, Mercedes Martínez Crespo.

Gracias, too, to the many Cubans who shared insights and shone the light on obscure issues (regretfully many must remain nameless to protect their identities) . . . to true believers who lived up to the values of the Revolution and helped restore my balance . . . to countless Cubans who despite their hardships displayed selfless hospitality, welcoming me into their hearts and homes and otherwise aiding in times of need . . . and to all Cubans, whose unequaled verve, virtue, charity, patience, and grace filled me with humility and taught me that I, and the world, have much to learn.

I offer my apologies to all others who, through my thoughtlessness or senility, have not been acknowledged but who in their own special ways helped make this project and my time in Cuba so rewarding.

Lastly, and above all, I offer my deepest gratitude and a lifelong *abrazo* to Daisy Frómeta Bartólome, whose gaiety, love, and affection filled my time in Cuba with sunlight and tropical warmth. Cuba may never be the same without her.

PREFACE

In October 1959 Fidel Castro spoke to the American Society of Travel Agents (ASTA) convention, held that year in the old Blanquita Theater (now the Karl Marx) in Havana. "We have sea," said Castro. "We have bays, we have beautiful beaches, we have medicinal waters in our hotels, we have mountains, we have game and we have fish in the sea and the rivers, and we have sun. Our people are noble, hospitable, and most important, they hate no one. They love visitors, so much in fact that our visitors feel completely at home."

Normal relations with United States still existed back then, and the U.S. ambassador, Philip Bonsai, also lauded Cuban tourism at the ASTA convention: "Cuba is one of the most admirable countries in the world from the point of view of North American tourism and from many other points of view."

Four decades have passed. Nothing has changed but the politics.

Cuba won its independence from Spain at the turn of the century only to be occupied militarily, politically, and economically by the United States. It was an uncertain independence: never fully under the United States' thumb, but never fully out from under it, either, until the Revolution wrote another chapter in Cuban history. Castro & Co. made a beautiful revolution that ousted a corrupt and brutal dictator but, alas, spun off into Soviet orbit and adopted their own ruinous authoritarian model. Four decades later, Cuba and the U.S. remain separated by 90 miles of shimmering ocean churned into a watery no-man's land by political enmity. Today, the Straits of Florida are the widest, deepest moat in the world.

Travelers visiting Cuba today do so at a fascinating historical moment, as Cuba is unwinding from its Marxist cocoon. A new Cuba is emerging. It is extending its hand to the rest of the world and inviting us to visit. Castro's welcome mat is plenty tattered, but foreigners are storming the beaches in droves. Four decades after Castro closed the doors to outsiders, his country is enjoying cult status again. About 1.7 million foreign visitors arrived in 1999, including more than 120,000 U.S. citizens, many of them fast-laners who traveled illegally to worship at the shrine of 1950s kitsch and savor the frisson of the forbidden.

The U.S. government, however, isn't listening, although it has eased restrictions on who may visit. An increasing number of U.S. citizens are circumventing the travel restrictions by entering Cuba through Canada, Mexico, or the Bahamas. It's remarkably easy to do. Cubans play their part by abstaining from stamping passports, so Uncle Sam need never know. Most yanquis harbor the misimpression that it's illegal for U.S. citizens to visit Cuba. It's not; it's merely illegal to spend dollars there.

With all the hoopla about politics, it's easy to overlook the sheer beauty of the place. Cuba is made for tropical tourism: the diamond-dust beaches and bathtub-warm seas the colors of peacock feathers; the bottle-green mountains and jade valleys full of dramatic formations; the ancient cities, with their flower-bedecked balconies, rococo churches, and palaces and castles evocative of the once mighty power of Spain; and, above all, the sultriness and spontaneity of a country called "the most emotionally involving in the Western hemisphere." No matter what the state of political tensions, there is *santería* and salsa, and sunny days on talcum beaches strolled by *señoritas* in tiny *tanguitas*. Whatever the temperature a fresh breeze is sure to be blowing, carrying tropical aromas through cobbled colonial plazas. There are *mojitos* and *cuba libres* to enjoy, and the world's finest cigars to smoke fresh from the factory as you rumble down the lonesome highways in a chrome-spangled '55 Cadillac to the rhythm of the rumba on the radio.

The country is blessed with possibility. Divers are delirious over Cuba's wealth of deep-sea treasures. Sportfishing is also relatively advanced, with several dedicated resorts and far more fish than fishhooks. Laguna del Tesoro, part of the swampy Zapata Peninsula National Park, is one of several premier birdwatching sites. There are crocodiles, too, lurking leery-eyed in well-preserved everglades. Horseback riding options abound. Cuba is a prime destination for bicycle touring. And hikers can head for the Sierra Maestra to tread trails trod by Fidel Castro and Che Guevara.

Cuba's greatest, most enigmatic appeal, however, is that traveling through it you sense you are living inside an unfolding drama. Cuba is still intoxicating, still laced with the sharp edges and sinister shadows that made Federico García Lorca, the Spanish poet, write to his parents, "If I get lost, look for me in Cuba," and that made Ernest Hemingway want "to stay here for ever."

Forty-odd years of ruinous economic policies have led many visitors to expect the worst—a fossilized shell of a country with a depauperate population with lips glued shut by fear. Yet those who simply point out Cuba's negatives—the inept bureaucracy, the shortages, the muffled press—do not see the smiling children, or notice the educated youths eager to quote you poetry or challenge you to a game of chess. Cuba, what Bill Bryson called " a Third World country with First World people," rightly brags about its educational network and its health system, which provides free care for everyone and has reduced infant mortality and raised life expectancy to a par with developed nations. And after several decades of not being caught up in the monied economy, there is a distinct lack of hype, an environment in which success is not measured by the level of consumption (although this is changing). Cubans can still take ample pleasure in rocking on a veranda watching laughing kids chase a hoop down a dusty street. Even the young retain fond memories of days before the Soviet Union collapsed, when Cubans had become accustomed to a quality of life that has only recently been pulled from under their feet.

Following the implosion of the Soviet Union, there was general agreement that things had gone terribly wrong, and the future remains full of uncertainty. Conditions are severely testing the Cubans' faith in human cooperation, a situation exacerbated by the tourism boom, which has hallmarks of a Faustian bargain. In the 1950s, Cuba—the third most developed country in the Americas—was considered the playground of the United States. The revolutionaries, however, scorned tourism for its bourgeois decadence: the gambling, prostitution, live sex acts, and drugs. Things are now coming full circle as the inequity between the dollar and the peso has created an inverted economy in which bellhops and *jiniteras* (prostitutes) make far more money than surgeons and college professors. An economic elite is once again becoming visible. Drugs are back, along with corrupt officials, beggars, and new resentments and tensions.

It doesn't take great imagination to envision how Havana could again become, in Somerset Maugham's piquant phrase, "a sunny place for shady people." The city's demimonde that continues to bubble beneath the surface is just waiting for someone to marshal it. What makes Havana so fascinating won't last forever. As the foreign influence spreads, the more Havana will be "spoiled," changing the face of the Malecón and the vision of a Havana skyline as hazy as Cuba's future.

Cuba today drifts somewhere between communism and capitalism. In the quest for survival, Castro's government has been forced to turn back to the entrepreneurial spirit it once eschewed. A new breed of relatively young, pragmatic, and market-savvy political leaders is seeking a homespun paradigm of socialism-cum-free-market economy that can restore economic growth while preserving social benefits and avoiding upheaval that could topple the government. Meanwhile, Castro continues to rule with his inimitable velvet-gloved iron hand.

Fidel retains his tactical skills and—whatever Washington would like to think—the affection of a large percentage of "his" people. Nonetheless, while support for Castro remains especially strong in the countryside, most Cubans long ago lost faith in Fidel (since 1959, one-tenth of the Cuban population has sought freedom and opportunity across the Florida Straits). Many even among the disaffected are reluctant to blame Castro entirely for the country's troubles, however. Since 1961, Cuba has been subjected to a punishing embargo that the U.S. government says is done in the name of democracy but which most Cubans consider only adds to their hardships brought about by four decades of ill-conceived policies.

The embargo serves Castro well (and he knows it: "Whenever Mr. Castro has sensed a thaw in relations, he has acted swiftly to refreeze them," says *The Economist*). Demonized by the U.S., *El Comandante* remains for Cubans a symbol of national dignity, despite the country's deteriorated circumstance. True, most Cubans desire change—especially a change of leadership—but when Cubans talk of "change," they speak of greater efficiency, more food on the table, a greater freedom to live their lives as they wish . . . but without compromising the accomplishments of their Revolution. Increasingly society is divided. Meanwhile, in Florida, politically ambitious and wealthy right-wing Cuban-Americans wait lustfully in the wings.

To the international visitor, the frustrations of life for the average Cuban need be no more than a slight inconvenience. Tourists are free to go wherever they wish, and there are few visible hallmarks of a totalitarian system (the secret police lurk in the shadows). Still, the government tries to erect barriers between tourists and Cubans. The traveler, wrote Mark Ottaway, is constantly "battling a system that prefers groups to individuals, and probably has little worse than failure to hide." The "real" Cuba isn't easy to fathom, and the casual visitor is easily beguiled. In this twilight land, everything appears twice: once as it seems, and once as it really is. Tourists riding in comfortable Toyota minivans may wind up with little more than a canned experience of the country (it is easy to recognize the incredible social gains without understanding the vast human toll). An open-minded visitor is torn two ways; Cuba—"so hard to embrace, impossible to let go," thought Tom Miller—is both disheartening and uplifting. You'll most probably fall in love with the country, while being thankful you don't have to live in it.

After all, you don't have to respect a government to fall in love with a country or its people. The compellingly warm-hearted Cubans relish a passion for pleasure despite (or because of) their hardships. Salsa and irresistible rumbas pulse through the streets, and throngs of people congregate at nightclubs and cabarets, including the Tropicana, the open-air extravaganza now in its sixth decade of stiletto-heeled paganism. Cubans you have met only moments previously may invite you into their homes, where rum and beer are passed around and you are lured to dance by narcotic rhythms. How often have I been carried away and even cried, laughing, flirting, dancing as it were with the enemy?

Everywhere, Cubans embrace and welcome you into their arms. Everything touches your heart. You come away feeling like my friend Stephanie Gervassi-Levin, who on her first visit to Cuba began dancing uncontrollably in a *casa de la trova*. The Cubans formed a line and, "like a diplomat," took her hand, kissed her cheek. As I set out to write this book, she implored, "Chris, bring your genuine feeling into your pages. Breathe the innocence and beauty of Cuba without castrating Castro and his revolution."

Ernest Hemingway, who loved Cuba and lived there for the better part of 20 years, once warned novice writer Arnold Samuelson against "a tendency to condemn before you completely understand. You aren't God, and you never judge a man," Hemingway said. "You present him as he is and you let the reader judge."

INTRODUCTION

THE LAND

Cuba lies at the western end of the Greater Antilles group of Caribbean islands, which began to heave from the sea about 150 million years ago. Curling east and south like a shepherd's crook are the much younger and smaller Lesser Antilles, a cluster of mostly volcanic islands that bear little resemblance to their larger neighbor.

Cuba is by far the largest of the Caribbean islands—at 114,524 square km. It is only slightly smaller than the state of Louisiana, half the size of the United Kingdom, and three times the size of the Netherlands. It sits just south of the Tropic of Cancer at the eastern perimeter of the Gulf of Mexico, 150 km south of Key West, Florida, 140 km north of Jamaica, and 210 km east of Mexico's Yucatán Peninsula. It is separated from Hispaniola to the east by the narrow, 77-km-wide Windward Passage, or Old Bahamas Channel, a major shipping lane between the North Atlantic Ocean and Caribbean Sea.

Cuba is actually an archipelago with some 4,000-plus islands, islets, and cays dominated by the main island (104,945 square km), which is 1,250 km long—from Cabo de San Antonio in the west to Punta Maisí in the east—and between 31 and 193 km wide; it averages 80 km wide. Likened in shape to everything from an alligator

to a phallus, Cuba is a crescent, convex to the north.

Slung beneath the mainland's underbelly is the Isla de la Juventud (2,200 square km), the westernmost of a chain of smaller islands—the Archipiélago de los Canarreos—which extends eastward for 110 km across the Golfo de Batabanó. Farther east, beneath east-central Cuba, is a shoal group of tiny coral cays sprinkled with beaches like powdered diamonds poking up a mere four or five meters from the sapphire sea—the Archipiélago de los Járdines de la Reina.

The central north coast, too, is rimmed by a necklace of coral jewels: dark green, limned by sand like crushed sugar shelving into bright turquoise shallows, with surf pounding on the reef edge. It's enough to bring out the Robinson Crusoe in anyone, perhaps with the trail of a tiny lizard leading up toward the scrubby pines as the only sign that any living creature has been here before.

TOPOGRAPHY

Cuban landscapes are soft and calming, epitomized by sensual waves of lime-green sugar-

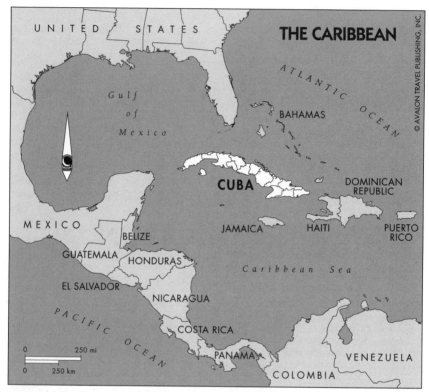

cane undulating like a great swelling sea—landscapes that Kenneth Tynan described in *Holiday* magazine in 1961 as "of soft Pissarro and Cézanne color, and the tropical intensity of Gauguin." Emerald greens flow into burning golds; soft, faded pastels and warm ochers are relieved by brilliant tropical colors, flower petals as red as lipstick, pavonine waters shading through dazzling jade, and, always, the chartreuse of the cane fields.

And yet it is rarely dramatic. Extended flatlands and rolling plains cover almost two-thirds of the island. Indeed, Cuba is the *least* mountainous of the Greater Antilles, with a median elevation of less than 100 meters above sea level. Its topography is dominated by *llanos,* the flatlands that at times seem to stretch forever, level as football fields and just as green, smothered in swampland inhabited by crocodiles or parceled into a checkerboard quilt of banana groves, pineapple farms, citrus orchards, rice paddies, and ubiquitous fields of sugarcane rippling in the breeze like folds of green silk. (In contrast, the upland plains of east-central Cuba are relatively infertile and the habitat of Cuban cowboys—*vaqueros*—who tend hardy cattle.)

Cuban Highs

The monotonously fecund flatlands are disjoined by three mountain zones, where the air is cool and inviting and the roads dip and rise through very untropical-looking countryside. Each of the three *alturas* offers its own compelling beauty, with cool pine forests and sparkling lakes.

The westernmost is the slender, low-slung Sierra del Rosarios and Sierra de los Órganos that together constitute the **Cordillera de Guaniguanico** forming a backbone along the length of northern Pinar del Río Province and rising to 692 meters atop sugarloaf-shaped Pan de Guajaibón. In their midst is the striking Valle de Viñales, a classic karst landscape of sheer-faced knolls called *mogotes,* theatrical formations that rise abruptly from the plain—antediluvian morphology riddled with caves.

The compact **Sierra Escambray** rise steeply from the coast of west-central Cuba, dominating eastern Cienfuegos and southern Villa Clara Provinces, with slender fingers extending east into Sancti Spíritus Province.

A third mountain zone, incorporating several adjacent ranges, overshadows the provinces of Granma, Santiago de Cuba, and Guantánamo and spills over into Holguín Province. To the west, the precipitous ranges of the Sierra Maestra rise steeply from the sea, culminating atop Pico Turquino at 1,872 meters. They extend from Cabo Cruz eastward 250 km to Guantánamo Bay, interrupted only by the small depression and bay in which nestles the city of Santiago de Cuba. To the east, the folded ranges of the Cuchilla de Toa, Sierra de Puriscal, and Sierra de Cristal are separated from the Sierra Maestra by the Nipe Plateau.

Earthquakes are common in eastern Cuba. The trees move as in a high wind, the birds stop calling, and huge chunks of unstable mountain cleave off and avalanche down the steep slopes. These mountains are rising in some places as much as one meter every 3,000 years, a result of the upheaving that has been going on for at least 150 million years, when the Caribbean plate, a free-floating piece of the earth's crust drifting northeastward at about 10 cm a year, first crumpled into the much larger, slow-moving North American plate, forcing the leading edge of the former under the latter and heaving up great amounts of volcanic material.

Down by the Shore

Depending on who is counting, Cuba has more than 400 beaches. They come in shades of oyster white, mulatto dark, golden, and taupe, and range in texture from talcum-fine to coarse-grained. The most breathtakingly beautiful are 20 km long, especially those on the ocean side of the innumerable coral cays beaded like pearls off the coast. Other beaches are unappealing, especially those of the south coast, despite being touted on tourist maps with tempting umbrella symbols; notable exceptions include Playa Girón and Playa Ancón.

What virtually all have in common is sandy bottoms shelving gently into lagoons protected by offshore coral reefs. The shallows are bright green, turning to aqua, azure, and then sapphire the farther out you go. Beyond that, the ocean gleams a deep indigo.

The coast is indented by dozens of huge bays shaped like deep flasks with narrow inlets. They are havens for shipping today as they were for pirates and Spanish galleons years ago (Cuba has 13 ports listed in the *World Port Index* as

beach at Sierra Los Galeones, in Santiago de Cuba Province

10 BEST BEACHES

PROVINCE	BEACH	LOCATION
Camagüey	Playa Los Pinos	Cayo Sabinal
Camagüey	Playa Santa Lucía	Santa Lucía
Archipiélago de los Canarreos	Playa Blanca	Cayo Largo
Archipiélago de los Canarreos	Playa Sirena	Cayo Largo
Ciego de Ávila	Playa Palma Real	Cayo Coco
Ciego de Ávila	Playa El Paso	Cayo Guillermo
Ciudad de la Habana	Playa Santa María del Mar	Playas del Este
Havana	Playa Jibacoa	Jucáro
Holguín	Playa Mayor	Guardalavaca
Holguín	Playa Pesquero	Guardalavaca
Matanzas	Playa Mayor	Varadero
Pinar del Río	Playa Levisa	Cayo Levisa
Sancti Spíritus	Playa Ancón	Trinidad
Villa Clara	Playa Santa María	Cayo Santa María

offering "excellent" shelter). Not least of these is Bahía de Habana, on whose western shores grew Havana.

Rivers

Cuba has over 500 rivers, most of them short, shallow, and unnavigable. The principal river, the 370-km-long Río Cauto, which originates in the Sierra Maestra and flows northwest, is navigable by boat for about 80 km. On the flatlands, especially those of the southern plains, the rivers loop lazily to the sea through a morass of mangroves.

Most rivers dwindle to trickles in the dry season, then often swell to rushing torrents, flooding extensive areas on the plains when the rains come (80% falls in summer). To assuage the deluge, Cuba is now studded with huge man-made reservoirs that help control water flow.

CLIMATE

Cuba lies within the tropics, though its climate—generally hot and moist (average relative humidity is 78%)—is more properly semi- or subtropical. There are only two seasons: wet (May to November) and dry (December to April), with regional variations.

The island is influenced by the warm Gulf Stream currents and by the North Atlantic high-pressure zone that lies northeast of Cuba and gives rise to the near-constant *brisa,* the local name for the prevailing northeast trade winds that caress Cuba year-round. Indeed, despite its more southerly latitude, Havana, wrote Ernest Hemingway, "is cooler than most northern cities in those months [July and August], because the northern trades get up about ten o'clock in the morning and blow until about five o'clock the next morning."

Temperatures

Cuba's mean annual temperature is 25.2° C, with an average of eight hours of sunshine per day throughout the year. There is little seasonal variation, with an *average* temperature in January of 22° C, rising (along with humidity) to an average of 27.2° C in July. Nonetheless, in summer the temperature can rise to 32° C or more, and far higher in the Oriente, especially the lowlands of Guantánamo Province (the hottest part of the country), where the thermometer rises inexorably until you may, like one 19th-century writer, be "forced to take off your flesh and sit in your bones." The southern coast is generally hotter than the north coast, which receives the trades. Hot winds sometimes rip across the central plains in summer, drawn by the rise of hot air off the land.

Midwinter temperatures can take a sharp dip, infrequently falling below 10° C, when severe cold fronts sweep down into the Gulf of Mexico. Atop the higher mountains temperatures may plunge at night to 5° C.

Sea temperature rises from 26° C in winter to 28° C in summer, although the northern coastal waters are often cooler due to varying influence of the Gulf Stream.

Rainfall

Some rain falls on Cuba an average of 85-100 days a year, totaling an annual average of 132 cm. Almost two-thirds falls during the May-October wet season, which can be astoundingly humid. Summer rain is most often a series of intermittent showers interspersed with sunshine, but lingering downpours and storms are common.

Central and western regions experience a three- to five-month dry period known as *La Seca*. February through April and December are the driest months. Nonetheless, heavy winter downpours are associated with cold fronts sweeping south from North America.

The Atlantic coast tends to be slightly rainier than the southern coast. The mountains receive the highest rainfall, especially the uplands of eastern Oriente (up to 400 cm fall in the Cuchillas de Toa). The mountains, however, produce regional microclimates, forming rain shadows along the southeast coast, so that pockets of cacti and parched scrub grow in the lee of thick-forested slopes.

Years of relative drought are common, when the cattle and sugarcane suffer. When it rains hard, sheets of water collect in the streets, waves crash over the Malecón, power snaps off, telephone lines go down, and taxis are impossible to find.

Hurricanes

Cuba lies within the hurricane belt. August through October is hurricane season, but freak hurricane-force storms can hit Cuba in other months, too. The **"Storm of the Century,"** for example, struck Cuba on 12 March 1993 and destroyed or damaged 40,000 homes and caused US$1 billion in damage.

Cuba has been hard-struck by several hurricanes in recent years. In October 1996, Hurricane Lili, moved north from the western Caribbean and battered the island. It dumped as much as 46 cm of rain in 48 hours, destroyed some 10,500 homes, and damaged at least 145,000 others. Hurricane Lili presaged Hurricane George in 1998; and Hurricane Irene struck Cuba in October 1999, slamming Havana.

When there are no hurricanes, midsummer weather is the best of all the year.

CUBA'S CLIMATE

Average temperatures are listed in degrees Celsius

	JAN.	FEB.	MARCH	APRIL	MAY	JUNE	JULY	AUG.	SEPT.	OCT.	NOV.	DEC.
National Average												
	26	26	27	29	30	31	32	32	31	29	27	26
Havana												
	22	22.5	23	25	26	27	28	28	27.5	26	24	22.5

DAYS WITH RAINFALL

	JAN.	FEB.	MARCH	APRIL	MAY	JUNE	JULY	AUG.	SEPT.	OCT.	NOV.	DEC.
Havana												
	6	4	4	4	7	10	9	10	11	11	7	6

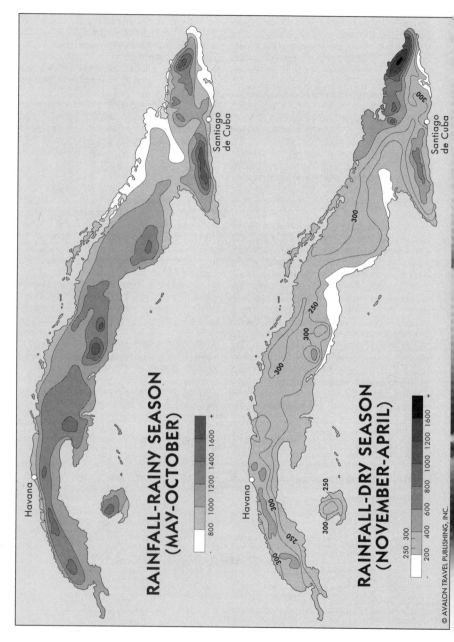

RAINFALL–RAINY SEASON
(MAY–OCTOBER)

800 1000 1200 1400 1600 +

RAINFALL–DRY SEASON
(NOVEMBER–APRIL)

250 300

200 400 600 800 1000 1200 1600 +

© AVALON TRAVEL PUBLISHING, INC.

Havana

Santiago
de Cuba

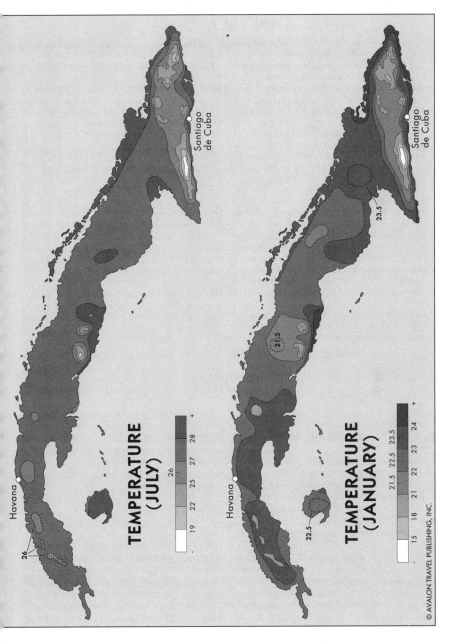

TEMPERATURE
(JULY)

26

- 19 22 25 27 28 +

Havana

26

Santiago
de Cuba

TEMPERATURE
(JANUARY)

23.5

21.5

22.5

- 15 18 21 21.5 22 22.5 23 23.5 24 +

Havana

Santiago
de Cuba

© AVALON TRAVEL PUBLISHING, INC.

HURRICANES

*I*n the warm air of the doldrums—the relatively calm reaches of the Atlantic Ocean south of the Tropic of Cancer—air made lighter by heat and by an infusion of water vapor begins to rise rapidly. The rising air leaves behind it a low-pressure area that draws more air in along the surface of the ocean, to become further moistened and warmed, and to rise skyward in its turn.

The rising air gradually cools. Its water vapor condenses into clouds that spread outward and sink toward the sea again. The central column of upwelling air thus acts like a chimney, pulling in a draft at the bottom from an ever-widening area and spewing warm air and moisture upward like smoke. As long as the source of warmth and moisture remains at the center of the storm, the process will accelerate. The condensing of water vapor atop the chimney releases heat, which further fuels the winds.

The force of the spinning of the earth—the Coriolis effect—acts on the air being drawn toward the chimney and causes it to spiral inward in a counterclockwise direction. When the air reaches the chimney where the winds converge, it spirals higher and higher around an area of relative calm. The inwardwheeling air has been gathering speed, while the growing whirlwind has moved ponderously into the path of the eastern trade winds.

The brewing storm swirls counterclockwise around a deepening low-pressure center, called a tropical depression. When the winds reach gale force (39 mph), the depression becomes a tropical storm. With a width up to 200 miles, its winds are much more dispersed than those of a hurricane. As pressure at the center continues to fall, the ring contracts, concentrating the energy into a much smaller diameter. At the energy-packed core, the hurricane's fury reigns supreme.

Several days before the hurricane hits land, the winds ahead of it begin to push up water until it is piled up against the shore. Then the maelstrom of screaming winds and churning waves bear down.

Even more dangerous is the bulging swell of ocean that the hurricane carries at its heart. At the center of the swirling maelstrom is a calm spot, the eye, which can mislead people into thinking that the storm has passed. Here, beneath the chimney. the dramatic drop in barometric pressure causes the surface of the ocean to rise: the sea's surface is literally sucked upward. As the dome of water approaches land, it rises even more as the ocean floor shelves gently upward. Then the great welling pours ashore as a storm surge—a vast wall of water that may be 30 feet or more above normal sea level and which the monster storm shoves along with all its furious energy.

FLORA

Cuba's ecosystems are less varied and less remarkable than those of many smaller destinations. Yet it touts the most impressive species diversity of any Caribbean island. Despite four centuries of devastating deforestation, extensive tracts remain cloaked in a dozen shades of tropical green. Coastal mangrove and wetland preserves, dry forest, scrubby pine forest, pockets of rainforest, and even montane cloud forest, almost desert-dry terrain supporting cacti, and other wild places are strewn like isles within an isle.

Cuba boasts more than 6,300 higher-plant species, of which some 3,180 (nearly 51%) are endemic and about 950 are endangered. The Sierra Maestra, for example, is one huge botanical garden, profusely smothered in everything from delicate orchids to prehistoric ferns. Above 2,000 meters, the vegetation changes abruptly to cloud forest. Some wind-battered elfin woods on exposed ridges are dwarfed, whereas more protected areas have majestically tall trees festooned with bromeliads, lichens, mosses, yellow-flowering *palo de cruz* vine, and all manner of lianas and creepers.

TREES

Indigenous tree species include mahogany, cedar, pine, rosewood, ebony, lignum vitae, cottonwood, logwood, *majagua, jagüey* (a relative of the weeping willow), and the deciduous, silvery *yagruma,* which shimmers as if frosted and bursts forth with huge lily-like blooms. Cuban craftsmen highly prize these timbers, many of which are now in short supply following centuries of logging to supply the furniture makers of Europe and to clear the land for King Sugar. The mountain ranges still have ecosystems typical of original Antillean vegetation.

Other archetypal species include the swollen baobab, which looks as if it has its roots in the air (for which it is sometimes called the "upside-down tree"), and the white-trunked *kapok,* or silk cotton, and revered *ceiba,* both of which have wide-spreading boughs.

The bully of trees is the strangler fig. It sprouts from the tops of trees from seeds dropped by birds or bats. It then sends roots to the ground, where they dig into the soil and provide a boost of sustenance. Slowly—it may take a full century—the roots grow and envelop the host tree, choking it until it dies and rots away, leaving the hollow, freestanding fig tree.

There are fruit trees, too, such as the alligator pear tree; the big, dark green *aguacates;* and the *zapote,* whose pulpy red fruit is the queen of Cuban fruits. One of Sierra del Rosarios' endemic species, *Psidium guayabita,* produces a berry from which sweet *licor de Guayabita* and dry *Guayabita seca* brandy are made. Sea grape trims the island's shores, as does the coastal manchineel, whose poisonous sap and tiny apple-like fruits should be avoided.

Many woody species are exotics, imports from far-off lands. Two examples are the eucalyptus from Australia and the cola nut from Africa.

Palms
Visually, the predominant species are the palms, of which Cuba has more than 30 types, including the rare cork palm, found in the western part of Cuba, and the bulging *barrigona,* or belly palm, so named because of its remarkable ability to store water. The coconut palm is severely outnumbered, although it holds its own in northeast Cuba around Baracoa, where an entire local cuisine has evolved from the nut.

The king of palms is the ubiquitous, silver-sheathed *Roystonea regia,* the royal palm with its swollen upper trunk, the indisputable symbol of Cuba (it's even part of the national emblem). It is protected by law, despite its ability to thrive almost anywhere. (Those palms with the swollen *lower* trunks are not mutations but *Bearrigona,* "belly palms.") The **Jardín Botánico Soledad,** at

Pepito Tey, 10 km east of Cienfuegos, has the island's most complete collection of Latin American palms. The **Jardín Botánico Nacional,** in the southern suburbs of Havana, also has palms from around the world.

Mangroves
Cuba's shorelines are home to five species of mangrove, which together cover four percent of Cuba. These pioneer land builders thrive at the interface of land and sea, forming a stabilizing tangle that fights tidal erosion and reclaims land from the water. The irrepressible, reddish-barked, shrubby mangroves rise from the dark water on interlocking stilt roots. Small brackish streams and labyrinthine creeks wind among them like snakes, sometimes connecting, sometimes pe-

---

THE ROYAL PALM

*T*he majestic royal palm (*palma royal* in Spanish) grows singly or in great elegant clumps. Its smooth gray trunk, which can tower 25 meters, resembles a great marble column with a curious bulge near the top. Long leaves droop sinuously from the explosive top, blossoming afresh with each new moon.

The royal palm is as useful as it is stately. Its fronds *(pencas)* make good thatch, and the thick green base—the *yagua*—of the *penca,* being waterproof, also makes an excellent roof or siding material. The trunk itself makes excellent timber. Bees favor palm honey; and pigs seem to like the seeds, which are used for pig feed. Humans devour the delicious, succulent palm-heart *(palmito),* from the center of the trunk. And birds love its black fruit and carry the seeds *(palmiche)* all over the country.

tering out in narrow culs-de-sac, sometimes opening suddenly into broad lagoons.

Mangroves—most wonderfully seen in Zapata or the northern cays—are halophytes, plants that thrive in salty conditions. Although they do not require salt (in fact they grow better in fresh water), they thrive where no other tree can. Cuba's rivers carry silt out of the mountains onto the coastal alluvial plains, where it is trapped by mangroves. The nutrient-rich mud generates algae and other small organisms that form the base of the marine food chain. Food is delivered to the estuaries every day from both the sea and the land so those few plants—and creatures—that can survive here flourish in immense numbers. And their sustained health is vital to the health of other marine ecosystems. The preservation of the mangroves has been taken on by the **Instituto de Ecológia y Sistemas** (Ecology and Systems Institute), Carretera de Varona Km 3.5, Capdevila, Havana, tel. (7) 57-8010.

Mangrove swamps are esteemed as nurseries of marine life and havens for water birds—cormorants, frigate birds, pelicans, herons, and egrets—which feed and nest here by the thousands, producing guano that makes the mangroves grow faster.

A look down into the water reveals luxuriant life: oysters and sponges attached to the roots, small stingrays flapping slowly over the bottom, and tiny fish in schools of tens of thousands. Baby black-tipped sharks—and other juvenile fish too—spend much of their early lives among mangrove roots, out of the heavy surf, shielded by the root maze that keeps out large predators. High tide brings larger diners—big mangrove snappers and young barracudas hang motionless in the water.

Mangroves build up the soil until they strand themselves high and dry. In the end they die on the land they have created.

EPIPHYTES AND PARASITES

On higher ground, palms and large-leafed undergrowth such as the "everlasting plant," whose large leaves form habitats for other plants, give way to ferns (including the ground frond, which curls away at your touch), bracken, pine trees,

feathery-leafed *palo de cotorra* (parrot tree), and parasitic *conde de pino* (Count of the Pine) vine, whose bright red berries add color to the trunks of its pine tree hosts.

Many trees play hosts, too, to epiphytes, arboreal nesters (epiphytes comes from the Greek, "upon plants") that attach themselves to tree trunks or branches. The epiphytic environment is a kind of nutrient desert. Thus bromeliads—brilliantly flowering, spiky leafed "air plants" up to 120 cm across—have developed tanks or cisterns that hold great quantities of rainwater and decaying detritus in the whorled bases of their stiff, tightly overlapping leaves. The plants gain nourishment from dissolved nutrients in the cisterns. Known as "tank epiphytes," they provide trysting places and homes for tiny aquatic animals high above the ground.

FLOWERS AND GARDENS

Monet Colors
The forests and grasslands flare with color, some flamboyantly. Begonias, anthuriums, "Indian laburnum," oleander, and poinsettia are common, as are the sensitive mimosa, hibiscus, blossoming hydrangea, bright pink morning glory, and bougainvillea in its rainbow assortment of riotous colors. Trees such as the vermilion African flame-of-the-forest, purple jacaranda, blue rosewood, and almost fluorescent yellow *corteza amarillo* all add their seasonal bouquet to the landscape.

Cuba's national flower is the brilliant white, heady-scented *mariposa,* a native species of jasmine that became a symbol of rebellion and purity at the time of the independence wars.

African golden trumpet is found everywhere. Water hyacinths, with their white and purple blooms, crowd the freshwater lakes. The brilliant scarlet Cupid's tears *(Lagrimas de Cupido)* speckles green meadows. Congea clambers up over houses. Fence posts cut from the piñon tree grow from a stick in the ground and burst into bright pink efflorescent blossom. And jasmine, orange *jubia d'oro,* and azalea flank major thoroughfares and run down the central divides.

Many herbs also grow wild in Cuba, though surprisingly few find their way into local stores and, hence, into cooking. An exception is mint *(yerba buena),* cultivated on the island since at least 1535. Pimento is an important cash crop that finds its way into local hot sauce. And locally produced vanilla flavors Coppelia ice cream.

Orchids

Cuba has several hundred known species of orchids, and countless others await discovery. In 1990, the purple Ames orchid (thought to be extinct) was discovered, as was another variety, *Marathrum cubanum,* which has no common name. At any time of year dozens of species are in bloom, from sea level to the highest reaches of the Sierra Maestra.

Not only are orchids the largest family of flowering plants, they're also the most diverse: poke around with magnifying glass in hand and you'll come across species with flowers less than one millimeter across. Others have pendulous petals that can reach more than half a meter. Some flower for only one day. Others will last several weeks. The greatest diversity exists in humid—not wet—mid-elevation environments, where they are abundant as tropical epiphytes (constituting 88% of orchid species). While not all orchids lead epiphytic lives—the Spanish called them *para-sitos*—those that do are the most exotic of epiphytes.

If you're serious in your study, check out *Flowers of the Caribbean,* by G. W. Lennox and S. A. Seddon, or *Native Orchids of the Eastern Caribbean,* by Julian Kenny; both are published by Macmillan Caribbean, Basingstoke, England.

Botanical Gardens

The **Jardín Botánico Nacional,** near Parque Lenin outside Havana, features dozens of orchid species. You'll find a splendid **Orquideria** (orchid garden) at Soroa, in Pinar del Río Province. There's also a large botanical garden a few kilometers east of Cienfuegos, and another outside Santiago de Cuba. Farther east, in Baconao, is a cactus garden, and set high atop Gran Piedra, at **Ave de Paraísos,** mists swirl through a series of gardens divided by topiary hedges. Here, bird of paradise *(ave de paraíso),* dahlias, chrysanthemums, and dozens of other colorful species are grown for domestic use.

A large collection of native plants can also be seen in the Zapata Swamp, the largest such ecosystem in the Caribbean. Close to one million hectares in size, the swamp is a repository for the greatest diversity of species in the island—750 botanical varieties, 116 native to Cuba, and six found only in Zapata.

FAUNA

No one is quite sure how many species of fauna Cuba possesses. The vast majority are invertebrates (mostly insects), with a great many species endemic to specific regions, plus dozens of unique species and subspecies, including the world's smallest frog *(Sminthillus limbatus)* and smallest bird (the bee hummingbird, also called the *pájaro mosco*—fly bird—for its diminutive size or *zunzuncito* for the swish of its wings); an endemic crocodile species; and unique, beautiful colored snails of the genus *Polymita,* most commonly found in northeast Oriente, around Baracoa.

Alfonso Silva Lee's *Natural Cuba* (St. Paul: Pangaea, 1996) is a beautifully written, lavishly illustrated book about Cuba's wildlife; you can order online from www.cubabooks.com.

BIRDS

Cuba has at least 388 species of birds, of which 21 are native to Cuba. About half the birds to be seen in Cuba never venture the 90 miles north to the United States. Many, however, are occasionals, who fly in for the winter. Birds that have all but disappeared in other areas still find tenuous safety in protected pockets of Cuba. The nation offers hope for such rare jewels of the bird world as the ivory-billed woodpecker, found in Cuchillas de Toa, in Holguín Province.

Cuba is a major stopover for migratory waterfowl, and more than a score of species of dove, duck, quail, mallard, snipe, and pigeon flock seasonally to the country's freshwater lakes and coastal lagoons. Spoonbills and flamingos are also common on the cays and among marshy lagoons. White egrets *(coco blanco)* are commonly found around cane fields and water flats, and their cousins the *coco negro,* or ibis, and blue heron (locally called *garza*) are also easily seen picking at a buffet of fresh delicacies that extends for miles. Black frigate birds, with their long scimitar wings and forked tails, hang like sinister kites in the wind and from this airborne perch harry other seabirds until the latter release their catch (birders have a name for such thievery: kleptoparasitism). *Gaviotas,* or gulls, needless to say, also prefer maritime regions, as does the *gincho* (the sea osprey), who performs aerial acrobatics. The *codorniz,* or diver, lives beside freshwater lakes, where it is frequently found alongside the *yagauza,* a cross between a goose and a duck. The shimmering kingfisher prefers moving water.

Of terrestrial species, the marabou stork can be seen in scrub areas. Such areas are also favored by the *cararia,* a goose-stepping ocher, black, and white hawklike relative of the Senegalese snakebird. Listen at night for the hoot of the barn owl, called the *susundamba* in Africa. Pygmy owls, with their old women's voices, perch in sapodilla trees. Like the owl, the endemic *siju* can rotate its head through 360°.

The *tocororo* (a member of the trogon family) is the national bird, perhaps because its brilliant blue, white, and red plumage copies the colors of the national flag. It wears a scarlet sash across its breast, like the one worn by the King of Spain. Listen for its tell-tale call: *có, co, có, co, có, có.*

Other birds you might expect to see include pelicans, the yellow-necked green finch, the wedge-tailed chuchinguaco, or the aura vulture wheeling and sliding on the thermals, Everglade kites soaring in hunt of carrion, and common house sparrows and blackbirds (Ernest Hemingway, in *Islands in the Stream,* wrote of the "flight of blackbirds going in towards Havana where they flew each night from all the countryside to the south and east, converging in long flights to roost, noisily, in the Spanish laurel trees of the Prado").

Tanagers, *oropendolas,* and woodpeckers brighten the forests. The woodpecker's short, stubby wings enable it to swerve and dodge at high speed through the undergrowth as it chases insects.

Alas, the island's parrot population has been severely depleted. There were so many parrots and macaws in the New World 500 years ago that the Americas were shown on maps as *Terra Psittacorum,* land of the free parrot. Even Columbus took home as a pet a Cuban red parrot (now on the road to extinction). The best place to spot parrots is the Los Indios forest reserve on Isla de la Juventud. Inhabited by 153 species of birds, including the Cuban grulla or sandbill crane, but most notably by the Cotorro—the Cuban parrot, emerald green with red throat, foreneck, and cheeks, a white spot on its head, blue primaries, and a maroon abdomen.

The Zapata Peninsula is also a tremendous spot for birding (18 of the nation's 21 endemic species can be seen here), as is Sierra Maestra National Park (favored by the *rabijunco,* a rare migratory bird that settles in these mountains).

Hummingbirds
Of all the exotic bird species in Cuba, the hummingbirds beat all contenders. More than 300

THE WORLD'S SMALLEST BIRD

*I*magine a bird that tips the scales at a mere two grams—less than a penny! It is easy to be fooled into thinking of *Mellisuga helenae* as an insect. In fact, it's the world's smallest bird, about the size of a large bee (hence its colloquial name: the bee hummingbird). This tiny jewel is endemic to Cuba.

At 2.5 cm (1.5-inch) long, the male hummer ranks as smallest bird in the world. The female is about 6 mm (0.25 inches) longer. The female's cotton-soft nest is barely bigger than a doll's teacup.

The solitary hummer guards its territory with a ferocity remarkable for its diminutive size. One scientist records having a seen a bee hummer "explode with rage" when a vulture had the nerve to perch too close. "The furious hummer attacked it so relentlessly that within minutes the chastened vulture flew off."

It forages on tiny spiders, flies, and other insects, but also takes nourishment from the nectar of plants such as trumpetvines, which depend symbiotically on the bird for pollination.

The bird's range has been gradually depleted, and it is now considered endangered.

species of New World hummingbirds constitute the family Trochilidae, and Cuba has 16. All are stunningly pretty and easy to spot. Their magnificent emerald and purple liveries shimmer iridescent in the sunlight as they sip nectar from the blooms and twirl in midair, their wings a filmy blur. Some males are beplumed with long streamer tails and glistening mustaches, beards, and visors.

These tiny high-speed machines are named after the hum made by the beat of their wings. At up to 100 beats per second, a hummingbird's wings move so rapidly that the naked eye cannot detect them. Alone among birds, they can generate power on both the forward and backward wing strokes, a distinction that allows them to fly sideways, hover, rise straight up, propel themselves upside down, and even fly backwards.

Typically loners, hummingbirds bond with the opposite sex only for the few seconds it takes to mate. Many are fiercely territorial. With luck you might witness a spectacular aerial battle between males defending their territories (if two hummers go zipping by, they're probably in a dogfight). Nests are often no larger than a thimble. Inside, the female will lay two eggs no larger than coffee beans.

Hummers earned a place in the mythology of the Taíno Indians, who called them *colibri,* meaning "god bird." They symbolized rebirth, since the Indians believed that the creature died when the weather turned dry and was born again when the rains came. They worshiped the bird as a *zemi,* a fetish idol representing the path of the sun across the sky. Legend lives on in folklore—some Cubans still believe that the most effective love potion is one made from dead hummers that have been dried and ground up.

Flamingos

For casual birders, seeing flamingos is a highlight of exploring the cays and lagoons of Cuba. There are six species of flamingos worldwide (four in the New World, and two in Africa). Standing over 1.2 meters tall, the roseate is the largest of the New World species. The ungainly yet beautiful bird—locally called the *Cabellero d'Italia* (Italian wig)—can be seen feeding in large congregations at Cayo Coco, Zapata, and other enclosed lagoons where evaporation keeps salinity much higher than in the sea. The

supersalty soup teems with larval brine flies and diatoms, blue-green algae—favorite foods of *Phoenicopterus ruber,* the roseate, or West Indian, flamingo. Their food supply contains canthaxanthin, a substance that give the birds their soft pink color (flamingos raised in zoos are fed synthetic canthaxanthin so as not to disappoint visitors).

The flock retreats en masse at the approach of a visitor. One step too far and the birds take off, webbed feet stamping the water surface to foam as the scarlet wings beat for lift in their ungainly take-off, when 10,000 flame-pink birds may suddenly be poured into the blue bowl of sky. Flamingos resemble the Concorde in flight, with reaching head and neck and trailing legs outstretched to counterbalance each other.

Flamingos do not breed every year. When they breed, they do so en masse. The mating instinct, once sparked, gathers steam until hundreds or even thousands of birds may be displaying in a tumult, parading up and down, marching stiff necked in great columns. Occasionally an individual will break step, stand bolt upright, and shoot out its wings, while others fluff up their feathers and drop their heads as surely as if their necks had been broken.

The birds build nests by ladling wet mud into miniature volcanoes, which the sun then hardens. Soon the forest of legs conceals tiny youngsters swaddled in gray fluffy plumage.

AMPHIBIANS AND REPTILES

The most common reptiles you'll see are any of 46 lizard species, especially the bright green Lagartija lizard, with its vermilion wattle, the comical curly-tailed lizard, chameleons, and quaint geckos—everyone's mosquito-eating friend.

With luck, you may spot the dragonlike iguana (particularly on Cayo Largo and other offshore cays), which can grow to two meters in length. It can be seen in coastal areas crawling through moist deciduous forest leaf litter or basking on branches that hang over water—its preferred route of escape when threatened. Its head is crested with a frightening wig of leathery spines, its heavy body encased in a scaly hide, deeply wrinkled around the sockets of its muscular legs. Despite its menacing *One Million Years B.C.* appearance, it is quite harmless, a nonbelligerent vegetarian.

Aquatic turtles (terrapins) are also common, particularly in the Zapata Peninsula, where you can see them basking in rows on logs.

The **amphibians** are primarily represented by the frogs and toads, most of which you're probably more likely to hear than to see—especially the horny bullfrogs, croaking their lusty two-tone serenade through the night. Spelunkers might even spot the axolotl, a blind, albino cave-dwelling newt.

Cuba is also home to 14 species of Neotropical **snakes.** None is poisonous. Among the more common snake species are the wide-ranging boas, which you might spot crawling across a cultivated field or waiting patiently on a bough of a tree in wet or dry tropical forest, savanna, or dry thorn scrub. The Cuban boa can grow to four meters in length. Its converse is the 20-cm-long pygmy boa, found solely in the caves of the Valle de Viñales. Wild boas vary in temperament. Larger ones are aggressive and quite capable of inflicting serious damage with their large teeth. Heaven forbid a full-grown adult should sink its teeth in sufficiently to get its constricting coils around you.

Crocodiles and Caimans

In Cuba, it's easy to spot crocodiles and caimans, the croc's modest-sized relative. The speckled caiman is still relatively common in parts of

crocodiles

Cuba's wet lowland—and in fact may be the most abundant in existence today. It is no more than two meters long—one of the smallest of western crocodilians. Another species, the non-native caiman or *babilla,* is found on the Isla de la Juventud.

The scales of the caiman take on the blue-green color of the water it slithers through. Their nests are heavily disturbed by dogs, foxes, lizards, and humans. And increasingly they are being sought for their skins, which are turned into trivia. Ironically, this is easing the pressure on the crocodiles, which are fast disappearing elsewhere as humanity takes their hides and habitats.

An endemic crocodile species, the rare yellow and black *Crocodylus rhombifer,* is found only in the Zapata Peninsula but is being reintroduced to the Lanier swamps, Río Cuato estuary, and other native areas. The crocodile, with a lineage going back 250 million years, was hunted to near extinction during colonial days and today has the most restricted geographical range of any crocodile species in the world. *Lagarto criollo* (as the Cuban croc is colloquially known) is much more aggressive than its cousin, the placid American crocodile, which inhabits many of the estuaries and coastal mangroves around the island and which interbred with the Cuban crocodile. Since the Revolution, Cuba has had an active and highly successful breeding program to save the indigenous species. Today the population is abundant and healthy (about 6,000 exist in the wild). In 1995, the Cuban government was authorized by the Convention of International Trade in Endangered Species to market the skins of the rare animals worldwide to be turned into shoes and handbags, with the money to be plowed back into conservation (only crocs in the captive-breeding program will be culled).

The creatures, which can live 80 years or more, spend much of their days basking on mud banks. At night, they sink down into the warm waters of the river for the hunt. While the American species is a fish eater, the omnivorous Cuban crocodile occasionally likes meat—wild boars, the occasional deer, unsuspecting fishermen. Pugnacious full-grown males will strike at humans. Crocodiles, who prefer stealth, can run very fast in short bursts. Crocs cannot chew. They simply snap, tear, and swallow. Powerful stomach acids dissolve everything, including bones. A horrible way to go! Beware that toothy leer.

Mating season begins in February. The polygamous males (who form harems) will defend their breeding turf from rival suitors with bare-toothed gusto. When estrous females approach, the ardent male gets very excited and goes through a nuptial dance, roaring intensely and even kicking up clouds of spray with his lashing tail. A curtsey by the damsel and the male clasps her ardently with his jaws, their tails intertwine, and the mating is over before you can wipe the steam from your camera.

A female crocodile selects a spot above the high-water mark and exposed to both sunlight and shade, then makes a large nest mound out of sticks, soft vegetation, and mud, which she hollows out to make room for her eggs (usually between 30 and 70). She will guard the nest and keep it moist for several months after laying. The rotting vegetation creates heat, which incubates the eggs. When they are ready to hatch,

the hatchlings pipe squeakily and she uncovers the eggs and takes the babies into a special pouch inside her mouth. She then swims away with the youngsters peering out between a palisade of teeth. The male assists, and soon the young crocs are feeding and playing in a special nursery, guarded by the two watchful parents (only 10% of newborn hatchlings survive in the wild; 90% survive in captive breeding programs). For all their beastly behavior, crocodiles are devoted parents.

Despite being relics from the age of the dinosaurs, croc brains are far more complex than those of other reptiles. They are sharp learners. They also have an amazing immune system that can even defeat gangrene. Cuba is looking at the commercial potential, including extraction and development of potential medicines and, purportedly, aphrodisiacs.

Marine Turtles

Marine turtles-notably the hawksbill and, to a lesser degree, the green, nest on Cuban beaches, mostly on Isla de la Juventud and southern cays.

One hundred years ago turtles were as abundant throughout the Caribbean as bison once were on the North American plains. They were highly prized for their meat by indigenous peoples, who netted and harpooned them. And British and Spanish fleets, buccaneers, and whalers counted on turtle meat to feed their crews while cruising in New World waters. They're easy to catch and easy to keep alive for weeks on their backs in a space no bigger than the turtle itself. The end of colonialism offered no respite. Large-scale green turtle export occurred about the turn of the century, when turtle soup became a delicacy.

Most of the important nesting sites in Cuba are now protected, and access to some is restricted. Despite legislation outlawing the taking of turtle eggs or disturbance of nesting turtles, adult turtles continue to be captured for meat by Cuban fishermen. Hawksbills are also hunted illegally in Cuba for the tourist trade—one often sees stuffed turtle specimens for sale, and shells are used in jewelry and ornaments.

Of the hundreds of eggs laid by a female in one season, only a handful survive to maturity. (As many as 70% of the hatchlings are eaten before they reach the water.) Turtles have hit on a formula for outwitting their predators, though, or at least for surviving despite them. Each female turtle normally lays an average of 100 eggs. Some marvelous internal clock arranges for most eggs to hatch at night when hatchlings can make their frantic rush for the sea concealed by darkness. Often baby turtles will emerge from the eggs during the day and wait beneath the surface of the beach until nightfall. They are programmed to travel fast across the beach to escape the hungry mouths. Even after reaching the sea they continue to swim frantically for several days—flippers paddling furiously—like clockwork toys.

No one knows where baby turtles go. They swim off and generally are not seen again until they appear years later as adults. Turtles are great travelers capable of amazing feats of navigation. Greens, for example, navigate across up to 1,500 miles of open sea to return, like salmon, to the same nest site, guided presumably by stars and currents from their faraway feeding grounds.

FISH AND SHELLFISH

The warm waters off Cuba's coast are populated by more than 900 species of fish and crustaceans—from octopus, crabs, turtles, and spiny lobsters the size of house cats to sharks, tuna, and their cousins the billfish, which aerodynamically approach swimming perfection with their long pointed snouts, tapered bodies, and crescent-shaped tails. Some billfish grow as long as 3.6 m and weigh as much as 650 kg, with eyes contoured so as not to bulge and interrupt the smooth streamlined head. These creatures breathe not with gills but by taking in huge amounts of water through wide-open mouths. Thus they swim at high speed in order to breathe. The sailfish (a type of billfish) has been timed swimming over short distances at 110 kph—which is faster than the cheetah, the fastest land mammal. Unlike other fish, they are also warm-blooded, with temperatures considerably higher than those of the water around them.

The lucky diver may also spot whale sharks (the largest fish in the world) and manta rays, which swim close to the surface and whose wings can be up to seven meters across. The manta ray uses the water for support, much as gliders use air. It flaps its wings and thus sails slowly through the water, gathering floating crustaceans and tiny fish by filtration in its immense slot-like mouth.

Smaller fish are as strikingly bejeweled as the damsels of an exotic harem: sapphire fins attached to sulfur bodies, chocolate brown spots scattered on a vermilion flank, sage green scales individually rimmed with ringlets of red, white, and black. The entire spectrum has been tapped in audacious permutations. Around the coral reefs, where variety and richness of life are most abundant, individual species have evolved the most vivid liveries to assist in identification.

Fish to avoid include the fatally toxic and heavily camouflaged stonefish and the beautiful, orange-and-white-striped lion fish, whose long spines can inflict a killer sting. The bulbous Jimenea and the puffer fish, which can blow itself up to the size of a baseball, are also poisonous. Jellyfish are common, too, including the lethal Portuguese man-of-war. And don't go probing around inside coral, where moray eels make their home—their bite can take your fingers off.

The sea's sandy bottoms are home to conch—snails the size of baseballs—betrayed by their beautiful horn-studded, pink-lined, ceramic-like shell. The animal oozes along the sea floor at a snail's pace, its golden eyes peeping from the ends of long stalks. The islanders enthusiastically eat the tasty conch (they pound the heck out of the flesh, then marinate it in vinegar until it acquires the taste and texture of veal). Tempting as they are, leave them alone. Collecting shells—and coral—is against both Cuban and international law; the Cuban government mandates that only 600 kg of black coral can be harvested annually, but much, much more is taken illegally to end up in *coral negro* jewelry.

Inland, Lago de Tesoro harbors the rare *manjuarí*, the Cuban "alligator gar."

Coral Reefs
Coral reefs—the most complex and variable community of organisms in the world—rim much of Cuba at a distance of usually no more than one km offshore. The reefs are an aquatic version of the Hanging Gardens of Babylon. On the sea floor sit the massive brain corals and

CONSERVATION

Cuba has been likened to the setting of Ernest Callenbach's novel *Ecotopia*, about an egalitarian and environmental utopia where the streets are clean, everything is recycled, and nothing is wasted; where there are few cars and lots of bicycles; where electricity is generated from methane from dung; where free health and education services reach the farthest rural outpost; and where city dwellers tend agricultural plots designed to make the island self-sufficient in food and break its traditional dependence on cash crops for export.

Though simplistic there's truth in this vision. Cuba, a leader in second-generation human rights (to food, shelter, education, and good health) can claim to be a standard-bearer in the quest for third-generation rights to a clean and safe environment. The Cubans are ahead of the times in coping with ecological problems the entire world will eventually face. Indeed, during the Rio Earth Summit in Brazil in 1993, Cuba was one of only two countries worldwide to receive an A+ rating for implementation of sustainable development practices.

Cuba: Red or Green?

One of the first proposals of Cuba's revolutionary government in the early 1960s was to create a greenbelt around Havana. Volunteers spent weekends planting trees, flowers, and ornamental shrubs before the plan died on the vine. In 1978 the government established the National Committee for the Protection and Conservation of Natural Resources and Environment, with responsibility to manage natural resources and wildlife and control air and water pollution, although it has done a poor job, and much of the self-congratulatory hype is propagandist rhetoric.

Much of Cuba's advances are recent, necessitated by the collapse of the Soviet bloc. The fuel shortage caused Cubans to relinquish their cars in favor of a more environmentally sound mode of transportation—the bicycle. Everything from solar power (neglected, despite the perfect climate) to windmills (encouraged since the mid-1970s) are now being vaunted as alternatives to fossil fuels. For example, more than 100 of Cuba's 160 or so sugar mills are now powered by *bagasse* (waste from cane processing), saving the island the equivalent of 3.5 million tons of oil. In 1999, almost 35% of Cuba's energy supply came from biomass conversion (experts suggest that with appropriate technology, Cuba could generate twice the electricity from sugar cane that it currently gets from burning oil).

In the 1980s, Cuba began to edge away from debilitating farming systems. It initiated sustainable organic farming techniques and an enormously successful soil conservation program, while experiments were undertaken to determine which plants had medicinal value (herbal medicine—known as "green" medicine in Cuba—is today a linchpin in the nation's besieged health system, and *curanderos* and their homegrown remedies are no longer scorned).

Today, red and green are complementary colors. Cuba even has its own ecologically minded pressure group—**Sendero Verde** (Green Path)—a small dissident organization. Nonetheless, there is a lack of public education about ecological issues and few qualified personnel to handle them. And despite fairly adequate environmental laws, Cuba suffers from horrific waste and pollution. Industrial chimneys cast deathly palls over parts of Havana, Moa, and other nickel-processing towns of Holguín Province where "Photography Prohibited" signs have gone up around devastated land hammered and sickled into a ghastly gangue. Then there are the Hungarian-made buses that, in Castro's words, "fill the city with exhaust smoke, poisoning everybody. We could draw up statistics on how many people the Hungarian buses kill." And Havana Harbor is indisputably one of the most polluted bodies of water in the world, as are the bays around Nuevitas and Moa.

Environmental sensitivity has been lacking, too, in urban planning, which throughout the Revolution has been almost entirely limited to imported designs from Eastern Europe—highly inefficient and sinfully ugly units that show little harmony with the environment, fostering anomie among the inhabitants.

THE ROUTE OF THE TREASURE FLEETS

OUTBOUND JOURNEY FROM SPAIN
HOMEWARD JOURNEY VIA HAVANA

0   250 mi
0   250 km

© AVALON TRAVEL PUBLISHING, INC.

Deforestation and Conservation

When Christopher Columbus arrived in Cuba, more than 90% of the island was covered in forest. Some 467 years later, on the eve of the Revolution, only 14% of the land was forested. Seven million hectares had been felled for sugar and cattle, most within this century! During 1945-60, indiscriminate logging reduced forested areas from more than 40% to less than 10% of Cuba's land area.

José Martí said that "a region without trees is poor. A city without trees is sickly, land without trees is parched and bears wretched fruit." Thus, the revolutionary government undertook a reforestation program in the mid-1960s; by the late 1970s, the program had increased the total wooded area to almost 20%. Since the collapse of the Soviet bloc, however, Cuba has had to replace more than 300,000 cubic meters of imported timber by felling its own trees. Castro called for a reinvigorated reforestation program. The government announced the Manatí Plan, named for the eastern province where the program was initiated. Since its inception, about 697,000 hectares have been planted (Cuba is one of the few countries in the world to have increased the amount of forested land area in recent decades). Virtually the entire reforestation program, however, is in firs, not diverse species. There is little effort to regenerate primary forest.

National Parks and Nature Reserves: In 1963, Cuba established four nature reserves: **El Verayl** and **Cabo de Corrientes** on the Peninsula de Guanahacabibes, in Pinar del Río

Province; **Jaguaní,** in Holguín; and **Cupeyal del Norte,** in Guantánamo. A fifth reserve, **Cayo Caguanes,** was established in the north of Sancti Spíritus Province in 1968. The parks—Cuba's first—covered four percent of Cuba and were created under the auspices of the Academía de Ciencias (Cuban Academy of Sciences), which still administers Cuba's burgeoning system of parks and reserves.

In addition, UNESCO has declared four regions to be biosphere reserves: **Sierra del Rosarios** and **Guanahacabibes** in western Piñar del Río Province and **Cuchillas del Toa** and **Baconao** in eastern Cuba—constituting an especially vital preserve of important forest watersheds (Desembarco de Granma National Park, for example, is 80% covered with endemic woodland). Other habitats, such as the vast swamplands of the Zapata Peninsula (the largest such ecosytem in the Caribbean), are also protected as vital havens for dozens of endemic species.

Cuba recently created a **National Ecotourism Group** to promote and develop the reserves as ecotourism destinations. Over 100 national parks and reserves are planned. About two dozen have made it onto the statute books, though tourist facilities are meager.

HISTORY

Cuba has a sunny geography shadowed by a dark, brooding history. The Castroite Revolution, which replaced the Batista regime with another brand of authoritarianism, is part of a continuum in the struggle for freedom from oppression and tyranny that began with the Indian chief Hatuey's revolt in 1513, evolved through the wars of independence in 1868 and 1895 to the revolutions of 1933 and 1959. A sound knowledge of the island's history is therefore integral to understanding Cuba today. To gloss over the nuance of detail is to easily misread the march of events. It is as fascinating a tale of pathos as that of any nation on earth—perhaps keener, suggests Frank Tannebaum, "because nature has been kind to the island."

hopped their way up Caribbean islands over the course of many centuries.

The earliest to arrive were the **Gauanajatabeys,** hunter-gatherers who lived in the west, in what is now Pinar del Río Province. They were followed by the **Ciboneys,** who settled along the south coast, where they established themselves as farmers and fishermen. Mostly, it appears, they lived in caves. Little is known of these pre-Ceramic peoples (3500 B.C.-A.D. 1200).

The pre-Ceramic tribes were displaced by the **Taíno,** who first arrived from Hispaniola around A.D. 1100 and again, in a second wave, in the mid-15th century, when they were driven from their homeland on Hispaniola by the barbarous,

PRE-COLUMBIAN HISTORY

Europeans settled Cuba less than 500 years ago—a drop in the bucket compared to the 3,500-year-long tenure of indigenous peoples. The aborigines numbered no fewer than 100,000 (some estimates suggest as many as 500,000) when Christopher Columbus chanced upon the island in 1492. The Spaniards who claimed the island lent the name *Arahuacos,* or Arawaks, to the indigenous peoples, but there were several distinct groups that had left the Orinoco basin of the South American mainland and island-

An Indian smoking a rolled tobacco leaf inhaled through the nose.

THÉVET, 1558

cannibalistic Caribs, who leapfrogged northward through the island chain with the ferocity of a forest fire.

A Peaceable Culture

The Taíno lived in *bohios,* thatched circular huts designed to withstand the severe storms that frequently lashed the island. Villages, which allied with one another, consisted of 15 or so families governed by a *cacique,* or clan leader. They were "the first and purest socialists," in the words of a contemporary Cuban historian: they shared property and looked after the ill and less fortunate.

Since the land produced everything, the indigenous peoples were able to live well and peaceably, dedicated to the production of children (the parents put pressure on the soft skulls of newborn infants to induce broad, flat foreheads, esteemed as a mark of beauty in adults). They cusped fish from the rivers (often using *guaicán* sucker fish tethered on lines to bait larger fish) and culled birds from the trees, which also produced tropical fruits and nuts in abundance. The Taíno also used advanced farming techniques to maximize yields of yucca (also called *manioc*) and corn, which they called *mahis* (maize), as well as yams and peppers.

Although the men went naked, the Taíno were skilled weavers who slept in tightly woven cotton nets (hammocks, really) strung from poles (the Spaniards would later use native labor to weave sailcloth). They were also skilled potters and boat builders who hewed canoes from huge tree trunks. It seems they had evolved at least basic astronomical charts, which can be seen painted on the walls of caves islandwide.

Columbus "Discovers" Cuba

After making landfall in the Bahamas in 1492 during his first voyage to the New World, Columbus took on indigenous guides and threaded the maze of islets and shallows that lay to the southwest. On the evening of 27 October 1492, Columbus first set eyes on the hazy mass of Cuba.

The explorer voyaged along the north coast for four weeks, touching land at various points and finally dropping anchor on 27 November 1492 in a perfectly protected harbor near today's Gibara, in Holguín Province. The bay that Columbus named Puerto Santo he described by its distinctive, tall, flat-topped mountain, which Cubans now call *El Yunque* (The Anvil). According to legend, he left a wooden cross that today can be seen in Baracoa.

"They are the best people in the world," Columbus recorded of the Indians, "without knowledge of what is evil; nor do they murder or steal. . . . All the people show the most singular loving behavior. . . and are gentle and always laughing."

The Spaniards would change that forever.

THE SPANISH TAKE OVER

In 1493 the Pope granted to Spain control of the lands Columbus had found and ordered that the Indians be converted to Christianity. In 1509 King Ferdinand gave Christopher Columbus's son, Diego, the title of Governor of the Indies with the duty to organize an expedition to further explore Cuba. To lead the expedition, he chose a distinguished and wealthy soldier, Diego Velázquez de Cuellar.

In 1511 four ships from Spain arrived carrying 300 settlers under Diego Columbus and his wife, María de Toledo (grandniece of King Ferdinand). Also on board was tall, portly, blond Velázquez, the new governor of Cuba, and —very dashing in a great plumed hat and a short velvet cloak tufted with gold—his secretary, young Hernán Cortéz, who later set sail from Havana for Mexico to subdue the Aztecs.

Velázquez founded the first town at Baracoa in 1512, fol-

Christopher Columbus

lowed within the next few years by six other crude *villas*—Bayamo, Puerto Principe (today's Camagüey), San Cristóbal de la Habana, Sancti Spíritus, Santiago de Cuba, and Trinidad—whose mud streets would eventually be paved with cobblestones shipped from Europe as ballast aboard the armada of vessels now bound for the Americas.

A Sordid Beginning

The Spaniards were not on a holy mission. Medieval Spain was a greedy, cruel, uncultured civilization that foreshortened its cultural lessons with the sword and musket ball. The Spaniards had set out in quest of spices, gold, and rich civilizations. Thus the once-happy indigenous island cultures—considered by the Spaniards to be a backward, godless race—were subjected to the Spaniards' ruthless and mostly fruitless quest for silver and gold.

A priest named Bartolomé de las Casas accompanied Velázquez and recorded in his *History of the Indies*:

> *The Indians came to meete us, and to receive us with victuals, and delicate cheere . . . the Devill put himselfe into the Spaniards, to put them all to the edge of the sword in my presence, without any cause whatsoever, more than three thousand soules, which were set before us, men, women and children. I saw there so great cruelties, that never any man living either have or shall see the like.*

Slavery was forbidden by papal edict, but the ingenious Spaniards immediately found a way around the prohibition. Spain parceled its new conquests—Hispaniola and Cuba—among the conquistadores. The Indians were turned into *peones*—serfs. Each landowner was allotted from 40 to 200 Indian laborers under a system known as the *encomienda* (from the verb to entrust). Those Indians not marched off to work in mineral mines were rounded up and placed on plantations, where they were forced to labor under the guise of being taught Christianity. Since the Indians were supposed to be freed once converted, they were literally worked to death to extract the maximum labor.

Understandably, word of the brutal treatment—first applied on Hispaniola—spread throughout the Indies. Thus when Velázquez landed near Guantánamo Bay, he was surprised at the ferocity of the Indians' reception.

The Indian resistance was led by Hatuey, an Indian chieftain who had fought the Spanish on the island of Hispaniola and fled to Cuba after his people were defeated. Hatuey was the first in a long line of Cuban rebels—down to Fidel Castro—who learned how to use the mountains for guerrilla warfare. Eventually the Spaniards captured the heroic Indian chief and burned him at the stake on 2 February 1512. As the flames crackled around Hatuey's feet, Father Juan de Tesín offered to baptize him, promising the chieftain that he would then go to heaven. Hatuey asked the priest whether the Spaniards also went to heaven when they died. When Tesín replied, "Yes," Hatuey scornfully replied that he did not want to go where there were "such cruel and wicked people as the Christians." Thus the Spaniards, in their inimically cruel fashion, provided Cuba with its first martyr to independence.

The indigenous culture was quickly choked by the stern hand of Spanish rule—condemned so that Jehovah and Mammon might triumph over the local idols. The 16th century witnessed the extinction of a race. Those Taíno not put to the sword or worked to death fell victim to exotic diseases. Measles, smallpox, and tuberculosis also reaped the Taínos like a scythe, for the Indians had no natural resistance to European diseases. Within 100 years of Columbus's landfall, virtually the entire indigenous Cuban population had perished. (Indian blood, however, still courses through the veins of several thousand Cubans near Baracoa.)

The Key to the New World

The Spanish found little silver and gold in Cuba. They had greater luck in Mexico and Peru, whose indigenous cultures flaunted vast quantities of precious metals and jewels. Cuba was set to become a vital stopover and the hub of trade and shipping for Spanish galleons and traders carrying the wealth of the Americas back to Europe. Havana's sheltered harbor became the key to the New World. With the establishment of Havana as capital in 1607, a political structure began to take shape: the country was

SLAVE SOCIETY

The majority of slaves who were shipped to Cuba came from highly developed West African tribes such as the Fulani, Hausa, and Yoruba (they came mostly from Senegal, Gambia, and Guinea at first, and later from Nigeria and the Congo). Distinct ethnic groups were kept together (unlike in North America); as a result, their traditions and languages have been retained and passed down.

After being rounded up and herded to African ports, slaves were loaded onto ships where they were scientifically packed like sardines. Space meant profit. Chained together body-to-body in the airless, dark, rancid hold, they wallowed in their own excrement and vomit on the nightmare voyage across the Atlantic. Dozens died.

Once ashore, the Africans were herded into *barracoons* to be stored until sold to plantation owners or to work in grand mansions. To avoid the expense of advertising, the Havana *barracoons* were located near the governor's summer palace at the western end of Paseo (now Avenida Salvador Allende), where citizens out for a stroll could view the merchandise like zoo-goers. No attention was paid to family relationships. Parents, children, and siblings were torn asunder forever.

House slaves, while treated poorly, experienced better conditions than slaves in the country, where plantation life was exceedingly cruel. Even so, urban slaves were not spared harsh punishment, which was carried out in public by trained experts.

Plantation Life

Most slaves lived in *barracoons,* where they were laid out in rows. They had only mud floors and little ventilation. The huts swarmed with fleas and ticks. A hole in the ground served as a communal toilet.

The slaves were awakened at 4:30 a.m. By 6 a.m. they were marching in file to the fields, where they worked until sunset, with only brief pauses for rest. At 8:30 p.m., the silence bell was rung, and everyone had to go to sleep. Slaves stopped working when they reached 60 years of age.

Men were issued sturdy, coarse linen clothes, and the women blouses, skirts, and petticoats. The women also wore gold jewelry and earrings bought from Moorish tinkers who traveled between plantations. Chinese peddlers also made the rounds, selling sesame seed cakes and other items. Small private plots were the slaves' salvation. Here, they could grow sweet potatoes, gourds, beans, yucca, and peanuts and raise pigs and chickens, which they often sold to whites who came out from the villages. Some plantation owners even allowed slaves to visit nearby taverns, where they were able to trade, drink rum, and play wager games such as "the biscuit," which was played by putting "hard salt biscuits on a counter and striking them with your prick to see who could break them," recalls Estefan Montejo, who related his life as a slave and runaway *(cimarron)* in 1963 at the age of 105. His *Autobiography of a Runaway Slave* is the most comprehensive account of plantation life.

Sunday was rest day. The drums began about midday, and the slaves dressed in their Sunday outfits and danced. Slaves were not allowed to marry and raise families, although certain slave owners bred slaves like cattle for sale. Strong males were picked out to mate with the healthiest women, who were expected to produce healthy babies every year. Wet nurses looked after the *criollitos,* who sometimes never saw their parents again.

---

divided into municipalities, each with a town council. To supply the fleets, the forests were felled, making room for cattle and tobacco (and, later, sugar) for sale in Europe. Meats, hides, and precious hardwoods were shipped to Europe alongside gold and silver.

With the Indian population devastated, the Spanish turned to West Africa to supply its labor. The first slaves had arrived in 1513 from Hispaniola. By the turn of the century, an incredibly lucrative slave trade had developed. After being herded into ships, slaves were shackled below and endured the most deplorable conditions at sea. They arrived in Cuba diseased and half-starved, and after being sold, they were worked as beasts of burden, blasting and pummeling stone for gold, and cutting sugarcane beneath the searing sun.

Cuba grew rich. The wealth from sugar and slavery grew exponentially, as did that from the Spanish treasure fleets, which seemed to multiply in Havana Harbor year by year. Landowners, slave traders, merchants, and smugglers were in their heyday (the Spanish Crown heavily taxed exports,

Many white men took mistresses among the slave populations. Their children were usually granted their freedom. Havana's free mulattas soon found their way to Europe and North America, where their combination of African exoticism and grace and Spanish hauteur found favor with discerning males. Occasionally a black mistress would be particularly favored and treated well, although there were limits to their upward mobility. (Read Cirilo Villaverde's marvelous and tragic novel *Cecilia Valdés,* whose namesake heroine's passion to be accepted in Havana's upper social echelons ends in a violent denouement).

Rebellions and Runaways

Understandably, rebellion was always around the corner. Slaves were considered dangerous barbarians. (Victor Patricio Landaluze's representations of 19th-century life, which hang in Havana's Palacio de Bellas Artes, vividly portray how Africans were regarded at the time, as do the series of 19th-century cigarette

labels on display in Havana's National Library.) The first slave revolt occurred in 1532 in Oriente. A few years later, Havana was sacked by slaves in the wake of an attack by French pirates. Many slaves chose suicide (particularly the Lucumí, for they believed that after death they would return to Africa). Other slaves chose to run away and flee to the mountains. While runaways on other islands developed fiercely independent communities, such as the Maroons of Jamaica, Cuba's *cimarrones* tended to be independent; runaways often captured and sold other runaways.

To track down runaways, the authorities used posses of *ranchadores,* cruel white peasants with specially trained hunting dogs. When a runaway was caught, it was standard procedure to cut off one ear as a warning to other slaves. However, slaves had the legal right to buy their and their relatives' freedom. Once free, they could even own and sell property. Most free slaves set up small businesses or hired themselves out as domestic staff.

which fostered smuggling on a remarkable scale). The Spaniards tried to regulate the slave trade, but it was so profitable that it resisted control. Daring foreigners—such as John Hawkins and his nephew Francis Drake—cut in on the trade.

The Period of Piracy

Lured by Cuba's vast wealth, pirates followed in the Spaniards' wake. In 1521 a ship laden with Aztec treasure was captured by the Florentine pirate Ciovanni da Verrazano; the next year, corsair Jean Florin seized a ship full of

gold. As early as 1526, a royal decree declared that ships had to travel in convoy to Spain (the crown had a vested interest; it received one-fifth of the treasure). En route, they gathered in Havana Harbor. In 1537, Havana itself was raided. One year later, Jacques de Sores sacked the capital and demanded a ransom. When a bid by the Spaniards to retake the city faltered, de Sores put men, women, and children to the sword before razing the city. French corsairs preyed mercilessly on smaller cities and plantations across the island.

Great fortresses arose to protect the cities, but to no avail. As daring leaders emerged among the pirates, they organized into powerful groups that were soon encouraged and eventually licensed by the governments of France, Holland, and England to prey upon Spanish shipping and ports as a prelude to challenging Spanish dominance in the Americas. In 1587 King Philip of Spain determined to end the growing sea power of England and amassed a great armada to invade her. Francis Drake, Hastings, and Sir Walter Raleigh assembled a fleet and destroyed the armada, breaking the power of Spain in the Old World.

No city was safe; Cuba was so narrow that pirates could easily ransack towns in the center of the island. There were hundreds of raids every year, severely disrupting the economy. Spain was impotent. In 1662, Henry Morgan, a stocky Welshman and leader of the Buccaneers (a motley yet disciplined group of pirates that would later operate under British license from Port Royal in Jamaica) ransacked Havana, pilfered the cathedral bells, and left with a taunt that the Spanish weren't equal to the stone walls that Spain had built: "I could have defended Morro Castle with a dog and a gun."

Only when the pirate attacks began to ease up towards the end of the 17th century, were the Spanish colonizers able to settle down to raise cattle, tobacco, and sugar.

The Spanish Crown treated Cuba as a cash cow to milk dry as it pleased. For example, it had monopolized tobacco trading by 1717. The restriction so affected farmers' incomes that the *vegueros,* (tobacco growers) marched on Havana and deposed the administrators, and burned the fields of growers who cooperated with the Crown. The rebellion, the first against Spain, was brutally crushed. In 1740, Spain created the Real Compañia, with a monopoly on all trade between Cuba and Spain (it bought Cuban products cheaply and sold necessities from Europe at inflated prices).

England Takes Over

While Spain repressed its colony, it had entered a war against a more enlightened nation: England. In 1762, an armada of 200 English warships landed 20,000 troops at Cojímar outside Havana, which fell to the English on 12 August

after a 44-day siege. The English immediately opened the island up to free trade (including unrestricted trade in slaves). Foreign merchant vessels flocked, and Cuba witnessed surging prosperity as a trading frenzy ensued.

Alas, within a year the British traded Cuba for Florida (sugar planters in Jamaica had pressured England to cede back to Spain what would otherwise become a formidable rival for the English sugar market). Meanwhile, Spain had acquired a more enlightened king, Charles III, who adopted a free-trade policy. The boom continued, encouraged a decade later when the newly independent United States began trading directly with Cuba. The North Americans' collective sweet tooth fostered the rapid expansion of sugar plantations in Cuba.

KING SUGAR RULES

Vast fortunes were being made in sugar—and therefore also in slaves. Wealthy Cuban and U.S. slave merchants funded planting of new lands in sugar by granting loans for capital improvements, all meant to foster an increasing need for slaves. Land planted in sugar multiplied more than tenfold by the turn of the 18th century. For the first time, sugar outstripped tobacco in importance. The massive expansion was significantly boosted with the Haitian rebellion in 1791 and subsequent demise of the sugar industry on Saint Domingue (Haiti), at that time the dominant sugar producer in the world. About 30,000 French planters washed up in Cuba, bringing their superior knowledge of sugar production.

Cuba's slave population had been slow to develop compared to that of neighboring Caribbean islands. The short tenure of British rule sent the slave trade soaring. British slave traders established themselves in Havana and remained thereafter to profit in the booming trade alongside Habaneros. Between 1791 and 1810, over 100,000 slaves arrived (countless more undocumented slaves were brought in illegally). By 1840 slaves constituted 45% of the population.

In 1817 Spain signed a treaty with England to abolish the slave trade. However, Cuban officials "from the governor down to the harbormaster" were so enriched by bribes from slave traders that the industry continued unabated for most of the century (legislation passed by Spain in 1789 to improve the harsh treatment of slaves also went entirely unheeded). The British government sent emissaries to ensure compliance, but they "might as well have tried to catch mercury in a sieve." By 1835, when the British and Spanish governments agreed by treaty that any ship carrying slaves could be seized, as many as 2,000 vessels a year were arriving in Havana with slaves (to outwit the British navy, the slave traders merely adopted foreign flags; others simply unshackled the incriminating evidence and tossed it overboard). Only in 1888 was slavery in Cuba abolished, and then only because of a crisis in the sugar industry.

The unrivaled prosperity encouraged development of the island. By 1760 Havana was already larger than New York or Boston. The first University of Havana had been established in 1728, the first newspaper in 1763, and the postal service in 1764. Cuba's citizenry were growing vastly wealthy on trade with North America, with the difference that now much of the prosperity flowed back to Cuba, changing the face of Havana, Santiago de Cuba, and other cities. Monuments and parks were erected, along with public libraries and theaters. Streets were paved, and beautiful colonial homes were erected. In 1790 street lamps went up in the city.

THE REVOLUTIONARY ERA

Spain, however, continued to rule Cuba badly. Spain's colonial policy, applied throughout its empire, was based on exploitation, with power centralized in Madrid, and politics practiced only for the spoils of office and to the benefit solely of *peninsulares*—native-born Spaniards. "The Spanish officials taxed thrift right out of the island; they took industry by the neck and throttled it," thought Frederic Remington on his visit in 1899. Spain's monopoly laws encouraged the migration to Cuba of a kind of Spanish carpetbagger. Cuban-born *criollos* resented the corrupt *peninsulares* who denied them self-determination. No Cuban could occupy a public post, set up an industry or business, bring legal action against a Spaniard, or travel without military permission. The *criollos* increasingly felt *Cuban,* not Spanish

(most carried some black blood in their veins). By the early 19th century, a new generation of young Cuban intellectuals and patriots began to make their voices heard.

The American Revolution had a profound affect on the incipient desire for freedom among the *criollos.* Nationalist feelings were fueled, aided by Thomas Paine's *Rights of Man,* which was then being surreptitiously passed around the island. The French Revolution added to the liberation zeal, as did the slave revolution on neighboring Saint Domingue.

Following the Napoleonic Wars in Europe, Spain's new royal family—the Bourbons—took over a weakened country. Spain's New World territories were wracked by wars of independence led by Simón Bolívar. By 1835 only Cuba and Puerto Rico had not gained independence from Spain. The Spanish initiated brutally repressive policies throughout the island to quell all rumblings of self-rule.

In 1843, Miguel Tacón became governor. The Spanish noble ordered the streets cleaned, drove out criminals, and whipped the idle and unemployed into action. He built fountains and a great theater, paved the streets, and began the first Cuban railway. But Tacón would brook no foolish sentiments for independence. He suppressed patriotic sentiment and exiled leading nationalists. Many *criollos* were shot for treason. Others suspected of self-rule sentiments were lashed to *La Escalera* (the staircase or the ladder) and whipped, often until they died.

Spain clung to its colony with despairing strength and the support of wealthy *criollos* (concentrated in Western Cuba), who feared that abolitionist sentiments in Europe would lead to abolition of slavery in Cuba. They looked to the United States, where slavery was thriving, for support. In 1850 they were answered by a Venezuelan, Narciso López, who found financial support in the United States for an invasion of Cuba. He arrived with a ragtag force of 500 mercenaries from Kentucky and Mississippi and landed near today's Varadero in 1850. Instead of supporting the invaders, the citizenry notified the Spanish officials. López had to flee ignominiously back to the US. He returned the following year and put up an equally pathetic showing. Among those executed by the Spanish was the nephew of the governor of Kentucky. Not for the last time, the North American press whipped up public sentiment for an invasion of Cuba.

Uncle Sam Stirs

Annexation sentiment in the United States had been spawned by the Louisiana Purchase of 1803. The Mississippi River became the main artery of trade and Cuba's position at the mouth of the Gulf of Mexico took on added strategic importance.

Thus in 1809 Thomas Jefferson wrote, "I candidly confess that I have ever looked upon Cuba as the most interesting addition that can be made to our system of States, the possession of which would give us control over the Gulf of Mexico and the countries and isthmus bordering upon it." Jefferson had attempted to purchase Cuba from Spain in 1808 (he was the first of four presidents

to do so). John Quincy Adams thought Cuba a fruit that would ripen until it fell into the lap of the United States. And President James Monroe, writing to Jefferson in 1823, stated, "I have already concurred with you in the sentiment, that too much importance could not be attached to the Island, and that we ought if possible, to incorporate it into our union, availing ourselves of the most favorable moment for it, hoping also it might be done, without a rupture with Spain or any other power."

Sentiment didn't come into it. By 1848, 40% of Cuba's sugar was sold to the U.S. market; manufactures began flowing the other way. Yankees yearned for expanded trade. Thus President James Polk (1845-49) offered Spain US$100 million for Cuba. President Franklin Pierce (1853-57) upped the ante to US$130 million. His successor, James Buchanan, tried twice to

JOSÉ MARTÍ

He is the most revered figure in Cuban history. His name has been appropriated by the Castro government *and* the fiercely anti-Communist exiles in Florida. He is José Martí, the canonical avatar of Cuba's independence spirit. There is not a single village or town in Cuba that does not have a street, a square, or a major building named in his honor.

Martí was born in 1853 in a small house on Calle Paula in Habana Vieja. Martí came from peninsular stock. His father was from Valencia, Spain; his mother was from the Canary Islands. He spent much of his youth in Spain before his parents returned to Cuba. When the War of Independence erupted in 1868, Martí was 15 years old. Already he sympathized with "the cause."

At the age of 16, he published his first newspaper, *La Patria Libre.* He also wrote a letter denouncing a school friend for attending a pro-Spanish rally. The letter was judged to be treasonous, and Martí was sentenced to six years' imprisonment, including six months hard labor at the San Lázaro stone quarry in Havana. In 1871 he was exiled to Spain, where he earned a law degree and gravitated to the revolutionary circles then active in Madrid.

In 1878, as part of a general amnesty, He was allowed to return but was then again deported. He traveled through France and, in 1881, to the U.S., where he settled for the next 14 years with his wife and son, working as a reporter in New York.

The Pen and the Sword

Dressed in his trademark black suit and bow tie, with his thick moustache waxed into pointy tips, Martí devoted more and more of his time to winning independence for Cuba. He wrote poetry heralding the liberation of his homeland during a "time of fervent repose," the years following the Ten Years' War. His writing wedded the rhetoric of nationalism to calls for social justice.

Prophetically, Martí's writings are full of invocations to death. It was he who coined the phrase *La Victoria o el Sepulcro* (Victory or the Tomb), which Fidel Castro has turned into a call for *Patria o Muerte* (Patriotism or death), and more recently, *"Socialismo o Muerte."*

Martí is revered as much for his poetry, which helped define the school of modern Latin American poetry. His voluminous writings are littered with astute critiques of U.S. culture and politics. He despised the expansionist nature of the U.S., arguing that U.S. ambitions toward Cuba were as dangerous as the rule of Spain. "It is my duty. . . to prevent, through the independence of Cuba, the U.S. from spreading over the West Indies and falling with added weight upon other lands of Our America. All I have done up to now and shall do hereafter is to that end."

Theory into Action

In 1892 Martí met with leading Cuban exiles and

purchase Cuba for the same price. But Spain wasn't selling.

If the United States couldn't have Cuba, it preferred to see it in the feeble but safe hands of Spain rather than in the hands of more powerful France or England. And an independent Cuba may possibly have been ruled by blacks—a potential stimulus of discontent for the southern slave states. Overnight the American Civil War changed the equation. With slavery in the U.S. ended, it became impossible for Spain to keep the lid on Cuba. In 1868 the pot boiled over.

The Wars for Independence

The planters of western Cuba were determined to forestall the abolition of slavery in Cuba. But the relatively poor, backward, and nationalistic eastern planters had little to lose. It was expensive to maintain a slave population that was largely redundant for half the year. Their estates were going bankrupt and falling into the hands of rapacious Havana moneylenders. On 10 October 1868, a lawyer, poet, and planter named Carlos Manuel de Céspedes freed the slaves on his plantation at La Demajagua, near Manzanillo, in Oriente. Fellow planters rushed to join him by freeing their slaves, and as the dawn broke over the dewy plantations of Oriente, they raised the *Grito de Yara* (Shout of Yara), the cry of liberty heard throughout the island. Within a week, 1,500 men had flocked to his calling. (Céspedes was eventually elected president; after later being deposed in an internal feud, he was killed in battle in 1873). The Spanish called them the *Mambí,* a Congolese word meaning "despicable." The Mambí quickly captured the town of Bayamo. When Spanish forces arrived to retake the town, the rebels razed it. For the next 10

presented his "Fundamentals and Secret Guidelines of the Cuban Revolutionary Party," outlining the goals of the nationalists: independence for Cuba, equality of all Cubans, and establishment of democratic processes. That year, Martí began publishing *Patria.* Through dint of passion and idealism, Martí had established himself as the acknowledged political leader. He melded the various exile factions together, formulated a common program, and managed to integrate the cause of Cuban exile workers into the crusade (they contributed 10% of their earnings to his cause). He founded a revolutionary center, Cuba Libre (Free Cuba), and La Liga de Instrucción, which trained revolutionary fighters.

In 1895 Martí presented the *Manifesto de Montecristi,* outlining the policy for the war of independence that was to be initiated later that year. Martí was named major general of the Armies of Liberation, while General Máximo Gómez was named as supreme commander of the revolutionary forces.

On 11 April 1895, Martí, Gómez and four followers landed at Playitas, in a remote part of eastern Cuba. Moving secretly through the mountains, they gathered supporters and finally linked up with Antonio Maceo and his army of 6,000. The first skirmish with the Spanish occurred at Dos Rios on 19 May 1895. Martí was the first casualty. He had determined on martyrdom and committed sacrificial suicide by riding headlong into the enemy line. Thus Martí brought the republic to birth, says Guillermo Cabrera Infante, "carrying a cadaver around its neck."

tomb of José Martí, Santa Ifigenia Cemetery, Santiago

years Cuba would be roiled by the bitter First War of Independence in which white and black *criollo* fought side by side against 100,000 troops shipped from Spain.

Guerrilla warfare seized the island. Led by two brilliant generals—one a white, General Maximo Gómez, and the other a mulatto, Antonio Macéo—the rebels liberated much of the island and seemed on the verge of victory. However, the movement collapsed, and in 1878 the forces signed the Pact of Zanjón. The rebels were given a general amnesty (slaves who had fought with the rebels were also given freedom) in exchange for surrender. The long, bloody war claimed the lives of 250,000 Cubans and 80,000 Spaniards. At least 100,000 Cubans were forced to flee; their lands were expropriated and given to loyalists. Among those arrested was a teenager named José Martí y Pérez. After a brief imprisonment, the young, gifted orator, intellectual, poet, and political leader was exiled to Spain.

Although U.S. President Ulysses Grant (1868-77) was sympathetic to the rebels' cause and shared his predecessors' enthusiasm for seeing Cuba in U.S. hands, he gave the Cuban patriots no assistance, thereby sowing early seeds of anti-American discontent. (To ensure that Spain would be bound by international law to protect U.S. assets, the U.S. government had declined to recognize a state of belligerency.)

The Cuban economy had been devastated by the war, and huge tracts of land lay abandoned. Amid the chaos, North American investors stepped in and bought up the ravaged sugar plantations and many of the sugar mills at ludicrously low rates (by some accounts, as much as US$100 million was invested in the wake of the war). Meanwhile, the Spanish reverted to the same old recipe of tyranny. Independence, the one dignified solution refused the *criollos,* was the cause which united the whole revolutionary population of Cuba.

Martí's Martyrdom

José Martí had been born in Havana in 1853. As a lad of 15 he had startled his mother, reportedly, with the words "To many generations of slaves must succeed one generation of martyrs." Somewhere in his boyish brain he tucked away that foreboding notion. Following his exile to Spain, the journalist and political thinker traveled to the

United States, where he settled and through his writings and indefatigable spirit became the acknowledged "apostle" and "intellectual author" of independence. In 1892 he formed the Cuban Revolutionary Party, and from New York, Tampa, Florida, and elsewhere he rallied support for his *compañeros* in Cuba.

Though ill and gaunt, Martí was determined to return to Cuba undercover, wearing his trademark black frock coat and tie. In 1895 Martí joined General Maximo Gómez in the Dominican Republic. Together they sailed to Cuba. On 11 April, they pulled away from their steamer and rowed ashore, landing amid a storm at a village called Playitas at the eastern end of the island. Martí kissed the Cuban soil he had not seen for 16 years. From here, they linked up with the great Cuban general Antonio Macéo and his ragtag army.

Barely one month after returning from exile, Martí martyred himself on 19 May 1895, at the age of 42. His motto was, "To die for the fatherland is to live."

Martí's death left Cuba without a spiritual leader. But the Cubans were determined to seize their freedom. Generals Gómez and Macéo led an army of 60,000 the full length of Cuba, smashing Spanish forces en route through guerrilla tactics and occasional face-to-face battles. Macéo's brilliant tactics earned worldwide acclaim until he was finally killed in battle in December 1896 (his father and 10 of his brothers also died for the cause).

After Macéo's death, the struggle degenerated into a destructive guerrilla war of attrition. In a desperate bid to forestall independence, the Spanish governor, Valeriano Weyler—a ruthless general known as The Butcher—began a rural pacification program in which virtually the entire *campesino* population was either slaughtered or herded into concentration camps called protectorates, where thousands starved to death (the vicious campaign, which claimed the lives of 10% of Cuba's population, was called the *reconcentración* and involved the use of "volunteers," vicious guerrilla mercenaries from Spain). Weyler erected barbed wire fences, entrenchments, and small forts across the entire width of Cuba. In turn, the rebels torched the sugarcane fields and kept them burning until the conflagration licked the suburbs of Havana.

In 1896 Weyler banned exports from Cuba in an attempt to ruin supporters of the Mambí. When, the following year, a more liberal administration took over in Spain, Washington finally forced the Spanish government to recall Weyler.

THE SPANISH-CUBAN-AMERICAN WAR

The ideal of *Cuba libre!* (Free Cuba!) had genuine support among the U.S. populace, which saw echoes of their own struggle for independence a century earlier. United States sugar and business interests also favored intervention.

The public hungered for information about the war, feeding sales of newspapers throughout North America. The *New York World* and *New York Journal* (owned by, respectively, Joseph Pulitzer and William Randolph Hearst) started a race with each other to see which newspaper could first reach one million subscribers. The press took on the job of inflaming Yankee patriotism and fanning war fever based on fabrication and lies. While Hearst's hacks made up stories from Cuba, the magnate himself worked behind the scenes to orchestrate dramatic events. He sent the artist Frederic Remington to Cuba in anticipation of the U.S.'s entering the war. At one point Remington wired Hearst: "There will be no war. I wish to return." Hearst hastily replied: "Please remain. You furnish the pictures and I'll furnish the war."

Remember the *Maine!*

McKinley desperately wanted to avoid a shooting war with Spain but was powerless to do so. Responding to public pressure, he sent a warship—the USS *Maine*—to Havana to protect U.S. citizens living there. On 5 February 1898, the ship mysteriously exploded and sank in Havana Harbor, killing 258 people. Evidence suggests this was an accident, but Hearst had his coup and rushed the news out in great red headlines and beating the *World* to the one million mark. He blamed the Spanish, and so did the public. His *New York Journal* coined the phrase "Remember the Maine, to hell with Spain." The paper belabored the jingoistic phrase. The reaction in the U.S. was furious. The public, egged on by Hearst and Pulitzer, was convinced that might was on the

side of right. Theodore Roosevelt, then Assistant Secretary of the Navy, also fanned the flames, seeing the venture as "good for the navy."

On 25 April 1898, Congress declared war against Spain (U.S. forces also invaded Guam, Puerto Rico, and the Philippines, which they captured in one day). The managing editor of the *World* boasted, "Between the *World* and the *Journal,* we barked President McKinley into a war that was none of our business."

The Cavalry Arrives

The U.S. government claimed it was fighting to liberate Cuba. The Cuban general, Máximo Gómez, did not want U.S. troops, however. He wanted arms and ammunition. The revolutionaries were on the verge of victory and would have undoubtedly won their independence before the close of the century. To placate the Mambí, the Teller Amendment was added to the war declaration. This smokescreen stated that U.S. intentions were to restore peace—"That the United States hereby disclaims any disposition or intention to exercise sovereignty, jurisdiction or control over said island except for pacification thereof, and asserts its determination, when that is accomplished, to leave the government and control of the island to its people."

Cuban freedom fighters soon found themselves forced into the back seat and mostly restricted to manual labor away from the brief fighting, which was restricted to Oriente. The Yanks thought the Cubans a dirty and decrepit lot—most of whom weren't even *white!* "A collection of real tropic savages," reported Hearst journalist Stephen Crane. Where the Mambí did fight, heroically, their part was dismissed, as at the pivotal engagement at San Juan Hill in Santiago de Cuba, where, on 1 July 1898, a cavalry charge ostensibly led by Theodore Roosevelt (who had resigned from government service to volunteer but apparently arrived at San Juan horseless after the action was over) supposedly sealed the war. In a decisive naval battle on 3 July, the U.S. Navy decimated the Spanish fleet as it attempted to escape Santiago Harbor. On 17 July, Spain surrendered. The Spanish flag was lowered and the Stars and Stripes raised, ending one of the most foolishly run empires in the world. The Secretary of State called it "a splendid little war."

Victors always write the history books. Virtually no credit was given to the years of heroic fighting on the part of the valiant Cubans. The U.S. military leaders refused to invite the Mambí to the victory ceremony and parade; the Cuban troops were even ordered to surrender their weapons. Fidel Castro and the Cuban people have never forgotten the slight.

Cuba ended the century as it had begun—under foreign rule.

Uncle Sam Takes Over

Washington could have annexed Cuba but chose not to. Instead, it "granted" Cuba "independence"—at the end of a short leash. The U.S. military occupation formally began on 1 January 1899, when 15 infantry regiments, one of engineers, and four of artillery arrived to "pacify" Cuba. They would remain for four years. Washington dictated the peace terms embodied in the Treaty of Paris, signed on 11 April 1899. Even the Cuban Constitution was written by Washington in 1901, ushering in a period known as the Pseudo-Republic. Rubbing salt in the wound of Cuban sensibilities was a clause called the Platt Amendment, named for Senator Orville H. Platt of Connecticut but written by Elihu Root, Secretary of War. Through it, Uncle Sam acquired the Guantánamo naval base and the right to intervene whenever the U.S. deemed

it necessary. Although the professed aim was to ensure law and order and stability, the U.S. served to protect its own economic interests and, perhaps unintentionally, the vested interests of the ruling Cuban elite. Even the governor-general, U.S. Army General Leonard Wood, wrote President McKinley that "there is, of course, little or no independence left in Cuba under the Platt Amendment."

On Ascencion Day (20 May) 1902, the Stars and Stripes was lowered and the lone-star flag of Cuba, designed by Narciso López, rose into the sunny sky. Havana broke out in a three-day spree of rejoicing. "It's not the republic we dreamed of," said Máximo Gómez.

THE ERA OF "INDEPENDENCE"

The pseudo-republic was an era of Yankee colonization and domestic acquiescence. Economically, North America held sway over the lives of Cubans through its control of the sugar plantations. Politically, Washington called the shots—and maintained a revolving door to the increasingly corrupt Cuban presidency. U.S. officers who spoke no Spanish, had never lived in a hot country, and had no notion of Spanish or Cuban history and ideals found themselves in charge of a tired, starving people and a devas-

destruction of the USS Maine in Havana Harbor

tated land wrecked by war. As Hugh Thomas suggests: "This continuous U.S. presence, benevolent though it often set out to be, paternalistic though it usually was in practice, fatally delayed the achievement of political stability in Cuba."

Under General Wood, the U.S. authorities set up schools, started a postal system, established a judiciary and civil service, organized finances, and managed within a few years to eradicate yellow fever in a campaign based on the discovery by a Cuban physician, Dr. Carlos Finlay, that the fever was spread by mosquitoes. "It would have been a poor boon to Cuba to drive the Spaniards out and leave her to care for herself, with two-thirds of her people unable to read and write, and wholly ignorant of the art of self-government," stated Elihu Root.

The United States installed its first president—Tomás Estrada Palma (the first in a long line of U.S. puppets)—who received his salary, as well as instructions, directly from Washington. Palma, though re-elected in 1905, was too honest and weak to hold greedy politicians in check.

Washington's intentions were mostly honorable: it firmly wanted to establish a stable, democratic government in the U.S. tradition. Unfortunately, Uncle Sam chose an Anglo-Saxon system unsuited to the Cuban mentality: the centuries of corruption and graft could not be eradicated overnight. (As Machiavelli said, "A corrupted people, having acquired liberty, can maintain it only with the greatest difficulty." After independence, politics "became a cynical game among dishonest men.") Political office was not sought in order to serve the newly independent country but rather to get rich—an idea heartily endorsed by powerful U.S. business interests, who also profited (the United Fruit Company ran its sugar domains on a virtual apartheid basis, and black field hands usually lived in poverty). The U.S. government was constantly influenced to support this or that Cuban who had given, or would give, opportunities to U.S. investors or had borrowed from North American banks. Year by year Cuba sank more deeply into its old corrupt ways.

Each Cuban president forged new frauds of their own, handed out sinecures (which the Cubans called *botellas*—milk bottles given to babies) to cronies. Through the successive ad-

landing of U.S. troops in Cuba

JOSEPH BOGGS BEALE

ministrations of José Miguel Gómez (1909-13), General Mario Menocal (1913-21), and Alfredo Zayas (1921-25), Cuban politics sank deeper into iniquity.

When U.S. economic interests were threatened, Uncle Sam sent in troops ("dollar diplomacy" it was called, a phrase coined by President Howard Taft). The U.S. landed Marines In 1906 to "restore order" when an armed rebellion attempted to topple the re-elected Estrada regime; in 1912, when black rage exploded into open revolt; and again in 1917, when workers called a general strike (that time, the troops remained until 1923). Dollar diplomacy was blind to the corruption, state violence, and poverty plaguing the country.

The sordid system would last six decades, until a bearded young rebel came down from the mountains to oust the *ancien regime*.

A U.S. Colony

The opening years of the Cuban republic were a time of great opportunity for everyone except Cubans—whose economy was in shambles. Agriculture was devastated; industry had been destroyed. Everything was up for grabs. Cuba witnessed a great influx of capital as U.S. companies invested in every major industry—tobacco, railroads, utilities, mining, and, above all, sugar. Several thousand U.S. citizens settled, bringing their North American style and sensibilities to the city. In short order, every major industry—tobacco, railroads, utilities, mining, and, above all, sugar—were U.S. owned (the Du Pont estate would grow so enormous it had its own private customs officer). U.S. interests in the sugar industry increased almost overnight from 15% to 75%. Hectares of precious forests and agriculture lands were cut down or plowed up to plant sugar. Up and down the island tall, brilliant green cane dusted by delicate white blossoms shimmered under the blazing tropical sun. Often land was acquired through legal suits in corrupt or prejudiced courts that robbed tens of thousands of Cuban small landholders of their property. Cuba had become a giant Monopoly board controlled by Uncle Sam.

Thanks to billions of dollars of investment, the Cuban economy bounced back with vigor, though the mass of rural families kept on struggling to survive. Although the sugar workers had no other way of earning a living, the sugar companies paid them wages for only half a year. Employment lasted only as long as the dry season—usually until May, when the rains and the downtime began. With no money, a decreased diet, and depressed life, the workers and their families suffered miserably for half the year.

Profits from sugar were so great that Cubans sold out their other properties and poured their money into the industry, deriving dividends from sweetening the desserts of the world. In the cities the rapidly expanding middle classes built fine houses, and grand edifices went up all over Cuba. The peak of the sugar boom—the "dance of the millions"—lasted from 1915 to 1920, when the price of sugar climbed to US$0.22.5 a pound. Then came the crash. By 1921, the price had plummeted to US$0.03.625 a pound. In 1924, Cuba produced more than 4.5 million tons of sugar. The next year it produced a million tons more—but the sugar sold for less than US$0.01 a pound.

Sugar money paid for massive civic constructions and public utilities and for the plush mansions in beaux arts and art deco style then blossoming in the rapidly expanding suburbs of Havana. "Havana's physical reaching out from cramped quarters to openness symbolized the optimism of a generation," wrote Rosalie Schwartz. The capital city—jewel of the Caribbean—wore a new luster, and "a healthful and pleasurable city unfolded before the tourists' eyes." Cuba of the 1920s was far and away the richest tropical country anywhere, with a per capita income equivalent to that of Ireland, two-thirds that of Britain, and half that of the U.S. Havana was the Pearl of the Antilles and soon vied with Florida for the title of America's Riviera. As Prohibition and a wave of morality swept through the United States, Yankees flocked to Havana where those who chose could wallow up to their noses in cocaine and sex.

The Machado Epoch

In 1924, President Alfredo Zayas, having made his millions, declined to run for re-election. General Gerardo Machado y Morales, who had cut his teeth as a cattle rustler, stepped into the breach. Machado acted on his promises to construct schools, highways, and a health care system, and initiated the most ambitious development plan for Havana since that of colonial governor Miguel Tacón in the 1830s. However, he was also a uniquely corrupt man susceptible to *la mordida* (literally, "the bite"—bribes), which undercut law and order. Machado's promise to keep his fingers out of the till seemed plausible: he had lost three fingers while working as a butcher. In 1928 Machado manipulated a phony election. Although he won, the move triggered a wave of opposition. Machado became a tropical Mussolini, supported by a personal police force of 15,000. His politics were to make himself rich and to protect U.S. investments. His method was to assassinate anyone who opposed his government. Thousands of Cubans were imprisoned, tortured, and executed. Cuba was mired in deep unrest and violence.

When the Great Depression hit, Cuba's one-crop economy was dealt a deathblow, bringing misery throughout the country. Meanwhile, the U.S. had raised its import tariffs on sugar, exacerbating Cuba's plight. The Cuban economy collapsed, and the nation soon disintegrated into mayhem and violent madness. Havana and other cities were swept by random bombings and assassinations. When a radio incorrectly announced that Machado had resigned, thousands of people poured into the streets to celebrate. Machado's henchmen taught them the truth with bullets.

Machado responded to a growing number of hunger marches, strikes, and antigovernment

GENERAL FULGENCIO BATISTA

Fulgencio (he was christened Rubén) Batista y Zaldívar was born out of wedlock and into dire poverty in 1901 at Veguitas, near Banes, a backyard region of Oriente. His father was a sugar field worker (and the son of an indentured Chinese laborer); his mother was black. He enlisted and became a professional soldier and, after learning stenography, was promoted to sergeant.

Batista, an insecure "fiery little bantam of a fella," rose to the top during a *golpe* in 1933, when Fidel Castro was only seven. He became chief of staff of the army and as such, took over the government, beginning a 25-year tenure as the most powerful man in Cuba. Batista, who ruled during a period of prosperity, was at first popular with the masses, perhaps also because of his lowly origins—he was blackballed by the social elite because he was mulatto (members of the Havana Yacht Club turned off the lights when he showed up; the Havana Biltmore, on the other hand, admitted Batista

General Batista

and enjoyed the valuable real estate it received in return). However, he gradually became despised by the masses because his government was immensely corrupt.

In 1944 he retired to Florida, having accumulated US$20 million during his 11-year tenure. Batista missed the limelight, however, and, after working out a deal with the Mafia, returned to Cuba, venal and gluttonous. In March 1952 he pulled off his second coup. Batista oversaw an economic boom for Cuba that included major civic works for Havana. But the general had come back to power to commit grand larceny hand in hand with the Mob. Corruption and terror on the streets rose to new heights under his tenure.

At midnight on New Year's Eve 1958, Batista fled with a group of followers. He eventually settled in Spain, where he lived a princely life until his death in 1973. The poor cane-cutter died as one of the world's wealthiest men—he had milked Cuba of almost US$300 million.

demonstrations with greater repression. The dictator even closed schools and universities and forbade public gatherings.

Machado remained in power only because he was supported by U.S. financial interests. President Calvin Coolidge, of course, thought that "under Machado, Cuba is a sovereign state. . . her people are free, independent, in peace, and enjoying the advantages of democracy." Finally, in the summer of 1933, a general strike brought the whole country to a halt. On 11 August, Machado fled the country—carrying a suitcase full of gold.

Batista Days

Diplomat Sumner Welles, sent to Cuba earlier that summer by Franklin D. Roosevelt, appointed Carlos Manuel de Céspedes (son of the hero of the Ten Years War) as Cuba's provisional president. Within the month he had been overthrown by an amalgam of students (a potent political force) and army officers, including a pivotal 32-year old sergeant named Fulgencio Batista y Zaldivar. Batista was at Camp Columbia in Havana on 4 September, the day he led other noncommissioned officers in a *golpe* (coup) called the Sergeant's Revolt, which ousted the senior officers. They handed power to a five-man civilian commission that named a leftist university professor, Dr. Ramón Grau San Martín, president.

Grau's slogan was "Cuba for Cuba." When Grau unilaterally revoked the Platt Amendment, the U.S. government refused to recognize him. Grau lasted only four months. His proposed worker's compensation law and regulation of utility rates were far too reformist for Washington. Batista, self-promoted to colonel and chief of the army, was under no illusions as to the intentions of the United States, which sent 30 warships to Cuba as a warning. On 14 January 1931 Batista ousted Grau and seized the reins of power. The upstart sergeant wielded control behind a veil of stooge presidents whom he selected and deposed in quick succession. Batista would have center stage until driven from power in 1959.

Impressed by Batista's fealty to Washington, in 1934 the U.S. agreed to annul the Platt Amendment—with the exception of the clause regarding the Guantánamo naval base. In exchange, the U.S. established the Reciprocal Trade Agreement, which gave the U.S. total control over Cuba's market. Following promulgation of a new and progressive constitution in 1940, Batista ran for the presidency himself on a progressive platform. Cuban voters gave him a four-year term (1940-44) in what was perhaps the nation's first clean election.

Despite his personal ambitions, Batista displayed relative benevolence and good sense. He maintained enlightened attitudes on elections, civil liberties, public welfare, and workers' rights, enacted progressive social reforms and a new, liberal constitution. The Cuban Communist Party, founded in 1925, had grown popular among trade unions and played a significant part in the resistance against Machado, who had outlawed the *Partido Comunista de Cuba*. For pragmatic reasons, Batista legalized it, and two leading Communists—Juan Marinello and Carlos Rafael Rodríguez—became ministers in his 1940-44 government. (The influence of the Communist Party ebbed and flowed during the next two decades; intriguingly, it opposed Fidel Castro's revolution, and Castro was never associated with the party until he usurped it following the Revolution.) Batista, however, sold the country short by agreeing to sell the entire 1941 sugar crop to the U.S. for US$0.03 a pound

In the 1944 election, Batista's hand-picked successor lost to Ramón Grau San Martín, the president Batista had deposed. Batista retired to Florida, leaving his country in the hands of men who permitted their administrations to again sink into chaos and corruption. Grau (1944-48) and his democratically elected successor, Carlos Prío Socarrás (1948-52), betrayed the public trust, allowing their administrations to sink into chaos and corruption. Street demonstrations, assassinations, and bombings were once again daily events on the streets of Havana. Two rival gangster groups—the Socialist Revolutionary Movement (MSR) and Insurrectional Revolutionary Union (UIR)—ruled the streets (there were 64 political assassinations during Grau's 1944-48 administration). Street demonstrations erupted, organized on behalf of the opposition *Ortodoxo* party led by Senator "Eddy" Chibás, revered for his rare honesty. His public suicide on 5 August 1951 brought together a broad spectrum of Cubans fed up with corruption and student gangsterism. "Gangster mobs pillaged the dark and moldy streets of Old Havana, killing one another for ideologies even more obscure than the streets themselves," wrote Guillermo Cabrera Infante.

In 1952 Batista again put himself up as a presidential candidate in the forthcoming elections. It soon became clear that he wouldn't win. On 10 March, only three months before the election, he upended the process with a bloodless predawn *golpe*. Batista dissolved the congress and canceled the election. One of the reform-minded candidates for congress whose political ambitions were thwarted by Batista's coup was a dashing young lawyer with a predilection for stylish suits and the limelight. His name was Fidel Castro. In 1952, the 25-year-old had risen to great prominence as the most outspoken critic of corrupt government and was being hailed as a future president. Fidel's "always lurking violence" was there, however. He was a student-gangster leader: in December 1946, according to biographer Georgie Ann Geyer, Castro appeared at the home of his brother-in-law, Rafael Díaz-Balart, and blurted out, "Rafael let me in. I just killed Leonel Gómez," referring to a fellow student and rival gang member.

To his shame, Harry Truman immediately recognized the infant regime. By recognizing the illegal government, the United States lost any semblance of moral influence. Had Truman acted with greater rectitude there may never have been a revolution in 1959. Batista's rule was so widely hated that it unified the Cuban people. "The character of the Batista regime in Cuba made a violent popular reaction almost inevitable," concluded a State Department White Paper in 1961.

Batista had forsaken his interest in the Cuban people. He had lingered too long in Miami with *mafiosi* and returned spoiled with ambition and greed.

To lure tourists, in 1948 President Francisco Prío had opened the doors to gambling. The ploy worked. Cuban developers rushed to put up new hotels in anticipation of a rush of Yankee vacationers. Batista initiated another dizzying round of progressive acts that conjured a tourist boom, spurring economic growth and fueling a period of prosperity. As the Batista epoch progressed, however, gangsters began to take over the hotels and casinos with Batista's blessing—for a cut of the proceeds, of course (it wasn't until the mid-1950s that an infusion of foreign capital built Havana's mobster-run Las Vegas-style hotel-casinos for which pre-revolutionary Havana will always be associated). "A few years of profitable frivolity ensured its lasting reputation as the premier pleasure island of the time and offered a rallying cry and a focal point for anti-government rebels," notes historian Rosalie Schwartz. However, "Casino owners did not strew North American garbage across a pristine Cuban landscape," adds Schwartz. "Foreign gamblers introduced neither gangsterism nor vice to the island, nor did they necessarily corrupt righteous islands. . . . The mob was playing ball with seasoned veterans, not second-stringers."

Havana became the coolest place because it was the hottest. Visitors flocked to carouse with "glamorous, lissome Latin lasses, black-eyed señoritas, languorously, enticingly swaying" in the words of one vintage tourist brochure selling "night-time in Havana." North Americans arrived by plane or aboard the *City of Havana* ferry from Key West to indulge in a few days of sun and sin. They went home happy, unaware that behind the scenes chaos and corruption were rife.

Batista got himself *elected* president in November 1954. But it made no difference. He maintained his cynical rule with a brutal police force. Throughout this sordid period, the United States reluctantly supported Batista. Neither Washington nor Batista understood the revolutionary forces at work. In the towns, Batista's secret police tortured suspected opposition members and hung them from trees while, says Schwartz, "militants of Castro's Twenty-Sixth of July Movement placed phosphorous bombs in movie houses, buses, nightclubs, theaters, and parks." In the countryside, night fell with a blackness made creepier by the awareness of mysterious forces. "The President's regime was creaking dangerously towards its end," wrote Graham Greene in *Our Man in Havana.*

THE GATHERING STORM

Almost immediately following Batista's *golpe,* Fidel Castro began to plot Batista's downfall. Castro possessed a vision of his place in Cuba's future that seemed pre-ordained. He was also ruthlessly focused. His plan: street protests and legal challenges to the Batista regime (the basis for justifying the planned revolution as a legal act against an illegal regime) and a secret conspiracy simmering underneath. Castro's powerful personality drew the politically disaffected to him. They realized that here was a man who would act. As Tad Szulc wrote, Castro "was now personally at war with the Batista dictatorship. . . Castro would never relent."

After the secret police came to arrest him within 24 hours of Batista's coup, Castro was forced underground. He organized the Movement (later known as the 26th of July Movement) and ran it with military discipline. With a hard core of perhaps one dozen members, the Movement's membership was composed mostly of intellectuals, students, labor-union leadership, and, later, poor workers. Washington's support of Batista ostensibly revolved around the issue of Communism—an entirely irrelevant question with regard to Cuba at the time. Castro had shunned the Communist Party, whose members were automatically excluded from the Movement. Even Castro's Communist brother, Raúl, was kept out for a time. Instead, political instruction centered on the nationalist philosophy of José Martí.

Soon the Movement was an army in training.

The Attack on the Moncada Barracks

Castro, then 26 years old, launched his revolution on 26 July 1953 with an attack on the Moncada barracks in Santiago de Cuba. Castro's plan was to seize arms. A simultaneous attack was planned on Bayamo barracks using 30 men. Since Batista's reinforcements would most likely come from Holguín, Castro figured on blowing up the bridges over the Río Cauto, isolating Oriente Province as a "liberated zone." Meanwhile, other members of the Movement would seize key radio stations and appeal for a national uprising against Batista (Castro's manifesto, called *The Cuban Revolution,* would offer the nation a nine-point plan of salvation).

Castro chose 26 July for the attack because the city would be caught up in Carnival on that day and most of Batista's troops would be away on weekend passes. The rebels relied on surprise, not firepower (they attacked using shotguns and a miscellany of aging rifles and submachine guns). Unfortunately, everything conspired to go wrong the moment the attack began. It quickly collapsed in a hail of bullets, as did the Bayamo attack.

Batista declared a state of emergency. His propaganda machine went to work to convince the nation that the rebels had committed all kinds of atrocities. Unknown to Batista, however, the torture and assassination of 64 rebels who had been captured had been photographed. When the gruesome photos were published, a wave of revulsion swept the land (thousands of Cubans attended a Mass for the dead martyrs). The Catholic hierarchy stepped in and negotiated a guarantee of the lives of any future captives.

Castro was eventually captured by an army detachment whose commander—tall, 53-year-old, black Lieutenant Pedro Sarría—disobeyed orders to kill Castro on sight (Batista later jailed Sarría, but Sarría would go on to become a captain in Fidel's Revolutionary Army and a hero of the Revolution). Once in Santiago jail, Fidel was safe from murder because of his enormous public stature. Reporters were even allowed to interview the prisoner, who told them in detail of the rationale for the Moncada attack—a public rela-

tions coup that sowed the seeds of future victory. Amazingly, Fidel was allowed to broadcast his story over the national radio to demonstrate to the Cubans how subversive he was. "Imagine the imbecility of these people!" Fidel later said; "At that minute, the second phase of the revolution began."

History Will Absolve Me

Castro, who acted as his own attorney, was sentenced in a sealed court that opened on 21 September 1953. Castro's goal was to establish the legitimacy of the Moncada attack. Castro never attempted to defend against the charges leveled at him and his fellow conspirators. He relied solely on attacking Batista's regime, and proudly defended his own actions. When asked who was the "intellectual author" of the attack—in Cuban law, the instigator of an armed assault against the state was as liable as the perpetrator—Castro answered, "José Martí!" Gradually the trial turned as evidence of the brutal tortures mounted.

Castro was sentenced on 16 October in a tiny closed room at the Santiago de Cuba hospital. Castro spoke for two hours in a mesmerizing oratory in which he devastatingly denounced the Batista regime, citing history's precedents for taking up arms against tyrants, and ending with the words, "Condemn me, it does not matter. History will absolve me!" (The Moncada attack parallels in many ways Hitler's failed Rathaus Putsch in 1924, suggests biographer Georgie Ann Geyer. Indeed, Castro had studied and memorized *Mein Kampf,* and his "History Will Absolve Me" speech was closely modeled on the words of Adolf Hitler at the end of his Putsch trial, which ended with the words, "You may pronounce us guilty, [but] history will smile. . . . For she acquits us!")

Just as the attack on Moncada was a milestone in modern Cuban history, his brilliant defense speech was a watershed that earned him immense national sympathy and legitimacy as the foremost opponent to the dictator. His speech became a basic document of the Cuban Revolution, and this call to social justice would become Castro's justification for all future revolutionary acts. He was cheered as he was led away in handcuffs to serve 15 years in jail on the Isle of Pines (now Isla de la Juventud, or Isle of Youth).

Plotting from Prison

Fidel was imprisoned with 25 other companions of the 26 July attack. (José Martí had also been imprisoned on the Isle of Pines, adding to Castro's symbolic association with the original revolutionary hero.) Fidel immediately organized the Abel Santamaría Ideological Academy to teach history, philosophy, political economics, classics, and languages to his fellow revolutionaries. The classes devoured hundreds of books. Later, Fidel was removed to solitary confinement, but he maintained secret communications with fellow inmates, at times using sign language which they all learned.

The media gave wide coverage to Castro, whose stature increased with each day in jail. A nationwide campaign to free Castro added to his now lustrous sheen.

In November 1954, Batista won the national presidential election. Though the elections were rigged, Washington quickly embraced the "constitutional" regime. In May 1955 Batista bowed to mounting public pressure and signed an amnesty bill passed by congress. Castro and the Moncada prisoners were free. When the train carrying Fidel reached Havana, he was hoisted aloft by a huge crowd and carried through the streets.

Immediately Castro launched his anti-Batista campaign. Soon Castro was banned from making public addresses, and newspapers that printed his articles were closed. Inevitably Fidel was forced to move constantly for his own safety. On 7 July 1955, he boarded a flight to Mexico. "From trips such as this, one does not return or one returns with the tyranny beheaded at one's feet," he stated in a message printed in the *Bohemia* newspaper.

Castro's Exile

Castro's goal in exile was to prepare a guerrilla army to invade Cuba. Fidel's enthusiasm and optimism were so great that he managed to talk aged revolutionaries such as Alberto Bayo, a hero of the Spanish Civil War, into giving up their careers and businesses to train his nascent army—now known as MR-26-7 *(Movimiento Revolucionario 26 Julio)*—in guerrilla warfare.

In a brilliant coup, Fidel sent a powerful message to the congress of the *Ortodoxo* party, in which he called for the 500 delegates to reject

working with Batista through congressional elections and to take the high road—"called revolution." The delegates jumped to their feet chanting "Revolution! Revolution!" Castro had won over the organization. The Communists continued to shun him—the "objective conditions" defined by Karl Marx didn't exist.

Castro also authored the Movement's "Manifesto No. 1 to the People of Cuba," laying out the revolutionary program in detail: "The outlawing of the *latifundia*, distribution of the land among peasant families. . . The right of the worker to broad participation in profits. . . Drastic decrease in all rents. . . Construction by the state of decent housing to shelter the 400,000 families crowded into filthy single rooms, huts, shacks, and tenements. . . Extension of electricity to the 2,800,000 persons in our rural and suburban sectors who have none. . . Confiscation of all the assets of embezzlers acquired under all past governments. . ." It was a long list.

In July 1955 Castro first met Ernesto "Che" Guevara, an Argentinean doctor, intellectual, and revolutionary. Their destinies merged.

Castro's plan called for a long-term war in both countryside and urban areas (Castro, however, eschewed random violence against the public). To raise money for the endeavor, he toured the United States, speechmaking to thousands of Cuban exiles and Yankees alike, inspiring them by invoking Martí's legend. Meanwhile violent opposition to Batista was mounting in Cuba. Castro remained constant headline news in Havana.

When an attempt to purchase a patrol torpedo boat replete with torpedoes and 40-mm cannon failed (the MR-26-7 lost US$20,000 in the transaction), Castro bought a 38-foot-long wooden luxury cruiser to launch his invasion. In the wee hours of 25 November, the *Granma* slipped out of Mexico's Tuxpán Harbor.

The *Granma* Landing

The near-disastrous crossing lasted seven days. Huge swells whipped the boat, and soon the 82 heavily armed men were violently seasick. (The vessel had been designed to carry only 25 people). One engine failed. The boat began to take on water. And the food and water rations ran out; for two days the men had neither. Finally, two days overdue, the boat ran aground in mud at Los Cayuelos, near Niquero in Oriente Province, one mile south of the beach where Castro had planned. The men had to abandon their heavy armaments and supplies and wade ashore through dense mangroves. Che Guevara called it a "shipwreck."

On 2 December 1956 Castro and 81 men were ashore, ready to take on Batista's 40,000-strong armed forces, newly equipped with U.S. armaments. An uprising in Santiago de Cuba, timed to coincide with the planned landings, had failed two days earlier, providing Batista with ample warning that an invasion was imminent. Batista was informed of the landing almost as soon as the *Fidelistas* reached dry ground. On 5 December, after a forced march through arduous terrain, the exhausted column was ambushed by Batista's Rural Guard. The Rebel Army was destroyed. Only 16 men survived, including, remarkably, Castro, Che Guevara, Raúl Castro, Camilo Cienfuegos, and other key leaders. "There was a moment when I was Commander in Chief of myself and two others," Castro later recalled.

THE CUBAN REVOLUTION

Soon men began joining the Rebel Army, mostly idealists keen to help oust a corrupt regime, but many of them, claims Jon Lee Anderson, "former rustlers, fugitive murderers, juvenile delinquents, and marijuana traffickers." Castro wasn't proposing a peasant revolution, although guerrilla warfare with peasant support lay at the center of his plan. On 16 January, his modestly armed force struck an army post for the first time since the attack on Moncada.

Batista responded with a ruthless campaign against the local populace, while B-26 bombers and P-47 fighter planes supplied by the U.S. strafed the Sierra Maestra. Batista managed to alienate the peasantry upon whom Castro's forces relied, while the Rebel Army—which was not without incidences of robbery, rape, and murder, claims Anderson—displayed greater kinship with them (at first the peasants wanted nothing to do with them, but later the rebels cemented the *guajiros'* support by assisting with the coffee harvest in May 1957).

Much of the Rebel Army's success was due to Celia Sánchez, a middle-class revolutionary who organized the support network that supplied arms, food, and volunteers. It was Sánchez who guided journalist Herbert I. Matthews into the Sierra Maestra in 1957 for his famous interview with Castro that broke like a bombshell in the *New York Times* (24 February, 1957), along with a photo showing the bearded guerrilla leader. Castro managed to fool Matthews into believing that he had scores of soldiers and mastery of the mountains by putting on a Potemkin theater. "From the look of things, General Batista cannot possibly hope to suppress the Castro revolt," wrote Matthews, who saw Castro as the T. E. Lawrence of the Caribbean.

Washington, meanwhile, continued to supply arms and full support to Batista, unaware of the implications of the portentous developments. The U.S. government fueled Castro's lifelong anti-Americanism by awarding the head of Batista's air force a Legion of Merit for its Sierra Maestra campaign.

War in the Cities and Countryside

While the Rebel Army nibbled away at its foes in the mountains, a war of attrition spread throughout the countryside and cities. Sugarcane fields were razed; army posts, police stations, and public utilities were destroyed. On 13 March, an attack on the presidential palace in Havana by the Student's Revolutionary Directorate—acting independently of Castro—failed (35 students died in the attack). Castro, far off in the mountains of Oriente, increasingly found himself in a battle for revolutionary leadership with the Movement's urban wings. Castro considered it the latter's duty to *support* the guerrilla war; the urban revolutionaries felt that they deserved equal say in conducting the fight to oust Batista. On 12 July, Castro committed himself to "free, democratic elections"—the central point of his Sierra Maestra Manifesto, designed to assuage the growing leadership crisis.

"We didn't speak of Marxism and communism in those days," Castro told biographer Tad Szulc, "but of a social revolution, of a true revolution, of the role of imperialism in our country." Not until several years later did Castro identify his revolution with socialism (Raúl's rebel group, however, was indoctrinated in communist philosophy as part of its guerrilla training). To forestall a deal behind his back, Castro issued a manifesto affirming the Movement's choice of a respected liberal judge, Manuel Urrutia Lleó, to head a provisional government after Batista's fall. Urrutia promptly left for exile in the U.S., where he was instrumental in Eisenhower's decision to stop arming Batista publicly. (However, Washington kept shipping arms secretly—a fact that Castro discovered and made him furious. Nonetheless, Washington no longer dominated Cuba, nor did it wholeheartedly support Batista; indeed, many American diplomats supported Fidel. Remarkably, the CIA was channeling funds—at least US$50,000—to Castro's Movement. Its clandestine operation is still classified by the U.S. government, and few tidbits have trickled out.)

By spring, the rebels controlled almost all the mountain regions of Oriente Province. Although he still had only 300 men at arms, on 1 April, Castro declared "total war" on the regime, including the demand that Cubans refuse to pay taxes (an "unpatriotic and counterrevolutionary" action). A general strike was called for 9 April. More than 100 Cubans were killed by police. The strike collapsed and with it the last potency of moderate elements. Castro reorganized the Movement's top command, leaving himself paramount.

Batista met the increasing storm with brutal violence. Finally he decided to launch an all-out offensive in the Sierra Maestra with 14 battalions and 10,000 men—Operation FF *(Fin de Fidel)*. The 320 or so *Fidelistas,* however, beat back the 76-day offensive and even captured two tanks and huge quantities of modern weapons. Radio Rebelde broadcast the victories to the rest of the nation from La Plata, Castro's secret headquarters.

In July Castro and eight leading opposition groups (excluding the Communists—Castro decided to co-opt the Communists separately) signed the Caracas Pact—an agreement to create a civic coalition and calling on the U.S. to cease all aid to the Batista regime. The writing now on the wall, Washington began negotiations with Castro while maneuvering to keep him from power. In September, Castro—fueled by massive contributions of finances and arms from the Venezuelan government—led an offensive to take Santiago de Cuba. On 30 December, Che Guevara captured Santa Clara. The scent of victory was in the air.

The Revolution Triumphs

Washington prompted Batista to hand over power to a civilian-military junta led by General Eulogio Cantillo. The U.S. ambassador persuaded Batista to leave. At midnight on New Year's Eve, Batista and his closest supporters boarded a plane for the Dominican Republic. On 1 January, Cantillo announced his junta. Castro immediately responded over Radio Rebelde, informing the country that "the history of 1898 will not be repeated," an allusion to the usurpation of Cuban independence by U.S. forces. On 2 January, the same day that the rebel armies of Camilo Cienfuegos and Che Guevara entered Havana, Castro's army took over Santiago de Cuba. That night he delivered a televised victory speech.

On 3 January 1959, the triumphant guerrilla army began a five-day Romanesque victory march to Havana, with crowds cheering Castro atop a tank, all of it televised to the nation. Finally he entered Havana and was mobbed by euphoric throngs. That night, 8 January, Castro bathed in spotlights while delivering his victory speech before the nation. Two white doves suddenly appeared, and one miraculously flew down to rest on his shoulders—a stupefying event that fulfilled an Afro-Cuban superstition (doves in Santería mythology represent life) and granted Fidel the protection of the gods. It was "one of those rare, magical moments when cynics are transformed into romantics and romantics into fanatics," wrote photojournalist Lee Lockwood.

Castro—now the "Maximum Leader"—was intent from day one on turning the old social order upside down. He played his cards close to his chest.

Fidel moved cautiously but vigorously to solidify his power under the guise of establishing a pluralist democracy (the first act was a purge that sent thousands of military men and Batista supporters to the firing squad), but his aim was clear: "As a boy, Fidel never really saw any semblance of a working democratic system: he saw a rural spoils system, with everybody in on the take and the winnings going to the strongest," suggests biographer Georgie Ann Geyer. "He could bring about a democracy or a Communist revolution. He opted for the latter because it offered him the opportunity of becoming the undisputed ruler of the country for the rest of his life."

Although Manuel Urrutia had been named president and a coalition cabinet had been formed, Castro—the real power-holder—immediately set up a "parallel" government behind the scenes (in public, however, he stressed that he had no political ambitions). He began secretly negotiating with the Communists, working to co-opt them and build a Marxist-Leninist edifice. Castro recognized that the Cuban people were not yet ready for communism; first he had to prepare public opinion. (Many of his wartime *compadres* who resigned over this issue were jailed for treason). He also had to avoid antagonizing the United States into intervention. Castro began to manipulate Urrutia, first by getting himself named Prime Minister with power to direct government policy. He also manipulated the public: speaking before large crowds, he molded and radicalized the public

mood, using this as a tool to pressure the Urrutia government, which he repeated must obey "the will of the people." Meanwhile, the old walls of the *cabaña* fortress echoed with the fusillades of firing squads as hundreds of Batista supporters and "enemies of the revolution" were dispatched following summary trials (Che Guevara was the supreme prosecutor), echoing the tribunals of the French Revolution.

Uncle Sam Decides to Oust Castro

Castro had conjured a storm, and like the sorcerer's apprentice, it soon became unclear whether he was directing it or being controlled by it.

Castro—determined to assert Cuba's total independence—feared the possibility that U.S. Marines would steal his revolution as they had stolen independence at the end of the Spanish-

THE CIA'S ATTEMPTS TO KILL CASTRO

The bitter taste left by the CIA's botched Bay of Pigs invasion led to an all-out secret war against Castro, an effort code-named Operation Mongoose, headed by Bobby Kennedy. Mongoose eventually involved 500 caseworkers handling 3,000 anti-Castro Cubans at an expense of more than $100 million a year. The CIA's attempts (now defunct) to oust Castro were set in motion by President Eisenhower as early as March 1959. In *Inside the Company: CIA Diary*, ex-CIA agent Philip Agee describes how the dirty-tricks campaign included bombings of public venues meant to discredit Cuba. The agency also invented protest demonstrations, sowed discord in Cuban intelligence by fingering top officials as CIA agents, and even recruited Cuban embassy staff by "dangling stunning beauties. . . exceptionally active in amorous adventures."

The CIA's plans read like a James Bond novel. . . or a comedy of errors. Some plots were straightforward, like the attempt to kill Castro with a bazooka. The CIA's Technical Services Division (TSD) was more imaginative. It impregnated a box of cigars with botulism (they were tested on monkeys and "did the job expected of them") and hoped—in vain—to dupe Castro into smoking one. No one knows whether they reached Castro or whether some innocent victim smoked them.

The spooks also tried to damage Castro's image by sprinkling his shoes with thallium salts (a strong

depilatory), hoping that his beard would fall out. Another box of Castro's favorite cigars was contaminated with a chemical that produced "temporary disorientation."

Eventually the CIA turned to the Mob. It hired assassins hand-picked by Johnny Rosselli, who had run the syndicate's Sans Souci casino in Havana. The killers were on both the FBI's 10-most-wanted-criminals list and Bobby Kennedy's target list of organized crime figures. The marksmen disguised as Marxmen didn't fool Castro, who correctly assumed the CIA would hire assassins, whom he considered inefficient (an assassin "does not want to die. He's waiting for money, so he takes care of himself"). Several assassins were caught and executed.

All this, of course, backfired miserably. The secret war to oust Castro caused the Russians to increase their military commitment to Cuba. In the end it provoked the missile crisis, bringing the world to the brink of nuclear disaster.

Havana's **Museum of the Ministry of the Interior**, Avenida 5ta y Calle 14, is dedicated to the inept deeds of the CIA. Also check out *CIA Targets Fidel: The Secret Assassination Report* (Ocean Press, 1996), and Gus Russo's *Live by the Sword*, which tells the tale of how the Kennedy's fanatical desire to get Castro backfired and ended with JFK's assassination in Dallas.

Cuban-American War in 1898. He saw conspiracy plots in every move Uncle Sam made. Moreover, an antagonistic relationship between a Castroite Cuba and the United States was inevitable. History ordained it. The Revolution was born when the east-west struggle for power was at its zenith, a circumstance that caused the Revolution "to be used as a Cold War weapon and joined it to the side that turned out to be the loser."

There was no way Uncle Sam could tolerate a left-leaning revolution beyond its control only 90 miles from Florida, especially one that was aligning itself with America's principal enemy and presented ominous potential for U.S. economic and national interests (this was, after all, the nation of which John Foster Dulles said, "The United States doesn't have friends; it only has interests"). Although the U.S. government had recognized the new Cuban government on 4 January 1959 (a recognition that has never been officially withdrawn), barely two months later the National Security Council had determined to oust Castro and had already authorized the CIA to mount a paramilitary operation.

Just as Washington became obsessed with the Communist issue without understanding or taking into account Cuban nationalism, Castro allowed himself to become obsessed with the United States and its Plattist mentality.

Cuban sovereignty was no longer an issue in which Uncle Sam had a say—a theme that underlay Castro's visit to the United States in March 1959. Vice President Nixon met with Castro and badly misread the Cuban leader (he considered Castro to be controlled by the Communists), with profound implications. Castro disingenuously promised not to expropriate foreign-owned property and repeated the mantra, "We are not Communists." He also affirmed that elections would *follow* "democracy," which he publicly defined as when all Cubans were employed, well fed, well educated, and healthy. "Real democracy is not possible for hungry people," he said.

Let the Reforms Begin!
On 6 March 1959, all rents in Cuba were reduced by 50%. Two months later, Cuba enacted an Agrarian Reform Law (acclaimed, at the time, by the U.N. as "an example to follow"). The large

sugar estates and cattle ranches were seized without compensation (in violation of Cuba's 1940 constitution and the reform law itself). The law established 391 hectares as the maximum permissible holding, though this would soon be radically reduced. To achieve it, Castro created the National Institute of Agrarian Reform, or INRA, which became an immensely powerful political tool headed by the Rebel Army.

The agrarian reform significantly upped the ante in the tensions between Cuba and Washington and established a still unresolved grievance: nonpayment for illegally seized land. The interests of Spanish, British, French, Canadian, and Dutch citizens were all affected. Over time, all claims with those governments except the United States were settled through bilateral agreements.

The Cuban peasants were ecstatic at the reforms (many would be less so a few years later, when a second Agrarian Reform transferred all tracts over 67 hectares to the state). Understandably, however, Miami received a flood of unhappy exiles. At first, these were composed of corrupt elements escaping prosecution—pimps, politicos, thugs, assassins, henchmen, political hacks and their accomplices, mafiosi, and the thousands of underlings that support a corrupt regime. As the reforms extended to affect the upper and middle classes, they, too, began to make the 90-mile journey to Florida. The trickle turned into a flood. About 250,000 Cubans left by 1963, most of them white, urban professionals—doctors, teachers, engineers, technicians, businesspeople, and others with entrepreneurial skills. (As Castro's Revolution turned blatantly Communist and authoritarian, many of his revolutionary cohorts also began to desert him. Later, intellectuals and homosexuals were persecuted, and they, too, joined the flood.)

On 13 July 1959, President Utturia denounced the growing Communist trend. Castro resigned as prime minister, then played a typically brilliant gambit. Castro understood that the key to the revolution was Cuban sentiment. At the time of Uturria's resignation, Castro had arranged for peasants to be brought to Havana from all over Cuba to celebrate the anniversary of the attack on Moncada. Castro then appeared on television and denounced Utturia, manipulating public sentiment through direct appeals to the masses. The streets of Havana erupted in calls for the President's resignation and pleas for Castro's return. He had carried out the world's first coup d'etat by TV! On 1 May 1960, Castro defaulted on his promise to hold elections within a year. The "people," he proclaimed, had declared them unnecessary, rationalizing the suspension of the Constitution and refusal to seek a popular mandate. Castro had become a classic *caudillo*.

Into Soviet Orbit

Castro understood that he needed the Soviets to survive in the face of growing U.S. antagonism and had decided on a profound new relationship. He knew, wrote Lee Anderson, "if he was ever to govern as he saw fit and achieve a genuine national liberation for Cuba, he was going to have to sever [U.S. tentacles] completely." The Kremlin had shared the Cuban Communists' views that Castro was his own man. He was too unreliable. By 1960, however, Cuba seemed like a perfect strategic asset. So Castro and Khrushchev signed a pact. It is unclear, however, whether Castro fully understood the geopolitical consequences of flirting with the Soviet bear.

The emerging Havana-Moscow axis chilled Washington. Ever fearful of a U.S. invasion and unsure as yet of the depth of Soviet assistance, Castro had decided to make the peasantry the basis of Cuba's defense. Hence, he initiated a massive militia training program, while emissaries began to purchase arms overseas. Although the U.S. government pressured the Europeans not to sell arms to Cuba, the first shipment arrived from Belgium on 4 March 1960 aboard the French ship *Le Coubre*. One week later, the steamship exploded in Havana Harbor with 700 tons of arms and munitions still in the hold. Over 82 Cubans were killed. One school supports Castro's contention that the CIA was responsible; another school believes Castro may have arranged the bombing. Whatever the truth, the event managed to rally the Cuban people around Castro at a time when he was facing increasing domestic opposition.

During the funeral ceremony for the victims, Castro uttered the rallying cry that would later become the Revolution's supreme motto: *¡Patria o muerte!* Recalls Nobel Laureate Gabriel García Márques:

The level of social saturation was so great that there was not a place or a moment when you did not come across that rallying cry of anger, written on everything from the cloth shades on the sugar mills to the bottom margin of official documents. And it was repeated endlessly for days and months on radio and television stations until it was incorporated into the very essence of Cuban life.

When Soviet oil began to arrive in May 1960, U.S.-owned refineries refused to refine it. In response, the Cuban government took over the refineries. (The dramatic occasion seems to have been carefully plotted by Che Guevara. The U.S.- and British-owned Shell refineries had been supplying Cuba with oil on credit and were owed US$50 million by the Castro government; Che, claims Jon Lee Anderson, "informed the American oil firms that in order for him to pay off the debt owed them, they each had to buy 300,000 barrels of the Soviet oil and process it.... In one fell swoop, Cuba had freed itself of a fifty-million-dollar debt and gained an oil-refining industry.") The United States then hit Cuba where it hurt most: in July, President Eisenhower refused to honor a purchase agreement for Cuban sugar. Cuba's biggest market for virtually its entire source of income had slammed the door. Washington couldn't have played more perfectly into the hands of Castro and the Soviet Union, which happily announced that it would purchase the entire Cuban sugar stock.

Hit with Eisenhower's right cross, Castro replied with a left hook: he nationalized *all* Yankee property, including 36 sugar mills, two utility companies, and two nickel mines. In October the Eisenhower administration banned exports to Cuba. (In March 1961 President Kennedy extended the embargo to include Cuban imports—the beginning of a trade embargo that is still in effect.)

By slamming the door to Cuban sugar and American goods, the U.S. had severed Cuba's umbilical cord. The island faced economic collapse. During that period of intense Cold War, there were only two routes for underdeveloped nations. One way led West, the other East. Lock one door and there ceases to be a choice. "That's stupid, and it's a result of the howls of zealous anti-Communists in the United States," said Khrushchev. "Castro will have to gravitate to us like an iron filing to a magnet." But Castro was ahead of the game. The Soviet deal had been initiated during Che Guevara's 1959 "goodwill mission" and was an integral part of Castro's step-by-step formula to conjure a complete break with Washington.

The Counterrevolution

Uncle Sam couldn't resist the urge to depose Castro. It's easy to understand why. The Iron Curtain was an impenetrable reality in 1961. The Cold War was part of the climate, and Cuba was embracing the Soviet bear.

President Kennedy (who in 1960 had recognized in his book *The Strategy of Peace* that "Castro is part of the legacy of [Simón] Bolívar [and]. . . of that earlier revolution which won its war against Spain but left largely untouched the indigenous feudal order") said, "Our objection is not to the Cuban revolution. It is to the fact that Castro has turned it over to the Communists." In January 1961 the Kennedy administration broke diplomatic ties with Cuba. Kennedy pressured Latin American governments to follow suit through the Alliance for Progress, using the carrot and stick (the promise of US$25 billion in aid, and the threat of taking it away). Every Latin American country except Mexico fell in line.

Meanwhile, internal opposition to Castro was growing as repression haunted the land. Bands of counterrevolutionary guerrillas had set up a front in the Sierra del Escambray, supported by the CIA. Many former Castroite supporters fought against him when they realized that he had turned Communist *caudillo* and that a personality cult was being erected. Alas, the anti-Fidelistas didn't have a Fidel. Nonetheless, the *"Lucha Contra Bandidos"* (Struggle Against Bandits) lasted until 1966; to eradicate local support for the counterrevolutionaries, peasants were forcibly evacuated en masse to "strategic hamlets" in Pinar del Río, claims Anderson.

Castro, with his highly efficient intelligence operation, knew that the CIA was plotting an invasion of Cuba by Cuban exiles and correctly figured that the invading force would attempt to link up with these groups. In mid-1960 Castro began to suppress the independent press. He also established the Committees for the De-fense of the Revolution (CDRs)—a countrywide information network for "collective vigilance."

On 31 December 1960, Castro ordered a general mobilization to defend Cuba against military attack. Since a U.S. invasion would rely on local support, Cuba's State Security began a nationwide sweep against suspected counterrevolutionaries (about 30,000 suspects were arrested in Havana alone; many more were arrested in the wake of the invasion).

The Bay of Pigs Fiasco

President Kennedy was assured that the Cuban people would rise up in arms. They did, and within 72 hours they had defeated the CIA-backed invasion at the Bay of Pigs on 17 April 1961. (See the special topic, The Bay of Pigs in the Matanzas chapter.)

Senator J. William Fulbright, chairman of the Senate Foreign Relations Committee, had warned, "To give this activity even covert support is of a piece with the hypocrisy and cynicism for which the United States is constantly denouncing the Soviet Union. . . The point will not be lost on the rest of the world." It wasn't. The Bay of Pigs, or Playa Girón as Cubans call it, was a smashing public relations coup for Cuba. Arthur Schlesinger predicted that it would "fix a malevolent image of the new Administration in the minds of millions."

The invasion brought a new sense of unity to Cuba. United States ambassador Bonsal declared that the Bay of Pigs "consolidated Castro's regime and was a determining factor in giving it the long life it has enjoyed." As Castro admitted: "Our Marxist-Leninist party was really born at Girón; from that date on, socialism became cemented forever with the blood of our workers, peasants, and students." U.S. politicians still can't seem to understand that the threat of external danger strengthens the Revolution because of the powerful impact of nationalism on popular reactions.

The debacle not only solidified Castro's tenure but also provoked a repressive house-cleaning of anyone thought to be too independent or deviant. As Castro saw it, you were either for the Revolution or against it. By 1965, at least 20,000 political prisoners—including homosexuals, practicing Catholics, and other "social deviants"—toiled in labor camps or languished in jails.

THE CUBAN MISSILE CRISIS

The Cuban Missile Crisis, which Cubans refer to as the Caribbean Crisis, was the result of the escalating tensions of the deepening Cold War. The Soviet Union felt severely threatened by the American deployment of intermediate-range ballistic missiles on the Turkish border with the USSR. To the Soviets, the Bay of Pigs fiasco provided an opening for them to establish bases at equally close range to the U.S., which could then be used as bargaining chips for a reduction of U.S. bases in Turkey.

Castro feared that the U.S. was planning to invade Cuba. And the Soviets told him they had intelligence confirming his fears. Fidel accordingly requested "strategic defensive weapons." The Soviets began their military build-up in Cuba in early 1962, then pressured the Cuban government to formally request that the Soviet Union install nuclear missiles.

Cuban ports were closed and a curfew enacted while the missiles were brought in. They were a public secret—everyone knew, including Cubans leaving the island for Florida. Soon enough, on 14 October, a U-2 spy plane over western Cuba discovered missile sites. President Kennedy demanded that they be removed. Khrushchev refused.

On 22 October Kennedy ordered the U.S. military to go from DefCon (Defense Condition) 5 to DefCon 3. That night, Kennedy went on national TV and announced, "I have directed. . . initial steps to be taken immediately for a strict quarantine on all offensive military equipment. . . . It shall be the policy of this nation to regard any nuclear missile launched from Cuba as an attack by the Soviet Union on the United States, requiring full retaliatory response on the Soviet Union."

As he began speaking, 54 Strategic Air Command (SAC) bombers took to the air, Polaris submarines put to sea, and the SAC prepared 136 Atlas and Titan ICBMs for firing. A U.S. naval task force set out to intercept Soviet vessels and blockade Cuba. That day, *Revolución* published the banner headline U.S. Prepares Invasion of Cuba.

A volatile exchange of messages between Kennedy and Khrushchev followed. Tensions mounted. On 24 October the U.S. military went to DefCon 2—for the first and only time in history. The two superpowers verged on full-scale nuclear war.

Rogue Elephants

Although Kennedy was unaware of it, Thomas Powers, commander of SAC, had the "authority [granted by Curtis LeMay, U.S. Air Force Chief of Staff] to order retaliatory attack. . . if time or circumstance would not permit a decision by the President." Missiles in 1962 did not have the locking and security mechanisms of modern times, and such an unauthorized launch was entirely feasible.

While Kennedy was looking at the regional implications, Powers and LeMay were thinking of—and apparently hoping for—a preemptive war. Powers and LeMay knew that the U.S. and USSR were moving toward a policy of mutual deterrence based on a pact of "no first-strike," a policy the two figures publicly abhorred. Their missiles would then be a "wasting asset." They pushed Kennedy to bomb Cuba and take out the missiles, believing the Soviets wouldn't dare to respond (at the time, the USSR had only 44 ICBMs and 155 heavy bombers, compared to the U.S.'s 156 ICBMs, 144 Polaris submarine-launched missiles, and 1,300 strategic bombers).

At the height of the crisis, on 26 October, Powers ordered an unsanctioned and potentially cataclysmic launch of an ICBM from Vandenberg Air Force Base. Although it was launched across the Pacific and hit the missile test range in Kwajalein atoll in the Marshall Islands, it was still a deliberate provocation. After

The Cuban Missile Crisis

The Bay of Pigs fiasco also unquestionably led to the Cuban missile crisis in October 1962. If the U.S. had not been thoroughly defeated by Cuban forces on the beaches in 1961, Nikita Khrushchev almost certainly would not have dared to precipitate the crisis. But the crisis was really of Castro's making: "From 1960 onward," wrote Ernest May and Philip Zelikow, "Castro repeatedly predicted horrific scenarios involving U.S. action against him, then took action that made his prophecies self-fulfilling."

On 1 December 1961, Castro informed Cuba and the world that Cuba was officially a Marxist-Leninist state. The news was a bombshell to the Kennedy administration, which in March 1962 launched Operation Mongoose—a six-phase program to oust Castro by instigating an open revolt (400 CIA agents were assigned full-time to the operation in Washington) and any other

Khrushchev complained that U-2 spy planes flying over Siberia "could be easily taken for a nuclear bomber, which might push us to a fateful step," Powers ordered SAC bombers to deliberately fly past their turnaround points into Soviet airspace. They were recalled at the eleventh hour when Khrushchev relented and ordered the missiles removed.

Rogue Comandante
Fidel—always the gambler—was equally reckless. According to Carlos Franquí, editor of *Revolución* at the time, Fidel "drove to one of the Russian rocket bases, where the Soviet generals took him on a tour [the missile sites were Russian territory]. . . . At that moment, an American U-2 appeared on a radar screen, flying low over the island. . . . The Russians showed him the ground-to-air missiles and said that with a push of a button, the plane would be blown out of the sky.

"Which button?" Fidel reportedly asked.

"This one," a general replied.

At that, says Franquí, "Fidel pushed it and the rocket brought down the U-2. Anderson, the American pilot, was the only casualty in that war. The Russians were flabbergasted, but Fidel simply said, 'Well, now we'll see if there's a war or not.'"

Castro has vigorously denied that he (or any Cuban) had shot down the U-2 on 27 October. "It is still a mystery how it happened," he claims. However, Soviet ambassador Alexeev had cabled Moscow on October 25 warning that Castro wanted "to shoot down one or two piratic American planes over Cuban territory." He had not only created a potential world catastrophe, he had wanted to pursue it to its most horrific consequences: in another cable sent to Moscow on 26 October, claiming that a U.S. invasion was imminent, he had urged the Soviets to make a preemptive nuclear strike at the U.S.: "However difficult and horrifying this decision may be, there is, I believe no other recourse," he wrote.

Castro learned of Khrushchev's decision to back down over the radio, along with the rest of the world. He was livid. When United Nations Secretary-General U Thant met Castro immediately after the crisis to arrange for verification that the missiles had been removed, Castro refused all cooperation: Castro was in "an impossible and intractable mood."

What If. . . ?
The majority of Cubans remained on combat alert for a month, prepared to face down the atomic bomb with rifles. "A New York telephone operator, at that time, told a Cuban colleague that people in the United States were quite alarmed over what might occur," recalls Nobel Laureate Gabriel García Márquez. "'We, on the other hand, are quite calm,' replied the Cuban operator. 'After all, the atomic bomb doesn't hurt.'" Maurice Halperin, in *Return to Havana,* recalls living in Havana in October 1962: "Unbelievably, the popular mood was defiance. '¡Patria o Muerte!' Fidel shouted, and the masses seemed almost eager to take on the Yankees. There was an air of celebration in the city. . . Havana was throbbing."

A conference sponsored by the Center for Foreign Policy Development at Brown University and held in Havana in January 1992 revealed that the Soviets had 45 nuclear missiles readily deployable in Cuba, including nine tactical missiles to be used at the discretion of Soviet field commanders in the event of a U.S. invasion of the island. The U.S. was by then fully mobilized for invasion. Once the invasion began, Soviet generals would have repelled it with the nine tactical missiles, which in turn would have spurred a U.S. nuclear strike against the Soviet Union. Or maybe not; Franquí, writing in 1984, made the remarkable claim that the Russians never tried to run the nuclear warheads through the U.S. blockade and therefore the missiles were entirely harmless.

means possible. The operation—which included secret efforts outside the CIA—was led by Bobby Kennedy, who despised Castro for the Bay of Pigs debacle and took his father's advice: "Don't get mad, get even." Plans included a full-scale U.S. military invasion set for October 20, 1962 . . . which Castro was aware of.

Kennedy's threat to do away with socialist Cuba virtually obliged Fidel to ask the Soviets for rockets to defend Cuba in the event of a U.S. invasion. The Soviets were pleased to assist. In August, Soviet personnel and MiG fighter-bombers began to arrive. Kennedy had warned the Soviets that the U.S. would not tolerate the installation of missiles. Khrushchev promised Kennedy that no "offensive weapons" were being supplied to Cuba. His deceit had near-calamitous consequences. Remarkably, many in the Kennedy administration naively thought Castro might want to ask for U.S. help to throw the Soviets out. They also still believed that the Cuban population might support a U.S. invasion—one year after the Bay of Pigs! No direct contact was made with Castro during the crisis, and the Kennedy tapes (see Ernest May and Philip Zeilkow's *The Kennedy Tapes,* in the Booklist) show that no one in the administration attempted to consider what Castro's part in the game of Russian roulette might have been.

To Cubans, Castro personified the heroic confrontation with Yankee imperialism. Yet the crisis not only brought the world to the brink of a nuclear holocaust, it was a black mark for Castro in the eyes of much of the rest of the world.

Castro may have correctly calculated that the threat of nuclear conflict could save him from a nonnuclear attack. The crisis had ended with a guarantee from Kennedy that the U.S. would not invade Cuba (though there is no public record of an *explicit* commitment by Kennedy, and the no-invasion pledge was withdrawn after Castro refused to permit verification). Nonetheless, the Kennedys had initiated another invasion plan for 1964—OPLAN 380-63. Before it could be implemented, the president was dead, shot by Lee Harvey Oswald. (The Cuban leader may have beaten JFK to the draw: evidence of possible Cuban complicity in the assassination and Washington's cover-up, intended to avoid World War III, is presented in *Live by the Sword: The Secret War Against Castro and the Death of JFK,* by Gus Russo; see Booklist.)

Castro was now free to move forward with his socialist revolution.

MAKING THE REVOLUTION

"The real question," said Sen. J.W. Fulbright in 1961, "is whether Castro can in fact succeed in providing a better life for the Cuban people."

Cuba in 1959 was comparatively advanced in socioeconomic terms. It had a huge middle class spread throughout the island (constituting between one-quarter and one-third of the population). Shops were full of produce cheap enough for mass consumption. And the island's per capita rankings for automobiles, telephones, televisions, literacy (U.N. sources suggest that as many as 80% of the population were literate), and infant mortality (32 per 1,000 live births)

were among the highest in the Western hemisphere. But hundreds of thousands of Cubans also lived without light, water, or sewage. Poverty was also endemic, and thousands of citizens lived by begging and prostitution.

Castro's government poured its heart and soul into improving the lot of the Cuban poor. First came health and education, where instant gains could be seen. Castro, for example, dubbed 1961 the Year of Education. On the eve of the Revolution, 43% of the population was illiterate according to government statistics and half a million Cuban children went without school. In 1960, "literacy brigades" were formed of university students and high school seniors, who left the cities and fanned out over the countryside with the goal of teaching every single Cuban to read and write. Within two years, the regime had added 10,000 classrooms. By the end of its first decade, the number of elementary schools had nearly doubled, from 7,567 in 1958 to 14,753 in 1968. The number of teachers had more than tripled, from 21,806 to 68,583. Castro also set up special schools for the indigent, the blind, deaf, and mute, and ex-prostitutes. Electricity, gas, and public transport fees were dramatically lowered, as were rents and other fees. Price controls were instituted on goods sold on the free market. The government poured money into health care. And the Revolution brought unparalleled gains in terms of racism and social relations.

However, Castro's reforms came at the cost of politicizing all private choices and the totalitarian insistence that doctrinal projects took precedence over individual liberties. The free-thinking entrepreneurial middle class was effaced, reminding one of Saint-Just, Robespierre's disciple, who thought the only way to build the republic was to destroy everything opposing it. Cuba's far-reaching social programs also had a price tag that the national economy could not support. Cuba's infant socialism was living off the wealth accumulated by Cuban capitalism. Reality was about to burst the bubble of the triumphalist rhetoric.

Mismanaging the Economy
The young revolutionaries badly mismanaged the Cuban economy, swinging this way and that as Castro capriciously tacked between Soviet

CHE GUEVARA AND THE "NEW MAN"

Ernest "Che" Guevara was born into a leftist middle-class family in Rosario, Argentina, in 1928. He received a medical degree from the University of Buenos Aires in 1953, then set out on an eight-month motorcycle odyssey through South America that had a profound influence on his radical thinking.

In 1954, he spent a brief period working as a volunteer doctor in Guatemala and was on hand when the Arbénz government was overthrown by a CIA-engineered coup. Guevara helped organize the leftist resistance (his experience left him intensely hostile to the U.S.). He fled Guatemala and went to Mexico where, in November 1955, he met Fidel Castro and, seeing in him the characteristics of a "great leader," joined the revolutionary cause.

The two had much in common. Guevara was a restless soul who, like Castro, was also daring and courted danger. They were both brilliant intellectuals (Guevara wrote poetry and philosophy and was probably the only true intellectual in Cuba's revolutionary leadership). Each had a relentless work ethic, total devotion, and an incorruptible character. Although the handsome, pipe-smoking rebel was a severe asthmatic, with an acute allergic reaction to mosquitoes, Che also turned out to be Castro's best field commander, eventually writing two books on guerrilla warfare that would become standard texts for Third World revolutionaries. He commanded the Third Front in the Sierra Escambray and led the attack that on 28 December 1958 captured Santa Clara and finally toppled the Batista regime. It was Che Guevara who took command of Havana's main military posts on New Year's Day 1959. And it was he who moved Fidel towards socialism.

Shaping the Revolution

The revolutionary regime declared Guevara a native Cuban citizen as an act of gratitude, rendering him legally entitled to hold office in Cuba. Che (the word is an affectionate Argentinean appellation, literally "you" but colloquially meaning "pal" or "buddy") became head of the National Bank of Cuba and Minister of Finance and, in 1961, Minister of Industry. He also led the execution squads that dispensed with scores of Batista supporters—Guevara never flinched from pulling the trigger himself—and was instrumental in the general repression that was meant to crush "counter-revolutionaries." To U.S. officials,

says biographer Jon Lee Anderson, he was "the fearsome Rasputin of the regime." His mystical influence on others attracted to him a crowd of fanatically loyal disciples, *los hombres del Che*. (Once, Che—a notoriously bad driver—rammed a car from behind. The driver leaped out, swearing, but seeing Che he turned craven: "Che, Comandante! What an honor it is to have been struck by you!" he exclaimed, caressing his dent.) Despite his popularity, he narrowly escaped an assassination attempt on February 24, 1961, outside his home on Calle 18 in Miramar.

Guevara supervised the radical economic reforms that swept through Cuba and, embracing the Soviet model with innocent fervor, negotiated the trade deals with the Soviet Union and COMECON countries and the carefully crafted maneuvering that led to the seizing of U.S. assets (Soviet representative, Alexandr Alexiev, said, "Che was practically the architect of our relations with Cuba").

Meanwhile, Guevara's grand ambition was to export peasant revolution around the world: Che "had become the high priest of international revolution," says Anderson. "Stealthily, Che was setting up the chessboard for his game of continental guerrilla war-
continues on next page

CHE GUEVARA AND THE "NEW MAN"
(continued)

fare, the ultimate prize being his homeland." He worked ceaselessly to goad a conflict between the Soviet Union and United States. The forces he helped set in motion in Latin America created a dark period of revolutionary violence and vicious counter-repression throughout the continent.

Creating the "New Man"

Guevara was a "complete Marxist" (he had an obsessive hatred of bourgeois democracy) who despised the profit motive and U.S. interests. He believed that the selfish motivations that determine behavior in a capitalist system would become obsolete when collective social welfare became the stated goal. Che set out his thoughts in an essay, "Man and Socialism in Cuba," in which he explained the difference in motivation and outlook between people in capitalist and socialist societies. He believed that the notion of material value lay at the root of capitalist evil. Man himself became a commodity. Meanwhile, liberty eroded moral values: individualism was selfish and divisive and essentially detrimental to social development. At the heart of the revolution was the elimination of individualism.

To build socialism, a new ethos and consciousness must be built. By removing market forces and profit or personal gain, replacing these with production for the social good and planning instead of market "anarchy," a new individual would emerge committed to a selfless motivation to help shape a new society. Castro agreed with Guevara, and a revolution to create the New Man was launched. It called for collective spartanism shaped

by Castro's personal belief in sacrifice. Che set the example and lived up to his own severe dictates: he was unrelentingly moralistic. He became austere and deadly serious, casting aside his trademark humor. He "brutalized his own sensitivities," said his father. If he could do it, so could others.

The government moved to censure work for personal benefit. Bonuses and other financial incentives were replaced with "moral incentives"; consumerism was replaced by the notion of "collective and individual satisfaction" from work. Private enterprise and trade were banned. Ideological debate was quelled. Apathy was frowned on. And psychological and other pressures bore down on anyone who refused to go along with the new values imposed from above.

For many Cubans, the idea of the New Man struck a resonant chord, because the Revolution came from the people themselves, not against their will or in spite of them. This nourished the concept of collective responsibility and duty, subordinating liberty (to do as one wishes) for the common good. There was nothing the Cubans wouldn't do. The state didn't even need to ask. "No one worked from eight to five," a 59-year-old woman told reporter Lynn Darling. "You worked around the clock. The horizons were open. We had a world to conquer, a world to give to our grandchildren."

An intrinsic sense of egalitarianism and dignity was nourished and seeped into the Cuban persona, as many individuals strove to embody the New Man ideal (not everyone agreed: more than a million

dictate and misguided personal whim. In 1960 Castro had created JUCEPLAN, a central planning agency modeled on the Soviet's GOSPLAN. Few of its concepts were given a chance to mature—Fidel kept jumping in. In confusedly searching for "truly original socialism," Castro committed economic errors that were worsened by bureaucratic mismanagement and abrupt reversals in direction, proving Karl Popper's Law of Unintended Effects, which operates most fiercely on occasions when politicians try to reform business. Sound economic decisions were sacrificed to revolutionary principles intended to advance the power of the state over private initiative. Che Guevara, president of the National Bank of Cuba

and Minister of Finance and Industry, sought to replace trained managers with communist cadres and market forces with "moral incentives."

The awesome brain drain, a lack of foreign exchange, CIA sabotage, bad administration, lack of economic incentives, and naive policy all conspired to reduce production. Gradually, inventories of imported goods and cash at hand were exhausted. As machinery wore down or broke down, no replacements could be ordered from the United States because of the trade ban enacted in 1961. Raw materials could not be bought. Soon the economy was in appalling shape. In 1962 rationing was introduced. The black market began to blossom.

Cubans opted to leave rather than be suffer the crushing suppression of individual freedoms). Cubans spread their spirit throughout the Third World, helping the poor and the miserable.

Fall from Grace

However, Guevara was greatly at odds with Castro on fundamental issues. Castro's scheme to institutionalize the Revolution hand-in-hand with the Soviets, for example, ran counter to Guevara's beliefs (Guevara considered the Soviet Union as rapacious as the capitalists).

Although they were intellectual equals, in many ways Che Guevara and Fidel Castro were ill-matched. Where Castro was pragmatic, Guevara was ideological. And Guevara was fair-minded toward Cubans critical of the Castro regime, unlike Castro. Guevara gradually lost his usefulness to Fidel's revolution. His frankness eventually disqualified him, forcing him into suicidal exile.

Guevara left Cuba in early 1965. He renounced all his positions in the Cuban government was well as his honorary Cuban citizenship. Guevara apparently severed his ties with Cuba voluntarily, although the reasons have never been adequately explained.

Death and Eternal Glory

Che fought briefly in the Congo with the Kinshasa rebels before returning briefly in secret to Cuba. He reemerged in 1966 in Bolivia, where he unsuccessfully attempted to rouse the Bolivian peasantry to revolutionary passions . . . reflecting his ambition, in his own words, "to create another Vietnam in the Americas" as a prelude to another—and, he hoped, definitive—world war in which socialism would be triumphant. He was betrayed to the Bolivian Army Rangers by the peasants he had hoped to set free. He died on 9 October 1967, ambushed and executed along with several loyal members of the Cuban Communist Party.

Castro has since built an entire cult of worship around Che. He has become an icon, exploited as a "symbol of the purest revolutionary virtue" and lionized for his glorious martyrdom and lofty ideals. Che Guevara became the official role model of the *hombre nuevo,* the New Man. The motto *seremos como Che* ("we will be like Che") is the official slogan of the Young Pioneers, the nation's youth organization. In 1997 Che's remains were delivered to Cuba and interred in Santa Clara.

His image is everywhere. The photographer Korda shot the famous image that will live to eternity—"The Heroic Guerrilla"—showing Guevara wearing a windbreaker zippered to the neck, in his trademark black beret with five-point revolutionary star, his head tilted slightly, "his eyes burning just beyond the foreseeable future," wrote Tom Miller.

Che has been turned into a modern myth the world over. He became a hero to the New Left radicals of the 1960s for his persuasive and purist Marxist beliefs. He was convinced that revolution was the only remedy for Latin America's social inequities ("revolution cleanses men") and advocated peasant-based revolutionary movements. He believed in the perfectibility of man, although his own mean streak and manically irresponsible actions are glossed over by leftists. The ultimate tribute perhaps came from the French philosopher Jean-Paul Sartre, who honored Guevara as "the most complete man of our age."

Sugar was a bitter reminder of U.S. imperialism; monoculture was held to blame for many of Cuba's ills. Castro and Che Guevara decided to abandon a sugar-based economy and industrialize. When the attempt to diversify away from sugar failed, Castro switched tack and mobilized the entire workforce to achieve a record sugar harvest: 10 million tons a year by 1970 (the all-time previous record was only 6.7 million tons). Castro swung a machete to inspire canefield workers. To achieve the goal, the country went onto a war footing. Tens of thousands of inexperienced "voluntary" workers left their jobs in the cities and headed to the countryside. Holidays were abolished. Every inch of arable land was turned over to sugar in the quest for a Pyrrhic victory. Castro was everywhere, leading the charge (one journalist likened him to the overseer of a huge cane plantation, "sticking his Hellenic nose into everything and enjoying it. Power is fun, and if it is absolute, it is absolute fun").

Nonetheless, the effort was a failure: only 8.5 million tons were harvested. And the economy was left in chaos; production elsewhere had been severely disrupted and output declined. (Castro blamed technical reasons for the mammoth failure. Unable to accept his blunder, he repeated the same mistake with other products, notably milk.) Cuba was kept afloat by massive amounts of Soviet aid.

By 1968 the Cuban economy was coming apart at the seams. To make matters worse, that year Castro nationalized the entire retail trade still in private hands. More than 58,000 businesses—from corner cafés and ice cream vendors to auto mechanics—were eliminated in the "Great Revolutionary Offensive," part of the plan to create the "New Man." As a result, even the most basic items disappeared from the shelves. Rationing became more severe. (In 1952, in social indicators, Cuba placed third in the Americas after land-rich Argentina and oil-rich Venezuela; by 1981, at the height of the "socialist progress," it had slipped to 13th in the Americas in the World Bank list.)

The Soviets saved the day. Bit by bit, Castro was forced to follow Soviet dictates (the relationship was always hot and cold; Castro's iconoclastic nature rubbed the Kremlin the wrong way). Castro's zealous experimentations gave way to a period of enforced pragmatism. In 1976, Cuba joined COMECON, the Soviet bloc's economic community. Cuba would henceforth supply sugar to the European socialist nations in exchange for whatever the island needed; sugar was even rationed in Cuba to meet obligations.

That year, the First Communist Party Congress initialed a new constitution that recognized Marxist-Leninism as the state's official ideology and the party as the sole representative of the people. Fidel Castro's tenure as head of state was written into the Constitution.

Adventurism Abroad

The Cuban economy limped along, with shortfalls made up by the Eastern bloc. Cuba received about half of all Soviet economic and military aid to the Third World. Oil, consumer goods, and foodstuffs were plentiful.

Castro could thus give more attention to world affairs. He was committed to exporting his Revolution abroad (he had been complicit in armed plots against several neighboring countries from the moment the Revolution succeeded, including support for a failed invasion of the Dominican Republic in June 1959). In 1962 Guevara launched a wave of Cuban-backed guerrilla activity throughout Latin America that was endorsed by Castro in his "Second Declaration of Havana," which made a tacit declaration of war on Latin American governments official policy.

This adventurism rankled the more cautious Soviet leadership, which tried to bring Castro to heel. But the U.S. invasion of the Dominican Republic in April 1965 to aid the rightist generals was a splendid propaganda coup for Fidel's "anti-imperialism" adventures.

Thus, at the Organization of Latin American Solidarity conference in Havana in August 1967, Castro launched his Fifth International, to "create as many Vietnams as possible" in defiance of the Soviet Union's policy of co-existence with the U.S. Said Castro: "The duty of every revolutionary is to make the Revolution." Cuban troops had already been sent to countries as far afield as Algeria and Zaire. Soon revolutionary fighters from Angola, Mozambique, and elsewhere were being trained at secret camps on Isla de la Juventud.

By the 1970s, Castro, aspiring to Third World leadership, was shipping politico-military mercenaries abroad in a mission of "near Napoleonic dimensions." In Ethiopia and Angola, Cuban troops fought alongside Marxist troops in the civil wars against "racist imperialism" (in Ethiopia they shored up a ruthless regime), and in Nicaragua, Cubans trained, armed, and supported the Sandinista guerrillas that toppled the Somoza regime. These were, in Castro's eyes, extravagant stages on which to fight Uncle Sam.

Cuba became an international power and a major executant of Soviet policy. More than 377,000 Cuban troops were rotated through Angola during the 15-year war (the last troops came home in May 1991), proportionally far greater than the U.S. troop commitment in Vietnam. Tens of thousands of Cuban doctors and technical specialists were also sent to more than two dozen Third World countries to assist in development (more than 50,000 Cuban civilians were rotated through Angola alone). While Cubans were, and still are, highly critical of the military efforts abroad, Castro, who devoted much time to the cause of development, was lauded throughout the Third World (in 1979 he was named Chairman of the Nonaligned Movement).

Meanwhile Castro was welcoming fugitives from U.S. law, such as convicted members of the Black Panther organization and, suggests Georgie Ann Geyer, in the "isolated Orwellian settlement of Barlovento, which opened to the sea but was wholly closed to Cuba. . . shadowy international buccaneers like Robert Vesco could come and go in a world without immigration laws or visas."

Castro's adventurism served to maintain a chill with Washington. El Jefe launched his African initiatives at a time when Washington was looking at rapprochement with Cuba, beginning with the Ford administration, which worked out several agreements with the Castro government (a gradual lifting of the embargo was approved). Castro's adventurism cooled Uncle Sam's enthusiasm. Likewise Castro acted to thwart President Carter's easing of the embargo that included and end to travel restrictions. When Carter announced that the U.S. welcomed Cuban political refugees with "open arms," Castro, in "a gesture of supreme personal rage," slammed the door shut by concocting the Mariel Boatlift.

The Mariel Boatlift

In 1980, 12 Cubans walked through the gates of the Peruvian embassy in Havana and asked for asylum. The Peruvians agreed and refused to hand them over to the Cuban police. Carter announced that the U.S. would welcome Cuban political refugees with "open arms." In a fit of pique, Castro removed the embassy guards, and 11,000 Cubans rushed into the embassy. When the foreign press gave the case prominence, Castro decided to allow them to leave, along with dissidents and other disaffected Cubans. Many were coerced to leave. Castro let them all leave and added to the swelling numbers by emptying his prisons of criminals and homosexuals and other "antisocial elements." The Cuban government called them *escoria* (scum), much as Goebbels called Jews *Ungeziefer* (vermin). Thus Castro disposed of more than 120,000 critics and disaffected.

The Carter administration was forced to accept the *Marielitos*. (In November 1987, Cuba agreed to take back about 2,500 *Marielitos* with histories of mental illness or criminal records, plus almost 4,000 Cubans convicted of crimes since their arrival in the United States.)

In the 1980s President Ronald Reagan took a much harder line. Castro's adventurism received its first bloody nose in 1983, when President Reagan ordered U.S. Marines to storm the Caribbean island of Grenada to topple Maurice Bishop's Cuban-backed socialist regime. The Reagan administration also spawned the Cuban-American National Foundation to give clout to the right-wing Cuban-American voice. In 1985 he established Radio Martí to broadcast anti-Castro propaganda into Cuba.

THE BUBBLE BURSTS

Meanwhile, Mikhail Gorbachev had become leader of the Soviet Union and was initiating fateful reforms—just as Castro turned more sharply toward Communist orthodoxy.

Castro's program of Rectification of Errors and Struggles Against Negative Tendencies was initiated in 1986 in response to Cuba's faltering economy. The decision resulted in the closure of free farmers' markets, a brief fling that had led to an increase in the food supply and placed unobtainable items such as garlic back on kitchen tables. Castro, however, was alarmed at the success of the free-market experiment and railed against "millionaire garlic growers." The basic structure of Soviet-style planning and management would not be altered. It was Castro's first warnings that *glasnost* and *perestroika,* Gorbachev's "heresies," would not be tolerated in Cuba.

By the late 1980s, dissent was sweeping through the Soviet Union and Eastern Europe, where the Communist order was crumbling. Castro reverted to revolutionary purity: the achievements of North Korea's Kim Il Sung were suddenly praised in the media. (Still, Castro sent an envoy to Mexico to being purchasing riot gear for Cuba's police.)

In 1989 the Berlin Wall collapsed and the Communist dominoes came tumbling down. However, the news in Cuba was dominated by a political show trial that made it clear that reform was not in the cards. General Arnaldo Sánchez Ochoa, a powerful and charismatic national hero with impeccable credentials going back to the Sierra Maestra, was accused of colluding with the Colombian drug cartel to smuggle drugs to the U.S. via Cuba. After a closed trial, Ochoa and 13 other high-ranking officers were convicted of treason and corruption. Ochoa and three others were executed. A massive purge followed, notably of the Ministry of the Interior (MININT), but also of dissidents and private entrepreneurs.

LIFE IN THE "SPECIAL PERIOD"

Life turned grim under what the Cubans call the "Special Period," which began when the Berlin Wall crashed and Cuba's Soviet lifeline was severed. Cuba went from down to destitute.

The lights went out on the Revolution—literally. After the last Soviet tanker departed in June 1992, the government began electricity blackouts. There were no fans, no air conditioning, no refrigeration, no lights. There was no fuel for transportation. Buses and taxis gave way to *coches*—homemade, horse-drawn carts. Human and animal labor replaced oil-consuming machinery everywhere. Without oil or electricity to run machines, or raw materials to process, or spare parts to repair machinery, factories closed down and state bureaucracies began transferring laid-off workers to jobs in the countryside. Nightclubs, restaurants, and hotels that were once full all closed. Gaiety on the streets was replaced with a forlorn melancholy.

Harvests simply rotted in the fields for want of distribution, undermining one of Castro's bedrock promises—that all Cubans would have enough to eat. People accustomed to a government-subsidized food basket guaranteeing every person at least two high-protein, high-calorie meals a day were stunned to suddenly be confronting shortages of almost every staple. The scarcities were manifest in long lines for rationed goods, a phenomenon that had nearly disappeared by the mid-1980s. A kind of line organizers' Mafia evolved, selling places *(turnos)* in the queue *(la cola)*. Cubans spent their days standing and waiting.

What began as inconveniences turned into real hardships as domestic purchasing power declined from an estimated US$8.6 billion to US$2.2 billion. Monthly allotments were greatly reduced. Even cigarettes were rationed—to three packs a month. First toiletries, then meats and other staples disappeared. Cubans had to resort to making hamburger meat from banana peels and steaks from grapefruit rinds. Many Cubans began rearing *jutías,* ratlike native rodents—and the most desperate resorted to rats. Black marketeers were said to be melting condoms and passing the rubber off as cheese on pizzas. Cuba, the only country in Latin America to have eliminated hunger, began to suffer malnutrition. Old problems resurfaced, such as the *buzos*—people who live off garbage bins. The hardship caused a rupture in the nation's ethics. Crime rose swiftly, and envy and anomie filled the vacuum left by the collapse of the egalitarian promise.

By 1994 a cautious sense of optimism began to emerge, an anticipation that things might soon change for the better. The awful *apagónes* (blackouts) had been trimmed from 18 hours in duration to four. Food crops no longer rotted in the fields. The legal availability of dollars eased life for those Cubans who had access to greenbacks, and farmers' markets eased life for those without.

For powerful descriptions of the harrowing living conditions during the Special Period, read Jacobo Timerman's *Cuba: A Journey,* Maurice Halperin's *Return to Havana,* or Andres Oppenheimer's *Castro's Final Hour.*

Rumors swept the island that Ochoa, who had been espousing reformist discontent, had been conspiring to oust Castro (see Andres Oppenheimer's *Castro's Final Hour* in the Booklist).

The Special Period

With the collapse of Eastern Europe, goods began to disappear from Cuban shelves. When East German powdered milk ceased to arrive, Cuba eliminated butter; when Czechoslovakian malt no longer arrived, Cuban beer disappeared. Soaps, detergents, deodorants, toilet paper, clothing . . . everything vanished.

In January 1990, Castro declared that Cuba had entered a Special Period in a Time of Peace. He also announced a draconian, warlike austerity plan. A new slogan appeared throughout Cuba: ¡Socialismo o muerte!" (Socialism or death!). Inevitably, rising political discontent boiled over on 21 April 1991, when clashes erupted against the police—the first act of spontaneous rebellion since 1959.

Then on 18 August 1991, on the last day of the highly successful Pan-American Games in Havana (which Cuba won with 140 gold medals), the Soviet Union began its dizzying unraveling. Reformer Boris Yeltsin took power. Subsidies and supplies to Cuba virtually ceased. The same year, General Noriega was ousted in Panama—Cuba's main source for Western goods. Cuba was cast adrift, a lone socialist island in a capitalist sea.

With the umbilical cords severed, Cuba's economy slipped into coma. Nonetheless, at the Fourth Congress of the Cuban Communist Party, in October 1991, Castro announced a "sacred" duty to save the Revolution. Hopes of reform were dashed. Although the politburo was expanded, with reformers holding half the seats, a new resolution granted the Central Committee absolute powers to overrule any other government body in "unpredictable situations," thereby legally empowering the committee to overrule any legislative vote to oust Castro.

Believing that Cuba was on the verge of collapse, Uncle Sam tightened the screws. In April 1992 President Bush closed U.S. airports and ports to third-country vessels "guilty" of carrying Cuban goods or passengers. Later that year Congress passed the Cuban Democracy Act, which reduced economic assistance to countries trading with Cuba; increased punitive action against individuals breaking the embargo; and prohibited U.S. subsidiary companies abroad from trading with Cuba. The Reagan administration had placed four conditions on improved relations with Cuba: a halt to Cuban support of revolution in Central America, withdrawal of its troops from Angola, a reduction of ties with the Soviet Union, and improved human rights. Cuba met all these conditions, to which the Bush administration responded with a new set of imperatives, including the development of a market economy, a reduction of Cuba's armed forces, and internationally supervised elections.

In February 1993 long-promised elections for the National Assembly were held. They were the first elections by secret ballot in four decades, but candidates had been nominated by party-controlled organizations. In March 1993 the new Assembly re-elected Castro to another five-year term as president. With riots breaking out on the streets of Havana, however, it was clear that things couldn't continue the way they were. While dissidents were being rounded up and jailed, the growing reformist movement found an unexpected ally in Raúl Castro, who argued for deregulating key sectors of the economy. Market-savvy reformers were elevated to positions of power and scrambled to nail together a long-term economic recovery plan led by tourism. The Revolution's ideological principles were turned on their head. Possession of the dollar was legalized. Private enterprise was permitted. Even *Playboy*—long banned—was invited to shoot a pictorial photographed in various resorts, while tourist posters flaunted bikini-clad *Cubanas* and the slogan: "Cuba, come and be tempted."

But the economic situation had deteriorated so much that malnutrition had reappeared. A growing human tide had begun washing across the Straits of Florida.

The *Balsero Crisis*

Leaving Cuba without an exit permit is illegal; Cubans are rarely granted such visas. Although back then the U.S. also routinely denied requests for entry visas, the U.S.'s 1966 Cuban Adjustment Act *guaranteed* residency to Cubans who stepped foot on U.S. soil. (The U.S. had agreed to accept an annual quota of 20,000 Cuban immigrants plus, but most Cubans who petitioned the U.S. for a visa were rejected. After Cuba relaxed its immigration laws in 1991 and issued thousands of exit visas, the number of visas issued by the U.S. fell sharply—to just 864 in 1993. The more difficult the economic circumstances became in Cuba, the fewer legal immigrants were accepted, while the greater the number of *illegals* who were taken in. "Clearly this was part of a strategy," claimed Castro. "They thwarted people's efforts to acquire a visa, and deliberately caused discontent; they purposefully left these people disappointed, waiting indefinitely for their visa. They try to invent reasons; that there weren't enough Cubans qualified. How is it that all those who enter illegally have the right qualifications?")

On 5 August 1994, crowds gathered along the Malecón in response to a rumor that a major exodus was to be permitted and that a flotilla of boats was en route from Florida. When police attempted to clear the boulevard, a riot ensued. Passions were running dangerously high, and two police officers were killed and 35 people injured. Castro saw a chance to defuse a dangerous situation and benefit. He declared that Cuba would no longer police the U.S. borders: if the U.S. would not honor its agreement to allow people to migrate legally, then Cuba would no longer try to prevent anyone from going illegally. The

U.S. was hoisted on its own petard as thousands of *balseros* fled Cuba on makeshift rafts. In one tragic episode, 38 Cubans lost their lives when Cuban officials rammed a tugboat filled with escapees, then turned their water cannons on mothers and children trying to keep their heads above water.

During the next three weeks, at least 20,300 Cubans had been rescued at sea and shipped to Guantánamo naval base, which was expanded to eventually house up to 65,000 refugees. President Clinton's major goal was to avoid a replay of the 1980 Mariel boatlift. By 9 September, when the two countries agreed to measures "to ensure that migration between the two countries is safe, legal, and orderly," another 11,060 Cubans had been rescued. Henceforth the Coast Guard would intercept Cubans heading for the U.S. and return them to Cuba.

Meanwhile, a Miami-based volunteer group called Brothers to the Rescue led by José Basulto had been operating rescue missions. When the flood of *balseros* stopped, pilots of the organization began buzzing Havana and dropping "leaflets of a subversive nature."

On 24 February 1996, three Brothers to the Rescue Cessnas took off from Opalocka airfield near Miami, Florida. The planes, led by Basulto, were cleared to fly to the Bahamas. Once airborne, they diverted to Cuba. Cuban jet fighters shot two Cessnas down, killing both pilots. The Cuban government claimed that the aircraft came down in Cuban territorial waters. An investigation by the independent International Civil Aviation Organization (ICAO) confirmed that Basulto, who had separated from the other two planes, *did* violate Cuban airspace. But it also confirmed that two Cessnas were downed 10.3 and 11.5 miles *north* of Cuban airspace (ICAO also found that the U.S. government had prior knowledge of the flights and that several U.S. agencies had been carefully monitoring the flights).

Cuban-American exiles and Republican presidential candidates campaigning for the mid-March Florida primary erupted in fury. The incident scuttled the Clinton administration's carefully calibrated policy on Cuba of promoting democratic change as a prelude to easing the embargo and forced the president to sign the the Helms-Burton act.

The Helms-Burton Legislation

In 1995 Sen. Jesse Helms and Rep. Dan Burton had introduced the Cuban Liberty and Democratic Solidarity Act, which would significantly tighten the embargo. Following the Brothers to the Rescue incident, Helms rode the wave of anti-Castro sentiment in Miami and Washington and steered the legislation through Congress. Clinton caved in. By signing the bill, Clinton significantly limited his own power to change U.S. policy toward Cuba in the future. He and future presidents must now seek congressional approval—a near impossible task, given the strength of the anti-Castro lobby—if they seek to modify or lift the embargo. Incredibly, Clinton surrendered his authority to Helms, Chairman of the Senate Foreign Relations Committee and one of the Senate's most recalcitrant reactionaries.

The law codified all executive orders in effect relevant to the embargo, which will remain in place until a "transition government" is in place in Cuba that meets U.S. criteria. The bill also withdraws funding from any international institution providing humanitarian aid to Cuba; provides for a $50,000 civil fine for any U.S. citizen who travels to and "trades with" Cuba; denies entry into the U.S. territory to anyone who has "trafficked" in or done business with people or businesses that have trafficked in property confiscated from U.S. nationals; and bars U.S. banks from lending to these companies. Finally, Helms-Burton will allow any U.S. citizen whose property was confiscated after the Revolution to sue any foreign corporation that has "benefited" from the property or from its use. This holds true even if the claimant was *not* a U.S. citizen at the time of expropriation—a requisite of international law.

Behind the bluster about toppling Castro, the law really represents the interests of very wealthy Cuban-Americans, such as the Bacardi Corporation and the Fanjul family (the legislation put a $50,000 minimum value on the property lost before a suit can be filed; you had to be *very* rich in 1959 to own $50,000 worth of property). In fact, the legislation—dubbed by some the "Bacardi Rum Protection Law"—was drafted with the help of lawyers representing Bacardi, the National Association of Sugar Mill Owners of Cuba, and the Cuban Association for the Tobacco Industry.

Castro had got Uncle Sam so furious, the

U.S. wound up socking itself in the jaw (former president Jimmy Carter said, "I think of all the things that have ever been done in my country, this is the stupidest"). The law has earned the wrath of the United States' leading allies, who have wholeheartedly taken the Cuban side. Canada even enacted retaliatory legislation. The law has been condemned by everyone from the Pope to the Organization of American States—"a stunning defeat for the United States," reported the *New York Times*—and clearly violates international law, including the General Agreements on Tariffs and Trade (GATT).

A conspiracy theorist might think the law was written by Castro, who figured out that Helms-Burton creates more problems for the U.S. than for Cuba while forestalling a lifting of the embargo, his ultimate ally (see the special topic, Fidel Castro, below). "To save his scapegoat," suggested the *Washington Times,* Castro "found the means in the small, civilian planes that had been buzzing Cuba for months. He shot two down on the assumption that doing so would send Congress and the White House into a frenzy of anti-Castro rhetoric and embargo tightening." The law was been well publicized in Cuba, helping unite Cubans behind the Castro government as nothing had done in years, allowing *el comandante* to revive flagging anti-Yankeeism and jail dissidents in the face of a new threat from U.S. imperialism.

Castro, who works hard to keep the anti-American flame alive, may well have planned the whole affair. In May 1999 U.S. federal agencies had finally pieced together the events leading to the shooting down of the two planes. Janet Reno, the U.S. Attorney General, issued indictments against 14 Cuban agents, including several spies rounded up in Miami plus "MX," the code name for the head of Havana's Directorate of Intelligence, and charged them with actively working to provoke the incident in a plot called Operación Escorpión.

Holy Smoke

In January 1998, Pope John Paul II made a highly publicized four-day visit to Cuba, glided into the Plaza de la Revolución in his Plexiglas popemobile, and delivered a sermon to 500,000 Cubans (for the occasion, Castro made Christmas an official holiday and festive lights went up in the streets for the first time in decades). Castro had invited the Pope in the hope that a papal embrace magnified by television exposure might diffuse much of the internal opposition and give the regime new legitimacy. Castro had been counting on air-play from the 4,000 journalists who descended on Havana to cover the event, including the major U.S. media, who promptly turned heel and fled when the Monica Lewinsky scandal broke as the Pope touched Cuban soil.

About the same time, a series of bombs planted by right-wing-sponsored exiles exploded in Havana's tourist zones with the aim of scaring off tourists. The campaign claimed the life of an Italian businessman. The Cubans arrested and sentenced to death two Salvadorans reputedly working on behalf of the Cuban-American National Foundation.

But the real enemy lay within. Serious crime such as muggings, which the Revolution had virtually eradicated, had returned to the streets of Cuba. An armored van was even robbed by armed youths (an unprecedented occurrence) in Guanabacoa, and two Italians tourists were killed in September 1998 during an armed robbery. Cocaine was being sold openly on the street and at discos. Thousands of young Cuban women had turned to quasi-prostitution as *jiniteras,* wedding the city's overt promiscuity with a boomlet of dollar-rich tourists. And low-level corruption among police and government officials was becoming entrenched.

The government sensed that it was losing control. When two Cuban women died of cocaine overdoses in December 1998, Havana's discos and bars were closed down, and thousands of young men and women were arrested on the streets.

LATEST DEVELOPMENTS

On 1 January 1999, Cubans celebrated the 40th anniversary of the Cuban Revolution. Commented *The Economist:* "There does not seem much to celebrate. . . . The grand promises of the past 40 years are in tatters. In some ways, Cuba seems worse off in 1999 than it was in 1959." Nonetheless, economically things were much improved: the economy was bouncing back, driven by dollars from tourism and was given a boost when in January when President Clinton eased the trade embargo, permitting U.S. citizens to send up to US$1,200 annually to Cuban individuals and non-government organizations. Castro called the move a "fraud" and announced draconian legislation—the Law for the Protection of Cuba's National Independence and Economy—while several thousand black-bereted police from the Special Brigade were deployed on street corners throughout Havana and major cities.

The policy was officially "a battle against disorder, crime, disrespect for authority, illegal business, and lack of social control." But the new law was also designed to chill relations between Cubans and foreigners by creating a new counterrevolutionary felony: "supporting" hostile U.S. policies. Anyone providing information to foreigners could face a 30-year sentence. Outlawed were the "supply, search or gathering of information" for and the "collaboration" with foreign media. To get the point across, in March 1999 four prominent dissidents—the Group of Four—were labeled "counterrevolutionary criminals" and received harsh sentences for sedition. One Cuban, Dr. Desi Mendoza Rivero, was even jailed for eight years for "disseminating enemy propaganda" after informing foreign journalists about an outbreak of dengue fever. The sentences signaled a harsh crackdown, resulting in the United Nations Commission on Human Rights condemning Cuba as a "significant violator."

The state was also reasserting control throughout the private economy. Castro, in an echo of King Canute, may have decided to pull back after realizing that his modest economic reforms could undermine the government's political control. Some savvy *jiniteros* and *jiniteras* had accumulated small fortunes, at least by Cuban standards, a modest economic success that posed a threat to the regime. Getting on well outside the state-controlled economy, thousands of Cubans had discovered they no longer needed the State to get by. Castro's new lurch to hard-line authoritarianism all but swept away the goodwill and hopes for wider reform generated by the visit of Pope John Paul a year before.

Meanwhile hundreds of *jiniteras* were arrested, as were scores of other hustlers; at least 10 convicted criminals were executed. Then in June 1999 dozens of high officials within the tourism and business sectors were fired and arrested for corruption, while a ministerial shake-up included Roberto Robaina's replacement with a 34-year-old loyalist, Felipe Perez Roque, as Foreign Minister. Drug traffickers now face the firing squad and prostitutes face a 24-year jail term. Police of the Special Brigade remain around-the-clock, checking IDs at random.

CHILD PAWN

*F*orty odd years ago, a Cuban father discovered that his estranged wife had left for the United States and taken their five-year-old son with her. The courts awarded custody of the son to the mother. But the father, who was enraged by the thought of his son being raised in Miami by relatives who were his sworn political enemies, refused to acknowledge his loss: "One day I'll get my son and my honor back—even if the earth should be destroyed in the process. . . . I am prepared to reenact the Hundred Years War. And I'll win it," he wrote to his sister. The man later talked the mother into letting the boy visit him in Mexico on his word "as a gentleman" that the boy would be returned in two weeks. Instead the boy was secreted away, so that the wife had to enlist the Mexican police to get her son back while he was being taken for a stroll in Mexico City's Chapultepec Park.

The mother remarried and returned with the boy to her new home in Havana. But Cuba turned communist and in 1964 she fled the island for Spain. Cuba's youthful leader Fidel Castro, however, wouldn't let the woman take her son with her (nor, apparently, has she been allowed to return). The boy was eventually sent to the Soviet Union, married a Russian, and today runs Cuba's nuclear power program.

The mother was Mirta Diaz-Balart, whose nephew, Lincoln Diaz-Balart, is a Republican Congressman for Florida and champion of the crusade to keep Elián González in the United States. The boy's name is Fidelito. . . his father is Fidel Castro.

Into the New Millennium

Fidel got a break in March 1999 when the Baltimore Orioles came to Havana and beat the

Cuban Sugar Kings, the national baseball team, 3-2 in the first meeting of a U.S. professional club and a Cuban squad since March 1959 (the 50,000-seat stadium was filled with loyal fans of Fidel; only party members were invited to attend the game). On May 3 the Cubans got their revenge in Oriole Park, trouncing the Baltimore team 12-6 in a game that had all Cuba glued to the TV. The streets were deserted.

In November 1999 Hurricane Irene—the second hurricane in a year—pounded Cuba, causing four deaths and significant damage. That month, the leaders of Spain, Portugal and 16 Latin American countries attended the Ibero-American summit in Havana. Dignitaries included Spain's King Juan Carlos and Queen Sofia, the first Spanish monarchs to visit Cuba since independence. Though snubbing the United States's four-decade-old attempt to isolate Cuba, many dignitaries, including the king, spoke out against Castro's repression and called for greater democracy (their comments went unreported in Cuba).

Also in November, a provincial court in Havana upheld a US$121 billion dollar lawsuit against the United States government for 40 years of terrorist aggressions against the island. The lawsuit was filed by eight Cuban mass organizations representing 3,478 Cubans purportedly killed and 2,099 incapacitated as a result of Washington's attacks against the Cuban Revolution since 1959.

Cuba saw the millennium in with a new battle with Uncle Sam, this one over a five-year-old boy, Elián González, saved by the U.S. Coast Guard after his mother and 10 other people drowned when their boat sank en route from Cuba to Florida during Thanksgiving 1999. Elián, plucked from his inner tube, launched a continuing soap opera. Miami's anti-Castroite Cubans and right-wing politicians turned the child into a poster boy for the American Way of Life—a "new Dalai Lama," thought Wayne Smith—and demanded that the boy remain in the U.S. against the Cuban father's wishes. Castro (who routinely denies permission for the children of Cuban exiles to join their parents abroad), responded by demanding that the "kidnapped" boy be returned and turned the issue into an anti-American crusade by organizing "Free Elián" protests and summoning Cubans to attend the nationwide rallies (some teenagers sang their own muffled version of the protest chant, "Elián, our friend! Cuba is with you!" chanting, "Elián, our friend! Take us with you!").

In January 2000, Castro vowed that protests would last "10 years, if necessary," while the case wound through the Florida courts. Meanwhile Elián, who was turned into a geopolitical pawn by the two warring factions, had achieved almost saintly status among Miami's defiant Cuban exiles, some of whom, believing he had the power to heal, gathered outside his home in the city's Little Havana district in the hope of touching his hand. Flouting the law and integrity, Elián's crazed custodians refused to hand him over to his loving father when the latter arrived in the U.S. in April 2000 to collect his son. In a dawn raid, the INS grabbed Elián and reunited him with his father, who seems happily reconciled with life in Cuba. Confounding pundits, Juan Miguel González refused to apply for asylum and affirmed his wish to return Elián to a nurturing life in Cuba—preferring to live in a peaceable society that treasures its children. In late June Elián and his father returned to Cuba after the U.S. Supreme Court affirmed the father's right to custody of his son.

GOVERNMENT

Cuba is an independent socialist republic. The Cuban Constitution, adopted in 1975, defines it as a "socialist state of workers and peasants and all other manual and intellectual workers." Dr. Fidel Castro Ruz is head of both state and government.

All power and initiative are in the hands of the Communist Party, which controls the labyrinthine state apparatus. There are no legally recognized political organizations independent of the party, which the Constitution recognizes as "the highest leading force of the society and of the state."

The Constitution, copied largely from the Soviet Constitution of 1936, guarantees the "freedom and inviolability of the individual" as well as freedom of speech, press, and religion—as long as these conform to the "goals of socialist society." In reality, no dissent is permitted.

STATE STRUCTURE

The Central Government
The Council of Ministers: The highest-ranking executive body is the Council of Ministers, headed by Fidel Castro and comprising several vice presidents and ministers. The council is empowered to conduct affairs of the state and draw up bills for submission to the Assembly.

The Executive Committee of the Council of Ministers administers Cuba on a day-to-day basis.

According to the Constitution, the council is accountable to the National Assembly of People's Power, which "elects" the members at the initiative of the head of state. The council has jurisdiction over all ministries and central organizations and effectively runs the country under the direction of Fidel Castro.

The National Assembly: The *Asemblea Nacional* (National Assembly of People's Power) is invested with legislative authority but exercises little legislative initiative. The Assembly is a stepping stone for ambitious individuals whose political future depends on going along with leadership decisions. Discussion is usually restricted to subjects introduced from the leadership. It is mostly a rubber-stamp legislature. It has been headed since 1993 by Ricardo Alarcón, Cuba's ambassador to the United Nations and tipped as a potential successor to Fidel.

The Assembly is elected for a five-year term but meets only twice annually (members are part-timers, not full-time legislators). There were 589 deputies in the 1993-98 *quinquenio* (five-year term). Prior to 1993, deputies were elected by the provincial assemblies. In 1993 they were elected directly by voters, although candidacies must first be approved by the Communist Party. Most deputies are drawn

*revolutionary wall
in Manzanillo*

from the party bureaucracy and are predominantly male and white. The Assembly elects high government officials and ratifies executive appointments.

The Council of State: The Council of State is modeled on the Presidium of the former Soviet Union, and functions as the Executive Committee of the National Assembly when the latter is not in session. It is presided over by Fidel Castro.

The Cuban Communist Party

The sole political party is the *Partido Comunista de Cuba* (PCC), of which Fidel Castro is head and his brother Raúl vice secretary. It is closely modeled on the party of the former Soviet Union,

The party's goal is "to guide common efforts toward the construction of socialism." In Marxist theory, the construction of socialism proceeds through the "dictatorship of the proletariat" toward the Communist utopia. En route, the working class takes the reins of state power and governs in its own name. The party assumes unto itself the leadership role and ostensibly represents the "vanguard of the proletariat" or "institutional expression of the people." The PCC determines the direction in which society is to move, and the state provides the mechanism for moving in that direction.

The PCC occupies the central role in all government bodies and institutions. It is led by the *Buró Político* (Politburo), made up at press time of 24 individuals (the number keeps changing). Steering the party is the *Comité Central* (Central Committee) of the PCC, whose members are selected by Castro, who—surprise!—is its chairman. The Comité elects members of the Politburo. It meets every six months and is the principal forum through which the party leadership disseminates party policy to lower echelons. The committee—downsized from around 225 members to 150 in October 1997—is organized into departments, such as the Department of Economy. Less than 20% of members are women; the share of the military has declined from 32% to 12% since 1975.

At the base of the PCC chain is the party cell of 10 members organized at work and educational centers. The cells recruit new members, who go through a six-month scrutiny as to their ideological purity. The youth organizations are the most common avenue for passage into the PCC. Current membership is about 600,000 (about five percent of the population).

The party was formed in 1965. Most of the original 100 committee members were only nominally Communists; but all were ardent *Fidelista* loyalists. (In the early years following the Revo-

---

CUBA'S VITAL STATISTICS

Area: 114,478 square km (42,804 square miles)

Population: 11,100,000 (1999 estimate)

Annual Population Growth: 0.9% (1990-99)

Urbanization: 75%

Capital: Havana, pop. 2,200,000

Principal Cities: Camagüey, 740,000; Ciego de Avila, 365,000; Cienfuegos, 370,000; Guantánamo, 495,000; Holguín, 985,000; Las Tunas, 420,000; Matanzas, 610,000; Pinar del Rio 695,000; Sancti Spiritus, 435,000; Santa Clara, 810,000; Santiago de Cuba, 990,000

Religion: secular; most of those who practice religion are Roman Catholic, but traditional Afro-Cuban paganism has a large following; 4% Protestant

Language: Spanish

Climate: subtropical, with a wet season from May to October and a dry season from November to April. Average annual temperature is 24°C, with little variation. January and February are the coolest months.

Time: GMT -5. Daylight saving time operates Apr.-Oct.

Currency: peso (official rate of exchange is 1 peso to US$1; unofficial exchange rate is approximately 20 pesos to US$1)

Business Hours: Government offices: Mon.-Fri. 8:30 a.m.-12:30 p.m. and 1:30-5:30 p.m., alternate Saturdays 8 a.m.-5 p.m. National banks: Mon.-Fri. 8:30 a.m.-noon and 1:30-3 p.m.; Saturday 8:30-10:30 a.m.

Literacy: 98%

Life Expectancy: 75 years

Annual Birth Rate: 16 per 1,000 (1998)

Mortality Rate: 7 per 1,000 (1998)

Infant Mortality Rate: 6.5 per 1,000 (1999)

HUMAN RIGHTS

*D*isobedience is the capital sin in Cuba. "It is fair to say that under Castro, Cubans have lost even the tenuous civil and political liberties they had under the old regime," claims Professor Wayne Smith, former head of the U.S. Interests Section in Havana. "Woe to anyone who gets on a soap box in downtown Havana and questions the wisdom of the Castro government." The Cuban penal code states that disrespect for authorities is good for one to seven years in prison. Castro is careful not to crack down too hard, but free speech is tightly controlled. As a result, Cubans talk in whispers when discussing the government, are fearful of mentioning Fidel by name, and live generally in a state of fear about police informers (known as *emboris siciñangas* and a score of other terms).

Writers and artists suffer systematic persecution for "deviations" and are regularly expelled from UNEAC, the Writers' Union, "as traitors to the revolutionary cause." Dissidents dismissed from their jobs are often put to work as gardeners—it's safer to poison garden insects than Cuban minds. Elizardo Sánchez, president of the dissident Cuban Commission of Human Rights and National Reconciliation and the most famous of Cuban dissidents, has since spent years in and out of jail.

The regime is not above jailing even its most loyal supporters if they renege on the Revolution. Carlos Franquí, leading revolutionary, founder of *Radio Rebelde,* and editor-in-chief of *Revolución,* was even expunged from photos (airbrushed into nonexistence) and made a nonperson until he was forced to flee surreptitiously to France. Even the most trivial comment or action can bring retribution. For example, Olga Andreu, the librarian of *Casa de las Américas,* was removed from her job simply for recommending Caberara Infante's *Tres Tristes Tigres.*

Plantados (dissidents who remain firm) are often taken to Villa Marista, the state security headquarters, where psychological abuse is said to be common. The unlucky ones are said to end up at either the Combinado del Este penitentiary, south of Havana, or the Carbó Serviá ward at the Mazorra, the Havana Provincial Psychiatric Hospital. Dissidents have reported electric-shock treatment and other physical abuses. *Against All Hope,* by former *plantado* Armando Valladeres, tells of his 22 years behind bars in Cuba.

In late 1995, some 130 dissident factions—most prominently the intellectual opposition movement *Criterio Alternativo* (Alternative Criterion Group), led by Cuban poet María Elena Cruz Varela—formed an umbrella group called the **Concilio Cubano.** Concilio represents the most significant political challenge to Castro in four decades; while not seeking to overthrow the government, the organization demands that free speech be permitted. The past few years have seen a dramatic increase in dissident activity . . . and a new round of repression.

Freeze and Thaw

Contemporary Cuba, however, is a far cry from the 1960s, when crushing sentences were imposed en masse following secret, often puppet, trials. In 1965 when the CIA was doing its best to overthrow the Cuban government, Castro admitted that there were 20,000 "counterrevolutionary criminals" in Cuban jails, including cultural and political dissidents. The true numbers were unquestionably far higher.

The U.S. Department of State's reports on human rights suggest that Cuba's record has improved steadily. By international standards, the numbers of political prisoners is now few, hovering somewhere around 300 Cubans in jail for strictly political offenses. The repression runs hot and cold, and the past few years have seen a chill, including harsh new laws that extend the death penalty for 112 offenses (79 for violations of state security). In 1999 a new gag law introduced jail terms for Cuban journalists writing for the foreign press and for any Cuban who provides information to the "enemy." The recent spate of repression resulted in the United Nations Human Rights Commission placing Cuba on its list of worst offenders in 1999, when Amnesty International—website: www.amnestyusa.org—named Cuba and Colombia the worse offenders in Latin America.

How Much Is the U.S. to Blame?

A small country persecuted by the most powerful nation on earth and living under a state of economic siege is not the best ground for freedom to flourish. The U.N. Special Rapporteur seriously criticized Cuba's human rights record but also condemned Washington's hostility to Castro's government as a contributing factor that provides a handy excuse for keeping a tight rein on the populace.

lution, Castro purged old-school Communist militants from the bureaucracy and political institutions, subordinating both in 1963 to the newly formed *Partido Unificado de la Revolución Socialista*—United Party of the Socialist Revolution—which was in turn replaced by the PCC.)

Castro has since drawn from "the elite of the elite" of the party to maintain his government. All top Cuban officials had to be graduates of the Ñico López Central School of the Cuban Communist Party, a university offering indoctrination in Marxist theory.

Key positions in government have been occupied by loyal revolutionaries from the ranks of M-26-7, a kind of elite club (even most Cubans are not aware of who constitutes the inner circle and how it works), although this has changed in recent years as most members of the old guard have been "retired" and replaced by young party stalwarts. Loyalty to Fidel takes precedence over all other considerations.

Policy emanates from Fidel Castro, who has used his own charismatic qualities and inordinate tactical skills to consolidate almost hegemonic authority. Although the Council of State and Council of Ministers ostensibly make the decisions, Castro shapes those decisions (it is claimed that no official in his right mind dares to criticize Castro and that constructive discussion is virtually impossible). The PCC has no program—Castro defines the flavor of the day.

In December 1975 the First Congress of the Communist Party adopted a new constitution (ratified in February 1976), which established the *permanent* character of the state and ruled out any ideological or structural changes in the future. It became unconstitutional to challenge Fidel Castro, who was effectively named leader for life. Total power was legally vested in him as first secretary of the Communist Party, president of the Republic, chairman of the State Council, chairman of the Council of Ministers, and commander in chief of the armed forces. (He is normally referred to as *Comandante-en-Jefe,* Commander in Chief.) His younger brother, Raúl, was named first vice president of both the Council of State and the Council of Ministers, the second secretary of the Communist Party, defense minister, and General of the Army.

Local Government
The country is divided into 14 provinces and 169 municipalities *(municipios),* dominated by the city of Havana (a separate province), with its population of two million people. Each province and municipality is governed by an Assembly of Delegates of People's Power, representing state bodies at the local level. Traditionally the councils elected members of the Provincial Assemblies; since 1992 members have been elected by popular ballot and serve two-and-a-half-year terms.

The first experiment in "elected" local government—*poder popular* (popular power)—began in 1974 and was designed to improve public administration through limited decentralization. The organs of poder popular also serve as forums for citizens' grievances and deal with problems such as garbage collection, housing improvement, and running day-care centers. When new legislation is pending, local officials go out to "discuss it with the people." They are not autonomous bodies, however, and are hampered by dependence on the vertical structure of economic planning. The Communist Party closely monitors their performance.

The country is also unofficially divided into three areas that are sometimes still referred to colloquially by their colonial titles: Occidente (the western region), Las Villas (the center), and Oriente (the east)

Committees for the Defense of the Revolution
The linchpins in maintaining the loyalty of the masses and spreading the Revolution at the grassroots level are the *Comités para la Defensa de la Revolución* (CDRs), created in 1960 as neighborhood committees designed to protect the Revolution from internal enemies. There are 15,000 CDRs in Havana, and 100,000 throughout the island. Every block has one.

On one hand, the CDRs perform wonderful work: they collect blood for hospitals, take retired people on vacations, discourage kids from playing hooky, organize graduation parties, etc. But they are also the vanguard in keeping an eye on the local population, watching and snitching on neighbors (the CDRs are under the direction of MININT, the Ministry of the Interior). Anyone nay-saying the Revolution, mocking

Castro, or dealing on the black market (economic crimes are political crimes, seen as a security threat to the state), is likely to be reported by the block warden, a loyal revolutionary who records what he or she hears from colleagues and neighbors.

People face harsh retribution if they cross the line into political activism. In 1991, Rapid Response Detachments were formed, ostensibly made up of volunteers from local CDRs but under the purview of MININT, to deal with public expressions of dissent. This they do through distasteful pogroms called *actos de repudios,* beating up dissidents, much as did Hitler's *Blockwarts.* Like Nazi street gangs, the brigades are said to be a spontaneous reaction of outraged Cubans.

A position as head of a CDR once earned respect, and weekly meetings could count on a good audience. Today, CDRs are disdained by the urban masses and attendance is minimal, "and these are mostly friends who come to help him save face and avoid ridicule," says author Jon Lee Anderson of a friend who is a party militant and head of his local CDR.

Other Mass Organizations

Citizen participation in building socialism is manifested through a number of mass organizations controlled by the PCC. Prominent among them are the **Federation of Cuban Women,** the **Confederation of Cuban Workers, Organization of Small Farmers,** and the **Union of Communist Youth.** Although ostensibly representing the interests of their members, the bodies subordinate these to national goals. Thus, for example, strikes are banned and workers have learned to subordinate their autonomy in return for benefits (pensions, holidays, guaranteed employment, etc.) from the state. No independent labor organizations are permitted.

Membership in various mass organizations is a virtual prerequisite for getting on in Cuban society. Promotions, access to university, even to vacations and material incentives for the average citizen rely upon being a "good revolutionary" through participation in an organization. Those who are not members become social outcasts. Over 80% of Cuban citizens are members (in contrast, a majority of those who have left Cuba were not members).

'Now for the evidence,' said the King, 'and then the sentence.' 'No!' said the Queen, 'first the sentence and then the evidence!' 'Nonsense!' cried Alice, so loudly that everybody jumped, 'the idea of having the sentence first. . . !'

The Judiciary

The highest court in the land is the People's Supreme Court in Havana. Its president and vice president are appointed by Fidel Castro; other judges are elected by the National Assembly. There are seven courts of appeal, 14 provincial courts, and 169 municipal courts for minor offenses. The provinces are divided into judicial districts with courts for civil and criminal cases.

Courts are a fourth branch of government and are not independent. The judiciary is not charged with protecting individual rights, as in democratic societies, but rather, according to Article 121 of the Constitution, with "maintaining and strengthening socialist legality." Thus they are subject to interference by the political leadership. The Council of State, for example, can overturn judicial decisions, and Castro frequently does so in political trials. And interpretation of the Constitution is the prerogative solely of the National Assembly, not the courts.

Private practice of law is not permitted, and the accused are denied recourse to defense counsel other than state-appointed officials. The penal code accepts a defendant's confession as sufficient proof of his guilt (there are many cases of individuals pressured into confessing to crimes they did not commit). Revolutionary Summary Tribunals enjoy wide powers. Due process is systematically flouted in political cases according to the apolitical Washington-based human-rights group American Watch.

Cuba, however, has a policy of criminal rehabilitation (except for political crimes). In meting out punishment, the penal system allows for amends and guarantees an individual's job upon release from prison. People considered a menace to society receive harsh sentences. Capital punishment by firing squad remains.

The Military and Security Apparatus

Cuba boasts a formidable military under the aegis of the Fuerzas Armadas Revolucionarias (FAR), commanded by Raúl Castro. Its military and militia are replete with battle-tested soldiers (as many as 350,000 Cuban troops served on active duty in Angola and Ethiopia during the 1970s and '80s). In 1993 over 180,000 men and women were on active duty (including 13,500 in the navy and 22,000 in the air force), although this number has since been scaled back to about 65,000 troops, according to a 1998 U.S. government report, which says the navy has shrunk to only one dozen ships and the air force to two dozen combat-ready planes. In addition, Cuba has 130,000 reservists supplemented by about 100,000 in the "youth labor army," 50,000 in the civil defense force, and 1.3 million in the territorial militias. All males between the ages of 16 and 45 are subject to conscription (conscripts complete a basic training program and are assigned to one of the regular armed forces). Women between 17 and 35 may volunteer for military service.

The key to defense, however, is the "Guerra de Todo el Pueblo" (War of All the People). In the event of an attack, the *entire* population of Cuba will be called into action. To this end, regular defense exercises are conducted for all segments of the civilian population. All Cuban citizens undergo compulsory military training one Sunday—called "Día de la Defensa"—each month, though this, too, has been scaled back. While traveling through Cuba, do not be surprised to see young women in high heels or old ladies with their hair in curlers tossing grenades and taking pot-shots at imaginary GIs. Small military training grounds are scattered along the roadsides throughout the island.

Spending for the armed forces has fallen sharply from its peak of US$2.24 billion in 1988. In 1991 the military was re-engineered to help the economy—a return to the model of the "civil soldier," who assists in construction and agriculture—and earn its way by virtue of what it produces from its investments in tourism, agriculture, and industry. As much as 70% of the armed forces' effort is involved in their own self-sustainment.

As recently as 1991, the Soviet Union maintained about 11,000 military personnel in Cuba; by mid-1993 every one had returned to the former Soviet Union. The Russians maintain a handful of staff at the former Soviet electronic surveillance facility at Lourdes.

State security is the responsibility of the Ministry of the Interior, which operates a number of intelligence-related services, plus the National Revolutionary Police (PNR), with paramilitary and military units under its umbrella. Other intelligence units—most notoriously, the much-feared Seguridad del Estado or G-2—are operated by the Department of State Security and the General Directorate of Intelligence. The repressive machinery, euphemistically known as "social controls," is all-encompassing. Ordinary Cubans face constant harassment, including on the streets by police demanding to see their *cédulas* (ID), which much be carried at all times. Secret police are everywhere, and the average citizen is ever fearful of informers, colloquially termed *embory siciñanga,* or "untrustworthy." There are more security-linked officials than meet the eye (as many as one in 27 Cubans, including informers, according to Guillermo Cabrera Infanta, the former editor of *Revolución*).

GOVERNMENT BY PERSONAL WHIM

Cuba is really a *Fidelista* state, one in which Marxist-Leninism has been loosely grafted onto Cuban nationalism, then tended and shaped by one man. The Cuban leader likes to leave his development choices wide open, allowing a flexible interpretation of the correct path to socialism. Ideological dogma is subordinated to tactical considerations. Castro's emotions, what Castro biographer Tad Szulc calls his *caudillo* temperament (that of a modernizing but megalomanical political strongman), are powerful factors in his decision-making.

Castro makes decisions about the minutest aspects of government (it was he, for example, who decided that nurses should wear trousers, not skirts, because a nurse in skirt leaning over a patient, he suggested impishly, might cause a man lying in a bed behind her to have a heart attack). Even minor decisions are delayed until they have received Castro's blessing.

In consequence most Cuban managers in the state-run economy lack the courage or authority to make decisions, a massive obstacle to the development of an efficient economy. Government officials must study Castro's speeches intently to stay tuned with his forever-changing

FIDEL CASTRO

hatever you think of his politics, Fidel Castro is unquestionably one of the most remarkable and enigmatic figures of this century, thriving on contradiction and paradox like a romantic character from the fiction of his Colombian novelist friend Gabriel García Márquez.

Fidel Castro Rúz, child prodigy, was born on 13 August 1926 at Manacas *finca* near Birán in northern Oriente, the fifth of nine children of Ángel Castro y Argiz. Fidel's mother was the family housemaid, Lina Ruz González, whom Ángel married after divorcing his wife (several biographers claim that Fidel's illegitimacy caused him great conflicts). Fidel weighed 10 pounds at birth—the first hint that he would always be larger than life. The early records of his family are sketchy, and Castro, who seems to have had a happy childhood, likes to keep it that way—much as he attempts to suppress the notion that he comes from a well-to-do family. (Fidel's father was an émigré to Cuba from Galicia in Spain as a destitute 13-year-old. In Cuba, he made money from the presence of the American-owned United Fruit Company and became a wealthy landowner who employed 300 workers on a 26,000-acre domain; he owned 1,920 acres and leased the rest from the United Fruit Company, to whom he sold cane.)

As a boy Fidel was extremely assertive, rebellious, and combative. He was a natural athlete and grew especially accomplished at track events and baseball. He was no sportsman, however; if his team was losing, he would often leave the field and go home. Gabriel García Márquez has said, "I do not think anyone in this world could be a worse loser" (in December 1999 Castro withdrew the Cuban boxing squad from the world amateur boxing championship in Houston because he disagreed with some of the referees' decisions). It became a matter of principle to excel—and win—at everything. His Jesuit teachers identified what Richard Nixon later saw in Castro: "that indefinable quality which, for good or evil, makes a leader of men." His school yearbook recorded that he was *excelencia* and predicted that "he will fill with brilliant pages the book of his life."

Star Rising

Fidel enrolled in Havana University's law school in October 1945, where he immediately plunged into politics and gained the limelight as a student leader. Castro earned his first front-page newspaper appearance following his first public speech, denouncing President Grau, on 27 November 1946. In 1947, when the foremost political opposition figure, Edward Chibás, formed the *Ortodoxo* party, Castro, at the age of 21, was sufficiently well known to be invited to help organize it. He stopped attending law school and rose rapidly to prominence as the most outspoken critic of the Grau government, including as head of his own revolutionary group, Orthodox Radical Action.

The period was exceedingly violent: armed gangs roamed the campus, and Fidel never went anywhere without a gun. As organizer of the street demonstrations calling for Grau's ouster, Castro was soon on the police hit list, and several attempts were made on his life. In February 1949, Fidel was accused of assassinating a political rival. After being arrested and subsequently released on "conditional liberty," he went into hiding.

He remained determined to stay in the limelight, however. In March he flew to Bogotá to attend the Ninth Inter-American Conference, where foreign ministers were destined to sign the charter of the Organization of American States. Soon enough Castro was in the thick of student demonstrations opposing the organization as a scheme for U.S. domination of the hemisphere. One week later, while he was on his way to meet Jorge Eliécer Gaitán (the popular leader of the opposition Progressive Liberal Party), Gaitán was assassinated. Bogotá erupted in spontaneous riots—the *Bogotázo*. Castro was irresistibly drawn in and, arming himself with a tear-gas shotgun and police uniform stolen from a police station, found himself at the vanguard of the revolution—with a police detachment under his command. Inevitably Castro again made headline news.

On 12 October 1949, Castro married a pretty philosophy student named Mirta Díaz-Balart, and they honeymooned for several weeks in the

United States. (Fulgencio Batista even gave the couple $1,000 for their honeymoon; Castro's father-in-law was Batista's attorney. The couple divorced in 1954.) Back home, Castro was once again in the thick of political violence. Gangsterism had soared under President Prío. In November Fidel gave a suicidal speech in which he denounced the gangster process, admitted his past associations with gangsterism, then named all the gangsters, politicians, and student leaders profiting from the "gangs' pact." Again in fear for his life, Fidel left Cuba for the United States.

He returned four months later to cram for a multiple degree. In September 1950 Castro graduated with the titles of Doctor of Law, Doctor of Social Sciences, and Doctor of Diplomatic Law (in the press, Fidel is often referred to as Dr. Castro). He then began a law practice, concentrating on "lost causes" on behalf of the poor (most of his legal work was offered pro bono publico—free).

Congressional Candidate

By 1951 Castro was preparing for national office. Fulgencio Batista, who had returned from retirement in Florida to run for president, even asked to receive Castro to get the measure of the young man who in January 1952 shook Cuba's political foundation by releasing a detailed indictment of President Prío. Castro's campaign was far ahead of his time. The imaginative 25-year-old utilized mass mailings and stump speeches with a foresight and veracity theretofore unknown. His personal magnetism, his brilliant speeches, and his apparent honesty aroused the crowds, who cheered him deliriously.

Castro was certain to be elected to the Chamber of Deputies. It was also clear that Batista was going to be trounced in the presidential contest, so at dawn on 10 March 1952, he effected a *golpe* (military coup) and, next day, moved back into the presidential palace he had vacated eight years before.

Says Tad Szulc: "Many Cubans think that without a coup Castro would have served as a congressman for four years until 1956, then run for the Senate, and made his pitch for the presidency in 1960 or 1964. Given the fact that Cuba was wholly bereft of serious political leadership and given Castro's rising popularity. . . it would appear that he was fated to govern Cuba—no matter how he arrived at the top job."

The rest, as they say, is history.

A Communist *Caudillo*

At 30 years old, Castro was fighting in the Sierra Maestra, a disgruntled lawyer turned revolutionary who craved Batista's job. At 32, he had it. He was determined not to let go—the last in a long line of self-proclaimed Cuban redeemers who have reneged on their promise. When he came down from the mountains, he was considered a "younger, bearded version of Magwitch: a tall outlaw emerging from the fog of history to make Pips of us all," wrote Guillermo Cabrera Infante, a brilliant novelist who, like thousands, supported Castro but later soured on him: "The outlaw became a law unto himself." Fidel used the Revolution to carry out a personal *caudillista* coup (a *caudillo* is a Spanish strongman leader). "Communist or not, what was being built in Cuba was an old-fashioned personality cult," wrote John Anderson.

Castro has since led Cuba through four decades of "dizzying experience." He has outlasted nine U.S. presidents, each of whom predicted his imminent demise and plotted to hasten it by fair means or foul. He shows no sign of relinquishing power and has said he will never do so while Washington remains hostile—a condition he thrives on and works hard to maintain (Graham Greene determined that Castro was "an empirical Marxist, who plays Communism by ear and not by the book").

Castro is consummately Machiavellian: masking truth to reach and maintain power. "He has lied all his life, although he does not see his 'lies' as lies," suggests biographer Georgie Ann Geyer. "Often the first person he deceived was himself," added historian Hugh Thomas. Castro is far from the saint his ardent admirers portray; nor is he the evil oppressor portrayed by Washington. Says Gabriel García Márquez: "He has the nearly mystical conviction that the greatest achievement of the human being is the proper formation of conscience and that moral incentives, rather than material ones, are capable of changing the world and moving history forward." He is also sincere in his desire to inspire a society motivated by kindness and generosity in others. Castro deserves full credit for the extraordinary gifts of national dignity and advances in health and education that the Revolution has bestowed upon Cuba and wishes to share with the underprivileged world.

Castro—who knew he could never carry out his revolution in an elective system—genuinely believes that disease, malnutrition, illiteracy, economic inadequacy, and dependence on the West are criminal
continues on next page

FIDEL CASTRO
(continued)

shames and that a better social order can be created through the perfection of good values. "Political ideas are worthless if they aren't inspired by noble, selfless sentiments," he has said. "I am sure that all the people could be happy—and for them I would be ready to incur the hatred and ill will of a few thousand individuals, including some of my relatives, half of my acquaintances, two-thirds of my professional colleagues, and four-fifths of my former schoolmates."

Despite the turn of events, Castro clings to the thread of his dream: "I have no choice but to continue being a communist, like the early Christians remained Christian. . . If I'm told 98% of the people no longer believe in the Revolution, I'll continue to fight. If I'm told I'm the only one who believes in it, I'll continue."

A Hatred of Uncle Sam

Castro turned to Communism mostly for strategic, not ideological, reasons, but his bitterness towards the United States undoubtedly also shaped his decision. He has been less committed to Marxism than to anti-imperialism, in which he is unwavering: he has chosen, suggests Geyer, a "classic Masada posture of eternal and suicidal confrontation against the Americans." He has cast himself in the role of David versus Goliath, in the tradition of José Martí, who wrote "my sling is the sling of David." Castro sees himself as Martí's heir, representing the same combination of New World nationalism, Spanish romanticism, and philosophical radicalism. His trump card is Cuban nationalist sentiment.

His boyhood impressions of destitution in Holguín province under the thumb of the United Fruit Company and later the 1954 overthrow of the reformist Arbenz government in Guatemala by a military force organized by the CIA and underwritten by "Big Fruit," had a profound impact on Castro's thinking. Ever since, Castro has viewed world politics through the prism of anti-Americanism. During the war in the Sierra Maestra, Castro stated, "When this war has ended, a much bigger and greater war will start for me, a war I shall launch against them. I realize this will be my true destiny."

He brilliantly used the Cold War to enlist the Soviet Union to move Cuba out of the U.S. orbit, and was thus able—with Soviet funds—to bolster his stature as a nationalist redeemer by guaranteeing the Cuban masses substantial social and economic gains.

Though the Cold War is over, he appears like Napoleon on St. Helena, thought Wendy Gimbel, a prisoner of his own fantasies, "playing on the floor with his tin soldiers, recreating his victories in battles ended long ago."

Castro, however, has no animosities towards North Americans. His many close personal contacts range from media maverick Ted Turner to actor Jack Lemmon and even the Rockefeller clan.

Many Talents

Castro has a gargantuan hunger for information, a huge trove of knowledge (Fidel is an avid speed-reader), and an equally prodigious memory (he never forgets facts and figures, a remarkable asset he nourished at law school, where he forced himself to depend on his memory by destroying the materials he had learned by heart).

There is a sense of perfection in everything he does, applied through a superbly methodical mind and laser-clear focus. He has astounding political instincts, notably an uncanny ability to predict the future moves of his adversaries (Castro is a masterly chess player). Castro's "rarest virtue," says his intimate friend Gabriel García Márquez, "is the ability to foresee the evolution of an event to its farthest-reaching consequences."

Castro is also a gambler of unsurpassed self-confidence. (Says Infante, "Castro's real genius lies in the arts of deception and while the world plays bridge by the book, he plays poker, bluffing and holding his cards close to his olive-green chest.") His daring and chutzpah are attributed by some observers to his stubborn Galician temperament—that of an anarchist and born *guerrillero* (guerrilla fighter). He has stood at the threshold of death several times and loves to court danger. For example, in 1981 he chose to run to the Mexican port of Cozumel in a high-speed launch just to see whether the U.S. Navy—then patrolling the Gulf of Mexico to stop Cuban arms shipments to Nicaragua—could catch him.

Above all, Castro has an insatiable appetite for the limelight and a narcissistic focus on his theatrical role. (His vanity is so monumental that on one of his rare visits to see his illegitimate and ignored daughter, Alina, he asked if she wanted to see a movie. She wanted to see *The Godfather,* but instead her father treated her to a screening of a film about his triumphal tour of Eastern Europe.) Fidel wears glasses but dislikes being seen in public in them, considering them a sign of weakness. His beard is also more than a trademark; he likes to hide his double chin. He never laughs at himself unless he makes the joke. And he assiduously avoids singing or dancing (he is perhaps the only male in Cuba who has never been seen to dance).

He nurtures his image with exquisite care, feigning modesty to hide his immense ego. "I am not here because I assigned myself to this job. . . I am here because this job has been thrust upon me," Castro told journalist Ann Louise Bardach in 1994. He also claims that his place in history does not bother him: "All the glory in the world can fit into a kernel of corn." Yet in the same breath he likens himself to Jesus Christ, one of his favorite allusions (the reason Castro didn't object to pictures of Jesus next to him, went a joke during the Pope's visit to Cuba in 1998, is that he thought it was another picture of himself). Castro has carefully cultivated the myth of Fidel the Christ-like redeemer figure. "He had the 'Jordan River syndrome,'" Cuban psychiatrist Dr. Rubén Darío Rumbaut told Geyer, "If people came to him, they would be purified."

Castro's revolutionary concept has been built on communicating with the masses (whom he sees and treats as his "children"), and he conducts much of his domestic government through his frequent public speeches, usually televised in entirety (Cubans joke that he always sits up slightly when talking into the camera because he has hemorrhoids). He understood at an early stage that he and television were made for each other. Castro—"one of the best television actors in the world"—is masterfully persuasive, an amazingly gifted speaker who holds Cubans spellbound with his oratory textured in rich, gilded layers, using his trademark combination of flattery and enigmatic language to obfuscate and arouse. Says the *Wall Street Journal:* "Say this for Fidel: the man knows spin."

His early speeches often lasted for hours; today he is more succinct. (Fidel's loquaciousness is legendary. When he and Raúl were imprisoned together on the Isle of Pines in 1954, Raúl complained that his elder brother "didn't let me sleep for weeks. . . he just talked day and night, day and night.") He is not, however, a man of small talk; he is deadly serious whenever he opens his mouth. He also listens intently when the subject interests him; he is a great questioner, homing immediately to the heart of the matter.

Adored or Hated?

A large segment of Cubans see Castro as a ruthless dictator who cynically betrayed the democratic ideals that he used to rally millions to his banner. To Miami exiles especially, *El Líder* is just a common tyrant. Nonetheless, Castro's longevity and success are due in great measure to the admiration of many among the Cuban people to whom he was and remains a hero. There persists an adulation for *El Máximo* or *El Caballo* (the horse—an allusion to the Chinese belief that dreams represent numbers to place bets on, and that the horse is number one). Traveling through Cuba you'll come across countless families who keep a framed photograph of him, though many do so to keep in Fidel's good books. You'll even hear of women offering themselves to Fidel, "drawn by his power, his unfathomable eyes."

Cubans' bawdy street wisdom says that Castro has various domiciles—a sane precaution in view of the CIA's numerous attempts on his life—so that he can attend to his lovers. Certainly many highly intelligent and beautiful women have dedicated themselves to Castro and his cause. But Fidel saves his most ardent passions for the Revolution, and the women in his life have been badly treated as *Havana Dreams,* the biography of his former lover, Naty Revuelta, reveals. (Delia Soto del Valle, Castro's wife of 30-odd years and with whom he has six sons, is rarely seen in public and never with her husband.) Nonetheless, he is a "dilettante extraordinaire" in esoteric pursuits, notably gourmet dining (but not cigars; Fidel quit smoking in 1985). His second love is deep-sea fishing. He is also a good diver and used to fly down frequently to spearfish at his tiny retreat on Cayo Piedra, where he dined on an offshore barge and slept in a rustic old caretaker's home while guests relaxed more luxuriously in a modern guesthouse.

Castro retains the loyalty of millions of Cubans, but he is only loyal to those who are loyal to him. His capacity for Homeric rage is renowned, and it is said that no official in his right mind dares criticize him. (Paradoxically, he can be extremely gentle and courteous, especially towards women, in whose company he is slightly abashed.) Cubans fear the consequences of saying anything against him, discreetly stroking their chins—an allusion to his beard—rather than uttering his name. He feels that to survive he must be "absolutely and undeviatingly uncompromising." In 1996 his biographer Tad Szulc wrote, "He is determined not to tolerate any challenge to his authority, whatever the consequences." You are ei-

continues on next page

FIDEL CASTRO
(continued)

ther for the Revolution or against it. Castro does not forget or pardon. Beneath the gold foil lies a heart of cold steel (Castro's former mentor at the Colegio de Belén, Father Armando Llorente, noted that he "had the cruelty of the Gallego . . . . The Spaniard of the north is cruel, hard"). Thus, while he has always shown solicitude for those who have served him or the Revolution, he demands, for example, that loyalists sever personal ties with family members who have turned their backs on Cuba (he routinely denies exit permits for children of Cubans who have fled the country and want their youngsters to join them). His policies have divided countless families, and Castro's family is no exception. His sister, Juanita, left for Miami in 1964 and is an outspoken critic of her brother's policies; and his tormented daughter, Alina Fernández Revuelta, fled in disguise in 1993 and vilifies her father from her home in Spain. Castro's long-suffering former wife, Mirta Díaz-Balart also lives in Spain, separated from her son and unable to return.

Castro denies that a personality cult exists. Yet Castro lives, suggests Szulc, "bathed in the absolute adulation orchestrated by the propaganda organs of the regime." The first page of newspapers and the lead item on the evening television news are devoted to Castro's public acts or speeches. Although there are no streets or public edifices named for him, monuments, posters, and billboards are adorned with his quotations and face, notably on May Day and other special holidays, when stooges work the crowds with chants of "Fi-del! Fi-del!"

Castro's hair and beard have grayed and his skin is dotted with sunspots, but when I last saw him in 1999 he looked in good health. Says writer Guy Talese: "His facial skin is florid and unsagging, his dark eyes dart around the room with ever-alert intensity, and he has a full head of lustrous gray hair not thinning at the crown." Rumors persist of ill health, but doctors say Castro maintains a mostly vegetarian diet and works out every day on an exercise bicycle. His family is renowned for longevity (one of his relatives recently returned to Cuba for the birthday party of his 105-year-old grandmother). Given his innate conviction of destiny and unquenchable thirst to lead, the indefatigable Cuban leader, who turned 74 in 2000 and has outlasted all other leaders of his time, could be around for many years.

views. The fear of repercussions from on high is so great that the bureaucracy—Cubans call it a "*burro*cracy"—has evolved as a "mutually protective society" (Cubans joke that the island *is* a two-party state—the Communist Party and the Bureaucratic Party). Says Gabriel García Márquez: "Beside the enormous achievements that sustain the revolution—the political, scientific, sports, cultural achievements—there is a colossal bureaucratic incompetence affecting nearly every order of daily life, and most particularly domestic happiness."

The result—besides an "endless labyrinth of errors committed and about to be committed" (in a speech in early 1987, Castro said, "We must correct the errors we made in correcting our errors")—is minimal accountability. Castro has been quick to admit the shortcomings of the system, which he blames on irresponsible managers, lack of discipline, and greed and corruption in high places (making, suggests Maurice Halperin, "the noticeable exception of his own performance."

Castro has built a new privileged ruling class based around top-level government officials, the security apparatus, and the military. Access to privilege has fostered a struggle to obtain political position; for every inept or corrupt bureaucrat, however, are many highly capable and dedicated Communists who have not taken advantage of their powerful positions to aggrandize themselves.

"The fundamental problem," says Tad Szulc, "remains Fidel Castro's psychological inability, rather than conscious refusal, to let go of any power . . . a state of affairs that paralyzes all initiative at lower levels." Political rivalry—even criticism—isn't welcome. Purges within the party and government are occasionally aimed against individuals allegedly trying to establish their own power bases or expressing disaffection. And apocalyptic slogans such as "Socialism or Death!" indicate that on the surface, Castro prefers obduracy over consent and political change.

"Direct Democracy"

Fidel Castro runs Cuba as much by charismatic as through institutional leadership: *personalismo* is central in *fidelismo*. Castro has called Western democracies "complete garbage." He prefers what he calls "direct democracy"—his appeals ("popular consultations") to the people. Castro has relied on his ability to whip up the crowds at mass rallies and elicit mass support through direct appeals to the Cuban people.

Castro uses persuasive arguments to keep revolutionary ardor alive. Images of destitution in neighboring countries are standard fare, as is the threat from the United States, which has spent four decades assiduously trying to undermine Castro and the Cuban Revolution. Despite his anti-embargo rhetoric, Castro works hard to maintain a state of tension, suggesting that he prefers relations just as they are.

For the first many years, Fidel bounced around the countryside in his jeep to learn firsthand what the people felt, identifying their problems and working to resolve them. Gradually, however, it is claimed, Fidel lost touch with what the average Cuban feels and became "caught in his own delusions," while apparatchiks and technocrats, who "form the loyal crowds at speeches," seek to protect or further their careers by telling Castro what he wants to hear.

A State of Acquiescence

Castro has engineered a state where an individual's personal survival requires a display of loyalty and adherence to the Revolution. Otherwise jail or "spontaneous" acts of repudiation by gangs of "citizens" quickly silence the dissident and serve to put others on notice. Castro maintains control through intimidation and repressive laws: the state is a domineering entity in every aspect of Cubans lives. "A margin of public criticism is allowed, to vent political pressure. The headiest steam is periodically allowed to leave for Florida on rafts and inflated inner tubes. A Cuban prefers to risk his life on the Straits of Florida than risk his life throwing a Molotov cocktail at some government office," says Lisette Bustamante, a former Cuban TV correspondent who fled to Spain.

The government maintains a file on *every* worker, a labor dossier that follows him or her from job to job. Cubans have to voice—or fake—their loyalty. To become *integrado* (integrated) is essential to get by. Transgressions are reported in one's dossier. It's advantageous to be a member of the Union of Young Communists or a similar organization in order to prove loyalty to the government. Most workplaces convene meetings in which workers discuss government poli-

cies and their effects on the people. Complaints are relatively few, to avoid inviting trouble. If "antisocial" comments are noted, the worker may be kicked out of his or her job, or blackballed.

Most Cubans have accommodated themselves to the parameters of permissible behavior set out years ago. The hardcore opponents left for Miami long ago. Most of the rest go along. The fear of the unknown, of losing one's benefits, of vengeance from the disaffected, are powerful factors in the inertia that pervades the country.

Nonetheless, dissidence and vocal opposition to both the state of affairs and the Castro government have grown markedly in recent years. A majority of Cubans are tired of sacrifice, foolhardy experiments, and the paternalism that tells them how to live their lives. The constant opening and closing of society has taken its toll, raising and then dashing Cubans' hopes.

Rising social discontent and divisions at the grassroots level have prompted the government to broaden and invigorate its structures to attract and maintain support and keep revolutionary fervor alive. Meanwhile expressions of discontent have risen markedly, as have harassment and jailing of dissidents, notably in spring 1996, again since 1999, when police initiated crackdowns on dissidents, freelancers, and Cubans having contact with foreigners.

From Marx to Martí

The sudden collapse of the Soviet bloc sent severe ideological shock waves through Cuba and forced Castro to make political changes that marked a break with the past. Fidel was clearly shaken by events in Eastern Europe and seemed to lose his self-confidence and footing. Castro recognized that the top-down process was out of sync with the social base. He embarked on his own version of the "Chinese model" for the survival of socialism: creating a market economy with the aid of foreign investment, while maintaining political control. Rather than move towards a multi-party system, Castro aimed to make the present one-party system more democratic and responsive to people's needs. Major political reform was out of the question: Castro believes that the Soviet Union collapsed because Mikhail Gorbachev allowed both economic and political reforms.

In March 1990 he called for the Fourth Communist Party Congress and initiated a grassroots program to collect recommendations from the populace—the first national public opinion survey in post-1959 history. More than 3.5 million Cubans spoke their minds before the meetings were abruptly called off. The people expressed overwhelming desire for reform. While Cubans aired their grievances, the Soviet Union collapsed. As a result the Fourth Congress—held in October 1991—ended up concentrating on how to save socialism, declaring its faith in the existing system, instead of how to embark on the next stage of the Revolution. The Congress closed with an announcement that Cuba would live under wartime conditions. Hopes for liberalization of the economy were dashed.

Nonetheless, the Congress enacted several key reforms. Elections by voice vote within the Communist Party were replaced by confidential ballots (leading to the first-ever votes—three—against Fidel Castro), and religious believers were again welcomed into the party. And delegates to Cuba's National Assembly would henceforth be elected by direct vote, rather than the indirect system in which provincial delegates elect national delegates. Direct elections for the presidency were not debated.

The result? The ideological values of Marxism-Leninism have been diluted, usurped by a new prominence for the ideas of José Martí: "patriotic" education and duty have been placed ahead of Communist tenets. New laws no longer necessarily reflect Marxist-Leninist ideology—a prerequisite for the welcoming of capitalist methods and (heavens!) even the endorsement of foreign private-property owners. The Cuban government ostensibly now acknowledges the family, not the state, as "society's fundamental cell."

Also in 1991, more than half of the 225 members of the Central Committee were replaced in a dramatic shakeup meant to inject youthful energy and new wisdom. Young charismatic reformers from within the Communist Party were elevated to important portfolios. The "best and the brightest" were going to organize things for a post-Soviet Cuba. Several mass organizations, such as the Union of Young Communists (no longer under the direction of the Communist Party), have also gained a limited measure of increased autonomy. New governmental institutions, such as the People's Councils *(Consejos Populares),* have assumed new responsibilities for solving grassroots problems. Independent organizations have evolved (many erstwhile state-employed journalists, for example, have formed their own union). And the right of Cuban nationals to travel abroad has been extended, although Castro decides who can leave his island. (In mid-1991 the government lowered the age eligibility for a Cuban passport to 20, though the document—good for a specified amount of time—costs US$800, plus US$175 a month for an extension.)

Going to the Ballot Box

In February 1993 legislative elections were the first in which voters also cast ballots directly for

revolutionary slogan

AFTER FIDEL?

Fidel Castro turned 74 in August 2000. He may last another decade, even two, but he can't live forever. What comes next?

Fidel's four-years-younger brother, Raúl Castro, the armed forces minister and number two in the Communist Party, is his hierarchical successor. However, he has none of his brother's charisma and is far less popular than Fidel, from whom he derives his political strength.

The prominent rise of influential young politicians suggests that Fidel may prefer his successor to be drawn from their ranks. The foremost contenders are Ricardo Alarcón, the National Assembly president and top emissary in dealings with the U.S., and Carlos Lage, the economics czar and vice president of the Council of State.

Meanwhile, Castro is standing fast inside his fortress, and the Cuban people trapped inside have no choice, writes Wendy Gimbel, "but to go along with him and wait for the future to reveal itself." He recently said that he would step down if the conditions were right ("Time goes by, and even marathon runners get tired"), but never while the U.S. maintains its aggressive posture—which he clearly strives to maintain.

A Cuban dissidents' movement has evolved as the most viable organized opposition to the current regime; it is treated by the government with a mixture of repression and scorn (Castro claims that Cuba cannot afford the potential instability of a multi-party system while the U.S. continues to undermine the current government). Most dissident leaders want to see a transition based on reforms that mobilize the system in the direction of social democracy. "Our system is so sick with hatred that any attempt to overthrow the current system would have a terrible effect. Blood would run in the streets," says Elizardo Sanchez, head of the Cuban Commission of Human Rights and National Reconciliation, a leading dissident group within Cuba.

The Potential for Civil War

A change of leadership could be traumatic. In a classified warning in August 1993, the CIA predicted that "tensions and uncertainties are so acute that significant miscalculations by Castro, a deterioration of his health, or plotting in the military could provoke regime-threatening instability."

The situation has improved since 1993, but Castro's leadership is so central to the regime's viability that his absence will create unprecedented dilemmas. The initial succession crisis will probably lead to political turmoil. The party may split into factions, while the populace may take to the streets to vent its pent-up desire for change. The potential for bloodshed is considerable—the island is saturated with weapons and virtually every adult knows how to use them.

The role of the military could be decisive. The military top brass is made up of loyal communists (purges get rid of the rest), but it is unknown where the military's loyalties may lie in Fidel's absence.

More U.S. Intervention?

Alas, Cuba is caught between the devil and the deep blue sea. The U.S. holds the key to Cuba's destiny. Since 1996, embodied in U.S. law is the *demand* that Cuba constitute a transition government and, within a year of establishing that government, hold "free and fair" democratic elections. In effect the U.S. policy has been aimed at destabilizing Cuba without concomitant efforts to establish a viable alternative to the Castro regime.

Once Pandora's box is opened, the U.S. government may feel compelled to intervene; the Clinton administration has already taken steps to deal with the ensuing chaos and confusion, which it considers "inevitable." At that point the U.S. might also assist radical Cuban-Americans in returning to Cuba to "liberate" their homeland—a scenario that is anathema to everyone now living in Cuba, including the opposition groups, and would doubtless be resisted tooth and nail. U.S. government studies suggest an invasion of Cuba would cost at least 50,000 U.S. casualties. "If they come, they'll experience another Vietnam!" warns Fidel.

It could happen. Since 1994 right-wing politicians led by Sen. Jesse Helms, Chairman of the Senate Foreign Relations Committee, have firmly taken the reins of U.S. policy toward Cuba. Helms, an unrepentant Cold Warrior who has threatened to take Castro out—either "in a horizontal or vertical position"—says, "Forget Haiti. Invade Cuba!" Let's hope he doesn't mean it.

candidates to the provincial and national assemblies. It wasn't democracy as Westerners know it. Candidates were not allowed to campaign beyond having their names and resumes published in the official press. Candidates are barred from proposing programs to deal with specific issues (on the pretext that such campaigning encourages "demagoguery and false promises"). The candidate selection process is largely party-controlled: nominations are decided by the party. And only the Communist Party is legally permitted to distribute propaganda or organize political meetings.

Still, the National Assembly went through an 84% turnover. "Only" two-thirds of candidates were Communist Party members; hence, the new legislature has a large contingent of non-Communist legislators, including two Protestant ministers. The election of Assembly members has no bearing on the selection of high government officials, which is two stages removed from popular accountability.

In April 1994 another major reorganization took place. The State's 21 Ministries, nine Committees, and 10 Institutions were reduced to 27 Ministries and five Institutions. Each had to reorganize internally to reflect current conditions and adapt to the evolving enterprise system. Reforms were also made further down as part of streamlining the People's Power System, intended to do away with duplicate functions, more clearly delineate who is responsible for what, and give more clout to local municipal assemblies. Local elected officials are now required by law to meet with voters and report back on what is being done to solve their problems.

RETRENCHMENT?

Cuba is not rushing to embrace the capitalist model, however much it appears so on the ground. The Castro government has been edging towards a "market dictatorship" (dubbed *capitalismo frío,* or cold capitalism) while behind the scenes a power play has played out between hard-liners and reformers over the pace of reform in Cuba.

The Cuban hierarchy fears losing control. It also fears that Cuba's dignity and sense of purpose has been lost, leading to a crisis of values. By 1995, as the Cuban economy began to rebound, hard-liners in the government expressed fears that change has come too quickly—too much too soon.

The full Central Committee of the Cuban Communist Party met in March 1996 (for only its sixth time ever) and signaled a retrenchment of communist ideals. The meeting confirmed that Cuba would continue its economic planning according to the tenets of Marxist-Leninist theory, while reaffirming its will to resist the Clinton administration's "Track II" policy of undermining the Castro regime through academic exchanges, support for dissidents, and other "fifth column" activities. Nongovernmental bodies and the self-employed sector came in for keen criticism, and rigorous efforts to suppress "the negative effects" of free enterprise were called for. The boom in tourism was considered a kind of Trojan horse that also spreads negative influences, including "the ideas of consumer society" (U.S. dollars aren't clean—they come tainted by decadent cultural values).

The convocation concluded that while harmful, economic changes are necessary under existing circumstances, while the need to protect socialism was paramount to maintain "revolutionary purity." Thus a harsh crackdown on political dissidents was implemented in spring 1996, followed in January 1999 by the introduction of draconian laws meant to discourage close interactions with foreigners. Meanwhile, Roberto Robaina and other key reformers were replaced with more hard-line loyalists.

Like China's Communist rulers, Castro has coupled modest economic reforms with strict social and political control, ostracizing or imprisoning government critics. Like the Chinese, Fidel appears to be betting that even modest economic progress will stifle demands for political change

THE ECONOMY

THE PREREVOLUTIONARY ECONOMY

For several decades prior to the Revolution, U.S. corporations virtually owned the island, with assets in Cuba of over a billion dollars. Most of the cattle ranches, more than 50% of the railways, 40% of sugar production, 90% of mining and oil production, and almost 100% of telephone and utility services were owned by U.S. companies.

Beginning in 1934, every year the U.S. Congress established a preferential quota for Cuban sugar. In exchange for a guaranteed price that was US$0.02 above the world market price—in effect, a "subsidy" to protect U.S. domestic sugar producers—Cuba had to guarantee tariff concessions on U.S. goods sold to Cuba (the island's manufacturers thereby found it impossible to compete with U.S. imports). The agreement kept Cuba tied to the U.S. as a one-commodity economy. It also bound Cuba to U.S. goods. Cuba was a classic case of a dependent nation. It exported sugar but was forced to import confections. It exported tomatoes but had to buy tomato paste. It supplied the fruits it later had to buy back in cans and the tobacco it had to purchase as cigarettes. In 1958 the U.S. imported more than 75% of all Cuban exports (mostly sugar) and supplied the island with more than 80% of its imports.

Nonetheless, U.S. firms had began to sell their Cuban sugar holdings to Cuban firms beginning in 1935 and by 1958, U.S. firms owned fewer than 40 of Cuba's 161 mills. They had also expanded their investments in other industries. As a result, Cuba had a vibrant economy. The country was relatively prosperous—fourth among the 20 Latin American nations on a per capita basis (its national income in 1957 was US$2.3 billion, topped only by that of the much larger countries of Argentina, Mexico, and Venezuela), with a large middle class and a mature market economy and banking sector. In 1958 Cuba had gold and foreign exchange reserves—a key measure of a healthy balance of payments—totaling US$387 million in 1958 dollars (worth US$1.9 billion in today's dollars), which according to IMF statistics were ranked third in Latin America, behind only Venezuela and Brazil.

Then Castro made a maverick swerve to the rest of the West.

COMMUNISM ON STEROIDS

Castro and Che Guevara, who became the Minister of Industry, might have been great revolutionaries, but they didn't have the sharply different set of skills and understanding necessary to run an efficient economy, which they had swiftly nationalized. (After the Revolution Che Guevara was named president of the bank and Minister of Finance. He loved to regale the joke of how he'd gotten the job. Supposedly at a cabinet meeting to decide on a replacement of bank president Felipe Pazos, Castro asks who among them is a "good *economista.*" Che raises his hand and is sworn in as Minister of head of the National Bank. Castro says: "Che, I didn't know you were an economist." Che replies, "I'm not!" Castro asks, "Then why did you raise your hand when I said I needed an economist?" to which Guevara replies, "Economist! I thought you asked for a communist.")

There were few coherent economic plans in the 1960s—just grandiose schemes that almost always ended in near ruin. The revolutionaries had zero experience in marketing, financing, and other mercantilist skills. Worse, they tried to buck the law of supply and demand. They replaced monetary work incentives with "moral" incentives, set artificially low prices, and got diminishing supplies in return.

The minimum wage allowed Cubans to buy all available necessities, but there was nothing else to purchase. Therefore there was no incentive to earn more. Rationing inhibited the work incentive that would in turn permit the elimination of rationing. Socialism had nationalized wealth but, says Guillermo Cabrera Infante, in a "Hegelian capriole" it "socialized poverty" too. Forty years of

WHAT U.S. CITIZENS CAN DO
TO HELP END THE EMBARGO

For four decades, Washington has clamped a strict trade embargo on Cuba in the expectation that economic distress would oust Castro or at least moderate his behavior. Since 1996 the U.S. embargo has been embodied in law. Here's what Uncle Sam says the failed embargo, enacted by President Kennedy in 1961, is all about:

The fundamental goal of U.S. policy toward Cuba is to promote a peaceful transition to a stable, democratic form of government and respect for human rights. Our policy has two fundamental components: maintaining pressure on the Cuban Government for change through the embargo and the Libertad Act while providing humanitarian assistance to the Cuban people, and working to aid the development of civil society in the country.

Noble sentiments perhaps, but critics call it a violation of the International Human Rights Law and Conventions that injures and threatens the welfare of Cuban people. Says Eloy Gutiérrez Menoyo, one of Cuba's foremost dissidents: "How to you explain to a Cuban mother who cannot find medication for her child . . . that the purpose of the embargo is the democratization of Cuba?"

Sen. Jesse Helms, sleepwalking though history, says: "Castro was able to withstand the pressure of the embargo because the effects were almost entirely offset by massive subsidies from the Soviet Union. Only with the collapse of the Soviet Union has the embargo begun to have an effect." However, Cuba's halting but unmistakable recovery in recent years is not what Washington expected. The embargo is increasingly under attack, and not just from the left. Even the U.S. Chamber of Commerce is pressing for its abolition.

U.S. citizens who oppose the embargo can make their views known to representatives in Washington.

Contact Your Senator or Representative in Congress: U.S. Congress, Washington, D.C. 20510, tel. (202) 225-3121—House switchboard—or (202) 224-3121 for the Senate switchboard. Write a simple, moderate, straightforward letter to your representative that makes the argument for ending the embargo and requests he/she co-sponsor a bill to rescind the Helms-Burton legislation.

Write or Call the President: The President, The White House, Washington, D.C. 20500, tel. (202) 456-1414. Also call or fax the **White House Comment Line,** tel. (202) 456-1111, fax (202) 456-2461, **National Security Advisor,** tel. (202) 456-2255, fax (202) 456-2883, and the **Secretary of State,** tel. (202) 647-6575, fax (202) 647-7120.

Publicize Your Concern: Write a simple, moderate, straightforward letter to the editor of your local newspaper as well as any national newspapers or magazines and make the argument for ending the embargo.

Senators and Representatives and their staffs religiously read and heed letters to the editors in hometown and home-state publications. Every letter on an important issue is deemed to express the views of 500 other constituents who don't take the trouble to write.

Support Solidarity Organizations: Humanitarian and solidarity organizations that work to normalize relations with Cuba are underfunded and welcome donations (see the Organizations To Know chart for a complete list of organizations).

Also visit the website of **USA*ENGAGE** at www .usaengage.org, an organization dedicated to lifting the embargo. It lists links to the White House, Congress, and other useful U.S. government and nongovernmental agency links at www.usaengage .org/resources/links.

---

fidelismo, reports *The Economist,* "has left Cubans with a ruined economy."

Dependency on Comrade Joe

"As early as 1981, it was calculated that since Castro took over Cuba it had experienced an annual average per-capita-growth-rate of minus 1.2 percent. By 1990 the minus growth-rate had increased to an average of over two percent," records historian Paul Johnson (Cuban government statistics, however, claim that economic growth averaged 7.3% annually in the early

1980s). Fortunately the Soviet Union acted as Cuba's benefactor, providing aid estimated at more than US$3 billion annually or around US$11 million per day.

The reemphasis on sugar production in the late 1960s represented a shift from a disastrous policy of rapid industrialization designed to diversify the economy. Eventually the reimposition of Soviet planning and management mechanisms allowed the Cuban economy to recover during the 1970s (the annual national budget, for example, was roughly in balance—about US$10.8 billion in both revenue and expenditure). The Soviet largesse, however, had a further deleterious effect on the domestic economy. Says P. J. O'Rourke, "The Cuban got the luxury of running their economy along the lines of a Berkeley commune, and like California hippies wheedling their parents for cash, someone else paid the tab."

The Soviet Union also sustained the Cuban economy by buying 85% of its foreign exports "at reasonable market prices." On the eve of the collapse of the Soviet Union, 84% of Cuba's trade was with the Soviet Union and Eastern Europe.

The End of Subsidies

After the fall of the Berlin Wall, imports from Eastern Europe fell by half in 1990 and virtually ceased in 1991. Imports from the Soviet Union fell from US$5.52 billion in 1989 (including 13 million tons of petroleum) to US$1.31 billion in 1991 (the October coup in Russia severed the gasoline pipeline; no oil whatsoever was delivered in December). By 1992, trade with Cuba's former Communist partners had shriveled to seven percent of its former value.

To compound the problem, the world market price of sugar (which in the 1980s accounted for 80% of Cuba's export earnings) also plummeted. In 1989, one ton of sugar bought seven tons of oil; in 1993, a time when Cuba *desperately* needed oil, it would buy just 1.3 tons. With the supply of fertilizers and pesticides also curtailed, the sugar harvest plummeted from 8.1 million tons in 1989-90 to 4.2 million tons in 1992. In 1993, the harvest—the lowest in 50 years—produced only 3.3 million tons (with an export value of only US$965 million, down from US$5 billion in 1986). It was an unmitigated disaster.

The Soviet Union's collapse cut Cuba's "rust-bucket" economy adrift. Between 1990 and 1994, the economy shrank 34% according to the Cuban government (the U.S.-Cuba Trade and Economic Council claims that the fall was as much as 70%). By the end of 1994, half the country's industrial factories had closed, as had 70% of its public transport network. Sugar mills were shut down and cannibalized for parts to keep more efficient mills operating. Power outages further disrupted industrial production. Lunch breaks were eliminated so that office workers could leave early to save on electricity. Ominously, inflation was running at 80-90%. Unemployment stood at 40%. The work force was left idle.

Cuba would have to do an about-face to survive.

A FAREWELL TO MARXISM

In October 1991 the Cuban Communist Party Congress adopted a resolution establishing profit-maximizing state-owned Cuban corporations that operate independently of the central state apparatus. They're free to engage in multinational commerce, and they enjoy independence in purchasing, marketing, and negotiating with foreign investors constituted for a period of 25 years with a one-time option for a 25-year extension. Each company must establish its own profit margin (they give to the state any profits remaining after reinvesting and paying dividends to shareholders). Foreign investors are exempted for 10 years from taxes on income—and, most important, they can repatriate all profits.

By 1993 a clearly defined model had evolved. The old Central Planning Board, which piloted the state-run economy, was abolished, and a Foreign Investment Ministry was created to aggressively woo foreign investors. In September 1995 the Cuban National Assembly passed a law allowing foreigners to have wholly owned businesses in all sectors of the economy except defense, national security, education, and public health. Foreign corporations (but not individuals) can even buy buildings (but not land, which is leased). Duty-free zones were also created around Havana and Santiago de Cuba with special tax, banking, tariff, and other incentives for foreign corporations.

Cuba stood between "an unworkable socialism and a voracious market economy, searching for alternatives in the midst of crisis," noted Cuban scholar Gail Reed.

Reinventing Capitalism

Cuba has sent some of its best and brightest abroad for crash courses in capitalist business techniques. The University of Havana has adapted its economics courses to include courses on capitalism. And an International Business Center of Havana opened in June 1993 to teach marketing and management seminars. That ultimate symbol of *Yanqui* capitalism, advertising, has also returned to Cuba.

Havana has even handed over large chunks of the economy to the military, which in July 1987 begun sweeping experiments in the management of its enterprises, including Western-style management techniques; military leaders began taking seminars on entrepreneurial methods, quality control, and worker incentives. Today generals in civilian clothes run quasi-private corporations such as Gaviota (which is partially owned by foreign investors), some of whose resort hotels are built by the army's construction company, Unión de Empresas Constructoras. TRD Caribe, a subsidiary of Gaviota, even runs the nationwide chain of stores selling Western goods.

By January 1994, 69% of state-run companies were operating in the red, kept from bleeding to death by massive state subsidies. The government proposed to cut its massive deficit by slashing subsidies, eliminating 700,000 jobs, imposing price increases, and reducing a huge excess of liquidity by taking up to nine billion pesos out of circulation (in 1994, 12.5 billion pesos were in circulation in Cuba). As of 1999, the effort to reduce the number of pesos in circulation had stalled.

The government also desperately needed to get hold of foreign currency floating freely in the black market. In 1993, economics minister Carlos Lage estimated that up to US$300 million in foreign currency was circulating illegally each year, usually coming into the country as aid from relatives abroad or as tips from foreign tourists. That year, therefore, Cuba legalized possession of that paramount capitalist tool, the *yanqui* dollar (the government also hoped to attract more

money from the million-plus Cuban exiles and to relieve shortages by making more foreign goods available). To soak up the dollars, the government opened up "foreign exchange recovery stores." Every item imaginable—from imported toothpaste to Japanese TVs—was made available. The dollar's legalization opened up a huge internal market, igniting trade that has fueled the economy: in 1994, Cubans spent an estimated US$1 billion in 600 state-run hard-currency stores across the island.

When dollars were legalized, the peso—which officially is at parity with the dollar but was floating at its real value on the black market—crashed, bottoming out at 150 to the dollar in 1994. By 1995 it had rebounded to 20 to US$1, a sure sign of a stronger economy. It has since stabilized at around 21 to US$1.

In September 1995 the government also announced that Cubans could open interest-bearing savings accounts or purchase certificates of deposits with dollars (the National Bank of Cuba would henceforth pay the market interest rate). Cuba even introduced its first investment fund—the Beta Gran Caribe Fund—in fall 1995, on the Irish Stock Exchange. (The old Havana Stock Exchange is—and is likely for the foreseeable future to remain—a workers' canteen.)

In the summer of 1993, Castro also opened up the service sector and agriculture to private enterprise on an individual basis. State farms were to be converted to private cooperatives run on the basis of profitability, individual citizens could lease land and cultivate it on their own, and produce markets were permitted. The government also legalized self-employment for plumbers, electricians, tailors, cobblers, barbers, photographers, and dozens of others who could—upon registration (self-employed people need a permit from the State Labor and Social Security Committee)—ply their trades freely, though they are restricted from having employees. By mid-1995, 210,000 Cubans (about five percent of Cuba's labor force) had officially registered as self-employed individuals, or *cuentapropistas.* Another 200,000 or so were engaged in similar activities without bothering about the legalities.

And in 1994, the National Assembly of People's Power approved the first tax law in Cuba—a bitter pill to swallow, since Cubans had not been subject to taxation since 1967. In addition, parliament approved fees for a range of items that had been free, such as school lunches and sporting events. In January 1996 personal foreign exchange income and various "profitable activities" became subject to taxation at rates from 10% to 50%, payable in pesos or hard currency, depending on how taxpayers made their income. Taxes are targeted primarily at the self-employed, who must pay a fixed monthly payment (and, at the end of the year, a progressive amount based on their actual income). To collect taxes, a new entity, the National Office of Tax Administration (ONAT), was created.

Back from the Brink

As a result of all these reforms, Cuba halted the slide. Cuba's GDP rebounded by an average of 4.2%, 1994-96. The economy stagnated again in 1997 and 1998 before inching towards continued recovery in 1999, when a 6.2% rise in GDP was reported, fueled primarily by robust growth in tourism—Cuba's biggest income earner—which generated gross revenues of about US$2 billion in 1999. And as of mid-1999, about 600 foreign companies had opened offices in Cuba (actual foreign investment is about US$4 billion). Meanwhile the island's trade deficit at the end of 1998 was officially reported at US$2.8 billion, and foreign debt has risen from US$2.8 billion in 1983 to US$11.2 billion in 1999.

Despite the economic recovery, the Cuban government was not planning to lift its "Special Period" status. As radical as these changes appear, Cuban authorities have hesitated about wholesale economic reforms: the state has no intention of ceding control of the economy to its citizens or foreign enterprises. Hence, after opening a Pandora's box, in 1995 the government began reversing itself on some of the reforms. That year Castro warned that the economic reforms "do not signify a return to capitalism, much less a crazy and uncontrolled rush in that direction. . . . We have swept away the capitalist system, and it will never return as long as there is a communist, a patriot, a revolutionary in Cuba. . . . Our main objective is to preserve the revolution, our independence, and the achievements of socialism"—and, he might have added, the single-party system or his own rule. In October 1997 the Communist Party's Fifth Congress dedicated itself to the status quo by rejecting new steps towards liberalizing the economy or easing up on political control. The activities of the foreign joint ventures, the new farmers' markets, the new self-employed sector, and the vast new black market had grown far larger and more vibrant than the official, socialist economy.

Thus the Cuban government began muscling its way into joint-venture businesses; while state-controlled firms began backing out of deals with foreign companies, delaying payments on their debts, and putting inappropriate pressures on foreign partners (in 1999 Castro warned: "We want the minimum of foreign ownership and capital in this little island"). Scores of companies have pulled out, accusing the Cuban government of reneging on deals and excessive government interference. As soon as something begins to work, it is halted. As soon as anything becomes profitable, it is stopped. Despite a nationwide efficiency campaign initiated in 1998, waste and mismanagement are ingrained. And many vaunted changes are just patches on an old tire.

Cuba's self-employed have also found Cuban-style capitalism bruising in the face of growing government regulation meant to edge them out of business. The self-employed (who earn far more than the average monthly salary of 214 pesos, equivalent to US$10) are no longer allowed to sell their products near schools, hospitals, tourist areas, government establishments, or on major streets. Nor can state enterprises buy their goods or services from the self-employed. An individual may sell only what he or she produces—no filthy middlemen! No one may hire workers. University graduates are not allowed to work on their own account in their own profession. And taxes, which have been steadily raised, says The Economist, "seem designed not to raise revenue from such businesses but to wipe them out." To that end, the state occasionally purges entrepreneurs it considers too prosperous by seizing their assets gained from "excess profits." By 2000, petty bizneros had virtually disappeared from the streets, as had many private restaurants, though artists, farmers, and arrendadores inscriptos (licensed renters of private rooms) have continued to thrive. Except for this tiny sector, the Cuban government has shrewdly kept retail commerce in state hands, opening hundreds of consumer outlets around the island. Together they pulled in about US$1 billion in 1999 from the one-third to one-half of the population with some form of access to dollars, or *fula,* as Cubans call it (a reference to the green-gray gunpowder used in *santería* to invoke the spirits).

The question is whether the tentative steps towards *capitalismo frío* will prove too slippery a slope for the government to turn back. Cuba's dollar economy is growing at an exponential rate. Foreign remittances have skyrocketed since 1999, when the Clinton administration increased the amount of money that Cuban American families can send to Cuba (the sum is estimated at US$1 billion annually). The billion-dollar marketplace is transforming the face of major cities, creating a dollar culture. Most of the money eventually ends up in state hands, absorbed through state stores and taxes. It goes to finance imports and the construction of new light industry, businesses, and consumer-oriented technology.

AGRICULTURE

"There must be much hunger," says one of Ernest Hemingway's characters in *Islands in the Stream.* "You cannot realize it," comes the reply. "No I can't," Thomas Hudson thought. "I can't realize it at all. I can't realize why there should ever be any hunger in this country ever." Traveling through Cuba, you'll also sense the vast potential that caused René Dumont, the outstanding French agronomist, to say that "with proper management, Cuba could adequately feed five times its current population."

Before the Revolution, Cuba certainly couldn't feed itself: the best arable lands were planted in sugarcane for export. Alas, the revolutionary government hasn't managed agriculture efficiently either. Thoughts of self-sufficiency were sacrificed to satisfy the Soviet sweet tooth. And management of agriculture has been dumb-foundingly inept.

After the Revolution, the lands were organized in a system of centralized, inefficient state farms dedicated to monoculture. Large farms supplanted small ones, machines replaced laborers, and Cuba followed "modern" agricultural practices, utilizing imported pesticides and fertilizers. Food distribution was also centralized and highly inefficient ("for every peso of fruits and vegetables on the stand, US$0.23 are lost to spoilage," reported journalist Gail Reed).

Compounding the problem, during the early 1980s Cuba had pushed toward the extremes of capital-intensive farming without regard to the consequent problems. Insecticides devastated natural insect predators, while many pests became resistant (and Cuba began to see infestations of "super-pests"). Meanwhile soils had been salinized by excessive irrigation and sterilized by fertilizers and pesticides and no longer produced a concomitant increase in yields. (Cuba is the only country in Latin America whose pro-

traditional agriculture, oxen plowing

duction of rice has fallen since 1958, when it ranked fourth in the region, with a yield of 2,400 kg per hectare. By contrast, Cuba's Caribbean neighbor, the Dominican republic, has increased its rice production fourfold since 1958, from 2,100 kg per hectare to 5,400 kg per hectare in 1996. Cuba's yields today are only 2,500 kg per hectare.)

Over 1.6 million hectares are given to sugarcane and 2.5 million to pasture. Only 1.5 million hectares are set aside for other crops. A mere 12% of the land under cultivation is planted in food crops; the rest is dedicated to export crops. More than 60% of Cuba's rice, grains, and other staples are imported, normally through food-for-sugar barter deals as, for example, with France, which in February 2000 renewed a contract to provide 70% of Cuba's wheat and flour needs in a US$180 million deal (in 1998-99 France exported 714,000 metric tons of cereals to Cuba).

Cuba's major obstacle to recovery remains agricultural production, which in the early 1990s collapsed due to a combination of factors, including lack of machinery, fertilizers, and labor incentives, plus a series of alternating droughts and torrential storms that conspired with a series of pest plagues to devastate crop harvests (in 1999, Cuba's worst drought in 40 years destroyed 42% of the nation's crops; Cuba received US$7 million in food aid from the U.N. World Food Program in addition to the US$3 million it gets annually from the United Nations). Deteriorating living conditions have also induced farmers and agricultural workers to put down their hoes to move in with better-off city cousins, leaving fewer and fewer laborers toiling in the fields. To forestall the movement, the virtues of returning to an agrarian lifestyle are being extolled.

The "National Food Self-Sufficiency Program"

In 1991-94 Cuba's population faced malnutrition on a massive scale. Cuba's number-one priority was to increase food production. Ground zero in the battle is the fertile agricultural land around Havana, where large tracts of land have been switched from export crops to food crops. Vacant land, such as that along roadsides, was cultivated. And vegetable gardens—previously a

SOYA WANNA INVEST IN CUBA?

*B*efore the economic crisis, Cuba provided all children under the age of 14 with one liter of dairy milk per day. Today the country can only provide milk for children under seven. The government's goal was to substitute soy yogurt for children between ages seven and 14. To help Cuba realize its potential, Global Exchange launched the Campaign to Exempt Food and Medicines from the Embargo (under existing U.S. law, trade in food and medicines to Cuba is illegal) by creating ¡Soy Cubano! in association with the Cuban Institute for Basic Research in Tropical Agriculture. ¡Soy Cubano! has entered into a joint venture with a Cuban factory that produces soy yogurt, soy ice cream, and soy cheeses. The joint venture directly contravenes the U.S. embargo—and is meant to do so—by encouraging U.S. citizens to invest in a Cuban enterprise that works towards ensuring that Cuban children receive a healthy, protein-rich diet. The money funds the purchase of raw materials and equipment, research, and the construction of soy factories in each province of Cuba, with the aim of producing two liters of soy yogurt drink per week for Cuban children who can no longer receive their previously guaranteed liter of milk per day due to the economic crisis.

A persuasive half-hour documentary video explains the issues (US$25, or US$50 to institutions). The video and shares can be purchased by contacting the ¡Soy Cubano! Company, c/o Global Exchange, 2017 Mission St. #303, San Francisco, CA 94110, tel. (415) 255-7296, fax (415) 255-7498, e-mail: info@globale change.org, website: www.globalexchange.org.

rare sight—sprouted in the urban centers.

Legions of "volunteers" and laid-off workers were shipped to the countryside to help boost production. The massive mobilization of city folk to farmlands did not solve the problem. The "national food self-sufficiency program" failed to meet basic needs, especially for vegetables and fruits. More dramatic reforms were called for.

The Breakup of State Farms

In September 1993 Cuba made dramatic changes in the organization of its agriculture. Prior to this, state farms and about 180 agro-industrial complexes cultivated 82% of Cuba's arable land. Cooperatives farmed an additional 10%, with the balance farmed by private farmers. The new law—Resolution 357—authorized the establishment of autonomous cooperatives (*unidades básicas de producción cooperativa*). These cooperatives own their production, administer their own resources, open their own bank accounts, elect their own managers, develop their own budgets, purchase their own equipment, and pay their own taxes. They farm government land but own the crop they harvest (by contrast, traditional cooperatives pool their plots for common land ownership). However, they are still obliged to follow state directives and sell all their production to the state at prices fixed by the latter.

In addition the law authorized the transfer of idle land to private owners. In 1994, 12,000 hectares of tobacco land were turned over to 5,835 families. Families have been granted land in mountainous areas. And small plots (less than half a hectare) of idle land have been leased to pensioners and others whose circumstances prevent them participating in "systematic" farming. Private farms currently utilize about 20% of Cuba's cultivable land (they, too, are obliged to sell 80% of their produce to the state).

As a result of the reforms, only 5.5% of sugarcane farmlands are now in state farms.

Reverting to Traditional Agriculture

Massive experiments in farming are taking place, based on traditional practices such as increased use of animals (since 1990, 100,000 oxen have been domesticated to plow the fields) and old-fashioned mulching combined with organic fertilizers such as fermented cane runoff.

Today Cuba is at the forefront of historic efforts to apply ecologically sound agricultural techniques. "Cuba has made what is probably the world's most immediate and far-reaching changeover from chemical-dependent agriculture to low-input, sustainable agriculture," says Medea Benjamin, co-author of *The Greening of Cuba: A National Experiment in Organic Agriculture.*

The Cubans began experimenting with alternative farming in the early 1980s. The demise of the Soviet Union has forced them to plunge in headlong, assisted by the U.N. Food and Agricultural Organization. Cuba has rediscovered traditional peasant methods and invented its own alternative technologies. The Mechanization Institute, which once developed tractor-drawn plows, now builds innovative implements pulled by oxen; and the use of biofertilizers (for example, legumes as green manures and free-living bacteria that make atmospheric nitrogen available for other crops) is said to be unrivaled in the world. And biological agents such as fungi and nematodes have been harnessed as pest control agents (today it has over 200 centers that produce biopesticides nationwide, headed by farmers trained in universities; while farmers in other Latin American countries are marginalized, in Cuba they are at the center of things and enjoy access to leading technology). A small worm-eating fly now guards the yucca crop; zillions of wasps are being bred to attack the sugarcane borer; and ants have been unleashed in the banana and sweet potato crops.

The Food Research Institute of Havana has also developed a technology for the production of food products (such as milk and yogurt) from soybeans. Fortunately soy food products are much less expensive to produce than meat and dairy products. Nutritionists have come up with a soy-enriched ground beef as a solution to the beef shortage. They've also invented Cerelac, a powdered milk substitute that today has replaced the liter of milk a day that every child once received. The government had to convince Cubans to eat the stuff (Cubans roll their eyes at the mere mention of soy—they do *not* like it).

By 1995 Cuba was beginning to see chemical-free food production rising to levels attained before the organic revolution. More than 2,730 government-operated gardens checkering the country's 169 municipalities have also eased the shortfalls. The gardens, or *agropónicos,* which usually feature modern irrigation systems, employ about 22,000 workers and sell two dozen varieties of vegetables and herbs directly to consumers at prices as much as half that of market levels. In addition to the urban plots, the program has given rise to several thousand larger and more intensive gardens, generally located on the outskirts of cities and towns and producing fruit in addition to vegetables and herbs. Overall, the government estimates that 117,000 people work in urban agriculture and that the gardens account for about half the vegetables grown in Cuba.

"The future elsewhere in the world will require Cuba's new model," says Dr. Peter Rosset, director of California's Institute for Food and Development Policy (popularly known as Food First), which has a collaborative project with the Cuban Association for Organic Farming and the Advanced Institute for Agricultural Sciences of Havana.

Global Exchange (see the Organizations To Know chart) offers study tours of Cuba's organic farming and agricultural development.

Food First, 398 60th St., Oakland, CA 94618, tel. (510) 654-4400 or (800) 888-3314; e-mail: foodfirst@igc.apc.org, website: www.foodfirst.org/cuba, also has occasional study tours featuring visits to agricultural cooperatives, biopesticide production centers, "organoponic" food gardens, and the Havana Agricultural University in San José de las Lajas.

Cattle

Cattle numbered more than 5.9 million on the eve of the Special Period. Cuba has always had a strong cattle industry, particularly in the provinces around Camagüey, which has been famous for beef and dairy production since before the Revolution. Castro has taken a lively interest, especially in the development of sturdier strains and artificial insemination. The central uplands are a focus for genetic breeding of cattle, such as Cuba's home-grown Charolais, Santa Gertrudis, and F1 strains. Zebu from India, for example, have been crossed with Canadian Holstein, producing offspring well adapted to the tropics yet capable, reportedly, of giving a whopping 9.5 liters or more of milk a day.

Development is hindered by mismanagement and a lack of water and nutritious feed; cattle forage on natural grasses, but owing to deforestation and a change to a more arid climate over the past 400 years, these have evolved to the point where they are no longer nutritious. Cuba has made advances in alternative cattle feeds (such as from bagasse), but not sufficient to sustain notably greater yields.

Unfortunately the dairy industry became reliant on imported feed grain. In 1990 Cuba could no longer afford to import feed for domestic livestock. Consequently, milk production has plummeted. (In 1994 the state therefore had to curtail the milk ration for children over seven. In mid-

1995 it limited rations to children under three-and-a-half years old.)

Killing cattle for private consumption or sale of meat is now illegal, and beef is virtually impossible to find, giving rise to a rash of cattle rustling (45,000 head of cattle were reportedly stolen in 1998). The Castro government replied by fining ranchers 500 pesos for each head of cattle they lose.

Citrus

In 1990 Cuba—the world's 14th-largest producer—exported 460,000 tons of citrus (down from 800,000 tons in 1989), mostly to the Soviet Union and Eastern Bloc countries. Since then, many of the citrus plantations have become overgrown with weeds. Most of Cuba's citrus fruits are not of sufficient quality to compete on world markets (the vast majority of fruits grown serve the domestic market for fruit juice). However, considerable effort is now being made to upgrade with investment from Chile and Israel. A 115,000-acre citrus operation at Jagüey Grande is the world's largest under one management; it is operated by an Israeli company as part of a US$22 million joint venture. The Jagüey Grande project (which accounts for more than 60% of domestic production) produced about 440,000 tons of oranges, grapefruits, limes, and tangerines in 1996-67, equivalent about one percent of total U.S. production (an Israeli engineer working on the project informed me that Cuban plantation managers vastly exaggerate the production figures).

Following the 1996-67 harvest of 690,000 tons, production fell but rebounded to 750,000 tons in 1998-99

Coffee

Cuba produces excellent coffee. The finest quality is the Crystal Mountain variety, grown mainly in the Sierra del Escambray, although most coffee is grown in the mountains of eastern Cuba. Most coffee is grown on small plots worked by hand in quasi-cooperatives that must sell their entire crop to the government at fixed prices.

Last century, Cuba was one of the world's leading coffee producers. In 1827 there were 2,067 coffee plantations *(cafeteles)*. Most, however, were destroyed during the 10-year War of Independence. The introduction of a tariff to protect Cuban coffee in 1927 prompted a revival, and

THE *ZAFRA*

ith the onset of the dry season, Cuba prepares for the *zafra*, the sugar harvest, which runs from November through June. Then the temperatures soars above 32° C, and the harvesters *(macheteros)* are in the fields from dawn until dusk, wielding their short, wide, blunt-nosed machetes.

First the cane stalks are burnt at ground level to soften them for the cut. The *macheteros* grab the three-meter-tall stalks, which they slash close to the ground (where the sweetness concentrates). Then they cut off the top and strip the dry leaves from the stalk.

Before the introduction of mechanical cane cutters in the 1970s, 350,000 laborers were required for the harvest, and workers used to come by tens of thousands from Haiti and Jamaica just for the season. In 1989, when three-quarters of the crop was harvested mechanically, only 60,000 workers were needed. The Cuban-designed combine-harvester can cut a truckload of cane (close to 7 metric tons) in 10 minutes, three times more than the most skilled *macheteros* can cut by hand in a day.

The cut cane is then delivered to one of the approximately 150 sugar mills in Cuba, which operate 24 hours a day, pouring bilious black smoke into the air. Here the sugarcane is fed to the huge steel crushers that squeeze out the sugary pulp called *guarapo* (drunk by Cubans cold or with rum), which is boiled, clarified, evaporated, and separated into molasses and sugar crystals. The molasses makes rum, yeast, and cattle feed. *Bagasse,* the fiber left after squeezing, fuels boilers or is shipped off to mills to be turned into paper and wallboard. The sugar is shipped by rail to bulk shipping terminals, such as the huge Tricontinental in Cienfuegos, for transport to refineries abroad.

sugarcane

Cuba enjoyed modest exports on the eve of the Revolution. The exodus of workers from the land, however, has had an impact on coffee production, which declined markedly since the Revolution—from 60,300 tons in 1961-62 to an annual average of 19,100 tons, 1976-80 (production rose to an average of 27,000 tons, 1981-90). Yields and total production have dropped even more steeply since 1990. Cuba produced 21,000 tons of coffee beans in 1997-98 (6,200 tons were exported, earning US$50 million), and only 13,500 tons in 1998-99 (the lowest in more than 50 years) when drought and hurricane devastated the crop.

A plan—*Plan Turquino*—was therefore conceived to motivate farmers and their families to remain in the mountains and train young people in coffee cultivation. More than 20,000 acres of poorly used or vacant state lands have been transformed into more than 10,000 privately-managed coffee farms and given to families in search of a home and work. And much of the 300,000 acres devoted to coffee production is being upgraded. The state-run Cuba-Café oversees production and export. (Japan and France account for almost 80% of Cuba's coffee exports).

Sugar

¡Azúcar! The whole country reeks of sweet, pungent sugar, Cuba's curse and her blessing. The

Cuban landscape is one of endless cane fields, lorded over by the towering chimneys of great sugar mills. Sugar is Cuba's bondsman. The nation's bittersweet calvary has been responsible for curses like slavery and the country's almost total dependence on not only the one product, but, as history as proven, on single imperial nations: first Spain, then the United States, and most recently the Soviet Union.

Due to Cuba's soil and climate, sugar thrives here as nowhere else in the world. The unusual depth (up to seven meters) and fertility of Cuba's limestone soils are unparalleled in the world for producing sugar—sugar plants can be raised without replanting for up to 20 years, a longer period than anywhere else in the world. And the sucrose content of Cuban sugar is higher, too.

Four decades ago the World Bank wrote of "the diabetic dangers of the dominance of sugar in her economic bloodstream." Cuba's economy reverberated whenever world sugar prices fell. Periods of prosperity were followed by periods of depression.

Cuba's traditional dependence on sugar exports changed little during three decades of socialism: sugar represented about 75% by value of Cuban exports on the eve of the Revolution; in 1989 it was about 80%. Cuba's newfound colonial role was to feed sugar to the Soviet bear. (The Soviets showed little interest in promoting Cuban diversification.) Production rose gradually from about five million tons a year in the early 1970s to 7.5 million tons on average in the late 1980s. About one-quarter of production went to capitalist markets to earn Cuba hard currency.

The collapse of the Soviet bloc rendered a triple whammy to Cuba's sugar industry. Not only did its main market collapse, but preferential prices guaranteed by the Soviet Union also vanished, forcing Cuba to sell its sugar at world market prices. Alas, world sugar prices fell from US$0.20 in 1980 to a measly US$0.04 in 1985—comparable to prices in the depression year of 1932. Cuba's sugar-dependent economy is still on a treadmill; it has had to produce more and more sugar to generate the same income. Moreover, Cuba has faced growing competition from Brazil and new producers such as India and the increasingly more efficient sugar *beet* producers. The sugar fields also had to go without fertilizer and herbicides, while a lack of

fuel and spare parts rendered harvesters (the harvest is 80% mechanized) and sugar processing plants useless. From seven million tons in 1991, the harvest plummeted in 1994 to a 50-year low of 3.3 million tons.

In 1993 the government reorganized the industry. Most state farms were abolished. Workers now work in cooperatives, earning profits for cane produced over state-set quotas. Cuba hopes to attract foreign investors to build sugar refineries (the country has traditionally exported raw sugar to countries that process the sugar in their own refineries; much of world demand is for refined sugar, which sells at a higher price). By May 1996 the harvest had attained the year's goal of 4.5 million tons before slipping back in 1998 to 3.2 million metric tons, a 50-year low. The 1999 harvest was a slight improvement: 3.78 million metric tons.

Ironically, sugar isn't easy to find in Cuba and is rarely available at government stores.

Tobacco

Tobacco has traditionally been Cuba's second most important agricultural earner of foreign exchange. About 50,000 hectares are given to tobacco, which is grown in rich valleys and slopes throughout Cuba, but predominantly in a 90-mile-long, 10-mile-wide valley—Vuelta Abajo—in Pinar del Río, incomparably the best spot in the world to grow tobacco. Cuban tobacco is grown on small properties, many privately owned by the farmers (the average holding is only 10 hectares, about 25 acres).

Annual production attained about 50,000 metric tons in the mid-1970s before a blight of blue mold infected the tobacco fields. Production gradually recovered and reached about 40,000 tons in 1990 (enough for 90 million cigars, worth about US$100 million). Unable to afford fertilizers and fungicides, and hit by adverse weather, Cuba experienced a series of disastrous harvests. Production fell by 50% in 1993 and markedly again in 1995. European importers rushed in to protect their source by offering short-terms loans. It worked. The 1996 harvest yielded 32,000 tons (70 million cigars' worth), up 25% from 1995. In 1999 cigar exports reached 160 million, valued at US$260 million (compared to 126 million in 1998, worth US$200 million), below the ambitious official target of 200 million.

Foreign investment continues. In December 1999 Altadis, the Franco-Spanish tobacco giant, signed off on a US$500 million deal to take a 50% stake in Cuba's state tobacco firm Habanos S.A.

INDUSTRY

The Castro regime has invested considerable money in metal processing, spare parts industries to service equipment installed prior

---

HOLY SMOKE!

"There is no substitute for our tobacco anywhere in the world. It's easier to make good cognac than to achieve the quality of Cuban tobacco."

—**Fidel Castro**

It seems ironic that Cuba—scourge of the capitalist world—should have been compelled by history and geography to produce that blatant symbol of capitalist wealth and power, the cigar. Yet it does so with pride. The unrivaled reputation of Cuban cigars as the best in the world transcends politics, transubstantiating a weed into an object capable of evoking rapture. And Cubans guard the unique reputation scrupulously.

"Havana" cigars are not only a source of hard currency—they're part and parcel of the national culture. Although Fidel gave up smoking in 1985 (after what he called a "heroic struggle"), Cubans still smoke 250 million cigars domestically every year. Another 160 million are exported annually through Habanos, S.A. Although some 20% of Cuban cigars are machine-made, only hand-rolling can produce the best quality.

An Early Beginning

This cigar tradition was first documented among the indigenous tribes by Christopher Columbus. The Taino Indians made monster cigars (at the very least, they probably kept the mosquitoes away) called *cohiba* (the word "cigar" originated from *sikar*, the Mayan word for smoking, which in Spanish became *cigarro*).

The popular habit of smoking cigars (as opposed to tobacco in pipes, first introduced to Europe by Columbus) began in Spain, where cigars made from Cuban tobacco were first made in Seville in 1717. Demand for higher-quality cigars grew and *Sevillas* (as Spanish cigars were called) were superseded by Cuban-made cigars. King Ferdinand VI of Spain en-

couraged production—a state monopoly—in the Spanish colony. Soon tobacco was Cuba's main export. After the Peninsula Campaign (1806-12) of the Napoleonic wars, British and French veterans returned home with the cigar habit, which soon became fashionable in their home countries. By the mid-19th century, there were almost 1,300 cigar factories throughout Cuba.

Soon, Cuban cigars were being imported into the U.S. Domestic cigar production also began, using Cuban tobacco (even the American cigars were known as Havanas, which by then had become a generic term). By the late 19th century, several U.S. presidents practiced the habit and helped make cigar smoking a status symbol. The demand fostered a full-fledged cigar-making industry in the United States (by 1905 there were 80,000 cigar-manufacturing businesses in the U.S., most of them mom-and-pop operations run by Cuban émigrés). But it was to Cuba that the cognoscenti looked for the finest cigars of all. "No lover of cigars can imagine the voluptuous pleasure of sitting in a café sipping slowly a strong magnificent coffee and smoking rhythmically those divine leaves of Cuba," wrote American pianist Arthur Rubenstein.

Bundled, Boxed, and Boycotted

Cuban cigars were sold originally in bundles covered with pigs' bladders, later in huge cedar chests. The banking firm of H. Upmann initiated export in cedar boxes in 1830, when it imported cigars for its directors in London. Later the bank decided to enter the cigar business, and the embossed cedar box complete with colorful lithographic label became the standard form of packaging. Each specific brand evolved its own elaborate lithograph, while different sizes (and certain brands) even evolved their own box styles.

The Montecristo was the fashionable cigar of choice. In the 1930s, any tycoon or film director worth the name was to be seen with a whopping Montecristo A in his mouth. Half of all the Havanas

to the U.S. embargo, and factories turning out domestic appliances (albeit of shoddy quality). Cement, rubber, and tobacco products, processed foods, textiles, clothing, footwear, chemicals, and fertilizers are the staple industries.

The government is keen to stimulate domestic manufacturing, funded by foreign capital. For example, while other factories were closing around it, the Antillana Steel Plant began operating in 1992, producing around 460,000 tons a year (doubling Cuba's steel production). The

---

sold in the world in the 1930s were Montecristos, by which time much of Cuba's tobacco industry had passed into U.S. ownership.

Among the devotees of Cuban cigars was President Kennedy, who smoked Petit Upmanns. In 1962, at the height of the Cuban missile crisis, Kennedy asked his press secretary Pierre Salinger to obtain as many Upmanns as he could. Next day, reported Salinger, Kennedy asked him how many he had found. Twelve hundred, replied his aide. Kennedy then pulled out and signed the decree establishing a trade embargo with Cuba (JFK didn't suffer from the embargo . . . he had his friend British Ambassador David Ormsby Gore bring in Cuban cigars in his diplomatic pouch). Ex-British premier Winston Churchill also stopped smoking Havanas and started smoking Jamaican cigars, but after a time he forgot about politics and went back to Havanas. During World War II, the Cubans had made him a gift of 10,000 top-quality cigars. His brand was Romeo y Julieta.

The embargo dealt a crushing blow to Cuba's cigar industry. Castro nationalized the cigar industry and founded a state monopoly, Cubatabaco. Many dispossessed cigar-factory owners emigrated to the Dominican Republic, Mexico, Venezuela, and Honduras, where they started up again, often using the same brand names they had owned in Cuba (today the Dominican Republic produces 47% of the handmade cigars imported into the U.S.). Experts agree, however, that these foreign "Cuban" brands are inferior to their Havana counterparts.

A Finer Choice

At the time of the Revolution, about 1,000 brands and sizes of Havanas existed. There are now about 35 brands and 500 cigar varieties. Only eight factories make handmade export-quality cigars in Cuba today, compared to 120 at the beginning of the century. All cigar factories produce various brands. Some factories specialize in particular flavors, others in particular sizes—of which there are no fewer than 60 standard variations, with minor variations from brand to brand.

Fatter cigars—the choice of connoisseurs—are more fully flavored and smoke more smoothly and

slowly than those with smaller ring gauges. As a rule, darker cigars are also more full-bodied and sweeter. The expertise and care expressed in the cigar factory determine how well a cigar burns and tastes.

Cigars, when properly stored, continue to ferment and mature in their boxes—an aging process similar to good wines. Rules on when to smoke a cigar don't exist, but many experts claim that the prime cigars are those aged for six to eight years. Everyone agrees that a cigar should be smoked either within three months of manufacture or not for at least a year (the interim is known as a "period of sickness").

A complete range of books about Cuban cigars is available at a discount online at www.cubabooks.com.

cigar factory, Trinidad

first bottling plant for natural juices and milk opened in November 1993, when Cuba announced plans for an electric motor factory, to be set up with assistance from China. It also opened its first paper-producing factory in 1994 (much of the production is earmarked for export), when it also launched its first animal feed factory.

Cuba's biggest problem is gross mismanagement and the fact that many factories date from the antediluvian dawn. A singular exception and one of Cuba's great hopes for increasing export earnings is in pharmaceuticals, where its investments in biotechnology are beginning to pay off (U.S. biotechnology expert Sam Dryden calls the Cuban program "world class").

In late 1994 the government also launched Coral Container Lines (with 65 merchant vessels) to expand its maritime links. The country is well served by eight major ports: Havana, with about 50 docks with full loading facilities, accommodates almost 40% of all cargo, including most grain and oil shipments.

Cuba's deep-sea fishing fleet consists of small independent operators banded into cooperatives. Many boats departed during the Mariel boatlift in 1980 and never returned. The fleet has dwindled ever since.

Mining

Cuba boasts an array of mineral resources, and most have yet to be exploited. Cuba is particularly wealthy in deposits of chromite, cobalt, and iron (up to 3.5 billion tons of ore), gold and silver (up to 600,000 tons), plus copper, manganese, lead, and zinc, all concentrated in northeastern Cuba. In February 1996, the Golden Hill Mining Co. of Canada announced "spectacular" results after drilling for gold in east-central Cuba. In recent years, Cuba has granted at least a dozen foreign companies prospecting rights.

By far the most important mineral is nickel. Cuba is the world's fourth-largest producer of nickel and has about 37% of the world's estimated reserves (about 19 million tons). The reserves are relatively easy and cheap to mine. Despite low world prices at the start of 1999, the island's nickel industry had not halted production at its three operating plants, and that year Cuba produced 66,600 metric tons, well short of the 73,000 target. In 2000, buoyant world prices and expected production of 74,000 metric tons lifted anticipated revenue above US$500 million.

Despite the U.S. government's attempts to disrupt Cuba's nickel sales to Europe, exports have quadrupled since 1990, mostly to Germany, Italy, and Sweden, as well as to India, Canada, and China. Mining has attracted 30% of all foreign business ventures on the island, although major investors have cooled their heels in recent years. In December 1999 the major international investor, Canada's Sherritt International Corp., which had planned to invest as much as US$475 million, pulled the plug as a result of human-rights abuses and "business complications."

Oil

In April 1960 the Soviet ship *Chernovci* arrived with a 70,000-barrel load of oil—the beginning of a 10,000-kilometer petroleum pipeline that was maintained for three decades. Cuba traded nickel, citrus, and sugar to the Soviet Union in return for 10-12 million tons of crude oil and petroleum per year (as much as half of this was re-exported for hard currency to purchase necessities on the world market; by the mid-1980s, oil surpassed sugar as the island's major moneymaker). Spared the hardship of oil shocks and price swings, Cuba became addicted to cheap oil and failed to divert its energy supply. Russia's decision to halt supplies of subsidized oil in 1991 triggered Cuba's desperate crisis. Between 1989 and 1992 the supply dropped from 13 million to 6.1 million tons. The inability to convert oil into cash was a crisis in itself. Worse, Russia now demanded hard currency for its oil—at world prices.

Cuba *does* have oil, and crude is currently being pumped from 20 oil fields. The five main producers are along the north coast concentrated near Varadero, which has estimated reserves of one billion barrels. Production began in 1988 and has risen steadily from 882,000 tons in 1992 to 1.68 million in 1998 (about 12 million barrels)—enough to cover one-sixth of the island's oil needs.

In 1990, foreign oil companies were invited to explore and invest, and Cubapetróleo formed Comercial Cupet S.A. to enter into contracts with foreign investors. Cuba's hopes to attract significant investments from the world's oil giants were scotched by threats from Washington. Nonetheless, more than a dozen companies have invested. Production contracts are for 25 years. Under the risk contracts, the foreign companies supply all the capital and technology for exploration. If oil isn't found, the company withdraws without any benefits. The Cuban government projected oil production to reach 2.1 million metric tons (about 17 million barrels) in 2000.

Russia has also resumed bartering oil for sugar through a triangulation deal whereby Russia delivers oil to Venezuelan-owned refineries in Europe, Venezuela ships an equivalent amount of its own oil to Cuba, and Cuba pays Russia with sugar.

Cuba's crude oil is heavy, with a high sulfur content that makes it hard to process. The majority is used unrefined for electricity generation in inefficient Eastern European systems that require high-grade crude oil. Cuba is thus upgrading its technology to take advantage of heavier, domestic high-sulfur fuel. Reportedly more than 40% of the Republic of Cuba's electricity was generated in 1999 from Cuban fuels.

Seeking higher-quality oil, in January 2000 the Cuban government opened up a 112,000 sq. km zone of the Gulf of Mexico for deep-water exploration by foreign companies, who expect to find enough domestic reserves for Cuba to become self-sufficient.

TOURISM

Before 1959 Cuba was one of the world's hottest tourist destinations. When Batista was ousted, most Americans (85% of foreign tourists before 1959) stayed home—visitation declined from 272,226 in 1957 to a scant 12,000 in 1974. Havana's former hot spots gathered dust. Apart from a handful of Russians, the beaches belonged to the Cubans throughout the 1960s and '70s, when tourism contributed virtually nothing to the nation's coffers.

One thing was clear at the 19th Cuba Tourism Convention held in May 2000 at Havana's Pabexpo: the U.S. government's attempts to pressure the international travel and tourism trade into staying home are disdained abroad. More than 200 journalists and more than 2,000 delegates showed up to take notes and negotiate a piece of Cuba's robust tourism pie.

How robust? Cuba posted a 19.8% *average* annual growth 1990-99, compared to 4.7% for the Caribbean as a whole.

Cuba's Comeback

Havana's view of tourism has profoundly shifted since the demise of the Soviet Union. Forsaken by his sugar daddy, Fidel established a no-holds-barred task force to bandage Cuba's hemorrhaging economy with hard currency culled from a once toxic source—Western consumer culture. Its five-year tourism industry plan for 1996-2000 called for investments of US$1.376 billion in hotel rooms. The challenge is whether Cuba can sell its sun and sand without selling its soul.

Cuba is successfully beating its swords into timeshares. It has quickly emerged as a major force in attracting non-U.S. tourists and is already well on the way to recapturing its 30% pre-Castro share of the Caribbean market. In 1999 the island received 1.7 million visitors, good for approximately US$2 billion, up from US$1.8 billion in 1998.

Cuba was gearing up to receive as many as two million tourists in 2000, and has set itself an ambitious long-term goal of seven million tourists annually by 2010, with an investment of US$11 billion. Says *Condé Nast Traveler:* "The goal will likely be met," thanks largely to packages that are immensely competitive (Cuba has no labor overhead, as workers are paid in worthless pesos). It's even cheaper for Mexicans to vacation in Cuba than Cozumel or Cancún. Canadians top the visitor chart, followed by Italians, Spaniards, and Germans, in that order.

Planning for the Invasion

Currently priority is being given to construction of new hotels and to refurbishment of existing hotels that don't meet international standards (the government planned on having 39,000 hotel rooms by 2001, and 45,000 hotel rooms by 2010, about equivalent with the Dominican Republic). Business, like nature, abhors a vacuum, and foreign companies are rushing in where Uncle Sam fears to tread. More than a dozen major foreign companies are involved in joint-venture agreements with Cuba's five major tour and hotel entities—Cubanacán, Gaviota, Gran Caribe, Horizontes, and Islazul. And in a move that is having profound implications, rooms-for-hire and private restaurants have been legalized and regulated. The government is even taking steps to promote residential tourism: deluxe apartments are being built for sale to foreigners.

Cuba's Tourism Development Master Plan is designed to avoid overbuilding and overdeveloping key areas. Although 67 areas have been earmarked for tourist development, the plan focuses on eight regions: the city of Havana (number one in tourist visits), Varadero (a beach resort in Matanza Province and number two in visitors), Cayo Largo (the largest island of the Canarreos archipelago), Cayo Coco (slated to be Cuba's second Varadero, with US$1.6 billion projected investment), Santiago de Cuba (Cuba's second largest city, in the far east of the country), Trinidad (a colonial gem named a UNESCO World Heritage Site), and both Santa Lucía and Northern Holguín (where beaches are being milked for their resort potential).

The Ministry of Tourism is positioning and promoting Cuba as a Caribbean destination offering diversity and value for money. New marketing efforts are focusing on higher-income travelers and on promoting broader vacation packages that expand beyond single locales. Cuban tourism operators are being encouraged to implement cooperative promotion campaigns. All-inclusive vacations, yacht-charter programs, full-service scuba diving centers, fly-drive vacations, ecotourism, and incentive travel are all destined to receive high priority. And the strategy gives a strong emphasis to developing multi-destination vacations hand in hand with neighboring islands and foreign tour operators.

Cruise terminals are also planned, as well as marinas, airport expansion, at least four new golf courses, and the replacement of Cubana's aging air fleet. And the U.S.-Cuban immigration accord signed in May 1995 has allowed Cuba to focus more attention on developing its water sports infrastructure (previously the Castro regime feared that the boats and jet skis would be used by Cubans eager to flee to Florida). Plans call for mitigating other weak links in the tourism industry, notably a shortage of "stand alone dining and entertainment facilities," limited domestic air transportation, substandard service, inept management, and awful food.

Cuba's Tourism Structure

The Ministry of Tourism oversees tourism development and acts as a watchdog over the operations of state-owned tourism agencies that operate autonomously and within a system of self-management and "healthy competition" that includes the authority to form associations with foreign capital.

The muscle behind Cuba's tourist trade is Cubanacán, which operates over 60 hotels and has shown significant profits since its founding (it also owns restaurants, marinas, buses, and rental cars, and has been at the forefront of the island's efforts to strike lucrative joint-management agreements with foreign hotel corporations). Gaviota has developed far more specialized programs than Cubanacán, including health tourism for wealthy foreigners, but also owns several dozen deluxe resorts and has positioned itself as a provider of VIP services. Many of its hotels are former R&R facilities enjoyed by the military until 1989. It, too, operates tour buses and offers car rentals. The company also uses former military planes and helicopters to move tourists around the island. Additional hotel groups include Gran Caribe for four-and five-star hotels; Horizontes, for three-star and less; and Islazul for two-star and domestic hotels that serve both Cubans and tourists. In addition, Rumbos outfits tourist areas with facilities and services with everything from restaurants, coffee shops, and highway rest stops, to airport services, excursions, and scooters for rent.

THE CUBAN PEOPLE AND SOCIETY

It is a rare visitor to Cuba who, exploring beyond the tourist circuit, does not at some time break down in tears. Everyone, everything, touches your heart. It is the way the Cubans embrace you with global innocence, how their disarming charm and irrepressible gaiety amid the heartrending pathos of their situation moves you to examine the meaning of life.

"It is not easy to describe the strength and enthusiasm of the Cubans," wrote Angela Davis after attending the 1962 World Youth Peace Festival in Helsinki, when the Revolution was only three years old. The cultural presentation given by the Cuban delegation illustrated for Davis the "infectious dynamism" that moves so many visitors to tears.

At the end of their show, the Cubans did not simply let the curtain fall. Their "performance" [which satirized the way U.S. capitalists had invaded Cuba and robbed it of sovereignty], after all, had been much more than a mere show. It had been life and reality. Had they drawn the curtain and bowed to applause, it would have been as if their commitment was simply "art." The Cubans continued their dancing, doing a spirited conga right off the stage and into the audience. Those of us openly enthralled by the Cubans, their revolution, and the triumphant beat of the drums rose spontaneously to join their conga line. And the rest—the timid ones, perhaps even the agents—were pulled bodily by the Cubans into the dance. Before we knew it, we were doing this dance—a dance brought into Cuban culture by slaves dancing in a line of chains—all through the building and on into the streets. Puzzled Finns looked on in disbelief at hundreds of young people of all colors, oblivious to traffic, flowing down the streets of Helsinki.

DEMOGRAPHY

Cuba's population is approximately 10.9 million (the 1989 census identified 10.5 million), of which 73% are classified as urban; 19.9% live in the city of Havana, with a population of about 2,200,000 (Santiago de Cuba, the second-largest city, has about 350,000 people). The annual average growth rate is 0.9%, down from 2.3% from 1953 to 1970 and 1.1% in the 1980s. More than two million Cubans have left the island since 1959.

Cuba's family-planning policies have helped the country reduce its birth rate from 4.2% in 1960 to 1.9% today—about the same as in the U.S. Cuba is in the company of the world's developed nations in respect to its aging population and low birth rates. Fertility rates are 1.9 children per woman, compared to 1.8 in both the U.S. and Great Britain, 1.7 in Canada and Japan, and 1.6 in Spain.

The declining birth rates are due to the population's cultural development, the high percentage of women engaged full-time as workers, and access to health care, including abortion services (88% of adults use contraceptive methods, though Cuban men and women alike shun Kohinoor, the heavy-duty Cuban-made condoms locally called *el quitasensaciones*—the killjoy—which in all senses of the word are hard to come by). Instead, Cuban women use abortion as a birth control: Cuba has a staggering 56.6 abortions for every 100 live births. The government has introduced a national "pro-infancy" program and increased sex education classes and is dis-

WHAT'S IN A NAME?

Spanish surnames are combinations of the first surname of the person's father, which comes first, and the mother's first surname, which comes second. Thus, the son of Ángel Castro Argiz and Lina Ruz González is called Fidel Castro Ruz. Married women add the husbands' surnames to their own family name.

old man and boy

tributing contraceptives with the aim of reducing the abortion rate by half.

Cuba's marriage rate is the world's highest: 17.7 per 1,000 people each year. Its divorce rate is also high: 4.2 per 1000, compared to 4.8 for the U.S. and 0.4 for Italy. Nonetheless, 60% of births are to unmarried mothers (Cuba has a high incidence of teenage pregnancy). This carries no social stigma, as the Family Code 1974 abolished the concept of illegitimacy, and Cuba has a long history in this regard (about one-quarter of children were born out of wedlock on the eve of the Revolution, simply because many people could not afford the marriage fees or the fees to register their children; both Fulgencio Batista and Fidel Castro were born out of wedlock).

An Aging Population

The reduced birth rate could lead to a real population reduction by the year 2022. The low birth and mortality rates and high life expectancy also mean a rapidly aging population. About 14% of the population is 60 years or older—an enormous social security burden for the beleaguered government. The number of elderly will triple by 2030, when the nonworking population will equal the working population.

The extremely high suicide rate (21.6 per 100,000 Cubans, double that of the United States) is also the greatest cause of death between the ages of 15 and 45. Cuba has few facilities or professionals trained to treat depression.

The Ethnic Mix

Officially about 66% of the population is "white," mainly of Spanish origin. About 12% is black, and 22% is mulatto of mixed ethnicity. In reality the percentage of mulattoes is far greater (Cuban lore claims there is some African in every Cuban's blood). Chinese constitute about 0.1%. While there are no pure-blooded native Indians left in Cuba, in the east—especially around Baracoa—genetic traces recall the indigenous culture. (Cubans—in fact, all Latin Americans—resent the way North Americans take to themselves the word America. "We, too, are Americans," they'll remind you.)

The population has grown markedly darker since the Revolution. About 10% of Cuba's population have emigrated since 1959, and the vast majority of exiles were white (98% of Miami's Cuban-exile community is white).

Race Relations

Slavery has burdened many countries of the Americas with racial and social problems still unresolved today. But Cuba has gone as far as any other to untangle the Gordian knot. Cuban society is as intermixed as any other on earth (interracial sexuality has been a central theme throughout Cuban history). Racial harmony is everywhere evident. Cubans feel proud of the racially liberating Revolution that has achieved what appears to be a truly color blind, multiracial society.

Despite slavery, by Caribbean norms Cuba has been a "white" society whose numbers were constantly fed by a steady inpouring of immigrants from Spain. After emancipation in 1888, the island was spared the brutal segregation of the American South, and as in the U.S., a black middle class evolved. A strong, separate black culture evolved, with its own social clubs, restaurants, and literature. There was significant mobility and opportunity. "Cuba's color line is much more flexible than that of the United States," recorded black author Langston Hughes during a visit in 1930: "There are no Jim Crow cars in Cuba, and at official state gatherings and less official carnivals and celebrations, citizens of all colors meet and mingle." Havana society of the time, wrote Hugh Thomas, was "one in which relations between black and white were of an extreme, if tolerant complexity, endogamy combined with joint preoccupation with Afro-Cuban cults as well as left wing politics. The prejudices which kept blacks from the new luxury hotels of the late 1950s were still things of the future."

Gradually, however, U.S. visitors began to import Southern racial prejudice to their winter playground. To court their approval, hotels that were formerly lax in their application of color lines began to discourage even mulatto Cubans. And the Biltmore Club, which had taken over Havana's only wide clean stretch of beach, began to charge a dollar for the privilege of its use (no small sum in those days) and introduced a color bar as well, although mulatto plutocrats and policemen still mingled.

Cuba on the eve of the revolution had adopted "whites only" clubs, restaurants, schools, hotels, beaches, recreation centers, housing areas, and, of course, discrimination in job hiring. When dictator Fulgencio Batista—who was a mixture of white, black, and Chinese—arrived at the exclusive Havana Yacht Club, they turned the lights out to let him know that although he was president, as a mulatto he was not welcome. And many blacks lived as described by Ernest Hemingway in Islands in the Stream: "The lean-to was built at a steep slant and there was barely room for two people to lie down in it. The couple who lived in it were sitting in the entrance cooking coffee in a tin can. They were Negroes, filthy, scaly with age and dirt, wearing clothing made from old sugar sacks."

Cuba's revolutionary government swiftly outlawed institutionalized discrimination and vigorously enforced laws to bring about racial equality. Castro said, "We can't leave the promotion of women, Blacks, and mestizos to chance. It has to be the work of the party: we have to straighten out what history has twisted."

There is no doubt that the Cuban government has achieved marvelous things. By replacing the social structures that allowed racism to exist, the Revolution has made it virtually impossible for any group to be relegated forever to racial servitude. Afro-Cubans are far healthier, better educated, and more skilled and confident than blacks in Brazil, Colombia, Panama, Jamaica, Haiti, or the urban underclass of the U.S. They enjoy the lowest rate of infant mortality in Latin America and the Caribbean—a rate vastly superior, it should be added, to that of blacks in the United States. Hence, blacks are, on the whole, more loyal to Castro than whites.

The social advantages that opened up after the Revolution have resulted in the abolition of lily-white scenes. Mixed marriages no longer raise eyebrows in Cuba. Everyone shares a Cubanness. Black novelist Alice Walker, who knows Cuba well, has written, "Unlike black Americans, who have never felt at ease with being American, black Cubans raised in the Revolution take no special pride in being black. They take great pride in being Cuban. Nor do they appear able to feel, viscerally, what racism is." A negative perspective is offered by Carlos Moore, an Afro-Cuban writer who left Cuba in 1963, in his Castro, the Blacks, and Africa (Center for Afro-American Studies, University of California, Los Angeles, 1988).

Behind the Veil

There are still cultural barriers, however. Some social venues attract an almost exclusively white crowd, while others are virtually all-black affairs (blacks still retain their religion, their bonds, their worldview). The most marginal neighborhoods still have a heavy preponderance of blacks. Most Cuban blacks still work at menial jobs and earn, on average, less than whites. And blacks are notoriously absent from the upper echelons of government and tourism, where there is a tendency to hire whites.

Nor has the Revolution totally overcome stereotypical racial thinking and prejudice. Black youths, for example, claim to be disproportionately harassed by police (though, ironically, blacks are well represented among the uniformed police). You still hear racist comments: many white Cubans, especially the former wealthy classes, still exist inside their heads in a lily-white Cuba that exists in particular enclaves of Miami. And many Cuban mulattoes still prefer to define their racial identity with whites rather than with blacks (prior to the Revolution, it was common for mulattoes with lighter skin to be referred to as *mas adelantados*—more advanced).

CHARACTER, CONDUCT, AND CUSTOMS

In a world full of cynicism and anomie, the Cubans' refreshing innocence and disarming charm is uplifting. Although a clear Cuban identity has emerged, Cuban society is not easy to fathom. Cubans "adore mystery and continually do their damnedest to render everything more intriguing. Conventional rules do not apply," thought author Juliet Barclay. "When it came to ambiguity, Cuba was the leader of the pack," added author Pico Iyer. "An ironist can have a field day."

The Cubans are somewhat schizoid. In the four decades since the Revolution, most Cubans have learned to live double lives. One side is spirited, inventive, irrepressibly argumentative and critical, inclined to keep private shrines at home to both Christian saints and African gods, and profit however possible from the failings and inefficiencies of the state. The other side commits them to be good revolutionaries and to cling to the state and the man who runs it.

The Cubans value context, and their philosophical approach to life differs markedly from North American or northern European values. Therefore, attempts to analyze Cuba through the North American value system are bound to be wide of the mark. Most important, most North Americans don't understand what the "Revolution" means. When Cubans speak of the "Revolution," they don't mean the toppling of Batista's regime, or Castro's seizure of power, or even his and the country's conversion to communism. They mean the ongoing process of building a society where everyone supposedly benefits. Their philosophical framework is different. Most

Cubans, regardless of their feelings for Castro, take great pride in the "Revolution." Though today Cuba suffers a pandemic of disaffection, a large percentage seems happy to accept the sacrifice of individual liberties for the notion of improving equality.

The Cuban people are committed to social justice, and the idea that democracy includes every person's right to guaranteed health care, education, and culture is deeply ingrained in their consciousness. This has less to do with an innate Cuban characteristic than with *fidelismo*, whose tenets call for puritanism and morality, which after four decades have seeped into the masses. The spartan effort reached extremes, as the following news story shows:

> *Premier Fidel Castro has decided to revise the rules of baseball, it was disclosed today.*
>
> *Last Sunday, after cutting cane at a nearby sugar mill, Dr. Castro pitched a sandlot game. But when a runner stole second base from him, the Premier ordered him back to first.*
>
> *"In the revolution," Dr. Castro said, "no one can steal—even in baseball."*

True, city folk crave the opportunity to better their lives materially, but Cubans are not concerned with the *accumulation* of material wealth. Unlike North Americans, they are not individual consumpto-units. Most Cubans are more interested in sharing something with you than getting something from you. (Cubans call each other *compañero* or *compañera*, which has a "cozy sound of companionship.") They are unmoved by talk of your material accomplishments. When Cuba's most famous doctor, Rodrigo Alvarez-Cambras, was given one million dollars for removing a malignant tumor from Iraqi leader Saddam Hussein, the esteemed black surgeon and dedicated socialist donated his gift to the Cuban state.

It is more important that everyone has more than the basic minimum—more important, too, to live life. Indeed, four decades of socialism has not changed the hedonistic culture of Cubans:

the traditional Afro-Cuban tropical culture has proved resistant to puritanical revolutionary doctrine. They are sensualists of the first degree. Judging by the ease with which couples neck openly, wink seductively at strangers, and spontaneously slip into bed, the dictatorship of the proletariat that transformed Eastern Europe into a perpetual Sunday school has made little headway in Cuba. The state may promote the family, but Cubans have a notoriously indulgent attitude to casual sex—the national pastime.

Cubans are also proud, and notoriously toilet- and fashion-conscious. Even the poorest Cuban manages to keep fastidiously clean and well dressed. It has been said that "to take away their soap would be Castro's greatest folly. Almost anything else can be tolerated, but take away their soap and the regime would fall!"

The women are astute and self-assured, and the men are very sentimental. The struggles of the past four decades have fostered a remarkable sense of confidence and maturity. As such, there's no reserve, no emotional distance, no holding back. Cubans engage you in a very intimate way. They're not afraid of physical contact; they touch a lot. They also look you in the eye: they don't blink or flinch but are direct and assured. They're alive and full of emotional intensity. You sense that Cubans are so chock-full of verve and chutzpah that Cuba will surely remain the same, though regimes may come and go.

The economic crisis and the collapse of socialism, however, have fostered an identity crisis; even the most dedicated communists admit their fears about the future. Particularly worrisome is a loss of values, morals, and solidarity. The principles of the New Man are being eroded. The New Man is the very essence of the Revolution, what the Cuban Revolution is all about. He or she is a person whose social conscience prevails over selfish material interest: an unalienated being, unsullied by the profit motive, living to serve the community, and preferring a virtuous existence over indulgent ways (see the special topic, Che Guevara, above).

Cuba today is a suffering and anxious nation, subject to the same horrendous forces that have caused the Third World such despair. Many people are alternately sad and high-spirited. Conditions are often heartbreaking, yet most Cubans don't get beaten down. They never seem to lose their sense of humor, reminding Pico Iyer of a statement by the 18th-century Englishman Oliver Edwards: "I have tried in my time to be a philosopher, but I don't know how, cheerfulness was always breaking in."

Social Divisions

The Revolution destroyed the social stratification inherited from Spanish colonial rule. Distinct delineations among the classes withered away. Not that prerevolutionary Cuba was entirely rigid—it was unusual in Latin America for its high degree of "social mobility" (Castro's father, for example, was a poor farm laborer when he emigrated from Spain but rose to become a wealthy landowner). Prerevolutionary life was not simply black and white, rich and poor. There was a huge middle class, although it has been argued that there was no characteristically middle-class way of life—no conscious middle-class ideal.

As an agrarian-populist movement pitted against Havana-based middle-sector interests, *fidelismo* warred against the middle class and destroyed it (the Castro government assiduously avoids reference to the middle class), eradicating the hard-earned wealth of tens of thousands and tearing families asunder: almost every family in Cuba has suffered emotional turmoil from the revolution, with friends and relatives driven into exile. The old privileged, entrepreneurial class was replaced by a *nueva clase* of senior Communist Party members who enjoy benefits unavailable to other Cubans; the old underclass has been replaced by a class of outcasts who do not support the revolutionary government and have thereby been deprived of social benefits.

Cubans lack the social caste system that makes so many Europeans walk on eggshells. There is absolutely no deference, no subservience. Cubans accept people at face value and are slow to judge others negatively. They are instantly at ease, and greet each other with hearty handshakes or kisses. Women meeting for the first time will embrace like sisters. A complete stranger is sure to give you a warm *abrazo,* or hug. Even the most fleeting acquaintances will offer you a meal, or go out of their way to help you however they can. As a foreigner, you'll meet with the warmest courtesies wherever you go. Every Cuban wants to open his or her home and is eager to please, uncommonly generous, extremely courteous and gracious, and self-sacrificing to a fault. (Cubans can't understand why foreigners are always saying, "Thank you!" Doing things for others is the expected norm.)

In the current crisis, however, society is unraveling, a stratified society is emerging, and the values and ethics are becoming strained. Prostitution is once again rampant. An economic elite of *masetas* (rich Cubans) is becoming visible, and so are class resentments and tensions. And low-level corruption, long a necessity for getting around Cuba's socialist inefficiencies, is blossoming into a more insidious high-level graft and racketeering. The Cubans who are loyal to Castro now get the last benefits, while those who are least loyal, those who shun the government or look to Miami, live the best. The *jiniteras,* the petty thieves on the streets, the children who now resort to begging: all these things are the result of Cuba's poverty. The New Man—one of the greatest gifts of the Revolution—is slowly dying. "The world is poorer for the loss of that intangible, optimistic, altruistic spirit," says Saul Landau. Indeed it is.

Cuban Curiosity

A sense of isolation and a high level of cultural development have filled Cubans with intense curiosity (in the country, few Cubans have ever traveled beyond a 50-mile radius of their homes). One reason why so many Cubans ask foreigners *"¿Qué hora es?"* is to strike up a conversation. Another reason is that they really do need to know the time in a country where time stopped years ago They will guess at your nationality and quiz you about the most prosaic matters of Western life, as well as the most profound. Issues of income and costs are areas of deep interest, and you may be questioned in intimate detail. Sexual relations arouse equally keen interest, and Cubans of both genders are often excited to volunteer their services to help guide Cupid's arrow.

Until recently, foreigners were approached constantly on the street (since the crackdown in 1999, they are more circumspect). Cubans are starved, and eager, to know about the outside world. In private, they pepper you with questions. They watch Hollywood movies and often converse with a surprising mix of worldly erudition and astounding naïveté.

If you tell them you are a *Yanquí,* most Cubans light up. They are genuinely fond of U.S. citizens. "Why do Americans not like us?" many naïve Cubans ask you, before expressing their hope that Cuba and the U.S. might soon again be friends.

Although Cubans thrive on debate, they are hesitant to discuss politics openly except behind closed doors, where they may open up to you with sometimes unexpected frankness. Only then will you be able to gauge how they really feel about Cuba and Castro.

Humor

Despite their hardships, Cubans have not lost the ability to laugh. Their renowned humor is called the "yeast for their buoyant optimism about the future." Stand-up comedy is a tradition in Cuban nightclubs. And *chistes*—jokes—race around the country.

Cubans turn everything into a *chiste,* most of which are aimed at themselves. Theirs is a penetrating black humor that spares no one—the insufferable bureaucrat, *jiniteras,* the Special Period. There are no sacred cows. Not even Fidel—perhaps *especially* not *El Jefe*—is spared the barbs, although his name is never used (the silent reference is usually communicated by the gesture of a hand stroking a beard), and no one in his right mind would tell such a joke in public. Other favorite targets of scorn are Russian-made Lada cars and Hungarian buses, which every Cuban agrees are all lemons and which the Hungarian government stopped making after selling the fleet to Cuba—hence, no spare parts.

Like the English, Cubans also boast a great wit. They lace their conversations with double entendres and often risqué innuendo. The Spanish-speaking foreigner is often left behind by subtle inflections and Cuban idioms.

The Nationalist Spirit

Cubans are an intensely passionate and patriotic people united by nationalist spirit and love of country. They are by culture and tradition politically conscious. The revolutionary government has engaged in consciousness raising on a national scale, instilling in Cubans—a people used to being underlings—that they can have pride as a nation. The national character is shaped by passionate struggles and a turbulent history rich in violent conquest, slavery, rebellion, dictatorship, revolution, and invasion.

Cubans are nationalists before they are socialists or even incipient capitalists. Cubans had not expected socialism from the Revolution but those who could accept it did so not simply because so many benefited from the social mobility the Revolution had brought but because, as Maurice Halperin suggests, "it came with nationalism; that is, an assertion of economic and political independence from the United States, the goal of Cuban patriots for a half century." This reality provides Cubans with a different perspective and viewpoint on history.

Labor and the Work Ethic

Cubans are distinct from all their Caribbean neighbors in one important respect. They combine their southern joy of living with a northern work ethic that makes them unique achievers. Through the centuries, Cuba has received a constant infusion of the most energetic Spanish people in the Caribbean, what author James Michener calls "a unique group, one of the strongest cultural stocks in the New World": the wealthier, better-educated, and most motivated colonizers fleeing rebellion and invasion on Haiti, Santo Domingo, and Jamaica. The entrepreneurial spirit isn't dead, as attested by the success of *paladares* and that of makeshift enterprises that sprang up in 1993 before being quashed.

The vast majority of Cubans work for the state. With few exceptions, the state dictates where an individual will work. Thus the degree of anomie is great. Many Cubans ask their doctor friends to issue *certificados* (medical excuses) so that they can take a "vacation" from the boredom of employment that offers little financial reward and little hope of promotion. (*Socio* is the buddy network, used to shield you from the demands of the state. *Pinche* and *mayimbe* are your high-level contacts, those who help you get around the bureaucracy, such as the doctor who writes a false note to relieve you of "voluntary" work in the countryside.)

The improvements in the standards of living among rural families in recent decades have not been enough to keep the younger generation on the land. There has been a steady transfer of workers from agricultural to industrial and service-oriented jobs. Since the Special Period, the migration from the *campos* has accelerated.

To make up for the labor shortfall, Castro invented "volunteer" brigades. Urban workers, university students, and even schoolchildren are shipped to the countryside to toil in the fields. Workers who refuse to work on *microbrigades* are subject to recrimination. Although the legal minimum working age is 17, the Labor Code exempts 15- and 16-year-olds to allow them to fill labor shortages. Volunteer workers get an *estímulo*, a reward, such as priority listing for apartments. There are moral rewards and material rewards—perhaps a week at Varadero, or the right to buy a refrigerator—for other workers. Nonetheless, very little work gets done in the fields (groups spend much of the day in dalliance, often carnally, until the time comes to go home).

Cuba has 6.6 million people of working age, of which 67% are in the labor force. Wages are according to a salary scale of 22 levels, with the top level getting six times that of the lowest. Highly trained professionals share the same struggles as unskilled workers. Though paid slightly more, doctors and engineers and lawyers are not a separate "class" as they are in the U.S., Europe, or even the rest of the Caribbean. Life is little different for those who earn 200 pesos a month and those who earn 850.

The Cuban government puts the average monthly salary in Cuba at 217 pesos (about US$10 at real exchange rates), although the "real wage" is considerably higher when subsidized housing, etc., are taken into account. Many workers receive no salary; instead they are paid in kind (a friend of mine—a model—is paid five bottles of rum per month). Nor does the government allow Cubans who work for foreign entities to be paid in dollars, though the foreign companies pay US$450 a month per worker to the state agency, Acorec, which pays the workers in worthless pesos.This policy is the source of a lawsuit filed in June 1999 on behalf of the Cuban Committee for Human Rights. The Castro regime goes out of its way to keep precious greenbacks out of the Cubans' empty pockets (for example, only after two years of negotiations did the government begrudgingly agree to permit Super-Clubs and Sandals, Jamaican hotel chains that do not permit tipping, to offer profit sharing to

SEX AND TOURISM

"'What effect is dollarization having on families and society?' asked one of [the journalists]. Said Maruetti [a Cuban economist], looking bureaucratically oblivious, 'Number One: foreign investment. Two: intensive development of tourism. Three: opening to foreign trade.' Sis had been out hitchhiking and someone made a foreign investment in her. It's all part of Cuba's intensive development of tourism. And, boy, is she open to foreign trade."

—P. J. O'Rourke

$\mathcal{B}$efore the Revolution, Batista's Babylon offered a tropical buffet of sin: Castro declared that there were 100,000 prostitutes in Havana, about ten times the true figure (Yankees were blamed for prostitution, although prostitution had preceded tourism to Cuba by several hundred years). In 1959 the revolutionary government closed down the sex shows and porn palaces and sent the prostitutes to rehabilitative trade schools, thereby ostensibly eliminating the world's oldest trade. Prostitution reappeared, however, within a few years of the Triunfo. And Fred Ward recorded in 1977 how "a few girls have been appearing once again in the evenings, looking for dates, and willing to trade their favors for goods rather than money." He thought it "more a comment on rationing than on morals."

Jiniteras—the word comes from *jineta,* or horsewoman, or jockey—have always been part of the postrevolutionary landscape, especially at em-

bassy functions. The Cuban government, claims Guillermo Cabrera Infante, has always made state *mulattas* available to foreign dignitaries (as a foreign diplomat quipped, "Cubans are better suited to make their living in bed than anyone else on earth."). Critics even claim that in the early 1990s the Cuban government sponsored the island's image as a cheap-sex paradise to kick-start tourism, charging, for example, that Havana's Comodoro Hotel sold special certificates permitting foreigners to take Cuban girls to their rooms. Tourism-related "prostitution" was soon proliferating beneath a general complacency. Soon the first worrisome signs of child prostitution appeared, with girls as young as 13 hanging around outside the Hotel Habana Libre. The situation reached its nadir when Rumbos, a Cuban tourist company, was stung by allegations of exporting "dancing girls" to Latin America, while in 1999 a Mexican company, Cubamor, was accused of operating organized sex tours with official connivance.

The Government's Response

"The state tries to prevent it as much as possible. It is not legal in our country to practice prostitution, nor are we going to legalize it. Nor are we thinking in terms of turning it into a freelance occupation to solve unemployment problems. [Laughter.] We are not going to repress it either," Castro told *Time* magazine, while also claiming that Cuba had the healthiest and best-educated prostitutes in the world.

Nevertheless, in 1996 Cuban women were barred from guest rooms in tourists hotels, and the police initiated a crackdown. In Varadero, *jiniteras* were swept from the streets. Then in January 1999, thousands of young women were picked up on the streets of Ha-

Cuban staff, while limiting payments to two percent). There are no independent labor unions in Cuba to fight for workers' rights.

Cuban Passivity

Cubans nationwide say that things cannot go on as they are: "We must have change!" When you ask them how change will come, most roll their eyes and shrug. Politically the majority of Cubans—those not firmly committed to the political apparatus—are weighed down with passivity. Open demonstrations against the gov-

ernment are extremely rare. Those who touch the third rail of government displeasure are swiftly dealt with. Few dare take such a step.

Silence, congruity, and complicity—pretending to be satisfied and happy with the system—are cultural reflexes that have been called indicative of cultural decay. Jacobo Timerman's *Cuba: A Journey* provides a baneful look at this passivity.

Sexual Mores

Cuba is a sexually permissive society. As journalist Jacobo Timerman wrote, "Eros is amply

vana and jailed, while those without an official Havana address were returned to their homes in the countryside. Several provinces have since banned Cuban girls from staying with tourists in private rooms. Nonetheless, sexual relations between tourists and Cubans (mostly women) continue. At night on dimly lit streets, perfumed *Cubanas* in high heels and tight Spandex smile and hiss at unaccompanied males.

Like everything in Cuba, the situation is complex and needs some explaining.

A Chance to Get Ahead—and Get Away

The women who form intimate relationships with tourists are a far cry from the uneducated prostitutes of Batista days. Most would laugh to be called *jiniteras*. Studies by the Federation of Cuban Women (FMC) have shown that even among *jiniteras*, "Most have the benefit of extensive economic and educational opportunity compared to the lot of their sisters before the Revolution. Most are not ashamed [and] few have low self-esteem. . . . With very few exceptions, they don't need to practice commercial sexual relations to survive. Instead, what motivates these women. . . is the desire to go out, to enjoy themselves, go places where Cubans are not allowed to go." They're seeking a *papiriqui con guaniquiqui* (a sugar daddy) as a replacement for a paternalistic government that can no longer provide. Says writer Coco Fusco, "on the street these women are seen as heroic providers whose sexual power is showing up the failures of an ailing macho regime."

A pretty *Cubana* attached to a generous suitor can be wined and dined and get her entrance paid into the discos, drinks included. Many women hook up with a man for the duration of his visit in the hope that a future relationship may develop. Many suc-

ceed in snagging foreign husbands. Their dream is to live abroad—to find a foreign boyfriend (usually considerably older) who will marry them and take them away. It happens all the time. Educated and morally upright *mulattas* smile at tourists passing by on the street or hang out by the disco doorways, seeking affairs—*lucha un yuma*—and invitations to be a part of the high life.

In a society where promiscuity is rampant and sex on a first date is a given, any financial transaction—assuredly, more in one night in *fula* (dollars) than she can otherwise earn in a month's salary in worthless pesos—is reduced to a charitable afterthought to a romantic evening out. In 1995 the Congress of the Federation of Cuban Women concluded that the rise in "prostitution" has an equal amount to do with Cuban youth's permissive attitudes towards sex. It recognized *jiniterismo* as an expression of a moral crisis and stressed the need to emphasize the role of the family, to help dissuade young women who have discovered the megaton power of their sexuality from living it out to the full.

Sex and Underage Partners

Sex is legal at the age of 16 in Cuba, but under Cuban and international law, foreigners can be prosecuted for sex with anyone under 18.

The **Center for Responsible Tourism,** 1765-D Le Roy Ave., Berkeley, CA 94709, e-mail: CRTourism @aol.com, publishes a leaflet, *What You Should Know About Sex Tourism Before You Go Abroad,* dealing with sex with minors.

If you know of anyone who is traveling to Cuba with the intent of sexually abusing minors, contact the U.S. Customs Service, International Child Pornography Investigation and Coordination Center, 45365 Vintage Park Rd., Suite 250, Sterling, VA 20166, tel. (703) 709-9700, e-mail: icpicc@customs.sprint.co.

gratified in Cuba and needs no stimulation." A joyous eroticism pervades Cuban men and women alike that transcends the hang-ups of essentially puritanical Europe or North America. Seduction is a national pastime pursued by both sexes—the free expression of a high-spirited people confined in an authoritarian world. After all, Cubans joke, sex is the only thing Castro can't ration.

In *Chronicles of the City of Havana* (1991), Uruguayan journalist Eduardo Galeano tells the following story.

One day at noon, guagua 68 screeched to a halt at an intersection. There were cries of protest at the tremendous jolt until the passengers saw why the bus driver had jammed on the brakes: a magnificent woman had just crossed the street.

"You'll have to forgive me, gentlemen," said the driver of guagua 68, and he got out. All the passengers applauded and wished him luck.

The bus driver swaggered along, in no hurry, and the passengers watched him approach the saucy female, who stood on the corner, leaning against the wall, licking an ice cream cone. From guagua 68, the passengers followed the darting motion of her tongue as it kissed the ice cream while the driver talked on and on with no apparent result, until all at once she laughed and glanced up at him. The driver gave the thumbs-up sign and the passengers burst into a hearty ovation.

Cubans had elevated eroticism into "national genius" long before 1959, but Cubans' overt sexuality owes much to the revolution. It would be, said Che Guevara, "a revolution with *buchango* (pizzazz)." Che's widow, Aleida March, told biographer Jon Lee Anderson that women were "throwing themselves" at the *barbudas* after the Triumph of the Revolution and that, "Well—with a big smile as if to indicate it was quite a scene—there had been a lot of "lovemaking" going on." Thus the tone was set early, noted Lois Smith and Alfredo Padula, by a "bacchanal in which the triumphant revolutionaries and euphoric nation celebrated between the sheets, causing a boom in business for Cuban prostitutes." Cuban sexuality has ever since defied the efforts of the Revolution to tame and control it.

Promiscuity is rampant. So are extramarital affairs. Love is not associated with sex. And both genders are unusually bold. Men and women let their eyes run slowly over strangers they find attractive. Long glances—*ojitos*—often accompanied by uninhibited comments, betray envisioned improprieties. Cuban women don't find the *piropo* (catcall or courtly overtures) demeaning. One *Cubana,* returning from a visit to Chicago, asked: "Doesn't anybody in the States stare at anybody? My body was so lonely to be watched." Even the women murmur *piropos* and sometimes-comic declarations of love. "Dark-eyed Stellas light their feller's panatelas," Irving Berlin once wrote of Cuba. And how!

In a country where consumer pleasures are few and far between, casual sex has become the most desirable and available leisure activity among youth. Teenagers become sexually active at an early age: girls at 13 on average, boys at

15, according to Cuba's National Center for Sex Education, which dispenses sex counseling to youths, along with condoms and birth control pills. Males and females old and and young alike insist that promiscuity is a natural attribute. "Cubans like sex," says the director of Baracoa's family planning clinic. "It's part of our daily meal. Here you have girls who at 13 are already experts in sex."

Homosexuality

Cuban gays must find pleasing irony that the heart of the homosexual world is Castro Street in San Francisco. It is assuredly not named in El Jefe's honor, as gays—called "queens," *maricónes,* or *locas* in the Cuban vernacular—were persecuted following the Revolution. Castro (who denies the comment) supposedly told journalist Lee Lockwood that a homosexual could never "embody the conditions and requirements of. . . a true revolutionary." Before 1959, the most visible expression of homosexuality was in prostitution, which led to support for the Stalinist notion that homosexuality was a product of capitalist decadence. Thus, homosexuals were among the groups identified as "undesirable."

Castro says that such prejudices were a product not of the Revolution but of the existing social milieu. "We inherited male chauvinism—and many other bad habits—from the conquistadores," he told Tomás Borge in *Face to Face with Fidel Castro* (Ocean Press, 1992). "That historical legacy. . . influenced our attitude toward homosexuality." At the time, the gay rights movement had not yet been born in the U.S. and the same prejudices that the revolutionaries inherited about homosexuals were prevalent elsewhere in the world, too.

Thus gays and lesbians met with "homophobic repression and rejection" in Cuba, just as they did in the U.S. In Cuba, however, it was more systematic and brutal. The pogrom began in earnest in 1965; homosexuals were arrested and sent to agricultural work and reeducation camps—UMAPA (Units for Military Help to Agricultural Production)—which gay filmmaker Néstor Almendros revealed in his documentaries *Improper Conduct* and *Nobody Listened.* (Echoing Auschwitz, over the gate of one such camp in Camagüey was the admonition: "Work Makes You Men.")

Many brilliant intellectuals lost their jobs because they were gay (or accused of being gay through anonymous denunciation). Homosexuality was also considered an aberration of nature that could weaken the family structure. Hence homosexuals were not allowed to teach, become doctors, or occupy positions from which they could "pervert" Cuban youth.

Although UMAP camps closed in 1968 (later, those who had lost their jobs were reinstated and given back pay), periodic purges occurred throughout the 1970s and early 80s. Understandably, many homosexuals left—or were forced to leave—on the Mariel boatlift. However, by the mid-1980s, Cuba began to respond to the gay-rights movement that had already gained momentum worldwide. Officially the new position was that homosexuality and bisexuality are no less natural or healthy than heterosexuality. Families are encouraged to go to therapy to learn to accept homosexuality within the family. In 1987, a directive was issued to police to stop harassment. And an official atonement was made through the release at the 1993 Havana Film Festival of *Vidas paralelas* (Parallel Lives) and *La Bella de Alhambra* (The Beauty at the Alhambra), and the hit movie *Fresa y Chocolat* (Strawberry and Chocolate), which dealt sympathetically with homosexuality. *Fresa y Chocolat*, which deals with the persecution of gays in Cuba and the government's use of informers, was officially approved by Cuba's Film Institute (headed by Alfredo Guevara, a homosexual and close confidante of Castro), offering proof that the government was exorcising the ghost of a shameful past.

Nonetheless, prejudice still exists throughout society, and there is still a restriction on gays joining the party. The gay community does not have representative organizations.

Gay Cuba, by Sonja de Vries, is a documentary film that looks candidly at the treatment of gays and lesbians in Cuba since the Revolution. You can order copies from Frameline, 346 Ninth St., San Francisco, CA 94103, tel. (415) 703-8654, fax (415) 861-1404; e-mail: frameline@aol.com, website: www.frameline.org. Also check out *Machos, Maricones, and Gays: Cuba and Homosexuality,* by Ian Lumsden (Philadelphia, PA: Temple University, 1996) for a study of the relationship between male homosexuality and Cuban society.

LIFE IN CUBA

On the eve of the Revolution, Cuba was a semi-developed country with more millionaires than anywhere south of Texas, a rapidly evolving capitalist infrastructure, and an urban labor force that had achieved "the eight-hour day, double pay for overtime, one month's paid vacation, nine days' sick leave, and the right to strike." On the other hand, in 1950, a World Bank study team reported that 40% of urban dwellers and 60% of rural dwellers were undernourished (rural dwellers relied on *malanga,* a nutritious—albeit tough—root, corn, sweet potatoes, plantains, and sugar; even beans and rice were beyond reach of the rural dweller, as were most vegetables). Over 40% of Cuban people had never gone to school; only 60% had regular full-time employment. The La Beneficencia orphanage in Havana even had a drop chute with flaps to facilitate the abandonment of babies by mothers who couldn't afford to bring them up.

The Revolution immeasurably improved the human condition of millions of Cubans, eliminating poverty and gross disparities, although at the cost of destroying the middle classes and imposing a general paucity on millions of others. But at least everyone had the essentials. Everyone enjoyed two two-week vacations a year at the beach. And the government provided five crates of beer as a wedding present and birthday cakes for kids under 10. (The state still issues a nightgown to a bride and also to pregnant women, "causing some irreverent wags to note that these were exactly the two times when a woman least needed one," says Georgie Ann Geyer.)

The 1990s have been devastating for a population accustomed to a much higher standard of living. In 1991 when Castro warned his people that they were entering a "Special Period," he was warning that their society was about to experience a special kind of collapse, and they were about to feel a special kind of pain. The worst year, 1993, was "so hard, so difficult, so terrible," said Castro. Only in 1995 did things begin to improve.

The Bare Essentials
Row upon row of citrus trees grow just 30 miles from Havana, but it is near impossible to find an

THE CUBAN-AMERICANS

"We see, then, how vain the faith and promises of men are who are exiles from their own country. . . . They naturally believe many things that are not true, and add many others on purpose. . . . They will fill you with hopes to that degree that if you attempt to act upon them you will incur a fruitless expense, or engage in an undertaking that will involve in your ruin. . . . A Prince therefore should be slow in undertaking any enterprise upon the representations of exiles, for he will generally gain nothing by it but shame and serious injury."

—*Niccoló Machiavelli,* Discourses

There are more than one million Cuban-born people in the United States, half of them naturalized citizens, according to the U.S. Census Bureau. They are concentrated in Dade County, Florida (over 500,000), and New Jersey. Their capital is Miami, just 140 miles from Havana—a distance protracted by a generation of despair, hubris, and bile. Their ambition, entrepreneurship, and investments have made Miami the gateway to Latin America. Along the way, Cuban-Americans have moved up through the political hierarchy and gained an inordinate amount of political clout. (Cuban-American political leaders have also disdained U.S. law, tainted Miami with unparalleled levels of corruption, and turned Miami into the nation's most repressive city for free expression.)

The majority of Cuban-Americans were forced to flee Cuba shortly after the Revolution, where they formed the wealthy and middle classes. In the immediate years following the Revolution, at least 230,000 *"gusanos"*—worms (as Castro called them)—left Cuba. A similar number left between 1965 and 1971, when the U.S. government chartered airlines for its Freedom Flights Program (including thousands of Cuban children spirited out in the Peter Pan Program). Another 120,000 left in 1980 on the Mariel boatlift, which ended in immigration accords. An additional 20,000 leave Cuba every year in a lottery for U.S. visas, while the most desperate are *balseros* (rafters) who risk their lives crossing the

Straits of Florida by whatever means they can find. . . the Cuban equivalent of jumping the Berlin Wall. . .

Almost every family in Cuba has a relative who has fled Cuba for a better life. Even Fidel has family in exile, and not just his errant daughter Alina, who has called her father a "tyrant" and "mediocrity," and his granddaughter, but also his sister Juana, who fled to Miami in the early 1960s and speaks out against the pain and turmoil her brother has caused.

Most Cuban Americans still dream of a Cuba that no longer exists—and maybe never did exist in the way they recall it. Many have grown militant with distance and time, cultivating delusion "like hothouse orchids," in the words of Cristina García. Nonetheless, fully 70% of Miami Cubans say they will never return to Cuba.

Cuban Americans are torn over the best approach to dealing with Fidel Castro. Moderates, such as Cambio Cubano (Cubans for Change), the Cuban Committee for Democracy, and the Cuban-American Alliance Education Fund, want to see a measured policy, including direct negotiations with Castro to encourage phased-in democracy and avoid a period of anarchy and civil war. These centrist groups have limited influence however; they can't get Washington's ear because the right wing has out-organized and outspent them.

The politically implacable Cuban-American National Foundation (CANF), the largest and by far the richest and most powerful of the exile groups, considers itself the Cuban government in exile and is more or less treated as such by U.S. administrations (it was created by the Reagan administration). Critics portray the CANF as vengeful and greedy extremists intoxicated by a cult of nostalgia and drunk on a dream of "liberating" Cuba. Many of the CANF's well-heeled leaders (who come from the Havana's former elite) have ties to the Batista regime. CANF's powerful founder and former chairman, Jorge Mas Canosa, made no secret of his desire to be president of post-Castro Cuba (he also boasted about having "kicked [the Americans] out of [Miami]"). His death in 1997 left the old anti-Castro faction in disarray, boosting the moderate voice. Nonetheless, the CANF continues to campaign relentlessly for toughening the embargo meant to worsen the havoc wreaked on the Cuban people by Fidel in the vain hope that they will finally rise up and rebel. Nonetheless, the Cuban-American community is also Cuba's second most important source of finance: as much as US$1 billion annually is sent as aid to family members in Cuba.

Hardball Politics

Contemporary U.S. policy toward Cuba is largely shaped by this hard-nosed constituency. The CANF has pumped more than US$4 million into the U.S. political system since 1979. Policymaking in Washington is held hostage to this lobby because of narrow political considerations. Democrats attempt to win their votes by appearing more anti-Castro than the Republicans.

Polls show that more than 40% of Cuban-Americans want open dialogue with Cuba. However, the CANF is dead set against any wide-ranging U.S.-Cuba talks and works hard to keep Washington from cutting a deal with Castro. Its fanaticism is so unyielding that U.S. Congressman Lincoln Diaz-Balart, (R-Florida), a Castro in-law whose father was Batista's attorney and head of security services, and fellow Cuban-American Republican Congresswoman Ileana Ros-Lehtinen even blocked a contribution of food aid to the U.N. World Food Program intended to stem critical food shortages caused by two years of severe drought in Cuba.

Extremist right-wing Cuban-American groups regularly intimidate individuals who favor a softer approach to the Castro government. According to a report in May 1996 by the New York-based Human Rights Watch, the atmosphere for dissenting views "remains marked by fear and danger." Anti-Castro terrorist groups such as Omega 7 and Alpha 66 have been responsible for a spate of bombings and assassinations in the United States since the 1970s. Anyone opposing *la causa* (the cause—i.e., the overthrow of Fidel Castro) is a potential target.

Cuban exiles also continue to launch sporadic raids into Cuban territory: their commandos train in the Everglades. The political power of the Cuban-American lobby is such that prosecutions are rarely made. Charges are routinely dropped, and Human Rights Watch charged Dade County's Cuban-American government officials and police with being "derelict" in prosecuting offenders.

The View from Cuba

Castro has been very successful in convincing Cubans that the extreme Batistiano element in Miami means trouble if they ever return. Cubans are fully versed in the antics of the "Miami Mafia," whom Castro blames for the embargo that worsens their lives.

The Cuba government portrays the exiles as the top rung of a class structure that left a racist society and carried their prejudice with them (CANF's 50 directors are all white). No Cubans see the CANF leadership defending free health or education or the interests of the elderly and poor. They also fear that their homes and land will be sold from under them if the ultra-conservative exiles ever return to power. It's a well-founded fear. Many Cuban-Americans are determined to gain back what they left behind (they maintain a register of properties), while others seem eager to make money from selling off Cuban assets; a favorite T-shirt among Cuban-Americans in Miami shows the Malecón lined with fast-food joints.

Nonetheless, the Cuban government appeared to reach out to exiles in the early 1990s. In 1994, it initiated the first of several conferences on democracy in Havana for exiles to examine measures for normalizing relations. Thus, *gusanos* (worms) became *mariposas* (butterflies), and Cuba's Foreign Ministry even launched a new quarterly magazine, *Correo de Cuba* (Mail from Cuba) for Cubans living abroad. In reality, Castro uses the Cuban-American lobby as a lever to maintain the U.S. embargo and he connives to keep the exile community on the boil: when the waters cool, he finds a rationale to keep them simmering.

Meanwhile, the exodus from Cuba continues. When the last lottery for U.S. visas was held in 1998, more than 500,000 Cubans applied. The 20,000 visas issued annually by Uncle Sam to Cubans is a safety valve for Castro: lottery applicants spend more time dreaming of a better life in the U.S. than plotting resistance at home ("If the wealthy, educated Cubans had remained in place," Cuban historian Guillermo Jiménez told journalist Wendy Gimbel, "if they hadn't put on their jewelry and run to the United States for cover, the country could have gotten rid of Fidel Castro a long time ago"). The agreement also earns millions of dollars a year for Cuba, which charges up to US$1,000 for health certificates and other documents that those granted a U.S. visa must provide to the Interests Section.

The story of the Cuban-Americans is one of anger, frustration, and sadness of two generations divided. As Cuban-American Cristina García wrote: "Cuba is a peculiar exile. We can reach it by a thirty-minute charter flight from Miami, yet never reach it at all."

For an intriguing, satirical look at the "mythomania" of the Miami exile community, read Roberto Fernandez's *Raining Backwards*. I also recommend Cristina García's *Dreaming in Cuban,* a splendid, almost surreal novel on a similar theme.

a loving Cuban couple

orange for sale. Vast acres of state farms and co-operatives go unfarmed, while cultivated land goes virtually untended. What happens to the food produced is a mystery. Hospitals, schools, and works canteens get priority, but almost nothing reaches the state groceries (almost 40% of produce is stolen as it passes through the distribution system known as *acopio*). The *campesinos* do okay. But many urban dwellers go without.

So much is allowed per person from the state grocery store per month—six pounds of rice, eleven pounds of beans, four ounces of coffee, four ounces of lard—but only when available. Candles, kerosene, and matches all appear in the ration books but are hardly ever in stock. Nor are cooking oil, household detergent, or soap—the items most direly felt (in some places, a bar of soap is more valued than a bar of gold). A wait for a new bra can take years! Take just a few steps from your tourist palace and you'll find heart-stopping absences of everything you've taken for granted in life.

Most Cubans rely on the underground economy—*los bisneros*—doing business illegally; on theft or fortuitous employment; or, for the exceedingly fortunate, a wealthy relative or a lover abroad. Cubans are no longer focused on issues of everyday survival as they were just a few years ago. Sure, few Cubans can eat in the dollars-only restaurants where the good food is served, but food is more plentiful in the cities, thanks to Chinese-style markets where farmers are allowed to sell food they produce in excess of government quotas directly to consumers. And daily necessities such as toilet paper and toothpaste and luxury goods such as TVs are available to those with access to U.S. dollars.

The Black Market and *Resolviendo*

The black market, known as the *bolsa* (the exchange), resolves the failings of the state-controlled economy. For four decades it has touched all walks of life. Gas-station attendants sell gasoline "stretched" with kerosene (the good stuff is siphoned off and sold on the black market), while store managers routinely set aside part of the state-supplied stock to sell on the *bolsa*.

Cubans have always survived by *resolviendo*—the Cuban art of barter, the cut corner, the gray market where much of Cuba's economy operates. What the black market can't provide, the Cubans often take for themselves. During the early 1990s, when things were dire, offices were plundered for light bulbs, and restaurants had to chain the tableware to the table to stop it from walking off.

In 1993 the government had no option but to legalize both farmers' markets *(mercados agropecuarios)* and the dollar. As a result, black market prices tumbled in response to the law of supply and demand, but market prices are high, and a typical Cuban salary buys little. The average monthly wage is about 217 pesos (about US$10 at market exchange rates), yet meat in the farmers' market can cost 25 pesos a pound, and black beans nine pesos (fortunately, rent, food, and utilities are so heavily subsidized that they are virtually free), and most household necessities, such as toothpaste, can only be bought with dollars.

A few years ago a peso income had some value. Today it is virtually worthless. Life has become organized around a mad scramble for dollars. The lucky ones have access to family cash, known as *fulla,* sent from Miami. Cuban economists reckon that about 62% of the population now has some form of access to dollars. The rest, including many professionals (doctors, engineers, architects, white-collar workers) have experienced downward mobility. Without access to U.S. dollars, Cubans must rely on their wits and faith (Cubans joke about getting by on *fe,* Spanish for faith, but today an acronym for *familia extranjera*—family abroad). The majority of Cubans have to simply *buscar la forma,* find a way.

Barter is common. So are time payments, verbal contracts for future delivery, and a hundred variations on the theme. Those with a few dollars might buy scarce products and then barter them to other Cubans who have no link to the dollar economy. One neighbor might bring another canned goods in exchange for fish. A third can get his car engine fixed in exchange for peanut butter.

Every morning people prepare to cobble together some kind of normalcy out of whatever the situation allows them. Cubans are masters at making the best of a bad situation. *Resolver*—to resolve, to overcome obstacles with ingenuity, spontaneity, and humor—is one of the most commonly used verbs on the island.

For all the training and education of its population, Cuban technology is virtually nonexistent. Everything is a hand-me-down from the Soviet bloc or North America—mummified American cars, taped-together Russian biplanes, and 45-pound Chinese bicycles that resemble armor-plated tanks. Almost everything is broken, canceled, or closed. The staple of transport in cities is the horse-drawn cart. The staple for inter-city travel is the open-topped truck, often with jerry-rigged seating, but often without seats altogether. Cubans are moved about like cattle. As P.J. O'Rourke once observed, Cuba is so poor and has so few cars, only a paranoid schizophrenic would look both ways before crossing a Havana street.

Having sacrificed for the Revolution for four decades, many Cubans are exhausted. Frustrations have set in. It's a remarkable testament to the spirit of the people that they have been able to withstand the upheavals without grave social and political consequences.

Simple Pleasures
Invited to Moscow in the 1960s, archivist of the Cuban Revolution Carlos Franqui tried gamely to define its essence for jaded Soviet apparatchiks. Finally he exclaimed, "Look, we Cubans try to have fun with everything—cyclones, demonstrations, hunger, even war!" Knitted brows. Fun with war? Well, when they were fighting Batista's men in the Sierra Maestra, he explained, there was a three-hour truce so they could all have a dance.

Cuba has no *fiesta* tradition. The Cubans are too industrious for that—too busy playing volleyball or baseball or practicing martial arts or

playing dominoes in Old Havana

making love while the other half whittles away the long, hot afternoons in the cool shade of arcaded balconies, playing dominoes or eking out a meager living mending cigarette lighters or resoling shoes. At night everyone gathers around the TV to watch *Te Odio, Mi Amor*—an immensely popular Brazilian *telenova* (soap opera) dubbed into Spanish—and life on the dimly lit streets disappears except for the occasional courting couple. In rural areas pleasures are simple: cockfights, rodeos, fiestas, cigars, cheap rum, and sex. Urban life is more urbane, offering movies, art galleries, trovas (traditional music gatherings), discos, cigars, cheap rum, and sex.

Cuban social life revolves around the family and, to a lesser degree, friends and neighbors. Cubans are a gregarious people, and foreigners are often amazed by the degree to which Cubans exist in the public eye, carrying on their everyday lives behind wide-open windows open to the streets as if no one were looking. To Cuban passersby, this is nothing remarkable, but the foreigner cannot resist the same insatiable curiosity that seizes you when your neighbors at home forget to draw their curtains at night.

For all its musical gaiety and pockets of passionate pleasure, life for the average Cuban is dreary, even melancholy. Life for the majority is reduced to making do and making out. Socialist equality can begin to look dismal as you contemplate Cubans rocking on their porches, waiting for something to happen.

Living Conditions

Until the Revolution, government expenditures were concentrated mostly in and around Havana and the provincial cities. The countryside was neglected and had few sewers or plumbing, few paved roads or electricity. Rural housing was basic. According to the 1953 census, only two percent of rural houses had piped water, 54% had no toilet whatsoever (85% of the rural population relied for their water on rivers and streams—many polluted), and 43% had no electricity.

Since the Revolution, the government has concentrated its energies on developing the countryside and replacing urban shantytowns with hideous apartment housing. Today virtually every house on the island has electricity (households are metered separately for use of electricity; payments are made directly to state authorities), although a large percentage do not have hot water. Many urban houses do not have water at all: hidden behind many streetside buildings are pockets of sobering poverty and as depressing in their squalor as the most sordid of Mexican shanties. As many as one million Cubans are "ill housed." By law, no renter can pay more than 10% of his or her salary in rent, and almost 80% of Cubans own their own homes ("Mrs. Thatcher's vision of a homeowners' society come true in communist Cuba," Martha Gellhorn noted, wryly. "Rents pile up like down payments year after year, until the sale price of the flat is reached, whereupon bingo, you become an old-fashioned capitalist owner."). Those who owned houses before the Revolution have been allowed to keep them; those who fled Cuba forfeited their property to the state. Cubans can swap their houses without state approval but cannot buy or sell them.

The typical country house is a low, one-story structure with thick walls to keep out the heat, built of adobe or porous brick covered with stucco painted blue, pink, green, or buff, and roofed with red tiles. It's often whitewashed within and has high ceilings; tall, barred, glassless windows; and cool stone or tile floors. But tens of thousands of rural dwellers still live in slum shacks of scrap tin and wood, woven bamboo, and, if they're lucky, a thick thatched roof to keep out the rains.

Conditions in the cities vary markedly, particularly in Havana, where most prerevolutionary housing is deteriorated to a point of dilapidation, though there *are* many fine, well-kept houses and every city has a section that resembles its middle-class American counterpart. Fifty percent of Havana's housing is rated "poor" to "bad." And everywhere the housing shortage is so critical that many Cubans live in a *barbecue,* a room divided in two. Due to lack of space, the high-ceilinged rooms of many old colonial buildings have been turned into two stories by adding new ceilings and wooden staircases. "A government that is more comfortable with twelve people living in one room than one person living in twelve rooms," thought Paul Goldberg.

Interiors often belie the dour impression received on the street. Rooms everywhere are kept spick-and-span and furnished with typically Cuban decor: family photos, kitschy ceramic animals, plastic flowers, and other effusive knick-knackery—and frequently a photo of Fidel, Che, or Camilo Cienfuegos, though often as a safeguard to keep in good standing. Always there is a large refrigerator (Russian or prerevolutionary Yankee) and at least one TV.

Most housing built since the Revolution (in both town and country) is concrete apartment block units of a standard Bulgarian design—the ugly Bauhaus vision of uniform, starkly functional workers' housing, which had the advantage of being cheap to build and, in theory, easy and cheap to maintain. Most have not been maintained and were jerry-built by unskilled volunteer labor, adding salt to the wound of the aesthetic shortfall.

Virtually every home in Cuba has its original, tattered prerevolutionary furniture. Most houses haven't seen a pot of paint in four decades and feature grimy walls and chipped tiles and often near-derelict bathrooms. Why is there no paint? Because the centralized planning process is intent on meeting production quotas, not on allocating scarce resources for maintenance and repair, which are not foreseen in their plans. Spare parts aren't ordered to maintain sewers or electrical boxes, so over time everything is jerry-rigged. Until 1993 it was illegal for Cubans to freelance as electricians, plumbers, or construction workers, so everyone relied on the state, which gave home and public-utility repair low priority.

Cuba today is littered with half-finished structures like the bones of dinosaurs. Materials are simply no longer available to finish the jobs. Squatting is common, and homelessness has begun to reappear.

CHILDREN AND YOUTH

One of the simplest pleasures for the foreign traveler is to see smiling children (Cuban children are always smiling) in school uniforms so colorful that they reminded novelist James Michener of "a meadow of flowers. Well nourished, well shod and clothed, they were the permanent face of the land." And well behaved, too! About 35% of the population is below 16 years of age.

Children are treated with great indulgence by the state as much as by family members. The government has made magnificent strides to improve the lot of poor children, though, to be

TURNING FIFTEEN

*F*our decades of socialism have killed off many traditional celebrations—but not *las fiestas de quince*—the birthday parties for 15-year-old girls. There is nothing like a *quince* party (a direct legacy of Spanish heritage) for a young *Cubana.*

Parents will save money from the day the girl is born to do her right with a memorable fifteenth—the day on which the *quinceañera* may openly begin her sexual life without family recrimination. A whole arsenal might be involved, from the hairdresser and dressmaker (a special dress resembling a wedding gown or a knock-'em-dead Scarlett O'Hara outfit is *de rigueur*) to the photographer and the classic American car with chauffeur to take the young woman and her friends to the party.

preparations for a quince *celebration*

sure, many are still so poor they go without shoes.

Once, when asked about the sister who turned her back on the Revolution, Fidel told TV interviewer Barbara Walters, "We have the same mother and father, but different ideas. I am a committed socialist. She is an enemy of socialism and that is why she says [bad] things about me. But let me tell you. I have five million brothers and sisters and between us we have millions of children. We love these children." There is no doubt he is sincere.

Children are sworn in at the age of six to become Communist Pioneers.

The *I Generation*

Today's Cuban youth have grown up in a mature Revolution—more than 60% of the Cuban population was born after the Revolution. The older generation had attempted to make the Revolution, had faced down the threat of U.S. invasion, and had witnessed astounding social achievements—all through collective endeavor. Although there is respectful communication between generations, clashes are becoming more common. Where their parents use "we," Cuba's youth use "I"—I want to do so and so. The majority are bored by the constant calls for greater sacrifice and tired of being treated as if they were stupid. They want to enjoy life.

Cuban youth are in a confusing limbo where neither the socialist role model nor its complete rejection is appropriate to the current circumstances. Young people growing up in the current era of hardship and economic opening are not necessarily abandoning revolutionary principles, though many of the young are angry and disaffected. The methods and ideas many are adopting alarm the authorities. As the quest for U.S. dollars tightens its grip, an increasing number of Cuban youth are asking, "What's the point in studying?" They are more concerned with their future than with the party's. Many youths realize they can get further through their own work and savvy and are going into business for themselves as *jiniteros* and *cuenta propistas* (freelancers), making a buck doing anything from driving taxis to repairing tire punctures.

The government worries that the increased association with foreign tourists helps foster nonconformism, such as the growing number of long-haired youths—*roqueros* and *frikis*—who sport ripped jeans and would look at home at a Metallica concert.

Cuban youth are expressing their individuality—they want to be themselves, which today means showing a marked preference for anything North American, especially in clothing. They wouldn't be caught dead in a *guayabera*, the traditional tropical shirt favored by older men. Instead young women dress in the latest fashion—tight jeans, halter tops, mini-skirts, short shorts, and diaphanous blouses, flared pants, and trendy platform shoes. Young men follow suit, though more conservatively, as well as their budgets allow. "Egotism" is flourishing. Consumerism is capturing the imagination of Cuban youth, spawned by the notion that the only way to advance is by making money. Teenagers are becoming sexually promiscuous at an earlier age, and their casual attitude to sex is fueling a rapid rise in prostitution.

More and more, youth feel there is no future in Cuba. "We can't wait forever," they say. They see Fidel Castro as "a benevolent idealist whose program has run out of steam."

Youth are served by their own newspapers, such as *Pioniero* and *Juventud Rebelde (Rebel Youth)*.

Global Exchange (see the chart, Organizations To Know) offers study tours to explore Cuban youth culture. Also look for a copy of *Cuba Va!*, a hour-long documentary in which Cuban youth express their fears and hopes; US$95; Cuba Va Video Project, 12 Liberty St., San Francisco, CA 94110, tel. (415) 282-1812, fax (415) 282-1798.

WOMEN AND MACHISMO IN CUBAN SOCIETY

According to Saul Landau, Cuba is the only "unisex" country in the world. The country has an impressive record in women's rights. A United Nations' survey ranks Cuba among the top 20 nations in which women have the highest participation in politics and business. Women make up 50% of university students and 60% of doctors (a review of the University of Havana yearbooks shows that women were well represented *before* the Revolution also), although they are still poorly represented in the upper echelons of government.

Cuba's solid achievements in the past four decades reflect Castro's own faith in the equal abilities of women and the belief that the Revolution cannot be called complete until women share full opportunities. The Revolution set the ambitious albeit ambiguous goal of "full sexual equality" and set its own path to follow. "Feminism was roundly denounced by the revolution for being a bourgeois indulgence and an imperialist tool to divert women from the more important class struggle by tricking them into rejecting men," note Lois M. Smith and Alfred Padula.

Women workers' rights are protected by Law 1263, passed in 1974, which guarantees women the same salaries as men. Women receive 18 weeks of paid maternity leave—six before the birth and the remainder after. Working mothers have the right to one day off with pay each month, or the option of staying home and receiving 60% of their full salary until the child reaches the age of six months. And every woman and girl can get birth control assistance, regardless of marital status.

The Cuban **Family Code** codifies that the male must share household duties. The Spanish heritage is patriarchal (under the Spanish Civil Code, which was extended into the Cuban Republic, the husband had exclusive rights to property, finances, and, legally, the obedience of his wife and children). The strict Spanish pattern has been broken down by the Revolution, but it still colors family life.

Prejudices and stereotypical behaviors still exist. Male machismo continues, and pretty women walking down the street are often bombarded with comments ranging from *piropos* (witty compliments) to forthright invitations to sex. And though the sexes may have been equalized, the Revolution has not been able to get the Cubanness out of Cuban women who, regardless of age, still adore coquetry.

Few Cuban women simply put on a dress and go out. Instead, they make a great show of expressing their bodily beauty. "Cuban women don't walk, they sway," Naty Revuelta, one of Castro's former mistresses (and the mother of his daughter), has said. "When they walk, everything is in motion, from the ankle to the shoulder.

The soldiers had a terrible time in the beginning, trying to teach them to march in the militia. They just couldn't get the sway out of them." Even the most ardent revolutionaries still paint their faces and attempt a toilette to heighten the femme fatale effect, as in their preference for minimalist and tight-fitting clothing. Women still routinely shorten and take in their uniforms to show their legs, outline their backsides, and be noticed.

Overt appreciation of the female form may seem sexist to "politically correct" North Americans, but in Cuba, rear ends have a value and meaning much more significant than in other cultures. Cuban literature overflows with references to *las nalgas cubanas*—the Cuban ass—usually plump and belonging to a well-rounded mulatta. Tom Miller synthesizes the longstanding fascination with *el culo*—the butt—in his marvelous travelogue, *Trading with the Enemy*. "I found enough material to keep a culophile busy for months."

Of course, these stereotypes belie the ongoing debate within Cuba about the "correct" role of women. A nongovernmental organization called **Association of Women Communicators**, MAGIN, Calle 11 #160 e/ K y L, Vedado, Havana, tel. (7) 32-3322, fax (7) 33-3079, organizes workshops designed to build self-esteem and develop a greater understanding of the concepts of gender and feminism. Likewise, **Casa de las Américas**, Av. 3ra y G, Vedado, Havana, tel. (7) 32-3587, fax (7) 32-7272, e-mail: casa@tinored.cu, works to broaden the area of women's studies in Cuba, and it too sponsors workshops and seminars on the status of women.

Women's interests are also represented by the **Federation of Cuban Women** (Federación de Mujeres Cubanas), Paseo #250, Havana, tel. (7) 30-6043, headed by Vilma Espín, wife of Raúl Castro and known as the First Lady of Cuba. It was founded to rouse women to be good revolutionaries but in recent years has devoted more effort to women's issues and rights, particularly the fight against a rising tide of teenage pregnancy (the *average* Cuban girl begins sexual activity at 13 and has her first baby at 18). Together, Vilma Espín and Fidel choose each year's "Miss Cuba" (Cuba has no such beauty pageant).

RELIGION

Cuba was officially atheist from the early 1960s until 1992, during which time proselytizing was illegal. Nonetheless, a recent government survey found that more than half of all Cubans are *creyentos,* believers of one sort of another. Since the collapse of the Soviet Union, the state has softened its approach to organized religion.

Christianity

Cubans have always been lukewarm about Christianity, and the church has never been strong in Cuba. In colonial times, there were few churches in rural districts, where it was often usual for a traveling priest to call only once a year, usually to perform baptisms and marriages. Even in towns, most Cubans would respond to the bell only on special occasions, usually when it pealed for births, marriages, and maybe Easter morning, when men milled by the door, piously half in and half out. The Catholic Church sided with the Spanish against the patriots during the colonial era. After independence the constitution therefore provided for separation of church and state, depriving the former of its political influence and state support.

Later, the Catholic Church had a quid pro quo with the corrupt Machado, Grau, and Batista regimes—You keep out of our business and we'll keep out of yours." When the Revolution triumphed, many of the clergy left for Miami along with the rich to whom they had ministered.

The Catholic Church grew concerned as the Revolution moved left. When Fidel nationalized the church's lands, it saw red (kind of). The church became a focus of opposition. In August 1960, the Catholic bishops issued a pastoral letter formally denouncing the Castro government; a second pastoral letter later that year urged Fidel to reject Communism. Fidel saw red, too. Many priests were expelled (few Cubans entered the priesthood; the Vatican had to look abroad for three-quarters of its priests in Cuba).

Although the Castro regime has never banned the practice of religion, the church was allowed to engage in only marginal social activities. Church attendance came to be considered antisocial. Religious education was eliminated from the school curriculum. Practicing Catholics were banned from the Communist Party. In 1965 Holy Week was even rechristened "Playa Girón Week." Consequently, religious believers declined from more than 70% of the population to less than 30% and attendance plummeted. Churches had to close down due to disrepair (many priests resorted to holding services in private homes).

In 1986 Fidel Castro performed an about face: religion was no longer the opiate of the masses. In 1990, he admitted that "believers" had been unjustly treated. That year, radio and television stations began transmitting religious music and songs. The following year, the Communist Party opened its doors to believers, and security agents disappeared from churches. It was a timely move, co-opting the shifting mood. The collapse of the Soviet Union proved the adage that "when the earth moves under the people's feet, they naturally look up to the sky." The collapse left a spiritual vacuum that has fed church attendance, while the number of seminarians has also skyrocketed.

Castro recognizes that the accelerating religious revival reflects a massive loss of faith in government. He has attempted to go with the rising tide, while recognizing, too, that the church has a valuable role to play in upholding ethical values in the face of flagging enthusiasm and growing doubt. The Cuban government and Protestant Church initiated a dialogue aimed at finding a strategy to unite atheists and believers (though Protestantism was only introduced at the turn of the century, prerevolutionary Cuba evolved the highest percentage—almost 15%— of Protestants of any Latin American nation; as of 1999 there were 49 Protestant churches with a membership of around 250,000).

Skirmishes continue, however. In spite of warming relations with the Protestant Church, the Catholic Church hierarchy has continued to be highly critical of the Castro government. In summer 1994, Cuba's 11 Catholic bishops issued a pastoral letter criticizing the government's monopoly on power and calling for reforms. It was the strongest criticism of Castro to date (Castro called it a "stab in the back"). The bishops have also condemned right-wing Cuban émigrés, the U.S. embargo, and U.S. interference in Cuban affairs, even though the embargo specifically exempts relief shipments to "nongovernmental organizations"—in effect, the church (such support permits the church to usurp the state's role as provider).

Papal emissaries began visiting Cuba in 1990—part of the Pope's agenda to help save Cuba from the dangers of a violent and bloody power transition. In November 1996, Castro met with Pope John Paul II in Rome. The pontiff's emotionally charged visit to Cuba in January 1998 was an extraordinary event that boosted the influence of the Catholic Church in Cuba and reignited an expression of faith among the Cuban people. An ensuing display of goodwill towards the church was reflected in an open-air celebration involving tens of thousands of Cuban Protestants in Plaza de la Revolución in June 1999, with Fidel Castro in attendance. (In December 1997 Castro declared Christmas a holiday as a goodwill gesture to the Pope, three decades after it was canceled; Xmas trees appeared in the stores for the first time in many years, and in 1999 even Santa Claus was to be seen acting as doorman outside Havana's Hotel Meliá Cohiba.)

Despite increased tolerance of the church, harassment continues. In April 1999, for example, the Communist Party arranged noisy street demonstrations to march outside cathedrals while Mass was being held over Easter Week and even ordered crucifixes removed from funeral cars donated by Italy. In December 1999 the Pope, disappointed with the meager progress since his visit, urged Castro to respect human rights and display "a more generous opening."

Santería

Santería, or saint worship, has been deeply entrenched in Cuban culture for 300 years. The cult is a fusion of Catholicism with the Lucumí religion of the African Yoruba tribes (several other Afro-Cuban cults emerged during the slave era, most notably the Bantu tribe's Palo Monte and the Abakuá secret societies). Since slave masters had banned African religious practice, the slaves cloaked their gods in Catholic garb and continued to pray to them to preserve a shred of their souls and strengthen them against the indignities of their bondage.

Thus, in santería, Catholic figures are avatars of the Yoruban orishas (divine beings of African animism worshiped in secretive and complex

---

SANTERÍA TERMS

Abakua – Secret all-male society in Cuba

Babalawo – High priest of Lucumi

Batá – Set of three drums of Yoruba origin—iya, itotele, and okonkolo—used in santería

Cajón – Crate or box having a predominantly bass tone, which is sat on and played during a rumba

Chango – The mighty orisha of fire, thunder, and lightning

Eleggua – Messenger of all orishas

Fundamento – A strict set repertoire of rhythms for each orisha and/or the essence of playing traditional *batá*

Obatala – Orisha king of the white cloth; symbol of peace and purity

Ogun – Orisha represented as an iron worker or warrior

Orishas – Deities of the Lucumi religion; most are symbolic of human qualities and aspects of nature

Palo – monte Syncretic religion based on the beliefs of the Bantu-speaking peoples brought to Cuba

Toque – Specific rhythm attributed to an orisha

---

rituals that may feature animal sacrifices along with chanting, dancing, and music). Gods change their sex at midnight: by day, adherents may pray in front of a figure of Santa Barbara and at night worship the same figure as Changó. There are several hundred gods in the pantheon, but only about 20 are honored in daily life.

It is thought that the *orishas* control an individual's life (a string of bad luck will be blamed on an *orisha*) and must therefore be placated. The gods are believed to perform all kinds of miracles on a person's behalf and are thus consulted and besought. They're too supreme for mere mortals to communicate with directly. Hence, *santeros* or *babalaos* (priests) act as go-betweens to honor the saints and interpret their commands.

Cubans are superstitious people. It's said that if you scratch a Cuban, Catholic or non-, you find a *santería* believer underneath. Almost every home has a statue of a santería god and a glass of water to appease the spirits of the dead. Even Fidel Castro, a highly superstitious person, is said to be a believer. He had triumphed on 1 January, a holy day for the *orishas*. The red and black flag of the revolutionaries was that of El-leguá, god of destiny. Then, on 8 January 1959, as Fidel addressed the nation from Camp Columbia, suddenly two doves flew over the audience and circled the brightly lit podium; miraculously, one of the doves alighted on Fidel's shoulder, touching off an explosion from the ecstatic onlookers: *"Fee-del! Fee-del! Fee-del!"* In *santería,* doves are symbols of Obatalá, the Son of God. To Cubans—and perhaps Fidel himself—the event was a supreme symbol that the gods had chosen Fidel to guide Cuba.

Over ensuing years, Castro's dogma of scientific communism attempted to convert *santería* into a folkloric movement. Religious rites were restricted. As Marxism lost its appeal in the late 1980s, *santería* bounced back, offering relief from the "propogandistic realism" of the socialist world. The desperate conditions of the Special Period have caused millions to visit their *babalaos*. In 1990 the Castro government began to co-opt support for the faith—it is said that Castro also encourages *santería* as a counterpoint to the rising power of the Catholic Church—by economically and politically supporting the *babalaos* (reportedly, many *babalaos* have been recruited by MININT, for they above all know people's secrets).

Santería is a sensuous religion. It lacks the arbitrary moral prescriptions of Catholicism—the *orishas* let adherents have a good time. The gods themselves are fallible and hedonistic philanderers, such as the much feared and respected Changó, god of war, fire, thunder, and lightning, whose many mistresses include Oyá (patroness of justice) and Ochún, the sensuous black goddess that many Cuban women identify as the *orisha* of love.

Throughout Cuba, you'll see believers clad all in white, having just gone through their initiation rites. Each person is "guarded" by a particular god. Followers of Changó wear collars decorated with red and white plastic beads; followers of Ochún wear yellow and white beads. Each saint also has his or her own dance. Each, too, has his or her "altar," such as the ceiba tree in the corner of Havana's Plaza de Armas, where good

charms and bad (fruits, rum-soaked cakes, pastries, and coins) are strewn near its trunk and the stirred earth near its sacred roots bulges with buried offerings. At other altars, caged pigeons await their fate at the end of a knife.

The government has set up *diplosanterías* where foreign visitors can consult with santería priests for dollars. Reservations can be made through any Infotur office (see Tourist Information, in the On The Road chapter). Or check with state tour agencies, such as Rumbos and Havanatur, which offer excursions to witness santería in Regla and Guanabacoa (see Organized Excursions, in the Getting Away section in the Havana chapter). Also contact the **Orisha Study Program,** P.O. Box 17323, Burlingame, CA 94011, tel. (510) 845-5843; and **La Peña Cultural Center,** 3105 Shattuck Ave., Berkeley, CA 94705, tel. (510) 849-2568, which has an Orisha Culture Series.

Judaism

Cuba's Jewish community once thrived. Today it is thought to number only about 1,300, about five percent of its prerevolutionary size, when Havana's Jewish community supported five synagogues, several schools, and a college.

The first Jews are thought to have traveled to Cuba with Columbus and were followed in the 16th century by Sephardic Jews escaping persecution at the hands of the Spanish Inquisition (many Jews fled to the Caribbean under assumed Christian identities). Later, Jews coming from Mediterranean countries felt at home in Cuba. They concentrated in southern Habana Vieja (Old Havana), many starting out in Cuba selling ties and cloth and gaining a monopoly based around Bernaza and Muralla Streets and across the bay in Guanabacoa. They were joined at the turn of this century by Jews from Florida, who founded the United Hebrew Congregation. Other Ashkenazic Jews emigrating from Eastern Europe passed through Cuba en route to the United States in significant numbers until the U.S. slammed its doors in 1924, after which they settled in Cuba. Arriving during a time of destitution, they were relatively poor compared to the earlier Jewish immigrants and were disparagingly called *polacos*. Many were sustained by the largesse of the United Hebrew Congregation.

Sephardic Jews came as families and were profoundly religious. They formed social clubs, opened their own schools, and married their own. By contrast, Ashkenazim most often were single men who went on to marry Cuban (Catholic) women and eventually were assimilated into Cuban society, says Robert M. Levine in his book *Tropical Diaspora: the Jewish Experience in Cuba* (University Press of Florida, 1993). The Ashkenazim were fired with socialist ideals and were prominent in the founding of both the labor and Cuban communist movements.

Cuba seems to have been relatively free of anti-Semitism (Batista was a friend to Jews fleeing Nazi Europe). Levine, however, records how during the late 1930s, the U.S. government bowed to isolationist, labor, and anti-Semitic pressures at home and convinced the Cuban government to turn back European Jews. It is a sordid chapter in U.S. history, best told through the tragic story of the SS *St. Louis* and its 937 passengers trying to escape Nazi Germany in 1939. The ship languished in Havana harbor for a week while U.S. and Cuban officials deliberated on letting passengers disembark; tragically, entry was refused, and the ship and passengers were sent back to Europe and their fate.

By the 1950s, Cuban Jews had prospered in the clothing trade and enjoyed a cosmopolitan life. The Revolution "had elements of tragedy for the Jewish community," writes Rosshandler, author of the autobiographical novel *Passing Through Havana* (St. Martin's Press, 1984). Castro gave them "the option of staying and keeping their homes. But they had devoted their energy to business and they could not bear to live in a society that looked down on what they prized." Jews became part of the Cuban diaspora, and only perhaps as many as 2,000 remained (a few joined the Castro government; two became early cabinet members). Some 500 Cuban Jews were secretly allowed to emigrate to Israel beginning in 1994.

"Castro's Jews" say that Jews have been better treated in Cuba than anywhere else in the world. Jewish religious schools were the only parochial schools allowed to remain open after the Revolution (the government provided school buses). The Cuban government has always made matzoh available and even authorized a kosher butcher shop in Habana Vieja to supply meat for observant Jews. The Jewish community also has its own cemetery, atop a hill in Guanabacoa, east of Havana, dating from 1910.

A renaissance in the Jewish faith is occurring. Synagogues are being refurbished and new ones opened. In 1994 the first bar mitzvah took place in over 12 years and the first formal bris in over five years. And the Hebrew Sunday School (for children and adults) in the Patronato (the Jewish community center on the ground floor of the synagogue in Vedado; see the Havana chapter) teaches Hebrew and Yiddish. Adela Dworin, the doyenne of the Patronato, is a font of knowledge.

To learn more, look for screenings of the documentary film *Havana Nagila: the Jews of Cuba* (57 minutes, 1995), directed by Laura Paull, which traces the history of Jews in Cuba. Also look for screenings of *Next Year in Havana,* a documentary by Lori Beraha about Havana's Jewish community; you can order copies from Lori, tel. (510) 527-3349, e-mail: loria@uclink4 .berkeley.edu.

The **Cuban-Jewish Aid Society,** P.O. Box 2101, Mill Valley, CA 94942, tel. (415) 388-2418, fax (415) 550-8009; and 44 Mercury Ave., Colonia, NJ 07607, tel. (908) 499-9132, sends medicines, humanitarian aid, and religious articles to Cuba. Donations should be sent to the New Jersey address. The society is licensed to take U.S. citizens on its annual tours of Cuba.

An organization called **Jewish Solidarity,** 2337 Coral Way, Miami, FL 33145, tel. (305) 856-0177, fax (305) 856-1210, website: www. jewishcuba.org/solidarity.html, delivers humanitarian aid to Cuba. (Also see www.jewishcuba .org, and the Getting There section of the On The Road chapter.)

EDUCATION

Despite its restrictions on individual liberty, Cuba has attempted to maximize its human potential, and its education system is justifiably a source of national pride. The country enjoys one of the greatest proportions of university graduates in the world, and it is a joy to hear everywhere the intelligent voices of an educated and evocatively philosophical people. In general, Cubans are highly knowledgeable, often displaying an astonishing level of intellectual development and

HOW CUBANS FEEL ABOUT THE REVOLUTION

The fall of the Berlin Wall and the disintegration of the Soviet Bloc brought expectations of a Ceausescu-like ending for Castro. Why, then, have Cuba's internal and external crises not produced Castro's downfall? The U.S. State Department sows the field with stories of a "one-party monopoly," "40 years of brainwashing," and the "grip of fear" imposed on Cubans by "the police state." All true. But what they do not take into account are the unifying power of national pride, the very real achievements of the Revolution, and, yes, Fidel's unique charisma.

National pride is alive and well, but Cubans are acutely aware of their struggles.

¡Viva Fidel!

For loyalists, Castro is a symbol of national dignity. After five centuries of humiliation, he gave Cuba pride in independence. Unlike Eastern Europe, Cuba's revolution was home-grown, not imposed by Soviet troops. It came from the Cubans themselves. Just as Yankees take pride in the men of 1776, Cubans take pride in *their* revolutionary heroes: they are the nation's embodiment of independence from Spain and the United States. For loyalists, Fidel is Cuba's George Washington.

Most Cubans who support the Revolution do so not from reading Karl Marx but because they believe they are infinitely better off than residents of neighboring countries. While the disaffected compare themselves to North America, loyalists prefer to compare Cuba to Mexico, Jamaica, Haiti, and the Dominican Republic—countries beset by true poverty. Countries where hordes of child beggars live in squalid slums. Instead, uniformed schoolchildren attend daycare centers and schools. Cuba has invested 40 years of resources to become one of the few underdeveloped nations with a system that protects all members of society from illiteracy and ill health. Everyone still eats—even if not well—and medical care, albeit stretched to the limit, is free and available to all. Loyal Cubans are acutely aware of all this.

"Our real problem," says Ricardo Alarcón, head of the National Assembly, "is comparing ourselves with the past," referring to the "golden years" of the 1980s. The social gains of the Revolution were achieved two decades ago and were taken for granted. Since the onset of the Special Period, Cuba has found it impossible to sustain its cradle-to-grave benefits. Nonetheless, in an independent Gallup poll (the only independent poll held in post-revolutionary Cuba) in November 1994, 58% of Cubans said the nation's successes in education and health care outweigh its failures. Eighty percent felt their food needs had been met, 90% felt the same about health, and 96% regarding education. When asked about "the principal failure of the Cuban Revolution," only three percent answered "no liberty" and a similar percentage

erudition. Their conversations are spiced with literary allusions and historical references. Even in the most remote Cuban backwater, you'll come across bright-eyed children laden with satchels, making their way to and from school in pin-neat uniforms colored according to their grades (younger ones wear short-sleeved white shirts, light-blue neckerchiefs, and maroon shorts or mini-skirts; secondary school children wear white shirts, red neckerchiefs, and ocher-yellow

answered "no rights." In response to the Gallup poll's question "In your opinion, what is the most serious problem facing Cuba?," the largest group, 31%, answered that it was the U.S. embargo. It is difficult to know how many answered honestly among a population where fear of criticizing the government is ingrained.

Living the Lie

The precise numbers are unclear. The Revolution has ruined as many lives as it has raised, and Cuba is a divided and schizophrenic society. "Whatever sense of shared cause once united Cubans has been eroded by a state that piles absurdities onto privations in the name of a generation-old revolution. An entire generation is learning to abandon hope," wrote Taras Grescoe. For the schoolboys in red bandanas who ask you for *un dollar* to buy candy, *socialismo o muerte* is already an empty formula.

Loyal *fidelistas* are today a minority. For the overwhelming majority of Cubans, Fidel Castro has outlasted his time (though no Cuban in his right mind would express such negative feelings openly). Those with a hate-hate relation are resigned to sullen silence, prison, or exile while the rest live the lie. Fatalists, they go along with the rote civic boosterism, pretending to support Fidel's socialist Revolution while harboring secret wishes for a radical change.

A majority of Cubans are anxious for a return to the market economy, even at the cost of privilege and inequity and risk—though not at the cost of the benefits of the Revolution. But they are confused by their perplexing dilemma. Despite the palpable discontent, many of those who do not actively support Castro are unsure of a viable alternative: they understand that their economy is in ruins, but they see no one who can lead them out of their present misery. It is as if they feel they are at least on familiar ground with Fidel. Hence, Cubans have a love-hate relationship with El Máximo. They speak of Castro with a combination of the respect and anger a son feels for an overbearing father who can't get with the times.

more on its army (it is claimed that not a single state-supported library existed on the eve of independence). Better education was one of the prime motivations for the Revolution that overthrew General Machado in 1933, but education made little progress in the post-war decades. And though the constitution of 1940 expressed lofty ideals—the budget of the Ministry of Education should not be smaller than that of any other ministry—educational funds became a huge source of graft (Aureliano Sánchez Arango, who took office in 1948 as a rare honest Minister of Education, described his ministry as a cave of entrenched bandits). The Castro government claims that those who could afford to sent their children to private schools while the majority went unversed. Official statistics are contradictory. On the eve of the Revolution, 43% of the population was illiterate according to government statistics and half a million Cuban children went without school, while the U.N. Statistical Yearbook suggests that as much as 80% of the population was literate.

Children are the Hope of the World is a 1998 video that takes a look at the Cuban educational system. It costs US$39.95 with shipping. Contact fax (305) 551-1202 or e-mail: farogroup@aol.com.

The Great Literacy Campaign

In December 1960 the government announced a war on illiteracy. On 10 April 1961, 120,000 literacy workers—*brigadistas*—spread throughout the island to teach reading and writing to one million illiterates. (To learn more about the campaign, check out the **Museum of Education** in Havana.) The government followed up by establishing about 10,000 new classrooms in rural areas and introducing traveling libraries. Today literacy is about 95.7%, according to UNESCO statistics, compared to 94.8% for Costa Rica, 85% for Jamaica, and 45% for Haiti. School is compulsory to age 15 (ninth grade). Children may then continue three years pre-university study or at technical schools. Anyone who has ever visited a Cuban classroom must remark on the enthusiasm displayed by willing, lively pupils. In rural areas, few schools have a library or gym or laboratory, yet teachers get on with the job. All education is free.

long pants or mini-skirts all the way up to the. . . twelfth grade. The neckerchiefs show that they are Pioneers, similar to Cub and Boy Scouts).

During Spanish colonial times, no country in Latin America spent less on education and

The University of Havana was founded in 1728.

The *average* Cuban has received nine years of schooling (94% of Cuban children complete five years of primary schooling, the minimum required for a child to have a chance of being literate and numerate). One in every 15 people is a college graduate. And about four percent—more than 400,000 people—hold university degrees, while another 1.3 million have graduated from technical schools. Cuba has four universities, plus 85 research centers. Opportunity is there for all children, but even Cuba's educational system is competitive. Children with special talents may opt to attend specialist schools that foster particular skills in art, music, or sports. The best pupils go to highly prized vocational schools—assuming, of course, that they display the correct behavioral attitudes. As a result, a UNESCO study of language and mathematics skills throughout Latin America found that Cuba was way ahead of all other nations (Cuban students scored an average 350 points out of a possible 500; other nations ranged from 80 to 280).

Before the Special Period, all schoolchildren went on two camping trips every year. They also spent a week at Varadero or a similar beach resort (top students from every school also spent a month together at Varadero as a reward for their efforts). Sadly, those days have ended. And truancy and illiteracy are rising.

The Downside

As the Brazilian economist Roberto Campos said, statistics are like bikinis: they show what's important but hide what's essential. For one, the hyper-educated population is hard pressed to find books, and not simply because of a shortage of paper, which has meant a dearth of children's textbooks. In schools nationwide, books and pencils are as rare as silk pajamas.

Schooling stresses linguistic and arithmetic skills at primary level and vocational and technical abilities at secondary level. (There is no doubt that Cuba's schools produce a people with inordinate literary abilities; gain a Cuban pen pal and you'll understand what I mean.) Many senior students, however, have little choice of professional study. A close friend, given no choice but to study civil construction, told me how she and her classmates hated the subject. Those who didn't want to study or wanted to flunk were allowed to volunteer to work on construction projects. No wonder Cuban construction is so bad!

And the literary panorama is severely circumscribed: only politically acceptable works are allowed. Cubans' understanding of world affairs is shaped by a system evolved following the Revolution to foster socialist thinking. In the hands of the state, schooling has been a key tool in promoting the "communist formation" of the next generation and the creation of the "New Man." The Marxist-Leninist conception of things has been embodied in education through Article 38 of the Constitution. The school syllabus is heavily doctrinaire: the U.S. is presented as an evil oppressor, and Fidel and Che are revered.

Work-Study

What is unique about the Cuban education system is its emphasis on combining learning with work. Cuban children are expected to be *estudiantes hoy, trabajadores mañana, soldados de la patria siempre*—students today, workers tomorrow, soldiers always—fulfilling José Martí's dictum: "In the morning, the pen—but in the afternoon, the plow."

The "Schools in the Countryside" program began in 1971. Secondary schoolchildren spend time each summer working in the countryside, where they live in boarding schools attached to 500-hectare plots of arable land and boasting names such as "the Juvenile Column of the Centenary." Half of all intermediate-level children also attend a rural boarding school for at least some of their education. Here, time is equally divided between study and labor, the latter most often in citrus plantations, where the kids bring in the harvest. Here, too, unintended by the state, children learn to be lovers. Promiscuity is a staple in the fields.

HEALTH

In prerevolutionary Havana, only the monied class could afford good medical care according to the Castro government, which has claimed that there were only 6,250 physicians in all of Cuba on the eve of the Revolution. Of these, 70% were in Havana (as were 60% of all hospital beds). Many people in rural areas went without medical services of any kind. However, according to the United Nations Statistical Yearbook, in 1957 Cuba ranked third in Latin America, behind only Uruguay and Argentina, in numbers of physicians and dentists per capita, with 128 physicians and dentists per 100,000 people (the same as the Netherlands, and ahead of the United Kingdom, with 122 per 100,000 people). And Cuba's infant mortality rate of 32 per 1,000 live births in 1957 was the lowest in Latin America and the 13th lowest in the world.

Whatever the truth, the Cuban Revolution forced half of Cuba's entire medical staff to flee the island by 1961, leaving Cuba critically short of doctors.

From the beginning, health care has assumed an inordinately prominent place in revolutionary government policies (in 1989, the government spent 12% of its budget on health care). Today some 21 medical schools churn out 4,000 doctors each year. In 1978, Fidel Castro predicted that Cuba would become the bulwark of Third World medicine, put a doctor on every block,

become a world medical power, and surpass the U.S. in certain health indices. In all four, he has been vindicated.

As a result, UNICEF puts Cuba four notches behind the United States in health indices and ahead of all other developing nations. Cuba's life expectancy of 74 years is on a par with Argentina and Chile, the two countries considered the most developed in Latin America (by comparison, Mexico has 73, Guatemala has 67, Haiti has 53), and its infant mortality rate the lowest. In mid-1996 Cuban authorities reported an infant mortality rate of eight per 1,000 births (compared to seven for Great Britain, Canada, and the United States). In January 2000 it reported that the rate had dropped to 6.5 per 1,000.

The Revolution's impressive accomplishment is due to its emphasis on preventive medicine and community-based doctors. The immediate need in 1959 was to stem the epidemics, infections, and parasitic diseases then plaguing Cuba. The first effort was to provide health services to poor rural areas that were without them. It has been notably successful. A near 100% immunization rate has ensured the total eradication of several preventable contagious diseases. The Pan American Health Organization declared Cuba the first polio-free country in the Americas. Cuba has the highest rate of immunization against measles in the world—better than the U.S.—says UNICEF, which uses the measles immunization rate as the most reliable barometer of a country's commitment to bringing basic medical advances to its people. Cuba has also eradicated malaria and diphtheria. And reportedly no one has died from tuberculosis since 1979.

Family Doctor Program

Castro also set out to train doctors en masse. By 1984, Cuba's ratio of doctors per 10,000 inhabitants was double the Latin American ratio, and its ratio of nurses was seven times higher than the norm. That year, the government established the family doctor program, calling for 75,000 doctors and 20,000 nurses to provide primary care—on every city block and in every hamlet—by the year 2000. In 1999 Cuban Health Minister, Carlos Dotres, claimed that Cuba had 65,800 doctors, 30,000 community doctors, and 84,000 nurses, with a total of 115,000 health care personnel: one doctor for every 170 inhabitants,

CUBA'S FLYING DOCTORS

Since 1963 when Cuba sent 56 doctors to newly independent Algeria, the country has provided medical assistance to third world countries regardless of its own economic straits. In 1985 the *New York Times* dubbed Cuba's international medical aid program "the largest Peace Corps-style program of civilian aid in the world." That year Cuba had 16,000 doctors, teachers, agronomists, and other technical specialists serving in 22 third world countries, including more doctors than the World Health Organization. After Hurricane Mitch in 1998 wiped out entire towns in Central America, Cuba deployed medical brigades across the region. Cuban doctors stayed on, working for free in remote hamlets that have never had regular medical care. In December 1999 it had 3,140 medical personnel serving in 58 countries, including more than 1,000 in Guatemala, Nicaragua, Belize, Honduras, and Haiti.

Cuba has also offered free medical care in Cuba for third world patients, most famously for child victims of the Chernobyl nuclear disaster in the Soviet Union. In addition, prior to the Special Period, Cuba offered more than 20,000 international scholarships a year to third world medical students (many times the number offered by the U.S.), all of whom were required to return to their home countries upon completion of their training. Cuba has even donated entire hospitals to third world countries. In November 1999 it opened a new Latin American School for Medical Sciences, offering free medical education to students from 18 countries in the region. At the Ibero-American summit in Havana in November, Latin leaders who strongly criticized Castro's human-rights record clamored for more spaces in the school for their students. Castro obliged, expanding plans to teach as many as 7,500 Latin American medical students over five years, 10 times the original number. In so doing, the Cuban leader is playing the humanitarian in a part of the world where Washington slashed economic aid by 83%, 1990-96.

---

twice as many per capita as the United States, which has one for every 352 inhabitants. The vast majority of people from Mexico south to Tierra del Fuego would weep with joy to have such medical care. (Dental care lags behind, with one dentist for about every 1,280 inhabitants; most Cubans have very bad teeth.)

The idea is for every Cuban to have his or her own doctor trained in comprehensive general medicine close by, living and working in the neighborhood, combining the duties of a family doctor and public health advocate (the doctor maintains the medical history of every community member and prepares a preventive medicine schedule for each patient). Foreign visitors are welcome to peek inside the three-story *casa del médico* (the family doctor's home), with a clinic on the ground floor, living quarters for the doctor's family on the second floor, and quarters for the nurse's family above.

Medical services are free to all citizens, regardless of medical attention and care required. Cubans have no fear of being turned away because they cannot pay (they also receive care from medical staff dedicated to their vocation). "We do not want to have private medicine because we have created a healthy system which

has rendered extraordinary results," Castro has said. "And we do not want to destroy it. It would be a historic crime to do so."

Every town and village also has a hospital, plus a maternity home and a home where the elderly can spend their days being cared for while sons and daughters work (the government also runs day-care centers for children 45 days to six years old throughout the island). Fifteen mobile laboratories travel the country performing pre-clinical diagnostics for breast cancer. All women get pap smears and, if pregnant, extensive prenatal care. Virtually the entire population has been screened for AIDS. And local clinics even provide sex education for youngsters and exercise classes for elderly persons.

Beyond Primary Care

Cuba also commands the kind of technology that most poor countries can only dream about: ultrasound for obstetricians, CAT scans for radiologists, stacks of high-tech monitors in the suites for intensive care. Cuba has performed heart transplants (since 1985), heart-lung transplants (since 1987), coronary bypasses, pacemaker implantations, microsurgery, and a host of other advanced surgical procedures. A 1988

Pan-American Health Organization assessment of Cuba's foremost hospital, the Hospital Hermanos Ameijeiras, concluded that it "conducts research and uses technology at the international cutting edge in the 38 specialties in which services are rendered." In 1992 *Science* magazine rated the Ibero-Latin American Center for Nervous System Transplants and Regeneration as the world's best for the treatment of parkinsonism through transplanting fetal brain tissue.

In addition, prior to the Special Period, the homegrown pharmaceutical industry supplied 80% of Cuba's needs. Cuba has made notable leaps in advancing the field of molecular immunology. It even manufactures interferons for AIDS treatment; a meningitis vaccine first "discovered" at the Finlay Institute; even a cure for the skin disease vitiligo, discovered by Cuban doctor Carlos Miyares Cao. Alas, the collapse of the Soviet Union and the U.S. embargo have prevented Cuba from being able to obtain the raw materials, equipment, or spare parts for their high-tech industry. The entire world is poorer for it. Nonetheless, Cuba continues to share its stupendous commitment with the rest of the world. In mid-1999 it opened a former naval academy as the Latin American Medical School to train doctors from throughout the continent.

MEDICAL AID FOR CUBA

You can make tax-deductible donations to the following relief organizations:

Cuba AIDS Project, 635 12th St., #12, Miami Beach, FL 33139, tel. (305) 531-3973, e-mail: cubaaidspr@aol.com, website: www.cubaonline.org, works to support the fight against AIDS in Cuba.

Cuba Medical Project, 36 E. 12th St., New York, NY 10003, tel. (212) 475-3232, fax (212) 979-1583, e-mail: disarm@igc.apc.org, has delivered more than $17 million in medicines and medical supplies to Cuba.

Medical Journals for Cuba is a project of the International Action Center (IAC), c/o Gloria La Riva, 2489 Mission St., #24, San Francisco, CA 94110, tel. (415) 476-3799, www.actionsf.org. The center accepts contributions of medical journals.

Operation USA: Cuba Medical Relief Project, 8320 Melrose Ave., Suite 200, Los Angeles, CA 90069, tel. (323) 658-8876, fax (323) 653-7846, e-mail: opusa@opusa.org, www.opusa.org, seeks donations plus volunteers (tel. 800-678-7255) to deliver them to Cuba.

The **U.S.+Cuba Medical Project,** One Union Square W #211, New York, NY 10003, tel. (212) 227-5270, fax (212) 227-4859, e-mail: uscubamed @igc.apc.org, www.igc.org/cubasoli/infomed.html, works through the Cuban Red Cross to deliver medical supplies to Cuba.

The **U.S.-Latin American Medical Aid Foundation,** P.O. Box 552, New York, NY 10025, tel. (888) 669-1400, fax (212) 749-7596, e-mail: hornung @medaid.org, www.medaid.org, delivers medical supplies to Cuba.

MADRE, 121 West 27th St., Room 301, New York, NY 10001, tel. (212) 627-0444; fax (212) 675-3704; e-mail: madre@igc.org, www.madre.org, delivers critical breast cancer screening equipment, preventive medicines, and treatment to the women of Cuba through its Share Hope Campaign.

Computers for Cuban Health

In 1994 Cuba's Ministry of Public Health lost its US$1 million budget for purchasing medical journals and books. It turned to computer communication with the help of the United Nations. Havana's Center for Medical Sciences Information (CNICM) initiated INFOMED, website: www.infomed.sld.cu, to link outlying doctors and rural clinics with regional and provincial hospitals, research centers, and medical schools, which, in turn, are connected to a central database in Havana. The U.N. provided Type 4986 servers. But Cuba is desperately short of end-user terminals at its key medical centers.

Project INFOMED collects old PC-XT or PC-AT computers for shipment to Cuba. If you have an old IBM-compatible machine collecting dust in your attic, why not donate it to INFOMED and allow it to be reincarnated as a life-saving instrument? Financial contributions are also needed to cover shipping costs. And medical supplies are welcome.

Contact INFOMED-USA, Peace for Cuba Task Force, P.O. Box 450, Santa Clara, CA 95052, tel. (408) 243-4359, fax (408) 243-1229; e-mail: jreardon@igc.apc.org; or via the caravan's website at www.igc.org/cubasoli. On the East Coast, contact Infomed-USA, 1870 Wyoming Ave. NW, Washington, DC, 20009, tel. (202) 667-3730, e-mail: bstiller@capaccess.org.

Many observers note that quality of service has been sacrificed to quantity, that the quality of medical services before the Revolution was far superior to that of most other Latin American nations, and that the improvements since 1959 have been built on accelerating gains made in the 1940s and '50s. True, most hospitals and clinics are basic by Western standards. But they are there, and fully staffed.

Cuba's Medical Crisis

Cuba's admirable health system has suffered a catastrophic setback since the collapse of the Soviet bloc. Even before the Special Period, Cuba's health system faced severe shortages and long waiting lists for operations. Since 1991 services have been vastly curtailed. Dissemination of medicines has plummeted. Nonessential operations have been postponed, and priority is given to those in most urgent need.

Doctors are writing prescriptions that the local pharmacy can no longer fill (the Cuban pharmaceutical industry has had to export many of its more sophisticated products to obtain foreign funds). Critical medicines are in such short supply that doctors have turned to herbal remedies. Herbal teas substitute for sedatives. Aloe is given as an anti-inflammatory. Doctors use acupuncture to anesthetize patients. Lacking sutures, many surgeons learned to sew using hemp. Materials for diagnostic tests have virtually disappeared. Faced with a severe shortage of X-ray film, radiologists have turned to more dangerous fluoroscopy. The absence of sulfa drugs, antibiotics, antibacterial medicines, and disinfectants has turned routine health problems into serious illnesses. Shortages of soap, toilet paper, chlorine, and other water treatment chemicals have made many drinking water supplies unsafe and brought a rise in diarrhea and hepatitis in health facilities and countrywide. And many hospitals even tell their patients to bring their own towels and bed sheets.

In addition, in the early 1990s Cubans' average caloric intake fell dramatically, leaving the population more susceptible to disease. Cuba ranked last in Latin America in per capita daily caloric consumption, according to U.N. Food and Agriculture Organization data (by comparison, the 1960 U.N. Statistical yearbook ranked pre-Revolutionary Cuba third out of 11 Latin

American countries in per capita daily caloric consumption). Cuba's per capita supply of cereals fell from 106 kg per year in the late 1940's to 100 kg in 1995. Per capita supply of tubers and roots fell from 91 kg per year to 56 kg; meat supplies have fallen from 33 kg per year to 23 kg per year. Thus the incidence of babies born with low birth weights and of anemia among expectant mothers rose. Beriberi (caused by Vitamin B deficiency), scurvy, typhoid, and tuberculosis—all eradicated since the Revolution—reappeared. And in 1993 about 50,000 Cubans were diagnosed with optic neuritis, a mysterious eye and nerve disorder leading to gradual blindness attributable to malnutrition and vitamin deficiency. (*Granma* even featured a story recommending that Cubans eat flowers, leaves, and seeds from pumpkins, sweet potatoes, beets, and manioc to supplement their vitamin intake).

Foreign public health experts say that the impact of the Special Period could have been catastrophic had Cuba not had such a superb health system nationwide.

Fortunately the situation has improved markedly, though the average calorific intake of tens of thousands of Cubans is still below the World Health Organization recommended minimum.

Uncle Sam's Shame

The situation was worsened in 1992, when the U.S. Congress passed the Torricelli Act, which banned all shipments of foods and medicines to Cuba except humanitarian aid (these items had previously been exempt from the embargo). Prior to the bill's passage, 70% of U.S. subsidiary trade with Cuba was in food and medicines. By barring such trade, the embargo forced Cuba to import medicines and medical supplies from Europe and Asia at vastly inflated prices. In addition, all medical equipment and supplies manufactured in the U.S. or under U.S. patent could not be exported to Cuba by third-country companies without a license from the U.S. Commerce Department.

The American Public Health Association has reported that "the embargo has exacerbated an already difficult situation in which nutritional deficiencies, unsafe water, deteriorating sanitation, overcrowding, and an absence of crucial medicines and supplies have attacked the formerly healthy population." Senator Jesse Helms and anti-Castroite Cuban-American Congressman Lincoln Diaz-Balart work hard to prevent any softening of these restrictions.

The U.S. embargo, however, provided a boon by forcing Cubans to innovate. "The embargo allowed for Cuban scientists to create their own space," says Dr. Jorge Gavilondo. Without the sanctions, Cuba might have been turned into a pill factory. "We would have been absorbed by the big [American] production companies."

The Clinton administration has eased some of the restrictions and approved certain licensed sales of food and medicines; in August 1999,

for example, it granted the Anglo-American drug company Smith Kline Beecham permission to commercially develop the Cuban meningitis vaccine, one of a growing number of licenses now being granted to U.S. health-care companies to trade with Cuba. A trade fair for U.S. medical suppliers was even held in Havana in January 2000. Ironically, in September 1998 when Washington committed US$7 million to the U.N. World Food Program's relief campaign for Cuba, Castro refused to accept it (in December 1999, he also turned away 55,000 pounds of desperately needed U.S. medical supplies meant for pediatric hospitals).

ARTS AND ENTERTAINMENT

Since the Revolution, the government's sponsorship of the arts has yielded a rich harvest in every field. The **Centro Nacional de Escuelas de Arte** (National Center of Schools of Art), created in 1960, has 41 schools under its umbrella, including the national Escuela de la Música, a national folkloric school, two ballet schools, two fine arts schools, and a school of modern dance, plus schools at the provincial level.

Cuba's Ministry of Culture works to expose every Cuban to as full a range of cultural offerings as possible. Visit a cigar factory and you'll hear the *lector* reading from the works of Ernest Hemingway, Nicolas Guillén, or Gabriel García Márquez. Nor is it unusual to hear of ballet being performed in factories or for a traveling puppet theater group to perform in a mountain village.

Cuba's wealth of arts venues is unrivaled within the Caribbean except, perhaps, for Venezuela. The local **Casa de la Trova** should be your second port of call, after finding a room, in every town. They are often free, though those near tourist hotels usually charge a dollar entrance. Local musicians drop in to jam, and you are as likely to hit a bum night as an unforgettable one. Every city has at least one *Casa de la Trova,* and a *Casa de la Cultura,* where movies, art exhibitions, and other cultural events are hosted. The local **UNEAC** (the Cuban Writers and Artists Union) will plug you into local life just as sweetly. Major cities also have ongoing music concerts, choral recitals, and art and sculpture exhibits. Virtually every town also has a theater, a movie

house, and at least one disco or *centro nocturno.* And *noches cubanas* take place in most towns on Saturday nights, when tables get moved into the streets, bars are set up, meals prepared alfresco, and then the street is cleared and dancing begins.

Cuba is one of the few tropical countries to have produced a *modern* culture of its own. During the first years of the Revolution, Castro enjoyed being the "bohemian intellectual." Artists and writers enjoyed relative freedom. As the romantic phase of the Revolution passed into an era of more dogmatic ideology, hard-line Marxists took over the Culture Council. In 1961 the government invited intellectuals to a debate on the meaning of cultural liberty at which Castro offered his "Words to the Intellectuals," which he summed up with a credo: "Within the Revolution, everything. Against the Revolution, nothing!" (It is ironic that one of the most brilliant of Cuban intellectuals should have so stifled intellectual freedom.) The government acquired full control of the mass media. Many talented intellectuals, writers, and artists were intimidated into ideological straitjackets. Thousands chose to leave Cuba.

Many talented individuals stayed, of course, and produced rich and lively works. But these were dark years of a relative spiritual vacuum. Social (socialist) analysis was always woven into the artistic tapestry. No politically incorrect works were allowed. The carryover is felt today, although it is no longer a punishable crime to possess music by the Beatles.

Despite ideological restraints, there is a genuine commitment on the part of the Cuban government to culture and the arts. Unfortunately schools suffer great shortages of instruments, sheet music, leotards, dance shoes, paints, brushes, and other materials. *Donations are welcome!*

Buoyed by commercial possibilities opened by tourism, artwork and entertainment have taken wing. Tourists are generally inured to the drought. Most major hotels, for example, have bars and discos. Take your pick between dollars-only haunts, where drinks will set you back at least US$3 a pop, to earthy discos (called cabarets) for locals, where *one peso* will buy a beer. At some places, only couples are admitted; many discos have a strange policy of not letting single women in (the opposite of Western discos). Few discos get in the groove before midnight; most go on until 4 a.m. or dawn.

The casinos and strip clubs, of course, were closed years ago.

Resources

In Havana, look for the weekly tourist newspaper *Cartelera,* which publishes information on exhibitions, galleries, and performances. It's available in many hotel lobbies. *Granma* also lists the forthcoming week's events.

The Ministry of Culture sponsors a bimonthly magazine, **Revolución y Cultura,** containing interviews, fiction, poetry, essays, photography and profiles on the arts, plus news on cultural events. It is hard to come by today; past issues—US$3 each—can be obtained from the Center for Cuban Studies (see the Organizations To Know chart).

And look for **ArteCubano: Revista de Artes Visuales,** a superb quarterly magazine published in both Spanish and English by Cuba's National Council of Fine Arts. You can order subscriptions ($56 in North America) from Ediciones Cubanas, Calle Obispo #527 esq. Bernaza, Havana, tel. (7) 63-1910, fax (7) 33-8943.

New Art of Cuba, by Luis Camnitzer, is a superb coffee-table book that profiles the evolution and protagonists in Cuba's flourishing contemporary art scene.

Paradiso: Promotora de Viajes Culturales, Calle 19 #560 esq. C, Vedado, Havana, tel. (7) 32-6928, fax (7) 33-3921, promotes artistic and cultural events, festivals, courses, seminars, workshops, and conferences in arts, sciences, and technology. It also arranges participatory courses for foreigners in cultural courses.

UNEAC (Union Nacional de Escritores y Artistas de Cuba), Calle 17 #354 e/ G y H, Vedado, tel. (7) 32-4551, fax (7) 33-3158, the national writers and artists union, hosts workshops and festivals spanning poetry to contemporary music.

For general information on the arts in Cuba online, visit www.Cubaarts.com.

FESTIVALS

The Special Period took its toll on popular festivals, cultural celebrations, and *cumbanchas,* street parties that might go on all night, with plenty of saucy rumba and saucier females to dance the hip-shaking rumba with. Festival such as those celebrating the beginning of the Revolution (25-27 July) and the triumph of the Revolution (1 January) were curtailed. However, festival life is rebounding Fortunately, festival life has rebounded, as with the newly rejuvenated **Cabildos** festival on 6 January, when the streets of Habana Vieja resound with festivities recalling the days when *cabildos* danced through the streets in vivid costumes and painted faces; for information, contact the City Historian's office at Calle Tacon #1, tel. (7) 33-8183. **Carnaval in Havana!** and **Carnival in Santiago,** too, were revived in 1995 after a five-year hiatus. Traditional *comparsas*—music and dance originally tied to slaves' tribes of origin—once again parade through the streets. The carnivals traditionally have been performed in July following the *zafra,* sugar harvest, but the Havana carnival is now held in February.

Folkloric and traditional music fiestas and specialist festivals are held throughout the island, ranging from "high culture," such as the **International Ballet Festival,** to purely local, down-to-earth affairs, such as the year-end *parrandas* of Villa Clara Province, where the townsfolk indulge in massive fireworks battles.

For a list of forthcoming conferences, symposiums, and events, contact the **Palacio de Convenciones,** Calle 146 e/ 11 y 13, Playa, tel. (7) 22-6011, fax (7) 21-9496, e-mail: palco@

MAJOR FESTIVALS

FESTIVAL/EVENT	MONTH	LOCATION	CONTACT
Havana Cigar Festival	February	Havana	tel. (7) 33-9509 fax (7) 33-8946
Classic Car Show	March	Havana and Matanzas	tel. (7) 61-5686 fax (7) 66-9281 e-mail: tamara@cultural.ohch.cu
International Percussion Festival	June	Havana	tel. (7) 23-8808 fax (7) 33-6633 e-mail: persuba@yahoo.com
Festival of Caribbean Culture	July	Santiago de Cuba	tel. (226) 42287 fax (226) 42387
Steam Train Festival	September	Havana	tel. (7) 24-4520 e-mail: eventos@rumvia.rumb.cma.ne
Festival of Contemporary Music	October	Havana	tel. (7) 32-0194 fax (7) 33-3158 e-mail: uneac@artsoft.cult.cu
Festival of Cuba	October	Bayamo	tel. (23) 42-4833 e-mail: pompa@comarit.com.cu
International Ballet Festival	October	Havana	tel. (7) 55-2948 fax (7) 33-3177
Festival of Latin American Culture	October	Holguín	tel. (24) 46-1673 e-mail: secthlg@tauronet.cult.cu
International Festival of New Latin American Cinema	November	Havana	tel. (7) 55-2854 fax (7) 33-3078
International Jazz Festival	December	Havana	tel. (7) 31-1234 fax (7) 33- 3176 e-mail: icm@artsoft.cult.cu

palco.get.cma.net, which publishes a *Schedule of International Events.*

Some of Cuba's annual festivals are world renowned, among them the **Havana Jazz Festival,** the **International Lyric Festival,** the **Guitar Festival,** Havana's **International Contemporary Music Festival,** and the **International Festival of New Latin-American Cinema,** held in Havana in mid-December.

When 1 May rolls around, the whole of Cuba takes to the streets to honor "workers" at **May Day Parades.** *The* place to be that day is the Plaza de la Revolución in Havana, where you'll be surrounded by up to 500,000 people waving colorful banners and placards and wearing T-shirts painted with revolutionary slogans. The sensation is uplifting as you are swept along in the tide making its way to the plaza to witness the military parade and to hear Fidel Castro and other leaders exhort Cubans to greater sacrifice. Scores of buses bring workers and children in from surrounding regions. Similar scenes are repeated islandwide.

Cuba, though nominally atheist, hosts a number of religious parades, such as the **Procession of the Miracles** each 17 December when hundreds of pilgrims—many of them dragging stones or crawling on their knees—make their way to the Santuario de San Lazaro, the "leper of the miracles," to give thanks to the saint (known as Babalu Aye in *santería*) for miracles they imagine he has granted. The sanctuary is at Rincón, on the outskirts of Santiago de las Vegas in Havana Province.

¡**Afrocubanismo!** is a major annual festival and workshop of Afro-Cuban music and dance hosted each August/September in Banff, Canada. Contact **The Banff Center for the Arts,** Office of the Registrar, P.O. Box 1020, Station 28, 107 Tunnel Mountain Dr., Banff, Alberta, Canada T0L 0CO, tel. (403) 762-6180.

The **Eleggua Project,** 7171 Torbram Rd., Suite 51, Mississauga, Ontario L4T 3WA, tel. (800) 818-8840, fax (905) 678-1421, e-mail: cancuba@pathcom.com, website: www.pathcom.com/~cancuba, sponsors the **Cuba Youth Jazz Festival** in February, and the **Cuban Youth Choral Festival** in April.

MUSEUMS AND GALLERIES

Few cities in Latin America can match Havana's showcase museums and galleries. Havana has almost 40 museums and at least 14 major art galleries and countless minor ones. Other museums and galleries are scattered throughout the province. You'll find many natural history museums and "decorative arts" museums, but by far the majority are dedicated in one form or another to the glories of the Revolution. Entrance for foreigners usually costs US$0.50-5. Almost always you are accompanied by a guide, who either trails a short distance behind or offers a sometimes stirring, sometimes turgid, précis of socialism.

THEATER

Havana has seven major theaters; Santiago de Cuba has eight. There are about 30 provincial theaters, many devoted to comedy, a Cuban staple. Nonetheless, Cuba is *not* a thespian's dream. Theater is the least developed of Cuba's cultural media. Many theaters host little drama and are used mostly for operatic, symphonic, and other concerts. Theater was usurped by the Revolution as a medium for mass consciousness raising. As such it became heavily politicized (the Teatro Escambray, for example, took to the hills to convey revolutionary ideals to the peasantry). In recent years, an avant-garde theater offering veiled political criticism has begun to evolve.

MUSIC AND DANCE

Author Norman Mailer scolded President Kennedy for the Bay of Pigs defeat by asking, "Wasn't there anyone around to give you the lecture on Cuba? Don't you sense the enormity of your mistake—you invade a country without understanding its music." These days it's Cuba that's invading the U.S. and the rest of the world. Says *Rhythm Music* magazine: "From Babalu to Bamboleo, a wealth of musicians is pouring out from under the Mango Curtain." Hardly a month goes by without some legendary Cuban

under the Mango Curtain, music "flows like river"

musician making his or her stateside debut, usually before a packed house of adoring fans (as long as the musicians are in good standing with the Cuban government). The rhythm juggernaut rolling across the U.S. is typified by the explosive 1999 success of the Grammy-winning *Buena Vista Social Club* and four-set album, *Cuba: I Am Time* (Blue Jacket Records). And no wonder. On the sleeve notes of the *Buena Vista Social Club*, Ry Cooder writes that in Cuba, "nurtured in an atmosphere sealed off from the fallout of a hyperorganized and noisy world. . . the music flows like a river. It takes care of you and rebuilds you from the inside out."

Music—the pulsing undercurrent of Cuban life—is everywhere. Dance, from the earliest *guaguanco* to the *mambo* craze, has always been a potent expression of an enshrined national tradition—Cuban sensualism. Girls are whisked onto the dance floor and whirled through a flurry of complicated steps and sensuous undulations, the intensity of which makes their North American counterparts look like butlers practicing the waltz. Young or elderly, every Cuban undulates with coquetry, swaying to the rhythm just a little closer than cheek to cheek. It's a wonder the birth rate isn't higher.

Cubans even enjoy the anguished, melancholy verses of the tango, which perfectly fits Cuba's mood today. Many Cubans listen to the radio broadcasts of María Luisa Macbeth—devoted to tango. Havana has two tango clubs, and you may find others around the country.

Folkloric Music and Dance

The development of Cuban music styles since 1800—from *contradanza* (the word is a colloquial translation of "country dance," brought from Jamaica), *danzón*, *habanera*, mambo, and *son* to *nueva trova*—is the story, writes Erroll McDonald, "of a swinging dialectic between West African choral and percussive genius and European melodic and harmonic sophistication." The earliest influence was Spanish. The colonists brought the melodies (such as the *bolero*), guitars, and violins from which evolved early *criollo* folk music. Most of Cuba's folk music, or *guajira* (such as the all-important *danzón*, the *punto*, and the *zapateo*, all popular in past centuries among white country people and accompanied by small accordions, kettledrums, gourds, and

THE BUENA VISTA SOCIAL CLUB

*I*n 1996, eclectic U.S. slide guitarist Ry Cooder made a musical pilgrimage to Cuba in search of a clique of legendary but largely forgotten veteran musicians to make a comeback album, the *Buena Vista Social Club*, named for a Havana venue where many of the artists performed in the 1950s. German film director Wim Wenders tagged along with his Beta steadicam to chronicle how Cooder rounded them up, ushered them into recording studios, cut an album of sepia-toned tunes and dispatched them on a world tour and runaway success. The documentary celebrates the musicians' performance on the world stage and offers a portrait of their life back in an impoverished Cuba.

The tender heart of the *Buena Vista* movie is crooner, Ibrahim Ferrer, a soft-spoken septuagenarian who had been a singer with the legendary Beny Moré band in the 1950s, but who was shining shoes at the time Cooder's team rediscovered him for the *Buena Vista* album. His weathered, yet still nimble voice is supported by the arthritic fingers of 76-year-old pianist Ruben González, creator in the early 1940s of the modern Cuban piano sound, flying into action after long retirement (his piano had been reduced to dust by termites when Cooder brought him back from obscurity); the slick guitar work of 90-odd-year-old Francisco Repalido, known as "Compay Segundo," the grandfather of *son* music, who plays in his trademark Panamá hat; guitarist Eliades Ochoa, a maestro of the *guajira* (country lament), easily recognized in his trademark cowboy hat; and the dulcet voice of Omara Portuono, who was once one of the leading bolero singers in Cuba.

This suave old bunch of codgers wowed the world when the documentary movie, produced by Cooder, was released in 1999, swept the U.S., and introduced it to the richness of *son*, danzón, and bolero. The result was a runaway success. In March 1998 the album (on the London-based World Circuit label) won the Grammy for Tropical Music and topped the charts among Latin albums, taking Cuban music international for the first time, and selling more than a million copies worldwide.

You can buy the CD at a discount at www.cubabooks.com.

calabashes) is European music that has been influenced through contact with black culture.

You can still witness such *punto campesinas* being performed in country towns, including the slow and sensual *yambú* and (especially in Matanzas Province) the *columbia,* a solo men's dance performed blindfolded with machetes. The melancholic love song *Guantanamera* is undoubtedly the most famous of Cuban *guajiras,* recorded by everyone from Pete Seeger to Júlio Iglésias. Look for performances by the **Conjunto Folclórico Nacional** (National Folklore Dance Group), which performs nationwide. The group was founded in 1962 to revive Cuban folk traditions because it was thought that the populace had lost touch with its folkloric past. Every major city has a performance group supported by the national umbrella body.

From Europe, too, came the *trovas,* poetic songs concerned with great historical events and, above all, with love. *Trovas,* which were descended from the medieval ballad, were sung in Cuba throughout the colonial period. *Trovadores* performed for free, as they still do at Casas de la Trova. The Matamoros Trio is perhaps the best known in the genre. This century has seen the evolution of *trovas nuevas,* songs about contemporary life. The movement has ties to the American folk-protest song movement of the 1960s and often includes outspoken criticism of current situations. The contemporary works of Pablo Milané and Silvio Rodríguez, for example, echo the revolutionary dreams and restlessness of the current generation.

The African Influence

Almost from the beginning, the Spanish guitar (from the tiny *requinto* to the nine-stringed *tres*) joined the hourglass-shaped African *bata* and *bongo* drum, *claves* (two short hardwood sticks clapped together), and *chequerí* (seed-filled gourds) to give Cuban music its distinctive form. Slaves played at speakeasies in huts in the slaves' quarters. Their jam sessions gave birth to the *guaguancó,* a mix of flamenco guitar and African rhythm that is the mother of Cuban dance music. Later, slaves would take the *guaguancó* a few steps further to create the sensuous rumba, a sinuous dance from the hips (the rumba has African roots, but the melody is very Spanish) and from which tumbled most other forms of

Cuban music; and the *tumba francesa,* a dance of French-African fusion.

Rumba: Rumba remains deliriously popular. On Saturday afternoons crowds of Cubans flock to the local Rumba Sabado (Rumba Saturday). Watch for performances by Los Muñequitos de Matanzas (literally, the dolls of Matanzas but signifying the "kings of rumba")—who tour worldwide but whose base is Matanzas, where you might catch them at the Casa de la Trova.

From rumba, which evolved around the turn of the century, came *son,* originally a sugar-workers' dance adopted by urban musicians for their large percussion and horn sections. Such contemporary groups as Los Van Van have incorporated the *son,* which has its own variants, such as the fast, infectious, overtly sexual *son changüí* from Guantánamo Province, typified by the music of Orquestra Revé.

Mambo: The mambo, like the cha-cha, which evolved from it, is a derivative of the *danzón,* jazzed up with rhythmic innovations. Mambo is a passé but still revered dance, like the jitterbug in the U.S., danced usually only by older people. Created in Cuba by Orestes López in 1938, mambo stormed the United States in the 1950s, when Cuban performers were the hottest ticket in town. Though the craze died, mambo left its mark on everything from American jazz to the old Walt Disney cartoons where the salt- and peppershakers get up and dance. People were titillated by the aggressive sexual overtures required of women in the elegant but provocative dance. Captivated by the earthy break from the more modest swing, Americans created a simpler but equally risqué spin-off—"dirty dancing."

A few years ago, the movie *The Mambo Kings* fueled the popularity of Cuban dancetorias across the U.S. Such clubs, however, lack the building sexual energy that fuels the dance in tattered, peeling Havana.

Filin: The mix of Cuban and North American sounds created blends such as *filin* ("feeling") music, as sung by Rita Montaner and Nat King Cole, who performed regularly in Havana; and *Cu-bop,* which fused bebop with Afro-Cuban rhythms, epitomized by Beny Moré—*el bárbaro de ritmo* (the Barbarian of Rhythms)—a theatrical showman who was considered the top artist of Cuban popular music but who drank himself into oblivion in the 1960s.

Modern Sounds

The Revolution put a crimp in the music scene. Foreign performers stayed away, while many top performers left Cuba, such as Celía Cruz, "queen of salsa." But even Cuba isn't able to escape the latest global pandemic—the omnipresent Céline Dion.

Salsa: Salsa (a derivative of *son*) has flourished since the 1980s, when the government began to lighten up. It is the heartbeat of most Cuban nightlife and a musical form so hot it can cook the pork. Los Van Van—one of Cuba's hottest big, brassy salsa-style bands, and Cuba's most popular dance band for the past three decades (in 2000 they won a Grammy for "Best Salsa" album: *Llego*)—and Irakere have come up with innovative and explosive mixtures of jazz, classical, rock, and traditional Cuban music that have stirred commotion in the music and entertainment circles. They regularly tour Europe and Latin America, earning the country scarce hard currency (most musicians are state employees). Isaac Delgado, ¡Cubanismo!, Orquesta Aragon, NG La Banda, and Vocal Sampling are other top-notch Cuban bands to watch out for.

The hottest sound of the moment is Bamboleo, which became a leader in the *timba* (new-wave Cuban salsa) when it debuted at the 1995 Cuban Jazz Festival and revitalized the hometown music scene with a fierce new energy. The bald-headed female singers also started a new craze in hairstyles.

Jazz: For a long time, the playing of jazz in Cuba was completely discouraged (it was seen as "representative of Yankee imperialism, the music of the enemy"). Cuban musicians missed out on the Latin Jazz effervescence of the 1960s. Paquito D'Rivera, for example, was discouraged from playing jazz when he became director of the Orquestra Cubana de Música Moderna in 1970. Today Cuba boasts wonderful jazz players of every stripe, though there is still a paucity of places where jazz can be heard.

Cuban jazz zigzags from bebop to fusion and European classical to Afro-Caribbean rhythms. It is "a bravura, macho form of jazz; trumpeters playing the highest notes and pianists going as fast as they can go." Cuban jazz musicians are admired the world over for their unique creativity and spirit. "When this is over and the musicians start coming out of Cuba, we'll all have to go back to school to catch up," says North American jazz maestro Tito Puente. Many leading international stars are Cuban. Celebrated trumpeter Arturo Sandoval left Irakere and Cuba in 1990. Juan Carlos Formell (son of Juan Formell, the leader of Los Van Van), who is at the vanguard of a new generation of young Cuban artists in exile, defected in 1993 for New York. And D'Rivera left Cuba for New York in 1980. (Like many artists, however, D'Rivera's departure had nothing to do with politics. "I fell in love with being a jazz musician in New York since first listening to a Benny Goodman record," he says. Nonetheless, his music was pulled from the shelves in Cuba, and for nine years Castro refused to let D'Rivera's son join him. Those who leave Cuba take their *Cubanidad* with them; they become nonpersons at home.)

Watch for pianists Chucho Valdés, Gonzalo Rubalcava, and Ruben González, the octogenarian star of the *Buena Vista Social Club.*

The **International Havana Jazz Festival** is held in mid-February in Havana.

Rock and Roll: Rock and roll was once officially banned. Today you'll see many long-haired youths—*roqueros*—wearing Led Zeppelin and Metallica T-shirts (heavy metal fans are known as *metálicos,* while "hippies" are called *frikis*). In recent years, the Young Communists have lassoed the popularity of modern-music to corral disaffected youth. Hence the state sponsors rock concerts, and state television and radio generously broadcast pirated videos of everyone from Nirvana to Sinéad O'Connor. However, the government keeps its own rock musicians (such as heavy-metal group Zeus) on short leashes. Playing unofficial venues can get *roqueros* arrested. To a large degree the state decides what music can be played. Electricity rationing also sometimes pulls the plug on rehearsals and concerts, which are advertised through the grapevine.

Many Cubans are also hip to hip-hop and World Beat, and the island has hosted an annual Cuban Rap Festival since 1995. You'll find many reggae fans sporting dreadlocks (such as Carlos Alfonso Valdés, the leader of a popular Cuban funk band, Sintesis, with dreadlocks nearly down to his waist) and Bob Marley T-shirts (Cuban youth have scarce resources but possess a dead-on fashion sense gleaned from MTV).

TUNING WITH THE ENEMY

When Benjamin Treuhaft first visited Cuba, he marveled at the ability of young musicians to raise beautiful sounds from decrepit pianos—Wurlitzer short uprights from the turn of the century, unpromising 1970s Russian Tchaikas, and pre-1959 U.S. instruments eaten by salt air and termites.

Treuhaft, a piano tuner who has tuned on behalf of Steinway, vowed to collect pianos and ship them to Cuba. He sent letters to piano dealers across the nation soliciting parts and soon had pledges for dozens of pianos. His mission of musical mercy, however, struck a dissonant note with the U.S. Commerce Department, which declared that pianos are not humanitarian aid and were therefore barred. When Treuhauft replied in jest that the Cubans might use the pianos for military purposes, the case was shifted to the department's Office of Missile and Nuclear Technology! Due considerations were presumably given to piano throw weights and trajectories before official permission was given to ship his pianos, providing that they were not "used for the purpose of torture or human rights abuse"—proof that U.S. policy toward Cuba is overdue for its own major tuning. Says lawyer Thomas Miller, "Our leaders in Washington now believe they can bring the Cuban people to their knees by forcing them to listen to out-of-tune pianos."

The first 22 pianos (plus an organ and half a ton of spare parts) reached Havana in December 1995, to be dispersed to deserving students and teachers by the Instituto Cubano de la Música (Cuban Institute of Music). More than 60 pianos have thus far been shipped, along with 20 piano tuners. Treuhaft has even installed a German wire-spinning machine in Havana.

Treuhaft needs piano wire, tuning pins, and tools, but most of all that old piano (in rebuildable condition) languishing in your basement. Monetary donations are also requested (make checks payable to Havapiano). Contact Benjamin Treuhaft, 39 E. St. #3, New York, NY 10003, tel. (212) 505-3171, e-mail: blt@igc.org.

Watch for *Tuning With the Enemy*, a hour-long documentary filmed in Havana and Berkeley about Treuhaft's project. It was made for English TV but does the rounds of the U.S.

Ben Treuhaft

Classical Music

"In the realm of classical music Cuba has been an inspirational locale rather than a breeding ground for great composers and instrumentalists," says noted pianist Daniel Fenmore. Nonetheless, it is astounding how many contemporary Cubans are accomplished classical musicians. Everywhere you go, you will come across violinists, pianists, and cellists serenading you for tips while you eat.

Cuba boasts several classical orchestras, notably the **Orquestra Simfónica Nacional**. It first performed in November 1960 and has a repertoire ranging from 17th-century works to the most contemporary creations, with a special emphasis on popularizing works by Latin American and Cuban composers, such as Amadeo Roldán and Alejandro García Caturla. It may not be on a par with the London Philharmonic or the San Francisco Symphony Orchestra, but a performance is stirring nevertheless. Watch, too, for performances by Frank Fernández, Cuba's finest classical pianist.

Ballet

Cubans love ballet, which is associated in Cuba with one name above all—Alicia Alonso. Alonso was a prima ballerina with the American Ballet Theater since its inception in the 1940s. She returned to Cuba and, sponsored by Batista (who hated ballet but considered her star status a propaganda bonus), founded the **Ballet Nacional de Cuba,** website: www.balletcuba.cubaweb.cu, in 1948. Alonso was outspoken in her criticism of the "Sordid Era," and she went into exile in 1956 when Batista withdrew his patronage. The Revolution later adopted her. Her company is renowned worldwide for its original choreography and talent. The season runs all year and Havana's Grand Theater and National Theater are regular venues for performances. The National Ballet company spends much of its time touring at home and abroad.

The **Camagüey Ballet**—founded since the Revolution by Alicia's husband, Fernando Alonso—is also renowned for its innovative streak, as is the Santiago-based **Ballet Folklórico de Oriente,** which lends contemporary interpretations to traditional themes.

Cabarets

Cabarets are a staple of Cuban life. Every town has at least one. The entertainment varies, but singers, magicians, acrobats, and comedians are usually featured. Sometimes, the term "cabaret" merely refers to a disco. More frequently it refers to Las Vegas-style *cabarets espectáculos,* or "shows," highlighted by long-legged women (usually mulattas) in high heels and skimpy costumes with lots of sequins, feathers, and frills and who gyrate their glistening copper-colored bodies into an erotic frenzy. Usually they are accompanied by smaller dance troupes of bare-chested male performers. Cuban couples delight in these shows.

Cabarets have also become a tourist staple. The largest and showiest, involving dozens of performers, are reserved for the upscale hotels. Outshining them all is the Tropicana, Cuba's premier Las Vegas-style nightclub, boasting over 200 performers. It has two outlets—one each

in Havana (run by Gran Caribe) and Santiago de Cuba (run by Cubanacán), and is a *de rigueur* night out for *every* tourist.

ARTS AND CRAFTS

Cuba has a prominent place in the world of arts. You'll find an incredible array of art, sculpture, and photo exhibitions—especially in Havana but also nationwide. The shows often draw top international artists as well as Cubans of stature. In Havana you can pick up a bimonthly program **(Galerías de Arte Programacion)** from the Centro de Desarrollo de las Artes Visuales, San Ignacio #352, Plaza Vieja, Havana 1. As for crafts, I'm in constant awe of the range and quality. And Cuba's poster and mural art is perhaps unrivaled in the world.

Cuba has made great efforts to display art from other countries, notably the Caribbean and Latin America, as for example the **Art of Our Americas** collection, housed in Havana's Casa de las Américas, a nongovernmental institution that has studied and promoted every aspect of Latin American and Caribbean culture since 1959. Similar institutions can be found islandwide. Even entire villages, such as **El Oásis** near Santiago, exist as art communities.

The prestigious **Havana Biennale** is an annual art show hosted by the Havana's Centro Wilfredo Lam each May.

Everyday Art portrays Cuba's folkloric traditions and contemporary art scene. This 50-minute video focuses on the everyday life of Cuban musicians, dancers, and artists and reflects the strong presence of folk art in social institutions such as religion and education. You can order it for US$30 from Caribbean Music and Dance Programs, 12545 Olive St. #241, St Louis, MO 63141, tel. (314) 542-3637 or toll free (877) 665-4321, fax (314) 469-2916, e-mail: caribmusic@igc.apc.org, website: www.caribmusic.com.

The Center for Cuban Studies (see the chart, Organizations To Know) maintains the **Cuban Art Space,** the largest collection of contemporary Cuban art in the United States, with more than 800 paintings, drawings, and graphics, plus about 5,000 posters. Originals and reproductions are offered for sale (Mon.-Fri. noon-8 p.m.;

CUBAN POSTER ART

*C*uba's strongest claim to artistic fame is surely its unique poster art, created in the service of political revolution. Cuban poster art has blossomed thanks to state support—a situation comparable to the United States in the 1930s, when the government paid artists to produce individual work.

The three leading poster-producing agencies—the Organization of Solidarity with the Peoples of Africa, Asia and Latin America; the Cuban Film Institute; and the Editora Política, the propaganda arm of the Cuban Communist Party—have produced over 10,000 posters since 1959. Different state bodies create works for different audiences: artists of the Cuban Film Institute (ICAIC), for example, design posters for movies from Charlie Chaplin comedies to John Wayne westerns; Editora Política produces posters covering everything from AIDS awareness, baseball games, and energy conservation to telling children to do their homework.

Cuba's most talented painters and photographers rejected Soviet realism and developed their own unique graphic style influenced by Latin culture and the country's geography. The vibrant colors and lush imagery are consistent with the physical and psychological makeup of the country, such as the poster urging participation in the harvest, dripping with psychedelic images of fruit and reminiscent of a 1960s Grateful Dead poster.

Cuban posters are typically graceful, combining strong simple concepts and sparse text with ingenious imagery and surprising sophistication. One poster, for example, warns of the dangers of smoking: a wisp of smoke curls upward to form a ghostlike skull.

The vast collection—acclaimed as "the single most focused, potent body of political graphics ever produced in this hemisphere"—provides a lasting visual commentary of the Revolution.

In the U.S., you can order posters—or a CD collection of posters—from the **Cuba Poster Project,** c/o Inkworks, 2827 7th St., Berkeley, CA 94710, tel. (510) 845-7111, fax (510) 845-6753, e-mail: lcushing@igc.apc.org, website: www.zpub.com/cpp.

Saturday and Sunday, noon-5 p.m.). On the West Coast, **Duvall Durand Gallery,** 432 Sutter St., San Francisco, CA 94108, tel. (415) 781-6440, fax (415) 781-6621, e-mail: DuvallGallery@aol.com, imports and sells fine art from leading Cuban painters. And you can buy superb lithographs of Cuban cigar art from **La Habana Gallery,** P.O. Box 1307 Burlingame, CA 94011-1307, tel./fax (650) 347-7410, e-mail: comandante@eltiburon.com, website: www.eltiburon.com.

The security staff at Havana's international airport check all artwork for its value. Anything deemed of antique value or of high value will be either confiscated or taxed. An export permit is required for all works of art not purchased from state galleries and shops where official receipts are given. If you buy from an independent artists, you'll need to buy a permit (good for up to five works of art) for US$10 from the National Registry of Cultural Goods, Calle 17 #1009 e/ 10 y 12, Vedado. Allow up to two days for processing. Without it you run the risk of Cuban Customs taking it. However, Customs seems more interested in guarding against precious works leaving the country, and for kitschy paintings sold on the street, you should be fine. Nonetheless, the Cuban government occasionally sells off art treasures on the sly. In 1990, for example, Sotheby's of London sold two painting by the Spaniard Joaquín Sorolla for US$2 million. The paintings belonged to the Oscar B. Cintas Foundation but were confiscated by the Castro government following the Revolution. The Cintas Foundation sued, claiming sale of stolen art. (See the Shopping section in the Havana chapter for regulations regarding purchasing and exporting works of art.)

The Artist in Cuba

Cuban artists express an intense Afro-Latin Americanism in their passionate, visceral, colorful, socially engaged art. Painters and other artists imaginatively stretch their limited resources to produce widely interpretive modern and postmodern works. The work is eclectic, but there is energy in it all.

In the late 1960s, the government tried to compel Cuban artists to shun then-prevalent decadent abstract art and adopt the realistic style of the party's Mexican sympathizers such as Diego Rivera and David Alfaro Siqueiros, who turned from easel painting to wall murals because, in the words of Siqueiros: "While it is technically possible to play a revolutionary hymn on a church organ, it is not the instrument one would prefer." The artists who grew up *after* the 1959 revolution—the "generation of the '80s"—have been given artistic encouragement, reflecting Cuba's liberal notion that artists are no less socially useful than masons, storekeepers, and bus drivers.

Cuba has 21 art schools, organized regionally with at least one per province. The **Instituto Superior de Arte** (Higher Institute of Art), Calle 120 #1110, Cubanacán, Havana, tel. (7) 21-0288, Cuba's premier art school, remains key as an educational center and gateway to the world of Cuban art.

The art educational system is both traditional and modern, with fundamental classical drawing and painting techniques at its core. The Cuban state has always fostered academic training in still life, landscape, and figure form (the nobility of sugarcane cutters and factory workers, of course, was emphasized). On attaining mastery of these skills, artists are encouraged to depart on experiments in expression to the extent of their imaginations (and without overstepping Castro's 1961 dictum to think more of the message than the aesthetic). As a result, says critic Tina Spiro, "most Cuban artwork, regardless of its style, is informed by a precision of line and a beautiful technical finish."

Upon matriculation from art school, artists receive the support of the **Fondo Cubano de Bienes Culturales,** Calle 36 #4702, Kohly, Havana, tel. (7) 66-9499, in marketing and presenting their work to the public. The Cuban Cultural Fund is organized regionally by province and offers gallery exhibitions, cataloging services, shipping, and transportation.

Until recent years, artists were employed by various Cuban state institutions and received a small portion of receipts from the sale of their work. In 1991 the government finally recognized that copyright belongs with the artist. It has created independent profit-making, self-financing agencies, such as ARTEX (Artistic and Literary Promotion), Av. 5ta #8010, Miramar, Havana, tel. (7) 24-2741, to represent individual artists on a contractual basis whereby the agency retains 15% of sales receipts. New regulations

provide that artists (including performers) can, ostensibly, retain up to 85% of earnings from the sale or licensing of copyrights abroad. A portion of the retained earnings goes to the Ministry of Culture's **Fondo de Desarrollo por Educación y Cultura** (Fund for Educational and Cultural Development), which provides resources for arts training and public arts programs.

The artists themselves are increasingly shaking off their clichés and conservatism. In 1980 when the Cuban government began to loosen up, it even sponsored a show of avant-garde work influenced by international formats. Artists began holding unofficial exhibitions in their homes. By the late 1980s the artists were overstepping their bounds (*The Orgasm on the Bay,*

WILFREDO LAM

Wilfredo Lam, a Cubist and student of Pablo Picasso, was one of the greatest painters to emerge from Cuba during this century. He was born in 1902, in Sagua La Grande, his heritage a mixture of Cuban, African, and Chinese blood. He studied at Havana's San Alejandro School of Painting. In 1936 he traveled to Paris and developed close ties with the surrealists. Picasso too k Lam under his wing and offered the young Cuban his studio to work in. Lam lived briefly in Marseilles before returning to Havana. In 1956 he returned to Europe, although he continued to visit Cuba periodically. He died in Paris on 11 September 1982.

Lam's work distills the essence of Afro-Antillean culture. He broke with the traditional rules and created his own style using the myths, rituals, customs, and magic of his background to explore a world of Caribbean negritude. His most important works are considered to be *La Silla,* painted in 1941, and *La Jungla,* painted in 1943. Many of his etchings, sketches, and canvases are exhibited in Havana's Bella Artes museum. His *La Manigua,* painted in Haiti in 1956, hangs in the Museum of Modern Art in New York. And one of his paintings, *La Mañana Verde,* sold at Sotheby's in 1995 for US$965,000. You can even walk on his work which is inset on the sidewalks of Calle 23 (La Rampa) in Vedado.

Lam is honored at the **Centro Wilfredo Lam,** San Ignacio, Habana Vieja, tel. (7) 61-2096 and 61-3419, fax (7) 33-8477, e-mail: wlam@art-soft.cult.cu.

Roberto Fernández Martinez in his studio

by Tomás Esson, for example, depicted an ejaculating cigar in Castro's mouth). Armando Hart, Minister of Culture, decided that the Cuban artists' enthusiasm should be promoted from afar. Mexico City was selected and a community of deported artists has evolved—quixotically, with official Cuban sponsorship. In recent years, Cuban artists have taken the Western art world by storm. Says *Newsweek,* "Like the German and Italian neoexpressionists who took over the scene in the 1970s and '80s, the Cuban artists may be on the brink of changing the face of contemporary art."

Eroticism—often highly graphic—is an integral component of contemporary Cuban art, in keeping with the culture's expressive sensuality and as exemplified by the works of Aldo Soler, with his evocatively symbolic nudes. A new religious element has also taken root (where Afro-Cuban faith was basic to art in the 1980s, religious art today is inclining toward Roman Catholicism). And much of current art subtly criticizes the folly of its socio-political environment, but

usually in a politically safe, universal statement about the irony in human existence—for example, Juan-Carlos Amador Machado has broken through the restrictions and paints the world of rotting Habana Vieja outside his door, expressing the hardships of daily life in a dark, surreal way. Within limits, this artistic dissent is not censored. Armando Hart has maintained this policy throughout his lengthy tenure from the Revolution to the present day.

Among Cuba's most revered contemporary artists is Alfredo Sosabravo—a painter, draftsman, engraver, and ceramist born in 1930—and the most versatile and complete artist among those making up the plastic-arts movement in Cuba today. You'll come across his works (and influence) everywhere, including a permanent exhibition at Havana's Museo Nacional and the Palacio de Bellas Artes. He is dramatically present in hotel lobbies and other tourist spots. Look, too, for the erotic art of Chago Armada and Carlos Alpizar, and the sensual landscapes of Lester Campa, painted in almost hallucinogenic detail. The most profound of foreign influences is that of the Spanish surrealist, Salvador Dali, whose fantastical and tortured imagery is reflected in contemporary works islandwide.

Carving and Crafts

You'll find many artists producing fantastic sculptural ceramics, such as those of Teresita Gómez or Roberto Fernández Martinez, whose works—often totemic—are heavily influenced by African myths. Look, too, for the works of women artists such as Antonio Eiriz and Amelia Peláez, and U.S.-born Jacqueline Maggi, now professor of engraving at the Advanced Institute of Art, in Havana, who "tackles the problem of women" in her woodcarvings and sculptures.

Lovers of Tiffany lamps should look for Gilberto Kindelán's transparent art nouveau lamps with bucolic landscapes featuring butterflies, which Kindelán describes as very visual and lending themselves well to poetry and movement in glass. The artist gets his glass, pewter, copper, and bronze from old mansions, recycling pieces rescued from beneath the wrecking ball.

You'll also find a resurgence of Cuban jewelry, some of which is quite stunning. Silver inset with black coral is the staple.

The **Asociació Cubana de Artesanos Artisticas** (Handicrafts Association of Cuba), Calle Obispo #411, Habana Vieja, tel. (7) 61-1167, sponsors crafts.

LITERATURE

Cubans are incredibly literate. They are avid readers, and not just of home-country writers. The works of many renowned international authors are widely read throughout Cuba: Ernest Hemingway, Tennessee Williams, Gabriel García Márquez, Günter Grass, Isabel Allende, Jorge Amado (one 21-year-old Cuban told me she enjoyed reading Agatha Christie, Tennessee Williams, and even Anne Rice). Finding books is a problem: bookstores are few and meagerly stocked, so that tattered antique editions do the rounds until they crumble to dust.

Cuba's goals and struggles have been a breeding ground for passions and dialectics that have spawned dozens of literary geniuses whose works are clenched fists that cry out against social injustice. Says writer Errol McDonald, "The confluence of the struggle against Spanish and American imperialism, the impact of the cultivation of sugar and tobacco, a high appreciation of the 'low-down' sublimities of Afro-Cuban and Hispanic peasant life, a deep awareness of European 'high' and American popular culture, and the shock of the revolution has resulted in a literature that is staggering for its profundity and breadth—its richness."

Cuba's early literary figures were mostly essayists and poets. Indeed, poets were being published in Cuba 100 years before the *Mayflower* landed in Massachusetts in 1620. The tensions of the 19th century produced some astounding writers, most notably José Martí, perhaps the greatest prose writer in Spanish during this period and epitomizing the emergence of a *criollo* style that marked a desire to find a myth to express the past and point to the future of an uncrystallized nation.

Cuban literature was born in exile. The most talented Cuban writers, such as Cirilo Villaverde (whose spellbinding novel *Cecilia Valdés* was written in exile in the 1880s), José María Heredia (1803-39), Julián del Casal (1863-93), Alejo Carpentier (1904-80), and José Martí, all produced their best works abroad. The promiscuous Cuban 19th-century woman of letters, Gertrudis Gómez de Avellaneda y Artega (1814-73), also flourished as a writer in exile. So, too, more recently, Virgilio Piñera, a brilliantly mordant literary man whose extraordinary brutal lyricism and grim evocation of the simple facts of life are captured in *Cold Tales*. Piñera was cast into purgatory in the 1960s, among the first intellectuals who became "contagious political bacteria" during the Revolution.

There also evolved in the 1930s and '40s a black poetry that drew heavily on the myths and memories of slavery, very socialist in content, as portrayed by the works of Nicolá Guillén, which spawned a sentimental fashion still prevalent in the works of contemporary poets.

Although post-revolutionary Cuba has had its literary figures of note, it has not produced a definable literature of its own.

The "Gray Five Years"

In the first years of the Revolution, literary magazines such as *Lunes* and *Casa* attained an extraordinary dynamism. In 1961 Castro reacted. The "debate" in 1961, when Castro dictated that only pro-revolutionary works would be allowed, evoked a vacuum. Ever since, the degree of "social responsibility" has determined who gets published (as well as who speaks on radio or television). The newspaper *Revolución* became a powerful organ that, says Infanta, "literally blasted many writers into submission—or oblivion" (later it was reborn as *Granma*). Writers, suggests Jacobo Timerman, "were crushed and immobilized by a tombstone."

The ice age lasted for a very long decade and came to a climax 1970-76, a period euphemistically called "the gray five years" *(quinquenia gris)*. Then, the communists attempted to force Cuba into the mold of Eastern European "socialist realism" to the detriment of Cuba's rich national culture. Most of the boldest and best writers (many of whom had been devoted revolutionaries) departed into exile. Among them were Carlos Franquí, Guillermo Cabrera Infante, Huberto Padilla, and playwright Antón Arrufat.

The worst years ended when the Ministry of Culture was founded in 1976, ushering in a period of greater leniency.

Post-Revolutionary Literature

Although much of the cream of the crop left Cuba, the country still maintained a productive literary output. Some contemporary novelists were uncritically complicit in Castroism. But the limitations imposed by strictures of orthodoxy have, for the most part, stifled emotion, sensibility, and a rich, fertile language. "What good is teaching millions to read when only one man decides what you read?" asks Infante, who was one of the first to leave and one of the greatest of Cuba's 20th-century writers.

Five notable exceptions are Alejo Carpentier; José Lezama Lima (1912-76), author of *Paradiso,* which was later made into a successful film; Nicolás Guillén (1902-86), the mulatto, communist, and literary grandee of the Cuban revolution who in the 1920s wrote *poesía negra* (black poetry) and whose later works are encapsulated in *The Great Zoo & Other Poems,* political poems of the common man; Dulce María Loynaz, Director of the Cuban Academy of Language and acclaimed as the leading Cuban poet; and the poet Eliseo Diego, who won Cuba's National Literature Award in 1986.

Carpentier (his name is pronounced in the French style) is known for his erudite and verbally explosive works with far-reaching symbolism. My favorite is "Journey Back to the Source," a brilliant short story chronicling the life of Don Marcial, Marqués de Capellanías, but told chronologically backwards from death to birth. Carpentier was born in Havana to a French father and Russian mother. In 1946 during the violent excesses of the Batista era, he had to flee Cuba for Venezuela where he wrote his best novels (one year before, he published a seminal work called *Music in Cuba*). When the Castro revolution triumphed, the gifted novelist and revolutionary patriot returned as an honored spiritual leader. Alas, Carpentier became a bureaucrat and sycophant; under his influence, the National Printing Press even reworked *Moby Dick* to make it palatable to the socialist masses (Captain Ahab, Ishmael, and Queequeg were still there but, says Infante, "you couldn't find God in the labyrinth of the sea").

Cuban writers prefer the short story. The influence of Kafka is abiding, claims J. M. Cohen in *The New Writers in Cuba,* reflecting the tussle between the solid liberalism of the writers'

union—UNEAC—and Casa de las Américas and the communist puritanism and petty persecution of non-conforming writers.

Many young writers born since 1959 have pushed the boundaries of expression further than ever before. Such writers as Reinaldo Arenas and José Camillo de la Cera also fled Cuba and became well known abroad. Others struggled on, facing harassment for their efforts. There were no independent publishing houses. Therefore many splendid writers found it difficult to get their books published because their works were too radical. Iginio Barrere Causse, who has won international awards (the checks have never arrived), has six unpublished manuscripts. Some authors have resorted to sending manuscripts with foreigners. Others become "official writers."

The New Thaw

The 1990s saw a considerable thaw from the 1960s and '70s, when all that writers were permitted to write was, *"Viva Cuba, Viva la Revolución."* The Cuban government began to salvage those artists and writers who, having produced significant works, were never allowed to publish. Now-dead writers of note are invoked and homage is paid to them, while those who remain alive now see their works dusted off, published, and awarded honorifics. Many writers previously reduced to "nonpersons" have been being treated with kindness and, often, post-mortem canonization.

Ironically, this new openness coincided with the hardships of the Special Period, which caused a severe paper shortage. By 1993 books were beginning to get as scarce as the food. Many state-employed writers found themselves among the ranks of the unemployed. Prompted by the economic and political openings of the early 1990s, they banded together to form the **Union of Freelance Writers and Artists.**

Alas, Cuba's political climate runs hot and cold. In spring 1996 the government began to cool authors down a bit, and freelancers continue to feel sharp tugs on the leash.

Resources

Virtually every town has a library *(biblioteca),* albeit usually meagerly stocked with books solely of a politically correct flavor. The Biblioteca

Political publishing flourished in the early 1990s, but has since faded with resumed government authority.

Nacional (National Library) in Havana contains more than 530,000 volumes. Literary and poetry readings are common events in Havana and other municipalities (most are free). Most towns also have at least one bookshop, though the always paltry stock is usually limited to Spanish-language texts by Fidel Castro, Che Guevara, José Martí, and classics of international literature by those on the right—or is that the left?—side of politics. Don't expect to see works that offer anything other than a sympathetic viewpoint of communism. English-language works are extremely hard to find, with the exception of leftist texts from Australia's Ocean Press. Most gift stores sell coffee-table books on Cuba, as well as a range of leftist, English-language texts and, occasionally, pulp fiction novels.

An excellent resource is the **Unión Nacional de Escritores y Artistas de Cuba,** UNEAC, Calle 17 #351, Vedado, Havana, tel. (7) 32-2391, the Writer's Union, housed in a beautiful old mansion not far from the Habana Libre. The mansion's porch is now the union's cafe, where you may mingle with Cuba's literati. UNEAC publishes a bimonthly magazine, *La Gaceta,* and subscriptions (US$40) are available through Pathfinder, 410 West St., New York, NY 10014, tel. (212) 741-0690, fax (212) 727-0150.

The **Havana Book Fair,** organized by the Cuban Book Institute and the Cuban Book Chamber, is usually held in February, attracting exhibitors, publishers, and booksellers. For information, contact either the Center for Cuban Studies (see the chart, Organizations to Know), or Buró de Convenciones, Calle M e/ 17 y 19, Vedado, Havana, tel. (7) 31-3600, fax (7) 33-4261, e-mail: buroconv@burconv.mit.cma.net

FILM

Cubans are passionate moviegoers, and the entire island is blessed with cinemas, including many of prerevolutionary art-nouveau grandeur. Entrance usually costs a single peso (foreigners are rarely charged in dollars), and the menu is surprisingly varied and hip. Leading Hollywood productions (classic and contemporary) and cartoons are shown, as are westerns, kung-fu flicks, and other foreign productions, particularly those of socially redeeming quality. Movies are often subtitled in Spanish (others are dubbed, to enjoy which you'll need to be fluent in Spanish). Adult films are banned, as are certain politically "offensive" movies (one movie you will not see in Cuba, for instance, is *The Wonderful Country,* starring Robert Mitchum; it was banned because the villains were called the Castro brothers).

In 1959 Cuba established a high-quality cinema institute to produce feature films, documentaries, and newsreels with heavy revolutionary content. All movies in Cuba—their production, importation/exportation, and distribution—are under the control of the **Instituto de Cinematografía** (Film Institute), Calle 23 #1109, Vedado, Havana, tel. (7) 33-4634, fax (7) 33-

3281, and **Cinemateca de Cuba,** Calle 23 #1155, Vedado, Havana, e-mail: cinemateca@icaic.inf.cu, website: www.cinecubano.cu.

Undoubtedly the most respected of Cuba's filmmakers is Tomás Gutiérrez Alea, one of the great masters of Cuban cinema, whose work is part of a general questioning of things—part of the New Latin American Cinema. The Film Institute has granted a relative laxity to directors such as Gutiérrez, whose populist works are of an irreverent picaresque genre. For example, *Memorías del Subdesarrollo* (Memories of Underdevelopment), made in 1968, traced the life of the bourgeoisie disrupted by the Revolution. He followed it with *Death of a Bureaucrat,* a satire on the stifling bureaucracy imposed after the Revolution; and *La última cena* (The Last Supper), which dealt with a member of the upper class confronting the emerging social phenomenon that was about to topple them.

Gutiérrez's finest film, a true classic of modern cinema, is *Fresa y Chocolate* (Strawberries and Chocolate), which when released in 1994 caused near-riots at cinemas in Cuba, for the crush for entry was so great. The provocative but humane comedy tells of the difficulties faced by a macho, homophobic Communist Party member in befriending a homosexual. It portrays the marginalization of intellectuals, the implementation of prejudices, the idealization of "norms" of behavior, the struggles to be different in a rigid revolutionary context. It is less an indictment than a social analysis of the purge against homosexuals that climaxed in the 1970s, when many actors and directors were fired. (The purge swept university classrooms, publishing, and public offices, profoundly affecting Cuba's cultural movement. Extremely talented homosexual artists languished in the anonymity of minor jobs. The Cuban theater, which had attained broad prestige, has never recovered in spite of strong support from the government in recent years.)

Fresa y Chocolat is understood as a universal plea for tolerance. It could not have been produced without official approval, and therefore exemplifies an acknowledgement of how the prejudice against homosexuals harmed Cuba's cultural life.

One of my favorite movies is *Soy Cuba* (I Am Cuba), Soviet director Mikhail Kalatozov's agonizingly serious black-and-white early-'60s Cold War agitprop made when the idealism and the promise of the Cuban Revolution were genuine. A classic of its kind, the movie depicts events of the Cuban Revolution through the eyes of one of Russia's most acclaimed directors and the words of leading Russian poet, Yevgeny Yevtushenko. Intended as the *Battleship Potemkin* of the 1960s, it brims with tales of oppressive reality and kitschy imagery of Americans pawing scantily clad Cuban beauties. The deep-focus cinematography of the Cuban landscape is stunning. However, Cubans apparently despised the film after its 1964 release in Havana. It was booed and swiftly disappeared, resurfacing in 1993 at the San Francisco International Film Festival to a stunned and delighted audience. Cuba never looked so fantastically exotic as through the radical camera techniques and surreal imagery à la Eisenstein. You can obtain copies of *Soy Cuba* from New York-based Milestone Film & Video, 2355 West 96th St. #28C, New York, NY 10025, tel. (800) 603-1104.

The annual **International Festival of New Latin American Cinema,** better known as the Havana Film Festival and held in December, as it has been since 1978, is esteemed throughout the world. The famous all-night parties with top Cuban performers were replaced in 1994 by more serious all-night conversations. But this is *the* event to see and be seen at in Cuba. Fidel is often on hand, schmoozing with Hollywood actors and directors in the lobbies of the Hotel Nacional and Habana Libre. For information, contact Alfredo Guevara, tel. (7) 55-2854, fax (7) 33-3078, in Cuba; or, in New York, the **Center for Cuban Studies,** which organizes tours to the film festival (see the chart, Organizations To Know). Its October 1999 issue of *Cuba Update* focuses on "40 Years of Cuban Film."

For general information on Cuban cinema online, check out www.cinecubano.com.

ON THE ROAD

Outside Cuba, all phone and fax numbers given here need to be preceded by "53-7," the codes for Cuba and Havana respectively, except where area codes otherwise noted in parentheses. Within Cuba, dial "7" before the telephone number when calling from outside Havana.

RECREATION

BICYCLING

The occasional sweat and effort make Cuba's spectacular landscapes and serenity all the more endearing from the seat of a bike saddle. Sure, you'll work for your reward—but you'll never get so close to so much beauty in a car.

Bicycle touring offers a chance to explore the island alongside the Cubans themselves. Since the demise of the Soviet Union severed the gasoline pipeline, the Cubans have taken to bicycling with zeal. The roads are little trafficked, although potholes and stray animals are a consistent problem (a helmet is a wise investment). Repairs are never a problem: thousands of Cubans make a living repairing bicycles and punctures *(poncheras)*. You should, however, bring essential spares.

Airlines generally allow bicycles to be checked free of charge (properly packaged) with one piece of luggage. Otherwise, a small charge may apply. Leave your racing bike at home and bring a mountain bike.

A good resource for cycling information is Cuba's **Federación de Ciclismo,** tel. (7) 68-3776 or 68-3661, in Havana. Competitive cyclers might try the **Club Ciclocaribe Olímpico,** Comité Olímpico Cubano, Calle 13 #601 esq. C, Vedado, Havana, Cuba CP 10400.

Organized Tours
In Cuba: Club de Cicliturismo "Gran Caribe," c/o Transnico, Lonja del Comercio, Oficina 6d, Habana Vieja, tel. (7) 66-9908, e-mail: transmail.insocom.etecsa.com, offers cycling tours. (Also see Bicycling in the Entertainment section of the Havana chapter.)

In the U.S.: Global Exchange offers a "bicycle adventure in Cuba" in association with the Cuban Bicycle Club (US$850, including airfare from Cancún). (See the chart, Organizations to Know under Media Resources.)

Lucie Levine, 15543 Maplewood Dr., Sonoma, CA 95476, tel./fax (707) 996-1731, also offers annual bike trips in association with the Havana Bicycle Club and the Instituto Cubano de Amistad con los Pueblos.

Wings of the World, 1200 William St. #706, Buffalo, NY 14240, tel. (800) 465-8687, fax (416) 486-4001, offers eight-day escorted bicycling tours to Cuba every month. The trip includes a warm-up ride through the colonial streets of Havana, then seven days venturing through eastern Cuba.

In Canada **Active Journeys,** 4891 Dundas St. W, Suite 4, Toronto, ON M9A 1B2, tel. (416) 236-5011 or (800) 597-5594, fax (416) 236-4790, e-mail: journeys@pathcom.com, also offers bicycle tours; as does **MacQueen's Adventures Tours,** 430 Queen St., Charlottestown, Prince Edward Island, Canada CIA 4E8, tel. (902) 368-2453 or (800) 969-2822, fax (902) 894-4547; e-mail: biketour@macqueen.com, www.macqueens.com.

In the U.K. **Hazel Pennington Bike Tours,** P.O. Box 75, Bath, Avon BA1 1BX, England, tel. (01225) 480130, fax (01225) 480132, offers bike tours of Cuba.

BIRDWATCHING

Wherever you travel in Cuba, you're sure to be surrounded by the calls and whistles of dozens of exotic species. Much of the Cuban landscape is relatively open and scrubby, making birds more easy to spot. Your best bet for seeing and learning about different species is to hire a qualified guide. Bring binoculars, although you can also buy them (expensive!) at Óptica Miramar, Av. 7ma y Calle 24, Miramar, Havana, tel. (7) 24-2269, or Óptica Miramar outlets nationwide.

The swampy Zapata Peninsula is one of the best birdwatching arenas in the Caribbean—87% of the island's 380-plus bird species (22 of them endemic) can be seen here—and has an **International Birdwatching Center** at Playa Larga. With luck you might spot the smallest hummingbird in the world (the *pájaro mosca*), the *tocororo* or Cuban trogon, and flamingos, which can also be seen on the northern cays. The cays are also favored nesting sites for scores of migratory species. Isla de la Juventud has Cuba's largest population of parrots. The Sierra del Rosarios and mountains of Ori-

ente are also superb birding sites, especially Baconao Biosphere Reserve and Cuchillas de Toa Biosphere Reserve, created when the endangered ivory-billed woodpecker was discovered there a few years ago.

The state agency **Cubatur,** Calle F #135, Vedado, Havana, tel. (7) 33-4037, fax (7) 33-3529, publishes a birdwatching brochure and recently introduced birding excursions.

Questers, 381 Park Ave. S, New York, NY 10016, tel. (800) 468-8668, fax (212) 251-0890, e-mail: quest1973@aol.com, website: www.questers.com, sometimes offers birding tours in the eastern provinces. **Wings of the World** also offers eight-day birding tours in January, February, and March. In Canada, **MacQueen's Adventures Tours** also offers guided birdwatching programs. (See Bicycling, above for both Wings of the World and MacQueen's.)

ECOTOURISM

Cuba has cliché beaches (i.e., tropical white sand), but it also has bush. Ecotourism has come late to the Caribbean, and not least to Cuba, which depends heavily on resort-based, sunseeking tourists. Despite its vast acreage in national parks and the diversity of its landscapes, Cuba's ecotourism potential remains virtually untapped. Cuba has very few naturalist guides. And so-called "eco-lodges" are mostly merely lodges set in wilderness areas. But a beginning has been made, and eco-reserves, trails, and trained guides are being introduced, such as at the **Moka Eco-Hotel,** at Las Terrazas in Pinar del Río Province. Ecotourism is beginning to rise on the neap of an eco-sensitive tide.

Wings of the World (see Bicycling, above) offers an 11-day ecotrip, "From Mountains to Forest." Departures are offered the third Sunday of each month. The tour visits the Sierra de Nipe mountains, Pinares de Mayarí, Baconao Biosphere Reserve, Zapata, Viñales, and Las Terrazas in Pinar del Río. **Global Exchange** (see the chart, Organizations to Know, in the Media Resources section) offers study tours that provide insights into Cuba's sustainable development projects. The trips focus on sustainable agriculture, traditional medicines, and renewable energy.

In Cuba, **Cubamar Viajes,** Paseo #206 esq. 15, Vedado, Havana, tel. (7) 66-2523, fax (7) 33-3111, e-mail: cubamar@cubamar.mit.cma .net, website: www.cubamar.cubaweb.cu, is developing camping and ecotourism. **Alcona S.A.,** Calle 42 #514 esq. Av. 7ma, Playa, Havana, tel. (7) 24-9227, has a series of weeklong ecotour packages to ecological reserves throughout Cuba. And **EcoTur S.A.,** Av. 5ra #9802 esq. 98, Playa, tel. (7) 24-5195, fax (7) 24-7520, offers a series of eco-oriented tours and excursions.

In Canada, **Magna Outdoors,** 163 Buttermill Ave. #3, Concord, ON F4K 3X8, tel. (905) 761-7330 or (800) 387-3717, fax (905) 761-0929, offers ecotours.

FISHING

So few anglers have fished Cuba during the past three decades that the fish populations are jostling for space. Cuba is a sleeper, with freshwater lakes and lagoons that almost boil with tarpon, bonefish, snook, and bass. And so many game fish run offshore, streaming through the Gulf Stream that Ernest Hemingway called his great blue river, that deep-sea fishing here has been compared to "hunting elk in the suburbs."

Freshwater Fishing
The star of the show is largemouth bass, the freshwater fish that is most attractive to millions of U.S. sport fishermen. Bass fishing is best at Lake Hanabanilla and neighboring Lake Granizo in the Sierra del Escambray; Lake Cuyaguatoje in Pinar del Río; and Lake Zaza in Sancti Spíritus Province. Nearby Lake Legrije, and Lake Redonda, near Morón in Ciego de Avila Province, are other good sites.

Americans fishing home waters apparently catch, on average, only one bass every two days of fishing. "During those same two days, a bass fisherman fishing at Lake Zaza in Cuba might expect to catch 100 bass of incredible quality," claims Dan Snow, a fishing expert who has spent more than a decade fishing in Cuba.

Trout fishing is particularly good at Presa Alacranes, in Villa Clara. The record catch at this freshwater reservoir is 7.1 kilograms.Lake Zaza and Lake La Redonda, which has the highest concentration of trout per square kilometer, are also good.

As for bonefish, few (if any) destinations can compare. Angling maestro Joe Brooks wrote glowingly of fishing Cuba's Isle of Pines (today's Isla de la Juventud) in the 1950s, when he and his angling pals, bonefish experts all, landed 31 bones on their best day. In 1995, an inexperienced angler named Oddvar Sessions landed 26 bonefish at Zapata—before 3:30 p.m. and in off-season! Light-tackle enthusiasts will also find shallow-water bonefish and tarpon in abundance off Cayo Largo, and in the Járdines de la Reina archipelago south of Ciego de Ávila Province. Maspotón, a dedicated hunting and fishing resort on the south shore of Pinar del Río, is also a popular spot to catch tarpon, as are Laguna del Tesoro and the brackish coastal lagoons of Zapata Peninsula. These "silver rockets" can reach up to 75 kg. You're sure to have your hands full: no other fish jumps, leaps, twists, and turns like the tarpon. When you tire of wrestling these snappy fighters, you can take on snook—another worthy opponent.

The best months for bass fishing are the colder months, when the temperature drops to an average of 25°C. Tarpon and snook are caught year-round.

You should take your own rods, reels, and tackle.

Cubatur and **Horizontes** publish brochures on fishing in Cuba and can arrange licenses and fishing guides (compulsory), included in the price of your fishing package.

Dan Snow publishes **CubaNews,** P.O. Box 5484, Kingwood, TX 77325, tel. (713) 358-2262, a monthly newsletter on fishing; subscription $50 per year.

Deep-Sea Fishing
You'll discover far more fish than fishhooks off the coast of Cuba, where snagging the *really* big one comes easy. Hardly a season goes by without some IGFA record being broken. Every year, the big run of marlin begins in May, when they swim against the Gulf Stream current close to the Cuban shore. In places, the stream begins only a quarter mile offshore with the depth sounder reading 1,000 feet; another quarter mile and the bottom plummets another 5,000 feet.

There is much to learn about tactics in fighting big fish, and no fishermen was ever so knowledgeable as Ernest Hemingway, who returned to Cuba year after year and reputedly became the first sportsman to fish marlin with rod and reel in Cuban waters. Unfortunately in this Cuba of food shortages, the Cubans aren't yet into tag-and-release, preferring to let you sauté the trophy (for a cut of the steak), but be sure to do the cooking yourself, as your skipper, like most Cubans, is sure to prefer his fish cooked until it resembles a sole (I'm talking shoes).

Fishing expeditions are offered from Marina Hemingway, Playas del Este, Varadero, and other marinas along the north coast. Other good spots are the Los Canarreos Archipelago (which includes Isla de la Juventud and Cayo Largo).

Spearfish such as the dorado, marlin, and striped tuna bite best on beetles. The barracuda, however, is so rapacious it will "even go for a shoestring." Not so the coronado, the grouper, or the *macabí,* which are more cautious eaters. Barracuda run year-round. The best months for spearfish are May-August.

Puertosol Marinas, Calle 1ra #3001, Miramar, Havana, tel. (7) 24-5923, fax (7) 24-5928, offers sport fishing excursions from most of its 18 marinas islandwide. Typical four-hour light-tackle excursions *(pesa a fondo)* cost US$15-30 per person; four-hour deep-sea excursions cost US$150-250 for up to four passengers. Likewise, **Clubnaútica,** Av. 5ta y Calle 248, Miramar, Havana, tel. (7) 24-1689, fax (7) 24-6653, e-mail: clubnau@comermh .cha.cyt.cu, offers excursions from Marina Hemingway, Varadero, Cayo Largo, and Marina Tarará. Its four-hour "Fishing the Hemingway Route" package from Havana's Marina Hemingway costs US$360 for four passengers, including lunch and drinks.

Fishing Tournaments

Cuba hosts several sport fishing tournaments. The big three competitions are based in Havana's Marina Hemingway. **The Currican Tournament** is held the first or second week of April, when the surface species take to Hemingway's "great blue river." **The Ernest Hemingway International Marlin Tournament** is the granddaddy of tournaments. It's held each May or June and offers trophies for the biggest marlin

and the highest score. The Ernest Hemingway Cup may well be the world's most sought-after fishing trophy. **The Blue Marlin Tournament** is held each August or September. For information, contact Comodoro José Díaz Escrich at Clubnaútica (see above).

Wings of the World (see Bicycling, above), offers eight-day fishing trips timed to coincide with each of the three tournaments. These trips are fully legal for all U.S. citizens. **Last Frontier Expeditions,** 4823 White Rock Circle, Suite H, Boulder, CO 80301, tel. (303) 530-9275, fax (303) 530-9275, e-mail: CopaBob@aol.com, also offers trips to the Ernest Hemingway tournament.

GOLF

Cuba is investing in its future as a golfing destination. The **Havana Golf Club,** Carretera de Vento, Km. 8, Capdevila Havana, tel. (7) 44-4836 or 44-8227, is a nine-hole course, but an additional nine holes is expected to open in 2000. See the Havana chapter for details. Varadero's new Canadian-designed 18-hole championship course has international standard facilities. Annual golf tournaments are hosted at the Havana Golf Club and at Varadero.

Two 18-hole championship courses are planned for Jibacoa, and another near Artemisa, both in Havana Province, with an 18-hole course in Havana city, plus other courses in Cayo Coco, Cayo Santa Lucia, and Santiago de Cuba.

Wings of the World (see Bicycling, above) and **Last Frontier Expeditions** (see the Fishing section, above) offer golf tours.

HIKING

Cuba has the potential to be a hiker's paradise. For now, organized hiking is relatively undeveloped. There is only a handful of trails developed specifically for hiking. Notable exceptions are the trails in Parque Nacional Pico Turquino in the Sierra Maestra, though at press time the park was closed to visitors. You can also head for the foothills of the Sierra del Rosarios, and Sierra Maestra and Cuchillas de Toa in Oriente, where trails lace the mountains. Pinares de Mayarí (in Holguín Province), El Saltón (in Santiago

Golf is becoming a popular tourist attraction.

Province), and Moka Hotel (in Pinar del Río) are all eco-resorts with hiking trails.

Don't forget to carry plenty of water and a shade hat. And you should stock up on snacks before setting out. You may be able to buy local produce from farmers, who'll generously offer whatever they have out of the goodness of their hearts. Common courtesy dictates that you should pay for hospitality. Camping wild is frowned on by authorities.

SAILING

The Cuban coastline extends 5,746 km, or 3,102 nautical miles, of which 2,400 km are along the 10-fathom line. The **northeast** coast is indented with deep, flask-shaped bays with few marina facilities. The **central north** coast is a maze of coral cays and islets with sheltered coves, with the resort of Varadero to the west; much of the water is too shallow for boating. West of Havana the **coast of Pinar del Río** is more easily navigated, with a few pocket bays and cays dispersed off the coast (but only one marina). The **south coast** has a handful of meager marinas, plus the attraction of scores of cays, most notably Cayo Largo (a good base for forays to or from the Cayman Islands). Along the entire **southeast coast,** surf pounds the base of dramatic steep mountains; there are tiny harbors evenly spaced.

For cruising, you'll need to register your boat upon arrival and receive a cruising permit called a *Permiso Especial de Navegación* (US$50 or more, depending on the length of your boat). You'll need an official clearance—a *despacho*— to depart for your next, and each and every, stop. Authorities will usually ask for a planned itinerary, but hold to your guns and insist on flexibility to cruise at random toward your final destination. A *Permiso de Salida* will be issued listing your final destination and possible stops en route. Simon Charles, in his *Cruising Guide to Cuba,* reports that the Ministry of the Interior (MINREX) has never denied or modified his requests; he recommends noting on the *permiso* any plans to scuba dive or anchor offshore at any of Cuba's zillion cays. Be patient! Official proceedings are always courteous but time consuming.

Puertosol Marinas de Cuba (see above) operates 18 marinas and dive centers, including 11 new "full-service" marinas currently being developed around the island. However, at press time only a few were up to international par. Some are very basic. All marinas offer freshwater, 110-volt electrical hook-ups, plus diesel and gasoline. Berthing fees range from US$0.25-0.45 a foot per night.

See the Getting There section in this chapter for information on sailing *to* Cuba. See regional chapters for information on sailing excursions.

Warning: Beware fishermen's nets, especially in the Gulf of Batabanó.

The famous **U.S.-Havana Regatta,** which was held every March from 1930 to 1959, was revived in 1994. In 1999, 250 boats took part in the race from Tampa, Florida, to Marina Hemingway, in Havana. The International Nautical Club of Havana hosts the annual race, whose date and start point varies year by year. Since Cuba foots the bill for docking and other fees, U.S. participants are not in violation of U.S. law. For information on future regattas, contact the Sarasota Sailing Squadron, tel. (941) 388-2355, or **Clubnaútica** (see the Fishing section, above) at Marina Hemingway.

Yacht Charters

Clubnaútica has facilities in Holguín, Varadero, Cayo Largo, and Marina Tarará. Its low season weekly charter rates range from about US$2,100 for an Elan 43 to about US$4,690 for an Oceanis 500 or similar. It also has catamarans for charter, as well as powerboats, such as Zuiderzee 30s (US$2,660). A deposit of US$2,000 or US$3,500 is required, depending on size of boat. Skippers cost US$65 a day plus meals. A hostess is US$50 extra. Bedding and cleaning service are provided. Diving equipment can be rented additionally. Deposits (35% on signing) can be paid by Euro-traveler's check, credit card, or cash. Rates increase as much as 60% in peak season (mid-December through mid-January).

Puertosol Marinas de Cuba (see the Fishing section, above) also rents yachts at most of its 18 marinas islandwide. Typical rates begin at about US$1,540 per week for small vessels in low season.

A French company, **Stardust Marine,** tel. (0535) 4-8320, fax (0535) 4-8321, e-mail: star2have@ip.etecsa.cu, VHF16; or 2 rue d'Athénes, 75009 Paris, tel. (01) 55-07-15-26, fax (01) 55-07-15-22, offers charter yachts for cruising the Archipíelago de las Canarreos. It's based at Cayo Largo. (See Cayo Largo, in the Isla de la Juventud chapter for details.)

SCUBA DIVING

Cuba is a diver's paradise. There are dozens of Spanish galleons and even U-boats sunk off the south coast. Many of the sites, particularly to the south, are unexplored. The best diving is on the south side, although the north coast has some splendid sites, including the 40-km-long reef off Santa Lucía, with countless cays and islets and wrecks. Visibility ranges from 15 to 35 meters. Water temperatures average 27° to 29° C.

The traditional critters of the Caribbean abound: barracuda, rays, sharks, tarpon, and turtles. The star-studded cast also includes angels, bigeyes, butterflies, damsels, drums, gobies, groupers, grunts, jacks, parrot fish, snappers, triggerfish, and wrasses, all of which seem perfectly content to ignore the human presence. Dozens of morays peer out from beneath rocky ledges.

Spearfishing is strictly controlled. Spearguns and gigs are *not* allowed through customs.

Cuba has developed four principal dive areas: the **Archipiélago de los Colorados,** on Cuba's extreme northwest shore; the **Sabana and Camagüey archipelagos,** two extended islet clusters centrally located on the northern coastline; **Járdines de la Reina,** a group of coralline limestone cays on the southeast coast; and the **Isla de la Juventud.** Many sites are also being explored near **Cayo Largo.** The so-called **"Blue Circuit"** east of Havana also has prime sites. And the waters off the tip of **Cabo de Corrientes,** at the westernmost point of Cuba, offer fantastic diving with dozens of sites accessible from the **María la Gorda International Diving Center.** Several dedicated dive boats have been introduced; you can even dive from Fidel Castro's protocol ship, the *Coral Negro,* a live-aboard which takes 20 passengers and is fully equipped.

At least 30 beaches have scuba facilities, and there are 11 decompression chambers (including three mobile chambers), with more planned (in Havana, the chamber is at the Luís Díaz Military Soto Hospital, Habana del Este, tel. 7-97-4251).

Many large beachside hotels offer diving programs and certification courses. Many also have modestly equipped dive shops. Cuban dive masters are all trained by internationally recognized organizations and are highly skilled. And the standard of equipment is good. Nonetheless, it's a good idea to bring your own equipment (leave tanks and weight belts at home, as all scuba diving centers have steel 12- or 15-liter tanks). If you need to replace O-rings, batteries, straps, etc., most supplies are available. Tank fittings and equipment in Cuba are both European and North American.

TURNING OUT CHAMPIONS

Tiny Cuba is one of the top five sports powers in the world, excelling in baseball, volleyball, boxing, and track and field. Cuba is by far the strongest Olympic power in Latin America, and took eighth place at the 1996 Olympic Games in Atlanta with nine gold medals (in 1992 it placed fifth in Barcelona). At the 1999 Pan-American Games in Canada it came second only to the U.S., beating the rest of the continent and reaping 69 gold medals.

Cuba's international success is credited to its splendid educational system. When the Revolution triumphed, sports became a priority alongside land reform, education, and health care. In 1964 the Castro government opened a network of sports schools—Escuelas de Iniciación Deportiva (EIDE)—as part of the primary and secondary education system, with the job of preparing young talent for sports achievement. There are 15 EIDE schools throughout Cuba. The island also has 76 sports academies and an athletic "finishing" school in Havana (the Escuela Superior de Perfeccionamiento Atlético).

In 1971, the Cuban government formed the National Institute for Sports, Physical Education, and Recreation. The state invested huge sums in bringing sports to the Cuban people. Sports training is incorporated into every school curriculum and many adult education programs. School Games are held islandwide every year. These mini-Olympics help Cuba identify talent to be selected for specialized coaching (for example, María Colón Rueñes was identified as a potential javelin champion when she was only seven years old; she went on to win the gold medal at the Moscow Olympics). Many of Cuba's sports greats have passed through these schools—track and field stars such as world-record-holding high jumper Javier Sotomayor, world-record sprinters Leroy Burrel and Ana Fidelia Quirot, and volleyball legends such as Jel Despaigne and Mireya Luís.

Little Cuba has always punched above its weight, and never more so than in the world of boxing: Cuba is a heavyweight and as of 1999 held 23 Olympic titles, 45 senior world titles, 42 junior world titles, and 25 world cups.

In August 1999, Castro announced an ambitious bid to host the Olympic Games in 2008, saying it was merited by the island's athletic record. However, Cuba's reputation was tarnished the following month at the Pan-American Games in Winnipeg, Canada, when Sotomayor and three Cuban gold medal winners were disqualified for drug use (Castro blamed the CIA), and in February 2000, Sotomayor and five other Cuban athletes were dropped from a meet in Greece for failing a cocaine test.

Amateurs or Professionals?
Sports figures are considered workers and "part of the society's productive efforts." As such, sports stars are paid a salary on a par with other workers, although most national team members also receive special perks, such as access to new cars.

Most Cuban sports stars are genuinely motivated by the love of accomplishment, representing the Revolution's model of a "new man." Alberto Juantorena, the only person to win Olympic 400- and 800-meter golds, demonstrates the unselfish attitude and fierce loyalty to his beleaguered island so typical of Cuba's athletes. Like dozens of Cuban superstars, he has turned down offers to earn big money abroad. However, scores of athletic stars have turned their backs on the island, including 11 athletes and a coach who defected during the 1999 Pan-American Games.

Cuba has a Sports Hall of Fame, in the **Sala Polivalente Ramón Font** sports hall on Avenida Independencia, Vedado, Havana, tel. (7) 81-4296.

For general information on Cuban sports online, check out www.cubasports.com.

Publicitur publishes a 60-page booklet, *The Cuban Caribbean: Scuba-Diving Guide,* by Feliberto Garrié Fajardo. However, serious divers should consult *Diving and Snorkeling Guide to Cuba,* by Diana Williams (Lonely Planet, 1999), which provides detailed accounts of major dive sites. Cubanacán and Marlin Marinas jointly publish a *Scuba Cuba* brochure with a section on Havana.

Organized Tours
In North America, **Scubacan International,** 1365 Yonge St. #208, Toronto, ON M4T 2P7, tel. (888) 799-CUBA, fax (416) 927-1257, e-mail: info@scubacan.com, website: www.scubacan.com, offers "fully-hosted" trips for U.S. travelers. **Wings of the World** (see Bicycling, above) offers weeklong diving packages to the Isle of Youth. And **Scuba in Cuba** 416 W. San Ysidro Blvd. #L, PMB-815, San Ysidro, CA 92173-2443,

tel. (310) 842-4148 (U.S. answering machine), or Av. Quintana Roo, Suite TIJ-1173, Zona Centro, Tijuana, Mexico 22000, tel. (066) 865298, e-mail: scuba@cubatravel.com.mx, website: www.cubatravel.com/mx/scuba, offers scuba packages in conjunction with the Caribbean Diving Center and Puertosol.

In the U.K., **Aquatours,** Milboa Lodge, Portsmouth Rd., Thames Ditton, Surrey KT7 0ESl, tel. (0181) 398-0505, fax (0181) 398-0570, e-mail: arnie@aquatours.com, website: www.aquatours.com, has scuba tours to Cuba. **Regal Holidays,** 22 High St., Sutton, Ely, Cambs. CB6 2RB, tel. (0353) 778096, fax (0353) 777897, e-mail: andy@regal-diving.co.com, website: www .regal-diving.co.uk, offers dive packages to the Isla de la Juventud and María la Gorda. And **Scuba en Cuba,** 7 Maybank Gdns., Pinner, Mddx. HA5 2JW, tel. (01895) 624100, fax (01895) 624377, e-mail: Diana_W_scubaenc@compuserve.com, website: www.scuba-en-cuba.com, has packages and tailor-made tours to sites throughout Cuba.

SPORTS

Cuba is a world superstar in sports and athletics—out of all proportion to its diminutive size. Virtually every conceivable sport and recreation are available. Rough basketball courts are everywhere, and most towns have a baseball stadium, gymnasium, and athletic facilities. Boxing is a passion for Cubans, and almost every town has a boxing gym and even open-air bouts. A few upscale hotels have gyms, but you'll also find at least one public gym in every town. Most facilities are basic by North American standards.

The Cuban calendar is replete with national and international sporting events, from fencing, tennis, and wrestling to badminton, sport fishing, and even motorcycle races and car rallies. The Ministry of Tourism is even said to be preparing a US$10 million, two-year, road repair project for Havana's Malecón seaside highway that will, when completed, result in a Monte Carlo-type of Formula One car race.

For a complete list of sporting events, contact the **Palacio de Convenciones,** Calle 146 e/ 11 y 13, Playa, tel. (7) 22-6011, fax (7) 21-9496, e-mail: palco@palco.get.cma.net, which publishes a *Schedule of International Events.*

Cubadeportes, Calle 20 #710, Miramar, Havana, tel. (7) 24-0945 or 24-1133, fax (7) 24-1914, manages Cuban sports and access to them for foreigners. For sporting events, call Cubadeportes at tel. (7) 24-7230.

Organized Tours

U.S.Tour Companies: Coaches, trainers, and sports enthusiasts can learn the secrets of Cuba's amateur sports success on an eight-day study tour offered by **Wings of the World** (see Bicycling, above). Basketball, volleyball, baseball, and boxing are all featured, including visits to the Sports Medicine Institute, the national baseball training center in Cienfuegos, plus visits to various national sports schools, where training sessions and formal matches are held.

Last Frontier Expeditions (see the Fishing section, above) offers a trip to the **Ernest Hemingway International Sports Classic** (Clásico Internacional Hemingway), a 10K race through Habana Vieja that the company helped initiate in 1995. The race occurs each May and is part of National Sports Week, which includes baseball, basketball, and volleyball, symposia on sports, and visits to sports-medicine clinics.

In Canada, the **Eleggua Project,** 7171 Torbram Rd., Suite 51, Mississauga, ONT L4T 3WA, tel. (800) 818-8840, fax (905) 678-1421, e-mail: cancuba@pathcom.com, website: www.pathcom.com/~cancuba, represents agencies and institutions of the Cuban sports institutions and provides travel services, including training and coaching sessions with Cuban teams.

ACCOMMODATIONS

The Institute of Physical Planning has developed a master plan that suggests Cuba can attain more than 150,000 hotel rooms; it planned to have 34,400 rooms in service by the year 2000, up from 23,467 in January 1996. The vast majority of hotels are concentrated in the major tourism zones. Outside these areas, hotels tend to be of poor quality, though usually not below tolerable levels (in the boondocks, you will have minimal choice).

Cuban hotels are graded by the conventional star system, although the rating is rather generous. Prior to 1987, virtually all hotel construction was for the use of Cubans. Most such hotels rate as one- or two-star on the international scale and are usually dreary post-Stalinist properties described as having "all the plaintiveness of an Olympic facility two decades after the games have ended." However, Cuba now boasts many world-class hotels, with more coming online every month.

Most cities have at least one or two older hotels (usually basic, with faded charm) around the central park, and a larger, concrete Bauhaus-era hotel on the outskirts. Following the Revolution, the Soviets infected the entire island with their architectural blight, melancholic enough to dampen even the most optimistic traveler's spirits. (You wonder if the architects have ever visited the sites; faceless factotums in Havana have, for example, ordered frosted glass for windows in rooms that would otherwise offer staggering views.) Many of these dowdy structures have been given a facelift, with potted plants, fresh paint, and new furnishings. Others, however, retain lumpy beds and dour utility furniture, despite the remake. The cash-strapped government continues to upgrade its hotels.

Hotels built in recent years reflect standards necessary to attract a foreign clientele and are up to Western standards in most regards. Niche hotels have begun to appear, including five-star deluxe properties in Havana and the main beach resorts. International hotel companies have made inroads in joint management ventures with the Cuban hotel groups. Jamaica's SuperClubs, for example, manages several deluxe hotels island-

wide. Even Club Med is in Cuba, having opened a 600-room luxury resort in Varadero in late 1996.

Many of the new upscale hotels have state-of-the-art energy-management and security systems, plus a panoply of services commensurate with first-rate hotels elsewhere in the world. Some have online access. That said, even the more upscale hotels are not entirely free of Cuban quirks.

In older hotels, rooms are generally small by North American standards. Carpeting is rare; cool, tiled floors are the norm. Lighting tends to be subdued (usually because the wattage is low). But virtually every hotel room has air-conditioning. Many use both 220 volt and 110 volt outlets (usually marked), often in the same room, so check before plugging any electrical appliances, or you could blow a fuse. Most hotels have both a "regular" restaurant (usually with buffet service) and a specialty restaurant. A swimming pool is usual, most often with a bar. Most hotels also supply towels and soap, but only top-line hotels usually provide shampoo and toiletries. Bring your own sink plug and face cloth for less expensive hotels.

Fawlty Towers?
Except for upscale options, Cuba's hotel foibles conjure up déjà vu for viewers of *Fawlty Towers*, the BBC's hilarious sitcom. Most hotels have a few petty annoyances. For example, after a hot, sticky day you return to your room to find no hot water—a plight for which you're supposed to get 10% off your bill. No running water at all? Twenty percent off. Ah! The water is running—but, alas, there's no plug. In theory, you're entitled to a well-defined refund for each such contingency. A sorry mattress is worth a 10% discount according to the State Prices Commission.

The number of faults is usually in inverse proportion to price. At properties that still await renovation, you'll find gurgling pipes, no toilet seat (quite likely), no bath plugs (virtually guaranteed), sunken mattresses (guaranteed). Be prepared for cold showers. You'll soon get used to it and may even come to look forward to a refreshingly cool shower. Even hot water may only be tepid—and available at certain times of day. Shower units are often powered by electric heater elements, which you switch on for the duration of your shower. Beware! It's easy to give yourself a shock from any metal objects nearby.

Though many of the staff are mustard keen, far too many hotels have abysmal service (Castro agreed: "Cubans are the most hospitable, friendly, and attentive people in the world. But as soon as you put a waiter's uniform on them, they become terrible.") Sometimes the opposite is true. Chambermaids, for example, often rearrange your belongings until you can no longer find them—which may be the whole point (I've "lost" several items of clothing this way).

Cuba is aggressively addressing the deficiencies and has set up hotel management training schools run by Austrians—world leaders in the hospitality industry. However, hotel management still has a very long way to go, and there never seems to be a manager on site when you need one.

It's enough to make you wonder if Basil Fawlty is running the show.

PRICES

Hotels in this book are classified as: **Budget** (less than US$35), **Inexpensive** (US$35-60), **Moderate** (US$60-85), **Expensive** (US$85-110),

Very Expensive (US$110-150), and **Luxury** (US$150 and above).

Prices at many hotels vary for low and high season. Usually low season is May-June and Sept.-Nov., and high season is Dec.-April and June-Aug. Peak-season rates (Christmas and New Year) sell at a premium. However, this varies. Some hotels have four rates according to peak high season and low low season. Usually single rooms cost about 20% less than double rooms. Cuba imposes no room tax or service charge to guests' bills (this may change, however).

To keep costs down, consider buying a charter package tour with airfare and hotel included (tour operators usually buy hotel rooms in bulk and pass the saving on to you). Also consider a villa (usually well furnished and an excellent bargain when sharing with other people) or, my recommendation, a *casa particular*—a private room.

It pays to book through a travel agent such as Cubatravel, tel. (310) 842-4148 (answering machine), e-mail: info@cubatravel.com.mx, website: www.cubatravel.com.mx, in Mexico (066) 865298, or any of Cubatour's or Havanatur's international representatives, since Cuban hotels offer discounts as much as 50% to wholesalers. Canadians and Europeans can keep costs down by buying a charter package tour with airfare and hotel included. They represent tremendous bargains, although standards vary widely. If you book your hotels from abroad, you'll be issued hotel vouchers that you exchange upon arrival in

Hotel El Castillo, Baracoa

Cuba for a coupon (usually through the Cubatur representative at the airport), or present at your hotel.

Oh, and American Airlines' gives 500 "Advantage Miles" if you stay in a Sol Meliá property—even in Cuba.

WHAT TYPE OF ACCOMMODATION

Camping

Cuba is not geared for camping, and tent sites are virtually nonexistent. That said, Cuba is replete with *campismos,* basic holiday camps built for Cubans, but with cabins not tents. By international standards, facilities are basic, but the previously dour sites are being gradually upgraded for foreign tourists. At press time they still received relatively few clients. Most sites are operated by **Cubamar Viajes,** Paseo 206, Vedado, Havana, tel. (7) 66-2523, fax (7) 33-3111, e-mail: cubamar@cubamar.mit.cma.net. You can also book through *campismo popular* offices *(carpetas)* in most towns.

You will require permission to camp "wild." Don't expect to find fresh water or food available at most places. Pack in *everything* you think you'll need.

Peso Hotels

Peso hotels cater to Cubans and are extremely cheap—usually the equivalent of less than US$1 for Cubans, who pay in pesos. Although a few are quite attractive, most are dour by Western standards. The worst are little more than mildewed nests of foul bedclothes.

You cannot book peso hotels through any state tourism organization; you will have to do this face-to-face in Cuba. Every town has a *carpeta* (central booking office) where hotel reservations are made. They'll make bookings by telephone for a small charge. Usually you're told the hotel is full. If the receptionist warms to you, a room can magically be found. But don't count on it, as things have tightened up in recent years, and very few peso hotels now take foreign guests.

Aparthotels, Villas, and *Protocolos*

Aparthotels are also a bargain, offering rooms with kitchens or kitchenettes (pots and pans and cutlery are provided), and sometimes small suites furnished with sofas and tables and chairs. One- or two-bedroom units are available. Aparthotels are particularly economical for families. Most are characterless: it's all a matter of taste. Many are linked to regular hotels, giving you access to broader facilities.

Some places feature fully staffed villas, including *protocolos*—special houses reserved for foreign dignitaries. Most of the *protocolos* are in splendid mansions in the Cubanacán region of Havana.

All-Inclusive Resorts

Cuba has recently cottoned to the runaway success of the all-inclusive concept elsewhere in the Caribbean. Many beach resorts are now run as all-inclusives: cash-free, self-contained properties where your room rate theoretically includes all meals and beverages, entertainment, and water sports at no additional fee. Standards vary. Properties managed by international name-brand hotel chains are preferred to the purely Cuban-run affairs. Grupo Sol Meliá's dozen or so beach resort properties are all well managed and offer great value, as do the Jamaican-run SuperClubs resorts, and beaches run by Jamaica's Sandals chain.

Check the fine print. Some all-inclusives charge for water sports.

Casas Particulares

My favorite way to go is to seek out a *casa particular* (literally, private house), a room in a family home. Since the triumph of the Revolution, the Urban Reform Law explicitly prohibited the rent of housing, despite which *casas particulares* began to blossom in the mid-1990s, when a ban was placed on Cuban guests in hotel rooms (foreign guests turned to private room rentals to consummate their unions). In 1996 the law was reformed: Cubans are now permitted to rent out up to two rooms. A new tax code was also introduced, regulating *casas particulares* to ensure that those renting out their houses "fulfill their social duty" by paying taxes (US$100 monthly per room in a non-tourist zone, and US$250 in a tourist zone (regardless of whether rooms are rented or not), plus 10% of annual earnings, and US$10 monthly for any street advertising. Your host now has to record your pass-

Accommodations range from humble to sumptuous, as at Hostal Casa Muñoz, Trinidad.

port number and, ostensibly, the particulars of any of your guests. Slightest infractions are dealt with harshly: a US$1,500 fine is standard.

Casas particulares have sprouted like mushrooms on a damp log, and you'll have no difficulty finding a place. Look for a tent-like blue *Arrendador Inscripto* symbol on the front doors of *casas particulares* (a red symbol indicates that the house accepts only Cubans). As of April 2000, however, no new applications for private room rentals were to be considered by the government. Conditions vary remarkably, so it's worth checking out several places before settling on your lodging. Be wary of hustlers, who often try to steer you away from a specific *casa* you might be seeking by claiming, for example, that it is full or that the family has moved or died.

The going rate in Havana is US$20-40, and US$10-20 outside Havana, often with breakfast and dinner included. Some families are willing to vacate their entire homes on a moment's notice. And your host can normally arrange for a *custodio* (guardian) for your car (the going rate is US$2 for the night).

The situation is fluid, however. For example, at press time it was illegal to rent rooms in Varadero.

Casa particular owners must report the name and passport details of every guest within 24 hours of the latter's arrival, so MININT is always abreast of foreigners' movements. If you have a computer, be cautious about sending e-mails, as all traffic is checked, and secret police have been known to make house calls to check up on guests traveling with computers.

CUBAN HOTEL GROUPS

Six Cuban hotel entities compete for business (operating in cooperative management agreements with foreign hotel groups). The corporations all publish directories available through Cuban tourist offices abroad. You may need to double-check telephone numbers—they change frequently.

Cubanacán, Av. 7ma #6624 e/ 66 y 70, Miramar, tel. (7) 24-6316, fax (7) 24-6313, e-mail: dirmark@reserva.cha.cyt.cu, website: www.cubanacan.cu, has about 12 hotels in Havana, from modest to luxury. Cubanacán also has about 60 islandwide hotels (representing 80% of all five-star hotels in Cuba).

Gaviota, Edificio La Marina, Av. del Puerto y Justiz, Habana Vieja, tel. (7) 66-6765, fax (7) 33-2780, e-mail: gaviota@nwgaviot.gav.cma.net, website: www.gaviota.cubaweb.cu, (a branch of the Cuban military!) owns three three-star hotels in Havana plus more than a dozen elsewhere.

Gran Caribe, Av. 7ma #4210 e/ 42 y 44, Miramar, tel. (7) 24-0575, fax (7) 24-0565, e-mail: armando@grancaribe.gca.cma.net, website: www.grancaribe.cubaweb.cu, operates about 35 hotels (mostly in Havana and mostly top-end, including the landmark Hotel Nacional).

Horizontes, Calle 23 #156 e/ N y O, Vedado, tel. (7) 33-4042, fax (7) 33-3161, e-mail: crh@horizontes.ht.cma.net, website: www.horizontes.cu, has nine hotels in Havana plus dozens islandwide, in the two- and three-star categories.

Hoteles Habaguanex, Calle Oficios #110 e/ Lamparilla y Amargura, Habana Vieja, tel. (7) 33-8693, fax (7) 33-8697, website: www.granma.cu/1999/publicidad/habaguanex, operates five historic hotels in Habana Vieja, with more being added.

Islazul, Malecón y G, Vedado, Havana, tel. (7) 57-1286, fax (7) 33-3458, e-mail: comazul@teleda.get.cma.net, website: www.islazul.cubaweb.cu, operates hotels primarily for national tourism (Cubans pay in pesos), but also accepts tourists (who pay in dollar equivalent). Islazul hotels offer some of the best bargains in Cuba. The company has been restoring its hotels to compete with other chains that charge two or three times more.

Local municipalities operate an additional 6,500 rooms. Most of the latter are very basic (many are also rapidly deteriorating).

RESERVATIONS

Officially, it's absolutely necessary to book at least two nights' accommodation prior to arrival, which you can do abroad through accredited tour agencies. Since 1997 Cuba immigration officials have been more assiduous in ensuring that arriving visitors have pre-booked rooms. However, in early 2000 this was not the case.

If you're asked, you can give a private address if you have reservations at a *casa particular*. (Tourist visas state that tourists must obtain permission from immigration authorities if wishing to stay at other than a hotel or "authorized accommodation," which includes *casas particulares*. Some immigration officials don't seem clear about this and attempt to force tourists to book a hotel room regardless. If this happens to you, point out that registered *casa particulares* pay taxes and are legal; stick to your guns.) Otherwise, expect to be directed to the tourist information booth to secure a hotel reservation.

Finding a hotel room without a reservation is hardly ever a problem. Still, many of the best hotels book solid at Christmas, New Year, and during Carnaval in Havana in mid-February and in Santiago de Cuba in July. It's wise to secure accommodation in advance. Many hotels in the provinces won't give a room without a reservation, even if they have one available, because they're tied in to the bureaucracy of central reservation agencies in Havana. It's potluck. You should pay in advance for all nights you intend staying; otherwise you might be asked to check out to make room for someone who just made a reservation. Crazy!

Don't rely on mail to make reservations—it could take several months to confirm. Call direct, send a fax or e-mail, or have a Cuban state tour agency or a tour operator abroad make your reservation. Normally a deposit will not be required. *But don't expect your reservation to be honored!*

Outside Cuba, phone and fax numbers need to be preceded by 53-7, the codes for Cuba and Havana respectively.

SECURITY

Many hotel lobbies now have MININT security agents in dark suits with microphones tucked in their ears. They were posted following the spate of bombs planted in Havana's hotels in 1997 and serve to prevent a repeat performance, but also do double duty to keep Cubans from slipping upstairs with foreign guests. Unfortunately they lend a prison-like atmosphere and are not above bothering hotel guests and their legitimate friends.

Theft is an issue, especially in budget hotels. Most tourist hotels have safe deposit boxes at the front desk or in individual guest rooms. Be sure to use one for any valuables, especially your passport, camera, and money. Clothing is often stolen. Consider locking *all* your items in your suitcase each time you leave your room. Before accepting a room, ensure that the door is secure and that your room can't be entered by someone climbing in through the window. *Always* lock your door.

GUEST CARDS

Upon registering, you'll be issued a *tarjeta de huesped* (guest card) at each hotel, identifying you as a hotel guest. Depending on your hotel, the card may have to be presented when ordering and signing for meals and drinks, when changing money, and often when entering the elevator to your room.

CUBAN GUESTS

The presence of young women on the arms of foreign men (and Cuban men with foreign women) became a fixture of most hotel lobbies in the early 1990s. In 1995 the government began to clear them out, and there are now strictures against young Cuban women (and men) entering hotel lobbies alone. At press time no Cubans were permitted in guest rooms in tourist hotels. *Period.* A kind of tourist apartheid is in force. Even Cubans with pockets full of *fula* (dollars) can't register in the better hotels, officially under the pretext of protecting tourists. In the event that you find a lover, you can now rest assured that the hotel staff will turn your partner away unless you can prove that he or she is your spouse.

Both Cubans and foreigners are allowed to stay at hotels run by Islazul, where the clientele is *primarily* Cuban; foreigners and Cubans generally come and go and interact without restriction. However, the policy is in flux as the government finesses its handling of *jiniteras* (goodtime girls) and *jiniteros* (illicit marketeers) in hotels, and at press time even Islazul hotels did not permit Cubans to enter the rooms of foreign hotel guests (staff are often posted in elevators to prevent such occurrences).

Fortunately, in most provinces it is still legal to have a Cuban as your guest if you're staying in a *casa particular.* Your Cuban partner must be 18 years of age. And your host is supposed to record his or her name and other pertinent details for inspection by authorities. Ostensibly he or she should be your steady *novio* or *novia* (boyfriend or girlfriend), not a *jinitera.* Your host may insist on this, but most hosts (being Cuban and thereby sexually liberal) will not blink an eye as to your sexual dalliances, as Cuban couples often rent rooms by the hour in someone else's home to consummate their love unions.

At press time, each province had a different approach to foreign guests having *chicas* (Cuban girls) in their rooms. Havana, Cienfuegos, and Santiago de Cuba, for example, were relatively permissive, but Sancti Spíritus and Camagüey had a firm no-go policy and MININT officials actively policed for transgressions.

Of course, the government is sensitive to the needs of every man and woman and has created state-run, 24-hour "love hotels," also known as *posadas.*

Posadas
Posadas exist to provide relief for the large numbers of Cubans who live together with aunts, uncles, parents, and even grandparents, along with the children, often in conditions in which rooms are subdivided by curtains. At these hotels, couples can enjoy an intimate moment together, although conditions are often dour. Most couples are married, sometimes to each other. (In most, conditions are modest to say the least. More upscale, congenial facilities have gardens, a/c, and music in the rooms, such as El Monumental—12 km west of Havana—which is favored by government officials). Rooms are usually rented for three hours, typically for five pesos (US$0.25), for which the state thoughtfully provides a bottle of rum by the bed.

Foreigners are often turned away, but many Cubans illegally rent rooms to lovers who need a place of convenience (US$15 was the going rate).

FOOD AND DRINK

A standing joke in Cuba is: What are the three biggest failures of the Revolution? Breakfast, lunch, and dinner. Cuba may be a culinary adventure but not one that will usually have you, like Oliver, asking for more. You're not going to Cuba to put on weight.

Before the Revolution, Cuba boasted many world-class restaurants. Alas, after 1959 many of the middle-and upper-class clientele fled Cuba along with the restaurateurs and chefs, taking their custom, knowledge, and entrepreneurship with them. In 1967 all remaining restaurants were taken over by the state. It was downhill from there. The blasé socialist attitude to dining, tough economic times, and general inefficiencies of the system are reflected in boring menus, poor standards, and lack of availability (don't be fooled by extensive menus, as many items will probably not be available). State-run restaurants come in grades one to seven, one being the best. Why does every menu in Cuba look the same? Because bureaucrats dictate things, not the chef or the restaurant manager.

There are usually plenty of local eateries in towns, but even here it can be a wearying experience trying to find somewhere with palatable food. Havana is an exception to the culinary rule, with wide options. In rural areas (ironically), eating can be a real challenge. Shortages are everywhere (a refrigerator in Cuba is called a *coco* because it has a hard shell on the outside and nothing but water inside). You may even feel twinges of capitalist guilt when asking a waitress for milk to go with your coffee.

Rationing has become a permanent fixture of the past three decades. The collapse of the Soviet Union made a bad situation much worse, since in 1989 an estimated 40% of rationed items were supplied by the former Soviet bloc. (Depending on your viewpoint, Cuba's rationing system proves either that the government is inept or that it is just. To critics it is "the most conspicuous indicator of a prolonged, systemic economic failure." Others point out that prior to the "Special Period," rationing had guaranteed the entire population sufficient proteins, carbohydrates, minerals, and vitamins to maintain good health. The Cuban government likes to blame the U.S. embargo, but after a sustained tour of the island you're likely to conclude that without the profit motive to oil the wheels, the inefficient communist system is mostly to blame.) Whatever, the paucity is a constant source of exasperation for foreigners traveling independently. Fortunately, everywhere you eat you're sure to be serenaded by troubadours to add cheer to even the dreariest meal.

Throughout the island you'll pass mile after mile of rich cultivated land growing produce, but when you arrive at your hotel you'll often find that the only vegetables on the menu are canned. After a while you'll be sick to death of fried chicken and *bocaditos* (ham sandwich) and vegetables either overcooked or from a can. Bite the bullet! As a tourist, you're privileged to get the best that's available. When touring, you should plan ahead. Stock up on sodas, biscuits, and other packaged snacks at dollars-only stores (there's always one at Cupet gas stations) before setting out each day.

Take a sweater—many restaurants have the a/c cranked up to freezing. And be relaxed about dining; expect service to take much longer than you may be used to. Sometimes the service is swift and friendly, sometimes protracted and surly. You can wait 10 minutes for a waiter, another half hour for the meal to arrive, 15 minutes for the bill, and another 10 for the change. Plan up to two hours for dinner in a state-run restaurant.

Most places serve *criollo* (traditional Cuban) food, but only a few restaurants truly excel in native Cuban cuisine. The more expensive places tend toward "continental" cuisine, at which even fewer excel. International cuisines are poorly represented. No restaurants come anywhere near close to winning awards. Even in Chinese, Italian, and other "international" restaurants, Cuban chefs have difficulty breaking out of their straitjackets. Things are slowly beginning to stir, but Formatur, which runs culinary training schools, continues to graduate chefs who haven't the foggiest clue of how to translate international influences into reality. The creative nouvelle dishes that now appear on some menus are sure to disappoint.

In the better restaurants waiters expect to be tipped 10%, even where a service charge (now the norm in expensive restaurants) has been added to your bill. Check your bill carefully, however—bread is usually delivered to your table but is often charged to your bill extra even if you didn't order it—one of several dastardly tricks frequently used to separate you from your dollars. Another is the *consumo mínimo* policy: a minimum-purchase charge applied in an increasing number of establishments (usually bars) and rife for abuse.

Eating in Cuba doesn't present the dire health problems associated with many other destinations in Latin America, but you still need to use common sense precautions (see the Health section, this chapter).

Breakfasts

Few places serve breakfast other than hotel restaurants, most of which serve variations on the same dreary buffets (*mesa sueca*—Swiss table): ham, cheese, boiled eggs, and an array of fruits and unappetizing cakes and biscuits. The variety is usually limited by Western standards, and presentation often leaves much to be desired. Fruits—mangoes, papayas, pineapples—are most often frozen overnight and thawed (barely) for breakfast, thereby destroying the pulp and flavor. Top-class hotels usually do a bit better. Nonguests are usually welcome; prices range US$4-12.

In more remote areas, you'd be wise to have a large breakfast—finding food during the day may be a withering chore. Don't leave breakfast (normally served 7-10 a.m.) until the last thing or you'll arrive to find only crumbs (I'm not kidding).

Hotel room rates rarely include breakfast, although members of tour groups usually have breakfasts (and most dinners) included in the cost of their tour. Refunds are not made for meals not taken.

Many hotels offer an *oferta especial* (special offer) that grants guests a discount up to 25% on buffet meals.

Peso Eateries

Most restaurants admit both Cubans and foreigners, and charge the former in pesos and the latter in dollars (the price in pesos is usually converted one-to-one into dollars, which translates into vastly overpriced meals for tourists without any commensurate preference in quality of food or service). However, you can still find basic *criollo* dishes at pesos-only restaurants that aim at Cubans. Food availability tends to be hit and miss (usually only one or two items are available) and the cuisine undistinguished at best. In some you may be refused service or asked to pay in dollars.

State-run *merenderos* (lunch counters)—the staple for local dining—and private roadside snack stalls display their meager offerings in glass cases. A signboard indicates what's available, with items noted on strips that can be removed as particular items sell out. These accept pesos from foreigners and are an incredibly cheap way of appeasing your stomach with snacks if you can stomach the sometimes appallingly dirty conditions (if squeamish, don't take a peek inside the kitchen).

You can still find plenty of *guarapos* throughout Havana producing fresh, sweet, empowering juice from crushed sugarcane.

Hotel Food

The majority of hotels have amateurs in the kitchens. With few exceptions, food quality seems to decline with distance from Havana. Away from tourist centers, hotels are often "oases in a consumer desert," and even the local populace flock to feast on meals of dubious quality. Fortunately, the situation is beginning to improve as Cuba focuses on training its culinary staff and the worst food deficiencies of the Special Period are being overcome.

In general, hotel fare leans heavily towards pork, eggs, canned vegetables, and baked goods. Smorgasbord (*mesa sueca*—Swiss table) buffets are popular. The variety is usually limited by Western standards, and presentation often leaves much to be desired. *À la carte* menus are offered in specialty restaurants in top-class hotels (meals here are rarely included in package prices). Many hotels have *Noches Cubana* (Cuban nights), featuring typical Cuban specialties.

In general, the best meals—and well worth a splurge—are served in the deluxe hotels.

Paladares

As everywhere in Cuba, the way to go is to eat at *paladares*—private restaurants whose owners often meld entrepreneurship with a sense for experimentation and culinary flair (the word means "palate," and comes from the name of the restaurant of the character Raquel, a poor woman who makes her fortune cooking, in a popular Brazilian TV soap opera, *Vale Todo*). Here you can fill up for US$5-15, usually with bloat-inducing meals. Usually the price includes a salad and dessert and, often, beer.

The owners put great energy into their enterprises, many of which are open 24 hours. Most serve both Cubans (often for pesos) and foreigners (always for dollars) and display an inventiveness in preparing good food and service that Fidel himself has often complained about with regard to State restaurants. However, Castro says that the *paladares* are "enriching" their owners and has refused to dine at them. (*Paladares* were legalized in September 1994 to help resolve the food crisis, but have always been fettered by onerous taxation and restrictive regulations.) *Paladares* are not allowed to sell shrimp or lobster (a state monopoly). Nevertheless most do, so ask: it's easy enough to find a huge lobster meal for US$10, including beer or soft drink. Restaurant owners are also allowed to serve only up to 12 people at one seating. Though relatives can assist, the owners cannot hire salaried workers.

At press time the crippling monthly licensing fee of U$100 had put many *paladares* out of business, as intended. As they come and go, it's often difficult to monitor their sanitary standards. Feel free to check out the kitchen (often a stomach-churning experience) before choosing to dine.

Many are open 24 hours; some are closed or operate at restricted hours during the summer off-season. Your Cuban friends will be able to recommend their favorite *paladares*. Look for Christmas lights (the unofficial advertisement) hanging outside.

Fast Food

Thank goodness there are as yet no McDonald's or KFCs in Cuba. However, in 1995 a chain of KFC-style, dollars-only fried-chicken joints called **El Rápido,** began to open, including a drive-in just off the Malecón with waitresses on roller skates (they proved too unstable and were short-lived). At most, the standard of fare makes KFC look like gourmet cuisine.

The McDonald's equivalent is **Burgui,** serving up uninspired burgers. It, too, has outlets throughout the major cities, open 24 hours. Hamburgers are popular, cheap, and usually not much worse than North American fast-food burgers (though some, to be sure, *are* much worse, such as those sold at roadside stands for one peso. "Are you *sure* that's meat?").

Self-Catering

Shopping for food for the average Cuban is a dismal activity. There are scant groceries, no roadside 7-Elevens. And the state-run groceries, called *puestos,* where fresh produce—often of questionable quality—is sold, can make Westerners cringe. Cuba's best fruits and vegetables are exported for hard currency or turned into juices. Meat is equally scarce. And count yourself lucky, for example, to find anywhere serving fresh milk. As a result, most Cubans are forced to rely on the black market.

Since 1994, when free trading was legalized for farmers, Cuba has sprouted **produce markets** or farmers' markets *(mercados agropecuarios),* where fruits, vegetables, and meats are sold privately. Every town has at least one, though it will often be hidden away off the beaten track. In 1998 the government opened its own fruit and vegetable markets to undercut the farmers. Fresh fish is harder to come by. The government-run **Pescaderias Especiales** sell fish and other seafoods. Each municipality has one.

You can purchase Western goods at dollars-only stores, open to foreigners and Cubans alike and stocked with packaged and canned goods from all over the world. Havana even has a few supermarkets, though these are rare outside the capital. Cupet gas stations usually have dollars-only stores attached, where Western snack goods are sold.

Most towns have bakeries serving sweet and tasty confections and Cuba's infamously horrible bread (most often served as buns or twisted rolls), which Maurice Halperin found, whether toasted or not, "formed a sticky mass difficult to dislodge from between cheek and gum."

(Cuba's reputation for lousy bread pre-dates the Revolution. "Why can't the Cubans make decent bread?" Che Guevara is reported to have asked. Of course, Cubans eat rice, not bread, as they have since the early 19th century, when it became the staple food of black slaves; only well-to-do Cubans ate bread.) To be fair, some hotels and restaurants serve excellent bread, and the situation has improved following the arrival of French expertise to run a new bakery chain (France also supplies most of the wheat).

Cafés and Snack Bars

Major cities have plenty of splendid sidewalk cafés, although most of the prerevolutionary *cafeterías*—coffee stands—that used to make coffee on every corner have vanished, as have most of the former tea shops *(Casas de Té or Casas de Infusiones)*. Most cafés are really uninspired snack bars-cum-restaurants; there are few in the purist Parisian tradition, and as of yet no U.S.-style coffee shops.

Rumbos S.A. has been opening roadside snack bars at strategic points all over Havana; of a uniform design with green-shade awnings, they serve a standard menu of *bocaditos, papa fritas,* and *criollo* staples such as fried chicken.

Health

Eating in Cuba doesn't present the health problems associated with many other destinations in Latin America. However, in February 1999 at least 14 people died in Matanzas after eating from an unlicensed street stall, so *caveat emptor!*

And the water? Well, Christopher Columbus noted the quality of Cuba's water in 1494 on his second voyage to the New World: "The water is so cold and of such goodness and so sweet that no better could be found in the world." But that was then. Today the state of urban plumbing is questionable, and tap water is best avoided. Bottled mineral water is widely available and usually delivered to your table automatically if you ask for water (usually US$1). Usually this is imported French or Italian water, or Ciego Montero Agua Mineral, produced by Cubagua and which comes from Manatial de Ciego Montero, in Palmira in Cienfuegos Province (it "stimulates the digestion and facilitates the urinary elimination of uric acid," says the label.)

WHAT TO EAT

Cuban Dishes

Ninety times out of a hundred, your options are *criollo, criollo,* or *criollo.* Cuban food is mostly peasant fare, usually lacking in sauces and spices.

Pork *(cerdo)* and chicken *(pollo)* are the two main protein staples, usually served with rice and black beans *(frijoles negros)* and fried banana or plantain *(platanos)*. *Cerdo asado* (succulent roast pork) and *moros y cristianos* (Moors and Christians—rice and black beans) and *arroz congrí* (rice with red beans) are the most popular

*two native products—
rum and oranges*

dishes. *Congrí oriental* is rice and red beans cooked together. *Frijoles negros dormidos* are black beans cooked and allowed to stand till the next day. Another national dish is *ajíaco* (hotchpotch), a stew of meats and vegetables.

By far the most common dish is fried chicken *(pollo frito)* and grilled chicken *(pollo asado)*. Grilled pork chops are also common. Beef is virtually unknown outside the tourist restaurants, where filet mignon and prime rib are often on the menu. Most steaks tend to be far below Western standards—often overcooked and fatty.

Another favorite dish is *conejo,* rabbit (it's commonly on the menu but rarely available; where they get rabbits from I don't know, as I've never seen one in Cuba). Meat finds its way into snacks such as *empanadas de carne,* pies or flat pancakes enclosing meat morsels; *ayacas,* a kind of tamale, corn tortilla filled with meat and spices; *piccadillo,* a snack of spiced beef, onion, tomato; and *bistec de palomilla,* fillet of steak, often cooked as an *empañada.* Crumbled pork rinds find their way into *fufu,* mixed with cooked plantain, a popular dish in Oriente. And ham and cheese, the two most ubiquitous foods, find their way into fish and stuffed inside steaks as *bistec uruguayano.*

Fish had never been a major part of the Cuban diet and has made its way onto the national menu only in recent years. As food shortages increased following the Revolution, Castro himself appealed to Cubans to eat fish; he said he would be seen eating only fish on TV until Cubans understood its nutritional value. Sea bass *(corvina),* swordfish *(filet de emperador),* and *pargo* (red snapper) are the most commonly eaten species. You can find some splendid fish dishes, but all too often Cuban chefs murder your fish steak. Dry, leathery, and zealously overcooked is the norm, with lots of bones for good measure.

Lobster is readily available virtually everywhere. State restaurants charge US$10-25 for lobster dishes, but you can enjoy a whole-lobster meal with trimmings and beer for US$10 at most *paladares,* although legally they're not supposed to serve shrimp or lobster.

International Influences

Cuba's culinary landscape has suffered for lack of international connections during four decades.

(Let's face it: what could the Soviets offer?) Foreign restaurateurs fled the island en masse after the Revolution, taking their know-how and entrepreneurship with them.

A few *chino* descendants still operate Chinese restaurants, however. You'll find one in almost every town, making do as best they can in the food shortages. With luck you'll also come across Spanish restaurants serving seafood *paella* (Las Terrazas in Cojímar and Hostal Valencia in Havana are two). And Italian restaurants are numerous, although their menus are mostly limited to bland spaghetti bolognese and pizzas. Street stalls sell tasty pizzas (usually five pesos per slice), though most Cuban pizzas are dismal by North American standards—usually with a bland base covered with a thin layer of tomato paste and a smattering of cheese and ham (English people will recognize it). Likewise, hamburgers are cheap but usually considerably worse than North American fast-food burgers.

Fortunately, several French and South American chefs have enlivened the Havana scene in recent years with cuisine approaching international standards (La Giraldilla and La Torre come to mind). And several deluxe beach resorts now have international chefs.

Vegetables

Cubans consider green vegetables "rabbit food." Fresh vegetables rarely find their way onto menus, other than in salads. Mixed salads *(ensaladas mixta)* usually consist of a plate of lettuce or cucumbers *(pepinos)* and tomatoes (often served green, yet sweet) with oil and vinaigrette dressing. *Palmito,* the succulent heart of palm, is also common as a salad. Often you'll receive canned vegetables. Sometimes you'll receive shredded cabbage *(col),* often alone. Beetroot is also common.

Plantain, a relative of the banana, is the main staple and almost always served fried. Yucca is also popular: it resembles a stringy potato in look, taste, and texture and is prepared and served like a potato in any number of ways. A popular side dish is *boniato* (sweet potato), and other root vegetables such as *malanga,* a bland root crop rich in starch grown by the native Indian population and a staple of rural families before the Revolution.

Vegetables are most often used in soups and stews, such as *ajíaco,* a popular and tasty soup made with yucca, malanga, turnips, and herbs. Another common soup is garbanzo. Beans are the most common vegetable and are used in many dishes.

Fruits

Cuba's rich soils and amicable climate nourish a panoply of fruits. . . at least, they should. Elsewhere in the Caribbean and Latin America, you can't drive around a bend without having someone selling a bunch of ripe bananas or handfuls of papayas, mangoes, or coconuts. Not so in Cuba. Fruits are rare jewels outside hotel restaurant buffets. You'll pass many fields of pineapples, although rarely will you find any available outside hotel restaurants, and the same is true of melons (increasingly, however, Cubans are taking to the sides of roads to hawk fruits). Even oranges and grapefruits, grown widely in Cuba, are about as common as gold nuggets: virtually the entire fruit harvest goes to produce fruit juice.

To buy fruits, head to the local *mercado agropecuario* (farmers' market). In addition to well-known fruits such as papayas, look for such lesser-known types as the furry *mamey colorado,* an oval, chocolate-brown fruit with a custardy texture and taste; the cylindrical, orange-colored *marañon,* the cashew-apple, whose seed grows *outside* the fruit; the oval, coarse-skinned *zapote,* a sweet granular fruit most commonly found in Oriente; and the large, irregular-shaped *guanábana,* whose thick skin is covered with briars (the pulp, however, is sweet and "soupy," with a hint of vanilla). *Canitel* (familiar to travelers to Jamaica as ackee) is also grown, through rarely found.

Count yourself lucky to get your hands on mangoes, whose larger versions are referred to in the feminine gender, *mangas,* because of their shape and size. And be careful with the word *papaya.* Habaneros refer to the papaya fruit as *fruta bomba* because in Cuba, "papaya" is a slang term for vagina.

The most common fruit is the *platano,* a relative of the banana but used as a vegetable in a variety of ways, including as *tostones,* fried green plantains eaten as a snack, much like thick chips or English crisps.

Surprisingly, coconuts are rare in the nation, except in eastern Cuba, around Baracoa, where the juice and meat find their way into the cuisine peculiar to the region (eastern Cuba boasts the nation's only real regional cuisine).

Desserts

Cubans make great desserts, often available for a few centavos at bakeries *(panaderías)* islandwide. Hotel confections tend toward biscuits and sponge cakes (usually rather dry) topped with jam and canned cream. *Flan,* a caramel custard, is also popular (a variant is a delicious pudding called *natilla),* as is marmalade and cheese. Also try *tatianoff,* chocolate cake smothered with cream; *chu,* bite-size puff pastries stuffed with an almost bitter cheesy meringue; and *churrizo,* deep-fried doughnut rings sold at every bakery and streetside stalls, where you can also buy *galletas,* ubiquitous sweet biscuits sold loose.

The best desserts are sold by the French-run **Paín de Paris** chain and sold for dollars. Look under *Tiendas—Alimentos* in the telephone directory for local outlets.

The many coconut-based desserts include *coco quemado* (coconut pudding), *coco rallady y queso* (grated coconut with cheese in syrup), and the *cucurucho,* a regional specialty of Baracoa made of pressed coconut and cocoa.

Of course, the best dessert of all is Cuban **ice cream,** most notably that made by Coppelia. Most cities have a Coppelia outlet. Before the Revolution, Howard Johnson's 28 flavors was the brand of choice. Fidel, however, had promised to outdo the Yanks with 29 flavors, a boast Cuba failed to achieve. Cubans use specific terms for different kinds of scoops. *Helado,* which means "ice cream," also means a single large scoop; two large scoops are called *jimagua;* several small scoops is an *ensalada;* and *sundae* is ice cream served with fruit. Want more? Ask for *adicionál.*

DRINKING

Nonalcoholic Drinks

Water is potable virtually everywhere, although a series of hurricanes in recent years has disrupted and contaminated supplies. Stick to bot-

There are three types of rum: clear, aged three years; golden, aged five years; and añejo, aged seven years and considered the highest quality. The Matusalem on the right is considered the finest añejo rum in Cuba.

tled mineral water, which is widely available. In restaurants it's normal to receive bottled water, usually Ciego Montero Agua Mineral, produced by Cubagua (it comes from Manatial de Ciego Montero, in Palmira in Cienfuegos Province, and "stimulates the digestion and facilitates the urinary elimination of uric acid," says the label.)

Coca-Cola and Pepsi (or their Cuban-made equivalent, Tropicola), Fanta (or Cuban-made Najita), and other soft drinks are readily available at hotels, restaurants, and dollar-stores. *Malta Caracas* is a popular nonalcoholic drink from Venezuela that resembles a dark English stout but tastes like root beer.

Far more thirst quenching and energy giving, however, is *guarapo,* fresh-squeezed sugarcane juice, sold cold at roadside *guaraperías.* Sugar even finds its way into water: *agua dulce,* a popular *campesino's* drink made of boiled water and brown sugar gives one energy for field labor. And look for *prú,* a refreshing soft drink concocted from fruit, herbs, roots, and sugar.

There's no shortage of canned fruit drinks (virtually the entire Cuban fruit crop is pulped for juices), sold for dollars. Occasionally you'll come across small bars selling fresh-squeezed orange juice (usually 20-50 centavos a glass) and *agua natural* (natural water; usually free). Another great way to beat the heat is by downing *batidos,* delicious and refreshing fruit drinks blended with milk and ice, and *refrescos,* chilled fruit juices that you can buy at roadside stalls, usually for 50 centavos or one peso.

Coffee: Cubans take frequent coffee breaks, and no home visit is complete without being offered a *cafecito.* Coffee also ends each meal. Cubans love it thick and strong, like espresso, served black in tiny cups, and heavily sweetened. *Delicious.* Unfortunately the prerevolutionary *cafeterías*—coffee stands—that used to make coffee on every corner have vanished. A few tea shops *(Casas de Té* or *Casas de Infusiones).*

Much Cuban domestic coffee has been adulterated—*café mesclado*—since the Special Period with other roasted products, usually chicory. Stick with Cubita, the export brand sold vacuum-packed.

Café con leche (coffee with milk) is served in tourist restaurants, usually at a ratio of 50:50, with hot milk. Don't confuse this with *Café americano,* which is usually diluted Cuban coffee.

Alcoholic Drinks

Beers: Cuba makes several excellent German-style beers, usually served just a little above freezing (US$0.75 -2, depending on where you drink). One of the best is Hatuey, Cuba's flagship beer. Cristal, Manacas, and Lagarto are lighter. Bucanero is a heavy-bodied lager that comes light or dark. You'll also find regional beers as well as the inexpensive and duller *Clara,* the rough-brewed beer for domestic consumption (typically one peso). Harder-to-find brews include the new Caribbean Ice, and Polar Bear, brewed in Camagüey since 1911.

Before the Special Period, most villages had *cervecerías,* beer dispensaries that were boisterous social centers. In some rural areas you may still find roadside dispensers on wheels where you can buy beer in paper cups for a few centavos.

You'll also find Heineken, and Canadian and Mexican brands for sale in dollar stores and tourist hotel bars. Prices range from US$1-3.

Rum: Cuba's specialty is rum and rum-based cocktails. About one dozen distilleries operate in Cuba today, producing some 60 brands of rum. They vary widely (the worst can taste like paint thinner). Cuban rums resemble Bacardi rums—which is not surprising, since several key rum factories in Cuba were originally owned by the Bacardi family. Each brand generally has three types of rum: clear "white rum," labeled *Carta Blanca,* which is aged three years and costs less than US$5 a bottle; the more asserting "golden rum," labeled *Dorado* or *Carta Oro,* aged five years, and costing about US$6; and *"añejo,"* aged seven years and costing US$10 or more.

The best in all three categories are undoubtedly Havana Club's rums, topped only by Matusalem Añejo Superior, described by a panel of tasting experts as showing "a distinctive Scotch whisky-like character, with peaty and smoky aromas and flavors accented by orange-peel notes dry on the palate and long in the finish." A few limited production rums, such as Ron Santiago 45 Aniversario (US$20) and the 15-year-old Havana Club Gran Reserva (US$80) approach the harmony and finesse of fine Cognacs.

A bottle of quality rum costs US$5-10 at **Tiendas Panamericanos** and hotel stores. In touristy nightclubs, the same bottle can set you back US$20 or more, though you can buy a bottle of rum in local discos for US$3-5. In nontouristy clubs, a shot *(trago)* of rum will cost about US$0.50, and in peso joints 50 *centavos.* Beware bottles of rum sold on the street—it may be bootleg rum.

Golden and aged rums are best drunk straight (although *campesinos* drink *tragos* of overproof *aguardente,* cheap white rum). White rum is ideal for cocktails such as a *piña colada* and, most notably, the *daiquiri* and the *mojito*—both favorites of Ernest Hemingway, who helped launch both drinks to world fame. And recalling the Andrews sisters' song, "Drinking Rum and Coca-Cola," you'll want to try a *cuba libre* on its home turf. Dark rums are also used in cocktails such as the appropriately named *mulata,* with lime and cocoa liqueur.

Other Alcoholic Drinks: Certain regions are known for unique liqueurs, such as *guayabita,* a brandy-like drink made from rum and guava and exclusive to Pinar del Río.

Wine lists have improved in recent years, and imported Chilean and French wines are a relative bargain, though storage is sometimes wanting. Some places even serve Californian wines. You might even try the local *vino,* a sweet and unsophisticated Cuban wine produced in Soroa, Pinar del Río, sold under the "Soroa" label, which I suspect is Spanish wine bottled in Cuba and blended with local grapes. Imported wines aren't cheap. Expect to pay US$4 and upward for a tiny glass, US$15 for a bottle. Sometimes it is watered down!

The Isla de la Juventud makes its own heavy, port-style wines, as does Villa Clara.

Forget hard liquors, which are readily available in touristy bars but usually very expensive. You can buy bottles of your favorite imported tipple at *diplotiendas.*

GETTING THERE

BY AIR

About 40 airlines service Cuba. Charters account for about 90% of arrivals. The vast majority of flights to Cuba arrive in Havana at the José Martí International Airport. Many leading international carriers have regular scheduled service from Europe, Canada, and Central and South America (the U.S. government bans flights between the U.S. and Cuba except Miami-Havana charters for licensed travelers; see the special topid, U.S. Law and Travel to Cuba).

Cuba has a well-developed air transport network, with six international airports: Camagüey (Ignacio Agramonte), Cayo Coco, Havana (José Martí International), Holguín (Frank País Airport), Santiago de Cuba (Antonio Maceo Airport), and Varadero (Juan Gualberto Gómez).

Cuba's national airline is **Cubana de Aviación,** Calle 63 #64, Vedado, Havana, tel. (7) 33-4949, fax (7) 33-4056, e-mail: ecacom@iacc3.get.cma.net, website: www.cubana.cu, which celebrated its 70th anniversary in 1999 and handles 30 percent of all traffic into Cuba from more than two dozen destinations worldwide. Cubana has been upgrading its fleet lately and leases DC-10s and A-320s that serve Europe and Mexico and offer business class and first class *(Clase Tropical)* service. However, the workhorses in the stable remain uncomfortable and poorly maintained Soviet-made aircraft (I've even seen cockroaches on board). Cubana's fares are generally lower than other airlines', but the airline is poorly managed: its attitude toward scheduled departures is cavalier (flight times change frequently, so double-check any published schedules); the airline is notorious for disposing of seats of passengers who arrive after the scheduled check-in time; nonsmoking regulations are rarely enforced; and its safety record is appalling. In 1999 it was named the airline with the worst safety record in the world, with a "fatal incident rate" of 18.2 incidents per million flights (compared to an average of 0.5 per million for U.S. airlines), and that was *before* a Cubana DC-10 crashed in Guatemala *and* a YAK-42 in Venezuela in December 1999. Says one tour operator to Cuba: "The horror stories we hear from clients will make your hair stand on end."

Many airlines operate a summer and winter timetable. Information below is based on winter (high-season) schedules.

Ensure that you make your reservation as early as possible (several months in advance would be ideal), especially during peak season, as flights are often oversold. Always reconfirm your reservation within 72 hours of your departure (reservations are frequently canceled if not reconfirmed, especially during Dec.-Jan. holidays), and arrive at the airport with at least two hours to spare. Avoid reservations that leave little time for connections—baggage transfers and customs and immigration procedures may take more time than planned. Check, too, to see what penalties, if any, are charged for changes to your tickets. Cubana, for example, charges US$80 to change your return date.

I recommend booking online (via internet websites such as Travelocity.com or Expedia.com) or through a travel agent (most do not charge a fee, but instead derive their income from commissions already figured into the airlines' fees). The agent's computer will display most of the options, usually including seat availability and current fares, and they have the responsibility to chase down refunds in the event of overbooking, cancellations, etc.

From the U.S.

At press time, no regular commercial flights were permitted between the U.S. and Cuba, except for certain licensed charters. Nor can any U.S. airline, tour operator, or travel agent make arrangements for flights to Cuba without a license from the Treasury Department.

Nonetheless, thousands of U.S. citizens take advantage of the many scheduled commercial airline services to Cuba from third countries. Getting to Cuba from the U.S. is no more difficult than flying, say, from Buffalo, New York, to Banff, Canada. The most popular routes are through Canada or the Bahamas for East Coast residents, and through Mexico—especially Cancún

CUBANA AIRLINES OFFICES OUTSIDE CUBA

EUROPE

Barcelona: Calle Fontanella 12B, Plaza Cataluña, Barcelona 08010, tel. (03) 318-8833, fax (03) 318-6091

Berlin: Frankfurter Tor 8-A, 10234 Berlin, tel. (030) 589-3409, fax (030) 589-2947; Airport, tel. (030) 678-8185

Brussels: Avenie Louise #272, BTE1, Brussels, tel. (02) 640-2050, fax (02) 640-0810

Cologne: Flughafen Kolh-Bonn Postfach 980151, 51129 Koln, tel. (02203) 402198, fax (02203) 412197

Frankfurt: An der Hauptwache 7, 60313 Frankfurt am Main, tel. (069) 913-0980, fax (069) 913-09840

Las Palmas: Calle Galicia #29, Las Palmas 35007, Gran Canaria, tel. (0928) 272408, fax (0928) 272419

London: 49 Conduit St., London W1R 9FB, tel. (0171) 734-1165, fax (0171) 437-0681

Madrid: Calle Princesa #25, Edificio Exágono, 28008 Madrid, tel. (01) 542-2923, fax (01) 541-6642; Airport, tel. (01) 205-8448

Milano: Via Paolo de Cannobio 2-21122, Milano, tel. (02) 801437, fax (02) 720016

Moscow: Karovit Val 7, Corpus 1, Sección 5, Moscow, tel. (095) 237-1901, fax (095) 237-8391; Airport, tel. (095) 578-7650

Paris: Tour Maine Montparnasse, 33 Avenue de Maine, B.P. 171, 75755 Paris Cedex 15, tel. (01) 45-38-31-12, fax (01) 45-38-31-10; Airport, tel. (01) 48-84-40-60

Rome: Via Barberini 86, 4 Piano, Rome 00187, tel. (06) 474-1104, fax (06) 474-6836

Santiago de Compostela: Doctor Tejeiro #20, Santiago de Compostela, tel. (0981) 581415

CANADA

Montreal: 4 Place Ville Marie #405, Montreal, Quebec H3B 2E7, tel. (514) 871-1222, fax (514) 871-1227

Toronto: Lester B. Pearson Airport, tel./fax (416) 676-4723

CENTRAL AMERICA AND CARIBBEAN

Cancún: Av. Yaxchilan #23, SM-24 M-22 retorno 3, e/ Nit-Cheaven y Tanchacte, Cancún, tel. (098) 860192, fax (098) 877373, Airport tel. (098) 860192

Fort-de-France: 50 Rue Schoelcher 97200, Fort-de-France, Martinique, tel. (596) 605200, fax (596) 603820

Kingston: 22 Trafalgar Road #11, Kingston 10, tel. (876) 978-3410 or 978-3406

Mexico City: Temistocles #246 esq. Homero, Colonia Polanco, C.P. 11550 Deleg. Manuel Hidalgo, Mexico D.F., tel. (05) 255-3776, fax (05) 255-0835; Airport, tel. (05) 571-5368

Nassau: Hotel British Colonial Beach Resort, Room 239, Nassau, tel. (242) 322-3301

Panama: Calle 29 y Av. Justo Arosemena # 4-14, tel. (507) 227-2122 or 27-2291, fax (507) 272-2241

San José: De Canal 7, Carretera á Pavas, San José, tel. (506) 290-5095, fax (506) 290-5101

in the Yucatán Peninsula—for everyone else. From here, Havana is only a hour away and flights leave twice a day (times vary slightly throughout the year). If you fly from Bahamas and are transferring to flights into the U.S., you'll be greeted by U.S. Immigration officers who have an office inside Nassau airport. If you are quizzed whether you've been to Cuba and you are not licensed by OFAC, you may have a problem explaining your trip.

It is *essential* to have completely separate tickets and reservations for your travel into and out of Cuba from any third country: under the terms of the embargo, U.S. citizens showing an airline reservation which includes an onward flight to Cuba must be refused boarding on the flight out of the U.S. However, you can reserve your ticket with a foreign carrier such as Air Jamaica (which serves Cuba from its North American gateways) but you have to pay for the Jamaica-Cuba leg upon arrival in Jamaica. You

Santo Domingo: Av. Tiradente esq. 27 de Febrero, Plaza Merengue, Local 209, Dominican Republic, tel. (809) 227-2040, fax (809) 227-2044; Airport, tel. (809) 549-0345

SOUTH AMERICA

Bogotá: Carrera 14 #7920, Bogotá, tel. (01) 621-0793, fax (01) 621-0785

Buenos Aires: Sarmiento 552 e/ Florida y San Martin, Buenos Aires, tel. (01) 326-5291, fax (01) 326-5294; Airport, tel. (01) 620-0011

Caracas: Av. Rómulo Gallegos con Primera, Edificio Pascal Torre B #133, Palos Grandes, Caracas, tel. (02) 285-3548, fax (02) 285-6313

Guayaquíl: Centro Comercial Las Vitrinas, Local 61, Calle H La Kenedy, Guayaquíl, tel. (04) 390727, fax (04) 289911

Lima: Jiron Tarata #250, Miraflores, Lima 18, tel. (01) 410554, fax (01) 471363

Montevideo: Boulevar Artigas 1147 #504, Montevideo, Uruguay, tel. (02) 481402

Quito: Avenida de los Shyris y 6 de Diciembre, Edificio Torre Nova Oficina 1A, Quito, tel. (02) 227463

Rio de Janeiro: Rua Teofilo Otono 81, CJ 901, CEP 20080, Rio de Janeiro, tel. (021) 233-0960

Santiago de Chile: Calle Fidel Oteiza 1971 #201, Providencia, Santiago de Chile, tel. (02) 274-1819, fax (02) 274-8207

São Paulo: Rua da Consolacao 232, Conjunto 1009, Centro São Paulo, tel. (011) 2144571, fax (011) 255-8660

can search online with ticketing agencies such as Travelocity (www.travelocity.com), although you can't actually purchase a ticket that involves a portion for travel to Cuba through a U.S. online company, even if you're a foreign citizen whose flight won't touch the U.S.

Non-licensed travelers should also refer to the sections on getting to Cuba from Canada, Mexico, and the Caribbean.

Licensed Charters: Licensed charter flights cater to travelers with permission to travel to

and spend money in Cuba (the flights aren't listed, and you are led to the plane as if a spy swap were taking place). Flights operate to Havana from Miami twice weekly (typically US$299 round-trip, US$195 one-way; children under 12, US$175 round-trip, US$115 one-way). Flights from New York's JFK airport depart every Friday at 8:35 p.m., with a return flight scheduled for before dawn every Saturday (the direct flights are flown by Grupo Taca, an alliance of Central American airlines), and cost $629 round-trip. Flights from LAX started in December 1999 every Saturday with a return on Sunday at a cost of around $750 round-trip.

Charter operators are only authorized to carry properly documented passengers as permitted by the U.S. Treasury Dept. Individuals who are hosted by the Cuban government are barred from taking these charter flights and must travel on a non-Cuban carrier from outside the U.S. Flights are authorized monthly, and once authorized they fill up almost immediately. (See special topic, U.S. Law and Travel to Cuba, in the Getting There section.)

The main licensed travel service provider (TSP) is **Marazul Charters,** Tower Plaza Mall, 4100 Park Ave., Weehawken, NJ 07087, tel. (201) 319-3900 or (800) 223-5334, fax (201) 319-9009, and—for Cuban-Americans only, in Miami, tel. (305) 232-8157), e-mail: info@marazultours.com, website: www.marazultours.com—which operates charter flights to Havana from Miami and New York.

Other licensed travel service providers include **Cuba Cultural Travel** 944 Dogwood St., Costa Mesa, CA 92677, tel. (949) 646-1229, e-mail: info@cubaculturaltravel.com, website: www.CubaCulturalTravel.com; U.S.-run **Cubatravel,** Rio Suchiate #10075, Suite 11, Col.Revolución, Zona Rio, Tijuana, Mexico 22000, tel. (066) 865298, in the U.S., tel. (310) 842-4148, e-mail: info@cubatravel.com.mx, website: www.cubatravel.com.mx; **Tico Travel,** 161 East Commercial Blvd., Ft. Lauderdale, FL 33334, tel. (954) 493-5335 or (800) 493-8426, fax (954) 493-8466, e-mail: tico@gate.net, website: www.destinationcuba.com, which makes reservations; **Airline Brokers Company,** tel. (305) 871-1260, fax (305) 447-0965, e-mail: tfre97a@prodigy.com; and **C&T,** P.O. Box 996091, Miami, FL 0351, tel. (305) 876-7660, fax (305)

U.S. LAW AND TRAVEL TO CUBA

*C*ontrary to popular belief, U.S. law does *not* prohibit U.S. citizens from visiting Cuba. However, to visit Cuba legally, you must either spend no money there, or qualify for a license issued by the U.S. Treasury Department in order to buy goods (a meal at a hotel, for example) or services (an airline ticket, tour package, or hotel room). In order to apply, you need a good reason. Except as specifically licensed by the Office of Foreign Assets Control (OFAC), payments in connection with any other travel to Cuba are prohibited, whether travelers go directly or via a third country such as Mexico, Canada, or another Caribbean island.

U.S. citizens and any person in the U.S. is subject to these restrictions, regardless of citizenship. Under these restrictions, spending money relating to Cuban travel is prohibited unless the traveler is licensed. The regulations change frequently and are open to interpretation by the understaffed office (interpretation often shifts with the political breeze). In May 1999 the Clinton administration announced new regulations that expanded travel opportunities. U.S. universities and nongovernmental organizations may now apply for two-year travel permits to Cuba that will allow any of its members to travel to Cuba without requiring individual certification.

To determine if you or your organization qualify for a **general license** (which does not require prior government authorization) or a **specific license** (which does require prior government authorization), contact the Licensing Division, Office of Foreign Asset Control (OFAC), U.S. Department of the Treasury, 1500 Pennsylvania Ave. NW, Washington, D.C. 20200, tel. (202) 622-2520 or (202) 622-2480, fax (202) 622-1657, website: www.ustreas.gov/ofac/ofactxt.

Request the *Cuban Assets Control Regulations.* Alternately, check with the U.S.-Cuba Trade and Economic Council, 30 Rockefeller Plaza New York, NY 10112-0002, tel. (212) 246-1444, fax (212) 246-2345, www.cubatrade.org, which stays abreast of latest regulations. Relevant information is contained within the Code of Federal Regulations (31 CFR Part 515).

The Office of Cuban Affairs (OCA), Department of State, Washington, D.C. 20520, tel. (202) 647-9273, fax (202) 736-4476, website: www.state.gov, establishes the policies by which the OFAC interprets the regulations by which laws are enforced.

The following regulations applied at press time (the regulations change frequently, so it is worth checking with OFAC):

General Licenses

The following categories of travelers are permitted to spend money for Cuban travel without the need to obtain special permission from OFAC, nor are they required to inform OFAC in advance of their visit to Cuba. Such individuals must sign a Travel Affidavit for travel on any of the direct flights from the U.S. declaring that they fall within one of the following categories.

Official Government Travelers: U.S. and foreign government officials, including representatives of international organizations of which the United States is a member, who are traveling on official business.

Journalists: Individuals who are regularly (full-time) employed by a news gathering organization (television network, television station, television production company, radio station, newspaper, newsletter, magazine, video production company, etc.). Travelers are advised to have company identification (with photograph), business card, and/or a letter from the company confirming full-time employment.

Persons who are visiting close relatives: People with close relatives in Cuba may visit them in circumstances of humanitarian need. This authorization is valid only once every 12 months.

Amateur or semi-professional athletes traveling to participate in athletic competition held under the auspices of an international sports federation.

Full-time professionals whose travel transactions are directly related to non-commercial, academic research and whose research will comprise a full work schedule in Cuba; plus full-time professionals whose travel transactions are directly related to attendance at professional meetings or conferences that do not promote tourism or other commercial activity involving Cuba or the production of biotechnological products.

University and secondary school students may travel to Cuba as long as their university or school has applied for a specific license, which is good for two years and covers any student or academic employee of that institution.

"Fully-Hosted" Travelers: Individuals subject to U.S. law traveling on a "fully hosted" basis can travel without a specific license so long as they do not spend any funds of their own while in Cuba. This includes travel on a prepaid, all-inclusive tour package with companies such as Wings of the World (see Organized Tours in the Transportation chapter). Funds used to make payments for hotels, meals, ground transportation, sundries, etc., must originate from: a) an entity within Cuba; b) an entity within another country or; c) an individual within another country. The use of indirect transfers is not permitted. A "fully-hosted" traveler may not travel on any direct flight between the U.S. and Cuba, and may pay for transportation only if aboard a non-Cuban carrier such as Mexicana, Air Jamaica, Lacsa, Iberia, etc. Travelers whose expenses are covered by a person not subject to U.S. jurisdiction may not bring back any Cuban origin goods, except for informational materials (books, magazines, posters, etc.) and an unlimited amount of artwork. Gifts from Cuba nationals may be brought into the U.S., but the gift must remain with the U.S. Customs Service at the point of entry; the traveler subject must then request a license from the OFAC to take possession of the gift.

("Fully hosted" travelers are subject to increased scrutiny. As of March 1998, there is no longer a presumption of innocence; there is now a presumption of guilt. A letter from an individual or entity not subject to U.S. law—or a letter from a U.S.-based law firm—confirming that the individual was "fully hosted" will not be accepted as "proof" that a visit was "fully hosted." "Fully-hosted" travelers are now required to produce receipts for all daily expenses within Cuba which demonstrate that all of the expenses were paid by an individual or entity not subject to U.S. law, and to submit a signed letter to that effect.)

Special Licenses

A specific license requires written government approval. Applicants should write a letter to OFAC stating the date of the planned visit and the length of stay; the specific purpose(s) of the visit; plus the name(s), title(s), and background(s) of the traveler. OFAC has been understaffed and is notoriously slow: allow two or three months. Special licenses are issued by OFAC on a case-by-case basis authorizing travel transactions by persons in connection with the following travel categories:

Humanitarian Travel: Persons traveling to Cuba to visit close relatives in cases involving hardship more than once in a 12 month period; persons traveling to

Cuba to accompany licensed humanitarian donations (other than gift parcels); or persons traveling in connection with activities of recognized human rights organizations investigating human rights violations.

Commercial "Opportunists": Individuals wishing to identify commercial opportunities in the fields of artwork, communications, entertainment, informational materials, medical equipment, medical instruments, medical supplies, medicated products, medicines, pharmaceuticals, and telecommunications; register trademarks and patents; organize and participate in trade shows; authorize consumer credit cards to be valid for use; and provide travel services and provide air transportation services.

Freelance Journalists: Freelance journalists need a special license, but it is good for multiple trips to Cuba. Many travelers have successfully been approved as "freelancers," particularly if traveling on arranged programs such as offered by the Center for Cuban Studies. If you want to go it alone and try the "journalist" or "researcher" angle, write to OFAC, which requires a written statement of why your proposed trip falls within the rules for permissible travel.

Others: Persons attending public performances, clinics, workshops, and exhibitions.

What You May Spend

Licensed travelers are authorized to spend up to US$185 per day. Exemptions to the US$185 per day authorization can be requested from OFAC. "Fully hosted" travelers are not subject to spending limits while within the Republic of Cuba. And journalists may spend more than $185 daily (the amount is unspecified) to cover expenses incurred in the reporting of a story.

Money may be spent only for purchases of items directly related to travel such as hotel accommodations, meals, and goods personally used by the traveler in Cuba, or for the purchase of $185 worth of Cuban merchandise to be brought into the United States as accompanied baggage. Purchases of services unrelated to travel, such as nonemergency medical services, are prohibited. The purchase of publications and other informational material is not restricted in any way.

Licensed travelers may return from Cuba with up to US$100 worth of Cuban products (such as cigars, rum, tee-shirts, crafts, etc.) for their personal use. For cigars, the U.S. Customs Service permits up to 100 cigars, but the total value must not exceed US$100. For example, if a traveler returns with 100

continues on next page

U.S. LAW AND TRAVEL TO CUBA

(continued)

cigars which cost US$1 each, the traveler would not be permitted to bring any other Cuban products (such as rum). Travelers should retain a receipt showing the amount paid for all Republic of Cuba-origin products.

Qualified Travel Service Providers

U.S. law states: "U.S. travel service providers, such as travel agents and tour operators, who handle travel arrangements to, from, or within Cuba must hold special authorizations from the U.S. Treasury Department to engage in such activities."

OFAC has licensed the following companies as authorized Travel Service Providers (TSPs) legally entitled to make commercial travel arrangements to Cuba: U.S.-run **Cuba Cultural Travel,** 944 Dogwood St., Costa Mesa, CA 92677, tel. (949) 646-1229, e-mail: info@cubaculturaltravel.com, website: www.CubaCulturalTravel.com; **Cubatravel,** Rio Suchiate #10075, Suite 11, Col.Revolucion, Zona Rio, Tijuana, Mexico 22000, tel. (066) 865298, in the US, tel. (310) 842-4148, e-mail: info@cubatravel.com.mx, website: www.cubatravel.com.mx; **Marazul Charters,** Tower Plaza Mall, 4100 Park Ave., Weehawken, NJ 07087, tel. (201) 319-9670 or (800) 223-5334, fax (201) 319-9009, e-mail: bguild@marazultours.com, website: www.marazultours.com; and **Tico Travel,** 161 East Commercial Blvd., Ft Lauderdale, FL 33334, tel. (954) 493-5335 or (800) 493-8426, fax (954) 493-8466, e-mail: tico@gate.net, website: www.destinationcuba.com.

TSPs can only make reservations for licensed travelers. You must obtain approval before proceeding with a reservation. Qualified travelers should begin preparations two months in advance of their travel date. After you have determined which license you need you must acquire a visa from the Cuban government (see Immigration and Customs, in the section on Information and Services, in the On The Road chapter).

However, referring to other travel agencies and tour operators (i.e., non-TSPs), "It is possible to provide travel services to U.S. persons legally able to travel to Cuba for family visits, professional research, or news gathering," says Michael Krinsky, a partner in the law firm of Rabinowitz, Boudin, Standard, Krinsky and Lieberman, which represents the Cuban government in the United States.

U.S. travel agencies can also provide services to third countries, from where a traveler makes his or her own arrangements for travel to and within Cuba. They may also be able to provide services, such as travel arrangements to Jamaica, where a component includes an excursion to Cuba. Treasury Department regulations do not "show a clear penalty against travel agents who book travel this way." *Travel agents should double-check the regulations,* however, with the U.S. Department of the Treasury, or with Krinsky, 740 Broadway, New York, NY 10003, tel. (212) 254-1111, fax (212) 674-4614, e-mail: mkrinsky@igc.apc.org.

Visas for Licensed Travelers

All licensed travelers to Cuba must have a visa from the Cuban government prior to reserving your flight. Tico Travel and Marazul (see above) can assist you in acquiring your visa. (Tico Travel charges US$120 for the visa and preparing the documents.) There are two different forms: one for those born in Cuba and one for those born outside Cuba; allow thirty days for processing.

Cubans and Cuban-Americans: Anyone who permanently left Cuba after 31 December 1970 must have a valid Cuban passport (people born in Cuba who left Cuba permanently before that date don't need a Cuban passport). If you don't have a Cuban passport and you left Cuba after 31 December 1970, you must contact the Cuban Interests Section in Washington D.C., tel. (202) 797-8609, to get the re-

871-1260. (The Miami-based commuter carrier Gulfstream International Airlines also operates one flight a week to Havana exclusively for staff of the U.S. Interests Section.)

By Private Aircraft: Owners of private aircraft, including air ambulance services, who intend to land in Cuba must obtain a temporary export permit for the aircraft from the U.S. Department of Commerce prior to departure.

You must contact the **Instituto de Aeronáutica Civil de Cuba,** Calle 23 #64 e/ Infanta y P, Vedado, tel. (7) 33-4445, fax (7) 33-3082, at least 10 days prior to arrival in Cuba and at least 48 hours before an overflight.

From Canada

Over 200,000 Canadians visited Cuba in 1999, and there are plenty of flights between Canada

quired paperwork. Cubans who left Cuba permanently prior to 1959 can acquire a slightly less expensive 359 Visa, acquired directly with the Cuban Interests Section.

Illegal Travel
More than 160,000 United States citizens traveled to Cuba in 1999. The majority did so legally (92 percent were Cuban-Americans with relatives there) while the rest slipped in through third countries and spent freely without a license. The U.S. government has recently sought to tighten control of unsanctioned travel. Since May 1998 persons subject to U.S. jurisdiction who travel to Cuba without a license bear a "presumption of guilt" and may be required to show documentation that all expenses incurred were paid by a third party not subject to U.S. law. Since 1994 OFAC has fined about 400 people. Trading with Cuba illegally is good for up to a US$55,000 fine, but most fines have been US$1,500 to US$5,000.

Freedom to Travel
In 1984, the Supreme Court agreed that U.S. citizens have a constitutional right to travel but that the right had to yield to national security concerns. Restrictions on travel to Cuba (actually currency controls, constituting a virtual ban on travel) were upheld within the bailiwick of executive (presidential) privilege. In September 1995 the **Freedom to Travel Campaign,** 2017 Mission St. #303, San Francisco, CA 94110, tel. (415) 255-7296, fax (415) 255-7498, e-mail: info@globalexchange.org, initiated a lawsuit challenging the constitutionality of the restrictions as a violation of First Amendment rights. The U.S. Circuit Court of Appeals, however, upheld the 1984 Supreme Court ruling. In 1996 Congress passed a resolution reaffirming the right of U.S. citizens to travel for educational, cultural, and humanitarian purposes.

and Cuba (although most fly to Cuba's beach resorts rather than Havana; the bulk of Canadian charters fly to Varadero, a three-and-a-half-hour flight from Toronto). Toronto-based charter tour operators are the driving force of the trade. You might find cheap airfares—about C$400 round-trip—through **Travel Deals,** tel. (416) 236-0125 or **Wholesale Travel Group,** tel. (416) 366-1000. **Canadian Universities Travel Service,** Travel Cuts, 187 College St., Toronto, ON M5T 1P7, tel. (416) 979-2406, website: www.travelcuts.com, sells discount airfares to students and has 25 offices throughout Canada.

Scheduled Flights: Cubana, (see Cubana International Offices chart for contact information) has three scheduled departures weekly using an A-320 from Montreal and Toronto to Havana (from about C$500 in low season and C$700 in high season). You can usually get rates lower than Cubana's published fares by booking with Canadian tour agencies that block large numbers of seats. (American Airlines gives 1200 "Advantage Miles" if you fly with **Canadian Airlines** to Cuba, which happens to use Cubana as a regional partner to operate the flight.) Cubana also flies from Toronto to Cienfuegos and Varadero.

Air Canada, tel. (800) 869-9000, website: www.aircanada.ca, flies three times weekly from Toronto to Havana, with connecting service to San José, Costa Rica. **Lacsa,** tel. (800) 225-2272, offers a similar service.

You can also fly with **Air Jamaica,** 4141 Yonge St. #104, Willowdale, ON MAP 2A8, tel. (416) 229-6024 or (800) 526-5585, fax (416) 229-6003, website: www.airjamaica.com, which offers connecting flights to Havana through Montego Bay, Jamaica.

Charter Flights: Air Canada Vacations, tel. (514) 422-5788, a division of Air Canada, has twice-weekly flights to Havana. Seven-night packages range from C$499 to C$1,099. **Air Transat,** tel. (514) 987-1616, fax (514) 987-9750 and **Canada 3000,** tel. (416) 674-2661, also offer charters to Havana, plus Varadero, Cienfuegos, and Santiago de Cuba. Tickets on both charter airlines are issued only via travel agencies.

Numerous air-hotel packages are offered by companies that utilize the above charter services. Such companies advertise in the travel sections of leading Canadian newspapers. For example, **Regent Holidays,** 6205 Airport Rd., Bldg. A, Suite 200, Mississauga, ON L4V 1E1, tel. (905) 673-3343 or (800) 263-8776, e-mail: general@regentholidays.com, website: www.regentholidays.com, offers charter flights and air/hotel packages using Air Transat, flying to Havana every Sunday.

From Europe

Direct air service to Cuba is available from most Western European counties. The cheapest fares are usually on direct flights, but you can also find cheap fares via Caribbean destinations or via Miami, from where you can take a flight to the Bahamas and then to Cuba (see below). American Airlines, British Airways, Continental, United Airlines, and Virgin Atlantic fly from London to Miami. Note, however, that if flying aboard a U.S. carrier, you must have your ticket for the Cuban portion issued on a separate ticket stock, plus you must make your reservation for the Bahamas-Cuba leg separately.

The cheapest *scheduled* fares are APEX (Advance-Purchase Excursion), which you must buy at least 21 days before departure and which limit your visit. From Europe you must stay a minimum of 14 days and return within 180 days. Penalties usually apply for any changes after you buy your ticket. Generally, the farther in advance you buy your ticket, the cheaper it will be. Buy your return ticket before arriving in Cuba, as flights are often full, and one-way tickets purchased in Cuba tend to be expensive (note, too, that if you miss a Cubana charter flight, you'll forfeit 100% of the fare and need to purchase a new ticket). Keep your eyes open for introductory fares.

Charter packages that include airfare and accommodations are often cheaper than many flight-only options; since you don't *have* to use the hotel portion, they can be the cheapest way to get to Cuba. Certain restrictions apply. If you're flexible, consider traveling **standby,** where you do not make a reservation but instead turn up at the airport and hope for an empty seat, preferably at a last-minute discount rate.

From France: Air France, tel. (0802) 80-28-02, www.airfrance.com.fr, flies from Paris's Charles de Gaulle airport to Havana on Wednesday and Saturday using a Boeing 747 (US$934 low season, US$1,034 high season round-trip, 30 day APEX). **AOM,** tel. (0803) 00-12-34, www.aom.com, flies to Havana from Paris daily (except Tuesday). I was quoted US$1,464 for a six-month advance purchase. **Cubana,** 41 Blvd. de Montparnasse, tel. (01) 53-63-23-23 or (01) 45-38-31-12, flies direct to Havana from Orly airport in Paris on Friday and Sunday, and via Holguín on Monday and Santiago de Cuba

on Thursday and Saturday; to Varadero on Saturday; and to Ciego de Ávila on Sunday, using a DC-10.

From Germany: Cubana, tel. (069) 913-0980, operates a DC-10 to Havana from Berlin via Frankfurt on Sunday. It also has charter service from Cologne to Havana on Friday. **LTU,** tel. (0180) 52065, fax (0180) 52075, e-mail: service@ltu.de, website: www.ltu.de, flies to Havana and Holguín from Berlin on Friday. **Condor,** Postfach 1164, 65440 Kelsterbach, tel. (06107) 939888, fax (06107) 939810, e-mail: information@condor.de, was planning on introducing charters from Germany.

A travel agency called **Die Reisegalerie,** Myliusstr. 68, 60323 Frankfurt, Germany, tel. (069) 972-06000, fax (069) 972-06002, e-mail: reisegal@aol.com, www.reisegalerie.com, specializes in flights to Cuba. Also try **Kubareisen,** v.-Ossietsky-Str. 25, 48151 Muenster, tel. (0251) 790077, fax (0251) 798363, e-mail: kubareisen@aol.com, www.cubatravel.web.com.

Discount fares are available through **Council Travel** in Dusseldorf, tel. (0211) 32-9088, and Munich, tel. (089) 895022; and from **STA Travel,** tel. (069) 430191, fax (069) 439858, in Frankfurt.

From Italy: Air Europe, tel. (02) 6711-8228, website: www.aireurope.it, flies from Milan to Havana via Rome on Sunday, and direct from Milan on Tuesday (US$800 round-trip). **Cubana,** tel. (06) 474-1104, flies from Rome to Havana on Monday, Wednesday, and Friday using a DC-10; and to Camagüey on Monday and Santiago de Cuba on Wednesday.

Lauda Air, e-mail: office@laudaair.com, website: www.laudaair.com, in Italy, Strada Provinciale 52, 21010 Vizzola Ticino, tel. (0331) 759-31, fax (0331) 230-467, flies charters from Milan to Havana on Wednesday and Saturday, to Cayo Largo on Saturday, and to Camagüey, Ciego de Ávila, Holguín, and Varadero on Sunday.

From The Netherlands: Martinair, website: www.martinair.com, flies direct from Amsterdam to Ciego de Ávila and Havana continuing to Cancún on Monday.

KLM, www.klm.com, has flights to Havana from Amsterdam on Wednesday and Sunday

From Russia: Aeroflot, 4 Frunzenskaya Naberezhnay, Moscow, tel. (095) 1568019, website: www.aeroflot.org, flies from Moscow to Havana via Varadero for US$600 one-way, US$810 round-trip. **Cubana** operates an Ilyushin once a week from Moscow.

From Spain: Cubana, flies direct to Havana from both Madrid, tel. (01) 542- 2923, and Barcelona, tel. (0343) 318-8833, once weekly using a DC-10, and from Santiago de Compostela on Friday and Las Palmas (Canary Islands) using an Ilyushin. **Iberia,** tel. (01) 587-8785, also flies to Havana from Madrid, daily except Friday.

Air Europa, tel. (01) 902-401501, www.aireuropa-online.com, flies from Madrid to Havana on Tuesday, Thursday, Saturday, and Sunday using a Boeing 767. One-way fare is US$480 low season, US$610 high season; round-trip costs US$800 and US$940 respectively.

From the U.K.: British Airways, tel. (0345) 222111, website: www.british-airways.com, flies from Heathrow to Havana via Nassau. Fares are from £472 return. **Cubana,** 49 Conduit St., London W1, tel. (0171) 734-1165, fax (0171) 437-0681, flies to Havana from Gatwick three times weekly using a DC-10, with a connecting flight from Manchester on Wednesday. One Havana flight is direct. A second flies via Cayo Largo, and the third via Ciego de Ávila.

Monarch flies charters to Holguín and Varadero twice weekly from Gatwick using an A-330. **Thompson Holidays,** tel. (0990) 502399, offers charter flights from Gatwick to Varadero from £755 including hotels. **Airtours,** tel. (01706) 240033, website: www.airtours.co.uk, was to introduce charters from Glasgow, Scotland, in 2000.

Captivating Cuba, tel. (0181) 891-2222, fax (0181) 892-9588, e-mail: info@captivating-cuba.co.uk, website: www.captivating-cuba.co.uk, is the U.K.'s largest tour agency handling air traffic Cuba. Also try **Journey Latin America,** 12 Heathfield Terr., London W4 4JE, tel. (0181) 747-3108, fax (0181) 742-1312, e-mail: flights@journeylatinamerica.co.uk, website: www.journeylatinamerica.co.uk, which offers round-trip flights between London and Havana from £407 low season, £468 high season on Iberia. And **Regent Holidays,** tel. (0117) 921-1711, fax (0117) 925-4866, website: www.cheapflights.co.uk, also offers inexpensive flights to Havana.

You may be able to save money by buying your ticket through a "bucket-shop," which sells discounted tickets on scheduled carriers. They usually have access to a limited number of tickets, so book early. "Bucket shops" advertise in London's *What's On, Time Out,* and leading Sunday newspapers. **Trailfinders,** 42 Earl's Court Rd., London W8 6EJ, tel. (0207) 938-3366, fax (0207) 937-9294, website: www.trailfinders.com, specializes in cheap fares throughout Latin America. **STA Travel,** 74 Old Brompton Rd., London SW7, tel. (020) 7361-6144, website: www.statravel.co.uk, specializes in student fares. STA also has offices throughout the U.K. Alternately, try **Council Travel,** 28A Poland St., London W1V 3DB, tel. (0171) 437-7767; or **Travel Cuts,** 295A Regent St., London, W1R 7YA, tel. (0207) 255-2082, fax (0207) 528-7532.

Online one of the best resources for airfares to Havana is www.cheapflights.co.uk/Havana.html, which at press time listed London-Havana round-trip airfares for £329-534.

From Elsewhere: Cubana flies to Havana from Copenhagen on Thursday, from Brussels on Saturday, and from Las Palmas on Friday and Lisbon once weekly using an Ilyushin.

From the Caribbean

From the Bahamas: Cubana, tel. (242) 322-3301, offers a daily charter flight to Havana from Nassau. The flights generally leave around 4:30 p.m. but change frequently. Cuba's **Aero Caribbean** also flies between Nassau and Havana daily, Wed.-Sun.

You can show up at the airport and purchase a Cubana seat and visa (US$201), but you run the risk that the plane might be full. More secure is to book Cubana flights for US$179 round-trip (plus US$20 visa and US$10 ticket tax) through **Bahatours,** based in the Graycliff Hotel, P.O. Box N-7078, Nassau, Bahamas, tel. (242) 361-6510, fax (242) 361-1336. Ask for Michael Larrow, whose services I've used several times: he'll meet you at the airport ticket counter with your ticket. Bahatours (also known as Havanatur Nassau) also offers two- to seven-night packages including airfare, transfers, and accommodations. You can guarantee your reservation with a credit card.

Likewise, **Cuba Tours,** P.O. Box N-1629, Nassau, tel. (242) 325-0042, fax (242) 325-3339, makes flight reservations and offers Cuba packages (its office is at Southland Shopping Centre, East St.), as does **Majestic Travel,** tel. (242) 328-0908, which has been recommended by a reader (US$208 round-trip, including tourist visa). You can pick up your ticket at the office once you arrive in Nassau (Majestic Travel has vans at the airport that offer free transfers to the office and back to the airport), but if you plan on departing for Cuba the day you arrive, be sure to allow two or three hours in Nassau for the transaction.

Innovative Travel & Tours, tel. (242) 325-0042, fax (242) 325-3339, doesn't accept credit card reservations and requires you to pay a deposit in advance through a wire transfer or certified check, which has to be mailed. Your ticket is delivered to you at the airport (one reader reports that her booking went smoothly). Round-trip tickets cost US$192 for up to 30 days (plus US$25 tourist visa); US$30 extra for an open-ended ticket.

Returning from Cuba, you pass through Bahamian immigration (there is no in-transit lounge). Bahamian Customs go "on notice" when the Cubana flight arrives and may search your bags (although they're really interested in Bahamian nationals with bags stuffed full of cigars). The departure terminal for flights to the U.S. is to the left of the exit from the arrivals hall. You must pass through U.S. Immigration and Customs here. They, too, go "on notice." If you're a U.S. citizen, they won't know that you've been in Cuba unless you tell them. However, U.S. officials may ask you outright if you've been to Cuba, or where you stayed in the Bahamas and how long. If you choose to tell the truth, expect to have your Cuban purchases confiscated. If you choose not to tell the truth, any hesitation may give the game away.

From the British Virgin Islands: Tour & Marketing, B.V.I, Wickhams Cay, Road Town, Tortola, e-mail: help@gocuba.com, website: www.gocuba.com; U.S. voicemail: (800) 863-3293, offers complete travel services to Cuba.

From the Cayman Islands: Cuba's **Aero Caribbean** flies between Grand Cayman and Havana on Wednesday, Friday, and Sunday. **Eddy Tours,** P.O. Box 31097, Grand Cayman, tel. (345) 949-4606, fax (345) 949-4095, operates charters.

From the Dominican Republic: Cubana, tel. (809) 227-2040, has charter service to Havana from Santo Domingo on Thursday (via Santia-

go de Cuba) and Sunday. Cuba's **AeroGaviota,** Calle 47 #2814 e/ 28 y 34 Reparto Kohly, Havana tel. (7) 81-3068, fax (7) 33-2621, also operates between Puerto Plata and Havana.

From Jamaica: Air Jamaica tel. (305) 670-3222 or (800) 523-5585 in the U.S.; in Jamaica, tel. (876) 922-4661 (Kingston) or (876) 952-4300 (Montego Bay), flies from Montego Bay to Havana on Monday, Thursday, and Saturday for US$156 one-way, US$188 round-trip. **Cubana,** tel. (876) 978-3410, has scheduled flights to Havana from Kingston and Montego Bay on Friday, with additional charter service from Montego Bay utilized by several Jamaican tour companies. And **Tropical Airlines,** tel. (876) 968-2473 in Kingston, (876) 979-3565 in Montego Bay, flies twice weekly to Santiago de Cuba and Varadero.

Caribic Vacations, 69 Gloucester Ave., Montego Bay, tel. (876) 953-2600 or 979-9387, fax (876) 979-3421, e-mail: carhouse@caribiconline.com, website: www.caribiconline.com, offers Cubana charter flights from Montego Bay to Havana (US$190 round-trip, including Cuban visa) and Varadero (US$270) on Friday and Sunday, and to Holguín (US$199) and Santiago de Cuba ($199) on Thursday. It also offers air-hotel packages.

Tropical Tours, tel. (876) 952-0440, fax (876) 952-0340, e-mail: tropical@cwjaimaica.com, website: www.marzouca.com, offers charters to Havana from Montego Bay and Kingston on Monday, Thursday, and Sunday using Air Jamaica Express; and to Santiago de Cuba on Thursday. A two-night "Weekend in Havana" package costs US$299.

From Elsewhere: Cubana operates service between Havana and Curacao (Monday), Fort-de-France in Martinique (Friday), Pointe-a-Pitre in Guadeloupe (Friday), Santo Domingo in Dominican Republic (Wednesday and Sunday), and Sint Maarten (Sunday). **Aero Gaviota** also offers charter flights from the Caribbean and Central and South America.

From Central America

From Belize: Cuba's **Aero Caribbean** flies between Belize and Havana on Monday.

From Costa Rica: LACSA tel. (506) 296-0909, in the U.S., 1600 NW LeJeune Rd. #20, Miami, FL 33126, tel. (305) 870-7500 or (800)

225-2272, part of Grupo Taca, website: www.grupotaca.com, flies from San José to Havana daily (US$265 one-way, US$399 round-trip), continuing to Toronto. Grupo Taca has a LatinPass (e-mail: mail@latinpass.com, website: www.latinpass.com) permitting multiple stops at cities throughout the Americas, including Havana. The cost varies according to number of cities and their zone.

Cubana, tel. (506) 290-5095, operates flights from San José to Havana on Thursday and Sunday (US$499).

Your best booking agent is U.S.-owned **Costa Rica's TravelnNet,** tel. (506) 256-7373, fax (506) 256-8412, e-mail: travelnet@central-america.net, website:www.centraolamerica.com, which specializes in Cuba. **Tikal Tours,** tel. (506) 223-2811, fax (506) 223-1916, e-mail: advtikal@sol.racsa.co.cr, also specializes in Cuba.

From El Salvador: Grupo Taca has flights from El Salvador to Havana three times weekly (US$280 one-way, US$399 round-trip).

From Guatemala: Grupo Taca flies from Guatemala to Havana three times weekly (US$280 one-way, US$399 round-trip). Cuba's **Aero Caribbean** flies between Guatemala and Havana on Wednesday and Friday.

From Mexico: Mexicana, tel. (05) 448-0990 or (800) 502-2000, website: www.mexicana.com.mx, flies from Mexico City to Havana daily, with a second flight each Thursday and Saturday stopping in Mérida (fares range from US$361 to US$601 round-trip).

Cubana, Temistocles #246 B esq. Av. Homero, Colonia Polanca, tel. (05) 255-3776, fax (05) 255-0835, also offers service from Mexico City on Wednesday and Saturday using a DC-10.

Far more popular among U.S. travelers are the flights from Cancún. **Cubana,** Av. Yazchilán #23 SM-24 M-22, Retorno 3 e/ Nir-Cheaven y Tan-Chacte, tel. (098) 87-73-33, flies daily from Cancún to Havana. Fares are about US$199 round-trip, plus US$25 tax. These flights on ancient dilapidated Russian jets are not for the weak hearted (see the paragraph on Cubana Airlines in the introduction to this chapter). A better alternative is **Aerocaribe,** Av. Cobá #5, Plaza América Local B, Cancún, Quintana Roo, tel. (098) 842000, fax (098) 841364; and c/o Merihabana, Calle 11 #114, local 7 e/ 26 y 28, Col. Itzimna, Merida, e-mail: merimid@mpsnet.com.mx, a re-

gional airline of Mexicana (not to be confused with Cuba's Aero Caribbean), which flies from Cancún to Havana twice daily using a DC-9 for US$166 one-way, US$257 round-trip. In the U.S. telephone (800) 531-7901, or book through Cubatravel. Aerocaribe also flies nonstop from Cancún to Varadero on Tuesday and Wednesday. It permits only 40 kilos of baggage, and only 20 kilos free (each extra kilo costs US$3).

Several companies offer charter flights and packages from Mexico. I recommend U.S.-run **Cubatravel,** Rio Suchiate #10075, Suite 11, Col. Revolución, Zona Rio, Tijuana, Mexico 22000, tel. (066) 865298; in the U.S., tel. (310) 842-4148, e-mail: info@cubatravel.com.mx, website: www.cubatravel.com.mx. Cubatravel makes flight arrangements for U.S. citizens from all points in Mexico serving Cuba. Cubatravel books a large number of travelers with Aerocaribe and is thereby able to offer discounted roundtrip fares of US$268 including tax, from Cancún to Havana.

Taino Tours, Av. Coyoacán #1035, Col. del Valle, CP 03100, México, D.F., tel. (05) 559-3907, fax (05) 559-3951, e-mail: taino@pceditores.com, website: www.pceditores.com/taino, offers Cuba charters from Tijuana, Cancún, and Merida. It has offices throughout Mexico.

Other wholesalers in Yucatán are **Merihabana Travel,** Calle 11 #114, local 7 e/ 26 y 28, Col Itzimina, Mérida, tel./fax (098) 22-6612, e-mail: merimid@mpsnet.com.mx; **Caribbean Tropical Tours,** tel. (098) 80-8160, fax (098) 80-8160, e-mail: cubatravel@mail.caribe.net.mx, website: www.cuba-travel.com.mx; and **Divermex,** Plaza Americas, Cancún, tel. (098) 842325, fax (098) 842325. Readers have complained about **Viñales Tours,** another local wholesaler.

A good option for folks in California is a weekly **Aeromexico,** tel. (051) 33-4000 or (800) 021-4010, charter that flies Tijuana to Havana using a MD-80 every Saturday at 5:30 p.m., returning Sunday morning (available through Cubatravel for US$535, including tax).

From Nicaragua: Cuba's **Aero Caribbean** flies between Managua and Havana on Friday.

From Panamá: COPA, Av. Justo Arosemena y Calle 39, Apdo. 1572, Zona 1, tel. (507) 227-2672, flies to Havana from Panamá City daily.

From South America
From Chile: Ladeco, tel. (02) 639-5053, fax (02) 639-7277, flies to Havana from Santiago de Chile, as does **Lan Chile,** tel. (02) 632-3442, website: www.lanchile.com, using a Boeing 767 every Monday. **Cubana,** tel. (02) 274-1819, flies from Santiago de Chile to Havana twice weekly.

From Ecuador: TAME, tel. (02) 509382, fax (02) 509594, e-mail: tamecom@impsat.net.ec, website: www.tame.com.ec, the national airline of Ecuador, flies to Havana from Quito on Thursday (from US$352 round-trip). **Cubana,** tel. (09) 227463, flies to Havana from Guayaquíl and Quito on Saturday using a chartered Boeing 727.

From Venezuela: Aeropostal, tel. (800) 284661 or (02) 708-6211, fax (02) 794-0702, flies from Caracas on Monday and Saturday (US$353). **Cubana,** tel. (02) 285- 3548, flies to Havana from Caracas on Monday and Wednesday.

From Elsewhere: Cubana has service to Havana from Bogotá (Tuesday), Buenos Aires (thrice weekly), Montevideo (Saturday), and Rio de Janeiro and Sao Paulo (Saturday).

From Asia
Cubanacá and JAL (www.jal.co.jp) were to initiate weekly flights between Tokyo and Havana beginning August 2000 using Boeing 747s.

Otherwise, there are no direct flights; travelers fly via London or the U.S. Flying nonstop to Los Angeles, then to Mexico City, Tijuana, or Cancún is perhaps the easiest. A round-trip economy ticket is about HK$16,000, depending on the agent. Hong Kong is a good source for discount plane tickets. Alternately, fly United or Malaysia Airlines to Mexico City (20 hours) and catch a flight next day to Havana (three hours).

From Macau you can fly with **Iberia,** e-mail: infoib@iberia.com, website: www.iberia.com, nonstop to Madrid and then on to Havana.

Travel Network, 11th Floor, On Lan Centre, 11-15 On Lan St., Central, Hong Kong, tel. (852) 2845-4545, fax (852) 2868-5824, has experience booking travel to Cuba. Ask for Alene Freidenrich, who can arrange visas. Or contact the Cuban Honorary Consul, Room 1112, Jardine House, 1 Connaught Place, Central, Hong Kong,

tel. (852) 2525-6320; allow seven working days; one visa costs HK$250).

STA Travel is a good resource for tickets, and has branches in Hong Kong, Tokyo, Singapore, Bangkok, and Kuala Lumpur. You'll find a listing of international offices at its website: www.sta-travel.com.

From Australia and New Zealand
You'll find no direct flights to Cuba and no bargain fares. The best bet is to fly to Los Angeles or San Francisco and then to Cuba via Mexico. Air New Zealand, tel. (02) 9223-4666 in Sydney, tel. (09) 366-2400 in Auckland; Delta Airlines, tel. (02) 9262-1777 in Sydney, tel. (09) 379-3370 in Auckland; Qantas, tel. (02) 9957-0111 in Sydney, tel. (09) 57-8900 in Auckland; and United Airlines, tel. (02) 9237-8888 in Sydney, tel. (09) 307-9500 in Auckland, offer direct service between Australia, New Zealand, and California. Fares from Australia to California begin at about A$1,600 for special fares; about A$2,300 for regular APEX fares. Fares from New Zealand begin at about NZ$2,495.

A route from Sydney via Buenos Aires or Santiago de Chile and then to Havana is also possible. And a round-the-world (RTW) ticket offers the option for additional stopovers at marginal extra cost.

Cubatours, 235 Swan St., Richmond, Victoria 3121, tel. (03) 9428-0385, specializes in airland packages to Cuba, as do Melbourne-based **Cuba World,** tel. (03) 9867-1200;
Caribbean Bound, 85 Goulbourn St., Sydney 2000, NSW, Australia, tel. (02) 928-144888, fax (02) 928-18578, e-mail: sales@caribbean .com.au, website: www.caribbean.com.au; and **Caribbean Destinations,** Level 4, 115 Pitt St., Sydney, tel. (800) 816717, and Level 1, North Tower, The Rialto, 525 Collins St., Melbourne, Victoria 3000, tel. (03) 9618-1128, fax (03) 9618-1199.

Specialists in discount fares include **STA Travel,** in Sydney tel. (02) 9212-1255, in Auckland, tel. (09) 309-9723, which has regional offices throughout Australia and New Zealand. Online visit STA's website at www.sta-travel.com for a complete listing of offices. One of STA's offices is—get this—207 Cuba St., Wellington, tel. (04) 385-0561.

BY CRUISE SHIP

Cuba is destined to become one of the biggest ports-of-call in the world once the U.S. embargo is lifted. (Most U.S. cruise companies have plans in place for Cuba, but under current U.S. law no U.S. company can operate cruises to Cuba, and because foreign-owned vessels cannot dock in the U.S. within six months of visiting Cuba or carrying Cuban passengers or goods, most foreign cruise companies shun the island.)

At press time, four cruise companies offered regular cruises to Cuba. U.S. citizens can *legally* take cruises as long as they don't spend any money in Cuba, or tip Cuban staff aboard the ships.

In the U.S., the **Cruise Line Industry Association,** 500 Fifth Ave. #1407, New York, NY 10110, tel. (212) 921-0066, may be able to provide up-to-date information on regulations regarding cruising to Cuba.

The Cruise Lines
The **Cuba Cruise Corporation,** 13 Hazelton Ave., Toronto, ON M5R 2E1, tel. (416) 964-2569 or (800) 387-1387, fax (416) 964-3416, website: www.cubacruising.com, launched the MV *La Habana* in November 2000, sailing from Nassau on Thursday year-round on four- and five-day voyages. *All* U.S. citizens can take the all-inclusive cruises legally on a "fully hosted" basis, as their Cuban expenses are paid by a Canadian-based non-profit organization (such passengers cannot buy any souvenirs; U.S. citizens traveling with licenses can return to the ship with up to US$100 worth of Cuban merchandise). Per person, double occupancy, rates start at US$595 for the "Classic Havana" three-day/four-night cruise.

Italian **Greta Line,** Via Piemonte 26, 00187 Roma, Italy, tel. (06) 428-84-370, fax (06) 420-83-540, e-mail: italia.prima@flashnet.it, website: www.4cubacruises.com/cruis, operates the 520-passenger *Italia Prima* on week-long cruises departing on Sunday from Havana to Playa del Carmen in Mexico, Montego Bay in Jamaica, and Grand Cayman. You can join the cruise in Mexico, and "exceptionally in Jamaica." You can also book in Italy through **Viajes Crucero,** Di-

CRUISING THROUGH SOCIALIST SEAS

The seas around Cuba have all the makings of a premier cruise region. With scores of beaches and dozens of colonial cities, the possible itineraries are endless.

In 1993, 8.5 million people took cruises in the Caribbean, saturating Caribbean ports of call. With almost 30 new cruise ships being introduced by the year 2000, cruise companies have set their sights on Cuba to relieve the pressure.

U.S. cruise companies are still barred from operating to Cuba. Although foreign-owned cruise ships are free to call, they fear the repercussions of the 1992 Torricelli Act, which prevents foreign vessels that berth in Cuba from berthing in U.S. territory within 180 days. Nonetheless, industry pundits predict Havana will once again become one of the world's busiest cruise ports, replacing Nassau as the most visited port in the Caribbean.

Cuba's strategic location 90 miles south of Florida makes it a natural cruise hub. A cruise ship sailing from south Florida in late afternoon could be in Havana by sunrise the following morning.

Cruise-ship companies hungry for a virgin destination are tripping over themselves to be first into Cuba. At least one company is studying the prospect of ferry service between Miami and Havana. Florida East Coast Industries even has plans to operate a rail-barge across the 90-mile-wide strait. And the Port of Miami has released details of a plan to build six new cruise-ship terminals in anticipation of the inevitable boom.

Cuba is already embracing the cruise industry in a big way. The island already has eight major ports and 44 minor ports capable of handling cruise ships. Port facilities that have been described by one cruise industry official as "not wonderful, but they're functional for cruise ships" are being upgraded. To accommodate the anticipated influx, the Cuban government has committed resources for the development of state-of-the-art cruise passenger terminals such as the "Terminal Sierra Maestra in Havana."

visión del Norte # 421-101, Colonia del Valle., tel. (06) 56-69-02-77, fax: (06) 56-82-97-98, e-mail: division@viajescrucero.com.mx, www.viajescrucero.com.mx/italia. In the U.K., you can book through Voyages Jules Verne, 21 Dorset Square, London NW1 6QG, tel. (0171) 616-1000, fax (0171) 723-8629, e-mail: sales@vjv.co.uk, www .vjv.co.uk, which has 15-night packages on the *Italia Prima* from £995.

A French company, **Nouvelle Frontieres,** www.nouvelles-frontieres.fr, operates the 650-passenger *Tritón,* a Greek vessel with departures from Havana on Sunday and calls at Grand Cayman, Montego Bay, Isla de la Juventud, and Calica in Mexico. Cruises are offered December through April only. (The company's website and brochure provide no contact information. You might have better luck at its Italian site—www.nouvelles-frontieres.it—where pages about the cruise were under construction at press time; e-mail: info@nouvelles-frontieres.it.). U.S. citizens can also book these all-inclusive cruises through Last Frontier Expeditions, 4823 White Rock Circle, Suite H, Boulder, CO 80301-3260, tel. (303) 530-9275, fax (303) 530-9275, e-mail: CopaBob@aol.com, website: www.cubatravel-experts.com, boarding in Mexico, which makes the trip legal if you don't spend any money ashore.

U.K.-based **Airtours,** tel. (01706) 240033, website: www.airtours.co.uk, operates the *Sundream.* (formerly the *Song of Norway*) on a similar round-trip itinerary mid-winter, departing Montego Bay for Cancún, Cozumel, Havana, Isla de Juventud, and Grand Cayman. The cruises are represented in Cuba by **Sunquest Cruises,** 130 Merton St., Toronto, ON M4S 1A4, tel. (416) 485-1700, e-mail: info@sunquest.ca, website: www.sunquest.ca. Seven-night cruises cost C$959, including air from Canada. **The Cruise People,** 1252 Lawrence Ave. E, Suite 202, Don Mills, ON M3A 1C3, tel. (416) 444-2410 or (800) 268-6523, fax

(416) 447-2628, e-mail: cruise@tcpltd.com, www.tcpltd. com, also books Cuban cruises.

The 439-passenger **Club Med II,** the world's largest sailing ship, operated by Club Mediterranee, visited Cuba in both 1998 and 1999. Club Med, tel. (800) 258-2633, www.clubmed.com, does not promote the cruises in the U.S.

A Belgian company, **Havanatour Benelux,** Av. Louise 335, B-1000 Brussels, tel. (02) 627-4990, fax (02) 627-4998, operates cruises in the Gardens of the Queen using a former Greenpeace and Dutch Royal Marine vessel. The main focus is scuba diving. (Also see the Gardens of the Queen section in the Camagüey chapter.)

BY YACHT

Cuba offers a warm reception to visitors arriving by sea. No advance permission is required. However, it is wise to give at least 72 hours' warning if possible by faxing complete details of your boat, crew, and passengers to the harbormaster's office at Marina Hemingway: fax (7) 24-3104, or to Marinas Puertosol, Calle 1ra #3001, Miramar, Havana, tel. (7) 24-5923, fax (7) 24-5928, e-mail: comerc@psol.mit.cma.net, website: www.puertosol.cubaweb.cu. (Anyone planning on sailing to Cuba should obtain a copy of Simon Charles's *Cruising Guide to Cuba,* and Nigel Calder's *Cuba: A Cruising Guide;* see the Booklist.)

The U.S. State Department advises that "U.S. citizens are discouraged from traveling to Cuba in private boats" and permits such travel "only after meeting all U.S. and

Cuban government documentation and clearance requirements." Since July 1998, private boats of less than 150 feet must obtain permits before leaving Florida and entering Cuban waters.

Nonetheless, scores of sailors—including U.S. citizens in U.S.-registered vessels—sail to Cuba each year without incident and without breaking the law (which for U.S. citizens means no spending money there). All persons subject to U.S. law aboard vessels, including the owner, must be an authorized traveler to engage in travel transactions in Cuba. If you are not an authorized traveler, you may not legally purchase meals, pay for transportation, lodging, dockage, or mooring fees, and you may not bring any Cuban-origin goods back to the U.S. Any payments to Cuban marinas would be considered a prohibited payment to a Cuban national and therefore in violation of the regulations. (Ostensibly, you'll need to find a non-U.S. citizen to pay your berth fees, and I presume you will cater yourself with food brought from the U.S. Get the picture?) Most U.S. skippers I've spoken to have had no problems when they return to the U.S.— as long as they don't have their holds full of Cuban cigars.

At the present time, the U.S. and Cuba do not have a Coast Guard agreement. Craft developing engine trouble or other technical difficulties in Cuban territorial waters cannot expect assistance from the U.S. Coast Guard. Cuba's territorial waters extend 19 km (12 miles) out. Alas, there are reports of increasing corruption among Cuban officials involving foreign yachters, abetted by the fact that Cuban authorities may impound your vessel as collateral against the cost of rescue or salvage.

Yacht Charters and Crewing

U.S. citizens should refer to Treasury Department regulations regarding chartering vessels for travel to Cuba. Charter companies in the Bahamas may permit travel to Cuba. Try **Nassau Yacht Haven,** tel. (242) 393-8173. In the U.K., contact Alan Toone of **Compass Yacht Services,** Holly Cottage, Heathley End, Chislehurst, Kent BR7 6AB, tel. (0181) 467-2450. Alan arranges yacht charters and may be able to assist in finding a crewing position. It is rar easier is to charter a yacht in Cuba.

Traveling with Private Skippers

It's possible to find private skippers sailing to Havana from Florida, New Orleans, and other ports along the southern seaboard, as well as from the Bahamas. Boats leave all the time from marinas along the Florida Keys. You can call various marinas for recommendations. Be flexible. Pinpointing exact vessel departure dates and times is nearly impossible, especially in winter. As Ernest Hemingway wrote, "Brother, don't let anybody tell you there isn't plenty of water between Key West and Havana!" A nasty weather front can delay your departure as much as a week or more.

In the U.S., if you plead your case sufficiently well, you might try a humanitarian organization called **Conchord Cayo Hueso,** 7 Higgs Ln., Key West, FL 33049, tel. (305) 294-0205, e-mail: jitters@aol.com. It has 47 registered vessels on call to carry humanitarian aid under license from the Treasury Department. Note, however, that they do *not* take ordinary citizens looking for a way to sneak into Cuba.

Warning: Vessel owners are prohibited from carrying travelers to Cuba who pay them for passage if the owner does not have a specific license from OFAC authorizing him or her to be a Service Provider to Cuba. There's nothing illegal if passengers don't spend money in Cuba and if skippers don't charge for passage to or from Cuba. You may be questioned about this by U.S. Customs or Immigration, who'll take a dim view of things. If a skipper asks for money, legally you must decline (the median cost of gas is about US$500). Consider negotiating a *free* passage; of course, diesel fuel is expensive, so you may feel charitably inclined.

Conchord Cayo Hueso runs an online coffeehouse (US$50 membership) that brings vessel owners and prospective travelers together. Transporting "friends sharing expenses" does not require a Treasury license. However, skippers are responsible for their passengers and crew while in Cuba, and each person may be required to sign an affidavit that he or she will not be spending any money in Cuba. Also, once in Cuba skippers may not be allowed to leave for the U.S. without their entire manifest of crew and passengers (this seems arbitrary however).

STUDY COURSES IN CUBA

Academic Exchanges

Wayne Smith, former chief of the U.S. Interests Section in Havana (and an outspoken critic of U.S. policy toward Cuba), heads the **Cuba Exchange Program** offered through the School of Advanced International Studies at Johns Hopkins University, 1740 Massachusetts Ave. NW, Washington, D.C. 20036, tel. (202) 663-5732, fax (202) 663-5737. Smith escorts scholars on learning programs.

Likewise, the **Cuban Studies Institute,** 6823 St. Charles Ave., New Orleans, LA 70118, tel. (504) 865-5164, fax (504) 865-6719, e-mail: cuba@tulane.edu, website: www.cuba.tulane .edu, operates "Tulane's Summer in Cuba Programs" for undergraduates, with such themes as Afro-Cuban culture and history, the business environment, social and work system, environment and society, historic preservation, and public health.

Also try **CamBas Association,** tel. (319) 354-3189, fax (319) 338-3320, associated with the University of Iowa.

In Cuba, **Mercadu S.A.,** Calle 13 #951, Vedado, Havana, tel. (7) 33-3893, fax (7) 33-3028, arranges study visits for foreigners at centers of higher learning and spanning a wide range of academic subjects. It also arranges working holidays and runs a summer school at the University of Havana.

The Arts

The **Ballet Nacional de Cuba,** Calzada #510 e/ D y E, Vedado, Ciudad de la Habana, C.P. 10400, tel. (7) 55-2953, fax (7) 33-3117, offers three-week and month-long intensive courses for intermediate and advanced level professionals and students (US$250 monthly).

The **Centro Nacional de Conservación, Restauración y Museologico,** Calle Cuba #610, e/ Sol y Luz, tel. (7) 61-3335, fax (7) 33-5696, offers residential courses for urban planners, conservationists, architects, etc., at the Convento de Santa Clara in Habana Vieja. Most courses are 12 days long and cost an average of US$300.

The **Instituto Superior de Arte,** Calle 120 #11110, Playa, Havana, tel. (7) 21-6075, fax (7) 33-6633, e-mail: isa@reduniv.edu.cu, offers courses spanning the gamut of the art world. Besides short-term courses, it also accepts foreigners for full-year study beginning in September (from US$2,000 for tuition).

The **Unión de Escritores y Artistas de Cuba,** Calle 17 #354 e/ G y H, Vedado, tel. (7) 55-3113, fax (7) 33-3158, e-mail: uneac@artsoft.cult.cu, offers a series of courses in the arts and Cuban culture, focusing on music.

In the U.S., **Caribbean Music & Dance,** 12545 Olive Rd. #241, St. Louis, MO 63141, tel. (314) 542-3637, toll-free (877) 665-432, fax (314) 469-2916, website: www.caribmusic.com, e-mail: caribmusic@igc.org, offers a series of cultural workshops in Cuba, where tour participants can learn to dance like a real Cuban!

In similar vein, the **Center for Creative Education,** in Stone Ridge, NY, tel. (914) 687-8890, e-mail: CCEdrums@aol.com, offers study tours in conjunction with Artes Escenicas and UNEAC with classes in dance and percussion (US$1,895 for two weeks, including airfare).

Maine Photographic Workshops, P.O. Box 200, 2 Central St., Rockport, ME 04856, tel. (207) 236-8581 or toll-free (877) 577-7700, fax (207) 236-2558, www.theworkshops.com/cuba, e-mail: info@theworkshops.com, offers 10-day courses in Cuba for photographers, writers, and artists. The 2000 roster included a photography workshop with *National Geographic* photographer David Alan Harvey.

In Canada, **Eleggua Project,** 7171 Torbram Rd., Suite 51, Mississauga, ON L4T 3W4, tel. (800) 818-8840, fax (905) 678-1421, website: www.pathcom.com/~cancuba, e-mail: cancuba@pathcom .com, offers a series of study courses, conferences, and field programs in ethnic studies and Afro-Cuban culture, plus music, dance, and arts, and cultural and social issues.

Culture

In Cuba, **Paradiso: Promotora de Viajes Culturales,** Calle 19 #560 esq. C, Vedado, tel. (7) 32-6928, fax (7) 33-3921, arranges visits and participation in cultural courses and programs, such as children's book publishing, theater criticism, contemporary visual art, ballet and modern dance, plus festivals such as the International Beny Moré Festival, the International Hemingway Colloquium, and the Artisans' Fair.

The **Conjunto Folclórico Nacional** (National Folklore Dance Group) and **Danza Contemporánea de Cuba** offer twice-yearly two-week courses in Afro-Cuban music and dance. Contact **ARTEX,**

Avenida 5ta #8010 esq. 82, Miramar, tel. (7) 24-2710, fax (7) 24-2033. ARTEX also sponsors other courses in the arts and literature, including seminars in *cutumba* (Franco-Haitian-Cuban song and dance) and courses at the Cuban School of Ballet (La Escuela Cubana de Ballet), the Instituto Superior de Arte, and the National School of Art (Centro Nacional de Escuelas de Arte).

Spanish Language Courses

Spanish language courses in Cuba offer options from beginner to advanced and usually include workshops on Cuban culture. The norm is three to five hours of instruction daily, more in intensive courses. Classes are best arranged from abroad via one of the following organizations:

Cubamar Viajes, Calle 15 #752 esq. Paseo, Vedado, tel. (7) 66-2523, fax (7) 33-3111, e-mail: cubamar@cubamar.mit.cma.net, offers courses in Spanish at the **José Martí Language and Computer Center for Foreigners,** Calle 16 #109 in Miramar. It offers four levels from basic to specialized, each either intensive (20-100 hours) or regular (120-160 hours).

Friendship Tours, 12883 98th Ave., Surrey, BC V3T 1B1, Canada, tel. (604) 581-4065, fax (604) 581-0785, e-mail: friendship@home.com, offers two- and four-week courses for C$1,499 and C$1,899.

Global Exchange, 2017 Mission St. #203, San Francisco, CA 94110, tel. (415) 255-7296 or (800) 497-1994, fax (415) 255-7498, e-mail: roberto@globalexchange.org, website: www.globalexchange.com, offers a Spanish language school with the University of Havana, including private tutors and group classes plus cultural activities. Two-week (US$1,200 including airfare from Cancún) and month-long (US$1,750) courses are offered monthly.

The **Grupo de Turismo Científico Educacional,** Avenida 5 #601, Miramar, tel. (7) 24-1567, offers intensive Spanish language courses at the José Martí Language Center.

You can also sign up for two-week to four-month Spanish language and Cuban culture courses offered by **Mercadu S.A.** (see above).

In the U.K., the **School of Latin American Spanish,** Docklands Enterprise Centre, 11 Marshalsea Rd., London SE1 1EP, tel. (0171) 357-8793, offers seven-week regular and intensive summer language courses in Cuba.

Maps and Charts

You'll need accurate maps and charts, especially for the reef-infested passage from the Bahamas. British Admiralty charts, U.S. Defense Mapping Agency charts, and Imray yachting charts are all accurate and can be ordered from **Bluewater Books & Charts,** 1481 S.E. 17th St., Ft. Lauderdale, FL 33316, tel. (954) 763-6533 or (800) 942-2583, fax (954) 522-2278, e-mail: nautical-charts@bluewaterweb.com, website: www.bluewaterweb.com.

You can also be order detailed National Oceanic & Atmospheric Administration charts from NOAA, Riverdale, MD 20737-1199, tel. (301) 436-8301 or (800) 638-8972, e-mail: distribution@noaa.gov, website: www.chartmaker.ncd.noaa.gov, or the Better Boating Association, P.O. Box 407, Needham, MA 02192. Most marine stores also stock U.S. government charts of the region.

In Havana, you can purchase nautical charts from **El Navigante** Calle Mercaderes #115, Habana Vieja; tel. (7) 61-3625, fax (7) 33-2869, but its stock is relatively limited. It sells a complete set of nautical charts, including a "Chart Kit" containing maps of the entire Cuban coast (charts I and VII cost US$40; charts II, III, and VI cost US$45; charts IV and V cost US$35). It's open Mon.-Fri. 8 a.m.-5 p.m., and Saturday 8 a.m.-1 p.m.

See regional chapters for information on specific marinas.

BY ORGANIZED TOURS

A wide range of organized tours to Cuba is offered from North America and Europe, and U.S. citizens are well catered for (see below). Most such tours focus on the cultural and historical experience, with Havana as a focus, but there are plenty of sports-oriented tours and just plain ol' fun tours. Believe it or not, even U.S. veterans are catered to.

Joining an organized tour offers certain advantages over traveling independently, such as the learning passed along by a knowledgeable guide. Tours are also good bets for those with limited time: you'll proceed to the most interesting places without the unforeseen delays and distractions that can be the bane of indepen-

INTERACTIVE ONLINE TRAVEL

The e-commerce boom makes it easy to plan and arrange your trip to Cuba online.

A good starting point is U.S.-run, **Cuba Travel,** Rio Suchiate #10075, Suite 11, Col.Revolución, Zona Río, Tijuana, Mexico 22000, tel. (066) 865298 (in the U.S., tel. 310-842-4148), e-mail: info@cuba-travel.com.mx, website: www.cubatravel.com.mx. Cubatravel books airfares, makes hotel reservations, and offers package tours to Cuba, including scuba programs, architecture tours of Havana, bicycle tours, and Jewish heritage tours.

Its affiliate, **Cuba Cultural Travel,** www.Cuba-CulturalTravel.com, is a licensed travel provider that assists licensed individuals and groups of U.S. travelers with travel arrangements to Cuba.

Another affiliate, Canadian-based **Cubahotels.com,** www.cubahotels.com, offers a complete online directory of hotels in Cuba and accepts reservations online with credit cards.

Don't confuse Cubatravel with **Cuba Travel USA,** P.O. Box 161281, Austin, TX 78716, tel. (512) 347-8952, fax (512) 306-1322, e-mail: cubatravel@writeme.com, run by Dan Snow, who has been running tours to Cuba for two decades, specializing in fishing but with a piece of literature promoting the allure of young Cuban women.

A British firm, **Tour & Marketing,** P.O. Box 24258,

London SE9 1WS, tel. (0800) 074-5010, e-mail: help@gocuba.com; in Spain, Aptos. Azahara, L-2 Los Cristianos, Arona, Tenerife, tel. (0922) 795864, fax (0922) 706652, offers complete travel services at www.gocubaplus.com and www.cubavip.com. The company, which is based in the British Virgin Islands, has an office in Havana and "assisted" 1,200 Americans in 1998, both with travel to and help on the island. U.S. citizens should check out www.uscubatravelcom, or call voice mail (800) 863-3293 (the call will be returned). It offers pre-paid ticket service for or from Tijuana, Cancun, Nassau, Grand Cayman, as well as cities in Europe. Other services include accommodation, excursions, city tours, car rentals, and airport transfers.

Likewise, **Cubalinda.com Inter-Active Travel,** e-mail: info@cubalinda.com, website: www.cubalinda.com, offers an interactive travel emporium featuring information and reservation services for travel to Cuba in partnership with Cuban state company Cubatur. The site was under development at press time, but will eventually list information on transportation, accommodation, and "a global offer of practically everything a foreigner can do in Cuba," including 21 activities. It has an office and ground service in Havana at Calle E #158, Suite 4-A, Vedado, tel. (7) 55-3980, fax (7) 55-3686.

dent travel. Everything is usually taken care of from your arrival to your departure, including transportation and accommodations. The petty bureaucratic hassles and language problems you may otherwise not wish to face are eliminated, too. And several companies buy hotel rooms and airline seats in bulk, then pass the saving on to you. However, you'll be almost entirely divorced from the real Cuban experience, gain little understanding of the local culture, be shepherded by guides and minders, and suffer daily from tantalizing glimpses remembered only in wistful backward glances as you are hauled off to the next official tourist site.

Check the tour inclusions carefully to identify any hidden costs such as airport taxes, tips, service charges, extra meals, and entertainment. Most tours are priced according to quality of accommodation, from deluxe to budget.

Operators in Canada and the United Kingdom offering tours to Cuba must by law guar-

antee full repayment in the case of default. Consider trip cancellation insurance. Paying for your tour by credit card is a good idea; in the event of a serious complaint you can challenge the charge.

Tours from the U.S.

U.S. citizens *can* legally travel to Cuba by qualifying for certain organized tours with non-profit organizations and other entities that arrange trips with special government authorized licenses in hand (see the special topic, U.S. Law and Travel to Cuba, in the Getting There section). Almost any type of special interest activity is now catered for, although most programs are "study" tours that provide an immersion in particular aspects of Cuban life and issues. There's usually plenty of time for relaxation. Participants usually have to demonstrate serious interest in the subject of study; in reality, this often proves a formality, especially in the realm of "arts," where

Uncle Sam accepts that it is difficult for artists to make a living as professionals. Tour operators tend to be fairly liberal about whom they consider researchers, and the government is equally loose about demanding proof. So a popular way to going to Cuba legally is to declare oneself a scholar or journalist and sign up for a licensed tour. Most U.S. organizations that offer trips to Cuba are *not* accredited tour and travel operators and do not offer consumer-protection programs.

Also see the Recreation section, this chapter, for details on bicycling, birding, and other special-interest tours offered by U.S. companies and organizations.

Cabas Associates, 4915 Broadway, Suite 41, New York, NY 10034, tel. (319) 354-3189 or (800) 446-1234, fax (319) 337-2045, offers study tours of contemporary Cuban society. The one-week itinerary includes visits to Havana, Matanzas, Varadero, and Trinidad (from US$895).

Caribbean Music and Dance Programs, 12545 Olive St. #241, St. Louis, MO 63141, tel. (314) 542-3637 or toll-free (877) 665-4321, fax (314) 469-2916, e-mail: caribmusic@igc.apc.org, website: www.caribmusic.com, offers a variety of music and dance study courses in Cuba under an OFAC license. For example, each February the organization offers a two-week Cuban Popular Music & Dance Workshop in association with the Havana Jazz Festival. Courses are taught at the prestigious Escuela Nacional de Arte (ENA). The dance workshops are open to everyone from beginners to professionals and includes lively tuition in *danzón, son, cha-cha-chá, mambo, rumba, salsa, larueda,* and the hip-swiveling *despolote.* Chucho Valdés and Irakere, Juan Formell and Los Van Van, Changuito, and legendary flautist Richard Esqúes are among the faculty who provide one-on-one tuition. Imagine learning guitar from Eric Clapton and you have the idea. Santiago de Cuba is also the venue for a "Cuban & Haitian Folkloric Dance & Music Workshop" and one-week packages to the "Festival of Fire" carnival.

The **Center for Cuban Studies,** 124 West 23rd St., New York, NY 10011, tel. (212) 242-0559, fax (212) 242-1937, e-mail: cubanctr @igc.org, website: www.cubaupdate.org, has an eclectic range of week-long and longer trips focusing on education and health care, urban issues, welfare, African roots of Cuba culture, sexual politics, architecture and preservation, and cultural events such as the Havana Film Festival. Most trips are a week to 10 days in duration and cost from US$900 to US$1,400, including round-trip airfare from Miami or Nassau. The center also offers an annual weeklong Jewish heritage tour in January, plus a one-week seminar on Cuban music in February. Participation is limited to "researchers and journalists," including arrangements for individual travel.

The **Cuban-Jewish Aid Society,** 44 Mercury Ave., Colonia, NJ 07067, tel. (908) 499-9132, offers annual trips Jewish heritage tours to Havana.

Global Exchange, 2017 Mission St. #303, San Francisco, CA 94110, tel. (415) 255-7296 or (800) 497-1994, fax (415) 255-7498, e-mail: globalexch@igc.org, website: www.globalexchange.com, sponsors study tours to Cuba focusing on different aspects of Cuban life, including health care, art, culture and education, religion, Afro-Cuban culture, women's issues, and music and dance. Most trips are 10 days long and cost an average of US$1,300, including round-trip airfare from Mexico or the Bahamas. The organization also has bicycle tours. It refuses to obtain an OFAC license on the grounds that to do so would acknowledge the legitimacy of the U.S. embargo.

Global Exchange, in association with Jim Long, a Vietnam veteran, P.O. Box 40430, San Francisco, CA 94140, e-mail: jimlong@sf.com, offers an annual trip to Cuba for U.S. veterans. The trips depart in early November and are timed to celebrate Veterans Day in the company of Cuban military veterans. Past programs have included visits to Guantánamo and the Bay of Pigs; military ceremonies honoring the war dead; plus meetings with Cuban military figures and a visit to the Cuban military command center and look-out over the U.S. naval base at Guantánamo. The trips are operated through a provision in U.S. legislation that permits such tours to be hosted by the Cuban government.

Last Frontier Expeditions, 4823 White Rock Circle, Suite H, Boulder, CO 80301-3260, tel. (303) 530-9275, fax (303) 530-9275, e-mail: CopaBob@aol.com; in Cuba, e-mail: last.frontiere @ip.etecsa.cu, website: cubatravelexperts.com, an Aruba-based company, offers packages for cigar lovers, plus hosted sports-related events such as the Ernest Hemingway International Sports Classic 10K race, the Ernest Hemingway Sportfishing Tournament, the Havana Open Golf Tournament, hunting and fishing trips, and baseball fantasy camps. It also has a Classic Car Rally tour, programs for a male audience (including an "Old Havana Nostalgia Tour"), Caribbean cruises, cigar tours, and a one-week "International Hemingway Centennial Tour."

Last Frontier Safaris, (same address as above), offers fishing, horseback riding, hiking, rafting, and jeep-driven tours. (It claims to support Cuba's "Wildlife Conservation Fund" and Cuban Federation of Wildlife, yet offers hunting trips!)

Marazul Tours, Tower Plaza Mall, 4100 Park Ave., Weehawken, NJ 07087, tel. (201) 319-9670 or (800) 223-5334, fax (201) 319-9009, e-mail: bguild@marazultours.com, website: www .marazultours.com, organizes special-interest tours and individual travel for those with OFAC licenses.

Queers for Cuba, 3543 18th St. #33, San Francisco, CA 94110, tel. (415) 995-4678, operates an annual "solidarity and education delegation" to Havana each December. The trip focuses on expanding understanding and expressing solidarity with Cuba's gay and lesbian population.

Wings of the World, 1200 William St. #706, Buffalo, NY 14240-0706, tel. (800) 465-8687, fax (416) 486-4001, actively—and legally—promotes its Cuban "cultural adventures" to *all* U.S. citizens, with weekly departures. Because the company's tours are "fully hosted and totally prepaid," including personal amenities, participants ostensibly "neither exchange nor spend money while in Cuba." Trips start at US$2,495, excluding airfare. The company also offers a wide range of special theme tours, including birding, cigars, classic cars, cycling, culture, ecology, medicine, sports, scuba diving, a Hemingway tour to coincide with the annual Hemingway Colloquium in Havana, and monthly "Cuban cigar adventures." The company claims that "not one of our American travelers has had any problems with the State Department" as the company "abides by all the legal requirements" (the legal key is that Wings is a private club; you're not "buying" a trip, but as a club member you are entitled to benefits, including a free trip). Available are 10- and 12-day tours of Cuba, de-

parting from Toronto, Nassau (Bahamas), or Cancún (Mexico). It handles groups as small as two people. Readers have written to complain that the company reneges on promises to return deposits.

WorldGuest Services, tel. (201) 861-5059 or (800) 873-9691, fax (201) 861-4983, website: www.worldguest.com, offers study tours billed as "humanitarian missions" to Cuba, such as delivering supplies to hospitals (US$1,960 for seven nights, including airfare). Themes for 2000 included photography, Jewish heritage, architecture, and culture.

In addition, many foreign companies accept U.S. travelers without licenses. Check their websites. Two places to start are www.cubatravel.com.mx and www.uscubatravel.com.

Tours from Canada

Canadians primarily book inexpensive beach vacation packages, and most of the travel and tour operators cater to this market (see the section on flights from Canada, above). Havana-based tours are few.

One of the leading Cuba specialist travel agencies is **Canada 3000 Holidays,** 31 Fasken Dr., Toronto, ON M9W 1K6, tel. (416) 679-3200, fax (416) 679-3503, website: www.c3holidays.com. Also try **Wings of the World,** 653 Mt. Pleasant Rd., Toronto, ON M4S 2N2 tel. (416) 482-1223 or (800) 465-8687, fax (416) 486-4011.

Friendship Tours, 12883-98th Ave., Surrey, BC V3T 1B1, tel. (604) 581-4065, fax: (604) 581-0785, e-mail: friendship@home.com, website: members.home.net:80/friendship, offers a variety of Havana-based tours—including a two-week "Explore Havana Plus" trip with one week each in Havana and Varadero (C$2,099 from Toronto; C$2,499 from Vancouver) and two- and four-week "Learn Spanish in Cuba" trips (C$1,499 and C$1,899)—primarily for people sympathetic to the goals of the Revolution.

The **Eleggua Project,** 7171 Torbram Rd., Suite 51, Mississauga, ON L4T 3WA, tel. (800) 818-8840, fax (905) 678-1421, e-mail: cancuba@pathcom.com, website: www.pathcom.com/~cancuba, is a cooperative partnership of North American and Cuban non-governmental agencies that provides travel services and tours, including training and coaching sessions with Cuban teams, plus study tours, courses, and conferences in the arts and culture, including ethnic studies such as Afro-Cuban music, Cuban cinema, and "indigenous legacies," and trips to festivals such as the "Cuba Youth Choral Festival."

And **Intra Kensington Travel,** tel. (403) 283-3383, www.intraken.ab.ca/cuba, offers package tours (it issues Cuban tourist visas to U.S. citizens as participants).

Tours from the U.K.

Interchange, 27 Stafford Rd., Croydon, Surrey CR0 4NG, tel. (0181) 681-3612, fax (0181) 760-0031, website: www.interchange.uk.com, represents Havanatur and offers special-interest group tours, plus tailor-made itineraries for independent travelers, including one- and two-week packages, escorted motor coach tours, and ecology and scuba diving packages. All holidays are fully flexible and you can mix and match resorts. A 2.25% service charge applies if you pay using a credit card. Likewise, contact **Cubanacán U.K.,** Skylines, Unit 49, Limeharbour, Docklands, London E14 9TS, tel. (0171) 537-7909, fax (0171) 537-7747.

Journey Latin America, 12 Heathfield Terr., London W4 4JE, tel. (0181) 747-3108, fax (0181) 742-1312, e-mail: flights@journeylatinamerica.co.uk, website: www.journeylatinamerica.co.uk, features Havana on its nine-day "Cuban Discovery" and two-week "Cubana Libre" trips, plus two-week fly-drive packages. JAL also has an office at 2nd Floor Barton Arcade, 51-63 Deansgate, Manchester M3 2BH, tel. (0161) 832-1441, fax: (0161) 832-1551, e-mail: man@journeylatinamerica.co.uk.

Captivating Cuba, tel. (0181) 891-2909 or (410) 511575 (mobile phone), website: www.cubawel.com, is an independent tour operator specializing exclusively in holidays to Cuba and offering a wide range of package holidays and individually tailored trips, including cigar tours, golfing, and scuba diving. It accepts U.S. citizens.

Caribbean Connection, Concorde House, Canal St., Chester CH1 4EJ, tel. (01244) 355-400, fax (01244) 355-419, e-mail: itc@itc-uk.com; and **Caribbean Expressions,** 104 Belsize Lane, London NW3 5BB, tel. (0171) 794-1480, fax (0171) 431-4221, also offer Cuba programs.

Regent Holidays, 15 John St., Bristol BS1 2HR, tel. (0117) 921-1711, fax (0117) 925-4866, e-mail: regent@regent-holidays.co.uk, specializes in customizing tours for independent travelers but also has package tours that include a seven-day "Pearl of the Caribbean" tour from £789.

Explore Worldwide, 1 Frederick St, Aldershot, Hants GU11 1LQ, tel. (01252) 760000, fax (01252) 760001, website: www.explore.co.uk, offers a 15-day "Cuba Libre!" trip that tours the entire island from Viñales to Santiago de Cuba and is focused toward adventurous, activity-oriented travelers.

Festival Tours International, 96 Providence Lane, Long Ashton, Bristol BS18 9DN, tel./fax (01275) 392953, offers packages to Carnaval and the Havana Jazz and Film Festivals. Also contact the **Britain-Cuba Dance Student Exchange,** Weekends Arts College, Interchange Studios, Dalby St., London NW5 3NQ.

A score of other companies offer tours. Many advertise in the travel sections of leading newspapers, plus *Time Out,* and *What's On* in London.

Tours from Europe

In Germany, contact **Kubareisen,** v.-Ossietsky-Str. 25, 48151 Munster, tel. (0251) 790077, fax (0251) 798363, e-mail: kubareisen@aol.com. In Switzerland, try **Carib Tours,** Malzstr. 21/Postfach, Zurich 8036, Switzerland, tel. (01) 463-8863, fax (01) 463-9261, and **Jelmoli Reisen,** tel. (01) 211-1357, and in France, **Havanatur,** tel. (01) 4742-5858.

Several Italian tour operators specialize in Cuba. Try **Cuba Italturist,** tel. (02) 535-4949, fax (02) 535-4901, in Milan; or **Ostiensis Viaggi,** Viale dei Romagnoli, 760 Ostia Antica, 00119 Roma, tel. (06) 565-2473, fax (06) 565-2399, e-mail: ostiensisviaggigroup@micanet.it. **Sol y Med,** Via Boezio #2, 0-0192 Roma, tel. (06) 688-07252, fax (06) 636700, e-mail: choa1@yahoo.com, specializes in medical tourism and special events. And **New Tibon Travel,** Piazza Arnaldo, 10/A, 25121 Brescia, tel. (030) 45002, fax (030) 290516, specializes in cycling, fishing, and ecology trips.

Cubanacán has offices at Tvisseringhlaan 24, 2288 ER Rijswijk, Netherlands, tel. (070) 390-5152, fax (070) 319-3452; Via Fabio Filzi 33, 20124 Milan, Italy, tel. (02) 667-1121, fax (02) 667-10839; and 7 Rue Perignon, 75015 Paris, France, tel. (01) 53-69-01-01, fax (01) 53-69-01-43.

Also see the information on charter airlines, this section, for companies offering tour packages.

Tours from Other Countries
Excursions from Jamaica, the Bahamas, and Central America are very popular with U.S. citizens. See the sections on air service from the Caribbean and Central America, above, for companies offering tour packages.

VOLUNTEER PROGRAMS

Cuba welcomes volunteer teams to work for 20-day stints in the countryside. The work is hard—mostly it consists of cutting sugar cane. Contact the Havana-based **Cuban Institute of Friendship with the Peoples** (Instituto Cubano de Amistad con los Pueblo), ICAP, Calle 17 #301 e/ H y L, Vedado, Habana, Cuba, tel. (7) 32-8017.

In the U.S.: U.S. law prohibits U.S. citizens from receiving remuneration for work in Cuba. You are permitted to work in Cuba if fully hosted.

The **American Friends Service Committee,** Human Resource, 1501 Cherry St., Philadelphia, PA 19102, tel. (215) 241-7000, fax (215) 241-7275, e-mail: afscinfo@afsc.org, website: www.afsc.org, is a Quaker organization which in the past has offered youth from the U.S. and other countries a chance to engage with Cuban youth on three-week summer programs. The program was not offered at press time but may be resurrected. The program involves summer work camps and conferences in which Christians and communists come together. Participants should be between 18 and 28 years old and fluent in Spanish.

Pastors for Peace-IFCO, 620 West 28th St, Minneapolis, MN 55408, tel. (612) 670-7121 or (612) 378-0062, fax (612) 870-7109 or (612) 378-0134, e-mail: p4p@igc.apc.org, delivers humanitarian aid to Cuba through the annual "U.S.-Cuban Friendshipment Caravan." The caravan moves through, and gathers aid in, 150 cities from the West Coast to Washington, D.C., before

traveling to Canada or Mexico, where the aid is shipped to Cuba. Volunteers can participate in the caravans, which openly defy the embargo and deliver aid to Cuba *without* a license. Pastors for Peace also supports community development projects in Cuba through the Martin Luther King Memorial Center in Havana. The organization also operates Work Brigades in which volunteers work to help construct houses. Research trips are also offered in which participants live in a working-class *barrio* in Havana as fully hosted guests.

The **U.S.-Latin American Medical Aid Foundation,** P.O. Box 552, New York, NY 10025, tel. (888) 669-1400, fax (212) 749-7596, e-mail: US-LAMAF@aol.com, website: members.aol.com/US-LAMAF, provides opportunities for individuals to travel to Cuba to hand deliver licensed medical supplies.

Cross-Cultural Journeys, P.O. Box 1369, Sausalito, CA 94666-1369, tel. (800) 353-2276, e-mail: info@crossculturaljourneys.com, offers volunteer programs, while the **Venceremos Brigade,** P.O. Box 7071, Oakland, CA 94601-0071, tel. (415) 267-0606, a leftist solidarity group, offers "workcamp brigades" for committed socialists, as does the **Brigada Antonio Maceo,** P.O. Box 248829, Miami, FL 33124, a Cuban-American organization.

Similar tours are offered by **Witness For Peace,** 1229 15th St., NW, Washington, DC 20005, tel. (202) 588-1471, fax (202) 588-1472, e-mail: witness@witnessforpeace.org, website: www.witnessforpeace.org, in which participants work alongside Cubans to assist with community development. The three-week trips are hosted by the Cuban Institute for Friendship with the People (ICAP) but coordinated by people in local communities.

In the U.K.: The **Cuban Solidarity Campaign,** The Red Rose Club, 129 Seven Sisters Road, London N7 7QG, tel. (0171) 263-6452, fax (0171) 561-0191, e-mail: cubasc@gn.apc.org, website: www.poptel.org.uk/cuba-solidarity, sends international work brigades to help in construction and the sugar harvest. The organization also publishes the *CubaSí* newsletter.

GETTING AROUND

Cuba is deceptively large. Contrary to popular notion, you can tour the island on your own without restriction by air, tour bus, public bus, bicycle, or car. I've even shipped my motorcycle to Cuba and traveled 11,000 km without a hiccup or raised eyebrow. Stick with tourist services and you're fine, but if you plan on using local transport, be warned. As Cuba's Transportation Minister, Alvaro Pérez, admitted in December 1999, the country's transportation system has suffered a "brutal deterioration." Four decades ago, Cuba had 15,600 buses; today it has 3,800. For Cubans, the daily grind of getting around is a nightmare.

BY AIR

The fastest way to get around is to fly. Fortunately, Cuba's air network is relatively well developed, and flying is economical. Most of Cuba's main cities have an airport, and virtually every major tourism destination is within a two-hour drive of an airport.

In 1998, **Inter Grupo Taca,** Hotel Habana Libre Tryp, Calle L, Vedado, tel. (7) 66-2703, fax (7) 33-3728, the Central American carrier, initiated flights within Cuba using modern 14-passenger Cessna Gran Caravans linking all major points of tourist interest. Alas, in late 1999 all service was suspended and it was unclear at press time whether it would be resurrected. This is by far a superior carrier to any domestic option.

Several poorly managed Cuban carriers also offer service using less trustworthy, beaten-about Russian aircraft, though the carriers are upgrading their fleets. **Aero Caribbean,** Calle 23 #64, Vedado, tel. (7) 33-4543, fax (7) 33-5016, e-mail: aerocarvpcre@iacc3.get.cma.net, operates flights between Baracoa, Cayo Coco, Cayo Largo, Havana, Isla de la Juventud, Holguín, Santiago, Trinidad, and Varadero. **Aero Gaviota,** Av. 47 #2814 e/ 28 y 34, Raparto Kohly, Playa, tel. (7) 23-0668, fax (7) 24-2621, offers charter flights in 30-passenger Yak-40s and 38-passenger Antonov-26s and "execu-tive" service in eight-seat helicopters. **Cubana,** Calle Infanta esq. Humboldt, Havana, tel. (7) 33-4949, the largest carrier, has service between all the major airports. Its fares are 25% cheaper if booked in conjunction with an international Cubana flight. However, its safety

---

CUBANA OFFICES IN CUBA

Baracoa: Calle Martí #181, tel. (21) 4-2171

Bayamo: Calle Martí #58 esq. Parada y Rojas, tel. (23) 42-3916

Camagüey: Calle República #400 esq. Correa, Camagüey, tel. (322) 9-2156 or 9-1338

Ciego de Ávila: Calle Chico Valdéz #83, Carretera Central e/ Maceo y Honorato Castillo, tel. (33) 2-5316

Guantánamo: Calle Calixto García e/ Aquilera y Prado 817, tel. (21) 3-4533 or 3-4789

Havana: (National) Calle Infanta esq. Humboldt, Plaza, tel. (7) 33-4949 or 33-4950, (International) Calle 23 #64, Vedado, Havana, tel. (7) 33-4949

Holguín: Calle Libertad esq. Martí, Policentro, tel. (24) 42-5707; Aeropuerto Frank País, tel. (24) 46-2512

Las Tunas: Calle 24 de Febrero esq. Lucas Ortiz, tel. (31) 4-2702

Manzanillo: Calle Maceo #70 e/ Villuenda y Merchá, tel. (23) 2800

Moa: Avenida del Puerto Reparto Rolo, Monterrey, Moa, tel. (24) 6-7916; Aeropuerto Capitán Orestes Acosta, tel. (24) 7370

Nueva Gerona: Calle 39 #1415 e/ 16 y 18, Nueva Gerona, Isla de la Juventud, tel. (61) 2-2531 or 2-4259

Santiago de Cuba: Calle Félix Pena #671 e/ San Basilio y Heredia, tel. (226) 2-4156, 2-0898, or 2-2290; Aeropuerto Antonio Maceo, tel. (226) 9-1014 or 9-1865

Varadero: Hotel Iberostar Barlovento, Calle 9 esq. 1ra, tel. (5) 66-7593; Aeropuerto Juan Gualberto Gómez, tel. (5) 61-1823

AEROTAXI OFFICES

CITY	ADDRESS	TELEPHONE	FAX
Bayamo	Aeropuerto	(23) 42-2186	(23) 42-3267
Cayo Coco	Aeropuerto	(33) 30-1245	
Cayo Largo	Aeropuerto	(5) 4-8100	
Havana	Calle 27 #102 e/ M y N, Vedado, Havana	(7) 33-4064	(7) 33-4063
Isla de la Juventud	Aeropuerto Nueva Gerona	(61) 2-2300	
Pinar del Río	Aeropuerto Borrego	(82) 63-196	
Sancti Spíritus	Aeropuerto	(41) 2-4316	
Santa Lucía	Aeropuerto	(32) 6-1573	
Santiago de Cuba	Aeropuerto	(23) 42-2186	
Trinidad	Aeropuerto	(41) 4-4406	
Varadero	Calle 24 y Avenida Playa	(5) 66-7540	

record is the worst of any airline in the world (see Getting There, above).

AeroTaxi, Calle 27 #102 e/ M y N, Vedado, Havana, tel. (7) 32-4460 or 33-4064, offers flights on old Russian Antonov 2s, a 12-passenger biplane with a sloping floor and, thought Alex Hamilton, "a cabin design like a garden shed." It too is upgrading its fleet to modern jets.

Reservations
Transportation is limited by lack of aircraft, so flights are frequently fully booked, especially in the Aug.-Dec. peak season, when Cubans take their holidays. Often you must make a reservation a week in advance. Fortunately, foreigners with dollars are usually given priority on waiting lists. Reservations usually have to be paid in advance and are normally nonrefundable. Forgo telephone reservations: make your booking *in person* at the airline office or through one of the major tour agencies. If you make your reservations before arriving in Cuba, you'll normally be given a voucher that you exchange for a ticket upon arrival in Cuba.

Be sure to arrive on time for check-in; otherwise your seat will likely be given away. If that happens, *don't expect a refund,* and bear in mind that you may not even be able to get a seat on the next plane out. Delays, flight cancellations, and changes in schedule are common. And don't expect luxury—be happy to get a boiled sweet.

BY BUS

Tourist Buses
Víazul, tel. (7) 81-1413, fax (7) 66-6092, e-mail: viazul@transnet.cu, website: www.viazul.cu, operates services for foreigners to key places on the tourist circuit using modern a/c Volvo and Mercedes buses. Most buses depart Havana for major tourist destinations, but the service also includes links between key destinations such as Varadero to Trinidad. Children travel at half price.

You can also book yourself onto an excursion bus operated by one of the state-run tour agencies. Every tourist hotel has at least one tour desk offering such excursions. Take a sweater; some buses are overly air-conditioned.

Transmetro, tel. (7) 81-6089, offers buses and minibuses for rent to groups.

Public Buses
Public buses serve almost every nook and cranny of the island. Virtually the entire population relies on the bus system for travel within and between cities. Many Cubans say bus travel is more reliable and faster than train travel, although they sometimes have to wait *weeks* to get a seat!

There are two classes of buses for long-distance travel: *especiales* are faster, air-condi-

TRANSPORTATION TELEPHONE NUMBERS

CITY	AIRPORT	RAILWAY STATION	BUS TERMINAL
HAVANA			
	(7) 45-3133	(7) 62-4888 (Estación Casablanca)	
		(7) 62-1920 (Estación Central)	
		(7) 78-4971 (Estación Cristina)	
		(7) 81-4431 (Estación 19 de Noviembre; Tulipán)	
HAVANA PROVINCE			
Artemisa	-	(63) 3-2193	(63) 3-2145 (national) (63) 3-3527 (municipal)
Batabanó	-	(62) 8-8555	(62) 8-4065
Camilo Cienfuegos (Hershey)	-	(692) 2-2065	-
Guines	-	(62) 2-2105	(62) 2-4567
Mariel	-	-	(64) 9-2208
San Antonio de los Baños	-	-	(650) 2737
Santa Cruz del Norte	-	-	(692) 8-3375 (692) 8-3422 (local)
CAMAGÜEY PROVINCE			
Camagüey	(322) 6-1525 (international) (322) 6-1010 (national)	(322) 9-2633	(322) 7-2302 (national) (322) 8-1525 (municipal)
Minas	-	(32) 9-6181	-
Nuevitas	-	-	(32) 4-3105
Santa Cruz del Sur	-	(32) 32-2228	-
CIEGO DE ÁVILA PROVINCE			
Cayo Coco	(33) 30-1165	-	-
Ciego de Ávila	(33) 2-5717	(33) 2-3313	(33) 2-5109 (national) (3) 2-3076 (municipal)
Júcaro	-	(33) 9-8101	-
Morón	-	(335) 3683	(335) 3398
CIENFUEGOS PROVINCE			
Cienfuegos	(432) 7994	(432) 5495	(432) 5720 (national) (432) 6050 (municipal)

continues on next page

TRANSPORTATION TELEPHONE NUMBERS

(continued)

GRANMA PROVINCE

Bartolomé Masó	-	-	(23) 59-5328
Bayamo	(23) 42-4502	(23) 42-4955	(23) 42-4036 (national)
			(23) 42-6892 (municipal)
Manzanillo	(23) 5-2800	(23) 5-2195	(23) 5-3404
Media Luna	-	-	(23) 59-3264
Niquero	-	-	(23) 59-2215
Pilón	-	-	(23) 59-4295

GUANTÁNAMO PROVINCE

Baracoa	(21) 4-2216	-	(21) 4-2239
Guantánamo	(21) 32-3564	(21) 32-5518	(21) 32-3713
Jamaica	-	(21) 9-8244	-

HOLGUÍN PROVINCE

Banes	-	-	(24) 8-3633
Cacocum	-	-	(24) 2-7194
Gibara	-	-	(24) 3-4215
Holguín	(24) 46-2512	(24) 42-2331	(24) 42-211 (national)
			(24) 42-2322 (municipal)
Mayarí	-	-	(24) 5-2170
Moa	(24) 6-4409	-	(24) 6-6323
Rafael Freyre	-	-	(24) 2-1040

ISLA DE LA JUVENTUD

Cayo Largo	(5) 4-8141	-	-
Nueva Gerona	(61) 2-2300	-	(61) 2-4270,
			(61) 2-3121 (local)

LAS TUNAS PROVINCE

Las Tunas	(31) 4-7902	(31) 4-8140	(31) 4-3060 (national)
			(31) 4-2117 (municipal)

tioned, and more comfortable than *regulares*. Long-distance travel us usually aboard noisy, rickety old Hungarian-made buses, with jammed windows, noxious exhaust fumes, and (often) arse-numbing seats. Upscale Mercedes and Volvo buses are gradually being added to the service.

Most towns have *two* bus stations for out-of-town service: a **Terminal de Ómnibus Intermunicipales,** for local and municipal service, and a **Terminal de Ómnibus Interprovinciales,** for service between provinces.

Interprovincial services: The state agency **Empresa Ómnibus Nacionales,** Av. Independencia #101, Havana, tel. (7) 70-6155, fax (7) 33-5908, operates all interprovincial services. Foreigners now pay in dollars and receive reserved seating. Reservations are essential; do *not* expect to show up at the station and simply board a bus.

For Cubans, demand so exceeds supply that there is often a waiting line in excess of one month for the most popular long-distance routes. Intercity buses rarely have a spare seat. Hence,

MATANZAS PROVINCE			
Cárdenas	-	-	(5) 52-1214 (5) 52-2528 (local)
Colón	-	(5) 3-2748	(5) 3-2808 (5) 3-3507 (local)
Jagüey Grande	-	(59) 2683	-
Matanzas	(52) 7015	-	(52) 9-1473 (national) (52) 9-2701 (municipal)
Pedro Betancourt	-	(5) 89-8104	(5) 89-8282
Varadero	(5) 61-3016	-	(5) 61-2626
PINAR DEL RÍO PROVINCE			
Bahía Honda	-	-	(86) 527 (national) (86) 740 (municipal)
Isabel Rubio	-	(84) 9-2144	-
Pinar del Río	(82) 6-3248	(82) 2272	(82) 2572 (national) (82) 2878 (municipal)
San Juan y Mártinez	-	(8) 9-8129	(8) 9-8227 (national) (8) 9-8121 (municipal)
SANCTI SPÍRITUS PROVINCE			
Sancti Spíritus	(41) 2-6011	(41) 7248	(41) 2-4142
Trinidad	(419) 2547	(419) 3348	(419) 4448
SANTA CLARA PROVINCE			
Caibarién	-	(42) 3-3150	(42) 3-3325 (national) (42) 3-3201 (municipal)
Remedios	-	(42) 39-5129	(42) 39-5185
Santa Clara	(422) 8-6183	(422) 2-2895	(422) 9-2114 (national) (422) 3470 (municipal)
Zuluetas	-	-	(42) 39-9133
SANTIAGO DE CUBA PROVINCE			
El Cobre	-	-	(22) 3-6131
Santiago de Cuba	(226) 9-1014	(226) 2-2836	(226) 5-2143 (reservations) (226) 2-3050 (national) (226) 2-4329 (municipal)

Cuban bus stations have been called "citadels of desperation." However, many Cubans say bus travel is more reliable and faster than train travel.

Only one-way tickets are available. Don't forget to book any return trip also as far in advance as possible. On the day of travel, arrive at the terminal at least one hour ahead of departure, otherwise your seat may be issued to people on the waiting list. You may be asked to reconfirm your booking.

If you don't have a reservation or miss your departure, you can try getting on the standby list— *lista de esperas*. Normally you'll receive a *número de espera,* a ticket that indicates your position on the waiting list (the *lista de espera* is posted in the waiting room and includes the numbers).

If you plan to travel like a Cuban, you should try to make your reservation as early as possible If you don't get shooed away to the dollars-only counter, expect a Kafkaesque experience. First, there's often a milling mob to contend with, with everyone clamoring to get his or her name on the list. Your name will be scrawled on a decrepit pile of parchment, added to the scores of names ahead of you. Ask to see the sheets for the destination you want so that you can gauge how many days' delay is likely.

Intermunicipal services: Usually no reservations are available for the short-distance intermunicipal services. You'll have to join the queue, but be prepared for a mad scrum as soon as the bus arrives. At other times, you'll be issued a *tike*

(a slip of paper, not a ticket) that records your destination and position in line. You board when your number is called, so don't wander off—and don't dally once it's called (you should learn Spanish numerals by heart; alternately, ask a neighbor to help identify when it's your turn). Fares are collected on board. Since buses are often full, try to board the bus at its originating point. Most intermunicipal terminals are chaotic. Buses are as-

VÍAZUL BUS SCHEDULE

FROM	TO	TIMES	COST
Havana	Bayamo	3 p.m. (Tuesday and Friday only)	US$44
Havana	Camagüey	3 p.m. (Tuesday and Friday only)	US$33
Havana	Ciego de Ávila	3 p.m. (Tuesday and Friday only)	US$27
Havana	Cienfuegos	8:15 a.m. (Tuesday and Friday only)	US$20
Havana	Holguín	3 p.m. (Tuesday and Friday only)	US$39
Havana	Pinar del Río	9 a.m. (alternate days only)	US$11
Havana	Playa Girón (Bay of Pigs)	7:45 a.m. (daily except Mon.)	US$15
Havana	Sancti Spíritus	3 p.m. (Tuesday and Friday only)	US$23
Havana	Santa Clara	3 p.m. (Tues. and Fri. only)	US$18
Havana	Santiago	3 p.m. (Tues. and Fri. only)	US$51
Havana	Trinidad	8:15 a.m.	US$25
Havana	Varadero	8 and 8:30 a.m. and 4 p.m.	US$10
Havana	Viñales	9 a.m. (alternate days only)	US$12
Playa Girón	Havana	4 p.m.	US$15
Santiago	Havana	5:30 p.m. (Mon. and Thurs. only)	US$51
Trinidad	Havana	3 p.m.	US$25
Trinidad	Varadero	2:30 p.m.	US$20
Varadero	Havana	8 a.m. and 4 and 6 p.m.	US$10
Varadero	Sancti Spíritus	8:15 a.m.	US$16
Varadero	Santa Clara	8:15 a.m.	US$11
Varadero	Trinidad	8:15 a.m.	US$20
Viñales	Havana	1:30 p.m. (alternate days only)	US$12

The Santiago-Havana bus stops in Bayamo, Holguín, Las Tunas, Camagüey, Ciego de Ávila, Sancti Spíritus, and Santa Clara.
The Trinidad-Havana bus stops in Cienfuegos.
The Trinidad-Varadero bus stops in Sancti Spíritus and Santa Clara

FOR INFORMATION AND RESERVATIONS:

Havana: Casa Matriz, Avenida 26 y Zoológico, tel. (7) 81-1413, fax (7) 66-6092, e-mail: viazul@transnet.cu, website: www.viazul.cu.

Sancti Spíritus: Viro Guirnart e/ Antonio Maceo y Gustavo Izquierdo, tel. (41) 9-2404.

Santiago: Avenida de los Libertadores esq. Yarayó, tel. (226) 2-8484

Varadero: Calle 36 y Autopista, tel. (5) 61-4886

PUBLIC BUS SERVICE FROM HAVANA

Pinar del Río	9 a.m. and 12:30, 2:20, and 5:30 p.m.	Regular	US$7
Viñales	9:50 a.m.	Regular	US$8
Matanzas	4:55 p.m.	Regular	US$4
Varadero	2:45 p.m.	Regular	US$6
Cardenas	8:45 a.m.	Regular	US$6
Playa Girón	11:40 a.m. (Fri.-Sun. only)	Regular	US$10.50
Santa Clara	6:30 and 8:40 a.m.	Regular	US$12
Cienfuegos	6:15 a.m. and 12:05, 4:15, and 7:30 p.m.	Regular	US$14
Trinidad	5:45 a.m.	Especial	US$21
Sancti Spíritus	4:40 a.m.	Regular	US$15.50
	3:50 p.m.	Especial	US$15.50
Camagüey	9:20 a.m. and 7:45 p.m.	Especial	US$27
Ciego de Ávila	12:25 p.m.	Especial	US$22.50
Morón	9:50 a.m. (Fri.-Sun. only)	Especial	US$24
Santiago de Cuba	12:15 and 7:20 p.m.	Regular	US$35
Las Tunas	8:45 p.m.	Regular	US$27
Holguín	9:15 a.m. (Fri.-Sun. only)	Regular	US$36
	6:25 p.m. (daily)	Especial	US$36
Bayamo	9:45 p.m.	Regular	US$30
Manzanillo	8:15 p.m.	Regular	US$32
Guantánamo	3:15 p.m.	Regular	US$38
Baracoa	10:45 a.m. (Fri.-Sun. only)	Especial	US$43

phyxiatingly crowded and interminably slow. These buses don't normally cross provincial boundaries; hence, you may be put down at a border in the middle of nowhere and have to mill around with everyone else, hoping that a connecting bus shows for the rest of the journey.

Practicalities: Don't rely on the validity of published schedules. Information about bus schedules is fragmentary. There are no published schedules; instead, since schedules change, they are normally written in chalk at bus stations. Beware pickpockets and don't display wads of money when purchasing your ticket. Get there at least an hour before departure for long-distance buses. Often the rush to get aboard can be furious.

Passengers are granted 22 kg baggage limit (plus one piece of hand luggage), although it seems not to be strictly enforced. Some buses have room for storage below; others do not, in which case luggage space will be limited to overhead racks. *Travel light!* Consider leaving some luggage at your hotel in Havana.

If possible, sit toward the front. Conditions can get very cramped and—if the air conditioner isn't working—very hot; the back tends to get the hottest (and often smelliest—from exhaust fumes). You'll want some water to guard against dehydration, but don't drink too much coffee or other liquids—toilet stops can be few and far between. *Bring plenty of snacks.* Long-distance buses make food stops, but often there isn't sufficient food for everyone.

Cubans relinquish their seats gladly to pregnant women, the handicapped, elderly people, and mothers with small children. Set a good example: do the same.

Within Towns

Most large towns have intracity bus service. Usually, they are cloyingly overcrowded. At least they only cost 10 centavos (the standard fare), which you normally drop into a fare box next to the driver. Many Cubans board through the rear door (although technically this is illegal), in which case, if the bus is jam-packed like a sardine can,

*When is a bus not a bus?
When it's a camiones,
of course!*

you can pass your fare to the front via other passengers. Be prepared for the *cola* (queue) to disintegrate when the bus arrives.

To stop the bus, shout ¡*Parada!*

A tourist shuttle service—**Vaivén Bus Turístico**—operates a circuit within Havana.

Makeshift "Buses"

In many areas, flatbed trucks—*camiones*—have been converted and have basic wooden seats welded to the floor. Often *camiones* are the only option for public transport, especially in the Oriente. Often there are no seats, and the local "bus" might be a converted cattle truck or a flatbed pulled by a tractor, with passengers crammed in and standing like cows. If you're hitchhiking, this is for you.

Camiones depart from transportation hubs in all towns and cities. Hawkers yell out destinations. You pay in pesos.

Fej Films, P.O. Box 24062, Lansing, MI 48909-4062, www.arrozconfrijoles.com, publishes a video—*Arroz con Frijoles: The Budget Traveler's Guide to Cuba*—that provides a good introduction to the ins and outs of travel by *camiones.*

BY RAIL

Exploring by train is the next step down the travel ladder—a great way to meet Cubans and see the country at a slow pace, but relatively unpredictable and, at times, uncomfortable.

Cuba was one of the few Latin American countries with a well-developed railway system in 1959 that reached into virtually every corner of the country. Rail transport, which was nationalized following the Revolution, has been largely neglected since 1959 in favor of truck transport. A major upgrading occurred in the 1970s, when the Central Railroad was rebuilt. New diesel locomotives (all of them relatively fuel inefficient) were imported from the Soviet Union, Czechoslovakia, and Argentina.

Some 5,300 km of the 14,640-km system constitute main line public railways. One main rail axis spans the country, connecting all the major cities, with major ports and secondary cities linked by branch lines. There is no rail service *within* cities, although quaint commuter trains (a little like the dinky English or Swiss two-carriage trains) called *Ferro-Ómnibus* provide suburban rail service in and between many provincial towns.

The loss of oil and spare parts since the collapse of the Soviet Bloc reduced the state-run railroad system to shambles. Most services, however, have been restored to their pre-Special Period schedules. Published schedules are subject to frequent change. Also check the arrival time at your destination carefully and plan accordingly, as many trains arrive (and depart) in the wee hours of the morning. Few trains run on time.

Two services operate between Havana and Santiago de Cuba: the fast *especial,* which takes

TRAIN SCHEDULES AND FARES FROM HAVANA

NO.	DESTINATION	ORIGIN STATION	DEPART	ARRIVE
11	Santiago (Especial)	Estación Central	7:30 p.m.	9:10 a.m.
13	Santiago	Estación Central	4:40 p.m.	6:40 a.m.
15	Holguín	Estación Central	2:05 p.m.	4:05 a.m.
17	Bayamo	Estación Central	8:25 p.m.	10:20 a.m.
17	Manzanillo	Estación Central	8:25 p.m.	11:40 a.m.
19	Santiago	Estación Central	10:40 a.m.	10:30 p.m.
21	Morón	Estación Central	8:45 a.m.	3:06 p.m.
25	Sancti Spíritus	Estación Central	9:25 p.m.	5:40 a.m.
67	Cienfuegos	Estación Coubre	1:25 p.m.	11:35 p.m.
313	Pinar del Río	Estación Coube	9:45 p.m.	3:26 a.m.
315	Güines Union	Estación Coubre	5:30 p.m.	9:25 p.m.

DESTINATION	FARE (REGULAR)	NO.
Aguacate	US$2	15, 25
Artemisa	US$2.50	313
Cacocum (Holguín)	US$23.50	13
Camagüey	US$19.50	13, 15
Ciego de Ávila	US$15.50	13, 15, 21
Cienfuegos	US$9.50	67
Colón	US$6	15, 25
Florida	US$18	15
Guantánamo	US$33	13
Holguín	US$27	15
Jatibónico	US$14	15
Jovellanos	US$5	15, 25
Las Tunas	US$23.50	13, 15
Matanzas	US$3.50	13, 15, 21, 25
Morón	US$24	21
Pinar del Río	US$6.50	313
Placetas	US$11.50	15, 25
Sancti Spíritus	US$13.50	25
Santa Clara	US$10	13, 15, 21, 25
Santiago de Cuba	US$30.50	12
Zaza del Medio	US$13	25

DESTINATION (IN ORDER OF STOP)	FARE (ESPECIAL)	NO.
Matanzas	US$10	11
Santa Clara	US$15	11
Ciego de Ávila	US$22	11
Camagüey	US$27	11
Las Tunas	US$37	11
Cacocum (Holguín)	US$37	11
Santiago de Cuba	US$43	11

16-20 hours for the 860-km journey and operates each two consecutive days but not the third; and the slow *regular.* The *especial* (which has a poorly stocked *cafetería* wagon, comfy seats, and bone-chilling a/c) stops at the major cities en route; the other (far less salubrious, but lazy and quite adequate) is colloquially called the *lechero*—the "milkman"—because it stops at virtually every village.

Bicycles are allowed on most trains in a special compartment. You usually pay (in pesos) at the end of the journey.

Reservations

The state agency **Ladis** (formerly Ferrotur), tel. (7) 62-4259, handles ticket sales and reservations for all national train service. Foreigners must now pay in dollars, for which you get a guaranteed seat. Commuter trains still charge foreigners in pesos.

In Havana you can normally walk up to the Ladis office at the central station, buy your ticket, and take a seat on board within an hour (see the Getting Away section in the Havana chapter). It is best to buy your ticket as far in advance as possible. And don't trust being able to book consecutive journeys "down the line" in advance—make a habit of buying your ticket for the next leg of your journey upon arrival in each destination.

Reservations can usually be made through Infotur offices, which saves the bother of waiting in line at the station. Some tour agencies will also make your booking for you. You'll need to show your passport.

Reservations for local services can't be made. You'll have to join the *cola* (queue) and buy your ticket on the day of departure (sometimes the day before; each station usually lists the allotted time for ticket purchase).

On the day of departure, get there early. The seating in the waiting room is comfortable. You'll need to listen attentively for announcements of departure, as the electronic information board is usually out of order.

Classes

Foreigners paying dollars are now expected to travel on the *especial,* which has reclining cushioned seats. Service in this "luxury class" includes a basic meal (usually fried chicken or beans and rice with soda to wash it down). Regardless, take snacks and drinks. Most branch line services are *clase segunda* (second class) only, which, though inexpensive, is arduous for long journeys and best suited to hardy travelers—they're typically dirty and overcrowded, with uncushioned wooden seats. *Clase primera* (first class) is marginally better, with padded seats, though still crowded and hardly comfortable. Some routes offer *clase primera especial,* which provides more comfort and, often, basic boxed meals.

Nonsmoking compartments haven't yet made it to Cuba.

Train Journeys

Transnico Train Tours, Lonja del Comercia, Oficina 6d, Plaza San Francisco de Asís, Habana Vieja, tel. (7) 66-9908, operates luxury train travel in the style of the Orient Express, using original American coaches pulled by a Canadian diesel train, with steam power for special occasions. Transnico also offers a "Narrow Gauge Adventure" on Baldwin Moguls and Consolidations, plus a "Sugar Mill Steam" trip.

For information and reservations in Canada contact: Canadian Caboose Press, Box 844, Skookumchuck, BC V0B 2E0, Canada, cellular tel. (250) 342-1421, website: www.cal.shaw. wave.ca/~hfinklem/GoodMed.htm; or Uniglobe Travel, tel. (250) 426-8975 or (888) 426-8975, fax (250) 426-8994, e-mail: wc.bakerst@uniglobe .com. In the U.K., contact Rob Dickinson, 5, Ash Lane, Monmouth, NP5 4FJ, tel./fax (01600) 713405, e-mail: steam@dial.pipex.com, website: www.ds.dial.pipex.com/ steam/americas .htm#Cuba. In Europe, contact Transnico, Avenue Montjoie, 114 -1180 Brussels, R.C. 579074, Belgium BE 447.460.901, tel. (02) 344-4690, fax: (02) 346-5665, e-mail: transnico.international.group@skynet.be, website: users. skynet .be/transnico/index.html.

Steam in Paradise, 3a Leamington Place, Hayes UB4 8Q2, England, also offers steam train tours from England.

Steam train excursions are also by local tour operators on the Rafael Freyre line, in Holguín Province (see the Rafael Freyre and Vicinity section in the Las Tunas and Holguín chapter).

BY TAXI

Cuba has a good taxi system, including long-distance taxis. Taxis serving tourists charge in dollars; those serving the local population—peso taxis—charge in pesos. During rainy periods, taxis are in high demand.

Tourist Taxis

Tourist taxis are inexpensive by U.S. or European standards, so much so that they're a viable option for short-haul touring, especially if you're traveling with two or three other people. Generally, taxis will go wherever a road leads. Most *turistaxis* (those serving tourists for dollars) in Havana and leading cities are radio-dispatched, although you can also find them at designated pick-up points and at tourist hotels. Most *turistaxis* are modern Japanese cars or Mercedes.

In Havana, **Panataxi** provides efficient radio-dispatched taxi service (mostly for Cubans but also for tourists) using Lada, the Russian-made Fiat described as "tough as a Land Rover, with iron-hard upholstery and, judging by sensation, no springs." They are far more economical than *turistaxis*. See the Havana chapter.

You can hire a *turistaxi* by the hour or day; the cost normally compares favorably to hiring a car for the day. By law, Cuban drivers must use their meters (not all taxis outside the main cities have meters). If you want to get the price down, you might be able to strike a bargain with the driver. Here's the deal. Your driver will stop the meter at so many dollars and you give him a slightly greater amount. Since his dispatcher records the destination, mile for mile, usually a dollar per mile, the taxi driver splits the excess with the dispatcher. Most taxi drivers are unscrupulously honest with passengers. If you think you're being gouged, contest the fee.

Outside Havana, you'll normally find taxis around the main squares of small towns. You do not normally tip Cuban taxi drivers.

At press time, official rates were pegged to distance. In towns, you can get almost anywhere for less than US$10. Nighttime fares cost about 20% more. Long journeys are usually charged at a pre-agreed fare.

Long-Distance Taxis: Several tourist taxi companies offer excursions. See regional chap-

MAKING SENSE OF ADDRESSES

*I*n most Cuban cities, addresses are given as locations. Thus, the Havantur office is at Calle 6 e/ 1ra y 3ra, Miramar, Havana, meaning it is on Calle 6 between (e/ for *entre*—between) First and Third Avenue (Avenida 1ra y 3ra).

Street numbers are occasionally used. Thus, the Hotel Inglaterra is at Prado #416 esq. San Rafael, Habana Vieja; at the corner *(esq.* for *esquina)* of Prado and Calle San Rafael, in Old Havana (Habana Vieja).

Piso refers to the floor level (thus, an office on *Piso 3ra* is on the third floor). *Altos* refers to "upstairs."

Most cities are laid out on a grid pattern centered at a main square or plaza (usually called Plaza Central, Parque Central, Plaza Mayor, or named for a local revolutionary hero), with parallel streets *(calles)* running perpendicular to avenues *(avenidas)*. Some towns, however, have even-numbered *calles* (usually north-south) running perpendicular to odd-numbered *calles* (usually east-west).

Many streets have at least two names: one pre-dating the Revolution (and usually the most commonly used colloquially) and the other a post-revolutionary name. For example, in Havana, the Prado is the old (and preferred) term for the Paseo de Martí. On maps, the modern name takes precedence, with the old name often shown in parentheses.

ters. For example, in Havana Taxi Transtur, Calle 19 #210 esq. J, Vedado, tel. (7) 33-6666, fax (7) 33-5535, e-mail: taxihab@transtur.com.cu, offers chauffeured excursions to Viñales (US$165/200 by car/minivan), Varadaro (US$120/150), and to Soroa (US$75/85). Hourly rates for a chauffeured taxi are generally on a sliding scale averaging from US$15 the first hour (20 km limit) to US$80 for eight hours (125 km limit), with US$0.70 per km for extra distance.

Freelance Cabs

Don't mind the possibility of breaking down in the boonies? Many Cubans with classic cars from the heyday of Detroit treat their prized possession as exotic cash cows—they rent them out (mostly illegally) for tourists. Says Cristina García, "Twenty dollars buys gas enough for a

ciclotaxis, *Havana*

although they are assigned to airports, hotels, and other key sites. Peso taxis (also called **colectivos**) also accept foreigners. They usually take as many passengers as they can cram in and are not supposed to pick up passengers between their designated departure and return points. The auto-taxis leave when the car is full. Look for a light lit up above the cab—it signifies if the taxi is *libre* (free). You should change dollars for pesos beforehand.

The base fare is one peso. Each km costs 25 centavos (35 centavos at night).

Maquinas also hang around outside railway and bus terminals and provide service between towns. The drivers yell out the names of destination. Often they won't depart until they fill up with passengers. Count on traveling about three km per peso.

Bicitaxis

Bicitaxis—the Cuban equivalent of rickshaws—patrol the main streets of most Cuban cities, where they are now the standard means of moving around. These tricycles have been cobbled together with welding torches or are conversions of Chinese imports, with abandoned car seats and shade canopies. Fares are negotiable.

Horse-Drawn Cabs

The clip-clop of hooves echoes through virtually every town and resort in Cuba. Horse-drawn cabs *(coches* or *calezas)* are the staple of local transport and have been given a new lease on life since the Special Period. In Havana, Varadero, and other beach resorts, elegant antique carriages with leather seats are touted for sightseeing. Elsewhere they're a utility and are often decrepit carts with basic bench seats pulled by fittingly scrawny mules (one peso is a standard fare).

You don't tip the driver, but *please* buy some food for the emaciated mule.

decent spin. Seventy dollars gets you a day in a top-of-the-line Cadillac convertible with fins so big they block the rear-view mirror. Forget about renting from Hertz or Avis ever again."

Your fare is negotiable, so ask around. Agree on the fare *before* getting in. Make sure you know whether this is one-way or round-trip. Don't be afraid to bargain. You may get a better deal if you speak Spanish and know local customs. The driver will usually be amenable to any request you make. I've hired a car and driver for as little as US$30 for a full day, plus gasoline (a common courtesy is also to buy your driver his or her lunch), but much depends on the quality of the car—and your negotiating skills.

Peso Taxis

Taxis—deprecatingly called *los incapturables* (uncatchable)—also serve the local population, usually along fixed routes within cities and charging in pesos at ludicrously low rates. These *maquinas,* are usually old Yankee cars. You'll normally find them around the main squares,

BY CAR

Cuba is a great place to drive. Exploring the island by car allows total freedom of movement (there are no restrictions on where you can go), and you can cover a lot of turf without the delays of public transport. There are so few vehicles on the roads

CUBA'S VINTAGE AMERICAN CARS

Magnificent finned automobiles cruise grandly down the street like parade floats. I feel like we're back in time, in a kind of Cuban version of an earlier America.

—Cristina García,
Dreaming in Cuba

Fifties nostalgia is alive and well on the streets of Havana. Stylish Chevrolets, Packards, and Cadillacs weave among the sober Russian-made Ladas and Moskovitchs, their large engines guzzling precious gas at an astonishing rate. Automotive sentimentality is reason enough to visit Cuba—the greatest living car museum in the world.

American cars flooded into Cuba for 50 years. During Batista's days, Cuba probably imported more Cadillacs and Buicks and DeSotos than any other nation in the world. Then came the Cuban Revolution and the U.S. trade embargo. In terms of American automobiles, time stopped when Castro took power.

Still, relics from Detroit's heyday are everywhere, ubiquitous reminders of that period in the 1950s when American cars—high-finned, big-boned, with the come-hither allure of Marilyn Monroe—seemed tailor-made for the streets of prerevolutionary Havana.

Imagine. A '57 Packard gleams in the lyrical Cuban sunlight. Nearby, perhaps, sits a '50 Chevy Deluxe, a '57 Chevrolet Bel Air hardtop, and an Oldsmobile Golden Rocket from the same year, inviting foreigners to admire the dashboard or run their fingers along a tail fin. More numerous are staid Chrysler New Yorker sedans, Ford Customlines, and Buick Centuries.

Lacking proper tools and replacement parts, Cubans adeptly cajole one more kilometer out of their battered hulks. Their intestinally reconstituted engines are monuments to ingenuity and geopolitics—decades of improvised repairs have melded parts from Detroit and Moscow alike. (Russian Gaz jeeps are favorite targets for cannibalization, since their engines were cloned from a Detroit engine.)

One occasionally spots a shining example of museum quality. The majority, though, have long ago been touched up with house paint and decorated with flashy mirrors and metallic stars, as if to celebrate a religious holiday. Some are adorned with multicolored flags to invoke the protection of Changó or another *santería* deity.

The mechanical dinosaurs are called *cacharros.* Normally, the word means a broken-down jalopy, but in the case of old Yankee classics, the word is "whispered softly, tenderly, like the name of a lost first love," says Cristina García in the introduction to *Cars of Cuba,* a beautiful little photo-essay book (New York: Harry N. Abrams, 1995); available from www.cubabooks.com.

The **Classic Car Show** is held in March in Havana, tel. (7) 61-5868, fax (7) 66-9281, e-mail: tamara@cultural. ohch.cu. To order a 30-minute video of the show (US$35.95 including shipping), telephone (253) 265-2073, e-mail: cheguevara @usa.net.

Last Frontier Expeditions, 4823 White Rock Circle, Suite H, Boulder, CO 80301-3260, tel. (303) 530-9275, fax (303) 530-9275, e-mail: CopaBob @aol. com, website: www.club havana.com, offers a classic car tour that includes a classic car rally. **Wings of the World,** 1200 William St. #706, Buffalo, NY 14240, tel. (800) 465-8687, occasionally offers a "Classic Car Adventure" in Cuba.

a cacharro, *a beloved survivor from the 1950s, before the Revolution and before the trade embargo*

ER, COMANDANTE . . . CAN I BUY A CAR?

$\mathcal{E}$ very Cuban dreams of owning a car, though the chances are slim. Virtually all cars imported since 1959—Polish Fiats, Czech Skodas, Soviet UAZs, and Jeep-like Romanian AROs—are owned by the state. Owners of pre-revolutionary cars can sell them freely to anyone with money to buy. And many top-level professionals have been given permission to buy Ladas or Moskviches from the state, although the cars can only be resold back to the government, which pays a pittance—in pesos. The government can seize any car sold illegally. New cars are leased out to high-level workers, and others who work for foreign companies, but the cars must be returned if they lose their jobs. Benighted workers such as sports stars and top artists have been gifted or allowed to buy cars they can freely sell, but permission to buy such a car is usually granted in writing from a vice president or even from Fidel Castro himself.

that you can travel all day and sometimes pass only a half dozen other vehicles. You can travel the entire length and breadth of the country in about two weeks, though this is pushing things. A drive from Havana into Pinar del Río, then east to the Zapata Peninsula and Trinidad, then back through the Sierra del Escambray allows you to see much of the nation's splendid scenery, history, and culture along with enough hairpins, dirt roads, and mountain passes to give drivers a sense of adventure. From Santiago, a route east to Guantánamo and Baracoa, then via Holguín, Bayamo, Manzanillo, and Chiviríco should suffice for a one-to two-week drive.

Cuba has some 31,000 km of roads, of which about 15,500 km are paved. Virtually every town, airport, and harbor is accessible by paved road, as are all the more popular beach destinations. In more remote areas, especially in the mountains and distant coastal regions, access is by unpaved road that can shake both a car and its occupants until their doors and teeth rattle. In the rainy season, such roads become quagmires or even totally flooded. Here you'll need a four-wheel-drive vehicle. The worst paved roads are in Holguín Province, whose municipal authorities have failed to maintain the appallingly

potholed highways. By contrast, many main roads in the western provinces had been repaired at press time and were in excellent condition. Most roads are in reasonably good condition. To bolster the road-repair budget, tolls—the first since the Revolution—were introduced in 1996 for specific roads, including the Matanzas-Varadero Expressway and the Cayo Coco bridge: foreigners pay US$2 per vehicle (buses and trucks pay US$4).

The main highway is the **Carretera Central** (Central Highway), built during the reign of General Machado. It runs along the island's spine for 1,200 km from one end of the country to the other. (Its construction, announced in 1926, was a classic tale of corruption. Chase National Bank financed the project to the tune of US$100 million, benefiting contractors, General Machado, and his cronies immensely. The U.S. construction company, Warren Bros., lobbied heavily to prevent the U.S. government from ousting Machado.) The road is an ordinary two-lane highway that leads through dozens of sleepy rural towns.

For maximum speed and minimum sightseeing, take the A-1, the country's main highway—six lanes wide and fast. Construction by the Soviets of this **Autopista Nacional** (National Expressway; sometimes called the *Ocho Vías*—eight-ways) came to a halt with the Special Period and has not been resumed. Unfinished concrete bridges still hang perilously over the road, linked to nothing but thin air. About 650 km have been completed, from Pinar del Río to a point just east of Santa Clara, and from Santiago de Cuba about 30 km northwestward. Travel time between Havana and Santa Clara is about four hours. Be cautious on the Autopista, where you are tempted to travel at high speed. Two ungated railway lines cross the highway in depressions that can bend your wheels if you hit 'em at high speed.

Traffic Regulations

To drive in Cuba, you must be 21 years or older and hold either an International Drivers' License (IDL) or a valid national driver's license. You must also have at least one year's driving experience. In North America you can obtain an IDL through any American Automobile Association office; and in the U.K. from the AA, Fanum

House, Basingstoke, Hampshire RG21 2EA, or RAC, P.O. Box 100, 7 Brighton Rd., Croydon CR2 6XW.

Traffic drives on the right, as in the U.S. The speed limit is 100 kph on freeways, 90 kph on highways, 60 kph on rural roads, 50 kph on urban roads, and 40 kph in children's zones. Speed limits are vigorously enforced by an efficient highway patrol. If you are issued a ticket, it will normally be taken care of by your car rental agency, which will deduct the sum from your credit card.

Seat belt use is not mandatory, nor are motorcyclists required to wear helmets. Insurance—a state monopoly—*is* mandatory. Note that it's illegal to 1) enter an intersection unless you can exit, 2) make a right turn on a red light unless indicated by a white arrow or traffic signal *(derecha con luz roja),* or 3) overtake on the right. Cars coming uphill have right of way.

Driving Safety

Driving is of as high a standard as you will find anywhere in the Caribbean or Latin America,

10 BEST SCENIC DRIVES

CIENFUEGOS AND VILLA CLARA PROVINCES

Trinidad to Manicuragua via Carretera 4-432   Mountain drive with steep climbs and hairpin bends winds through forests (south side) and rolling tobacco country (north side).

GRANMA PROVINCE

Bartolomé Masó to Marea del Portillo   A 4WD challenge, with steep, looping road in awful condition, but the staggering mountain vistas are topped by views down over the coast and sea.

GRANMA AND SANTIAGO PROVINCES

Marea del Portillo to Santiago de Cuba   A lonesome drive with awesome coastal scenery, with the jade-colored sea hemmed in by cloud-tipped mountains.

GUANTÁNAMO PROVINCE

Cajobabo to Baracoa via Carretera Centra   An awesomely steep ascent through the pine-clad Sierra Cristal, with snaking bends and occasional pullouts for savoring the vistas. On the north side of the mountain, the looping road loops down through more jungly terrain.

HOLGUÍN PROVINCE

Rafael Freyre to Floro Pérez   Wheel-bending potholes don't deter from the enjoyment of this drive past dramatic *mogotes* (limestone formations), palm-shaded *bohios,* and tobacco fields tended by *guajiros* in straw hats and linens.

Guardalavaca to Banes via Carretera 6-241   This road wends between soaring *mogotes,* with stands of royal palms in the vales, and more ox-drawn plows and endearing rusticity than you can shake a stick at.

PINAR DEL RÍO PROVINCE

Quiebra Hacha to Bahía Honda via Circuito Norte   Winding ridge-top drive between mountain and sea, with quintessential rural scenery.

Viñales to Guane via Sumidero   Mountain drive through a valley farmed with tobacco. Rural Cuba at its best. The road is badly potholed.

SANCTI SPÍRITUS PROVINCE

Chambas to Caibarién via Circuito Norte   Classic rural scenery: tobacco fields tended by ox-drawn plows, shaded by royal palms, with rustic *bohios* in the lee of mountains.

Trinidad to Sancti Spíritus via Circuito Sur   Roller-coaster ride through sugarcane fields in the Valle de los Ingenios and farther east past the rugged heights of the Alturas de Banao.

SUGGESTED ITINERARIES

The itineraries below assume you will spend at least three days in Havana, a recommended minimum.

A 7-DAY DRIVE FROM HAVANA

DAY 1 Drive the Circuito Norte via Mariel, enjoying the quintessential rural scenery. At San Diego de Nuñez, turn south for Las Terrazas. Hike, swim the local cascades, explore the village, visit Lester Campo's art gallery, dine at the old coffee *finca*. Overnight at the Hotel Moka.

DAY 2 Return to San Diego de Nuñez and continue west along the Circuito Norte to Viñales. Visit a tobacco farm and the Cueva del Indio. Overnight at Hotel La Ermita or *casa particular*.

DAY 3 Drive to Pinar del Río, and visit the cigar factory. Head east along the Autopista, turning inland for Parque Nacional la Güira to visit the Cuevas de las Portales. Continue east to Soroa to visit the orchid garden and cascade. Overnight at Villa Soroa or *casa particular*.

DAY 4 Visit the Cafetal Angarora in Artemisa and then continue east via the Autopista to Australia. Turn south for the crocodile farm at La Boca, and Museo Playa Girón at Playa Girón (Bay of Pigs). Continue via Yaguarams to Cienfuegos. Overnight at the Hotel Yagua or *casa particular*.

DAY 5 East via the Circuito Sur to Trinidad. Overnight in this colonial gem at a *casa particular*.

DAY 6 Full day exploring Trinidad, with an afternoon break on the beach at Playa Ancón.

DAY 7 Head north through the Sierra Escambray via Topes de Collantes, Manicaragua, and Santa Clara. Visit to the Museo de Che in Santa Clara, then return to Havana via the Autopista.

A 14-DAY DRIVE FROM HAVANA (extension of 7-day drive)

DAY 7 Head north through the Sierra Escambray via Topes de Collantes, with time for hiking or a horseback ride. Return to Trinidad.

DAY 8 Continue east through the Valle de Ingenios, briefly calling in at Sancti Spíritus to roam the historic plazas. Continue along the Carretera Central via Ciego de Ávila (no need to stop); turn north for Morón and Cayo Coco. Overnight at Cayo Coco or Cayo Guillermo.

DAY 9 Full day to relax on the beach or go scuba diving.

---

partly due to the very difficult driving test (all Cuban drivers attend a two-month driving course that includes four weeks of theoretical classes). Cubans rarely display typical Latin tendencies behind the wheel. They drive relatively slowly (far *too* slowly sometimes, but you can't blame them in their four-decades-old clunkers). They also obey traffic signals, mostly, and for the most part are respectful. But then again, there are traffic police everywhere.

Keep your speed down. The main cause of traffic deaths in Cuba is collisions with bicycles and wayward livestock that wander freely onto highways. Oxen, farmers driving ox-carts and bicyclists all have a tendency to turn into your path at the moment you decide to pass (Cubans in the boonies are not used to seeing other traffic, so it isn't on their minds). Driving at night is perilous—most roads are unlighted, few have side rails or painted markings at the margins, and there are always pedestrians and animals to contend with.

Sticks jutting up in the road usually indicate a huge pothole. Slow down if you see the sign *topes* or *túmulos*, meaning "road bumps." The first time you barrel over them heedlessly will serve notice to respect the warning next time.

Even on the darkest of days, with torrential rains falling, Cubans will forego using headlights, perhaps because headlights by day are illegal except for emergency vehicles. Still, use yours and be seen! Every second Cuban you pass will raise their hands and make a motion like a quacking duck to let you know. *Quack! quack!*

Vamos por el camino corecto—in essence, "Drive Safely!"

DAY 10 Return to Morón and head west along the Circuito Norte via Yaguajay, perhaps stopping at Sendero Ecoturístico Pelú de Mayijagua to hike the Sierra de Jatobónico. Just east of Caibarién take the causeway to Cayo Las Brujas or Cayo Santa María.

DAY 11 Full day to relax on the beach or go scuba diving.

DAY 12 Continue west to Remedios, with the morning to explore the colonial streets. Then on to Santa Clara to visit the Tren Blindado and Museo de Che. Overnight at Hotel Los Caneyes or a *casa particular*.

DAY 13 West along the Carretera Central to Matanzas via San Miguel de los Baños. Either continue to Havana or overnight at Casa del Valle or at Jibacoa.

DAY 14 Return to Havana.

A 10-DAY SOJOURN IN AND AROUND SANTIAGO

DAY 1 Explore the histÍoric center, taking in Calle Heredia, main plazas, and museums. In the evening, check out the Casa de la Trova.

DAY 2 Visit the cigar factory, Santa Ifigenia cemetery, Plaza de la Revolución (including the Museo de Antonio Maceo), and the Moncada barracks. In the evening, visit the Tropicana nightclub.

DAY 3 Take a taxi to the Morro castle, then visit Cayo Granma for lunch. Return to town and explore Reparto Vista Alegre.

DAY 4 Hire a car and drive out to El Cobre. Continue to El Saltón for hiking. Overnight in the mountains.

DAY 5 Continue west to Bayamo, with full day to explore. Overnight in Bayamo.

DAY 6 West via Bueycito to Bartolomé Maso and—with a 4WD—transcend the Sierra Maestra via Las Mercedes to Marea del Portillo. Overnight in Marea del Portillo.

DAY 7 Return to Santiago along the coast road via Chivirico.

DAY 8 Drive up to Gran Piedra for hiking, and the Ave de Paraíso garden. Descend and continue to Granjita Siboney, the Spanish-American War Museum, Valle de la Prehistória and El Oasis. Overnight at Hotel Bucanero or in Siboney.

DAY 9 Full day to relax on the beach.

DAY 10 Return to Santiago.

Accidents and Breakdowns

One of the most common sights in Cuba is to see a car stalled in the road with females sitting stoically to the side while the males toil to jury-rig a repair. If your car breaks down, there will be no shortage of Cubans willing to offer advice and consummate fix-it skills. If the problem is minor, fine. However, rental car agencies usually have a clause to protect against likely damage to the car from unwarranted repairs. For major problems, call the rental agency; it will arrange a tow or send a mechanic.

You should also call the agency in the event of an accident. After an accident, *never* move the vehicles until the police arrive. Get the names, license plate numbers, and *cedulas* (legal identification numbers) of any witnesses. Make a sketch of the accident. Then call the **transit po-**lice, tel. (7) 82-0116 in Havana; tel. 116 outside Havana.

Do *not* offer statements to anyone other than the police. In case of injury, call the **Red Cross** (unfortunately, there is no national emergency telephone number to summon an ambulance, although several cities are served by calling 118). Try not to leave the accident scene, or at least keep an eye on your car; the other party may tamper with the evidence. And don't let honking traffic pressure you into moving the cars.

The *tráficos*—traffic police—are usually level-headed. However, as a foreigner with deep pockets, the blame might be assigned to you in the event that it cannot be proved otherwise. Don't expect much help from locals. Cubans are loath to involve themselves where the police are con-

DISTANCES FROM HAVANA

All figures represent kilometers.

Baracoa 1,069
Bayamo 842
Camagüey. 570
Cárdenas. 152
Ciego de Ávila 461
Cienfuegos 336
Guantánamo. 971
Holguín 771
Isla de la Juventud 138
Las Tunas 694
Matanzas. 101
Pinar del Río 176
Rancho Boyeros. 17
Sancti Spíritus 386
Santa Clara 300
Santiago de Cuba 876
Soroa 95
Surgidero de Batabanó 56
Trinidad 454
Varadero 140
Viñales. 188

cerned. Show the police your license and car rental documents, but make sure you get them back (if you suspect the other driver has been drinking, ask the policeman to administer a Breathalyzer test—an *alcolemia*). The *tráfico* cannot levy a fine on the spot. If someone is seriously injured or killed and you are blamed, you should immediately contact your embassy for legal assistance. **Asistur,** Paseo de Martí #254, Havana, tel. (7) 33-8930 or 57-1314, can also offer legal and other assistance.

Gasoline

Gasoline (petrol) is sold at **Servi-Cupet** stations nationwide. Virtually every town has a Cupet station, plus at least one other station serving gas for pesos to locals; otherwise, gas stations are few and far between. In 1998 a second company began opening state-of-the-art, dollars-only gas stations under the nomenclature **Oro Negro.** Gasoline is readily available everywhere. Still, it's wise to not let your gas tank get below half full, especially since occasional electrical blackouts shut the pumps down. If you run out of gas, there's sure to be someone willing to sell from private stock.

Gasoline costs US$0.90 per liter—about US$3.40 a gallon. (Cupet stations accept U.S. dollars only. "Regular" and "Superior" grades are available, but as yet unleaded gas is not.)

Cubans without dollars have a harder time of things. Gas station attendants do a brisk business by siphoning off a liter of gas here and there for sale on the black market.

Insurance

If you rent a car, you will be responsible for any damage or theft. Hence you should purchase insurance offered by the rental agency. It costs US$8-15 daily with a deductible (you pay the first US$200-500 or so), or US$12-20 for fully comprehensive coverage. Inspect your car thoroughly for damage and marks before setting off; otherwise, you may be charged for the slightest dent when you return. On the diagram you'll be given to sign, note even the most innocuous marks. Don't forget the inside, as well as the radio antenna. Defrosters often don't work (you'll need to bring a rag to wipe the windows, since they will tend to fog up). **Note:** you can use your a/c to clear up condensation only briefly, after which it cools the windows too much, causing condensation. Don't assume the car rental agency has taken care of tire pressures or fluids. Check them yourself before you set off.

If you have your own vehicle, the state-run organization **ESEN,** Calle 18 e/ Aves. 5ta y 7ma, Miramar, Havana, tel. (7) 29-6510 or 24-1763 (ask for Maritza Naranjo), insures automobiles and has special packages for foreigners. It offers a choice of all risks, including theft, roll-overs, "catastrophes," and "partial theft." I insured my motorbike for a premium of US$8,000; the policy cost US$228, including theft, fire, accident, and a small medical premium (my policy was valid for three months at 40% of the annual premium).

Maps and Directions

Cuban roads are very well signed. However, many signs are where you'd never think of looking or are otherwise obscured. Ask directions whenever you're in doubt. However, it's extraordinary how little Cubans know of regions outside their own locale. You may as well ask them directions to the far side of the moon. In the countryside, you'll need to phrase your questions so as not to preempt the answer. For example, rather than asking, "Does this road go to so-and-so?" (which will surely earn you a reply, *"Sí, señor!"*), ask "Where does this route go?"

You should acquire as many maps as you can lay your hands on. The best resource is the *Guía de Carreteras,* a complete atlas in booklet form for drivers, published by Editorial Limusa, Balderas 95, Mexico DF, CP 06040, tel. (05) 521-2105, fax (05) 512-2903. It can be purchased in Cuba from tour desks and souvenir outlets. The best general map of Cuba is *Kuba/Cuba,* published by Cartographia of Budapest. The 1:250,000-scale map is fairly accurate. So, too, is the one published by Freytag & Berndt. Both feature streets maps of leading cities on the reverse sides. You can order it online from www.cubabooks.com.

Otherwise look for *Automapa Nacional,* published by Ediciones Geo and available for sale at many tourist souvenir outlets. Cuba's Instituto Cubano de Geodesia y Cartografía publishes a road map *(mapa de carreteras)* for each province. They're quite detailed. Most maps published in Cuba are several years out of date. And even the best maps show paved roads that are in fact dirt roads—or mere figments of cartographic imagination.

Traffic Police
Traffic police, or *tráficos* (mostly motorcycle cops), patrol the main highways. Often there's a cop at the entrance and exit of a town. Oncoming cars will flash their lights to indicate, "Slow down—police ahead." Cuban traffic cops are generally very scrupulous and courteous with foreigners (they'll usually greet you and send you on your way with a salute), though usually Hitlerite with Cubans.

If you're stopped, the police will ask to see your license, passport, and rental contract. Speeding fines are usually paid through the car rental agency. Don't think you can get away without paying a fine. Delinquent fines are reported to the immigration authorities, who may catch you as you attempt to exit the country. The best advice is: don't speed!

Throughout Havana and on major country highways, you'll pass *puntos de control*—control points—manned by police and looking like tiny air-traffic-control towers. You are expected to slow down. Signs give advance warning.

Car Rentals
No, you can't book Avis or Hertz in Cuba and must make do with the badly managed Cuban car rental agencies that offer ill-maintained, albeit modern, cars. You can rent a car at the airport upon arrival. If you're tired or jet-lagged, this is not a good idea: relax for a day or two, and then rent your car. The demand is so great that even in off-season many rental outlets have no small cars available. If you're planning on traveling to Cuba during peak Christmas and New Year season, you'll absolutely need to make reservations. Make sure you clarify any one-way drop-off fees, late return penalties, etc. If you book from abroad, ask for a copy of the reservation to be faxed to you and take this copy with you to Cuba. The companies accept payment by Visa, MasterCard, Eurocard, Banamex, Carnet, and JCB, as well as in cash and travelers' checks. You will normally be required to pay a deposit of US$500 (perhaps more).

Be sure to book a current-year model only. Most Cuban car rental agencies fail to budget for adequate maintenance and let their cars go to ruin quickly—often dangerously so! Don't accept a car without thoroughly inspecting it, including a test drive. Insist on this. And note every scratch and dent in the car on the rental form before leaving, or you could end up being charged for damage that already existed. This scam is frequent.

The range of vehicle options is extensive. You can usually choose manual or automatic, although the particular agency (or the specific location where you book) may not have the model you request. Normally it can arrange for the model you want to be delivered. Agencies will deliver and pick up from your hotel (larger upscale tourist hotels have their car rental desks on-site).

If your car is broken into or otherwise damaged, you must get a police statement—otherwise, you may be charged for the damage (check the fine print on the contract).

Most agencies offer a **chauffeur service** for US$30 a day.

In the U.K., you can book cars in advance through **Havanatur U.K.,** 27 Stafford Rd., Croydon, Surrey CR0 4NG, tel. (0181) 681-3613, fax (0181) 760-0031. Rates begin at £30 per day for a Daewoo Tico, £37 for a convertible Daihatsu Jeep, and £43 for a Nissan Sentra, based on a one-week rental.

Rates: Expect to pay about US$45-100 per day, plus insurance, depending on the size of the vehicle. Substantial discounts apply for rentals over seven days. You will normally be required to pay a deposit of US$250. Most companies offer a choice of Type A insurance (with a deductible of US$250) or Type B (fully comprehensive, except car radio and one tire). If you plan on doing considerable mileage, take the unlimited mileage option. *(Jiniteros on Calle 23 and La Rampa, in Havana, will offer to alter your odometer to avoid excess mileage charge. ¿Kilometraje?)*

Note that if you extend over the return period, you'll be billed on an *hourly* basis for additional time (make sure the time recorded on your contract is that for your *departure with the car,* not the time you entered into negotiations). Also check the fuel level carefully *before* setting off. If it doesn't look full to the brim, point this out to the rental agent; otherwise, you could be the victim of an impending scam (if you return the car with the same amount of fuel, you may be charged for the extra gas needed to top up the tank—and the agent will no doubt be pocketing the difference, having recorded a full tank when you rented the car).

Rental Companies: Most of the following car agencies based in Havana also have regional offices. Most are badly managed, cars are ill-maintained, and scams are common. See regional chapters for details on local service.

The largest agency, **Havanautos,** Edificio Sierra Maestra, Calle 1ra y O, Miramar, Havana, tel. (7) 23-9815 or 24-0646 reservations, fax (7) 24-0648, website: www.havanautos.cubaweb.cu, offers a range of Japanese cars in all categories, from a small Daewoo Tico (US$50 per day with unlimited mileage; less for seven days or more, on a sliding scale) to a five-passenger Daewoo Leganza for US$77 daily, a Daihatsu Tenios jeep for US$70 daily, and a six-passenger Dodge Caravan for US$120 daily. "Special Weekend" package rates are offered, but they don't pro-

vide any extra savings. Insurance is additional—US$9 per day with US$250 deductible, US$15 with no deductible. See Scams, below.

Micar, 1ra y Paseo, Vedado, Havana, tel. (7) 55-2444, fax (7) 33-6476, rents five models of Fiats. The Cinquecento, Uno, Panda, and Punto are all small and perfect for nippy commuting in Havana or for two people for touring. Rates are US$35-45 daily (with a 100 km limit; US$0.20 per extra km) or US$45-55 for unlimited mileage. A larger Fiat Brava costs US$65 or US$77.

Palcocar, tel. (7) 33-7235, fax (7) 33-7250, serves the convention business and rents Subaru Vivio's (US$35 daily, US$45 with unlimited mileage) and Mitsubishi Lancers (US$50 per day; US$65 with unlimited mileage).

Panautos, Linea y Malecón, Vedado, Havana, tel. (7) 55-3286, fax (7) 55-657, e-mail: panatrans@dpt.transnet.cu, specializes in diesel vehicles and rents seven-seat Mitsubishi jeeps (US$130) and Ssangyong Musso jeeps (US$95), plus Citroën sedans (from US$51). Prices include limited mileage.

Rex Limousine Service, Av. de Rancho Boyeros y Calzada de Bejucal in Plaza de la Revolución, Havana, tel. (7) 33-9160, fax (7) 33-9159, e-mail: rex@ceniai.inf.cu, website: www.rex-limousine.com, rents Audi A4s and A6s from US$65 daily plus US$20 insurance; Volvo sedans from US$150 per day, US$750 weekly plus insurance (US$25 daily); and Volvo limousines for US$325 daily, US$1,625 weekly including insurance and chauffeur. Hourly rentals are available.

Via Rent-a-Car, Av. del Puerto #102, between Obrapía and Justiz, Havana, tel. (7) 33-9781 or 66-6777, fax (7) 33-2780, e-mail: dtor _rc@nwgaitov.gav.cm.net, a division of Gaviota, rents Peugeots (US$40-80 daily depending on model for 100 km, then US$0.35 per km extra; US$48-92 unlimited mileage); Suzuki jeeps (US$38 daily for 1997 models, US$48 for 1999 models; US$46-60 unlimited mileage); and Ssangyong sedans. Each additional designated driver costs US$10 (US$15 if the driver is Cuban). Chauffeurs cost US$30 daily.

Other car rental agencies include **Cubacar,** Av. 5ta y 84, Miramar, tel. (7) 24-2718, fax (7) 33-7233; **Fenix,** Calle Cuba #66, Habana Vieja, tel. (7) 63-9720, fax (7) 66-9546; and **Transauto,** Calle 3ra #2605 e/ 26 y 28, Miramar, tel. (7) 24-

5532, fax (7) 24-4057. Cubacar rents the Suzuki X-90, a sprightly 4WD two-seater with poptop roof—a fun car as surprisingly capable off-road as on.

Four-Wheel Drive: For most exploring, you don't need a 4WD. You'll want one, however, for exploring the Sierra Maestra, Sierra Cristál, Sierra del Purial, and Cuchillas de Toa, many of the roads leading to and along virtually the entire southern shore, the extreme northwest coast, the Peninsula de Guanahacabibes, and the extreme south of Isla de la Juventud. This is especially true in rainy season, when dirt roads become veritable morasses.

Fly-Drive Packages: Viajes Horizontes, Calle 23 #156 e/ N y O, Vedado, tel. (7) 33-4042, fax (7) 33-4361, e-mail: crh@s1.hor. cma .net, website: www.horizont.cu, part of the Hoteles Horizontes group, offers a "Flexi Fly & Drive" prepaid package combining car rental and hotel vouchers that offers the freedom to follow your whims. You simply pick up your car at any of the international airports in Havana, Varadero, Holguín, or Santiago de Cuba and hit the road armed with vouchers good at any of Horizontes' 70-plus hotels islandwide. The standard six- or 13-night package includes a stick-shift Audi A4 or Volvo plus double room with EP plan. The package offers unlimited mileage and the flexibility of traveling wherever you wish without hotel reservations (except for the first night, which is reserved in advance). Another benefit is that you can drop the car off at any of the other locations at no additional charge. Nor do you have to pay a deposit for the car rental. Children under 12 travel free. Horizontes has 24-hour service.

Cubanacán, Av. 146 y 9na, Miramar, Havana, tel. (7) 33-6044, fax (7) 33-6702, has a "Fly-Drive & Diving" program, as does **Havanatur,** Calle 6 #117 e/ 1 y 3, Miramar, Havana, tel. (7) 24-2424.

In the U.K., **Journey Latin America** (see the By Air section under Getting There, above), offers two two-week fly-drive programs with set itineraries, departing London's Stansted airport on Thursday year-round. The first includes nights in Havana, Sancti Spíritus, Camagüey, Santiago de Cuba, and Holguín; the second is a shortened version—Havana to Holguín.

Campervans: Campervans have come to Cuba courtesy of an Italian company—**Cubamar Campertour,** Via Ghibbellina 110, 1-50122 Firenze, Italy, tel. (055) 239-6293, fax (055) 238-2042, e-mail: lucia99@ats.it, working in association with Cubamar and using imported BRIG 670s, which sleep six people. The vehicles are powered by Mercedes turbo diesel engines and contain all the services of a small apartment: bathroom with flush toilet and shower, kitchen with fridge and three-burner stove, wardrobes, and even a security box. No prices had been established at press time.

Guides: You can request a personal guide from most of the car rental offices nationwide. Most are familiar with at least two languages. They're also extremely well versed in history. For example, contact **Havanatur,** Calle 6 #117 e/ 1 y 3, Miramar, Havana, tel. (7) 24-2424.

Scams: Several car rental agencies have been accused of scams. There are many tricks and ploys, including renting cars with partially filled gas tanks, attempts to charge for damage your didn't cause, "not returning the car on time," failing to service the car. For example, Havanautos' Isla de la Juventud office claimed that it was not authorized to rent me a car with a full tank of gas. I had to pay for 30 liters, which was just sufficient to cover the distance I intended to travel. I was encouraged to buy more gas at the gas station. Inevitably you return the car with gasoline that you've paid for, but for which you cannot receive a refund. Another common trick is to try to charge you when you return the car claiming, for example, that you failed to "maintain" the car (this scam is often used if the odometer passes a significant mileage, such as 10,000 km, during your journey).

Motorcycles and Scooters: At press time, you could not rent motorcycles in Cuba. Maybe you can negotiate to rent a Ural or MZ or—heavens!—an old Harley from one of Havana's *harlistas.* However, small Japanese and Italian scooters can be rented from Rumbos stands at virtually all the main resorts. Rates are about US$30 a day, plus insurance. They're highly unstable, especially in the sand-blown streets of resorts. If you opt for a scooter, drive slowly and cautiously.

Taking Your Own Motorcycle: Yes, you can take your own motorbike, although this is not as easy as it was few years ago when I did it. Outside the U.S., you can ship your motorcycle air freight with most scheduled carriers. You would be wise to contact a motorcycle shipping broker, who can usually get better rates and can take care of freighting insurance, etc. In Germany, contact **MHS Motorradtouren GmbH,** Donnersbergerstrasse 32, D-8000 Munich 19, tel. (089) 168-4888, fax (089) 166-5549.

Getting there from the U.S. is more of a problem. Legally, you require an export license from the U.S. Commerce Department to take a vehicle to Cuba. Unless you can show sufficient cause, your request will be denied. Hence if you travel unlicensed, you could run afoul of authorities, who could seize your motorbike. Nonetheless, many U.S. sailors take their motorbikes into Cuba. Alternately, consider freighting by sea from Canada or Tampico (Mexico) aboard **Coral Container Lines,** Calle Oficios #170, Havana, tel. (7) 57-0925, fax (7) 33-8115, e-mail: info@coral.com.cu, website: www.coral. cubaweb.cu, Cuba's freight service. And Cubana charges about US$1,000 one-way from Mexico aboard its DC-10. However, the Mexican route is a Kafkaesque experience.

THE BICYCLE REVOLUTION

*I*n 1991, when the first shipment of Flying Pigeon bicycles arrived from China, there were only an estimated 30,000 bicycles in Havana, a city of two million people. The visitor arriving in Havana today could be forgiven for imagining he or she had arrived in Ho Chi Minh City. Bicycles are everywhere, outnumbering cars, trucks, and buses 20 to one. The story is the same across Cuba.

Cynics have dubbed Cuba's wholesale switch to bicycles since the collapse of the Soviet bloc as a socialist failing, a symbol of the nation's backwardness. Others acclaim it an astounding achievement, a two-wheel triumph over an overnight loss of gasoline and adversity. *Granma,* the Cuban newspaper, christened it the "bicycle revolution."

American cars had flooded the island for half a century. Then came the U.S. trade embargo. The 1960s saw the arrival of the first sober-looking Lada and Moskovitch sedans, imported in the ensuing decades by the tens of thousands from the Soviet Union, along with Hungarian and Czech buses, which provided an efficient transport network. The Eastern bloc buses were notorious for their lack of comfort, as were the stunted Girón buses that Cuba began producing in 1967. But they carried millions of Cubans for years despite their defects. Professor Maurice Halperin, who taught at the University of Havana, does not "recall seeing a single adult Cuban on a bicycle in Havana during the entire period of my residence in the city, from 1962 to 1968."

Goodbye to Gas
The collapse of the Soviet Union severed the nation's gasoline pipeline. Transportation ground to a halt, along with the rest of the Cuban economy.

In November 1990 the Cuban government launched sweeping energy-saving measures that called for a "widespread substitution of oxen for farm machinery and hundreds of thousands of bicycles for gasoline-consuming vehicles." Cuba's program of massive importation, domestic production, and mass distribution was launched as a "militant and defensive campaign," symbolized on 1 May 1991 when the armed forces appeared on bicycles in the May Day parade.

The government contracted with China to purchase 1.2 million bicycles, and by the end of 1991, 530,000 single-gear Chinese bicycles were in use on the streets of Havana.

Cuba: Bicycle Capital of the Americas
Overnight, Cuba transformed itself into the bicycle capital of the Americas. "The comprehensiveness and speed of implementation of this program," said a 1994 World Bank report, "is unprecedented in the history of transportation." The report noted that about two million bicycles were in use islandwide.

"Today, we can say that the bicycle is as much a part of the Cuban scenario as the palm tree," says Narciso Hernández, director of Empresa Claudio Arugelles Fábrica de Bicicletas, in Havana. Hernandez's factory is one of five established in 1991 by the Cuban government to supplement the Chinese imports. Each of the factories produces a different model. Cuba imports parts such as small bolts, chains, spindles, and brakes, but makes the frames, forks, and handlebars.

The bicycles are disbursed through MINCIN (Ministerio de Comercial Interior), which parcels them out to schools, factories, and workers' associations. Others are sold at special stores. Lucky recipients can purchase their bicycles outright or pay for them

Documentation in Cuba: Upon arrival in Cuba (presumably at Marina Hemingway), you'll be given a letter from Cuban Customs (make sure it has an official stamp), which grants you one week in which to register with the main Customs office at Terminal Sierra Maestra in Habana Vieja (it was scheduled to move at press time). Here you're given another official form that grants you the right to import your motorbike for 30 days (you'll need to return to this office to have it extended, in increments of 30 days), but I am informed that you must now post a bond equivalent to 100% of the value of the motorcycle. You then go to the main Transit Police office at Avenida 1ra e/ 12 y 14 in Miramar to have your motorbike inspected and receive a *chapa* (license plate). You'll need to take a special 10-peso stamp, which you purchase at any post office. The whole process will cost US$0.50. The inspectors will make an imprint of your vehicle registration number.

If you wish to renew your *chapa* for an additional 30 days, you have to visit the *tránsito* office at Via Blanca and Aguas Claras, rather than at

---

in monthly installments. Workers pay 125 pesos—equivalent to about half the average monthly salary—while students pay 65 pesos.

The Chinese bicycles were cumbersome, hard-to-pump beasts—true antediluvian pachyderms with only one gear. Worse, they weighed 48 pounds. The Cubans redesigned the chunky models with smaller frames, thereby lopping off 15 pounds. Cubans manage to coax great speed from their sturdy steeds. Young men zigzag through the streets, disdainful of all other traffic, while old men and women pedal painstakingly down the middle of the road with leisurely sovereignty, like sacred cattle. During the early phase of the bicycle revolution, hospital emergency rooms were flooded with victims. Most Cubans had never ridden bicycles before. They teetered en masse through the potholed streets, often with passengers, even whole families, hanging onto jury-rigged seats and rear-hub extenders. Due to the paucity of cars, cyclists rode the wrong way down major boulevards, which they crisscrossed at will. Few *bicis* had rear reflectors, and the brakes on the Chinese-made models barely worked. Handlebar warning bells chirp incessantly.

Cuban planners like Gina Rey, of the Grupo para el Desarrollo Integral de la Capital (Group for the Integral Development of the Capital), Calle 28 #113 e/ 1ra y 3ra, Miramar, tel. (7) 22-7303, (7) 22-7322, fax: (7) 24-2661, e-mail: gdic@ceniai.inf.cu, were challenged to reorganize Havana's transportation network to prevent turmoil on the streets. The plan called for many colonial streets in Habana Vieja to be closed to motorized traffic. Bicycle lanes were created. The city government initiated classes in bicycle safety. Bicycle parking lots were cleared throughout the city. Ferryboats threading their way across Havana harbor were equipped for bicycles. And special buses *(Ciclobuses)* were detailed to carry cy-

clists through the tunnel beneath the bay.

"We've entered the bicycle era," Castro has noted. "But after this Special Period disappears we mustn't abandon this wonderful custom." Bicycles would solve many of the country's energy quandaries—and pollution and health problems, too. "With bicycle, we will improve the quality of life in our society," Castro claims. Anyone who has seen Hungarian buses coughing fitfully through the streets of Cuba, belching thick black clouds, would agree.

aboard a ciclobus, wheels on wheels

Avenida 1ra. First, though, you'll need to receive a 30-day extension from customs (if you landed your vehicle at Marina Hemingway, you'll need to get a letter from the Customs office there). Fortunately, the extension costs nothing—but it does have to be obtained in Havana.

BY BICYCLE

I've bumped into a handful of foreigners cycling independently through Cuba. You'll need to take your own bike, as there are no rentals in Cuba. One essential item: a sturdy lock. Always take precautions against theft (keep your bicycle in your hotel room). You can even buy mountain bikes in Cuba at dollar stores, but they're cheap Chinese crap. (Also see the Recreation section, above.)

Although they do not have sections on Cuba, *Latin America by Bike: A Complete Touring Guide,* by Walter Sienko (Seattle, WA: The Mountaineers, 1993), and *Latin America by Bike,* by J.P. Panet (New York: Passport Press, 1987) provide good insight into preparing for cycling in the Americas.

HITCHHIKING

Stoics among stoics can travel the Cuban way. Four decades of fidelismo have had such a traumatic effect on the transportation system that the populace now relies on anything that moves. The roadways of Cuba are lined with hundreds of thousands of hitchers, many of them so desperate after hours in the sun that they wave peso bills at passing cars. *Hitchhiking is how the majority of Cubans get around.*

So many Cubans rely on hitching that the state has set up *botellas* (literally bottles, but colloquially used to signify hitchhiking posts) on the edge of towns. Here officials of the Inspección Estatal, wearing mustard-colored uniforms (and therefore termed *coges amarillas,* or yellow-jackets) are in charge. They wave down virtually anything that comes rolling along, and all state vehicles—those with red license plates—must stop to pick up hitchers. Many *botellas* even have rain shelters and steps to help you climb into trucks. Early morning is easiest for hitching, when there's more traffic.

A queue system prevails: first come, first serve. The Cubans will be honored and delighted by the presence of a foreigner and may usher you to the front of the line. You, they realize, have restricted time; they have all the time in the world.

Cuba is probably the safest place in the world to hitch, though it may be excruciatingly slow going. In Cuba if buses don't go where you're going, don't expect to see many cars. And sticking out your thumb won't do it. Do things the Cuban way, try to wave down the vehicle—whether it be a tractor, a truck, or a motorcycle. If it moves in Cuba it's fair game. Open-

Hitchhiking is an accepted mode of public transportation.

CUBAN TOUR OPERATORS

AGENCY	ADDRESS	TELEPHONE	FAX
Agencía San Cristóbal	Oficios #110 e/ Lamparilla y Amargura, Habana Vieja	(7) 33-9585	(7) 33-9586
Cubadeportes	20 #706 e/ Calle 7ma y 9na, Miramar, Havana	(7) 24-0945	(7) 24-1914
Cubamar	15 #752 esq. Paseo, Vedado, Havana	(7) 66-2423	(7) 33-3111
Cubanacán Viaje Tours	Calle 146 e/ 9 y 11, Playa, Havana	(7) 33-6042	(7) 33-0107
Cubatur	Calle 15 #410 e/ F y G, Vedado, Havana	(7) 33-4121	(7) 33-3104
Gaviota Tours	Av. 49 esq. Calle 36A, Reparto Kohly, Havana	(7) 24-4781	(7) 24-9470
	16 e/ 5ta y 7ma, Miramar, Havana	(7) 66-6765	(7) 33-2780
Havanatur's Tours & Travel	Calle 0 y 1ra, Miramar, Havana	(7) 23-9783	(7) 24-1760
Mercadu	13 #951 esq. Calle 8, Vedado, Havana	(7) 33-3893	(7) 33-3028
Paradiso	19 #560 esq. C, Vedado, Havana	(7) 32-9538	(7) 33-3921
Rumbos	Casa Matriz, Linea y M, Havana	(7) 66-9713	(7) 24-4520
Sol y Son	Calle 23 #64, Vedado. Havana	(7) 33-3162	(7) 33-5150
Viajes Horizontes	Calle 23 #156 e/ N y O, Vedado, Havana	(7) 33-4042	(7) 33-4361

bed trucks are the most common vehicles (no fun if it rains).

If you receive a ride in a private car, politeness dictates that you offer to pay for your ride: *"¿Cuando lo debo?"* after you're safely delivered. Even Cubans pay a few coins, and so should you. Expect to be asked for dollars as a foreigner.

Picking up hitchhikers is normal and integral to showing your goodwill.

ORGANIZED EXCURSIONS

If your time is limited and you like the idea of a smooth-running itinerary, book an excursion with one of the national tour agencies. This gives you the added flexibility of making your own tour arrangements once you've arrived in Cuba and gained a better sense of your options and desires.

This is one area where Cuba runs a world-class operation. Most are up to Western levels of efficiency and service. Cuba has a surprisingly large and modern fleet of buses and minibuses for transfers, excursions, and touring. English-speaking guides, private transportation, meals, and accommodations are standard inclusions. You can book excursions at the tour desk in the lobby of virtually any tourist hotel. See the Havana and regional chapters for details. Also see the Recreation section, this chapter.

Foreign Pastures: Cuba is actively promoting multi-destination travel, combining Cuba with a visit to one or more neighboring countries. For example, **Havanatur Multidestino,** Av. 1ra y 0, Miramar, Havana, tel. (7) 24-2090, promotes multi-destination "Vacation Plus!" packages combining excursions in Cuba with a choice of Cancún, Mérida, Nassau, Jamaica, Costa Rica, Panamá, Guatemala, and other destinations served by Cubana Aviación. And **Italturist,** tel./fax (7) 33-3977 in Havana, tel. (02) 535-4949 and fax (02) 535-4901 in Milan, offers five-day eco-archaeological excursions from Havana to Campeche.

IMMIGRATION AND CUSTOMS

DOCUMENTS AND REQUIREMENTS

Tourist Visas

A valid passport is required for entry. Citizens of Japan, Malaysia, Peru, and Singapore need a visa to enter Cuba obtainable from Cuban consulates. For other foreign visitors, including U.S. citizens, a tourist visa will suffice. No tourist visa is required for a stay of less than 72 hours.

Tourist visas (US$25, or £15 in the U.K.) are issued by approved tour agencies abroad (see the tour operators listed under the Getting There section in this chapter). Normally the visas will be issued at the ticket counter of the airline providing travel to Cuba when you check in. In some cases they are issued at an airport upon arrival within Cuba, but don't count on it. If you apply for a tourist visa through a Cuban consulate, it can take six or more weeks (go in person if possible). Many commercial agencies charge a fee for issuing tourist visas.

Foreigners are limited to a 60-day stay. Your initial tourist visa is good for one entry for 30 days only, but you can request a single 30-day extension, or *prórroga,* (US$25) from the Ministerio del Interior (MININT). Alas, in Havana the immigration table in the lobby of the Hotel Habana Libre has been supplanted by the need to visit the immigration office on Calle 17, e/ J y K (open Mon.-Fri. 10 a.m.-1 p.m. and 2-4 p.m.) You're thrown in with Cubans, so expect a long wait to be processed. Later in the day is best. Extensions can also be obtained at Marina Hemingway for people arriving by private vessel. If traveling in the provinces, it may be easier to visit a regional immigration office.

Don't list your occupation as journalist, police, military personnel, or government employer, as the Cuban government is highly suspicious of anyone with these occupations. Listing yourself as such can cause problems. "Consultant" is a far safer gambit.

U.S. Citizens: Officially, U.S. citizens need a visa, although in practice a tourist visa is all you'll need. Visas can be obtained in advance from the Cuban Interests Section, 2630 16th St., NW, Washington, D.C. 20009, tel. (202) 797-8518, fax (202) 797-8521, e-mail: cubaseccion@igc.apc.com. Visas may take months to obtain. Even then, you're not guaranteed a reply. It is far easier to obtain a tourist card from whichever licensed travel service provider makes your arrangements (see the special topic, U.S. Law and Travel to Cuba, in the Getting There section). If you're traveling with an organized group, the organization will obtain your visa in about two weeks.

In the past, Cuban authorities didn't stamp your passport, but they have taken to doing so with greater frequency, including arbitrarily yet "in a precise way" stamping a tiny, almost invisible, stamp on page 16 of some U.S. passports.

The U.S. government recommends that its citizens arriving in Cuba register at the U.S. Interests Section, located in the Swiss Embassy in the former U.S. Embassy building in Havana, on Calzada (Calle 5ta), e/ L y M in Vedado, tel. (7) 33-3551 to 33-3559, fax (7) 33-3700.

Cuban Émigrés: U.S. citizens of Cuban origin are required to enter and leave Cuba with Cuban passports (you will also need your U.S. passport to depart and enter the United States). No visa is required, but an entry permit (US$100) valid for a 21-day stay was necessary, issued by tour agencies or the Cuban Interests Section or any other Cuban embassy or consulate. Cuban émigrés who have "not demonstrated any hostile attitude toward Cuba and who do not have a criminal record in their country of residence" can obtain a **Multiple Entry Travel Visa** *(vigencia de viaje)* good for two years and entry to Cuba as many times as desired for periods of up to 90 days. A nonrefundable deposit of US$50 is required, plus a US$150 fee payable upon receipt of the permit (you'll need a valid Cuban passport, six passport pictures, and proof that you do not have a criminal record).

Uncle Sam permits Cuban-Americans to visit Cuba only once per year and only for reasons of extreme family hardship.

(Cuba does not recognize dual citizenship for Cuban citizens who are also U.S. citizens; Cuban-born citizens are—according to the U.S.

EMBASSIES AND CONSULATES IN CUBA

The following nations have embassies/consulates in Havana (additional countries can be found in the local telephone directory under *Embajadas*). Phone numbers and addresses change frequently. Call to confirm address and opening hours.

Argentina: Calle 36 #511 e/ 5ta y 7ma, Miramar, tel. (7) 24-2972, fax (7) 24-2140

Austria: Calle 4 #101 esq. 1ra, Miramar, tel. (7) 24-2394, fax (7) 24-1235

Belgium: Av. 5ta # 7408 esq. 76, Miramar, tel. (7) 24-2410, fax (7) 24-1318

Brazil: Calle 16 #503 e/ 5ta y 7ma, Miramar, tel. (7) 24-2139, fax (7) 24-2328

Canada: Calle 30 #518 esq. 7ma, Miramar, tel. (7) 24-2516, fax (7) 24-2044; emergency tel. (7) 24-2516

Chile: Av. 33 #1423, Miramar, tel. (7) 24-1222, fax (7) 24-1694

China, People's Republic of: Calle C #317 e/ 13 y 15, Vedado, tel. (7) 33-3005, fax (7) 33-3092

Colombia: Calle 14 #515 e/ 5ta y 7ma, Miramar, tel. (7) 24-1246, fax (7) 24-1249

Costa Rica: Calle 46 #306, Miramar, tel. (7) 24-6937

Czech Republic: Av. Kohly #259, Nuevo Vedado, tel. (7) 33-3467, fax (7) 33-3596

Denmark: Paseo de Martí #20, Habana Vieja, tel. (7) 33-8128, fax (7) 33-8127

Ecuador: Av. 5ta #4407 e/ 44 y 46, Miramar, tel. (7) 24-2034, fax (7) 24-2868

Finland: Calle 140 #3121 e/ 21 y 23, Miramar, tel./fax (7) 24-0793

France: Calle 14 #312 e/ 3ra y 5ta, Miramar, tel. (7) 24-2143, fax (7) 24-2317

Germany: Calle 13 #652, Vedado, tel. (7) 33-2460, fax (7) 33-1586

Greece: Av. 5ta #7802 esq. 78, Miramar, tel. (7) 24-2995, fax (7) 24-1784

Hungary: Calle G #458, Vedado, tel. (7) 33-3365, fax (7) 33-3286

India: Calle 21 #202 esq. K, Vedado, tel. (7) 33-3169, fax (7) 33-3287

Italy: Paseo #606 e/ 25 y 27, Vedado, tel. (7) 33-3378; e-mail: ambitcub@ceniai.inf.cu

Jamaica: Av. 5ta #3608 e/ 36 y 36A, Miramar, tel. (7) 24-2908

Japan: Calle N #62 esq. 15, Vedado, tel. (7) 33-3454, fax (7) 33-3172

Mexico: Calle 12 #518 e/ 5ta y 7ma, Miramar, tel. (7) 24-2909, fax (7) 24-2719

Netherlands: Calle 8 #307, e/ 5ta y 7ma, Miramar, tel. (7) 24-2511, fax (7) 24-2059

Nicaragua: Calle 20 #709, Miramar, tel. (7) 24-1025, fax (7) 24-6323

Norway: Paseo de Martí #20, Habana Vieja, tel. (7) 33-8128, fax (7) 33-8127

Panama: Calle 26 #109, Miramar, tel. (7) 24-1673, fax (7) 24-1674

Peru: Calle 36 #109 e/ 1ra y 3ra, Miramar, tel. (7) 24-2474, fax (7) 24-2636

Poland: Av. 5ta #4407, Miramar, tel. (7) 24-1323

Portugal: Av. 5ta #6604 e/ 66 y 68, Miramar, tel. (7) 24-2871, fax (7) 24-2593

Romania: Calle 21 #307, Vedado, tel. (7) 33-3325, fax (7) 33-3324

Russia: Av. 5ta #6402 e/ 62 y 66, Miramar, tel. (7) 24-1749, fax (7) 24-1074

Spain: Calle Cárcel #51 esq. Agramonte (Zulueta), Habana Vieja, tel. (7) 33-8025, fax (7) 33-8006

Sweden: Av. 31A #1411 e/ 14 y 18, Miramar, tel. (7) 24-2563, fax (7) 24-1194

Switzerland: Av. 5ta #2005 e/ 20 y 22, Miramar, tel. (7) 24-2611, fax (7) 24-1148

Turkey: Calle 20 #301, Miramar, tel. (7) 24-2933, fax (7) 24-2899

Ukraine: Av. 5ta #4405, Miramar, tel. (7) 24-2586, fax (7) 24-2341

United Kingdom: Calle 34 #708, Miramar, tel. (7) 24-1771, 24-1049, fax (7) 24-1772

United States: (Interests Section) Calzada e/ L y M, Vedado, tel. (7) 33-3551 to 33-3559, fax (7) 33-3700

Uruguay: Calle 14 #506 e/ 5ta y 7ma, Miramar, tel. (7) 24-2311, fax (7) 24-2246

Venezuela: Calle 36A #704 e/ 7ma y 42, Miramar, tel. (7) 24-2662, fax (7) 24-2773

Vietnam: Av. 5ta #1802, Miramar, tel. (7) 24-1042, fax (7) 24-1041

Yugoslavia: Calle 42 #115, Miramar, tel. (7) 24-2982, fax (7) 24-2982

Zimbabwe: Av. 3ra #1001, Miramar, tel. (7) 24-2137, fax (7) 24-2720

State Department—thereby denied representation through the U.S. Interests Section in the event of arrest).

Journalist Visas

Journalists are permitted a 90-day stay and must enter on a journalists' D-6 visa (US$60). Officially these should be obtained in advance from Cuban embassies, and in the U.S. from the Cuban Interests Section in Washington, D.C., 2630 16th St. NW, Washington, D.C.

CUBAN CONSULATES AND EMBASSIES ABROAD

Australia: 9-15 Bronte Rd. #804, Sydney NSW 2026, tel. (070) 354-1417

Canada: 388 Main St., Ottawa K1S 1E3, tel. (613) 563-0141, fax (613) 540-2066

China: 1 Xiushui Nanjie, Beijing 100600, tel. (10) 6532 2822, fax (10) 6532 1984

France: 16 rue de Presles, 75015 Paris, tel. (01) 45 67 55 35, fax (01) 45 66 80 92

Germany: Kennedy Allee 22-24, 5300 Bonn 2, Godesberg, tel. (0228) 885733

Greece: Sophokleoys 5, Athens, tel. (01) 6842807

Italy: Via Licinia 7, 00153 Rome, tel. (06) 575-5984

Mexico: Presidente Masarik 554, Colonia Polanco, Mexico 5 DF, tel. (05) 259-0045

Netherlands: Mauritskade 49, Den Haag, 2514 HG, tel. (070) 3606061

Portugal: R. Pero Covilha, 14, Lisbon 1400, (01) 301-5317, fax (01) 301-1895

Spain: Paseo de la Habana 194, Madrid 28071, tel. (01) 359-2500

Switzerland: Seminarstrasse 29, 3006 Bern, tel. (031) 444-834

United Kingdom: (Embassy) 167 High Holborn, London WC1V 6PA, tel. (0171) 240-2488

United Kingdom: (Consulate) 15 Grape St., London WC2H 8DR, tel. (0171) 240-2488

U.S.A: (Interests Section) 2630 16th St. NW, Washington, D.C. 20009, tel. (202) 797-8518, fax (202) 797-8512

20009, tel. (202) 797-8518, fax (202)797-8521, e-mail: cubaseccion@igc.apc.com. If you enter on a tourist visa and intend to exercise your profession, you must register for a D-6 visa at the **Centro de Prensa Internacional** (International Press Center), on La Rampa between N and O, tel. (7) 32-0526, fax (7) 33-3836. The *Accreditaciones de Prensa Extranjeras*—Foreign Journalist's Accreditation—office is to the rear of the *telecorreos* to the right of the entrance. A journalist's visa costs US$60. You'll need passport photos, which you can have taken at the Photo Service store adjoining the Press Center.

Other Visas

A commercial visa is required for individuals who are traveling to Cuba for business. These must be obtained in advance from Cuban embassies or from the Cuban Interests Section in Washington, D.C. (see above). If you wish to enter using a tourist visa and then, while within Cuba, change your visa status, contact the **Ministry of Foreign Affairs** (Ministerio de Relaciones Exteriores, or MINREX), Calle Calzada #360 y Avenida de los Presidentes, Vedado, tel. (7) 30-5031, fax (7) 31-2314, which handles immigration issues relating to foreigners.

Other Documentation and Considerations

All tourists may be required to demonstrate an outbound ticket and adequate finances for their proposed stay upon arrival. This is normally requested of travelers planning on staying 30 days or more. Cuban immigration authorities do not require travelers to show proof of immunizations or an international vaccination card.

The law requires that you carry your passport or tourist card with you at all times during your stay. It's a good idea to make photocopies of *all* your important documents, including your passport, and keep them separate from the originals, which you can keep in your hotel safe along with other valuables. It's wise, too, to take half a dozen passport-size photographs (you can have photos taken at most Photo Services stores throughout Cuba; and, in Havana, at the Centro de Prensa Internacional, see above). In the event of a problem, you should contact your embassy or consulate, plus MINREX (see above).

DRUGS

*C*uban law prohibits the possession, sale, or use of narcotic substances, including marijuana. Laws are strictly enforced, and Cuba vigorously prosecutes drug traffickers caught in Cuban territory. Nonetheless, drugs are finding their way to the island, and foreign visitors are often asked if they wish to buy marijuana and even cocaine. You may be dealing with a plain-clothes policeman. If you're caught, you will receive no special favors because you're foreign. A trial could take many months, in which case you'll be jailed on the premise that you're guilty until proven innocent.

Cuban officials are sensitive to incursions into the country by CIA agents, right-wing Cuban exiles, and other "antisocial" characters. They are also sensitive to your appearance, so be aware that you can help your own cause by looking neat and tidy. If you look like you'd be a "bad influence," you might be turned around and put on the next plane home.

CUSTOMS

Cuban airports have the international two-zone system (red, for items to declare) and green (nothing to declare). The customs regulations are complicated and open to interpretation by individual customs agents. Visitors to Cuba are permitted 20 kilos of personal effects plus "other articles and equipment depending on their profession," all of which must be re-exported. In addition, up to 10 kilos of medicines, 200 cigarettes, 50 cigars, 250 grams of pipe tobacco, and up to three liters of wine and alcohol, plus US$50 of additional goods are permitted tax free. An additional US$200 of "objects and articles for non-commercial use" can be imported, subject to a tax equal to 100 percent of the declared value (you must fill out a customs form and use the red zone), but this applies mostly to Cubans and returning foreign residents bringing in electrical goods, etc. Most electrical goods are banned, including video-cassette recorders, though the latter restriction is not enforced for tourists. (A sign in Havana airport reads: "For-bidden articles: freezers, refrigerators, air-conditioning units, video recorders, toasters, irons. . ." Suggests *The Economist,* "That a country desperately in need of any and all of the above items should ban them altogether sums up Mr. Castro's Cuba nicely.") Cuban authorities will seize fruits, weapons, and "counterrevolutionary" and "obscene and pornographic" materials are also banned, as are playing cards. A nominal limit of six rolls of film is rarely enforced.

A customs declaration need not be filled out. However, if you're carrying valuable items such as laptop computers or video cameras, you may be asked to provide a written declaration. If for whatever reason you must leave some items with customs authorities, make sure that you obtain a signed receipt to enable you to reclaim the items upon departure.

Your hand-carried baggage will be X-rayed upon arrival at the Havana airport.

The headquarters of Cuban Customs **(Aduana General de la República)** is at Plaza de la Revolución #6, Nuevo Vedado, tel. (7) 55-5466.

Don't lose your baggage claim tag issued at your originating airport. You'll need to show this upon exiting the airport in Cuba.

Returning to the U.S.

U.S. citizens who have traveled *legally* to Cuba are allowed to bring back no more than US$100 of Cuban goods as accompanied baggage, plus up to US$10,000 of artwork and an unlimited amount of literature, posters, and other informational materials protected under the First Amendment of the Constitution. Sculpture created by Cubans may be licensed for importation provided it is lower than $25,000 in value. Uncle Sam's quixotic rules also state that if you are *legally* permitted to visit Cuba, you are also allowed to bring back a "reasonable" amount of Cuban cigars—as long as you purchased them in Cuba. "Reasonable" means up to two boxes per person. Uncle Sam quirkily forbids you to bring cigars back if bought anywhere other than in Cuba. Be sure to get a receipt, even if you buy from a street seller. No goods of Cuban origin may be imported to the U.S. unaccompanied, either directly or through third countries, such as Canada or Mexico.

All other U.S. citizens are liable to have any Cuban goods confiscated, however innocuous and however acquired. Don't tempt fate by flaunting your Cuban T-shirt or shaking your Cuban maracas.

Restrictions on importing Cuban-made goods to the U.S. apply to citizens of *any* country arriving from any other country, including in-transit passengers.

The Office of Foreign Assets Controls publishes a pamphlet, *What You Need to Know about the U.S. Embargo,* U.S. Department of the Treasury, 1500 Pennsylvania Ave. NW, Washington, D.C. 20220, tel. (202) 622-2520, fax-on-demand (202) 622-0077, website: www.treas.gov/ofac. Alternately, contact the U.S. Customs Service, 1300 Pennsylvania Ave. NW, Washington, DC 20229.

Returning to Canada

Canadian citizens are allowed an "exemption" of C$300 annually (or C$100 per quarter) for goods purchased abroad, plus 1.1 liters of spirits and 200 cigarettes.

EXITING CUBA

Travelers exiting Cuba are charged US$20 departure tax on international flights. No charge applies for travelers leaving by private boat. Cuba prohibits the export of valuable antiques and art without a license, as well as (ostensibly) as endangered wildlife products.

It goes without saying that trying to smuggle drugs through customs is not only illegal but also stupid. Trained dogs are employed to sniff out contraband at U.S. airports as well as at Cuban airports and ports.

You may not export more than US$5,000 in cash.

TOURIST INFORMATION

TOURIST OFFICES

Cuba's **Ministerio de Turismo,** Calle 19 #710, Vedado, Havana, tel. (7) 33-4202, or 33-0545 for international relations, is in charge of tourism. However, Cuba's tourist offices abroad are represented by other state tourism agencies, most notably Cubatur, Havanatur, and Cubanacán. There is no such office in the U.S.; however, **Cubanacán,** 55 Queen St. E, Suite 705, Toronto, ON M5C 1R5, tel. (416) 362-0700, fax (416) 362-6799, e-mail: cuba.tbtor@sympatico.ca, will provide information and mail literature to U.S. citizens.

The office of the Cuban tourism agency, **Cubatur,** Calle F #157 e/ Calzada y Calle 9 in Vedado, tel. (7) 33-4155, provides information and can make arrangements for independent travelers, as can the headquarters of **Havanatur,** Calle 6 #117, Miramar, Havana, tel. (7) 24-2424, and Havanatur's **Tour & Travel,** Av. 1ra y 0, Miramar, Havana, tel. (7) 24-1549, fax (7) 24-2074, or at La Rampa y Calle P, tel. (7) 70-5284.

Publicitur, Calle 19 #60 e/ M and N, Vedado, tel. (7) 55-2826, fax (7) 33-3422, e-mail: public@public.mit.cma.net, is the agency responsible for publishing and disseminating tourism literature.

Tourist Information Bureaus

Infotur (Información Turística), the government tourist information bureau, operates **Palacios de Turismo** (tourist information booths) throughout the island. It has three information centers in Havana, including in the arrivals lounge at José Martí International Airport, tel. (7) 66-6112 or 45-3542. Staff can make reservations for car rentals, accommodations, and bus transfers, as well as sell prepaid telephone cards. However, they stock only a limited range of tourist literature and maps.

Virtually every hotel has a **buro de turismo** in the lobby. Most of the bureaus are geared to selling package excursions, but you'll usually find the staff willing and conscientious, if not always chock-full of information. The best ensemble of bureaus is in the lobby of the Hotel Habana Libre Tryp, in Vedado, Havana. (Also see the section on Tourist Information under General Information And Services in the Havana chapter.)

Other Information Bureaus

Información Nacional dispenses information about virtually every aspect of Cuba. Its main office is at Calle 23 #358, two blocks west of the Hotel Habana Libre, in Vedado, Havana, tel. (7) 32-1269. The **Oficina Nacional de Es-**

tádisticas, on Paseo e/ 3ra y 5ra, one block south of the Meliá Cohiba, can provide all manner of statistics on Cuba.

TRAVEL PUBLICATIONS AND RESOURCES

Tourist Guides and Publications
Before You Go: Occasional features on Cuba appear in leading travel magazines such as *Islands* and *Caribbean Travel & Life,* website: www.caribbeantravelmag.com. An equivalent in the U.K. is *Caribbean World,* Albert Hall Magazines, 84 Albert Hall Mansions, Prince Consort Rd., London SW7 2AQ, published quarterly. Subscriptions in the U.K. cost £10; overseas subscriptions cost £21.70.

In Cuba: *Sol y Son,* Graphic Publicidad, Calle 14 #113, e/ 1ra y 3ra, Miramar, Havana, tel. (7) 24-2245, fax (7) 24-2186, is the slick in-flight magazine of Cubana airlines, published in English and Spanish. It provides profiles and news information on destinations, culture, and the arts.

The 300-page plus *Directorio Turístico de Cuba* (Tourist Directory of Cuba, US$40) is published once per year as a venture between a Cuban and Mexican company and includes names, addresses, telephone and facsimile numbers for ministries, hotels, airports, airline offices, etc., plus maps and other information. You can order it from the U.S.-Cuba Trade & Economic Council, 30 Rockefeller Plaza New York, NY 10112-0002, tel. (212) 246-1444, fax (212) 246-2345, website www.cubatrade.org.

Travel agents are also catered to by *Travel Trade Cuba,* Hotel Deauville, Hab. 207, Galiano y Malecón, Centro Habana, tel. (7) 33-6268, fax (7) 66-2398, e-mail: ttccuba@ip.etecsa.cu, website: ttc.cubaweb.cu. published in English and Spanish. Albeit useful, unlike international counterparts in the Italian-based Travel Trade Gazette group, this glossy publication is simply a PR tool for Cuban travel companies and avoids investigative journalism. (Also see the General Information and Services section in the Havana chapter.)

Maps
Before you go: Two of the best road maps are the 1:250,000 topographical map produced

USEFUL GOVERNMENT TELEPHONE NUMBERS

MINISTRY OF FOREIGN RELATIONS

Reception	tel. (7) 30-5031
Passports and Visas	tel. (7) 32-4908
Europe	tel. (7) 32-1895
North America	tel. (7) 32-5791
U.S.	tel. (7) 32-3359

CUBAN INSTITUTE FOR FRIENDSHIP WITH THE PEOPLE (INSTITUTO CUBANO DE AMISTAD CON LOS PUEBLOS)

Reception	tel. (7) 55-2395
Foreign residents (living in Cuba)	tel. (7) 55-2409
Cuban residents abroad	tel. (7) 55-2421
Europe	tel. (7) 32-7449
North America	tel. (7) 55-2414

OTHER ORGANIZATIONS

Conventions Buruea	tel. (7) 66-2015
Federation of Cuban Women	tel. (7) 55-2771
Institute of National Parks	tel. (7) 29-0523
Institute of Sports and Physical Education	tel. (7) 40-3581

The following numbers are for the **international relations** offices of the following ministries (all in Havana):

Communications	tel. (7) 78-2860
Economy and Planning	tel. (7) 81-9354
Education	tel. (7) 61-5147
Foreign Investment	tel. (7) 23-8573
Health	tel. (7) 33-4341
Justice	tel. (7) 55-2436
Science and Technology	tel. (7) 57-0606
Sports and Physical Education	tel. (7) 40-5366
Superior Education	tel. (7) 55-2363
Tourism	tel. (7) 33-0545

by Kartografiai Vallalat of Hungary, and a virtually identical map by Freytag & Berndt. Both show main tourist attractions and feature street maps of key cities. You can buy or order from

CUBAN TOURIST BUREAUS ABROAD

Argentina
Virrey del Pino #1810, Buenos Aires, tel. (01) 4786-9383, e-mail: oturcuar@tournet.com.ar

Brazil
Av. São Luis 50-39 Andar, CEP 01046 São Paulo SP, tel. (011) 259-3044, fax (011) 258-8818

Canada
55 Queen St. E, Suite 705, Toronto, Ontario M5C 1R5, tel. (416) 362-0700, fax (416) 362-6799, e-mail: cuba.tbtor@sympatico.ca
440 Blvd. René Lévesque Ouest, Bureau 1402, Montreal, Quebec H2Z 1V7, tel. (514) 875-8004, fax (514) 875-8006, e-mail: mintur@generation.net

France
24 rue du Quatre Septembre, 75002 Paris, tel. (01) 45-38-90-10, fax (01) 45-38-99-30, e-mail: ot.cuba@wanadoo.fr

Germany
Steinweg 2, 6000 Frankfurt Main 1, tel. (069) 28-83-22/23, fax (069) 29-66-64, e-mail: gocuba@compuserve.com

Italy
via General Fara 30, Terzo Piano, 20124 Milano, tel. (02) 6698-1463, fax (02) 6738-0725, e-mail:ufficioturisticodicuba@interbusiness.it

Mexico
Insurgentes Sur no. 421, Complejo Aristo, Edif. B, 06100 Mexico D.F., tel. (05) 255-5897, fax (05) 255-5866, e-mail: otcumex@mail.internet.cma.net

Russia
Hotel Belgrado, Moscow, tel./fax (095) 243-0383

Spain
Paseo de la Habana #28, 1ed 28036, Madrid, tel. (01) 411-3097, fax (01) 564-5804, e-mail: otcuba@develnet.es

United Kingdom
161 High Holborn, London WC1V 6PA, tel. (0171) 836-3606, fax (0171) 240-6655, e-mail: Cubatouristboard.london.@virgin.net

---

travel bookstores or online from www.cuba-books.com.

SouthTrek, 1301 Oxford Ave., Austin, TX 78704, tel. (512) 440-7125, fax (512) 443-0973, e-mail: sotrek@onr.com, specializes in maps of Latin America, and sells a 250:000 scale map of Cuba. Likewise, **Omni Resources,** P.O. Box 2096, Burlington, NC 72160, tel. (800) 742-2677, fax (910) 227-3748, website: www.omnimap.com, and **Treaty Oak,** P.O. Box 50295, Austin, TX 78763, tel. (512) 326-4141, fax (512) 443-0973, e-mail: maps@treatyoak.com, sell Cuba maps. Another excellent online map source is www.gonetomorrow.com.

In Canada, **ITMB Publishing,** 736A Granville St, Vancouver, BC V6Z 1G3, tel. (604) 687-5925, is the best resource.

In the U.K., try **Stanford's,** 12-14 Long Acre, London WC2E 9LP, tel. (0171) 836-1321, fax (0171) 836-0189, and the **Ordnance Survey International,** Romsey Rd., Maybush, Southampton SO9 4DH, tel. (0703) 792000, fax (0703) 792404.

In Australia, try **The Map Shop,** 16a Peel St., Adelaide, SA 5000, tel. (08) 231-2033; in New Zealand, try **Specialty Maps,** 58 Albert St., Auckland, tel. (09) 307-2217.

Grupo Noriega Editores, Baldreas 95, Mexico DF, CP 06040, tel. (05) 521-2105, fax (05) 512-2903, publishes a splendid tourist pocket atlas—*Guía de Carreteras*—that offers the most accurate and complete maps of Cuba in a handy little booklet. You can buy it at souvenir stalls in Havana.

In Cuba: The **Instituto Cubano de Geodésia y Cartografía** produces a *Mapa Turístico de Cuba* as well as regional and city maps, plus detailed maps of individual attractions, such as Cementerio Colón. They vary in scope, but some are extremely accurate and detailed. The institute doesn't sell maps, but you can buy them through Infotur offices and souvenir stalls. Maps of specific sites, such as Parque Lenin, can often be bought at the attraction itself. The institute also publishes a series of provincial road maps (*mapas de carreteras*).

Cuba's **Ediciones Geo** produces a series of pocket-size tourist maps of regions and cities. They have a handy index and brief information in six languages. Cuban tour and hotel outfits also produce their own maps.

Detailed maps of the island's infrastructure are produced by the **Instituto de Planificación Física,** Laparilla 65, Habana Vieja, tel. (7) 62-9330, fax (7) 61-9533. They don't normally sell maps.

Infotur and Rumbos S.A. souvenir stalls in Havana and elsewhere usually have maps for sale. In Havana you should also try **Tienda de las Navegantes,** Mercaderes 115, Habana Vieja, tel. (7) 61-3625, fax (7) 33-2869 (for boaters, VHF channel 16 CMYP3050). This store has the widest array of tourist maps and nautical charts available in Cuba, covering the entire island. If you're planning on touring farther afield, you should definitely head here.

Telecorreos (telephone and post centers) in the provinces sell regional and city maps.

Travel Videos

You can get a rosy overview of Cuba by ordering *Cubanacán's Cuba* from **Sam-Sher Enterprises,** 9040 Leslie St., Suite 6, Richmond Hill, ON L4B 1G2, tel. (416) 771-9752, fax (416) 771-9741; and *Cuba & Haiti* (one hour; US$19.95; £12.99), Lonely Planet, 155 Filbert St., Oakland, CA 94607, tel. (510) 893-8555, fax (510) 893-8563, e-mail: info@lonelyplanet.com.

Also in Canada, **Martz Travel** has produced a 60-minute video—*Cuba Now*—specifically for travel agents and tourism industry personnel, US$29.95; Cuba Now, Box 2517, Wilkes-Barre, PA 18702, tel. (570) 825-0973.

Fej Films, P.O. Box 24062, Lansing, MI 48909-4062, www.arrozconfrijoles.com, publishes a video—*Arroz con Frijoles: The Budget Traveler's Guide to Cuba*—that provides a panoply of information for the impecunious, no-frills traveler wanting to discover the non-touristed Cuba. It covers accommodation, transportation, and food issues; US$39.95 (indicate PAL or NTSC).

Travel Clubs

The **South American Explorers,** 126 Indian Creek Rd., Ithaca, NY 14850, tel. (607) 277-0488, fax (607) 277-6122, e-mail: explorer@samexplo.org, website: www.samexplo.org, publishes the quarterly *South American Explorer* magazine, containing a list of guidebooks, maps, trip reports, and resources for sale, as well as feature articles and advice for travelers and explorers. Annual membership costs

In the U.K., the **Latin American Travel Association,** 1-7 Windmill Mews, Chiswick, London W4 1RW, tel. (0181) 742-1529, fax (0181) 742-2025, promotes Cuba and the rest of Latin America as a tourist destination on behalf of its members, most of whom are tour operators and travel suppliers.

Cuba is a member of both the **Caribbean Tourist Organization** (CTO), 80 Broad St., 32nd Floor, New York, NY 10004, tel. (212) 635-9530, fax (212) 635-9511, e-mail: get2cto@dorsai.org, website: www.caribtourism.com, and the **Caribbean Hotel Association,** 18 Marseilles St., Suite 2B, San Juan, PR 00907, tel. (809) 725-9139, fax (809) 725-9108, e-mail: wpina @caribbeanhotels.org, website: www.caribbeanhotels.org, both of which are barred under U.S. law from promoting tourism to Cuba in the United States. In Canada, the **Tourism Industry Association of Canada,** 1016-130 Albert St., Suite 1016, Ottawa, ON K1P 5G4, tel. (613) 238-3883, fax (613) 238-3878, e-mail: TIAC@resudox.net, suffers no such restraint. The CTO has a Canadian office at Taurus House, 512 Duplex Ave., Toronto, ON M4R 2E3, tel. (416) 485-7827, fax (416) 485-8256; and in the U.K. at 42 Westminster Palace Gardens, Artillery Row, London SWIP 1RR, tel. (0171) 222-4335, fax (0171) 222-4325.

MEDIA RESOURCES

NEWSPAPERS AND MAGAZINES

Before You Go

There's no end of publications and coverage on Cuba outside Cuba. Mainstream U.S. publications often report negatively and are unduly influenced by information provided by the U.S. government. Says much-loved newsman Walter Cronkite, "The American people are being denied the free flow of information to and from Cuba that would enable them to intelligently par-ticipate in the decisions on our future policy there. The culprit is the U.S. government." It pays to broaden your reading to gain a truer picture of Cuba—never an easy country to understand. (See Organizations To Know chart for more a concise listing of many concerned organizations.)

One of the best sources is *Cuba Update,* published quarterly by the Center for Cuban Studies. It covers arts, economics, politics, women's and race issues, and travel and is strongly sympathetic to Cuba's socialist perspectives.

ORGANIZATIONS TO KNOW

Canadian-Cuban Friendship Association, P.O. Box 743, Station F, Toronto, Ontario M4Y 2N6, tel. (406) 654-5585. Promotes "friendship, understanding, and cooperation" between the peoples of Canada and Cuba. It offers cultural exchanges, lectures, and cultural events, and sends medicinal and material aid to Cuba, as well as publishing the *Amistad* newsletter.

Center for Cuban Studies, 124 W. 23rd St., New York, NY 10011, tel. (212) 242-0559, fax (212) 242-1937, e-mail: cubanctr@igc.apc.org, website: www.cubaupdate.org. Supports educational forums on Cuba, publishes the splendid quarterly *Cuba Update,* organizes study tours, and distributes a wide range of books and videos on Cuba. It also has an art gallery and the largest research library on Cuba in North America.

Conchord Cayo Hueso, 7 Higgs Ln., Key West, FL 33049, tel. (305) 294-0205, e-mail: jitters@aol.com. Carries humanitarian aid to Cuba using 47 registered private vessels. It also organizes athletic, cultural, religious, and other exchanges.

Cuban American Alliance Education Fund, 614 Maryland Ave. NE #2, Washington, DC 20002-5825, tel. (202) 543-6780, fax (202) 543-6434, e-mail: caaef@igc.org, website: www.cubamer.org. Represents moderate Cuban-Americans who wish for dialogue with Cuba. In particular, it sponsors efforts at family reunification and an end to travel restrictions imposed by Washington on Cuban-Americans wishing to visit Cuba. It also has a program to assist in the physical rehabilitation needs of children at the Julito Díaz Hospital (donations of medicines and medical equipment are needed).

Cuban American National Foundation, 7300 N.W. 35th Terr., Miami, FL 33122, tel. (305) 592-7768, fax (305) 592-7889, e-mail: canfnet@icanect.net, website: www.canfnet.org. An ultra-conservative lobbying group dedicated to the overthrow of Fidel Castro and replacement by a self-appointed government formed of CANF leaders, many with ties to the Batista regime.

Cuban Solidarity Campaign, The Red Rose Club, 129 Seven Sisters Road, London N7 7QG, tel. (0171) 263-6452, fax (0171) 561-0191, e-mail: cubasc @gn.apc.org, website: www.poptel.org. uk/cuba-solidarity. This socialist friendship organization works to support "Cuba's right to self-determination" by sending work brigades, offering study tours, and delivering medical and other aid to Cuba.

Global Exchange, 2017 Mission St. #303, San Francisco, CA 94110, tel. (415) 255-7296, fax (415) 255-7498, e-mail: info@globalexchange.org, website: www.globalexchange.org. Organizes monthly study tours to Cuba on an eclectic range of themes. Global Exchange has launched a Campaign to End the Cold War Against Cuba, and the Campaign to Exempt Food and Medicines from the Embargo. Has

Contributors include leading experts on Cuban issues, both in and outside Cuba. Subscriptions cost US$35 a year, or US$50 a year including membership in the center.

CubaINFO is a triweekly news digest on U.S.-Cuban relations and economic and foreign affairs, published by the Cuba Exchange Program of the School of Advanced International Studies at Johns Hopkins University. Subscriptions cost US$50 individuals, US$200 corporate (add US$25 for international orders). Write SAIS, 1755 Massachusetts Ave. NW, Washington, D.C. 20036-1984, tel. (202) 232-0290, fax (202) 232-0316, e-mail: cubainfo@igc.apc.org. In a similar vein is *La Alborada,* a monthly newsletter published by the Cuban American Alliance

Education Fund, and representing the perspectives of moderate Cuban-Americans.

The U.S.-Cuba Trade and Economic Council's website: www.cubatrade.org/eyeon.html, provides weekly economic updates on Cuba.

CubaNews, P.O. Box 81, Spencerville, MD 20868, tel. (301) 421-1491, fax (301) 421-9810, also serves private investors and claims to be the "authoritative guide to Cuban business, politics, and economic development." Subscriptions cost US$349 yearly.

Global Exchange publishes an annual *Cuba Reader,* a 100-page compendium of current articles on Cuba's political and economic system, health care, human rights, U.S. relations, etc. (US$9, plus US$1.50 shipping). Global Ex-

---

also sponsored "Freedom to Travel Challenge" tours for those who want to challenge the legality of U.S. travel restrictions.

Hermana a Hermana/Sister to Sister, 2017 Mission St. #303, San Francisco, CA 94110, tel. (415) 255-7296, fax (415) 255-7498, e-mail: globalexch@igc .apc.org, is a coalition of Canadian, Mexican, and Caribbean women's groups formed to create "peaceful and just relations between the U.S. and Cuba" through cultural, professional, religious, and education exchanges between American, Latin American, Caribbean, and Cuban women. It also leads women's delegations to Cuba.

IFCO/Pastors for Peace, 402 West 145th St., New York, NY 10031, tel. (212) 926-5757, fax (212) 926-5842, e-mail: ifco@igc.apc.org, website: www.if-conews.org. Organizes the U.S.-Friendshipment Caravans to Cuba, challenging the embargo by traveling with vehicles filled with donations of humanitarian aid. Also has study tours and organizes work brigades to assist in community projects in Cuba. IFCO stands for Interreligious Foundation for Community Organization.

Peace for Cuba Task Force, P.O. Box 450, Santa Clara, CA 95052, tel. (408) 243-4359, fax (408) 243-1229, e-mail: jreardon@igc.apc.org or dwald@igc. apc.org. Devoted to improving relations with Cuba. It sponsors speaking forums and accepts donations of medicines, foodstuffs, and educational materials for the U.S.-Cuba Friendshipment Caravans. It also runs Project INFOMED to supply desperately need-

ed computers to medical centers in Cuba. Donations of computers and peripherals are requested.

U.S.-Cuba Labor Exchange, P.O. Box 39188, Redford, MI 48239, tel./fax (313) 561-8330. This trade unionists' organization promotes socialist solidarity with Cuban workers and the Revolution. It organizes labor exchanges to Cuba.

U.S.-Cuba Medical Project, P.O. Box 206, 408 Thirteenth St., Oakland, CA 94612, tel. (510) 869-5655; and One Union Square West #211, New York, NY 10003, tel. (212) 227-5270, fax (212) 227-4859, e-mail: uscubamed@igc.apc.org. Provides medical and humanitarian aid to Cuba, working through the Cuban Red Cross. Leads caravans that deliver medical supplies to hospitals in Cuba.

U.S.-Cuba Trade and Economic Council, 30 Rockefeller Plaza, New York, NY 10112, tel. (212) 246-1444, fax (212) 246-2345, e-mail: council@cuba-trade.org, website: www.cubatrade.org. A nonpartisan business organization that publishes the newsletter *Economic Eye on Cuba.* It claims not "to take positions with respect to U.S.-Republic of Cuba political relations," but it favors trade.

USA*ENGAGE, website: www.usaengage.org. This a broad-based coalition representing U.S. business and agriculture exists to persuade Washington to lift economic sanctions. Members include 40 national and state associations and organizations plus such corporations as AT&T, Boeing, Citibank, Dow Chemical, and 400 other heavy hitters.

change also publishes books on Cuba's political economy and U.S.-Cuban relations.

Information Services Latin America (ISLA), 1904 Franklin St. #900, Oakland, CA 94612, tel. (510) 835-4692, e-mail: isla@datacenter.org, website: www.igc.org/isla, maintains a clipping service of news regarding Cuba, emphasizing politics, the economy, culture, and foreign affairs.

The *Cuban Daily News Digest,* P.O. Box 30003, North Vancouver, BC, Canada V7H 2Y8, tel. (604) 929-9694, fax (604) 929-3694, e-mail: jhitchie@direct.ca, website: www.smallcapcenter.com, is a daily compilation of news articles about Cuba from various news sources, available online. It is available online. The same organization also publishes **Cuban Investment Letter.**

Cuba-L is a daily clippings service on Cuba produced by the Cuba Research & Analysis Group and the Latin American and Iberian Institute at the University of New Mexico, 801 Yale NE, Albuquerque, NM 87106, tel. (505) 277-2501, e-mail: nvaldes@unm.edu. For US$60 annually (US$30 for students) you get a daily package of Cuba-related news items culled from leading publications, government agencies, tourism bureaus, and think tanks covering the political spectrum.

In England, the Cuban Solidarity Campaign, 129 Seven Sisters Rd., London N7 7QG, tel. (0171) 263-6452, fax: (0171) 561-0191, e-mail: cubasc@gn.apc.org, website: www.poptel.org .uk/cuba-solidarity, publishes the *CubaSí* newsletter. Subscriptions cost £4 (unwaged), £12 (waged), or £15-50 (organizations).

See Tourist Information, above, for publications relevant to tourism.

Foreign Publications in Cuba

In Havana, upscale hotel gift stores sell a small selection of leading international newspapers and magazines (including *Newsweek, Time, USA Today, The New York Times, Le Figaro,* and *Das Spiegel*), as well as a minuscule selection of consumer magazines (even *Cosmopolitan* has been banned as "pornographic and sensationalist"). Such publications are scarce elsewhere in Cuba and they seem to disappear from shelves whenever there's a major international tiff that pits Cuba against the U.S., as during the NATO Kosovo campaign of spring 1999, when Cuba supported Yugoslav thug Slobodan Milosevic. Foreign publications are distributed in Cuba through **World Services Publications,** Calle 33 #2003, e/ 20 y 22, Vedado, tel. (7) 33-3002, fax (7) 33-3066. Expect to pay up to three times what you'd pay at home.

In 1998 the U.S. government allowed 11 U.S. news organizations to set up shop in Cuba, but as of 1999 the Cubans had only allowed CNN and Associated Press to establish bureaus (in the Hotel Habana Libre Tryp and Lonja del Comercio, respectively).

Cuban Publications

Pre-Castro Cuba had a vibrant media sector, with 58 daily newspapers of differing political hues. The Castro government closed them all down. Today domestic media is entirely state controlled (in October 1999 the Inter-American Press Association listed Cuba as one of the worst violators of press freedoms in the hemisphere) and subject to what Maurice Halperin refers to as "the self-righteous and congratulatory monotony of the Cuban propaganda machine." What you read in Cuba's state-controlled media usually hides as much as it reveals (the Spanish word *media,* remember, means half—as in half the story). The Cuban populace has virtually no access to foreign publications and is starved for unbiased news reporting.

The most important publication and virtually the sole mouthpiece of international news is *Granma,* the cheaply produced, eight-page official Communist Party propaganda piece published daily. It focuses heavily on profiling a daily succession of victories in the building of socialism; "lingo sludge," and "a degradation of the act of reading" are among the accusations hurled at it. It's essential reading if you want to get the Cuban take on international events, and it has some quality reporting on the arts, culture, and medicine. But its triumphalist tone is often a bit Alice-in-Wonderlandish, often inspired by Castro's determination to denigrate the U.S. at every turn (some of the unsigned editorials are written by Fidel Castro, whose colorful style, highlighted with subtle invective, is unmistakable). No opportunity is lost; thus, Saddam Hussein, Slobodan Milosevic, and similar international hoodlums are portrayed as heroes acting in defiance of a villainous, imperialistic Uncle Sam. A weekly edition is also published in Spanish, English, and French. You'll find it in the glove pocket of Cubana Airlines' flights, plus many hotel gift stores and at the editorial offices, at Av. General Suárez y Calle Territorial, Plaza de la Revolución, Havana, tel. (7) 81-6265 or 70-6521, fax (7) 33-5176, e-mail: granmai@tinored.cu, website: www.cubaweb.cu/granma. You can buy *Granma* at streetside kiosks, but they rapidly run out (many Cubans make some extra money by re-selling their newspapers once the last issue runs out; others—seriously—stand in line to take *Granma* home to use as toilet paper). U.S. subscriptions cost US$40, Pathfinder Press, 410 West St., New York, NY 10014, tel. (212) 741-0690.

Granma is also available online in various languages at www.granma.cu.

Juventud Rebelde, General Suárez, e/ Ayesteran y Territorial, tel. (7) 6-9876, is the evening paper of the Communist Youth League and echoes *Granma.* (The Communist Party also publishes the monthly *El Militante Communista.*). Similar mouthpieces include the daily *Tribuna de la Habana; Trabajadores,* the newspaper of the trade unions; *Mujeres,* Av. Rancho Boyeros y San Pedro, Havana, tel. (7) 70-1000, a monthly magazine for women; and *Contactos,* published bimonthly by the Chamber of Commerce. *Opciones* is a weekly serving the business, commercial, and tourist sectors, aiming at foreign businessmen in Cuba.

Cuba also produces some excellent magazines focusing on the arts and culture, such as *Habanera,* a monthly magazine about Havana, and *Prisma,* an English-language, bimonthly magazine covering politics, economics, travel, and general subjects on Cuba and the Americas published by Prensa Latina. In a similar vein is the weekly magazine *Bohemia* (you can order copies through the Center for Cuban Studies), while *Tropicana Internacional* is a bimonthly covering the Cuban music scene, *Mar y Pesca* is a monthly magazine on maritime issues, including water sports. And the Casa de las Américas publishes a splendid eponymous bimonthly about the arts (in Spanish only), as well as the *Conjunto: Revista de Teatro Latinamericano.*

BOOKS

You'll find hundreds of books on Cuba. The best online resource is www.cubabooks.com.

(The chart, Organizations To Know, is also very helpful.)

New York's **Center for Cuban Studies** (see the), publishes a catalog of books, posters, and other informational materials available for mail-order purchase. The Center maintains the **Lourdes Casal Library,** which has a collection of over 5,000 books on Cuba, as well as subscriptions to *Granma, Bohemia,* and other Cuban journals. It's open Mon.-Fri. 10 a.m.-6 p.m. and Saturday by appointment. The Center also sells from a huge collection of videos on Cuba, Cuban feature films on video, plus short films made by the Cuban Institute of Cinematic Arts and Industries. Most are in Spanish with English subtitles. It has a free catalog.

Two publishers of leftist books on Cuba are **Ocean Press,** GPO Box 3279, Melbourne, Victoria 3001, Australia, or P.O. Box 020692, Brooklyn, NY 11202; and **Pathfinder Press** (see above), which has distributors worldwide: in the U.K. and Europe, Pathfinder, 47 The Cut, London SE1 8LL, tel. (0171) 261-1354, fax (0171) 928-7970; in Australia and New Zealand, c/o Baker & Taylor International, 80 Chandos St., St. Leonard, NSW 2065, tel. (02) 436-2666, fax (02) 436-2170.

Ediciones Universal, P.O. Box 450353, Miami, FL 33245, e-mail: ediuniver@aol.com, publishes books on Cuba in Spanish, including classic novels such as the works of Hemingway and José Martí. It has scores of titles on all themes.

Macmillan Caribbean, Houndmills, Basingstoke, Hampshire RG21 2XS, England, tel. (1256) 29242, fax (1256) 20109, publishes a series of special-interest titles on Cuba.

Travel Tips for Travelers to Cuba is published by the U.S. State Department's Bureau of Consular Affairs (DOS Publication #9232, DCA). It's available from the Superintendent of Documents, U.S. Government Printing Office, Washington, D.C. 20402, tel. (202) 783-3283.

The CIA's *World Factbook* book includes data on the people, politics, geography, and economies of numerous countries, including Cuba. It can be ordered from the Superintendent of Documents, P.O. Box 371954, Pittsburgh, PA 15250-7954, tel. (202) 512-1800, fax (202) 512-2250, website: www.access.gpo. gov/su_docs, or www.cia.gov. It is also available on CD-ROM from the National Technical Information Service, 5285 Port Royal Rd., Springfield, VA 22161, tel. (800) 553-6847, or (703) 605-6000 outside U.S., fax (703) 605-6900, website: www.ntis.gov, for US$30.

For a list of recommended reading, see the Booklist.

ONLINE RESOURCES

There are dozens of Cuba-specific internet sites. A key starting point should be the Republic of Cuba's Havana-based **CubaWeb,** website: www.cubaweb.cu, which carries information direct from Havana reflecting the views of the Cuban government. It has links to individual sites in the following categories: news, travel and tourism, politics and government, business and commerce, Internet and technology, health and science, culture and arts, and festivals and events.

The similarly-named **CubaWeb,** website: www.cubaweb.com, is a U.S.-based site that acts as a clearing house for information on Cuba, but it is weak on up-to-date information.

Your second stop should be **El Web de Cuba,** website: www3.cuba.cu, with categorized links. It has a link to **Paginas Amarillas de Cuba** (Cuba Yellow Pages), website: www.paginasamarillas.cu, a telephone directory that at press time was threadbare in its listings and amateur in its construction.

Cubanacán, the state-run tourism entity, maintains a website at www.cubanacan.cu with information on all aspects of tourism from auto rentals to marinas and health tourism, plus links to Cubana Aviación, the Buro de Convenciones, and more than a score of tourism-related sites, It includes "tourist bulletins."

Another starting point should be www.cubanet.org, which offers breaking news and news reports from the leading wire services, and is particularly good for hard-hitting info on Cuba's darker side. The **Latin American Network Information Center,** website: www.lanic.utexas.educ, is a well-organized reference site with links to many internet resources on Cuba, as well as a database of Castro's speeches. Likewise the **Cuban Studies Institute** at Tulane University has an excellent links site at www.cuba.tulane.edu/res.

USA•ENGAGE, www.usaengage.org, offers a listing of feature articles and other news items on Cuba relating to economics and politics, and has a superb list of government and non-governmental agency links at www.usaengage.org/resources/links.

California-based Boulevards News Media maintains a Havana site—www.lahabana.com—featuring updates on travel, arts, culture, and news.

General searches on Yahoo, Excite, and other major search engines will pull up hundreds of other sites related to Havana and Cuba, as will www.caribbeansupersite.com/cuba.

A British firm, **Tour & Marketing,** e-mail: help@gocuba.com offers complete travel services at www.gocubaplus.com, plus VIP travel services at www.cubavip.com, and broad-based information on arts, culture, sports, etc., at www.cubavip.com. The Mexican company, **Cuba Travel Service** maintains a useful list of Cuba links at www.cuba-travel.com.mx. Likewise, Latin American Travel Consultants, e-mail: LATC@pi.pro.ec, has a **Latin American Travel Resource Center** with a list of Cuba links at www.amerispan.com; it also publishes the *Latin American Travel Advisor* online at www.amerispan.com.

La Casa del Habano has www.cubamall.com, with links to numerous Cuba-related sites.

For information on all things related to Afro-Cuban affairs, from music to conferences, check out **AfroCuba Web,** at www.afrocubaweb.com.

Uncle Sam has a website devoted to Cuba at www.state.gov/www/regions/wha/cuba/index with information on such themes as human rights, people-to-people contacts, and travel. It's a none-too-flattering, highly biased picture. Another rightist news service is **Latin American News Syndicate,** P.O. Box 781464, San Antonio, TX 78278, tel. (210) 699-0381, fax (210) 699-1675, e-mail: lans@txdirect.net, www.latamnews.com.

The CIA provides the *World Factbook* at www.cia.gov/cia/publications/factbook/cu, good for statistics and general information on Cuba. Go to www.odci.gov/cia for everything you ever wanted to know about the CIA (well, perhaps not everything).

RADIO AND TELEVISION

The state-owned **Instituto Cubano de Radio y Televisión,** tel. (7) 32-9544, controls all broadcast media.

Television

Virtually every home has a TV, and Cubans are addicted to television, especially Brazilian *telenovelas* (soap operas). Reception is limited to the two national TV networks—**Canal 6: Cubavision** and **Canal 2: Tele Rebelde**—and one provincial station in Oriente.

Most tourist hotels provide satellite or cable access, including HBO, ESPN, Cinemax, CNN, VH1—a rival to MTV—and the international service of TV España. (Many hotels that claim to have "satellite" TV can only provide a half dozen fuzzy U.S. stations). The Cuban government supposedly pirates foreign cable TV stations by stealing a signal captured by a government satellite dish mounted on the Habana Libre Hotel and retransmitted to other tourist hotels.

Tele Rebelde features national and international news at 12:30 and 8 p.m. Most programming is communist pablum, such as narrow, self-righteous newscasts. However, Cuban TV also has some very intelligent programming, with an emphasis on science and culture, sports, Hispanic soaps, and foreign movies, which Cubavision shows every Saturday night. Cartoons are heavily moralistic and aim to teach Cuban youth proper behavior, and educational shows have a broadly internationalist focus. There is none of the mindless violence that dominates contemporary American cartoons, although insidious elements of Yankee culture, such as gangsta-rap, are seeping in. Advertisements typically inveigh against abortions *("Aborción no es un metodo anticonceptivo"),* exhort Cubans to work hard, or call for their participation in important political events.

The weekly tourist publication *Cartelera,* available free at hotel newsstands, lists television programming for the coming week.

Radio

Cuba ranked eighth in the world in number of radio stations in 1958. Today it has only five national radio stations, all government run. **Radio Liberación** offers mostly cultural programs; **Radio Musicál** airs classical music; **Radio Progreso** features light entertainment; **Radio Rebelde** and **Radio Reloj** both report news from a highly slanted perspective. There are also provincial and local stations, such as **Radio Havana Cuba.** In Havana and along the northwest coast, you can tune in to radio stations from southern Florida; on the south coast, to stations from Jamaica; and in Oriente, to the American Forces Network (AM 1340 or FM 102.1), broadcast from Guantánamo naval base. However, in much of the countryside you can put your car radio onto "scan" and it will just go round and round without ever coming up with a station.

Radio Martí and **TV Martí** attempt to broadcast anti-Castro programming into Cuba from the U.S. The Cuban government manages to block this right-wing propaganda (funded by the U.S. government to the tune of US$20 million a year). The only people able to receive TV Martí are the folks in the U.S. Interests Section.

The *Christian Science Monitor* beams into Cuba, as does the *BBC World Service;* call the BBC in London for frequencies: tel. (0171) 257-2685. Reception is spotty at best.

For Tourists

Radio Taíno (AM 1160) is geared for tourists and airs in both English and Spanish 1-3 p.m. daily. It promotes Cuban culture and plays middle-of-the-road music. **TV Taíno** is the television equivalent. *Cánal de Sol* is available in many hotels, providing viewing for foreigners (everything from foreign soccer matches to kitschy travelogues). Watch, too, for screenings of *Walking in Havana* (a guided tour with the City Historian, Eusebio Leal).

HEALTH AND SAFETY

As long as you take appropriate precautions and use common sense, you're not likely to incur serious illness. If you do, you have the benefit of knowing that the nation has the best health system outside the "developed" world and one that guarantees treatment. There are English-speaking doctors in most cities, and you will rarely find yourself far from medical help.

There are local pharmacies everywhere, but they are meagerly stocked and medicines are hard to find away from key tourist spots (*turno regulares* are open 8 a.m.-5 p.m., *turnos permanentes* are open 24 hours).

Facilities for Foreigners

Cuba offers specialized services to foreign tourists. Most major cities and resort destinations have 24-hour **international clinics** *(clínicas internacionales)* staffed by English-speaking doctors and nurses. A number of international pharmacies *(farmacías internacionales)* in Havana and key tourist centers cater to foreigners and supply a large range of Western drugs for not much more than the same price you'd pay in the U.S. (You may be approached by Cubans outside tendering dollars and begging you to purchase desperately needed medicines on their behalf.)

The larger, upscale tourist hotels have nurses on duty. Other hotels will be able to request a doctor for in-house diagnosis and treatment for minor ailments. Payment is made in foreign currency (non-U.S. credit cards are accepted).

Ópticas Miramar, Av. 7ma y 22, Marianao, Havana, tel. (7) 24-2269 or 24-2990, fax (7) 24-2803, provides optician services and sells contact lenses and spectacles at prices comparable with the U.S. It has several outlets in Havana, as well as most major cities, including in Varadero at Av. 1ra #4204, e/ 41 y 43, tel. (7) 66-7525. I had my spectacles stolen in Cuba—a reminder to take a spare pair.

The Cuban agency **Servimed,** Calle 18 #4304, e/ 43 y 47, Miramar, tel. (7) 24-2658, fax (7) 24-2948, operates facilities throughout Cuba that are geared to providing medical and health services to foreigners, including a wide range of beauty- and spa-related services. In Havana,

these include the **Clínica Cira García,** tel. (7) 24-2811, ext. 14, a full-service hospital; **Farmacía Internacionál,** tel. (7) 24-2051, a pharmacy stocked with Western pharmaceuticals; **Óptica Miramar,** (see above); and **Instituto Pedro Kouri,** which specializes in treatment of HIV/AIDS, hepatitis, and other contagious and parasitic diseases. Servimed even offers such programs as drug rehabilitation and treatment for alcoholism. See regional chapters for details.

An excellent online resource is **Infomed,** at www.infomed.sld.cu.

With a few exceptions, facilities and standards, however, are not up to those of North America.

U.S. citizens should note that Uncle Sam's concern for your welfare is such that even if visiting Cuba legally, payment for "nonemergency medical services" is prohibited. Developing an ingrown toenail? Sorry, buddy. . . endure!

BEFORE YOU GO

Dental and medical checkups may be advisable before departing home, particularly if you intend to travel for a considerable time, partake in strenuous activities, or have an existing medical problem. Take along any medications, including prescriptions for eyewear; keep prescription drugs in their original bottles to avoid suspicion at customs (a letter from your physician explaining the need for any prescription drugs in your possession might also be a good idea). If you suffer from a debilitating health problem, wear a medical alert bracelet. Pharmacies can prescribe drugs (be wary of expiration dates, as shelf life of drugs may be shortened under tropical conditions).

A basic health kit is a good idea. Pack the following (as a minimum) in a small plastic container: alcohol swabs and medicinal alcohol, antiseptic cream, Band-Aids, aspirin or painkillers, diarrhea medication, sunburn remedy, antifungal foot powder, calamine and/or antihistamine, water-purification tablets, surgical tape, bandages and gauze, and scissors. **Adventure Medical**

HEALTH TOURISM

*T*he need for foreign currency has resulted in some health-care resources being diverted to "health tourism" (originally developed for an Eastern bloc clientele), where foreign patients come to Cuba for advanced treatment.

Cuba's "sun and surgery" program is run by **Servimed,** Calle 18 #4304 e/ 43 y 47, Playa, tel. (7) 24-2023, fax (7) 24-1630, a division of Cubanacán, which offers everything from spas and health resorts offering "stress breaks" to advanced treatments such as eye, open-heart, and plastic surgery. It is acknowledged as a world leader in orthopedics, and the **Frank País Orthopedic Hospital** recently had to double the capacity of its 40-bed ward for foreigners to meet demand. Cuba has even established the **International Placental Histotherapy Center** for treating vitiligo. And the **International Neurological Restoration Center** is claimed to be the only center in the world devoted entirely to the field of "neuro-restoration" (it offers treatments for Parkinson's disease, Alzheimer's disease, multiple sclerosis, epilepsy, etc.). Treatment for stress, asthma, hypertension, obesity, and alcohol control are also provided. Even silicon boob jobs are available (foreigners are charged about US$4,500 for implants)!

Kits, 5555 San Leandro, Oakland, CA 94624, tel. (510) 261-7414 or (800) 324-3517, fax (510) 261-7419, e-mail: amkusa@aol.com, website: www.adventuremedicalkits.com, has the most comprehensive range of travel medical kits, which come with handy medical booklets.

Information on health concerns can be answered by **Intermedic,** 777 Third Ave., New York, NY 10017, tel. (212) 486-8974, and the **Department of State Citizens Emergency Center,** tel. (202) 647-5225. In the U.K., you can get information, innoculations, and medical supplies from **British Airways Travel Clinics,** tel. (01276) 685040, website: www.british-airways.com/travelqa/fyi/health/docs/clinfone.shtml, which has branches nationwide, or the **Thomas Cook Vaccination Center,** 3-4 Wellington Terrace, Turnpike Lane, London N8 0PXX, tel. (0181) 889-7014.

The **International Association for Medical Assistance to Travellers** (IAMAT), 417 Center St., Lewiston, NY 14092, tel. (716) 754-4883, website: www.cybermall.co.nz/NZ/IAMAT; in Canada, 40 Regal Rd., Guelph, ON N1K 1B5, tel. (519) 836-0102, e-mail: iamat@sentex.net; in Europe, 57 Voirets, 1212 Grand-Lancy, Geneva, Switzerland, publishes helpful information, including a list of approved physicians and clinics. An indispensable pocket-sized book is *Staying Healthy in Asia, Africa, and Latin America,* Moon Publications, 5855 Beaudry St., Emeryville, CA 94608, tel. (510) 595-3664, website: www.moon.com, which is packed with useful information.

The U.S. **Centers for Disease Control and Prevention,** tel. (404) 332-4559 or (877) 394-8747 (travelers' hotline), fax (888) 232-3299, website: www.cdc.gov, issues latest health information and advisories by region.

Travel Insurance

Travel insurance is highly recommended. Travelers should check to see if their health insurance or other policies cover for medical expenses while abroad—and specifically in Cuba. Traveler's insurance isn't cheap, but it can be a sound investment. Travel agencies can sell you traveler's health and baggage insurance, as well as insurance against cancellation of a prepaid tour.

International: If you're concerned about things going wrong, consider purchasing insurance through **Assist-Card,** an international company, 15 rue du Cendrier, 1201 Ginebra, Switzerland, tel. (022) 738-5852, fax (022) 738-6305, website: www.assist-card.com, which offers travel assistance with everything from tracking lost luggage and finding medical, legal, and technical services to emergency transfers and repatriation, which you can request 24 hours a day. It has Regional Assistance Centers worldwide, including in Cuba (yes, even for U.S. citizens). Insurance premiums cost from US$40 for five days, US$70 for 10 days, US$80 for 16 days, and US$100 for 30 days (US$6 per day for additional days), and cover up to US$12,000 in medical costs plus other benefits. A premium package costs more. Assist-Card International has regional headquarters in the following locations: **Argentina**–Suipacha 1109, 1008 Buenos Aires, tel. (011) 4312-6801, toll free (0800) 81981, fax (011) 4311-2971; **Spain**–Calle Silva 2, Madrid, tel. (01) 559-0500, fax (01) 542-4680;

and the **U.S.**–1001 South Bayshore Dr. #2302, Miami, FL 33131, tel. (305) 381-9959, fax (305) 375-8135. For assistance in Cuba, call Asistur (see below); if you have difficulty, you can call the regional office in Miami.

In the U.S.: U.S. citizens are in luck: some insurance programs guarantee coverage for Cuba. These include **American Express,** P.O. Box 919010, San Diego, CA 92190, tel. (800) 234-0375; **Travelers,** 1 Tower Square, Hartford, CT 06183, tel. (203) 277-0111 or (800) 243-3174; and **TravelGuard International,** 1145 Clark St., Stevens Point, WI 54481, tel. (715) 345-0505 or (800) 782-5151.

In the U.K.: The **Association of British Insurers,** 51 Gresham St., London BC2V 7HQ, tel. (0171) 600-3333, website: www.abi.org.uk, and **Europe Assistance,** 252 High St., Croyden, Surrey CR0 1NF, tel. (0181) 680-1234, can provide advice for obtaining travel insurance in Britain. Inexpensive travel insurance is offered through **Campus Travel,** tel. (0171) 730-8111, **Endsleigh Insurance,** tel. (0171) 436-4451, and **STA Travel,** tel. (0171) 361-6262.

In Cuba: You can obtain insurance once you arrive in Cuba through **Asistur,** Paseo del Prado #254, Habana Vieja, tel. (7) 33-8920, 33-8527, 33-8339, fax (7) 33-8087, e-mail: seguro@asist .sid.cu, in association with the Cuban insurance agency, **Aseguradora del Turismo La Isla S.A.,** Calle 14 #301 esq. Calle 3ra, Miramar, tel. (7) 24-7490, fax (7) 24-7494. The basic package covers up to US$400 of baggage, US$7,000 in medical expenses, US$5,000 for repatriation, plus additional coverage.

The Cuban agency **ESEN,** Av. 5ta #306, Vedado, tel. (7) 32-2508, fax (7) 33-8717, also offers medical insurance for foreign travelers (US$10 per US$1,000 of treatment). Another Cuban company, **ESICUBA,** Seguros Internacionales de Cuba, Calle Cuba #314, e/ Obispo y Obrapía, tel. (7) 57-3231, fax (7) 33-8038, e-mail: esicuba@sic.get, offers travelers' insurance, although most of its policies are oriented toward the needs of companies, not individuals. ESICUBA insures all kinds of risks. Premiums are expensive and can be paid in any convertible foreign currency (indemnities are paid in the same currency). It's open 8 a.m.-3 p.m. Both ESEN and ESICUBA are independent companies, although the Cuban government is the major shareholder. They're rated by Insurance Solvency International and reinsure through Lloyds and other major insurers.

Vaccinations

No vaccinations are required to enter Cuba unless visitors are arriving from areas of cholera and yellow fever infection (mostly Africa and South America), in which case they must have valid vaccinations. Epidemic diseases have mostly been eradicated throughout the country. Cuba's achievements in eliminating infectious disease are unrivaled in the world. It is the only country to have totally eliminated measles, for example.

Consult your physician for recommended vaccinations. Travelers planning to rough it should consider vaccinations against tetanus and infectious hepatitis.

Infectious hepatitis (hepatitis A) is reported only infrequently in Cuba. Main symptoms are stomach pains, loss of appetite, yellowing skin and eyes, and extreme tiredness. Hepatitis A is contracted through unhygienic foods or contaminated water (salads and unpeeled fruits are major culprits). A gamma globulin vaccination is recommended. The much rarer Hepatitis B is usually contracted through unclean needles, blood transfusions, or unsafe sex.

You do *not* need an International Certificate of Vaccinations. Plan ahead for getting your vaccinations.

HEALTH PROBLEMS

Infection

Even the slightest scratch can fester quickly in the tropics. Treat promptly and regularly with antiseptic and keep the wound clean.

Intestinal Problems

Cuba's tap water is safe to drink in most places. However, serious deficiencies in water treatment chemicals in recent years have made many regional water supplies unsafe. Drink bottled mineral water *(agua mineral),* which is widely available. Remember, ice cubes are water, too. Always wash your hands before eating, and don't brush your teeth using suspect water.

Food hygiene standards in Cuba are very high. Milk is pasteurized, so you're not likely to encounter any problems normally associated with dairy products. However, the change in diet—which may alter the bacteria that are normal and necessary in the bowel—may briefly cause diarrhea or constipation (in case of the latter, eat lots of fruit). Fortunately, the stomach usually builds up a resistance to unaccustomed foods. Most cases of diarrhea are caused by microbial bowel infections resulting from contaminated food. Common-sense precautions include not eating uncooked fish or shellfish (which collect cholera bugs), uncooked vegetables, unwashed salads, or unpeeled fruit (peel the fruit *yourself*). And be fastidious with personal hygiene.

Diarrhea is usually temporary, and many doctors recommend letting it run its course. I prefer to medicate straight away with Lomotil or another antidiarrheal. Rest and drink lots of liquid to replace the water and salts lost. Avoid alcohol and milk products. If conditions don't improve after three days, seek medical help.

Diarrhea accompanied by severe abdominal pain, blood in your stool, and fever is a sign of **dysentery.** Seek immediate medical diagnosis. Tetracycline or ampicillin is normally used to cure bacillary dysentery. More complex professional treatment is required for amoebic dysentery. The symptoms of both are similar. **Giardiasis,** acquired from infected water, is another intestinal complaint. It causes diarrhea, bloating, persistent indigestion, and weight loss. Again, seek medical advice. **Intestinal worms** can be contracted by walking barefoot on infested beaches, grass, or earth.

Sunburn and Skin Problems
The tropical sun is intense and can fry you in minutes. It can even burn you through light clothing or while you're lying in the shade. The midday sun is especially potent. Even if you consider yourself nicely tanned already, use a sun cream or sunblock at least SPF 8. Zinc oxide provides almost 100% protection. Bring sun lotions with you; they're not always readily available in Cuba, although most hotel stores sell them. If you're intent on a tan, have patience. Build up gradually, and use an aloe gel after sunbathing; it helps repair any skin damage. The tops of feet and backs of knees are particularly susceptible to burning. Con-

sider wearing a wide-brimmed hat, too. Calamine lotion and aloe gel will soothe light burns; for more serious burns, use steroid creams.

Sun glare—especially prevalent if you're on water—can cause conjunctivitis. Sunglasses will protect against this. **Prickly heat** is an itchy rash, normally caused by clothing that is too tight or in need of washing. This and **athlete's foot** are best treated by airing out the body and washing your clothes.

Dehydration and Heat Problems
The tropical humidity and heat can sap your body fluids like blotting paper. You'll sweat profusely, especially in the Oriente, where summer temperatures are extreme. Leg cramps, exhaustion, dizziness, and headaches are possible signs of dehydration. Although your body may acclimatize to the heat gradually, at the same time dehydration can develop slowly. Diarrhea will drain your body of fluids swiftly.

Drink regularly to avoid dehydration. Avoid alcohol and caffeine, which process water in the body.

Excessive exposure to too much heat can cause **heat stroke,** a potentially fatal result of a failure in the body's heat-regulation mechanisms. Excessive sweating, extreme headaches, and disorientation leading to possible convulsions and delirium are symptoms. Emergency medical care is essential! If hospitalization is not possible, place the victim in the shade, cover him with a wet cloth, and fan continually to cool him down.

Don't be alarmed if your ankles and legs get puffy. It's the tropical climate. When you rest, keep your feet higher than your head (a cold Epsom salts footbath also helps).

Many tourists come down with colds *(catarro Cubano),* often brought on by the debilitating effects of constantly shifting from icily air-conditioned restaurants and hotels to sultry outdoor heat. A more serious ailment is **bronchitis,** which should be treated with antibiotics.

Snakes, Scorpions, and Crocodiles
Snakes are common in Cuba. Fortunately, they're not poisonous but they can bite. The worst you'll usually suffer is puncture marks and some bruising and swelling, but who needs that? You should always watch where you're treading or putting your hands in the wilds.

Scorpions *(alacrán)* exist in Cuba, although they are not very numerous and you are not likely to see them. Their sting is painful and can cause nausea and fever but is not usually as frightening as the horror stories would have you believe. If you get stung, drink lots of liquids and take lots of rest. Don't forget to shake out your shoes and clothing each morning. Trying to pick up a scorpion by hand is foolish; if the bugger refuses to leave your room, a hard, hefty object (and something to clean up the mess) is the best defense.

A saucepan, however, won't work on the aggressive Cuban crocodile. Something bigger is called for—like a big stick to jam between top and bottom jaws. Fortunately, most areas inhabited by crocodiles, such as the Zapata swamps, are off-limits to foreigners without guides. Don't go wading in swampland.

Insects and Arachnids

The most common bugs you'll see will be cockroaches, which are found virtually everywhere and are harmless, albeit they carry disease (you don't want them crawling over your food).

At some stage during your visit to Cuba you'll probably be the victim of rapacious **mosquitoes.** Varadero, the cays, Zapata, and other coastal flatlands are particularly noted for mosquitoes, as is the waterfront region of Miramar in Havana. Their bites itch, sure, but you need have no fear of malaria—it's not present in Cuba. Fortunately, mosquitoes are mostly nocturnal; when they awake from daylight slumber they are demonically hungry and will drool over your blood-suffused body. To keep them at bay, turn on your a/c or overhead fan as high as is comfortable.

scorpion (alacán)

However, mosquitoes (particularly those active by day) *do* transmit **dengue fever,** which *is* present, although extremely rare, in Cuba. The illness can be fatal (death usually results from internal hemorrhaging). Its symptoms are similar to those for malaria, with additional severe pain in the joints and bones, for which it is sometimes called "breaking bones disease." Other symptoms include severe headaches and high fever. Unlike malaria, it is not recurring. Clothing can be sprayed with the insecticide permethrin. There is no cure. Dengue fever must run its course. In the unlikely event you contact it, have plenty of aspirin or other painkillers on hand. Drink lots of water.

Tiny, irritating **"no-see-ums,"** truly evil blood-sucking sand flies about the size of a pinpoint, inhabit a few beaches and marshy coastal areas in Cuba. This nuisance is active only around dusk, when you should avoid the beach. You can pour sulfur powder on your shoes, socks, and ankles.

Repellent sprays and lotions are a must for moist areas. Take lotion to apply to the body and aerosol spray for clothing. Avon Skin-So-Soft oil is such an effective bug repellent—especially against "no-see-ums"—that U.S. Marines use it by the truckload ("Gee, private, you sure smell nice—and your skin's so soft!"). The best mosquito repellents contain DEET (diethyl-metatoluamide), although it leaves "no-see-ums" unfazed. DEET is quite toxic; avoid using it on small children, and avoid getting it on plastic or Lycra—which it will melt. Use mosquito netting at night in the lowlands (you can obtain good hammocks and "no-see-um" nets in the U.S. from **Campmor,** P.O. Box 997, Paramus, NJ 07653, tel. (800) 526-4784. A fan over your bed and mosquito coils *(espirales,* which are rarely sold in Cuba) that smolder for up to eight hours also help keep mosquitoes at bay. Citronella candles may help, too.

Long-sleeved shirts and long pants will help reduce the number of bites you collect.

There are wasps and bees in Cuba; otherwise, Cuba is relatively free of biting insects. Even ants are a relative rarity. The most common bugs you'll see will be cockroaches, which are found virtually everywhere. Check your bedding before crawling into bed. Keep beds away from walls. And, for true paranoids, look underneath the toilet seat before sitting down.

AIDS IN CUBA

Cuba has one of the world's most aggressive and successful campaigns against AIDS. The World Health Organization (WHO) and the Pan-American Health Organization have praised the program as exemplary. Cuba's unique response to the worldwide epidemic that began in the early 1980s was to initiate mass testing of the population and a "mandatory quarantine" of everyone testing positive. By 1994, when the policy of *mandatory* testing was ended, about 98% of the adult population had been tested. Voluntary testing continues.

The program has stemmed an epidemic that rages only 50 miles away in Haiti and kept the spread of the disease to a level that no other country can equal. By the end of 1997, Cuba had recorded 1,408 cases of HIV, and 373 people had died of AIDS. A recent report by WHO's Global Program on AIDS showed Cuba with 7.3 cases per million population; in comparison, the U.S. had 241.2 cases per million.

At first, the purpose was to keep the disease from spreading. The objective was to develop AIDS sanatoriums throughout the island, where people who test HIV-positive could be evaluated medically and psychologically and educated in the ethics and biology of AIDS prevention—then go out and lead a normal life, using the sanatorium as an outpatient facility. Twelve sanatoriums exist on the island. Residents live in small houses or apartments, alone or as couples (straight or gay). Cuba has defended its sanatorium policy as a way of guaranteeing first-class health care for patients while protecting the rest of the population.

Mandatory confinement was ended in early 1994. Instead, an outpatient program has been implemented. (Anyone who tests HIV-positive has his or her job and salary assured, whether or not he or she is able to work).

Unlike the United States, the primary source of contamination in Cuba has been heterosexual relations, initially attributable to Cuba's military involvement in Angola and Ethiopia. The rapid growth of tourism is throwing a new variable into the equation: WHO statistics show a 150% increase in sexually related diseases in Cuba since 1990, a trend strongly implicating the foreign invasion. The Cuban state now emphasizes personal responsibility. The Ministry of Health has established the **Centro Nacional de Educación Sexual,** Calle 19 #851, Vedado, tel. (7) 55-2529, to offer safe-sex workshops. And the **Centro Nacional de Educación de Salud,** Calle 1 #507, Vedado, Havana, tel. (7) 32-1920, has an AIDS Information Drop-In Center.

Despite Cuba's laudable success, today it has little money to spend on AIDS programs that go beyond the barest essentials. Nonetheless, in late 1997 Cuba started testing an anti-AIDS vaccine.

The **Cuba AIDS Project,** 465 S.W. 62nd Court, Miami, FL 33144, tel. (305) 531-3973, e-mail: cubaidspr@aol.com, delivers medications to Cubans who suffer from HIV/AIDS on the islands. Donations and couriers are needed.

Fortunately, only a few people have fierce reactions to insect and spider bites. However, bites can easily become infected in the tropics, so avoid scratching! Treat with antiseptics or antibiotics. A baking-soda bath can help relieve itching if you're badly bitten, as can antihistamine tablets, hydrocortisone, and calamine lotion.

Chiggers *(coloradillas)* inhabit grasslands, particularly in dry areas favored by cattle. Their bites itch like hell. Mosquito repellent won't deter them. If you plan on hiking through cattle pastures, consider dusting your shoes, socks, and ankles with sulfur powder. Sucking sulfur tablets *(azufre sublimado)* apparently gives your sweat a smell that chiggers find obnoxious. **C&C Laboratories,** P.O. Box 7779, Dallas, TX 75209, tel. (214) 748-7953, sells Chigarid, for relief of chigger bites. Nail polish apparently works, too (over the bites, not on the nails) by suffocating the beasts.

Ticks hang out near livestock. They burrow headfirst into your skin. Extract a tick by gripping it with tweezers as close to the head as you can get and pulling it gently out. Be careful not to pull the body—you'll snap their bodies off, leaving their heads in your flesh, where they'll fester.

Some insect larvae, once laid beneath your skin, can cause boils (you'll often see a clear hole in the middle of the boil or pimple). Completely cover with Vaseline and a secure Band-Aid or tape and let it dry overnight. You should be able to squeeze the culprit out next day.

Scabies: Since the onset of the Special Period, the lack of hygiene products and generally harsher conditions under which many Cubans are now forced to live have led to a rapid increase in the incidence of scabies (a microscopic mite) and lice. Infestation is possible if you're staying in unhygienic conditions or sleeping with people already infested. A casual sexual liaison is the most common way to become contaminated. If you're unfortunate enough to contract scabies, you'll need to use a body shampoo containing gamma benzene hexachloride or one percent lindane solution (lindane is a highly toxic pesticide). At the same time, you must also wash all your clothing and bedding in very hot water—and throw out your underwear. Your sexual partner will need to do the same. The severe itching caused by scabies infestation appears after three or four weeks (it appears as little dots, often in lines and sometimes ending in blisters, especially around the genitals, elbows, wrists, lower abdomen, nipples, and on the head of the penis). A second bout of scabies usually shows itself within 48 hours of re-infestation. Treatment in the U.S. is by prescription only. However, you can obtain *Scabisan* or *lindane* (one percent solution) from Cuban pharmacies, including the **Farmácia Internacional** in Havana.

Avoid **beehives**. If you disturb a hive, running in a zigzag is said to help in fleeing. If there's water about, take a dunk and stay submerged for a while.

If any bites you receive become infected, it's best to have them treated locally (and certainly promptly); doctors back home might have difficulty diagnosing and treating the condition.

AIDS and Sexually Transmitted Diseases

The risk of contracting AIDS in Cuba is relatively minor. The rate of infection is among the world's lowest and the Cuban government conducts an exemplary anti-AIDS campaign. Cuba even manufactures AIDS diagnostic kits as well as interferons for treatment. However, the incidence of AIDS is already showing signs of rapid increase due to the growing prevalence of sexual liaisons between Cubans and foreigners.

Gonorrhea, syphilis, and other sexually transmitted diseases are fairly common. Avoidance of casual sexual contact is the best prevention. If you do succumb to the mating urge, use condoms, which can be purchased at dollar stores. However, don't rely on condoms (*preservativos*)

being available locally. You should purchase a supply before departing for Cuba. Practice safe sex.

Gynecological Problems

Travel, hot climates, and a change of diet or health regime can play havoc with your body, leading to yeast and other infections. A douche of diluted vinegar or lemon-juice can help alleviate yeast infections. Loose, cotton underwear may help prevent infections such as candida, typified by itching and a white, cheesy discharge. A foul-smelling discharge accompanied by a burning sensation may indicate trichomoniasis, usually caught through intercourse but also by contact with unclean towels, etc.

Other Problems

Rabies, though rare in Cuba, can be contracted through the bite of an infected dog or other animal. It's always fatal unless treated. You're extremely unlikely to be the victim of a vampire bat, a common rabies carrier that preys on cattle. Still, if you're sleeping in the open, keep your toes covered.

MEDICAL EMERGENCIES

In emergencies, call 116 for the police. Unfortunately, there is no single emergency telephone number for the Red Cross or ambulance.

You will never be far from a hospital or Red Cross service in Cuba. All hospitals in the country provide free emergency health care for foreigners.

A Swiss-based company called **Assist-Card** provides emergency services in Cuba, including arranging doctor's visits to your hotel and even emergency evacuation. It works in conjunction with **Asistur**. See the section on Travelers Insurance, above.

Medical Evacuation

Uncle Sam has deemed that even U.S. emergency evacuation services cannot fly to Cuba to evacuate U.S. citizens without a license from the Treasury Department. The rules keep changing, so it is worth checking the latest situation with such companies as **Traveler's Emergency Network,** P.O. Box 238, Hyattsville, MD 20797,

HOSPITALS AND CLINICS *(POLICLÍNICOS)*

For a complete list of hospitals and clinics, see the Cuba telephone directory.

HAVANA

(7) 55-2197	Hospital Calixto García
(7) 24-0330	Hospital Cira García (international clinic)
(7) 57-6077	Hospital Hermanos Ameijeiras

HAVANA PROVINCE

Artemisa	(63) 3-3011 Hospital
Batabanó	(62) 8-3385 Clinic
Guines	(686) 2-3557 Hospital
Mariel	(64) 9-2011 Hospital
San Antonio de los Baños	(650) 2892 Hospital
Santa Cruz del Norte	(692) 8-4124 Hospital

CAMAGÜEY PROVINCE

Camagüey	(322) 6-1011 Hospital, (322) 8-2012 Hospital
Florida	(32) 5-4713 Hospital
Nuevitas	(32) 4-3014 Hospital
Playa Santa Lucía	(32) 3-6203 International clinic, (32) 3-6294 Clinic
Santa Cruz del Sur	(32) 32-2246 Hospital

CIEGO DE ÁVILA PROVINCE

Ciego de Ávila	(33) 2-4015 Hospital
Júcaro	(33) 9-8181 Clinic
Morón	(335) 3530 Hospital

CIENFUEGOS PROVINCE

Cienfuegos	(432) 3911 Hospital

GRANMA PROVINCE

Bartolomé Masó	(23) 366 Doctor, (23) 367 Clinic
Bayamo	(23) 42-6598 Hospital, (23) 42-2144 Clinic (emergencies)
Manzanillo	(23) 5-4011 Hospital, (23) 5-2861 Clinic (emergencies)
Niquero	(23) 59-2627 Hospital
Pilón	(23) 59-4412 Hospital

GUANTÁNAMO PROVINCE

Baracoa	(21) 4-2502 Hospital, (21) 4-2739 Clinic (emergencies)
Guantánamo	(21) 38-1012 Hospital (general), (21) 38-2106 Clinic (emergencies)

HOLGUÍN PROVINCE

Banes	(24) 8-3302 Hospital
Gibara	(24) 3-4193 Hospital
Guarvalavaca	(24) 3-0291 International clinic
Holguín	(24) 48-1477 Hospital, (24) 42-5302 Hospital
Moa	(24) 6-6012 Hospital
Rafael Freyre	(24) 2-0135 Hospital

ISLA DE LA JUVENTUD

Cayo Largo	(5) 4-8238 Clinic
Nueva Gerona	(61) 2-3002 Hospital

LAS TUNAS PROVINCE

Las Tunas	(31) 4-5012 Hospital

MATANZAS PROVINCE

Cárdenas	(5) 52-4011 Hospital
Colón	(5) 3-3011 Hospital
Jagüey Grande	(59) 2151 Hospital
Matanzas	(52) 7016 Hospital
Pedro Betancourt	(5) 89-8363 Clinic
Playa Girón	(5) 9-4196 Clinic
Playa Larga	(5) 7134 Clinic
Varadero	(5) 61-7710 International clinic, (5) 61-3464 Clinic

PINAR DEL RÍO PROVINCE

Bahía Honda	(86) 239 Hospital
Pinar del Río	(82) 2010 Hospital, (82) 6-2046 Clinic
San Juan y Mártinez	(8) 9-8207 Clinic
Viñales	(8) 9-3348 Clinic

SANCTI SPÍRITUS PROVINCE

Sancti Spíritus	(41) 2-4017 Hospital
Topes de Collantes	(42) 4-0384 Hospital
Trinidad	(419) 4012 or 3201 Hospital

SANTA CLARA PROVINCE

Caibarién	(42) 3-3011 or (42) 3-5657 Hospital
Manicuragua	(42) 49-1552 Hospital
Remedios	(42) 39-5230 Hospital
Santa Clara	(422) 7-2016 Hospital
Zuluetas	(42) 39-9163 Clinic

SANTIAGO DE CUBA PROVINCE

El Cobre	(22) 3-6300 Hospital
Santiago de Cuba	(226) 4-2016 Hospital

tel. (800) 275-4836, and **International SOS Assistance,** Box 11568, Philadelphia, PA 19116, tel. (215) 244-1500 or (800) 523-8930, fax (215) 244-0165, e-mail: individual@intsos.com, website: www.intsos.com, both of which provide worldwide ground and air evacuation and medical assistance.

The insurance packages sold by **Aseguradora del Turismo La Isla S.A.** (see Travelers Insurance, above) include US$5,000 coverage for repatriation in the need of medical evacuation.

The Office of Overseas Citizens Services provides emergency information for U.S. citizens, tel. (202) 647-5225; or (202) 647-4000 after hours.

SAFETY

All the negative media hype sponsored by Washington has left many people with a false impression that Cuba is unsafe. Far from it. Few places in the world are as safe for visitors.

Frankly, most visitors are no more likely to run into problems in Cuba than they are in their own backyards. The vast majority of Cubans are honest and friendly. Rape and other violent crimes are virtually unknown. In rural towns many residents still say they can hardly remember the last time a crime was committed. But that was when there was nothing to steal. The sudden influx of wealthy tourists and the hardships faced by Cubans in their daily life have fostered a growing problems.

Traffic is perhaps the greatest danger, despite a relative paucity of vehicles on the road. Be especially wary when crossing the streets in Havana. Stand well away from the curb—especially on corners, where buses often mount the sidewalk. Cyclists are everywhere, making insouciant turns and weaving with leisurely sovereignty, like Brahmin cattle. And sidewalks are full of gaping potholes and tilted curbstones. Watch your step! Outside Havana, oxen, mules, and other livestock wander along the roads. Use extra caution when passing tractors and trucks, which without warning tend to make sweeping turns across the road.

In the countryside you need to take some basic precautions. Hikers straying off trails can easily lose their way in the mountain forests.

Remember that atop the higher mountains, sunny weather can turn cold and rainy in seconds, so dress accordingly. And be extra cautious if crossing rivers; a rainstorm upstream can turn the river downstream into a raging torrent without any warning. Ideally, go with a guide.

Uncle Sam issues **Travel Warnings and Consular Information Sheets,** tel. (202) 647-5225, fax (202) 647-3000, website: www.travel.state.gov. Its Cuba sheet is chillingly negative and to some degree, skews realities to scare the dickens out of you.

Theft and Scams

Cuba's many charms can lull visitors into a false sense of security. The country has more than its fair share of economic and social problems, with rising street crime among them. The recent economic crisis has spawned a growing number of petty thieves and purse snatchers. Theft from hotel rooms is increasing. Corruption—until very recently virtually unknown in revolutionary Cuba—has reared its ugly head, too, and has got a grip at the highest levels of government. And the seed of an organized Mafia can be sensed. An armed attack on an armored van in December 1998 was a dramatic first, and two Italians were killed during an armed robbery in September 1998. Most crime, however, is opportunistic; thieves seek easy targets. Don't become paranoid. A few common-sense precautions, though, are in order.

Your biggest irritant—besides bureaucratic stalling and idiocies—will probably be *jiniteros*—hustlers—touting everything from fake cigars *("son real, señor!")* to a night of bliss with their beautiful cousin. You'll also find kids imploring you for pencils and Chiclets (*sheek-lays;* Cuba does not make chewing gum).

Your biggest problem will probably be the persistent scams pulled by restaurants, hotels, and other tourist entities (the Cuban government doesn't want tourists: it wants your dollars). Insist on an itemized bill at restaurants, add it up diligently, and count your change. Be prepared for charges for things you didn't consume or which didn't materialize, and for higher charges than you were quoted in the first place. Car rental companies and their employees are particularly adept at scams (see the car rentals section in

Getting Around, this chapter). Cuban tour agencies aren't above the same. You pay for a deluxe hotel, say, on a package to Cayo Largo but are told when you arrive that the hotel in question doesn't honor such packages. You're then fobbed off to the cheapest hotel. When you return to Havana to request a refund, you're plain out of luck, as the documents relating to your trip can't be found. And the *consumo mínimo* charge in many bars and nightclubs is an invitation to fleece you (if you have an expensive drink followed by, say, a water, watch for the latter being charged first at the minimum charge, usually US$5).

Often if you challenge the charges, the employee will unapologetically say "it was a mistake" but expect you to pay anyway. Rarely is there a manager available, and usually they also say there is nothing that can be done about it. However intransigent the staff, be politely persistent. Emotional pleas often help. If the scam amounts to outright theft, as with rental car scams, take the staffer's name and threaten to report him or her to the head office and police. That usually does the trick.

Common-Sense Precautions

Don't wear jewelry, chains, or expensive watches. Leave them with your ego at home. Wear an inexpensive digital watch. And never carry more cash than you need for the day. The rest should be kept in the hotel safe. If you don't trust the hotel or if it doesn't have a safe, try as best you can to hide your valuables and secure your room. The majority of your money should be in the form of traveler's checks, which can be refunded if lost or stolen.

Crowded places are the happy hunting grounds of crafty crooks. If you sense yourself being squeezed or jostled, don't hold back—elbow your way out of there immediately. Better safe than sorry. Never leave your purse, camera, or luggage unattended in public places (don't leave items on the beach unattended if you go for a swim). And always keep a wary eye on your luggage on public transportation, especially backpacks (sneak thieves love their zippered compartments).

Never carry your wallet in your back pocket. Instead, wear a secure money belt. Alternative-

Capitolio, Havana, Cuba's pre-Revolution Senate and Chamber of Republics

ly, you can carry your bills in your front pocket. Pack them beneath a handkerchief. Carry any other money in an inside pocket, a "secret" pocket sewn into your pants or jacket, or hidden in a body pouch or an elasticized wallet below the knee. Spread your money around your person.

Don't carry more luggage than you can adequately manage. Limit your baggage to *one* suitcase or duffel. And have a lock for each luggage item. Purses should have a short strap (ideally, one with metal woven in) that fits tightly against the body and snaps closed or has a zipper. *Always* keep purses fully zipped and luggage locked.

Don't leave anything of value within reach of an open window. Don't leave anything of value in your car. Don't leave tents unguarded. And be particularly wary after cashing money at a bank, or if doing a deal with a street-changer or *jinitero*.

EMERGENCY TELEPHONE NUMBERS

Cuba is slowly introducing a single number system for emergencies. At press time, most calls were still placed direct to regional service providers.

CITY	AMBULANCE	FIRE	POLICE
NATIONAL	114	115	116
HAVANA			
Ciudad de la Habana	(7) 40-5093, 40-5094	(7) 81-1115, (7) 57-5291	(7) 82-0116
Santiago de las Vegas	(683) 2248	(683) 2666	(683) 3734
HAVANA PROVINCE			
Artemisa	(63) 3-2597	(63) 3-3300	(63) 3-3153
Batabanó	(62) 8-5335	(62) 8-3545	(62) 8-5375
Mariel	(63) 9-2444	(63) 9-2321	(63) 9-2441
Santa Cruz del Norte	(692) 8-3158	(692) 8-3310	(692) 8-3306
San Antonio de los Baños	(650) 2781	(650) 2225	(650) 2111
CAMAGÜEY			
Camagüey	(322) 9-2860	115	116
Nuevitas	(32) 4-2227	115	116
Playa Santa Lucía	(32) 3-6294	-	(32) 3-6225
Santa Cruz del Sur	-	(32) 32-2122	(32) 32-2238
CIEGO DE ÁVILA			
Cayo Coco	-	(33) 30-8167	(33) 30-8107
Ciego de Ávila	185	115	116
Morón	(335) 3151	115	116
CIENFUEGOS			
Cienfuegos	(432) 5019	115	116
GRANMA			
Bayamo	185	115	116
Bartolomé Masó	(23) 59-5448	-	(23) 59-5441
Manzanillo	118	115	116
Pilón	(23) 59-4261	(23) 59-4524	(23) 59-4493
GUANTÁNAMO			
Baracoa	(21) 4-2472	115	(21) 4-2623
Guantánamo	-	115	116

Make photocopies of all important documents: your passport (showing photograph and visas, if applicable), airline ticket, credit cards, insurance policy, driver's license. Carry the photocopies with you, and leave the originals along with your other valuables in the hotel safe where possible. If this isn't possible, carry the originals with you in a secure inside pocket. Don't put all your eggs in one basket. Prepare an "emergency kit" to include photocopies of your documents and an adequate sum of money to tide you over if your wallet gets stolen.

CITY	AMBULANCE	FIRE	POLICE
HOLGUÍN			
Banes	(24) 8-2727	115	116
Gibara	-	(24) 3-4539	(24) 3-4248
Holguín	185	115	116
Moa	(24) 6-6432	115	(24) 6-6243
ISLA DE LA JUVENTUD			
Cayo Largo	(5) 4-8238	(5) 4-8247	(5) 4-8253
Nueva Gerona	(61) 2-4170	115	116, (61) 2-2652
LAS TUNAS			
Las Tunas	(31) 4-2073	115	16
MATANZAS			
Cárdenas	196	115	116
Jagüey Grande	2414	115	116
Matanzas	(52) 2337	115	116
Playa Girón	(5) 9-4133	115	116
San Miguel de los Baños	(5) 89-6117	-	(5) 89-6163
Varadero	(5) 61-2950	115	116
PINAR DEL RÍO			
Bahía Honda	(86) 565	(86) 241	(86) 243
Consolación del Sur	(8) 8-2383	115	(8) 8-2121
Pinar del Río City	(82) 6-2317	115	116, (82) 2525
Viñales	-	-	(8) 9-3124
SANCTI SPÍRITUS			
Trinidad	(419) 2362	115	116
Sancti Spíritus	(41) 2-4462	115	116
SANTIAGO DE CUBA			
El Cobre	(22) 3-6105	-	(22) 3-7116
Santiago de Cuba	185	115	116
Siboney	-	-	(22) 3-9116
VILLA CLARA			
Caibarién	(42) 3-3888	115	116
Remedios	(42) 39-5149	-	(42) 39-5218
Santa Clara	(422) 3965	115	116

For credit card security, insist that imprints are made in your presence. Make sure any imprints incorrectly completed are torn up. Don't take someone else's word that it will be done. Destroy the carbons yourself.

In Havana and other major cities, be wary of darker back streets at night (very few streets have lights). And note that some local bars can get rowdy after the *aguardente* (cheap rum) has been flowing a while. Cubans are an uncommonly decent lot in general. You'll see plenty of drunks on weekends and at street carnivals.

DEALING WITH OFFICIALS

Bribery and Corruption

Cuba is one of the few places in the Third World where you can get yourself into serious trouble by offering a bribe. Castro's government has differed greatly from other countries receiving billions of dollars in foreign aid—most of which has ended up in officials' pockets. It also ended overt corruption, where an elite ruling class plundered the national treasury.

However, during major financial straits, otherwise upright honest people will do unscrupulous things, and the integrity of Cuban officials has begun to show serious cracks. Many have turned to the black market to augment their salaries. And the reemergence of a dollar-based market economy is fostering a rapid rise in corruption. A local Mafia is slowly but surely evolving. Castro blames the growth in bribery and corruption on "economic relations with capitalism" (see Andres Oppenheimer's *Castro's Final Hour* for an opposing viewpoint). There have been isolated reports of tourists being shaken down for money, although most corruption seems to be in black-market activities that are hardly likely to affect you.

Never pay a policeman money. If a policeman asks for money, get his name and badge number and file a complaint to the Ministry of Foreign Relations.

Police

The **Nacional Revolucionario Policía** (National Revolutionary Police) are a branch of the Ministry of the Interior. Their presence is ubiquitous. Uniformed Cuban policemen perform the same functions as uniformed police officers in other countries. However, they also exist to enforce revolutionary purity and it is upsetting to foreign visitors to witness the constant and petty harassment by policemen of everyday Cubans on the streets.

Police are under instructions not to stop or harass tourists unless they have broken, or are suspected of breaking, the law. If you are stopped by policemen wanting to search you, insist on the search being done in front of a neutral witness—*"solamente con testigos."* If at all possible, do *not* allow an official to confiscate or walk away with your passport (you should always carry a copy of your passport and tourist card with you at all times to verify your identity). Don't panic. Tell as little as circumspection dictates—unlike priests, policemen rarely offer absolution for confessions.

Cuba is a paranoid nation that zealously guards against threats to the state's integrity (with good reason; Uncle Sam is still bent on toppling the Castro regime by fair means or foul). The state security apparatus is fine-tuned to keep an eye on foreigners. Plainclothes policemen and informers are abundant, and the CDRs are also alert. Remember that freedom of speech is relative and does not include the right to go around criticizing the Cuban system or you-know-who. Obey all laws and customs. Journalists and others in "sensitive occupations" may be assigned specific rooms—which may be bugged—or otherwise kept an eye on. Be circumspect about what you say, especially to anyone you do not implicitly trust, even, or especially, the beautiful *cubana* (or *cubano*) too eager to be your lover.

Never attempt to photograph police officers or military figures without their permission.

Dealing with Bureaucrats

Cuba has an insufferable bureaucracy as portrayed in the trenchant black comedy *Death of a Bureaucrat.* Behind every office door is a desk or counter behind which is a woman—preferably middle-aged and the very "cornerstone of bureaucracy"—whose job it is to keep people out.

The island is riddled with Catch-22s, and working with government ministries (I almost wrote "mysteries") can be a perplexing and frustrating endeavor. Civil servants in Cuba are always civil but usually servants only to their master, in the words of Guillermo Cabrera Infante. Very few people have the power to say, "Yes"—but everyone is allowed to say, "No." Finding the person who can say "Yes" is the key.

Ranting at Cubans gets you nowhere. Getting apoplectic with charming-faced Cuban officialdom only results in "negatives given more positively, broader and more regretful smiles, a rueful elevation of palms, eyes, and shoulders." Logical arguments count for little; charm, even romantic *priopos* or a gift of chocolate, seem to work better.

IF TROUBLE STRIKES

If things turn dire, you should contact **Asistur**, which exists to provide assistance to tourists in trouble. Its services include providing insurance, medical assistance, funeral repatriation, and legal and financial aid. Asistur also helps obtain new travel documents and locate lost luggage and may even indemnify against loss (assuming you already have travelers' insurance). The main office is at Calle 4 #110, e/ 1ra y 3ra, Miramar, tel. (7) 24-8835, fax (7) 24-1613 or 33-8088, e-mail: comercia@asistur.get.cma.net, website: www.asistur.cubaweb.cu. It has an **alarm center** at Prado #212 esq. Trocadero in Habana Vieja, open 24 hours, 365 days a year: tel. (7) 33-8920, fax (7) 33-8087, e-mail: asisten@asisten.get .cma.net. You'll also find Asistur outlets in Cienfuegos, Varadero, and Santiago de Cuba and other key tourist centers.

You should also contact your embassy or consulate. Consulate officials can't get you out of jail, but they can help you locate a lawyer, alleviate unhealthy conditions, or arrange for funds to be wired if you run short of money. They may be able to authorize a reimbursable loan while you arrange for cash to be forwarded, or even lend you money to get home (the U.S. State Department hates to admit this).

If you're robbed, immediately file a police report. You'll need this to make an insurance claim. You'll receive a statement *(denuncio)* for insurance purposes (and to replace lost tourist cards, traveler's checks, etc.) and which you should make sure is dated and stamped. (The Cuban police usually energetically investigate theft against foreigners. At press time there was no special unit responsible for pursuing thefts from tourists.)

U.S. Citizens: U.S. citizens shouldn't expect the **U.S. Interests Section,** c/o Embassy of Switzerland, Calzada, e/ L y M, Vedado, tel. (7) 32-0551 or 32-9700, to bend over backward; it exists for political reasons, not to help citizens. Nonetheless, one reader has written to says that the staff were very helpful and issued a new passport immediately after his money and passport were stolen, though he was traveling in Cuba without a license (nor was he reported to the Treasury Department). The *Handbook of Consular Services,* Public Affairs Staff, Bureau of

ASISTUR OFFICES

MAIN OFFICE (HAVANA)

Calle 4 #110 e/ 1ra y 3ra, Miramar,
tel. (7) 24-8835, fax 24-1613 or 24-8088

Paseo del Prado #254, e/ Animas y Trocadero, Habana Vieja, tel. (7) 33-8527 or 62-5519, fax (7) 33-8087

OTHER LOCATIONS

Cienfuegos: Hotel Jagua, Calle 37 #1, Punta Gorda, tel. (432) 6362 or 66-6190

Guardalavaca: Centro Comercial,
tel. (24) 3-0148

Santiago de Cuba: Hotel Santiago, Av. de las Américas y Calle M, tel. (226) 33-5015, ext. 3128, fax (226) 33-5805, and Calle General Lacret, Parque Céspedes, tel. (226) 63-8284 or 62-5519, fax (226) 33-8087.

Varadero: Calle 31 #101, e/ 1 y 3,
tel. (5) 33-7277

EMERGENCY HELP

In the event of an emergency, the following may be of help:

Citizen's Emergency Center, U.S. State Department, tel. (202) 647-5225, fax (202) 647-3000.

International Legal Defense Counsel, 1429 Walnut St. #800, Philadelphia, PA 19102, tel. (215) 977-9982.

International SOS Assistance, 8 Neshaminy Interplex, P.O. Box 11568, Philadelphia, PA 19116, tel. (215) 244-1500.

Consular Affairs, U.S. Department of State, Washington, D.C. 20520, provides details of such assistance. Friends and family can also call the Department of State's **Overseas Citizen Service,** tel. (202) 647-5225, website: travel.state.gov/acs.html, to check on you if things go awry. Remember, however, that the U.S. does not have *full* diplomatic representation in Cuba, and its tapestry of pullable strings is understandably threadbare. If arrested, U.S. citizens should ask Cuban authorities to notify the U.S. Interests Section. A U.S. consular officer will then try to arrange regular visits, at the discretion of the Cuban government. (Cuba does not recognize dual citizenship for Cuban citizens who are also U.S. citizens; Cuban-born citizens are—according to the U.S. State Department—thereby denied representation through the U.S. Interests Section in the event of arrest.)

Legal Assistance: Asistur (see above) provides legal assistance. The **Consultorio Jurídica Internacional** (International Judicial Consultative Bureau), Calle 18 #120 esq. Av. 3ra, Miramar, Havana, tel. (7) 24-2490, fax (7) 24-2303; and Av. 1ra #2008 esq. Calle 21, Varadero, tel. (7) 33-7077, fax (7) 33-7080, e-mail: cji@imagenes.get.cma.net, website: www.cji.cubaweb.cu, also provides legal advice and services regarding all aspects of Cuban law—from marriages and notarization to advising on the constitutionality of business ventures. It can assist travelers, including those who lose their passports or have them stolen (for U.S. citizens, Cuban officials can produce documents—US$175—that preclude needing to have a new U.S. passport issued in the U.S. via the U.S. Interests Section).

MONEY

CURRENCY

Dollars
All prices in this book are quoted in U.S. dollars unless otherwise indicated.

Cuba wants *dollars! dollars! dollars!* Take as much as you want—there is no limit to the amount of convertible currency you can bring into Cuba (however, Cuba does not permit more than US$5,000 to be exported; an exception is if you're bringing in over that amount and anticipate leaving with more than US$5,000, in which case you must declare it). All hotels, car rental agencies, resort facilities, restaurants, and other places dealing with international tourists accept *only* foreign currency, notably U.S. dollars (sometimes called *moneda efectiva* or *divisa*, and colloquially known as *fula, guano, guaniquiqi, varo,* and *verde*). Most European currencies are also accepted in a pinch, as are Mexican pesos and Canadian dollars, but having U.S. dollars will make life considerably easier. Note that Cuban banks buy foreign currency in exchange for U.S. dollars, not for pesos (see Cuban Currency, below).

A large quantity of counterfeit US$100 bills are in circulation (printed in Colombia, apparently), and Cubans are wary of these. You'll usually have to supply your passport number or other ID that will be recorded when paying with a US$100 bill (and sometimes with a US$50 bill). You'll usually be able to change a US$100 bill, even if someone has to make the rounds to find someone to break it down. Nonetheless, it's always best to have plenty of small bills, especially for the boonies. Supposedly, only post-1962 bills are now legal tender, but you'll find greenbacks going back to the 1930s still circulating.

(Cuba pays about US$260 million in commissions to foreign institutions for changing dollars into foreign currencies. To save money and move Cuba away from dollar dependency, in March 1999 the Cuban government began preparations to embrace the euro. Stay tuned.)

Cuban Currency
The Cuban currency is the peso, which is designated $ and should not be confused with the U.S. $ (to make matters worse, the dollar is sometimes called the peso). Cuban currency is often called *moneda nacional* (national money).

The Cuban peso is not traded on international markets as a convertible currency. Nonetheless, the Cuban government establishes its value at parity with the U.S. dollar. However, the *unofficial* exchange rate—the black market rate—is used by almost everyone to set the peso's true value, and that of goods and services. The rate has been relatively stable since 1996 and at press time stood at 21 pesos to one U.S. dollar.

Very few state-run entities will accept pesos from foreigners. In reality, there is very little that most foreigners will need pesos for. Exceptions are if you want to travel on Cuban buses, hang out at local bars and restaurants not normally frequented by tourists, or buy *refrescoes, batidos,* or other snacks on the street. Otherwise, spending pesos is nigh impossible.

Bills are issued in denominations of one (olive), three (red), five (green), 10 (brown), 20 (blue), and 50 (purple) pesos; a one-peso coin is also issued. The peso is divided into 100 *centavos,* issued in coin denominations of one, two, five, 10, and 20 centavos (which is also called a peseta).

You can also purchase special gold and silver **Cuban Mints** (not candy) at banks, airports, and other locations, including the **Cuban Mint Store,** Calle 18 #306, e/ 3 y 5, Miramar, Havana, tel. (7) 29-6693, fax (7) 22-8345. The bright red three-peso note with Che Guevara's portrait makes a good souvenir (US$3).

Tourist Currency

Although they're now being taken out of circulation, you may occasionally be given rainbow-colored notes and flimsy coins that look like Monopoly money. They're called *pesos convertibles* (convertible pesos), or "B Certificates," and flimsy coins stamped "INTUR" that are valid in lieu of dollars for all transactions. This currency is widely accepted. Bills are issued in the following denominations: one, two, five, 10, 20, 50, and 100 pesos, on a par with U.S. dollar denominations. You can use them as you would U.S. dollar bills and can exchange them for hard currency at the airport on the day of departure.

Exchanging Currency

You can exchange your foreign currency for the necessary U.S. dollars at banks or hotel cash desks (arriving, you can change money upon arrival at international airports in Cuba).

Legally, foreign currency can be changed for pesos only at a bank or an official *casa de cambio* (exchange bureau) run by **Cadeca S.A.** (an acronym for *casa de cambio*). Cadeca has exchange booths at key points throughout Havana and in most large cities. Most are aimed at culling dollars from the local economy, rather than from tourists. Nonetheless, foreigners can exchange dollars for pesos here (you *cannot* change any unused pesos into dollars, however, even at the airport upon departure). Cadeca buys and sells at the approximate black market rate. Exchange only small amounts of dollars for pesos as pocket change for local buses etc. And spend all your local currency before leaving.

Street Changers

The creation of Cadeca has taken the wind out of the sails of *jiniteros* who change cash illegally on the streets (and face heavy fines if caught). You'll be offered about the same deal as Cadeca offers. Many tourists are ripped off during the deal, so due caution is urged. Even muggings have been reported. A few ripoff artists work as pairs. Always count your pesos before handing over your U.S. dollars; otherwise, you could find yourself holding a bunch of newspaper clippings wrapped inside a wad of real notes. *It ain't worth it!*

Banks

The most important of the relatively few banks in Cuba catering to foreigners is the autonomous, state-run **Banco Financiero Internacional,** which offers a full range of banking services, including currency exchange services at free-market rates. The branches are all open Mon.-Sat. 8 a.m.-3 p.m., but 8 a.m.-noon only on the last working day of each month. Its main outlet is in the Hotel Habana Libre in Vedado, tel. (7) 33-4011

The state-controlled **Banco de Crédito y Comercio** (formerly the Banco Nacional de Cuba) is the main commercial bank with numerous outlets island-wide (most are open weekdays 8:30 a.m.-3 p.m.). The **Banco Internacional de Comercio** primarily caters to foreign businesses. The **Banco Popular** caters mainly to Cubans, but provides foreign transaction services.

A number of foreign banks have opened offices in Havana in recent years. However, at press time foreign banks could not offer banking services to foreign travelers.

Credit Cards and ATMs

Most hotels, car rental companies, and travel suppliers, as well as larger restaurants, will accept credit card payments, as long as the cards are not issued by U.S. banks (the U.S. Treasury Department forbids U.S. banks to process transactions involving Cuba). The following credit cards are honored: Access, Banamex, Bancomer, Carnet, Diners Club International, JCB, MasterCard, and VISA International. You can use your non-U.S. credit card to obtain a cash advance up to US$5,000 (US$100 minimum) at most banks.

WESTERN UNION REPRESENTATIVES IN CUBA

Western Union's headquarters is in the prerevolutionary Western Union building at Calle Obispo #351, Havana, tel. (7) 62-0011. All regional offices share the same telephone number—tel. (7) 24-1399—and are open Mon.-Fri., 10 a.m.-5 p.m., and Saturday 10 a.m.-noon.

HAVANA

Casablanca	Av. 1ra y 36 Playa, Miramar
Compas	Av. 101 esq. 18, Cotorro
Dandy	Calle 14 e/ 4 y 6, Santiago de Las Vegas
Danubio	Av. 26 esq a 23, Vedado
Festival	Calle 28, e/ 281 y 283, Calabazar
Filosofía	Neptuno esq. San Nicolas, Centro
Focsa	Calle 17 esq. M, Vedado
Moure	Neptuno esq. Zulueta, Habana Vieja
Santa Fe	Calle 1ra., e/ 294 y 296, Santa Fe
Servicentro Boyeros	Av. Rancho Boyeros y Ayestaran, Plaza
Servicentro Boyeros	Av. Rancho Boyeros (in front of Hospital Psiquiatrico), Mazorra
Sol	Calle 3ra. #340, Zona 1, Alamar
Villa Panamericano	Edif. 34, Habana del Este

CAMAGÜEY

El Encanto	Calle Maceo #52 esq. General Gómez, Camagüey

CIEGO DE ÁVILA

El Trópico	Independencia #70 e/ Honorato del Castillo y Maceo, Ciego de Ávila

Don't rely entirely on credit cards, however, as often you may find that no vouchers are available to process transactions.

U.S. Travelers: In general, U.S. citizens must travel on a cash-only basis. At press time, however, several entities had begun accepting payment with U.S.-issued MasterCard and Visa (Rex Limousines, for examples, accepts U.S. MasterCard for car rentals). And the **Bank of Nova Scotia** in Havana was reputedly giving cash advances against U.S. MasterCards (but not Visa). If you have a foreign bank account, you can try to obtain a credit card, which you can then use without restraint (aside from your credit limit). You'll still be breaking U.S. laws, but the Cubans make no distinctions.

In 1999 automated teller machines (ATMs) began popping up in major cities, dispensing U.S. dollars to Cubans with cash cards sent from relatives abroad and used to cull money wired into accounts in Canada, Europe, or Latin America. The Cuban state entity, **Fincimex,** Calle 2 #302 esq. 3ra, Miramar, Havana, tel. (7) 24-4823; from the U.S., tel. (416) 296-0738, issues the **Tran$card,** which you can use to send money to Cuba from anywhere in the world.

Traveler's Checks

Traveler's checks (unless issued by U.S. banks) are accepted in most tourist restaurant and hotels, and in some foreign-goods stores, although with more hesitancy than credit cards. Traveler's checks can also be cashed at most hotel cashier desks, as well as at banks. They can be in any foreign currency, but non-U.S. dollar denominations can cause problems. Thomas Cook traveler's checks are best. And on last visit, American Express travelers' checks were being accepted at most Cuban banks.

You should *not* enter the date or the place when signing your checks—a Cuban requirement.

CIENFUEGOS	
Casa Mimbre	Av. 60 esq. Calle 35, Cienfuegos
GRANMA	
Las Novedades	Av. Frank Pais 35 esq. Calle 2da, Reparto Jesús Menéndez, Bayamo
GUANTÁNAMO	
La Sucursal	Calixto García #967 e/ Emilio Girot y Carretera Central, Guantánamo
HOLGUÍN	
Tienda El Encanto	Libertad #213 e/ Martí y Luz Caballero, Holguín
LAS TUNAS	
Servicentro Puerto Padre	Av. Libertad #156, e/ Donato Marmol y Bartolomé Maso, Puerto Padre
Tienda La Nueva	Vicente Garcia #28 esq. Franco Julian Santana, Las Tunas
MATANZAS	
La Mina	Calle Medio #28810, e/ Ayuntamiento y Santa Teresa, Matanzas
Puerta Del Sol	Calle Ruiz #568 e/ Calzada y Coronel Verdugo Cardenas, Cardenas
PINAR DEL RÍO	
El Fuego	Calle Martí esq. Osmani Arenado, Pinar Del Río
SANCTI SPÍRITUS	
La Habana	Calle Céspedes esq.Comandante Fajardo, Sancti Spíritus
SANTIAGO DE CUBA	
La Violeta	Santo Tomas, e/ San Geronimo y Enramada, Santiago De Cuba
VILLA CLARA	
Variedades Riviera	Carretera Central y Banda Esperanza #452, Santa Clara

Money Transfers

In June 1999 President Clinton granted permission for **Western Union,** tel. (800) 325-6000, website: www.westernunion.com, to handle wire transfers to Cuba, permitting anyone in the U.S. to send up to US$300 every three months, but not to Cuban officials or government entities. Each transfer costs US$29. Only designated Western Union offices are permitted to handle such transactions, which in Cuba are handled by CIMEX at 30 locations on the island (mostly Tiendas Panamericano and Cupet gas stations).

Citizens of other countries can arrange a "wire transfer" through the Banco Financiero Internacional (see above). You'll need to telex your home bank. It's a good idea to carry full details of your home account with you in Cuba, including your bank's telex number. The process can take many days. **DHL** reputedly is trustworthy for sending money in the form of travelers' checks.

Quickcash, e-mail: paymaster@careebecons.com, website: quickcash.careebecons.com, lets you make money transfers from your Visa or MasterCard account online through the Internet. Deliveries are made in U.S. dollar cash (or the currency of your choosing) in one to five days through banks in Havana, although the processing is via the Canadian banking system and transfers are settled on your account in Canadian dollars. Each transaction is limited to a maximum of C$450, but you can make as many transactions as you wish. A posting on Cuba's own web page—www.cubaweb.cu—also lists information. (Additional online information is also available at www.duales.com.)

Also in Canada, **Antilles Express,** 9632 Charlton Ave., Montreal, Quebec H2B 2C5, tel. (514) 385-9449, can also forward money to Havana in five days (longer elsewhere in Cuba) for a hefty commission.

In an emergency, you can also arrange money transfers or even a cash advance through **Asistur,** (see If Trouble Strikes, above).

COSTS

The Cuban government—which enjoys a virtual monopoly on services—is guilty of gouging and in danger of overpricing itself in its greed to cull dollars at every turn. Without competition to regulate the market, the state has jacked up prices in recent years to sometimes ridiculous levels. Hotels and restaurants are, on average, at least 50% more expensive than they deserve to be, and often much more.

Still, Cuba can be as expensive or inexpensive as you wish, depending on how you travel. If you get around on public transport, rent rooms with Cuban families, dine on the street at *paladares* and peso snack bars, and keep your entertainment to nontouristy venues, then the truly impecunious may be able to survive on as little as US$40 a day, with your room taking the lion's share. However, by being so frugal you'll have to rough it and be prepared for a basic food regimen. If you want at least a modicum of comforts, then budget *at least* US$60 a day. The majority of travelers will need double this, especially in Havana.

Accommodation in Havana costs US$25-200 per night. Meals average US$5-15 with a beer; although lunch or dinner at the best restaurants will usually cost upward of US$20 and can easily run to US$50 or so per person. Entrance to a cabaret or disco will cost US$5-25, plus drinks (a visit to Tropicana will set you back US$60). Day tours featuring sightseeing and meals average US$35-50. Taxis average about US$1.50 per mile.

Be prepared, too, for lots of extra expenses for minor services that are provided free of charge in North America and most European nations.

If you plan on touring, take enough cash to leave deposits for a rental car. And don't forget: that if you run out of money, you may have difficulty getting more money forwarded quickly and easily, particularly if you're a U.S. citizen. Bring items you think you'll need; you don't want to start shelling out for toiletries and the like. And don't forget that you'll want to buy some Cuban cigars, souvenirs, and artwork.

Note that virtually everywhere on the tourist circuit, where Cubans pay in pesos, you'll be charged at parity in dollars, or even greater.

Discounts
Cuba is not in the business of offering discounts. Quite the opposite. It is intent on extracting the maximum from you. However, **Interchange,** (also known as Havanatur U.K.), Interchange House, 27 Stafford Rd., Croydon, Surrey RO 4NG, tel. (0181) 681-3613, fax (0181) 760-0031, offers a **Discount Card** good for a 10% discount on all optional tours and excursions and meals at selected restaurants in Havana and elsewhere.

COMMUNICATIONS

The **Ministry of Communications,** Avenida de Independencia y 19 de Mayo, Plaza de la Revolución, tel. (7) 57-4124, controls all communications, including mail, telephone, and online services (open Mon.-Fri. 8 a.m.-5 p.m.).

MAIL

Correos de Cuba operates the Cuban postal service. However, Cuba's mail system is terminally slow and delivery is never guaranteed (much mail is censored or for other reasons disappears en route; *never* send cash).

International airmail *(correo aereo)* averages about one month each way (to save time, savvy Cubans usually hand their letters to foreigners to mail outside Cuba). Don't even think about seamail. When mailing from Cuba, it helps to write the country destination in Spanish: England is *Inglaterra* (use this for Wales and Scotland also, on the line below either country); France is *Francia;* Italy is *Italia;* Germany is *Alemania;* Spain is *España;* Switzerland is *Suiza;* and the U.S. is *Estados Unidos.*

Post Offices: Most major tourist hotels have small post offices and philatelic bureaus and will accept your mail for delivery. There are post offices *(correos)* throughout Cuba (to buy stamps, go to the *sellos* counter; you'll need pesos for domestic mail). If you use those in residential districts, expect a long wait in line.

Most post offices are open weekdays 10 a.m.-5 p.m. and Saturday 8 a.m.-3 p.m. You can send a fax, telex, or telegram at most post offices.

Rates: Within Cuba, letters cost from 15 centavos (20 grams or less) to 2.05 pesos (up to 500 grams); postcards cost 10 *centavos.* An international postcard costs US$0.50 to all destinations; letters cost US$0.75.

Parcels: The Ministerio de Comunicaciones requires that parcels to be mailed from Cuba should be delivered to the post office *unwrapped* for inspection. It is far better to send packages through an express courier service. If mailing to the U.S., remember that Uncle Sam is ever vigilant for parcels from Cuba. Don't try mailing Uncle Fred a box of Cohibas for Christmas. They'll be smoked all right—on the U.S. Customs funeral pyre!

Online Mail: Want your mail to be delivered within seconds? You can write online and send letters, postcards or telex to friends and family in Cuba using **E-sriba,** e-mail: info@e-scriba.com, website: www. e-scriba.com. Content is printed and sent from an E-scriba distribution center. Letters cost US$2 for up to 800 words (80 lines). Telegrams cost US$4 per 10 words (one line). You can pay with Visa, MasterCard or American Express, or with bank draft or money order payable to E-scriba Inc., 1 Yonge Street #1801, Toronto, ON M3E 1E5, Canada. You must buy credit for a minimum of six cyberstamps (US$2 each) to be deducted from your account as you use them.

Receiving Mail: Getting incoming mail is time-consuming. You can receive mail in Havana by having letters and parcels addressed to you using your name as it appears on your pass-

port or other I.D. for general delivery to: "c/o Espera [your name], Ministerio de Comunicaciones, Avenida Independencia y 19 de Mayo, Havana 6, Cuba." To collect mail *poste restante,* go to the **Ministry of Communications,** Avenida de Independencia y 19 de Mayo, Playa, tel. (7) 57-4109, on the northeast corner of the Plaza de la Revolución. The names of people who have received mail are posted. Keep incoming mail simple—parcels are less likely to make it. It may be more efficient to have incoming mail addressed *"Espera" [your name]* at your hotel or embassy (but, please, not the U.S. Interests Section).

Express Mail
DHL Worldwide Express has offices in most major cities throughout Cuba. The main offices are in Havana at Av. 1ra y Calle 26, Miramar, tel. (7) 24-1578 or 24-1876, fax (7) 24-0999, open weekdays 8 a.m.-8 p.m. and Saturday 8 a.m.-4 p.m. See regional chapters for other locations. DHL acts as customs broker and offers daily door-to-door pickup and delivery service at no extra charge. It guarantees delivery in Havana in less than 24 hours. It offers international service between Cuba and foreign countries, plus domestic service between towns throughout Cuba. The minimum cost to send *to* Cuba by DHL is US$60. Packages sent from Cuba cost less. It offers four options: *Express,* for sending documents with no commercial value; *International,* for documents to anywhere in the world; *International Packages,* for commercial samples; and *National* (still in its promotional stage), for sending documents and packages between towns throughout Cuba.

Cubapost, Calle 21 #10099, e/ 10 y 12, in Vedado, tel. (7) 33-0485, fax (7) 33-6097, offers an international express mail service (EMS) to virtually every country in the world except the U.S. Rates begin at US$27 (0.5 kg) to Canada and Mexico, and US$34 for the rest of the world. Service within Havana costs US$4 for the first

SENDING FLOWERS TO CUBA

ant to surprise your Cuban lover with a bouquet of roses? Easily done through Swiss-based Interflora, e-mail: info@fleurop.com, website: www.fleurop.com, which handles requests online and can deliver to Cuba within 48 hours, worldwide. A bouquet of 12 red roses costs US$48.50, delivered to the addressee's door.

five kg, and delivery is guaranteed within 24 hours. Domestic service within Cuba costs US$5-9 (up to five kg) according to zone. Open Mon.-Fri. 8 a.m.-5 p.m., and Saturday 8 a.m.-noon.

Cubapacks, Calle 22 #4115, Miramar, tel. (7) 24-2134 or 33-2817, fax (7) 24-2226 (open Mon.-Fri. 8:30 a.m.-noon and 1:30-5:30 p.m.), and **Cuba Express,** Av. 5ta #8210, e/ 82 y 84, Miramar, tel. (7) 24-2331, fax (7) 24-2584 (open Mon.-Fri. 8 a.m.-5 p.m.), also offer express mail services.

Restrictions

Uncle Sam restricts what may be mailed to Cuba from the U.S. Letters and literature can be mailed without restriction. Gift parcels can be "sent or carried by an authorized traveler" to an individual or religious or educational organization if the domestic retail value does not exceed US$200. Only one parcel per month is allowed. And contents are limited to food, vitamins, seeds, medicines, medical supplies, clothing, personal hygiene items, and a few other categories. All other parcels are subject to seizure. Don't think you can skirt around this by sending by DHL. Your package will either be returned or seized.

Likewise, the Cuban government is highly sensitive to incoming and outgoing mail, which is likely to be read by censors and confiscated if deemed "counter-revolutionary" or "pornographic."

TELECOMMUNICATIONS

Telephones

Cuba's telephone system is the responsibility of the Empresa de Telecomunicaciones de Cuba (ETECSA), headquartered in the Lonja del Comercio, Plaza de San Francisco, Habana Vieja. ETECSA, set up in 1992, is a joint venture with the Italian telecommunications company, ILTE, and has the awesome task of upgrading Cuba's inept and derelict phone system. Much of the telephone network predates the Revolution (the ITT system, installed long before the Revolution, was replaced in the 1960s by "fraternal Hungarian equipment"—Castro's words—and it was downhill from there). ETECSA plans to eventually replace Havana's analog system with digital system, and a fiber-optic network is being installed. But there's an awful long way to go. And phones are scarce: Cuba has one of the lowest rates of telephones per capita in Latin America: only 5.4 per 100 people (placing it 14th out of 20 Latin American countries).

The business card of Elizardo Sánchez, a leading dissident, has a caveat next to his phone number: *"If it works."* Service has never been good, and unless you're making a call from a modern international hotel, calling can be a wearying experience. Phones in international hotels and *centros telefónicos* tend to be modern and up to par; private phones and those in most state-run enterprises are usually antiques and perform like something from a Hitchcock movie. Getting a dial tone is the first obstacle. You may get a busy signal (though this does not necessarily mean that the line is engaged) or a series of squeaks and squawks. You just have to keep trying. And a telephone line that is working one minute may simply go dead the next. Some days are better than others.

Cubans usually answer the phone by saying either *"¡Oigo!"* (I'm listening!) or *"¡Dígame!"* (Speak to me!). It sounds abrupt, but they're not being rude.

Public Phone Booths: ETECSA operates modern, efficient, glass-enclosed telephone kiosks called *centros telefónicos* (*telecorreos* where they combine postal services) throughout Cuba. They utilize phone-cards—see below—as well as coins. These telephone bureaus do not accept collect or incoming calls.

There is also no shortage of stand-alone public phones. Some are modern and take phone cards. Others are older and can only be used for local calls; they take five-centavo coins. When you hear the "time-up" signal (a short *blip*), you must *immediately* put in another coin to avoid

TELEPHONE AREA CODES

To call Cuba, dial 53, then the city code, then the telephone number. Within Cuba, if calling to a number outside the area code where you are, dial 0, then wait for a tone before dialing the city code and number. A complete list of city and provincial codes is provided in the national telephone directory.

HAVANA CITY (CIUDAD DE LA HABANA)

All numbers use the prefix "7"
Exceptions:
Cotorro: 6820
Guanabo: 687
Santiago de las Vegas: 683

HAVANA PROVINCE

Artemisa: 63
Batabano: 62
Bejucal: 66
Boca de Jaruco: 6929
Guines: 62
Jaruco: 64
Mariel: 63
San Antonio de las Vegas: 64
San Antonio de los Baños: 650

CAMAGÜE

Camagüey: 322
Florida: 32
Nuevitas: 32
Santa Cruz del Sur: 32
Most other towns use the prefix "32"

CIEGO DE ÁVILA

Ciego de Ávila: 33
Cayo Coco: 33
Morón: 335
Most other towns use the prefix "33"

CIENFUEGOS

Cienfuegos: 432
Cruces: 433
Most other towns use the prefix "43"

GRANMA

All towns use the prefix "23"

GUANTÁNAMO

All towns use the prefix "21"

HOLGUÍN

All towns use the prefix "24"

ISLA DE LA JUVENTUD AND CAYO LARGO

Cayo Largo: 5
Nuevo Gerona: 61
All other towns use the prefix "61"

LAS TUNAS

All towns use the prefix "31"

MATANZAS

Jagüey Grande: 59
Matanzas: 52
Playa Larga: 59
Cienega de Zapata: 59
Varadero: 5
Most other towns use the prefix "5"

PINAR DEL RÍO

Bahía Honda: 86
Candelaria: 85
Guane: 84
Isabel Rubio: 84
Pinar del Río: 82
Most other towns use the prefix "8"

SANCTI SPÍRITUS

Arroyo Blanco: 48
Jatibónico: 41
Playa Ancón: 418
Sancti Spíritus: 41
Topes de Collantes: 42
Trinidad: 419
Most other towns use the prefix "41"

SANTIAGO DE CUBA

Cruce de los Baños: 225
El Cruce: 22
Palma Soriano: 225
Santiago de Cuba: 226
Siboney: 22
Most other towns use the prefix "22"

VILLA CLARA

Caibarién: 42
Manicaragua: 42
Remedios: 42
Santa Clara: 422
Most other towns use the prefix "42"

being cut off. Newer public phones also take 20-centavo coins and can be used for long-distance calls also (you get any change back when you hang up).

International Calls: When calling Cuba from abroad, dial 011 (the international dialing code), then 53 (the Cuba country code) followed by the city code and the number. For direct outbound international calls from Cuba, dial 119, then the country code (for example, 44 for the U.K.), followed by the area code and number. For the international operator, dial 0, wait 30 seconds for the tone; then dial 9. For operator-assisted calls to the U.S., dial 66-1212. (Using a Cuban telephone operator can be a Kafkaesque experience, as many do not speak English. In the U.S., AT&T has a "language line" that will connect you with an interpreter, tel. (800) 843-8420; US$3.50 per minute.)

Some of the large, upscale tourist hotels now have direct-dial telephones in guest rooms for international calls. Others will connect you via the hotel operator. Or you can call from ETECSA's *centros telefónicos.* The main international telephone exchange is in Vedado in the lobby of at the Hotel Habana Libre Tryp; a receptionist links you with the international operator (it can take forever, so leave plenty of time).

Calls are charged per minute and keep getting hiked. At press time, the following charges applied: US$3.50 to the U.S. and Canada, US$4.50 to Central America and Caribbean countries, US$6 to South America, US$8 to Europe and the rest of the world. Operator-assisted calls cost more.

Domestic Calls: For local calls in the same area code, simply dial the number you wish to reach. To dial a number outside your area code, dial 0, then *wait for a tone* before dialing the local city code and the number you wish to reach. For the local operator, dial 0. Rates range from 30 centavos to three pesos and 15 centavos for the first three minutes, depending on zone (tourist hotels and ETECSA booths charge in U.S. dollars: from US$1-2.75 per minute, depending on province).

Prepaid Phone Cards: All ETECSA *telecorreos* and an increasing number of streetside public phones take prepaid phone cards (you insert the card into the phone and it automatically deducts from the value of the card according to period of time of your conversation). You can buy phone cards at tourist hotels, ETECSA outlets, certain restaurants, and several dozen other outlets listed in the telephone directory, as well as from **Intertel,** Calle 33 #1427, e/ 14 y 18, Miramar, Havana, tel. (7) 24-2476, fax (7) 24-2504. Cards can be bought in denominations of US$10, US$25 or. They can be used for domestic and international calls. You'll be able to see the diminishing value of the card displayed during your call (if it expires, you can replace it with a new one without interrupting your call by pushing button C and inserting a new card).

Cellular Phones: Cubacel (a joint agreement between Mexico's TIMSA and Emtelcuba) provides cellular phone service. Its main office is at Calle 28 #510, e/ 5 y 7, Miramar, tel. (7) 33-2222, fax (7) 80-0000 or 33-1737, website: www.cubacel.com; open Mon.-Fri. 8 a.m.-5 p.m. and Saturday 8 a.m.-noon. It also has an office at José Martí International Airport, tel. (7) 80-0043, fax (7) 80-0400 (Terminal 2), and tel. (7) 80-0222, fax (7) 80-0445 (Terminal 3); and in Varadero at Av. 1ra #2 e/ 42 y 43, tel./fax: (5) 80-9222; in Cienfuegos, at Cuatro Caminos, Carretera a Palmira Km 2, tel. (0432) 45-8222, fax (0432) 45-8037; and in Santiago de Cuba at the Hotel Santiago, tel. (0226) 87-199, fax (0226) 88-122.

Cubacel rents cellular phones for US$7 daily (plus a US$3 one-time activation fee). You also have to pay a US$410 security deposit, plus US$100 per day deposit for use. Air time costs US$0.90 per minute in addition to relevant long-distance charges. Long-term service costs US$40 monthly (plus US$120 activation and US$0.30-0.40 per minute air time). Cubacel sells cellular phones at outrageous markup. Far better is to bring your own cellular phone into the country; Cubacel will activate it and provide you with a local line for US$12.

Telephone Directories: ETECSA publishes four comprehensive regional directories, (Ciudad de la Habana, Zona Occidental, Zona Central, and Zona Oriental) that can be obtained (US$10) from ETECSA headquarters in the Lonja del Comercio (see above). A national directory costs US$25. Cuba has made an amateurish stab at an online directory: website: www.paginasblancas.cu and www.paginasamarillas.cu. They're frustratingly poor. Good luck!

Telephone numbers change with dizzying regularity as ETECSA tries to rationalize the old system. Even the 1998 telephone directory is out-of-date. Trying to determine a correct number can be problematic as many entities have several numbers and rarely publish the same number twice. Often you'll receive a recorded message saying the number doesn't exist *("Este numero no existe por ningún or nada"),* but keep trying.

Most commercial entities have a *pizzara,* or switchboard. Call 113 for directory inquiries.

Telex, Fax, and Telegram

You can send telexes and faxes from most tourist hotels, usually for a fee slightly more than the comparable telephone charge. You can also transmit from most *telecorreos.*

ECTESA offers 24-hour "telegram by telephone" service by calling tel. (7) 81-8844 or going through its *telecorreo* offices. International telegraphic service is charged per word: 75 centavos to North America, 80 to Europe, 85 to the rest of world. Domestic rates are posted in *telecorreos.* In Havana, telegrams may be also sent from **Cuba Transatlantic Radio Corporation (RCA),** Calle Obispo y Aguiar.

Online Service in Cuba

In October 1996, Cuba connected to the Net. The Cuban government declared access to the Net a "fundamental right" of the Cuban people, then promptly changed the rules, making it virtually illegal for Cubans to buy a computer (nor are Cubans permitted to own a computer without authorization; and computer programmers are banned from teaching their skills outside state-run entities). Computer communications are tightly controlled by the government. Very few individuals have access to a computer or modem (call it the Digital Revolution versus the Cuban Revolution). Only Cuban government officials and foreigners with passports can buy computers, and other computers in private hands are routinely seized.

The Cuba government is behind the times in its application of online services, although most state entities now have websites and e-mail connections. The Centro Nacional de Intercambio Automatizado de Información (Center for Automated Interchange of Information, CENIAI) of the Cuban Academy of Sciences administers the Net in Cuba and provides a Web gateway (www.ceniai.inf.cu), using a server that is part of the state-run ETECSA telephone company. At least twice a week they receive a dial-up call from Toronto for two-way UUCP-based data transmission of files. In addition to its own use, CENIAI acts as a hub, receiving traffic from the University of Havana, the Ministry of Higher Education, and a Unix-based PC belonging to the main UJC computing club in Havana, which is supposed to become a collection point for traffic from other clubs. Unfortunately, the poor international telephone lines make this a fragile, slow, and expensive process. The e-mail link through CENIAI (ceniai.cu) is reported to be the most effective means of communicating with the island.

In Cuba, travelers can send and receive e-mail at **Infotur** offices and in the **Hotel Habana Libre** (see Online Services in the Communications section, in the Havana chapter). And most upscale tourist hotels, particularly in Havana, now have business centers with online access for guests. A few also feature modem outlets in guest rooms. Tourists are permitted to bring laptop computers, which must be declared and may not be left behind in Cuba.

All e-mail is passed to CENIAI where it can loiter for days until there is room on the satellite uplink (it is routinely read by MININT and may be "disappeared" if considered too critical). Be careful what you send, or the secret police may come knocking. Seriously.

There are numerous computer clubs and formal classes in computer technology in Cuba, centered in the **Palacio Central de Computación y Electrónica,** tel. (7) 63-3349 or 61-7555, in the old Sears building on Calle Reina No. 2 at Calle Amistad in Centro Habana, which also houses the e-mail network, *tinored.* The administrative contact is Pedro Espineira, e-mail: peter%tinored@apc.org.

GENERAL PRACTICALITIES

WHEN TO GO

Cuba has distinct summer and winter periods, despite its subtropical location. The winter period, Nov.-April, is most pleasant, with relatively little rain and temperatures averaging a balmy 75-80° F. Surprisingly cool spells are possible, however, as cold fronts move south from Florida, bringing the chance of brief periods of rain. This is also the busy season, and many hotels in Havana and favored resort destinations can be fully booked, especially during Christmas, New Year, and Easter. Consider making advance reservations for the first few nights during these periods.

Traveling off-season (May-Oct.) has benefits, although you should be prepared for the possibility of prolonged rains, severe storms, and even a slim chance of hurricanes. This period is also the hottest, with average temperatures rising to about 30-32° C in midsummer. The hottest weather is in the eastern part of the country, which can be stifling. Some unpaved roads may become impassable for short periods of time due to mud and flooding. Most hotels charge lower rates in the summer low season, usually 20-40% below winter rates, and it often easier to find rooms in the most popular hotels.

Spring and autumn are preferable. *Cartelera*, the weekly tourist newspaper, publishes a weather forecast on page two. Cuban TV newscasts feature weather forecasts (in Spanish).

Also consider whether you want to attend specific festivals and events (many are now timed for the peak season).

WHAT TO TAKE

Pack light. A good rule of thumb is to lay out everything you wish to take—then cut it by half. Most often, I've regretted packing too much, not too little. Remember, you'll need some spare room too for any souvenirs you plan on bringing home. Leave your jewelry at home—it invites theft.

Most important, don't forget your passport, airline tickets, traveler's checks, and other documentation. You'd be amazed how many folks get to the airport before discovering this "minor" oversight.

Many items are scarce in Cuba. You can usually find a full range of Western toiletries available in hotel stores and dollar stores in major towns islandwide. However, don't depend on it. Take all the toiletries you think you'll need. Don't forget a towel and face cloth—upscale hotels will provide them, but not so less expensive hotels. Women should pack extra tampons (those you don't use will make good gifts to Cuban women). T-shirts also make good giveaways. Most Western medicines and pharmaceuticals can be purchased at special pharmacies and clinics for foreigners in Havana and major cities, but you should bring any specific medications you think you'll need. Be sure to take toilet paper. Supplies are so short in Cuba (even in dollar stores) that locals have to resort to soap and water or newspapers.

Independent travelers will find it a good idea to pack at least a half dozen extra passport photographs for any unforeseen official paperwork that might arise.

The Basic Rules

Limit yourself to *one* bag (preferably a sturdy duffel or garment bag with plenty of pockets), plus a small day pack or camera bag. If using public transport, note that space on domestic buses and planes is limited. If you travel by bus or train, forgo suitcases and backpacks with external frames or appendages—they catch and easily bend or break. One of the best investments you can make is a well-made duffel bag that doubles as a backpack and can be carried by hand or on the back. A small day pack allows you to pack everything for a one- or two-day journey. You may even be able to leave the rest of your gear in the storage room of a Havana hotel.

Limit the number of changes of clothing. However, remember that you'll sweat often. Pack items that work in various combinations—preferably darker items that don't show the inevitable dirt and stains you'll quickly collect on your travels. Note, though, that dark clothes tend to be hotter than light clothing, which reflects the sun's rays. Pack khakis and subdued greens if you plan on much close-up nature viewing.

Some people recommend packing just two sets of clothes—one to wash and one to wear. Two sets of clothing seem ascetic. Three T-shirts, two dressier shirts, a couple of tank tops, a sweatshirt and sweatpants, a polo shirt, a pair of Levi's, "safari" pants, two pairs of shorts, and a sleeveless "safari" or photographer's jacket with heaps of pockets suffice for me. Women may wish to substitute blouses and mid-length skirts. Don't forget your bathing suit.

Be resigned in advance to the fact that the climate takes the wave out of your hair. Simplify your hairdo before you leave home.

Pack plenty of socks and undergarments—you may need a daily change. Wash them frequently to help keep athlete's foot and other fungal growths at bay. Better yet, rely on sandals as much as possible.

Coping with the Climate

Cuba is mostly hot and humid. You'll want light, loose-fitting shirts and pants. And if you plan on hiking, a loose-fitting cotton canvas shirt and pants will help protect against thorns and biting bugs. But Cuba can occasionally get chilly in midwinter, especially at night. It's always a good idea to pack a sweater and/or a warm windproof jacket. You'll need one to cope with the bone-chilling a/c in hotels and restaurants. Parts of Oriente and the extreme west are parched, hot, and dry most of the year. At higher altitudes, it can get very chilly and wet if clouds set in. (Whenever you move from, say, relatively cool upland areas to hot, humid lowlands, *take a shower*. This leaves the human body at the *local* temperature. You'll be amazed at how much more quickly you'll adjust.)

In the wet season, plan on experiencing rain. An inexpensive umbrella is best (they're in short supply, so it's best to bring one with you). Raincoats are heavy and tend to make you sweat. Breathable Gore-Tex rainproof jackets work fine. A hooded poncho is also good.

Note that denim jeans take forever to dry when wet. I always pack a pair of light cotton-polyester safari-style pants, which are cooler, dry quickly, and have plenty of pockets. Ideally, everything should be drip-dry, wash-and-wear.

If visiting in the wet season, protect your spare clothing in a plastic bag inside your backpack.

Jackets, Ties, and Cocktail Dresses?

Cubans do not stand on ceremony, and most travelers will not need dressy clothes. Cubans dress informally but always very neatly (they rarely go out in the evening without first changing into fresh clothes). Even Cuban businesspeople and officials dress simply, usually with a *guayabara* shirt worn outside the trousers, even at official functions. Nonetheless, at the very least, pack a pair of slacks and a dressy shirt. You may wish to take a jacket and tie or cocktail dress for dinners in more expensive hotels and restaurants—or, for the lucky few, an impromptu meeting with Fidel or at other diplomatic functions. Shorts are acceptable wear. Save shorter-style runner's shorts for the beach.

Some restaurants and discos have a dress code; T-shirts and shorts are not permissible.

Footwear

You'll need a comfortable pair of low-heeled walking shoes. Lightweight sandals are de rigueur. Normally, sneakers will do double duty for most occasions. In the wet season—and if you plan on any nature activities—your shoes will get wet. Rubber boots *(botas de hule)* are a godsend on tropical trails. In fact, they're standard wear for *campesinos.* Buying them in Cuba is virtually out of the question, however, so you might want to invest in a pair of waterproof hiking shoes.

Other

If you bring prescription drugs, be sure the druggist's identification label is on the container. Writing materials are extremely hard to come by: take pens, pencils, and notepads (and lots of extras to give away).

FILM AND PHOTOGRAPHY

Cuba is a photographer's dream. Photographer John Kings, who accompanied James Michener to illustrate his book *Six Days in Havana,* called Havana "one of the most photogenic cities in the world. . . . It was captivating and challenging and for the next five days my finger barely left the shutter of my little German eye." You'll agree, so come prepared.

You are never denied access to anything you wish to photograph (except military and industrial installations, airports, and people in uniform).

Equipment and Film

Officially, you are allowed to bring two cameras plus six rolls of film into Cuba (don't worry about the official film limit; I've never heard of it being enforced). Film is susceptible to damage by airport X-ray machines. Usually one or two passes through a machine won't harm it, but the effect is cumulative. You should *always* request that your film (including your loaded camera) be hand-checked by airport security.

Decide how much film you think you'll need to bring—then triple it. I recommend one roll per day as a minimum if you're even half-serious about your photography. If you do need to buy film in Cuba, check the expiration date; it may be outdated. And the film may have been sitting in the sun for months on end—not good.

Film—almost exclusively Kodak or Agfa—is sold at most tourist hotels and at Photo Service stores, located in towns islandwide. Very rarely will you find slide (transparency) film. Most Photo Service stores also sell a few Nikon, Minolta, and Canon instant cameras, as well as a meager stock of batteries. *Take spare batteries* for light meters and flashes, and bring all filters and other accessories as you will not be able to buy them in Cuba.

Keep your film out of the sun. If possible, refrigerate it. Color emulsions are particularly sensitive to tropical heat, and film rolls can also soften with the humidity so that they easily stretch and refuse to wind in your camera. Pack film in a Ziploc plastic bag with silica gel inside to protect against moisture.

Keep your lenses clean and dry when not in use. Silica gel packs are essential to help protect your camera gear from moisture; use them if you carry your camera equipment inside a plastic bag. Never turn your back on your camera gear. Watch it at all times.

Film Processing

You can have your print film processed at most Photo Service outlets. Photo Serve also makes color prints and copies up to 50 by 60 inches and offers framing. However, Cuba faces a chemical shortage, and there is no guarantee that the processing chemicals are clean. For this reason you should consider waiting until you get home (try to keep your film cool). You can also buy film with prepaid processing—each roll comes with a self-mailer and you can simply pop it in a mailbox; the prints or slides will then be mailed to your home. However, given the vicissitudes of the Cuban mail system, you're more likely to arrive home first (and your film may never show up).

Videos

Officially, video cameras may not be brought in, but the restriction is rarely, if ever, applied to tourists. It's best to ensure that you have fresh batteries before arriving, although camcorder batteries can be found in Havana and major tourist resorts at Photo Service outlets. The same rule holds true for blank tapes, which are not always readily available outside major tourist locales.

Cuba uses the same broadcast standard as North America.

Photo Etiquette

Cubans of every shade and stripe will ham for your camera and will generally cooperate willingly. However, never assume an automatic right to take a personal photograph. If you come across individuals who don't want to be photographed, honor their wishes. It's a common courtesy, too, to ask permission to photograph what might be considered private situations. Use your judgment and discretion. Don't attempt to photograph members of the police or military—they are under strict instructions not to allow themselves to be photographed.

Many children will request money for being photographed. So, too, will the mulattas dressed in traditional costume in Plaza de la Catedral in Habana Vieja. The latter are officially sanctioned to do so, but the government discourages its other citizens from "begging." Whether you pay is a matter of conscience. If they insist on being paid and you don't want to pay, don't take the shot. In markets, it is considered a courtesy to buy a small trinket from vendors you wish to photograph. And don't forget to send photographs to anyone you promise to send to.

Warning: Several foreigners have been arrested and deported in recent years for filming pornography. The Cuban government defines it fairly broadly—and keeps a strict watch for such illicit use of cameras.

Military posts are off-limits, as is the land around the metal-processing factories of Nuevitas and Moa (one suspects not because of industrial espionage, but because of the sobering pollution and devastation).

WEIGHTS AND MEASURES

Cuba operates on the metric system. Liquids are sold in liters, fruits and vegetables by the kilo. Distances are given in meters and kilometers.

Vestiges of the U.S. system and old Spanish systems remain, however, such as the *pulgada* (2.54 cm), *cordel* (20.35 meters), or, more commonly, the *caballeria* (about 324 square *cordeles,* the amount of land deemed sufficient to support a mounted soldier and his family). Old units of weight still heard include the *onza* (about one ounce), *libra* (about one pound), *saco* (a measure of coffee), and *quintal,* (a hundredwieght, about 100 pounds).

TIME

Cuban time is equivalent to U.S. eastern standard time: five hours behind Greenwich mean time, the same as New York and Miami, three hours ahead of the U.S. west coast. There is little seasonal variation in dawn. However, Cuba has daylight saving time May-October.

BUSINESS HOURS

Hours are flexible. Government offices usually open Mon.-Fri. 8:30 a.m.-12:30 p.m. and 1:30-5:30 p.m. and every second Saturday 8:30 a.m.-noon. Banks are usually open Mon.-Fri. 8:30 a.m.-noon and 1:30-3 p.m. and Saturday 8:30-10:30 a.m. Post offices are usually open Mon.-Sat. 8 a.m.-10 p.m. and Sunday 8 a.m.-6 p.m.

NATIONAL HOLIDAYS

1 January	Liberation Day (Día de la Liberación)
2 January	Victory Day (Día de la Victoria)
28 January	José Martí's birthday
24 February	Anniversary of the Second War of Independence
8 March	International Women's Day (Día de las Mujeres)
13 March	Anniversary of the students' attack on the presidential palace
19 April	Bay of Pigs Victory (Victoria del Playa Girón)
1 May	Labor Day (Día de las Trabajadores)
26 July	National Revolution Day (anniversary of the attack on the Moncada barracks)
30 July	Day of the Martyrs of the Revolution
8 October	Anniversary of Che Guevara's death
10 October	Anniversary of the First War of Independence
28 October	Memorial day to Camilo Cienfuegos
2 December	Anniversary of the landing of the *Granma*
7 December	Memorial day to Antonio Maceo

Most shops are open Mon.-Sat. 8:30 a.m.-5:30 p.m., although many remain open later, including all day Sunday. Museum opening times vary widely (and change frequently), although most are closed on Monday. Most banks, businesses, and government offices close during national holidays.

Many Cubans still honor the *merienda,* coffee breaks taken usually at about 10 a.m. and 3 p.m.

Cubans like to dine late. Many *paladares* and restaurants are open 24 hours; others stay open until midnight. However, local eateries serving Cubans often run out of food by mid-evening—don't leave dining too late.

ELECTRICITY

Cuba operates on 110-volt AC (60-cycle) nationwide, though 220-volt is found in places. Most outlets use U.S. plugs: flat, parallel two-pins, and three rectangular pins. A two-prong adapter is a good idea (take one with you; they're hard to come by in Cuba). **Magellan's,** P.O. Box 5485, Santa Barbara, CA 93150, tel. (800) 962-4932, e-mail: sales@magellans.com, website: www.magellans.com, can supply plugs and adapters, as well as dozens of other handy travel items.

At press time, parts of Cuba were still suffering occasional electricity blackouts. Take a flashlight and spare batteries. A couple of long-lasting candles are also a good idea.

If possible, do not allow your personal computer or disks to pass through an airport X-ray machine. The magnets supposedly can wipe out all your data and programs (however, I've never had any such problem). Insist on having it hand-checked. You'll need to turn your computer on to show that it's not a bomb.

SPECIAL NOTES

NOTES FOR MEN

What do men want to know about? Women! It doesn't take the average male visitor long to discover that Cuban woman are hot-blooded. True, they like being romanced but they're also much more aggressive than foreign men may be used to, displaying little equivocation and a keen interest in foreign males. They often call foreign men timid ("They touch you like you're crystal"). Such overt sexuality can be thrilling to males raised in a Protestant or Catholic culture. On the beaches, languorous Lolitas in tiny *tangas* sashay along the sands blowing kisses at foreign men twice or three times their age. Tourism-generated relationships are proliferating. So, too, are marriages between Cubans and foreigners. The government takes a glum view of both.

Although there are many exceptions, it is often not any animal magnetism that makes Cuban women want to share your bed. It is the bulge in your pocket—a wallet filled with greenbacks. Many women who seek out foreigners would laugh to be called prostitutes (*jineteras,* from *jineta* meaning jockey), the term used for women who hang out at the entrances of hotels and discos or parade the beaches, seeking invitations for drinks, a meal, a taste of the high life, and—*"por Dio!"*—a romantic liaison that may even end, who knows, in a proposal of marriage to a wealthy *pepe* (slang for foreigner). But the Castro regime sees things differently. In 1996 it began a crackdown on *jiniterismo,* including attempts to regulate visits by Cubans in private apartments rented by foreign tourists and the arrest of at least two groups of foreign males involved in "pornography." (See the special topic, Sex and Tourism, in the Government section of the Introduction chapter.)

Cuba is not free of the kind of scams pulled by good-time girls in other countries, such as muggings by male accomplices, and even drugging and robbery. Petty robbery (your paramour steals your sunglasses or rifles your wallet while you take a pee) is common and such liaisons require prudence. Most women, however, count themselves lucky to have found a foreigner's acceptance and are happy to accept whatever comes their way.

Men in "sensitive" occupations (journalists and government employees) should be aware that there is always a possibility that the femme fatale who sweeps you off your feet may be in the employ of Cuba's state security.

NOTES FOR WOMEN

Most women stress the enjoyment of traveling in Cuba. With few exceptions, Cuban men treat women with great respect and, for the most part, as equals. Postrevolutionary political correctness is everywhere. True, Cuba is a mildly macho society, but sexual assault of women is unheard of. It is hard to imagine a safer place for women to travel. This is especially true in the countryside, where the Cuban male is much more conservative than his urban counterpart. *Women Travel: Adventures, Advice, and Experience,* by Niktania Jansz and Miranda Davies (Rough Guides), is full of practical advice for women travelers.

If you do welcome the amorous overtures of men, Cuba is heaven (many Stellas travel to Cuba to get their groove back). The art of gentle seduction is to Cuban men a kind of national pastime—a sport and a trial of manhood. They will hiss in appreciation from a distance like serpents, and call out *piropos*—affectionate and lyrical epithets that, in general, Cuban women encourage.

Take effusions of love with a grain of salt; while swearing eternal devotion, your Don Juan may conveniently forget to mention he's married. Be aware, too, that while the affection may be genuine, you are assuredly the moneybags in the relationship. There are even Cuban men who earn their living giving pleasure to foreign women looking for love beneath the palms.

Cuban men are used to relations with Cuban women, who revel in expressing their megaton sexuality. My female friends report that Cuban men are diligent in the role of pleasing a woman.

If you're not interested in love in the tropics, simply pretend not to notice advances and avoid eye contact; a longing stare is part of the game. You can help prevent these overtures by dressing modestly, especially in rural areas where shorts, tube tops, or strapless sundresses invite attention.

A good resource is the **Federación de Mujeres Cubanas,** Cuban Women's Federation, Paseo #260, Vedado, Havana, tel. (7) 55-2771, which sponsors forums and acts to promote the interests of women. In the U.S., the **Federation of Women's Travel Organizations,** 4545 N. 36th St. #126, Phoenix, AZ 85018, tel. (602) 956-7175, might be useful.

Global Exchange leads a Women's Delegation to Cuba study tour, in which participants meet women workers and members of women's and neighborhood organizations. The **Center for Cuban Studies** also has similar study tours occasionally. (The chart Organizations to Know provides information on more groups.)

NOTES FOR GAYS AND LESBIANS

Cuba is schizophrenic when it comes to homosexuality. Following the Revolution, homosexuals were treated harshly. During the late 1960s, scores of gays were purged from government posts and sent to work camps, and purges continued sporadically through the next decade. (Even Castro's guest Allen Ginsberg, the homosexual poet, was kicked out of Cuba for remarking that Fidel Castro must have had homosexual experiences as a boy and for stating that he would like to make love with Che Guevara.)

In the past decade, the Cuban government has attempted to make amends. The interior of the country, more wed to traditional machismo and antigay sentiment, is also liberalizing. Discrimination still exists, but there are still instances of police harassment, and derogatory terms persist. Gays, *jiniteros,* and Cuban "liberals" who befriend foreigners often fall afoul of the law of *peligrosidad,* which declares as "dangerous" anyone who acts in an antisocial manner and against the norms of socialist morality. Still, things have never been so open.

Gay Cuba, by Sonja de Vries, is a documentary film that looks candidly at the treatment of gays and lesbians in Cuba since the Revolution. You can order copies from Frameline, 346 Ninth St., San Francisco, CA 94103, tel. (415) 703-8654, fax (415) 861-1404; e-mail: frameline@aol.com, website: www.frameline.org. Also check out *Machos, Maricones, and Gays: Cuba and Homosexuality,* by Ian Lumsden (Philadelphia, PA: Temple University, 1996) for a study of the relationship between male homosexuality and Cuban society. (Also see Homosexuality in Cuba in the Introduction chapter.)

Meeting Places
Many Cuban homosexuals remain in the closet. Still, the new sense of freedom for gays is finding its outlet in an increasing number of gay gathering places, notably in Havana. See the Havana chapter for details.

Organizations
I am not aware of any lesbian organization (Cuban machismo is still so strongly entrenched

that it is inconceivable to many that lesbianism actually exists). The first gay men's group on the island, called **Cubans in the Struggle Against AIDS,** was recently formed. And gays and lesbians from Cuba and the U.S. joined hands in February 1994 to form a networking group—**Queers for Cuba**—based out of the **Cuban National Commission on Sex Education,** Calle 23 #177, Vedado, Havana, tel. (7) 30-2679, and intended to build solidarity with Cuban lesbians, bisexuals, and gays. It sponsors educational forums about the reality of gays in Cuba and organizes delegations to the island. The group is requesting donations of gay literature, school and office supplies, and safe sex materials. Donations can be sent to Queers for Cuba, 3543 18th St., Box 33, San Francisco, CA 94110, tel. (415) 995-4678, which also offers solidarity trips to the island.

The **Center for Cuban Studies** offers occasional "update" study tours of lesbian and gay issues in Cuba. It also requests donations of condoms, safe sex materials, literature, medicines, etc. **MADRE,** 121 West 237th St. #301, New York, NY 10001, tel. (212) 627-0444, fax (212) 675-3704, e-mail: madre@igc.org, website: www.madre.org, also accepts donations of material aid (condoms, literature, etc.) for distribution in Cuba.

Useful resources include the **Gay & Lesbian Travel Services Network,** 2300 Market St. #142, San Francisco, CA 94114, tel. (415) 552-5140, fax (415) 552-5104; e-mail: gaytvlinfo@aol.com; **Odysseus: The International Gay Travel Planner,** P.O. Box 1548, Port Washington, NY 11050, tel. (516) 944-5330 or (800) 257-5344, fax (516) 944-7540, e-mail: odyusa@odyusa.com, website: www.odyusa.com; the **International Gay Travel Association,** P.O. Box 4974, Key West, FL 33041, tel. (800) 448-8550; and the **International Gay & Lesbian Association,** 208 W. 13th St., New York, NY 10011, tel. (212) 620-7310; international headquarters, 81 Kolenmarkt, B 1000, Brussels, Belgium, tel./fax (02) 5022471, e-mail: ilga@ilga.org, website: www.ilga.org.

NOTES FOR STUDENTS AND YOUTH

Cuban students receive discounts for entry to many museums and other sites. This may apply to foreign students, too, although at press time the **International Student Identity Card** (ISIC) was not accepted in Cuba. Things change. The card entitles students 12 years and older to discounts on transportation, entrances to museums, and more. When purchased in the U.S. (US$15; tel. (800) 438-2643), ISIC even includes emergency medical coverage (although this won't apply in Cuba) and access to a 24-hour emergency hotline. Students can obtain an ISIC at any student union. Alternately, in the U.S., contact the **Council on International Educational Exchange (CIEE),** 205 E. 42nd St., New York, NY 10017, tel. (212) 661-1414, fax (212) 972-3231, website: www.ciee.org or www.counciltravel.com In Canada, cards (C$13) can be obtained through **Travel Cuts,** 187 College St., Toronto, ON M5T 1P7 tel. (416) 979-2406. In the U.K., students can obtain an ISIC from any student union.

The U.S. government permits academic exchanges with Cuba, and students can enroll at Cuban universities. The **Cuban Exchange Program,** School of Advanced International Studies, Johns Hopkins University, 1740 Massachusetts Ave. NW, Washington, D.C. 20036, tel. (202) 663-5732, fax (202) 663-5737, can provide information.

Transitions Abroad, 18 Hulst Rd., Box 344, Amherst, MA 01004, tel. (413) 256-3414, e-mail: business@TransitionsAbroad.com, website: www.transabroad.com, provides information for students wishing to study abroad. Another handy resource is the *Directory of Study Abroad Programs,* contact Renaissance Publications, 7819 Barkwood Dr., Worthington, OH 43085, tel. (614) 885-9568, fax (614) 436-2793, and **CIEE's Work Abroad Department,** 205 E. 42nd St., New York, NY 10017, tel. (212) 661-1414, ext. 1130, website: www.councilexchanges.org.

The **Union de Jovenes Comunistas** (Young Communists' Union) has an international relations office at Calle 17 #252, Vedado, Havana, tel. (7) 32-3906.

NOTES FOR SENIORS

Cuba treats its own senior citizens with honor, and discounts are offered for entry to museums, etc. Again, this may apply to foreign seniors in a few instances.

Global Exchange (see the chart, Organizations To Know) occasionally offers an "Elders in Cuba" study tour.

Useful resources include the **American Association of Retired Persons** (AARP), 601 E. St., Washington, D.C. 20049, tel. (202) 434-2277 or (800) 424-3410, e-mail: member@aarp.org, website: www.aarp.org, which has a "Purchase Privilege Program" offering discounts on airfares which you may be able to use for flights to a third country en route to Cuba. **Elderhostel,** 75 Federal St., Boston, MA 02110, tel. (617) 426-7788 or (805) 426-8056, website: www.elderhostel.org, offers educational trips for seniors, as does Toronto-based **ElderTreks,** tel. (416) 588-5000 or (800) 741-7956, website: www.eldertreks.com. Neither organization offered trips to Cuba at press time, but they may be useful resources.

Other handy sources include *The Mature Traveler,* P.O. Box 50820, Reno, NV 89513, a monthly newsletter; and *The International Health Guide for Senior Citizen Travelers,* by Robert Lange, M.D. (New York: Pilot Books).

NOTES FOR TRAVELERS WITH DISABILITIES

Cuba has made great advances in guaranteeing the rights of the disabled, and Cubans go out of their way to assist travelers with disabilities. However, you'll need to plan your vacation carefully—few allowances have been made in infrastructure.

The **Asociació Cubana de Limitados Físicos y Motores** (Cuban Association for Physically-Motor Disabled People, ACLIFIM), Ermita #213, e/ San Pedro y Lombillo, Plaza de la Revolución, CP 10600, Havana, tel. (7) 81-0911, fax (7) 33-3787, e-mail: aclifim@informed.sld.cu, can be of assistance. In the U.S., contact **Marazul Tours,** Tower Plaza, 4100 Park Ave., Weehawken, NJ 07087, tel. (201) 319-3900 or (800) 223-5334, fax (201) 319-9009, e-mail: info@marazultours.com, website: www.marazultours.com, which arranges trips to the Cuban conferences on disabled people's rights.

In the U.S., the **Society for the Advancement of Travel for the Handicapped,** 347 Fifth Ave. #610, New York, NY 10016, tel. (212) 447-7284, fax (212) 725-8253, e-mail: sathtravel@aol.com, website: www.sath.org, publishes a quarterly newsletter entitled *Access to Travel.* Another handy newsletter is *The Wheelchair*

Traveler, 23 Ball Hill Rd., Milford, NH 03055, tel. (603) 673-4539. Don't expect them to have much information on Cuba, however.

TRAVELERS WITH CHILDREN

Generally, travel with children poses no special problems. Cubans adore children and will dote on yours. There are few sanitary or health problems to worry about. However, children's items such as diapers (nappies) and baby food are very difficult to obtain in Cuba. Bring cotton swabs, diapers (consider bringing cotton diapers; they're more ecologically acceptable), Band-Aids, and a small first-aid kit with any necessary medicines for your child. If you plan on driving around, bring your own children's car seat—they're not offered in rental cars.

Children's hospitals are located in all major cities; Havana has seven children's hospitals, including the **Pediatrico Centro Habana,** Calzada de Infanta y Benjumeda, Centro Habana, tel. (7) 79-6002.

Children under the age of two travel free on airlines; children between two and 12 are offered special discounts (check with individual airlines). Children under 16 usually stay free with parents at hotels, although an extra-bed rate may be charged.

Cuban TV features a few children's programs, and you can find kiddies' books in Spanish at

BITE YOUR TONGUE!

*B*ig Brother keeps a close watch on Cubans, who have to account to the state for their every move. And many foreigners are not above surreptitious surveillance. But you're free to roam wherever you wish without hindrance or a need to look over your shoulder.

That said, you can be sure that nay-saying the Revolution or you-know-who in public can land you in trouble swiftly. Criticism of the government is defined as "antisocial behavior" and, for Cubans, is punishable by law. Cuban authorities do not look favorably on foreigners who become involved in political activity, especially with known dissidents. Secret police and informers are everywhere. Avoid making inflammatory or derogatory comments; otherwise you could well find yourself on the next plane home.

leading bookstores. Many hotels feature children's amusements, including water slides. Some also offer babysitting. There are children's amusement parks *(parques diversiones)* in every town, although most are run-down. Several have carousels, small roller coasters, and other rides.

The equivalent of the Boy and Girl Scouts and Girl Guides is the **Pioneros José Martí,** Avenida de la Presidencia #503, Vedado, Havana, tel. (7) 32-1111, which has chapters throughout the country. Its main focus is instilling youth with revolutionary correctness and civil responsibility. Having your children interact would be a fascinating education.

Travel with Your Children, 45 W. 18th St., New York, NY 10011, tel. (212) 206-0688, publishes the *Family Fun Times* newsletter. It also operates an information service. **Great Vacations with Your Kids** (New York: E.P. Dutton), by Dorothy Jordan and Marjorie Cohen, is a handy reference guide to planning a trip with children, as is *Travel with Children,* by Maureen Wheeler (Lonely Planet).

PERSONAL CONDUCT

Cubans are immensely respectful and courteous, with a deep sense of integrity. Politeness is greatly appreciated, and you can ease your way considerably by being both courteous and patient. Always greet your host with *"¡Buenas días!"* (morning) or *"¡Buenas tardes!"* (afternoon). And never neglect to say, *"Gracias."* Honor local dress codes as appropriate. Topless and nude bathing are neither allowed nor accepted, except at key tourist resorts. For men, short shorts should be relegated to beachwear, although longer shorts are now gaining acceptance on urban streets for men. Cuban women, however, expose a lot of flesh in their everyday dress.

Cubans are extremely hygienic and have an understandable natural prejudice against anyone who ignores personal hygiene, for which the Russians—*bolos*—were despised.

Respect the natural environment. Take only photographs, leave only footprints.

HAVANA

INTRODUCTION

Winston Churchill, approaching Havana by sea in 1895, wrote that he felt "delirious yet tumultuous. . . . I felt as if I sailed with Long John Silver and first gazed on Treasure Island. Here was a place where anything might happen. Here was a place where something would certainly happen. Here I might leave my bones."

Countless writers have commented on the exhilarating sensation that engulfs visitors to this most beautiful and beguiling of Caribbean cities. The potency of Havana's appeal is owed to a quality that "runs deeper than the stuff of which travel brochures are made. It is irresistible and intangible," writes Juliet Barclay—as if, adds Arnold Samuelson, recalling his first visit to Havana in 1934, "everything you have seen before is forgotten, everything you see and hear then being so strange you feel. . . as if you had died and come to life in a different world." The city's ethereal mood, little changed today, is so pronounced that it finds its way into novels. "I wake up feeling different, like something inside me is changing, something chemical and irreversible. There's a magic here working its way through my veins," says Pilar, a Cuban-American character from New York who returns to Havana in Cristina García's novel *Dreaming in Cuban*. Set foot one time in Havana and you can only flee or

succumb to its enigmatic allure. It is impossible to resist the city's mysteries and contradictions.

Walking Havana's streets you sense you are living inside a romantic thriller. You don't want to sleep for fear of missing a vital experience. Before the Revolution, Havana had a reputation as a place of intrigue and tawdry romance. The whiff of conspiracy, the intimation of liaison, is still in the air.

Your first reaction is of being caught in an eerie colonial-cum-1950s time warp. Fading signs advertising Hotpoint and Singer appliances evoke the decadent decades when Cuba was a virtual colony of the United States. High-finned, chrome-spangled dowagers from the heyday of Detroit are everywhere, conjuring images of dark-eyed temptresses and men in Panama hats and white linen suits. Havana, now Communist but still carnal, is peopled in fact as in fiction by characters from the novels of Ernest Hemingway and Graham Greene. All the glamour of an abandoned stage set is here, patinated by age. For foreign visitors, it is heady stuff.

Profile of the City

Havana (pop. 2.2 million), political, cultural and industrial heart of the nation, contains one-fifth of Cuba's population. It has a flavor all its own; a

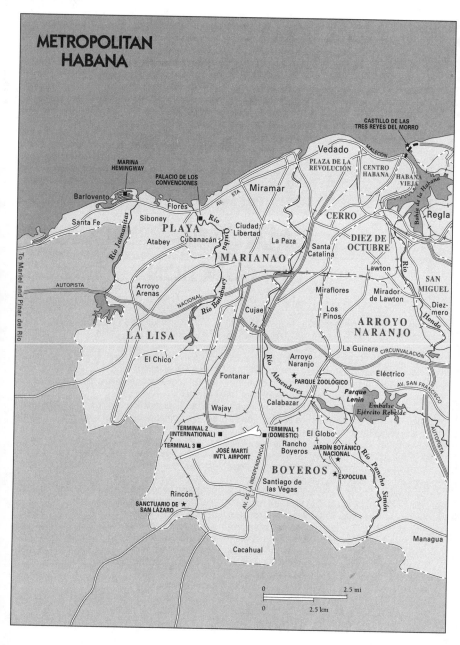

METROPOLITAN HABANA

CASTILLO DE LAS
TRES REYES DEL MORRO

MARINA
HEMINGWAY

PALACIO DE LOS
CONVENCIONES

Vedado

PLAZA DE LA
REVOLUCIÓN

MALECÓN

CENTRO
HABANA

HABANA
VIEJA

Barlovento

Flores

AV. 5TA.

Miramar

Santa Fe

Siboney

PLAYA

Río Quibú

Ciudad
Libertad

CERRO

Regla

To Mariel and Pinar del Río

Atabey

Cubanacán

La Paza

DIEZ DE
OCTUBRE

MARIANAO

Santa
Catalina

Bahía de la Habana

AUTOPISTA

Arroyo
Arenas

NACIONAL

Río Banabuey

Cujae

Miraflores

Lawton

Río

Mirador
de Lawton

SAN
MIGUEL

Diez-
mero

Hondo

LA LISA

Los
Pinos

ARROYO
NARANJO

El Chico

Fontanar

Río Almendares

Arroyo
Naranjo

La Guinera

CIRCUNVALACIÓN

Eléctrico

AV. SAN FRANCISCO

Wajay

Calabazar

PARQUE ZOOLÓGICO

Parque
Lenin

Embalse
Ejército Rebelde

AUTOPISTA

TERMINAL 2
(INTERNATIONAL)

TERMINAL 1
(DOMESTIC)

El Globo

TERMINAL 3

JOSÉ MARTÍ
INT'L AIRPORT

Rancho
Boyeros

JARDÍN BOTÁNICO
NACIONAL

Río Pancho Simón

AV. DE LA INDEPENDENCIA

BOYEROS

★EXPOCUBA

Rincón

Santiago de
las Vegas

SANCTUARIO DE ★
SAN LÁZARO

Managua

Cacahual

0   2.5 mi

0   2.5 km

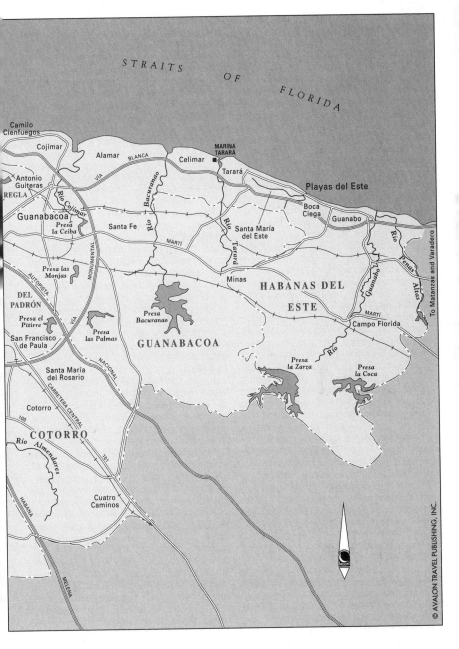

STRAITS OF FLORIDA

Camilo Cienfuegos

Cojímar

Alamar

BLANCA

Celimar

MARINA TARARÁ

Tarará

Playas del Este

Antonio Guiteras

REGLA

VÍA

Río Cojímar

Río Bacuranao

Boca Ciega

Guanabo

Río Peñas Altas

Guanabacoa

Presa la Ceiba

Santa Fe

MARTÍ

Río Tararà

Santa María del Este

To Matanzas and Varadero

Presa las Monjas

MONUMENTAL

Minas

HABANAS DEL

ESTE

Guanabo

AUTOPISTA

DEL PADRÓN

Presa el Pitirre

VÍA

Presa las Palmas

Presa Bacuranao

GUANABACOA

MARTÍ

Campo Florida

San Francisco de Paula

Santa María del Rosario

NACIONAL

Presa la Zarza

Río

Presa la Coca

Cotorro

CARRETERA CENTRAL

COTORRO

100

Río Almendares

101

HABANA

Cuatro Caminos

MOON

MELENA

© AVALON TRAVEL PUBLISHING, INC.

strange amalgam of colonialism, capitalism, and communism merged into one.

One of the great historical cities of the New World, Havana is a far cry from the Caribbean backwaters that call themselves capitals elsewhere in the Antilles. It is obvious, as you walk tree-lined boulevards and eerily Neapolitan streets that are the most tranquil and unthreatening of any you will find in Latin America, that Cuba was wealthy years ago to a degree that most South American and Caribbean cities were not. Havana is a city, notes architect Jorge Rigau, "upholstered in columns, cushioned by colonnaded arcades."

The Spanish colonial buildings hard up against the Atlantic are handsome indeed. They come in a spectacular amalgam of styles—from the academic classicism of aristocratic homes, rococo residential exteriors, Moorish interiors, art deco and art nouveau public buildings, and "internationalist" housing and other Communist carbuncles that reflect Cuba's gravitation into the Soviet orbit.

At the heart of the city is enchanting Habana Vieja (Old Havana), a living museum inhabited by 60,000 people and containing perhaps the finest collection of Spanish colonial buildings in all the Americas. Baroque churches, convents, and castles that could have been transposed from Madrid or Cádiz still reign majestically over squares embraced by the former palaces of Cuba's ruling gentry and cobbled streets still haunted by Ernest Hemingway's ghost.

Hemingway's house, Finca Vigía, is one of dozens of museums dedicated to the memory of great men and women. And although most of the older monuments—those of politically incorrect heroes—were pulled down, at least they were replaced by dozens of grandiose monuments to those on the correct side of history.

Street names may have been changed, but balmy city streets with walls in faded tropical pastels still smolder gold in the waxing sun. Sunlight still filters through stained-glass *mediopuntos* to dance on the cool marble floors. And time cannot erase the sound of the "jalousies above the colonnades creaking in the small wind from the sea," in the words of Graham Greene. "True, [Havana] was disheveled and shabby," wrote Brenda Loree, "but in the manner of a beautiful woman who had let herself go. You could still tell that she had good bones."

Faded Glory

It has been fashionable among foreign journalists of late to portray Havana as a slum, a crumbling city of "tattered colonnades and peeling paint, shadowed by a somnolent remorse." True enough, Havana aches with penury and pathos. The sultry seductress of prerevolutionary days needs a million gallons of paint (political humorist P. J. O'Rourke has written, "Half an hour in Havana is enough to cure you of a taste for that distressed look so popular in Crate & Barrel stores"). Four decades of official neglect have left Havana's buildings in various stages of decay. But at least they're still standing and haven't been swept away by a gaudy wave of tourist hotels, shopping malls, and marinas.

Havana has been "a city in lamentable decline" for more a century, but policies since the Revolution have only hastened the tragic decay. Soon after Castro took power, his government announced a policy emphasizing rural development over urban improvement. The countryside had long been neglected, and a significant portion of the rural population lived in abject poverty. But the putative triumphs of the Revolution in the countryside could not stem migration to the cities, particularly Havana, which suffered ongoing neglect and impoverishment. Little new construction has taken place in the past 30 years. As a result, Havana has faced an acute housing shortage. The Revolution "democratized" the former haunts of the ruling and middle classes—many of their mansions in the once all-white suburbs of Vedado and Miramar, like the housing in working-class regions, were divided into smaller and smaller apartments.

"The unhealthy shanty towns, which had disappeared during the early years of the Revolution, have reappeared," Castro declared in 1989, speaking of the *ciudadelos,* the decrepit tenements "where families live in one or two little rooms, with very little space." Castro estimated that 300,000 people in Havana live in slum conditions and that only 50% of inhabitants have proper sewage (in a 1999 report by the Havana municipal authorities, some 9,000 people were living in shelters and another 100,000 in houses officially considered unsafe; 60,000 houses are slated for demolition). Local residents have virtually no access to paint or other desperately needed materials with which to improve their living conditions, and governmental authorities have shown only minimal concern to invest in such improvements.

In certain areas, conditions are now truly depressing. Many Habaneros cling tenaciously to family life behind crumbling façades festooned with makeshift wiring and inside tottering buildings that should have faced the bulldozer's maw long ago. Many buildings have fallen masonry and piles of plaster on the floor, unpainted walls mildewed by the tropical climate, and stairs so dilapidated one is afraid to step onto them. Once pleasant strolls in Cerro and Habana Vieja have become obstacle courses over piles of rubble and beneath wooden braces propping up one building after another. At least garbage collection is efficient. And fortunately most of the sewers still work and although when it rains the streets fill with puddles, they are free of the pestilent aromas of so many other cities elsewhere in the tropics.

A City Rekindled

Havana has rebounded from the grim days of the early 1990s. Gasoline is again plentiful and reports of Cuba's transport system having come to a virtual standstill are now outdated. The streets are thrumming to motor traffic, including a new fleet of buses (cast-offs imported from Europe) and taxis (for foreigners). And the notorious power outages that plagued Havana nightly in the early 1990s have now become occasional and brief-lasting inconveniences.

Habana Vieja—a treasure trove of ancient palaces and cathedrals and castles—is in the midst of a stunning restoration that has been ongoing for over a decade. The commercial district of Vedado is again on the rise with foreign-funded construction. Scores of mansions in Miramar are being restored to haughty grandeur and turned into posh boutiques and restaurants. And deluxe hotels are sprouting like mushrooms on a damp log, along with a new aquarium and an international trade center. Even deluxe apartments for sale to foreigners are going up.

GEOGRAPHY

Havana lies 145 km due south of Florida, on Cuba's far northwest coast. It is built on the west side of a sweeping bay with a narrow funnel entrance—Bahía de Habana—and extends west 12 km to the Río Jaimanitas.

The city slopes gradually inland from the shore. Habana Vieja and Central Havana, however, are mostly flat and slope almost imperceptibly. Vedado and Miramar also slope gradually to the south, where Cerro and Plaza de la Revolución extend across gently rolling hills.

Municipios and Districts

Ciudad de la Habana (City of Havana) is a sprawling city. The metropolitan area covers 740 sq. km and incorporates 15 *municipios,* or municipalities, subdivided into distinct districts. The urban center mostly lies west and south of the harbor, or Bahía de la Habana, and encompasses almost 15,000 blocks or *manzanas.* Like all fine cities, Havana is a collection of neighborhoods, each with its own distinct character that owes much to the date that each developed.

The *municipio* of **Habana Vieja** (the oldest part of the city) lies immediately west of the harbor, and with neighboring **Regla** across the harbor, dates from the 16th and 17th centuries, though most structures are of the 17th and 18th centuries.

Centro Habana, west of Habana Vieja, and Casablanca, the fishing village facing Havana to the north (and part of the *municipio* of Regla), date from the 18th century and were the first residential areas outside the ancient city walls.

Residential Vedado, the modern heart of the city, and Nuevo Vedado to the south, form the *municipio* of **Plaza de la Revolución** and blend neighborhoods of the 19th and 20th centuries. Plaza de la Revolución extends west from Centro to the Río Almanderes.

The now-decrepit residential districts of **Cerro** and **Diez de Octubre,** which includes La Vibora district, lies south of Plaza de la Revolución and Centro Habana, respectively, and date from the 19th century.

Playa extends west of the Río Almanderes and includes, in order, the districts of Miramar and (to its south) Buena Vista, with once glamorous Cubanacán, and Flores, Siboney, Atabey, and Santa Fe beyond. These areas date from the late 19th and early 20th centuries.

The suburban, residential *municipios* of **La Lisa** and **Marianao** lie south of Playa and offer little of touristic interest.

Encircling the core are the expansive and mostly rural outrider *municipios* of **Boyeros, Arroyo Naranjo, Cotorro,** and **Guanabacoa,** each pinned by their respective 17th-century eponymous villages. These *municipios* combine historic villages such as Santiago de las Vegas and San Francisco de Paula, as well as more modern industrial enclaves.

Habana del Este extends east from the harbor for some 30 miles along the shore as far as the beaches of the Playas del Este. Between the city and Playas del Este are the postrevolutionary urban enclaves of Ciudad Panamericano, Ciudad Camilo Cienfuegos, Alamar, and Celimar, and the 18th-century fishing village of Cojimar.

HISTORY

Foundation of a City

Today's Havana began life in July 1515 as the westernmost of the seven cities established under Diego Velázquez. The city, called San Cristóbal de la Habana, was first located on the south coast, where Batabanó stands today. The site was an unmitigated disaster. Within four years the settlers had moved to the north coast, where they erected rough huts at the mouth of the Río Chorrera (now Almendares). A few years earlier, the expeditionary Sebastian de Ocampo had discovered a more promising site—Puerto de Carenas, so named because the site was ideal for careening ships—a few km farther east, and on 25 November 1519, the date of the second founding of San Cristóbal de la Habana, the settlers moved to the shore of a flask-shaped, deep-water bay surrounded by rolling hills and hidden within a cliff-hung narrow channel.

The first houses stood facing the sea in a row between the present sites of the Plaza de Armas and the Plaza de San Francisco. Initially, life was extremely spartan. But Puerto de Carena's proximity to the deep channel between Cuba and the shallow seas of the Bahamas was highly advantageous.

The Early Years

Throughout the 16th century, an ever-increasing number of ships called in Havana's port as the New World began to yield up its riches. Staggering amounts of treasure were transported to Spain. In 1508 the prize amounted to 8,000 *ducados;* by 1512, it rose to 90,000. When Mexico and Peru were conquered, the quantities rose to astronomical heights. The city gained such prominence that in July 1553 the governor of Cuba, Gonzalo Pérez de Angulo, moved the capital (and his residence) from Santiago de Cuba in the east of the island.

In 1564 a Spanish expedition reached the Philippines. The next year it discovered the northern Pacific trade winds that for the next 250 years propelled ships laden with Chinese treasure to Acapulco, from where the booty was carried overland to Veracruz, on the Gulf of Mexico, and loaded onto ships bound for Havana and Europe. Oriental perfumes, pearls, silks, and ivories passed through Havana. To these shipments were added silver from Bolivia, alpaca from Peru, and rare woods from central America, plus Cuban tobacco, leather, fruit, and its own precious woods. Havana could never have imagined such wealth! The fleet of 1583 had to leave one million pesos behind because there was no more room in the ships' holds.

Every spring and summer, all the ships returning from the Americas crowded into Havana's harbor before setting off for Spain in an armed convoy. To provision them, an aqueduct was built to bring water down to the harbor, fruit and vegetables came from small holdings outside Havana, and the citizens made soup and *tasajo* (salted meat) from the vast quantities of crabs and tortoises that overran the city. Havana's air reeked, and the city itself overflowed with drunken sailors, packs of wild dogs, cutthroats, and whores—at night, few citizens dared venture out unless heavily armed.

Building for Posterity

While the British went out to their colonies to grow rich and return, the Spanish went to grow rich and stay. They brought a permanence of design and planning to their New World cities that other colonial powers never achieved. "The Spanish built cities where they settled, but the English just let cities grow. The poorest street of Havana had dignity compared to the shanty towns of Kingston," wrote Graham Greene.

By the turn of the 18th century, Havana was the third-largest city in the New World (after Mexico City and Lima). The 17th and 18th centuries saw a surge of pious energy and ecclesiastical construction as the ever-powerful bishops brought their influence to bear in statuary and stone. Most notable of the "builder-bishops" was Diego Evelino de Compostela, a vigorous ecclesiastic who arrived from Spain in November 1687. In short order, he initiated the Convento de Belén, Convento de Santa Clara de Asís, Iglesia Santa Teresa de Jesús, and Iglesia del Santo Ángel Custodio. Compostela's work was continued by an equally dynamic bishop, Gerónimo Valdés, who founded the University of Havana.

The wealth of the Americas helped fill the churches and convents with gold and silver. Havana's wealth increased as the tobacco industry prospered from European noses, which reverberated with satisfied sneezes induced by Cuban snuff. Industries were established, and the city was renowned for building the best galleons in the Indies. The goods of the hinterlands, especially precious leathers and timber, flowed out from the harbor, while the black gold of slaves and the fineries of Europe flowed in.

Spanish ships also unloaded builders and craftsmen, hired to help citizens display their earnings—legitimate and ill-gotten alike—in an outpouring of architectural sophistication. They brought with them a Moorish aesthetic, which they translated into what Juliet Barclay calls a unique "tropical synthesis of column, courtyard, and chiaroscuro."

The British Take Over
On 4 January 1762, George III of England declared war on Spain. Some years before, the British governor of Jamaica, Charles Knowles, had been hosted on an official visit to Havana, where he spent much of his time reconnoitering the city's defenses. Knowles was consulted, and a plan drawn up for an attack on Havana.

Though the city of about 40,000 inhabitants was heavily defended, its Achilles' heel was the Cabaña, a long ridge overlooking Morro Castle and Havana's harbor. On 6 June, a British fleet of 50 warships—carrying 11,000 troops—arrived off Cojímar. The next day they put ashore—and Havana erupted in panic. The Spanish scuttled three ships in the harbor mouth, ineptly trapping their own warships inside the harbor. That night, when Spanish guards atop the Cabaña began firing at British scouts, the Spanish warships began blasting the ridge, causing their own troops to flee. The British took the ridge and laid siege to Havana. On 29 July sappers blew an enormous hole in the Castillo de Morro, and the flag of St. George was raised over the city.

The English immediately lifted the trade restrictions. Merchant ships from many nations raced to Havana, which overnight became what Abbé Guillaume Raynal called the "boulevard of the New World." To his discredit, however, the English commander, George Keppel, Earl of Albermarle, milked the city dry by imposing usurious levies, especially upon the Catholic Church. After the British commandeered the Iglesia San Francisco de Asís for Protestant worship, the church was never again used for service by Havana's citizens.

The citizens were relieved of further indignities on 10 February 1763, when England exchanged Cuba for Florida in the Treaty of Paris, which

French pirates attacking Havana

ended the war. On 6 July, the last British troops departed Havana. The Spanish lost no time in building an enormous fortress—San Carlos de la Cabaña, the largest fortress in the Americas—atop the Cabaña ridge. The British invasion ensured that Havana would never again be neglected by Spain.

Havana Comes of Age

Havana prospered, growing every year more elegant and sophisticated. Under the supervision of the new Spanish governor, the Marqués de la Torre, it attained a new focus and rigorous architectural harmony. The elegant Prado (the first broad boulevard outside the city walls) was laid, great warehouses went up along the harbor, the Plaza de Armas was reconstructed with the grand dimensions (and a grandiose governor's residence) familiar to visitors today, and a baroque cathedral was built and new buildings erected in the Plaza de Cienaga (today's Plaza de la Catedral). The first public gas lighting arrived in 1768, along with a workable system of aqueducts. Most of the streets—which had by now been given the names they possess today—were cobbled. Fine theaters arose alongside bustling casinos and bars.

The wealthy merchants and plantation owners erected beautiful mansions graced with baroque stonework painted in every conceivable combination of pastel colors and fitted inside with every luxury in European style. Such households were maintained by slaves—often in great numbers, for the slave trade through Havana had grown astronomically as sugar began to dominate the slave-based agricultural economy, contributing even vaster sums to Havana's coffers.

Whirligig Life on the Streets

Life coursed through Havana's plazas like a storm of sweetpeas: peasants leading mules bearing baskets of fruit and vegetables, farmers adding to the great crush as they drove cattle and pigs to market, acrobats and clowns doing tricks for handouts, musicians serenading, lottery-ticket sellers bearing down on anyone who looked as if he deserved some good luck that day, water vendors hawking foul-smelling water, goats being milked door-to-door, and volantas—carriages with light bodies suspended as if in midair between enormous wheels—rac-

ing around the streets, each pulled by a well-groomed horse ridden by a black calesero (postilion) in resplendent livery. (Habana Vieja's system of one-way streets dates to this period. Many of the street signs embedded in the walls of in Habana Vieja still bear a pointing hand in a frilly cuff pointing the way for passing caleseros.)

The city must have resembled a grand operatic production—especially at night, with the harbor, crosshatched by masts and spars, shining under the glint of soft moonlight while coquettish maidens wearing white ball gowns and necklaces of giant fireflies—cocullos—gathered on Sunday for the brilliant masked balls eagerly anticipated by Habaneras.

The City Bursts Its Seams

By the mid-19th century, Habana Vieja harbored 55,000 people. New buildings were going up, and the city was bursting with uncontainable energy. Soon there was not a square centimeter left for building within the city walls. In 1863, the walls came tumbling down—less than a century after they were completed. A new upscale district called Vedado rose behind the shore west of Habana Vieja. Graceful boulevards pushed into the surrounding hills and countryside, lined with a parade of quintas (country houses) fronted by classical columns. The baroque bowed out as architects harked back to the heyday of Greece.

Havana owes much of its modern face to Governor Miguel Tacón y Rosique, who initiated a brisk program of urban reform that included creation of a fire brigade, a police force, street cleaning, street signs, a drainage system, and unbridled construction. Tacón supported the first railroad in the Spanish colonies, linking Havana with Bejucal in 1837. Fortunately for latter-day tourists, Tacón had a rival: the Conde de Villanueva, the criollo (Cuban-born) administrator of the royal estates.

The elitist Peninsulares (native Spaniards) ran Cuba as a fiefdom, and criollos were allowed no say in administration of the island. Unquenchable animosity had arisen between them, firing the wars of independence but also fueling a contest to erect public and rival edifices as expressions of Spanish and disaffected criollo pride. We owe the Templete, the neo-baroque Gran Teatro on Parque Central, and the contemporary face of the Prado to this war.

Alas, while Havana matured in grandeur, the surrounding countryside was being laid waste by the wars of independence. Spanish authorities in Havana meted out harsh sentences against anyone who declared himself against Spain. La Cañana became a jail, and many famous nationalist figures, including José Martí, were imprisoned here. By the late 1880s, many of the wealthy land-owning Habaneros were forced to sell their crippled estates to U.S. citizens, many of whom had begun to flock to the island for other pleasures selected from more than 200 brothels.

The U.S. government had long coveted Cuba, and found its pretext on 15 February 1898, when the USS *Maine* exploded in Havana harbor. The hulk of the *Maine* lay in the harbor until 1912, when the rusting symbol of *norteamericano* interference in Cuban affairs was raised, hauled far out to sea, and sunk.

Into the 20th Century

When the war ended, in 1898, the U.S. military administration initiated far-reaching reforms, including a campaign that eradicated the yellow-fever epidemics then common in Havana, and the capital city entered a new era. The Malecón was laid out; wealthy *Yanquis* and *Cubanos* built their posh mansions side-by-side in the western suburbs of Vedado and Miramar, where the first country clubs were opened; the older residential areas settled into an era of decay; and many cherished old buildings were demolished. Apartment buildings and hotels went up, and many of the once-fashionable houses along the Prado and in Habana Vieja were converted for commercial use.

By the mid-19th century, Chinese immigrants had occupied the marshy lowlands in the valley west of Habana Vieja, which they drained, and established market gardens to supply Habaneros. As the city expanded, land values rose and the Chinese were squeezed out. A massive public works initiated in 1907 moved millions of tons of earth into the valleys, which were raised for residential development, while surveyors laid out the roads that would link Habana Vieja with the rapidly expanding areas of Vedado, Cerro, Vista Alegre and other suburbs beyond the Río Almendares, where the middle classes were building dwellings in eclectic, neo-

classical, and revivalist styles. Electricity and new water supplies were extended westward, local merchants soon followed, and Marianao saw a boom. The crowded narrow streets and tight, shade-giving colonial quarters of older sections gave way to broad sidewalks and shaded porches facing onto broad lawns as the city began to spread out, its perimeter enlarged by grid extensions *(ensanches)* incorporating parks, boulevards, and civic spaces.

Meanwhile, many colonial mansions disappeared, leveled by the wrecking ball and replaced by commercial establishments such as banks. Many other once-grand colonial homes were subdivided and rented to less affluent Habaneros who could not afford the upkeep, while the real estate boom sponsored further spatial fragmentation, so that homes that once belonged to single families were turned into beehives. The communities of *solares* expanded, with humble, unsanitary dwellings crowded within patios and back lots of buildings and hidden from view from the street.

Despite the slums, Havana continued to prosper in the wake of World War I. President Gerardo Machado (1925-33) and Céspedes envisioned Havana as a model modern city on the grand European theme using a city-beautification plan based on Jean-Claude Nicolas Forestier's beaux-arts scheme. Forestier, an internationally acclaimed landscape designer who had reshaped Paris, led an interdisciplinary team of Cuban designers that would pay homage to Havana's history while reshaping the city with landscaped malls, tree-lined avenues, parterres, and a gigantic park at the heart of a new metropolitan center. In 1920 the new Presidential Palace was opened and the presidency of Cuba relocated from the Palace of the Captains-General. In 1929 the ribbon was cut on the statuesque Capitolio, and the legislature took its seats. But Cuban politics had sunk into a spiral of corruption and graft, and in the ensuing decades Havana attracted the good and the bad in about equal measure. Havana, wrote Juliet Barclay, filled with "milkshakes and mafiosi, hot dogs and whores (when U.S. naval vessels entered Havana harbor, the narrow harbor mouth beneath the Morro Castle was "jammed with rowboats full of clamoring prostitutes!" recalls one sailor). Havana's women had turned in their lace man-

THE MOB IN HAVANA

For three decades the Mafia had dealings in Cuba, and though they never had the run of the house as claimed, prerevolutionary Havana will forever be known for their presence.

During Prohibition (1920-33), mobsters such as Al Capone had contracted with Cuban refineries to supply molasses for their illicit rum factories. When Prohibition ended, the Mob turned to gambling. The Mafia's interests were represented by Meyer Lansky, the Jewish mobster (as a Jew he could never be a full-time member of the Mafia) from Miami who arrived in 1939 and struck a deal with Fulgencio Batista, Cuba's strongman president ("the best thing that ever happened to us," Lansky told national crime syndicate boss Salvatore "Lucky" Luciano). Lansky, acting as lieutenant for Luciano, took over the Oriental Park race track and the casino at Havana's Casino Nacional, where he ran a straight game that attracted high rollers. The Cuban state was so crooked that the Mob didn't even need to break the law.

World War II effectively put an end to the Mob's business, which was relatively small scale at the time. Lansky returned to Florida, followed by (in 1944) by Batista, when he lost to Ramón Grau in the national election.

After the U.S. deported Luciano to Italy in 1946, he immediately moved to Cuba, where he intended to establish a gambling and narcotics operation and regain his status as head of the U.S. Mob. He called a summit in Havana's Hotel Nacional (the meeting was immortalized in *The Godfather,* and the official cover, records Alan Ryan, "was that it was meant to honor a nice Italian boy from Hoboken called Frank Sinatra," who went down to Havana to say thanks). The U.S., however, pressured Grau to deport Luciano back to Italy. Before leaving, Luciano named Lansky head of operations. Lansky's aboveboard operation, however, had withered in the Mob's absence, replaced by rigged casinos. Havana's gambling scene had developed a bad reputation: Cuban casinos rented space to Cuban entrepreneurs who, says Stephen Williams, ran "wildly crooked games with the only limit to their profit being the extent of their daring."

Meyer Lansky

tillas for stockings and marched out the door in sling-back heels. Yanquí Doodle had come to town and was having martini-drinking competitions in the Sevilla Bar."

Wealthy business folk (17,000 foreign merchants, bankers, etc., lived in Havana) also flocked to play golf at the Havana Country Club, or gamble at Marianao's Oriental Park racetrack and Grand Nacional Casino. The club became the place to be, and Country Club Park became the most exclusive address in town—Havana's Beverly Hills—with architecturally distinctive homes of the Cuban elite, who danced the *danzón* and Charleston at afternoon teas on the country club terrace. Private clubs proliferated during the Republican era. The Lyceum Lawn Tennis Club and Vedado Tennis Club dated from the pre-WWI years, followed by the Havana Yacht Club (founded in 1888) and similar clubs west of the Río Almendares predominantly utilized by the Cuban elite.

By the 1950s Havana was a wealthy and thoroughly modern city on a par with Buenos Aires and Montevideo, and had acquired skyscrapers such as the FOCSA building and the Hilton (now the Habana Libre). Ministries were being moved to a new center of construction, the Plaza de la República (today the Plaza de la Revolución), inland from Vedado. Hotels were booming. Gambling found a new lease on life, and casinos flourished. (It wasn't until the mid-1950s, however, that an infusion of foreign capital built the Havana's Las Vegas-style hotel-casino for which prerevolutionary Havana will always be associ-

Lansky's return to Havana coincided with Florida voters' decision to outlaw gambling, followed by a federal campaign to suppress national crime syndicates. Mobsters decided Cuba was the place to be. A new summit was called at Fulgencio Batista's house in Daytona Beach, attended by Cuban politicians and military brass. A deal was struck: Batista would return to Cuba, regain power, and open the doors to large-scale gambling. In return, he and his crooked pals would receive a piece of the take.

A gift of US$250,000 (personally delivered by Lansky) helped convince President Grau to step aside, and on 10 March 1952, Batista again occupied the Presidential Palace. New laws were quickly enacted to attract investment in hotels and casinos, and banks were set up as fronts to channel money into the hands of Cuban politicos. In the United States, the Mafia faced certain limitations. In Cuba, anything was permissible: gambling, pornography, drugs. Corruption and self-enrichment occurred on a colossal scale. Organized crime became one of the three real power groups in Cuba (the others being Batista's military regime and American business). Still, there was never any doubt that Batista was in control and he kept the Mob on a tight chain.

One "family" headed by Cuban-Italian Amleto Batistti controlled the heroin and cocaine routes to the United States and an emporium of illegal gambling from Batistti's base at the Hotel Sevilla. A second, headed by Tampa's Mafia boss, Santo Trafficante Jr., operated the Sans Souci casino-nightclub and the casinos in the Capri, Comodoro, Deauville, and Sevilla-Biltmore Hotels. Watching over them all was Lansky, who ran the Montmarte Club and the Internacional Club of the Hotel Nacional.

Lansky again cleaned up the gambling to attract high-stakes gamblers from the States. No frivolities were allowed. Games were regulated, and card sharps and cheats were sent packing. Casinos were extensively renovated, and cocaine and prostitutes were supplied to high rollers. (Trafficante claimed to have supplied three prostitutes for Senator John F. Kennedy and then watched the foursome through a one-way mirror—but forgot to film it.)

The tourists flocked. Lansky's last act was to built the ritziest hotel and casino in Cuba—the US$14 million Hotel Riviera and Golf Leaf Casino, which opened on 10 December 1958. Three weeks later, on New Year's Eve, the sold-out floor show at the Riviera's Copa Room nightclub had 200 no-shows: Batista and his crooked henchmen had fled the country. The Mob's whirlwind honeymoon was over. Ironically, Trafficante and the Mafia had considered Castro "a joke" but were hedging their bets for all eventualities by secretly funding the rebels as well as Batista. To no avail. Once Castro took power the casinos were closed down (only after they had paid their employees), and in June 1959 Lansky, Trafficante, and other "undesirable aliens" were kicked out of Cuba. Said Lansky: "I crapped out."

The Mob, an autobiography by Mob lawyer Frank Ragano, makes good reading and supplies the scoop on the Mafia's involvement in Havana.

ated.) The city's large, financially comfortable middle class had likewise developed a taste for American TV and cars, went to Coney Island and the newly developed beach resorts on weekends, and enjoyed the same restaurants, bars, and cabarets as tourists. "The future looks fabulous for Havana," said Wilbur Clarke, the croupier who operated the casino in the Hotel Nacional, little knowing what the course of history had in store. (See the Machado Epoch and Batista Days sections in History section of the Introduction for a discussion of the period of violence and political mayhem.)

The Postrevolutionary Era

Fidel Castro arrived in Havana on 9 January 1959 to a tumultuous welcome. One of the first acts of the government was to close the strip clubs, casinos, and brothels. As time unveiled the communist nature of the Castro regime, a mass exodus of the wealthy and the middle class began, inexorably changing the face of Havana. Tourists also got the message, dooming Havana's hotels, restaurants, and other businesses to bankruptcy.

In 1959 Havana was a highly developed city— one of the most developed in Latin America— with a large wealthy and prospering middle class, and a vigorous culture. Nonetheless, the city faced a tremendous housing shortage. Festering slums and shanty towns marred the suburbs. The government ordered them razed. Concrete high-rise apartment blocks were erected on the outskirts, especially in Habana del Este. And the

Presidential Palace and Capitolio—ultimate symbols of the "sordid era"—were turned into museums, while the new government moved into buildings surrounding the Plaza de la Revolución.

That accomplished, the Revolution turned its back on the city and gave its attention instead to the countryside. Resources were diverted from Havana. Left to deteriorate, thousands of older homes collapsed (almost 100 important colonial houses a year collapse by one estimate), forcing their occupants into temporary jerry-built shelters that eventually became permanent, while "pragmatism invaded tall rooms," says Nancy Stout, "forcing them to yield their height to additional sleeping quarters popular labeled *baracoas*." The city was relayered horizontally as tens of thousands of migrants poured into Havana. Some estimates suggest that as many as 400,000 *palestinos,* immigrants from Santiago and the eastern provinces, live in Havana, their presence resented by a large segment of Habaneros. Havana's aged housing and infrastructure, much of it already decayed, have ever since suffered benign neglect. Cuba's

---

SIGHTSEEING HIGHLIGHTS: HAVANA

HAVANA

Cañonazo: Nightly firing of a cannon by men in 18th-century military garb from the ramparts of the Fortaleza de la Cabaña.

Cojímar: Old fishing village where Ernest Hemingway berthed the *Pilar:* A memorial to Hemingway and the Las Terrazas bar and restaurant recall his presence.

Maqueta del Centro Histórico: Superb scale-model of Old Havana, with guide to provide a historical overview.

Maqueta de Habana: Detailed 1:1,000 scale model of Havana. Provides a bird's-eye perspective of the entire city.

Monument y Museo Martí: Towering marble and granite statue dominates Plaza de la Revolución. All-around views of Havana from the *mirador*. Contains a splendid museum honoring Cuba's National Hero.

Museo Ernest Hemingway (Finca Vigía): "Papa's" former home on a hill southeast of Havana is preserved as it was on the day he died. His sportfishing boat—the *Pilar*—stands in the grounds.

Museo de la Revolución: Former presidential palace now tells the tale of the Revolution in gory detail. A visit is *de rigueur.*

Parque Histórico Morro y Cabaña: Imposing castle complex containing the restored **Castillo de los Tres Reyes del Morro** and massive **Fortaleza de San Carlos de la Cabaña,** with cannons in situ, the **Museo Che Guevara** and **Museo de Fortificaciones y Armas,** containing armor and weaponry spans the ages.

Plaza de Armas: Beautifully restored plaza at the heart of Old Havana, with a castle, museums, and lots of vitality.

Plaza de la Catedral: Small, atmospheric plaza hemmed in by colonial mansions and one of the New World's most exquisite cathedrals.

Playas del Este: Beautiful miles-long beach within a 30-minute drive of the city, drawing locals on weekends.

Tropicana: Spectacular cabaret with more than 200 performers—predominantly tall mulattas in fantastical costumes. Havana at its most sensual. Don't miss it!

---

socialist achievements are now little more than vast slums. Even the Mayor of Havana has admitted that "the Revolution has been hard on the city."

Havana's vitality was slowly drained. Says journalist Wendy Gimbel: "Most Cubans will tell you that Havana actually died in March 1968, when Fidel Castro closed the small businesses that lent their color and texture to the life of the city: the cafés, the pawnshops, the laundries and hardware stores, the shops where people gathered to tell their stories, and the bars where they had a beer or a Bacardi rum."

The city was honored in 1977 when the Cuban government named Old Havana a national monument and formalized a restoration plan endorsed in 1982 by UNESCO's Inter-Governmental Committee for World Cultural and Natural Protection, which named Habana Vieja a "World Heritage Site" worthy of international protection. The revolutionary government established a preservation program for Habana Vieja and the Centro Na-

HAVANA'S MUSEUMS

You can purchase a one-day ticket for US$9 good for all the museums in Habana Vieja; it's available from the Museo de la Ciudad, in the Palacio de los Capitanes Generales.

The following are the major museums:

Museo y Archivo de la Música: (Music Archives and Museum) Calle Capdevilla #1, e/ Aguiar y Habana, Centro Habana, tel. (7) 80-6810.

Museo Antropológico Montane: (Anthropological Museum) Universidad de La Habana, Calle L y San Lázaro, Vedado, tel. (7) 79-3488.

Museo de Arte Colonial: (Museum of Colonial Art) Casa del Conde de Bayone, Plaza de la Catedral, Habana Vieja, tel. (7) 62-6440.

Museo de Artes Decorativos: (Museum of the Decorative Arts) Calle 17 #502, Vedado, tel. (7) 32-0924.

Museo Casa Abel Santamaría: (House of Abel Santamaría) Calle 25 #154, Vedado, tel. (7) 70-0417.

Museo Casa Natal de José Martí: (Birthplace of José Martí) Calle Leon Peréz, Habana Vieja, tel. (7) 61-3778.

Museo de Ciencias Naturales: (Museum of Natural Sciences) Calle Obispo, Plaza de Armas, tel. (7) 63-2687

Museo de la Ciudad de Habana: (City Museum of Havana) Calle Tacón #1, Habana Vieja, tel. (7) 61-2876.

Museo de la Danza: (Museum of Dance) Linea y Avenida de los Presidentes.

Museo de la Educación: (Museum of Literacy) Calle Obispo esq. Mercaderes, tel. (7) 61-5468.

Museo de la Perfumeria: (Perfume Museum) Calle Oficios e/ Obispos y Obrapía, Habana Vieja.

Museo Ernest Hemingway: (Ernest Hemingway Museum) San Francisco de Paula, tel. (7) 91-0809 or 55-8015.

Museo Histórico de las Ciencias Carlos Finlay: (Carlos Finlay Historical Museum of Sciences) Calle Cuba #460, Habana Vieja, tel. (7) 63-4824.

Museo de Ciencias Naturales Felipe Poey: (Felipe Poey Museum of Natural Sciences) Universidad de La Habana, Calle L y San Lázaro, Vedado, tel. (7) 32-9000.

Museo Máximo Gómez: (Máximo Gómez Museum) Avenida Salvador Allende, Centro Habana, tel. (7) 79-8850.

Museo Municipal de Guanabacoa: (Municipal Museum of Guanabacoa) Calle Martí #108, Guanabacoa, tel. (7) 97-9117.

Museo Municipal de Regla: (Municipal Museum of Regla) Calle Martí #158 e/ Facciolo y La Piedra, Regla, tel. (7) 97-6989.

Museo Nacional del Aire: (National Air Museum) Av. 212 y La Coronela, Cubanacán.

Museo Nacional de Bellas Artes: (National Fine Arts Museum) Calle Animas e/ Agramonte y Monserrate, Habana Vieja, tel. (7) 63-9042.

Museo Nacional de Cerámica: (National Ceramics Museum) Castillo de la Real Fuerza, Plaza de Armas, Habana Vieja, tel. (7) 61-6130.

Museo Nacional de Música: (National Music Museum) Calle Capdevila #1, Habana Vieja, tel. (7) 61-9846.

Museo Napoleónico: (Napoleonic Museum) Calle San Miguel #1159, Vedado, tel. (7) 79-1412.

Museo Numismático: (Numismatic Museum) Calle Oficios #8 e/ Obispo y Obrapía, Habana Vieja, tel. (7) 61-5857.

Museo Postal Cubano: (Postal/Philatelic Museum) Avenida Rancho Boyeros, Plaza de la Revolución, tel. (7) 70-5581.

Museo del Pueblo Combatiente: (Museum of the Fighting People) Avenida 5ta #7201, Miramar, tel. (7) 29-1497.

Museo de la Revolución: (Museum of the Revolution) Calle Refugio #1, Habana Vieja, tel. (7) 62-4091.

Museo de Ron: (Rum Museum) Calle San Pedro, e/ Churruca y Sol.

Museo de Tábaco: (Cigar Museum) Calle Mercaderes #120, Habana Vieja, upstairs, tel. (7) 61-5795.

Parque Histórico Militar El Morro-La Cabaña: (El Morro-La Cabaña Historical Military Park) Carretera de la Cabaña, Habana del Este, tel. (7) 62-0607.

cional de Conservación, Restauración y Museologia was created to inventory Havana's historic sites and implement a restoration program that would return much of the ancient city to pristine splendor without displacing the residents.

SIGHTSEEING

The city core is divided into three regions of tourist interest: Habana Vieja, Centro Habana (Central Havana), and Vedado and Plaza de la Revolución (Vedado is administratively a part of Plaza). To the west, beyond the Río Almendares, is a fourth important district, Miramar. Outside these four regions are the suburbs, which extend for a radius of about 20 km from the center.

Since the main sights are so spread out, it is best to explore Havana in sections, beginning with Habana Vieja, where the vast majority of historical sites are located and the narrow streets lend themselves to pleasure-filled perambulation. All touristed areas are patrolled by police, which in early 2000 were on virtually every other corner on a 24-hour basis.

A guided city tour is a good way of getting your bearings. The best option is to hop aboard the **Vaivén Bus Turístico,** which circles Havana on a continual basis, taking in most sites of tourist appeal route. A US$4 ticket is good all day for as many stops and times as you wish. See Tourist Bus under Getting Around. (Also see City Tours in the section on Organized Excursions under Getting Around, this chapter.)

HABANA VIEJA~THE OLD CITY

Evocative Habana Vieja (4.5 square km; pop. 105,000) is colloquially defined by the limits of the early colonial settlement that lay within fortified walls. Today the legal boundary of Habana Vieja includes the Paseo de Martí (Prado) and everything east of it. The vast majority of sites of interest are concentrated here. Don't underestimate how much there is to see in Habana Vieja. At least three days are required, and one week isn't too much.

The original city developed along an axis that extended roughly north-south from Castillo de la Real Fuerza to Plaza Vieja. Here are the major sites of interest, centered on two plazas of great stature: the Plaza de Armas and the smaller but more imposing Plaza de la Catedral. The old squares concentrate the past into an essence that is so rich, suggests Juliet Barclay, "that it is indigestible unless taken in small sips." Each square has its own flavor, which seems to change with the hours and light: melancholic in the rain, bustling and alive in the sun, and "voluptuous when a hot midnight is illuminated by lamps and vibrates with guitar music and the muffled heartbeat of an African drum." The plazas and surrounding streets shine after a complete restoration, their structures newly painted and seeming like confections in stone.

The much-deteriorated southern half of Habana Vieja is given short shrift by most visitors.

The restoration has yet to reach the area, although a fistful of gems are worth a peek and several now gleam after being restored. The area east of Avenida de Bélgica and southwest of Plaza Vieja, between Calles Brasil and Merced, was the great ecclesiastical center of colonial Havana and is replete with churches and convents. The area around Calle Belén was also the site of the first community of Sephardic Jews in Cuba following their expulsion from Castile and Aragon in 1492. A Jewish community became well established, and this century many Polish and Lithuanian Jews settled here after fleeing Nazi persecution. The Cuban government proposes to reconstruct the Jewish settlement, and has made a start by rehabilitating the regional synagogue.

Habana Vieja is a living museum and suffers from inevitable ruination brought on by tropical climate, hastened since the Revolution by years of neglect. The grime of centuries has been soldered by tropical heat into the chipped cement and faded pastels. Beyond the restored areas, Habana Vieja is a quarter of sagging, mildewed walls and half-collapsed balconies festooned with laundry seemingly held aloft by telegraph cords and electrical wires strung across streets in a complex spider web.

You'll frequently find humble and haughty side by side, since for most of the colonial period, areas were socially mixed. Slaves lived in separate quarters or their masters' mansions. Merchants lived above their warehouses, where the slaves also lived. The best stores in colonial days were along Calles Obispo and O'Reilly, seething Oriental bazaars that were once covered in colorful awnings that softened the glare of the sun. They were Aladdin's caves of European fineries, incense, crystal and china, muslin and ribbons, and *piña* cloth, a silky gauze made of pineapple fiber and dyed in radiant colors. Obispo is still the lifeline connecting Centro Habana with Habana Vieja.

The maze of narrow one-way streets is purgatory for anyone with a motor vehicle, so *walk.* In any event, the main plazas and the streets between them are barred to traffic by huge artillery shells in the ground.

Many important street names in Habana Vieja betray a feature of historical note. For example, the ecclesiastics who strolled down Calle Obispo gave it its name: Bishop Street. Similarly, Calle Inquisidor was named for the member of the Spanish Inquisition who lived here; and Calle Mercaderes is so-named because many merchants lived here. Empedrado ("cobbled") was named thus because it was the first paved street in the city; Lamparilla means "small lamp" as first street lamps in the city went up along here; likewise, Calle Tejadillo is named for the tiles that graced its façades, another first in Havana.

Orientation

Habana Vieja is roughly shaped like a diamond, with the Castillo de la Punta its northerly point. Its western boundary, Paseo de Martí (colloquially called the Prado) runs south at a gradual gradient from the Castillo de la Punta to Parque Central and, beyond, Parque de la Fraternidad, from where Avenida de la Bélgica runs southeast, tracing the old city wall to the harborfront at the west end of Desamparados. East of Castillo de la Punta, Avenida Carlos Manuel de Céspedes (Avenida del Puerto) runs along the harbor channel and curls south to Desamparados.

PARQUE CENTRAL AND VICINITY

Spacious **Parque Central** is ground zero, the social epicenter of Habana Vieja, and an appro-

priate point from which to begin your perambulation. Its position is pivotal. From here the Prado spills north to the harbor channel and the Malecón, and south past the Capitolio to Parque de la Fraternidad. Calle Obispo slopes one km east to Plaza Armas and the heart of the old city.

The park—bounded by the Prado (Paseo de Martí), Neptuno, Agramonte, and San Martín—is presided over by stately royal palms, poinciana, and almond trees shading a Carrara marble **statue of national hero José Martí,** inaugurated in 1905 as the first such monument built in his honor in Cuba. Baseball fanatics gather near the Martí statue at a point called *esquina caliente* ("hot corner") to discuss and argue the intricacies of the sport.

The ocher-colored **Hotel Plaza,** built as a triangle in 1909, sits on the northeast face of the square, while the façade of the recently constructed **Hotel Parque Central,** due north of the park, blends historic components into a contemporary guise. Much of the action happens in front of the **Hotel Inglaterra,** on the west side: the café beneath the shady portal facing onto the boulevard in front of the hotel, known as the Acera del Louvre, provides a splendid vantage for watching the to-ing and fro-ing.

Immediately south of the Inglaterra is the exquisitely detailed **Gran Teatro,** tel. (7) 62-9473, built in 1837 as a social club for the large Galician community with an exorbitantly baroque façade graced with caryatids. It has four towers, each tipped by an angel of white marble reaching gracefully for heaven. It still functions as a theater for the National Ballet and Opera, and patrons still plump their bums into plush velvet seats of the two theaters within: the Teatro García Lorca and the Teatro Tacón, in its time considered to be one of the three finest theaters in the world. Operatic luminaries from Enrico Caruso and Sarah Bernhard performed in its heyday. Entrance costs US$2 with guide.

The less imposing **Teatro Payret** (built in 1878) faces the square from the south. Today it functions as a cinema. The building on the southeast side of the square with a tower at each of its corners is the **Centro Asturiano,** erected in 1885 and until recently housing the postrevolutionary People's Supreme Court, where a questionable version of justice was dispensed. The **Museo Nacional de Bellas Artes,**

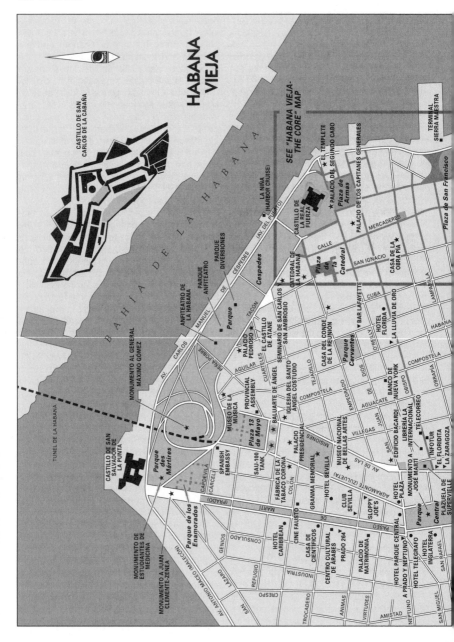

HABANA VIEJA

CASTILLO DE SAN CARLOS DE LA CABAÑA

BAHIA DE LA HABANA

TUNEL DE LA HABANA

CASTILLO DE SAN SALVADOR DE LA PUNTA

MONUMENTO DE ESTUDIANTES DE MEDICINA

MONUMENTO A JUAN CLEMENTE ZENEA

AV. ANTONIO MACEO (MALECON)

Parque des Mártires

SPANISH EMBASSY

SAU-100 TANK

Plaza 13 de Mayo

MUSEO DE LA MÚSICA

PALACIO PRESIDENCIAL

FABRICA DE TABACO CORONA

GRANMA MEMORIAL

HOTEL SEVILLA

MUSEO NACIONAL DE BELLAS ARTES

MONUMENTO AL GENERAL MAXIMO GOMEZ

Parque Anfiteatro

ANFITEATRO DE LA HABANA

Parque Diversiones

LA NIÑA (HARBOR CRUISE)

(AV. DEL PUERTO)

CASTILLO DE LA REAL FUERZA

PALACIO PEDROSO

EL CASTILLO DE ATANÉ

SEMINARIO DE SAN CARLOS SAN AMBROSIO

CASA DEL CONDE DE LA REUNION

Parque Cervantes

CATEDRAL DE LA HABANA

Plaza de la Catedral

CASA DE LA OBRA PIA

EL TEMPLETE

PALACIO DEL SEGUNDO CABO

PALACIO DE LOS CAPITANES GENERALES

Plaza de Armas

SEE "HABANA VIEJA- THE CORE" MAP

TERMINAL SIERRA MAESTRA

Plaza de San Francisco

MERCADERES

SAN IGNACIO

PROVINCIAL ASSEMBLY

BALUARTE DE ANGEL

IGLESIA DEL SANTO ANGEL COSTUDIO

BANCO DE NUEVA YORK

EDIFICIO BACARDI

LIBRERIA LA INTERNACIONAL

MONUMENTO A JOSÉ MARTI

TELECORREO

INFOTUR

EL FLORIDITA

LA ZARAGOZA

Parque Central

PLAZUELA DE SUPERVIELLE

HOTEL PLAZA

HOTEL PARQUE CENTRAL

MONUMENTO A PRADO Y NEPTUNO

HOTEL TELEGRAFO

HOTEL INGLATERRA

CLUB SEVILLA

SLOPPY JOE'S

HOTEL CARIBBEAN

CINE FAUSTO

CASA DE CIENTIFICOS

PRADO 264

PALACIO DE MATRIMONIA

CENTRO CULTURAL DE ARABES

BAR LAFAYETTE

HOTEL FLORIDA

LA LLUVIA DE ORO

O'REILLY

OBISPO

OBRAPIA

COMPOSTELA

AGUACATE

VILLEGAS

HABANA

LAMPARILLA

CUBA

SAN IGNACIO

AV. DE LAS MISIONES

AGRAMONTE (ZULUETA)

MARTI (PRADO)

PASEO DE

CONSULADO

INDUSTRIA

CRESPO

ANIMAS

VIRTUDES

SAN MIGUEL

SAN RAFAEL

NEPTUNO

AMISTAD

TROCADERO

REFUGIO

GENIOS

LAZARO

SAN

COLON

CARCEL

CAPDEVILA

PEÑA POBRE

AV. CARLOS MANUEL DE CESPEDES

CUARTELES

AGUILAR

COMPOSTELA

TEJADILLO

EMPEDRADO

CALLE

TACON

SAN JUAN DE DIOS

Parque de los Enamorados

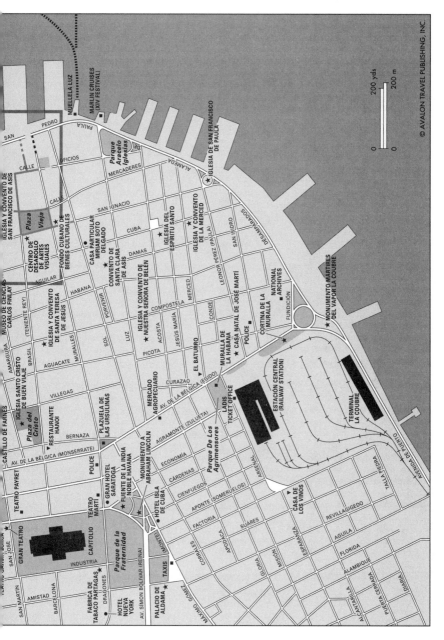

© AVALON TRAVEL PUBLISHING, INC.

200 yds

200 m

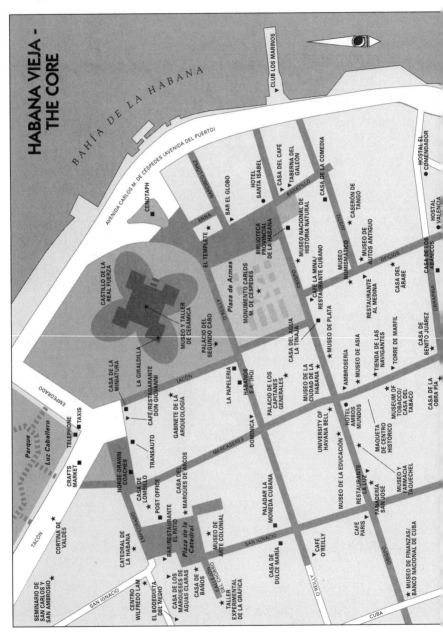

HABANA VIEJA – THE CORE

BAHÍA DE LA HABANA

AVENIDA CARLOS M. DE CÉSPEDES (AVENIDA DEL PUERTO)

CLUB LOS MARINOS

CENOTAPH

CASA DEL CAFÉ
TABERNA DEL GALEÓN

BAR EL GLOBO

HOTEL SANTA ISABEL

CASA DE LA COMEDIA

HOSTAL EL COMENDADOR

CASTILLO DE LA REAL FUERZA

EL TEMPLETE

BIBLIOTECA PROVINCIAL DE LA HABANA

MUSEO NACIONAL DE HISTORIA NATURAL

CASERÓN DE TANGO

HOSTAL VALENCIA

Plaza de Armas

MONUMENTO CARLOS M. DE CÉSPEDES

MUSEO NUMISMÁTICO

MUSEO DE AUTOS ANTIGUO

LA GIRALDILLA

MUSEO Y TALLER DE CERÁMICA

PALACIO DEL SEGUNDO CABO

CAFÉ LA MINA/ RESTAURANTE CUBANO

RESTAURANTE AL MEDINA

CASA DEL ÁRABE

CASA DE LOS ABANICOS

CASA DE LA MINIATURA

CAFÉ/RESTAURANTE DON GIOVANNI

GABINETE DE LA ARQUEOLOGÍA

CASA DEL AGUA LA TINAJA

MUSEO DE PLATA

MUSEO DE ASIA

TIENDA DE LAS NAVIGANTES

TORRE DE MARFIL

CASA DE BENITO JUÁREZ

CASA DE LA OBRA PÍA

TACÓN

LA PAPELERÍA

HABANOS S.A. (HQ)

PALACIO DE LOS CAPITANES GENERALES

MUSEO DE LA CIUDAD DE LA HABANA

AMBROSERÍA

EMPEDRADO

Parque Luz Caballero

TELEPHONE

TAXIS

HORSE-DRAWN COACHES

CASA DE LOMBILLO

TRANSAUTO

POST OFFICE

DOMINICA

MERCADERES

UNIVERSITY OF HAVANA BELL

HOTEL AMBOS MUNDOS

MAQUETA DE CENTRO HISTÓRICO

MUSEUM OF TABACO/ CASA DEL TABACO

TACÓN

CORTINA DE VALDÉS

CASA DEL MARQUÉS DE ARCOS

MUSEO DE ARTE COLONIAL

MUSEO DE LA EDUCACIÓN

RESTAURANTE LA LUZ

PALADAR LA MONEDA CUBANA

MUSEO Y FARMACIA TAQUECHEL

SEMINARIO DE SAN CARLOS Y SAN AMBROSIO

CENTRO WILFREDO LAM

EL BODEGUITA DEL MEDIO

CATEDRAL DE LA HABANA

BAR/RESTAURANTE EL PATIO

Plaza de la Catedral

CASA DE LOS MARQUESES DE AGUAS CLARAS

CASA DE BAÑOS

CALLEJÓN DEL CHORRO

TALLER EXPERIMENTAL DE LA GRÁFICA

SAN IGNACIO

PANADERÍA SAN JOSÉ

CASA DE DULCE MARÍA

CAFÉ O'REILLY

SAN IGNACIO

CAFÉ PARÍS

EMPEDRADO

O'REILLY

MUSEO DE FINANZAS/ BANCO NACIONAL DE CUBA

OBISPO

CUBA

OBISPO

O'REILLY

OFICIOS

BARATILLO

ENNA

FRANCISCO LÓPEZ

INQUISID

MERCADERES

TACÓN

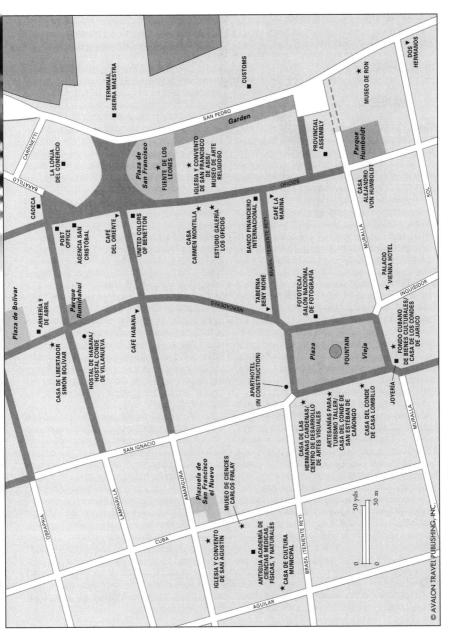

TERMINAL SIERRA MAESTRA

CUSTOMS

DOS HERMANOS

MUSEO DE RON

SAN PEDRO

Garden

PROVINCIAL ASSEMBLY

Parque Humboldt

CARPINETTI

LA LONJA DEL COMERCIO

Plaza de San Francisco

FUENTE DE LOS LEONES

IGLESIA Y CONVENTO DE SAN FRANCISCO DE ASÍS/ MUSEO DE ARTE RELIGIOSO

BARATILLO

CADECA

POST OFFICE

AGENCIA SAN CRISTÓBAL

CAFÉ DEL ORIENTE

UNITED COLORS OF BENETTON

CASA CARMEN MONTILLA

ESTUDIO GALERÍA LOS OFICIOS

BANCO FINANCIERO INTERNACIONAL

CAFÉ LA MARINA

OFICIOS

CASA ALEJANDRO VON HUMBOLDT

SOL

MURALLA

Plaza de Bolívar

ARMERÍA 9 DE ABRIL

Parque Rumiñahui

CASA DE LIBERTADOR SIMÓN BOLÍVAR

HOSTAL DE HABANA/ HOSTAL CONDE DE VILLANUEVA

CAFÉ HABANA

TABERNA BENY MORÉ

FOTOTECA/ SALÓN NACIONAL DE FOTOGRAFÍA

MERCADERES

BRASIL (TENIENTE REY)

PALACIO VIENNA HOTEL

INQUISIDOR

APARTHOTEL (IN CONSTRUCTION)

Plaza Vieja

FOUNTAIN

FONDO CUBANO DE BIENES CULTURALES/ CASA DE LOS CONDES DE JARUCO

JOYERÍA

MURALLA

SAN IGNACIO

CASA DE LAS HERMANAS CÁRDENAS/ CENTRO DE DESARROLLO DE ARTES VISUALES

ARTESANÍAS PARA TURISMO TALLER/ CASA DEL CONDE DE SAN ESTEBAN DE CAÑONGO

CASA DEL CONDE DE CASA LOMBILLO

AMARGURA

Plazuela de San Francisco el Nuevo

MUSEO DE CIENCIES CARLOS FINLAY

LAMPARILLA

CUBA

OBRAPHIA

IGLESIA Y CONVENTO DE SAN AGUSTÍN

ANTIGUA ACADEMIA DE CIENCIAS MEDICAS FÍSICAS, Y NATURALES

CASA DE CULTURA MUNICIPAL

BRASIL (TENIENTE REY)

AGUILAR

50 yds

50 m

0

0

© AVALON TRAVEL PUBLISHING, INC.

the Fine Arts Museum, was due to move here following a restoration. The **Teatro Martí** (dating from 1884), two blocks south of Parque Central, on Dragones at Agramonte, was likewise being restored.

PASEO DE MARTÍ (PRADO)

Paseo de Martí, colloquially known as the Prado, is a kilometer-long tree-lined boulevard that slopes northward downhill from Parque Central to the harbor mouth and Castillo de San Salvador de la Punta. The Prado is a smaller but no less courtly version of the Champs-Elysées and a splendid place to linger and watch Havana's life unfold.

The beautiful boulevard lay *extramura* (outside the old walled city of San Cristóbal de la Habana) and was initiated by the Marquis de la Torre in 1772 and completed in 1852. Until the end of the last century, it was Havana's most notable thoroughfare. The mansions of aristocratic families rose on each side, and it was a sign of distinction to live on Prado Promenade. In time the Prado lost its luster as the rich moved into exclusive new neighborhoods. During the "sordid era," the Prado and the area immediately west of it—the infamous Colón borough of Centro Habana—became famous for sleazy shows and gambling houses such as La Central, where President Prío held "his infamous nights of white women and tall showgirls."

Two bronze lions guard its upper, southern end. The Prado's central median is an elevated walkway. An ornate wall borders the path, with alcoves inset into each side containing marble benches carved with scroll motifs. At night it is lit by old brass gas lamps with big globes atop dark green wrought-iron lampposts in the shape of griffins. Schoolchildren sit beneath the shade trees, listening attentively to history or literature lessons presented alfresco. Midway down the Prado, between Calle Colón and Refugio, the laurel trees provide a shady gathering place for those seeking apartments or homes for swap or rent. Pinned to the trees and trestled notice boards are announcements for *Se Permuta* (For Exchange).

One block north, at Prado #207, between Colón and Trocadero, is the **Academía Gimnástico,** where budding homegrown Olga Korbuts train

for a potential Olympic career. Visitors are occasionally welcomed inside this converted old mansion to see pre-teens practicing on the ropes and vaulting horses surrounded by fluted columns and a baroque stucco ceiling. It was featured in the movie, *Buena Vista Social Club,* with Ruben González at the piano. It's open Mon.-Fri. 8:30 a.m.-5:30 p.m. and Saturday 8 a.m.-noon.

Up and down the Prado you'll see tiled mosaics reflecting the Moorish style that has influenced Havana's architecture through the centuries. Note, for example, the mosaic mural of a Nubian beauty on the upper wall of the **Centro Cultural de Árabe** (between Refugio and Trocadero), and the façade of the former Hotel Regis on the corner of Refugio, combining art nouveau and arabesque flourishes. The most stunning example, however, is the lobby of the **Hotel Sevilla** (at Calle Trocadero), which is like entering a Moroccan medina. It was inspired by the Patio of the Lions at the Alhambra in Granada, Spain. The Sevilla was the setting for the comical intrigues of Wormold in Graham Greene's *Our Man in Havana*. The hotel opened in 1908 with the novelty of telephones and private baths in every room. The gallery walls are festooned with black-and-white photos of famous figures who have stayed here, from singer Josephine Baker (who was refused at the Hotel Nacional because she was black) and boxer Joe Louis to Al Capone, who took the entire sixth floor for himself and his bodyguards (Capone occupied Room 615).

Another resplendent building worth a browse is the **Casa de los Científicos,** on the west side of the Prado at Trocadero, now a budget hostel that offers the benefit of superlative if albeit slightly chipped architectural surroundings. Also note the **Ciné Fausto,** a simple yet powerful rectangular modernist building with an ornament band on its upper façade harking back to art deco. At Prado #306 esq. Animas, is Habana Vieja's **Palacio de Matrimonia,** where wedding ceremonies are performed.

The bronze statue at the base of the Prado is that of Juan Clemente-Zenea, a patriotic poet shot for treason in 1871. Others who suffered at the hands of the Spanish colonialists are honored immediately to the right in the Martyr's Park and Park of the Lovers.

Parque de Mártires and
Parque de los Enamorados

The parkland at the base of the Prado occupies the ground of the former Tacón prison, built in 1838. Nationalist hero José Martí was imprisoned here in 1869-70 and never recovered from the hard labor he was forced to perform. The prison was demolished in 1939 and the park dedicated in memory of all those who suffered for their ideals. Preserved for posterity, however, were two of the punishment cells and the chapel used by condemned prisoners before being marched to the firing wall.

The park is divided in two by **Avenida de los Estudiantes,** with the Park of the Lovers to the south and Martyr's Park to the north. The most important monument here is the **Monumento de Estudiantes de Medicina,** a small Grecian-style temple shading the remains of a wall used by Spanish colonial firing squads. Here on 27 November 1871, eight medical students met their deaths after being falsely accused of desecrating the tomb of a prominent loyalist, Gonzalo Castañón. A trial found them innocent, but enraged loyalist troops—the Spanish Volunteers—held their own trial and shot the students. The monument stands at the juncture of the Prado and the Avenida del Puerto, facing the Castillo.

Castillo de San Salvador de la Punta

This small, low-slung fortress guards the entrance to Havana's harbor channel. It was initiated in 1589 directly across from Morro Castle so that the two fortresses might catch invaders in a crossfire. Between them a great chain was slung each night to secure Havana harbor in colonial days; you can still see the cannons embedded in the reefs and to which the chain was attached. Originally it stood upon an outcrop that jutted out into the harbor channel. Its site remains pivotal, and from the plaza overlooking the channel (a favorite spot for trysting lovers at night), you may revel in the sweeping vista westward along the Malecón toward the statuesque façade of Vedado. The fortress was in the final stages of restoration at press time, when a handsome park with benches and a statue of D'Iberville had been laid out to the east.

PARQUE DE LA FRATERNIDAD
AND VICINITY

This large tree-shaded square two hundreds meters south of Parque was laid out in 1892 on an old military drill square, the Campo de Marte, to commemorate the fourth centennial of Columbus' discovery of America. In olden times a bullring also stood here, and the plaza was a setting for the city's festivities. By the mid-1850s it was the site of the city's railway station, terminating the railway that ran along today's Zanja and Dragones. The current layout dates to 1928 with a redesign to celebrate the sixth Pan-American Conference, held in Havana that year. The streets around the park are a major start and drop-off point for urban buses and for peso taxis, which congregate in vast numbers, forming a veritable auto museum of 1950s Americana.

The most important site is the **Árbol de la Fraternidad Americana**—the Friendship Tree— planted at its center in 1928 to cement goodwill between the nations of the Americas. Each delegate to the conference brought soil from his or her home country. Busts of outstanding American leaders such as Simón Bolívar look out over the comings and goings, including a **statue to Abraham Lincoln.**

Another monument of interest is the **Fuente de la India Noble Habana,** in the middle of the Prado. The fountain, erected in 1837, is surmounted by a Carrara marble statue of *La Noble Havana,* the legendary Indian queen, coyly clad in fringed drapes, a feather headdress, and palm leaves. In one hand she bears a cornucopia, in the other a shield with the arms of Havana. Four great fish lie at her feet and spout water when the tap is turned on.

The **Palacio de Aldama,** on the park's far southwest corner at Amistad y Avenida de Bolívar, was built in neoclassical style in 1844 for a wealthy Basque, Don Domingo Aldama y Arrechaga, with a façade lined by Ionic columns and an interior of colored marbles and murals of scenes from Pompeii. Duly restored, it houses the **Instituto de Historia del Movimiento Comunista y de la Revolución Socialista de Cuba** (Institute of the History of the Communist

Movement and the Socialist Revolution), tel. (7) 62-2076. Hardcore lefties might get a thrill.

Capitolio

This building, on the north side of Parque de la Fraternidad and one block south of Parque Central, dominates Havana's skyline. It was built between 1926 and 1929 as Cuba's Chamber of Representatives and Senate and was obsequiously designed after Washington's own Congress building, reflecting the United States' expanding influence in the early 1900s. The 692-foot-long edifice is supported by flanking colonnades of Doric columns, with semicircular pavilions to each end of the building. The lofty stone cupola rises 61.75 meters and is topped by a replica of 16th-century Florentine sculptor Giambologna's famous bronze Mercury in the Palazzo de Bargello.

A massive stairway—flanked by neoclassical figures in bronze representing Labor and Virtue—leads steeply up to a 40-meter-wide entrance portico with three tall bronze doors sculpted with 30 bas-reliefs that depict important events of Cuban history up to the Capitolio's inauguration in 1929. (You can have your photo taken at the base of the stairs by any of several official photographers whose antique cameras sit atop wooden tripods.)

The pristine, recently restored building is constructed of local Capellania limestone, hinting at the overwhelming opulence and beauty within. The stunning Great Hall of the Lost Steps is almost entirely of marble, with bronze bas-reliefs all around and massive lamps on tall carved pedestals of glittering copper. Facing the door is a massive bronze statue—**Statue of the Republic**—of Cuba's voluptuous Indian maiden resembling Liberty and representing the Cuban Republic. At 17.54 meters tall, she is the world's third-largest indoor statue and weighs 49 tons. In the center of the floor is a 24-carat diamond that marks km 0—the starting point from Havana for the country's highways. The diamond, alas, is a replica (rumor has it that the original is kept securely in Fidel's office). Above your head is the dome and gilt-covered barrel-vaulted ceiling carved in refulgent relief.

Two long lateral galleries lead from this entrance vestibule. The semi-circular Senate chamber and the former Chamber of Representatives at each end are quite stunning.

It's open Mon.-Sat. 9 a.m.-5 p.m. Entrance is US$3. A breeze-swept veranda café serves sandwiches and refreshments and offers grand views down over the Prado.

In 1960 the Capitolio became the headquarters of the **Academy of Sciences.** The library—the **Biblioteca Nacional de Ciencias y Naturales**—is still here (open Mon.-Sat. 8 a.m.-5 p.m.), on the ground floor on the south side of the Capitolio; but the science and natural history museums recently moved to Plaza de Armas.

Fábrica de Tabaco Partagas

Be sure to visit the Partagas Cigar Factory (officially named Fábrica Francisco Pérez Germán), behind the Capitolio at Industria #502, tel. (7) 33-8060, and where you can see Cuba's premium cigars being hand rolled for export. The fabulous exterior is capped by a roofline of baroque curves topped by lions and bearing the words in large block letters, "1845 PARTAGAS REAL FÁBRICA DE TABACOS," proudly testifying that it has been making cigars for more than 150 years.

The factory, built in 1845, specializes in full-bodied cigars such as the spicy, strongly aromatic La Gloria Cubana, Ramón Allones, the Montecristo, and, of course, the Partagas, one of the oldest of the Havana brands, started in 1843 by Don Jaime Partagas. Partagas turns out five million cigars a year, among them no fewer than 40 types of Partagas brand (many are machine-made and of inferior quality). The factory's showroom displays a cigar measuring 50 inches.

The humidor to the right of the entrance serves as an information booth and sales room, and cigar aficionados might pop into the "secret" air-conditioned lounge, replete with plump leather lounge chairs, TV, coffee bar, and its own humidor.

Guided tours are offered daily at 10 a.m. and 2 p.m. (US$10).

CALLE AGRAMONTE (ZULUETA)

Calle Agramonte, more commonly referred to by its colonial name of Zulueta, slopes gently from the northeast side of Parque Central to the Monumento al General Máximo Gómez and the harbor channel. Agramonte parallels the Prado. Traffic runs one-way uphill.

One block north of Parque Central, at the corner of Agramonte and Animas, a mosaic on the paving (on the west side of the street) announces your arrival at **Sloppy Joe's,** "a high-ceilinged, bottle-encrusted, tile-floored oasis" formerly known as La Victoria. The bar became an institution among partying tourists during Prohibition after an inebriated journalist sought a $50 loan, was rebuffed by the owner, and wrote a vengeful editorial accusing the saloon owner of running an unsanitary place, claiming it should be called "Sloppy Joe's." There's no such thing as bad publicity, and the crafty owner changed the name. Dedicated drinkers flocked and continued to do so through the decades. In spring 2000 the near-derelict building was still shuttered, its interior a dusty shambles awaiting the restoration now sweeping Habana Vieja. It is slated to be restored as a bar and (possibly) a hotel.

Across the way is the diminutive **Museo de Bomberos,** in the old Cuartel de Bomberos fire station. The museum exhibits turn-of-the-century firefighters' uniforms plus three vintage fire engines, including a 1901 horse-drawn machine made by Shand, Mason & Co., London. (In 1999 the museum moved from its former location at Calle Oficios and Lamparilla, where it was housed on the site of the worst day in Havana's fire fighting history and the cause of the largest funeral of the 19th century. On 17 May 1890 a devastating fire broke out in that building and 28 firefighters and numerous bystanders were killed when an enormous explosion took place; the owner had defied a ban on storing explosives within the ancient city, but had failed to notify the fire department. A mausoleum to the firefighters can be seen in Cementerio Colón, in Vedado.)

The **Museo Nacional de Bellas Artes,** the National Museum of Art (Cuba's most important art museum), is housed in the Palacio de Bellas Artes, on Trocadero between Zulueta and Monserrate, tel. (7) 63-9042 or 61-2332. The museum contains a fabulous collection of Cuban paintings (on the second floor), plus European collections (ground floor) that include works by Goya, Murillo, Rubens, and Velázquez, as well as the works of impressionists. English painters such as Reynolds, Gainsborough, and Turner are represented. It also boasts Latin America's richest trove of classical antiquities including Roman, Greek, and Egyptian statuary and artworks. Rotating exhibits display the works of Cuba's leading contemporary artists. A three-year reorganization of the museum is planned, and at press time the works had been dispersed. It was previously open Tues.-Sun. 9 a.m.-5 p.m. (US$2).

Fifty meters north of the museum is the three-story green façade of the **Fábrica de Tabaco La Corona,** dating from 1888, when this cigar factory, at Agramonte #106 e/ Refugio y Colón, tel./fax (7) 62-6173, was built by the American Tobacco Company. Today it is officially called the Miguel Fernández Roig, but colloquially La Corona. It's a favorite on the tourist circuit and provides a splendid exposé on the intricacies of cigar manufacture, as well as a heady experience thanks to the cigar aromas. Odalys Lara, a well-known Cuban TV presenter, acts as reader. Imagine having Barbara Walters or Thora Hurd read to you while you work! It's open to the public Mon.-Sat. 7 a.m.-5 p.m.

Fronting the former Presidential Palace (see below), on Refugio, is a **SAU-100 Stalin tank,** illuminated at night on its lofty pedestal. It was supposedly commanded by Fidel Castro at the Bay of Pigs. To the north is a wide-open park, **Plaza 13 de Mayo,** leading down to a Calle Carcél and, beyond, the General Máximo Gómez monument (see below). The ornate building at the base of Agramonte, on the west side of Carcél, is the **Spanish Embassy,** housed in the one of the most flamboyant of Havana's structures in art nouveau style.

Palacio Presidencial

This ornate palace, at Refugio, e/ Agramonte y Monserrate, was initiated in 1913 to house the provincial government. Before it could be finished, it was earmarked as the Presidential Palace, and Tiffany's of New York was entrusted with its interior decoration. It was from here that a string of corrupt presidents, ending with Fulgencio Batista, spun their webs of dissolution.

Following the Revolution, the three-story palace was converted into the **Museo de la Revolución,** tel. (7) 62-4092; open Tues. 10 a.m.-6 p.m. and Wed.-Sun 10 a.m.-5 p.m.; entrance US$3 (cameras US$5 extra). The marble staircase in the foyer leads upstairs to a massive

THE INSIDE STORY ON CIGARS

*Y*ou'll forever remember the pungent aroma of a cigar factory, a visit to which is de rigueur. The factories, housed in fine old colonial buildings, remain much as they were in the mid-19th century. Though now officially known by ideologically sound names, they're still commonly referred to by their prerevolutionary names, which are displayed on old signs outside. Each specializes in a number of cigar brands of a particular flavor (the government assigns to certain factories the job of producing particular brands. And revolutionary slogans exhort workers to maintain strict quality—"Quality is respect for people."

To learn more, refer to Nancy Stout's *Habanos,* a splendid coffee-table book on the subject (Rozzoli, New York, 1997).

From Leaf to Cigar
The tobacco leaves, which arrive from the fields in dry sheets, are first moistened and stripped. The halves

a cigar factory in Havana, circa 1900

are then graded by color and strength (each type of cigar has a recipe). A blender mixes the various grades of leaves, which then go to the production room where each *tabaquero* and *tabaquera* receives enough tobacco to roll approximately 100 cigars for the day.

The rollers work in large rooms, where they sit at rows of workbenches—*galeras*—resembling old-fashioned school desks. Two workers sit at each desk, with piles of loose tobacco leaves at their sides. The rollers take great pride in their work, and it's a treat to marvel at their manual artistry and dexterity. The rollers' indispensable tool is a *chaveta,* a rounded, all-purpose knife for smoothing and cutting leaves, tamping loose tobacco, "circumcising the tips," and sometimes banging a welcome to factory visitors on their desks in rhythmic chorus like a percussion orchestra. Most workers are born to their tasks, following in the footsteps of other family members, carrying on their traditional skills from one generation to the next.

While they work, a *lector* (reader) reads aloud from a strategically positioned platform or high chair. Morning excerpts—beginning promptly at 8 a.m.—are read from the *Granma* newspaper; in the afternoon, the *lector* reads from historical or political books or short stories and novels (Alexander Dumas, Agatha Christie, and Ernest Hemingway are favorites; Dumas' novel *The Count of Monte Cristo* was such a hit in the 19th century that it lent its name to the famous Montecristo cigar). The practice dates back to 1864, when the unique institution was set up to alleviate boredom and help the cause of worker education. *Lectores* are auditioned and hired on their reading ability and the tradition has for over a century carried great political weight, while serving to produce astutely versed workers. Says city architect Mario Coyula: "In Cuba before the Revolution, men who were completely illiterate knew the classics, the plays of Shakespeare, and most modern novels. And even though they could not read or write, they were well versed in current political issues."

Rolling the Cigar
The cigar roller—*torcedore*—fingers his or her leaves and, according to texture and color, chooses two to four filler leaves, which are laid end to end and gently yet firmly rolled into a tube and then enveloped by the binder leaves to make a "bunch."

The rough-looking "bunch" is then placed with nine others in a small wooden mold that is screwed down to press each cigar into a solid cylinder. Next, the *tabaquero* selects a wrapper leaf, which he or she trims to size. The "bunch" is then laid at an angle across the wrapper, which is stretched and rolled around the "bunch," overlapping with each turn. A tiny quantity of flavorless tragapanth gum (made from Swiss pine trees) is used to glue the *copa* down. Now the *tabaquero* rolls the cigar, applying pressure with the flat of the *chaveta.* Finally, a piece of wrapper leaf the size and shape of a quarter is cut to form the cap; it is glued and twirled into place, and the excess is trimmed.

The whole process takes about five minutes. A good cigar maker can roll about 100 medium-sized cigars a day (the average for the largest cigars is far less).

Cigar rollers serve a nine-month apprenticeship (each factory has its own school). Many fail. Those who succeed graduate slowly from making petit corona cigars to the larger and specialized sizes. Rollers are paid piece rates based on the number of cigars they produce. They receive on average 350-400 pesos for a six-day workweek. In addition, they can puff as much as they wish on the fruits of their labor while working.

Today the majority of rollers are women. Prior to the Revolution, only men rolled cigars; the leaves were selected by women, who often sorted them on their thighs, giving rise to the famous myth about cigars being "rolled on the dusky thighs of Cuban maidens."

Cigars Go to Market

The roller ties cigars of the same size and brand into bundles—*media ruedas* (half-wheels)—of 50 using a colored ribbon. These are then fumigated in a vacuum chamber. Quality is determined by a *revisador* according to eight criteria such as length, weight, firmness, smoothness of wrappers, and whether the ends are cleanly cut. *Catadores,* professional smokers, then blind test the cigars for aroma, draw, and burn, the relative importance of each varying according to whether the cigar is a slim panatela (draw is paramount) or a fat robusto (flavor being more important). The *catadores* taste only in the morning and rejuvenate their taste buds with sugarless tea.

Once fumigated, cigars are placed in cool cabinets for three weeks to settle fermentation and remove any excess moisture. The cigars are then graded according to color and then shade within a particular color category.

A trademark paper band is put on by an *anillado.* (A Dutchman, Gustave Bock, introduced the band to distinguish his cigars from other Havanas last century. Later, bands served to prevent gentlemen smokers from staining their white evening gloves.) Finally, the cigars are laid in pinewood boxes with the lightest cigar on the right and the darkest on the left (cigars range from the very mild, greenish-brown *double claro* to the very strong, almost black *oscuro.*) The boxes are inspected for alignment and uniformity. A thin leaf of cedar wood is laid on top to maintain freshness, and the box is sealed with a green-and-white label guaranteeing the cigars are genuine Havanas, or *puros Habanos* (today *puro* is a synonym for cigar).

VISITING HAVANA'S CIGAR FACTORIES

The five major cigar factories in Havana (there are others) all now welcome visitors. Unfortunately, the tours are not well organized and often crowded with tour groups, few of whom have any appreciation for cigars. Explanations of tobacco processes and manufacturing procedures are also sparse. Tours usually bypass the tobacco preparations, alas, and begin in the rolling rooms, or *galeras,* and pass to the quality-control methods. Visitors therefore miss out on seeing the stripping, selecting, and dozens of other processes that contribute to producing a handmade cigar.

Although the government has considered banning tours (it did so briefly in 1997 at the Partagas and La Corona factories), the income comes in handy and includes a portion given to the factories and used to improve workers' conditions.

You can book through tour desks in major hotels or call the factories direct. Be sure to book ahead, for every entrance is guarded by an ever-present, stern-faced female concierge determined to stop you from entering. Says Nancy Stout: "These women are tougher than the civil guard nearby, in his green khakis with a tie-on red armband and pistol around his waist."

Habanos S.A. has its headquarters at **Empresa Cubana del Tabaco,** 104 O'Reilly e/ Tacón y Mercaderes, Habana Vieja, tel. (7) 62-5463; open 7:45 a.m.-3:45 p.m.

(continues on next page)

THE INSIDE STORY ON CIGARS
(continued)

Fábrica La Corona, Calle Agramonte #106 e/ Refugio y Colón, Habana Vieja, tel./fax (7) 62-6173, is open to the public Mon.-Sat. 7 a.m.-5 p.m.

Fábrica Partagas, Calle Industria #520 e/ Dragones y Barcelona, Habana Vieja, tel. (7) 62-4604, offers guided tours daily at 10 a.m. and 2 p.m. (US$10).

Fábrica H. Upmann, one block west of Partagas, at Calle Amistad #407 e/ Dragones y Barcelona, Centro Habana, tel. (7) 62-0081, is open Mon.-Fri. 8 a.m.-4 p.m. for drop-in visitors. Tours are offered at 10:30 a.m. and 1:30 p.m. (US$10)

Fábrica Romeo y Julieta, on Padre Varela e/ Desague y Peñal Verno, Centro Habana, tel. (7) 78-1058, is open for visits by permission only, Mon.-Fri. 7 a.m.-4 p.m. Permission must be requested from the Empresa Cubana del Tabaco, O'Reilly #104 e/ Tacón y Mercaderes, Habana Vieja, tel. (7) 62-5463.

Fábrica El Laguito, at Calle 146 #2302, Cubanacán, tel. (7) 21-2213. Visits by permits only. Permission must be requested from the Empresa Cubana del Tabaco (see above).

Organized Tours
Cuban Adventures, 4823 White Rock Circle, Suite H, Boulder, CO 80301-3260, tel. (303) 530-9275, fax (303) 530-9275, e-mail: CopaBob@aol.com, website: www.clubhavana.com, operates cigar tours to Cuba, including tours of the legendary cigar factories. Likewise, **Wings of the World Travel,** 1200 William St. #706, Buffalo, NY 14240-0706; or 1636 Third Ave. #232, New York, NY 10128, tel. (800) 465-8687, fax (416) 486-4001, offers a Cuban Cigar Adventure.

In the U.K., Peter Lloyd, a Havana cigar merchant, 25 Terrace Rd., Aberystwyth SY23 1NP, Wales, tel. (01970) 612254, e-mail: A_E_LLOYD@compuserve.com, website: www.cubawe1.com and **Captivating Cuba** collaboratively offer cigar tours (the trips are fully hosted in Cuba, so U.S. citizens can legally join; from US$980).

The Moncada Room displays the bloodstained uniforms of the rebels who attacked the Moncada barracks in Santiago in 1953. Another section is dedicated to the revolutionaries who lost their lives in an assault on the palace on 13 March 1957 (Batista escaped through a secret door to a secure apartment reachable only by a private elevator, frustrating an action that turned into a bloody debacle). Che Guevara is there in the form of a lifelike statue, sweating, rifle in hand, working his way heroically through the jungle. Notice Ronald Reagan satirized in Western sheriff's outfit alongside other notable adversaries of the Cuban state in the museum's "Corner of Cretins."

At the rear, in the former palace gardens, is the **Granma Memorial,** preserving the vessel that brought Fidel Castro, Che Guevara, and other revolutionaries from Mexico to Cuba in 1956. The *Granma,* a surprisingly muscular launch that embodies the powerful, unstoppable spirit of the revolutionary movement, is encased in an impressive glass structure—a simulated sea—with a roof held aloft by great concrete columns, rather like Lenin's tomb. It is surrounded by vehicles used in the revolutionary war: strange armored vehicles, the bullet-riddled "Fast Delivery" truck used in the student commando's assault on the Presidential Palace in 1957, and Fidel's green Land Rover with *Comandancia General Sierra Maestra* stenciled in red on the door. There's also a turbine from the U-2 spy plane downed during the missile crisis in 1962, a naval Sea Fury, and a T-34 tank supposedly used by Castro himself against the counter-revolutionaries at the Bay of Pigs.

You can take photos of the exhibits from the street, but to get closer to the *Granma* you must enter the museum through the main entrance.

---

lobby with a fabulous muraled ceiling and, beyond, vast salons, notably the Salón de los Espejos (the Mirror Room), a replica of that in Versailles, and the Salón Dorado (the Gold Room) decorated with yellow marble. The building contains fine works of art.

Rooms are divided chronologically, from the colonial period to the modern day. It is necessary to follow the route room by room through the mazelike corridors. Detailed maps describe the battles and progress of the revolutionary war. Hundreds of guns and rifles are displayed alongside grisly photos of dead and tortured heroes.

Monumento al General Máximo Gómez

This massive monument of white marble supported by classical columns dominates the waterfront at the base of Agramonte. The monument, erected in 1935, honors the Dominican-born hero of the Cuban wars of independence who led the Liberation Army as commander-in-chief. Although a foreigner, Gómez (1836-1905) dedicated himself to the cause of Cuban independence and displayed Napoleonic brilliance in his tactics. Generalissimo Gómez is cast in bronze, bare headed and head aloft, shown reining in his horse. It was designed and made by the sculptor Aldo Gamba and at its base has three reliefs depicting the Fatherland, the People, and Freedom.

The access road to the Havana harbor tunnel that leads to Parque Morro—Cabaña (and also to Playas del Este, Matanzas, and Varadero) curls and nosedives beneath the monument.

Monumento al General Máximo Gómez

CALLE MONSERRATE

Calle Monserrate—Avenida de Bélgica—parallels Agramonte one block to the east (if driving, Monserrate is one-way downhill), and follows the space left by the ancient city walls after they were demolished last century. A semi-derelict watchtower—**Baluarte de Ángel**—erected in 1680 still stands in front of the Presidential Palace at Refugio and Monserrate as a lone reminder of the fortified wall that once surrounded Habana Vieja.

At the base of Monserrate, at its junction with Calle Tacón, is the **Museo de la Música,** tel. (7) 61-9846 and 63-0052, housed in the sober Casa de Pérez de la Riva, built in Italian Renaissance style in 1905 and which briefly served as a jail. The museum traces the evolution of Cuban music since early colonial days; many antique instruments are displayed, including a beautiful collection of venerable pianos and the huge collection of drums once owned by Fernando Ortíz, a renowned Africanist. There is even a separate room where you can listen to old scores drawn from the record library. Concerts are also hosted. Open Mon.-Sat. 9 a.m.-4:45 p.m. Entrance is US$2.

Immediately east of the Presidential Palace is the **Iglesia del Santa Ángel Custodio** sitting atop a rock known as Angel Hill. There's a virginal purity to this shimmering white church with a splendid exterior. Actually, the lavishly Gothic façade is the rear of the church. The church was founded in 1687 by builder-bishop Diego de Compostela. The tower dates from 1846 when a hurricane toppled the original, while the façade was reworked in neo-Gothic style in the mid-19th century. It's immaculate yet simple within. Gray marble floor. Modest wooden Gothic altar. Statues of saints all around. Pristine stained-glass windows. Splendid! Cuba's national hero, José Martí, was baptized here on 12 February 1853. The church has appeared in several movies and was the setting for the tragic marriage scene that ends in the violent denouement on the steps of the church in the 19th-century novel *Cecilia Valdés,* by the nationalist Cirilo Villaverde. A bust of the author stands in the *plazuela* outside the church entrance on the corner of Calles Compostela y Cuarteles, on the east side.

It's worth continuing along Cuarteles one block to a junction known as **Las Cinco Cuarteles de El Ángel,** (Five Corners of the Angel), where you can admire an agglomeration of ancient houses, some with beams of round trunks that attest to their age.

Monserrate continues south three blocks to **Plazuela de Supervielle,** commemorating Dr. Manuel Fernández Supervielle, mayor of Havana during the 1940s and whose principal election promise—to resolve the city's on-going water supply problem—went unfulfilled (the allocated money ended up in private pockets), causing him to commit suicide. The plazuela is shadowed on its north side by the uniquely inspired **Edificio Bacardi,** former headquarters of the Bacardi rum empire. Finished in December 1929, this magnificent art deco edifice is clad in Swedish granite and local limestone. Terra-cotta of varying hues accents the design, with motifs showing Grecian nymphs and floral patterns. It is crowned by a Lego-like bell tower topped in turn by a wrought-iron, brass-winged gargoyle that is the famous Bacardi motif. The building is difficult to appreciate at street level: to better admire it, nip inside the Hotel Plaza, where it is best seen from the *azotea*— the rooftop plaza. The Edificio Bacardi, surely one of the world's finest art deco inspirations, was receiving a much-needed restoration at press time.

Plazuela de Albear, a tiny plaza on Monserrate one block east of Parque Central at the west end of Calle Obispo, is hallowed ground. Not because of the bust to Francisco de Albear, who engineered the Malecón and Havana's first water drainage system last century (still in use). Rather, here—on the southwest corner—is El Floridita.

El Floridita

This famous restaurant and bar has been serving food at this location since 1819, when it was called Pina de Plata. Its name was later changed to La Florida, and then, more affectionately, El Floridita. This bar is haunted by Ernest Hemingway's ghost. The novelist's seat at the dark mahogany bar is preserved as a shrine. His bronze bust watches over things from its pedestal beside the bar, where Constante Ribailagua once served frozen daiquiris to Hemingway (he immortalized both the drink and the

THE DAIQUIRI

*T*he daiquiri is named for a Cuban hamlet 16 miles east of Santiago de Cuba, near a copper mine where the mining firm's chief engineer, Jennings S. Cox, first created the now world-famous cocktail that Hemingway immortalized in his novels. Cox had arrived in 1898, shortly after the Spanish-American War, to find workers at the mines anxious about putatively malarial drinking water. Cox added a heartening tot of local Bacardi rum to boiled water, then decided to give his mixture added snap and smoothness by introducing lime juice and sugar.

The concoction was soon duplicated, and within no time had moved on to conquer every highlife watering hole in Havana. It is still most notably associated with El Floridita, and Hemingway's immortal words: *"Mi mojito en La Bodeguita, mi daiquiri en El Floridita."*

Shaved—frappéd—ice, which gave the drink its final touch of enchantment, was added by Constante Ribailagua, El Floridita's bartender, in the 1920s. The frozen daiquiris, "the great ones that Constante made," wrote Hemingway, "had no taste of alcohol and felt, as you drank them, the way downhill glacier skiing feels running through powder snow and, after the sixth and eighth, felt like downhill glacier skiing feels when you are running unroped."

A daiquiri should include all of Cox's original ingredients (minus the water, of course). It may be shaken and strained, or frappéd to a loose sherbet in a blender and served in a cocktail glass or poured over the rocks in an old-fashioned glass. The "Papa Special" that Constante made for Hemingway contained a double dose of rum, no sugar, and a half-ounce of grapefruit juice.

The Perfect Daiquiri

In an electric blender, pour half a tablespoon of sugar, the juice of half a lemon, 1.5 ounces of white rum. Serve semi-frozen blended with ice (or on the rocks) in a tall martini glass with a maraschino cherry.

venue in his novel *Islands in the Stream*) and such illustrious guests as Gary Cooper, Tennessee Williams, Marlene Dietrich, and Jean-Paul Sartre. (Rum authority Francisco Campoamor's book, *The Happy Child of Sugar Cane,* tells the tale of El Floridita.)

El Floridita was recently spruced up for tourist consumption with a 1930s art-deco polish. Waiters hover in tux jackets and bow ties. You expect a spotlight to come on and Desi Arnaz to appear conducting a dance band, and Papa to stroll in as he would every morning when he lived in Havana and drank with Honest Lil, the Worst Politician, and other real-life characters from his novels. They've overpriced the place. But, what the hell—sipping a daiquiri at El Floridita is a must.

CALLE TACÓN AND THE HARBOR CHANNEL

Throughout most of the colonial era, sea waves washed upon the beach that lined the southern shore of the harbor channel and was known as the Playa de las Tortugas for the marine turtles that came ashore to lay eggs. The beach lined what is today **Calle Tacón,** which runs along the site of the old city walls forming the original waterfront. In the early 19th century, the area was extended with landfill, and a broad boulevard—**Avenida Manuel de Céspedes** (Avenida del Puerto)—was laid out along the new harborfront, with a wide, shady park separating it from Calle Tacón. To the west is **Parque Anfiteatro,** with an open-air theater in Greek fashion and a *parque diversiones* (children's fairground); to the east is **Parque Luz Caballero,** pinned by a statue of José de la Luz Caballero, "teacher of Cuban youth, 1800-62."

At the western end of Tacón, at the foot of Calle Cuarteles, is the **Palacio de Artesanía** housed in a magnificent mansion—originally the Palacio Pedroso—built in Moorish style for a nobleman, Don Mateo Pedroso, around 1780. Pedroso's home—a profusion of patterned tiles and foliate door arches—was a center for Havana's social life well into the 19th century. Today, duly restored, it houses craft shops and a bar where you can soak up live music and soothing rum while enjoying a pronounced whiff of the *Arabian Nights.* Folkloric and other entertainment is offered by night and on weekends (see the Entertainment section).

Amazingly, no maps make any mention of the splendid little medieval-style fortress—**El Castillo de Atane**—a stone's throw east, at the foot of Chacón. This is because the *fortaleza* today houses a police headquarters, as it has since it was built in 1941 for the former Havana Police Department. Yes, it is only a pseudo-colonial confection.

Fronting the "castle," in the middle of Tacón, is a watchtower—a rare remnant of the original city wall. Waves once beat against this sentry box, now landlocked since construction of the Avenida del Puerto. During the English attack on Havana in 1762, this section of wall bore the brunt of the British assault on the city, fired on from the heights of El Morro and La Cabaña after those fortresses had been conquered.

The jewel in the crown of Tacón is the **Seminario de San Carlos y San Ambrosio** a massive seminary, due east of El Castillo de Atane, between Chacón and Empedrado, established by the Jesuits in 1721 and ever since a center for young men studying for an ecclesiastical career. The seminary was built in an irregular polygon during the second half of the 18th century with a three-story gallery in varying styles, and features a massive banister of caoba wood with elaborate carvings. Its dramatic baroque façade —which amazingly dates from the 1950s when its remodeled in neo-baroque style in the style of the Havana cathedral—can be admired, but the serenity of the inner courtyard, alas, is off-limits to public viewing.

A large artisans' market takes up the length of Tacón directly in front of the seminary, where an excavated site shows the foundations of the original seafront section of the city walls—here called the **Cortina de Valdés**—against which the sea once lapped, no more than 10 yards from the seminary.

Tacón ends at a tiny *plazuela* at the foot of Empedrado, where a bevy of colorful old fishing boats that could have fallen from a painting by Hockney sit on the cobbled curbside in front of the **Casa de la Miniatura,** a former mansion that now sells exquisite miniature soldiers and pirates, although the range (once vast) is now motley. Horse-drawn open-air cabs called *calezas* gather here, offering guided tours to tourists (see Getting Around in the Transportation section).

Around the corner to the south, on a narrow extension of Tacón that leads to Plaza de Armas, another restored mansion now houses **Bar y**

RESTORING OLD HAVANA

Old Havana has been called the "finest urban ensemble in the Americas." The fortress colonial town that burst its walls when Washington, D.C., was still a swamp is a 350-acre repository of antique buildings. More than 900 of Habana Vieja's 3,157 structures are of historic importance. Of these, only 101 were built in the 20th century. Almost 500 are from the 19th; 200 are from the 18th; and 144 are from the 16th and 17th. But only one in six buildings is in good condition. Many are crumbling into ruins around the people who occupy them.

In 1977 the Cuban government named Habana Vieja a national monument. The following year it formalized a plan to rescue the city from centuries of neglect under the guidance of Eusebio Leal Spengler, the charismatic city historian, thanks to whose efforts Havana was proclaimed a UNESCO World Heritage Site in 1982. The ambitious plan stretches beyond the year 2000 and concentrates on the five squares, Plaza de Armas, Plaza de la Catedral, Plaza Vieja, Plaza de San Francisco, and Plaza del Cristo. The most important buildings have received major renovations; others are being given facelifts—symbols of triumph over horrendous shortages of materials and money. Today the heart of Habana Vieja gleams magnificently once again, as if new.

To satisfy a mix of needs, structures are ranked into one of four levels according to historical and physical value. The top level is reserved for museums; the second level for hotels, restaurants, offices, and schools; and the bottom levels for housing. Priority is given to edifices with income-generating tourist value, usually the oldest buildings, many of them stupendous art nouveau structures quietly sinking into ruin (Havana contains as many splendid art deco buildings as Miami—perhaps more—plus countless art nouveau houses)

A government-run company, **Habaguanex,** Calle Oficios #110, on Plaza de San Francisco, tel. (7) 33-8693, fax (7) 33-8697, website: habaguanex. cubaweb.cu/habaguanex.html, has responsibility for restoring and opening hotels, restaurants, cafés, shops, etc., in Habana Vieja. Leal selects sites for renovation, supervises the construction teams, and chooses the hotels and restaurants that will occupy the restored buildings. Habaguanex caters primarily to the tourist trade. The profits (US$70 million, 1993-98) help finance infrastructural improvements throughout Habana Vieja and elsewhere in the city, with 33% of revenues devoted to social projects. It's an awesome task. In southern Habana Vieja, where there are relatively few structures of touristic interest, far more houses are collapsing than are being restored. The inflow of tourist dollars is but a trickle in a desert of need.

Florida-based Cuban-Americans, including architects and art historians, have formed **Asociación del Patrimonio Nacional Cubano** (Cuban National Heritage), 1625 Colony Ave., Kissimmee, FL 34744, tel. (407) 847-7892, fax (407) 847-2986, e-mail: sales@fbj.com (type "Heritage" in the subject line), website: www.fbj.com/heritage, as a trust-in-exile to protect Cuba's art and architectural heritage, including from powerful southern Florida developers who are hungrily eyeing the island and are likely to bulldoze historic areas.

Restaurante D'Giovanni, with a fabulous inner courtyard graced by three tiers of balustraded balconies (note the stunning mural in the entranceway). Also worth a visit is the building next door, **Gabinete de la Arqueología,** the Archaeological Department of the Office of the City Historian, at Calle Tacón 12, tel. (7) 61-4469. Remarkably, the beautiful mansion (first mentioned in documents in 1644) was inherited in 1700 by a mulatta whose owner, Doña Lorenza de Carvajal, had granted her freedom (Doña Lorenza's own daughter had brought disgrace upon herself by becoming pregnant and was shuttled off to a convent). The mansion's most remarkable feature is a series of eccentric murals depicting life in bold Technicolor as it was lived in Havana centuries ago (the murals, painted between 1763 and 1767, were revealed during a recent restoration from beneath 26 layers of paint and whitewash). It's open Tue.-Sat. 10 a.m.-5 p.m., and Sunday 9 a.m.-1 p.m.

PLAZA DE LA CATEDRAL

You'll find yourself returning again and again to this exquisite cobbled square dominated by the intimate but imposing and decadently baroque 18th-century "Columbus Cathedral"—and, on the other three sides, aristocratic *palacios,* the

Casa de Lombillo, Casa del Marqués de Arcos, Casa del Conde de Bayona, and Casa de Marqués de Aguas Claras.

This was the last (and finest) square to be laid out in Habana Vieja, for it occupied a lowly quarter where rainwater drained (it was originally known as the Plazuela de la Cienaga—Little Square of the Swamp). Its present texture dates from the 18th century, before which it served as a fish market and cattle watering station. A cistern was built here in 1587, and only in the following century was the area drained for construction.

The square is Habana Vieja at its most quintessential, the atmosphere enhanced by mulattas in traditional costume who will happily preen and pose for your camera for a small fee. Be sure to visit by night also, when the setting is enhanced by the soft glow of wan lanterns and the plaza is moody and dreamy. One night per month the plaza is venue for **Noches en la Plaza de la Catedral,** when tables are laid out in the square, dinner is served, and you get to witness a folkloric *espectáculo* with a stunning backdrop (see Entertainment section for details).

Catedral de la Habana
This splendid edifice is the maximum exemplar of Cuban baroque. Known colloquially as Catedral Colón and Catedral de San Cristóbal, it has an official name—Catedral de la Virgen María de la Concepción Inmaculada (her statue is installed in the High Altar), tel. (7) 61-7771. The cathedral was initiated by the Jesuits in 1748. The order was kicked out of Cuba by Carlos III in 1767, but the building was eventually completed in 1777 and altered again in the early 19th century by Bishop José Díaz de Espada, who found many of the elements not to his liking. Thus, the original baroque interior is gone, replaced in 1814 by a new classical interior.

Describing the cathedral's baroque façade, adorned with clinging columns and rippled like a great swelling sea, Cuban novelist Alejo Carpentier wrote that it was "music turned to stone." The façade, which derives from Francisco Borromini's 1667 San Carlo alla Quattro Fontane in Rome, is so simple yet magnificent that a royal decree of December 1793 elevated the church to a cathedral because "the beautifully carved stones of the church. . . are clamoring from their walls for the distinction of cathedral."

On either side of the façade are mismatched towers (one fatter and taller than the other) containing bells supposedly cast with a dash of gold and silver which is said to account for their musical tone. Officially, the eastern bell tower is closed to tourists. However, for a small tip Marcelino the *campanero* (bell-ringer) may lead you up the timeworn stairs of the tower where, like Quasimodo, you may run your fingers over the eight patinated bells of different sizes and peer down over the square. Take care up here, as nobody thinks to clean up the debris underfoot, and there are no guard rails!

Columns divide the rectangular church into three naves, with a marble floor, and two side aisles supported by great pillars, with eight chapels off to the side. The interior is in excellent condition, although the murals (the work of the renowned Italian painted Giuseppe Perovani) above the main altar are mildewed. Vermay is also represented. The main altar is very simple and of wood. More impressive is the chapel immediately to the left, with several altars including

Plaza de la Catedral

one of Carrara marble inlaid with gold, silver, onyx, and carved hardwoods. Look, too, for the wooden image of Saint Christopher, patron saint of Havana, dating to 1633 and originally composed of 170 pieces.

The Spanish believed that a casket which had been brought to Havana with due pomp and circumstance from Santo Domingo in 1796 and resided in the cathedral for over a century held the ashes of Christopher Columbus. Casket and ashes—a "pile of dust and a bit of bone"—were returned to Spain in 1899. All but the partisan Habaneros now believe that the ashes were those of Columbus' son Diego. The stone statue of Columbus—the *Gran Almirante*—that stood outside the cathedral is gone also (Graham Greene, in *Our Man From Havana,* thought it looked "as though it had been formed through the centuries under water, like a coral reef, by the action of insects"), transferred to Spain with the casket.

At press time, the cathedral was open Mon.-Sat. 10 a.m.-3:30 p.m., and Sunday 9 a.m.-10:30 p.m.

Casa de los Marqueses de Aguas Claras
If the heat and bustle of the square get to you, you should settle on the patio beneath the soaring *portal* of this splendid old mansion on the west side of the plaza. Here you can sip a cool beer or heady *mojito* and watch the comings and goings while being serenaded by musicians. The mansion was owned during the 16th century by Governor General Gonzalo Pérez de Angulo and has since been added to by subsequent owners. The inner courtyard, which has a fountain and a grand piano amid lush palms and clinging vines, today houses the Restaurante La Fuente del Patio.

The restaurant extends upstairs, where members of the middle classes once dwelled in apartments (since converted for diners' pleasure, enhanced by *mediopuntos* which by day saturate the floors with shifting fans of red and blue light). You can steal out onto the rickety balconies to look down on the colorful action, noting the patterned cobbles.

Casa del Conde de Bayona
For the best view and photos down over the square, ascend the steps to the upper level of Casa del Conde de Bayona, the simple two-story structure that faces the cathedral on the south side of the square. The house dates to 1720 and is a perfect example of the traditional Havana merchant's house of the period, with side stairs and an *entresuelo* or mezzanine of half-story proportions tucked between the two stories and used to house servants and slaves. It was built in the 1720s for Governor General Don Luís Chacón and today houses the **Museo de Arte Colonial,** tel. (7) 62-6440. The museum is an Aladdin's cave of colonial furniture, glass, porcelain, Baccarat crystal, ironwork, musical instruments, and other sumptuous artifacts from the colonial period. One room is devoted to the stunningly colorful stained-glass *vitrales* and *mediopuntos* unique to Cuba. There's even an array of chamber pots—handy if you get taken short. Open daily except Tuesday 9:30 a.m.-7 p.m.; entrance costs US$2 (cameras cost US$2, guides cost US$1).

Other Sights
On the southwest corner of the square, at the junction with Calle San Ignacio, is the **Callejon de Chorro,** a tiny cul-de-sac with a plaque denoting where a bathhouse was once located at the terminus of the Zanja Real (the "royal ditch," a covered aqueduct that brought water from the Río Almendares, some 10 km away). A small sink and spigot are all that remain. At the end of Callejon de Chorro is the **Taller Experimental de la Gráfica,** where you can watch art students making prints. The **Casa de Baños** sits at the corner of the square and Callejon, looking quite ancient but built this century in colonial style on the site of a 19th-century bathhouse erected over an *aljibe*—water reservoir—fed by the Zanja Real. Today the latter contains the **Galería Victor Manuel,** tel. (7) 61-2955, which sells exquisite quality arts.

On the plaza's east side is the **Casa de Lombillo.** Built in 1741, this former home of a slave trader still houses a small post office (Cuba's first), as it has since 1821. Note the postbox set into the outside wall; it is a grotesque face—that of a tragic Greek mask—carved in stone, with as its slit a scowling mouth that looks as if it might take your fingers or at least spit back your letter. At press time the Oficina del Historidades de la Ciudad (office of Eusebio Leal Spengler, the city historian) was due to move here.

Casa de Lombillo adjoins the **Casa del Marqués de Arcos,** built in 1740s for the royal treasurer. The two houses are fronted by a wide gallery *(portal)* supported by thick columns.

CALLE EMPREDADO

Cobbled Calle Empredado leads west from the north side of the Plaza de la Catedral.

Anyone with an interest in art should call in at the **Centro Wilfredo Lam,** on San Ignacio, tel. (7) 61-2096 and 61-3419, fax (7) 33-8477, e-mail: wlam@artsoft.cult.cu, immediately west of the cathedral at the corner of Empedrado and San Ignacio, in the restored former mansion of the Counts of Peñalver. The center is named for the noted Cuban artist and displays works by Lam, other Cuban artists, and artists throughout the third world. The center is a cultural institution that studies, researches, and promotes contemporary art from around the world. It sponsors workshops and the biennial Havana Exhibition, in which up-and-coming artists have a chance to exhibit. It also has a library on contemporary art, as well as a collection of 1250 art pieces. Open Mon.-Fri. 8:30 a.m.-3:30 p.m., but Mon.-Sat. 10 a.m.-5 p.m. for guided visits.

La Bodeguita del Medio

No visit to Havana is complete without at least one visit to Ernest Hemingway's favorite watering hole, at 207 Calle Empedrado, tel. (7) 62-6121, half a block west of the cathedral. This neighborhood hangout—Hemingway's "little shop in the middle of the street"—was originally the coach house of the mansion next door. Later it was a *bodega*, a mom-and-pop grocery store where a Spanish immigrant, Ángel Martínez, served drinks and food over the counter. According to Tom Miller in *Trading with the Enemy*, Martínez hit upon a brilliant idea: he gave writers credit. The writers, of course, wrote about their newfound hangout, thereby attracting literati and cognoscenti from around the world. (After the Revolution, Martínez stayed on as manager.)

You enter through a saloon-style swinging door. The bar is immediately on your right, with the restaurant behind (note the beautiful tile work along the passageway wall). The bar is usually crowded with tourists. Troubadours move among the thirsty *turistas*. Between tides, you can still savor the proletarian fusion of dialectics and rum. The house drink is the *mojito,* the rum mint julep—US$3—that Hemingway brought out of obscurity and turned into the national drink; alas, it is insipid, about as bad as you'll find in Havana.)

The rustic wooden bar is carved with names. Miscellaneous bric-a-brac adorns the walls: posters, paintings, and faded black-and-white photos of Papa Hemingway, Carmen Miranda, and other famous visitors. The sky-blue walls look as if a swarm of adolescents has been given amphetamines and let loose with crayons. The most famous graffiti is credited to Papa: "Mi Mojito En La Bodeguita, Mi Daiquiri En El Floridita," he supposedly scrawled. Errol Flynn thought it "A Great Place To Get Drunk." They are there, these ribald fellows, smiling at the camera through a haze of cigar smoke and rum. Stepping from La Bodeguita with rum in your veins, you may feel an exhilarating sensation, as if Hemingway himself were walking beside you through the cobbled streets of this most literary of Havana's terrain.

Other Sights

The **Casa del Conde de la Reunión,** at Empredado #215, 50 meters west of La Bodeguita, was built in the 1820s, at the peak of the baroque era. The doorway opens onto a courtyard surrounded by rooms in which Alejo Carpentier, Cuba's most famous novelist (and a dedicated revolutionary), once worked. A portion of the home, which houses the **Centro de Promoción Cultural,** is dedicated to his memory as the **Museo Carpentier,** tel. (7) 61-5500. One entire wall bears a display with sloping glass of Carpentier's early works. His raincoat is thrown stylishly over his old desk chair, suggesting that the novelist might return home at any moment. It's open weekdays 8:30 a.m.-4:30 p.m. Entry is free.

Two blocks west, you'll pass **Plazuela de San Juan de Díos,** a small, unkempt plaza between Calles Habana and Aguiar and centered on a white marble monument—erected in 1906—with a life-size facsimile of Miguel de Cervantes, the great Spanish author of *Don Quixote,* sitting in a chair, book and pen in hand, looking contemplatively down upon rose bushes, lending the plaza its colloquial name: Parque Cervantes.

CALLE O'REILLY AND VICINITY

Calle O'Reilly runs from the northwest corner of Plaza Armas and although today quite sedate, was before the Revolution a major commercial thoroughfare: "The bells were ringing in Santo Christo, and the doves rose from the roof in the golden evening and circled away over the lottery shops of O'Reilly Street and the banks of Obispo," wrote Graham Greene in *Our Man in Havana*. It is named not, as you may suspect, for an Irishman but rather for a Spaniard, Alejandro O'Reilly, who arrived to represent the Spanish crown after the British returned the city to Spain in 1763.

Catercorner to Plaza de Armas, at the corner of O'Reilly and Tacón, is a plaque inset in the wall and that reads, "Two Island Peoples in the Same Seas of Struggle and Hope. Cuba and Ireland." The building is the **Empresa Cubana del Tabaco,** O'Reilly #104, tel. (7) 61-5759, fax (7) 33-5463, the headquarters of Habanos S.A., which oversees Cuba's production and sale of cigars. Visitors are welcomed into the lobby to admire an exhibition.

Walking west you'll pass **Calle San Ignacio,** a narrow, picturesque cobbled thoroughfare leading 50 meters north to Plaza de la Catedral. Half a block west of Calle San Ignacio is **Café O'Reilly,** O'Reilly #205, an atmospheric streetside café with an ornate cast-iron spiral staircase that leads up to a tiny bar where you may sit on a balcony and sip a coffee or beer while watching the tide of people flooding O'Reilly.

Worth a look, too, is the neoclassical **National City Bank of New York,** at O'Reilly and Compostela, where, "passing through great stone portals, which were decorated with four-leaf clovers," Greene's Wormold was reminded of his meager status.

O'Reilly continues westward without buildings of further note.

PLAZA DE ARMAS

The most important plaza in Habana Vieja, and the oldest—originally laid out in 1519—is this handsome square at the seaward end of Calles Obispo and O'Reilly, opening onto Avenida del Puerto to the east. Plaza de Armas was the early focus of the settlement and later became its administrative center, named Plaza de Iglesia for the church that once stood here (demolished in 1741 after it was destroyed when an English warship, the ill-named HMS *Invincible,* was struck by lightning and exploded, sending its main mast sailing down on the church). The square was later used for military exercises: hence, Plaza de Armas.

The square seems still to ring with the cacophony of the past, when military parades, extravagant fiestas, and musical concerts were held under the watchful eye of the governor, and the gentry would take their formal evening promenade. The lovely tradition has been revived on Sunday, when at night the plaza hosts musical concerts. A secondhand book fair is held here daily. The square is lent a romantic cast by its verdant park shaded by palms and tall trees festooned with lianas and epiphytes and lit at night by beautifully filigreed lamps. At its center is a statue of Manuel de Céspedes, hero of the Ten Years' War, with a tall palm at each corner.

It is still rimmed by four important buildings constructed in the late 18th century. The following are described in clockwise order around the plaza, beginning at the Palacio de los Capitanes Generales.

Palacio de los Capitanes Generales
Commanding the square is this somber, stately palace fronted by a cool loggia shadowed by a façade of Ionic columns supporting nine great arches. The tall loggia boasts a life-size marble statue of Fernando VII with a scroll of parchment in one hand that from the side appears jauntily cocked (pardon the pun) and is the butt of ribald jokes among locals. In his other hand he holds a plumed hat.

Spain's stern rule was enforced from here: the Palacio de los Capitanes Generales was home to 65 governors of Cuba between 1791 and 1898 and, after that, the early seat of the Cuban government (and the U.S. governor's residence during Uncle Sam's occupation). Between 1920 and 1967, it served as Havana's city hall. Originally the parish church—La Parroquial Mayor, built in 1555—stood here: the holy structure was demolished when the mast

El Templete and Hotel San Isabel, Plaza de Armas

and spars of the *Invincible* came through the roof in what was termed an unfortunate "act of God."

The palace is a magnificent three-story structure surrounding a courtyard (entered from the plaza) which contains a statue of Christopher Columbus competing for the light with tall palms and a veritable botanical garden of foliage. Don't be alarmed by any ghoulish shrieks—a peacock lives in the courtyard. Arched colonnades rise to all sides, festooned with vines and bougainvillea. Several afternoons each week an orchestra plays decorous 19th-century dance music, while pretty girls in crinolines flit up and down the majestic staircase, delighting in the ritual of the *quince,* the traditional celebration of a girl's 15th birthday. On the southeast corner you can spot a hole containing the coffin of an unknown nobleman, one of several graves from the old Cementerio de Espada (a church that once stood here was razed to make way for the palace); note the plaque—the oldest in Havana—commemorating the death of Doña María de Cepero y Nieto, who was felled when a blunderbuss was accidentally fired while she was praying.

Today the palace houses the **Museo de la Ciudad de Habana,** the City of Havana Museum, 1 Calle Tacón, tel. (7) 61-2876. The entrance is to the side, on Calle Obispo. The great flight of marble stairs leads to high-ceilinged rooms as gracious and richly furnished as those in Versailles or Buckingham Palace. The throne room (made for the King of Spain but never used) is of particularly breathtaking splendor

and is brimful of treasures. There is also a Hall of Flags, plus exquisite collections illustrating the story of the city's (and Cuba's) development and the 19th-century struggles for independence. Even here you can't escape the ubiquitous anti-Yankee expositions: one top-floor room contains the shattered wings of the eagle that once crested the Monumento del Maine, in Vedado (see the Vedado section, below), along with other curios suggestive of U.S. voracity.

The museum also has a model of an early 20th-century sugar plantation at 1:22.5 scale, complete with steam engine, milling machines, and plantation grounds with workers' dwellings, a church, and a hotel—all transporting you back in time on the world's smallest sugar plantation. A railroad runs through the plantation, with two steam locomotives pulling sugarcane carriers, water tanks, and passenger carriages.

It's open daily 9:30 a.m.-6:30 p.m. Entrance costs US$3 tourists (US$2 extra for cameras; US$10 for videos; US$1 for a guide). You can purchase a US$9 ticket here, good for *all* museums in Havana. The museum also offers guided tours of the plaza and Old Havana (US$5, or US$6 with the museum entry).

Palacio del Segundo Cabo
The quasi-Moorish, pseudo-baroque, part neoclassical Palace of the Second Lieutenant, on the north side of the square, on Calle O'Reilly, dates from 1770, when it was designed at the city post office. Its use metamorphosed several times until it became the home of the vice-governor

general (Second Lieutenant) and, immediately after independence, the seat of the Senate. Today, it houses the Instituto Cubano del Libro (the Cuban Book Institute) and, appropriately, a Bella Habana bookstore. The Institute hosts occasional public presentations, but is otherwise generally not open to public perusal.

Castillo de la Real Fuerza

This pocket-size castle, begun in 1558 and completed in 1582, is the second oldest fort in the Americas and the oldest of the four forts that guarded the New World's most precious harbor. Built in medieval fashion, it was almost useless from a strategic point of view, being landlocked far from the mouth of the harbor channel and hemmed in by surrounding buildings that would have formed a great impediment to its cannons in any attack. With walls six meters wide and 10 tall, the castle forms a square with enormous triangular bulwarks at the corners, which slice the dark waters of the moat like the prows of galleons. The governors of Cuba lived here until 1762.

Visitors enter the fortress on the northeast corner of Plaza de Armas via a courtyard full of patinated cannons and mortars. Note the royal coat of arms (of Seville in Spain) carved in stone above the massive gateway as you cross the moat by a drawbridge to enter a vaulted interior containing suits of armor. Stairs lead up to the storehouse and battlements, now housing an impressive **Museo y Taller de Cerámica**, tel. (7) 61-6130, featuring pottery both ancient and new.

You can climb to the top of a cylindrical tower rising from the northwest corner: the tower contains an antique brass bell gone mossy green with age and weather. The bell was rung to signal the approach of ships, with differing notes for friends and foes. The tower is topped by a bronze weathervane called La Giraldilla de la Habana. It's a pathetic looking thing, but much is made of it (it's the symbol of Havana and also graces the label of Havana Club rum bottles). The vane is a copy—the archetype, which was toppled in a hurricane, resides in the city museum. The original was cast in 1631 in honor of Inéz de Bobadilla, the wife of Governor Hernando de Soto, the tireless explorer who fruit-lessly searched for the Fountain of Youth in Florida. Soto named his wife governor in his absence, and she became the only female governor ever to serve as such in Cuba. Every afternoon for four years she climbed the tower and scanned the horizon in vain for his return, and it is said that she died of sorrow. In memory of his widow, the residents of Havana commissioned the weathervane and placed it atop the tower. The Giraldilla is a voluptuous albeit small figure with hair braided in thick ropes, bronze robes fluttering in the wind. In her right hand she holds a palm tree and in her left a cross.

The castle is open daily, 8 a.m.-7 p.m.; entry costs US$1.

The Northeast Corner

Immediately east of the castle, at the junction of Avenida del Puerto and O'Reilly, is an obelisk to the 77 Cuban seamen killed during World War II by Nazi submarines (five Cuban vessels were sunk by German U-boats).

A charming copy of a Doric temple—**El Templete**—sits on the square's northeast corner. It was built in the early 19th century on the site where the first mass and town council meeting were held in 1519, beside a massive ceiba tree. The original ceiba was felled by a hurricane in 1828 and replaced by a column fronted by a small bust of Christopher Columbus. The tree has since been replanted and today still shades the tiny temple, which wears a great cloak of bougainvillea. Its interior, with black and white checkerboard marble floor, is dominated by triptych wall-to-ceiling paintings depicting the first Mass, the first town council meeting, and the inauguration of the Templete. In the center of the room is a bust of the artist, Jean Baptiste Ver May, whose ashes (along with those of his wife, who also died—along with 8,000 other citizens—in the cholera epidemic of 1833) are contained in a marble urn next to the bust. Entry costs US$1 with interpretive guide.

The Southeast Corner

The grand building immediately south of El Templete is the former Palacio del Conde de Santovenia, built in the style of the Tuileries Palace in France and today housing the **Hotel Santa Isabel,** on Calle Barratillo. The *conde* (count) in question was famous for hosting elaborate parties, most notoriously a three-day bash in 1833 to celebrate the accession to the throne of Isabel II and which climaxed with an ascent of a gaily decorated gas-filled balloon (he was less popular with his immediate neighbors, who detested the reek of oil and fish that wafted over the square from his first-floor warehouses). In the late 19th century, it was bought and sanitized by a colonel from New Orleans who reopened it as a resplendent hotel, a guise it resumed in 1998.

Half a block east of the hotel, on narrow Calle Baratillo, is the **Casa del Café,** tel. (7) 33-8061, serving all kinds of Cuban coffees, and, next door, the **Taberna del Galeón,** tel. (7) 33-8476, better known as the House of Rum. Inside, where it is as cool as a well, you can taste various rums at no cost, although it is hoped you will make a purchase from the wide selection (a free *mojito* awaits your arrival). The place is popular with tour groups, which ebb and flow like sardines. It's open Mon.-Sat. 9 a.m.-5 p.m., and Sunday 9 a.m.-3 p.m. The door is usually closed, but only to keep the air-conditioned air chill.

The South Side

On Calle Obispo, on the east side of the square is the **Biblioteca Provincial de la Habana,** Havana's spanking new provincial library housing a surprisingly paltry (and dated) array of books. Next to it is a small art gallery—**Galería Villena**—showing changing exhibitions.

Adjoining to the west is the **Museo de Ciencias Naturales,** tel. (7) 63-2687, which shows off the collection of the Academía de Cíencias and encompassing the Museo de Ciencias Naturales (Museum of Natural Sciences) and the Museo de Ciencias y Técnicas (Museum of Science and Technology). The museum houses superb collections of Cuban and international flora and fauna, many in clever reproductions of their natural environments, plus stuffed tigers, apes, and other beasts from afar. It has monthly lectures and videos, and features a natural history library. It's open Tue.-Sun. 9:30 a.m.-6:30 p.m.; US$3.

The Southwest Corner

Facing the plaza, at the junction with Calle Oficios, is **Restaurante Cubano,** housed in a green

and ocher 17th-century mansion that was originally the college of San Francisco de Sales for orphan girls. Its central patio is surrounded by galleries of stocky columns and wide arches enclosing slatted doors and *mediopuntos* and now roamed by peacocks who beg tidbits from diners. The outside patio facing the plaza is occupied by the lively **Café Mina,** where you may sit beneath shady canopies while Cuban musicians entertain. The **Casa del Agua la Tinaja,** next door, sells mineral water (US$0.25 a glass—the source was discovered in 1544, and early explorers made use of the water; in 1831, an aqueduct was built to carry it to the burgeoning town, thereby solving the water shortage).

Facing the south side of the Palacio de Capitanes Generales, along a 50-meter-long cobbled section of Calle Obispo, is a series of gems, beginning at Obispo #113, where massive metal-studded doorways open into what was once a stable now containing a bakery—**Dulcería Doña Teresa**—selling custards, ice creams, and other delights. Next door is the **Museo de Plata,** crammed with silver and gold ornaments from the colonial era, and including old clocks, coins, medals, and plates and, upstairs, candelabras, a dining set that includes a massive silver punch bowl *(ponchera),* a beautiful replica in silver of Columbus's *Santa María,* walking sticks, and a splendid collection of swords and firearms. Downstairs a silversmith is occasionally on hand to demonstrate his skills. Entry costs US$1 (plus US$1 for a guide, optional).

Next door is the **Oficina del Historidades de la Ciudad** (office of the city historian; Obispo #117-119), with a copper galleon hanging above its door and an old cannon standing upright outside. Appropriately, this is the oldest house in Havana, dating from around 1570. Inside, behind a grilled gate, is a *quitrín,* a two-wheeled conveyance with a movable bonnet to protect passengers from the elements, made to be pulled by a single horse (usually ridden by a *calesero,* a black slave dressed in high boots, top hat, and a costume trimmed with colorful ribbons). The office was due to move to a new location in Plaza de la Catedral.

Opposite, look closely at the two cannons outside the south side of the Palacio de Capitanes Generales and you'll note the monogram of King George III. They're relics of the brief English occupation of Cuba in 1762.

At the end of the cobbled pedestrians-only block is a fabric store in a beautiful blue-and-cream mansion, the former Casa del Marques de Casa Torre (Obispo #121); and, around the corner, on Mercaderes, the **Casa de las Infusiones,** still selling refreshing cups of tea today as it has since 1841.

CALLE OBISPO

Calle Obispo has been one of the city's busiest thoroughfares since its inception in the early colonial era. The name means "Bishop's Street" and supposedly derives from the use of the path by ecclesiastics of the 18th century. It became Havana's premier shopping street early on and was given a boost when the city walls went up in the mid-1700s, linking the major colonial plaza with the Monserrate Gate, the main entranceway to the city built into the city wall. Calle Obispo is still Habana Vieja's bustling thoroughfare, linking Plaza de Armas with Parque Central. The most important structures date from the 1920s, when Obispo became a center for banking: a kind of Cuban Wall Street.

On the corner of Calles Mercaderes and Obispo is the rose-pink **Hotel Ambos Mundos,** tel. (7) 66-9592, built in the 1920s and recently reopened after a long restoration. Off and on throughout the 1930s, Hemingway laid his head in Room 511, where the plot of *For Whom The Bell Tolls* formed in his mind. After the Revolution, the hotel was turned into a hostelry for employees of the Ministry of Education across the way. Hemingway's room—"a gloomy room, 16 square meters, with a double bed made of ordinary wood, two night tables and a writing table with a chair," recalled Colombian author Gabriel García Márquez—has been preserved down to an old Spanish edition of *Don Quixote* on the night table. His room is open to view Mon.-Sat. 10 a.m.-5 p.m. (entrance US$1).

Across the street, on the northwest corner of Obispo and Mercaderes, is the **Museo de la Educación,** tel. (7) 61-5468, dedicated in part to telling the tale of the remarkable and inspirational literacy campaign of 1961, when university students and teachers went to the far corners of Cuba to create a "territory free of illiteracy." Open. Mon.-Fri. 8:15 a.m.-4:45 p.m. Entry is free.

Note the **antique bell** held aloft by modern concrete pillars immediately east of the museum. Its plaque in Spanish commemorates the fact that this was the original site of the University of Havana, founded in January 1728 and housed in a convent that once stood here. It was demolished in the mid-19th century, and all that remains is the bell that once tolled to call the students to class.

Havana is replete with dusty old apothecaries, but the **Museo y Farmácia Taquechel,** at Obispo #155, tel. (7) 62-9286, immediately south of the Maqueta, is surely the most interesting with its colorful ceramic jars decorated with floral motifs full of herbs and potions. It dates from 1898 and is named for Dr. Francisco Taquechel y Mirabal. The place sparkles behind modern glass doors after a recent restoration.

Another site of interest is the **Banco Nacional de Cuba,** in a splendid neoclassical building—that of the Comité Estatal de Finaza—fronted by fluted Corinthian columns and portals decorated with four-leaf clovers. It's three blocks west of Plaza de Armas, at Calle Cuba. He was true to his beliefs and was determined to do away with money altogether. When new banknotes were issued, it was Che's job to sign them, which he did dismissively by simply scrawling "Che." Today the old bank houses in its basement vaults the **Museo de Finanzas,** dedicated to telling a version of the history of banking in Cuba from the colonial era to the tenure of Che Guevara's reign as the bank's president in the early 1960s, and featuring the enormous safe within which—when Cuba had such—the nation's gold reserves were held for more than half a century.

The most resplendent building along Obispo is the former Palacio de Joaquín Gómez, cater-corner to the bank, between Calle Cuba and Aguiar, and now the **Hotel Florida,** with a stunning lobby dating from 1838. Also worth a peek is **La Casa del Consomé La Luz,** five blocks west of Plaza Armas, at Calles Obispo and Havana, another moody apothecary with a white marble floor and old glass cabinets faded with age, filled with chemists tubes, mixing vases, and mortars and pestles, and lined with bottles of oils, herbs, and powders.

CALLE OFICIOS

Calle Oficios leads south from Plaza de Armas three blocks to Plaza de San Francisco. Its newly restored colonial buildings are confections in stone, and walking this street you may fall under a spell from which you may never escape.

The first noteworthy building is **Casa del Árabe** (Arab House) at Oficios #12, tel. (7) 61-5868. This mansion, an appropriately fine example of Moorish-inspired architecture, is the only place in Havana where Muslims can practice the Islamic faith. It now houses a museum dedicated to all things Arabic. You enter into a beautiful place bursting with foliage—a softly dappled courtyard radiating ineffable calm. The prayer hall is decorated with hardwoods inlaid with mother-of-pearl, tempting you to run your fingers across the floral and geometric motifs to sense the tactile pleasure. The museum displays exquisitely crafted camel saddles and Oriental carpets, an exact replica of a *souk* (market), models of Arab *dhows,* (the traditional sailing vessels), and a superb collection of Arab weaponry. Open daily 9 a.m.- 7 p.m. Entrance costs US$1. Cultural activities are hosted in the evenings.

Coin lovers should call in next door at the **Museo Numismático,** the Coin Museum, in the former 17th-century bishop's residence at Oficios #8, tel. (7) 61-5811. The fascinating collection of coins dates back to the earliest colonial days and includes "company store" currency printed by the sugar mills. Open Tues.-Fri. 10 a.m.-5 p.m., Saturday 10 a.m.-4 p.m., and Sunday 9 a.m.-1 p.m.

Across the street, at Calle Oficios 13, Havana's **Museo de Autos Antiguo** includes an eclectic range of antique automobiles from a 1905 Cadillac to a 1960s-era Daimler limousine, plus Che Guevara's jeep and Cuban novelist Alejo Carpentier's Volkswagen Beetle. Classic Harley-Davidson motorbikes are also exhibited. Open daily 9:30 a.m.-7 p.m. Entrance costs US$1 (US$2 extra for cameras, US$10 for videos).

Make sure to call in at **Hostal Valencia,** a picturesque Spanish-style *posada* that looks as if it's been magically transported from some Manchegan village. It originated in the 17th century as the home of Governor Count Sotolon-go, an aristocrat of pure Spanish pedigree. The hotel, on the corner of Oficios and Obrapía, could have been used as a model by Cervantes for the inn where Don Quixote was dubbed a knight by the bewildered innkeeper. The *hostal* sets out to attract tourists with a liberal coating of green and white paint, various bits and pieces of armor, a handsome bar and courtyard, and a splendid restaurant looking onto Oficios through full-length *rejas*—turned wooden rails. One look and you may want to check in.

PLAZA DE SAN FRANCISCO

The cobbled Plaza de San Francisco, at Oficios and the foot of Amargura, faces onto Avenida del Puerto and the inner shore of Havana harbor, of which it was once an inlet. During the 16th-century, long before the Franciscan convent and church were built here, the area was the great waterfront of the early colonial city and Iberian emigrants disembarked with their dreams, slaves were unloaded, and Spanish galleons, their holds groaning with treasure, were replenished with water and victuals for the passage to Europe. A market developed here and the square became the focus of the annual Fiesta de San Francisco. In the 17th century, the customs house and prison were built here, while nobles built their homes on surrounding streets. The plaza has been fully restored including the cobbles, relaid in 1999.

At its heart is the **Fuente de los Leones**—Fountain of the Lions—erected in 1836, moved to different locations at various times, but finally ensconced where it began life. The muscular five-story neoclassical building on the north side is the **Lonja del Comercio,** the "Goods Exchange," dating from 1907, when it was built as a center for trading in food commodities. It now sparkles after a complete restoration: the shell is original but the interior is state-of-the-art futuristic and houses offices of international corporations, news bureaus, and tour companies. Note the beautiful dome crowned by a bronze figure of the god Mercury.

Across the way, where Spanish galleons once tethered, the **Terminal Sierra Maestra** cruise terminal faces onto the plaza.

THE COLONIAL STYLE

Cuba's colonial mansions—with their tall, generously proportioned rooms and shallow-stepped staircases—were usually built on two main floors (the lower floor for shops and warehouses, the upper floor for the family) with a mezzanine between them for the house servants. Colonial homes typically featured two small courtyards, with a dining area between the two, parallel to the street. Life centered on the inner courtyard, or *traspatio*, hidden behind massive wooden doors often flanked by pillars. The homes were heavily influenced by traditional Spanish and *mudejar* (Moorish) styles, and evolved quintessential Cuban features, such as:

Alfarjes: Pitched wooden roofs combining parallel and angled beams to create additional definition for interiors, providing a conceptual shift in emphasis to enhance the sense of space. They were normally found in churches and smaller homes and adopted a star pattern.

Antepechos: Ornamented window guards flush with the building façade

Cenefas: Italianate bands of colored plasterwork used as decorative ornamentation on interior walls.

Entresuelo: Shallow mezzanine levels between ground and upper stories, usually housing slaves' living quarters.

Lucetas: Long rectangular windows that run along the edges of doorways and windows and usually contain stained or marbled glass.

Mamparas: Double-swing half-doors that serve as room dividers or as partial outer doors to protect privacy while allowing ventilation. The *mampara* was described by the 20th-century Cuban novelist Alejo Carpentier as "a door truncated to the height of a man, the real interior door of the Creole home for hundreds of years, creating a peculiar concept of family relations and communal living."

Patio: An open space in the center of Spanish buildings—a Spanish adaptation of the classic Moorish inner court—which permits air to circulate through the house. The patios of more grandiose buildings are surrounded by columned galleries.

Persianas: Slatted shutters in tall, glassless windows, designed to let in the breezes while keeping out the harsh light and rains.

Portales: Galleried exterior walkways fronting the mansions and protecting pedestrians from sun and rain. The grandest are supported by stone Tuscan columns and have vaulted ceilings and arches. Later, North American influences led to a more sober approach, with square wooden posts (à la the porch).

Postigos: Small doors set at face level into massive wooden doors of Spanish homes

Rejas: Wooden window screens of rippled, lathe-turned rods called *barrotes* that served to keep out burglars (later *rejas* were made of metal)

Vitrales: Arched windows of stained glass in geometric designs that fan out like peacock's tails and diffuse the sunlight, saturating a room with shifting color. A full 180-degree arch is called a *mediopunto*.

Iglesia y Convento de San Francisco de Asís

Dominating the plaza on the south is the great church whose construction was launched in 1719. It began humbly but was reconstructed in 1730 in baroque style with a 40-meter bell tower—one of the tallest in all the Americas, crowned by St. Helen holding the Holy Cross of Jerusalem. The church was eventually proclaimed a Minorite Basilia, and it was from its chapel that the processions of the *Vía Crucis* departed every Lenten Friday, ending at the Iglesia del Santo Cristo del Buen Viaje. The devout passed down Calle Amargura (Street of Bitterness), where stations of the cross were set up at street corners and decorated with crucifixes and altars. You can still see the first of the stations—**Casa de la Cruz Verde**—at the corner of Calles Amargura and Mercaderes; it's shaded beneath the eave, above the Mudejar-style balcony.

The church and adjoining convent were recently restored. During the restoration, I watched muralists painting the marvelous trompe l'oeil that extends the perspective of the nave. Note the Tiffany grandfather clock (in working order), dating to the 1820s, on the far right. On the left side, inset into the walls, are the morbid remains of Teodoro—a Franciscan brother of high regard—pickled in glass jars next to a statue of St. Francis. Members of the most aristocratic families of the times were buried in the crypt, visible through a glass window in the terra-cotta tile floor.

Alas, the sumptuously adorned altars are gone, replaced by a huge crucifix suspended above a grand piano. Yes, the nave has metamorphosed into a concert hall; the music program is posted in the entrance. Performances (usually classical) are given each Saturday at 6 p.m. and Sunday at 11 a.m.

The nave opens to the right onto the cloisters of a convent, to which the church belonged (it had 111 cells for members of the religious community). Today it contains the **Museo de Arte Religioso** with fabulous silverwork, porcelain, and other treasures of the Spanish epoch, including a room full of ornately gilded hymnals of silver and even mother-of-pearl displayed in glass cases. A music school occupies part of the building. The church and museum are open daily 9 a.m.-7 p.m. Entrance costs US$2 plus US$1 extra for the campanile, which offers marvelous views over the city (cameras cost US$2 extra; videos cost US$10).

South of the Plaza

The beautiful colonial buildings on Calle Oficios south of the plaza date from the 16th century and possess a marked Mudejar style, exemplified by the wooden balconies. The entire block has been magnificently restored and many of the buildings converted into art galleries. What a remake! One of the gems is the pink and green **Casa de Carmen Montilla,** 50 meters south of the square. Only the front of the house remains, but the architects have made creative use of the empty shell. Through the breezy doorway you can catch sight of a fabulous 3-D mural by famous Cuban artist Alfredo Sosabravo at the back of an open-air sculpture garden. Fabulous art is portrayed in the two-level art gallery, and next door at the **Estudio Galería Los Oficios,** offering revolving art exhibitions; open Mon.-Sat. 9:30 a.m.-5 p.m. Entry is free.

Further south, the 19th-century building housing the **Asemblea Provincial Poder Popular,** or local government office, whose lobby is striking for its ornate baroque and neoclassical stucco

work. An antique railway carriage—the *Mambi*—is parked on rails on the narrow lane between the convent and the Asemblea.

Opposite the Asemblea, at the corner of Oficios and Muralles, is **Casa Alejandro Von Humboldt,** where the famous German explorer (1769-1854) lived and made his botanic and mineral investigations of Cuba during his travels in 1800-01. The restored building is now a museum dedicated to the scientist and features botanical specimens and prints, navigational instruments such as sextants, exhibits on slavery, and tracts from Humboldt's books. It's open Tue.-Sat. 9 a.m.-5 p.m. Entrance costs US$1.

CALLES MERCADERES

Intimate Calle Mercaderes links Plaza de Armas with Plaza Vieja, four blocks south. Now restored to grandeur, it is brimming with handsome buildings and museums of interest.

The block immediately south of Calle Obispo and the Hotel Ambos Mundos includes the **Maqueta de Centro Histórico,** opened in early 2000. This stunning model features a 1:500 scale model of Habana Vieja measuring eight by four meters, with buildings color coded by use and accurate to the ventilator ducts on the roofs. It's housed in a darkened room with floodlights illuminating the model. Guides give a spiel. This a *must visit* (don't confuse it with the Maqueta de la Habana, in Miramar). It's open daily 9 a.m.-6:30 p.m. Entrance costs US$1 (plus US$1 for the guide; US$3 for a camera, and US$10 for videos).

Across the way is the **Tienda de las Navegantes** (Mercaderes #117), a beautiful wood- and glass-fronted building with a ship's wheel inlaid with a copper galleon above the door. This incongruously positioned store sells maps and nautical charts, including the best selection of road and city maps available in Cuba. A hearse-size glass case contains a three-meter-long scale model of the *Juan Sebastian Elcano,* made in 1928 for La Compañia Transatlántica de Barcelona.

Across the street are the **Casa de Puerto Rico** and **Casa del Tabaco,** both at Mercaderes #120. Besides a fine stock of cigars, the latter also houses the **Museum of Tobacco,** tel. (7) 61-5795, upstairs. The first room, part of which is decorated as a typical middle-class sitting room with rocking chairs and a cigar displayed on a silver ashtray, contains a collection of lithos from cigar-box covers. Other exhibits include pipes and lighters from around the world. Note the silver cigar box engraved with script that reads: "To my godfather Dr. Fidel Castro Ruz from Fidel Charles Getto, August 9, 1959." Open Tues.-Sat. 10 a.m.-5:30 p.m. and Sunday 9 a.m.-1 p.m.; no entrance charge.

At the end of the block, at the corner of Obrapía, the pink building with wraparound wrought-iron balustrade and Mexican flag fluttering above the doorway is the **Casa de Benito Juárez,** housing the Sociedad Cubano Mexicana de Relaciones Culturales, tel. (7) 61-8166, marvelously displaying artwork and costumes from different Mexican states. Open Tue.-Sat. 10:30 a.m.-5:30 p.m. and Sunday 9 a.m.-1 p.m. Entrance costs US$1. The house faces a tiny landscaped *plazuela* with a larger-than-life bronze statue of Simón Bolívar atop a marble pedestal and a fabulous mural behind.

On the next block is the **Museo de Asia,** tel. (7) 63-9740, which downstairs seems unimpressive: a few inlaid bowls, rugs, musical instruments, and a marble model of the Taj Mahal. The best rooms are upstairs, containing an astonishing array of carved ivory, silverware, mother-of-pearl furniture, scimitars, kukris, and other Oriental armaments, plus exquisite kimonos. Most of the collection comprises gifts to Fidel from Asian nations. The foyer contains an engraved rock—a gift from the citizens of Hiroshima. The museum also includes a small bonsai garden, and one of the rooms downstairs doubles as a school class, a crafty ploy to remind visitors of the success of Cuba's education program. Open Tue.-Sat. 10 a.m.-5:30 p.m., and Sunday 9 a.m.-1 p.m. Entry costs US$1 (plus US$2 for a camera, US$10 for video).

Half a block south is a sign for the **Armería 9 de Abril,** at Mercaderes #157, tel. (7) 61-8080, no longer a museum (the collection is now incorporated into the Museo de la Revolución) but important in contemporary history: here four members of MR-26-7 were killed in an assault on the armory on 9 April 1959. A sign outside reads, "Armaments Company of Cuba, hunting supplies and explosives." The company was a subsidiary of Dupont, the U.S. munitions giant.

Across the street is **Casa del Libertador Simón Bolívar,** Mercaderes 156, tel. (7) 61-3988, housing the Venezuelan embassy and containing the **Museo de Simón Bolívar,** which displays cultural works and art from Venezuela (open Tues.-Sat. 10 a.m.-5 p.m., US$1).

If heading down to Plaza Vieja, check out the stunning lobby—a mix of art nouveau and neo-classical—with dramatic skylight in the building on the southwest corner of Mercaderes and Amargura.

CALLE OBRAPÍA

The two blocks of Calle Obrapía between Oficios and San Ignacio contain several beautifully restored buildings of historic appeal. The street is named for the *obra pía*—pious act—of Don Martín Calvo de la Puerta, who devoted a portion of his wealth to dowering five orphan girls every year.

The most important is the **Casa de la Obra Pía,** Obrapía 158, tel. (7) 61-3097. This splendid mansion with lemon-meringue-yellow walls on the northwest corner of Obrapía and Mercaderes was owned by the Calvo de Puertas family, one of the most important families in Cuba in early colonial days. It dates from the early 17th century, with additions such as voluptuous moldings and dimpled cherubs as late as 1793 in baroque style. Visitors can see the arms of the Castellón family (who bought the house after Martín Calvo de la Puerto's death), surrounded by exuberant baroque stonework, emblazoned above the carved entrance of regal proportions. As much as any house in Habana Vieja, Casa de la Obra Pía exemplifies the Spanish adaptation of a Moorish inner courtyard, with a serene, scented coolness illuminated by daylight filtering through *mediopuntos* fanning out like a peacock's tail. It features a permanent exhibition of works by Alejo Carpentier in the foyer; other rooms contains miscellaneous art. Open Tue.-Sun. 9:30 a.m.-2:30 p.m. Entrance costs US$1.

Across the way is the **Casa de África,** tel. (7) 61-5798. When flung open wide, its large wooden doors reveal breezy courtyards full of African artwork and artifacts, masks, and cloth. On the third floor you'll find a fabulous collection of paraphernalia used in *santería,* including statues of the leading deities in the Yoruban pantheon, dancing costumes of the Abakuá, and *otanes* (stones) in which the *orishas*—the gods of *santería*-are said to reside. Open Mon.-Sat. 10:30 a.m.-5 p.m. and Sunday 9:30 a.m.-1 p.m. Entrance costs US$2.

One block further west, at the corner of Calle Cuba, the **Casa de Gaspar Riveros de Vasoncelos** is esteemed for its corner balcony with delicately curved balustrades and though restored in 1985, it is not open to the public. Between Mercaderes and Oficios, at Obrapía 111, is the **Casa Guayasamú,** housing a museum of plastic arts and photographs from Ecuador, with changing exhibitions of art from other Latin American countries. A huge dugout canoe sits in the entrance lobby. Open Tue.-Sat. 10:30 a.m.-5:30 p.m., and Sunday 9 a.m.-1 p.m. Entrance costs US$1.

To the east, between Calle Mercaderes y Oficios is the **Casa de los Abanicos,** where traditional Spanish fans *(abanicos)* are still handmade and painted. The reception area sells the fans (from US$1.40 to US$144). It's open Tue.-Sat. 9 a.m.-5 p.m. and Sunday 9 a.m.-1 p.m.

PLAZA VIEJA AND VICINITY

The last of the four resplendent main squares in Habana Vieja is Plaza Vieja, the old commercial square (bounded by Calles Mercaderes, San Ignacio, Brasil, and Muralla), surrounded by mansions and apartment blocks from where residents could look down on processions, executions, bullfights, and wild fiestas. The plaza originally hosted a market where peasants and free blacks sold all manner of produce. A stone fountain pinned its center, with a wide bowl and four dolphins that gushed "intermittent streams of thick, muddy liquid which Negro water vendors eagerly collected in barrels to be sold throughout the city," recorded a French visitor in the 19th century.

Alas, President Machado built an underground car park here in the 1930s, and the cobbles and fountain fell afoul of the wrecking ball. Time and neglect brought near-ruin this century, and many of the square's beautiful buildings sank into a sorry state of repair. Fortunately, Eusebio Leal

and his maestros have waved a magic wand over the plaza. Even the fountain has reappeared, now gurgling clear water. *A magnificent restoration!* The square is renowned for its acoustics and is often used for concerts.

A café, a fashion boutique, and a classy bar **(Taberna Beny Moré)** featuring the personal effects of the renowned composer and singer Beny Moré have opened, and two hotels and a cinema **(Cine Habana)** were to be added. **Fototeca,** tel. (7) 62-2530, the state-run agency that promotes the work of Cuban photographers, has its headquarters on the east side of the square and offers international photo exhibitions in the Salón Nacional de Fotografia (open Tue.-Sat. 10 a.m.-5 p.m.).

The most important building, on the south side of the square, is the **Casa de los Condes de Jaruco,** an impressively restored 18th-century structure highlighted by mammoth doors opening into a cavernous entrance hall. The building was built between 1733 and 1737 by the father of the future Count of Jaruco, who gave it its name. Today it houses several *galerías* under the umbrella of the **Fondo Cubano de Bienes Culturales** (BFC), tel. (7) 62-3577, the organization responsible for the sale of Cuban art. The BFC headquarters is upstairs. Whimsical murals are painted on the walls, touched in splashy color by the undulating play of light through *mediopuntos* and by the play of shadow through *rejas.* Upstairs, various galleries sell an eclectic range of creative arts and crafts. The downstairs is occupied by three galleries.

On the northwest corner is the **Casa de las Hermanas Cárdenas,** recently restored with faux brickwork and marble. The building—named for two sisters, María Loreto and María Ignacia Cárdenas, who lived here in the late 18th century—houses the **Centro de Desarrollo de Artes Visuales,** tel. (7) 62-3533. Through the towering doors, immediately on the left, is a craft workshop where young women can be seen making cloth dolls and naive animals gaudily painted in the pointillist fashion now common throughout the Caribbean. The inner courtyard is dominated by an intriguing sculpture—a kind of futuristic skyscraper in miniature—crafted by Alfredo Sosabravo. Art education classes are given on the second floor, reached via a wide wooden staircase that leads to the top story, where you'll find an art gallery in a wonderfully airy loft. If the tiny yellow door is locked, ask for the key downstairs. Open Tue.-Sat 10 a.m.-5:30 p.m.

Next door is the **Casa del Conde de San Estéban de Cañongo,** at San Ignacio #356. This former mansion of a nobleman today houses an intriguing artisans' factory—**Artesanías Para Turismo Taller**—where workers use stems of the *malanbueta* plant to weave baskets, wall hangings, and dozens of other items. You can watch the acid being squeezed from the thick reeds, which are pressed into flat yet flexible fibers woven into durable mats on simple looms worked by foot pedals. Other workers sit to the side conjuring the stems into baskets, purses, *zapatas* (shoes), and intriguing wall hangings depicting scenes of old Havana.

The old **Palacio Vienna Hotel** (also called the Palacio Cueto), on the southeast corner of Plaza Vieja, is a phenomenal piece of Gaudiesque art nouveau architecture, fabulously ornate and dating from 1906. The frontage is awash in surf-like waves and ballooning balconies. It was scheduled for renovation.

Physicians and scientists inclined to a busman's holiday might walk one block west and one north of the plaza and check out the impressive **Museo de Ciencias Carlos Finlay,** at Calle Cuba #460, tel. (7) 63-4824, between Amargura and Brasil. The building, which dates from 1868 and housed the Royal Academy of Sciences, today contains a pharmaceutical collection and tells the tales of various Cuban scientists' discoveries and innovations. The Cuban scientist Dr. Finlay is honored, of course, for it was he who discovered that yellow fever is transmitted by the Aedes aegipti mosquito. The museum also contains a medical library of 95,000 volumes. Open Mon.-Fri. 8:30 a.m.-5 p.m. and Saturday 8:30 a.m.-3 p.m. Entrance is US$2.

The church immediately north of the museum, across Lamparilla, is the **Iglesia de San Agustín,** built in 1633 but much altered since and consecrated anew in 1842 when it was given to the Franciscans after they lost their tenure at the Church of Saint Francis of Assisi in the eponymous square. Unlike other churches in Havana, this one bears the influence of the Augustine monks who came to Cuba from Mexico and imbued their own style, with rich Mexican murals. The curves and counter-curves of the undulating

pinion façade likewise are of Mexican influence. It also boasts a fine organ and six altars.

PLAZA DEL CRISTO

The disheveled Plaza del Cristo lies at the west end of Amargua, between Lamparilla and Brasil, two blocks east of Avenida de Bélgica (Monserrate). It was here that Wormold, the vacuum-cleaner salesman turned secret agent, was "swallowed up among the pimps and lottery sellers of the Havana noon" in Graham Greene's *Our Man in Havana.* Wormold and his wayward daughter Millie lived at 37 Lamparilla. Alas, the house was fictional.

The square which was slated to receive a complete restoration, is dominated by the tiny, utterly charming **Iglesia de Santo Cristo Buen Viaje.** The church is one of Havana's oldest, dating from 1732, but with a Franciscan hermitage—called Humilladero chapel—dating from 1640. Buen Viaje was the final point of the *Vía Crucis*—the Procession of the Cross—held each Lenten Friday and beginning at the Iglesia de San Francisco de Asís. The church, which is in a splendid state of repair and has an impressive cross-beamed wooden ceiling and stained-glass windows, was named for its popularity among sailors and travelers, who used to pray in it for safe voyages. Open daily, 9 a.m.-noon.

If hungry, call in at the **Restaurante Hanoi,** on Calle Brasil (Teniente Rey) and Bernanza, at the southwest corner of the square, tel. (7) 57-1029. The restaurant is housed is in one of the oldest houses in Havana and is colloquially known as La Casa de la Parre (Grapevine House) for the luxuriant grapevine growing in the patio.

THE ECCLESIASTICAL CORE

Southern Habana Vieja is worth visiting for its enclave of 18th-century ecclesiastical buildings concentrated within a few blocks in the heart of the region.

Closest to the colonial core to the north, midway along Calle Brasil, at Compostela, two blocks east of Plaza del Cristo, you'll find the handsome **Iglesia y Convento de Santa Tere-**

sa de Jesús, the third of Havana's monasteries, built by the Carmelites in 1705 with separate church and convent, both with outstanding baroque doorways. The church has ever since performed its original function (call in on Saturday afternoon, when Afro-Cuban music and dance is hosted in the courtyard), although the convent ceased to operate as such in 1929 when the nuns were moved out and the building was converted into a series of homes.

Across the road, on the east side of Compostela, is the **Farmácia Roturno Permanente** (formerly the Drogerría Sarrá), whose magnificently carved wooden shelves seem more fitting as the altar work for the church across the way. The paneled shelves bear painted glass murals and are stocked with herbs and pharmaceuticals in colorful old bottles and ceramic jars.

Three blocks south on Compostela is the **Iglesia y Convento de Nuestra Señora de Belén**, a huge complex occupying the block between Calles Luz and Acosta and Compostela and Aguacate and until recently a derelict shell. The convent was built to house the first nuns who arrived in Havana in 1704. Construction took from 1712 to 1718. This was the first baroque religious structure erected in Havana, and it served as a refuge for poor convalescents under the tenure of Bishop Compostela. Spanish authorities ejected the religious order—the Order of Bethlehem—in 1842 and turned the church briefly into a government office before making it over to the Jesuits. They in turn established a college for the sons of the aristocracy here. It is linked to contiguous buildings across the street by an arched walkway—the **Arch of Bethlehem,** unfortunately in decrepit condition—spanning Acosta. As you enter, note the ornate façade decorated with a nativity scene set in a large niche framed with a shell. The church, which was being restored at press time,

Iglesia y Convento de Nuestra Senora de Belen

will supposedly become a religious community again, part of the building will house a home for the aged, while the cloisters are slated to become a hotel.

Two blocks east of Belén, on Calle Cuba between Luz and Sol, you'll discover the **Convento de Santa Clara de Asís,** tel. (7) 61-3335, fax (7) 33-5696, a massive nunnery—the first founded in Havana—begun in 1638 and completed in 1644. It was a refuge for girls unlucky enough to possess an insufficient dowry to attract suitors. Only thus could the unfortunate females preserve their self-respect. It is a remarkable building, with a lobby full of beautiful period pieces and an inner and outer cloistered courtyard awash in divine light and surrounded by columns, one of which is entwined by the roots of a *capulí* tree, whose fruits resemble large golden pearls and taste ambrosial. Steady yourself before gazing up at the breathtaking cloister roof carved with geometric designs: a classic *alfarje.* Indeed, stunning wooden carvings abound. It's open Mon.-Fri. 9 a.m.-4 p.m.; entrance US$1.

The convent has been restored to pristine condition and now, fittingly, houses the **Centro Nacional de Conservación y Museología,** plus nine charming rooms for rent (see Accommodation). The center offers courses for architects, planners, conservationists, and the like. Peek inside the **Salon Plenario,** a marble-floored hall with a lofty beamed wooden ceiling of imposing stature.

The **Iglesia Parroquial del Espíritu Santo,** Havana's oldest church, lies two blocks south of Santa Clara de Asís, at the corner of Calles Cuba and Acosta. The church, which dates from 1638 (the circa 1674 central nave and façade and circa 1720 Gothic vault are later additions) was originally a hermitage "for the devotions of free Negroes." Later, continuing in liberal tradition, King Charles III issued a royal decree giving the right of asylum here to anyone hunted by the authorities (a privilege no longer bestowed). The church reveals many surprises, including a gilded, carved wooden pelican in a niche in the baptistery. The sacristy (where parish archives dating back through the 17th century are preserved) boasts an enormous cupboard full of baroque silver staffs and incense holders. Catacombs to each side of the nave are held up by subterranean tree trunks and boast between niches (still containing the odd bone) a series of paintings of skeletons crowned with tiaras and holding miters, almost erased by time and damp, They represent the dance of death. The body of Bishop Gerónimo Valdés had been laid to rest in the church. He remained in a kind of limbo, his whereabouts unknown, until he turned up, buried under the floor, during a restoration in 1936. Today he rests in a tomb beside the nave, which boasts a carved wooden altar. The sturdy tower holds four bells. Steps lead up to the gallery, where you may turn the handle of a carillon.

Finally, two blocks south on Calle Cuba is another small handsome church—**Iglesia y Convento de Nuestra Señora de la Merced**—tucked into the corner of Cuba and Calle Merced. Trompe l'oeil frescoes add color to the ornate interior, which contains romantic dome paintings (added during a remodeling in 1904) and an alcove lined with fake stalactites in honor of Nuestra Señora de Lourdes. It is one of the most resplendent of the city's church interiors. The church, begun in 1755, has strong Afro-Cuban connections, and it is not unusual to see devotees of *santería* kneeling in prayer. In its heyday it was the favored church for weddings of the aristocracy. Try to time your visit for 24 September, when scores of gaily colored worshipers cram in for the Virgen de la Merced's feast day. More modest celebrations are held on the 24th of every other month.

AVENIDA SAN PEDRO (DESAMPARADOS)

Southward of the Plaza de San Francisco, Havana's waterfront boulevard swings along the harborfront, overshadowed by portside warehouses and sailors' bars and changing names as it curves from Avenida San Pedro to Leonor Pérez.

HAVANA'S CITY WALLS

*C*onstruction of Havana's fortified city walls began on 3 February 1674. They ran along the western edge of the bay and, on the landward side, stood between today's Calle Egido, Monserrate, and Zulueta according to a plan by the Spanish engineer Cristóbal de Rodas. To pay for construction, the Court of Spain voted an annual budget from the Royal Chests of Mexico and even decreed a tax on wine sold in Havana's taverns.

Under the direction of engineer Juan de Siscaras, African slaves labored for 23 years to build the 1.4-meter-thick, 10-meter-tall city wall that was intended to ring the entire city using rocks hauled in from the coast. The 4,892-meter-long wall was completed in 1697, with a small opening for the mooring of ships, and a perimeter of five km. The damage inflicted by the British artillery in 1762 was repaired in 1797, when the thick wall attained its final shape. It formed an irregular polygon with nine defensive bastions with sections of wall in between, and moats and steep drops to delay assault by enemy troops. It was protected by 180 cannons and garrisoned with 3,400 troops. In its first stage it had just two entrances (nine more were added later), opened each morning upon the sound of a single cannon and closed at night the same way.

As time went on, the *intramuros* (the city within the walls) burst its confines. In 1841, Havana authorities petitioned the Spanish Crown for permission to demolish the walls. Just 123 years after the walls went up, they came down again. The demolition began in 1863, when African slave-convicts were put to work to destroy what their forefathers had built under hard labor. The demolition wasn't completed until well into the 20th century.

Alas, only fragments remain, most notably at the junction of Calle Egido and Avenida del Puerto, near the railway station at Avenida del Puerto and Egido, and at Calles Monserrate and Teniente Rey. Sentry boxes still stand in front of the Presidential Palace, between Calles Monserrate and Zulueta, and at the west end of Calle Tacón.

The Fundación Destilera Havana Club, or **Museo de Ron,** was under construction at press time in a harborfront colonial mansion on San Pedro, between Churruca and Sol. It will host an audio-visual presentation on the history and production of Cuban rums, with a free rum sampling to boot. A mini-production unit was to be installed to demonstrate the process from the growing of sugarcane and fermentation to the distillation and aging process that results in some of the world's finest rums. A bar—**Bar Havana Club**—will let you tipple the wares. Open 9:30 a.m.-6 p.m. (the bar will be open 11 a.m.-2 a.m.).

Be sure to call at **Dos Hermanos,** the simple bar at the foot of Sol and once favored by Ernest Hemingway: see the Entertainment section. A strong *mojito* will steel you for a close look at the harbor, named by the United Nations as one of the world's ten most polluted bodies of water. When the tides ebb sufficiently to draw out the harbor waters, petroleum scums the ocean fronting the Malecón and the stench hangs over the port city like Banquo's ghost. The plight dated back to prerevolutionary days, when "the smoke blew straight across the sky from the tall chimneys of the Havana Electric Company and . . . the water was as black and greasy as the pumpings from the bottom of the tanks of an oil tanker . . . and the scum of the harbor lay along the sides blacker than the creosote of the pilings and foul as an unclean sewer." A clean-up is supposedly slated.

Farther south, at the junction with Calle Oficios, San Pedro takes a name change: Leonor Pérez, which runs alongside the **Alameda de Paula,** a 100-meter-long raised promenade lined with marble and iron street lamps, and the setting on weekdays for alfresco tuition and physical education for school kids. Midway along the Alameda is a carved column with a fountain at its base, erected in 1847 to pay homage to the Spanish navy, although it bears an unlikely Irish name: **Columna O'Donnell,** named for the Capitán-General of Cuba, Leopoldo O'Donnell, who dedicated the monument. It is covered in relief work on a military theme and crowned by a lion with the arms of Spain in its claws.

Leonor Pérez leads south to **Plazuela de Paula,** a small circular plaza with the recently restored **Iglesia de San Francisco de Paula** in the middle of the road. This twee little place was abandoned ages ago as a church and today houses a little museum full of oil paintings and oversize photographs of early 20th-century bands. Note the national hymn—La Bayamesa —inscribed in metal on the interior wall to the left.

West of the plazuela, at the foot of Calle San Isidro, were the old P&O docks where the ships from Miami and Key West used to dock and where Pan American Airways had its terminal when it was still flying the old clipper flying-boats. Before World War II, when the U.S. Navy took over the docks, San Isidro had been the great whorehouse street of the waterfront. According to Ernest Hemingway, many of the women were Europeans. After the war, the Navy closed the brothels and "shipped all the whores back to Europe. Many people were sad after the ships had gone and San Isidro had never recovered. There were gay streets in Havana and there were some very tough streets and tough quarters, such as Jesús y María, which was just a short distance away. But this part of town was just sad as it had been ever since the whores had gone."

South of the plazuela, the waterfront boulevard becomes Desamparados, which runs south to the **Cortina de la Habana,** a remnant section of the old fortress wall enclosing Habana Vieja in colonial days. Desamparados continues south from here past the docks to the Vía Blanca, the road for San Francisco de Paula, Regla, and Playas del Este. One hundred meters south of the Cortina you'll see a monument made of twisted metal parts—fragments of *La Coubre,* the French cargo ship that exploded in Havana harbor on 4 March 1960 (the vessel was carrying armaments for the Castro government, and it is generally assumed that the CIA or other counterrevolutionaries blew it up). The **Monumento Mártires del Vapor La Coubre** honors the seamen who died.

AVENIDA DE BÉLGICA (EGIDO)

Avenida de Bélgica, colloquially called Egido, follows the hollow once occupied by the ancient walls of Habana Vieja. It is a continuation of Monserrate (see Calle Monserrate, above) and flows downhill from two blocks east of Parque de la Fraternidad to the harbor. It has the appearance of being run-down, but a closer look reveals that it is lined with beautiful buildings constructed during the urbanization that followed demolition of the walls. Though built during the mid-19th century they have the appearance of being much older, as with the **Palacio de la Contesa de Villalba,** a Renaissance-style edifice facing onto the **Plazuela de los Ursulinos.** Similarly, the **Palacio de los Marqueses de Balboa,** one block south, speaks of erstwhile beauty through a layer of grime and decay.

The street's masterpiece is the **Estación Central de Ferrocarril,** Havana's impressive Venetian-style railway station, at the corner of Calle Arsenal, and containing, sitting on rails in its lobby, an 1843-model steam locomotive—*La Junta*—said to have been Cuba's first. The station was designed in 1910 by a North American architect, blending Spanish Revival and Italian Renaissance styles. It is built atop what was once the Arsenal, or Spanish naval shipyard.

On the station's north side is a small shady plaza—**Parque de los Agrimensores** (Park of the Surveyors)—pinned by a large remnant of the old city wall.

A shining star in southern Habana Vieja's constellation is the **Casa Natal de José Martí,** a simple house—painted ocher, with green windows and door frames and terra-cotta tile floors—at Leonor Pérez #314 (also called Calle Paula), tel. (7) 62-3778, at the junction with Egido and facing the railway station. The house is a shrine for Cuban schoolchildren, who flock to pay homage to Cuba's national hero, who was born on 28 January 1853 and spent the first four years of his life here. The entrance lobby displays letters from Martí in glass cases and a bronze bust on a simple wooden pedestal. Many of his personal effects are here, too, including a lacquered *escritorio* (writing desk) and a broad-brimmed Panama hat given to him by Ecuadorian President Eloy Alfaro (Panama hats don't come from the country of Panama—they're made next door but one, in Ecuador). Many of his original texts and poems and sketches are displays. There's even a lock of the hero's hair from when he was only four years old. There are more guides (one per room) than you can shake a stick at. They follow you around eerily, although at a discreet distance. Open Tues.-

Sat. 9 a.m.-5 p.m. and Sunday 9 a.m.-1 p.m. Entrance US$1 (US$1 extra for guides, US$2 for cameras, US$10 for videos). The building across the street houses a *Salón de Expocisiones,* where piano recitals and other cultural activities are hosted.

Egido slopes south to the Cortina de la Habana (see above) at the junction with Desamparados, and is lined with remnants of the **Murallas de Habana,** the original city walls. Just north of Desamparados is the **Puerta de la Tenaza,** the only ancient city gate still standing. Here a plaque inset within a still extant remnant of the old wall shows a map of the old city and the extent of the original walls and fortifications.

PARQUE HISTÓRICO MORRO Y CABAÑA

Looming over Habana Vieja, on the north side of the harbor channel, is the rugged cliff face of the Cabaña, dominated by two great fortress-

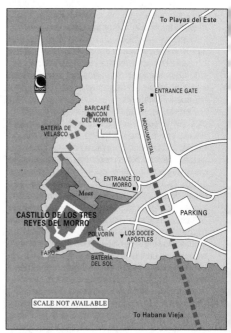

es—the Castillo de los Tres Reyes del Morro and the Castillo de San Carlos de la Cabaña—that constitute **Morro-Cabaña Historical Park,** tel. (7) 62-7653, and are must-sees by both day and night. Together they comprise the largest and most powerful defensive complex built by the Spanish in the Americas and are maintained in a superb state.

The Cabaña looms over the village of **Casablanca,** which clings to the shore on the northeast side of Havana harbor, in the easterly lee of the Castillo de San Carlos de la Cabaña. Casablanca's narrow main street is overhung with balconies. And from here tiers of houses rise up the hillside. Today a few rusting freighters sit in dry dock, and fishing boats bob along the waterfront. Casablanca is also fascinating as the departure point for the "Hershey Train," a three-car passenger train once belonging to the Hershey-Cuban Railroad (see the special topic, the Hershey Train, in the Havana Province chapter).

Getting There: Visitors arriving by car reach Loma Cabaña via the tunnel (no pedestrians) that descends beneath the Máximo Gómez Monument off Avenida de Céspedes. The well-signed exit for the Morro and Castillo San Carlos is immediately on your right after exiting the tunnel on the north side of the harbor. Buses from Parque de las Fraternidad pass through the tunnel and will drop you by the fortress access road (the *ciclobus* permits bicycles).

You can also get there by day by taking the little ferry that bobs its way across Havana harbor to Casablanca every 20 minutes or so from the Muelle la Luz (10 centavos) on the south side of the Terminal Sierra Maestra, at the foot of Calle Santa Clara. From here you can walk uphill (it's a steep 10-minute climb) to an easterly entrance gate to the Foso de los Laureles in the Cabaña. However, the latter gate closes at dusk, so don't take this route if you plan on seeing the *cañonazo.*

Casablanca is also reached by car from the Vía Monumental: the exit is marked about one km east of the tunnel. The road follows the eastern ridge of the *cabaña* and switchbacks down to Casablanca.

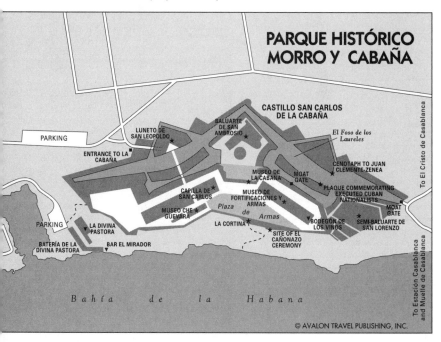

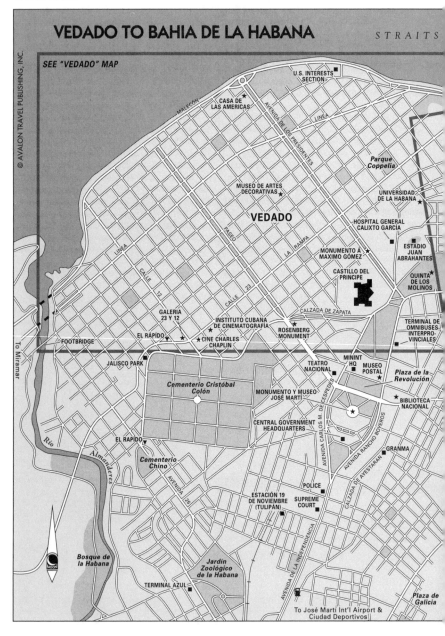

VEDADO TO BAHIA DE LA HABANA

STRAITS

© AVALON TRAVEL PUBLISHING, INC.

SEE "VEDADO" MAP

MALECÓN

AVENIDA DE LOS PRESIDENTES

U.S. INTERESTS SECTION

CASA DE LAS AMERICAS

LINEA

Parque Coppelia

MUSEO DE ARTES DECORATIVAS

UNIVERSIDAD DE LA HABANA

VEDADO

PASEO

LA RAMPA

HOSPITAL GENERAL CALIXTO GARCIA

ESTADIO JUAN ABRAHANTES

LINEA

CALLE 12

CALLE 23

MONUMENTO A MAXIMO GÓMEZ

CASTILLO DEL PRINCIPE

QUINTA DE LOS MOLINOS

CALZADA DE ZAPATA

GALERIA 23 Y 12

INSTITUTO CUBANA DE CINEMATOGRAFÍA

ROSENBERG MONUMENT

TERMINAL DE OMNIBUSES INTERPRO- VINCIALES

To Miramar

FOOTBRIDGE

EL RÁPIDO

CINE CHARLES CHAPLIN

TEATRO NACIONAL

MININT HQ

MUSEO POSTAL

Plaza de la Revolución

JALISCO PARK

Cementerio Cristóbal Colón

MONUMENTO Y MUSEO JOSÉ MARTÍ

AVENIDA CARLOS M. DE CESPEDES

BIBLIOTECA NACIONAL

CENTRAL GOVERNMENT HEADQUARTERS

AVENIDA RANCHO BOYEROS

Río Almendares

EL RÁPIDO

Cementerio Chino

AVENIDA 26

GRANMA

CALZADA DE AYESTARAN

POLICE

ESTACIÓN 19 DE NOVIEMBRE (TULIPÁN)

SUPREME COURT

AVENIDA DE LA INDEPENDENCIA

Bosque de la Habana

Jardin Zoológico de la Habana

TERMINAL AZUL

Plaza de Galicia

To José Martí Int'l Airport & Ciudad Deportivos

MOON

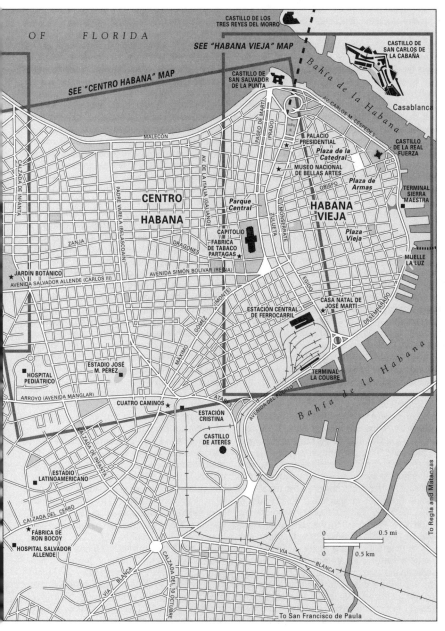

OF FLORIDA

CASTILLO DE LOS
TRES REYES DEL MORRO

SEE "HABANA VIEJA" MAP

CASTILLO DE
SAN CARLOS DE
LA CABAÑA

SEE "CENTRO HABANA" MAP

CASTILLO DE
SAN SALVADOR
DE LA PUNTA

Bahía de la Habana

Casablanca

MALECÓN

PASEO DE MARTÍ (PRADO)

PALACIO
PRESIDENCIAL

*Plaza de la
Catedral*

CASTILLO
DE LA REAL
FUERZA

AV. CARLOS M. CÉSPEDES

AV. DE LA ITALIA (GALIANO)

PADRE VARELA (BELASCOAÍN)

CALZADA DE INFANTA

MUSEO NACIONAL
DE BELLAS ARTES

OBISPO

*Plaza de
Armas*

TERMINAL
SIERRA
MAESTRA

CENTRO

HABANA

*Parque
Central*

MONSERRATE

ZULUETA

**HABANA
VIEJA**

ZANJA

CAPITOLIO

DRAGONES

FÁBRICA
DE TABACO
PARTAGAS

*Plaza
Vieja*

EGIDO

MUELLE
LA LUZ

JARDÍN BOTÁNICO

AVENIDA SIMÓN BOLÍVAR (REINA)

AVENIDA SALVADOR ALLENDE (CARLOS III)

MÁXIMO GÓMEZ (MONTE)

CASA NATAL DE
JOSÉ MARTÍ

DESEMPARADO

ESTACIÓN CENTRAL
DE FERROCARRIL

ESTADIO JOSÉ
M. PÉREZ

HOSPITAL
PEDIÁTRICO

ARROYO (AVENIDA MANGLAR)

CUATRO CAMINOS

ATARES

AVENIDA DEL PUERTO

TERMINAL
LA COUBRE

Bahía de la Habana

ESTACIÓN
CRISTINA

CASTILLO
DE ATERÉS

CALZADA DE INFANTA

ESTADIO
LATINOAMERICANO

CALZADA DEL CERRO

To Regla and Matanzas

0   0.5 mi

0   0.5 km

FÁBRICA DE
RON BOCOY

HOSPITAL SALVADOR
ALLENDE

VÍA BLANCA

CALZADA DEL 10 OCTUBRE

VÍA
BLANCA

To San Francisco de Paula

Entrance to the park costs US$1 (entry to the castles is extra).

Castillo de los Tres Reyes del Morro

This handsome, ghost-white castle, tel. (7) 63-7941, is built into the rocky palisades of Punta Barlovento, crowning a rise that drops straight to the sea at the entrance to Havana's narrow harbor channel. Canted in its articulation, the fort—whose construction began in 1589—follows a tradition of military architecture established by the Milanese at the end of the Middle Ages, forming an irregular polygon that follow the contours of the rocky headland on which it was built, with a sharp-angled bastion at the apex, stone walls 10 feet thick, and a series of batteries stepping down to the shore. Hundreds of slaves toiled under the lash of whip and sun to cut the stone *in situ,* extracted from the void that forms the moats. El Morro took 40 years to complete and served its job well, repelling countless pirate attacks and withstanding for 44 days a siege by British cannon in 1762.

The castle has been marvelously restored to former glory and has lost none of its commanding composure, with plentiful cannons on trolleys in their embrasures. A still-functioning lighthouse was constructed beside the fortress in 1844.

Originally the castle communicated with the exterior principally by sea, to which it was linked via the **Plataforma de la Estrella,** the wharf at the southern foot of the cliff. Today you enter via a drawbridge across the deep moat that leads through a long tunnel—the **Tunel de Aspillerado**—to the vast wooden gates. The gates open to the **Camino de Rondas,** a small parade ground (Plaza de Armas) with, to the right, a narrow entrance to the **Baluarte de Austria** (Austrian Bastion), a covered area with cannon embrasures for firing down on the moat (it is named for the period when the Austrian House of Hapsburgs ruled Spain). A cobbled ramp—also to the right—leads up from the plaza to the **Baluarte de Tejeda,** a wide windswept platform with further embrasures and a splendid view east past the **Batería de Velasco** (with cannons added in the 19th century) and along the coast. On the seaward side of the Tejeda bastion (named for the governor and military leader who began work on the castle), you can look down into the crevasse caused by the explosion that breached the Caballero del Mar wall in the 1762 siege by the British. Various plaques inset in the bastion commemorate heroic figures of the siege: even the Royal Navy is honored on a plaque placed by the British Embassy. From here you can walk the curtain wall where rusting cannons of the **Morrillo,** or High battery, are in place; with the Low Battery on the level below. Do not be tempted to walk the wind-battered battlements, which are canted seaward and have no guardrails. One false step and you could easily tumble onto the wave-swept rocks below.

To the left of the Plaza de Armas is the **Surtida de los Tinajones,** where giant earthenware vases are inset in stone. They once contained rapeseed oil as fuel for the 15-meter-tall lighthouse, reached by a small ramp over the *surtida.* The original lantern was replaced in 1928, by acetylene and, finally in 1945, an electric lantern that still flashes its light every 15 seconds, sending a beam 18 miles.

The Camino de Rondas surrounds a central building built in 1763 atop the cisterns that supplied the garrison of 1,000 men with water. The galleries of this two-story structure are given to exhibition rooms, including the **Museo Navigación** with expositions on the colonial sea-voyages of Portugal and Spain. Another room exhibits relics recovered from the bottom of Havana harbor, including mementos from the USS *Maine,* which mysteriously exploded in the harbor on 5 February 1898, providing a pretext for U.S. entry into the Spanish-Cuban war.

All maritime traffic in and out of Havana harbor is controlled (as it has been since 1888) from the **Sala de la Estación Semafórica,** the semaphore station atop the castle, accessed via the Baluarte de Tejeda. With luck you may be invited in to scan the city using 20x120 power Nikon binoculars. The flagpole outside was used to signal information to the city fortresses and harbormasters about approaching traffic. It was here, too, that the English raised the Union Jack to proclaim their capture of Cuba . . . and the Spanish flag was raised again one year later. The flagpole came to take on political significance, and it was here that the Stars and Stripes replaced the flag of Spain when the latter came down for the last time in 1898. Today the tradition of adorning the flagpole with multicolored signal flags is continued on public holidays.

Below the castle, facing the city on the landward side and reached by a cobbled ramp, is the **Battery of the Twelve Apostles,** with massive eponymous cannons, and a splendid little bar—El Polvorín ("The Powderhouse")—and restaurant attached (see the Food section).

The Morro is open daily 9 a.m.-8 p.m. (entrance US$2, plus US$1 for a guide, and US$2 for photos, US$5 for video). Entry to the lighthouse ostensibly costs US$2 extra.

Castillo de San Carlos de la Cabaña
This massive fortress lining Cabaña hill half a kilometer east of the Morro enjoys a strategic position with a sloping vantage to the north out to sea, and a cliff-top balcony over the city and harbor to the south. It covers 10 hectares, stretching 700 meters in length. It was built 1764-74 following the English invasion, and cost the staggering sum of 14 million pesos (costly enough, thought the king after whom it is named, that when told the cost he reached for a telescope; surely, he said, it must be large enough to see from Madrid). From the very beginning the castle was powerfully armed and could count in the mid-19th century some 120 bronze cannons and mortars, plus a permanent garrison of 1,300 men (the castle was designed to hold 6,000 troops in times of need). Still, it was never used in battle, and for that reason it has been claimed that its dissuasive presence won all potential battles—a tribute to the French designer and engineer entrusted with conception and construction. It has been splendidly restored.

The fortress is reached from the north. You pass through two defensive structures before reaching the monumental baroque portal (flanked by great columns and a pediment etched with the escutcheon of King Charles III and plaques dedicated to various colonial governors) and massive drawbridge over a 12-meter-deep moat, one of several moats carved from solid rock and separating individual fortress components.

Beyond the entrance gate, a paved alley leads to the **Plaza de Armas,** centered on a grassy, tree-shaded park fronted by a 400-meter-long curtain wall. Immediately ahead upon entering the plaza is the **Comandancia de Che,** where Che Guevara had his headquarters in the months following the Triunfo del Revolution (his guerrilla army occupied the fortress on 3 January

1959). The small structure now houses the **Museo Che Guevara.** To the west, the cobbled street leads past a small **chapel** with a charming vaulted interior containing a beautifully-carved wooden altar, plus a spired bell tower and an even more impressive baroque façade surrounding blood-red walls. Venerated here were three saints: Santa Carlos, patron saint of the fortress; Santa Barbara, patron saint of artillerymen; and Nuestra Señora del Pilar, patron saint of sailors.

Immediately west, on the north face of the plaza, is a building that contains a **history museum** tracing the castle's development, including a room containing various torture instruments and dedicated to the period when political executions took place; and another with uniforms and weaponry from the colonial epoch (including a representation of the *cañonazo* ceremony; see below). A portal here leads into a garden—**Patio de Los Jagüeyes**—that while today a place of repose, once served as a *cortadura,* a defensive element once packed with explosives that could be ignited to foil the enemy's attempts to gain entry.

A long building runs west from here, following the slope of the plaza. Today the various rooms make up the impressive **Museo de Fortificaciones y Armas,** containing an impressive collection of suits of armor and weaponry that spans the ancient Arab and Asian worlds and stretches back through medieval times to the Roman era. Never seen a battering ram or ballistic catapult? Check 'em out here. A model of the Cabañana helps in understanding the concepts that made this fortress so formidable.

To the rear of the armaments museum is the **Calle Marina,** a handsome cobbled street lined with former barracks, armaments stores, and cells of condemned prisoners. The former vaults have been converted and now contain two worthy restaurants (see the Food chapter). Another of Havana's finest restaurants—**La Divina Pastora**—lies below and 200 meters west of the Morro, by the wharf where supply ships once berthed.

Midway down Calle Marina, a gate leads down to the **El Foso de los Laureles,** the massive Moat of the Laurels containing the execution wall where hundreds of nationalist sympathizers were shot during the wars of independence, when the fortress dungeons were used as a prison for Cuban patriots, a role that Generals Machado and Batista continued. Following the Revolution, scores of Batista supporters and "counter-revolutionaries" met the same fate: Che Guevara commanded the execution squads. Today goats nibble the grass that grows richly in the blood-soaked soil.

On the north side of the moat is a separate fortress unit, the **San Juliá Revellin,** recently reopened and today containing examples of the missiles installed during the Cuban Missile Crisis (called by the Cubans, the October 1962 Crisis): among them a Soviet nuclear-tipped R-12 rocket.

At the north end of the Plaza de Armas, a covered path leads to the **Semi-baluarte de San Lorenzo,** an expansive maze-like fortification offering vast views over the harbor from the cannon embrasures.

The curtain wall—**La Cortina**—runs the length of the castle on its south side and formed the main gun position overlooking Havana. It is still lined with ceremonial cannons engraved with lyrical names such as *La Hermosa* (The Handsome). Here, every night at 9, a small unit assembles in military fashion, dressed in scarlet 18th-century garb and led by fife and drum. Soon enough, you'll hear the reverberating crack of the *cañonazo*—the nightly firing of a cannon, which used to signal the closing of the city gates and the raising of the chain to seal the mouth of the harbor (see Entertainment). Today it causes unsuspecting visitors to drop their drinks.

The castle is open daily 10 a.m.-10 p.m. Entry costs US$3 (plus optional US$1 for guide, US$2 for a camera, US$10 video) and includes the *cañonazo* (you can visit the castle by day and return at night on the same ticket). Kids are charged half price. The rest of the fortress grounds are still used as a military base, and most of the surrounding area is therefore off-limits.

Excursions are available to witness the *cañonazo,* usually followed by dinner at La Divina Pastora. You can make reservations through any of the tour agencies listed in the Getting Around section of the Transportation chapter.

El Cristo de Casablanca

A great statue of Jesus Christ looms over Casablanca, dominating the cliff face immediately east of the Castillo, with the domed National Observatory behind. The 15-meter-tall statue, erected in 1958, stands atop a three-meter-tall pedestal and was hewn from Italian Carrara marble by noted female Cuban sculptor Jilma Madera. The figure stands with one hand on his chest and the other raised in a blessing. From the viewing platform *(mirador)* surrounding the statue, you have a bird's-eye view of the deep, flask-shaped harbor. The views are especially good at dawn and dusk, and it is possible, with the sun gilding the waters, to imagine great galleons slipping in and out of the harbor, a conduit for the wealth of a hemisphere.

The statue is accessible by a 10-minute uphill walk from Casablanca by either a staircase beginning in the plazuela 100 meters north of the ferry terminal; or by a winding roadway that leads west from the *plazuela.*

CENTRO HABANA

Centro Habana (Central Havana—pop. 175,000) lies west of the Prado and Habana Vieja. Centro is laid out in a near-perfect grid and is mostly residential, with few sites or sights of note. Much of Centro is so dilapidated that the region conjures up images of what Dresden must have looked like after the bombing.

In prerevolutionary days, Centro was the heart of Havana's red-light district, and scores of prostitutes roamed such streets as the ill-named Calle Virtudes (Virtues). Today southern Centro is the great commercial heart of the city—if a bit faded from the days when there were more goods to sell. Still, the main shopping streets of San Rafael, Neptuno, and Galiano have sprung back to life, and modern U.S.-style shopping centers have opened, stocked with mostly imported goods for dollars only.

Believe it or not, there's also a small Chinatown—Barrio Chino—delineated by Calles Zanja, Dragones, Salud, Rayo, San Nicolás, and Manrique.

The two major west-east thoroughfares are the Malecón to the north, and the Zanja and Avenida Salvador Allende though the center; plus two important shopping streets—Calles Neptuno and San Rafael between the Malecón and Zanja. Three major thoroughfares cut south from the Malecón: Calzada de Infanta, forming the western boundary; Padre Varela, down the center; and Avenida de Italia (Galiano) farther east.

MALECÓN AND VICINITY

When questioned by an immigration official as to why he had come to Cuba and stayed for 10 years, Costa Rican composer Ray Tico replied: "I fell in love with Havana's seafront drive." The Malecón (more properly the Muro de Malecón; literally "embankment," or "seawall") was designed as a jetty wall in 1857 by the Cuban engineer General Francisco de Albear but not laid out until 1902 (by the U.S. governor General Woods) and fronts sinuously and dramatically along the Atlantic shoreline between the Castillo de San Salvador de la Punta and Río Almendares, almost five miles to the west.

"Silver lamé" was what composer Orlando de la Rosa called the six-lane seafront boulevard. The metaphor has stuck, although it is today only a ghostly reminder of its former brilliance—what Martha Gellhorn called a "19th-century jewel and a joke." The Malecón is lined with once-glorious houses, each exuberantly distinct from the next. Unprotected by seaworthy paint during four decades, they proved incapable of withstanding the salt spray that crashes over the seawall in great airy clouds and then floats off in rainbows. Their façades—green trimmed with purple, pink with blue, yellow with orange—became decrepit, supported by wooden scaffolding, while the broad limestone walkway became now pitted and broken.

At press time a restoration was underway. A new seawall had been completed, and about half the buildings had been renovated, including the interiors, though the workmanship seems iffy.

All along the shore are the worn remains of square baths—known as the "Elysian Fields"—hewn from the rocks below the seawall, originally with separate areas for white men, white women, and Negroes. Since the Revolution they are more democratic. These Baños de Mar precede construction of the Malecón and were cut into the steps of rock alongside the Calzada de San Lazaro. Each is about 3.7 meters square and 1.8-2.4 meters deep, with rock steps for access and a couple of portholes through which the waves of this tideless shore wash in and out.

The Malecón is the city's undisputed social gathering spot and offers a microcosm of Havana life: the elderly walking their dogs, the shiftless looking for tourists; the young passing rum among friends; fishermen tending their lines; and always scores of entwined couples. All through the night, lovers' murmurings mingle with the crash and hiss of the waves.

The intriguing building fronted by weathered caryatids one block west of the Prado is the old Club Unión casino. Newly restored, it now houses the **Centro Cultural de España,** Malecón #17, tel. (7) 66-9189. The former gaming rooms offer art and cultural exhibits honoring Spain, and cultural events are hosted daily, including flamenco. It's open Mon.-Fri. 10 a.m.-5 p.m. and Saturday 10 a.m.-3 p.m.

Literature buffs may be intrigued by the **Museo Lezama Lima,** three blocks inland from the Malecón at Trocadero 162, e/ Crespo y Industria, two blocks west of the Prado. The museum is in the former home of José Lezana Lima, author of *Paradiso,* which was made into a renowned movie.

Dominating the Malecón to the west is the massive bronze **Monumento Antonio Maceo,** atop a marble base in a plaza in front of the **Hospital Hermanos Ameijeiras** (the hospital was built atop what was intended to be the Banco Nacional de Cuba, but Che Guevara, as the revolutionary Minister of Finances, nixed the plans, despite which local rumor has it that the vaults still contain Cuba's meager gold reserves). The motley tower that stands at the west end of the plaza is the **Torreon de San Lazaro,** a military redoubt with loopholes for snipers aiming along the Malecón.

Barrio Cayo Hueso

Immediately west of the Plaza Antonio Maceo is a triangular area formed by the Malecón, Calle San Lazaro, and Calzada de Infanta, forming the northwest corner of Centro Habana. The *barrio* dates from the early 20th century, when tenement homes were erected atop what had been the Espada cemetery (hence the name, Cay of Bones). Some 12,000 homes are squashed into the compact and deteriorated region, accessed by a warren of irregular alleyways.

In 1995, because of its deteriorated state, Cayo Hueso became the first area of Havana earmarked for an experimental program to halt its decline based on a humanistic and manageable approach to public housing. A new microbrigade effort was launched to renovate existing buildings, providing experts to guide inhabitants in the rehabilitation of their own units and utilizing supplies that are placed in their hands. Almost 20 government agencies are involved in the restoration (each agency has adopted a street), and an effort has been made to educate the local community as to its history and culture.

CENTRO HABANA

© AVALON TRAVEL PUBLISHING, INC.

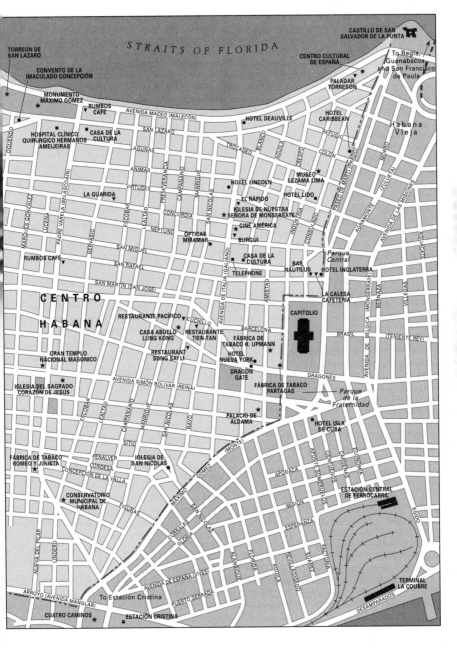

STRAITS OF FLORIDA

CASTILLO DE SAN
SALVADOR DE LA PUNTA

TORREON DE
SAN LAZARO

CONVENTO DE LA
IMACULADO CONCEPCIÓN

CENTRO CULTURAL
DE ESPAÑA

To Regla,
Guanabacoa
and San Francisco
de Paula

MONUMENTO
MÁXIMO GÓMEZ

RUMBOS
CAFÉ

AVENIDA MACEO (MALECÓN)

PALADAR
TORRESON

HOTEL DEAUVILLE

HOTEL
CARIBBEAN

Habana
Vieja

HOSPITAL CLÍNICO
QUIRÚRGICO HERMANOS
AMEIJEIRAS

CASA DE LA
CULTURA

SAN LÁZARO

LAGUNAS

TROCADERO

BLANCO

AGUILA

CRESPO

REFUGIO

COLÓN

OQUENDO

ANIMAS

VIRTUDES

LA GUARIDA

PRESERVANCIA

CAMPANARIO

MANRIQUE

SAN NICOLAS

HOTEL LINCOLN

MUSEO
LEZAMA LIMA

EL RÁPIDO

HOTEL LIDO

MARQUES GONZÁLEZ

LUCENA

PADRE VARELA (BELASCOAIN)

GERVASIO

ESCOBAR

LEALTAD

CONCORDIA

NEPTUNO

IGLESIA DE NUESTRA
SENORA DE MONSERRATE

CINE AMÉRICA

INDUSTRIA

CONSULADO

PASEO DE MARTI (PRADO)

MORRO

ZULUETA

AGRAMONTE

AVENIDA DE LAS MISIONES

ÓPTICAS
MIRAMAR

BURGUI

RUMBOS CAFÉ

SAN MIGUEL

SAN RAFAEL

SAN MARTIN (SAN JOSE)

AVENIDA DE ITALIA (GALIANO)

CASA DE LA
CULTURA

AMISTAD

BAR
NAUTILUS

Parque
Central

HOTEL INGLATERRA

MONSERRATE

BERNAZA

VILLEGAS

HABACUY

CENTRO

HABANA

TELEPHONE

LA CALESA
CAFETERÍA

RESTAURANTE PACÍFICO

CUCHILLO

CASA ABUELO
LUNG KONG

RESTAURANTE
TIEN-TAN

BARCELONA

CAPITOLIO

BRASIL

AVENIDA DE BELGICA

(TENIENTE REY)

GRAN TEMPLO
NACIONAL MASONICO

RESTAURANT
SONG SAI LI

FÁBRICA DE
TABACO H. UPMANN

HOTEL
NUEVA YORK

IGLESIA DEL SAGRADO
CORAZON DE JESÚS

AVENIDA SIMÓN BOLIVAR (REINA)

DRAGON
GATE

DRAGONES

FÁBRICA DE TABACO
PARTAGAS

Parque
de la
Fraternidad

ESCOBAR

LEALTAD

CAMPANARIO

MANRIQUE

SAN NICOLAS

RAYO

PALACIO DE
ALDAMA

HOTEL ISLA
DE CUBA

SITIO

GOMEZ

FÁBRICA DE TABACO
ROMEO Y JULIETA

PEÑALVER

CONDESA

CONCEPCIÓN DE LA VALLA

IGLESIA DE
SAN NICOLAS

APONTE

SOMERUELOS

CIENFUEGOS

CARDENAS

ECONOMÍA

FACTORÍA

APODACA

CONSERVATORIO
MUNICIPAL DE
HABANA

FIGURAS

MÁXIMO

SAN NICOLAS

MISIÓN

ESTACIÓN CENTRAL
DE FERROCARRIL

NUEVA DEL PILAR

LINDERO

CORRALES

GLORIA

ALAMBIQUE

ESPERANZA

FLORIDA

SUAREZ

REVILLAGIGEDO

AGUILA

EGIDO

AVENIDA DE ESPAÑA (VIVES)

ARROYO (AVENIDA MANGLAR)

To Estación Cristina

PUERTO CERRADA

TERMINAL
LA COUBRE

CUATRO CAMINOS

ESTACIÓN CRISTINA

DESAMPARADOS

The area, indeed, is a cultural treasure. On Calle Hornos, the first cultural center dedicated to tango was formed. Today it still hosts tango dancing, while other cultural events are hosted on Callejon de Hamel (also known as "Salvador's Alley"), located one block south of San Lazaro, where the renowned artist Salvador González has adorned walls with evocative murals in sun-drenched yellow, burnt orange, and blazing reds, inspired by *santería,* reflecting his religious beliefs and ties to Afro-Cuban culture. The authorities tried to close González's project when it was nascent, but locals came into the streets to protect the now-precious heritage. González, a bearded artist with an eye for self-promotion, has an eclectic art gallery where he sells his works for US$500 and up.

The plazuela at the junction of Infanta, between Calles Jovellar and San Lazaro, honors students of the University of Havana who were murdered or otherwise lost their lives during the fights against the Machado and Batista regimes. San Lazaro rises to the *escaleras,* the wide staircase at the entrance to the university that was the center for student demonstrations, and the junction of Infanta and San Lazaro was an important scene of battles between students and police. A memorial plaque in the plazuela recalls that it was from Calle Jovellar 107 that Fidel Castro set out for Santiago de Cuba on 25 July 1953 in a blue Buick sedan, initiating the attack on the Moncada barracks that would launch his revolution.

CALLES SAN RAFAEL AND NEPTUNO

The major commercial thoroughfare of Centro is **Calle San Rafael,** which for five blocks leads west from Parque Central as a pedestrian precinct lined with department stores, many of which still bear prerevolutionary neon signs promoting U.S. brand names from yesteryear. The pedestrian precinct stretches to Galiano, where it reverts to traffic and the stores give way to residences.

Calle Neptuno parallels San Rafael to the south and is a secondary shopping node for several blocks west of Galiano. Fans of tango might check out the **Casa del Tango,** at 303 Neptuno, honoring the tradition of the Argentinian dance and run by an elderly couple who

keep no regular hours. Within it is festooned with magazine covers, record covers, and other mementos to tango.

Be sure to pop into the **Cine América,** tel. (7) 62-5416, at the junction of Galiano. Dating from 1941, the interior is a model of art deco grace, with tiers of ballooning balconies and curvilinear box seats melting into the walls of the vaulted auditorium that boasts a moon-and-stars ceiling. The foyer features a terrazzo floor with zodiac motifs and an inlaid map of the world with Cuba, which lies at the very center, picked out in polished brass. Albeit severely deteriorated and crying out for restoration, it remains one of the world's great modern-style theaters.

Another tiny gem is the **Iglesia de Nuestra Señora de Monserrate,** dating from 1843, on Galiano one block north of Neptuno.

BARRIO CHINO AND VICINITY

After the end of slavery in 1886, landowners imported 150,000 Chinese as indentured laborers to work the fields. They were contracted to labor for eight years for miserable wages insufficient to buy their return. Most stayed and many intermarried with blacks. The Sino-Cuban descendants of those who worked off their indenture gravitated to Centro Habana, where they settled in the zones bordering the Zanza Real, the aqueduct that channeled water to the city. Here they worked as domestics or opened vegetable shops, laundries, and restaurants and were later joined by other Chinese fleeing persecution in California, including a wealthy group of California Chinese who arrived with investment opportunities in mind. In time, Havana's Chinese quarter (Barrio Chino) became the largest in Latin America, a mini-Beijing in the tropics.

During the "sordid era" it was a center of opium dens, prostitution houses, and the infamous Shanghai theater, where for US$1.25 one could see a "nude cabaret of extreme obscenity with the bluest of blue films in the intervals," wrote Graham Greene, who "watched without much interest Superman's performance with a mulatto girl (as uninspiring as a dutiful husband's)," then "smoked marijuana, and [saw] a lesbian performance at the Blue Moon," before snorting a little cocaine. Superman—also

OUR MAN IN HAVANA

No contemporary novel quite captures the tawdry intrigue and louche of Batista's Havana than does Graham Greene's *Our Man in Havana,* published in 1958 on the eve of the Revolutionary triumph and set amid the torrid events of Havana in 1957.

The comic tale tells of Wormold, an English vacuum salesman based in Havana and short of money. His daughter has reached an expensive age, so when approached by Hawthorne, he accepts the offer of £300 a month and becomes Agent 59200/5, MI6's man in Havana. To keep his job, he files bogus reports based on Lamb's *Tales from Shakespeare* and dreams up military apparatus from vacuum-cleaner designs. Unfortunately, his stories begin to come disturbingly true and Wormold becomes trapped by his own deceit and the workings of a hopelessly corrupt city and society.

Graham Greene (1904-91) was already a respected author when he was recruited to work for the Foreign Office, serving the years 1941-43 in Sierra Leone, in Africa. In the last years of the war, he worked for the British Secret Service dealing with counterespionage in the Iberian Peninsula, where he learned how the Nazi Abwehr (the German Secret Service) sent home false reports—perfect for his novel, in which he also poked fun at the British intelligence services. He traveled widely and based many of his works, including *Our Man in Havana,* on his experiences. He visited Havana several times in the 1950s and was disturbed by the mutilations and torture practiced by Batista's police officers and by social ills such as racial discrimination: "Every smart bar and restaurant was called a club so that a negro could be legally excluded." But he confessed to enjoying the "louché atmosphere" of Havana and seems to have savored the fleshpots completely. "I came there. . . for the brothel life, the roulette in every hotel. . . I liked the idea that one could obtain anything at will, whether drugs, women or goats," he later wrote.

Castro condoned *Our Man in Havana* but complained that it didn't do justice to the ruthlessness of the Batista regime. Greene agreed: "Alas, the book did me little good with the new rulers in Havana. In poking fun at the British Secret Service, I had minimized the terror of Batista's rule. I had not wanted too black a background for a light-hearted comedy, but those who had suffered during the years of dictatorship could hardly be expected to appreciate that my real subject was the absurdity of the British agent and not the justice of a revolution." Nonetheless, Castro permitted the screen-version starring Alec Guinness as Wormold to be filmed in Havana in 1959.

Greene returned to Cuba in the years 1963-66. Although initially impressed by Castro's war on illiteracy (he called it "a great crusade"), he later soured after witnessing the persecution of homosexuals, intellectuals, and Catholics. Perhaps for this reason, the author isn't commemorated in Cuba in any way.

---

known as El Toro (the Bull)—had a 14-inch penis and earned US$25 nightly and became so famous that he was immortalized in *The Godfather II* when the mobsters are in Cuba watching a live sex show. Greene made the Shanghai a setting in *Our Man in Havana,* when Wormold wisely opts to take Beatrice to the Tropicana instead.

Today Barrio Chino is a mere shadow of its former self, with about 400 native-born Chinese and perhaps 2,000 descendants still resident in the area. The vast majority of Chinese left Cuba in the years immediately following the Revolution. Barrio Chino has since lost much of its personality along with its colorful characters, who were encouraged to become "less Chinese and more Cuban." Nonetheless, there's enough to remind you of how things once were. Chinese lanterns still hang outside the doorways, alongside signs written in Chinese. You'll recognize Chinese features, too, in the lively free market held daily (except Wednesday) on tiny Calle Cuchillo. In 1995 the government of China agreed to help rebuild Havana's Chinatown and funded a dragon gate across Calle Dragones, announcing your entry from the east.

The most overtly Chinese street is diminutive, pedestrian-only **Calle Cuchillo,** which runs less than 100 meters and is lined with a dozen genuine Chinese restaurants. Be sure to visit at night when the Chinese lanterns are aglow. The most interesting of restaurants is **Restaurante Pacífico,** on Calle San Nicolas and Cuchillo. Ernest Hemingway used to eat here, on the top floor of the five-story building to which Fidel Castro is still an occasional visitor. "To get there," recalls Hemingway's son, Gregory, "you had to go up in an old elevator with a sliding iron grille for a door. It stopped at every floor, whether you wanted it to or not. On the second floor there was a five-piece Chinese orchestra blaring crazy atonal music. . . . Then you reached the third floor, where there was a whorehouse. . . . The fourth floor was an opium den with pitifully wasted little figures curled up around their pipes."

Perhaps the most interesting contemporary site in Barrio Chino is the **Casa Abuelo Lung Kong,** at Manrique y Dragones. The social club exists to support elders in the Chinese community and offers a genuine Chinese ambience. Oldsters sit in their rockers in the front *sala,* gossiping and reading newspapers, while in a basic restaurant at the rear, others dine on free breakfasts and lunches of Chinese fare using *parrillas* (chopsticks). You could be in Hong Kong. It has a more elegant restaurant upstairs. Visitors are usually made welcome, but it's a common courtesy to ask permission before putting your nose inside. Similarly, check out the **Sociedad Chung Shan,** another Chinese cultural society on Dragones between San Nicolas and Rayo.

If you can, time your visit to coincide with Chinese New Year at the end of January into early February, when the streets are charged with the staccato pop of firecrackers meant to scare away evil spirits and the lion comes out to leap and dance through the streets of Barrio Chino.

Fábrica de Tabaco H. Upmann

This cigar factory, on Calle Amistad e/ Barcelona y Dragones, tel. (7) 62-0081, one block west of the Capitolio, and officially known as the José Martí factory, was begun by the erstwhile London-based banking house of H. Upmann in 1844, when it registered its name as a cigar brand. In its heyday at the turn of the century, it was by far the largest producer of cigars in the country. The Upmann name remains synonymous with the highest quality Havana cigars—mild to medium-flavored, very smooth and subtle, and available in over 30 sizes (not to be confused with H. Upmanns made in the Dominican Republic). Cigar connoisseurs consider that the best Montecristos come from this factory, including the mammoth Montecristo A and Cohiba Robusto

and Esplendido. The factory's almost 50 rollers are all rated "grade seven," the highest ranking a cigar roller can possess in Cuba, although only three rollers possess the skills and strength to roll the whopping Montecristo A, of which only about 15,000 are made annually.

It's open Mon.-Fri. 8 a.m.-4 p.m. Tours are offered at 10:30 a.m. and 1:30 p.m. (US$10)

AVENIDAS SALVADOR ALLENDE AND VICINITY

This wide boulevard was laid out in the early 19th century by Governor Tacón, when it was known officially as Carlos III and colloquially as the Paseo, running east-west as a westerly extension of Avenida Reina (today's Avenida Simón Bolívar), which connects it to Parque de la Fraternidad. The governor built his summer house on Carlos III and was copied by many of Havana's nobility.

The few sites are of interest only in passing. One such is the **Gran Templo Nacional Masonico,** the Grand Masonic Temple established on 25 March 1951 and though no longer a Freemason's lodge, still retaining a fading mural in the lobby depicting the history of Masonry in Cuba. It competes for attention with a larger-than-life statue of José Martí.

Further west, at Salvador Allende y Arbol Seco is the **Casa del Cultura Centro Habana,** hosting cultural activities for the local community and containing the **Galeria Kahlo** in a colonial mansion of note. An intriguing curiosity one block west, at Hospital #707, one block north of Salvador Allende, is an **Evangelical temple** that draws a crowd of curious onlookers who crowd at the windows to witness Cuban believers clutching their Bibles within.

Avenida Salvador Allende continues its march westward of Calzada de Infanta through the Vedado district.

Luring you north along Calzada de la Infanta is the distant warbling of birds, and at the junction of San Rafael you'll discover a tiny enclosed plaza where members of the Asociación Nacional Ornithológica de Cuba, colloquially termed the **Canary Cultivators of Havana,** gather to make bird-talk and buy cages and seed. Their headquarters is half a block away, at Infanta

#402, tel. (7) 33-5749. Here ANOC members display and buy and sell their rainbow-hued birds, and the place is full of the shrilling of finches and parakeets. The members breed birds, which the association exports. It's open Mon.-Fri. 8:30 a.m.-5:30 p.m.

Eastward, Avenida Simón Bolívar slopes to Parque de la Fraternidad, with a sweeping view down the scalloped avenue. Simón Bolívar is lined with once-impressive colonial-era structures gone to ruin. One of the few structures not seemingly on its last legs is the **Iglesia del Sagrado Corazón de Jesús,** a Gothic inspiration in stone that could have been transported from medieval England, with a beamed ceiling held aloft by great marbled columns. The stained-glass windows rival the best in Europe. The church, one of the most active in Cuba, also boasts a fabulous soaring altar of carved wood. Services are offered Mon.-Sat. at 7 a.m. and 4:30 p.m. and Sunday at 7 and 9:30 a.m. and 4:30 p.m.

CALLE PADRE VARELA

Calle Padre Varela is sadly diminished since it was laid out last century with tall buildings to each side. Many edifices are ready for the wrecking ball, but there are at least two structures of contemporary note.

The first, four blocks down from Salvador Allende, is the **Fábrica de Tabaco Romeo y Julieta,** the famous cigar factory founded in 1875 and officially today the Antonio Briones Montoto factory, in an exquisite three-story building with ironwork balconies on Padre Varela, e/ Desague y Peñal Verno, tel. (7) 78-1058 and 79-3927. Green glazed tiles cover the interior walls of the lobby, and an iron staircase twirls gracefully toward the ceiling, decorated with classical moldings with pink and green laurel wreaths. It specializes in medium-flavored brands such as El Rey del Mundo (King of the World) and, since 1875, the fine Romeo y Julieta. It also makes the heavyweight, high-quality, and limited quantity Saint Luís Rey cigars favored by actor James Coburn and the late Frank Sinatra. Like most Havana cigar factories, duties vary by floor, with leaf handing on the ground floor, and stemming, sorting, rolling, box decorating, and ringing on the upper two floors. The factory is open for visits by permit only, Mon.-Fri. 7 a.m.-4 p.m. Permission must be requested from the Cubatabaco (the Empresa Cubana del Tabaco), O'Reilly #104, e/ Tacón y Mercaderes, Habana Vieja, tel. (7) 62-5463.

Another cigar factory—**Fábrica El Rey del Mundo**—is hidden behind the Romeo y Julieta factory at Calle San Carlos 816, tel. (7) 70-9336.

One block south of Fábrica de Tabaco Romeo y Julieta, on Padre Varela and Carmen is the **Conservatorio Municipal de Habana,** a music conservatory boasting a well-preserved classical façade, gleaming white and quite a shocker amid the decay and dishevelment.

Padre Varela continues south four blocks to Cuatro Caminos, an all-important junction where six major thoroughfares meet (see Cerro, below).

CERRO

South of Centro, the land rises gently to Cerro (pop. 130,000), a separate administrative district (the word means "hill") that last century developed as the place to retire during the torrid midsummer months; many wealthy families maintained a home in town and another on the cooler hill. The region is terribly deteriorated and the majority of buildings transcend sordid, reminding you of the worst tenements of New York or Glasgow. Cerro spreads out expansively and is renowned for some of the more disreputable areas of the city, including centers of drug trading. Avoid the Barrio Canal and Sucel districts.

The district is anchored by Avenida Máximo Gómez (popularly called Monte or Calzada de Cerro), which snakes southwest from Parque de la Fraternidad and is surely one of the saddest streets in all Havana. During the 19th century scores of summer homes were erected in classical style, each more extravagantly Italianate than the next. Many of the luxurious houses went up along Avenida Máximo Gómez. The avenue—lined with colonnaded mansions like an endless Greek temple—ascends gradually, marching backward into the past like a classical ruin. Alas, today it looks as Herculaneum must have looked during its decline. Monte's once-stunning arcades are now in desperate condition, and houses are decaying behind lovely façades. To my mind, it is the saddest sight in Havana.

Novelist James Michener, exploring Cerro while looking for a house in which to set the Cuban portion of a novel on the Caribbean, was told "in elegiac tones" by his guide, "The steps went down by decades. 1920s the mansions are in full flower. 1930s the rich families begin to move out. 1940s people grab them who can't afford to maintain them, ruin begins. 1950s ten big families move into each mansion, pay no rent, and begin to tear it apart. 1960s during the first years of the Revolution, no housing elsewhere, so even more crowd in, ruin accelerates. 1970s some of the weakest begin to fall down. 1980s many gone beyond salvation." Heartrending.

Supposedly façades are to be renovated and building materials distributed to residents according to the housing conditions with the aim of restoring Monte as one of the city's major shopping streets. To date there is little sign that local residents had received any assistance.

One of the few buildings of interest is the **Cuatro Caminos** farmers' market, at the junction of Máximo Gómez with Manglar and Cristina (also called Avenida de la México), in a much-dilapidated 19th-century market hall that still functions as such and is worth a visit for its bustling color and ambience.

At the other end of Máximo Gómez, one block south of the avenue, on Calle Peñon, is the tiny **Plaza de Galicia** shaded by venerable ceiba trees and bougainvillea bowers, with the diminutive **Iglesia de Peñon** at its heart. The church bears a Corinthian frontage and is topped by a round spire. It is open most afternoons and for Mass on Sunday. The plaza was dedicated in 1991 to the Pueblo Gallego (the Galician people).

Fábrica de Ron Bocoy

The most intriguing site in Cerro is this venerable former home-turned rum factory with a two-tone pink façade and the legend "BOCOY" above the wide, handsome door, on Máximo Gómez between Patrio and Auditor, tel. (7) 70-5642, immediately east of Hospital Salvador Allende. Its façade is decorated with four dozen cast-iron swans painted blue and white and marching wing to wing, "each standing tall and slim, its long neck bent straight down in mortal combat with an evil serpent climbing up its legs to sink its fangs," wrote James Michener. Michener, chose this building for the house in which lived "once-intimate liberal relatives" of a conservative Cuban exile family living in Miami in his book, *Caribbean.*

Beyond the swan-adorned portico, the mansion is one of Havana's most important distilleries, containing great oak casks up to seven meters tall stacked in dark recesses—"something out of Piranesi, a ghostly affair with a single unshaded light bulb"—and containing Cuba's famous (albeit least prestigious) Legendario rums. The distillery manufactures five types of rum, three brandies, sweet wine *(vinos dulces),* and liqueurs made of plantain, anise, cacao, mint, and coffee.

Bocoy, however, manufactures one of the choicest rums in Cuba, intended solely for Fidel Castro to give as gifts to notable persons and packaged in a bulbous earthenware bottle inside a miniature pirate's treasure chest labeled La Isla del Tesoro (Treasure Island). The bottles are guarded assiduously.

A guide leads free tours. It has a showroom upstairs and a separate bar for tippling the goods as a prelude—it is hoped—to buying. Open Mon.-Sat. 9 a.m.-5 p.m., and Sunday 9 a.m.-2 p.m.

VEDADO AND PLAZA DE LA REVOLUCIÓN

The conclusion of the brief Spanish-American-Cuban War in 1898 brought U.S. money rushing in to Havana, and a new age of elegance to Cuba's capital evolved, concentrated in hilly Vedado, between Centro Habana and the Río Almendares. Fine parks and monuments were added, along with the Malecón, the wide promenade anchoring the waterfront. Civic structures, large hotels, casinos, department stores, and lavish restaurants sprouted alongside nightclubs displaying fleshly attractions.

Vedado—today's commercial heart of Havana—has been described as "Havana at its middle-class best." The University of Havana is here. So are the fabulous cemetery Cementerio de Colón, many of the city's prime hotels and restaurants, virtually all its main commercial buildings, and block after block of handsome mansions and apartment houses in various states of decay or repair. (While exploring, watch for stone lions flanking the gates of large mansions. These revered symbols denote the home of a nobleman. Alas, some time late last century, a commoner who had amassed a fortune bought himself a title and erected lions. The proper grandees of Spain were so outraged that they tore theirs down in a protest known as *La Muerte de los Leones*—the Death of the Lions.) The streets are lined with jagüey trees dropping their aerial roots to the ground like muscular tendrils.

Vedado is administered as part of Plaza de la Revolución (pop. 165,000), which includes Nuevo Vedado, a distinct district south of Vedado: the area, much of which has been rebuilt since the Revolution, is centered on the Plaza de la Revolución, surrounded by ministry buildings, the Palacio de la Revolución (the seat of government), and the towering José Martí monument, now containing a museum named for the hero.

For a grand view of Vedado, head to the top of the Habana Libre. Alternately, take time for a cocktail or meal at La Torre, atop the 35-story **Focsa,** a prerevolutionary apartment building that later was used to house East European and Soviet personnel and has since reverted to its former role.

ORIENTATION

The sprawling region is hemmed to the north by the Malecón, to the east by Calzada de Infanta, to the west by the Río Almanderes, running in a deep canyon, and to the southeast by the Calzada de Ayestaran and Avenida de la Independencia.

Vedado follows a grid pattern aligned NNW by SSE and is laid out in quadrants. Odd-numbered streets (calles) run east-west, parallel to the shore. Even-numbered calles run perpendicular. (To confuse things, some "calles" are "avenidas," although there seems to be no logic as to which these are; and west of Paseo calles are even numbered, while east of Paseo calles run from A to P). The basic grid is overlain by a larger grid of broad boulevards averaging six blocks apart. Dividing the quadrants east-west—running through the heart of Vedado—is the all-important Calle 23, which rises (colloquially) as La Rampa from the Malecón at its junction with Calzada de Infanta to the northeast. Paralleling it to the north is a second major east-west thoroughfare, Calle 9 (Linea), five blocks inland of the Malecón, which it also intersects to the northeast. Four major roadways divide the quadrants north-south: Calle L to the east, and Avenida de los Presidentes, Paseo, and Avenida 12 farther west. Vedado slopes gently upwards from the shore to Calle 23 and thence gently downward toward Cerro.

Nuevo Vedado has an irregular pattern. Avenida de los Presidentes, Paseo, and, to the west, Avenida 26, connect Vedado to Nuevo Vedado. Most roadways converge on the Plaza de la Revolución, which is bounded by Avenida Carlos M. de Céspedes on its north side and Avenida de Rancho Boyeros on its south side. The two meet southwestward to form Avenida de la Independencia, which runs to the international airport.

THE MALECÓN

The Malecón runs along the bulging, wave-battered shorefront of northern Vedado, curling

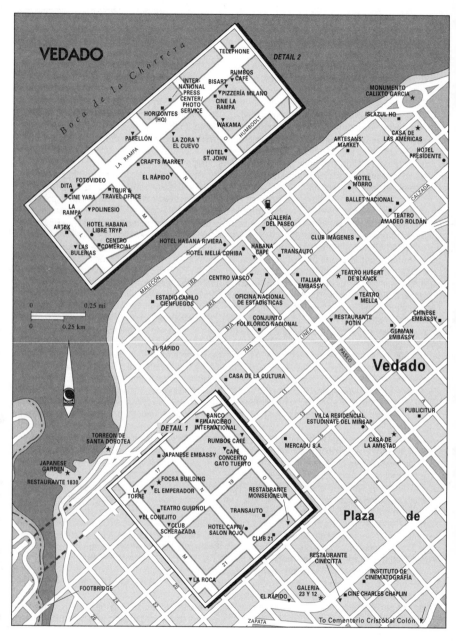

VEDADO

Boca de la Chorrera

DETAIL 2

TELEPHONE

RUMBOS CAFÉ
BISART

INTER-NATIONAL PRESS CENTER/PHOTO SERVICE
PIZZERÍA MILANO
CINE LA RAMPA

HORIZONTES (HQ)

WAKAMA

PABELLÓN
LA ZORA Y EL CUEVO

CRAFTS MARKET
HOTEL ST. JOHN

LA RAMPA

EL RÁPIDO

DITA
FOTOVIDEO
CINE YARA
TOUR & TRAVEL OFFICE

LA RAMPA
POLINESIO

ARTEX
HOTEL HABANA LIBRE TRYP

LAS BULERÍAS
CENTRO COMERCIAL
HOTEL HABANA RIVIERA

MONUMENTO CALIXTO GARCIA

ISLÁZUL HQ

ARTESANS' MARKET
CASA DE LAS AMÉRICAS
HOTEL PRESIDENTE

HOTEL MORRO

BALLET NACIONAL

CALZADA

TEATRO AMADEO ROLDÁN

GALERÍA DEL PASEO

CLUB IMÁGENES

HABANA CAFÉ
HOTEL MELIÁ COHIBA
TRANSAUTO

CENTRO VASCO

ITALIAN EMBASSY
TEATRO HUBERT DE BLANCK

MALECÓN
ESTADIO CAMILO CIENFUEGOS

OFICINA NACIONAL DE ESTADÍSTICAS

18A
3RA
5TA

TEATRO MELLA

CONJUNTO FOLKLÓRICO NACIONAL

RESTAURANTE POTÍN

CHINESE EMBASSY

GERMAN EMBASSY

LÍNEA

7MA

PASEO

EL RÁPIDO

0   0.25 mi
0   0.25 km

CASA DE LA CULTURA

Vedado

11

MOON

13
VILLA RESIDENCIAL ESTUDIANTE DEL MINSAP

PUBLICITUR

BANCO FINANCIERO INTERNATIONAL

DETAIL 1

TORREON DE SANTA DOROTEA

RUMBOS CAFÉ

JAPANESE EMBASSY
CAFÉ CONCERTO GATO TUERTO

17

MERCADU S.A.

CASA DE LA AMISTAD

JAPANESE GARDEN
RESTAURANTE 1830

FOCSA BUILDING
EL EMPERADOR

LA TORRE

TEATRO GUIGNOL
EL CONEJITO
CLUB SCHERAZADA

19

RESTAURANTE MONSEIGNEUR

TRANSAUTO

HOTEL CAPRI/ SALON ROJO
CLUB 21

Plaza   de

21

RESTAURANTE CINECITTA

INSTITUTO DE CINEMATOGRAFÍA

FOOTBRIDGE

24

22

20

LA ROCA

GALERIA 23 Y 12

EL RÁPIDO

CINE CHARLES CHAPLIN

26

ZAPATA

To Cementerio Cristóbal Colón

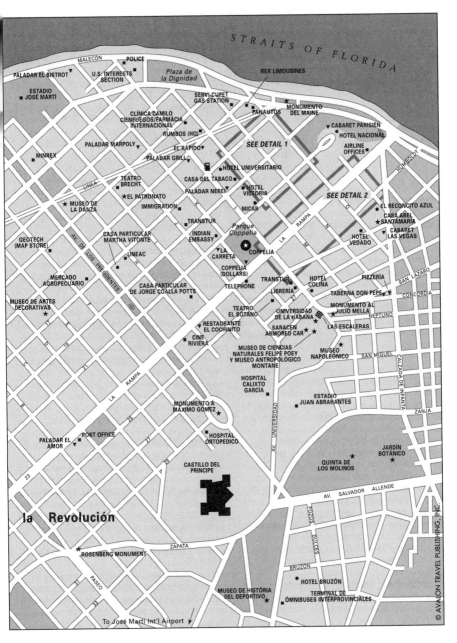

the Malecón
looking toward Vedado

east-west from La Rampa in the east to the Río Almandares in the west, a distance of three miles, where the seafront boulevard meets Calzada (7ma) and dips under the tunnel that links it with Miramar. This portion of the Malecón is less dramatic than that along the shoreline of Centro Habana. However, there are several important sights, not least the **Hotel Nacional,** dramatically perched atop a small cliff at the junction of La Rampa and the Malecón (entrance is on Calle O). This grande dame hotel—now a national monument—is worth a peek, not least for its Moorish-influenced architecture. The hotel was designed by the same architect who designed The Breakers in Palm Beach, which it closely resembles. It opened on 30 December 1930, in the midst of the Great Depression. The elaborately detailed, Spanish-style hotel was badly in need of refurbishment when mobster Meyer Lansky persuaded General Batista to let him built a grand casino and nightclub, which opened in 1955, drawing society figures from far and wide. Luminaries from Winston Churchill and the Prince of Wales to Marlon Brando have laid their heads here, as attested by the photos in the lobby bar. The sweeping palm-shaded lawns to the rear slope toward the Malecón, above which sits a battery of cannons from the wars of independence, and a network of defensive tunnels built in modern times.

Fronting the hotel on the shorefront is the **Monumento al Maine,** dedicated by the republican Cuban government to the memory of the 260 sailors who died when the U.S. warship exploded in Havana harbor in 1898, creating a prelude for U.S. intervention in the wars of independence. Two rusting cannons are laid out beneath 40-foot-tall Corinthian columns dedicated in 1925 and originally topped by an eagle with wings spread wide. Back then relations between the two nations were warm, and when a hurricane toppled the eagle, it was replaced by a more aerodynamic sibling (the original now resides in the former residence of the U.S. Ambassador, in the Cubanacán district, still occupied by the head of the U.S. Interests Section). Following the Revolution, the monument was a point for anti-Yankee rallies and immediately after the failed Bay of Pigs invasion in 1960, was desecrated by an angry mob that toppled the eagle from its roost and broke its wings (its body is now in the Museum of the City of Havana, while the head hangs on the wall of the cafeteria in the U.S. Interests Section). Fidel asked Picasso to replace the eagle with a dove, but Picasso refused (he couldn't top a neoclassical column with a cubist bird, he replied). The Castro government later dedicated a plaque that reads, "To the victims of the *Maine,* who were sacrificed by imperialist voracity in its eagerness to seize the island of Cuba." Recent evidence, however, suggests that the explosion was an accident.

Three blocks west, at the bottom of Calle L, is the unmarked **U.S. Interests Section,** (formerly the U.S. Embassy) where low-profile U.S. diplomats and CIA agents serve Uncle Sam's whims behind a veil of mirrored-glass windows.

In January 2000, the Cuban government tore up the grassy knolls in front of (east of) the U.S. Interests Section and sent in work crews around the clock to lay out the **Plaza de la Dignidad**, in honor of Elián González, the six-year-old Cuban boy rescued at sea after his mother and 10 other people died when their craft sank during a desperate bid to flee to the U.S. The fronts of buildings in view of the TV cameras were spruced up also for public consumption. . . the consummate Potemkin village. A giant billboard showing Elián caged behind wire went up also, replacing what must have been Havana's most photographed site: a huge, brightly painted billboard showing a fanatical Uncle Sam growling menacingly at a Cuban soldier who is shouting, *"Señores Imperialistas: ¡No les tenemos absolutamente ningún miedo!"* ("Imperialists: You don't scare us at all!"). A statue of José Martí holds a bronze effigy of little Elián in his arms. The plaza is dominated by the José Martí Anti-Imperialist Platform, a high-tech affair used for ongoing harangues of Uncle Sam.

The building is well-guarded by Cuban military figures who will shoo you away if you attempt to sit on the seawall within 100 meters or so of the U.S. Interests Section. Nor are you permitted to walk past the U.S. Interests Section on the inland side of the road.

Westward, the Malecón curls in much denuded state past an open-air sports stadium, the **CVD José Martí,** of a strange Bauhaus design in concrete. Immediately to the west, at the foot of Avenida de los Presidentes, is the **Monumento Calixto García,** with a tall bronze figure of the 19th-century rebel general on horseback atop a black marble pedestal. The statue is surrounded by a wall with verdigris bronze plaques

COPPELIA

C oppelia is the name of a park in Havana, the flying saucer-like structure at its heart, and the brand of excellent ice cream served there.

In the good old, bad old days, the trendy area at the top of La Rampa was full of ice-cream parlors. But, it is claimed, the lower classes and blacks weren't welcome, so in 1966 the government built a big, lush park with a parlor in the middle as the ultimate democratic ice-cream emporium—surely the biggest ice creamery in the world, serving an estimated 30,000 customers a day. Cuba's rich diversity is to be found standing in line at Coppelia on a sultry Havana afternoon.

Before the Revolution, Cuba relied on its northern neighbor for much of its ice cream supply and Baskin and Robbin's twenty-eight flavors was the brand of choice. Fidel, however, promised to outdo the Yanks with twenty-nine flavors (a boast that Cuba failed to achieve). Before the Special Period, you used to be able to choose anything from a one-scoop cone to complex sundaes as well as more than two dozen flavors, including exotic tropical fruits that Ben and Jerry have never heard of. Today it can manage only one or two flavors a day, and everyone swears the quality is not what it was.

The strange concrete structure that looms over the park, suspended on spidery legs, shelters a marble-topped diner-bar where Cubans seated atop tall bar stools slurp ice cream from stainless steel bowls.

A series of circular rooms is arranged overhead like a four-leaf clover, offering views out over three open-air sections where *helados* can be enjoyed beneath the dappled shade of lush yagüey trees. Each section has its own *cola* (line) proportional in length to the strength of the sun. Even on temperate days the *colas* snake out of the park and onto nearby streets like lethargic serpents. The *colas* move forward at a pace barely distinguishable from rigor mortis. Trying to make sense of the lines is a puzzle. Cuban lines are never static. Habaneros wander off willy-nilly to sit in the shade while others disappear from view completely lending the impression of having given up. But always they reappear at the critical moment, and your *cola* will coalesce in perfect order thanks to some unfathomable and puissant osmosis. Waitresses serve you at communal tables made of local marble. Coppelia is a family diner.

Coppelia featured in Tomás Gutierrez Alea's trenchant classic movie, *Fresa y Chocolate,* which was based on Senel Paz's short story, "The Woods, the Wolf, and the New Man," and is named for the scene at Coppelia where Diego, the homosexual, had ordered strawberry ice cream, much to the consternation of David, the loyal Fidelista: "Although there was chocolate that day, he had ordered strawberry. Perverse." After the success of the movie, Cuban males, concerned with their macho image, had taken a cue from the movie and avoided ordering *fresa*.

showing battle scenes from the wars of independence. Cannons lie amid an intriguing grotto-like landscape.

Immediately to the west is a massive apartment tower dating from 1967, interesting as one of the most sophisticated built since the Revolution although its atrocious construction standards are evident. Continuing, you'll reach the spic-and-span **Hotel Cohiba,** a late-1990s edifice whose contemporary face launched Havana toward the millenium; and the **Hotel Riviera,** the Mafia's last and most ambitious attempt to eclipse Las Vegas. Mobster Meyer Lansky owned the hotel but was registered as the kitchen manager to evade taxes. When opened in 1958 it was considered a marvel of modern design. It boasted an egg-shaped, gold-leafed casino and a nightclub whose opening was headlined by Ginger Rogers. Recently restored, it still functions as one of Havana's leading hotels.

The last bend of the Malecón brings you to the mouth of the Río Almandares, guarded by a small fortress, the **Torreon de Santa Dorotea,** built to guard the western approaches to Havana following the English invasion in 1762. Today it houses a restaurant.

LA RAMPA AND VICINITY

Millionaires, mafiosi, presidents, paupers, and pimps all once walked the five blocks of Calle 23, which rises steeply—and heavily American in style—from the Malecón to the Hotel Habana Libre. La Rampa was the setting of *Three Trapped Tigers,* Guillermo Cabrera Infante's famous novel about swinging-1950s Havana, for it was here that the ritziest hotels, casinos, and nightclubs were concentrated in the days before the Revolution.

Not until the 1950s did La Rampa begin to acquire its present look (prior to that, it was a shantytown). In 1963 multicolored granite tiles created by Cuba's leading artists—Wilfredo Lam, René Portocarro, and others—were laid at intervals in the sidewalks. It is art to be walked on—or not to be, as Hamlet would say.

La Rampa's flavor is that of a tree-lined boulevard in Buenos Aires or even Spain, with its candy-stripe awnings shading faded restaurants

and nightclubs from the heyday of sin. It is modern, vital, and busy and climbs steadily past the offices of Cubana, Havanatur, the television station, and art deco apartment buildings mingling with high-rise office buildings, cresting at Calle L, pinned by Coppelia parque, Cine Yara, and the **Hotel Habana Libre,** the national landmark hotel that was once *the* place to be after it opened in 1958 on the eve of the Revolution. Castro even had his headquarters here briefly in 1959, and for years the hotel teemed with shady foreigners—many of them, reported *National Geographic,* "not strictly tourists. . . watched by secret police agents from the 'ministry,' meaning MININT, the Ministry of the Interior." The lobby contains many fine contemporary art pieces, including a mosaic mural by René Portocarro. The hotel is fronted by a spectacular contemporary mural—*Carro de la Revolución* (the Revolutionary Car)—by ceramist Amelia Peláez, made of 525 pieces in the style of Picasso.

Anyone interested in Cuba's revolutionary history should step south one block to Calle 25 164, e/ Infanta y O and the **Casa Abel Santamaría,** tel. (7) 70-0417, where the martyr—brutally tortured and murdered following the attack on Moncada barracks in 1953—once lived. The simple two-room apartment (no. 603) was used prior to the attack as the headquarters of Fidel Castro's nascent revolutionary movement, the M-26-7. The original furnishings are still in place: a roped-off sofa bed, a small bookcase, Fidel's work desk with a statue of José Martí, and a kerosene fridge. You'd have to be a serious leftist or student of history to thrill to this place, but it's interesting in passing. The adjoining room (no. 604) has a small exhibition—mostly photos—of Abel's sister Haydee Santamaría, Fidel, and other revolutionaries (curiously, the only photo of Abel is as a two-year-old). Open Mon.-Fri. 9 a.m.-12:30 p.m. and 1-5 p.m., Saturday 9 a.m.-1 p.m. Entry costs US$1, or US$2 with the guide, who gives an enthusiastic spiel.

Catercorner to the Hotel Habana Libre, at the top of the hill at Calle L, is **Parque Coppelia,** an entire block devoted to the consumption of ice cream, of which Cubans are consummate lovers.

Universidad de la Habana

Follow Calle L south from La Rampa three blocks and you arrive at an immense stone staircase at

Calle 27—the famous *escalinata*—that leads up to the university. The 50-meter-wide steps are topped by a porticoed, columned façade beyond which lies a peaceful square surrounded by more columned arcades. The tree-shaded campus was loosely modeled on that of New York's Columbia University and is centered on a quadrant surrounded by classical buildings. A patinated statue looks down upon the *escalinata,* which in Batista days was famous as a setting for political rallies and riots.

During this century the university was composed of 13 schools, each with its own president. The presidents elected the president of the University Students' Federation, the pillar of student political activity and an extremely influential group amid the jungle of Cuban politics. The university was an autonomous "sacred hill," that neither the police nor the army could enter (although gangsters and renegade politicians roamed the campus). Its most notable of many notable students was Fidel Castro, who enrolled in the law school in October 1945 and was involved in the gangsterism. A Saracen armored car sits in the quadrant: it was captured in 1958 by students in the fight against Batista.

The dour modernist monument of concrete across the street at the base of the steps contains the ashes of Julio Antonio Mella, a student leader (and founder of the Cuban Communist Party) assassinated by the Machado regime in 1929.

Today it is a peaceful place. Visitors are allowed to stroll the grounds, although peeking into the classes requires advance permission. The campus is off-limits on weekends, and access is restricted by conscientious *custodios* to Mon.-Fri. 8 a.m.-6 p.m. The campus and museums are closed in July.

The university contains two museums, foremost the **Museo Antropológico Montane,** the Montane Anthropology Museum, tel. (7) 79-3488, on the second floor of the Felipe Poey Science Building, to the left (south side) of the quadrant beyond the portico at the top of the *escalitas.* The museum contains a valuable collection of pre-Columbian artifacts, including carved idols and turtle shells. Open Mon.-Fri. 9 a.m.-4 p.m. Entry costs US$1.

The **Museo de Ciencias Naturales Felipe Poey,** or Felipe Poey Museum of Natural Sciences, downstairs in the same building, tel. (7) 32-9000, fax (7) 32-1321, displays an excellent array of pre-Columbian artifacts and the inert remains of dozens of endemic species stuffed or pickled for posterity within glass cases. There's even a pilot whale suspended from the ceiling, while snakes, alligators, and sharks float in suspended animation on the walls. The museum—the oldest in Cuba—dates from 1842 and is named for its French-Cuban (1799-1891) founder. Poey was versed in every field of the sciences and founded the Academy of Medical Sciences, the Anthropological Society of Cuba, and a half dozen other societies. Open Mon.-Fri. 9 a.m.-4 p.m. Entry costs US$1.

Museo Napoleónico

Who would imagine that so much of Napoleon Bonaparte's personal memorabilia would end up in Cuba? But it is, housed in the splendid three-story Ferrara mansion on the south side of the university, at Calle San Miguel 1159, tel. (7) 79-1412. The collection was the private work of a politician, Orestes Ferrara, who brought back from Europe such precious items as the French emperor's death mask, toothbrush, and the pistols Napoleon used at the Battle of Borodino (other items were seized from Julio Lobo, the former National Bank president, when he left Cuba for exile). A library on Napoleon is organized chronologically to trace the life of the "Great Corsican." Open Mon.-Fri. and alternate Sundays 9 a.m.-noon and 1-4 p.m. Entry costs US$5.

Other Sights

The Gothic **Iglesia San Juan de Letran,** on Calle 19, e/ I y J, is hidden away in the residential district southwest of Coppelia. It dates from the 1880s and is one of Havana's most impressive ecclesiastical edifices with fine stained-glass windows.

One block west of the church is a small and charming park (between 21 and 19, and I and H) centered on a pergola and with a memorial to Leanor Pérez Cabrera, mother of José Martí, on its northeast corner. One block north, at the corner of 17 and I, is **UNEAC,** the Unión Nacional de Escritores y Artistes de Cuba, tel. (7) 32-4551, fax (7) 33-3158, with a stunning stained-glass window on the staircase and a patio where the intellectual elite gather to banter and debate.

Cuba's Jewish heritage is maintained with a passion, as demonstrated by the dedication of Adela Dworin—the doyenne—and her staff at **El Patronato,** otherwise known as the Casa de la Comunidad Hebrea de Cuba, which works to preserve Hebrew traditions and pride. The edifice at Calle I between 13 y 15, tel. (7) 32-8953, abuts the **Bet Shalon Sinagogo** (where you might witness services with permission) and contains an active community center and a large library on Judaica, Israel, and related themes. Tom Miller provides a splendid review of the *patronato* and Jewish heritage in Havana in his *Trading with the Enemy* (see Bibliography).

The black marble column at the corner of Linea and L was erected in 1931 to commemorate Havana's *chinos* who fought for Cuban independence.

AVENIDA DE LOS PRESIDENTES AND VICINITY

Avenida de los Presidentes is a wide boulevard that might be considered Vedado's backbone. It runs perpendicular to Avenida 23 and flows downhill to the Malecón. A wide, grassy, tree-lined median runs down its center, dividing separate roadways running uphill and downhill.

One of the most extravagant of the many mansions that line the boulevard is on Calle 17, two blocks west of Avenida de los Presidentes e/ D y E. Once owned by a Cuban countess, the villa now houses the **Museo de Artes Decorativos,** or Museum of Decorative Arts, tel. (7) 32-0924, which brims with a lavish collection of furniture, paintings, textiles, and chinoiserie from the 18th and 19th centuries. Most of the furniture, however, is European, not Cuban. No matter, it's staggering in its sumptuous quality. Upstairs, where the landing is festooned with ivory figures, you'll find a boudoir decorated Oriental style, with furniture inlaid with mother-of-pearl. Open Tues.-Sat. 11 a.m.-6:30 p.m. Entrance costs US$2 (cameras cost US$5 and videos US$10).

Following the Avenida de los Presidentes north, note the handsome bronze statue of Alexandro Rodríguez y Velasco on a granite pedestal, guarded by a bronze figure of Perseus at Linea and Avenida de los Presidentes.

The **Museo de la Danza,** in a restored mansion at the corner of Linea and Avenida de los Presidentes, opened on the 50th anniversary of the Ballet of Cuba, with diverse salons dedicated to Russian ballet, modern dance, the National Ballet of Cuba, and other themes. Exhibits include wardrobes, recordings, manuscripts, and photographs relating to the history of dance. Alicia Alonso, founder and *prima ballerina absoluta* of the Ballet of Cuba, gave her valuable personal collection, including her first ballet shoes and costume she wore in *Carmen.* The museum contains a library and video archives.

Near the base of Avenida de los Presidentes is the **Casa de las Américas,** at Av. 3ra esq. Calle G, tel. (7) 55-2706, fax (7) 33-4554, e-mail: casa@artsoft.cult.cu, a cultural center formed in 1959 by the revolutionary heroine, Haydee Santamaría, to study and promote the cultures of Latin America and the Caribbean. It has a large library and exhibits in two nearby galleries—the **Galeria Haydee Santamaría,** Av. 5ra y G, and the **Galería Mariano,** 15 #607, e/ B and C, containing the Art Collection of New America, comprising more than 6,000 pieces of sculpture, engravings, paintings, photographs, and popular art. The gallery contains a silk-screening shop and a small bookstore. Concerts, film screenings, and theater and dance programs are hosted. Open Mon.-Fri. 10 a.m.-5 p.m.

Midway between Avenidas de los Presidentes and Paseo is the recently restored **Parque Villalon,** between 5ra y Calzada (7ma) and C y D, surrounded by some important edifices including, on its southeast side, the grandiose Romanesque **Teatro Amadeo Roldán** recently restored to grandeur as a concert hall. Next door, at Calzada #1510, is the headquarters of the **Ballet Nacional de Cuba,** tel. (7) 55-2946. Understandably, the ballet school is closed to visitors (who might disturb the concentration of dancers), but sometimes you can spot the dancers practicing their pirouettes if you peek through the gate.

South of Calle 23, Avenida de los Presidentes climbs to the **Monumento al José Miguel Gómez** topped by nubile figures in classical style. The road then drops down to meet the westward extent of Avenida Salvador Allende through a canyon lined with ancient and giant jagüey trees forming a fantastical glade over the road. Hidden from site on the bluff above (to the west) is the **Castillo del Principe,** built in the 1770s following the English invasion. The castle is off-limits and rarely mentioned in Cuban literature because it houses a prison.

On the north side of Salvador Allende, about 100 meters east of Avenida de los Presidentes, is the unkempt **Jardín Botánico** (botanic garden). This was a popular recreation spot in colonial days, when it was the site of the pleasure gardens of the governor's summer palace. Slaves newly arrived from Africa were kept here in barracoons, where they could be displayed to passersby. The gardens surround the once-graceful **Quinta de los Molinos,** reached via a decrepit drive. The old mansion is named for the royal snuff mills that were built here in 1791. You can still see part of the original Zanza Real aqueduct (inaugurated in 1592) to the rear of the time-worn *quinta,* which now houses the **Museo de Máximo Gómez,** tel. (7) 79-8850, honoring the Dominican-born hero of the Cuban wars of independence. The collection is motley and poorly presented. Open Tue.-Sat. 9 a.m.-5 p.m., and Sunday 9 a.m.-1 p.m. (US$1).

PASEO AND WESTERN VEDADO

Paseo parallels Avenida de los Presidentes seven blocks to the west. It, too, is a linear park flanked by two avenues considered as one, being one-way in either direction. Although a pleasant stroll, Paseo offers little of touristic interest. An exception is the **Casa de la Amistad,** on Paseo between 17 and 19. This old mansion of generous proportions is run by the Cuban state as a "friendship house" with rooms for entertaining, plus a Casa del Tabaco and a meager snack bar out back overlooking the unkempt gardens. It makes a good spot to break your perambulations with a cool drink.

At the southern end of Paseo, at the junction of Paseo and Zapata, at the top of the rise that continues southeast to Plaza de la Revolución is the **Rosenberg Monument,** a curiosity in passing. Here a small park is pinned by a tree shading an inconspicuous red-brick wall bearing cement doves and an inset sculpture of Julius and Ethel Rosenberg, the U.S. couple executed for passing nuclear secrets to the Soviet Union. An inscription reads, "Murdered June 19, 1953." Julius' final words are engraved, too: "For Peace, Bread, and Roses, We Face the Executioners."

Paralleling Paseo six blocks to the west is Calle 12. **Galeria 23 y 12,** at the corner of Calle 23 and 12, marks the spot where on 16 April 1961, Fidel Castro announced on the eve of the Bay of Pigs invasion that Cuba was henceforth socialist. The anniversary of the declaration of socialism is marked each 16 April, when Fidel speaks on the corner. The façade bears a patinated bronze plaque showing Fidel in his usual defiant pose surrounded by the heroes who were killed in the U.S.-sponsored strike on the airfield at Marianao that was a prelude to the invasion. Today the building houses an art *salón.*

While walking down Calle 12 you'll pass one of Fidel Castro's "safe houses," between Linea and 13, where the road is cordoned off as a "Zona Militar."

One block south, at the junction of Calle 12 and Zapata (a sinuous westward extension of the Zanja, following the course of the ancient aqueduct) is Vedado's pride and joy, the Cementerio de Colón.

Cementerio de Colón

Described as "an exercise in pious excesses," Havana's Necrópolis Cristóbal Colón is renowned worldwide for its flamboyant mausoleums, vaults, and tombs embellished with angels, griffins, cherubs, and other ornamentation, with poppies, hibiscus, and bougainvillea and other cut flowers adding notes of bright color. The cemetery, which covers 56 hectares, contains over 500 major mausoleums, chapels, family vaults, and galleries (in addition to countless gravestones). It was laid out between 1871 and 1886 in sixteen rectangular blocks or *insulae* like a Roman military camp, with a Greek Orthodox-style, ocher-colored, octagonal church—the **Capillo Central**—at its center. The cemetery was divided by social status, with separate areas for non-Catholics and for victims of epidemics. It was originally open only to nobles, who competed to build the most elaborate tombs, with social standing dictating the size and location of plots.

Here the wealthy vied for immortality on a grand scale. The cemetery, a national monument, is a petrified version of society of the times, combining, says the *Guía Turística* (available at the entrance gate), a "grandeur and meanness, good taste and triviality, popular and cosmopolitan, drama and even an unusual black humor, as in the gravestone carved as a double-three, devoted to an emotional elderly lady who died with that domino in her hand, thus losing both game and life at a time." The "double three" *(doble tres)* was that of Juana Martin, a domino fanatic who indeed died as described.

Famous *criollo* patricians, colonial aristocrats, and war heroes such as Máximo Gómez are buried here alongside noted intellectuals, merchants, and corrupt politicians (as well, of course, as the rare honest one, too, such as Eduardo Chibás). The list goes on and on: José Raúl Capablanca, the world chess champion 1921-27; Alejo Carpentier, Cuba's most revered contemporary novelist; Hubert de Blanck, the noted composer; the Conde de Rivero, known for his pursuit of young women and who rests attended by marble maidens; and Celia Sánchez, Haydee Santamaría, and a plethora of revolutionaries killed for the cause. You'll even find Greco-Roman temples in miniature, an Egyptian pyramid, and medieval castles; baroque, romantic, Renaissance, art deco, and art nouveau art, allegories, and metaphors of human life by a pantheon of Cuba's leading sculptors and artists. You could take all day to discover all the gems. Fortunately, benches are provided beneath shade trees.

The most visited grave is the flower-bedecked tomb of Amelia Goyri de Hoz, revered as *La Milagrosa* (The Miraculous One) and to whom miraculous healings are attributed as a protector of sick children. According to legend, she died during childbirth in 1901 and was buried with her stillborn child at her feet. When her sarcophagus was later opened, the baby was supposedly cradled in her arms. Ever since, superstitious Cubans have paid homage by knocking three times on the tombstone with one of its brass rings before touching the tomb and requesting a favor (one must not turn one's back

on the tomb when departing). Many childless women pray here in hopes of a pregnancy.

The **Tobias Gallery** is one of several underground galleries; this one, 100 meters long, contains 256 niches containing human remains.

The impressive Romanesque-Byzantine entrance gate of locally quarried coral stone is at the top of Calle 12 and Calle Zapata, which runs along its north face. The triple-arched gate was inspired by the Triumphal Arch in Rome that alludes to the Holy Trinity, with reliefs in Carrara marble that depict the crucifixion and Lazarus rising from the grave. It is embellished with a marble sculpture for the coronation stone representing *The Theological Virtues:* Faith, Hope, and Charity. The major tombs line the main avenue that leads south from the gate.

An information office is to the right of the entrance; you must pay an entrance fee here (US$1). Guided tours are available free of charge, but tips would be welcome. You can buy a guidebook and map (US$5). Open 7:30 a.m.-5 p.m.

Chinese Cemetery

Immediately southwest of Cementerio Colón, on the west side of Avenida 26, the Chinese built their own cemetery, with graves that appeal to an Asian culture. The circular gateway derives from the *pai lou,* the monumental Chinese arches erected by custom at the entrance to processional ways, palaces, and tombs. Traditional lions stand guard over hundreds of graves beneath highly-pitched burial chapels with upward-curving roofs of red and green tile in the traditional *xuan-shan* (hanging mountain) gabled style. There's no charge to enter, but the gates are usually locked.

PLAZA DE LA REVOLUCIÓN

Havana's largest plaza is a must-see for two defining edifices, although the plaza itself is a rather ugly tarred square accurately described by P. J. O'Rourke as "a vast open space resembling the Mall in D.C., but dropped into the middle of a massive empty parking lot in a tropical Newark." You can't blame the Revolution. The trapezoidal complex measuring one kilometer in length was laid out during the Batista era, when it was known as the Plaza Cívica, and all the major edifices (including the José Martí monument and statue) date back to the 1950s.

On the plaza's northwest corner, across Avenida Céspedes, is the modern but run-down **Teatro Nacional,** with a glass-plated façade. The theater is underutilized—"waiting," wrote novelist Donald Westlake, "for a theatrical season that had never quite arrived."

The plaza is the center of government, highlighted by the **Palacio de la Revolución,** tel. (7) 79-6551, immediately behind the José Martí monument (see below) to the south. This is where Castro and the Council of Ministers and their underlings work out their policies of state. The labyrinthine, ocher-colored Palace adjoins the buildings of the Central Committee of the Communist Party and is fronted by a broad staircase built by Batista for the Cuban Supreme Court and national police headquarters. No visitors are allowed.

To the north and east are government ministries in soulless post-Stalinist style, including, on the northwest side, the tall **Ministerio del Interior** (the ministry in charge of national security) with a windowless wall bearing a soaring black-metal "mural" of Che Guevara and the words "Hasta la Victoria Siempre." To the east of the Ministry of the Interior is the **Ministerio de Comunicaciones** containing the **Museo Postal** (on the ground floor), tel. (7) 70-5581. Philatelists will find it fascinating. The well-cataloged collection is kept in vertical pull-out glass file drawers. A complete range of Cuban postage stamps (including the first, dating to 1855) is on display, plus a large collection of stamps from almost 100 other countries. Check out the little solid-propellant rocket that was launched in 1936 by a group of enthusiastic philatelists eager to promote rocket propulsion to speed up mail delivery. Hello! The museum has a well-stocked shop—*filatelica*—selling stamps. Open Mon.-Fri. 9 a.m.-4 p.m. (US$1 entrance).

Across Avenida Rancho Boyeros, on the southeast, is the **Ministerio de Defensa** and, behind, the headquarters of *Granma,* the national daily newspaper of the Cuban Communist Party. On the northeast corner of the square, is Cuba's largest library, the **Biblioteca Nacional.**

One block north, in the Sala Polivatente Ramón Fonst sports stadium on Rancho Boyeros between 10 de Mayo and Bruzón, you'll find the **Museo de História del Deportivo,** tel. (7) 81-4696, which tells the history of Cuban sports. Open Tues.-Sun. 10 a.m.-5 p.m. Admission is US$1.

Parking is strictly controlled at Plaza de la Revolución, with a designated parking zone on the east side of the plaza. If you park on the plaza or along the road, soldiers will quickly move you along.

Monumento y Museo José Martí

This spectacular monument, made entirely of gray granite and marble, sits atop a 30-meter-tall base that spans the entire square and acts as a massive reviewing stand and podium from which Fidel tutors, harangues, and encourages the masses. To each side, great arching stairways lead to a huge granite statue of the National Hero sitting in a contemplative pose, like Rodin's *Thinker.*

Behind looms a slender, 109-meter-tall Babylonian edifice stepped like a soaring ziggurat from a sci-fi movie. The tower—the highest point in Havana—is made entirely of gray marble quarried from the Isle of Youths. The top bristles with antennas. Vultures soar overhead and roost on the narrow ledges, lending an added eerie quality to the scene. Its construction is said to have cost every citizen in Cuba one centavo.

Until early 1996, soldiers barred the way up to the monument, from where sentries surveyed passersby—and often icily shooed them away. The guards have since departed, and the edifice has been opened as a museum dedicated to José Martí, within the base of the tower. The museum, tel. (7) 82-0906, is splendid, depicting everything you could wish to know about Martí. Predictably, the largest photograph of all depicts Fidel, shown in saintly homage on the beach at Cojababo, the site in Guantánamo Province where Martí put ashore in 1896 after a 16-year exile. New Age music plays in the background, drawing you to a multi-screen broadcast on the wars of independence and the Revolution. One of the four exhibition rooms is dedicated to traveling exhibits, which change every three months. To one side is a small art gallery featuring portraits of Martí by leading artists.

The museum is open Mon.-Sat. 10 a.m.-6 p.m. and Sunday 10 a.m.-2 p.m. Entrance costs

US$5 (plus US$5 for a camera, US$10 for videos). For an additional US$5, you can take the elevator to a viewing gallery at the top (open Mon.-Sat. 9 a.m.-4 p.m., Sunday 2-4 p.m.). From above, you can see that the entire structure is designed as a five-pointed star. Each star in the *mirador* contains windows on each side, providing a 360-degree view over Havana. On a clear day it is possible to see 50 miles. Inset in the floor of each point is a compass showing the direction and distance of national and international cities (New York, for example, is 2,100 km away, and the North Pole is 7,441 km away).

NUEVO VEDADO

Nuevo Vedado is a sprawling complex of mid-20th-century housing, including ugly high-rise, postrevolutionary apartment blocks, arrayed in irregular grids.

The main site of interest is the **Jardín Zoológico de la Habana,** Havana's provincial zoo (not to be confused with the national Parque Zoológico on the outskirts of the city), on Avenida 26 and Zoológico, tel. (7) 81-8915. The zoo is a sad affair that suffers from poor management and lack of attention. The hippopotamus, crocodiles, caimans, flamingoes, and other water-loving species wade and wallow in polluted lagoons. It has many monkeys and chimpanzees but tragically they are kept apart and though their cages abut each other, they are separated by walls so that no monkey or ape has a view of its neighbors. Other species include Andean condors, water buffalo, jaguars, leopards, lions (thankfully in a large pit), and a gorilla, which suffered a stoning from a child when I was last there. Animals and visitors alike are further tormented by modern music piped over loudspeakers at deafening levels. A children's playground offers pony rides. There's a basic snack bar. Open Tue.-Sun. 9:30 a.m.-5:30 p.m. (US$2).

From the city zoo you can follow Avenida Zoológica west to the bridge over the Río Almendares and by turning right at the end, enter the **Bosque de la Habana.** This woodsy parkland—recently cleaned up and renamed **Parque Metropolitano de la Habana**—stretches along the canyon and plain of the river, and can still be enjoyed in a virtually untouched state, for which it is popular with lovers—a veritable Garden of Eden. To the south, the woods extend to **Los Jardines de la Tropical,** a landscaped park built 1904-10 on the grounds of a former brewery and designed by the Tropical beer company for promotional purposes (a free round of drinks was offered to picnickers). The park was paid for by Catalonians resident in Cuba and, appropriately, found its inspiration in Antoni Gaudí's Parque Güell in Barcelona.

PLAYA (MIRAMAR AND BEYOND)

West of Vedado and the Río Almendares stretches a vast and vital region where prior to the Revolution, the wealthy and middle classes lived in low-rise apartments and columned and balustraded mansions. The *municipio*—called Playa—extends west to the far reaches of Havana, beginning in the east with the seaside district of Miramar extending west about four miles as far as the Río Quibu. The rich who were forced to depart left their grand homes and classy apartments as valuable "gifts" to the Revolutionary government, which seized the properties and turned many into clinics, kindergartens, and clubs. Those for which no public use could be found were divided up into private apartments and communal dwellings for multiple families flooding in from the countryside.

Miramar is at the forefront of Cuba's quasi-capitalist remake. Even upscale condominiums had gone up in 2000 for sale to foreigners (Cubans, however, are not permitted to buy or sell property, not that they have the money). Cuba's future can be seen here, writ in stone, with dozens of cranes and construction crews at work erecting new hotels and offices and, in spring 2000, the **Miramar Trade Center,** a 27,000-square-meter complex with adjoining offices opposite the gleaming new Meliá Habana hotel on Av. 3ra. This area, an undeveloped flatland between Calles 70 and 84, was also being developed with Havana's largest hotel complex—the Hotel Miramar (on Av. 5ra) and Hotel Panorama (on Av. 3ra), both well under way at press time.

Inland of Avenida 5ra—the main east-west boulevard—Miramar slopes south, uphill to the suburban Marianao district (see the Suburban Havana section, below), accessed from Vedado via Avenida 31, which begins at the junction of Avenida 7ma and Calle 10 and runs southwest to the famous Tropicana nightclub at Calle 70. (See the special topic, The Tropicana Nightclub, in the Entertainment and Recreation section.). From downtown, access to Miramar is via tunnels under the Río Almendares at the west end of both the Malecón (at its junction with Calle 7, or Calzada) and Calle 9; and via a steel bridge—**Puente de Hierro**—at the west end of Calle 9, that is closed to vehicular traffic during certain hours.

West of Miramar, Playa boasts the city's beach resorts or *balnearios*, which line the shore of the Naútico and Flores districts, cut through by Avenida 5ta. Playa also boasts Havana's most luxurious residences, concentrated along the leafy boulevards of the hilly Cubanacán district, on the slopes inland of the shore. Adjacent Siboney is now a center for biogenetic research.

AVENIDA 1RA (PRIMERA)

Avenida 1ra (Primera) runs along the Miramar seafront. It's a lively spot, popular with Havana's youth. It's Havana's answer to Santa Monica—without the sand and the pier, but, yes, you may occasionally see girls in skin-tight hot pants being pulled along on roller-blades by their dogs. Even surfing has come to Cuba: the surfing crowd find its waves in the coastal section fronting the Hotels Neptuno/Tritón on Av. 1ra between 70 and 84.

Avenida 1ra is witnessing a boom, with many embassies, restaurants, and commercial entities opting for a locale by the sea, although the shoreline is grotesque and lacks beaches.

Decrepit *balnearios* (bathing areas) are found all along Miramar's waterfront, cut into the coral shore. Most are concentrated west of the Hotel Comodoro, beginning at Calle 84. More appealing beaches—the Playas del Oeste—begin half a km further west in the Naútico district and extend west to Flores (Jaiminito); see Avenida 5ta, below. A stroll along the avenue is pleasant (don't underestimate its length: about two miles), but there are only two sites of interest.

Maqueta de la Habana

The must-see *maqueta* (model) is a 1:1,000 scale replica of the city housed in an a/c building—the Pabellón—at Calle 28 #113 e/ Aves 1ra y 3ra, tel. (7) 33-2661. The 144-square-meter model represents 144 square km of Havana and its environs. It is impressive—but, more important, a visit here puts the entire city in accessible 3-D perspective. There's a balcony for viewing the model from on high.

The *maqueta*—one of the largest city models in the world—took nine experts more than 10 years to complete (it's made from recycled cigar boxes) and shows Havana in the most intimate detail. Every contour is included, every building, every bump on every hill, even the balconies on buildings are there. It is color-coded by age: historic buildings are painted crimson; postrevolutionary buildings are in ivory. The model is made of sections that can be moved on rails to allow access for changes. It's open to the public Tues.-Sat. 10 a.m.-5:30 p.m. Entrance costs US$3 (US$1 for students, seniors, and children).

The Pabellón also contains the offices of the **Grupo para el Desarrollo Integral de la Capital,** the government institution responsible for overseeing the integrated development of Havana. is, tel./fax (7) 33-2661, e-mail: gdic@tinored.cu.

Acuario Nacional

On weekends, Cuban families flock to the National Aquarium on Av. 1ra and Calle 60, tel. (7) 23-6401, fax (7) 24-1442. It has an impressive array of tanks (with educational motifs in Spanish) with all manner of sea life, from anemones to corals and exotic tropical fishes in their natural environments; as well as a shark tank, another tank with hawksbill turtles, plus sea-lions and dolphins. More than 300 species of marine life are displayed. Shark-feeding and a sea lion act are offered as entertainment. Alas, some of the tanks are aged and ill-kept and may not be deemed "politically correct" in our modern times, but new tanks were being built as part of a massive expansion at press time.

The highlight is the **dolphin show,** offered eight times daily (determining the times has proven difficult: the public relations manager read me one timetable, which contradicted the published schedule she gave me, and the schedule posted at the gate offered yet different times). Call ahead for times. The show lasts 20 minutes and features four trained dolphins

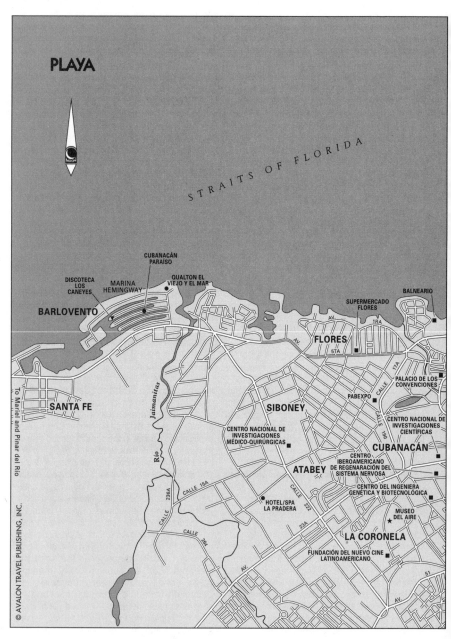

PLAYA

STRAITS OF FLORIDA

CUBANACÁN
PARAÍSO

DISCOTECA
LOS
CANEYES

MARINA
HEMINGWAY

QUALTON EL
VIEJO Y EL MAR

SUPERMERCADO
FLORES

BALNEARIO

BARLOVENTO

AV.

1RA

FLORES

AV.

5TA

17A

PALACIO DE LOS
CONVENCIONES

PABEXPO

CALLE

SANTA FE

SIBONEY

CENTRO NACIONAL DE
INVESTIGACIONES
CIENTÍFICAS

CALLE 190

CENTRO NACIONAL DE
INVESTIGACIONES
MÉDICO-QUIRÚRGICAS

CUBANACÁN

ATABEY

CENTRO
IBEROAMERICANO
DE REGENARACIÓN DEL
SISTEMA NERVOSA

CALLE 236A

CALLE 15A

CENTRO DEL INGENIERA
GENÉTICA Y BIOTECNOLÓGICA

CALLE

HOTEL/SPA
LA PRADERA

CALLE 222

MUSEO
DEL AIRE

LA CORONELA

CALLE 23A

CALLE 264

FUNDACIÓN DEL NUEVO CINE
LATINOAMERICANO

AV.

AV.

51

Río Jaimanitas

To Mariel and Pinar del Río

© AVALON TRAVEL PUBLISHING, INC.

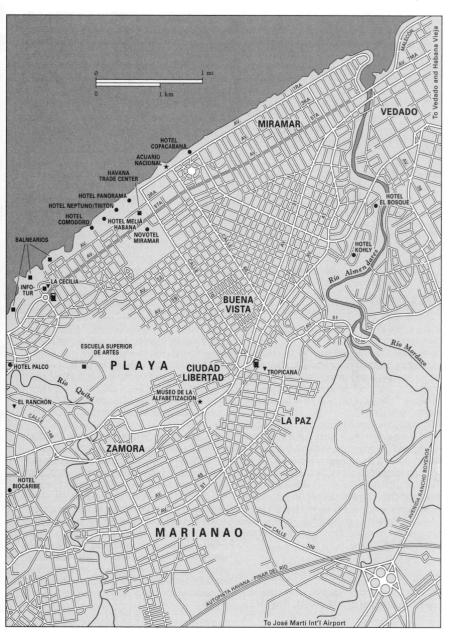

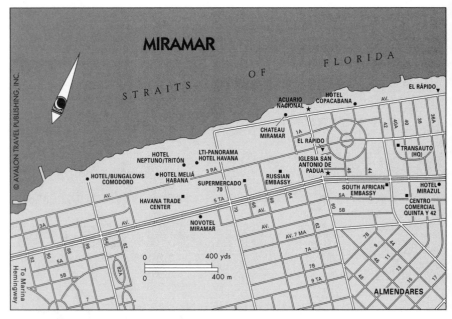

that belong to the species *Tursiop trucaus,* commonly known as "mule" dolphins. The dolphins belie that misnomer by performing synchronized leaps through hoops, dances to music, and other enthralling tricks while a commentator offers an educational program in Spanish. Take the kids, who have an opportunity to participate.

A small library upstairs caters to marine topics; open Monday 10 a.m.-1 p.m., Tue.-Fri. 10 a.m.-5 p.m., and Saturday 10 a.m.-9 p.m. Facilities include public toilets and a basic snack bar.

The aquarium is open Monday 6-11 p.m., Tue.-Thu. 10 a.m.-6 p.m., Friday 10 a.m.-10 p.m., and Saturday and Sunday 10 a.m.-6 p.m.

Rumbos S.A., tel. (7) 66-9713 or 24-9626, offers an evening at the aquarium, with sea lion and dolphin shows and shark-feeding on Monday and Friday, 6-10 p.m.

AVENIDA 5TA (QUINTA)

Miramar's main thoroughfare (and Havana's busiest boulevard) and "Embassy Row" is the wide boulevard called Avenida 5ta, lined by stately jagüey trees and flanked by mansions, many of which have been restored to an earlier grandeur and are now occupied by various Cuban commercial agencies or leased (or sold) to foreign corporations. A curiosity is the monstrous **Confederation of Independent States' Embassy,** a peculiar Cubist tower—formerly the Soviet Embassy; now the Russian Embassy, looking, thought Jon Lee Anderson, "like a glassy-eyed robot with amputated arms"—in the middle of Avenida Quinta between Calles 62 and 66. Construction began in 1978 and was ongoing at the time of the Soviet collapse. The church one block east is **Iglesia San Antonio de Padua,** in modernist style and dating from 1951 and quite simple yet peaceful within.

On Calle 18 e/ 5ta and 7ma, is **Che Guevara's former home,** where the revolutionary icon narrowly escaped assassination on 24 February 1961 when a gun-battle erupted outside his home a few moments after he had set out for work.

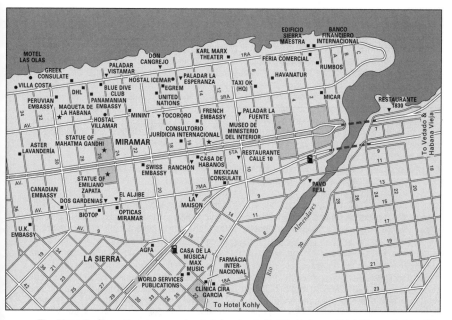

The **Plaza Emiliano Zapata,** spanning Avenida 5ta between Calles 24 and 26, is shaded by massive jagüey trees, seemingly supported by their aerial roots dangling like cascades of water. On the south side of the road is a life-size stone statue of Zapata, Mexico's revolutionary hero, appropriately surrounded by cacti; on the north side is a parthenon and behind it a bronze bust to Mahatma Gandhi.

The **Museo Marcha del Pueblo Combatiente,** housed in the former Peruvian embassy at 5ta and 72, tel. (7) 29-1497, and tells the official version of the events that took place here in April 1980, culminating in the Mariel boatlift, when some 120,000 Cubans—the Castro regime calls them *gusanos,* or worms—fled the island for Florida, causing President Carter no end of grief. Open Mon.-Sat. 9:30 a.m.-5:30 p.m.

The intriguing Byzantine-style church immediately to the west is the **Iglesia Jesús de Miramar.**

Museo de Ministerio del Interior

The Museum of the Ministry of the Interior, tel. (7) 23-4432, is dedicated to the CIA's 30 years of inept efforts to dethrone Fidel. The seal of the CIA looms over a room full of photos and gadgets—oddities straight from a spy movie—used in the agency's no-holds-barred attempts to kill Castro during the 1960s (see the special topic, The CIA's Attempts To Kill Castro, in the History section). It displays lots of small arms, bazookas, and the like. It also has displays honoring MININT's good work in solving homicides (there's even a stuffed German shepherd that was used by police in their sleuthing). A police helicopter and speedboat stand in a lot across the road. Open Tue.-Fri. 9 a.m.-5 p.m. and Saturday 9 a.m.-4 p.m. Entry costs US$2 (plus US$1 for a guide).

Playas del Oeste and Marina Hemingway

Avenida 5ta continues west beyond the Río Quibu and passes into the old Flores district, a shorefront region lined with *balnearios* (bathing areas). These beaches are small and most are nothing to write home about, but they're extremely popular with Cubans on weekends, when they get crowded. Most of the aging *balnearios* date from prerevolutionary days (many went up in the 1920s and '30s during the early years of Havana's tourist heyday when there was even a mini-version of New Jersey's famous Coney Island theme park).

The shining star is **Club Habana,** Av. 5ta, e/ 188 y 192, in Reparto Flores, Playa, tel. (7) 24-5700, fax (7) 24-5705. This palatial private "nautical and social club" is operated by Palco (the Conference Center agency) and managed by Spain's Sol Meliá, and was formerly the famous Havana Biltmore Yacht and Country Club, dating back to 1928. It covers 10 hectares and boasts a fine beach of white sand, plus a handsome pool with sundeck. The regally appointed main clubhouse has a business center, elegant restaurant, plush bar with marble floors, separate piano bar, and a Casa del Tabaco and cigar lounge. A fitness center offers sauna and massage. A nursery takes care of the kids. Sports facilities include yacht rental, scuba diving, surfboards, Aqua bikes, sea kayaks, a golf range, and beach volleyball. And it offers shows and cabarets on Saturday night. The club serves its members (US$1,500 per year), made up mostly of foreign diplomats and businessmen, but nonmembers are welcome: entrance costs US$10, Mon.-Fri.; US$15, Saturday and Sunday.

You can also swim at **Marina Hemingway,** Av. 5ta y Calle 248, tel. (7) 24-1150, fax (7) 24-1149, e-mail: comercial@comermh.cha.cyt.cu, one km west of Club Habana in the Santa Fe district, 15 km west of downtown, where there are several swimming pools sprinkled about the vast yachting marina. The best pool is that of the Hotel El Jardín del Edén. Take your pick of numerous restaurants and bars that get lively with Cubans on weekends, drawing flirty *Cubanas* eager to find positions as captains' mates (by day entry costs US$3; a US$10 *consumo mínimo*—minimum purchase charge applies on weekends). Deafening music is played constantly! The cabaret hosts shows at night (see the Entertainment section).

Additional beaches lie west of the marina along the Santa Fe waterfront.

CUBANACÁN AND VICINITY

Cubanacán is—or was—Havana's Beverly Hills, a rolling area on the west bank of the Río Quibu.

It was developed in the 1920s in a "garden-city" style, with winding tree-lined streets and enormous lots on which grandiose mansions and houses arose. A 18-hole golf course at the Havana Country Club served Havana's middle and wealthy classes, lending the name Country Club Park to what is now called Cubanacán, then as now the most exclusive address in town.

Bus no. 32 operates between La Rampa in Vedado and Cubanacán (five pesos), as does the **Vaivén Bus Turístico** (see By Bus in the Getting Around section, in the Transportation chapter).

Following the Revolution, most of the owners decamped and fled Cuba. Many mansions have since fallen into ruin, reminding novelist James Michener of "an Arthur Rackham painting of a country in which a cruel king has laid waste the mansions of his enemies." Some mansions were dispensed to Communist Party officials, many of whom still live in glorious isolation. Others have been splendidly maintained amid neatly trimmed lawns and serve either as "protocol" houses—villas where foreign dignitaries and VIPs are housed during visits to Cuba—or as foreign embassies and immaculately kept ambassadors' homes. Among them is the U.S. Residency, heavily-guarded for obvious reasons, in immaculate and spacious grounds in which, at the end of a long promenade, the eagle that once stood atop the Monumento del Maine on the Malecón spreads its magnificent wings. Fidel maintains several homes here, too, and security is sharp.

The erstwhile exclusive Havana Country Club was confiscated following the Revolution and converted to house a Cuban national arts institute: the **Instituto Superior de Arte,** featuring the School of Music (Escuela de Música), Ballet School (Escuela de Ballet), School of Modern Dance (Escuela de Baile Moderno), and School of Fine Arts (Escuela de Bellas Artes). The assemblage began life as the Castro government's first, and last, foray into serious architecture. The regime commissioned a team of leading architects to design a campus (built on the old golf course) meant to exemplify the possibilities of communist architecture. It proved too hedonistic, however, for the Castroite regime. Says Paul Goldberger: "The school had an earnest, determined aestheticism that did not sit well with a

GENETIC ENGINEERING

*C*uba is a biotech minipower. In 1965 there were said to be only 12 research scientists in Cuba; today there are more than 25,000. Under Fidel Castro's personal patronage, Cuba has evolved one of the world's most advanced genetic engineering and biotechnology industries, with large-scale investment coming from public sources such as the Pan American Health Organization and the World Food Program.

The program is led by the **Centro de Ingenieria Genética y Biotecnología** (Center for Genetic Engineering and Biotechnology, Avenida 31 y 158, in the Havana suburb of Cubanacán, tel. (7) 21-6022. The center, perhaps the most sophisticated research facility in the Third World, opened in 1986 as one of more than two dozen Cuban institutes dedicated to the biological sciences. Together they supply state-of-the-art health products to the world (sold through the marketing entity Heber Biotec), bringing in over US$100 million annually.

Cuba has developed nearly 200 products, both innovative and derivative. It invented and manufactures vaccines for cerebral meningitis, cholera, hepatitis B, interferon for the treatment of AIDS and cancer, and a skin-growth factor to speed the healing of burns. For years Cuba has touted a cure for the skin disease vitiligo. Recently it developed PPG, a "wonder drug" that reputedly washes cholesterol out of blood and, incidentally, is said to increase sexual potency (the source of a brisk black market for peddlers selling the drug to tourists). In 1996 CIGB scientists even began testing a vaccine to prevent HIV infection, and in 1999 a Cuban-developed cancer vaccine was undergoing clinical trials in Canada.

---

regime increasingly influenced by the harsh Leninism of the Soviet Union." In typical quixotic fashion, it abandoned the project and turned it into a classic of communist folly. You are welcome to wander the campus. Access is from Av. 5ta via Calle 120.

The **Palacio de las Convenciones**—Havana's impressive convention center—is also here, on Calle 146 e/ 11 y 13, tel. (7) 22-6011, fax (7) 21-9496, e-mail: palco@palco.get. cma.net, website: www.cubaweb.cu/palco. It was built in 1979 for the Non-Aligned Conference, and the main hall (one of 15 halls), seating

2,200 delegates, hosts meetings of the Cuban National Assembly. Nearby, at Avenida 17 y 180, is **Pabexpo,** with four exhibition halls for hosting trade fairs.

Cuba's admirable biotechnology industry is centered south and west of Cubanacán in the districts of La Coronela and Siboney respectively (dozens of ugly high-rise apartment blocks have also risen during the past four decades). The **Centro de Ingeniería Genética y Biotecnología,** for example, is at Avenida 31 and 190, tel. (7) 21-6022, fax (7) 21-8070; the **Centro Nacional de Investigaciones Científicas** is nearby at Avenida 25 and 158, tel. (7) 21-8066, and it was here that PPG, or Ateromixol, Cuba's homespun anti-cholesterol wonder drug was developed. You can arrange visits that will duly impress you with Cuba's phenomenal commitment to—and success with—cutting-edge research in the field.

La Coronela offers the **Museo del Aire,** the Air Museum on Avenida 212. The gamut of civilian and military aircraft displayed includes helicopters, missiles, bombers, and fighter planes, including Soviet MiGs and a turn-of-the-century biplane hanging from the ceiling. The museum also has a restoration program, plus three main rooms that are an Aladdin's cave of aviation mementos. A section dedicated to the Bay of Pigs battle evokes poignant memories; remnants of planes destroyed in the fighting and black-and-white photos speak with mute eloquence of the memory of Cuban pilots who died defending the island. There's also a collection of model aircraft, and a space section honoring Yuri Gagarin and Col. Arnaldo Tamayo Méndez, the first Cuban cosmonaut. An artisans' shop and a restaurant are planned. Open Tues.-Sun. 9 a.m.-5 p.m. Entrance US$2. The museum is hard to find: from Avenida 5ta take 17-A south to the roundabout; take the first exit to the right, heading west on Avenida 23; then the first left, onto 198; then the first right onto 212, disregarding the sign that reads 27; the museum is 100 yards on your left.

About 100 yards down Avenida 212 is the **Fundación del Nuevo Cine Latinamericano,** the Havana branch of the film institute presided over by Gabriel García Márquez.

For a swim and refreshments, call in at **Complejo Turístico La Giradilla,** at Calle 272, e/

37 y 51 in the La Coronela district, tel. (7) 33-0568, fax (7) 33-6390, e-mail: gerencia@giralda.cha.cyt.cu. Popular with the Cuban elite, this restaurant and entertainment complex occupies a huge 1920s mansion in expansive grounds that feature a huge swimming pool and sundeck plus a covered stage for floor shows and disco at night. See the Food and Entertainment sections, this chapter.

Fábrica El Laguito

This cigar factory, in a fabulous turn-of-the-century mansion at Av. 146 #2302, Cubanacán, tel. (7) 21-2213, one block south of the Palacio de los Convenciones, was opened in 1966 as a training school in the former home of the Marquez de Pinar del Río—adorned with 1930s art deco glass and chrome, a spiral staircase, and abstract floral designs in the stucco detailing. El Laguito makes Montecristos and the majority of Cohibas, *the* premium Havana cigar. It is common lore that Che Guevara initiated production while in charge of the Cuban tobacco industry: his objective was to make a cigar that surpassed every other prerevolutionary cigar. However, Nancy Stout (in her splendid book, *Habanos*) says that it was started by revolutionary heroine Celia Sánchez as a place of employment for women (men have been employed as rollers here only since 1994), while Che had his own little offshoot factory in the Cabaña fortress.

Since Cohibas are made from only the finest leaves, El Laguito is given first choice from the harvest ("the best selection of the best selection," says factory head Emilia Tamayo). About 3.4 million Cohibas are produced annually—about one percent of Cuban production. El Laguito also makes the best cigar in the world—the Trinidad, a seven-and-a-half-inch-long cigar until recently made exclusively for Fidel Castro to present to diplomats and dignitaries (the factory also made Fidel's own cigars in the days when he smoked).

Call ahead for an appointment if you wish to visit.

MARIANAO

This untouristed *municipio,* on the heights south of Miramar, began life as an old village. By the mid-19th century, wealthy Spaniards began to built fine summer homes along newly laid streets on the breeze-swept slopes. Sections still bear the stamp of the colonial past. Following the U.S. occupation of Cuba in 1898, the U.S. military governor, General Fitzhugh Lee, established his headquarters here and called it Camp Columbia. During the 1920s, Cuban developers promoted the area and established the Marianao Country Club, the Oriental Park race track, and Grand Nacional Casino; and Marianao became a center of tourism, being given a boost on New Year's Eve 1939 when the Tropicana nightclub opened as the ritziest thing Havana had ever seen. Marianao remained a center for pleasure until the Revolution, when **Las Fritas,** Marianao's erstwhile three-block-long strip of restaurants, beer parlors, shooting galleries, peep shows, and cabarets was shut down.

Camp Columbia later became the headquarters for Batista's army, and it was from here that the sergeant effected his *golpes* (coups d'etat) in 1933 and 1952. Camp Columbia—re-named Ciudad Libertad following the Revolution—continued to operate as a military airstrip, although Castro, true to his promise, had since turned Batista's barracks into a school. The airstrip was bombed on 15 April 1960 by B-26 light bombers (falsely painted in Cuban colors) during the run-up to the CIA-run Bay of Pigs invasion in an attempt to destroy Castro's air force. The attack failed, although five of Castro's planes were destroyed. The bombers had struck houses in the densely packed neighborhood of Ciudad Libertad, killing seven people and wounding 52, giving Castro a grand political victory in his calls for solidarity against U.S. aggression (one of the dying men wrote Fidel's name in blood on a wall).

Today the former Campamento Columbia army camp houses the **Museo de la Alfabetización,** at the junction of Calle 31 and Av. 100, tel. (7) 20-8054, and dedicated to the literacy campaign of 1961. Open weekdays 8 a.m.-5 p.m.; US$1. A tower outside the entrance is shaped like a syringe in honor of Carlos Finlay, the Cuban who in 1881 discovered the cause of yellow fever.

A nocturnal visit to the **Tropicana,** off Calle 72 between 41 and 45, tel. (7) 27-0110, fax (7) 27-0109 is a *must!* The whirlwind show opened in 1939 in an open-air theater and became Havana's top nightclub, boasting the most beautiful female dancers in Cuba. Most of the structures date from 1951 in modernist style. However, visitors are not welcome by day, when the dancers practice. You must visit at night, when the lavishly costumed, statuesque showgirls perform beneath the stars. (For details on the show, see the Entertainment section.)

SUBURBAN HAVANA

In addition, a number of metropolitan Havana's prime attractions lie on the city's outskirts and are well worth the drive. The following are presented in counter-clockwise order, beginning with southern Havana.

BOYEROS

Boyeros, south of the Playa district and southwest of Havana, is a vast, mostly undeveloped area with few sites of touristic appeal. It is accessed from downtown Havana via Avenida de Independencia, which runs south through the industrial area of **Rancho Boyeros** to the José Martí International Airport, south of which it become Avenida de los Mártires and you suddenly find yourself in Santiago de las Vegas, a colonial-era rural town in the midst of the country.

The **Havana Golf Club** is hidden east of Avenida de la Independencia in the industrial-residential area call Capdevila, midway between Havana and Santiago de las Vegas. The golf club opened in 1948 as the Rover's Athletic Club, built by British residents who felt homesick for Turnberry and was maintained by the British Embassy until given to the Cuban government in 1980. The place is popular on weekends with Cuban families, who flock for the swimming pool, not the golf. See the Culture and Entertainment chapter for details.

Santiago de las Vegas

This small town, 20 km south of Havana, is the nearest provincial town to Havana and is steeped in sleepy bucolic charm. It straddles Avenida de los Mártires (Avenida Rancho Boyeros), about three km south of the airport. Its allure lies in strolling the narrow streets lined with red-tile-roofed colonial houses painted in faded pastels. Take time to sit on the tiny main square, where children play hoop and senior citizens gather to debate and gossip beneath shade trees. At its core is a marble statue of a local Mambí hero, Juan Delgado Gonzales and other local citizenry who formed a regiment of Mambí (insurgent nationalist troops) during the wars of independence. A quaint whitewashed church faces onto the plaza from the west.

Santiago's streets are horrendously potholed with huge troughs big enough to swallow Cuba's hefty homegrown cattle.

The main road rises abruptly south of Santiago de las Vegas and soon you find yourself amid pine forests in an area utilized by the Cuban military, with several camps. At **El Cacahual,** about two km south of Santiago de las Vegas, General Antonio Maceo Grajables (1845-96)—the black general and hero of the wars of independence—slumbers in an open-air mausoleum in a circular park the size of a football field and shaded by trees full of birdsong. Two tombs for the memorial stand near here: Maceo's and that of Capitán Ayudante (Captain-Adjutant) Francisco Gómez Toro (1876-1896), son of General Máximo Gómez, who gave his life alongside Maceo at the Battle of San Pedro on 7 December 1896. The granite tombs are engraved in the style of Mexican artist Diego Rivera. An adjacent pavilion has a small exhibit with photos and maps showing the black general's route during the war.

The park forms a giant traffic circle on the east side of which stands a monument in bronze to Coronel (colonel) Juan Delgado, chief of the Santiago de las Vegas regiment, who recovered Maceo's body. The tiny hamlet of **Cacahual** lies hidden from sight no more than 200 yards east, behind the pine trees.

Getting There, Away and Around: A train runs to Santiago de las Vegas from the Estación Cristina at Avenida México and Arroyo in southwest Habana Vieja, tel. (7) 78-4971, (40 centavos) at 6:05 and 10:40 a.m., and 2:50 and 7 p.m. Return trains depart Santiago de las Vegas for Cristina at 7:57 a.m. and 12:30, 4:54, and 8:40 p.m.

Turistaxi has an office on General Peraza, tel. (683) 3007.

Sanctuario de San Lazaro

One of Cuba's most important pilgrimage sites is the Sanctuary of San Lazaro, half a kilometer west of the village of Rincón, three km southwest of Santiago de las Vegas. The well-maintained complex comprises a leprosarium, the **Los Cocos** AIDS sanatorium, and a church with gray marble floor and various altars (the main one is a popular roosting site for local birds). The church draws mendicants, especially on Sunday when Cubans come in droves to have their children baptized, while others fill bottles with holy water from a fountain behind the church.

San Lazaro is the patron saint of the sick, and as such the **Procession of the Miracles** takes place 17 December, when hundreds of pilgrims—up to 50,000 in some years—make their way to the sanctuary to give thanks for miracles they imagine he granted. The villagers of Rincón do a thriving business selling votive candles and flowers to church-goers. Limbless beggars, lepers, and other mendicants crowd at the gates and plead for a charitable donation while penitents crawl on their backs and knees as others walk ahead of them and sweep the road with palm fronds. "A man inched along painfully on his back, with cinder blocks tied to his feet," wrote Andrei Codrescu in *Ay Cuba!* "I asked the man coiling and uncoiling on his back with the cinder blocks tied to his feet what he was going to ask San Lazaro. 'To help me walk,' the man replied."

Getting There and Away: Bus no. M2 runs from Parque de la Fraternidad in Havana and stops on the southeast corner of the square. The *terminal de autobus* is on the southwest side of town, at Calle 12 y Avenida 17, on the road to Rincón and Santiago de los Baños. If driving, follow the signed road that leads west from El Cacahual, or take Carretera Santiago de las Vegas that begins at the bus station on the southwest edge of town.

Parque Zoológico

Cuba's national zoo is about 10 miles south of central Havana, at the west end of Avenida Soto, one km west of Calzada de Bejucal, in Boyeros, tel. (7) 44-7613 or 57-8054, fax (7) 24-0852. It was opened in 1984, covers 340 hectares, and has more than 800 animals and more than 100 species.

Tour buses (4 centavos) depart the parking lot about every 30 minutes and run through the African wildlife park—**Pradera Africano**—and lion's den, but you can also drive your own car farther into the park. The guided bus trip is the highlight and takes you through an expansive area not unlike the savanna of east Africa. Elephants come to the bus and stick their trunks in through the window to glean tidbits handed out by tourists. There are rhinos and two species of zebra, plus wildebeest, ostrich, and two hippos that spend most of their daylight hours wallowing in a deep pool. Gawkers gather at the low wall where you can simply reach over and stroke the elephants. Amazingly there's no security fence or moat, and you sense that the animals could simply leap or step over the four-foot-tall wall any time they wanted. Scary! No park staff is on hand, so visitors feed the animals all manner of junk food.

The lion pit—**Foso de Leones**—is a deep quarry on the north side of the park. The bus makes a quick loop through the pit, but you can also sit atop the cliff in a viewing platform and look down upon the lions fornicating, which is all they seem to do when they're not snoozing.

A walk-through section houses a leopard, tiger, chimps, monkeys, and birds, but conditions are deplorable and many of the animals look woefully neglected.

The zoo also raises more than 30 endangered species, plus there's a taxidermist's laboratory. There's a map of the zoo posted at the entrance gate, where there's a snack bar. A kiddy's area provides pony rides. It's open Wed.-Sun. 9:30 a.m.-4:30 p.m. Entrance costs US$3 per person (US$2 children, US$5 for a vehicle).

Getting There: By car the quickest way to the park is via Avenida de la Independencia (Avenida Rancho Boyeros) to Avenida San Francisco—the Parque is signed at the junction—which leads to the village of Arroyo Naranjo. The main entrance gate is off Calzada de Bejucal, which runs south through Arroyo Naranjo. A taxi will cost about US$12 each way.

Buses no. 31, 73, and 88 operate between La Vibora and Arroyo Naranjo.

ARROYO NARANJO

This *municipio* lies due south of Havana and offers three sites of appeal.

Parque Lenin

Parque Lenin, tel. (7) 44-2721, at Calle 100 y Carretera de la Presa, southeast of the village of Arroyo Naranjo, was created from a former hacienda and landscaped mostly by volunteer labor from the city (and maintained by inmates from a nearby psychiatric hospital). The vast complex, open Wed.-Sun. 9 a.m.-5:30 p.m., features wide rolling pastures and small lakes surrounded by forests and pockets of bamboo, ficus, and flamboyants, *güira,* from which maracas are made. What Lenin Park lacks in grandeur and stateliness, it makes up for in scale and scope. You'll need a long study to get an idea of the full scope of the park, which is laid out around the large lake, **Presa Paso Sequito.** with a huge reservoir—Ejército Rebelde— to the east. Cuban families flock to the park on weekends for the children's park, with carousels and fairground pleasures, horse riding, rodeos, and all the fun of the fair.

The park is bounded by the Circunvalación to the north and Calzada de Bejucal to the west. The official entrance to the park is off Calzada de Bejucal. A second road—Calle Cortina de la Presa—enters from the Circunvalación and runs ruler-straight down the center of the park; most sites of interest lie at the south end of this road, south of the lake. Calle Cortina is linked to Calzada de Bejucal by a loop road that passes most of the recreational sites north of the lake.

Sites, Galleries, and Museums: The sights of interest are concentrated on the south side of the lake. Begin with a visit to **Galería del Arte Amelia Peláez,** at the south end of Calle Cortina. It displays Paláez's works (she was responsible for the ceramic mural on the fascia of the Hotel Habana Libre, in Vedado) along with changing exhibitions of other artists. Behind the gallery is a series of bronze busts in rocks.

Nearby is the **Monumento Lenin,** a huge granite visage of the communist leader and thinker in Soviet-realist style. Moving west, you'll pass an **aquarium** displaying freshwater fish and turtles, including the antediluvian garfish *(marijuarí)* and a couple of Cuban crocodiles, Pepe and Rosita. Open Wed.-Sun. 9 a.m.-5 p.m. Entry costs US$1.

About 400 meters further west is the **Monumento a Celia Sánchez.** with a trail that follows a wide apse of large natural slabs to a broad amphitheater lined with ferns. At its center is a bronze figure of Sánchez ("the most beautiful and endemic flower of the Revolution") inset in a huge rock. A small museum exhibits portraits of the heroine alongside her personal items. (See the special topic, Celia Sánchez, in the Granma chapter.)

You might also visit the **Taller Cerámica** (ceramic workshop); **Casa de la Amistad Cubano Soviético** (Cuban-Soviet Friendship House), farther west; and the **Che Guevara Pioneer Palace,** full of stainless-steel sculptures of the revolutionary hero.

Activities, Recreation, and Entertainment: *Horseback riding:* There's an equestrian center—**Centro Ecuestre** (often called Club Hípico—immediately east of the entrance off Calzada de Bejucal. It offers riding lessons (a course of 10 one-hour riding lessons costs US$102), one-hour horseback trips (US$15), and even trips in a *coche* (colonial horse-drawn coach). You can rent horses also. The riding club covers 20 hectares and has stables for 30 horses, a training race track and paddock, several dressage paddocks, a smithy, veterinary clinic, changing rooms, showers, and even sauna and massage facilities. Open 9 a.m.-4:30 p.m.

Train Rides: A narrow-gauge railway circles the park, dropping passengers at various sites. The old steam train dates to 1870 and departs the **Terminal Inglesa** daily at 8 and 10 a.m., noon, and 2 and 4 p.m. (three pesos), and takes 30 minutes to circle the park. Another old steam train dating to 1915 is preserved under a red-tiled canopy in front of the station.

For Children: A *parque diversiones* (amusement park) is located in the northwest quarter and includes carousels, a miniature "big dipper," and pony rides.

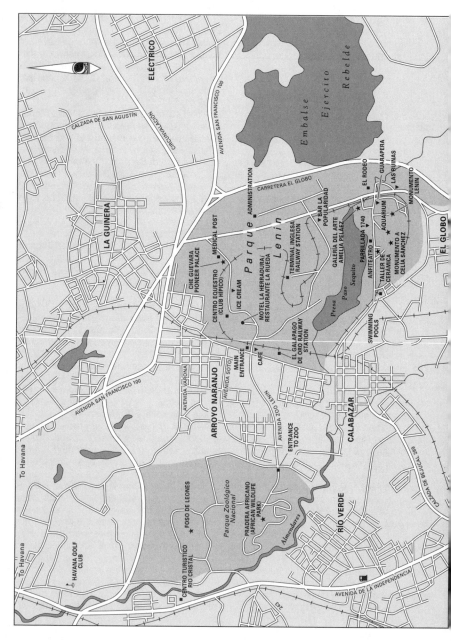

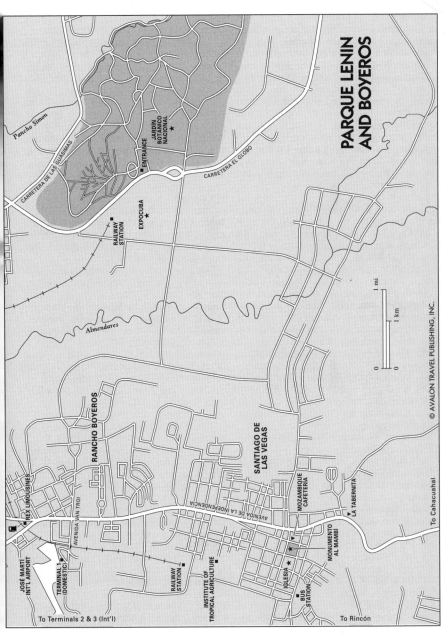

PARQUE LENIN
AND BOYEROS

Pancho Simon

CARRETERA DE LAS GUASIMAS

JARDÍN
BOTÁNICO
NACIONAL ★

ENTRANCE ■

CARRETERA EL GLOBO

EXPOCUBA ★

RAILWAY
STATION ■

Almendares

1 mi

1 km

0

0

© AVALON TRAVEL PUBLISHING, INC.

RANCHO BOYEROS

SANTIAGO DE
LAS VEGAS

AVENIDA VAN TROI

AVENIDA DE LA INDEPENDENCIA

MOZAMBIQUE
CAFETERIA ■

LA TABERNITA ■

To Cahacuahal

REX LIMOUSINES ■

JOSÉ MARTI
INT'L AIRPORT

TERMINAL 1
(DOMESTIC)

To Terminals 2 & 3 (Int'l)

RAILWAY
STATION ■

INSTITUTE OF
TROPICAL AGRICULTURE ■

IGLESIA ★

MONUMENTO
AL MAMBI ★

BUS
STATION ■

To Rincón

Rodeo: You can watch cowboys lasso cows at **El Rodeo,** which offers *rodeo cubano* in a horse ring (entry costs three pesos).

Rowboat Rental: You can rent rowboats on the lake at El Rodeo (see Other Facilities, below).

Theater and Music: Classical and other concerts are held at the **Anfiteatro,** a magnificent setting formed of a raised amphitheater facing down over the lake from its south side. Patrons sit in steeply banked seats hollowed from natural rock. The bands play on a floating stage.

Other Facilities: There's also a doll museum (Colina de los Muñecos), a drive-in movie theater (Ciné Césped; not operating at press time), and even a motocross circuit (not operating at press time).

Casa de la Popularidad is an information center with a small bar and restaurant. It's just off Calle Cortina at the junction with the loop road that leads along the north shore of the lake from Calzada de Bejucal. A tourist map of the park (US$1) will prove handy: you may be able to buy one at Tienda las Navigantes in Habana Vieja.

Getting There: See Parque Zoológico, above, for instruction on getting there by car (the official entrance—signed—is opposite the turnoff for the zoo on Calzada de Bejucal, south of the village of Arroyo Naranjo). However, the easiest route is to take the Avenida San Francisco 100 highway and turn south directly into the park. In addition to the Arroyo Naranjo entrance to the west, the Circunvalación runs past the north side of Parque Lenin, with a spur road running south through the park. A taxi will cost about US$15 each way.

Buses no. 31, 73, and 88 operate between La Vibora and the park entrance.

A train runs hourly from the Estació Cristina in Havana to Galápago de Oro station (on the northwest side of the park), which is served by bus no. 31.

Taxi Transtur, tel. (7) 33-6666, fax (7) 33-5535, e-mail: taxihab@transtur.com.cu, offers a chauffeured excursion for US$/40 (car/minivan). **Palcocar,** tel. (7) 33-7235, fax (7) 33-7250, charges US$25 for a chauffeured excursion, including two free hours.

Tours & Travel, Av. 1ra y 0, Miramar, tel. (7) 24-0993, and Calle 23 y M, Vedado, tel. (7) 33-4082, fax (7) 33-4084, has a guided excursion to Parque Lenin and the botanical garden (US$25).

ExpoCuba

ExpoCuba lies three km south of Parque Lenin, 25 km south of Havana, on the Carretera del Globo (the official address is Carretera del Rocío Km 3.5, Arroyo Naranjo), tel. (7) 44-6251, fax (7) 33-5307. It houses a permanent exhibition of Cuban industry, technology, sports, and culture. It's a popular venue for school field trips and conventioneers. The facility covers 588,000 square meters and is a museum, trade expo, World's Fair, and entertainment hall rolled into one. It has 34 pavilions, including provincial booths that display the crafts, products, music, and dance of each of Cuba's provinces. Railroad buffs might check out the vintage rolling stock (including turn-of-the-century carriages) on the entrance forecourt. Booth #9—the maritime booth—displays an armored motor-launch, among other vessels. Booth #25 exhibits old carriages and cars. It's open Wed.-Sun. 9 a.m.- 6 p.m. Entry costs US$1.

There's a information office at the entrance, alongside a bureau de change and a branch of Banco de Crédito y Comercio.

Getting There: ExpoCuba is three km south of Parque Lenin—take the Calle Cortina de la Presa south through the park—and immediately south of the village of El Globo.

Buses no. 88 and 113 leave for ExpoCuba (and the Jardín Botánico) from the north side of Havana's main railway station weekends at 10 a.m., noon, and 3 p.m. and from Havana's Terminal de Ómnibus at 9 and 11 a.m. and 4 p.m. Bus no. 80 also serves the park, from Lawton.

A three-car train runs to ExpoCuba, opposite the garden, from the 19 de Noviembre (Tulipán) station on Calle Tulipán, in Nuevo Vedado, tel. (7) 81-4431, Wed.-Sun. at 9:05 a.m. and 12:35 p.m.; it departs ExpoCuba at 10:50 a.m. and 3:50 p.m. (US$1 one-way).

Jardín Botánico

This huge (600 hectare) botanical garden, directly opposite ExpoCuba, doesn't have the fine-trimmed herbaceous borders of Kew or Butchart, but nonetheless is worth the drive for enthusiasts. Thirty-five km of roads lead through the park, which was laid out between 1969 and 1984. The expansive garden consists mostly of wide pastures planted with copses of trees and shrubs divided by Cuban ecosystems (from coastal thicket to Oriental humid forest) and by regions of the tropical world. Over 100 gardeners tenderly prune and mulch such oddities as the *satchicha* tree, with pendulous pods that certain African tribeswomen rub on their nipples in the belief that it will give them large breasts.

The geographic center has a fascinating variety of palm trees from around the world. But the highlight is the **Japanese garden,** beautifully landscaped with tiered cascades, fountains, and a jade green lake full of koi. This little gem was donated by the Japanese government for the 30th anniversary of the Revolution. There is even an "archaic forest" containing species such as *Microcyca calocom,* Cuba's cork palm, from the antediluvian dawn.

The **Rincón Eckman,** a massive glasshouse named after Erik Leonard Eckman (1883-1931), who documented Cuban flora between 1914 and 1924, is laid out as a triptych: cactus house; a room full of epiphytes, bromeliads, ferns and insectivorous plants; and a third with tropical mountain plants, a small cascade, and a pool.

The glasshouse (which has wheelchair access) boasts a souvenir stall and café, plus toilets. And the **Bambú Restaurant,** which overlooks the Japanese garden, serves as the best vegetarian restaurant in Havana (lunch only; Wed.-Sun., noon-3 p.m.). A museum, motel, amphitheater, and scientific center were planned.

Open daily 8:30 a.m.-4:45 p.m. Entrance costs US$0.60 per person, or US$3 with guide. Private vehicles are *not* allowed through the park except with a guide. Reservations can be made by calling tel. (7) 44-2516 or 44-8743. It's open Wed.-Sun 9 a.m.-5 p.m. You can buy a tourist map of the garden for US$1.

Getting There: See ExpoCuba, above. Also, **Tours & Travel** (see Parque Lenin, above) has a daily excursion to the garden (US$15, or US$25 with lunch).

SAN MIGUEL DE PADRON

The *municipio* of San Miguel de Padron extends south of the Bahía de la Habana and is mostly residential. The sole draw, beyond the suburb of Luyano, is **San Francisco de Paula,** on the outskirts of the city, 12.5 km south of Havana (about 20 minutes from Habana Vieja). San Fran-

cisco de Paula moves at a bucolic pace befitting its small wooden houses of colonial vintage. Rising above the village, but hidden from view, is Ernest Hemingway's must-see former home, Finca Vigía

Finca Vigía

In 1939, Hemingway's third wife, Martha Gellhorn, was struck by Finca Vigía (Lookout Farm), a one-story Spanish-colonial house built in 1887 and boasting a wonderful view of Havana. They rented it for US$100 a month. When Hemingway's first royalty check from *For Whom The Bell Tolls* arrived in 1940, he bought the house for US$18,500 because, like his character Ole Anderson in "The Killers," he had tired of roaming from one place to another. In August 1961 his widow, Mary Welsh, donated the 20-acre hilltop estate and most of its contents to the Cuban state, according to Hemingway's will.

On 21 July 1994, on the 95th anniversary of Papa's birthday, Finca Vigía reopened its doors as a museum, tel. (7) 91-0809, following nearly two years of repairs and remodeling. The house is preserved in suspended animation, just the way the great writer left it. His presence seems to haunt the large, simple home. No one is allowed inside—reasonably so, since every room can be viewed through the wide-open windows, and the temptation to pilfer priceless trinkets is thus reduced. (Two years after Hemingway died, someone offered US$80,000 for his famous Royal typewriter, which sits on a shelf beside his workroom desk; today you can buy it for US$7—inscribed in gray on a T-shirt that reads "Museo Ernesto Hemingway, Finca Vigía, Cuba").

Through the large windows you can see trophies, firearms, bottles of spirits, old issues of *The Field, Spectator,* and *Sports Afield* strewn about, and more than 8,000 books, arranged higgledy-piggledy the way he supposedly liked them, with no concern for authors or subjects. The dining room table is set with cut crystal, as if guests were expected.

It is eerie being followed by countless eyes—those of the guides (one to each room) and those of the beasts that had found themselves in the cross-hairs of Hemingway's hunting scope. "Don't know how a writer could write surrounded by so many dead animals," Graham Greene commented when he visited. There are bulls,

ERNEST HEMINGWAY AND CUBA

rnest Hemingway first set out from Key West to wrestle marlin in the wide streaming currents off the Cuban coast in April 1932. Years later, he was to sail to and fro, on the Key West-Havana route dozens of times. The blue waters of the Gulf Stream, chock-full of billfish, brought him closer and closer until eventually, "succumbing to the other charms of Cuba, different from and more difficult to explain than the big fish in September," he settled on this irresistibly charismatic island.

Hemingway loved Cuba and lived there for the better part of 20 years. It was more alluring, more fulfilling, than Venice, Sun Valley, or the green hills of Africa. Once, when Hemingway was away from Cuba, he was asked what he worried about in his sleep. "My house in Cuba," he replied, referring to Finca Vígia, in the suburb of San Francisco de Paula, 15 kilometers southeast of Havana.

The Cult of Hemingway
Havana's city fathers have leased Papa's spirit to lend ambience to and put a polish on his favorite haunts. Havana's marina is named for the prize-winning novelist. A special rum, "El

Ron Vígia" was even introduced to coincide with the author's 95th birthday, on 21 July 1994. Hemingway's room in the Hotel Ambos Mundos and Finca Vígia are preserved as museums. His name is attached to fishing tournaments and to sugar-free daiquiris. And his likeness adorns T-shirts and billboards.

Yet the cult of Hemingway is very real. Cubans worship him with an intensity not far short of that accorded Che Guevara and nationalist hero José Martí. The novelist's works are required reading in Cuban schools. His books are bestsellers. "We admire Hemingway because he understood the Cuban people; he supported us," a friend told me. The Cuban understanding of Hemingway's "Cuban novels" is that they support a core tenet of Communist ideology—that humans are only fulfilled acting in a "socialist" context for a moral purpose, not individualistically. (Many of Hemingway's novels appear to condemn economic and political injustices.)

"All the works of Hemingway are a defense of human rights," claims Castro, who knows Papa's novels "in depth" and once claimed that *For Whom the Bell Tolls*,

too, everywhere bulls, including paintings by Miró and Klee, photographs and posters of bullfighting scenes, and a chalk plate of a bull's head, a gift from Picasso.

Here is where Hemingway wrote *Islands in the Stream*, *Across the River and into the Trees*, *A Moveable Feast* and *The Old Man and the Sea*. The four-story tower next to the house was built at his fourth wife's prompting so that he could write unmolested. Hemingway disliked the tower and continued writing amid the comings and goings of the house, surrounded by papers, shirtless, in Bermuda shorts, with any of 60 cats at his feet as he stood barefoot on the hide of a small kudu.

Hemingway's legendary cabin cruiser, the *Pilar*, is poised loftily beneath a wooden pavilion on the former tennis court, shaded by bamboo

and royal palms. Nearby are the swimming pool (where Ava Gardner swam naked) and the graves of four of the novelist's favorite dogs.

The museum is headed by a trained curator, and free tours are offered. Entrance costs US$3 for foreigners. Open Mon.-Sat. 9 a.m.-4 p.m. and Sunday 9 a.m.-noon. Closed Tuesday and rainy days. A gift shop sells portraits, T-shirts, and other souvenirs.

Getting There: By Car: From Havana, begin at the foot of Calzada de Infante, at its junction with Vía Blanca. From this junction, take Calzada Diez de Octubre south half a km to Calzada de Luyano, which leads east to the Calzada de Güines, the Carretera Central that leads south to San Francisco de Paula. The museum is signed. Alternately, you can take the Circunvalación (Vía Monumental), which circles Havana and runs

Hemingway's fictional account of the Spanish Civil War, inspired his guerrilla tactics. Castro has said the reason he admires Hemingway so much is that he envies him the adventures he had. In July 1961, after Hemingway's death, his widow, Mary Welsh, returned to Finca Vígia to collect some items she wanted. Fidel came to visit. Recalls Welsh: Fidel "headed for Ernest's chair and was seating himself when I murmured that it was my husband's favorite. The Prime Minister raised himself up, slightly abashed."

The two headstrong fellows met only once, during the Tenth Annual Ernest Hemingway Billfish Tournament in May 1960. As sponsor and judge of the competition, Hemingway invited Cuba's youthful new leader as his guest of honor. Castro was to present the winner's trophy; instead, he hooked the biggest marlin and won the prize for himself. Hemingway surrendered the trophy to a beaming Fidel. They would never meet again. One year later, the great writer committed suicide in Idaho.

Papa and the Revolution

There has been a great deal of speculation about Hemingway's position toward the Cuban Revolution. Cuba, of course, attempts to portray him as sympathetic (Gabriel García Márquez refers to "Our Hemingway" in the prologue to exiled Cuban novelist Noberto Fuente's *Hemingway in Cuba*). Hemingway's Cuban novels are full of images of prerevolutionary terror and destitution. "There is an absolutely murderous tyranny that extends over every little village in the country," he wrote in *Islands in the Stream*.

"I believe completely in the historical necessity of the Cuban revolution," he wrote a friend in 1960. Papa was away from Cuba all of 1959, but he returned in 1960, recorded *New York Times* correspondent Herbert Matthews, "to show his sympathy and support for the Castro Revolution."

Hemingway's widow, Mary, told the journalist Luís Báez that "Hemingway was always in favor of the Revolution," and another writer, Lisandro Otero records Hemingway as saying, "Had I been a few years younger, I would have climbed the Sierra Maestra with Fidel Castro." The truth of these comments, alas, can't be validated. Papa even used his legendary 38-foot sportfishing boat, the *Pilar,* to run arms for the rebel army, claims Gregorio Fuentes, the weather-beaten sailor-guardian of the *Pilar* for 23 years. In his will, the great author dedicated his home and possessions—including his Nobel prize—to the Cuban state; but the *Pilar* he left to Fuentes.

Nonetheless, with the Cold War and the United States' break with Cuba, Hemingway had to choose. Not being able to return to Cuba contributed to Hemingway's depression, says his son Patrick: "He really loved Cuba, and I think it was a great shock to him at his age to have to choose between his country, which was the United States, and his home, which was Cuba." But Hemingway's enigmatic farewell comment as he departed the island in 1960 is illuminating. *"Vamos a ganar. Nosotros los cubanos vamos a ganar.* [We are going to win. We Cubans are going to win.] I'm not a Yankee, you know." But what would he have made of the outcome?

---

through San Francisco de Paula, linking it directly with Cojímar, too.

By Bus: Bus no. 7 departs from Parque de la Fraternidad in Habana Vieja. Bus no. 404 departs from Avenida de Bélgica (Monserrate) and Dragones. Both travel via San Francisco de Paula en route to Cotorro and Havana.

By Train: Trains run from Estació Cristina at Avenida de México and Arroy, Cuatro Caminos, in Cerro Habana, tel. (7) 78-4971. Take the train for Cotorro (four times daily) via San Francisco de Paula.

Organized Excursions: Promotora de Viajes Culturales, Calle 19 #560 esq. C, Vedado, tel. (7) 32-6928, fax (7) 33-3921, e-mail: paradis@turcult.get.cma, website: www.cult.cu/paradiso\index.html, offers a five-hour guided excursion to Finca Vigía (US$35, including lunch).

Cubanacán, Calle 146 esq. 9na, Playa, tel. (7) 33-9884, fax (7) 33-0107, also has a "Reencounter with Hemingway" trip.

REGLA

Regla, on the east side of Havana harbor, developed into a smugglers' port in colonial days, a reputation it maintained until recent days, when pirates (who made their living stealing off American yachts anchored in the harbor) were known as *terribles reglanos*. It was also the setting for Havana's bullfights. Today the main electricity-generating plant for Havana is here, along with petrochemical works, both of which pour insipid black and yellow plumes over the town. Regla is also a center of santería, and walking its streets

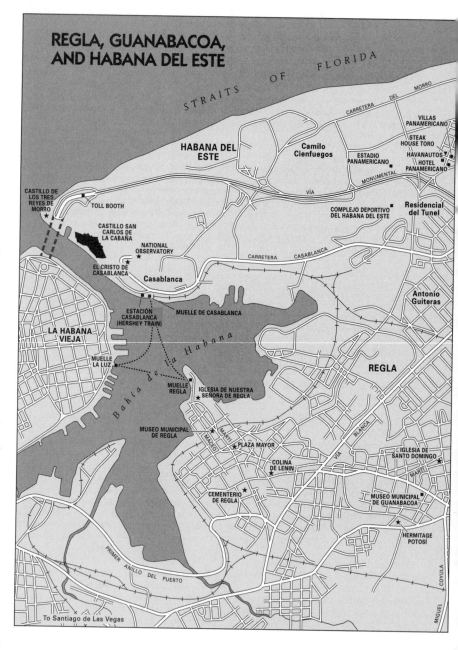

REGLA, GUANABACOA, AND HABANA DEL ESTE

STRAITS OF FLORIDA

CARRETERA DEL MORRO

VILLAS PANAMERICANO

STEAK HOUSE TORO

HAVANAUTOS

HOTEL PANAMERICANO

HABANA DEL ESTE

Camilo Cienfuegos

ESTADIO PANAMERICANO

MONUMENTAL

VÍA

CASTILLO DE LOS TRES REYES DE MORRO

TOLL BOOTH

COMPLEJO DEPORTIVO DEL HABANA DEL ESTE

Residencial del Tunel

CASTILLO SAN CARLOS DE LA CABAÑA

NATIONAL OBSERVATORY

EL CRISTO DE CASABLANCA

CARRETERA CASABLANCA

Casablanca

Antonio Guiteras

ESTACIÓN CASABLANCA (HERSHEY TRAIN)

MUELLE DE CASABLANCA

LA HABANA VIEJA

Bahía de la Habana

MUELLE LA LUZ

REGLA

MUELLE REGLA

IGLESIA DE NUESTRA SEÑORA DE REGLA

MUSEO MUNICIPAL DE REGLA

PLAZA MAYOR

COLINA DE LENIN

IGLESIA DE SANTO DOMINGO

CEMENTERIO DE REGLA

MUSEO MUNICIPAL DE GUANABACOA

HERMITAGE POTOSÍ

PRIMER ANILLO DEL PUERTO

MARTI

MACEO

VÍA BLANCA

MARTI

MIGUEL

COYULA

To Santiago de Las Vegas

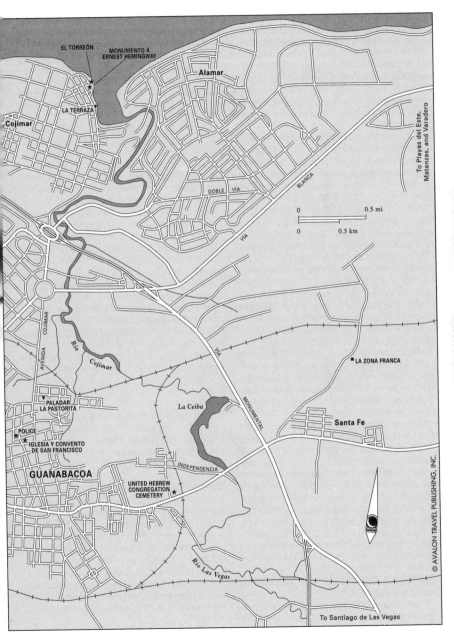

EL TORREÓN
MONUMENTO À
ERNEST HEMINGWAY

Alamar

LA TERRAZA

Cojímar

DOBLE VÍA

VÍA

BLANCA

To Playas del Este,
Matanzas, and Varadero

0   0.5 mi

0   0.5 km

AVENIDA COJÍMAR

Río

Cojímar

VÍA

LA ZONA FRANCA

PALADAR
LA PASTORITA

La Ceiba

MONUMENTAL

Santa Fe

POLICE

IGLESIA Y CONVENTO
DE SAN FRANCISCO

INDEPENDENCIA

GUANABACOA

UNITED HEBREW
CONGREGATION
CEMETERY

Río Las Vegas

© AVALON TRAVEL PUBLISHING, INC.

To Santiago de Las Vegas

you may note tiny shrines outside many houses. Calle Calixto García has many fine examples. Check out #116 (which has a small Madonna enclosed in glass in the wall, with fresh flowers by its side) and #114, whose large altar in the middle of the house is easily seen from the street. A **Fiesta de los Orishas,** a quasi-religious ceremony featuring Afro-Cuban music and dance, has been held in the past but was not offered at press time.

The harborfront hermitage of **Iglesia de Nuestra Señora de Regla** was built in 1810 and is one of Havana's loveliest churches. Visit on Sunday when devout Habaneros flock to pay homage to the black Virgén de Regla, patron saint of sailors (and Catholic counterpart to Yemayá, the African goddess of the sea in the Yoruba religion). The ocher-colored church is well preserved. Its inner beauty is highlighted by a fabulous gilt altar beneath an arched ceiling. On holy days, the altar is sumptuously lit with votive candles. Dwelling in alcoves in the wall are figurines of miscellaneous saints, which devotees reach up to touch while reciting silent prayers. Check out the vaulted niche on the left side of the nave, which contains a statue of St. Anthony leading a wooden suckling pig wearing a dog collar and a large blue ribbon.

Masses are held Tuesday and Sunday at 8 and 9 a.m. If you can, time your visit for the seventh of each month, when large Masses are held—or, better yet, 8 September, when the Virgin is paraded through town. The church is open daily 7:30 a.m.-6 p.m.

Outside, 20 meters to the east and presiding over her own private chapel, is the statue of the Virgén del Cobre, Cuba's patron saint, enveloped in a robe adorned with embroidered roses. Nearby is a **"water altar"** with—in miniature—a convoy of tiny ships, plus a wooden rowboat containing tiny effigies of the three Indian fishermen who supposedly found the statue of the black Virgin in Nipes Bay. Another altar is dedicated to St. Barbara, goddess of war. It is adorned with tin soldiers and toy tanks, and other pint-size military hardware—all appropriately painted red—Chango's ritual color. With luck, you may arrive to witness an Afro-Cuban *batá*-drum recital being pounded out beneath the altar.

From the harborfront plaza, the tidy, well-preserved main street (Calle Martí) leads two blocks east past a small plaza to the **Museo Municipal de Regla,** at #158, tel. (7) 97-6989. It tells the tale of the Virgin of Regla and of the city's participation in revolutionary struggles and presents an intriguing exhibit on Regla's santería associations. Open Mon.-Sat. 9 a.m.-6 p.m. and Sunday 9 a.m.-1 p.m. Entry costs US$2. The museum hosts cultural activities such as poetry recitals.

Continuing east you'll reach **Parque Guaycanamar,** the main plaza fronting a splendidly preserved Georgian edifice with columns. From here Calle Martí continues east about one km to **Cementerio de Regla,** at the junction with 10 de Octubre. It contains many fascinating tombs and headstones dating back over a century.

Immediately beyond the bridge about 400 meters north of the cemetery (but reached more directly from Parque Guaycanamar via Calle Calixto García), steps lead uphill to **Colina de Lenin** (Lenin Hill), where a three-meter-tall bronze face of the communist leader is carved into the cliff face, with a dozen life-size figures (in cement) cheering him from below. More cement figures attend an olive tree dedicated to Lenin's memory that grows above the cliff. A small museum atop the hill is dedicated to the life of Lenin and various martyrs of the Cuban revolution. It's a good vantage point from which to survey the town. (Bus no. 29 will also take you there from the ferry).

Services

There's a **Banco de Crédito y Comercio** on Calle Martí between 27 de Noviembre and Arangura. The **police station** is at the east end of Martí at the corner of Juan Gualberto Gómez.

Getting There

The little Regla ferries, tel. (7) 97-9130 (in Regla), bobbing like green corks, are magic carpets across Havana harbor. The ferries run constantly between Regla and the wharf on Avenida San Pedro at the foot of Santa Clara; it's a five-minute crossing (10 centavos). Other ferries depart Regla's wharf for Casablanca.

You can catch buses from Habana Vieja. Bus no. 6 departs from Agramonte (Zulueta) and Genios; bus no. 106 departs from Agramonte and Refugio.

GUANABACOA

Guanabacoa, about three km east of Regla, developed in colonial days as a major landing area for slaves for over a century. A strong Afro-Cuban culture developed. Guanabacoa remains Cuba's most important center of santería, and there are plentiful sign of this on the streets. As such, it is a popular pilgrimage site for Habaneros, but its various touristic attractions await restoration, and it is currently of interest only to those with a serious interest in santería or a bent for ecclesiastical history. Cuba's recently established **La Zona Franca,** Carretera de Berroa, Km 1, Municipio del Este, Ciudad de la Habana, AP 6965, tel. (7) 33-8137, fax (7) 33-8140, website: www.zfranca. cubaweb.cu, the "free trade zone," has been built three km east of Guanabacoa, with the hope of luring foreign industry.

The sprawling town is centered on a small square: the tree-shaded **Parque de Guanabacoa,** dominated by the columned **Palacio Municipal** and by **Iglesia Parroquial Mayor,** the recently restored church, which has a beautiful baroque gilt altar dripping with gold, with pink walls and a lofty wooden roof painted sky blue.

The **Museo Municipal de Guanabacoa** (Municipal Museum of Guanabacoa), Calle Martí #108, e/ San Antonio y Maceo, tel. (7) 90-9117, on the west side of the church, tells the tale of Guanabacoa's development. The museum outlines the evolution of Afro-Cuban culture, with emphasis on the slave days and santería. Open Mon.-Sat. 8 a.m.-6 p.m. and Sunday 2-6 p.m. If the museum is closed, try the **Bazar de Reproduciones Artísticas** down the road at Calle Martí 175, with a shrine to Yemaya and rooms brimming with santería regalia. It's open Mon.-Sat. 9:30 a.m.-5:30 p.m.

The list of religious sites is long: **Convento de Santo Domingo,** at Calles Santo Domingo and Lebredo; **Convento de San Francisco** (still used to train priests, apparently, two centuries after its founding; it lost a side tower however in 1884, knocked off by a hurricane); and **Iglesia Los Escolapios;** and **Iglesia de Santo Domingo,** at Bertemati between Jesús María and Lebredo, designed in 1728 and constructed by artisans from the Canary Islands, with one of the most complicated *alfarjes* (intricately pieced,

Moorish inspired, ceilings layered with geometric and star patterns) in Cuba, comprising thousands of fitted wooden pieces without nails. Also check out the **Palacio de Gobierno,** at Pepe Antonio and Jesús María.

Most touted sites are not worth the walk, however, as with the tiny, red-tiled **Hermitage Potosí** and its overgrown cemetery, atop a hill at Calzada Vieja Guanabacoa and Potosí, being in a sad state of neglect despite its tremendous potential. The hermitage dates back to 1644—one of the oldest in Cuba.

At the corner of San Juan Bosco and San Joaquín is a small shrine to Santo Lazarus beneath a fulsome bougainvillea bower. Pilgrims flock each 17 December bearing flowers and *promesas.* Mirella Acosta, who lives at San Juan Bosco #118, catercorner to the shrine, will happily recite details in Spanish.

Last but not least, Guanabacoa boasts a Jewish necropolis—the **United Hebrew Congregation Cemetery**—on the eastern outskirts of town, on Avenida Martí, entered by an ocher-colored Spanish-colonial frontispiece with a Star of David and Hebrew spelling on the pediment giving the game away. A **Holocaust memorial** stands in somber memory of the millions who lost their lives to the Nazis, with emotionally stirring text: "Buried in this place are several cakes of soap made from Hebrew human fat, a fraction of the six million victims of Nazi savagery in the 20th century. May their remains rest in peace."

If you linger through the afternoon and evening, call in at the **Casa de la Trova,** Martí, e/ San Antonio y Versalles, to see if any Afro-Cuban music and dance is happening.

The **Dirección Municipal de Cultura,** at the juncture of San Andres and Martí, can offer information on the town's culture.

Services
East of town, the **Banco Financiero Internacional** has a branch on Carretera de Berroa, Km 1.

Getting There
Bus no. 3 departs for Guanabacoa from Parque de la Fraternidad in Habana Vieja, and bus no. 95 from the corner of Corrales and Agramonte (Zulueta). From Vedado, you can take bus no. 195; from the Plaza de la Revolución, take bus no. 5.

HABANA DEL ESTE

Beyond the tunnel under Havana harbor you pass through a toll booth (no toll is charged), beyond which the six-lane Vía Monumental divided highway leads east to Ciudad Panamericano and Cojímar. One km east of the second (easternmost) turnoff for Cojímar, Vía Monumental splits awkwardly. Take the narrow Vía Blanca exit to the left to reach Playas del Este, Matanzas, and Varadero; the main Vía Monumental swings south so that you'll end up circling Havana on the *circunvalación.*

The coastal vistas along the Vía Blanca soon open up with some splendid views to the south as you drive along the coast road between Havana and Matanzas and look down upon wide valleys with rolling hills, tufts of royal palms, and *mogotes* far to the south.

Warning: The tunnel is monitored by cameras and watchful police eyes, and fines are dispensed to tourists for the slightest transgression. *Keep your speed down to the posted limits!* Motorcycles are not allowed through the harbor tunnel; if you're on two wheels, you'll have to take the Vía Blanca from its origin in Havana, which skirts around the bay.

CIUDAD PANAMERICANO

Three km east of Havana you'll pass the Ciudad Panamericano complex, built at great cost in 1991 for the Pan-American Games. A high-rise village was built to accommodate the athletes, spectators, and press. Today, it is a residential community for Cubans: built in the hurried, jury-rigged style of postrevolutionary years and although but a decade old, crumbling concrete, rusting metal doorframes, etc., hint that it is on its way to becoming a slum.

Ciudad Panamericano is pushed prominently in tourist literature, despite its ugly countenance. It offers nothing but regret for tourists. There's no reason to visit unless you have an abiding interest in sports or want a base close to the funky fishing village of Cojímar nearby.

Avenida Central is the main boulevard, sloping down towards the shore. Everything you'll need is to be found along here.

If you're staying here and need entertainment, the night spot of choice is the disco of the Hotel Panamericano (open 10 p.m.-6 a.m.).

Services
A **Banco de Crédito y Comercio** is on the right, 100 meters downhill from the hotel (open Mon.-Fri. 8:30 a.m.-3 p.m., and Saturday 8:30-11 a.m.). **Cadeca,** on the east side of the street, one block downhill from the hotel, changes dollars for pesos. The **post office** (open 7 a.m.-10 p.m.) Is at the bottom of the main street.

You can make calls from the *telecorreo* on the east side of the main street, two blocks downhill from the hotel. The **post office** is next door (open Mon.-Fri. 8 a.m.-noon, and 2-6 p.m., and Saturday 8 a.m.-noon).

There's a pharmacy and **Óptica Miramar** one block downhill of the hotel. The **medical center** is one block east of the main street, 50 meters downhill of the hotel.

Several supermarkets on the main street sell Western goods.

Getting There and Around
From the Vía Monumental heading east, take the first exit to the right—marked Cójimar—which will take you back over the freeway into the Pan-American complex and the Hotel Panamericano. (Another exit, two km farther, leads directly to the old village of Cójimar). Ciudad Panamericano is well served by buses from Havana. bus no. 204 arrives and departs from the main street in Ciudad Panamericano, bus no. M1 from the Vía Monumental.

A free shuttle departs the Hotel Panamericano (see the Accommodation chapter) for Havana at 9:30 and 11:30 a.m. and 2:30 and 5:30 p.m., dropping off downtown at the Hotel Caribbean on the Prado (20 minutes), and Hotel Capri in Vedado (40 minutes). The bus for Ciudad Panamericano departs the Hotel Capri at 10:20 a.m. and 12:20, 3:20, and 6:20 p.m., and from the Hotel Caribbean 20 minutes later.

The **Vaivén Bus Turístico** route was to be extended to include the Hotel Panamericano (see Tourist Buses in the Getting Around section, this chapter).

Havanautos tel. (7) 33-8113, has a car rental office near the post office. **Transauto,** tel. (7) 33-8802, has an office in Villa Panamericana. **Rent-a-Scooter** opposite the coffee shop, one block west of the Hotel Panamericano, rents Italian scooters (US$10 per hour, US$24 per day) and Yamaha Razzes (US$8 per hour, US$24 per day). A US$50 deposit is required.

The Hotel Panamericano offers a "Hemingway Tour" (US$3, including sandwich), on Monday, Wednesday, and Saturday.

COJÍMAR

For Hemingway fans, a trip to the fishing village of Cojímar is a pilgrimage. Here Ernest Hemingway berthed his legendary sportfishing boat, the *Pilar.*

The forlorn village spreads out along the shore and rises up the hill behind it; an old church on the hilltop has seen better days. The waterfront is lined with weather-beaten, red-tile-roofed cottages with shady verandas. White-caps are often whipped up in the bay, making the Cuban flag flutter above **El Torreon,** the pocket-size fortress guarding the cove's entrance. It was here in 1762 that the English put ashore their invasion army and marched on Havana to capture Cuba for King George III. The fortress, built in the 1760s to forestall another fiasco, is still in military hands, and you will be shooed away from its steps if you get too close. Alas, Hurricane George did a number on the fort when it ripped through in 1998, tearing away much of the foundations.

When Hemingway died, every fisherman in the village apparently donated a brass fitting from his boat. The collection was melted down to create the bust of the author—**Monumento Ernest Hemingway**—that has stared out to sea since 1962 from atop a large limestone block within a colonnaded rotunda at the base of El Torreon. A plaque reads: *"Parque Ernest Hemingway. In grateful memory from the population of Cojímar to the immortal author of* Old Man and the Sea, *inaugurated 21 July 1962, on the 63rd anniversary of his birth."* The royal blue sky and hard windy silence make for a profound experience as you commune alone with Papa.

After exploring, you should appease your hunger with fisherman's soup and paella at Hemingway's favorite restaurant, **La Terraza,** tel. (7) 65-3471, on the main street 200 meters south of El Torreon. After Hemingway's death, the restaurant went into decline. Apparently Fidel, passing through in 1970, was dismayed to learn of its condition and ordered it restored. The gleaming mahogany bar at the front, accepting dollars only, gets few locals—a pity; what a hangout it could be. You sense that Papa could stroll in at any moment. His favorite corner table is still there. He is there too, patinated in bronze atop a pedestal; adorning the walls in black-and-white, sharing a laugh with Fidel. See the Food chapter.

Cojímar's most famous resident is Gregorio Fuentes, Hemingway's old pal and skipper after

El Torreon and Hemingway bust

THE OLD MAN: GREGORIO FUENTES

Gregorio Fuentes, born in 1897, no longer has his sea legs and now walks with the aid of a crutch. But his memory remains keen, particularly when it comes to his old fishing companion, Ernest Hemingway. "His absence is still painful for me," says Fuentes, the now-ancient captain who from 1938 until Hemingway's death was in charge of the writer's boat, the *Pilar.*

Fuentes was the model for "Antonio" in *Islands in the Stream,* and is considered by many—albeit more contentiously—to be the model for Santiago, the fisherman cursed by *salao* (the worst form of bad luck) in *The Old Man and the Sea,* a simple and profound novel that won Hemingway the Nobel Prize for Literature. Fuentes—who says that the "Santiago" in the novella was partly modeled after another Cuban fisherman, Anselmo Hernández—looks the part: "The old man was thin and gaunt with deep wrinkles in the back of his neck. The brown blotches of the benevolent skin cancer the sun brings from its reflections on the tropic sea were on his cheeks. . . . Everything about him was old except his eyes and they were the same color as the sea and were cheerful and undefeated."

Fuentes claims not to have read any of Hemingway's works. "What for?" he says in a disdainful tone. "I've lived them with him."

Fuentes started his sea life at Lanzarote, in the Canary Islands, when he was four years old. He came to Cuba at age 10 and met Hemingway in 1931 on Tortuga, in the Bahamas, when the two men were sheltering from a storm (Fuentes was captain of a smack). The two men were virtually inseparable from 1935 to 1960. During World War II, they patrolled the coast for German U-boats. Years later, says Fuentes, he and Hemingway patrolled the same coast to assist Castro's rebel army. Their birthdays were 11 days apart and, reports Tom Miller, the two would celebrate each together with a bottle of whiskey. Fuentes kept the tradition alive after Hemingway's death by pouring a whiskey over the latter's bust down by the harbor.

The old skipper is regarded with awe by Cubans. He dines daily at Las Terrazas, where his meals have been free since 1993, courtesy of Castro, who named him a national treasure and gifted him a color TV and a doubling of his pension. In 1999, he celebrated his 102nd birthday and was still going strong.

the man himself

whom the novelist modeled the proud fisherman in *The Old Man and the Sea.* Travelers come from far and wide to hear Fuentes recall his adventures. When I last saw him, in May 1999, the centenarian was frail but still going strong. He will be delighted to smile for your camera and answer questions; however, please refrain from knocking on his front door at Calle Pesuela #209. The old man can often be found regaling travelers in La Terraza, and this is where you should arrange any meeting with him. Regardless, you should toast his good health with a turquoise cocktail—"Coctel Fuentes." His grandson, Rafael Valdés, charges visitors US$50 for 15-minute "consultations" with the Old Man, although haggling can cut the price more than half.

Cojímar is fascinating by night, too, with every house door and window wide open; families sitting on sofas watching TV; dogs roaming for morsels; figures gently rocking, suffused by the soft glow of 40-watt lights; the moonlight reflecting on the bay. Zigzagging through these streets one evening, I chanced upon a garden full of villagers sitting beneath the stars watching a movie projected onto a house wall.

The post office is two blocks west on Calle 98; open Mon.-Sat. 8-11 a.m. and 2-6 p.m.

Getting There

By car, the exit from the Vía Monumental is well marked (coming from Havana, take the *second* exit marked Cojímar).

You can catch **Buses** no. 58, 116, 195, 215 and 217 from the bottom of the Prado, at the junction with Avenida de los Estudiantes (10 centavos). Bus 58 departs from the west side of Parque de la Fraternidad, two blocks west of the Capitolio.

Virtually every major hotel in Havana offers **excursions** to Cojímar through its tour desk. **Paradiso: Promotora de Viajes Culturales,** Calle 19 #560 esq. C, Vedado, tel. (7) 32-6928, fax (7) 33-3921, e-mail: paradis@turcult.get.cma, website: www.cult.cu\paradiso\index.html, includes Cojímar on a five-hour guided excursion—Hemingway: the Mystery of a Footprint—offered daily from Havana.

ALAMAR AND CELIMAR

Immediately east of Cojímar you'll pass a modern, self-contained dormitory city conceived by Castro in April 1959 as the first revolutionary housing scheme in postrevolutionary Cuba and touted as an example of the achievements of socialism. Alamar (pop. 100,000) covers four square miles and is a vast sea of ugly concrete high-rise complexes—what Martha Gellhorn considered "white rectangular factories"—jerry-built with shoddy materials by microbrigades of untrained "volunteer" workers borrowed from their normal jobs and taught onsite. Alamar sprawls east to a sister-city: Celimar. Today the contiguous cities wear a patina of mildew and grime and, by any standards, are virtual slums. Refuse litters the potholed roadsides, and the roadside parks are untended. There are no jobs here, either, few stores, and no proper transportation. It is difficult to find any redeeming features.

The singular saving grace is **Playa Bacuranao,** a small horseshoe cove with white sand beach backed by sea grape and palms at the east end of Celimar. It's popular on weekends with Habaneros escaping city life for a day by the sea in the sun. The Spanish built a watchtower here (still extant), where they could watch for pirate ships and signal to Havana with smoke fires. Ernest Hemingway also used to berth his

Pilar here, and it was here that his fishermen in *To Have and Have Not* squeezed "the Chink's" throat until it cracked. A tourist resort here is now closed.

The area is good for **scuba diving.** The wreck of an 18th-century galleon lies just off the tiny beach and there's another wreck farther out (a popular playpen for turtles). Coral grows abundantly on both sides of the bay, so if you have **snorkeling** gear, bring it.

Getting There

Plenty of *camellos* leave from Parque de la Fraternidad: look for the M1. Buses no. 62 and 162 pass by Bacuranao, departing from Parque Central in Havana.

Most residents hitch. The junctions of the two major access roads off the Via Blanca are major *botellas* (hitching points).

TARARÁ

Two km farther east, you'll cross the Río Tarará and pass by the village of Tarará, at Vía Blanca Km 19. Tarará is famous as a health resort, with a splendid beach. Before the Special Period, it was used by Cuban schoolchildren who combined study with beachside pleasures and stayed at Tarará's **José Martí Pioneer City,** replete with soccer pitch, cinema, and other services. Here, too, several thousand young victims of the Chernobyl nuclear disaster in the Ukraine in 1988 were treated free of charge, as they still are: blonde, blue-eyed children still abound.

It was here, too, that Fidel Castro operated his secret government in the early stage of the Revolution. Che Guevara was convalescing here after his debilitating years of guerrilla warfare in the Sierra Maestra, and the location away from Havana proved perfect for secret meetings to shape Cuba's future while Fidel played puppeteer to the weak and demoralized "official" democratic government of President Urrutia.

Today Servimed operates Tarará as a health tourism facility with limited success. The place fell on hard times in recent years, but in spring 2000 a far-reaching renovation was almost promising to bring life back to the villas in the hopes that Tarará can be promoted as a tourist resort. The land slopes gently down to the shore. The upper half of the complex remains forlorn, but the lower half nearer the shore offers a pleasing albeit lonesome ambience.

There are two beaches. To the west is a delightful pocket-size beach that forms a spit at the river mouth. It's popular with locals and has a volleyball court and shady *palapas*. The channel is renowned for its coral—great for snorkeling and scuba diving, as large groupers and snappers swim in and out of the river mouth. A second, larger, white-sand beach spreads along the shoreline farther east. It, too, is popular with locals and a few tourists and also has a sand volleyball court, shade umbrellas, and lounge chairs.

Entry is free, but gaining access exemplifies the worse form of petty Cuban bureaucracy. Cubans and tourists alike must show ID. Tourists must bring their passports (a photocopy will *not* suffice): the two mule-minded female *custodios* refused my two photo IDs and turned me away!

Marina Tarará

Marina Puertosol Tarará, tel. (7) 97-1510, fax (7) 97-1499, channel VHF 77, is behind the spit, on the east side of the river. The marina, whose formerly impressive facilities were beginning to look threadbare in early 2000, has 50 berths with water and electricity hookups, plus diesel and gas. It also has a dry dock. (The Marina Puertosol head office is in Edificio Focsa, Calle 17 y M, Vedado, tel. (7) 33-4705, fax (7) 33-4703.)

The marina hosts the **Old Man and the Sea Fishing Tournament** each July. Registration costs US$200 for up to three *pescadores* (fishermen). Boats are made available for US$180 - 300 per day, depending on size. It also hosts the **La Hispanidad Fishing Tournament** in October (registration costs US$250, but boat charter fees are the same).

Boat Rental: Yachts can be rented for US$250 for nine hours. You can also rent three live-aboard motorboats. Weekly rentals range from US$2,100 (May-Oct.) to US$2,800 (mid-Dec.-mid-Jan.). Hobie-Cats are for rent on the beach. And pedal-boats can be rented at the marina for forays along the river estuary (US$4 per 30 minutes).

Scuba Diving: The *buceo* (scuba diving) office, tel. (7) 97-1501, ext. 239, faces the marina.

Trips cost US$30 (one dive) or US$50 (two dives). A four-day certification program costs US$400. Initiation dives (three hours) are also offered, and equipment rental costs US$10.

Sportfishing: You can charter a boat for four hours' sportfishing for US$200-250 depending on vessel (one to four people). Other fishing trips cost US$20.

Snorkeling: Three-hour **snorkeling** excursions cost US$30 based on a minimum of four people per boat.

Yacht Cruises: Excursions are offered, including six-hour "seafaris" that departs at 9:30 a.m. and cost US$50 including fishing, snorkeling, and lunch on board based on a minimum four passengers. A three-hour nocturnal cruise costs US$15 with dinner on board, plus music and dancing.

Other: Banana boats, jet skis, and catamaran trips are also available.

Services and Entertainment

The **Discoteca La Sirena,** near the marina, offers disco, Wed.-Sun. 10 p.m.-4 a.m. onwards. There's a **go-kart** track beside the Via Monumental at the turn-off for Tarará. A six-minute spin on a zesty 260 cc Honda costs US$5, and 13 minutes costs US$10. And a *parque diversion* (amusement park) on the west side of the Río Tarará offers carousels and other rides; access is by a separate exit from the Via Monumental west of the river.

Getting There

Tarará is at Km 17 Vía Blanca, 27 km east of Havana. It is signed off the Vía Blanca. A taxi will cost about US$17.

PLAYAS DEL ESTE

"A sense of the island's racial history and diversity wasn't to be culled from the telephone directory," wrote Carlo Gébler in *Driving Through Cuba,* "but was to be seen at first hand on the sand by the edge of the sea." Cubans are great beach goers, and nowhere on the island proves the case more than the Playas del Este. On hot summer weekends, all of Havana seems to come down to the beach (well, at least they did

Playa Santa María del Mar, Playas del Este

before the Special Period, when gas and money were more widely available). The beaches of Playas del Este are temples of ritual narcissism: young Cubans congregate here to meet friends, tan their bodies, play soccer or volleyball, and flirt. The beach action concentrates in front of the main hotel, the Tropicoco.

A nearly constant tropical breeze is usually strong enough to conjure surf from the warm turquoise seas—a perfect scenario for lazing, with occasional breaks for grilled fish or fried chicken from thatch-roofed *ranchitas,* where the drinks are strong and you can eat practically with your feet in the water.

Playas del Este is pushed as a hot destination for foreign tourists and in the mid-1990s enjoyed some success, bringing tourists (predominantly Italian and male) and Cubans (predominantly young and female) together for rendezvous under *palapas* and palms. A police crack-down on Cuban females in recent years has knocked the wind clear out of Playas del Este's sails. As a result, Italians canceled their vacation plans in droves and tourists are few and far between.

By international standards it's a nonstarter other than for a day visit. Upscale villas are available, but the hotels are dour. The nightlife and services are desultory. And though the beautiful beach offers bars and water sports, forget any other hopes of aesthetic appeal. The place is run-down and several buildings were derelict at last visit.

The beaches of Playas del Este stretch unbroken for six km east-west. The area is divided into the purely touristy Mégano and Santa María del Mar district to the west of the Río Itabo, with Boca Ciega (comprising mostly rental units for Cubans) and the village of Guanabo (a Cuban village with many plantation-style wooden homes) to the east. Separating these two distinct regions is a large mangrove swamp area where egrets, herons, and other waterfowl can be admired. The mosquitoes are fierce: by day, you're usually okay, but lather up with insect repellent at night.

The main beach—Playa Santa María—is several km long, with light golden sand shelving into stunning aquamarine and turquoise waters. Playa Boca Ciega is also beautiful, and backed by dunes. Playa Guanabo is the least-attractive beach. Local Cubans use it for recreation, including old men looking like salty characters from a Hemingway novel standing bare-chested, reeling in silvery fish from the surf.

The village of Santa María Loma is one km inland, atop the hill that parallels the shore.

See the Accommodations and Food sections, this chapter, for information on hotels and restaurants.

Dude Ranches
About four km inland, near Minas, are two *fincas de recreo*—falsely termed "dude ranches" by Rumbos, which operates them—in the heart of the Cuban countryside: **Hacienda Guanabito,**

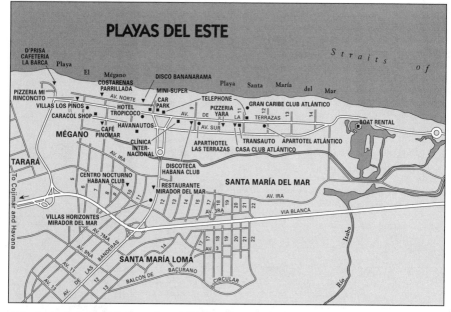

Calzada de Jústiz, km 3.5, Guanabo, tel. (687) 96-4610, and about 400 meters south, **Rancho Mi Hacienda,** Calzada de Jústiz, km 4, Guanabo, tel. (687) 96-4711. The former is no more than a thatched restaurant with a swimming pool and a few farm animals. The latter is a 13-hectare *finca* that offers horseback riding, boat rides on a lake, plus bloodless cockfights (in deference to tourists' politically correct modern tastes, the birds' spurs are covered to prevent them seriously hurting each other). Rancho Mi Hacienda hosts an Afro-Cuban cultural show once a week. Accommodation is provided in six handsome albeit rustic cabins connected by suspension bridges on the banks of the Río Itabo, plus three rooms in what was once a posh mansion. Each a/c unit has telephone, satellite TV, and minibar. There's a dining hall and swimming pool amid lush gardens.

Recreation
Several outlets on the beach rent **jet skis** (US$15 for 15 minutes) and **Hobie-Cats** (US$20 per hour). You can also rent shade umbrellas (US$3 per day) and beach chairs and lounge chairs (US$2 per day). **Horses** can be rented on the beach in front of Tropicoco. If the kids tire of the beach, take them to the basic kiddies' playground—**Parque Diversiones**—on Avenida Quinta and Calle 470 in Boca Ciega. The kids (and adults) can take pot shots at cutouts of soldiers (*yanquis,* perhaps?) at a fairground rifle range one block east, at Calle 472.

Scuba Diving is available from the water sport stand on the beach in front of the Hotel Tropicoco. A coral reef runs offshore at a depth of no more than 20 feet, with lots of brain, elkhorn, and staghorn formations.

Services
You can purchase postage stamps and make international calls at the Hotel Tropicoco. There's also a post office in Boca Ciega, on Avenida 5ta and Calle 448; and one in Santa María in Edificio Los Corales, on Avenida de las Terrazas at Calle 11, open 8 a.m.-1 p.m.

There are plenty of ETECSA phone booths. Servimed operates the Clínica Internaciónal, on Avenida de las Terrazas, 100 yards east of the Hotel Tropicoco, tel. (687) 97-1032. It's open 24

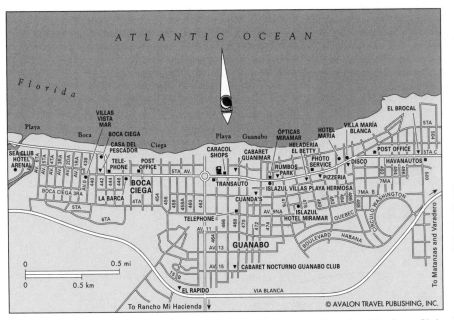

hours. A visit to the clinic costs US$25 (US$30 at night). The doctor also makes hotel visits if needed (US$50). It boasts a well-stocked pharmacy and even a clinical laboratory and an ambulance. Asistur can arrange credit payment if you're in financial straits.

The Tropical Travel Agency can make travel arrangements. It's in Edificio Los Corales, next to the post office on Avenida de las Terrazas in Santa María. There's also a tourism desk in the lobby of the Hotel Tropicoco.

Photo Service, in the lobby of the Hotel Tropicoco and on Avenida 5ta in Guanabo at Calle 480, sells instant cameras, batteries, and film.

Entertainment

There's not much nightlife. The hottest thing is the **Disco Bananarama,** a palenque bar-cum-disco right on the beach in Santa María. The **Hotel Tropicoco** also has a late-night disco (entrance free to hotel guests, US$2 to others). **Aparthotel Atlántico** offers entertainment at 1 p.m., which at press time included an "Afro-Cuban" show on Thursday, a "campesina" show on Tuesday, and a "Carib-

bean" theme on Saturday. The **Casa Club Atlántico** has a pool hall and dance club upstairs with a bar, TV, and karaoke. Open 2 p.m.-2 a.m. It offers a *cabaret espectáculo* on the weekend, with free entry.

Several down-to-earth places cater to the local Cuban populace. Try **Centro Nocturno Habana Club,** on Calle 10, e/ 1 y 3ra; **Cabaret Nocturno Guanabo Club,** on Calle 468; **Cabaret Guanimar,** Av. 3ra y Calle 468; or **Cabaret Pino del Mar,** on Av. del Sur, e/ Calles 5 y 7ma.

Western camp classic films dubbed in Spanish are shown at **Cine Guanabo** on Calle 480, one peso.

Getting There and Away

Playas del Este is well served by bus from Havana. Buses no. 62, 162, and 262 operate from Parque Central; bus no. 219 departs from the main bus terminal, and bus no. 400 departs from near the railway station, at the junction of Agramonte and Glória (one peso). You can also hire a *maquina* (a *colectivo* taxi) from outside the railway station and at Dragones, in Havana. They'll charge anywhere upward of US$5 to Playas del

Este, depending on the number of passengers.

Licensed taxis cost about US$20 one-way. Taxi and car rental companies offer chauffeured excursions. For example, **Palcocar,** tel. (7) 33-7235, fax (7) 33-7250, charges US$69 for an excursion with hotel pick-up and five free hours at the beach.

A train runs six times daily to Guanabo from Estación Cristina, at Avenida de México and Arroyo, in Habana Vieja, tel. (7) 78-4971.

Cubatur and Havanatur, in the Hotel Tropicoco, offers excursions to Havana and further afield.

Getting Around

You can walk virtually anywhere in Mégano/Santa María or Boca Ciega/Guanabo, although you will want wheels to get between them.

In Santa María, **Havanauto** has a car-rental office in the parking lot of Hotel Tropicoco. It also rents scooters for US$10 per hour, US$24 per day (with a US$50 deposit). **Transauto** has a scooter-rental office in the Aparthotel Atlántico, renting Suzuki scooters for US$15 per day (gas costs US$5.50 extra).

In Guanabo, **Havanauto** has two offices on Avenida 5ta, next to the gas station at Calle 464, and also at Calle 500, tel. (687) 96-2694. **Transauto** rents scooters from its office next to the Hotel Gran Via and opposite Havanauto on Avenida 5ta at Calle 464, tel. (7) 33-2917.

There's a **Cupet gas station** on Avenida 5ta, two blocks east of the traffic circle at the foot of Calle 462.

ACCOMMODATIONS

Havana is blessed with accommodations of every stripe. The motley and dowdy hostelries of a few years ago have been upstaged by a blossoming of deluxe and boutique hotels, with more coming online every year. However, Havana also has some appallingly dreary options, and at press time, of Havana's so-called luxury hotels (designated as such below by virtue of pricing), only one—the Novotel—would be considered deluxe by international standards. None is entirely free of Cuban quirks. All of which makes the unduly high prices doubly annoying (prices have shot up in recent years and Havana no longer represents a bargain). Upkeep and lousy management are the main problems, so that hotels rapidly deteriorate, and a newly constructed or renovated hotel today might appear run-down a year or two later. Says *Cigar Aficionado:* "A number of hotels in Havana still look like low-income housing or urban crack houses." You can go horribly wrong in your choice of hotel. It pays to do your research.

Havana is in the midst of a tourism boom, and many hotels are often fully booked during peak winter season. Don't worry: there are countless private room rentals *(casas particulares).*

Which District

Location is important in choosing your hotel.

In **Habana Vieja** you're in the heart of the old city, within walking distance of most major sites. Here you'll find three Spanish-style *posadas,* two exquisite colonial palaces-turned-hotel, and (around Parque Central) a fistful of turn-of-the-century hotels that have all been, or are being, upgraded.

Vedado's mid-20th-century offerings tend to be larger and still well situated for sightseeing. There are several first-class hotels from which to choose. In eastern Vedado you'll be in the midst of Havana's re-energized nightlife,

with Old Havana a 30-minute walk along the Malecón. Farther out, in western Vedado, are the Riviera and the tony Cohiba, beloved of cigar-chomping businessmen. Vedado also has plenty of *casas particulares* (private rooms for rent in family-run homes). Habana Vieja is a 10-15-minute taxi ride.

Playa (Miramar) has a number of hotels popular with tour groups, such as the Comodoro, Copacabana, and Kohly, plus several moderate to upscale business hotels, but all are far away from the main tourist sights, leading to whopping taxi bills. Several deluxe hotels are slated to open in coming years. You're well over a one-hour walk to Old Havana and will need wheels to get around. Habana Vieja is a 15-20-minute taxi ride.

The Suburbs are represented by the hotels of Ciudad Panamericano and Playas del Este. Avoid these at all costs unless you're determined to have a second-rate beach holiday (in Ciudad Panamericano you'll find yourself out on a limb, without even a beach to amuse).

Prices

Hotels in this book are classified as: **Budget** (less than US$35), **Inexpensive** (US$35-60), **Moderate** (US$60-85), **Expensive** (US$85-110), **Very Expensive** (US$110-150), and **Luxury**

TOP TEN HOTELS

Here's my top-ten list of places to stay in Havana.

Hostal El Comendador	Inexpensive	Habana Vieja
Hostal Valencia	Inexpensive	Habana Vieja
Hotel Ambos Mundos	Moderate	Habana Vieja
Hostal Conde de Villanueva	Moderate	Habana Vieja
Hotel Florida	Expensive	Habana Vieja
Hotel Cohiba	Luxury	Vedado
Hotel Golden Tulip Parque Central	Luxury	Habana Vieja
Hotel Santa Isabel	Luxury	Habana Vieja
Hotel Victoria	Luxury	Vedado
Novotel Miramar	Luxury	Miramar

(US$150 and above). Each price category is divided by district: **Habana Vieja, Centro Habana, Vedado, Miramar,** and **Suburban Havana.** All prices refer to double rooms, high season.

HABANA VIEJA

Habaguanex (Calle Oficios #110 e/ Lamparilla y Amargura, Habana Vieja, tel. (7) 33-8693, fax (0) 33-8697), the state corporation that administers tourist commercial enterprises in Habana Vieja, is slated to open 16 hotels in Habana Vieja in the next few years: the **Hotel Telégrafo** was due to open in 2000 adjacent to the Inglaterra on the west side of Parque Central; the 150-room **Gran Hotel Saratoga** was scheduled to open opposite the Capitolio, on the corner of Dragones and the Prado; an apartment hotel is to be built behind the Hotel Parque Central; and a residential complex with villas and a hotel is planned for the Parque Morro-Cabaña.

Casas Particulares

I have yet to find an agreeable *casa particular* in Habana Vieja, where so much of the housing is in decrepit condition. Touts will approach you on the street.

One option to trust is Margot and Amalia Urrutia's large apartment in an art deco building at Prado #20, Piso 7 Apto. A e/ San Lázaro y Cárcel, tel. (7) 61-7824. The sisters, who speak English, have two rooms with private bathrooms with hot water. The smaller single room costs US$25; a larger room with double bed costs US$35. A balcony offers views.

A reader recommends the home of Miriam Soto Delgado at Calle Cuba #611, Apto 4 e/ Santa Clara y Luz, tel. (7) 62-7144, for $20 per night.

A few others to consider include Aguacate #356 e/ Amargura y Lamparilla, tel. (7) 63-7448 (Leonardo Mayor); Galiano #564, Apt. H25 e/ Salud y Reina; Calle San Juan de Ríos #102, Apt. 4C e/ Aguacate y Compostela; Prado #20, Apto. 6A e/ San Lazaro y Carcel, tel. (7) 61-7932 (Guidelia y Estanislao); and San Ignacio #78, tel. (7) 61-9277 (Salvador Guiterrez Trujillo).

Budget (Under US$35)

One of the best bargains in town is the simple **Residencia Académica Convento de Santa Clara** in the former convent on Calle Cuba between Luz and Sol, tel. (7) 61-3335, fax (7) 33-5696. The restored building is beautiful and today houses the National Center for Conservation and Museology (Centro Nacional de Conservación y Museología), which offers residential courses to foreign and Cuban academics. It has nine charming, modestly furnished but well-kept rooms for US$25 s/d. A café serves basic refreshments.

A good bare-bones bet is the **Hotel Isla de Cuba,** an Islazul property on Máximo Gómez on the south side of Parque de la Fraternidad, tel. (7) 57-1128. It is used almost entirely by Cubans and is usually full. It was not accepting foreigners at press time, when it was scheduled to receive a facelift. However, it has accepted foreigners in the past and may do so again. The atmospheric colonial building is aged and gloomy but has antique charm. Beyond the massive 10-meter-tall mahogany doors, its narrow, soaring atrium has balconies and is surrounded by 64 simple but adequate rooms (two with a/c, the rest with fans). Rooms have telephones and clean bathrooms (with cold water only).

Alternately, consider the **Hotel New York,** on Dragones, one block west of Parque de la Fraternidad, tel. (7) 62-5260. This Islazul property serves mostly a Cuban clientele and has 75 rather dour rooms with ceiling fans, private bathrooms, and cold water (US$9.80 s, US$12.05 d, US$15.45 t, US$18 q high season); a small bar and restaurant in the lobby; and a popular patio bar and restaurant on the corner outside the hotel.

Inexpensive (US$35-60)

You may be excused for having a flashback to the romantic *posadas* of Spain the moment you walk into **Hostal Valencia,** Oficios #53 e/ Obrapía y Lamparilla, tel. (7) 57-1037, fax (7) 33-5628. Appropriately, this quaint 12-room hotel is run by a Spanish firm in partnership with the government. The recently restored 18th-century mansion (Casa de Sotolongo) exudes splendid charm, with its lobby—entered through a tall doorway—of hefty oak beams, Spanish tiles, magnificent wrought-iron chandeliers, and hardwood colonial seats. The inner courtyard is surrounded by a lofty balcony. The 12 spacious rooms have cool marble floors but are furnished, alas, in modern utility style. All have private bathrooms and TVs, telephones, refrigerators, and walls decorated with pretty ceramic plaques. Some have French doors that open onto the street. To the left as you enter is the equally atmospheric La Paella restaurant, and to the right the charming Bar Entresuelo. It has a well-stocked Casa del Tabaco. Rates were US$40 s, US$52 d, US$65 suite. *Recommended!*

Immediately behind the Hostal Valencia is the **Hostal El Comendador,** Calle Obrapía e/ Baratillo y Oficios, c/o (7) 57-1037, fax (7) 33-5628, another endearingly restored colonial home that opened in February 2000. Its 14 exquisite rooms feature marble floors, iron-frame beds, antique reproduction furnishings, security boxes, local TVs, old-style phones, and mini-refrigerators. The thoroughly modern bathrooms have claw-foot bathtubs, hair driers, and toiletries. Rooms on the mezzanine are cramped; take an upper story room with lofty ceiling. To the rear of the lobby is an **Exposición Arqueológica** containing pre-Columbian graves and skeletons discovered during restoration work. Rates were to be announced.

The **Hotel Caribbean,** Paseo de Martí #164, a Horizontes hotel on the corner of Colón and Prado, tel. (7) 33-8233 or 66-9479, is a favorite of budget travelers, and rightly so after a splendid renovation. It has 38 rooms (five with a/c), small and meagerly yet adequately furnished in pleasing Caribbean colors, with silent a/c, tiny TVs, telephones, in-room safe-boxes, and small yet nicely renovated bathrooms with all-new plumbing. It has a small, simple bar. Rates were US$33 s, US$43 d low season, US$36 s, US$48 d high season. There's no sign for the hotel: the entrance is immediately next to the Café del Prado (open 7 a.m.-3 a.m.), which serves the hotel and passers-by with pizzas, sandwiches, and spaghettis.

Nearby is the **Casa de Científicos** at Prado #212 e/ Calles Trocadero y Colón, tel. (7) 62-4511, fax (7) 33-0167. This lofty-ceilinged, four-story colonial mansion—the old Casa José Miguel Gómez—is a mini-Versailles, sumptuously adorned with rococo ceilings and marble floors and magnificent stained-class atrium ceiling. A rickety elevator and a marble staircase lead upstairs to 12 a/c rooms modestly furnished with a medley of antiques and utility furniture,

plus satellite TVs, and large, well-lit bathrooms with white tile work. The vast suite boasts a bathroom in black marble. A rooftop bar sometimes hosts entertainment. Downstairs, the elegant Restaurant Los Vitrales is replete with exquisite antiques. Rates were US$25 s, US$31, US$37 t with shared bathroom with cold water only, US$45 s, US$55 d, US$64 t with private bathrooms.

Moderate (US$60-65)
Want to rest your head where Ernest Hemingway found inspiration? Then try the **Hotel Ambos Mundos,** splendidly situated one block west of Plaza de Armas on Calle Obispo e/ San Ignacio y Mercaderes, tel. (7) 66-9530, fax (7) 66-9532. The hotel, which originally opened in 1920, reopened in 1997 after an interminable restoration. The compact lobby is airy and breezy, with tall French doors running the length of its walls. A pianist plays, adding notes to the tinkling fountain, and the mahogany lobby bar is always lively. The hotel offers 49 a/c rooms and three junior suites arranged atrium-style, each with cable TV and international telephone lines. Most rooms are small and dark, but feature modern albeit undistinguished furnishings. Some have windows looking out; others face the interior courtyard, which are quieter in early morning when the street cacophony can intrude. Facilities include a modest rooftop restaurant and solarium with views over Habana Vieja. Hemingway's room—511—is preserved in suspended animation. Avoid the fifth floor, which is a thoroughfare for sightseeing gawkers, who fill the single, rickety old elevator (the wait is interminable) and amble up and down the narrow marble stairs. The food in the rooftop restaurant is fairly good, but breakfast is said to be "weak" (there's a splendid bakery a one-minute walk away). Rates were US$65 s, US$90 d, US$110 t, US$120 suite.

Hostal Conde de Villanueva is an intimate posada-style hotel in the former home of the Count of Villanueva at Calle Mercaderas esq. Lamparilla, tel. (7) 62-9682. A splendid remake has restored the colonial mansion to former grandeur. Breezes waft through lofty doors, cooling the spacious lobby-lounge, with its bottle-green sofas and blood-red cushions, terra-cotta floor, and beamed ceiling with chandeliers. Beyond is an intimate courtyard, with caged birds, tropical foliage, and rockers beneath *porticos.* The eight large, airy, and simply appointed rooms and one suite (with jacuzzi) are arranged all-around on two levels, with *ventrales* on the upper balcony diffusing sunlight in rainbow hues. A small restaurant and bar to the rear has a fountain and TV. The hotel aims at cigar smokers with a Casa de Habanos outlet and a sumptuous smokers' lounge. Rates were US$53 s, US$68-77 d, US$135 suite, but I expect these will be jacked up. For now it remains one of the few real bargains in town. *Recommended!*

Expensive (US$85-110)

Parque Central is a privileged location offering several options. The first is the atmospheric **Hotel Plaza,** Calle Agramonte #267, tel. (7) 33-8583, fax (7) 33-8869, built in 1909 in the grand old style. The small entrance lobby is quite stunning with its lofty ceiling supported by Corinthian columns and festooned with plaster motifs. A venerable marble stairway leads upstairs to the 186 lofty-ceilinged a/c rooms (18 suites) furnished with dark hardwood antiques and reproductions, TVs (with U.S. cable channels), radios, safe deposit boxes (US$5), and heaps of closet space. The sky-high ceilings help dissipate the heat. Some rooms are rather gloomy, and rooms facing onto the street can be noisy. The gracious lobby bar is lit by day by four stained-glass skylights, and by gilt chandeliers at night when a pianist hits the ivories. The Restaurant Real Plaza serves superior cuisine in a classically chic setting. To the left, tucked away, is another restaurant serving grim breakfasts and set buffet meals. The top (fifth) floor has a terrace restaurant offering views over the city. The fifth-floor *azotea* has a gift store and a solarium with lounge chairs. Alas, prices have skyrocketed of late without justification. Rates were US$75 s, US$100 d low season, US$80 s, US$120 d high season.

On the west side of Parque Central, is the **Hotel Inglaterra,** Paseo del Prado #416, tel. (7) 33-8993 or 62-7071, fax (7) 33-8254, with its ornate wedding cake façade. It was a particular favorite of visitors in the 19th century, although travelers' accounts—such as those of Winston Churchill, who laid his head here in 1895—"reverberate with wails about the hard mattresses

and the offhand service." The hotel has been named a National Monument and prior to its recent price hike was very popular with younger, independent travelers, for whom it became the unofficial meeting point in Havana; the stiff rate increases are unjustified despite a recent renovation. The extravagantly decorated lobby is loaded with atmosphere. Musical interludes emanate from the lobby bar and restaurant, cool havens of stained glass and patterned tiles that whisk you off to Morocco with their arabesque archways and mosaics of green, blue, and gold. Of the 83 a/c rooms, three have panoramic views from their balconies. Noise from the square can be a problem, especially in the early morning. All rooms have telephones, satellite TV, safe deposit boxes, hair driers, and minibars, but they remain dark and musty. Take time to sip a *mojito* on the entrance patio bar or at the rooftop **La Terraza** bar, where cabaret is performed at night. Rates were US$75 s, US$100 d low season, US$80 s, US$120 d high season. *Overpriced!*

An intimate and resplendent option is the **Hotel Florida,** in a stunning colonial building—the Casa de Joaquín Gómez, built in 1835 for a wealthy merchant—at Calle Obispo #252 esq. Cuba. The compact hotel, with a soaring atrium with exquisite stained-glass skylight, was opened in late 1999 by Habaguanex (see Cuban Hotel Groups, above) and is aimed primarily at businesspeople. It is sumptuously furnished and features 25 rooms with wrought-iron beds and a tasteful contemporary interpretation off colonial decor, and each with satellite TV, phone, minibar, and security box. Rates were US$65 s, US$75 d low season, US$90 s, US$105 d high season.

Luxury (US$150+)

One peek inside the lobby of the **Hotel Sevilla,** Trocadero #55, between the Prado and Zulueta, tel. (7) 33-8560, fax (7) 33-8582, and it could be love at first sight, despite its outrageous pricing. The landmark hotel—famous as the setting for Graham Greene's *Our Man in Havana* (Wormold stayed in room 501)—has filigreed balconies and a newly touched up façade straight out of *1,001 Arabian Nights.* You enter via a lofty arched doorway of Gaudiesque proportions to what may strike you as a Moroccan medina, with spiral columns augering up from a marble floor. French louvered windows open fully so that the breeze blows freely, mingling with piped music and the sunlight pouring in through tinted *vitrales.* The hotel was built in 1924, and at press time its uninspired rooms and filthy walls suggested that it hasn't had a spring-cleaning all the while, despite a recent remake. The 178 rooms are disappointing: small, low on light, and furnished with tacky outdated furniture, although each has a safe, minibar, telephone, and satellite TV. The top-floor restaurant is a sumptuous gem (the food was until recently abysmal but has improved markedly with the arrival of a French chef). The French Accor group recently took over management, and things are gradually improving. A tour and car-rental desk are on-site, as are a swimming pool, four bars, beauty parlor, and shops. Taxi service can be slow, particularly at night. Room rates are US$84 s, US$128 d low season, US$97 s, US$154 d high season. *Overpriced!*

The **Golden Tulip Parque Central,** tel. (7) 66-6627, fax (7) 66-6630, e-mail: sales@gtpc.cha.cuy.cu (in The Netherlands, Golden Tulip, Stationsstraat 2, P.O. Box 619, 1200 AP Hilversum, tel. (031) 35-284588, fax (031) 35-284681; in Canada, tel. (800) 344-1212; in the U.K., tel. (0181) 770-0333), a joint venture of Cubanacán and the Dutch Golden Tulip hotel chain, sits at the top of the Prado, on Neptuno and Agramonte (Zulueta), on the north side of Parque Central. This ultramodern hotel is one of the best in town, with a management and staff that seem to understand the concept of service. The exterior is hardly inspirational, but the gracious lobby offers a surfeit of marble and lively decor in ocher and bottle green, blending a contemporary style with colonial hints. It has 281 rooms done up in a fashionable vogue with a soothing color scheme of soft greens and creams. They come with satellite TV, plus antique reproduction furnishings, and king-size beds (a deluxe rarity in Havana), plus marble bathrooms with separate tub and shower, vanity mirrors, ceilings inset with halogen bulbs, and heaps of fluffy towels. Avoid the second- and third-floor rooms on the southwest corner, with tiny windows at waist level (the integration of the colonial frontage into the design of guest rooms is ill conceived). Many rooms have no views whatsoever: be sure to ask for an exterior room. The suites are vast. An art gallery was to be added. A mezzanine has an upscale cigar lounge-bar with plump leather seats, plus executive meeting rooms, a business center, and a top-class restaurant. Topping it all is a rooftop swimming pool and jacuzzi in a rotunda with glass walls offering views over the city. Here, too, are a fitness room and a splendid rooftop grill in Italianate style serving snacks, including a traditional Dutch dish called *bitterballen.* Introductory rates were US$115 s, US$165 double, US$250 suite. Expect these to rise.

The Plaza de Armas provides a fabulous setting for the **Hotel Santa Isabel,** Calle Baratillo #9 e/ Obispo y Narciso López, tel. (7) 33-8201 or 66-9619, fax (7) 33-8391, a small and intimate hostelry recalling days of yore when it was *the* place to be. The splendid building, facing both westward onto the plaza and eastward onto the harbor, began life as a lodging at the end of the 17th century and, recapturing the colonial ambience, is today regarded as the most elite hotel in Habana Vieja. Decor includes plush velvet sofas, antiques, and modern art in the marble-floored lobby. The hotel has 27 lofty-ceilinged, a/c rooms (10 of them suites) arrayed around an airy atrium with fountain, with sunlight streaming in rainbows through stained-glass *mediopuntos.* The standard rooms occupy the third floor; 10 suites occupy the second floor. Rooms are furnished in pink and blue, with marble or stone and ceramic floors, poster beds, reproduction antique furniture, satellite TVs, direct-dial phones, and safe deposit boxes, plus leather recliners on wide balconies. Choose from twin or king-size beds. Suites have jacuzzi tubs. There's an elegant restaurant, a small lobby bar with a fountain, and a rooftop *mirador.* The Bar El Globo offers a pleasant spot to relax beneath the shade of the *portico* facing the square. A rooftop swimming pool was planned. However, management is abysmal (I witnessed several faults, including the most disturbing treatment of a guest I've ever encountered in two decades of travel reporting), and two readers have written to complain about reservations not being honored. Rates: US$110 s, US$150 d, US$135 s and US$190 d for junior suites, including breakfast.

CENTRO HABANA

Casas Particulares

One of the best *casas particulares* in Havana is located at Barcelona #56 e/ Aguila y Amistad, tel. (7) 63-8452. Jesús Deiro Raña, the host, offers one antique-filled room upstairs in his well-kept home, with a lofty ceiling and private bathroom with hot and cold water. He charges US$20, representing a great bargain. Call ahead. (Jesús and his family may move to San Rafael #312 e/ Galiano y San Nicolas, same telephone. He promises that this house is even better.)

A neighbor, Augusto Estanque, also offers three rooms for rent in his home at Barcelona #304, tel. (7) 63-0122 or 40-7471. Rooms are relatively small and dark, and share a clean but simple bathroom with hot and cold water. They can be rented singly for US$25 or you can take the entire house, which has lofty ceilings and *vitrales,* plus TV lounge. It had minimal furniture when I visited, but Augusto claims that more furniture is to be put in, along with a/c and a second bathroom. Guests can use the meager kitchen.

A reader has recommended a "comfortable" *casa* run by Orlandito and Tati at Industria #270 e/ Neptuno y Virtudos, tel. (7) 63-5690, on the sixth floor and conveniently placed close to Parque Central. Another recommends a house at Calle Escobar #413, close to Barrio Chino, where the English-speaking owner, Patricia, charges US$25 ("a bit overpriced"). And a third recommends Ana Maria's home at Avenida Salvador Allende #1005, with a large room and private kitchen and bathroom for $15.

In western Centro, near Vedado, try the following *casas particulares:* Juana Duran's at San Rafael #967, Apt. 75 (seventh floor) e/ Espado y Hospital, tel. (7) 79-4241; Pila Cotero's, in the same building at San Rafael #967, Apt. 83 (eighth floor) e/ Espada y Hospital, tel. (7) 70-7920; Jacobo León's at Infanta #113, Apt. 1 e/ San Francisco y Espada; Ninfa Milian Cruz's at Espada #5, Apto. 211 e/ Infanta y 25, tel. (7) 78-2478; Dr. Alejandro Oss's on the Malecón #163, Apto. #1 e/ Aguila y Crespo, tel. (7) 63-7359; Celia y Fidel's at Calle 25 #9, Apto. 7, tel. (7) 78-5355; and Miriam Rodríguez's at San Lazaro #621, altos e/ Gervasio y Escobar. I've not reviewed any of these.

Inexpensive (US$35-60)

The basic **Hotel Lido,** near the Prado at Animas and Consulado, tel. (7) 57-1102, fax (7) 33-8814, awaits a renovation and is overpriced at US$25 s, US$35 d low season. The modest a/c rooms feature utility furniture, telephones, radios, and tiny balconies. The bathrooms have cold water only. Safe deposit boxes are available (use them—the Lido has a reputation for theft), and a bar serves snacks in the dreary lobby. The fifth-floor *azotea* (rooftop) bar is open until 4 a.m. and has a view over Havana. This Islazul hotel serves both Cubans and tourists.

A better bet is the **Hotel Lincoln,** Galiano esq. Virtudes, tel. (7) 33-8209, an Islazul hotel also open to both Cubans and foreigners and famed as the spot where world-champion racecar driver Fangio was kidnapped by Castro's revolutionaries in 1958. This modest 139-room hotel dates from 1926 and has graceful public arenas, including a lobby boasting chandeliers and Louis XVI-style furnishings. It also has 16 suites. The a/c rooms are clean and pleasant and have radios and telephones, satellite TV, and mini-refrigerators (in suites). Facilities include the elegant Restaurant Colonial in the lobby, a rooftop terrace bar, and nightly entertainment that runs from Afro-Cuban cabarets to dance classes. Foreign guests are reminded that no *chicas* are permitted in their rooms, to which effect an attendant is imprisoned in the tiny elevator to prevent any subterfuge. Rates were US$22 s, US$29 d low season; US$27 s, US$36 d high season.

Moderate (US$60-85)

Though utilized by package-tour groups, the **Hotel Deauville,** tel. (7) 33-8812, fax (7) 33-8148, is a dour cement tower that journalist Martha Gellhorn called "a postwar, prerevolutionary blight on the Malecón." Gellhorn "came to dote" on the hideous hotel, though I'm not sure why. It lies in limbo at the foot of Avenida Italia (Galiano), midway between Habana Vieja and Vedado and is as ugly within as without. The 148 a/c rooms have TVs, radios, and telephones but dreary furnishings. Facilities include a rooftop swimming pool, with a disco, and a cabaret on Saturday. And service is terrible. At least the views over the city are splendid from upper-level rooms. The exterior was undergoing a facelift at press time, and hopefully the interior will receive the same. Until then, it's best avoided. Rates were US$40 s, US$52 d, US$67 t low season; US$48 s, US$62 d, US$78 t high season.

VEDADO AND PLAZA DE LA REVOLUCIÓN

Casas Particulares

The majority of private rooms for rent in Havana are concentrated here.

I've rented four or five *casas particulares* and inspected a score of others and eventually settled on a pleasing ground-floor unit in a modern apartment block with a large, well-lit, well-furnished bedroom with ceiling fan, a/c, telephone, and refrigerator, and a beautifully tiled bathroom with hot water, a secure garage for my motorcycle, and the company (whenever I choose) of a wonderful family—for US$25-30 daily. Contact Jorge Coalla Potts, Calle I #456, Apto. 11 e/ 21 y 23, tel. (7) 32-9032. His apartment is superbly situated two blocks from Coppelia and the Habana Libre. Jorge speaks broken English. *Recommended!*

Another splendid option is a three-room, two-bath apartment run by Martha Vitonte, Av. of the Presidentes #301, tel. (7) 32-6475, e-mail: rida@jcce.org.cu. Her apartment takes up the entire 14th-floor with wrap-around glass windows on a balcony that offers fabulous views over the city. Her lounge has plump leather sofas and lounge chairs and antiques. The three rooms are clean and beautifully kept and feature antique beds and en-suite bathrooms. Martha—a retired civil servant (she formerly worked in Havana's International Press Center) and an engaging conversationalist who speaks fluent English and has an answering machine—charges US$35 per room. The only drawback is the rickety elevator.

Octavio Fundora and Moraima Arébalo rent two a/c rooms in a nicely furnished apartment at Calle 5ta #717, Apto. 1 e/ 8 y 10, Vedado, tel. (7) 3-9769 or (7) 30-3290, e-mail: ofundora @yahoo.com, website: www.geocities.com/blue-building, with TV, VCR, stereo, and private bathrooms with hot water, plus use of a kitchen for US$25-30. The hosts speak English.

In far east Vedado, try **El Rinconcito Azúl,** run by Doña Tata, at Calle P #110 e/ Humboldt y Infanta, tel. (7) 70-4239. She has two a/c rooms with a shared bath with hot water for US$20 apiece. The rooms are simple and dark, but boast plentiful furnishings, and a kitchen and tiny lounge with TV.

Around the corner is **Casa Particular #156,** on Calle 25 and Infanta, tel. (7) 70-7613. Here Dolores Lopez offers four rooms with fans in a house with lofty ceilings, a kitchen; and a patio out back. Two rooms have private baths, two share a bath. The place is always busy with family members shooing in and out.

The *casa* at Calle 21 #203, between J and K, tel. (7) 32-1066, is in a timeworn house of

Jorge's Room for Rent

palatial proportions and full of antiques, but with filthy walls screaming for a fresh pot of paint. The owners offer one room in the house with a firm mattress and a shared bathroom with hot water and a bidet. Two other rooms are in a more modern addition upstairs and reached by an outside stairway. They're not particularly attractive and have tiny bathrooms, but also have a/c and telephone, and a refrigerator in the small kitchenette. Each room costs US$25.

Casa Blanca, Calle 13 #917 e/ 8 y 6, Vedado, tel. (7) 3-5697, e-mail: duany@casa.caspar.net, website: www.caspar.net/casa/, has an a/c room with hot water, terrace, phone, and e-mail service for US$20 per night (US$3 for breakfast).

Many of the occupants of the seven-story edifice at the corner of O and 21, opposite the entrance to the Hotel Nacional, advertise *casas particulares* for rent. Their signs hang above the front door.

A reader recommends Mercedes González's house at Calle 21 #360 Apto. 2A e/ G y H, Vedado, tel. (7) 32-5846. Her two rooms have a/c and ceiling fans, plus hot water and are described as "very clean" and "safe and secure." Another reader recommends Aleida García at Calle 28 #270 e/ 21 y 23, for US$20 with a/c. The place is said to be clean. A third recommends an unidentified *casa* with TV and VCR, a/c, and safe deposit box plus "electronic security" (e-mail: la_superabuela@hotmail.com).

In western Vedado, a North American friend who lives in Havana recommends Teresa Isidrón's at Calle 28 between 21 and 23, tel. (7) 3-9732, near Cementerio Colón. It's described as a "family environment," and Teresa hosts musicians on the rooftop terrace. She's "very plugged into the music and dance scene." She prepares meals and charges US$20-25.

Budget (Under US$35)

If you're on a serious budget and don't mind being a one-hour walk from things, consider the modest **Hotel Bruzón,** an Islazul property between Pozos Dulces and Boyeros, just north of the Plaza de la Revolución, tel. (7) 57-5684. There's nothing appealing about this 46-room hotel, with bare-bones utility furniture, a/c, small TVs and radios (local stations only), and basic bathrooms with cold water only. Still, it will do in a pinch for hardy budget travelers. It has a

small bar and a disco (with cabaret on Thursday). Rooms cost US$14 s, US$18 d low season; US$18 s, US$23 d high season.

The Ministry of Public Health runs **Villa Residencial Estudiantil del MINSAP,** on Calle 2 between 15 and 17, tel. (7) 30-9830 and 30-8411, in an old mansion with simple rooms for about US$20 s, US$25 d. It has a small restaurant and a broad, breeze-swept veranda with rockers.

Inexpensive (US$35-60)

The **Hotel Morro,** at Calles D and 3ra, tel./fax (7) 33-3907, is a no-frills property run by Horizontes. Each of its 20 a/c rooms has basic utility furniture plus a TV, telephone, and refrigerator, and a clean bathroom boasting two rarities: hair driers and plenty of towels. The louvered windows have frosted glass. The small Bar Arrecife serves snacks, and the hotel offers laundry service. Rates were US$21 s, US$28 d, US$37 t low season, US$29 s, US$38 d, US$47 t high season.

The Ministry of Education runs the **Hotel Universitario,** at Calle L y 17, tel. (7) 33-3403 or 32-5506, fax (7) 33-3022, formerly open to Cuban and foreign teachers (it had separate dining rooms for Cubans and foreigners) but today solely for foreign tourists. It's a basic, wood-paneled affair with a gloomy student-union-style bar and a pleasant restaurant downstairs behind the glum lobby. It has 21 rooms that offer the essentials but lack ambience. Rates were US$30 s, US$40 d, US$50 t year-round.

A popular bargain in the thick of Vedado is Horizontes' **Hotel St. John's,** on Calle O one block south of La Rampa, tel. (7) 33-3740, fax (7) 33-3361. Beyond the coldest air-conditioned lounge in the world, this 14-story property has 96 recently renovated a/c rooms, each with radio, telephone, and TV. A cabaret is offered in the Pico Blanco Room (Tues.-Sun.), and there are a rooftop swimming pool and a tourism bureau. It was receiving ongoing restoration at press time. Rates were US$25 s, US$33 d, US$45 t low season, US$32 s, US$43 d, US$54 t high season.

Moderate (US$60-85)

The recently renovated 194-room **Hotel Vedado,** tel. (7) 33-4062, at Calle O e/ 23 y 25, is of reasonable standard, albeit overpriced. It has a tiny, uninspired a/c lounge and minimal facilities, including a small tour desk. Rooms (done up in pastels) are small but adequate, with satellite TV, phone, tile floors, and small bathrooms. The El Cortijo Restaurant specializes in Spanish cuisine, and there's a disco and cabaret. Rates were US$44 s, US$58 d low season, US$53 s, US$70 d high season, including breakfast.

In a similar vein, try the modest 79-room **Hotel Colinas,** on Calle L, tel. (7) 33-4071, fax (7) 33-4104, two blocks south of the Habana Libre, one block from the University of Havana. The a/c rooms are depressingly hokey, but feature TV and phones. Facilities include a small tour desk, a modest mezzanine restaurant, and a patio snack bar good for watching the world go by. A renovation was slated. Rates were US$38 s, US$50 d, US$65 t low season, US$46 s, US$60 d, US$78 t high season, including breakfast.

Expensive (US$85-110)
In central Vedado is the charmless **Hotel Capri,** Calle 21 y N, tel. (7) 33-3747, fax (7) 33-3750. The airy lobby is flooded with light from plate-glass windows, as are the 215 a/c rooms, which are dowdily furnished but have TVs, telephones, and safe deposit boxes. The 18th-floor *azotea* swimming pool and La Terraza Florenta restaurant both offer spectacular views. The Capri was built by mobster Santo Traficante, Jr. Its gambling casino was, until 1959, run by George Raft, the mobster-movie actor. (A favorite hangout of the Mafia, the Capri was the setting for a scene in Mario Puzo's *The Godfather.*) When revolutionaries arrived on 1 January 1959 to destroy the gaming tables, Raft stood at the door and snarled, "You're not comin' in my casino!" The casino is long gone (it is now a drab dining room), but the hotel features the Salon Rojo cabaret *espectáculo*. It was slated for refurbishment. Rates were US$65 s, US$80 d low season, US$78 s, US$94 d high season. *Overpriced!*

Farther out, at the foot of Avenida de los Presidentes, is the **Hotel Presidente,** tel. (7) 33-4074, a tall, 144-room, art deco-style 1930s property with a maroon exterior and a carnal red and pink interior lent jaded elegance by its sumptuous Louis XIV-style furnishings and Grecian urns and busts that rise from a beige marble floor. The hotel was due to reopen in 2000 after a complete renovation.

Luxury (US$150+)
The grandest of Havana's Old World-style hotels, and Gran Caribe's flagship, is the **Hotel Nacional,** on Calle O, off La Rampa, tel. (7) 33-3564, fax (7) 33-5054. Luminaries from Winston Churchill and the Prince of Wales to Marlon Brando have stayed here, and this city icon—which dates from the 1930s—still dominates important events, when celebrities flock. The property recently emerged from a restoration that revived much of the majesty of the 60-plus-year-old neoclassical gem perched haughtily on a cliff overlooking the Malecón, with a postcard view of Havana Harbor. It is entered via a long, palm-lined driveway, while to the rear the hotel's magnificent greensward, studded with slender royal palms and pale ceibas, is perfect for a romantic stroll. The vast vaulted lobby with mosaic floors boasts Arab-influenced tile work and lofty wood-beamed ceilings, Moorish arches, and extravagant nooks and crannies where whispered confidences were once offered. Most of the 457 a/c rooms (15 are suites) have ocean views. They are large and appointed with cable TV, telephone, safe, and self-service bar; however they don't live up to the billing (nor high prices) and could do with more regal furnishings. The hotel was being renovated floor by floor at press time, when the only floor that was complete was the sixth floor, termed an Executive Floor, housing 63 specially appointed rooms and suites (for which a US$30 premium applies). The Comedor de Aguiar restaurant serves good Cuban and continental dishes. The top-floor cocktail lounge in the turrets offers a magical view; and the lobby-level bar offers a yellowing collage of luminaries including Mob titans Lansky, Santo Trafficante, and others. There are five bars, two swimming pools, and a full range of facilities, including upscale boutiques, beauty salon, spa, tennis courts, and a tour desk, plus the Cabaret Parisien—one of the hottest cabarets in town. Service is reasonably attentive by Cuban standards. Rates were US$100 s, US$140 d low season, US$120 s, US$170 d high season. Suites cost US$180-260 low season, US$215-315 high season. Special suites are US$400-1,000 year-round.

The landmark high-rise **Hotel Habana Libre Tryp,** at Calles L e/ 23 y 25, tel. (7) 33-4011, fax (7) 33-3141, e-mail: comer@rllibre.com.cu, is synonymous with the heyday of Havana. It was

Hotel Nacional

built in the 1950s by the Hilton chain and soon became a favorite of mobsters and high rollers. After the Revolution, Castro set up his headquarters here in January 1959. You used to hear that the whole place was bugged. The good ol' bad ol' days are long gone, and it is now managed by the Spanish Tryp group. The Habana Libre is still popular with foreigners and Cuban VIPs and, despite the security, with *jiniteras* prowling for foreign dates. It recently emerged from a recent renovation that included replacing the formerly capricious plumbing. The atrium lobby now shines beneath its glass dome and features a fountain and popular bar with a hip 1950s retro feel. The 533 rooms come equipped with satellite TV, direct-dial phone, minibar, safe deposit box, and hair drier in the bathrooms. It also offers 36 junior suites, and three suites, plus 24-hour room service. The hotel is loaded with facilities—all-important tour desks, a bank, airline offices, boutiques, post office, international telephone exchange, as well as a snack-bar-style cafe, two full-service restaurants, a patio bar under a futuristic 1950s-era skylight, a bar with cabaret on the 25th floor, and an all-important underground parking lot. The swimming pool is at mezzanine level. Rates were US$90 s, US$130 d low season, US$106 s, US$163 d high season. Overpriced?

A good bet and one favored by business travelers is the small and charming **Hotel Victoria,** Av. 19 y Calle M, tel. (7) 33-3510, fax (7) 33-3109, e-mail: reserva@gcvicto.gca.cma.net,

website: www.hotel-victoria.cubaweb.cu. This Victorian-style, neoclassical building began life in the 1920s as a small guesthouse and retains its personal feel. It has only 31 elegant, albeit somewhat small a/c rooms refurbished with 1970s decor, with hardwoods and antique reproduction furnishings. Relaxation is offered in a small swimming pool and an intimate lobby bar. The elegant restaurant is one of Havana's finest. Rates were US$80 s, US$100 d low season, US$90 s, US$120 d high season.

The **Melía Cohiba,** on Paseo e/ Calles 1 y 3, tel. (7) 24-3636, fax (7) 33-3939, e-mail: sec_com_mlc@cohiba1.solmelia.cma.net, is a hotel of international standard, bringing Havana squarely into the 21st century with its handsome postmodern European design and executive services, adding a shine to the drab grays at the base of Paseo. The 22-story, 462-room hotel is *the* hotel of choice for foreign businesspeople, who gather to smoke their stogies in the El Relicario bar. It is run by the Spanish Grupo Sol Meliá. There's no Cuban ambience whatsoever, except in the traditional cuisine of the Abanico de Cristal restaurant—one of four eateries in the hotel. The spacious lobby hints at the luxury within, with its marble, splendid artwork, and magnesium-bright lighting. The spacious and elegant rooms feature brass lamps, marble floors, Romanesque chairs with contemporary fabrics, a mellow color scheme of beige, gold, and rust, and mirrored walls behind the bed; they looked a bit tired at press time, however, despite the hotel's youth. The bathrooms are dazzling, with bright halogen lights and huge mirrors. Bidets and hair driers are standard, as are fluffy towels and piping hot water in torrents. There are three standards of suites. Facilities include two swimming pools, a gym, solarium, shopping center, a business center, four restaurants, five bars, and the Habana Café—Havana's take on the Hard Rock Café. Service is far better than in any other Havana hotel, though it doesn't quite reach deluxe billing. Rates were US$155 single, US$190 double, US$235-350 suites on "standard" floors; US$200 s, US$235 d, US$300-550 suites on the "executive floor."

The **Hotel Habana Riviera,** on the Malecón at the base of Paseo, tel. (7) 33-4051, fax (7) 33-3739, now operated by Gran Caribe, is one of the more famous legacies from the heyday of sin. Meyer Lansky's old hotel recently underwent restoration to recapture its 1950s class, *sans* casino (his 20th-floor suite, stripped of memorabilia, is available for US$200 a night). The idiosyncratic 1950s lobby was replaced with contemporary vogue and a pleasant cocktail lounge, and features acres of marble and plate glass. The spacious rooms received a total remake in 1998 and now come up to international standards, although one still has to ask if the hotel is worth the price. Room decor is in soothing pastels, with conservative contemporary furniture, satellite TVs, safe deposit boxes, and minibars. The 20-story hotel boasts a large seawater pool, tour desk, boutique, modest restaurant, coffee shop, a Casa de Habanos, and the newly renovated Salón Internacional (formerly the Palacio de Salsa) nightclub for entertainment. Rates were US$84 s, US$127 d low season, US$93 s, US$154 d high season. *Overpriced!*

PLAYA (MIRAMAR AND BEYOND)

Miramar's hotels are utilized by tour groups and businessmen. You're a long way from the sightseeing action, so expect to fork out plenty of *dinero* for taxi fares into town. Although many of the hotels sit on the shore, this section of Havana's coastline has few beaches and is ugly and barren (although the beaches of Playas del Oeste lie close at hand).

Miramar is slated to receive many new upscale hotels over the next few years. **Hotel Casa Habana** is a 175-room business hotel going up at press time on the south side of Avenida 5ra at Calle 96. The German LTU company's **LTI-Panorama Hotel Havana,** on the shorefront next to the Hotel Neptuno/Triton, will have 306 rooms when completed in 2000 opposite Havana's new World Trade Centre. And Leisure Canada's **Monte Barreto,** one block east, will include a five star oceanfront hotel with a conference center, world-class spa, and timeshare buildings surrounding a sheltered tropical garden courtyard.

Casas Particulares

Casa Miramar, Calle 30, #3502 e/ 35 y 37, Miramar, tel. (7) 29-5679; in Canada (604) 874-4143, e-mail: mail@casamiramar.com, website: www.casamiramar.com, is a colonial-style 1926 home with original marble floors and vaulted ceilings plus dark hardwood antiques and which owners Marco and Daulema are restoring to its original character and form (aided by Dualema's Vancouver-based sister and her Canadian architect-husband). It has two a/c rooms upstairs with shared bathroom with piping hot water and new fixtures. Each room has its own character and is furnished with early 1900s art nouveau furnishings, new queen-size box spring and mattress, goose down pillows, and a private balcony. Bedding and towels are changed daily. Breakfast is served on the terrace, and dinner is available by request (Marco cooks up an awesome baked Pargo). There's even a safe deposit box that you can program with your own PIN. A one-car garage is available for parking. Alas, Marco and Daulema chain smoke, and the street is noisy. Rates were US$35 per room, or US$38 including breakfast.

Jorge Pérez and his family offer a/c room with private entrance, TV, phone, mini-refrigerator, a private bathroom with hot water, plus garage in western Miramar at Calle 96 #535 e/ 5ta y 7ma, tel. (7) 80-2313, fax (7) 22-4136, e-mail: borbone@mail.infocom.etecsa.cu. Three generations of the Pérez family live here, and Jorge is fluent in English and Italian.

Ana Ortíz, Calle 172 #134 e/ 1ra y 3ra, tel. (7) 23-3465, has rooms in Reparto Flores, handy for Marina Hemingway, Club Havana, and Pabexpo. She can arrange rooms elsewhere.

Budget (Under US$35)
Motel Las Olas, overlooking the ugly shore on Av. 1ra at Calle 32, tel. (7) 29-4531, serves Cubans and impecunious foreigners. The meagerly appointed rooms cost US$20 s, US$30 d, US$42 t, US$52 q. Despite its "motel" status, it's not a love hotel: it's a workers' hotel and has a small pool, video games, and bar. It offers a meal plan for US$31 daily, but you'll do better dining elsewhere. The constant din of piped music in the pool forecourt may prove too much to bear. *Overpriced!*

Inexpensive (US$35-60)
Students will fit right in at the modest **Hostal Icemar,** Calle 16 e/ 1 y 3, tel. (7) 29-5471, fax (7) 22-1244, operated by MINET, the Ministry of Education, and mostly utilized by foreign students. However, anyone can check into this 1950s Miami-style hotel that was renovated in 1998. It has 54 large a/c rooms with TV and hot water. Check out several rooms, and take one facing the sea; they have more light. Rates were US$27 s, US$44 d, and US$66 t high season. It also offers a meal plan. You can also select any of six apartments across the road (same rates as rooms). They're huge (some sleep up to eight people) but some are rather gloomy and minimally furnished.

Two similar options are **Hotel Universitaria Ispaje,** Av. 1ra y Calle 22, tel. (7) 23-5370, eight rooms with private baths, US$25 s, US$35 d, including breakfast, and **Villa Universitaria Miramar,** at Calle 62 #508 esq. Av. 5ta, tel. (7) 32-1034, 25 rooms with private baths for US$15 s, US$18 d. There's a bar with pool table, popular with Cuban students and expats.

The **Villa Costa,** Av. 1ra e/ Calles 34 y 36, just east of the Hotel Copacabana, tel. (7) 29-2250, fax (7) 24-4041, is a handsome seafront villa with louvered windows topped by *ventrales* filtering the sunlight into rainbow colors. Caged songbirds chirp and chatter, adding their musical tones. The rooms are simply furnished, though roomy and adequate (US$27, including breakfast). You can also choose a nicely furnished a/c suite with a spacious bathroom (US$37). There's a nice lounge with a TV and VCR. It even has a swimming pool and a sundeck of sorts overlooking the ocean. The elegant little restaurant serves set meals for US$5.

Also worth considering is the **Hostal Villamar,** Av. 3ra esq. 24, tel. (7) 23-3778, in a castle-style colonial mansion. The four upstairs a/c rooms are spacious and nicely furnished with modern accoutrements, plus TVs (local stations only), radio, and spacious tiled bathrooms. It has a rustic bar and restaurant with wood-beamed ceilings and a fireplace, serving *criollo* food and open 24 hours. Rates were US$29 s, US$48 d.

Moderate (US$60-85)
The dreary **Hotel Kohly,** Av. 49 esq. 36A, Reparto Kohly, Playa, tel. (7) 24-0240, fax (7) 24-1733, e-mail: reserva@kohly.gav.cma.net, run by Gaviota, is a modest 1970s-style property popular with tour groups. Its out-of-the-way location offers no advantages. The 136 a/c rooms are pleasant enough, though modestly furnished, with satellite TVs, radio, phones, minibars, safe deposit boxes, and spacious showers. Most have balconies. The patio restaurant serves rice and beans, pork or chicken, and brothy shallots for US$4. The main restaurant is less appealing. Facilities include a tour desk, car rental, and a bar popular with the local youth, who come for the live music and to play pool on the full-size pool tables and tenpin bowling in the automated bowling alley. It was scheduled to be refurbished. Rates were US$50 s, US$62 d low season, US$54 s, US$68 d high season.

You can also choose any of five Mediterranean-style houses next to the hotel, with three to six bedrooms.

Gaviota also runs the recently refurbished and attractive **Hotel el Bosque,** sitting above the Río Almandares in the Reparto Kohly district of Miramar, on 28A one block east of Avenida 47, tel. (7) 24-9232, fax (7) 24-5637, e-mail: reservas@bosque.gav.cma.net. The breezy lobby has a bar with pool tables and opens to the rear onto a hillside patio where snacks are served. Its 61 rooms are pleasingly albeit modestly furnished with bamboo, and have a/c, satellite TVs, phones, safe deposit boxes, and large, louvered French windows opening to balconies (some rooms only), plus small bathrooms with modern glass-enclosed showers. The outside patio has a Mediterranean feel. There are taxis and rent-a-car, plus laundry, and tour desk. Rates were US$49 s, US$61 d low season, US$49 s, US$61 d high season.

Also try **Hotel Mirazul,** Av. 5ta y Calle 36, tel. (7) 33-0088, fax (7) 33-0045. This Wedgewood blue mansion is owned by the Ministry of Higher Education, which offers 10 rooms of varying sizes for tourists as well as educators and students. Rooms vary but most are spacious and have modest bamboo furnishings, satellite TVs, a/c, telephone, and hot water in bathrooms. Facilities include a restaurant, pool table, and rooftop sauna and sundeck. It's popular with expats in the know. Rates were US$40-60 s, US$50-70 d, depending on the room. A suite costs US$50 s, US$60 d, US$70 t, and US$80 q. Rates are lower rates for students and teachers.

The **Hotel Bellocaribe,** in Cubanacán at Calle 158 e/ 29 y 31, tel. (7) 33-9906, fax (7) 33-6838, predominantly serves the nearby Convention Center and biotech facilities, and is too far out from tourist attractions to appeal to the general traveler. It's a faceless modern property in drab communist style, with 120 pleasantly yet modestly furnished a/c rooms (including 15 suites) featuring satellite TV, radio, telephone, safe deposit box, and minibar. A full range of facilities includes car rental, tour desk, tennis court, shops, a Casa del Tabaco, and beauty salon, and there's an attractive pool and sundeck with separate kiddies' pool, plus the appealing La Estancia restaurant (see below). Rates were US$45 s, US$64 d, US$77 suite low season; US$57 s, US$81 d, US$93 suite high season.

Cubanacán also runs the **Mariposa,** an uninspired hotel on the Autopista del Medidodía midway between the airport and downtown Havana, in Arroyo Arenas west of the Cubanacán district, tel. (7) 33-6131 or 20-0345. It's handy for the Havana Convention Center but too far out to consider otherwise. The 50-room hotel has four junior suites, US$28 s, US$40 d, year-round.

Expensive (US$85-110)

A favorite of tour groups is the **Hotel Comodoro,** Av. 1ra y Calle 84, tel. (7) 24-5551, fax (7) 24-2028, e-mail: comercia@comodor.cha.cyt.cu, website: www.cubanacan.cu, a Spanish-Cuban joint venture at the west end of Miramar. It was originally built for the Cuban armed forces, was revamped, and is now a training school for apprentice Cuban hotel staff. The much-troubled 1960s hotel has 134 a/c rooms including 15 suites with satellite TV and telephone. Some rooms have a balcony. Safe deposit boxes cost US$2 per day. At press time the hotel had deteriorated markedly and was in the early stages of yet another much-needed renovation. It has a bathing area in a natural ocean pool protected by a pier, with its own little beach and spacious, elevated sun terrace shaded by almond trees. Facilities include a selection of bars and restaurants, and the famous Havana Club disco. There's a travel agency, clothes boutique, Red Cross clinic, and beauty salon. Scuba diving and jet skis are available. Rates were US$65 s, US$90 d, US$135 suite low season, US$80 s, US$110 d, US$155 suite high season.

Far better are the Comodoro's bungalows, which are recommended. See Very Expensive, below.

A recent restoration of the **Hotel Neptuno/Triton,** Av. 3ra y Calle 72, tel. (7) 33-1483 or 33-1606, fax (7) 33-0042, has done little to assuage the dreary nature of this ugly twin-tower highrise complex run by Gran Caribe. It has 524 a/c rooms and suites, all with modest furnishings, satellite TVs, telephone, radio, safe deposit box, and refrigerator. The tennis courts and large pool and sun terrace with funky plastic furniture lack appeal, as does the ugly shoreline. At least the hotel has shops, a pleasant bar, and three restaurants. Rates were US$55 s, US$70 d, US$90 t low season, US$70 s, US$90 d, US$110 t high season.

Further west in Barlovento, on the fringe of the city, Marina Hemingway offers the **Qualton El Viejo y el Mar,** tel. (7) 24-6336, fax (7) 24-6823, e-mail: reservas@oldman.cha.cyt.cu, a modern hotel with 186 rooms boasting modern furnishings, and each with satellite TV, phone, radio, minibar, security box, and balcony. It has an attractive lobby with piano-bar, shop, tour desk, and a restaurant serving ho-hum food. The marina offers plenty of facilities, including water sports. Rates were US$68 s, US$95 d low season, US$84 s, US$105 d high season; junior suites cost US$95/116 s/d low season, US$100/121 s/d high season; suites cost US$118/138 s/d low season, US$129/149 s/d high season; bungalows cost US$93/124 s/d low season, US$93/124 s/d low season, US$103/144 high season.

Cubanacán's new and appealing **Hotel El Jardín del Edén,** tel. (7) 24-7628, fax (7) 24-4379, e-mail: comercial@comermh.cha.cyt.cu, on Intercanal B at Marina Hemingway, has 314 a/c rooms including eight suites and 12 junior suites, all with satellite TVs, phones, radio, minibar, safe deposit box, and balconies. Facilities include a buffet restaurant, a café, and two bars, a splendid swimming pool, games room, bicycle rental, shop, and tour bureau. Rates were US$60 s, US$80 d, US$95 junior suite, US$110 suite low season; US$70 s, US$90 d, US$110 junior suite, US$130 suite high season.

Cubanacán's **Spa La Pradera,** at Calle 230 y 15, tel. (7) 24-7473, fax (7) 24-7198, e-mail: aloja@pradera.cha.cyt.cu, in Reparto Siboney, offers an advantageous position for conventioneers and scientists visiting the local bio-tech facilities, but is otherwise out-of-the-way. The modern, 164-room low-rise hotel is attractive however, and looks out over a large pool and gardens. All rooms feature a/c, satellite TV, phone, minibar, and security box. The resort hosts entertainment and features squash, basketball, and volleyball courts plus tiny gym with sauna. The hotel specializes in medical and spa treatments focusing on "life enhancement" and holistic treatments.

Very Expensive (US$110-150)

European tour groups favor the modern **Hotel Copacabana,** Av. 1ra e/ Calles 34 y 36, tel. (7) 24-1037, fax (7) 24-2846, whose oceanfront location offers a unique advantage. The hotel was opened in 1955 by a fervent admirer of Brazil. The atmosphere still has a Brazilian flavor and uses names from that country—the Itapoa steak house, the Do Port pizza and snack bar, the Caipirinha bar and grill. Not surprisingly, the place does a healthy trade with package groups from Brazil and Argentina. The 170 rooms boast hardwood furnishings, floral bedspreads, small TVs, telephones, and safe deposit boxes. The Restaurant Tucano (prix-fixe meals cost US$15) looks out over the huge swimming pool—popular with Cuban day visitors—and the ocean. A separate bar serves the pool, and there's a pizzeria. A discotheque, tourism bureau, car-rental office, and boutique round out the facilities, and scuba diving is offered. Rates were US$75 s, US$110 d low season, US$80 s, US$120 d high season. *Overpriced!*

The most appealing apartment villas in town are the **Comodoro Bungalow Apartments,** in an aesthetically striking Spanish-style village to either side of the Hotel Comodoro, Av. 1ra y Calle 84, tel. (7) 24-5551, 24-2028, website: www.cubanacan.cu. Set amid lush foliage are 320 beautiful posada-style, two-story, one-, two-, and three-bedroom villas facing onto two massive amoeba-shaped swimming pools. Very atmospheric! Rooms have balconies or patios, plus kitchen, living room, and minibar. Facilities include a 24-hour coffee shop, a business center, Photo Service outlet, upscale boutiques, travel agency, pharmacy, restaurant, and a cabaret *espectáculo* and other entertainment are offered. Rates were US$89 s, US$118 d low season, US$98 s, US$137 d high season, one bedroom; US$153-184 low season, US$180-216 high season, two bedrooms; and US$188-204 low season, US$220-248 high season, three bedrooms.

Chateau Miramar, is a Cubanacán property on the ugly coral shorefront next to the aquarium, Av. 1ra y Calle 62, tel. (7) 33-1915 or 33-0224, fax (7) 24-0224. The handsome five-story, 50-room hotel was recently refurbished but cannot justify its room rates. Rooms, albeit a bit sterile, are neatly furnished and feature satellite TV, minibar, radio, and safe deposit box. Nine of the rooms are one-bedroom suites with jacuzzi tubs. Facilities include a seaside pool, elegant restaurant, two bars, and executive office, a small shop, Casa del Tabaco, massage, plus entertainment. The sea spray reaches up to the top-floor windows. It's popular with business folk. Rates were US$106 s, US$130 d, US$190 suites.

Aiming at businessmen and conventioneers is the **Hotel Palco,** Av. 146 e/ 11 y 13, tel. (7) 33-7235, fax (7) 33-7250 or 33-7236, e-mail: info@hpalco.gov.cu, website: www.cubaweb.cu/palco, adjoining the Palacio de Convenciones (Convention Center). This purpose-built, five-story hotel has an expansive lobby and stylish modern décor—and hints of second-rate construction). The 180 rooms include 36 junior suites, and are arrayed around an atrium with a skylight roof with stained glass and, at the base, a botanical garden and still-water pool with carp (and mosquitoes). Rooms are spacious and up to par, with modern decor in calming ochers, a/c, satellite TVs, phones, minibars, safe de-

posit boxes, tile floors, and large, attractive bathrooms with hair driers. Facilities include a business center, elegant restaurant, outdoor snack
bar, a split-level pool, small sauna, and a smaller gym. Rates were US$74 s, US$94 d low season; US$91 s, US$111 d high season; US$130-
150 junior suite year-round.

You can rent attractive two-story waterfront
apartments, bungalows, and villas in the
Cubanacán Paraíso complex in Marina Hemingway, tel. (7) 24-1150, ext. 85. It has about
100 houses and bungalows with one, two, or
three bedrooms. All have terraces, TVs and
video, safe deposit boxes, and kitchens. In a
touch of strange Cuban logic, the *carpeta* (reception office) is the *last* building at the far end of
Pier 1. Rates were US$130 s/d for a one-room
bungalow; *casas* cost US$140 s/d one room,
US$200 two rooms for up to four people, and
US$250 three rooms for up to six people.

Luxury (US$150+)
The **Hotel Meliá Habana,** haughtily perched
atop a man-made mound on Avenida 3ra 200
meters east of Calles 84, tel. (7) 24-8500, fax
(7) 24-8505, e-mail: depres@habana. solmelia
.cma.net, is a recent addition to the luxury hotel
market and aims squarely at a business clientele.
Although its concrete and plate-glass exterior
jars, the expansive lobby is beautiful, with a surfeit of gray and green marbles and ponds, and a
sumptuous lobby bar plus the elegant Bosque
Habana restaurant. The 405 a/c rooms and four
suites are arrayed in a sinfully ugly complex
fronting the shore. All have balconies and ocean
views, plus satellite TVs, phones with fax and
modem lines, and safe deposit boxes, and come
up to international standards. The executive floor
offers more personalized service. Facilities include four restaurants, five bars, a pool, tennis
courts, hairdresser, gym, and a business center,
plus up-to-date meeting facilities. Rates were
US$140 s, US$175 d, and US$185 s, US$220 d
on the executive floor (US$15 extra with ocean
view; suites US$15 extra). *Overpriced!*

The ritzy **Novotel Miramar,** Av. 5ta e/ 72 y
76, tel. (7) 24-3584 or 62-8308, fax (7) 24-3583
or 62-8587, in North America, tel. (800) 221-
4542, is a joint project with Gaviota and the
French Accor group that opened in January
2000 as Havana's only true deluxe hotel. This
sublimely decorated property features a surfeit
of limestone, marble, and gracious neoclassical
wrought-iron furniture in the vast lobby where
Escher-style murals abound. It has 427 cavernous rooms, including eight suites, and five
rooms fully rigged for handicapped travelers.
All are done up on regal dark blue and gold
decor, with artwork. Glorious! The master suite
has a rooftop terrace. To the rear is a huge
swimming pool and terrace where "animations"
(cabaret) are held. A commercial gallery features a beauty salon, plus there's a squash
court and full health center. Introductory rates
were US$100 s, US$130 d, US$180 t low sea-
son, US$120 s, US$155 d, US$205 t high sea-
son for standard rooms. The complex will eventually include the **Apartotel Monteverde** and
the **Sofitel Quinta Avenida,** all squarely aiming
at a business clientele.

SUBURBAN HAVANA

Budget (Under US$35)
Parque Lenin: The **Motel La Herradura,** tel. (7)
44-1058, on the south side of the Centro
Ecuestre, has seven a/c rooms with TVs (local
stations only) and utilitarian decor for US$17 s/d.

HABANA DEL ESTE

Many places are ugly concrete carbuncles built
for Cubans and don't serve current tourism
needs well. Some are terribly run-down. The entire complex is divided into *zonas,* each with a
carpeta or reservations office for rental units.
Horizontes runs the show in Santa María; Islazul has a monopoly in Boca Ciega and Guanabo.

Casas Particulares
Playas del Este, Boca Ciega and Guanabo:
There are many *casas particulares* (private
homes) from which to choose. Look for the signs
or ask for a recommendation on the street. The
best I saw was an attractive colonial home at
the corner of Avenida 7ma and Calle 472. Also
try Angela Rico Terrera, tel. (687) 96-2885; and
Marisela Dieguez at Calle 490 #5C.

Budget (Under US$35)

Alamar: Villa Bacuranao, on the eastern shore of the cove at Playa Bacuranao, was closed at press time. No restoration was slated but stayed tuned.

About one km east of Celimar is a dour tourist complex called **Campismo Popular Celimarina,** with small and basic self-catering huts sprinkled amid pasture nibbled by goats. The shore isn't particularly appealing.

Playas del Este, Boca Ciega and Guanabo: Islazul's **Boca Ciega,** at the east end of 1ra, tel. (687) 96-2771, has 10 simple houses for rent: US$16 s, US$21 d. It has no facilities but rents volleyballs and footballs.

Hotel Gran Vía, another Islazul property, Av. 5ta y 462, tel. (687) 96-2271 offers five rooms for Cubans and five for foreigners: US$21 s/d low season, US$26 d high season. It has an a/c restaurant adjacent.

Also check out the simple **Islazul Hotel Miramar,** Av. 9na y Calle 478 in Guanabo, tel. (687) 96-2507, with 23 rooms with cold water only, plus balconies for US$20 s/d low season, US$26 d high season; and the **Islazul Villas Playa Hermosa,** Av. 5ta e/ 472 y 474. It has cabaret on Fri.-Sun. nights.

Guanabo also has several extra-budget hotels (US$5 or so) that say they no longer accept foreigners. Among them are **Hotel María** and **Hotel Vía Blanca,** opposite each other, Av. 5ta y Calle 486. You may have better luck at the very basic **Villa María Blanca.**

Inexpensive (US$35-60)

Ciudad Panamericano: The **Hotel Panamericano Resort,** Calle A y Av. Central, tel. (7) 95-1242, fax (7) 95-1021, features a hotel and two apartment complexes. The hotel's unappetizing lobby, full of dowdy utility furniture, is your first hint that a reservation here is a grave error. The rooms cry out for a refurbishment and are outfitted with modern albeit poorly made furnishings and maroon fabrics. Telephones and satellite TVs are standard. The hotel has a large swimming pool that is a popular social scene on weekends. There's also a large gym plus sauna, car and moped rental, and tourism bureau. It offers a beach excursion to Playas del Este for US$20.

The only other option is to rent a meagerly furnished apartment in the **Aparthotel Panamericano Resort,** opposite the hotel. It offers 421 two- and three-bedroom apartments popular with budget European charter groups. Facilities are meager, even dour, reminding me of a students' union in a low-end polytechnic. The lobby has a small bar and there's a basic restaurant. Rates were US$46 low season, US$54 high season for a two-bedroom apartment; US$58 low season, US$68 high season for a three-bedroom unit.

Playas del Este, Santa María: Horizontes runs the **Aparthotel Atlántico,** on Avenida de las Terrazas, tel. (687) 97-1494, fax (687) 97-1203, offering pleasantly furnished a/c apartments with TVs and telephones. Facilities include a restaurant, swimming pool with bar, scooter rental, tour desk, tennis courts, and entertainment. One-room units rent for US$24 s/d low season, US$36 high season; two-room units cost US$32 low season, and US$48 high season.

Inland on the hill, a 10-minute walk from the beach, is **Villas Horizontes Mirador del Mar,** tel. (687) 97-1354, fax (687) 97-1262, with one- to five-bedroom a/c units in a self-contained complex with a hilltop swimming pool, restaurant, and medical service that extends to massage in its *centro recreativo* (recreation center). Each has cable TV. It also rents rooms for US$36 d low season, US$40 d high season with breakfast. Villa rates run from US$45 for one bedroom to US$198 for five bedrooms, low season; US$52 to US$224 high season.

Villa Mégano, midway down Avenida de las Terrazas, tel. (687) 97-1610, at the far west end of Playas del Este, is a Horizontes property, a 10-minute walk from the beach. The ambience and decor of the a/c cabins is simple yet appealing, with tile floors, tiny satellite TVs, bamboo furnishings, small tiled baths with showers, and plate-glass doors opening to verandas. Larger cabins cost US$34 s, US$46 d low season; US$44 s, US$58 d high season; smaller cabins *(chicas)* cost US$28 s, US$38 d low season, US$36 s, US$48 d high season.

Another Horizontes option is **Aparthotel Las Terrazas,** Av. Las Terrazas y Calle 9, tel. (687) 4910, fronting the shore. It has 144 a/c apartments with kitchens, TVs, radios, and telephones for US$28 s, US$35 d. There's also a swimming pool.

Playas del Este, Boca Ciega and Guanabo: If you want a private villa in Boca Ciega, you can book one through **Villas Vista Mar,** Av. 1ra y Calle 438 in Boca Ciega. It has 69 *casas,* from US$44 for a two-bedroom, US$63 for a three-bedroom unit.

Cabañas Cuanda's, one block south of Av. 5ta y Calle 472, tel. (687) 2774, has 37 a/c rooms, most with double beds and showers with tepid water. Rooms are overpriced at US$25 d.

Moderate (US$60-85)
Cojímar: In 2000, Gran Caribe opened **Villa Cojímar,** a grand colonial mansion at the top of the hill at the entrance to the village. Rates were US$105 s, US$169 d.

Playas del Este, Santa María: The most popular place in town is the rather gloomy **Hotel Tropicoco,** between Avenidas Sur and Las Terrazas and facing Playa Santa María, tel. (687) 97-1371, fax (687) 97-1389. The uninspired, communist-style, five-story building was recently renovated (you'd never know it), but no amount of tinkering can improve the appallingly designed and unwelcoming lobby. It remains popular with Canadian tour companies (but, one suspects, not their clientele). It has 188 a/c rooms with uninspired decor, telephones, and radio. Services include a restaurant, bar, tour desk, shop, Casa del Tabaco, post office, and car rental. Rooms cost US$40 s, US$53 d low season; US$52 s, US$65 d high season.

Much nicer is the **Sea Club Hotel Arenal,** on Laguna Itabo in the midst of the lagoon between Playas Santa María del Mar and Boca Ciega, tel. (687) 97-1272, fax (687) 97-1287 (in Europe, Pantravel, C. so Pestalozzi, 4a, 6900 Lugano, Switzerland, tel. (91) 923-2043, fax (91) 922-6286, e-mail: srosso@pantravel.ch). It relies mostly on Italian, German, and Austrian charters. However, this all-inclusive property doesn't quite live up to the images presented in the slick brochure. Red-tile-roofed units surround a massive pool and lush lawns with thatched restaurant and bar. Rooms are spacious and offer eye-pleasing decor and furnishings. It has a few shops, and the staff try hard to keep guests amused with canned *animación* (entertainment).

Rates were US$65 standard, US$75 superior, Jan.-July and Sep.-Dec; and US$75 standard, US$95, superior, July-Aug., based on per person (double occupancy); a single supplement costs U$20 and US$30 respectively.

Very Expensive (US$110-150)
Tarará: Cubanacán Tarará, Via Blanca, Tarará, tel. (687) 97-1057, offers a range of one- to four-bedroom villas—*casas confort.* Most belong to Cubanacán. Others belong to Puerto Sol, and others to Islazul, which rents out to Cubans and tourists alike. The facility was in the midst of much-needed renovation at press time, when about half of the villas had been brought up to modern standards, although the grounds remain in need of a spruce up. Each has a radio, satellite TV, telephone, and private parking. Nonregistered guests are strictly proscribed (none may stay overnight without authority of the management, which even requires a list of guests attending "a social gathering"). A grocery, laundry service, and restaurants are onsite. Two-bedroom units cost US$160 low season, US$200 in high season without a pool; US$200 and US$250 with pool. Three-bedroom units cost US$240/300 low/high season without pool; US$280/350 with pool. Four-bedroom units cost US$320/400 and US$360/450 respectively. The *carpeta* (booking office), tel. (687) 97-1462, fax (687) 97-1499 or 97-1313, is 100 meters east of the marina.

Playas del Este, Santa María: A dreary option, but offering the advantage of being atop the beach, is the **Gran Caribe Club Atlántico** tel. (687) 97-1085, fax (687) 80-3911. It was until recently leased entirely for use by an Italian tour company (Going One) but the crack-down on *jiniteras* pulled the plug on the Italian market, forcing it to open its doors to all-comers. This all-inclusive is lowly by international standards and is dour in its public amenities. It has 92 rooms with a/c, satellite TVs, radios, and minibars. Facilities include a restaurant and snack bar, swimming pool, tiny gym, a tennis court, and a shop. Entertainment staff try to put a bit of pep into the scene. It's overpriced—even with meals included—at US$78 s, US$125 d low season, US$87 s, US$142 d high season.

The most elegant options are the **Villas los Pinos,** Av. Las Terrazas y Calle 4, tel. (687) 97-

1361, fax (687) 97-1524, e-mail: informatica@pinos.gca.cma.net, run by Gran Caribe, which offers 46 two-and three-room villas. Some appear a bit fuddy-duddy, others are impressive and up to international standards, with their own private pools. Villa #35 even has its own squash court. They all have TVs, VCRs, radios, telephones, and kitchens. Rates were US$175-375 low season, US$200-425 high season for up to four people, including housekeeping service. Other staff is on hand, and baby-sitters can be arranged.

FOOD

Cuba's dismal restaurant scene is even echoed in the capital city. You have to search hard for cuisine of international standard (some are deplorably bad: Restaurante 1830, for example). However, international standard restaurants are beginning to appear with the aid of foreign—primarily French—chefs who have arrived in recent years (for example, La Torre). Many are in the top-class hotels, although most would give the Japanese a nasty case of sticker shock.

Havana's restaurant scene is in a constant state of flux. Many of the establishments listed below may have changed by the time you read this (so, too, their prices). And sadly, the many *paladares* (private restaurants) that once existed are dwindling, purposely driven out of business through heavy taxation.

Havana's erstwhile Chinese population has left its culinary legacy on city streets. A fistful of restaurants boast genuine Oriental decor, although the cuisine is usually disappointing—more like Cuban cuisine with bamboo sprouts. Most offer chopsticks—*parritas.*

You can dine for a pittance at streetside snack bars, which still accept pesos from tourists. Havana has plenty of sidewalk cafés. Rumbos S.A., for example, has been opening up roadside snack bars at strategic points all over Havana; of a uniform design with green-shade awnings and serving a standard menu of *bocaditos, papa fritas,* and *criollo* staples such as fried chicken.

Havana is blessed with numerous bakeries selling a wide range of desserts. The best are **Pain de Paris: Croissants de France,** tel. (7) 33-7669, fax (7) 33-7671, run with French instruction, with an increasing number of outlets throughout the city. Notable are those in Habana Vieja next to the Hotel Inglaterra and on Calle Obispo, just off Plaza de Armas. Most cafés, however, are really snack- bars-cum-restaurants; there are few in the purist Parisian tradition, and the prerevolutionary *cafeterías—* coffee stands—that used to make coffee on every corner have vanished, as have most of the former tea shops *(Casas de Té* or *Casas de Infusiones).*

Always check your bill carefully!

Self-Catering

In addition to numerous farmers' markets *(mercados agropecuarios),* where fruits, vegetables, and meats are sold in both dollars and pesos, you can purchase Western goods at dollars-only stores, open to foreigners and Cubans alike and stocked with packaged and canned goods from all over the world. Havana even has a few supermarkets stocked with everything you'd expect to find in a Safeway or Sainsbury's.

Fresh fish is harder to come by. The government-run **Pescaderias Especiales** sell fish and other seafoods. Each municipality has one. The one in Vedado is next to the Hotel Vedado on Calle 25 between N and O and was selling shrimp for 22 pesos per pound, snapper *(pargo)* at 35 pesos per pound, and squid for 25 pesos per pound.

TOP TEN PLACES TO EAT

Here's my top ten list of places to eat in Havana.

La Bodeguita del Medio	Habana Vieja
El Floridita	Habana Vieja
Roof Garden Restaurant, Hotel Sevilla	Habana Vieja
Paladar La Guarida	Centro Habana
Coppelia	Vedado
Paladar Le Chansonnier	Vedado
Paladar Amor	Vedado
La Torre	Vedado
El Aljibe	Miramar
La Giraldilla	Playa

HABANA VIEJA

Peso Eateries

Peso pickings are slim in Havana's touristy heartland. The dingy and austere **Casa de los Vinos,** tel. (7) 62-1319, at the corner of Esperanza and Factoria, five blocks south of Parque de la Fraternidad and five west of the railway station, began life as a workers' canteen in 1912. With luck, you'll find sausage and bean soup—two of its specialties—although it has fallen on hard times of late and offered a meager menu when I last visited. The decor is highlighted by walls inlaid with tiles inscribed with love poems and proverbs such as "The wind and women change by the minute."

La Casa Arencibia, on Calle San Miguel at Amistad, near the Capitolio, offers *platas* of chicken liver for US$1.

Paladares

My favorite *paladar* is the pocket-size **La Moneda Cubana,** at San Ignacio #77, one block south of Plaza de la Catedral, tel. (7) 61-0401. Although tiny, it's well run, service is speedy, and the portions are huge. The menu offers the usual Cuban staples such as grilled chicken or fried fish (US$9) and even pork chops (US$10) served with rice and beans, mixed salad, and bread. It offers omelettes for US$8. Open daily, noon-11 p.m.

Try *La Rejita Mayéa,* Calle Habana #405 e/ Obispo y Obrapía, tel. (7) 62-6704. It has set meals—basic fare—for US$8. Open daily noon-11 p.m.

Breakfasts

Hotel restaurants welcome nonguests: I recommend the Hotel Parque Central Most serve meager buffets for US$8-15. Budget travelers should check out **Monserrate** Av. de Bélgica (Monserrate) y Obrapía. It offers bacon and eggs (US$1.50), toast (US$1), and American-style coffee (US$0.75).

Criollo

No visit to Cuba is complete without a meal at **La Bodeguita del Medio,** 207 Empedrado, one block west of Plaza de la Catedral, tel. (7) 62-4498, e-mail: reserva@bodem.gca.cma.net. La Bodeguita was honored in 1992 with the "Best of

the Best Five Star Diamond Award" by the North American Academy of Gastronomy. The restaurant specializes in traditional Cuban dishes—most famously its roast pork, steeped black beans, flat-fried bananas, garlicky yucca, and sweet guava pudding—which are, as Nicolás Guillén (Cuba's national poet) once put it, "overflowing with surges of aged rum." Alas, the *mojitos* long ago lost their edge (be sure to ask for *añejo* rum). You may have to wait for an hour or more to be seated. The service is relaxed to a fault, and the atmosphere bohemian and lively. *Soneros* (popular dance-music performers) and troubadours (poet-musicians) entertain. The food is generally fresher at lunch than at dinner, for which you'll pay US$10-20 (a US$10 minimum applies). Reservations are advised.

Virtually every foreigner passing through the Plaza de la Catedral also plunks his or her derriere at the **Restaurante El Patio,** tel. (7) 57-1034 or 61-8504, if only to enjoy a refreshment in the El Portal patio bar. In addition to its bar and patio café it has four dining rooms (one a folkloric dining room specializing in Mexican cuisine), open noon-11 p.m. The patio bar is open 24 hours and serves snacks such as an El Patio sandwich (US$3.50), a hamburger (US$3), and steak palomilla with fries (US$2.75). Drinks are expensive. The main restaurant has three set menus and serves overpriced (US$16-28) dishes such as shrimp *al ajillo* (in garlic) and even T-bone steak. But it is worth the price for the fabulous surroundings and the views over the plaza from upstairs.

Café/Restaurante La Mina, facing onto Plaza de Armas on Calle Obispo, tel. (7) 62-0216, is atmospheric and offers shaded patio dining out front where snacks and salads (US$3-5) and Cuban dishes (US$4-10) are served. To the rear you'll find the **Restaurante Cubano** where you dine in a courtyard with an arbor and free-roaming peacocks, caged birds, and saddles and other country artifacts for decor. Troubadours add to the ambience.

Around Parque Central a favorite of budget travelers is the **Colonial Restaurant,** on the ground floor of the Hotel Inglaterra. It has a wide-ranging menu of Cuban dishes, such as shrimp *en salsa roja* (US$11), *pollo asado* (US$4.50), and fried beef in creole sauce (US$5.25).

Prado 264 on the Prado at Calle Animas, serves pizzas and soups, plus the normal range of undistinguished Cuban fare for US$3-7. Cubans have their own menu in pesos. Nearby, in the Casa de Científicos at Prado #212, is **Restaurant Los Vitrales,** impressive for its exquisite rococo decor, colorful *vitrales,* and fine antiques, though the menu is less distinguished, with the usual Cuban fare running to chicken, fish, and steaks (US$6-26). Nearby, on Avenida de Bélgica (Egido), between Jesús María and Acosta, is **Puerto de Sagua,** tel. (7) 57-1026 or 63-6186, a humble yet pleasant restaurant designed on a nautical theme and also beloved of local Cubans.

La Zaragoza, Calle Monserrate e/ Obispo y Obrapía, tel. (7) 57-1033, open 24 hours, is a dark and moody Spanish-style bodega that maintains its Spanish ties with regional flags and soccer memorabilia. It serves *criollo* fare and specializes in seafoods such as squid rings (US$6), garlic shrimp (US$12), and *ceviche peruano* (US$2.50), but also serving lamb stew (US$9), tortillas (US$3), and pizzas (from US$2).

Nearby is the **Castillo de Farnés,** also on Monserrate at #361 esq. Obrapía, tel. (7) 57-1030. This Havana landmark has been famous since its founding as a Spanish restaurant in 1896 (Fidel Castro used to frequent it while a student). Its menu includes omelettes (US$4), garlic shrimp (US$9), and lobster and steak (US$15-20). Take a sweater. It has a patio snack bar out front. Next door, the simpler **La Monserrate,** popular with Cubans and budget tourists, also has a grill open to the street and serves burgers, pizzas and the like for US$1-2. Try its *Coctel Monserrate.* Open 11-3 a.m.

The *posada*-style **Los Doces Apóstoles,** tel. (7) 63-8295, squats at the base of Morro Castle. Here an African purée soup costs US$2, and creole chicken costs US$5.50. Open noon-11 p.m. Adjacent, the **El Polverín Bar** offers a charming little bar plus grand vistas from a breeze-swept patio beside the Twelve Apostles (the giant cannons guarding the harbor entrance). It's a perfectly lonesome spot to relax, and one popular with Cubans.

Arabic

Aiming mostly at tourists is **Restaurante al Medina,** in the Casa de los Árabes on Calle Oficios, one block south of Plaza de Armas, tel. (7) 57-1041. When I first called in, the menu was limited to standard *criollo* items. On my last visit, couscous and lamb dishes (US$6) had been added, as had kebabs (US$5) and kibbe (minced meat balls, US$4), and hummus (US$2.20).

Also try the **Restaurante Internacional Oasis,** in the Centro Cultural de Árabe on the Prado e/ Calles Refugio y Trocadero. Open 9 a.m.-midnight. Cabarets—often with transvestite shows—are hosted nightly (US$5).

Continental

You should be sure to eat at the huge, high-ceilinged, marble-floored **Roof Garden Restaurant** atop the Hotel Sevilla, tel. (7) 33-8560, not least for the sublime decor. Tall French doors open to balconies overlooking the city. Kemal Kairus, a Lebanese Cuban, plays piano. And the food—once mediocre at best—has improved by leaps since French chef Jean-Paul Gulotta took the helm in the kitchen, fusing Cuban into French, with mouth-watering recherché dishes for US$5-30.

The **Restaurante Real Plaza,** on the ground floor of the Hotel Plaza, is elegant, with gilt fittings and marvelous high-backed modern chairs. Here I've enjoyed grilled fish for US$7.50.

In the heart of the old city, try the **Café Mercurió,** tel. (7) 66-6188, facing onto Plaza de San Francisco at the base of the Longa del Comercio. This elegant restaurant and bar—open 24 hours—offers a wide-ranging menu of continental and Cuban fare, including lobster (US$25) and grilled fish (US$8). It offers air-con seating, or shaded dining alfresco on the cobbled plaza. And the regal **Restaurant El Condado** in the Hotel Santa Isabel on Plaza de Armas offers adventurous fare such as shrimp in mango sauce (US$19), and pork loin fried with orange and garlic (US$12).

Italian

The eponymous **A Prado y Neptuno,** which speaks of its location, is a modern, air-conditioned place popular with Cubans and serving a range of pizzas and pastas (US$3.50-7), plus steaks, fish, and chicken dishes (US$4-25). It has a *heladería* (ice-creamery) to the rear.

The **Cantiluomo,** at the west end of Obispo, shares the kitchen with the Floridita (see Seafoods, below) and offers a simple Italianate ambience and unambitious pasta dishes from

US$4. It has a good wine list. Farther down Obispo, **Via Venetto,** between Villegas and Aguacate, is a basic and gloomy Italian restaurant serving an exclusively Cuban clientele. Foreigners can pay in *pesos.*

The **Dominica,** at the east end of Calle Tacón, tel. (7) 66-2917, serves pastas and pizzas (US$6-12) in elegant surroundings and offers the unusual distinction of Mexican mariachi music some nights. It is popular with Cubans.

Oriental
Torre de Marfil, Mercaderes #121 e/ Oficios y Obrapía, tel. (7) 57-1038, has all the trappings: the Chinese lanterns, screens, and even a banquet table beneath a mock temple. It's staffed by Chinese waiters, but the service is disorganized and excruciatingly slow. The menu includes chop suey, chow mein, won ton (US$1.50), and shrimp and lobster dishes. Entrées range US$5-15. It serves set dinners from US$6.

Also consider **Restaurante Hanoi,** Calle Teniente Rey at the corner of Bernaza, tel. (7) 57-1029, also known as La Casa de la Parre (Grapevine House) for the luxuriant grapevine growing in the patio. The restaurant—a symbol of friendship with the people of Vietnam—is in one of the oldest houses in Havana. It has rattan furniture, Chinese lanterns, and lacquered wooden wall hangings inlaid with mother-of-pearl. Alas, the menu is more Cuban than Chinese, but no single dish costs more than US$3.50, and it offers "combination specials" for below US$3. Open 9 a.m.-11 p.m.

Surf and Turf
You *must* visit **El Floridita,** Monserrate y Obispo, Habana Vieja, tel. (7) 63-1063, e-mail: reserva@flori.gca.cma.net, the favorite watering hole of one of America's favorite drinkers—Ernest Hemingway—who immortalized the restaurant in *Islands in the Stream.* The circular restaurant to the rear wears a Romanesque livery of red and gold—plus an original mural of the old port—and still has a fin de siècle ambience, although today it is overly air-conditioned and rather sterile, cleansed of the heady atmosphere of the days when Papa drank here (it has been called a "glitzy huckster joint" in *Travel & Leisure*). In 1992, El Floridita received the "Best of the Best Five Star Diamond Award" by the North American Academy of Gastronomy. Most of the dishes, alas, are disappointing. The menu is mostly overpriced seafood. The house special is *langosta mariposa* (lobster grilled with almonds, pineapple, and butter) chased with the "Papa special" (a daiquiri), but it is best to stick with simple dishes such as prawns flambéed in rum. A shrimp cocktail costs US$15; oyster cocktails cost US$5. You can even have frog's leg soufflé (US$19). Lobster costs a whopping US$36-42. The cheapest dish is grilled chicken (US$11). The wine list is perhaps the best in the city, and choice cigars are offered, A string trio serenade in the bar. Your daiquiri will set you back a stiff US$6 (be sure to ask for the connoisseur's *daiquiri natural,* shaken, without the brain-numbing ice).

At the other extreme is **La Casa del Escobeche,** a simple bar with flagstone floor and *rejas* open to the street, at the corner of Calles Obispo and Villegas, serving a mostly Cuban clientele and, as its name suggests, offering delicious *escovitch* (cube chunks of fish marinated with lime and salsa) for pennies.

One of the nattiest eateries in town is the **Café del Oriente,** at the corner of Oficios and Amargura on the west side of Plaza de San Francisco, tel. (7) 66-6686. The ritzy marble-top bar, waiters in tux, and a jazz pianist add to the regal tone downstairs in the Bar Café (heck, you could be in New York or San Francisco). The upstairs restaurant is yet more elegant, with sparkling marble and antiques, French drapes, and a magnificent stained-glass ceiling. It offers mostly steaks and seafood dishes (US$12-30) and is open 24 hours.

For views toward Havana head to **La Divina Pastor,** tel. (7) 33-8341, 200 meters east of and below the Morro castle, directly across the harbor from Castle de la Real Furze. It's housed in a handsome hacienda-style structure fronted by a battery of cannons, and offers traditional entertainment such as bolero and cha-cha-cha. The atmosphere is splendid, especially on the patio in late afternoon. The menu includes such appetizers as Peruvian civet (US$4.50) and lobster cocktail (US$), and such entrées as lobster creole (US$20) and grilled shellfish (US$25). Parking costs US$1. It's open noon-11 p.m. Behind the restaurant, on the harborfront, is a wonderful little bodega-type bar—**Bar la Tasca**—with a breezy balcony offering fabulous views over the harbor. It's a great place to sit on a hot day. It has lances and medieval armor on the walls. The simple menu includes lobster and seafood dishes from US$8. It was closed for renovation at press time.

Spanish

My favorite Spanish restaurant in Havana is **La Paella** in the Hostal Valencia on Calle Oficios, one block south of Plaza de Armas in Habana Vieja, where you'll dine beneath colonial chandeliers, surrounded by antique dark-wood furnishings, with large open windows to provide a cooling breeze. It serves various paellas (ostensibly for two people only, although I have been served paella when dining alone) for US$7-15. The *caldo* (soup) and bread is a meal in itself (US$3). You can also choose steak, grilled fish, and chicken dishes (US$4-10) and wash them down with Spanish wines (US$6-13). Try the excellent vegetable house soup. However, during my most recent visits, the restaurant was serving minuscule portions.

Also in Habana Vieja, try modestly priced **La Tasca**, on the ground floor arcade of the Hotel Sevilla. Its decor replicates a Spanish bodega. The chef will whip up a good omelette. Likewise, the newly renovated **El Baturro** Av. de la Bélgica (Egido) y Merced, tel. (7) 66-9078, offers *tapas* (US$0.25) and *escabeche* shrimp (US$3.50) and other Spanish and Cuban dishes amid Spanish surrounds: barrels, a bull's-head, bullfight posters, ceramic murals, and brass lamps. The bar serves a full range of liquors.

The **Bodegón de los Vinos** in the Castillo de San Carlos de la Cabaña offers the most genuinely Spanish experience in Havana. It's built into the vaults of the castle and has traditional *mantegan* (from La Mancha) decor. It serves *tapas,* sausages, and other Spanish dishes (US$2-17) washed down by sangria (US$3). Flamenco dancers entertain. It occasionally fills with tour groups.

Cafés and Snack Bars

Most restaurants serve *cafecitos*—the thick, sweet Cuban version of espresso. Few serve coffee American-style. For a wider range, head to **Restaurant La Luz**, on Calle Obispo between San Ignacio and Mercaderes, selling cappuccinos, espressos, and various coffees. The **Casa del Café,** on the southeast corner of Plaza de Armas, tel. (7) 33-8061, also sells cappuccinos (US$2) plus various grades of Cuban coffees. It's open Mon.-Sat. 10 a.m.-6 p.m., and Sunday 9 a.m.-3 p.m.

Doña Isabel Cafetería, on Calle Tacón #4 esq. Empedrado, one block north of Plaza de Armas, tel. (7) 63-3560, serves sandwiches, pizzas, and other snacks. Next door, in a similar vein, is **Don Giovanni,** tel. (7) 57-1036, a café-restaurant in a beautiful colonial mansion. You can dine on the lower courtyard or upstairs in more elegant surroundings and look down over Calle Tacón and the harbor. It mostly serves snacks but also has a choice of pizzas and seafoods (US$4-15).

Another popular option for tourists is **El Patio Colonial,** on the Plaza de la Catedral. Its appeal is neither its ambience, the drinks, nor musicians, but rather that sitting beneath the cool *portrale* held aloft by tall columns, you can gaze out upon the whirligig of life on the plaza.

Café O'Reilly, on O'Reilly and San Ignacio, one block south of Plaza de la Catedral, has gone downhill in recent years and no longer serves cappuccinos or espressos, but remains a good place to relax over Cuban coffee and simple snacks (mostly tapas and tortillas) on the upstairs balcony, which looks down over Calle O'Reilly. It's popular with the gay crowd and has a strong local clientele.

While exploring Plaza de Armas, you should relax at **Café Mina,** facing onto the square and a good place to sip a cool beer or *mojito* (US$1.50) beneath shady umbrellas. It has lemonades. Bands and troubadours perform alfresco. Next to it (part of the same complex) is the **Al Cappuccino** coffee house serving homemade pastries and custard for US$1.

The **Café Paris,** on the corner of Calles Obispo and San Ignacio, is a very lively social scene for both Cubans and tourists. You'll sit at rustic wooden furniture and look out through open trellised windows on life flowing down Obispo. Lively Latin music is usually playing from a jukebox. Fare includes fried chicken (US$2.50), hamburger (US$2), Spanish sausage with potato (US$2.50), and various sandwiches. Beers cost $1. It's open 24 hours.

Another bar-cum-restaurant popular with Cubans is **La Lluvia del Oro,** at Obispo #316, on

Try an agropecuario
*(farmer's market)
for self-catering.*

the corner of Calle Habana. La Lluvia is expressive of the rising bohemian life of the city and remains lively into the wee hours (it, and Café Paris, remain the two major pick-up spots for foreign male tourists and flirty *Cubanas*). It serves snack food and pizzas.

Cubans congregate at **Café Habana** on Calle Mercaderes and Amargura; this pleasant little corner coffee shop sells cappuccinos and *cafecitos.*

The patio bar—the **Galeria La Acera del Louvre**—of the Hotel Inglaterra is the best place for coffee or snacks around Parque Central. It serves sandwiches, tortillas, tapas, and burgers (US$3-8), plus desserts and coffees. Service is slow.

Desserts and Ice Cream

Helado Tropical has small outlets throughout Havana, including an air-conditioned outlet at Calle Obispo #467, on the corner of Habana. The ice cream is nowhere near the quality of Coppelia, but quite acceptable.

The **Pasteleria Francesca,** a bakery due north of the Hotel Inglaterra on the west side of Parque Central, sells a marvelous array of confections for US$0.10 upwards. Likewise, you'll also find a bakery—**Panaderia San José**—cater-corner to Café Paris, at Calles Obispo and San Ignacio. It, too, sells a tempting array of confections from US$0.10. A few blocks east is **Dulcería Doña Teresa,** selling custards, ice creams, and other delights.

Self-Catering

The largest *agropecuario* (farmer's market) is **Cuatro Caminos,** in an old Mercado building at Manglar and Cristina (also called Avenida de la Mexico) in the far southwest corner of Habana Vieja. You may not want to buy a pig's head, or live ducks and chickens trussed on a pole, but if these—or herbs, vegetables, and fresh fruit or fish catch your fancy, you're sure to find it here. Watch for pickpockets.

Another large open-air market can be found on Avenida de la Bélgica (Egido) e/ Apodada y Corrales. It has separate section for meats, fish, and produce.

Imported salamis and meats are sold at **La Monserratte,** an air-conditioned butcher shop on Monserrate e/ Brasil y Muralles, near the Egido *agropecuario.*

CENTRO HABANA

Paladares

Private restaurants are few and far between in residential Centro, but ironically the area boasts the best *paladar* in town: **La Guarida,** on the third floor of an 18th-century townhouse on Calle Concordia #418 e/ Gervasio y Escobar, tel. (7) 62-4940. It's a trendy albeit vastly overpriced option that draws the cognoscenti for its cozy bistro ambience suggesting Soho (you may recognize it as a setting for scenes in the Oscar-nominated 1995 movie, *Fresa y Chocolate*).

Don't be put off by the dilapidated, funky staircase. Owners Enrique and Odeysis Nuñez oversee the kitchen that delivers such dishes as fillet of snapper with orange sauce, though portions are meager. Skip the limp Caesar salad (US$6). Wines are served by the half glass. And fries, rice, etc., are all charged extra. Budget US$25 apiece.

Nearby, **Paladar Torresón,** on the Malecón one block west of the Prado, tel. (7) 61-7476, has a balcony offering views along the seafront boulevard. It's fabulous at night, although food is standard *criollo* fare.

Criollo

The **Restaurant Colonial** in the Hotel Lincoln, is one of the better restaurants in Centro and serves a mostly Cuban clientele with soups, fish, shrimp, and chicken dishes for less than US$4. The service is surprisingly swift and conscientious. A pianist tickles the ivories.

Fast Food

El Rápido, Cuba's fried chicken chain, has an outlet on Calzada de Infanta at San Rafael. There's a **Rumbos** snack bar on the Malecón and Padre Varela.

Italian

Try **El Italiano,** at Calzada de Infanta and Allende, an unsophisticated place serving a local Cuban clientele.

Oriental

Barrio Chino boasts a score of restaurants, many staffed by Chinese waitresses in traditional costumes. The most famous is **Restaurante Pacífico,** on Calle San Nicolas, tel. (7) 63-3243, boasting genuine Chinese furniture and Cantonese favorites such as lobster or shrimp chow mein (US$7) and lobster chop suey (US$7). There are restaurants on all five floors, though the main restaurant is on the third. More exclusive guests gather on the fifth (Fidel is an occasional visitor), where Ernest Hemingway used to eat.

Calle Cuchillo is lined its 50-meter length with Chinese restaurants. The best is **Restaurante Tien-Tan,** cellular tel. (7) 80-6198, which offers more than 100 dishes—plus Tsing Tao beer from China. The menu includes such tantalizing offerings as sweet and sour fried fish balls with vinegar and soy (US$7), and pot-stewed liver with seasoning (US$7). This is probably the most genuinely Chinese cuisine in Cuba, and the only place that I've ever had highly spiced food on the island, though it still falls short of Chinese cuisine in New York or San Francisco. Tao, the *jefe,* hails from Shanghai and speaks English. If he befriends you he might offer a rice wine, but it is rough stuff. Stick to beer.

Also on Calle Cuchillo, consider **Restaurante Flamboyan** (entrées for US$1-3), **Restaurant Hueng-Hu** (entrées for US$15-20, though there is nothing special to justify these inordinate prices), and **Restaurant El Gran Dragon.**

The **Casa Abuelo Lung Kong,** at Manrique y Dragones, has a restaurant upstairs open to Cubans (pesos) and tourists (dollars). *Maripositas china* cost 10 pesos; chop suey and other entrées range 10-60 pesos. This is the real McCoy: Chinese staff, Chinese ambience, Chinese patrons.

One block east at Dragones 313 is the **Restaurant Song Sai Li,** tel. (7) 62-2757 with an authentic Chinese ambience in its upstairs restaurant. Balconies offer views along Dragones. It's simple Chinese menu offers *maripositas china* for 10 pesos and chow mein for 43 pesos.

Cafés

La Calesa Cafetería, one block west of Parque Central, on Calle San Rafael, is very popular with Cubans. You can sit in the open air beneath a shady canopy and watch the tide of shoppers flooding down San Rafael.

VEDADO AND PLAZA DE LA REVOLUCIÓN

Breakfast

One of the best buffet breakfasts is served in the **Hotel Cohiba.** Another good option (although the food is ho-hum) is the 24-hour **Café La Rampa,** occupying the terrace outside the Hotel Habana Libre and offering a breakfast special of coffee and toast for US$2, with eggs, bacon, coffee, and juice for US$7. It serves meager American-style breakfasts (US$2-6), plus tortillas (US$2.50-4), and has a breakfast special. The hotel also offers a breakfast buffet (US$9) in its mezzanine restaurant, 7-10 a.m.

Paladares

For creative fare with French-inspired food, try **Le Chansonnier,** at Calle 15 #306 e/ H y I, tel. (7) 32-3788, the best *paladar* in Vedado, where the owners try hard to recreate a French bistro, with simple yet tasty fare such as roasted rabbit in mustard sauce, or cream chicken with wine and mushroom sauce, served with superb french fries. All entrees cost US$10. A full list of French liqueurs is sold. You dine under an arbor in the patio of a handsome colonial home.

And **La Casa,** hidden away at Calle 30 #865 e/ 26 y 41 in Nuevo Vedado, tel. (7) 81-7000, is worth the drive according to *Cigar Aficionado,* which offers this description: "Located in a 1950s-style house with a modish decor, La Casa serves such delicious dishes as fresh prawns sautéed in butter with garlic, and juicy roasted pork with beans and rice."

Another of my favorites is **Paladar El Amor,** on the third floor of an old mansion on Calle 23 e/ B y C, tel. (7) 3-8150. This former mansion of a *condesa* (countess) is full of fading antiques. It is now owned by Amor, a well-known pop singer, and run by members of her family. Try the superb *pescado agridulce* (battered fish pieces with a sweet-and-sour sauce) served with salad and boiled potatoes for US$4.50, or fish leonesa cooked in white wine and onions (US$8.50). You'll dine off real Wedgewood china. Check your bill carefully: I got stiffed!

A steadfast bargain is the tiny **Paladar Restaurant Monguito** on Calle L directly opposite the Hotel Habana Libre and for that reason almost always full. The proprietor, China, serves simple but filling Cuban dishes such as *pollo asado,* grilled fish, and pork dishes (US$3-6).

The once-superb **Paladar Marpoly,** tel. (7) 32-2471, in a colonial home at Calle K #154 (one block north of Linea), has gone downhill. The home is full of religious icons and other intriguing knick-knacks. You can dine in the parlor, or to the rear, where a make-shift *bohio* is roofed in thatch. The creative menu includes a house special of seafood with pineapple and melted cheese served in a pineapple (US$11, with salad and side dishes). Alas, the place has been turned

into a menagerie: watching you eat are two monkeys, a dozen or so exotic dogs, a score of parrots and other birds, and—tragic!—a giant Galapagos turtle tethered to the wall. If ever Cuba offered a surreal dining experience, this is it. Hygiene is now questionable. It's open noon to midnight. It's tricky to get to because of the one-way streets (refer to the map). Look for a house with rust-red pillars and a mural of Santa Barbara on the wall, illumined at night.

A reasonable bet is **El Balcón del Edén,** near Coppelia, on Calle K e/ 19 y 21, tel. (7) 32-9113. It has dining upstairs on an open balcony. Try the superb *marisco enchilada* in spicy tomato sauce (US$10, including accompanying dishes). Servings are plentiful. It's open 24 hours. At night look for the red light illuminating the balcony.

Paladar Nerei at the corner of 19 y I, tel. (7) 32-7860, serves unremarkable but filling soups, tuna salad (US$3.50), spaghettis, grilled fish (US$7.50), calamari (US$8), and *criollo* dishes on a shaded terrace in a colonial home. It has a more wide-ranging menu than most *paladares,* including creative dishes such as duck with onions (US$7.50) and lamb in tomato sauce (US$7.50). Open Mon.-Fri. noon-midnight, and Saturday and Sunday, 6 p.m.-midnight.

Also try **El Bistro,** facing the Malecón at the base of Calle K, tel. (7) 32-2708. It's decorated with tasteful artwork, and you can dine on a balcony. Ostensibly it serves French food; in reality, it's Cuban cuisine with a quasi-French twist, such as *filete Roquefort* (US$12).

A friend recommended **El Helecho,** at Calle 6 e/ Linea y Calle 11, and the **Festivál** at the corner of Calle D and 27, tel. (7) 30-9549. And a reader recommends **Bon Appetit,** at Calle 21 esq. M, tel. (7) 32-2072, near the Hotel Capri; here Ruben Pérez and his family make decent food, with dinners for US$4. **Paladar Yiyo's,** Calle L #256 e/ 17 y 19, tel. (7) 32-8977, on the second floor, is run by a retired doctor and his wife and is recommended by a reader, as is **Restaurante Capitolio,** Calle 13 #1159 e/ 16 y 18, tel. (7) 3-4974.

Criollo

A safe bet is the **Restaurante El Barracón,** in the Hotel Habana Libre Tryp. It serves *criollo* dishes (especially pork dishes such as roast pork; US$12) and more adventurous fare (such as "jerked horsemeat stew" for US$10) in atmospheric surroundings, with entrées US$7-15; open noon-midnight. Setting higher standards is the hotel's top-floor **Sierra Maestra** restaurant, offering splendid views over Havana. Food quality is acceptable at a reasonable price. Diners get free entrance to the Cabaret Turquino.

The **Polinesio,** on Calle 23 and also part of the Hotel Habana Libre Tryp, tel. (7) 33-4011, ext. 131, has plenty of Tahitian-style ambience, and hints of the South Seas find their way subtly into the menu (it used to be a Trader Vic's back in the 1950s). A meal will run upward of US$20, but it offers a lunch special for US$15 with *mariposas chinas,* cheese balls with sweet-and-sour sauce, barbecued chicken (mediocre), plus cocktail, dessert, and coffee. Open noon-midnight.

El Conejito, Calle M #206 esq. Av. 17, tel. (7) 32-4671, is a good option, not least for its Old English or Teutonic ambience. A pianist plays while you dine on rabbit *(conejo)* served any of a dozen ways. Entrées average US$7. It also has fish and lobster dishes. Around the corner is the **Casona del 17,** (formerly the Don Armagemnon) in an old mansion on Calle 17 e/ Calle K y L, tel. (7) 33-4529. It presents a tasty paella (US$7), lobster enchilada (US$10), and such staples as grill fish and pork, to be enjoyed on a breezy outdoor patio or within the a/c room neoclassical building showing off contemporary art on the walls.

Taberna Don Pepe, at San Lazaro and Infanta, is a rustic bodega-style bar and restaurant where simple fare such as pollo frito averages US$2 a plate. And **La Carreta,** next to Coppelia on 21 e/ Calles J y K, offers similarly rustic ambience and simple Cuban fare, mostly to Cubans (in pesos; you'll pay dollars). At the other extreme, the **Wakama,** on Calle O, between La Rampa and Humboldt, and once a famous prerevolutionary nightclub, has been turned into an ascetic restaurant-bar.

Continental

One of my favorite restaurants in Vedado is **La Roca,** on 21 at M, tel. (7) 33-4501, with modern stained-glass windows all around (no views). The French-inspired menu offers such intriguing appetizers as smoked salmon with escovitched grouper (US$7) and apple in red wine (US$3), plus lobster with coconut (US$25), creative

seafood dishes, and pastas for the main course. The house specialty is Bavarian-style lobster. The results are hit-and-miss, but I've enjoyed some of the more pleasing dishes in town here and the service has consistently been good. It has a large wine selection, but the wines are poorly kept and I swear that my house wine—an Italian Chianti—was watered-down. A pianist entertains, and a separate bar has been described as "the sort of place that Dean Martin and Frank Sinatra would have loved." Officially La Roca is open noon-1:45 a.m., but tends to close at midnight.

A good bargain is the classy **Restaurante Monseigneur,** tel. (7) 32-9884, opposite the entrance to the Hotel Nacional at the corner of Calle 21. Its elegant decor—a bit gauche for some tastes—is aided by violin and piano music. The large menu is heavy with seafoods. Entrées are reasonably priced, with shrimp and lobster at US$12, but soups, salads, and tortillas are a bargain at US$2-3. Bring a sweater. If you have a few more bucks to spend, try the acclaimed **Comedor de Aguiar,** in the Hotel Nacional. It serves international cuisine, highlighted by shrimp with rum flambé.

Another elegant, albeit expensive, option is the **Restaurante Hotel Victoria,** at Calles 19 and M. The place is conducive to romance, with lots of hardwoods and brass lamps and gilt place settings. The menu—with an extensive wine list—offers grilled lobster (US$22), roasted snapper (US$12), filet mignon (US$11), and spaghetti with seafood (US$4).

The soaring FOCSA Building, at Calle 17, e/ Calles M y N, boasts two acclaimed restaurants. **El Emperador,** tel. (7) 32-4998, on the ground floor, is favored by Cuban VIPs, but I find its Vincent Price decor—blood-red curtains, Louis XIV-style furnishings, and off-tune pianist—a bit OTT (over the top). It serves soups and tortillas (US$2-4), plus Cuban staples and continental dishes such as filet uruguayano (US$8-25), but has lackluster service. Open 7-11 p.m.

The FOCSA building also boasts the equally costly but far more notable **La Torre,** tel. (7) 55-3089, a rooftop restaurant with splendid all-around views over the city and perhaps the best cuisine in the city. This restaurant has come a long way since iconoclastic French chef Frank Picol took over the kitchen. He's hampered by the difficulty of obtaining fresh ingredients, but his creative menu offers such tempting treats as roasted leg of lamb with garlic and rosemary (US$16), and filete de beef in pastry with onion confilore and red wine (US$27), backed by a large selection of wines. Open noon-midnight (the bar is open 11:30 a.m.-12:30 a.m.). *Recommended!*

An expensive disappointment touted as a dining highlight is **Restaurante 1830,** in a 1920s mansion just east of the Almendares tunnel on Avenida 7ma (Calzada), tel. (7) 33-4521, at the junction with the Malecón. You can choose any of four plush dining rooms with huge bay windows overlooking the ocean. Service is often slow and surly, and the food can be equally bad. Open noon-11 p.m.

Italian
In Vedado, check out the **Terraza Florentino,** the famous rooftop restaurant of the Hotel Capri, at Calle 21 y N, tel. (7) 33-3571. The pastas and risottos are inexpensive and tasty. Try the tangy spaghetti with shrimp in a white wine garlic sauce.

Don't be fooled by the **Terraza Restaurante Italiano Cinecittá,** at Av. 23 y 12. It serves pizzas, sure, but the menu is otherwise *criollo.*

Spanish
First and foremost head to **Centro Vasco,** at the corner of 3ra and 4, tel. (7) 3-9354, near the Meliá Cohiba and Riviera hotels, which was opened by a Basque in 1954 and retains its original modestly elegant decor, including a wall-to-wall mural showing Basque mountain scenes. It claims Basque cuisine, such as escovitched octopus (US$6), paella (US$8.50), and seafoods (US$5-20), but the preparation varies little from the usual Cuban fare.

The **Mesón La Chorrera** in the old fortress at the mouth of the Río Almendares at the west end of the Malecón, tel. (7) 33-4504, also specializes in Spanish cuisine and offers intriguing decor of ancient weaponry on the walls. The **El Cortijo Restaurant** in the Hotel Vedado offers paella and sangria (US$8) and a few other Spanish dishes in its mostly *criollo* menu.

Surf and Turf
The **Steak House Mirador Habana** on the 20th floor of the Hotel Habana Riviera offers all kind of meat dishes, from steaks to sausage, pork, and hams. It has a "Special Steak Porky" for US$10. It's open 6 p.m.-6 a.m.

Cafés and Snack Bars
To call the **Habana Café** either a café or snack bar is to call a Rolls-Royce merely a "car." This is Havana's version of the internationally renowned Hard Rock Café, but with a distinctly Cuban twist. (See the Entertainment section for a description.) It serves tasty and good-sized burgers (from US$5) delivered American-style, with ketchup and mustard, plus sandwiches (US$6.50), Caesar salad (US$7.50), filet mignon (US$17), and such desserts as a banana split (US$5). Entertainers amuse on the stage at lunchtime as well as at night. Entry is free but a *consumo minimo* policy applies (US$5 at the bar; US$10 at a table, per person). Check your bill carefully, as the staff *twice* tried to scam me!

The **Café La Rampa,** outside the Habana Libre, is popular with Cubans and tourists alike. It has a special offer: sandwich or pizza or burger with soft drink for US$5. And the shaded patio of **Las Bulerias** nightclub, facing the Hotel Habana Libre on Calle L, serves *bocaditos, papas fritas* and other simple fare for (US$2-5). **Club Sofia,** on La Rampa at Calle O, is a modern snack bar with windows open to the street.

Café 21, on Calle 21 opposite the Hotel Capri, has a shaded patio and serves sandwiches, tortillas, etc., for a few dollars. The dark, a/c restaurant next door—**Club 21**—has a dress code (no shorts) and serves soups, salads, and *criollo* dishes.

Desserts and Ice Cream
The granddaddy of *heladerias* (ice cream stores) is **Coppelia,** at La Rampa and Calle L in Vedado (catercorner to the Hotel Habana Libre), which serves ice cream in stainless steel bowls and that even last century traveler Albert Norton "thought especially fine" (however, Cubans complain that the quality has deteriorated in recent years). Tourists are usually steered to a dollar-only section, although foreigners are still permitted to pay in pesos in any of half a dozen communal peso sections. Forsake the dollar section and instead join the *cola* (line) to savor your ice cream with the Cubans—a far more rewarding experience. Be prepared for a lengthy

wait on hot days. Although the small dollar section offers the advantage of immediate service, an *ensalada* here costs US$2.60 while the peso sections offer larger *ensaladas* (five scoops) for less than 10% that amount. A *jimagua* (two scoops) costs two pesos, and a *marquesita* (two scoops plus a sponge cage) costs 2.50 pesos. (I could never fathom the pricing, which seems to change day by day.) It's open daily 11 a.m.-11 p.m., closed Monday. (See the special topic, Coppelia, in the Vedado sights section.)

Self-Catering

There's an *agropecuario* (farmer's market) selling fruits and vegetables at Calle 19, e/ F y Avenida de los Presidentes, and a much smaller one at Calle 21 esq. J.

There's a grocery stocking Western goods, plus a bakery, on the north side of the FOCSA building, on Calle 17 e/ M y N.

PLAYA (MIRAMAR AND BEYOND)

Paladares

My favorite here is the well-known **La Cocina de Lillam,** at Calle 48 #1311 e/ 13 y 15, offering consistently tasty Cuban fare with a creative twist—call it nouvelle Cuban. Lillam, who is superattentive, conjures up splendid appetizers such as a tuna-and-onion tartlet and a chick pea-and-onion dish with three types of ham, plus fresh fish dishes and oven-roasted meats. You can opt to dine in the plant-filled garden or in the a/c dining room. Budget US$5-15 apiece.

Likewise, try **Paladar La Fuente,** in an atmospheric old mansion with mezzanine terrace at Calle 10 #303 e/ Aves. 3ra y 5ta, tel. (7) 29-2836. It specializes in fish dishes with cheese and ham, including *filete uruguayano* (US$6). The portions are huge, the preparation is creative, and the food tasty and filling.

Nearby is **Restaurante Calle 10,** in a floodlit mansion on Calle 10 e/ 3ra y 5ta tel. (7) 29-6702. The menu includes ho-hum pizza (US$2), filete uruguayano (US$7), and fish with ham and cheese (US$5.50).

The **Paladar Vistamar,** at 1ra #2206, between 22 and 24, is popular. It serves continental fare as well as Cuban staples in a modern house on the seafront. Likewise, **Paladar Ris-**

torante El Palio at 1ra #2402, one block west at the corner of 24, serves Italian-*criollo* cuisine and is one of the most popular *paladares* in town for elite Cubans. Pastas, fettucines, and seafood dishes average US$5. You dine on a shaded patio to the rear, with suitably Italian decor. No telephone. It's open noon-midnight.

One of the best private options is **Paladar La Esperanza,** tel. (7) 22-4361, opposite the Hotel ICEMAR on Calle 16, between 3ra and 5ra; it's open daily (except Thursday) 8 a.m.-4 p.m. and 7-11:30 p.m.

Criollo

I find myself returning time and again to **El Aljibe,** Av. 7ma, e/ 24 y 26, tel. (7) 24-1583, serving the best Cuban fare in town. It has recently been discovered by tour groups, but is also popular with the Havana elite and foreign businessmen showing off their beautiful Cuban girlfriends. This atmospheric charmer is run by Sergio and Pepe García Macías, former owners of the famous prerevolutionary Rancho Humo restaurant. You dine beneath a soaring bamboo roof. The superb house dish, the *pollo asado el aljibe,* is standard, but far from ordinary—glazed with a sauce the ingredients of which are closely guarded, then baked and served with fried plantain chips, rice, french fries, and black beans served liberally until you can eat no more. Feel free to take away what may be left over. It's a bargain at US$12 (desserts and beverages cost extra). Other *criollo* dishes are served (US$10-20). For dessert, try the flan, coconut pie, or chocolate cake. Check your bill carefully, however—the bread and salad side dish delivered to your table will be charged to your bill even if you didn't order it, and a 10% service charge is automatically billed. The service is prompt and ultra-efficient (even when the tour groups are in), so feel free to tip extra. It's open noon-midnight,

Next to El Aljibe, at Calle 26, is the Dos Gardenias complex, tel. (7) 24-2353, a restored colonial mansion with the modest **Restaurante Criollo.** You can enjoy a whole meal for US$4, including bread, salad, beer (or refresco) and main course of chicken, *aporreodo de ternera,* or *picadillos à la criolla.* Soups and salads—a plate of cucumber—cost US$1. Dos Gardenias is open noon-midnight and offers chilly a/c interior or outdoor patio dining.

A more expensive option is the **Ranchón,** at Av. 5ta esq. 16, tel. (7) 24-1185, acclaimed as one of Havana's best restaurants, although it serves traditional Cuban cooking, notably grilled fish and meats (the grilled pork chops are particularly good). More creative dishes include a delicious appetizer of stuffed red peppers with tuna. Chef Juan Luís Rosalas prepares a daily special, from roast beef to lamb chops. It has good mixed salads. The food is well prepared and the portions are huge. Open noon-midnight. Don't confuse it with El Ranchón Palco.

El Ranchón Palco, Av. 19 y Calle 140, tel. (7) 23-5838, in jungly surroundings in the heart of the tony residential district of Cubanacán, is a handsome, open-sided *bohio* with terra-cotta floor, Tiffany-style lamps at the tables, and decor featuring saddles, umbrellas pendant from the thatch roof, and wooden toucans and parrots on swings. An octagonal bar pins its heart. You can opt to dine on a patio or beneath thatch, or in a separate, more elegant dining room. It serves meat dishes (US$10-30) and seafoods (US$12-26), and the usual *criollo* fare, but the food is undistinguished at best; canned vegetables, frozen fries, and your standard grilled fare, for example. It offers floor shows at night. Managed by the Palacio de Convenciones, it is popular among the government elite.

La Estancia Restaurant adjoins the Hotel Biocaribe, tel. (7) 33-7835, and offers a variety of frigid a/c rooms in an elegant colonial mansion. I prefer the tables arrayed around the intimate courtyard. It serves *criollo* fare, plus boneless chicken (US$8), filet mignon (US$12), and such rarities as blood sausage (US$2) and tuna salad (US$4). It offers a lunch and dinner special (US$14 and US$20) ·

Seafood

Don Cangrejo, Av. 1ra, e/ 16 y 18, tel. (7) 24-4169, offers some of the finest seafood in town (it should; it's overseen by the Ministry of Fisheries), served in a converted colonial mansion with glass windows offering views over the flagstone patio—good on calm days for alfresco dining—toward the Straits of Florida. The large menu features such appetizers as crab cocktail (US$6), crab-filled wontons (US$3), plus such house specialties as crab claws (US$15), garlic shrimp (US$12.50), plus paella, lobster, and fish

dishes. However, the canned vegetables are dismaying! The wine list runs to more than 150 labels, and René Garcia is one of the few professional wine waiters in town. It's popular with the dollar-bearing Cuban elite and has been described as "a take on Joe's Stone Crab in Miami."

Argentinian

Meat lovers might try **La Pampa,** in the Hotel Comodoro, Av. 3ra y Calle 84 in Miramar, tel. (7) 33-2028, fax (7) 33-1168. It specializes in Argentinian dishes such as *morcillas* (blood sausage) and *chinchulines* (grilled tripe stuffed with garlic).

Continental

A real treat is **La Giraldilla,** at Calle 222, e/ 37 y 51, tel. (7) 33-0568, fax (7) 33-6390, in the La Coronela district of La Lisa. It serves recherché nouvelle dishes under the baton of a French chef and management. Choose from a selection of dining rooms, including a Spanish *bodega* serving tapas and wines, the **Bistro Gourmet,** with a stunning beamed ceiling and National Heritage furnishings, and an Italian pizzeria and outside grill. It offers a US$30 dinner special, including rum and cabaret. Prices are reasonable. I enjoyed a superb creamed vegetable soup (US$4), sautéed prawns in garlic (US$17), and sautéed salmon (US$19). It's popular with Cuban models and political elite, who also flock for the bar, disco, and cabaret. A cigar store and Las Vegas-style cabaret followed by Havana's best disco guarantee postprandial pleasures.

The elegant a/c **Villa Diana** on Calle 28A in Reparto Kohly, tel. (7) 24-9232, ext. 621, offers an all-you-can-eat buffet for US$12. The fare, which claims to be continental, is really *criollo* with a hint of Europe. It has live music and is popular with Cubans. It's open noon-6 a.m.

Prepare yourself for sticker shock if you dine at **Tocororo,** housed in a neoclassical mansion on the corner of Calle 18 y Av. 3ra, tel. (7) 33-4530. This exquisite restaurant—an elitist luxury where ordinary Cubans can't even think of setting foot—is known as Gabriel García Márquez's favorite eatery (the Colombian novelist is known for his fondness for fine food, but here seems to have missed the beat). The walls bear the signatures of the rich and famous, although the reputation for fine food is undeserved. More fulfilling is the decor. The lobby is a cross between a museum, an art gallery, and a middle-class Victorian parlor full of rich treasures. Tocororo extends out into a garden patio—a delightfully tropical and relaxed place to eat, replete with rattan furniture, Tiffany lamps, and heaps of potted plants, painted wooden toucans and parrots hanging from gilt perches, and real *cotorros* (parrots) in cages. A pianist and a jazz ensemble entertain. The food is typical Cuban fare with an international twist. Or is it international with a *criollo* twist? Try the grilled lamb chops and mixed seafood brochette and local favorites such as *frijoles*. But it ain't worth the outrageous price (expect to pay from US$25 for a run-of-the-mill grilled steak; and watch for the 10% service charge), and the wines, reputedly, are "normally in bad condition." Open noon-midnight.

A less-expensive option is **La Cecilia,** Av. 5ta #11010 e/ 110 y 112, tel. (7) 33-1562, 22-6700, another elegant and romantic restored mansion in the middle of a large garden. Most of the tables are outdoors and lit by Tiffany lamps surrounded by bamboo. It serves typical Cuban dishes such as *tasajo* (jerked beef), *churrasco* (broiled steak), and *pollo con mojo* (chicken with onion and garlic), as well as grilled lobster. Entrées range US$10 and up. The place has a lengthy wine list at reasonable prices. At night it hosts a *cabaret espectáculo.* Open noon-midnight (and Thurs.-Sun. 9:30 p.m.-3 a.m. for cabaret).

In a similar vein is **La Ferminia,** at Av. 5ta #18207 e/ 182 y 184, tel. (7) 21-0360, in a house full of anthuriums, chandeliers and antiques. It has six private rooms, each in a separate color scheme (the pink room is full of Meissen porcelain), and you can also dine on an outside patio beneath a timbered roof. The menu includes soups (US$3), grilled chicken (US$8), and fish dishes (US$12); the house specialty is a mixed grill (US$28) with shrimp, lobster, fish, chicken, and scallops. (The chefs, alas, have learned their vegetable preparation from the English—boiled to death.) Open noon-midnight.

If you'd like to watch a fashion show while you dine, try the touristy **La Maison,** Av. 7ma y Calle 16, tel. (7) 33-1543 or 33-0126. It offers a series of packages that include dinner; the cheapest is US$25 without alcohol. Open Mon.-Sat. 7 p.m.-1 a.m.

Italian

The **Ristorante Gambinas** in the Dos Gardenias complex, Av. 7ma y 26, offers undistinguished pizzas, spaghettis, and raviolis for less than US$5. Take your sweater! Nearby, the Quinta y 42 commercial complex houses the flashy looking **Ristorante Italiano Rossini.**

For pizza check out the **El Tucano** snack bar in the Hotel Copacabana. It's nothing to write home about, but the pizzas (average US$5) are the best I've had in Havana. Try the vegetarian pizza. It also has a buffet lunch for US$15. Alternately, try the **Pizzeria La Pérgola** in the Club Almandares on Avenida 49C in Reparto Kohly, where you can dine alfresco under an arbor or inside, where the a/c is cranked up (open noon-midnight).

By some accounts, **La Cova Pizza Nova,** in Marina Hemingway, Av. 5ta y 248, tel. (7) 24-1150, has the best pizza in town.

Oriental

Your best bet is **Pavo Real,** Av. 7ma #205, e/ Calle 2 y 4, tel. (7) 24-2315, a little corner of China. Look for the huge Chinese neon sign outside. It also boasts Chinese decor, including art deco stained-glass doors. It serves undistinguished classics such as chow mein dishes for US$7 and up, plus Japanese tempura (US$9 and up), and Thai chicken (US$6.50). Try the spring rolls. Open noon-midnight.

A better bargain is the **Fonda China,** in Los Gardenias, Av. 7ma y Calle 26. I recommend the chop suey de camarones (US$8). Entrées are US$4-9, complete meals US$8-10.

Hankering for grilled eels, *kim ch'i, chu'sok,* and other Korean specialties? Then head to **El Morambón,** Av. 5ta y 32, tel. (7) 23-3336. The cuisine is lackluster and overpriced, but you can eat it until 2 a.m.

Cafés and Snack Bars

Miramar lacks cafés. The **Parrillada La Fuente,** abutting the Casa de la Música on Calle 20 between 33 and 35, has an outdoor snack bar with shade trees; sandwiches and burgers cost below US$2, and fried chicken, steaks, and fish dishes run to US$16.

Desserts

You can buy delicious pastries, loaves, and iced cakes at **Nonaneli Pandería Dulcería,** a bakery in the Quinta y 42 complex at Av. 5ta y Calle 42.

Self-Catering

The huge *supermercado* on Avenida 3ra y Calle 72 (100 meters east of Hotel Triton) in Miramar is Cuba's largest supermarket. It's like walking into a Safeway and has all the same Western consumer goods (at a hefty markup). It also has Cuba's best stock of fresh vegetables and fruits, canned goods, and other food items.

SUBURBS

Restaurants are listed below by region, rather than by type of fare as above.

Boyeros (El Chico)

La Rueda, tel. (684) 25, a rustic yet acclaimed restaurant on a Ministry of Agriculture goose farm, on the Carretera de Guajay, at Calle 294 in the village of El Chico. Not surprisingly, the menu offers goose-this and goose-that. Accompany your *foie gras* with the house cocktail of rum and fruit juice. Set meals cost US$20. Despite its distance from the city, the place gets full. Reservations are recommended. Cockfights are hosted. Open noon-8 p.m.

Boyeros (Santiago de las Vegas)

The nicest place is **La Tabernita,** a *complejo turístico* (tourist complex) on Doble Vía Cacahual, tel. (683) 2033, on the main road to Cacahual, at the south end of town. It has a thatched restaurant serving *criollo* fare and is popular with Cuban families on weekends. In a similar vein is **Rincón Criollo,** about one km south of town, amid pine trees.

In town, try the **Mozambique Cafetería,** on the northeast corner of the town plaza.

Arroyo Naranjo (Parque Lenin)

The park boasts the noted **Las Ruinas** restaurant, tel. (7) 44-3336. It's well worth the drive, if only to admire the fabulous decor and setting. The building, which looks like something Frank Lloyd Wright might have conceived, was designed in concrete encasing the ruins of an old sugar mill, with remnant free-standing walls overgrown with epiphytes and mosses (however, in communist fashion it is also designed without any thought for patrons' safety; beware the lip at the top of the stairs, which have no guard rails). Downstairs is a bar and modestly elegant restaurant where a pianist plays and the tables are lit by Tiffany lamps. Upstairs features stained-glass panels by the Cuban artist Portocarrero and louvered wooden French windows all around. Decor is elegant, with linens, silverware, classical urns full of flowers, and dozens of crystal chandeliers. It describes itself as serving international haute cuisine (lobster Bellevue—US$20—is a specialty). The food has been described by readers as both "reminiscent of school dinners" and "the best in Havana." I enjoyed a tasty shrimp *enchilada* (US$12). Other dishes include pizzas (US$4.50), blue cheese soup (US$2), shrimp brochette (US$12), and grilled fish uruguayano (US$11).

The **Restaurante Herradura** at the Centro Ecuestre, offers a pleasant a/c ambience and serves garlic shrimp, pizzas, lobster, and *criollo* dishes for US$4-20. Abutting it is an outdoor grill—**La Rueda Parrillada**—with a pleasant patio.

The Mexican-style former home of the estate owner now houses a small and pleasing restaurant, the **Parillada 1740,** next to the Galeria de Arte. There are several other snack bars serving *bocaditos,* fried chicken, and the like. For a resuscitating fresh-squeezed cane juice, head to the **guarapera** opposite the entrance to El Rodeo.

Arroyo Naranjo
(ExpoCuba and Jardín Botánico)

A fistful of restaurants and cafés provide refreshment at ExpoCuba. The best is the elegant **Don Cuba Restaurant,** built around an inner courtyard with neoclassical Roman-cum-Arabic architecture. Flautists and singers perform in the courtyard. I enjoyed a tasty grilled fish with rice and spiced vegetables (US$8).

The **Bambú Restaurant** overlooks the Japanese garden in the botanical garden. It bills itself as an "eco-restorán" and sells ice creams and sodas. I've not eaten here, but it is considered as the best—perhaps the only—vegetarian restaurant in Havana. It serves lunch only: Wed.-Sun, noon-3 p.m.

Regla

There are plenty of basic eateries to choose from, though nothing stands out. Most are concentrated along Martí. Two pleasant restaurants sit on the southwest corner of Parque Guaycanamar, where an ice cream shop can help you beat the heat, and **Pizzeria Puerto Bello** in on the southeast corner. At Calle Martí and Pereira is a small bar, **La Casa del Daiquirí,** selling daiquiris for a few pesos.

Guanabacoa

Pickings are slim. Try **Pizzería Bambino,** on the northwest corner of the main plaza, where there're also **Coppelia** and **Helado Tropical** outlets for ice cream. You're best bet is **Paladar La Pastorita,** on Calle 18 #21, tel. (7) 97-3732, in Reparto Guiteras (also known as the Bahía district) of northern Guanabacoa, serving huge portions.

Ciudad Panamericano

On the main street, **Steak House Toro,** tel. (7) 33-8545, offers clean, modern, a/c surrounds and serves rib steak, filet mignon, T-bone steak, etc., and has an all-you-can-eat roast beef special for US$10. The village's other eateries are all dreary affairs, if not in decor then in their menus. That of the hotel's **Restaurante Trópical** features soups (US$2), lobster and shrimp (US$13-21), and chicken roasted in fruit juices (US$6); breakfast at the hotel's buffet is a lackluster affair. **Restaurante Allegro** offers pizzas and spaghetti for US$3-5, and **Restaurant Beit-Jing** makes a pitiful stab at Chinese food.

For ice-cream desserts and shakes, head for the **Cremería,** 20 meters uphill from Tapatio. The **coffee shop** one block west of the hotel has a cool patio and is the hippest place to hang. A bakery is on the main street, 20 meters downhill from the hotel.

Cojímar

At **La Terraza** the food is good, with a wide-ranging menu that includes paella (US$7), grilled shrimp and fish (US$22), fish cocktail (US$2.50), shrimp cocktail (US$8). Open noon-11 p.m. The bar is open 10:30 a.m.-11 p.m.

If you're feeling impecunious, there's a good paladar—**Restaurante Claro de Luna**—a few blocks north of the Hemingway statue. And the basic **El Torreón** serves unremarkable criollo fare.

Tarará

At the west end of Tarará, **Restaurante Cojímar,** next to the marina office, serves basic criollo fare, as does a handsome, thatched restaurant immediately west of the swimming pool near the marina. A juice bar serves the east end of the beach, where there's also a restaurant 100 meters inland.

Prefer Chinese? Try **Restaurante El Chino** on the Via Monumental at the turn-off for Tarará.

Playas del Este (Santa María del Mar)

Most of the hotels have uninspired restaurants. Several thatched bars and eateries can be found on the beach, including two rustic places serving basic criollo fare in front of the Hotel Tropicoco. **Bar/Restaurante Bonanza,** on Playa Santa María, has a patio bar and modestly elegant indoor dining, too. You'll pay upward of US$5 for seafoods and fried chicken dishes. It also has burgers and pizza noon-5 p.m. Dinner is served 6-9:45 p.m.

Another beach option is the **D'Prisa Centro Turístico,** at the west end of Playa El Mégano, with a thatched bar and grill. **Mi Casita de Coral,** 100 meters east of the Hotel Tropicoco, serves criollo fare 24 hours daily. Likewise **Casa Club Atlántico** has a snack bar offering seafoods, criollo dishes, and spaghettis (US$3.50), plus a chicken oferta especial (lunch special) for US$2. **Costarenas Parrillada,** overlooking the beach on Avenida Norte, serves inexpensive grilled fare.

Pizzeria Mi Rinconcito, towards the west end of Avenida de las Terrazas, offers slices of pizza from US$1. Also catering to Italian tastes is **Pizzeria Yara,** Avenida las Terrazas y Calle 10, (the latter has its own swimming pool). **Café Pinomar,** Av. Sur y Calle 5, also serves pizzas and burgers and is open 24 hours.

For a breeze-swept view over the beach scene, head uphill to the **Restaurante Mirador del Mar,** Calle 11, e/ Aves. 1ra y 3ra.

Playas del Este (Boca Ciega and Guanabo)

El Bodegón, on 1ra in Boca Ciega, is a simple seafront restaurant with criollo fare served on a breeze-swept patio. Two blocks east is the handsome, thatched **Los Caneyes** open 24 hours, and also serving *criollo* dishes.

The most atmospheric place in Boca Ciega is **Casa del Pescador,** Av. 5ta esq. 442, a Spanish-style bodega. It has fishing nets hanging from the ceiling. Fish dishes average US$7, and shrimp and lobster start at US$8. The house specialty is *escabeche* (US$3.50). It's open 10 a.m.-10 p.m.

In Guanabo, the simple **D'Prisa Cafeteria La Barca,** Av. 5ta y 448, is popular with Cuban locals, perhaps for its stained glass windows as its *criollo* fare is undistinguished. Another **D'Prisa Cafeteria,** Av. 5ta y 476, is a modish, pocket-size place serving sandwiches and basic Italian dishes from US$1.

One of the nicer eateries is **El Brocal,** Av. 5ta C esq. 500, in eastern Guanabo. This red-tile-roofed restaurant offers rustic ambience for enjoying simple *criollo* fare. And nearby **Pizzeria Italiano Piccolo,** 504 y Av. 1ra, likewise offers colonial ambience near the shore.

Five km south of town, Rumbos' **Hacienda Guanabito** and **Mi Rancho Hacienda,** about 400 meters farther south, serve *criollo* food.

The sparse **Cuanda's,** 474 y Av. 5ta, serves salads for US$0.80, rice dishes from US$1, and pastas for US$4.

For ice cream, head to the **Heladería El Betty,** Av. 5ta y Calle 480. There's a **bakery** next door.

ENTERTAINMENT AND RECREATION

Don't believe anything you've read about communism having killed the capital city's zest. Habaneros love to paint the town red (so to speak). You can still find as much partying as party line in Havana—a city of spontaneity and the undisputed cultural epicenter of the Caribbean, especially in the realm of music, although restrictions imposed by police in recent years put a severe damper on Havana's nightlife for locals, who were forced to be more creative, which means that the birth rate will leap upward.

At night, the pace quickens and Havana pulsates with the Afro-Latin spirit, be it energy-charged musical sessions or the sacred chantings of *santería.* Nowhere else in the Caribbean has as many discotheques, cinemas, and cabarets to choose from. Sure, the city has lost the Barbary Coast spirit of prerevolutionary days, when, according to Graham Greene, "three pornographic films were shown nightly between nude dances" in the Shanghai Theater. Most of the famous clubs from the "sordid era," which ended in the 1950s, remain in name, their neon signs reminders of what was. Many—those still used by Cubans—are more seedy in decay (albeit without the strippers) than they were four decades ago, and often made more surreal because in many the decor hasn't changed.

During the 1980s, Havana was a rest-and-relaxation capital for the Latin Left. It is still popular with South Americans, who flock for the Latin American Film Festival and other world-class annual cultural extravaganzas, or to polish their reputations as lovers. Ballet is much appreciated by Habaneros. Each region has a *Casa de la Trova,* where you can hear traditional ballad-style *trova* (love songs rendered with the aid of guitar and drum), often blended with revolutionary themes; and a *Casa de la Cultura,* where movies, art exhibitions, and other cultural events are hosted. And Havana has ongoing music concerts, choral recitals, and art and sculpture exhibits. The only fault to be found is the quality of theater, although there's plenty of comedy theater.

On the bar scene, a fistful of atmospheric spots recall the heyday of the 1950s, such as Dos Hermanos, La Bodeguita del Medio, and El Floridita, all haunted by Hemingway's ghost. Hip cigar lounges, trendy bistro-bars, and take-offs on the internationally-renowned Hard Rock Café are beginning to blossom (Gato Tuerto and the Habana Café come to mind). Overall, however, the bar scene is dull. The city is devoid of the lively sidewalk bars that make Rio de Janeiro buzz and South Beach hum. Most major hotels have bars: some, such as the lobby bar of the Hotel Ambos Mundos, are splendid. Most bars have live music, everything from salsa bands to folkloric trios. Romantic crooners are a staple, wooing local crowds with dead-on deliveries of Beny Moré classics while sensual all-female bands woo tourists with the ubiquitous *"Beseme, beseme mucho. . ."* and the "Che song"—*"Querido Comandante Guevara/La transparencia de su presencia. . ."* Take your pick between dollars-only haunts, where liquors will set you back at least US$3 a pop, to grim local bars where *one peso* will buy a beer. Havana also offers earthy discos (called cabarets) and *centros nocturnos,* open-air discotheques, often with laser light shows, serving the locals, who in 1999 had (with the exception of Cuba's nouveau riche) been driven from tourist spots by high dollar prices.

The scene is fluid. Many venues herein described may have closed or be operating on a threadbare budget due to the Special Period; others, to which entrance was once free, now charge.

More and more clubs and discos have begun to apply a minimum charge policy *(consumo minimo),* which sometimes applies to the entire evening and sometimes to the first purchase. Watch out for abuses: for example, if a US$5 *consumo mínimo* applies for your first purchase and you order several beverages during the evening, be sure that the first drink you order is a more expensive drink—you'll be charged US$5 even for a mineral water—and that any inexpensive item you might order later in the evening doesn't get reversed and appear as the first drink on your bill.

Resources
The best resource is *Guia Cultural de la Habana,* published monthly by Centro de Desarrollo y Comunicación Cultural (CREART), Calle 4 #205, e/ Linea 11, Vedado, tel. (7) 32-9691, fax (7) 66-2562. It provides up-to-date information on what's-on in town. You can pick up free copies at tour desks in leading hotels.

The weekly newspaper *Cartelera* publishes similar information on exhibitions, galleries, and performances. It's available in many hotel lobbies. *Granma,* the daily Communist Party newspaper, also lists the forthcoming week's events.

And the Ministry of Culture sponsors a bimonthly magazine, *Revolución y Cultura,* containing interviews, fiction, poetry, essays, photography and profiles on the arts, plus news on cultural events. It is hard to come by today (past issues—US$3 each—can be obtained from the Center for Cuban Studies.

Dance classes for the casual tourist are offered at the Hotel Lincoln on Tuesday, 4-6 p.m. Alternately give Gilberto Capote, Calle O'Reilly #362, Apto. 6, 3ra piso (third floor) e/ Habana y Compostela, tel. (7) 61-7080. He's been recommended as a one-on-one dance instructor.

FESTIVALS AND EVENTS

The Special Period took its toll on popular festivals, cultural celebrations, and *cumbanchas,* the Cuban equivalent of street parties or sprees that might go on all night, with plenty of saucy rumba and saucier females to dance the hip-shaking rumba with. Fortunately, festival life is rebounding.

Religious parades are very few. The noted exception is the **Procession of the Miracles** each 17 December, when hundreds of pilgrims—many of them dragging stones or crawling on their knees—make their way to the Santuário de San Lazaro, the "leper of the miracles," to give thanks to the saint (known as Babalu Aye in *santería*) for miracles they imagine she has granted. The sanctuary, a national monument, is at Rincón, southwest of Havana, on the outskirts of Santiago de las Vegas. See the Sightseeing chapter.

For a list of forthcoming, conferences, and events, contact **Paradiso** (see Resources, above), or the **Palacio de Convenciones,** Calle 146, e/ 11 y 13, Playa, tel. (7) 22-6011, fax (7) 21-9496, e-mail: palco@palco.get.cma.net. The Cuban Convention Bureau, Edificio Focsa, Calle M, e/ 17 y 19, Vedado, Havana, tel. (7) 31-3600, fax (7) 33-4261, e-mail: burocon@buroconv. mit.cma.net, website: www.buroconv.cubaweb. cu, publishes an annual catalog listing events, fairs, and festivals.

Daily Events
Be sure to attend the **Ceremonia del Cañonazo** (Cannon Ceremony), held nightly at 9 p.m. at the Castillo de San Carlos de la Cabaña (see the Sightseeing chapter), when troops dressed in 18th-century military garb light the fuse of a cannon to announce the closing of the city gates, maintaining a tradition going back centuries. You are greeted at the castle-gates by soldiers in traditional uniform, and the place is lit by flaming lanterns. Very atmospheric! About 8:50 p.m. a cry rings out announcing the procession of soldiers who march across the Plaza bearing muskets, while a torch-bearing lights flaming barrels. The sol-

diers ascend to the cannon, which they prepare with ram-rod, etc. (Latter-day soldiers have pre-prepared the explosives and are on hand to guard the show.) When the soldier puts the torch to the cannon you have about three seconds before the thunderous boom. Your heart skips a beat, but it's all over in a millisecond and the troops promptly march off.

You can visit on your own; your US$3 entrance to the castles includes the ceremony and museums. Be sure to get there no later than 8:30 p.m. if you wish to secure a seat close to the cannon. The ceremony is popular with Cuban families and the place gets jam-packed. Latecomers (there are usually several hundred) are relegated to the lawns or the roof a good distance away.

You can book excursion tours from any hotel tour desk. Several tour agencies combine an excursion to witness the *cañonazo*. For example, Tours & Travel, tel. (7) 24-9200 or 24-9199 in Miramar, tel. (7) 24-7541 in Vedado, charges US$15 (or US$25 with dinner). Some agencies combine the ceremony with a cabaret.

Weekly Events

The place to be on Sunday at noon is **Salvador's Alley** (officially known as Callejon de Hamel), e/ Aramburo y Hospital, a narrow alley linking Calzada de Infanta and San Lazaro in Cerro. Here, Salvador González Escalona, tel. (7) 78-1661, e-mail: callejondehamel@hotmail.com, hosts a *rumba* each Sunday at noon, with exotic music and dance in an alley painted from pavement to sky in gaudy tropical murals. González also hosts a traditional music night every last Friday of the month at 8:30 p.m., plus a children's program the third Saturday of each month at 10 a.m.

Monthly Events

Habaguanex puts on the **Noche en la Plaza de la Catedral** on the third or fourth Saturday of every month. It's a glorious evening in the plaza, when a *criollo* dinner is served and a folkloric *espectáculo* takes place on the steps of the cathedral. The wide-ranging entertainment includes the Conjunto Folklórico JJ, ballet, and *boleros* (ballads). Tickets cost US$30 and can be booked in advance at tour agencies throughout the city; at the Restaurante El Patio in the plaza,

tel. (7) 57-1034; or at Habaguanex's office at Calle Oficios #110, e/ Lamparilla y Amargura, tel. (7) 33-8693, fax (7) 33-8697, website: www.habaguanexc.cubaweb.cu/habaguan.hml.

Annual Events

January: Recently reintroduced to kick off the year is the **Cabildos** festival on 6 January, when the streets of Habana Vieja resound with festivities recalling the days when Afro-Cuban *cabildos* danced through the streets in vivid costumes and painted faces. Contact the City Historian's office at Calle Tacon #1, tel. (7) 33-8183; or Habaguanex (see above).

February: The star-studded annual **International Havana Jazz Festival** is held in mid-February, highlighted by the greats of Cuban jazz, such as Chucho Valdés and Irakere, Los Van Van, Juan Formell, Silvio Rodríguez, and Grupo Perspectiva. Concerts are held in the Hotel Riviera's Salón Internacional (formerly the Palacio de Salsa), the Casa de Cultura de Plaza (an open-air courtyard with bleacher seating at Calzada #909 esq. 8, in Vedado, tel. 7-31-2003), and at José Echeverría Stadium, which hosts the All Stars Concert. You can buy tickets in pesos at the Casa de Cultura. Prearranged group tours to the festival are offered through **Caribbean Music and Dance Programs,** 12545 Olive St. #241, St. Louis, MO 63141, tel. (314) 542-3637 or toll-free (877) 665-4321, fax (314) 469-2916, e-mail: caribmusic@igc.apc.org, website: www.caribmusic.com. **Wings of the World,** 1200 William St. #706, Buffalo, NY 14240-0706; or 1636 Third Ave. #232, New York, NY 10128, tel. (800) 465-8687, fax (416) 486-4001, also offers an annual weeklong tour to the festival. Both programs include jazz workshops and reserved seating at jazz concerts.

Carnaval in Havana! was revived in 1995 after a five-year hiatus. Held in mid-February, thousands of Habaneros take to the streets. For an entire week, the Malecón becomes a stage for the island's hottest folkloric, salsa, and jazz groups. Tourists throw inhibitions to the wind and join local residents in colorful pre-Lenten revelry as traditional *comparsas*—music and dance troupes originally tied to slaves' tribe of origin—parade through the streets. The party mood is highlighted by outdoor concerts, street fairs, conga lines, and colorful parades. While many folks go lavishly gowned, others ecstatically flaunt their freedom, having cast off customary controls along with most of their clothing. For information, contact Roberto Labrada, tel. (7) 62-3883, fax (7) 33-5135, e-mail: rosalla @cimex.com.cu. Caribbean Music & Dance Programs (see above) offers seven-day group study programs to Carnival.

Literati and bookworms should time their visit to coincide with the **Havana Book Fair,** also held in February, organized by the Cuban Book Institute and the Cuban Book Chamber. For information, contact either the Center for Cuban Studies or Cámara Cubana del Libro, Feria Internacional del Libro Habana, Calle 15 #604, Vedado, Havana, Cuba, tel. (7) 32-9526, fax (7) 33-8212.

April: April 4 is the **Day of Children,** when various venues throughout the city host special entertainment for kids.

May: When 1 May rolls around, Habaneros head to the Plaza de la Revolución for the **May Day Parade.** Supposedly the day is meant to honor workers and is intended to appear as a spontaneous demonstration of revolutionary loyalty, although in reality it is a carefully choreographed affair and scores of buses bring workers and children from surrounding regions. Cuban stooges use loudspeakers to work up the crowd with chants of "Viva Fidel!" The military parade of yesteryear has been replaced; in recent years the overriding theme has reflected the political flavor of the day (thus the 1999 parade was heavily imbued with denunciations of NATO's bombing campaign in Yugoslavia). You'll be surrounded by as many as 200,000 people waving colorful banners and placards and wearing T-shirts painted with revolutionary slogans, and everyone eager for a glimpse of Fidel, who applauds lightly in saintly fashion. The disaffected scoff and stay at home.

Each May the city hosts the prestigious **Havana Biennale,** hosted by the Centro Wilfredo Lam, on San Ignacio, tel. (7) 61-2096 and 61-3419, fax (7) 33-8477, e-mail: wlam@ artsoft .cult.cu. The show features artists from more than 50 countries around the world and is hosted in almost two dozen venues throughout Habana Vieja. Practical workshops in printmaking and other disciplines are offered, as well as soirées and other activities.

The **Havana Cup** is an annual boat race from Florida to Havana and goes back to 1930 (with a respite 1960-94, when it was revived). In 1999 some 250 yachts competed from Tampa to Havana's Marina Hemingway.

June: The **International Boleros Festival** (Festival Internacional Boleros de Oro) is held in June and is sponsored by UNEAC, the National Union of Writers and Artists of Cuba, and featuring traditional Cuban folk music.

July: The **International Hemingway Colloquium** takes place in early July every two years. Contact Danilo Arrate, at the Cuban tour operator Paradiso, tel./fax (7) 55-8015.

August: Every second August (odd years) sees the **Festival Internacional de Música Popular Beny Moré,** named for the popular Cuban composer-singer referred to as *lo mas barbaro del ritmo* ("the guy with the most terrific rhythm") and featuring a panorama of popular Cuban music. The festival takes place in Havana concurrently with events in Cienfuegos.

September: The biennial **International Theater Festival of Havana** is sponsored by the National Council of Scenic Arts and features international theater companies covering drama, street theater, musicals, and contemporary and traditional dance.

October: The annual **Havana Festival of Contemporary Music** traditionally spans a week in early October. Venues include the Teatro Nacional, Gran Teatro, La Casa de las Américas, the Basilica de San Francisco de Asís, with a focus on chorale and orchestral works by Cuban and international performers.

The **International Festival de Ballet** is an established part of the annual calendar, and in 1998 dancers and choreographers from more than 26 countries—including from the Bolshoi, the New York City Ballet, and Opera de Paris—helped the Ballet Nacional de Cuba celebrate its 50th anniversary. Performances are held at the Gran Teatro, Teatro Nacional, and Teatro Mella. Contact the Ballet Nacional de Cuba, Calzada #510, e/ D y E, Vedado, Ciudad de la Habana, C.P. 10400, tel. (7) 55-2953, fax (7) 33-3117, website: www.balletcuba.cubaweb.cu.

November: The annual **Festivities of San Cristóbal de la Habana** celebrates the anniversary of the founding of the city with a wide range of musical, theatrical, and other performances. Also in November the **"Wemilere" African Roots Festival** takes place at venues throughout Guanabacoa and honors African folkloric traditions. Contact Ada Rosa Alfonso Rosales at Paradiso, tel. (7) 97-0202, e-mail: paradis@turcult.get.cma.net.

December: At the **International Festival of New Latin-American Cinema** (also known as the Latin American Film Festival), a star-spangled guest list is no longer wined and dined at the Cuban State's expense, as in days of yore, and the all-night parties for which the festival had earned fame were replaced in 1994 by more sober soirées. Still, Fidel is usually on hand, schmoozing with Hollywood actors and directors in the lobbies of the Hotel Nacional and Habana Libre. The menu of movies—shown at more than 20 cinemas and theaters across the city—includes films from throughout the Americas and Europe. For further information, contact the Instituto de Cinematográfía in Havana, tel. (7) 55-2841, fax (7) 33-4273, e-mail: festival@icaic.inf.cu, or the Center for Cuban Studies.

FOLK MUSIC AND DANCE

Habana Vieja
If your visit coincides with the once-per-month (usually the third or fourth Saturday) *Noches en la Plaza de la Catedral,* be sure to attend. See Festivals and Events, above.

One of the more active **casa de la culturas** is that in Habana Vieja at Aguilar #509 esq. Teniente Rey (also called Brasil), tel. (7) 63-4860, with entertainment nightly. It offers *peñas* on Tuesday, dancing on Wednesday, plus *boleros y poesia,* comedy, and even karaoke. Performances of Afro-Cuban rumba by Grupo Saranbanda are offered on Tuesday (free), plus folk music is offered on Friday. The performances, which begin at 8 p.m., are given in the courtyard of the Iglesia San Agustín, where every Saturday at 3 p.m. the Compañia "JJ" Túrarte also performs rumba and popular music and dance. This is traditional Cuban entertainment at its best. You'll probably be the only tourists there to watch the mulatta dancers dressed in daffodil yellows, flamboyant reds, and morning-sky blues whirling and shaking to the rhythms of a band dressed in magenta shirts and white shade hats. Entrance costs US$1.

Each Monday and Friday night, Dulce María hosts a soirée called **Encounter with Cuban Music,** at Calle San Ignacio #78, tel. (7) 61-0412. Climbing a rickety staircase to the top of the dilapidated three-story building, you emerge on her apartment *azuela* (rooftop) overlooking the Plaza de la Catedral. Hands are extended. You are hugged warmly by Cubans you do not know. Dulce's band, Son de Cuba, gears up with a rumba. The rhythms of the marimbas, bongos, and a guitar called a *tres* pulse across the rooftops of Habana Vieja. Rum and beer are passed around, and soon you are clapping and

Each district has its own casa de la culturas *offering captivating folk music and dancing.*

laughing while Dulce belts out traditional Cuban compositions, her hips swaying to the narcotic beat. The ice is broken. The infectious beat lures you to dance. It is like the plague—you can only flee or succumb. Each song is introduced, with the history and meaning behind the song explained. You're invited to bring your own instrument. Says Dulce: "If we don't know it, we'll invent it." Entry costs US$5, including a drink.

The **Palacio de las Artesanias,** at the west end of Tacón, also offers a *noche Afrocubana* Fri.-Mon. at 9:30 p.m. (US$3), plus what it calls *salsa espectáculos* (US$4).

The **Casa de 10 Octubre,** at Calzada de Luyanó and Calle Reforma, in the Luyanó district, south of Habana Vieja, is active on weekends.

Centro

The **Casa de la Trova** at San Lazaro #661, in Centro Habana, tel. (7) 79-3373, is especially active on weekends, as is the **Casa de la Cultura** on San Miguel, one block east of Avenida de Italia. It has a lively bamboo bar to the rear that draws a more mature Cuban crowd for live music.

The **Galeria Kahlo** of the Casa de Cultura, #720 Salvador Allende, tel. (7) 78-4727, hosts *peñas* and posts a list of forthcoming events on the outside wall. It's open Mon.-Sat. 11 a.m.-6 p.m. (except Friday).

Vedado

My favorite nightspot is **Café Concerto Gato Tuerto** ("one-eyed cat"), Calle O, e/ 17 y 19, tel. (7) 55-2696 or 66-2224, playing *música filin* ("feeling music"). Here a former colonial home has been restored with a contemporary decor. It has *trova* and *bolero* nightly featuring Havana's leading performers, including Alden Naigt, a dramatic story-teller and poet. Occasionally Carlos, one of the barmen, breaks out his trumpet and plays a superb rendition behind the bar while the barmaids demonstrate with choreographed and exquisite care the correct formula for making a drink called an *orgasmo.* Gato Tuerto is popular with a sophisticated, monied Cuban crowd; foreign males and their Cuban consorts fill the empty seats. There's no cover charge, but it has a *consumo mínimo* policy: you're charged US$5 for your first drink, regardless. If you order a *mojito,* be sure to ask for a *mojito interna-*

cionál made from two types of rum, including *añejo.* It has music nightly until 4 a.m. The restaurant upstairs serves until 2 a.m., and the grilled fish and *criollo* meals are good.

In a similar vein, try **Club Imágenes,** a stylish piano-bar at the corner of Calzada y C, tel. (7) 33-3606. Open 3 p.m.-4 a.m.

Cabaret Pico Blanco, in the Hotel St. John's, features traditional Cuban *trova* nightly, 10 p.m.-4 a.m. And the **Bar Hurón Azul,** of the Unión Nacional de Escritores y Artistes de Cuba (UNEAC, or Union of Writers and Artists), Calle 17 esq. I, tel. (7) 32-4551, fax (7) 33-3158, hosts *boleros* and *trovas* on Saturday nights (US$3). A listing of forthcoming events is posted on the gate. It's a great place to meet Cuban intellectuals.

Traditional Afro-Cuban dance is also the focus of **Sábado de Rumba,** held each Saturday afternoon, beginning about 2 p.m., in the inner courtyard of the **Conjunto Folclórico Nacional,** Calle 4 e/ Calzada y Linea, tel. (7) 31-3467. Entrance costs US$1. The National Folklore Dance Group performs nationwide and was founded in 1962 to revive Cuban folk traditions because it was thought that the populace had lost touch with its folkloric past (every major city has a performance group supported by the national umbrella body).

Also check out the **Riviera Azúl,** in the Hotel Deauville, on the Malecón and Galiano. The Afro-Cuban folkloric group Oni Ire performs on Friday at 10 p.m., preceding the disco. Entrance costs US$5.

A friend has recommended **Joya's,** the eponymous home of the host, who puts on *peñas* with dancing at her home at the corner of San Lazaro and Infanta, on Friday, Saturday, and Sunday nights. Apparently she's a Josephine Baker type and has been described as "a bit of a character" and a "mix between Marilyn Monroe and Muhammad Ali."

Playa (Miramar and Beyond)

For a bit of melancholy, head to **Boleros,** in the Dos Gardenias complex, Av. 7ma y Calle 26. Here, Isolina Carrillo hosts some of the best singers of the *bolero* nightly 10:30 p.m.-3 a.m. Carrillo was a cinema pianist at the age of 10, entered the conservatory at 13, and composed the famous song "Dos Gardenias" after which the complex is named.

CABARETS *(ESPECTÁCULOS)*

Habaneros love showy spectacles and overt displays of flesh—the bread-and-butter of cabarets, which are a staple of Cuban entertainment (the term "cabaret" is used by Cubans to refer to a medley of entertainment, such as comedy and vocalists; the term "show" or *"espectáculo"* is used to denote a Las Vegas-style review). By far the most spectacular cabaret is that at the Tropicana. Most of the larger hotels have their own *espectáculos,* as do a number of major restaurants. Several tour agencies offer visits to a cabaret in association with the **cañonazo** cannon ceremony (see above). You can also book excursions to the cabarets through hotel tour desks.

One of the best ways to enjoy them is to go with a group and to reserve a table. Have your hotel concierge call ahead. Otherwise a tip to the maitre d' should do the trick. A bottle of Havana Club rum, cans of Coke, and ice bucket and glasses will be delivered to your table when you arrive. They are usually followed by discos.

Habana Vieja
Most nights, the rooftop bar of the **Hotel Inglaterra** has live music, often with a small cabaret *espectáculo* (US$5). Weekend evenings are good.

Centro Habana
Habaneros without dollars to throw around get their cabaret kicks at **El Colmao,** Calle Aramburu, e/ San José y San Rafael, in Centro Habana. The traditional floor show is highlighted by Spanish flamenco. Open 8 p.m.-2 a.m. Cubans pay in pesos, but you may be required to pay in dollars.

Vedado
The most lavish show in Vedado is the **Cabaret Parisien,** in the Hotel Nacional, tel. (7) 33-3564, second only to the Tropicana. Shows are offered Fri.-Wed. at 10 p.m. with a smaller show at 12:30 a.m. Entrance costs US$30. Although the show ostensibly starts at 9 p.m., the real show doesn't start until about 10:30 p.m.

Slightly cheaper, but still exotic, is the Cabaret Capri, tel. (7) 33-3747, fax (7) 33-3750, in the **Salon Rojo,** in Vedado's Hotel Capri, Calle N y 21, nightly except Monday at 10 p.m. (US$10).

Salón Turquino, in the Hotel Habana Libre, tel. (7) 33-4011, offers a medley of entertainment varying nightly, with a *cabaret espectáculo* on Wednesday and Thursday (US$10, but US$5 for hotel guests), followed by a disco. Open 10:30 p.m.-4:30 a.m.

And there's no entry fee to the **Habana Café,** tel. (7) 33-3636, aside the Hotel Meliá Cohiba, at the foot of Paseo, which offers cabaret nightly and is one of the better touristy nightspots in town. See Bars, below.

Many discos also have cabaret, such as **Club 1830,** which hosts its flurry of flesh and feathers outdoors at midnight. It's a small affair but draws many Cubans, and is particularly popular with models from La Maison and a coterie of *jiniteras,* who hang out at the gates hoping to score with male tourists. Entrance costs US$10.

A smaller, cheesier alternative is the **Cabaret Las Vegas,** Infanta e/ Calles 25 y 27, tel. (7) 70-7939, with a show at 10 p.m. followed by a disco (US$5 per couple). The *espectáculo* is a feeble, short-lived affair with a five-member dance troupe and not worth the billing ("The *chicas,*" wrote Tom Miller, "danced in earnest but seldom in sync, their tattered fishnet stockings running before our eyes" while the solo singer "singing off-key into her cordless mike . . . would have been better served had she carried a mikeless cord"). And the set-up can take an excruciatingly long time. *Mojitos* cost a whopping US$5! The gloomy bar—the hangout for the protagonist in Guillermo Cabrera Infante's bawdy *Three Trapped Tigers*—has a pool table and is by day a local hangout. Why go? For the seedy charm.

Cubans also have access to the **Disco Tango** at the Hotel Bruzón, where a small *espectáculo* is presented on Thursday at 11 p.m. Foreigners pay US$5. And the seedy **Centro Nocturno La Red,** Calle 19 esq. Calle L, has a small *espectáculo* at midnight; US$2.

Playa (Miramar and Beyond)
The shining star in Havana's cabaret constellation is the **Tropicana,** at Calle 72, e/ 41 y 45, Marianao, tel. (7) 27-0110, fax (7) 27-0109, e-mail: reserva@tropicana.gca.cma.net. Cuba's premier Las Vegas-style nightclub, boasting over 200 performers, has been described as "like looking at a Salvador Dali painting come to life" and is a *must* night out for every tourist wanting

THE TROPICANA

*T*he prerevolutionary extravaganza now in its sixth decade of Vegas paganism—girls! girls! girls!—has been in continuous operation since New Year's Eve 1939, when it opened (in the gardens of a mansion—Villa Mina—that once housed the U.S. ambassador) as the most flamboyant nightclub in the world. The casino has gone, but otherwise neither the Revolution nor the recent economic crisis has ruffled the feathers of Cuba's most spectacular show.

Tropicana, the club to which Wormold took Millie on her seventeenth birthday in *Our Man in Havana,* quickly won the favor of the elite of society and soon eclipsed all other clubs in the grandeur and imagination of its productions. The Congo Pantera revue, which simulated a panther's nocturnal hunt in lush jungle, established the Tropicana's trademark, with dancers in the thick vegetation illuminated by colored spotlights and the panther, performed by Tania Leskoya, coming down from a majestic tree.

In the 1950s the club was owned by Martín Fox, who held a legal monopoly on the installation and maintenance of slot machines *(máquinas traganickeles).* Fox restored the property in modernist style, with a new showroom—the Salon Arcos de Cristal (Crystal Bows)—with a stupendous roof of five arcing concrete vaults up to 30 meters in span and curving bands of glass to fill the intervening space. A stone statue of a ballet dancer by the renowned Cuban sculptor Rita Longa was added, shown pirouetting on the tips of her toes. The statue, which has become Tropicana's motif, is joined by bacchants of the Fountain of Nymphs, with Greek maenads performing a wild ritual to Dionysius amid the lush foliage in front of the entrance.

In its heyday during the 1950s, the Tropicana spent more than US$12,000 nightly on its flamboyant shows, which ranged from the "Asian Paradise" portraying the exotic Orient to choreographed Haitian voodoo rituals. International celebrities such as Nat "King" Cole, Josephine Baker, and Carmen Miranda headlined the show, which was so popular that a 50-passenger "Tropicana Special" flew nightly from Miami for an evening of entertainment that ended in the nightclub's casino, where a daily US$10,000 bingo jackpot was offered and a new automobile was raffled for free every Sunday.

Then as now, however, the key attraction was the sensual mulatta parade; talent scouts scoured Cuba for the most beautiful models and dancers. The more than 200 performers are still hand-picked from the crème-de-la-crème of Cuba's dancers and singers. And famous international entertainers still occasionally perform, enhancing the superbly choreographed skits of *danzón, son,* salsa, Brazilian *ya-tratá,* Latin jazz, Afro-Cuban legends, and romantic ballads, interspersed with astonishing acrobatic feats.

The "paradise under the stars," which takes place in the open air, begins with the "Dance of the Chandeliers," when a troupe of near-naked showgirls parades down the aisles wearing glowing chandeliers atop their heads. Then a troupe of besequined males and long-legged showgirls rush onto the stage in a high-kicking flurry of flesh and feathers. The sexually charged show consists of creative song and dance routines and a never-ending parade of stupendous mulattas gyrating their glistening copper-colored bodies into an erotic frenzy. Patrons watch mesmerized as rainbow-hued searchlights sweep over the hordes of showgirls, and mocha-skinned mulattas, gaudily feathered, parade 20 feet up among the floodlit palm trees, quivering beseechingly like the most exotic of tropical birds. Between numbers they rush offstage and reappear in sexy outfits from a Frederick's of Hollywood catalog: tasseled thongs with ruffled tails, sequined bikinis with bras of coiled foil tipped by fake rubies, skin-tight bustiers with pull-ring zippers, bejeweled chokers, elbow-length gloves, and sensational headdresses more ostentatious than peacocks. *Marvelous!*

The top dancers, singers, and musicians in the country offer an unmatched evening extravaganza.

a jaw-dropping treat. The show, enhanced by a fabulous orchestra, takes place in the open-air Salón Bajo Las Estrellas nightly at 10:30. Entrance costs US$60, including a Cuba libre. You're charged US$5 for cameras; US$15 for videos. Cocktails cost US$3. Patrons supposedly get their money back if it rains (if the rains are intermittent, the show merely takes a break, then resumes). You can purchase tickets at the reservation booth, tel. (7) 27-0110, open 10 a.m.-6 p.m., or directly at the entrance from 8:30 p.m. (call ahead to check availability), but it's best to book in advance through your hotel tour desk, as the show is often sold out. A second, smaller show at the Tropicana opened in February 2000 in the recently renovated **Arco Cristal** cabaret room featuring dancers in flamboyant 1950s costumes.

Tropicana features two eateries: the elegant skylit **Los Jardines** (named for its surfeit of tropical plants, harboring mosquitoes) serving tasty continental fare and beef tenderloin with lobster as the house specialty (US$14.50; open 6 p.m.-1 a.m.); and the 1950s-diner-style **Rodney Café** serving salads, soups, burgers, tortillas, etc., to a mostly Cuban crowd (open noon-2 a.m.).

Macumba Habana, in the La Giraldilla complex, Calle 222, e/ 37 y 51, tel. (7) 33-0568, fax (7) 33-6390, in the La Coronela district of La Lisa, offers a top-class, albeit small *espectáculo* at 10:30 p.m. followed by Havana's first world-class disco. A fashion show is held on Monday. Entry costs US$10; US$15 on Friday and Saturday. A dinner special costs US$30.

The **Hotel Comodoro,** on Av. 1ra y Calle 84, tel. (7) 33-2703, features an *espectáculo* as part of its entertainment for guests. It's very good. **Discoteca Habana Club,** behind the Hotel Comodoro, tel. (7) 24-2902, also has a cabaret. You might also try the **Club Ipanema,** tel. (7) 24-1037, adjacent to the Hotel Copacabana, with a "Noches Azules" *espectáculo.* And the **La Cecilia** restaurant complex, Av. 5ta e/ 110 y 112, tel. (7) 24-1562, has a small *espectáculo* Thu.-Sun. at 9:30 p.m. with disco to follow.

Likewise, the *'Espectáculo Dos Gardenias'* in the **Salon Bolero** of the Dos Gardenias complex, Av. 7ma esq. 26, has shows at 9 p.m. and 11 p.m. (US$10; cameras cost US$5 extra, videos cost US$10). The program changes nightly. Call ahead. The **Salon La Tarde,** adjacent in

the same complex, has nightly entertainment from 7:30 p.m. (US$5).

Cabaret Chévere, at Club Almendares on Avenida 49C in Reparto Kohly, tel. (7) 24-4990, has an open-air cabaret with a band and fashion parade (but no *espectáculo*) Fri.-Sun. 10 a.m.-6 a.m. (US$5). The bar is open 24 hours. And there's a pool hall (US$1 per game).

Young adult Cubans flock to **Cabaret Marina,** at Marina Hemingway, tel. (7) 24-1150, ext. 120, which hosts shows Tue.-Sun. 10 p.m.-4 a.m. (a US$10 cover applies, and there's a US$15 *consumo mínimo* policy). It has a laser disco.

DISCOTHEQUES AND DANCING

There's no shortage of discos in dance-crazy Havana. The "best" are money-milking machines serving well-heeled foreigners but also popular with Cuban females. Male foreigners can expect to be solicited outside the entrance to these dollars-only discos: Cuban women take a stranger's arm and beg to be escorted in *("por favor!"),* because entry is beyond their means. At some places, only couples are admitted; many discos have a policy of not letting single women in (the opposite of Western discos).

Most of the hotel discos are open 10 p.m.-5 a.m. There's little point in arriving before midnight, when things get going. Most discos play a mix of Latin, techno, and world-beat music.

Drink prices in the touristy discos can give you sticker shock. The best bet is usually to buy a bottle of rum—as little as US$3 in discos catering mostly to Cubans, but expect to fork out at least US$20 for a bottle in ritzier places.

There are always taxis hovering outside the entrances of the best discos, and freelancers are on hand to run you home for a negotiable fare.

All the *cabaret espectáculos* feature discos following the show.

Habana Vieja

Marlin S.A., Calle 184 #123, Flores, Havana, tel. (7) 33-6675, operates a floating disco with karaoke aboard the *XIV Festival,* which departs the wharf on San Pedro at the foot of Luz, Tue.-Sun. 8:30 and 10:30 p.m. and 12:30 a.m. (US$5).

The old *Galeón,* a replica pirate ship, no longer sails after Cubans attempted to hijack it to Florida.

Centro

The **Casa Abuelo Lung Kong,** at Manrique y Dragones in Barrio Chino, has a disco upstairs on weekends on the outside patio.

Cuban youth without dollars head to **Cabaret Las Olas,** tel. (7) 70-3735, on the Malecón, 100 meters east of La Rampa, with an outdoor disco Fri.-Sun. 9 p.m.-1 a.m. (10 pesos). It's operated by UjoteCa, the Union of Communist Youth.

La Pampa, opposite the Torreon de San Lázaro at the Malecón and Vapor, has dancing nightly except Monday; US$1; including cabaret. It's on the edge of the rough Cayo Hueso district and has a decidedly earthy appeal. Leave your jewelry at home! Another earthy favorite of locals is **Palermo,** at San Miguel y Amistad (nightly except Wednesday).

Vedado

The **Salón Internacionál** (formerly the Palacio de Salsa), tel. (7) 33-4051, in the Hotel Havana Riviera specializes in the Latin beat and often features the top names in live Cuban music. I haven't checked it out, but as the Palacio de Salsa it was *the* place for serious salsa fans. It's open daily 10 p.m.-3 a.m. Also try the **Pico Blanco,** on the top floor of the Hotel St. John's on Calle O (US$5). It has salsa on Monday and rumba on weekend afternoons. And the ritzy **Salón Turquino,** atop the Hotel Habana Libre, is

THE GAY SCENE

*C*uban gays must find irony that the heart of the homosexual world is Castro Street in San Francisco. It is assuredly not named in El Jefe's honor, as gays—called "queens," *maricónes,* or *locas* in the Cuban vernacular—were persecuted following the Revolution. Castro (who denies the comment) supposedly told journalist Lee Lockwood that a homosexual could never "embody the conditions and requirements of . . . a true revolutionary."

However, by the mid-1980s, Cuba began to respond to the gay-rights movement that had already gained momentum worldwide. Officially, the new position was that homosexuality and bisexuality are no less natural or healthy than heterosexuality. The reckoning with the past was underscored in 1994 by the release of Tomas Gutierrez Alea's Oscar-nominated film, *Fresa y Chocolate.* The movie is understood as a universal plea for tolerance. It could not have been produced without official approval, and therefore exemplifies an acknowledgment of how the prejudice against homosexuals harmed Cuba's cultural life. Nonetheless, prejudice still exists throughout society, and there is still a restriction on gays joining the party. The Cuban gay community does not have representative organizations, although the first gay men's group on the island, Cubans in the Struggle Against AIDS, was recently formed.

Gay Cuba, by Sonja de Vries, is a documentary film that looks candidly at the treatment of gays and lesbians in Cuba since the Revolution. You can order copies from Frameline, 346 Ninth St., San Francisco, CA 94103, tel. (415) 703-8654, fax (415) 861-1404, e-mail: frameline@aol.com, website: www.frameline.org. Also check out *Machos, Maricónes, and Gays: Cuba and Homosexuality,* by Ian Lumsden (Philadelphia, PA: Temple University, 1996) for a study of the relationship between male homosexuality and Cuban society.

Gay Gathering Spots

Gay life in Havana has expanded noticeably in recent years, and male homosexuals act with more demonstrable confidence (lesbianism has not become quite so accepted). There are cruising sections, such as on the Malecón opposite the Fiat Café two blocks east of La Rampa, where the party spreads along the seafront boulevard in the wee hours. The corner of La Rampa and L, outside the Cine Yara, is a lesser cruising spot. The Café Monseigneur, on Calle O between La Rampa and 21, is a gay hangout. Parque de la Fraternidad has a late-night cruising scene. There are also private gay parties, known as *fiestas de diez pesos,* which charge a 10 peso cover.

A good place to find out that night's happening spot is to ask the gay crowd that congregates at night outside the Cine Yara.

For gay beaches, head to the Boca Ciega section of Playas del Este, east of town. In town, try Playita de 16, the rocky *balneario* at Calle 16 in Miramar; and Playa Tritón, in front of the Hotel Neptuno/Tritón.

a snazzy dance spot with magnificent views (US$10 entrance).

The tiny **Las Bulerias,** on Calle L opposite the Hotel Habana Libre is a smoky, moody place that plays a lot of reggae. It's popular mostly with black *Cubanas* (there are few Cuban males). It doesn't get in the groove until about 11 p.m. Entrance costs US$3; beers are US$1.

An in-vogue in-spot is **Johnny's,** also called "Club Rio," where young Cubans "gyrate ecstatically to songs by the Backstreet Boys and Ricky Martin."

UjoteCa, the Union of Communist Youth, runs the **Pabellón,** on La Rampa at Calle N. The Pabellon features a gamut of activities, Wed.-Sun.: typically salsa on Wednesday, disco and rap Thu.-Sat. (US$5), and disco with rock music on Sunday (US$7).

Cubans also kick up the dust at the **Café Cantante Mi Habana,** in the Teatro Nacional at Paseo, one block west of the Plaza de la Revolución, tel. (7) 33-5713 or 79-6011. Entry costs US$3. And **Club Scherazada,** a small, dingy, and smoky basement bar on the southwest side of the FOCSA building, at the junction of Calle 19 y M, offers a medley of musical offerings each night from 6 p.m., with *trovas* and *boleros* plus more lively sounds. It has a US$2.50 per person cover (the sign outside says *"US$5 por pareja"* but the doorman sometimes tries to con solo guests who don't know that this means "per pair"). It has a *peña yoruba* with rumba and other Afro sounds on Saturday, 3-8:30 p.m. A disco cranks up at 10:30 p.m.

Farther west, the **Turf Club** Calzada (Av. 7ma) y F, is a popular nightclub among the locals.

Cuban rock fans head to **Patio de María,** on Calle 37 y Paseo, near the Teatro Nacional, where the disco combines Latin sounds with rock on Friday and Saturday nights. Rock concerts are hosted on Sunday evenings.

Outdoors, I recommend the **Club 1830,** on an oceanside terrace behind the Restaurante 1830. The nightly disco is popular on weekends and includes a fashion show and undistinguished cabaret *espectáculo.* Entrance costs US$10. It's open 10 p.m.-4 a.m., but doesn't start jumping until well past midnight. It's a popular pick-up spot for *jiniteras.* Adjacent, the **Torreón La Chorrera,** also has a disco popular with Cuban youth.

Other spots to consider include **Salón Caribe,** tel. (7) 33-4011, in the Hotel Habana Libre (open Wed.-Mon. 9 p.m.-4 a.m.); and **Centro Vasco,** at the corner of Avenida 3ra and 4, tel. (7) 3-9354, near the Meliá Cohiba and Riviera hotels, with an upstairs disco and video-bar popular with Cubans.

Playa (Miramar and Beyond)

Absolutely the hippest spot in Havana at press time is **Macumba Habana,** in the La Giraldilla complex at Calle 222, e/ 37 y 51, tel. (7) 33-0568, fax (7) 33-6390, in the La Coronela district of La Lisa. This superchic open-air disco, under French management, boasts fabulous decor and great music and draws the chic crowd (mostly well-heeled foreign males and beautiful Cuban models). It has a selection of superb dining options attached, and a cigar store and features pre-disco cabaret. The disco goes on until 5 p.m. It has a dress code. Only couples *(parejas)* are allowed entry, though this can include two women. Entry costs US$10; US$15 on Friday and Saturday. A dinner special costs US$30.

If you have money to blow, the classiest disco by far is **Discoteca Habana Club,** behind the Hotel Comodoro on Avenida 1ra and Calle 84 at the west end of Miramar, tel. (7) 33-2703. Ostensibly it's open 10 p.m.-5 a.m., but it stays open later. Entrance costs US$10. Drinks are outrageously priced (Cokes and beers cost US$5; fruit juices cost US$7; a Cuba libre will set you back US$10). It attracts a blend of Cubans, Mexicans, and other Latins who bop to yester-decade's Abba tunes and pop hits (with a hint of salsa) played at top volume between cabaret floor shows.

The **Club Ipanema,** tel. (7) 29-0601, at the Hotel Copacabana, plays mostly techno music (or it did when I was last there). The clientele is mostly Cuban, and the atmosphere subdued. There's no entry charge, but a *consumo mínimo* of US$6 applies. It's open 10 p.m.-4 a.m.

Farther out, **Salón Rosado Beny Moré,** on Luís Duvalon, e/ Aves. 41 y 42, tel. (7) 29-0985, is an open-air concert arena famous for its wicked salsa concerts and sudden knife fights on weekends; top-billed Cuban singers perform. Police patrol the lines to get in: one for women, one for men. It gets packed; expect to wait in line for a hour or more. **La Cecilia,** tel. (7) 33-1562, on Avenida 5ta y 110, in Miramar, also hosts salsa and other music and dance after the restaurant closes (Thurs.-Sun. 9:30 p.m.-2 a.m.). And **Papa's** and the **Cabaret Marina,** way out west at Marina Hemingway, Av. 5ta esq. Calle 248, tel. (7) 33-1150, are discos popular with young Habaneras seeking to match as mates with foreign seafarers.

Cubans without dollars find their fun at such spots as **Juventud 2000 Discoclub,** tel. (7) 30-0720, in the Karl Marx Theater Complex at Av. 1ra y 10, (open Fri-Sun. 9 p.m.-2 a.m.), or the open-air amphitheater on the Malecón, 200 meters west of the Hotel Meliá Cohiba. This popular spot gets thronged with a mostly black crowd. There is usually a heavy police presence due to the frequent fights.

TANGO AND FLAMENCO

Into tango? The **Caserón de Tango** at Calle Justíz #21, one block south of Plaza de Armas in Habana Vieja, highlights the Argentinian music and dance form. Also in Habana Vieja, **La Zaragoza,** on Monserrate at Obrapía, offers tango, boleros, and flamenco on Thursday and Saturday night at 9:30 p.m.

Fans of tango might also check out the **Casa del Tango,** a tiny shop at Neptuno #303, where scratchy old recordings and tapes are played. Dance is not hosted here. Nearby, the **Centro Cultural de España,** Malecon #17, tel. (7) 66-9189 hosts midday flamenco.

JAZZ VENUES

Habana Vieja
A jazz trio perform in the **Café del Oriente,** at the corner of Oficios and Amargura on the west side of Plaza de San Francisco, tel. (7) 66-6686, where you can enjoy cocktails at the ritzy marble-top bar.

Centro
Cine América, tel. (7) 62-5416), on Galiano at Neptuno, is a run-down place that hosts jazz and ballet.

Vedado
The **Jazz Café** on the third floor of the Galeria del Paseo, facing the Hotel Meliá Cohiba at the base of Paseo, is a classy (albeit smoke-filled) joint with some of the best jazz in town, including from resident maestro, Chucho Valdés. A US$5 cover on weekends includes a cocktail.

The basement **La Zora y el Cuevo,** at the bottom of La Rampa e/ N y O, offers jazz of modest standard in English-pub style surrounds (the entrance is a giant English phone booth). Occasional foreign bands perform. It's open 10 p.m.-4 a.m. (US$5).

Jazz and salsa are staples at the **Jazz Cafetería,** in the Casa Cultura in Vedado at Calle 7 e/ Av. 4 y 6. The Casa Cultura is one of the venues for the annual **International Havana Jazz Festival** (see Festivals And Events, above).

Cuba's particularly vivacious version of jazz can also be heard at the **Salón Internacionál** (formerly the Palacio de Salsa) in the Hotel Riviera, and **Café Turquino Salsa Cabaret,** in the Habana Libre Hotel. The lobby bar of the Hotel Copacabana also has a jazz trio that performs nightly.

Playa (Miramar and Beyond)
A jazz group performs at the **Tocororo** restaurant, on the corner of Calle 18 y Av. 3ra, tel. (7) 33-4530.

BARS

Habana Vieja
The lobby piano bar in the **Hotel Ambos Mundos,** at Calle Obispo and Mercaderes, is lively and pleasant. **Taberna Beny Moré,** on the northeast side of Plaza Vieja, is an upscale and bohemian affair, with walls festooned with the personal effects of Cuban's renowned singer-composer, for whom the bar is named. There's live music.

And no visit to Havana is complete without sipping a *mojito* at **La Bodeguita del Medio,** Calle Empredado #207, tel. (7) 62-4498, e-mail: reserva@bodem.gca.cma.net, as Ernest Hemingway did almost daily. However, the *mojitos* are abysmally weak, the mint usually wilted, and the glass far too small for the US$4 tab, and unfortunately served by consistently surly bar staff! No cigars are sold here—bring your own.

Far better (and cheaper; US$2.50) *mojitos* are served in the **Dos Hermanos,** a wharf bar where Hemingway bent elbows with sailors and prostitutes at the long wooden bar, open to the street through wooden *rejas*. The down-to-earth bar, at San Pedro and Sol, is perfect for unpretentious tippling with locals, although it draws the occasional tour group, and offers the advantage of being open 24 hours The staff is friendly and there's often live music, plus bar snacks.

Hemingway enjoyed his daily daiquiri at **El Floridita,** at the corner of Calle Obispo and Monserrate, tel. (7) 63-1060, e-mail: reserva@flori .gca.cma.net, a fabulous place to sit at the bar smoking a premium *habano* and listening to the jazz quartet. Be sure to ask for the "Daiquiri Nature," a hand-shaken version (the regular daiquiris are today made in an electric blender). It may not quite live up to its 1950s aura when *Esquire* magazine named it one of the great bars of the world, but to visit Havana without sipping a daiquiri here would be like visiting France without tasting the wine.

The moodily atmospheric wood-paneled **Bar Monserrate,** just south of El Floridita at Avenida de Bélgica (Monserrate) and Obrapía, has long been popular with Cubans and is noted for its *Coctel Monserrate* (one teaspoon of sugar, two ounces of grapefruit juice, five drops of grenadine, two ounces of white rum, ice, and a sprig of mint).

The **Galería La Acera del Louvre** patio bar of the Hotel Inglaterra is a good spot to sip a beer or *cuba libre* and watch the to-ing and fro-ing around Parque Central. A Mexican *mariachi* band performs on Sunday at 8:30 p.m.

La Lluvia de Oro and always buzzing **Café Paris,** both on Obispo (at Calle Habana and San Ignacio, respectively), are lively, down-to-earth bars popular with a mix of Cubans and wayward foreigners, who frequent these bars to sample the live music and pick up wayward *Cubanas.* If you follow Obispo west to Villegas, you can even purchase takeout daiquiris for one and a half pesos, served in cardboard cups from a small shop—**El Huevino**—on the corner.

Another favorite of locals is the **Bar Lafayette,** on Aguilar between O'Reilly and Empedrado. Its house cocktail is rum and tomato juice.

Across the harbor channel, I recommend the atmospheric **Bar La Tasca,** on the harborfront facing Havana between the Morro and La Cabaña fortresses. It's an intimate oak-beamed

---

MOJITO: THE BODEGUITA'S CLASSIC DRINK

Here's the official version of how to make a killer *mojito:*

With a stirrer, mix half a tablespoon of sugar and the juice of half a lime in a highball glass. Add a sprig of *yerba buena* (mint), crushing the stalk to release the juice; two ice cubes; and 1.5 oz. of Havana Club Light Dry Cuban rum. Fill with soda water. *Salud!*

---

place, full of Spanish weaponry, with a friendly barman and a terrace where you can sip your *mojito* while enjoying the views. Nearby, and in a similar vein, are the **Mesón de los Doce Apóstoles** and **El Polvorín,** at the foot of the Morro castle. I love El Polvorín, offering patio dining with a view past the cannons and across the harbormouth toward Havana. Inside is as cool as a well, and early-colonial-atmospheric to boot.

For a truly down-to-earth experience, check out **Bar Actualidades** on Monserrate, behind the Hotel Plaza. This compact and dingy little bar is favored by Cubans and offers an insight into the nocturnal pleasures of impecunious Cubans. Its red light and raffish Afro-Cuban quality might have appealed to Sammy Davis Jr. and the Rat Pack.

The **Club Los Marinos,** tel. (7) 57-1402, overhanging the harbor on Avenida Carlos M. Céspedes one block east of Plaza de Armas, is popular with a younger Cuban crowd that flocks for karaoke. It offers music on the juke box and has a large-screen TV. Open nightly 7 p.m.-2 a.m. Entry costs US$1 (US$2 for karaoke). Karaoke is also the forte of the **Disco Karaoke** in the Hotel Plaza, packing the Cubans in thick as sardines, 10:30 p.m.-5 a.m. (US$4).

Centro

There are few bars of note. To commune with locals, try **Bar Nautilus,** a moody and gloomy place, quite lively to boot, with fish tanks in the wall. It's on Calle San Rafael, one block west of Parque Central.

Vedado

An in-vogue hot spot is the **Habana Café,** tel. (7) 33-3636, beside the Hotel Meliá Cohiba, at the foot of Paseo. Havana's homespun version of the

Hard Rock Café is a must-visit at least once, rekindling the zesty (but tamer) spirit of the 1950s, and luring everyone from tour groups to cigar-chomping bigwigs taking a stab at one-Upmannship with slender *Cubanas* on their arms. Seating is theater-style around the stage. The 1950s decor includes walls festooned with musical instruments and photos of famous performers from the era. A classic Harley-Davidson, an old Pontiac, and a 1957 open-top canary-yellow Chevy add a dramatic effect, as do period gas pumps, and a small airplane suspended from the ceiling. Suddenly the car horns beep and the headlamps flash, you hear the roar of an airplane taking off, then the curtains open and—voilá—the show begins. This is a classic nightclub, with non-stop entertainment 8 p.m.-3 a.m., including a small Tropicana-style cabaret, drummers, a splendid juggling act, and a Benny Goodman-style band. A group plays traditional music noon-4 p.m., and a pianist and *bolero* music keep patrons amused 4-8 p.m. The dress code is casual, but a suit is not out of place. *Mojitos* cost US$5.50. Try an *afrodisíaco* made of egg yolk, honey, milk, and vanilla (US$4.50). A *consumo mínimo* applies: US$5 at the bar, US$10 at a table—but be careful that you don't get ripped off. This "minimum consumption" charge (plus 10% service charge) applies to the first drink, for which you'll be charged US$5.50 even if it's a glass of soda water, so it pays to order a more expensive drink or food item first. The bar staff tried to scam me, and followed it up with a heavy-handed Mafia-style treatment from the bouncers and manager!

The ground-floor **El Relicario Bar** of the Hotel Meliá Cohiba is popular with a monied, cigar-loving crowd and offers an elegant Edwardian-themed ambience and relative serenity. In an entirely different vein is the cramped and raffish **La Roca,** on Calle 21 esq. M, tel. (7) 33-4501, the kind of dark yet appealing dive where the Rat Pack might have hung out in the 1950s.

The **Bar Vista del Golfo** in the Hotel Nacional has music on an old jukebox, and walls festooned with famous figures such as Errol Flynn, Johnny Weismuller, and mobsters.

The sparkling new **Bar Elegante** in the Hotel Riviera, adjacent to the Meliá Cohiba, now features the Disco Karaoke, nightly 8 p.m.-4 a.m.

More radical youth elements congregate at the **Casa de los Infusiones,** at Calles 23 y G in Vedado, where *aguardente* (neat rum) shots cost US$0.50 each.

Several bars offer superb views of the city: try the rooftop bar at the Hotel Nacional as well as those at the Hotel Inglaterra and Hotel Riviera, and La Torre, atop the FOCSA Building at Calles 17 y M (entrance, US$1). The best, perhaps, is the **Turquino,** on the 25th floor of the Hotel Habana Libre—fabulous views! The US$2 admission includes one drink.

Playa (Miramar and Beyond)

The hotels all have bars, although none stands out. The **Dos Gardenias** complex, on Avenida 7ma at 26, features a piano bar. And the bars in the **Novotel** promise to make a splash.

I like the tasteful bar of the elegant skylighted **Los Jardines** in the Tropicana nightclub, Calle 72, e/ 41 y 45, Marianao, tel. (7) 27-0110, fax (7) 27-0109, although it gets few patrons, despite the popularity of the cabaret. The fish-tanks behind the black marble-topped bar can keep you amused.

CINEMA

Cubans are passionate moviegoers, and Havana is blessed with cinemas—by one account more than 170—showing current Hollywood movies (normally within one year of release) plus Cuban films. Hollywood culture saturated the Havana of the 1930s, and the bloom of movie houses coincided with the heyday of art deco and modern styles. Overnight Havana was blessed with a crop of streamlined, futuristic façades suggestive of fantasy. Most striking, perhaps, is the 1941 Cine América, on Calle de Italia, tel. (7) 62-5416, in streamlined design, with curvilinear box seats melting into the walls of the vaulted auditorium: see Sightseeing.

Entrance usually costs two pesos (foreigners are rarely charged in dollars), and the menu is surprisingly varied, albeit a bit campy. Leading Hollywood productions (classic and contemporary) and cartoons are shown, as are westerns, kung-fu flicks, and other foreign productions, particularly those of socially redeeming quality. Movies are often subtitled in Spanish (others are dubbed, to enjoy which you'll need to be fluent in Spanish). Age restriction is 16 years. Children and youths can attend screenings at the **Cinemateca Infantíl y Juvenil,** at Cinema 23 y 12, every Saturday at 2:30 p.m. The latest issue of *Granma* will list what's currently showing.

In 1959 Cuba established a high-quality cinema institute to produce feature films, documentaries, and newsreels with heavy revolutionary content. All movies in Cuba—their making, importation, exportation, and distribution—are under the control of the **Instituto de Cinematográfía,** Film Institute, Calle 23 #1109, Vedado, Havana, tel. (7) 33-4634, fax (7) 33-3281, next to the Charlie Chaplin movie house (called the largest cinema in the world), and which has preview screenings of new Cuban releases in its studios.

The most important cinemas are:

Cine Acapulco: Av. 26, e/ 35 y 37, Vedado, tel. (7) 3-9573; daily from 4:30 p.m.

Cine Charles Chaplin: Calle 23, e/ 10 y 12, Vedado, tel. (7) 31-1101; daily except Tuesday at 5 and 8 p.m. (box office opens 30 minutes prior). Also here is **Video Charlot** (same times), also showing first-run movies.

Cine Payret: Prado y Calle San José, Habana Vieja, tel. (7) 63-3163; daily from 12:30 p.m.

Cine La Rampa: Calle 23, e/ O y P, Vedado, tel. (7) 78-6146; daily except Wednesday from 4:40 p.m.

Cine Riviera: Calles 23 y H, Vedado, tel. (7) 30-9564; daily from 4:40 p.m.

Cine Yara: Calle 23 y Calle L, Vedado tel. (7) 32-9430; daily from 12:30 p.m.

French films are shown on Saturday at 2 p.m. at the **Alliance Française,** Calle G #407, e/ 17 y 19 in Vedado, tel. (7) 33-3370. Entrance is free.

THEATER AND CLASSICAL PERFORMANCES

Havana has seven major theaters and numerous smaller locales. Although legitimate theater has yet to take off, Cubans are enthusiastic lovers of ballet and classical music.

The most important theater is the baroque **Gran Teatro de la Habana,** on the west side of Parque Central, tel. (7) 62-9473. It is the main stage for the acclaimed Ballet Nacional de Cuba

Gran Teatro de la Habana

(Calzada #510, e/ D y E, Vedado, tel. (7) 55-2953, fax (7) 33-3117) as well as the national opera company. The building has two theaters—the **Sala García Lorca,** where ballet and concerts are held, and the smaller **Sala Antonin Artaud,** for less-commercial performances. Jazz and other performances are often given, and most weeks throughout the year you can even see Spanish dance here Thurs.-Sat. at 8:30 p.m. and Sunday at 5 p.m. (US$10). A dress code (no shorts) applies for performances.

Look, too, for performances of the National Symphony—the orchestra is excellent if you excuse the occasional pings of dropped bows and triangles—and other classical and contemporary performances at the modern **Teatro Nacional,** on Avenida Carlos M. de Céspedes, one block west of the Plaza de la Revolución, tel. (7) 79-6011. It also has two performance halls—the **Sala Avellaneda,** for concerts and opera, and the **Sala Covarrubias.** It also hosts important Communist Party functions and revolutionary celebrations.

The **Basílica de San Francisco de Asís,** in Habana Vieja, also hosts classical concerts, normally on Thursday at 6 p.m.

The **Teatro Mella,** on Linea (Calle 7) y A, tel. (7) 3-5651, is noted for its contemporary dance and theater, including performances by the **Danza Contemporánea de Cuba.** Many of Cuba's more contemporary and avant-garde plays are performed here.

The **Casa de la Música,** Calle 17 y E in Vedado, offers concerts by soloists and chamber ensembles—and so does the **Casa de la Música,** Calle 20, e/ Av. 33 y 35, in Miramar, tel. (7) 24-0447, which has different performances nightly at 10 p.m. except Monday in the *sala de espectáculos* (US$10 cover). And the **Museo de la Música** at the north end of Monserrate, at its junction with Cuba, in Habana Vieja, offers classical concerts on Saturday and Sunday at 4 p.m. (US$2).

The **Teatro Amadeo Roldán,** Parque Villalon, e/ 5ra y Calzada (7ma) and C y D, was recently restored to grandeur and will feature classical concerts year-round. Nearby is the **Teatro Hubert de Blanck,** Calzada, e/ Calles A and B, tel. (7) 30-1011, and known for both modern and classical plays.

Watch, too, for performances by Xiomara Palacio, a puppet-show artist recognized as Cuba's leading figure in children's theater. And one of Cuba's premier choral groups, Schola Cantorum Coral, known also as Coralina, trains children and youth in chorale.

Comedy

Comic theater is popular with Cubans. It is considered part of the national culture and was an important element in 19th-century life. However, you'll need to be fluent in Spanish to get many giggles out of the shows, which are heavy on burlesque. Most cabaret shows also feature stand-up comedy. Look for announcements of forthcoming shows posted outside the Cine Yara in Vedado.

In Habana Vieja, head to **Casa de la Comédia** (also called Salón Ensayo), at the corner of Calles Justíz and Baratillo, tel. (7) 63-1160, one block southeast of Plaza de Armas. It hosts comic theater on weekends at 7 p.m., performed by the Teatro Anaquillé (US$2).

In Vedado, the **Teatro Brecht** specializes in comedy, which it offers every Tuesday at 8:30 p.m. The **Teatro Guiñol** on the west side of the FOCSA building, on M, e/ 17 y 19, also offers comedy; as does the **Teatro El Sótano,** Calle K #514, e/ 25 and 27, every Thursday evening.

The **Salón Internacional** in the Hotel Habana Riviera, Av. Paseo y Malecón, tel. (7) 33-4051, presents a weekly "Gran Fiesta" of comedy and music (US$5 cover). And **Cabaret Las Olas,** a simple outdoor facility on the Malecón, a block east of La Rampa, hosts comedy on Wednesday at 8 p.m.

Comedy is also sometimes performed at the **Café Cantante Mi Habana,** in the Teatro Nacional at Paseo, one block west of the Plaza de la Revolución, tel. (7) 33-5713 or 79-6011, and in the bar beside Casona del 17 at Calles 17 and M, in Vedado.

MUSEUMS AND GALLERIES

Havana has almost 40 museums and at least 14 major art galleries and countless minor ones. Typically you'll find at least 30 major exhibitions in Havana at any one time.

The bimonthly *Galerías de Arte Programación,* available from the **Centro de Desarrollo de las Artes Visuales,** at San Ignacio #352, in Plaza Vieja, lists openings. Likewise, the *Guia Cultural de la Habana, Cartelera,* and *Granma* publish current information on exhibitions and galleries, as does the bimonthly magazine *Revolución y Cultura.* See Resources, above, for contact information.

Museums

You'll find many natural history museums and "decorative arts" museums, but by far the majority are dedicated in one form or another to the glories of the Revolution. Almost always you are accompanied by a guide, who either trails a short distance behind or offers a sometimes stirring, other times turgid précis of socialism. Many museums support a variety of cultural activities, such as theater and ballet.

Art Galleries

You'll find an incredible array of revolving art, sculpture, and photo exhibitions. The shows often draw top international artists as well as Cubans of stature. And although official proscriptions keep a tight rein on avant-garde exhibitions, things had loosened enough in 1998 for an exhibition of nude photography by Roberto and Oswaldo Salas, Havana's first such exposition in many decades (surprisingly, a government that endorses a mature liberalism with regard to sexuality and sensuality has for long prohibited photographic explorations of the nude).

Cuba makes great efforts to display art from other countries, notably the Caribbean and Latin America, as for example the **Art of Our Americas** collection, housed in Havana's Casa de las Américas, Calle 3ra y G, tel. (7) 55-2706, fax (7) 33-4554, e-mail: casa@artsoft.cult.cu, a nongovernmental institution, which has studied and promoted every aspect of Latin American and Caribbean culture since 1959. The collection comprises more than 6,000 pieces encompassing sculpture, engravings, paintings, photographs, and popular art.

Likewise, the **Centro Wilfredo Lam,** at the corner of Empedrado and San Ignacio in Habana Vieja, tel. (7) 61-2096 and 61-3419, fax (7) 33-8477, e-mail: wlam@artsoft.cult.cu, has a collection of 1,250 contemporary art pieces from Cuba and around the world. Open Mon.-Fri. 8:30 am.-3:30 p.m., but Mon.-Sat. 10 a.m.-5 p.m. for guided visits. If you can, time your visit for May to coincide with the prestigious **Havana Biennale,** an annual art show hosted by the Centro Wilfredo Lam.

Needless to say, the **National Arts Museum** in Havana's Palacio de Bellas Artes, houses a tremendous collection of both classical and modern art featuring works by Renoir, Picasso, Rodin, and other masters. But there are dozens of other smaller galleries.

HAVANA ART GALLERIES

Centro Wilfredo Lam: San Ignacio #22 esq. Empedrado, Habana Vieja, tel. (7) 61-2096; Mon.-Sat. 10 a.m.-5 p.m.

Galeria del Arte Galiano: Calle Galiano #258 esq. Concordia, Centro Habana, tel. (7) 62-5365; Tue.-Sat. 10 a.m.-4:30 p.m.

Galeria del Arte Latinoamericano: Calle G e/ 3ra y 5ta, Vedado, tel. (7) 32-4653; Mon.-Fri. 10 a.m.-5 p.m.

Galeria Forma: Calle Obispo #255 e/ Cuba y Aguiar, Habana Vieja, tel. (7) 62-2103; Mon.-Sat. 10 a.m.-4 p.m.

Galeria Habana: Calle Linea e/ E y F, Vedado, tel. (7) 32-7101; Mon.-Sat. 10 a.m.-4:30 p.m., and Sunday, 9 a.m.-1 p.m.

Galeria Haydee Santamaría: Calle G e/ 3ra y 5ta, Vedado, tel. (7) 32-4653; Mon.-Fri. 10 a.m.-5 p.m.

Galeria Horacio Ruíz: Calle Tacón #4 esq. Empedrado, Habana Vieja; Mon.-Sat. 10 a.m.-5:30 p.m.

Galeria Francisco Javier Baez: Plaza de la Catedral, Habana Vieja; Mon.-Fri. 10 a.m.-5 p.m.

Galeria La Acacia: Calle San José #114 esq. Consulado y Industria, Centro Habana, tel. (7) 63-9364; Mon.-Sat. 10 a.m.-4 p.m.

Galeria Marinao: Calle 15 #607, e/ B y C, Vedado; Mon.-Fri. 10 a.m.-5 p.m., and Saturday 10 a.m.-3 p.m.

Galeria Nelson Dominguez: Calle Obispo #166, e/ Amargura y Churruca, Habana Vieja, tel. (7) 63-9407; Mon.-Sat. 10 a.m.-5:30 p.m.

Galeria Plaza Vieja: Calle Muralla #107 esq. San Ignacio, Habana Vieja, tel. (7) 62-6295; Mon.-Fri. 9 a.m.-3:30 p.m.

Galeria Roberto Diago: Muralla #107 esq. San Ignacio, Habana Vieja, tel. (7) 33-8005; Mon.-Sat. 10 a.m.-5:30 p.m.

Galeria UNEAC: Calle 17 esq. H, Vedado, tel. (7) 32-4551; Mon.-Fri. 9 a.m.-5 p.m.

Galeria Victor Manuel: Plaza de la Catedral, Habana Vieja, tel. (7) 61-2955; Mon.-Sat. 10 a.m.-4 p.m.

Taller de Seregráfia Rene Portocarrero: Calle Cuba #513, e/ Teniente Rey y Muralla, Habana Vieja, tel. (7) 62-3276; Mon.-Fri. 9 a.m.-4 p.m.

Taller Experimental de la Gráfica: Callejón del Chorro, Plaza de la Catedral, Habana Vieja, tel. (7) 62-0979; Mon.-Sat. 10 a.m.-4 p.m.

OTHER ENTERTAINMENT

Aqua Espectáculos

Swimming-pool *espectáculos* (also called *aquáticas danzas*) are choreographed water ballets with *son et lumière* and are offered at the Hotel Cohiba on Wednesday night, and the Hotel Nacional, which offers *Swan Lake* nightly at 9:30.

The **Qualton El Viejo y el Mar,** in the Marina Hemingway complex in the Barlovento district of western Havana, also offers an *aquática danza* on Tuesday at 9 p.m.

Fashion Shows

La Maison, Calle 16 #701 esq. Av. 7ma, Miramar, tel. (7) 24-1543, fax (7) 24-1585, offers fashion shows—*presentación de modas*—beneath the stars in the terrace garden of an elegant old mansion, on a stage lit by a *son et lumière*. Live music is provided. It's enjoyable, albeit a bit strained. Reservations are recommended. Entrance costs US$10 (US$15 including transportation and a bottle of rum). A 4 p.m. show is offered on weekends. Meals are served alfresco beneath the flame-of-the-forest trees. There's a piano bar in a separate a/c building (US$2), open after the show.

The disco at **Club 1830** also hosts a fashion show, included in the US$5 entrance price.

Poetry Readings and Literary Events

Prior to the Special Period, prominent writers and poets gathered at **La Moderna Poesía** bookstore, at the west end of Calle Obispo, each Saturday at noon to sign copies of their latest releases. Literary events have begin to appear again.

Literary readings are offered at the **Unión Nacional de Escritores y Artistas de Cuba** (UNEAC, or Union of Writers and Artists), at the corner of Calle 17 and I UNEAC, tel. (7) 32-4551, fax (7) 33-3158. The mansion's porch is now the union's cafe, where you may mingle with Cuba's literati.

Poetry readings are also given at the **Casa de las Américas,** Calle 3 and G, in Vedado, tel. (7) 55-2706, fax (7) 33-4554, e-mail: casa@artsoft.cult.cu,; the **Fundación Alejo Carpentier,** at Empedrado #215 in Habana Vieja, tel. (7) 61-3667; and **La Madriguera,** a popular hangout for university students, on Avenida Salvador Allende and Calles Luaces. The **Museum of Fine Arts,** on Tracadero and Agramonte (Zulueta), also hosts literary events, as well as film screenings and musical presentations.

Dolphin Show

A dolphin show is offered eight times daily at the National Aquarium, at Avenida 1ra and Calle 60 in Miramar, tel. (7) 23-6401 (US$2, children US$0.50; in addition to US$5 entrance to the aquarium). Shark feeding and a sea lion are also offered on a scheduled basis. (See the Playa sightseeing section above.)

Transvestite Shows

Cubans have a tremendous sense of satire and transvestite humor is a staple of any comedy show. Dedicated transvestite shows are hosted upstairs in the **Centro Cultural de Árabe** on the Prado, e/ Calles Refugio y Trocadero, on Friday, Saturday, and Sunday, 9 a.m.-midnight (US$15). Cabarets are hosted nightly (US$5). Another *tranvestis* show is hosted at the **Rosalia Castro,** around the corner from the Restaurant Hanoi, on Plaza del Cristo.

FOR GAYS

Gay life in Havana has expanded noticeably in recent years, and male homosexuals act with more demonstrable confidence (lesbianism has not become anywhere near so accepted). There are cruising sections, such as on the Malecón opposite the Fiat Café two blocks east of La Rampa, where the party spreads along the seafront boulevard in the wee hours. The corner of La Rampa and L, outside the Cine Yara, is a lesser cruising spot. The Café Monseigneur, Calle O, e/ La Rampa y 21, is a gay hangout. And Parque de la Fraternidad has a late-night cruising scene. There are also private gay parties, known as *fiestas de diez pesos,* and which charge a 10-peso cover.

For gay beaches, head to Boca Ciega section of Playas del Este, east of town. In town, try Playita de 16, the rocky *balneario* at Calle 16 in Miramar; and Playa Tritón, in front of the Hotel Neptuno/Tritón.

SPORTS

Havana has many sports centers *(centros deportivos)*, although most are very run-down or otherwise dour. The largest is the **Panamericano** complex, in Habana del Este, tel. (7) 97-4140. It includes an Olympic athletic stadium, tennis courts, swimming pool, and even a velodrome for cycling.

Organized Tours
Agencia de Viajes Cubadeportes (see the Sports section in the On The Road chapter) specializes in sports tourism and arranges visits to international sport events, training facilities, etc., including lodging, transfers, etc.

Last Frontier Expeditions (see Organized Tours in the On The Road chapter) specializes in trips to Cuba for sporting enthusiasts. For example, it offers a trip to the **Ernest Hemingway International Sports Classic** *(Clásico Internacional Hemingway)*, a 10K race through Habana Vieja that the company helped initiate in 1995. The race occurs each May and is part of National Sports Week, which includes baseball, basketball, and volleyball, symposia on sports, and visits to sports-medicine clinics. Last Frontier also offers the Ernest Hemingway Sportfishing Tournament, the Havana Open Golf Tournament, hunting and fishing trips, and baseball fantasy camps.

In Canada, **Eleggua Project,** (see Organized Tours section in the On the Road chapter) specializes in athletic and sports study programs to Cuba and provides travel services.

PARTICIPATORY ACTIVITIES

Bicycling
Bicycling offers a chance to explore the city alongside the Cubans themselves. The roads are a bit dodgy, with bully-boy trucks and buses pumping out fumes, plus potholes and other obstacles to contend with (a helmet is a wise investment). Repairs are never a problem: scores of Habaneros now make a living repairing bicycles and punctures *(poncheras)*. You should nevertheless bring essential spares.

If you're interested in joining groups of Cuban students, mostly English-speaking, contact or **Club Nacional de Cicliturismo Gran Caribe,** Lonja del Comercio, Calle Oficia, Havana, fax (7) 66-9908, e-mail: trans@mail.infocom.etecsa.cu, (alias the Havana Bicycle Club) of the University of Havana, which welcomes foreigners to join students on weekend cycle trips into the countryside surrounding Havana. Contact club president Ignacio Valladares Rivero, tel. (687) 98-9193 (home) or 78-3941 (Estadio Juan Abrantes).

The only place I'm aware of currently renting bicycles in Havana is at the Hotel Jardín del Eden in Marina Hemingway, tel. (7) 24-1150, ext. 371 (it charges US$1 per hour, or US$12 per day for mountain bikes).

Bowling
You can practice your tenpin bowling at an alley in the **Hotel Kohly,** at Avenida 49 esq. 36A, Reparto Kohly, in Vedado, tel. (7) 24-0240, fax (7) 24-1733, e-mail: reserva@kohly.gav.cma.net; or at the **Havana Golf Club** (see below), which has a fully mechanized two-lane bowling alley and full-size pool tables. They're very popular with local youth.

Golf
Havana offers golf at the **Havana Golf Club,** tel. (7) 55-8746 or 33-8919, fax (7) 33-8820, hidden east of the Avenida de la Independencia, at Carretera de Vento Km 8, Capdevila Havana, near Boyeros, about 20 km south of Havana. Of four courses in Havana in 1959, this is the only one remaining. Also called the "Diplo Golf Course," the nine-hole course—with 18 tees and 22.5 hectares of fairway—is a bit run-down, despite a recent facelift. The two sets of tees, positioned for play to both sides of the fairway, make the holes play quite differently. A second set of nine holes was to be open by the year 2001, when it will be a 6,257-yard course (the layout of the current nine holes will be changed) to be called Havana Diplomat Golf & Tennis Club. The course, a "woodland parkland-style layout" that is compared to Pinehurst in North

Carolina, starts off badly but the fifth and sixth holes are described as "well-designed holes that could hold their own on almost any course of the world."

'Golfito'—as the locals know it—has a minimally stocked pro shop, plus five tennis courts, a swimming pool, and two restaurants set amid landscaped grounds. The pleasant Bar Hoy 19 (19th Hole), with a small TV lounge, overlooks the greens. The club hosts golf competitions. Membership costs US$70 plus US$45 monthly (US$15 for additional family members). A round costs nonmembers US$20 for nine holes (US$30 for 18). You can rent clubs for US$10. Caddies cost US$3 per nine holes. A US$3.50 fee is charged to use the pool, US$2 for the tennis facilities. Jorge Duque, the affable resident golf pro, charges US$5 per 30 minutes of instruction.

The **Club Habana,** Av. 5ta 188 y 192, in Reparto Flores, Playa, tel. (7) 24-5700, fax (7) 24-5705, has a practice range. The club serves its members, made up mostly of foreign diplomats and businessmen, but nonmembers are welcome (entrance costs US$10 Mon.-Fri., and US$15 Saturday and Sunday).

A championship 18-hole course was slated for Havana.

Gymnasiums

Only a few tourist hotels have gyms. The best are at the Hotel Cohiba and Hotel Parque Central. Havana, however, is replete with gymnasiums and other sports centers. Contact Cubadeportes, Calle 20 #705 e/ 7 y 9, Miramar, tel. (7) 24-0945 or 24-7230, fax (7) 24-1914, for information.

Horseback Riding

Club Hípico, tel. (7) 33-8203 or 44-1058, fax (7) 33-8166, in Parque Lenin, in the *municipio* of Arroyo Naranjo on Havana's southern outskirts, is an equestrian center—*centro ecuestre*—that offers horseback rides plus instruction in riding, jumping, and dressage. A course of 10 one-hour riding lessons costs US$102. You can take one-hour horseback trips (US$15) and rent horses if you're already proficient. Open 9 a.m.-4:30 p.m.

Horseback riding is also offered near Playas del Este at **Finca de Recreo Guanabito,** Calzada de Jústiz, km 3.5, Guanabo, tel. (7) 96-4610,

and nearby at **Rancho Mi Hacienda,** Calzada de Jústiz, km 4, Guanabo, tel. (7) 96-4711, near Minas. These working "dude ranches" offer you a chance to get covered with dust and manure.

Running

The Malecón is a good place to jog, although you need to beware the uneven surface and occasional pothole. I use the bicycle lane. For wide-open spaces, head to Parque Lenin, where the road circuit provides a perfect running track. Serious runners might head to the track at the Panamericano complex, tel. (7) 97-4140; the **Estadio Juan Abrahantes,** on Zapata, south of the university; **Centro Deportivo Claudio Argüellos,** at the junction of Avenida de la Independencia, Avenida 26, and Vía Blanca; or **CVD José Martí** stadium, at the base of Avenida de los Presidentes in Vedado.

Sailing

Yachts and motor vessels can be rented at **Marina Hemingway,** Av. 5ta y Calle 248, Santa Fe, Havana, tel. (7) 24-1150, fax (7) 24-1149, e-mail: comercial@comermh.cha.cyt.cu, which has 27- and 33-foot *Piraña* yachts and larger motorboats for bare-boat or crewed rental.

Club Habana, Av. 5ta, e/ 188 y 192, in Reparto Flores, Playa, tel. (7) 24-5700, fax (7) 24-5705, also offers yacht rental.

Marina Puertosol Tarará, tel. (7) 97-1510, fax (7) 97-1499 (in Havana: Marinas Puertosol, Av. 1ra #3001 esq. 30, Miramar, tel. (7) 24-5923, fax (7) 24-5928), rents yachts for US$250 for nine hours. It also offers live-aboard motorboats. Weekly rentals range from US$2,100 (May-Oct.) to US$2,800 (mid-Dec. to mid-Jan.).

Scuba Diving

There's also good diving offshore of Havana. The Gulf Stream and Atlantic Ocean currents meet west of the city, where many ships have been sunk through the centuries, among them the wreck of the *Santísimo Trinidad,* off Santa Fé, west of Marina Hemingway; a merchant ship called the *Coral Island;* and the *Sanchez Barcastegui,* an armored Spanish man-o'-war that foundered in 1895. Their wooden and iron hulls make for fascinating exploration. This western shore is known as **Barlovento** and is unusual in that the island shelf drops by steps into the abyss, each forming a prairie with corals, gorgonians, sponges, and caves in addition to shipwrecks.

Also, the so-called **"Blue Circuit"** is a series of dive sites (with profuse coral and shipwrecks) extending east from Bacuranao, about 10 km east of Havana, to the Playas del Este. Visibility ranges from 15 to 35 meters. Water temperatures average 27° C to 30° C. The traditional critters of the Caribbean abound: barracuda, rays, sharks, tarpon, and turtles. The star-studded cast also includes angels, bigeyes, butterflies, damsels, drums, gobies, groupers, grunts, jacks, parrot fish, snappers, triggerfish, and wrasses, all of which seem perfectly content to ignore the human presence. Dozens of morays peer out from beneath rocky ledges.

Dive Centers: Marina Hemingway offers scuba diving from **La Aguja Scuba Center,** tel. (7) 21-5277 or 33-1150, fax (7) 33-6848 or 33-1536, which has professional guides and also rents equipment. La Aguja charges US$28 for one dive, US$50 for two dives, US$60 for a "resort course," and US$360 for an open-water certification. It offers dive excursions to Playa Girón (Bay of Pigs) and Varadero for US$70, and rents equipment for US$5. It's open daily 8:30 a.m.-4:30 p.m.

The **Blue Reef Diving Center** at the Hotel Cocomar, at Caimito, 23 km west of Havana, tel./fax (7) 80-5089, also has a scuba facility, as does **Club Habana**, Av. 5ta, e/ 188 y 192, in Reparto Flores, Playa, tel. (7) 24-5700, fax (7) 24-5705, also offers scuba diving (entrance costs US$10 for non-members; Mon.-Fri., and US$15 Saturday and Sunday).

The Hotel Copacabana, Av. 1ra, e/ Calles 44 y 46 in Miramar, tel. (7) 33-1037, fax (7) 33-3846, offers beginning and advanced scuba diving lessons as well as trips. The water sports concession here rents underwater video and photography equipment.

Marina Puertosol Tarará (see Sailing, above), at Tarará, near Playas del Este, has a scuba center, tel. (7) 97-1501, ext. 239, offering one-dive (US$30) and two-dive (US$50) trips, and four-day certification program (US$400), plus three-hour initiation dives. Equipment rental costs US$10.

The **Blue Dive Club,** tel. (7) 62-67349, is at Avenida 1ra and 24 in Miramar.

Havanatur offers a "scuba in Cuba" program, tel. (7) 23-9783, fax (7) 24-1760, e-mail: adolfov@cimex.com.cu.

Sportfishing

Marlin S.A., tel. (7) 24-1150, ext. 735, on Canal B at Marina Hemingway, offers sportfishing using a variety of boats (US$130-290 for four hours, US$185-470 six hours, depending on craft).

Puertosol (see Sailing, above) offers sportfishing excursions. Typical four-hour light-tackle excursions *(pesa a fondo)* cost US$15-30 per person; four-hour deep-sea excursions cost US$150-250 for up to four passengers.

Also see Tarará in the Habana del Este section, and Marina Hemingway in the Playa section.

Swimming

Most large tourist hotels have pools that are open for the use of nonguests. My favorite in Habana Vienna is the small rooftop pool in the **Hotel Parque Central.** Nearby is **Club Sevilla,** which offers access the ground-floor, open-air figure-eight pool to the rear of the Hotel Sevilla. Entry costs US$5 (US$2.50 for children and guests of the Hotel Plaza), plus a gym (US$2) and sauna (US$3.50), and massage (US$15-25). The entrance in on the corner of the Prado and Animas.

One of the best pools in Vedado is at the **Hotel Nacional** (US$5 per nonguest). Nonswimmers need to beware the sudden steep drop to the deep end, which plunges to three meters (a common fault in the design of Cuban swimming pools). Also try the small rooftop pool of the **Hotel Capri,** and the attractive, outdoor mezzanine pool in the **Hotel Habana Libre Tryp.**

In Miramar, the **Club Almendares,** on Avenida 49 C in Reparto Kohly, tel. (7) 24-4990, has a large, well-kept pool (US$3 adults, US$1 children) with sundeck and proves popular with Cuban families. Two other favorites are the pools at the **Hotel Copacabana** and the large, freeform pools in the **Hotel Comodoro** bungalow complex.

The best facility in Havana, however, is **Club Habana,** Av. 5ta, e/ 188 y 192, in Reparto Flores, Playa, tel. (7) 24-5700, fax (7) 24-5705, a private members-only club that opens its doors to

BEISBOL: CUBA'S NATIONAL PASTIME

*B*eisbol (or *pelota*) is as much an obsession in Cuba as it is in the U.S.—more so, in fact; in 1909, Ralph Estep, a salesman for Packard, journeyed through Cuba and thought it "baseball crazy." The first officially recorded baseball game was played in Cuba in 1874, at what is now the world's oldest baseball stadium still in use.

Just watch Cuban kids playing, writes author Randy Wayne White, "without spikes, hitting without helmets, sharing their cheap Batos gloves, but playing like I have never seen kids play before. It wasn't so much the skill—though they certainly had skill—as it was the passion with which they played, a kind of controlled frenzy." No wonder Cuba traditionally beats the pants off the U.S. team in the Olympic Games.

Needless to say, the U.S. professional leagues are well aware of this enormous talent pool. Many black Cubans found positions in the U.S. Negro leagues. (The flow went both ways. Tommy Lasorda, for example, played five seasons in Cuba and in 1959 pitched the national team into the Caribbean World Series.) Players who make the Cuban national team and barnstorm the Olympics earn about 400 pesos (US$20) a month, and it's not surprising that many are still tempted by the prospect of riches in the U.S. More than 30 Cuban baseball stars have fled Cuba since 1991, such as Livan Hernández,

who left in 1996 and was snatched up for US$4.5 million by the Florida Marlins.

The defection of Hernández so rankled Castro that in a fit of pique, Livan's half-brother Orlando "El Duque" Hernández, one of the world's greatest pitchers, was barred from playing for life (Castro even forbade the Cubans to watch the 1997 World Series that year); Hernández was relegated to work in the Havana Psychiatric Hospital for US$8 a month. Understandably, in January 1998 he fled Cuba on a homemade raft and was signed by the Yankees for US$6.6 million. Imagine the fury of Fidel, who, says Andrei Codrescu, "has railed against Yankee imperialism for years."

Still, not every player is eager to leave. In 1995, Omar Linares, slugging third baseman for the Pinar del Río team and considered to be one of the best amateur baseball players in the world, rejected a US$1.5 million offer to play for the New York Yankees. "My family and country come first," said Linares. "I'm aware of what a million-and-a-half dollars means, but I'm faithful to Fidel."

Ah, yes, Fidel. Cuba is led by a sports fanatic. In the early years of power, Castro would often drop in at Havana's Gran Stadium (in 1971 it was renamed Estadio Latinoamericano and holds 55,000 people; it was state-of-the-art when opened in 1946 with 35,000 seats) in Cerro in the evening to pitch a few

non-members for US$10 weekdays and US$15 on weekends. It has a splendid beach shelving gently into calm waters, as well as a large pool to Western standards. The pool complex at the new **Hotel Novotel**, Av. 5ta, e/ 72 and 76, tel. (7) 24-3584 or 62-8308, fax (7) 24-3583 or 62-8587, is another stunner.

The **Marina Hemingway** is very popular with Cubans as well as foreign sailors who arrive by private yacht. It has two pool complexes, the best being that of the Hotel Jardín del Eden. And the **Complejo Turístico La Giradilla**, at Calle 272, e/ 37 y 51 in the La Coronela district, just west of Cubanacán, tel. (7) 33-6062, offers a splendid swimming pool.

Further afield, there are public swimming pools in Parque Lenin, and also an Olympic pool— **Piscina Olímpica**—at Avenida 99 #3804, in Lotería, southeast of Havana in the *municipio* of Cotorro. In Habana del Este, try the **Hotel Panamericano** pool.

Forsake joining the locals who bathe and snorkel in the waters off the Malecón. The rocks are sharp, and the waters often rough and badly polluted (when the ebbing tide sucks Havana harbor, the sea off the Malecón can seem like pure gasoline). Far better is to head out to Bacuranao, Tárara, or Playas del Este, where you can swim in the warm sea; or to the *balnearios* of the Playa del Oeste extending from western Miramar to Barlovento. Care should always be taken when swimming in the waters off Tarará and Playas del Este, where the waves are often powerful and rip currents are common.

SPECTATOR SPORTS

Rough, often weed-covered basketball courts are everywhere, and Havana is replete with baseball stadiums, gymnasiums, and athletic facilities.

balls at the Sugar Kings' batters. And everyone knows the story of how Fidel once tried out as a pitcher for the old Washington Senators. How different history might have been had his curveball curved a little better! Says Tommy Lasorda: "Instead of a Senator he became a dictator."

Cuba's stars play more than 100 games a season on regional teams under the supervision of the best coaches, sports doctors, and competition psychologists outside the U.S. big leagues. Each province has a team on the national league *(Liga Nacional),* and two provinces and the city of Havana have two teams each, making 18 teams in all. The last game of every three-game series is played in a *pueblo* away from the provincial capital so that fans in the country can see their favorite team play live. The season runs Dec.-June. The teams play a 39-game season, with the top seven teams going on to compete in the 54-game National Series.

Stadiums are oases of relaxation and amusement. There are no exploding scoreboards or dancing mascots and beer and souvenir hawkers are replaced by old men wandering among the seats with thermoses, selling thimble-size cups of sweet Cuban espres-

so. Spam sandwiches replace hot dogs in the stands, where the spectators, being good socialists, also cheer for the opposition base-stealers and home-run hitters. Balls (knocked out of the field by aluminum Batos bats made in Cuba) are even returned from the stands, because everyone understands they're too valuable to keep as souvenirs.

Minor League Sports, 10216 Cozycroft Ave., Chatsworth, CA 91311, tel. (818) 349-1592, fax (818) 886-7224, e-mail: mlsport@aol.com, sends baseball supplies to Cuba and has offered baseball clinics on the island: "U.S.-Cuba Baseball Experiences."

Estadio Juan Abrahantes, Havana

Baseball
The baseball season runs Dec.-June at the 60,000-seat **Estadio Latinoamericano,** the main baseball stadium, hidden in Cerro on Avenida 20 de Mayo and Calle Pedrosa, tel. (7) 70-6526. Games are played Tues.-Thurs. at 8 p.m., Saturday at 1:30 and 8 p.m., and Sunday at 1:30 p.m. (three pesos). The entrance is at Calle Zequeira.

You can also watch games being played at the **Estadio Juan Abrahantes** (also called Estadio Universitario), below the university at the end of Zanja, at Avenida 27 de Noviembre.

Boxing and Martial Arts
The main boxing training center is the **Centro de Entrenamiento de Boxeo** at Carretera Torrens in Wajay, in the *municipio* of Boyeros, tel. (7) 22-0538, southwest of the city.

You can watch boxing and martial arts at the **Gimnasio de Boxeo Rafael Trejo,** at Calle Cuba #815, in Habana Vieja, tel. (7) 62-0266,

and at **Sala Polivalente Kid Chocolate,** on the Prado opposite the Capitolio, tel. (7) 62-8634. It's intriguing to pop inside to watch kids and adults sparring. They may even welcome you onto the court or into the ring! Likewise, martial arts are hosted at the **Sala Polivalente Ramón Font** on Avenida de la Independencia y Bruzón, in Plaza de la Revolución, tel. (7) 82-0000; and at the **Estadio Universitario Juan Abrahantes,** at San Rafael y Ronda, Vedado, tel. (7) 78-6959.

The week-long **International Conference on Olympic Style Boxing,** held at Havana's Instituto Superior de Cultura Física Manuel Fajardo in November 1999 was intended to become an annual event. Contact Agencia de Viajes Cubadeportes, Calle 20 #705 e/ 7ma y 9na, Miramar, tel. (7) 24-0945, fax (7) 24-1914,

Other Sports
Volleyball and basketball are hosted at the **Sala**

Polivalente Kid Chocolate and **Sala Poliva-lente Ramón Font** (see boxing).

For **fencing,** head to **ExpoCuba,** tel. (7) 44-6251, in the *municipio* of Arroyo Naranjo (see Suburban Havana in the Sightseeing section).

For **hockey,** head to the **Terreno Sintético de Hockey,** in Santiago de las Vegas (see Suburban Havana in the Sightseeing section).

The **Complejo de Pelota Vasca y Patinodromo,** at the junction of Avenida de la Independencia, Avenida 26, and Vía Blanca, tel. (7) 81-9700, has a **roller-skating** track.

And **soccer games** are played at the **Estadio Pedro Marrero** at Avenida 41 #4409, e/ 44 y 50, in Cerro, tel. (7) 23-4698.

FOR THE KIDS

Pony rides are offered in Parque Luz Caballero, between Avenida Carlos M. Céspedes and Tacón, in Habana Vieja. Immediately west is a *parque diversione* (children's fairground) in front of the Castillo de Atane on Calle Tacón. It offers electric train ride plus all the fun of the fair.

There are plenty of other *parques diversiones* in town. In Vedado, try **Jalisco Parque** on Calle 23 at 18. **Club Almendares,** on Avenida 49 C in Reparto Kohly, tel. (7) 24-4990, offers mini-golf and a kiddies' pool. And **Parque Lenin** has plenty of attractions to keep the kids amused—from an old steam train ride and pony rides to a *parque diversion* with a miniature roller coaster and other rides.

Casa de la Comédia, on Calle Justíz in Habana Vieja, hosts children's theater and comedy events on weekend afternoons.

Both the **Jardín Zoológico de la Habana** (Havana's zoo), in Vedado, and the **Parque Zoológico** (the national zoo) offer pony rides, *parque diversiones,* and, of course, the animals.

SHOPPING

Havana is a trove of bargain buys. True, you don't come here for factory outlets of designer boutiques. But for high-quality art and crafts, Havana is unrivaled in the Caribbean. The two big-ticket items are, of course, cigars and rum, readily available throughout the city, with the world's best cigars selling for one-third or less of their sale price in North America. Other great bargains include dolls, musical instruments (although few are made in Cuba), and music cassettes and CDs. And silver and gold jewelry belies Cuba's images as a stodgy vacuum of creativity.

You're not going to find anything of interest in peso stores, half-full (or half-empty) of shoddy Cuban-made plastic and tin wares. . . nor at the Cuban pawn shops, called *casas comisionistas* where Cubans place items for sale on consignment and pocket a commission (the State takes the rest). If your curiosity runs to it, check out a Cuban take on the modern department store or one of the illicit shops run by Habaneros, often concentrated along streets colloquially named *Calle Ocho* for the famous Eighth Street in Miami, where Cuban exiles established their businesses during the first years of exile. For obvious reasons, their existence is advertised by word of mouth.

ANTIQUES

Havana's museums and private homes are brimful of colonial-era antiques—to the degree that armed robbers have been known to raid houses and make off with the family jewels. Alas, there are few antique stores, partly because the government is keen to prevent a wholesale exodus of the country's treasures (however, it has been buying up antiques and gold from its own populace for a fraction of their market value, and it sometimes puts confiscated art works up for sale abroad on the sly). Nonetheless, you *can* find antiques for sale. Perhaps the best place is **Galería la Acacia,** 114 San José, Centro Habana, tel. (7) 63-9364 (open Mon.-Sat. 9 a.m.-4:30 p.m.), whose trove includes everything from 18th-century ceramics to grand pianos. Some of it is merely kitschy, and much is in a sorry state. But for the knowledgeable, there are some gems certified by the National Heritage Office, Calle 4 #251, Vedado, tel. (7) 55-2272, from which you'll need an export license.

You can buy traditional Spanish fans *(abanicos)* at the **Casa del Abanicos,** Calle Obrapía #107 e/ Mercaderes y Oficios. The hand-made and hand-painted fans cost US$1.40 to US$144. It's open Tue.-Sat. 9 a.m.-5 p.m. and Sunday 9 a.m.-1 p.m.

ARTS AND CRAFTS

Cuba's strong suit is arts and crafts, sold freely for dollars by artisans at street stalls, and also in art and craft stores by state agencies such as the Fondo de Bien Culturales and ARTEX. The best stuff is sold in the gift stores of the upscale hotels, which mark up accordingly; often you can find identical items on the street at half the price (as with *papier-mâché* baseball figures).

The shortest walk through Habana Vieja can be a magical mystery tour of homegrown art. In recent years, art has been patronized by the tourist dollar, and the city is overflowing with whimsical Woolworth's art: cheap canvas scenes, busty cigar-chomping ceramic mulattas, kitschy erotic carvings, *papier-mâché* masks and vintage Yankee cars, and animal figurines painted in pointillist dots. But there is plenty of true-quality art ranging from paintings and tapestries to hand-worked leather goods and precious wood carvings in Afro-Cuban realism running as high as US$100 but representing a solid investment. You'll also see *muñecitas* (dolls) everywhere, mostly representing the goddess of the *santería* religious (Cuban women are great doll collectors, and often keep their childhood dolls into late adulthood).

Pottery runs from small, rough, clay ashtrays with a clay cigar attached and Fidel in figurine form, to creative vases and ceramic ware. Also look for artfully delicate, copper-toned wind chimes and high-quality graphics printed on recycled paper, including reproductions of classic Cuban painters: Wilfredo Lam, Victor Manuel, Mariano Rodríguez, and Amelia Peláez. Keep your eyes peeled for originals by up-and-coming talent such as Tomás Sanchez, Manuel Mendive, and Zaida del Río, with their very Cuban vision of landscapes, myths, and reality; and the erotic works of Aldo Soler and Carlos Alpízar.

Souvenir Stores
ARTEX shops stock postcards, books, music cassettes and CDs, T-shirts, arts and crafts, rum, cigars, and other souvenirs. In Vedado,

check out the shop at the junction of Calle L and La Rampa. Nearby, at La Rampa and P, is a **Bisart** store with a similar range of goods.

Manzana de Gómez, a shopping complex on the northeast side of Parque Central, in Habana Vieja, has several souvenir stores selling carvings, leather goods, and intriguing wall hangings, belts, purses, and posters. The store called **Monsieur** is particularly good. Several souvenir stores cluster around Plazuela de Albear, immediately east of the Manzana de Gómez.

Open-Air Markets
Artists sell their works freely on the streets, often for unreasonably low prices. A limited amount of bargaining is normal at street markets. However, most prices are very low to begin with, and Cubans are scratching to earn a few dollars. Be reasonable. Don't bargain simply to win a battle. If the quoted price seems fair—and it usually is—then pay up and feel blessed that you already have a bargain. Feel free to

A fan being decorated by hand at Casa de Abanicos.

visit the artists' studios. Calle Obispo, in Habana Vieja has several.

There are plenty of markets to choose from. The best is the arts-and-crafts market held on Calle Tacón, in Habana Vieja, selling everything from miniature bongo drums and **papier-mâché** figures of Cuban baseball players to ceramics of busty, pipe-smoking mulattas.

In Vedado, a small open-air flea market on La Rampa e/ Calle M y L sells woodcarvings, jewelry, shoes, and leather goods. It's open daily 8 a.m.-6 p.m. A better bet is the larger **Carnaval de la Calle** market, on the Malecón e/ Calles D y E, where about 300 artisans exhibit and sell handicrafts ranging from corals delicately spun into bracelets (note, however, that coral is endangered), beaten copper pieces, quality leather sandals, woodcarvings, paintings, quaint ceramics, carved ox-horns, plates showing 3-D landscapes and, alas, stuffed marine turtles and turtle heads—which should be avoided!

Galleries

Havana is home to a dizzying galaxy of galleries, most with both permanent and revolving exhibitions and art for sale. Pick up a copy of the weekly tourist guide *Cartelera* for complete listings. You can also pick up a bimonthly program—*Galerías de Arte Programación*—from the **Centro de Desarrollo de las Artes Visuales,** at San Ignacio #352 in Plaza Vieja. Its calendar of openings usually lists at least 30 major exhibitions taking place in Havana at any given time. For more complete information on workshops and galleries, contact the **Fondo Cubano de Bienes Culturales,** also in Plaza Vieja at Muralla #107, tel. (7) 33-8005, fax (7) 33-8121, with excellent artwork for sale in its galleries (see Casa de los Condes de Jaruco, below). Most galleries are open Mon.-Sat. 10 a.m.-4 p.m.

One of the best places is **Galería la Acacia,** 114 San José e/ Industria y Consulado, Centro Habana, tel. (7) 63-9364, an art gallery with top-class contemporary works. Expect to pay US$1,000 or more for the best works. Other top-quality art is sold a short distance away at **Galería del Centro Gallego,** next to the Gran Teatro on Parque Central. This Aladdin's cave includes superb bronzes by Joel del Río, imaginative ceramics, some truly stunning silver and gold jewelry, Cuban Tiffany-style lamps, and wooden and papier-mâché animals painted in bright Caribbean colors and pointillist dots, in Haitian fashion. This is high-quality work, priced accordingly. Bring your US$100 bills.

Of a similar standard is the **Galería Victor Manuel,** tel. (7) 61-2955, on the west side of Plaza de la Catedral, displaying fine landscapes and ceramic pieces. Around the corner, on Calejón del Chorro, is the **Taller Experimental de la Gráfica,** which traces the history of engraving and has exclusive prints for sale.

The galleries in the **Casa de los Condes de Jaruco,** on Plaza Vieja, tel. (7) 62-2633, sell work of unparalleled beauty and quality. Upstairs, and most impressive of all, is **Galería de la Casona** with, among its many treasures, fantastic *papier-mâché* works of a heavily spiritualist nature. Be sure to walk through into the back room, where the works on display include Tiffany lamps, sculpted wooden statues, ceramic pieces, jewelry of truly mesmerizing creativity, and superb leatherwork in a uniquely Cuban style. Also upstairs is **Galeria de la Plaza Vieja,** where you will find some of the strongest statements in Cuban art. Similarly, you'll find experimental art for sale at the **Centro de Desarrollo de las Artes Visuales,** in the Casa de las Hermanas Cárdenas, on the west side of Plaza Vieja, tel. (7) 62-3533 or 62-2611.

Calle Obispo is famed for its art galleries. The highest quality works are displayed at **Galería Forma,** Calle Obispo #255, tel. (7) 62-0123, fax (7) 33-8121, selling artwork of international standard, including intriguing sculptures and ceramics and copper pieces. At Obispo #515, you'll find the studio of experimental ceramist Roberto Fernández Martinez, a lively old man with a spreading white beard, who explores the influences of African and Indo-Cuban mythology. His eclectic paintings range through a variety of styles from Klee to Monet. The **Asociación Cubana de Artesana Artistas** has a store on Obispo where individual artists have small booths selling jewelry and arts and crafts. Check out the fantastical, museum-scale wall hangings and fabulous statuettes in the gallery at the rear. Open Tues.-Fri. 1-6 p.m. and Saturday 10 a.m.-4 p.m.

The **Palacio de Artesanía Cubana,** on Calle Tacón, tel. (7) 62-4407, is replete with quality arts and crafts. You can also buy cigars and rum here. Open daily 9 a.m.-6 p.m.

The **Galeria Horacio Ruíz,** in the Palacio del Segundo Cabo, on the north side of Plaza de las Armas, has a large selection of *muñecas* (dolls) and papier-mâché masks.

The **Centro Wilfredo Lam,** on San Ignacio, tel. (7) 61-2096 and 61-3419, fax (7) 33-8477, e-mail: wlam@artsoft.cult.cu, exhibits works by the great Cuban master as well as other artists from around the Americas. It hosts the famous Havana Arts Biennial each May, when leading works are for sale. Likewise, the **Casa de las Américas,** on Calle 15 e/ B y C, Vedado, tel. (7) 55-2706, hosts exhibitions with works for sale. Also in Vedado, check out **Galeria Mariano,** part of the Casa de las Américas.

The small gallery in the lobby of the Hotel Nacional also exhibits and sells paintings by the Cuban masters. And the Hotel Cohiba's **Galeria Cohiba,** tel. (7) 33-3636, is another good source.

Jewelry

Most of the open-air markets have silver-plated jewelry at bargain prices. Check out the weekend market at Calle 25 e/ Calles I y H, in Vedado; some of the simple pieces for sale here (especially the necklaces) display stupendous creativity and craftsmanship. . . at low prices.

Most upscale hotels have *joyerías*—jewelry stores—selling international quality silver jewelry, much of it inlaid with black coral and in a distinctly contemporary vogue.

In Habana Vieja, head to the *joyería* in the **Casa de los Condes de Jaruco,** on Plaza Vieja, tel. (7) 62-2633, where the stunning works by Raúl Valladeres are for sale. Other good places to find upscale jewelry include the store in the **Museo de Plata,** on Calle Obispo in Habana Vieja; and the **Palacio de las Artesanias,** at the west end of Calle Tacón, in Habana Vieja. Also try the **Galeria del Centro Gallego** and **Galeria Victor Manuel.**

In Vedado, try the **Joyería La Habanera,** at Calle 12 #505 e/ Ave. 5ta y 7ma in Vedado, tel. (7) 33-2546, fax (7) 33-2529, which has an exquisite array of gold and silver jewelry.

One of the best upscale jewelry stores in town is the **Joyería Balla Cantando** in the Club Habana, west of Miramar in the Playas district. Likewise, the jewelry store upstairs in the **Casa de Habana,** Ave. 5ra y Calle 16, Miramar, offers top-notch creations.

Much jewelry, sadly, is of tortoiseshell, in spite of the fact that there's an international ban on the sale and transport of turtle products. *Don't buy it!*

Ceramics

You'll find many artists producing fantastic sculptural ceramics, such as those of Teresita Gómez or Roberto Fernández Martinez, whose works—often totemic—are heavily influenced by African myths. Look, too, for the works of women artists such as Antonio Eiriz and Amelia Peláez, and U.S.-born Jacqueline Maggi, now professor of engraving at the Advanced Institute of Art in Havana, who "tackles the problem of women" in her woodcarvings and sculptures. **Galeria Vilena,** on the south side of the plaza, sells ceramic works by leading artists such as Alfredo Sosabravo, Amelia Palaez, and Carballo Moreno.

More down-to-earth, whimsical pieces are a staple of the craft markets (see above).

Miscellany

Miniaturists and military buffs will find a few tiny soldiers, pirates, and other figurines in the **Casa de la Miniatura,** on Tacón, one block east of Plaza de la Catedral, but the collection is not what it once was. (Those that were antiques certified by the National Heritage Office are no longer for sale).

Lovers of Tiffany lamps should look for Gilberto Kindelán's transparent art nouveau lamps with bucolic landscapes featuring butterflies, which Kindelán describes as very visual and lending themselves well to poetry and movement in glass. The artist gets his glass, pewter, copper, and bronze from old mansions, recycling pieces rescued from beneath the wrecking ball.

BOOKS

For a city of two million literate and cultured people, Havana is appallingly short of books, which are severely restricted by the Cuban government (see Literature in the Arts and Entertainment section in the On The Road chapter). Havana is desperately in need of a Barnes & Noble.

Two stores stand out, but don't get your hopes up. The first is **Librería La Internacional,** at the top of Calle Obispo #528, Habana Vieja, tel. (7) 61-3238. It stocks a reasonable selection of historical, sociological, and political texts in English, plus a small selection of English-language novels. It's open Mon.-Sat. 9 a.m.-4:30 p.m. The city's largest bookstore is **Fernando Ortíz,** near the university on Calle L esq. 27, Vedado, tel. (7) 32-9653. Its stock spans a wide range of subjects in Spanish, plus a limited range of pulp fiction, English dictionaries, and sightseeing books on Cuba. It also sells a smattering of international magazines. Open Mon.-Fri. 10 a.m.-5 p.m. and Saturday 9 a.m.-3 p.m.

You'll also find a small selection of English-language novels at **La Bella Habana,** in the former Palacio del Segundo Cabo on the north side of Plaza de Armas, Habana Vieja, tel. (7) 62-8092. Open Mon.-Sat. 9 a.m.-4:30 p.m.

Others small outlets include **Librería Casa de las Américas,** at Calle G esq. 3ra, Vedado, tel. (7) 32-3587, open Mon.-Fri. 9 a.m.-5 p.m.; **Librería de la UNEAC,** in the Cuban Writers' and Artists' Union at Calle 17 esq. H, Vedado, tel. (7) 32-4551, open Mon.-Fri. 8:30 a.m.-4:30 p.m.; and **Librería Internacional José Martí,** at Calzada #259 e/ J y I, Vedado, tel. (7) 32-9838, open Mon.-Fri. 9 a.m.-4 p.m.

The **La Moderna Poesia** bookstore, opposite Librería La Internacional on Calle Obispo, promotes works by lesser-known Cuban authors. Readings and book signings are held here on Saturday. Also here is the **Librería Cervantes,** a venerable but depressing second-hand bookstore.

For books on art and film, check out **Tienda Chaplín,** on Calle 23 e/ 10ma y 12, tel. (7) 31-1101; it specializes in works related to the cinema but also has books on art and music, as well as posters and videos. Open Mon.-Sat. 2-9 p.m. **Centro de Desarrollo de Artes Visuales,** in the Casa de las Hermanas Cárdenas on Plaza Vieja, tel. (7) 62-3533 or 62-2611, sells artwork, posters, and art and photography books.

If all else fails, you can pick from the dreary collection of faded Spanish-language texts at the secondhand book fair in Plaza de Armas. (In Cuba, books are recycled until they fall apart. Books are so hard to come by that the law of supply and demand is at work. You'll gasp at the sticker-shock prices for tattered works so browned and wafer-crisp that they threaten to crumble in your hand, like palimpsests in an *Indiana Jones* movie). You'll find all kinds of antiquarian bric-a-brac, including atlases of Cuba, books on and by Ernest Hemingway, and the panoply of works by and about Che Guevera and Fidel Castro. Look for the *Album de la Revolución Cubana,* a bubble gum picture-card album that replaced baseball heroes with revolutionary heroes—primarily Fidel (tattered old copies sell from about US$40).

The only stationery store I know of is **La Papeleria,** at 102 O'Reilly, catercorner to the Plaza de las Armas. It sells pens, paper stock, and other basic office supplies.

CIGARS

Cigars are among the most coveted Cuban products for tourists. Quality cigars can be bought at virtually every restaurant, hotel, and shop that welcomes tourists. There are now more than two dozen **Casas de Tabaco** throughout the city, plus scores of other cigar outlets. The best shops now offer the type of selection previously only available in top stores in London or Geneva—everything from cedar boxes of 100 Hoyos de Monterrey Double Coronas to five-packs of Corona Lanceros. A good bet is to combine your purchase with a visit to a cigar factory.

Street Deals

Street deals are no deal. Everywhere you walk in Havana, *jiniteros* will offer you cigars at discount prices. You'll be tempted by what seems the deal of the century. Forget it! You might get lucky and get the real thing, but the vast majority are low-quality, machine-made cigars sold falsely as top-line cigars to unsuspecting tourists. Don't be taken in by the sealed counterfeit box, either. Fortunately a crackdown by police initiated in early 1999 has significantly reduced the problem.

You can buy inferior domestic cigars, called "torpedoes," for about one peso—US$1—in bars and restaurants and on the street.

Where to Buy

There are hundreds of outlets for cigars in Havana, but most shops have poorly informed and disinterested clerks who know little about *tabacos* (the Cuban term for *habanos*). Your best

BUYING CUBAN CIGARS

Taking home a box of premium stogies beats all other options for impressing your buddies back home. It pays to know the ins and outs.

The quality of Cuban cigars declined significantly in the mid-1990s as the government set to boost production (160 million handmade premium cigars were produced in 1998, more than double the number produced in 1995). By 1999 the quality and consistency had recovered, although the government was aiming for 240 million cigars in 2000. And prices have increased in recent years, although reported the June 1999 issue of *Cigar Aficionado:* "On the bright side, cigars purchased in Havana are anywhere from one fourth to one half the price of similar cigars in London or Geneva and about 15 percent less than prices in Spain."

Several of Cuba's 42 factories might be producing any one brand *simultaneously,* hence quality can vary markedly even though the label is the name. Cigars produced in Havana's La Corona, El Laguito, and Romeo y Julieta factories are considered the best. The source is marked on the underneath of the box using a code. And quality varies from year to year, which is also shown in the box code.

If you're buying for speculation, buy the best. The only serious collectors' market in cigars is in prerevolutionary cigars, according to Anwer Bati in *The Cigar Companion.* Older cigars produced before the 1959 Revolution are commonly described as "pre-Castro." Those made before President Kennedy de-clared the U.S. trade embargo against Cuba in February 1962 are "pre-embargo." Pre-Castro or pre-embargo cigars are printed with "Made in Havana—Cuba"on the bottom of the box instead of the standard "Hecho en Cuba" used today. Since 1985, handmade Cuban cigars have carried the Cubatabaco stamp plus a factory mark and, since 1989, the legend "Hecho en Cuba. Totalmente a Mano" (Made in Cuba. Completely by Hand). If it reads "Hecho a Mano," the cigars are most likely hand-*finished* (i.e., only the wrapper was put on by hand) rather than handmade. If it states only "Hecho en Cuba," they are assuredly machine-made.

In addition, there are styles, sizes, and brands of cigars that have not been made in Cuba since shortly after the Revolution. They're the most valuable (a Belinda corona from the late 1930s will sell for $100 or more). It's not unusual for a box of 100 Montecristo No. 1s from the late 1950s to sell for $4,500 or more. Connoisseurs opt for "cabinet cigars," which come in undecorated cedar boxes.

In 1998, the Cuban government upped the export allowance to US$2,000 worth of cigars with documentation (you'll need receipts). If you don't have your receipts, Cuban Customs permits only two boxes. In 1999 the U.S. government also upped *its* allowance: persons with licenses to travel to Cuba may purchase US$185 of Cuban cigars or other goods, but the cigars may only be purchased in Cuba.

bet if you're a serious smoker is to buy at a serious outlet. Most of the upscale hotels now feature a **Casa del Tabaco,** notably the Hotel Parque Central and the Hostal de Habana, in Habana Vieja; the Hotel Meliá Cohiba, Hotel Habana Libre, Hotel Riviera, and Hotel Nacional, in Vedado; but there are a score of others.

Most shops sell by the box only. Due to high demand, cigars are often on back order. For example, Cohibas were rare abroad in 1996 (one major London cigar merchant told me that the Cubans were holding back supply to raise prices). Prices can vary up to 20% from store to store, so shop around. If one store doesn't have what you desire, another surely will. You should inspect your cigars before committing to a purchase. Most shops don't allow this, but the best shops do.

My top ten list of outstanding cigar shops would include eight endorsed by *Cigar Aficionado:*

Habana Vieja: La Casa del Habanos in the Partagas factory at Industria #520 e/ Barcelona y Dragones in Habana Vieja, tel. (7) 33-8060, has a massive walk-in humidor and accounted for the largest percentage of the 14 million cigars sold by Cuban tobacconists to tourists in 1998. The store has a front room catering to the busloads of tourists; hidden away to the rear is a lounge with a narrow humidified walk-in cigar showcase for serious smokers. Manager Abel Díaz oversees service-oriented staff.

Palacio del Tabaco, in the Fábrica La Corona, at Agramonte #106 e/ Colón y Refugio, tel. (7) 33-8389, offers rare cigars such as figurados and double coronas. It has a small bar.

CRACKING THE CODE

The code printed as a series of letters underneath each cigar box tells you a lot about the cigars inside. If you know the code, even a novice can determine the provenance and date of cigars, the quality of which varies markedly between factory and year.

The first two or three letters usually refer to the factory where the cigars were made (for example, FPG refers to the Partagas factory), followed by four letters that give the date of manufacture (OASC, for example, means 0697, or June 1997). The 0 in front of single digit months is often omitted, however.

Newly created cigars will have a different code.

Date Code

1	N
2	I
3	V
4	E
5	L
6	A
7	C
8	U
9	S
0	O

Factory Code

BM	Romeo y Julieta (Briones Montolo)
CB	El Rey del Mundo (Carlos Balino)
EI	El Laguito
FR	La Corona (Fernandez Rey)
FPG	Partagas (Francisco Perez German)
HM	Heroes de Moncada
JM	H. Upmann (José Martí)
PL	Por Larrañaga (Juan Cano Sainz)

La Casa del Habano below the Museo de Tabaco at Mercaderes #120 esq. Obrapía, tel. (7) 61-5795, has a fairly limited selection but of high-quality. There's no smoking onsite.

La Casa del Tabaco y Ron, at Calle Obispo esq. Monserrate, tel. (7) 33-8911, is to the rear of this rum store. The sales staff is knowledgeable and friendly, and prices are the best in town. You can smoke upstairs in the bar.

La Casa del Habano, in the Hostal Condanueva at Calle Mercaderas esq. Lamparilla, tel. (7) 62-9682, aims (as does the hotel) to lure serious cigar smokers. It offers a large range of quality cigars and a sumptuous smoker's lounge with TV and plump leather seating.

La Casa del Tabaco Parque Central, at Neptuno e/ Prado y Zulueta, tel. (7) 66-6627, a small outlet in the recently opened Hotel Parque Central, has "the potential to be one of the best." Manager Emilio Amin Nasser oversees friendly staff, and the hotel offers one of the finest smoking lounges in Cuba upstairs.

Vedado: At press time Habaguanex was restoring an old mansion opposite the Hotel Victoria, on Calle 19 in Vedado, and converting it into a Casa del Habano. Until then, try the **Casa del Tabaco** in the forecourt of the Hotel Habana Tryp, and those in the Hotel Nacional and Hotel Meliá Cohiba.

Playa (Miramar and Beyond): La Casa del Habana, Ave. 5ra esq. 16, tel. (7) 24-1185, is perhaps the flashiest place in town. This impressive colonial mansion recently received a facelift that includes stained-glass windows of cigar label motifs. It boasts a vast humidor, executive rooms, bar and lounge, and good service. Manager Pedro Gonzalez will be happy to offer his recommendations.

La Casa del Habano, in Marina Hemingway on Avenida 5ta y 248 in the Santa Fe district, tel. (7) 24-1151, has "a good selection of cabinet cigars" plus "helpful and friendly" young staff. No smoking onsite.

Suburbs: A new **La Casa del Habano** was due to open at Ave. 5ta e/ 188 y 192, tel. (7) 24-5700, to be run by Enrique Mons, whom *Cigar Aficionado* has termed "the maestro of cigar merchants in Havana," and who for most of the 1970s and '80s was in charge of quality control for the Cuban cigar industry.

CLOTHING

Cuba isn't renowned for its fashions and offers little in the way of boutiques. Most likely, if you're male, you'll want to purchase a *guayabera,* Cuba's unique short-sleeved, embroidered shirt worn outside the pants, draped to hide any figure flaw. It is designed of light cotton to weather tropical heat, with eight to 10 rows of embroidered tucking, and is outfitted with four pockets to stock enough robustos for a small store. This cultural icon was designed in Cuba more than two centuries ago and represents a symbol of masculine elegance, although it is disdained by Cuban youth for its associations with government figures, (it has become a virtual uniform for State employees). You can buy *guayaberas* at any ARTEX store, or for pesos in the Cuban department stores along Calle San Rafael or Galiano.

La Belleza Cubana, on the west side of Plaza de San Francisco, is a woman's fashion boutique specializing in wedding wear. Next door, on Oficios at the foot of Amargura, is a **United Colors of Benetton** outlet where I bought a hip Italian jacket for $150.

Casa 18, also called Exclusividades Verano, Calle 18 #4106 e/ 41 y 43, Miramar, tel. (7) 23-7040, sells Cuban-designed clothes, including beautiful one-of-a-kind Verano dresses and straw hats. Nearby, at Calle 6ta y Ave. 11, is **La Flora,** which sells fine Cuban crafts and clothing, including *guayaberas* with the Pepe Antonio label and Verano dresses (other quality items include leather ware, stained-glass lamps, carved statues, and ceramic tableware).

The most famous fashion stores are found in **La Maison,** Calle 16 esq. 7ma Ave., Miramar, tel. (7) 24-1543, with stores selling upscale imported clothing and deluxe duty-free items such as perfumes and jewelry. There's a shoe and clothes store upstairs.

For embroideries and lace, head to **El Quitrín,** at the corner of Obrapía and San Ignacio, in Habana Vieja.

You can even buy military uniforms—a Soviet sailor's jacket, perhaps?—at **El Arte,** on Avenida Simón Bolívar, on the east side of Parque de la Fraternidad.

Lost those Ray-Bans? Then head to **Ximeres** on the forecourt of the Hotel Habana Libre in Vedado; it stocks a range of Western designer shades.

DEPARTMENT STORES AND *DIPLOTIENDAS*

All foreign goods are imported by Cimex, headquartered in the former Hotel Sierra Maestra on Avenida 1ra in Miramar. You may be amazed by the number of department stores and shopping malls that Cimex is opening up all over

town, selling all manner of Western goods, from Nikes and Reeboks to Japanese electronics. A guard at the door will usually search your bags and correlate the contents against your itemized receipt after purchase.

Once known as **diplotiendas,** the original dollars-only outlets were originally exclusively for diplomats and other foreigner residents. Today Cubans are also welcome—as long as they have dollars to spend. One of the original complexes is **Quinta y 42,** Ave. 5ta y Calle 42, which includes a sporting goods store, toy store, bakery, and general supermarket. Larger, more modern malls include the **Galerias de Paseo,** facing the Malecón at the foot of Paseo in Vedado. It even has a car showroom with new Fiats and Japanese cars (but it's for show, as Cubans can't legally buy new vehicles; that's the prerogative of the state agency, Cubalse).

A new **Centro Comercial Sierra Maestra** was under construction at press time at Avenida 1ra and Calle 0. Need a TV, microwave oven, or diesel-powered lawnmower? This is the place to come.

Havana's most important commercial thoroughfares have traditionally been Calles San Rafael and Neptuno, immediately west of Parque Central. This is where the major department stores were located in Cuba's heyday before 1959. They remained open throughout the Revolution, each year growing more dour and minimalist in what they sold until, by the mid-1990s, their shelves were bare. The vitality is coming back, however, and several department stores have reopened, stocked with imported goods for dollars.

If you need toiletries and general supplies, head for any of the smaller **Tiendas Panamericanos** that serve Cubans with dollars. You'll find them all over Havana, including at the foot of the FOCSA building on Calle 17 e/ M y N, in Vedado.

MUSIC AND MUSICAL INSTRUMENTS

You'll find cassettes and CDs for sale at every turn, at rates comparable to the U.S. and Western Europe. Few outlets offer bargains. Musicians in restaurants will offer to sell you cassette tapes of their music for US$5-15.

You can buy a quality guitar for US$200, or a full-size conga drum for US$100. But check that they're Cuban made. You'll be amazed how many stores sell drums made in the U.S.

In Habana Vieja, **Longina,** at Calle Obispo #360, tel. (7) 62-8371, offers a splendid collection of drums (a *bata*—set of three—costs about US$400), plus guitars, and even trombones (from China). It offers a large CD collection. The **Museo de la Música** at the junction of Calle Cuba and Monserrate, in Habana Vieja, also has a wide selection of CDs.

In Miramar, check out the **Estudios de Grabaciones,** the recording studio of EGREN, the state recording agency at Calle 18 e/ 1ra y 3ra. It has a large music store, tel. (7) 24-1473. However, for the widest selection, head to **Max Music,** at Calle 33 #2003 e/ 20 y 22, in Miramar, tel. (7) 24-3002, fax (7) 24-3006; or **Casa de la Música,** at Calle 20 #3309 esq. 35. Both have huge collections of cassettes and CDs running the gamut of Cuban, plus musical instruments. Instruments are sold upstairs in the Casa de la Música, but don't expect those drums (they're all made in the U.S.) or guitars (Japanese) to be Cuban. Only the claves and maracas are island-made.

Farther out, **Imágenes S.A.,** 5ta Av. #18008 esq. 182, Reparto Flores, Playa, tel. (7) 33-6136, fax (7) 33-6168, also has a large stock of CDs and cassettes, plus videos of live performances.

Better yet, you can visit the **Industria de Instrumentos Musicales Fernando Ortiz,** Pedroso #12, Cerro, tel. (7) 79-3151, fax (7) 33-8043, the workshop where guitars, drums, claves, and other instruments are made. Conga drums begin at $129

POSTERS

Posters make great souvenirs. Cuba is the world leader in political art and you can find stunning examples for sale at ARTEX and similar stores throughout the city. Check out the shop at **Cinemateca,** Calle 23 e/ 10ma y 12, Vedado: it sells superb film posters.

For reproduction prints, head to the dowdy **Galería Exposición,** in Manzana de Gómez on Calle San Rafael, tel. (7) 63-8364. It has famous pictures of Che plus a huge range of posters

and prints representing works by Cuba's best painters (US$3 to US$10). Likewise, try the **Galería de la Solidaridad OSPAAL,** Calle Bernaza #108 e/ Obrapía y Lamparilla, tel. (7) 63-1445, fax (7) 33-3995. (See the special topic, Cuban Poster Art in the Introduction.)

RUM AND LIQUOR

Two stores in Habana Vieja specialize in rums and offer tastings before you buy. The first is **Casa de Ron,** above El Floridita restaurant at the top end of Calle Obispo, tel. (7) 63-1242. It's open daily 10 a.m.-8 p.m. The second is the **Taberna del Galeón,** tel. (7) 33-8061, off the southeast corner of Plaza de Armas. The tavern—a favorite of tour groups—offers samplers in the hope that you'll purchase a bottle or two. But you can tipple upstairs in solitude. Try the house special, *puñetazo,* a blend of rum, coffee, and mint.

Another preferred spot for a tipple, albeit a bit out of the way, is the **Fábrica de Ron Bocoy,** at Calzada de Cerro (Máximo Gómez) e/ Patrio y Auditor, in Cerro, tel. (7) 70-5642. It makes the famous Bocoy and disappointing Legendario rums, and has a showroom upstairs and a separate bar for tasting the goods as a prelude to buying. Open Mon.-Sat. 9 a.m.-5 p.m., and Sunday 9 a.m.-2 p.m.

At press time, the **Museo de Ron** was under construction on Avenida del Puerto (San Pedro) e/ Churruca y Sol. It will feature the Bar Havana Club, where you can taste the wares after visiting the museum and mini-distillery. It will have a well-stocked store. Open 9:30 a.m.-6 p.m. (the bar will be open 11 a.m.-2 a.m.).

FOR CHILDREN AND THE CHILD WITHIN

The past few years has seen a blossoming of stores selling children's wear and toys. Most **Tiendas Panamericanos** sell a limited range of kiddies' toys and supplies. In Habana Vieja, try the **Tienda Pedagógica** on Calle O'Reilly at Mercaderes. In Vedado, try the kiddies' store in the gallery of the Hotel Habana Libre Tryp. Most of the toys are made in China and shoddy.

El Mundo de los Niños (Children's World) is a small, sparsely stocked children's store on Calle San Rafael and Oquendo, six blocks east of Calzada de Infanta, in Centro Habana.

Bombanera "La Ambrosia," Calle Mercaderes e/ Calle Obispo y Obrapía, sells boxed chocolates made in Cuba. The La Ambrosia factory opened in 1852 and was followed in 1881 by a rival company, La Estrella. The shop sells La Estrella chocolates, plus Peter's chocolate bars from Baracoa. A box of 18 chocolates costs US$6.95. You can have your chocolates gift wrapped.

INFORMATION AND SERVICES

MONEY

Banks

The most important of the relatively few banks in Havana catering to foreigners is the autonomous, state-run Banco Financiero Internacional, which offers a full range of banking services, including currency exchange services at free-market rates. The branches are all open Mon.-Sat. 8 a.m.-3 p.m., but 8 a.m.-noon only on the last working day of each month. Its main outlet is in the Hotel Habana Libre in Vedado, tel. (7) 33-4011, at the end of the corridor past the airline offices. This branch has a special cashier's desk handling travelers checks and credit card advances (Mon.-Sat. 9 a.m.-7 p.m., and Sunday 9 a.m.-2 p.m.).

Other BFI branches are located at Calle Brasil and Oficios, in Habana Vieja; Linea (Avenida 7ra) #1 and O, Vedado, tel. (7) 33-3003 or 33-3148, fax (7) 33-3006; and in the forecourt of the Edificio Sierra Maestra, Avenida 1ra y 0, Miramar.

The state-controlled Banco de Crédito y Comercio (formerly the Banco Nacional de Cuba) is the main commercial bank with numerous outlets citywide. In Vedado, the branch at Calle M and Linea has a foreign-exchange desk (open Mon.-Fri. 8:30 a.m.-1 p.m.), as does the branch at the base of La Rampa, immediately west of the Malecón (open Mon.-Fri. 8:30 a.m.-3 p.m.).

The Banco Internacionál de Comercio, Avenida 20 de Mayo y Ayestarán, Havana 6, tel. (7) 33-5115, fax (7) 33-5112, open Mon.-Fri. 8 a.m.-1 p.m., primarily caters to foreign businesses, as does the Dutch-owned **Netherlands Caribbean Banking,** Avenida 5ta #6407 esq. 76, Miramar, tel. (7) 24-0419, fax (7) 24-0472, open Mon.-Fri. 8 a.m.-5 p.m.

Credit Cards

Most hotels, car rental companies, and travel suppliers, as well as larger restaurants, will accept credit card payments as long as the cards are not issued by U.S. banks. However, Rex Limousines accepts U.S.-issued MasterCards.

You can use your non-U.S. credit card to obtain a cash advance up to US$5,000 (US$100 minimum) at the Banco Financiero Internacionál, in the Hotel Habana Libre in Vedado. The Bank of Nova Scotia in Habana Vieja reportedly gives cash advances against U.S.-issued MasterCards (but not Visas).

COMMUNICATIONS

Most major tourist hotels have small post offices and philatelic bureaus and will accept your mail for delivery. Havana is also well served by post offices, which are relatively efficient. If you use those in residential districts, expect a long wait in line. Far quicker is to use the small post office inside the lobby of the Hotel Habana Libre in Vedado (open 24 hours). In Habana Vieja, try the post office on the northeast corner of the Plaza de la Catedral. Others are found on the west side of Plaza de San Francisco; at 518 Calle Obispo, tel. (7) 63-2560; open daily 9 a.m.-7 p.m.; next to the Gran Teatro on Parque Central; and on the north side of the railway station on Avenida de Bélgica.

Express Mail Services

DHL Worldwide Express is headquartered at Avenida 1ra y Calle 26, Miramar, tel. (7) 24-1578 or 24-1876, fax (7) 24-0999, open weekdays 8 a.m.-8 p.m. and Saturday 8 a.m.-4 p.m. It has offices at Calle 40 and Avenida 1, and in the Hotel Habana Libre. DHL acts as Customs broker and offers daily door-to-door pickup and

USEFUL TELEPHONE NUMBERS

EMERGENCY

Ambulance	tel. (7) 40-5093/4
Fire	tel. (7) 81-1115
Police	tel. (7) 82-0116

MEDICAL

Clínica Cira García (international clinic, Havana)	tel. (7) 24-0330
Farmácia Internacional (24-hour pharmacy, Havana)	tel. (7) 24-2051
Hospital Hermanos Almeijeiras	tel. (7) 57-6077

FINANCIAL AND LEGAL

Asistur	tel. (7) 62-5519 or 33-852 (emergency)
Consultório Jurídica Internacional	tel. (7) 24-2490

EMBASSIES

Canada	tel. (7) 24-2516, or 24-2516 (emergency)
France	tel. (7) 24-2143
Germany	tel. (7) 33-2460
Italy	tel. (7) 33-3378
Spain	tel. (7) 33-8025
United Kingdom	tel. (7) 24-1771
United States (Interests Section)	tel. (7) 33-3551 to 33-3559

TRANSPORTATION

Cubana de Aviación Reservations (national)	tel. (7) 33-4446 or 70-9391
Cubana de Aviación Reservations (international)	tel. (7) 33-4446 or 78-4961
José Martí International Airport	tel. (7) 45-4644
Casablanca Railway Station	tel. (7) 62-1920
Central Railway Station	tel. (7) 62-1920
Cristina Railway Station	tel. (7) 78-4971
19 de Noviembre (Tulipán) Railway Station	tel. (7) 81-4431
Bus Terminal (Terminal de Ómnibus Nacionales)	tel. (7) 79-2456
Hydrofoil (kometa) for Isla de la Juventud	tel. (7) 78-1841
Ferry for Isla de la Juventud	tel. (7) 81-3642

delivery service at no extra charge. It guarantees delivery in Havana in less than 24 hours. (See Express Mail in the Communications section in the On The Road chapter for information on other express mail services.)

Telephone and Fax Service
See the On The Road chapter for general information on Cuba's telephone system.

The Empresa de Telecomunicaciones de Cuba (ETECSA) is headquartered in the Lonja del Comercio, Plaza de San Francisco, Habana Vieja, tel. (7) 70-5237. The main international telephone exchange is in Vedado in the lobby of at the Hotel Habana Libre Tryp; a receptionist links you with the international operator (it can take forever,

ETECSA operates modern, efficient, glass-enclosed telephone kiosks called *centros telefónicos* (*telecorreos*) where they combine postal services). Key ETECSA kiosks in Habana Vieja are on the ground floor of the Lonja del Comercio, on Plaza de San Francisco; and in Vedado at the base of La Rampa (Calle 23), on the north side of the street at P; at the top of La Rampa, facing Coppelia between K y L; in the Centro de Prensa Internacional, tel. (7) 32-0526/27/28, on La Rampa and Calle O; and outside the Hotel Meliá Cohiba at the foot of Paseo.

There are also plenty of stand-alone public phones, many of which take phone cards. Avoid these if possible; they tend to be on noisy street corners.

You can buy phone cards at tourist hotels, ETECSA outlets, certain restaurants, and several dozen other outlets listed in the telephone directory, as well as from **Intertel,** Calle 33 #1427 e/ 14 y 18, Miramar, Havana, tel. (7) 33-2476, fax (7) 33-2504.

Cellular Phones: Cubacel's main office is at Calle 28 #510 e/ 5ta y 7ma, Miramar, tel. (7) 33-2222, fax (7) 80-0000 or 33-1737, website: www.cubacel.com; open Mon.-Fri. 8 a.m.-5 p.m. and Saturday 8 a.m.-noon. It also has an office at José Martí International Airport, tel. (7) 80-0043, fax (7) 80-0400 (Terminal 2), and tel. (7) 80-0222, fax (7) 80-0445 (Terminal 3).

Telex and Fax: You can send telexes and faxes from most tourist hotels, most *telecorreos* (notably the main international telephone center in the Hotel Habana Libre), and the International Press Center (Centro de Prensa Internacionál), on La Rampa and Calle O, Vedado, tel. (7) 32-0526/27/28; open 8:30 a.m.-5 p.m. A fax costs US$6.50 minimum plus $1 per minute to the U.S. and Canada.

Telegrams: In Havana, telegrams may be also sent from Cuba Transatlantic Radio Corporation (RCA), Calle Obispo y Aguiar.

Online Service

Most upscale tourist hotels have business centers with online access for guests. A few, such as the Hotel Parque Central, also feature modem outlets in guestrooms. You can also send and receive e-mail at the Infotur offices at Avenida 5ra esq. 112 in Miramar, tel. (7) 24-7036, fax (7) 24-3977, e-mail: infomire@teleda.get.cma.net (US$1 per message), and Calle Obispo e/ Villegas y Bernazas, tel. (7) 62-4586, fax (7) 33-3333. Similar service was to be extended to the other Infotur offices. And Internet access is provided in the Hotel Habana Libre Tryp, on the 20th floor. You can also plug in your laptop in the international telephone center in the in hotel lobby and use its ISP to connect.

If you need technical assistance or computer parts, try DITA, Calle 23 e/ L and M, tel. (7) 55-3278.

Photography

Several small outlets sell cameras and a limited range of supplies. The best source is Foto Habana, next to the Centro Wilfredo Lam, on San Ignacio, 20 meters north of Empredado. It sells Fujichrome and Kodachrome. Also try the Photo Service next to the Centro Internacional de Prensa, at the base of La Rampa, or that inside the lobby of the Hotel Habana Libre Tryp.

GOVERNMENT OFFICES

Immigration and Customs

All immigration issues relating to foreigners are handled by the Ministerio de Relaciones Exteriores (Ministry of Foreign Relations), at Calle Calzada #360 e/ G y H, Vedado, tel. (7) 30-5031, fax (7) 31-2314.

You can have **passport photos** taken at the Photo Service store adjacent to the International Press Center. You can also have photos for visas,

passports etc., taken at Fotógrafa, Calle Obispo #515, a tiny hole-in-the-wall open 10 a.m.-4 p.m.

The main Customs office is on Calle San Pedro, opposite the Iglesia San Francisco de Asís; it's upstairs, to the right.

Consulates

Most consulates and embassies are located in Miramar. The U.S. Interests Section, the equivalent of an embassy but lacking an ambassador, faces the Malecón at Calzada (Calle 5ta) e/ L y M in Vedado, tel. (7) 33-3551 or 33-3559, fax (7) 33-3700. The staff is said to be helpful.

The Canadian Embassy is open weekdays 8:30 a.m.-5 p.m. except Wednesday 8:30 a.m.-2 p.m.

TRAVEL AGENCIES

Most hotels have tour bureaus that can make reservations for excursions, car rental, and flights, as do the Cuban-state tour companies. However, there are no independent travel agencies familiar to the rest of the world. For international airline reservations, you should contact the airlines directly. The best ensemble of tourist bureaus is in the lobby of the Hotel Habana Libre Tryp, in Vedado.

A British company, Tour & Marketing, has a travel office at Hotel Jardin del Eden, Suite 3541, Marina Hemingway, Havana, tel. (7) 29-7922, fax: 24-3546, website: www.gocuba.com. Cubalinda.com, Calle E #158, Suite 4-A, Vedado, tel. (7) 55-3980, fax (7) 55-3686, e-mail: info@cubalinda.com, website: www.cubalinda.com, operates in partnership with Cubatur to offer a gamut of special interest tours. It's owned and run by ex-CIA spy Philip Agee, author of *Inside the Company* (see Booklist) and employs European travel staff. (For details on the various tour entities, see Organized Tours and Excursions in the Getting Around and Getting Away sections.)

TOURIST INFORMATION

Information Bureaus

Infotur (Información Turística) has several information centers in Havana, including in the arrivals lounge at José Martí International Airport, tel. (7) 66-6112 or 45-3542. The Habana Vieja office is on Calle Obispo e/ Villegas y Bernazas, tel. (7) 62-4586, fax (7) 33-3333. There's another, smaller Infotur booth on Calle Obispo, at the corner of San Ignacio. There's a fourth office in Miramar on Avenida 5ra on the north side of the traffic circle at Calle 112, tel. (7) 24-7036, fax (7) 24-3977, e-mail: infomire@teleda.get.cma.net.

In Habana Vieja, Habaguanex, Calle Oficios #110, on Plaza de San Francisco, tel. (7) 33-8693, fax (7) 33-8697, website: habaguanex. cubaweb.cu/habaguanex.html, can provide information on hotels, restaurants, and other places under its umbrella.

Olivia King Carter, Calle 35 #168 e/ 6ta y Loma, tel. (7) 66-6471, e-mail: Olivia@ip.etecsa.cu, a U.S. student living in Havana, is a fountain of local knowledge. She welcomes calls.

Tourist Guides and Publications

Cartelera is a free weekly tourist publication for Havana that offers up-to-date listings of the forthcoming week's events, including TV programming, theater, music and dance, and other entertainment. You can pick up a copy at most tourist hotels or from the editorial office at Calle 15 #602 e/ B y C, Vedado, tel. (7) 33-3732.

Guía Cultural de la Habana is published monthly by Centro de Desarrollo y Comunicación Cultural (CREART), Calle 4to #205 e/ Linea y 11, Vedado, tel. (7) 32-9691, fax (7) 66-2562, and provides a tremendous up-to-date resource for what's on at cinemas, theaters, etc. You'll find fee copies at tour desks in leading hotels and at Palacios de Turismo

Look, too, for Infotur's "touristic and commercial guide" called *La Habana,* which lists the addresses and telephone numbers of hotels, restaurants, bars, shopping centers, and a full range of services. It contains a foldout map. You can pick it up at any or hotel tour bureau.

Maps and Nautical Charts

You'll find maps of Havana for sale at most Infotur offices and many hotel gift stores and souvenir stalls, as well as at various *telecorreos* (post offices and telephone exchanges).

However, the best source is Tienda de las Navegantes, Calle Mercaderes #115 e/ Obispo y Obrapía. Habana Vieja, tel. (7) 61-3625 or 66-6763 (for boaters, VHF channel 16 CMYP3050),

which has a wide range of tourist maps of Havana and provinces as well as specialized maps such as *Cementerio Colón: Map Turístico.* If you're planning on touring farther afield, you should definitely head here. Don't count on being able to buy maps covering your destination once you leave Havana.

Two of the best maps are *Mapa de la Habana Vieja: Patrimonio de la Humanidad* and *Ciudad de la Habana: Mapa Turística,* both produced by the Instituto Cubano de Geodesía y Cartografía. The road maps are very detailed. The map of Habana Vieja even includes pictures and details of most historic buildings of importance, plus other sites of interest. The Instituto also produces a road map *(mapa de carreteras)* to Habana Province, as well as maps of individual tourist attractions such as Parque Lenin. The road map isn't very good.

Look for the excellent little booklet *La Habana Antigua* (also published by the Instituto Cubano de Geodesia y Cartografía), which contains the most detailed maps of Habana Vieja available.

Detailed specialist maps are produced by the Instituto de Planificación Física, Laparilla 65, Habana Vieja, tel. (7) 62-9330, fax (7) 61-9533. It doesn't normally sell maps.

MEDICAL SERVICES

The larger upscale tourist hotels have nurses on duty. Other hotels will be able to request a doctor for in-house diagnosis and treatment for minor ailments.

Hospitals

Tourists needing medical assistance are usually steered to the **Clínica Cira García,** Calle 20 #4101 y Ave. 41, Miramar, tel. (7) 24-2811, fax (7) 24-1633. The gleaming full-service hospital is entirely dedicated to serving foreigners. It is staffed by English-speaking doctors and nurses. You pay in dollars—credit cards are acceptable unless they're issued on a U.S. bank (in which case, greenbacks are required, *muchas gracias*).

In Vedado, the **Centro Internacional Oftalmológica Camilo Cienfuegos,** on Calle L between Linea and 13, tel. (7) 32-5554, fax (7) 33-3536, e-mail: cirpcc@infomed.sid.cu, specializes in eye disorders but also offers a range of medical services running from optometry to odontics. Similarly, the recently opened **Instituto Pedro Kouri,** in Marianao, is devoted to "international medical care," especially HIV/AIDS, hepatitis, and contagious and parasitic diseases.

Havana is blessed with dozens of other hospitals for Cubans, notably the 24-story, 1,000-bed **Hospital Hermanos Almeijeiras,** at the corner of Padre Varela and San Lazaro, in Centro Habana, tel. (7) 70-7721.

Pharmacies

In Vedado, there's a small *farmácia internacional* in the **Centro Comercial** adjoining the Hotel Habana Libre on Calle 25. **Centro Internacional Oftalmológica Camilo Cienfuegos,** Calle L e/ Linea y 13, tel. (7) 32-5554, fax (7) 33-3536, e-mail: cirpcc@infomed.sid.cu, has a well-stocked international pharmacy.

In Miramar, **Clínica Cira García** has a similar 24-hour pharmacy at the rear, tel. (7) 24-2811, ext. 14; and the **Farmacía Internacional,** across the street on Avenida 41, tel. (7) 24-2051, is also fully stocked with Western pharmaceuticals and toiletries. It's open Mon.-Fri. 9 a.m.-5:45 p.m. and Saturday 9 a.m.-noon. **Biotop,** at Avenida 7 #2603 in Miramar, tel. (7) 24-2377, fax (7) 33-2378, also contains a smaller international pharmacy, open 9 a.m.-6:30 p.m.

A licensed medicinal herbalist operates at Obrapía #212, Mon.-Sat. 9 a.m.-6 p.m.

Opticians

Óptima Miramar, Ave. 7ma y Calle 24, Miramar, tel. (7) 24-2990, fax (7) 24-2803 provides full-service optician and optometrist services, and sells imported products such as solutions for contact lenses. It has outlets throughout the city.

You'll find other opticians serving Cubans under *Ópticas* in the phone book. (I had my spectacles stolen in Cuba—a reminder to take a spare pair!)

Gyms and Massage

Need an invigorating massage or beauty treatment? Try **Biotop** Ave. 7ma #2603 Miramar, tel. (7) 24-2377, fax (7) 33-2378, which has a poorly equipped gym (US$5), a sauna (US$5), two outdoor jacuzzis (not in use during my visit), and salt and algae baths. It's run by Servimed. It

offers health and beauty treatments, but the uninspired facility gets few visitors and looked a bit run-down when I last visited. A massage costs US$10. It's open 10 a.m.-8 p.m.

Spa La Pradera, Calle 230 e/ 15 y 17, Reparto Siboney, tel. (7) 33-7467, fax (7) 33-7198, e-mail: aloja@pradera.cha.cyt.cu, is a Cubanacán spa-hotel specializing in health treatments. It has a sauna, gym, hydro-massage, massages, paraffin and mud treatments, ozone therapy, and the like.

Most luxury hotels offer massages and have tiny gyms and/or spas. Most are a letdown, but those of the **Novotel Miramar, Hotel Cohiba,** and **Hotel Parque Central** are well stocked with modern equipment and mirrored walls.

Specialized massages are also offered by Dulce María in the Hostal Valencia, on Calle Oficios in Habana Vieja, tel. (7) 62-3801. She offers acupressure and reflexology using both Japanese *yumeiho* and Chinese techniques. She also offers massages at her home on Calle San Ignacio #78, tel. (7) 61-0412. "After an hour of massage you will feel like a teddy bear," she says. Dulce charges US$8 for 45 minutes.

SAFETY

You'll face very few hassles while walking the streets of Havana: the rash of muggings and petty crime that erupted a few years back has been nipped in the bud since January 1999, when thousands of "Special Brigade" policeman took to the streets on a 24-hour basis. Still, Havana is not entirely safe despite this remarkable policing. Most crime is opportunistic, and thieves seek easy targets. Be wary of darker back streets at night (very few streets have lights).

Be cautious and circumspect of all *jiniteros*—hustlers—seeking to sell you cigars or otherwise make a buck. (See the section on Safety in the On The Road chapter for general precautions.)

Where to Avoid?

Several muggings and nonviolent robberies have occurred near key tourist sites. Particular spots to be wary are around the Capitolio and Parque Central, the Paseo de Martí, the Plaza de Armas, and Plaza 13 de Marzo in front of the Museo de la Revolución, which has witnessed several nocturnal muggings. Other areas that require special caution by night are the back streets of southern Habana Vieja, anywhere in the Cerro district, and the Cayo Hueso and neighboring areas of Centro Habana. And roughneck bars and discos are best avoided on weekends, when no-holds-barred brawls break out.

Traffic

Be especially wary when crossing the streets in Havana. Stand well away from the curb—especially on corners, where buses often mount the sidewalk. Cyclists are everywhere, making insouciant turns and weaving with a lackadaisical disdain for safety. And sidewalks are full of gaping potholes and tilted curbstones. Watch your step!

MISCELLANEOUS SERVICES

Haircuts

There's no shortage of *peluquerias* and *salons de belleza*. A reader has recommended Papito, at Aguiar #10 e/ Peña Pobre y Ave. de los Misiones, Habana Vieja, tel. (7) 61-0202. He charges $3 and is very popular.

Laundromats

The only modern self-service laundry I know is the **Aster Lavandería,** on Calle 34 e/ 3ra y 5ta, in Miramar tel. (7) 24-1622. You can leave your clothes here and pick them up the same day. It costs US$3 per load for wash and dry. It's open Mon.-Sat. 8 a.m.-3 p.m. It also offers dry cleaning (US$2 for pants, US$1.50 for shirts). It's easy enough to find locals willing to wash your clothes for a few dollars. Ask around.

Most upscale hotels offer dry-cleaning and laundry service. It's expensive and usually takes two days, and the results are sometimes questionable.

The telephone directory lists several dozen other laundries throughout Havana, including more than a dozen self-service *(auto servicio)* locales, most in outlying area. Look under the heading: **Tintorerías y Lavanderias.**

Libraries

Havana has many libraries, although all are poorly stocked and largely devoid of international texts. The main one is the **Biblioteca Nacional,** on the east side of Plaza de la Revolución, tel. (7) 81-8780, fax (7) 35-5442. It's open Mon.-Sat. 8:30 a.m.-6:30 p.m. You can use the reference room.

The **Biblioteca Provincial de la Habana** opened in 1999 on the east side of Plaza de Armas, to much ballyhoo. However, it's a meagerly stocked affair (on a par with a rural village in the U.S. or U.K.), with only a modest supply of mostly out-of-date encyclopaedias and texts, mostly from the 1960s. It also has a small magazine room, plus a small musical library. It's open Mon.-Fri. 8:10 a.m.-9 p.m. and Saturday 9 a.m.-5:30 p.m., but is closed the first Monday of each month.

There are several specialized libraries, too. The **Biblioteca del Instituto de Literatura y Lingüística,** Ave. Salvador Allende #710 e/ Castillejo y Soledad, tel. (7) 7-5405, for example, has a huge collection of novels and foreign-language texts (open Mon.-Fri. 8 a.m.-5 p.m. and Saturday 8 a.m.-2 p.m.); and the **Biblioteca de Medicinas** on La Rampa at Calle N, tel. (7) 32-4317, offers medical texts (open Mon.-Sat. 7:45 a.m.-7:45 p.m.). The **Biblioteca Nacional de Ciencias y Tecnología,** in the Academy of Sciences in the Capitolio in Habana Vieja, tel. (7) 60-3411, ext. 1329, has books on sciences and technology. It's open Mon.-Sat. 8 a.m.-5 p.m.

Toilets

Public toilets are as rare as four-leaf clovers. Exceptions include at Obispo #511, where the facilities cost US$0.20, and near the Capitolio at Dragones #57.

Most hotels and restaurants will let you use their facilities, but expect to have a security guard follow you in to check that you're not planting a bomb. Seriously. An attendant usually sits outside the door: note the bowl with a few coins meant to invite a tip.

GETTING THERE

BY AIR

See the Transportation chapter for information on flights to/from Havana.

Havana's airport is the **José Martí International Airport** (see below), which in 1999 was served by more than two dozen airlines. The airport is 25 km southwest of downtown Havana, in the Rancho Boyeros district. The airport has four terminals spaced well apart from each other and accessed by different roads (nor are they linked by a connecting bus service).

Terminal 1: This terminal serves domestic flights; see the Getting About section below.

Terminal 2: Charter flights originating in Miami arrive at Terminal Two, tel. (7) 44-3300, carrying passengers with OFAC licenses. Services include car rental outlets.

Terminal 3: All international flights (except Miami-Havana charters) now arrive at the ritzy new Terminal Three, tel. (7) 33-5777 or 33-5666, at Wajay, on the north side of the airport and linked to downtown Havana by a four- and six-lane freeway (only halfway complete at press time). This terminal is built to international standards and receives about 30 international airlines. Long-term plans call for two further expansions, each of which will permit the airport to serve another three million passengers annually (in 1998 the airport handled 2.5 million passengers). For information on arrivals and departures, call (7) 45-3133 or (7) 70-7701.

Immigration and Customs: Immigration procedures are straightforward and no more daunting than when arriving at any other Caribbean destination. Anticipate a long delay, however, as immigration proceedings are slow and long lines often develop. Personal carry-on baggage is X-rayed upon arrival.

Travelers arriving without pre-booked accommodations are sometimes hassled and made to book—and pay for—at least two nights' hotel stay before being granted entry (see Accommodation and Food chapter for details).

Information and Services: There's an **Infotur** tourist information office immediately on the left after exiting the customs lounge, tel./fax (7) 66-6101. It's poorly stocked with information and maps, but is staffed 24 hours. You should check in here if you have prepaid vouchers for accommodations or transfers into town.

There's a **foreign exchange** counter in the baggage claim area, but this serves mostly to change other foreign currency into U.S. dollars. You'll not need Cuban pesos.

Getting into Town: There is no public bus service from either of the international terminals. Independent travelers must take a taxi (US$15-20 depending on destination), which wait outside the arrival lounges. With luck you might find a minibus operated by a tourist agency such as Cubanacán. Normally they serve arriving tour groups, but often they're also happy to act as a shuttle service. You'll be charged about US$15 to get to downtown hotels. Most people arriving on package tours will have been issued prepaid vouchers for the shuttle.

A **public bus** marked "Aeropuerto" departs from **Terminal One** for Vedado and Parque Central about 15 minutes after the arrival of domestic flights (one peso). Alternately, you can catch a "camel bus" (no. M-2 originating in Santiago de las Vegas) from the east side of Avenida de la Independencia, about 200 yards east of the terminal. The bus goes to Parque de la Fraternidad on the edge of Habana Vieja. The journey takes about one hour, but the wait can be just as long. You can also take a private (albeit illegal) taxi for a negotiable fee (usually about US$8); touts will approach you.

Car Rental: Havanautos, tel. (7) 33-5197, **Panautos,** tel. (7) 33-0306 and 33-0307, **Transauto Rent-a-Car,** tel. (7) 33-5177, and **Vía Rent-a-Car,** tel. (7) 33-5155, have offices outside the arrival halls of both Terminals 2 and 3. **Cubacar,** tel. (7) 33-5546, also has an office at Terminal 3. And **Rex,** tel. (7) 33-9160, fax (7) 33-9159, which offers Volvos and limousine service, has offices at Terminals 2 and 3, and near Terminal 1 at the junction of Avenida Independencia and Avenida Van Troi.

Check your car thoroughly before driving away. Many of the cars rented here are poorly maintained (in spring 1999, Havanautos gave me a battered 1996 model Daewoo with a faulty gas gauge and a dangerous gasoline leak). If you find a problem later on and want to exchange cars, you'll have to return to the airport office where you rented—and could well find yourself being charged for the problem. (See the Car Rental section in the Getting Around section of the On The Road chapter.)

BY SEA

By Cruise Ship

At press time, three cruise companies offered regular cruises to Havana, which is destined to become one of the biggest ports-of-call in the world once the U.S. embargo is lifted. See the Transportation chapter for details on existing cruises that call on Cuba.

Havana has a relatively new cruise terminal, **Terminal Sierra Maestra,** tel. (7) 33-6607, fax (7) 33-6759, inaugurated in December 1995. The facility is a natty conversion of the old Customs building on Avenida San Pedro. Passengers step through the doorways directly onto Plaza de San Francisco and find themselves in the heart of Habana Vieja. The facility—owned and operated jointly by Cubanco S.A. (part of the Cuban Ministry of Transport) and a Curaçao-based Italian company called Milestone—is world-class, combining colonial-style architecture with ultramodern aluminum and plate glass. Pier 1 has two floors, each 8,000 square meters. Downstairs is a parking lot and bus terminal. Passengers are processed upstairs, which has wooden boardwalks outside and hardwood parquet floor inside, and a 1948 Dodge De Luxe D24 and a 1958 Lincoln Continental on display. Facilities include a craft and souvenir store. Eventually Pier 1 will also have an Italian restaurant and disco upstairs.

Pier 3 currently serves as a ferry terminal. Plans include converting the pier at Mariel, west of Havana, into an international ferry terminal serving Florida.

By Private Vessel

See the Transportation chapter for general information on travel to Cuba by private boat.

Private yachts and motor cruises berth at **Marina Hemingway,** Av. 5ta y Calle 248, Santa Fe, tel. (7) 24-1150, fax (7) 24-1149, e-mail: comercial@comermh.cha.cyt.cu, on the western edge of metropolitan Havana, in Barlovento, 15 km west of downtown. The marina is a self-contained village and duty-free port with its own accommodations and restaurants and complete services. The preferred currency is U.S. dollars, but all convertible currencies are accepted, as are credit cards (except those issued in the U.S.). If you'd like, you can register your credit card and charge everything to your account while berthed.

The harbor coordinates are 23° 5'N and 82° 29'W. The seven-beam searchlight located five feet east of the entrance canal is visible for 17 miles. You should announce your arrival on VHF Channel 16, HF Channel 68, and SSB 2790 (expect a long wait for the reply). Arriving and departing skippers should watch for snorkelers and surfers both within and outside the narrow entrance channel. Skippers are advised to give at least 72 hours' warning if possible by faxing complete details of their boat, crew, and passengers to the harbormaster's office at fax (7) 24-3104. This is not a requirement, however.

Upon arrival, you must clear Immigration and Customs at the wharf on the left just inside the entrance channel. If you plan to dock for less than 72 hours, visas are not required (your passport will suffice). The harbormaster's office will facilitate your entry and exit (ext. 2884), and visa extensions can also be arranged for US$25. Be patient!

The marina has four parallel canals—each one km long, 15 meters wide, and six meters deep—separated by *Intercanales* with moorings for 100 yachts. Docking fees, which include water, electricity, and custodial services, cost US$0.35 per foot per day. Gasoline and diesel are available 8 a.m.-7 p.m., tel. (7) 24-1150, ext. 450, a mechanic is on hand, and your boat can be hauled out of the water if needed.

The marina has a tourism information center (8 a.m.-8 p.m., tel. (7) 24-6336 or tel. (7) 24-1150, ext. 733) and harbormaster's office in Complejo Turístico Papa, the main service area at the end of channel B. The 24-hour medical post is here (ext. 737), as are a 24-hour coin laundry (ext. 451), bathrooms with showers, soda bar, and TV lounge, storage room, ship chandler (or *avituallamiento*, ext. 2344), plus a beach-volleyball court and four tennis courts. The post office is at the entrance of Intercanal C (open 24 hours; ext. 448), where you'll also find the Hemingway International Nautical Club (ext. 701), which offers fax and telephone facilities, bar, and a quiet reading room. The shopping mall is at the east end of Intercanal B (ext. 739). Security boxes can be rented.

Many skippers bring their own bicycles, mopeds, or motorbikes to move around the marina and travel into Havana. Rental cars are also available (ext. 87), as are microbuses and taxis (ext. 85). The marina even has a scuba diving center (ext. 735) at Complejo Turístico Papa's at the west end of Intercanal B, where jet-skis can be rented (8:30 a.m.-4:30 p.m.).

Accommodation is provided at Qualton El Viejo y Mar, plus a series of condominiums, apartments, and villas (ext. 385 and 85; see the Accommodations section for details). And there were six restaurants at press time, plus four bars, and the Discoteca Los Caneyes (ext. 7330), open 10 p.m.-4 a.m.

GETTING AROUND

ON FOOT

Havana is a walker's city par excellence and one easily and best explored on foot (most of the sightseeing highlights are concentrated in Habana Vieja). You'll probably want to restrict your walking to a single district, such as Habana Vieja—whose compact, narrow, warren-like lanes are no place for vehicular traffic—or the Malecón, or Vedado. Only when traveling beyond and between these districts, you will need transport.

Sidewalks are generally in reasonably good repair, but beware potholes and dog shit underfoot.

BY BUS

Tourist Bus
Rumbos S.A., Casa Matriz, Linea y M, Vedado, tel. (7) 66-9713 or 24-9626, operates a minibus service for tourists. The **Vaivén Bus Turístico** makes a circuit of Havana on a continual basis (*vaivén* means "round-trip" or "to go and return") between Club Habana and Marina Hemingway in the west and Parque Morro-Cabaña in the east (the route may be expanded east to Hotel Panamericano, in Ciudad Panamericano). Four separate buses operate 9 a.m.-9:40 p.m. every 40-50 minutes, and stop at 23 bus stops (*parradas*) at key locations along the route. A US$4 ticket is good all day for as many stops and times as you wish. Each bus has a guide.

TRANSPORTATION TELEPHONE NUMBERS

AIR

Cubana de Aviación Reservations (national)	tel. (7) 55-1022
Cubana de Aviación Reservations (international)	tel. (7) 55-1046
José Martí International Airport (information)	tel. (7) 45-3133

BUS

Terminal de Ómnibus Nacionales (bus terminal: information for Cubans)	tel. (7) 79-2456
Terminal de Ómnibus Nacionales (bus terminal: information for foreigners)	tel. (7) 70-3397
Vía Azul Bus Terminal	tel. (7) 81-1413

RAIL

Estación Central de Ferrocarril (Central railway station: information)	tel. (7) 57-2014
Estación Central de Ferrocarril (Central railway station Ladis ticket office)	tel. (7) 62-4259
Estación 19 de Noviembre	tel. (7) 81-4431
Estación Cristina	tel. (7) 78-4971

TAXI

Panataxi	tel. (7) 55-5555
Taxis-OK	tel. (7) 24-1446

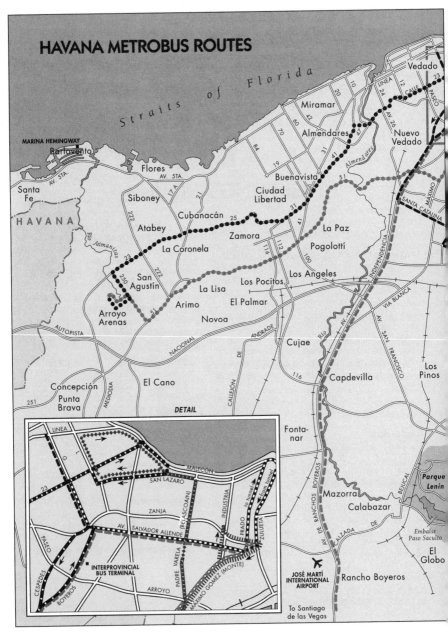

HAVANA METROBUS ROUTES

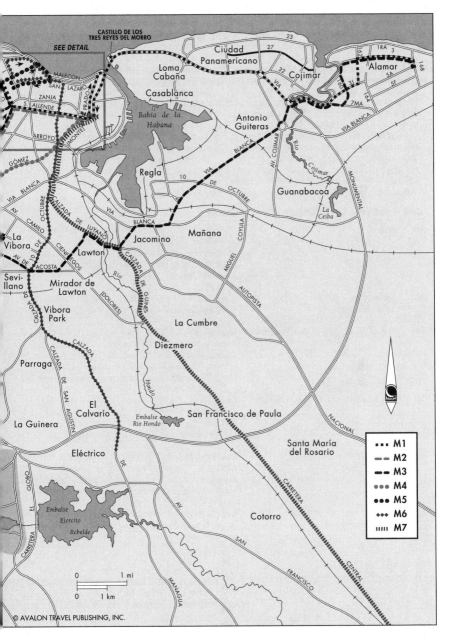

CASTILLO DE LOS
TRES REYES DEL MORRO

SEE DETAIL

MALECÓN

SANTA LAZARO

ZANJA

S. ALLENDE

PRADO

ARROYO

MONTE

GÓMEZ

VÍA BLANCA

AV. CAMILO

CALZADA DE LUYANÓ

CIENFUEGOS

La Víbora

AV. DE 10 DE OCTUBRE

ACOSTA

Sevillano

Lawton

Mirador de
Lawton

(DOLORES)

Víbora
Park

CALZADA

CALZADA DE SAN AGUSTÍN

Parraga

El
Calvarío

La Guinera

Eléctrico

EL GLOBO

Embalse
Ejercito
Rebelde

CARRETERA

DE

AV.

MANAGUA

0   1 mi
0   1 km

© AVALON TRAVEL PUBLISHING, INC.

Loma
Cabaña

Casablanca

Bahía de la
Habana

Regla   10

Ciudad
Panamericano   27   23

32   Cojimar   Alamar   3

VÍA   1RA   168
5A

AV. COJIMAR   64   3T   5E

Antonio
Guiteras   VÍA BLANCA   7MA

VÍA   DE   OCTUBRE

Río
Cojimar

Río   Cojimar

Guanabacoa

La
Ceiba

MONUMENTAL

VÍA   BLANCA

Jacomino   Mañana

CALZADA DE GÜINES

La Cumbre

Diezmero

Hondo

Embalse
Río Hondo   San Francisco de Paula

Santa María
del Rosario

MIGUEL COYULA

AUTOPISTA

NACIONAL

CARRETERA   CENTRAL

Cotorro

SAN

FRANCISCO

··· M1
– – M2
━ ━ M3
●●● M4
●●● M5
◆◆◆ M6
||||| M7

CAMELS IN CUBA!

*Y*es, camels roam the streets of Havana. These giant buses—*camellos*—were designed locally to save the day during the gasoline crisis, when ingenious engineers added bodies to articulated flatbed trucks. They're named for the shape of the coach: sagging between two humps like a Bactrian camel.

About half of the one million trips that *Habaneros* make daily are aboard the rumbling, crudely constructed behemoths, which carry the "M" designation (for Metro-bus) on bus routes. Designed to carry 220 people, they are usually stuffed with more than 300, so many that the true number can't be untangled. The "camel" is a warehouse on wheels: officially a *supertrenbus,* in which the packed ensemble sways in exhausted silence.

About 220 camels roam the streets of Havana. More are being added each week, made in a factory in Havana for about US$30,000 apiece and weighing in at more than 20 tons. Of course, the Mack trucks that pull them weren't designed for stop-and-start work, so maintenance is an ongoing problem.

Seven routes span Havana and the most distant suburbs. Most begin operation 4 a.m. with the last departure at 10 or 11 p.m. A standard 20 centavo fare applies.

LINE	ORIGIN	DESTINATION	ROUTE
M1	Alamar	Vedado	Calle 168 (e/ 5taE y 7taF) - Avenida 5ta - Calle 168 - Avenida 3ra - Calle 162 - Avenida Los Cocos - Avenida 7ma - Vía Monumental - Tunnel - Agramonte - Máximo Gómez (Monte) - Simón Bolívar (Reina) - Salvador Allende - Calle G
M2	Santiago las Vegas (Boyeros)	Parque Fraternidad	Avenida 349 (y Final) - Calle 17 - Calle 2 – Avenida de Boyeros - Salvador Allende - Simón Bolívar (Reina)
M3	Alamar	Ciudad Deportiva	Calle 168 (e/ 5taE y 7taF) - Avenida 5ta - Calle 168 - Avenida 3ra - Calle 160 - Avenida 7ma - Avenida Cojímar - Vía Blanca - Calzada de Guanabacoa - Lindero - Calzada de Luyanó - Porvenir - Acosta - Mayía Rodríguez - Santa Catalina - Avenida Boyeros
M4	San Agustín (Lisa)	Parque Fraternidad	Calle 270 (e/ 25 y 27) - Avenida 27 - Calle 264 - Ave 31 - Calle 250 - Avenida 51 - Calzada de Puentes Grandes - Calzada de Cerro - Máximo Gómez (Monte) - Prado (return to Monte via Dragones and Zulueta)
M5	San Agustín (Lisa)	Vedado	Calle 270 (e/ 25 y 27) - Avenida 27 - Calle 264 - Avenida 31 - Calle 250 - Avenida 23 - Avenida 26 - Avenida 31 - Avenida 41 - Calle 28 - Calle 23 - Malecón - Marina (return to Calle 23 via San Lázaro and Calle L)
M6	Calvario (Arroyo Naranjo)	Vedado	Calzada de Managua (e/ Camilo Cienfuegos y 1ra) - 10 de Octubre - Cristina - Belascosín - San Lazaro - Calle L (return to San Lazaro via Calle L, Linea, Malecón and Marina)
M7	Alberro (Cotorro)	Parque Fraternidad	Avenida 99 (y Final) - Carretera de Alberro - Avenida 101 - Calzada de Güines - Lindero - Calzada de Luyanó - 10 de Octubre - Cristina - Máximo Gómez (Monte) - Industria (return to Monte via Dragones and Prado)

You can pick up a map at the Rumbos head-quarters in Casa Matriz. Use the published map with caution, however, as the route has already changed since the service was introduced in 1998.

Public Bus

Havana's public buses, or *guaguas* (pronounced "wah-wah"), are for stoics. Habaneros are in-ured and would rather take a bus than walk under almost all circumstances, even if this means traveling like sardines in a can. Note, however, that no buses operate within Habana Vieja except along the major peripheral thor-oughfares. Fares are ridiculously cheap, but most buses are usually packed to the gills, es-pecially during rush hours—7-10 a.m. and 3-6 p.m. Beware of pickpockets on crowded buses.

Bus service is the responsibility of three agen-cies: **Asociación de Transportes de Servi-cios de Omnibus** (Astro), **Transmetro,** and **Omnibus Metropolitano,** which has introduced some modern Mercedes buses to its fleet. Most buses are either hand-me-down Yankee school buses (imported via Canada or Mexico), horribly uncomfortable Hungarian buses that belch out black fumes, poorly-made and equally uncomfy Cuban Giróns, or *Tren Buses* (also called *came-los*—camels), which are lengthy, truck-pulled passenger cars that sag in the middle, like the rolling stock on U.S. railways. These ships of the desert—isn't that appropriate?—are now the workhorses of the city bus system. Two key "camel" routes to know are the M1 (Parque de la Fraternidad to Habana del Este) and M2 (Parque de la Fraternidad to Santiago de las Vegas via the international airport).

Expect to wait in line for from 10 minutes to an hour, depending on the route. Cuban lines (queues, *colas*) are always fluid but tend to re-form when the bus appears, so you should follow the Cubans' example and identify the last person in line ahead of you (ask for *el último?*). Be pre-pared to push and jostle if the line devolves into a scrum. You'll undoubtedly be the only foreigner aboard and may find yourself being ushered aboard and offered a seat as a honored guest.

Buses stop frequently, but when full the driver may stop only when requested to do so. Bus stops—*paradas*—are usually well marked. Shout *Pare!* (Stop!), or bash the box above the door in Cuban fashion. You'll need to elbow your way to the door well in advance, however. Don't dally, as the bus driver is likely to hit the gas when you're only halfway out.

Schedules and Fares: Most *guaguas* run 24 hours, at least hourly during the day but on re-duced schedules 11 p.m.-5 a.m. The standard fare is 10 centavos (exact change only), which you deposit in the box beside the driver. Fares into the suburbs range from 10 to 50 centavos. You'll also find lots of smaller, red-and-cream-col-ored, buses called *omnibuses ruteros,* which charge 40 centavos and have the benefit of being uncrowded.

Routes and Route Maps: Many buses follow a loop route, traveling to and from destinations along different streets. Most buses display the bus number and destination above the front win-dow. If in doubt, ask. Many buses arrive and de-part from Parque Central and Parque de la Fraternidad in Habana Vieja and La Rampa (Calle 23) in Vedado, especially at Calle L and at Calzada de Infanta.

BY TRAIN

Intra-city service is provided to a limited num-ber of suburban destinations on commuter trains from the following two stations.

Local service aboard a two-car commuter train operates to ExpoCuba and the provincial town of San Antonio de los Baños from **Estación de 19 Noviembre** (also called Estación Tuli-pan) on Calle Tulipán and Hidalgo, 200 meters west of Avenida de la Independencia, south of Plaza de la Revolución, tel. (7) 81-4431. Trains depart for San Antonio at 6:05 and 9:45 a.m. and 12:10, 3:50, 5:55, and 8:40 p.m. Departures from San Antonio are at 5:45, 7:35, and 11:50 a.m. and 2:45, 5:36, and 7:45 p.m.

The *Servicio ExpoCuba* departs Estación de 19 Noviembre at 9:20 a.m. via Vibora (50 min-utes). Return trains depart ExpoCuba at 17:17 p.m.

Estación Cristina, at Cuatro Caminos in southwest Habana Vieja, tel. (7) 78-4971, serves Santiago de las Vegas, on the southern outskirts of Havana, and Batabanó on the south coast (the ferry and hydrofoils—*kometas*—to Isla de la Juventud depart from Batabanó). It has a snack bar. Trains also run from here to Parque Lenin and Playas del Este in summer only.

Trains depart for Santiago de las Vegas (40 centavos) at 6:05 and 10:40 a.m., and 2:50 and 7 p.m.; and for Batabanó (two pesos) at 7:45 a.m. and 12:25 p.m. Return trains depart Santiago de las Vegas for Cristina at 7:57 a.m. and 12:30, 4:54, and 8:40 p.m.; and Batabanó at 3:35 and 5:10 p.m.

BY TAXI

Havana has a superb taxi system. Hundreds of taxis serve both the tourist trade and the local population. If you use a tourist taxi four or five times a day, the cost may approach that of renting a car—especially if you're traveling between, say, Miramar and Habana Vieja.

Dollar Taxis

Licensed *turistaxis* are operated by state organizations, all of which charge in dollars. The cheapest is **Panataxi,** tel. (7) 55-5555, fax (7) 55-5461, which provides efficient radio-dispatched taxi service using new Peugeots. It's used by Cubans and foreigners alike. I've rarely had to wait more than 15 minutes for a taxi to arrive. A ride from the Habana Libre in Vedado to Habana Vieja will cost about US$4.

Taxis exclusively serving the tourist trade use modern Japanese and European sedans. These hang around outside tourist hotels, but can also be radio dispatched. The following companies operate tourist taxis: **Habanataxi,** tel. (7) 41-9600; **Taxis-OK,** tel. (7) 24-1446 and 24-9518; **Taxi Transtur,** tel. (7) 33-5539 or 33-6666, fax (7) 33-5535, e-mail: taxihab@transtur.com.cu, and (in Playas del Este) tel. (7) 96-3939; **Transgaviota,** tel. (7) 20-4650 or 33-9780, fax (7) 27-1626 or 33-0742; and **Turistaxi,** tel. (7) 33-5539.

Micar, 1ra y Paseo, Vedado, tel. (7) 55-2444, fax (7) 33-6476, offers minibuses at hourly rates on a sliding scale (US$40 four hours, US$70 eight hours, US$90 for 10 hours) but charges US$0.85 per km for the first 50 km (US$0.70 per km thereafter).

Tourist taxis are slightly more expensive than Panataxi cabs. Prices vary slightly according to size: the larger the more expensive. By international standards, however, Havana's taxis are relatively cheap, and you will rarely pay more than US$10 or so for any journey within town. Taxis are metered and strictly controlled; drivers are assiduous in using their meters, which begin at US$1. Expect to pay about US$5 from La Rampa to Habana Vieja, double that from Miramar. Nighttime fares cost about 20% more.

The taxi companies all offer special long-distance and hourly rates (the cost normally compares favorably to hiring a car for the day). Although relatively expensive, they are a value option for three or four passengers sharing the cost. If you want to get the price down, you might be able to strike a bargain with the driver. Here's the deal. Your driver will stop the meter at so many dollars and you give him a slightly greater amount. Since his dispatcher records the destination, mile for mile, usually a dollar per mile, the taxi driver splits the excess with the dispatcher. Most taxi drivers are unscrupulously honest with passengers. If you think you're being gouged, contest the fee.

Classic Cars

Fancy tootling around in an old Studebaker? You can rent classic cars for a city tour through **Gran Car,** tel. (7) 33-5647 or 40-1955, for US$15 per hour (20 km limit the first hour, with shorter limits per extra hour). Day rates decline from US$90 for one day to US$70 daily for five days (120 km daily limit). Set prices apply for provincial touring. One or two such cars can usually be found outside the major hotels, notably the Hotel Inglaterra, Hotel Nacional, and Meliá Cohiba.

HAVANA TAXIS

Gran Car	tel. (7) 33-5647, or 40-1955
Habanataxi	tel. (7) 41-9600
Panataxi	tel. (7) 55-5555
Taxis OK	tel. (7) 24-1446 and 24-9518
Taxi Transtur	tel. (7) 33-5539 or 33-6666
Transgaviota	tel. (7) 23-7000, 33-1730, or 81-0357
Turistaxi	tel. (7) 33-5539/40/41/42

Peso Taxis

Peso-only taxis—deprecatingly called *los incapturables* (uncatchable)—serve Cubans and until recently were not supposed to give rides to foreigners, although many did so (especially for a dollar gratuity). Recently there seemed to be no restriction. They are radio-dispatched, tel. (7) 70-1326 or 79-0443, and charge in pesos at ludicrously low rates using Ladas, the Russian-made Fiat described as "tough as a Land Rover, with iron-hard upholstery and, judging by sensation, no springs." They're painted black and yellow (with a strange Hebrew-type logo on the sides); most also have meters. Drivers may require foreigners to pay in dollars, in which case negotiate the price (expect to pay about half the fare you'd pay in a turistaxi). You'll find plenty around Coppelia in Vedado and Parque Central and Parque de la Fraternidad in Habana Vieja. Look for a light lit up above the cab—it signifies if the taxi is *libre* (free). With luck you might be able to pay in pesos (you should change dollars for pesos beforehand). The base fare is one peso. Each km costs 25 centavos (35 centavos at night).

The workhorses of the taxi system for Cubans are the *colectivos* (shared cabs that pick up anyone who flags them down, often until they're packed to the gills) that which generally run along fixed routes. Most are old Yankee jalopies. Ostensibly they're not supposed to pick up foreigners, but I've rarely had a problem. Most *colectivos* have a taxi sign above the cab and markings on the side, but follow the local example—wave down any large Yankee behemoth coming your way. Avenida 5ta and the Malecón linking Miramar with Habana Vieja are favorite routes. The south side of Parque de la Fraternidad is their preferred gathering spot. They depart from here on set routes throughout the city.

"Gypsy" Cabs

Illegal "gypsy" cabs driven by freelance chauffeurs are everywhere, too. Most are beat-up Ladas or American jalopies. You'll find freelance driver-guides outside the largest tourist hotels—especially the Hotel Inglaterra on Parque Central, and the Hotel Habana Libre Tryp and, to a lesser degree, the hotels Riviera and Cohiba, in Vedado—and outside discos late at night. Fares

TAXI FARES FROM HAVANA

The following are sample fares from Havana.

DESTINATION	ONE-WAY	ROUNDTRIP
Cienfuegos	US$130	US$250
Matanzas	US$70	US$120
Pinar del Río	US$90	US$160
Soroa	US$50	US$90
Trinidad	US$180	US$300
Viñales	US$95	US$170
Varadero	US$80	US$120

are negotiable, and it's often possible to hire a car and driver for the whole day for, say, US$30. But you'll often end up paying *more* than you would in a tourist taxi! Educate yourself about *turistaxi* fares to your destination beforehand, as many drivers attempt to gouge you. Beware of scams.

The drivers are constantly wary of the police. *Jiniteros* work on commission and will approach you and whisper under their breath—*"Hey, friend . . . taxi?"*

Ciclotaxis

Hundreds of tricycle taxis ply the streets of Habana Vieja and Vedado. They offer a relaxing (and cheap) way of sightseeing and getting around if you're in no hurry. You can go the full length of the Malecón, from Habana Vieja to Vedado, for US$3. You can hire them by the hour for about US$5. Most have fashioned their seats from car seats and offer shade canopies.

Cocotaxis

It could be the strangest taxi you'll ever take in your life. These bright yellow motorized tricycles look like scooped-out Easter eggs on wheels, like something out of a children's picture book. Most depart from outside the Hotel Inglaterra on Parque Central. They charge US$5 per hour for up to three people.

Horse-Drawn Cabs

Horse-drawn *calezas,* open-air coaches, offer a popular way of exploring the historic quarter of Old Havana, although they are barred from en-

CAR RENTAL LOCATIONS

CUBACAR

Main Office: Avenida 5ta, e/ B y Miramar	tel. (7) 24-2718, fax (7) 33-7233
José Martí International Airport (Terminal 2)	tel. (7) 33-5546
Avenida 1ra #16401, Miramar	tel. (7) 24-2277
Hotel Bellocaribe	tel. (7) 33-6032
Hotel Chateau Miramar	tel. (7) 24-0760
Hotel Comodoro	tel. (7) 24-1706
Hotel La Pradera	tel. (7) 24-7473
Hotel Meliá Cohiba	tel. (7) 33-4661
Hotel Meliá Habana	tel. (7) 24-8500
Hotel Parque Central	tel. (7) 66-6627
Marina Hemingway	tel. (7) 24-1707

FÉNIX

Main Office: Calle Cuba #66, Habana Vieja	tel. (7) 63-9720, fax (7) 66-9546

GRANCAR (AUTOS CLASICOS)

Main Office: Vía Blanca y Palatino, Cerro	tel. (7) 33-5647, fax (7) 33-5647

HAVANAUTOS

Reservations:	tel. (7) 24-0647
Main Office: Avenida 1ra, e/ 2 y 0, Miramar	tel. (7) 23-9658, fax (7) 24-0648
Apartotel Atlántico, Playas del Este	tel. (7) 80-2946
Calle 462 y 5ta, Playas del Este	tel. (7) 80-2946
Malecón y 11, Vedado	tel. (7) 33-4691
Hotel Habana Libre	tel. (7) 33-3484
Hotel Nacional	tel. (7) 33-3192
Hotel Neptuno/Tritón	tel. (7) 24-2921
Hotel Riviera	tel. (7) 33-3577
Hotel Sevilla	tel. (7) 33-8956
Hotel Tropicoco (Playas del Este)	tel. (7) 80-2952
José Martí International Airport (Terminal 1), (Terminal 2)	tel. (7) 33-5215 tel. (7) 33-5197
Villa Panamericana (Ciudad Panamericano)	tel. (7) 33-8113

MICAR (CUBALSE)

Main Office: Calle 13 #562, Vedado	tel. (7) 33-6725
Calle O #306, Miramar	tel./fax (7) 24-2444

PANAUTOS

Main Office: Calle Linea y Malecón, Vedado	tel. (7) 30-4763, fax (7) 55-5657
Servicentro La Copa, Calle 42 esq. 3, Miramar	tel. (7) 22-7684
José Martí International Airport (Terminal 2)	tel. (7) 80-3921
Avenida Zoológico y 26, Vedado	tel. (7) 66-6226
Calle 42 esq. 3ra, Miramar	tel. (7) 22-7684

REX

Main Office: Avenida Independencia y Calzada de Bejucal, Boyeros	tel. (7) 33-9160, fax (7) 33-9159
Calzady 15, Vedado	tel. (7) 33-7788, fax (7) 33-7789
José Martí International Airport (Avenida Van Troi) (Terminal 3)	tel. (7) 66-6074

TRANSAUTO

Main Office: Calle 40-A esq. 3ra, Miramar	tel. (7) 24-5552
José Martí International Airport (Terminal 3) (Terminal 2)	tel. (7) 33-5765 tel. (7) 33-5764
Avenida 3ra y Paseo, Vedado	tel. (7) 33-5763
Hotel Capri	tel. (7) 33-4038
Hotel Copacabana	tel. (7) 24-0621
Hotel Nacional	tel. (7) 33-5910
Hotel Neptuno	tel. (7) 29-0881
Hotel Neptuno/Tritón	tel. (7) 24-0951
Hotel Riviera	tel. (7) 33-3056
Playas del Este	tel. (7) 96-2917
Villa Panamericano	tel. (7) 33-8802

VIA RENT-A-CAR

Main Office: Edificio La Marina, Avenida del Puerto #102, Habana Vieja	tel. (7) 33-9781, fax (7) 33-9159

tering the pedestrian-only quarter. They're operated by Agencia San Cristóbal, Calle Oficios #110 e/ Lamparilla y Amargura, tel. (7) 33-9585, fax (7) 33-9586. Their official starting point is the junction of Empedrado and Tacón, but you can hail them wherever you see them. Others can be hailed outside the Hotel Inglaterra, on Parque Central. Expect to pay US$3 per person per hour in low season, US$5 in high season (October-April).

BY RENTAL CAR

I recommend renting a car only if you anticipate exploring the suburbs or if you intend touring beyond Havana. Virtually every tourist hotel either has a car rental desk or can arrange for a rental car to be delivered. The five state-owned car rental companies have main offices in addition to outlets in leading hotels.

Habaneros' standard of driving is, in general, admirable (certain taxi drivers excepted), although in recent years Cubans with newer cars have begun to drive faster and more aggressively than a few years ago. In Havana there are no bottlenecks. Havana is probably the only Latin American city without rush-hour traffic. Traffic police do an efficient job. Traffic signage is very good. And most of the traffic lights work—and are even obeyed! Havana's streets show deterioration but in general the roads are superior to, or at least no worse than, those of most other Caribbean or Latin American cities. (Road crews had even begun to re-lay roadbeds and patch holes at last visit.)

Roads to Avoid: Two notable exceptions to the generally high standards are busy Vía Blanca, which (south of Havana harbor) is in terrible shape and dangerous; and the divided highway **Autopista Circular**, or route Calle 100, which forms a semicircle south of the city, linking the arterial highways into Havana. The latter has little traffic and, frankly, it's too far out from the city to serve a useful function unless skirting the city entirely when traveling, say, between Pinar del Río and Matanzas. Be careful! It has treacherous potholes, and some are deathtraps—massive hollows invisible until you're upon them. They're usually at intersections.

Car Rental Companies: See the Getting Away section, below, for car rental companies, plus further details on car rentals.

Parking

A capital city without parking meters? Imagine. Parking meters were detested during the Batista era, mostly because they were a source of *botellas* (skimming) for corrupt officials, despite their introduction as a policy to restrain excessive traffic in the city center. After the triumph of the Revolution, Habaneros rampaged through the city smashing the meters.

Finding parking is rarely a problem, except in Habana Vieja (you should avoid driving in Habana Vieja, anyway, east of Monserrate). No-parking zones are well marked. Avoid these like the plague, especially if it's an officials-only zone, in which case a policeman will usually be on hand to blow his whistle. Havana has an efficient towing system for the recalcitrant. You can pay your parking ticket through your car rental agency (and be sure to do so before leaving the country).

Theft is a serious problem. As such, Habaneros prefer to park in *parqueos,* parking lots found throughout the city, with a *custodio* to guard against thieves 24 hours. Expect to pay US$1-2 overnight. In questionable areas I recommend paying a kid some pocket change to keep an eye on your vehicle during the day.

In central Vedado, the Hotel Habana Libre has an underground car park (US$0.80 for one hour, US$0.50 each additional hour; US$4 maximum for 24 hours).

Car Repairs

Your car rental company can arrange repairs. However, if you need emergency treatment, **Diplogarage** has centers open 24 hours at Av. 5ta esq. 120, Playa, tel. (7) 33-6159, and at Calle 2 esq. Av. 7ma, tel. (7) 23-5588, 33-1906.

BY SCOOTER

Transtur Rent-a-Car, Calle 19 #210 esq. J, Vedado, tel. (7) 33-8384, fax (7) 55-3995, e-mail: webmaster@transtur.com.cu, rents Suzuki scooters for US$10 for one hour, US$15 three hours, US$23 per day, or US$147 weekly.

BY BICYCLE

The perfect way to get around! Habaneros do it—almost one million bicycles wheel through the streets of the Cuban capital—so why not you? Be careful—there are plenty of potholes, and at night many of the streets are unlit. Cuban cyclists are notoriously lackadaisical on the roads, and traffic accidents kill an average of two cyclists in Havana every three days.

Cyclists are not allowed to ride through the tunnel beneath Havana harbor. The municipal government provides specially converted buses—the sky-blue **Ciclobus**—to ferry cyclists and their *bicis* through the tunnel (10 centavos). Buses depart from Parque de la Fraternidad, but the location is subject to change (the *ciclobus* formerly departed from Avenida de los Estudiantes at the base of La Rampa).

The only place I'm aware of that currently rents bicycles is at the Hotel Jardín del Eden in Marina Hemingway, tel. (7) 24-1150, ext. 371 (it charges US$1 per hour, or US$12 per day for mountain bikes).

In prior years Panataxi has rented bicycles through a division called **Panaciclo,** Avenida Rancho Boyeros y Santa Ana, near the main bus station in Plaza de la Revolución, tel. (7) 81-4444 or 45-3746. It has ceased doing so at press time.

BY FERRY

Tiny ferries (standing room only—no seats) bob across the harbor between the Havana waterfront and Regla (on the east side of the bay) and Casablanca (on the north side of the bay). The ferries leave on a constant yet irregular basis 24 hours, from a wharf called Muelle Luz on Avenida San Pedro at the foot of Calle Santa Clara in Habana Vieja, tel. (7) 97-9130 (in Regla); 10 centavos; five minutes.

ORGANIZED EXCURSIONS

City Tours

A city tour is a great way to get an initial feel for Havana. All the hotel tour bureaus offer guided city tours through the major tour agencies aboard a/c buses. For example, **Tours & Travel,** Av. 1ra e/ Calles 0 y 2, Miramar, Havana, tel. (7) 24-7541, fax (7) 24-2074, and La Rampa y Calle M, Vedado, tel. (7) 33-4082, fax (7) 33-4084, a division of Havanatur, offers a city tour (US$15), plus excursions to the botanical garden. It has an office in Vedado on La Rampa y Calle M, one block downhill from the Hotel Habana Libre.

Tropical Travel Agency, tel. (7) 24-9626, fax (7) 24-4520, a division of Rumbos, has a three-and-a-half-hour city tour departing daily at 9 a.m. and 2 p.m. and including Habana Vieja, Vedado, and Miramar (US$10).

deboarding a ciclobus

Agencía San Cristóbal, Calles Oficios #110 e/ Lamparilla y Amargura, tel. (7) 33-9585, fax (7) 33-9586, offers guided walking tours of Habana Vieja and excursions farther afield, plus books festivals, and makes other travel arrangements. Open Mon.-Sat. 8:30 a.m.-6 p.m., Sunday 8:30 a.m.-4 p.m.

Amistur S.A., Calle Paseo #4606 e/ 17 y 19, Vedado, tel. (7) 33-4544, fax (7) 33-3515, website: www.igc.apc.org/cubasol/amistur.html, is a Cuban tour agency handling specialized tourism.

Private Guides: Hotel tour bureaus and tour agencies can arrange personal guided tours. **Cubatur,** Calle F #157 e/ Calzada y 9ra, tel. (7) 33-4155, fax (7) 33-3104, offers guides for US$25 per day (up to 12 hours) in Havana, US$30 outside Havana. You can also hire a guide weekly (US$200). **Agencía San Cristóbal,** (see above), also arranges guides.

A U.S. resident student in Cuba, Olivia King Carter, Calle 35 #168 e/ 6 y Loma, tel. (7) 66-6471, e-mail: Olivia@ip.etecsa.cu, has proved useful in pointing the way to guides, etc. She's a fountain of local knowledge. She welcomes your calls and will be happy to assist.

Aerotaxi, Calle 27 #102 e/ M y N, Vedado, Havana, tel. (7) 33-4064, fax (7) 33-4063, offers sightseeing tours by Russian biplane.

Harbor Cruises
Marlin S.A., Calle 184 #123, Flores, Havana, tel. (7) 33-6675, offers a harbor cruise taking in the Morro headlands aboard *La Niña* from the wharf on Avenida Carlos M. Céspedes at the foot of O'Reilly, one block east of Plaza de Armas. The boat departs Mon.-Fri. at 1 p.m., plus Saturday at 10 a.m., 1 and 5 p.m. (US$2).

Marlin also offers a coastal cruise aboard the *XIV Festival* from the wharf on San Pedro at the foot of Luz, Tue.-Fri. at 10 a.m. and 4 p.m. (US$10). A kiddies' matinee cruise is hosted on Saturday and Sunday at 10 a.m., noon, and 2 p.m. (US$2).

And the *Gitana* (Gypsy) leaves Marina Hemingway. The boat was built in 1928 with art deco styling. It offers daily excursions along the coast to Playa El Salado, where guests are taken ashore in small boats for a buffet lunch and activities on the beach. Nocturnal cruises pass by Morro Castle.

You can make reservations for all three cruises at your hotel tour desk or via Puertosol, tel. (7) 66-7117 or 33-2161, fax (7) 66-7716 or 33-2877.

GETTING AWAY

DEPARTING CUBA

By Air
Those airlines serving Havana usually depart Havana the same day (see the Transportation chapter for details).

Cubana, Calle 23 #64, tel. (7) 33-4949 or 33-4446, has a fully computerized reservation system. You can pick up printed timetables of Cubana's domestic and international service at the information desk in the lobby of the Cubana office (open Mon.-Fri. 8:30 a.m.-4 p.m. and Saturday 8 a.m.-1 p.m.). Double check departure times, which change frequently and at short notice. Cubana is especially notorious for canceling the reservations of those who don't reconfirm on time. Cubana's office gets crowded, and you can often wait an hour or more before being attended. Allow plenty of time.

Tickets for Cubana **charter flights** must be purchased through Havanatur's **Tours & Travel,** at Calle 6 e/ Aves. 1ra y 3ra, Miramar, tel. (7) 33-2712, or below the Hotel Habana Libre Tryp on Calle L at the top of La Rampa, tel. (7) 33-4082. Don't expect to be able to purchase a ticket at the airport. You may be able to purchase tickets at the airport, but don't count on it. If you miss your flight and want to buy another ticket, you will have to go to the Miramar or Vedado offices.

José Martí International Airport
The airport, 25 km southwest of downtown Havana, in the Rancho Boyeros district, is accessed by Avenida de la Independencia. A new freeway was under construction at press time, paralleling Independencia about two miles west (the southernmost, six-mile-long section was complete; eventually it will be extended into the heart of Havana).

Remember that the airport has four terminals spaced well apart from each other and accessed by different roads (nor are they linked by a connecting bus service). See Getting There, above. *Make sure you arrive at the correct terminal for your departure.*

Terminal 1: Terminal One, on the south side of the runway, on Avenida Van Troi, off Avenida de la Independencia (Avenida Rancho Boyeros), tel. (7) 33-5177/78/79 or 79-6081, in Reparto Rancho Boyero, handles Cubana's domestic flights. The terminal has a snack bar and restaurant, but car rental companies have pulled out and relocated to the new international terminal. (Rex Limousines, however, has an outlet on Avenida de los Boyeros, next to the Cupet gas station, 400 meters from the terminal.)

Terminal 2: Terminal Two, or Terminal Nacional, on the north side of the runway about one km east of the international terminal, handles Miami charter flights.

Terminal 3: All international flights (except Miami-bound charters) depart from the main terminal, tel. (7) 45-1424, fax (7) 33-9164.

The **departure tax** (US$20 at press time) must be paid at a separate counter after you've checked in with the airline. The foreign exchange bank refuses to accept Cuban pesos, so you should spend these in Havana (or give them to a needy Cuban) before leaving for the airport.

Listen carefully to the boarding announcements; they are easy to miss, especially over the sound of the live band! Don't linger when your flight is called.

Terminal 4: Terminal Four (also called Terminal Caribbean), about 600 meters west of the international terminal, handles small-plane flights (mostly domestic) offered by Aero Caribbean, tel. (7) 55-8722. Flights to Cayo Largo also depart from here.

The following airlines have offices in the airport: **Aeroflot,** tel. (7) 33-5432; **Air France** tel. (7) 66-9708; **Aero Caribbean** tel. (7) 33-5958 or 45-3013; **Grupo Taca** tel. (7) 33-0112, fax (7) 33-0113; **Iberia,** tel. (7) 33-5234; **LTU,** tel. (7) 33-5339; and **Mexicana,** 33-5051.

Getting to the Airport: No buses serve the international terminals. Buses marked "Aeropuerto" operate to Terminal Nacional—the domestic terminal—from the east side of Parque Central in Habana Vieja (the *cola* begins near the José

Martí statue). The journey costs one peso. The journey takes about one hour and is very unreliable. Allow plenty of time. You can also catch bus no. M-2 from the west side of Parque de la Fraternidad. It goes to Santiago de las Vegas via the domestic terminal. Make sure you wait in the line for people wanting seats *(sentados);* the other is for stoics willing to stand. Ask.

A licensed taxi to the airport will cost about US$13-16 from Havana (about US$10 for an unlicensed taxi). You can also arrange a shuttle through one of the tour agencies (US$10-15).

EXPLORING BEYOND HAVANA

Special bus and train services have been laid on for foreigners, with seat availability virtually guaranteed. All other public transport out of Havana to towns far afield is usually booked solid for weeks in advance: if you plan on traveling by air, bus, or train, make your reservations as far in advance as possible.

By Air
The fastest way to get around is to fly, although you'll miss out on the *real* fun of Cuba—exploring the countryside serendipitously. Most of Havana's main cities have an airport, and virtually every major tourism destination is within a two-hour drive of an airport. Domestic flights depart Terminal 1 at José Martí International Airport.

Cubana, Calle Infanta esq. Humboldt, Havana, tel. (7) 33-4949, plus several other poorly managed Cuban carriers also offer service to all the major cities.

By Bus
Tourist Buses: Víazul, tel. (7) 81-1413, fax (7) 66-6092, operates bus services for foreigners to key places on the tourist circuit, using modern a/c Volvo and Mercedes buses. Buses depart **Terminal Víazul** at the corner of Avenida 26 and Zoológico, opposite the entrance to the zoo in western Vedado. It has a small café and a/c waiting room and offers free luggage storage. (See the Víazul Bus Schedule chart.)

Havanatur, Calle 6 #117 e/ 1ra y 3ra, Miramar, Havana, tel. (7) 33-2712 or 33-2090, fax (7) 33-2601, and other Cuban tour agencies offer seats on tour buses serving Varadero,

AIRLINE OFFICES

INTERNATIONAL

The following have offices in the Hotel Habana Libre, Calle L e/ 23 y 25, Vedado:

Aeropostal: tel. (7) 54-4000, fax (7) 55-2148

Air Europa: tel. (7) 66-6918 (open Mon.-Sat. 9 a.m.-6 p.m.)

Air Europe: (open Mon.-Fri. 9 a.m.-5 p.m., and Saturday 9 a.m.-1 p.m.). Air Europe's main office is in La Lonja del Comercio, Plaza de San Francisco, Habana Vieja, tel. (7) 66-6743.

Air Jamaica: tel. (7) 66-2447, fax (7) 66-2449

Grupo Taca: tel. (7) 66-2702, fax (7) 33-3728 (open Mon.-Fri. 9 a.m.-4 p.m., and Saturday 9 a.m.-1 p.m.).

The following have offices at Calle 23 #64, at the base of La Rampa in Vedado e/ Calles P y Infanta:

Aero Caribbean: tel. (7) 79-7524 or 33-3621, fax (7) 33-3871 (open Mon.-Fri. 9 a.m.-5 p.m. and Saturday 9 a.m.-1 p.m.).

Aeroflot: tel. (7) 33-3200, fax (7) 33-3288 (open Mon.-Fri. 8:30 a.m.-12:30 p.m. and 1:30-4 p.m.)

Air France: tel. (7) 66-2642, fax (7) 66-2634; open Mon.-Fri. 8:30 am.-4:45 p.m.)

ALM Antillean Airlines: tel. (7) 33-3730, fax (7) 33-3729

AOM: tel. (7) 33-4098 or 33-39997, open Mon.-Fri. 9 a.m.-1 p.m. and 2:30-5 p.m.

COPA: tel. (7) 33-1759

Cubana: tel. (7) 33-4446/7/8/9; open Mon.-Fri. 8:30 a.m.-4 p.m.

Iberia: tel. (7) 33-5041, fax (7) 33-5061

LTU: tel. (7) 33-3524, fax (7) 33-3590

Martinair: tel. (7) 33-4364, fax (7) 33-3729; open Mon.-Fri. 9 a.m.-4 p.m.

Mexicana: tel. (7) 33-3531 or 33-3532, fax (7) 33-3077

TAAG: tel. (7) 33-3527

Tame: tel. (7) 33-4949, fax (7) 33-4126

DOMESTIC

Aero Caribbean: Calle 23 #64, e/ Calles P y Infanta, Vedado, tel. (7) 33-5936

Aero Gaviota: Calle 47 #2814, Reparto Kohly, tel. (7) 81-3068

Aero Taxi: Calle 27 #102, Vedado, tel. (7) 32-8127

Aero Varadero: Calle 23 #64, e/ Calles P y Infanta, Vedado, tel. (7) 33-0012

Cubana: Calle 23 #64, e/ Calles P y Infanta, Vedado, tel. (7) 33-4949

Trinidad, and other key destinations. Check with tour desks in hotel lobbies.

Public Buses: See the Transportation chapter for general information on travel by public bus.

Most buses to destinations outside metropolitan Havana leave from the **Terminal de Ómnibus Nacionales** (also called Terminal de Ómnibus Interprovinciales) on Avenida Rancho Boyeros, two blocks north of Plaza de la Revolución at Calle 19 de Mayo, tel. (7) 70-3397. Buses leave from here for virtually every town throughout the country. The **information booth** for Cubans, tel. (7) 70-9401, is downstairs but there is no posted bus schedule and the service is often surly. Facilities include a post office and snack bars. The terminal is served by local bus no. 47 from the Prado (at Calle Animas)

in Habana Vieja; by bus no. 265 from the east side of Parque Central; and by buses no. 67 and 84 from La Rampa in Vedado.

Foreigners, however, now pay in dollars and receive preferential seating. The booking office for foreigners is to the right of the entrance and has an a/c lounge with TV.

If you plan to travel like a Cuban, you should try to make your reservation as early as possible either at the bus terminal or at the **Buro de Reservaciones** (also called the Oficina Reservaciones Pasajes), at Calles 21 y 4 in Vedado. It's open Mon.-Fri. 7 a.m.-2 p.m. and Saturday 7 a.m.-noon. If you don't get shooed away to the dollars-only counter, expect a Kafkaesque experience. First, there's often a milling mob to contend with, with everyone clamoring to get his or her name on the list. Your name will be scrawled on a decrepit pile of paper, added to the scores of names ahead of you. Ask to see the sheets for the destination you want so that you can gauge how many days' delay is likely.

If you don't have a reservation or miss your departure, you can try getting on the standby list—*Lista de Esperas*—at **Terminal La Coubre,** tel. (7) 78-2696, on Avenida del Puerto at the foot of Avenida de Bélgica (Egido) in southwest Habana Vieja. Interprovincial buses that have unfilled seats call in here after departing the Terminal de Ómnibus Nacionales to pick up folks on the standby list. The eastern end of the terminal is slated to provide train service; the bus service is at the western end.

Also see the By Bus section in the section on Getting Around in the On The Road chapter for general information on bus service.

By Rail

Traveling from Havana by train is increasingly a viable option. There are four railway stations:

Estación Central de Ferrocarril: The most important station is the Central Railway Station at Avenida de Bélgica (Egido) and Arsenal, in Habana Vieja, tel. (7) 57-2041, 61-2807, or 61-8382. Trains depart here for most major cities, including Pinar del Río, Cienfuegos, Santa Clara, Sancti Spíritus, Ciego de Ávila, Camagüey, Las Tunas, Santiago and Guantánamo, and Bayamo and Manzanillo. Two services operate between Havana and Santiago de Cuba: the fast *especial,* which takes 16-20 hours for the 860-km journey, and the slow *regular.* See the Transportation chapter for further details.

In 1999 certain trains began operating from the **Terminal La Coubre,** 100 meters south of the main railway station at the foot of Avenida de Bélgica (Egido). Trains depart for Cienfuegos at 1:25 p.m. (train #67; arrive 11:35 p.m.), and for Pinar del Río at 9:45 p.m. (train #313; arrive 3:26 a.m.).

Estación 19 de Noviembre: The railcar *(ferro-ómnibus)* to ExpoCuba and Santiago de las Vegas departs from the 19 of November Station (also called Tulipán), tel. (7) 81-4431, located southwest of the Plaza de la Revolución, at Calles Tulipán and Hidalgo. See the Getting Around section, above.

Estación Cristina: The Cristina Station, tel. (7) 78-4971, at Av. de México y Arroyo, facing Cuatros Palmas, on the southwest side of Habana Vieja, serves outer Havana, including Parque Lenin and Playas del Este in midsummer only. See the Getting Around section, above.

Estación Casablanca: An electric train—the famous **Hershey Train**—tel. (7) 62-4888, operates to Matanzas from a harborfront station at Casablanca, on the north side of Havana harbor. It's a splendid journey (three hours each way), which you can take either with the locals or on a tourist junket. (See the special topic, The Hershey Train, in the Havana Province chapter.)

Purchasing Tickets: The state agency **Ladis,** tel. (7) 62-4259, handles ticket sales and reservations for all national train service. Foreigners must now pay in dollars, for which they get a guaranteed seat (for departures from Estación Cristina and Estación 19 de Noviembre, tickets can be bought onsite in pesos by foreigners). The Ladis office serving foreigners is at Calles Arsenal and Zulueta (open daily 8:30 a.m.-6 p.m.), on the north side of the main railway station in Habana Vieja. Tickets can be purchased up to 30 minutes prior to departure, but you must purchase your ticket that day for a nighttime departure.

By Taxi

Touring far from Havana by taxi can be inordinately expensive. It's certainly an option, however, for places close at hand, such as Cojímar or even Playas del Este. Beyond that, you're probably better off renting a car or hiring a private freelance driver.

Taxi Excursions Taxi Transtur, Calle 19 #210 esq. J, Vedado, tel. (7) 33-6666, fax (7) 33-5535, e-mail: taxihab@transtur.com.cu, offers chauffeured excursions by car or minivan. For example, an excursion to Viñales costs US$165/200 (car/minivan); to Varadero, US$120/150; and to Soroa, US$75/85.

Palcocar, tel. (7) 33-7235, fax (7) 33-7250, offers chauffeured excursions to places within a 150-mile radius of Havana. A trip to Varadero costs US$180; US$85 to Soroa; US$320 to the Bay of Pigs (Playa Girón); and US$252 to Viñales. Hourly rates for a chauffeured taxi are on a sliding scale from US$15 the first hour (20 km limit) to US$80 for eight hours (125 km limit), with US$0.70 per km for extra distance.

Freelance Cabs: Don't mind the possibility of breaking down in the boonies? Many Cubans with classic cars from the heyday of Detroit treat their prized possession as exotic cash cows—they rent them out (mostly illegally) for guided tours. Says Cristina García, "Twenty dollars buys gas enough for a decent spin. Seventy dollars gets you a day in a top-of-the-line Cadillac convertible with fins so big they block the rearview mirror. Forget about renting from Hertz or Avis ever again."

Your fare is negotiable, so ask around. Agree on the fare *before* getting in. Make sure you know whether this is one-way or roundtrip. Don't be afraid to bargain. You may get a better deal if you speak Spanish and know local customs. The driver will usually be amenable to any request you make. I've hired a car and driver for as little as US$20 for a full day, plus gasoline (a common courtesy is also to buy your driver lunch), but much depends on the quality of the car—and your negotiating skills.

Penny-pinchers might try finding a *colectivo* taxi at Parque de la Fraternidad or near the central railway station, where drivers are used to making long-distance runs to Playas del Este or even Pinar del Río and Viñales. You'll need to negotiate a price—be patient and firm. The days when *colectivo* drivers would take pesos from foreigners are over. With luck, however, you can still find someone who might run you to Playas del Este for as little as US$40-50.

Maquinas, the intercity taxis, are usually big Yankee cars. Most depart from Parque de la Fraternidad for destinations far and wide. Others wait outside the main railway and bus terminals. Often they won't depart until they fill up with passengers. Count on traveling about three km per peso.

By Rental Car

For lengthy exploring outside Havana, I recommend renting a car for the ease, freedom, and control it grants (there are no restrictions on where you can go), plus you can cover a lot of turf without the time delays of public transport. The following agencies have outlets in Havana:

Havanautos, Edificio Sierra Maestra, Av. 1ra y O, Miramar, tel. (7) 23-9815, fax (7) 24-0648, reservations, tel. (7) 24-0646, website: www.havanautos.cubaweb.cu; **Micar,** 1ra y Paseo, Vedado, tel. (0+7) 55-2444, fax (0+7) 33-6476, has an office at the airport plus various offices in

Havana and one in Boca Ciega in Playas del Este, tel. (687) 96-2130; **Palcocar,** tel. (7) 33-7235, fax (7) 33-7250; **Panautos,** Linea y Malecón, Vedado, tel. (7) 55-3286, fax (7) 55-657, e-mail: panatrans@dpt.transnet.cu, has several offices in Vedado and Miramar; **Rex Limousine Service,** Avenida de Rancho Boyeros y Calzada de Bejucal in Plaza de la Revolución, tel. (7) 33-9160, fax (7) 33-9159, and Linea y Malecón in Vedado, tel. (7) 33-7788, fax (7) 33-7789; **Vía Rent-a-Car,** Av. del Puerto #102 e/ Obrapía y Justiz, tel. (7) 33-9781 or 66-6777, fax (7) 33-2780, e-mail: dtor_rc@nwgaitov.gav.cm.net, also has offices at the airport, and in the Hotel Bosque, Hotel Kohly, Hotel Habana Libre, and Hotel Tropicoco (in Playas del Este).

Other car rental agencies include **Cubacar,** Av. 5ta y 84, Miramar, tel. (7) 24-2718, fax (7) 33-7233; **Fénix,** Calle Cuba #66, Habana Vieja, tel. (7) 63-9720, fax (7) 66-9546; and **Transauto,** Calle 3ra #2605 e/ 26 y 28, Miramar, tel. (7) 24-5532, fax (7) 24-4057. (See the Getting Away section in the On The Road chapter for details on cars and rates, as well as for **fly-drive packages** and **campervans**.)

Guides: *Jiniteros* will offer to guide. I recommend José "Pepe" Alvarez, a bilingual chap who has been running a personal guide service for 10 years. Contact him at Lazada Norte I #182, Santa Catalina, Habana 13400, tel. (7) 41-1209, fax (7) 33-3921, e-mail: americuba@yahoo.com, or visit his website at hometown.aol.com/cuba-tours/home.html.

Warning: Several car rental outlets have been accused of scams. Several readers have complained about Havanautos (see details in the section on car rentals under Getting Around in the On The Road chapter).

Organized Tours and Excursions

You can book excursions and tours at the tour desk in the lobby of virtually any tourist hotel.

Popular one-day excursions (and typical prices) include to Cayo Coco (US$143), Cayo Largo (US$109), Soroa (US$29), the Valle de Yumurí (US$32), Varadero (US$35), and Valle de Viñales (US$44). Typical overnight trips include to Trinidad (US$195) and Viñales (US$79).

Cubanacán Viajes Tour, Calle 146 esq. 9na, Playa, tel. (7) 33-9884, fax (7) 33-0107, or Calle

160 #1107 esq. 11, tel. (7) 33-6044, fax (7) 33-6233, offers a gamut of excursions and tours to destinations throughout Cuba, as well as multi-destination excursions to Jamaica, the Dominican Republic, the Cayman Islands, and Mexico.

Havanatur's **Tours & Travel,** Avenida 5ta e/ 84 y 86, Miramar, tel. (7) 24-9200 or 24-9199, fax (7) 24-1547, has a wide range of excursions. It also offices in the lobbies of leading hotels, plus outside the Hotel Habana Libre on La Rampa y Calle M, tel. (7) 24-7541, fax (7) 24-2074.

Gaviota Tours, Avenida 49 esq. 36A, Reparto Kohly, tel. (7) 24-4781, fax (7) 24-9470, e-mail: gavitour@gaitur.gav.cma.net, acts as a full-service inbound tour operator and travel agency and offers a series of day excursions to Soroa and Viñales in Pinar del Río, plus Trinidad and Cienfuegos, and Varadero.

Rumbos S.A., Casa Matriz on Linea y M, tel. (7) 66-9713 or 24-9626, offers one-day excursions to Pinar del Río (four hours) and to "dude ranches" near Playas del Este, as well as multi-day tours to Viñales, Playa Girón, and Trinidad.

Sol y Son, on La Rampa #64, Vedado, tel. (7) 33-3162, fax (7) 33-5150, e-mail: solyson@ceniai.inf.cu, is the tour operator of Cubana Aviación. It has offices at the airport and in the Hotel Neptuno/Triton and offers a wide range of one-day and longer excursions.

Paradiso: Promotora de Viajes Culturales, Calle 19 #560 esq. C, Vedado, tel. (7) 32-6928, fax (0) 33-3921, e-mail: paradis@turcult.get.cma, website: www.cult.cu\paradiso\index.html.

Cuba has been slow off the mark to develop ecotourism but is beginning to catch on. **Eco-Tur S.A.,** Av. 5ra #9802 esq. 98, Playa, tel. (7) 24-5195, fax (7) 24-7520, offers a series of eco-oriented tours and excursions. The guides have very little knowledge of ecotourism, however, and the planning and execution of trips is a far cry from those of, say, Costa Rica.

Veracuba, Casa Matriz, Calle 146 #1002, Miramar, Havana, tel. (7) 33-6619, fax (7) 33-6312, has 350 buses. **Transtur,** Av. de Santa Catalina #360, Vibora, Habana, tel. (7) 41-3906, 40-4754, or 41-8571, has been around for more than 30 years, is the biggest transport provider specializing in ground transportation for tourists. **Tropical Travel Agency** offers a full-day guided excursion to Varadero Beach daily (US$27, US$37 with lunch). It has a similar full-day tour to Trinidad, including a visit to Playa Ancón (US$112, including breakfast and dinner).

Viajes Horizontes at Calle 21 e/ N y O, tel. (7) 66-2160, fax (7) 33-4585, is part of the Hoteles Horizontes chain and was created in 1997 to introduce ecotourism, trekking, bicycling, and more than 20 other types of travel programs. It also acts as a general travel agency for car, hotel, and tour bookings. It's open Mon.-Fri. 8:30 a.m.-12:30 p.m. and 1:30-5:30 p.m., and Saturday 8:30 a.m.-1 p.m.

And **Viñales Tours,** Calle 1 #2210 e/22 y 24, Miramar, tel. (7) 33-1051, fax (7) 33-1054, specializes in tours to Pinar del Río Province.

Also see the Organized Excursions section the On The Road chapter.

HAVANA PROVINCE

There is comparatively little of interest in the namesake province that extends 65 km east and west and 40 km south of Havana's city limits. Havana is ringed with provincial colonial towns, small, anonymous, timeworn, yet with a dusty charm underscored by the low, rich light of late afternoon. Tucked away from the road, hidden in folds of hills, are small fishing and farming villages shaded by royal palms, thorny *marabú* trees, and two-toned *yagruma* trees. Inland much of the northern province is hilly and pocked with reservoirs that supply fresh water to Habaneros.

Most of Havana Province is agricultural, especially the low-lying southern plain—the food basket of the capital city—whose rich red soils feed fruit trees and vegetables. The southern shore is a soggy no-man's-land of swamp and mangroves, where lowly fishing villages are among the most deprived and down-at-heels in Cuba. No road runs along the southern shore.

> ## SIGHTSEEING HIGHLIGHTS: HAVANA PROVINCE
>
> **Cafetal Angarora, Artemisa:** Ruins of a sugar plantation with slave barracks and other buildings amid the cane fields.
>
> **Hershey:** Charming old trains and the **Central Camilo Cienfuegos** sugar-processing factory still operate in the former plantation-estate of the Hershey chocolate company. Quintessential wooden homes.
>
> **Jibacoa:** Stunning white-sand beach with a burgeoning resort complex.
>
> **Puente Bacunayagua:** Stunning views over a dramatic gorge from Cuba's tallest bridge.
>
> **San Diego de los Baños:** Dusty provincial town with colonial edifices in reasonable state of repair, including the **Museo de la Comedia** (Museum of Humor).

WEST OF HAVANA

ALONG THE COAST

Avenida 5ta leads westward from Havana and becomes the coast road—Autopista La Habana-Mariel (route 2-1-3)—to Pinar del Río Province. Just beyond the city limits, you'll pass two places marked on maps as "resorts." Don't be fooled by the umbrella symbols. Neither **Santa Fe,** immediately west of Marina Hemingway, nor **Bara-**

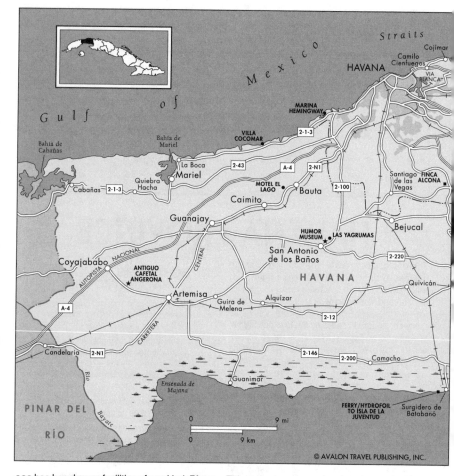

© AVALON TRAVEL PUBLISHING, INC.

coa has beaches or facilities of any kind. **Playa Salado,** five km farther west, is a tad more appealing. It's a tranquil spot where waves wash up onto a pebbly shore with pocket-size beaches beside a river estuary.

Here Cubanacán operates **Villa Cocomar,** Carretera Panamericano, Km 23.5, Caimito, tel./fax (7) 80-5089, looking quite run-down in early 2000. It has 47 a/c bungalows amid palms, casuarinas, and lawns—22 doubles with refrigerators, 25 singles with coolers—all with color TVs, telephones, and safety boxes (US$28 small, US$43 large). Facilities include the La Riviera restaurant, an open-air disco, shop, car rental and tour bureau, a swimming pool, and a sundeck. The **Blue Reef Dive Center** is here.

There's a **go-kart** track next to Villa Cocomar, and the beach has a snack bar and store.

Beyond Caimito, the sea glows an almost impossibly pavonine blue, as in a Maxfield Parrish painting. The route is lined with fields of spiny sisal.

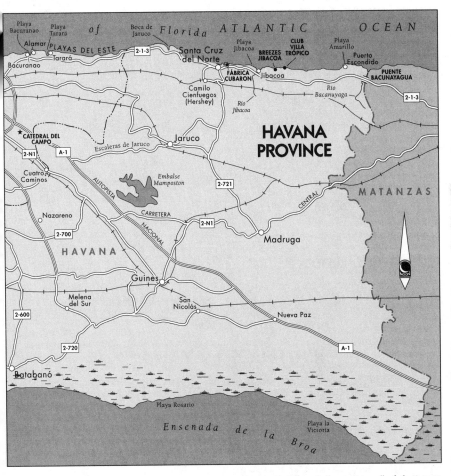

MARIEL AND POINTS WEST

This port city, deep inside a flask-shaped bay 45 km west of Havana, is best known as the site of the famous "boatlift" in April 1980, when 120,000 Cubans departed the island and sailed away to Florida. It's a small and sleepy town despite its port status. Mariel is ringed by docks and factories, including the largest cement factory in Cuba, whose main contribution to the

common welfare is to cast a pall of dust over everything for miles around. In 1999 Cuba signed a deal with the Dutch port of Moerdijk to develop and modernize the port.

The town evolved as a fishing village during the late 17th century. Then the British arrived and established a naval station here in 1762 (there is still a naval academy). Look for the Moorish-inspired building atop the hill on the outskirts north of town, a vision from *Beau Geste* amid the tousled palms. The **Museo Histórico,**

Calle 132 # 6926, tel. (63) 9-2554, tells of the city's development

If you decide to overnight, you're limited to the **Motel La Puntilla,** Calle 128, tel. (63) 9-2108, a 21-room peso hotel with swimming pool and bar. Buses depart and drop off at a "terminal," on Calle 71, tel. (63) 9-2104.

Route 2-1-3 continues west to **Cabañas,** beyond which you pass into Pinar del Río Province... a stunning drive. Soon you're amid quintessentially Cuban landscapes, with distant sugar mills *(centrales)* belching out black smoke above sensuously rolling green hills of cane, with mountains—the Sierra del Rosarios—in the distance. It is a special treat to take this little-traveled route during the cane harvest, when you'll share the winding road with creaky wooden carts pulled by oxen, dropping their loads of sugar as they go.

ALONG THE CARRETERA CENTRAL

An alternate route to Pinar del Río is along the freeway known as the Autopista, which begins at Avenida Rancho Boyeros on the southern edge of Havana. The freeway runs clean through the countryside, giving a wide berth to towns. Paralleling the Autopista is the old Carretera Central—route 2-N1—which was the main thoroughfare before the freeway was built. It offers a more compelling journey, passing through four modestly intriguing small towns.

Bauta has a historical museum on Calle 251 #14613, tel. (680) 2058, and the **Museo Antonio Maceo,** tel. (680) 3533. The **Motel El Lago,** on the Carretera Central just south of town, tel. (680) 3434, is a popular hostelry for Cubans, who flock to the swimming pool., but foreigners can't overnight in the 1950s-era mansion. You may have better luck at the dour **Hotel Machurrucuto,** off the Autopista, three km north of Punta Brave, tel. (680) 2971, US$10 s, US$20 d.

Caimito is worth the visit, if only to photograph the intriguing mural displaying a fierce bald eagle painted in the Stars and Stripes voraciously attacking a noble Cuban Indian and peasant. An attractive ocher-colored colonial-era church forms a backdrop.

You might pause in **Guanajay** to peek inside the dramatically baroque theater—Teatro Vicente Mora—on the north side of the town square.

SOUTH OF HAVANA

The entire landscape of southern Havana Province is rich agricultural land, intensively farmed. The area is modestly wealthy, with houses that are comfortable by Cuban standards (there are few rustic *bohíos*) and plenty of cars further hint at the regional prosperity. The southern coast is depressingly opposite. Maps show several *playas,* such as **Guanimar** and **Playa del Cajío,** but you can skip them. Guanimar is typical—a down-at-heels, one-street waterfront hamlet that stretches along the marshy waterfront. There's no beach to speak of, just small rowboats jury-rigged from aluminum, tin, and polystyrene and as melancholy as the hamlet itself.

A network of roads fans out south from Havana, crisscrossed by minor B-roads that form a complicated spiderweb linking a number of small towns of unpretentious appeal. A coast road parallels the shore about 10 km inland. East of Batabanó, it passes through miles of banana plantations around El Junco, before giving way to sugarcane. Stick to the main road; the secondary road system is an unfathomable labyrinth.

SAN ANTONIO DE LOS BAÑOS

The small town on the banks of the Río Ariguanabo, 30 km south of Havana, is appealing, despite its ramshackle state. There is considerable charm to its tiny triangular plaza, its ocher church, and its main street lined with colonnaded arcades.

The town boasts a **Museo de História,** on Calle 66, tel. (650) 2539, and a **Museo de la Comedia,** in a beautiful colonial home on Calle 60 and Avenida 45. The humor museum opened in 1979, when the city hosted the first **Humor Bienal Internacional** as a tribute to homegrown humorist Marcos Behemaras. The festival is still held here every two years and draws some of the best cartoonists from around the world (mostly Cuba, Russia, South America, and a few third world nations; the anti-imperialist theme is popular). It's well worth the US$2 entrance and the works, many of them quite brilliant, need no translation. Open Tues.-Sat. 10-5 p.m. and Sunday 9 a.m.-1 p.m.

The prestigious **Escuela Internacional de Cine y Televisión** (International Cinema and Television School), Carretera Villa Nueva Km 4.5, tel. (650) 3152, sponsored by the New Latin American Cinema Foundation, is also here, presided over by the great Colombian writer and Nobel prizewinner Gabriel García Márquez. The school trains cinema artists from throughout the third world.

You can hire a rowboat or speedboat at Las Yagrumas (see below) for excursions to the **Ojos de Agua,** the source of dozens of springs that feed the river, and to **Sumidero Cave,** where the river disappears underground.

Accommodation, Food, and Entertainment

Las Yagrumas, tel. (7) 33-5238 (in Havana), fax (7) 33-5239, overlooks the banks of the Ariguanabo one km northeast of town on the N2-100, the main road that leads south from the Playa district of western Havana. This contemporary colonial-style, red-tiled, two-story property is operated by Islazul. It has 120 pleasantly decorated a/c rooms (US$30 s, US$40 d year-round). Facilities include two grills and a café, a huge pool and sundeck, two tennis courts, two squash courts, a game room, a tour desk, and taxi service. Bicycle rentals cost US$1 per hour. Boat excursions on the river are offered (US$3), and you can rent boats for US$1 per person per hour. Lunch in the *parrillada* grill costs US$7, but US$14 in the a/c restaurant.

A good place to stop for a snack is the **Cuba Libre** restaurant, 200 meters west of the church (it's open Thurs.-Mon. 11:15 a.m.-5:45 p.m.). Equally appealing is **Restaurante Brisas del Caney,** a stone's throw away. Both serve *criollo* food under thatch. The latter has cabaret at night.

Traditional entertainment is hosted at the **Casa de la Cultura** on Calle 37, tel. (650) 2738, and occasionally at the **Casa de Bienes Cul-**turales, on Calle 41, tel. (650) 3194. A livelier scene on weekends is the **Taberna del Tío Cabrera** nightclub on Calle 56 and Avenida 39.

Transport

You can arrive or depart by bus; the **Terminal de Ómnibus,** is on Avenida 55, tel. (650) 2737.

ARTEMISA

Largest of the four towns is Artemisa, which dates from the early 19th century. The town, 60 km southwest of Havana, has a particularly active **Casa de la Cultura,** and wandering the streets you may come across a number of plaques and a bronze cube monument honoring the many citizens who participated in the attack on the Moncada barracks in Santiago in 1953 (24 of the original 150 Castroite rebels came from Artemisa. Check out the **Museo de Historia,** next to the Casa de la Cultura on Calle Martí, and the **Mausoleo a las Mártires,** east of the Carretera, on Avenida 28 de Enero (open Tues.-Sat. 8 a.m.-5 p.m. and Sunday 8 a.m.-noon). The mausoleum features a mural of Fidel and other revolutionaries and a quotation by Fidel.

The town's wide main street is colored by the faded pastels of neoclassical houses fronted with verandas supported by Doric and Ionic columns—appropriately, as the town is named for the Greek goddess of fertility, Artemis.

A residential golf complex was in the works at press time.

Antiguo Cafetal Angerona

A white marble statue of Artemis guards the ruins of an early-19th-century mansion five km west of Artemisa. Novelist James Michener used the site, part of an old coffee plantation—Cafetal Angerona, which went out of business about 1910 and is now a national monument—as the setting for his sugar plantation in his novel *The Caribbean.* Following a stream, Michener records in *Six Days in Havana,* how he found himself among a collection of "gigantic subterranean cisterns into which the copious supplies of water required in handling coffee beans were collected; it was like a scene from Dante. But it was when I climbed out of the cisterns and onto the plateau above that I came upon the salient fact of this

Artemis watches over the ruins of Cafetal Angerona.

great operation: the immense fenced-in area in which the slaves were kept, an area so vast that five or six football fields could have been fitted in. . . . The mournful place, called a *barracón,* had only one gate, beside which rose a tall stone tower in which men with guns waited day and night for any sign of incipient rebellion."

The watchtower and statue and ruins are still in place, and it is fascinating to explore the huge cisterns. There's no entrance fee, but you should tip any guide.

You might also consider a visit to the Central Abraham Lincoln, the local sugar mill that rises above the surrounding cane fields, to see how King Sugar is processed today.

Getting There

Bus no. 215 operates to Artemisa from Havana's main bus terminal. The **Terminal de Ómnibus** is on the Carretera Central, at Km 58, tel. (63) 3-3527. Trains run four times daily from Havana to the station on Avenida Héroes del Moncada, five blocks west of the plaza (US$2.50). Trains also run regularly to Pinar del Río (US$4).

BEJUCAL

This town, about 10 km south of Santiago de las Vegas and a 30-minute drive from Havana, is perhaps the prettiest in Havana Province and well worth an hour or so to admire its freshly painted colonial façades. At its heart is a tidy lit-tle square with an ocher-painted colonial church and Cine Martí. There's another attractive square two blocks farther west containing a bronze bust of Martí.

If the heat gets to you, imbibe a cup of refreshing tea at the **Casa Infusiones de Té,** on the main square, where you'll also find *criollo* dishes available at the **El Gallo Restaurant.**

On fine nights, join locals for an outdoor screening on Plaza Martí, claimed by locals as the setting for the movie *Paradiso,* based on the novel by José Lezama Lima.

BATABANÓ

This funky town (pop. 15,000) was one of the original seven cities, founded in 1515 (by Pánfilo de Narváez, a lieutenant of Diego Velázquez) and named San Cristóbal de la Habana. The settlers lasted only four years before uprooting and establishing a new city on the north coast—today's Havana, 51 km away. Batabanó is surrounded by ugly suburbs that are dormitories for agricultural field hands. I'm hard-pressed to say anything redeeming about it.

About three km south of Batabanó is **Surgidero de Batabanó,** the port town from which the ferries depart for Isla de la Juventud. Surgidero is a run-down, utterly depressing place. The road from Batabanó divides into a Y as you enter Surgidero; the left fork leads to the ferry terminal, the right to the railway station.

Accommodations
If you miss the ferry, take a deep breath. The only hotel in Surgidero de Batabanó is the **Hotel Dos Hermanos,** close to both the railway station and the ferry terminal at the southern end of Calle 68. It accepts foreigners but gets my vote as the most sordid hotel in Cuba. Fortunately, the price is only 10 pesos (more for a/c), which is about all it's worth.

Getting There and Away
Surgidero de Batabanó is served twice daily (Thursday, Friday, and Saturday) by train from Havana's Estación Tulipán. The rail station, whose platform is guarded by a huge cannon from the War of Independence, is at the end of Calle 68. Trains depart for Havana at 8 a.m. and 5 p.m. (two pesos).

The bus station is next to the rail station. A bus from Havana takes 90 minutes and costs 2.10 pesos. There's another station in Batabanó, about two miles from the port.

See the Isla de la Juventud chapter for information on ferry and hydrofoil services.

There's a **Cupet gas station** in Batabanó, at the junction of Calle 64 (the main street) and Avenida 73.

EAST OF HAVANA

ALONG THE AUTOPISTA

The Autopista (route A-1) runs southeast from Havana ruler-straight to the border with Matanzas Province, where it continues east as far as Sancti Spíritus. It's wide, fast, and devoid of traffic. However, watch for tractors, ox carts, and even cattle crossing the freeway.

The freeway runs parallel to and north of the old Carretera Central (route 2-N1). It skirts the towns and villages that line the old road. The most interesting town is **Santa María del Rosarío,** just east of the *circunvalación* (Havana's ring road), on the southeast outskirts of Havana. The town boasts a number of 18th- and 19th-century buildings, many of which were restored by a wealthy patron in the years preceding the Revolution. The town is centered on a large baroque church, a national monument colloquially called the **Catedral del Campo,** with a resplendent carved ceiling and wooden altar dripping with gold leaf. Santa María is served by bus no. 97 from Guanabacoa.

The most important town is **Güines,** an industrial town (pop. 30,000) and major rail junction of no particular charm 35 km southeast of Havana. It sits in the lee of forested hills to the north that include a well-known beauty spot called **Lomas de Amores** (Lovers' Hill).

Tourist maps show a series of beaches along the coast south of Güines, but they have little to offer.

There's a **Cupet gas station** on the main street in Güines, and another (along with a restaurant) at **Servicentro El Jagüey,** on the Autopista 35 km east of Güines.

Escaleras de Jaruco
These rolling hills rise east of Havana are popular among Habaneros escaping the heat for walks and horseback rides. The hills are composed of limestone terraces denuded in places into rugged karst formations laced with caves. Take the turnoff for **Tapaste** from the Autopista, about 15 km east of Havana. **Parque Escaleras de Jaruco** is six km west of Jaruco village and makes a scenic day trip, especially if you return via Playas del Este.

There are basic campsites (now very run-down), a motel—**Hotel Escaleras de Jaruco**—and two restaurants, most notably a brick-and-tile mansion called **El Árabe,** tel. (64) 3-8285, that sits atop the highest hill and specializes in lamb dishes. In recent years it has been hard-pressed to produce most of the dishes on the menu, such as lamb *en brochette* known as *lashe mischwuy.* Open Sunday only, in the afternoon.

ALONG THE CARRETERA CENTRAL

The Carretera Central runs southeast through the Havana suburbs of San Francisco de Paulo and Cotorro. You can follow it east through the rolling hills of the **Alturas de Habana-Matanzas** to Matanzas via the provincial town of Madruga. A few villages en route boast aged churches.

THE HERSHEY TRAIN

*R*ail journeys hold a particular magic, none more so in Cuba than the Hershey Train, which runs lazily between Casablanca and Matanzas year-round, four times a day. This fascinating electric railway has its origin in a chocolate bar.

In its heyday, before the Revolution, the Hershey estates belonging to the Pennsylvania-based chocolate company occupied 69 square miles of lush cane fields around a modern sugar-factory town (now called Camilo Cienfuegos), with a baseball field, movie theater, and amusements, and a hotel and bungalows for rent next to the mill.

At its peak, the estate had 19 steam locomotives. Their sparks, however, constituted a serious fire hazard, so they were replaced with seven 60-ton electric locomotives built especially for the Hershey-Cuban Railroad. Milton Hershey also introduced a three-car passenger train service between Havana and Matanzas every hour, stopping at Hershey. Alas, the diminutive vermilion MU-train locomotive that looked as if it could have fallen from the pages of a story about Thomas, the little "live" engine, was replaced in 1998 with a spiffy fleet of more comfortable, antique Spanish cars.

A Sugar of a Journey

The train departs Casablanca on the north side of Havana harbor and stops at Guanabacoa and dozens of little way stations en route to Matanzas. Two minutes before departure, the conductor gives a toot on the horn and a mad rush ensues. The train shudders and begins to thread its way along the narrow main street that parallels the waterfront of Casablanca. The rattle of the rails soon gathers rhythm, with the windows remaining wide open, providing plenty of breeze.

The train winds in and out among the palm-studded hills, speeds along the coast within sight of the Atlantic, then slips between palms, past broad bands of sugarcane, and through the Yumurí Valley. Two hours into the journey, you'll arrive at a blue station still bearing the Hershey sign. You are now in the heart of the old Hershey sugar factory, where the train pauses sufficiently for you to get down and capture the scene for posterity. Bring some snacks to share with locals, who willingly share from their meager packages unfolded on laps.

After a mesmerizing four-hour journey, you finally arrive at the sky-blue Matanzas station.

The train—which makes about 40 stops en route—departs Casablanca station, tel. (7) 62-4888, at 4:10 and 8:32 a.m. and 12:30, 4:22, and 9 p.m., arriving Matanzas 3.5 hours later. Two additional return journeys depart and arrive Havana's La Coubre station, avoiding the boat travel to and from Casablanca. Tickets cost $2.80 to Matanzas (foreigners can pay in pesos) and go on sale one hour in advance. Kids ride half-price. Passengers are assigned seat numbers. Ask for a window seat.

Five of the spiffy-clean Spanish coaches were intended for tourist service, to be pulled by a steam train—a Brill 3008—that ran for the first time in 1922. **Transnico** will market the tours. You can order a 60-minute VHS video, ***Hershey Electric: Adios to the Brills,*** from Canadian Caboose Press, Box 844, Skookumchuck, BC V0B 2EO, Canada (US$29.95).

Madruga was the setting in halcyon years for a *santería* procession held each 12 September that would culminate in a wild orgy of dancing and licentious behavior. Take time to stop at the **Ethnographic Museum**—the "House of Fredi"—in the home of the former *Santero Mayor* or *babalawo* (chief priest of the santería religion), where he initiated believers into the mysteries of the *Regla de Ocha.*

Finca Alcona

This farm raises *gallos* (cockerels) for combat. Apparently buyers come from all over the world to choose a prize Cuban cock. You, too, can visit and watch a cockfight. A grand **Feria de Gallos de Lidia** is held in early June. *Criollo* cuisine is served in the restaurant **El Gallo de Oro,** where a minstrel band performs popular *campesino* songs.

The farm is 17 km south of Havana, on the Carretera de Managua, outside the village of **Managua.** The easiest route is to take the Carretera Central to Cuatro Caminos, then turn west on the Carretera a Portugaletes for Managua, 15 km west (midway to Santiago de las Vegas). You can book an excursion (US$20, including lunch) direct with Finca Alcona, tel. (7) 22-2526 or 22-2527, fax (7) 33-1532, or through their office on Calle 42 #514 esq. Avenida 7, Miramar.

SANTA CRUZ DEL NORTE

East of the Playas del Este, the northern shore is hemmed in by low hills. Precious, albeit sulfur-rich, oil lies deep underground, and you'll begin to pass small oil derricks bobbing languidly atop the coral cliff tops.

Santa Cruz is a ramshackle industrial town steeping in a miasma of photo-chemical fumes and fronted by badly polluted waters. Cuba's largest rum factory, **Fábrica Cubaron,** also known as Ronera Santa Cruz, is here, producing the famous Havana Club rums and flavoring the air with its own heady aromas. Visitors are permitted by pre-arrangement with Cubaron in Havana. An even older factory, dating from 1919, stands down by the shore and may also open its doors to visitors eventually.

About four km south of Santa Cruz and worth the detour is **Camilo Cienfuegos,** formerly called Hershey and built as a model town by the Hershey Chocolate Company, which owned the sugar mill now called **Central Camilo Cienfuegos.** Hershey's town had a baseball field, movie theater, an amusement park, and scores of wooden homes for workers. Tourists could stay at the Hershey Hotel for $6, room and board, or rent one of two hundred bungalows located in the tropical park. The facilities still stand, now utilized by the Cuban state and forming a kind of lived-in museum made more intriguing by the quaint trains that serves the town and deliver visitors from Casablanca, north of Havana, and Matanzas. Visits to the sugar mill can be arranged through Juan Hernández, tel. (692) 27-335, at the mill.

The hardy and the impecunious may opt to sleep at the pesos-only **Motel Ferrocariarío,** next to the railway station at Hershey.

Buses no. 217 and 70 run from Havana to Santa Cruz del Norte, as does bus no. 699, from Calle Apodaca via Guanabo.

PLAYA JIBACOA

This beautiful beach, also known as **Playa Amarillo,** about four km east of Santa Cruz, extends east of the Río Jibacoa for several km. A smaller beach—**Playa Arroyo Bermejo**—lies tucked between cliffs at the mouth of the Río Jibacoa, about three km east of Santa Cruz del Norte, bracketed by rocky headlands. Coral reefs lie close to shore, perfect for snorkeling and scuba diving. The waters are of every shade of jade and blue. A series of white and reddish sand beaches extends further east.

Both beaches are popular with Cubans. The master plan for Jibacoa calls for 11 luxury hotels, two 18-hole championship golf courses, health spas, and time-share villas, to be developed by Leisure Canada and Gran Caribe.

You can reach Jibacoa on bus no. 126 from Santa Cruz, or from Casablanca near Havana (or Matanzas, or points between) on the Hershey Train (get off at Jibacoa Pueblo, about five km south of Jibacoa).

Accommodations and Food

Basic *campismos* line Playa Jibacoa. Most are restricted to Cubans, but foreigners are catered to at **El Abra,** tel. (692) 8-5120, a holiday camp with 87 small concrete cabanas with fans and promoted as an "eco-camp" by Cubamar, Calle 15 #752, Vedado, Havana, tel. (7) 66-2523, fax (7) 33-3111, e-mail: cubamar@cubamar.mit.cma.net. The recently renovated facility draws few vacationers but offers a huge swimming pool, horsebake riding, and bicycle rentals, and hiking trails lead into the nearby hills. Rates are US$10 s, US$14 d, US$18 t. Two a/c *casas* rent for US$21 s, US$30 d.

Farther east at Playa Amarillo is **Club Villa Trópico,** Carretera de Jibacoa, Vía Blanca, Arroyo Bermejo, tel. (7) 33-5651, an all-inclusive resort solely for Italians arriving on package tours run by the Italian company Ventaclub. It has 51 a/c rooms in cabanas.

Villa Jibacoa Loma is an Islazul property featuring attractive all-stone, two-story bungalows marvelously situated atop the headland overlooking the river mouth. It's rustic but full of ambience. Facilities include a small pool plus a restaurant. Some villas are modest, with small bedrooms; others are huge, with a pleasing contemporary feel (US$15 s and US$20 d low season, US$19 s and US$24 d high season per bedroom). Each features TV, a/c, telephone, refrigerator, and hot water. Some have kitchens. A bargain! Islazul also offers **Villas Los Jucaros,** alpine cabins amid pines behind Playa Jibacoa.

The award-winning Jamaican all-inclusive chain, SuperClubs, runs **Breezes Jibacoa,** Vía Blanca Km 60, tel. (692) 85-122, fax (692) 85-150; in North America, tel. (800) 467-8737; in the U.K., tel. (01749) 677200, a splendid four-star resort with 250 rooms and 10 suites on 19 acres of lush landscaped grounds with 300 meters of beach. This beautiful resort, with a contemporary take on classical architecture, is centered on a vast swimming pool. The spacious and tastefully decorated rooms are in two-story units and have king or twin beds, a/c, satellite TV, telephone, hair-dryer, tea and coffee-making facilities, safe deposit box, and iron, and large bathrooms with marble and plenty of high-pressure hot water. Suites have separate living areas and minibar. Choose from five bars, two restaurants, a café, grill, and room service. Martino's Italian restaurant (nonsmoking) offers an ambitious menu that includes excellent crepes stuffed with cottage cheese and spinach, and shrimp cooked in olive oil, garlic, and chili. The entrées hold their own on the international circuit and for Cuba prove exceptional. The resort's "Super-Inclusive" policy includes free everything, from booze to water sports, including scuba. It has an impressive gym, basketball and volleyball courts, a beauty store, a souvenir store, and a well-stocked humidor and rum store, plus massage (from US$7), medical center. And the staff is mustard-keen and personable. Introductory rates in December 1999 were US$85 s, US$75 d per person, US$106 s, US$94 d suite, but expect these rates to double. *Highly recommended!*

Entertainment
VentaClub and Breezes offer their own entertainment. You can join the locals at **Discoteca Jibacoa,** about one km west along the coast road; open Tue.-Sun. 9 p.m.-4:20 a.m.

PUERTO ESCONDIDO

The Vía Blanca moves away from the coast beyond Santa Cruz del Norte. About eight km east of the Río Jibacoa, a road leads north to the small coastal village of Puerto Escondido, a "wonderfully cool inlet a few miles down the Cuban coast," wrote Ernest Hemingway, who arrived aboard the *Pilar* to escape the hot summer nights. The spectacular setting—within a wide bend of a deep ravine—is occupied today by Puertosol's **Puerto Escondido Aquatic Center.** It offers windsurfing, waterskiing, and excursions by yacht and catamaran, plus diving and deep-sea fishing.

It was closed when I last passed by because a Cuban had recently fled to Florida in one of the marina's boats.

PUENTE BACUNAYAGUA

Camera at the ready? Then take a deep breath for your stop at this lofty bridge over the River Bacunayagua, 106 km from Havana and 10 km east of Puerto Escondido (about two km after crossing the Havana-Matanzas provincial boundary; it's 14 km from here to Matanzas). The 313-meter-long bridge, at 112 meters above the river—the highest in Cuba—spans the gorge of the Río Bacunayagua, which slices magically through the narrow coastal mountain chain. The Yumurí valley rolls away to the south, fanning out spectacularly as if contrived for a travel magazine's double-page spread. The views are spectacular, with the valley tufted with royal palms and framed in the hazy distance by dramatic *mogotes* (flat-topped limestone formations). Turkey vultures wheel and slide like kites on the thermals that rise up through the gorge.

The bridge is a favorite stop for tour buses, and there are facilities on the west bank to cater to the hordes. A *mirador* atop the cliff above the bridge offers the best views. There's a bar and restaurant here, and a souvenir shop. Police are usually stationed at either side of the bridge to catch speeding cars; stick to the 50 kph limit.

A road about one km east of the bridge winds downhill to **Villa Turística Bacunayagua,** a *campismo* for Cubans, with basic cabanas beside a rocky cove.

PINAR DEL RÍO
INTRODUCTION

Pinar del Río, the tail of the shark-shaped island, is Cuba's westernmost province. In the valleys here the world's most exquisite tobacco is nurtured and tenderly harvested on small plots by *guajiros,* Cuban peasants in straw hats, usually mustachioed, carrying a *machete,* and each with a cigar between his teeth. Ox-drawn plows transport you back in time amid quintessentially Cuban landscapes that attain their most dramatic beauty in Viñales Valley, tobacco country par excellence—and one of the most beautiful parts of the country, with incredible limestone formations looming over tobacco fields, plus caves for exploring, and a bucolic setting that Hollywood might have conceived for your camera.

Fernando Ortíz, author of *Cuban Counterpoint,* speculates that it is tobacco itself, the region's staple, that has blessed the local culture with a delicate warmth and finesse. Sugar, suggests Ortíz, is utterly masculine and fosters machismo in spite of its sweetness. Tobacco, in contrast, typifies Cuba's gentle, feminine side, despite the phallic shape into which it will be rolled.

The eastern lowlands are smothered in endless oceans of green sugarcane billowing like a great ocean, mile upon mile. A sweet, cloying odor of molasses wafts across the countryside,

and thick blue-black smoke billows from the tall chimneys of busy *centrales*. Following the Carretera Central or Circuito Norte, you may pass long lines of oxen and carts waiting patiently in the sun for their loads of cane to be unloaded. The sleepy town of Viñales is one of the most charming in all Cuba.

Other attractions in the pine-forested mountains include Soroa, known for its orchid garden; Las Terrazas, a model community with a first-rate eco-resort, plus artists' and artisans' studios, nature trails, cascades, and the ruins of 19th-century coffee *fincas* (farms) to explore; the thermal spas of San Diego de los Baños; and, nearby, La Gúira National Park, great for birding and for history buffs investigating the history of Che Guevara.

The town of Pinar del Río holds just enough to interest for a one-day visit, including a small cigar factory open for visits.

Land
Pinar del Río, is dominated by a low, ancient mountain chain—the Guanicuanjico—which forms an east-west spine through the province. The chain is divided by the Río San Diego into two mountain ranges—the Sierra del Rosario in the east and the Sierra de los Organos in the

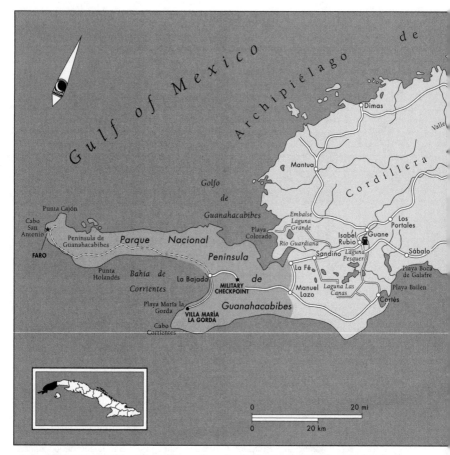

west—which cup stunning valleys. The mountains reach a height of 699 meters atop Pan de Guajaibón. The mountains edge up close to the narrow, undulating north coast, where a necklace of cays—the Archipiélago de los Colorados—lies protected by a coral reef. There are beaches, though few of great appeal. The star attraction is Cayo Levisa, off the central north coast.

The broader southern plains are covered with inferior soils that support expansive rice plantations, cattle pastures, and swamps that harbor hunting grounds and lakes stocked with bass and game fish. A slender pencil of uninhabited land—the Guanahacabibes Peninsula—hangs loosely off the southern tip, jutting west 50 km into the Gulf of Mexico. The peninsula is smothered in dense brush and cactus—a sharp contrast to the pine forests that cover much of the mountain slopes (the Peninsula de Guanahacabibes receives a mere 146 cm of precipitation per year). The peninsula is a nature reserve with a section where hunters may track down wild pig and deer. Fishermen and hunters are also served by several lakes and preserves. Playa María la Gorda, in Bahía de Corrientes, at the extreme southwest tip

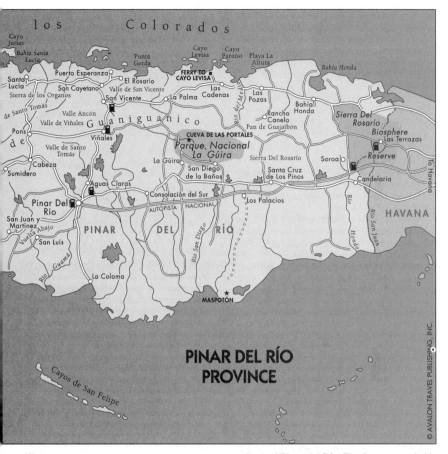

**PINAR DEL RÍO
PROVINCE**

© AVALON TRAVEL PUBLISHING, INC.

History
Pinar was settled by Europeans late in the tenure of Spanish colonial rule, when it was considered Cuba's "Cinderella" province.

The area was inhabited at least 4,000 years ago by the Guanahatabey, the initial aboriginal settlers. Later the region became a last refuge for the Ciboney Indians, who retreated before the advance of the Taíno Indians and, in turn, devastated the Guanahatabey.

The first Spanish settlement occurred only after 1717, when tobacco growers pulled up stakes in Havana Province and moved to the valleys of Pinar del Río. The farmers and citizens were beyond the pale and, guarding their independence jealously, engaged freely in smuggling. Later in the century, French coffee growers established *fincas* on the higher, easterly slopes, while sugar farmers established plantations below. Pinar del Río figured little in the war of independence and at the turn of the century remained a backward province.

Following the Revolution, counterrevolutionaries formed bands in the mountains and were suppressed only after several years' fighting.

Modernity overlays a way of life that has changed little since the end of the 19th century.

Which Route?

There are three routes from Havana to Pinar del Río. I recommend following a circle, combining two routes.

Most tourists follow the six-lane **Autopista,** the national highway linking the capital city with the town of Pinar del Río. It heads west almost ruler-straight and is in good condition the entire way. There's relatively little traffic, and the route is pleasingly scenic, with the Sierra del Rosarío off to the north. Be cautious of the many pedestrians seeking rides beside the road (they tend to wander onto the highway), particularly at night when the Autopista is unlit.

A second, more interesting, option is to follow the old **Carretera Central** through sleepy provincial towns such as Candelaria, Santa Cruz de los Pinos, and Consolación del Sur—towns memorable for their old churches, faded pastel houses, and covered walkways with neoclassical pillars. The two-lane highway parallels the Autopista along the southern edge of the mountains.

A far more scenic route is the lonesome **Circuito Norte,** which follows the picturesque north shore all the way west from Mariel to Mantua. Here's the scoop.

SIGHTSEEING HIGHLIGHTS: PINAR DEL RÍO

Cayo Levisa: Small offshore island with gorgeous white-sand beach, turquoise waters, and coral formations for diving.

Las Terrazas: Intriguing rural community with a splendid hotel. Local artists' studios, hiking trails, coffee *finca* (now a restaurant), and mineral springs and cascades.

Marea la Gorda: Top-notch scuba diving close to shore, making amends for a modest beach. Whales sharks are often seen.

Parque Nacional la Güira: Rugged, forested formations riddled with caverns, including **Cuevas de la Portales,** Che Guevara's headquarters during the Cuban Missile Crisis.

Soroa: An eco-retreat with cascade, orchid garden, and trails through the mountains.

Valle de Viñales: Beautiful valley dominated by dramatic limestone formations with caves. Quintessential rural landscapes. Center of tobacco farming.

THE NORTH COAST

The coast road west from Havana between Mariel and San Vicente is one of the most scenic in Cuba: a gentle roller-coaster ride with seductive glimpses of the sea to the north and, to the south, velvety, steep-sided mountains. There are simple *campismos* (holiday cabins) at **Playa Herradura,** north of Sandino, and **Playa San Pedro,** north of Pablo de la Torriente Brau.

West of San Vicente, the villages thin out, the road is lonesome, and there is little to hold your attention except the deep-shadowed Sierras, plump and rounded. The road runs a few miles inland of the coast. Side roads lead north to the shore itself, but there are few, if any, beaches of vital appeal. Side roads also lead inland to Soroa and the Valle de Viñales.

BAHÍA HONDA

Bahía Honda, 20 km west of Mariel, is very scenic. The town of the same name sits at the head of the bay. You can admire the vista from the hilltop **Motel Punta de Piedra,** tel. (86) 341, north of town. Otherwise, it's basic. Rooms cost US$15-20. A similar option is **Motel La Mulata,** 28 km west of Bahía Honda, with a terrace overlooking the bay.

Pan de Guajaibón

Just east of Las Pozas, you may be drawn from the highway to follow a side road south into the Sierra del Rosarios, lured by the sensuously rounded purple peak, Pan de Guajaibón (692 meters; 2,294 feet). The dramatic peak lies within a protected area known as Mil Cumbres (18,160 hectares), part of the Sierra del Rosarios Biosphere Reserve.

The road twists and loops for 15 km, growing ever more scenic as you rise gradually up and over undulating hillocks. Soon you are edging along beneath the *mogotes,* still rising, with slopes now covered with coffee bushes shaded by royal palms, and Pan de Guajaibón looming ahead like the Sugarloaf of Rio de Janeiro. Alas, the road gradually deteriorates and finally fizzles out at the hamlet of **Rancho Canelo,** from where a rough, overgrown track (4WD is recommended) probes the final few miles to the base of the soaring mountain.

Continuing along the Circuito Norte, beyond **Las Pozas** the land turns deep rust red. This is cattle country, with some sugarcane, bananas, and coffee plants for good measure.

Services

There are no gas stations, no stores, nowhere to buy even a soda or bottle of water along the coast road. Keep your eyes peeled for any little roadside stalls with signs for *refrescos* and *batidos.*

At Las Pozas, you'll find **Restaurante El Mambí.** It's the first eatery for miles. The pleasant though basic eatery is open 11 a.m.-2 p.m. and 6-8 p.m. It sells sweet, clear natural orange juice *refrescos* (10 centavos), salads, soups, and pork and chicken dishes. A meal and drinks will cost about 10 pesos (US$0.50)!

ARCHIPIÉLAGO DE LOS COLORADOS

West of Las Pozas you'll see the first cays of the Archipiélago de los Colorados beckoning seductively offshore, extending west all the way to the western tip of Cuba and beginning with Cayo Paraíso. Scuba diving is said to be sensational.

Cayo Paraíso

Ernest Hemingway had a fondness for beach-fringed, tousled-palm-shaded Cayo Paraíso. His presence has been venerated by the Provincial Commission of Monuments, which in 1989 erected a small monument beside the small wooden dock in his memory, on the 90th anniversary of his birth. It reads:

From the beginning of the 1940s, this place was the refuge of the great North American author Ernest Hemingway, who visited it assiduously, sometimes remaining on the cay for up to 20 days at a time. Here he wrote, rested, roamed the beach, swam, and loved it so much he used it as a base for antisubmarine operations from his yacht the Pilar *during the Second World War.*

A marina is planned at Cayo Paraíso for scuba divers and visiting yachters. The coral is superb, and there's a sunken vessel to explore eight meters down off the northeast of the island. You'll need a boat to get here.

Cayo Levisa

About 10 km west of Cayo Paraíso is a larger, more seductive coral cay ringed by 3.5 km of stunning sugar-white beaches two km offshore. It is the only cay in the archipelago that has accommodations. Cayo Levisa is popular with divers for its abundant black coral. There's a 30-meter-long dock on the south side.

A boat leaves for Cayo Levisa at 11 a.m. and 5:30 p.m. (US$15 per person, including cocktail; US$25 with seafood lunch) from the coast guard station at Palma Rubia (the turnoff from the Circuito Norte is 15 km west of Las Pozas, just west of the village of Las Cadenas).

Accommodations

Villa Cayo Levisa is a resort and diving center run by Horizontes, tel. (8) 33-4042, fax (8) 33-3161, e-mail: crh@horizontes.ht.cma.net, website: www.horizontes.cu. Horizontes. It's popular with Italians and Spaniards, particularly in midsummer. The 20 rustic yet pleasantly furnished, a/c cabanas face onto the beach. Water sports include sea kayaking, windsurfing, catamaran boating, and waterskiing. There's also a lively bar, a communal buffet restaurant serving good meals, and a small boutique. Excursions are offered via Horizontes. Rates were US$45 s, US$60 d, US$78 t low season; US$52 s, US$70 d, US$94 t high season, including transfer.

There were plans to add a hotel.

WEST OF CAYO LEVISA

Continuing west, you reach **La Palma,** the only town of consequence in the area, with a tiny museum and shops—the first I saw in 200 km. A road leads south from here over the mountains to La Gúira National Park and San Diego de los Baños. The scenery continues to inspire, with lonesome *bohios* and oxen working the palm-studded fields, the sea to the north, tantalizingly blue, and—to the south—low rolling hills backed by round-topped *mogotes.*

Ten km west of La Palma is the junction for Viñales and the town of Pinar del Río. Continue straight, though, and you reach **San Cayetano,** with a **Cupet gas station.** A turnoff leads north from here to the little fishing village of **Puerto Esperanza.**

West of San Cayetano the land begins to takes on a new look, strongly reminiscent of the Gold Country of California, with pine forests and, farther west, where the land flattens out, citrus orchards. From San Cayetano it is 22 km to the small port of **Santa Lucía.** The shallow *esteros* northeast of Santa Lucía are said to attract large numbers of hammerhead sharks in breeding season. Out beyond Bahía Santa Lucía is **Cayo Jutía,** currently being developed for tourism. It offers superb scuba diving and scintillating beaches. **Rumbos S.A.,** Maceo #117 Oeste e/ Galiano y San Juan, Pinar del Río, tel. (82) 4160, offers an excursion to Cayo Jutía from Pinar del Río.

West of Baja the road rises straight and as steady as a mathematical equation. The earth is rose pink and swathed in young pines. There's not a soul for miles. Then you arrive at **Dimas,** a pretty hamlet neatly arranged along a single street divided by a central median. At the end is a little pier where lobster boats unload.

Accommodations and Food

In all these miles there is only one restaurant and one hotel, the former at Puerto Esperanza. At El Rosarío, four km east of Puerto Esperanza, there's a villa, **Villa Rosarío,** tel. (8) 93828—a colonial mansion now a modest hotel with four rooms (two with shared bath) and a restaurant where lobster dishes are served.

DIMAS TO MANTUA

South of Dimas you pass around the western edge of the Sierras de los Organos as the road veers south to Mantua. This is a lonesome drive. The parched land is scrub covered and boring, and gazing upon the azure waters offshore you might wish that you were sailing, not driving. Scattered wrecks lie offshore, caught amid the coral reefs that scuttled 'em.

Five miles north of Mantua is a T-junction, with Mantua to the left and **Los Arroyos de Mantua** to the right, at the end of a road lined with banana plantations. Los Arroyos is a fishing village whose fleet works the Gulf of Mexico and Gulf of Guanahacabibes.

Mantua is a pleasant little town, which in 1896 was the site of a major battle during the War of Independence. The only note of appeal is a square at the south end of town dominated by fig trees surrounding a tall granite column topped by a bronze sculpture of a horse and warrior, *Al Soldado Invasor.* There's a **bank.** Buses arrive and depart in front of the **Casa de Cultura.**

ALONG THE AUTOPISTA

After leaving Havana, the six-lane concrete highway cuts through rolling plains planted in sugarcane. Then palm-thatch **bohios** and tobacco fields begin to appear alongside man-made lakes created for irrigation and recreation. Turnoffs lead north into the Sierra del Rosarios, replete with attractions. To the south, the land is as flat as a billiard table. These coastal flatlands can be skipped unless you have an abiding interest in hunting, fishing. There's nothing of visual appeal and few settlements.

There are two refreshment stops, one about one km east of the turn-off for Las Terrazas, about four km west of Coyajabos, and a second at Las Barrigonas, 27 km east of Pinar del Río. The latter features thatched *bohios* with tourist souvenirs, a café, and a sugarcane *trapiche* for freshly pressed juice.

There's a Cupet gas station at the turn-off for Soroa. The highway ends at the town of Pinar del Río, a two-hour drive from Havana.

SIERRA DEL ROSARIOS BIOSPHERE RESERVE

This 25,000-hectare (61,775-acre) reserve covers the easternmost slopes of the Sierra del Rosarios, with most of the area lush, prime forest. Much of the mountain slopes had been transformed by logging following the Spanish arrival. As time progressed, erosion and infertility contributed to abandonment of coffee farms and further denudation by impoverished peasants seeking income through logging. Today the land is given over predominantly to forestry, but raising cattle is also important. The area was named a biosphere reserve by UNESCO in 1985, following a decade of efforts at reforestation by the Cuban government.

Nature trails and ecotourism facilities are meager, though the potentials are great. The reserve protects close to 600 endemic higher plant species and 250 lower plant species (34% of the growth is native to the region). The reserve is covered by semi-deciduous, mid-elevation montane forest of pine and spruce. In springtime the thickly forested slopes blaze with bright red blossoms of *flamboyans,* and *poma rosa* grows wild by the roadside, which is also lined in season with white *yagruma* and the fiery blossoms of *popili.* At any time, the air smells piney fresh.

The 98 bird species (including 11 of Cuba's 24 endemic species) include Cuban trogons, *pedorreras,* woodpeckers, hummingbirds, parrots, and the national bird, the *tocororo.* Terrestrial turtles and frogs are common (pack your magnifying glass to search out the smallest frog in the world—*Sminthilus limbatus*). There's an outlandish looking water lizard, found only here, along with bats (five species), deer, and *jutías.*

It can get cool at night—bring a sweater. And bring repellent.

SOROA

Most famous of the Biosphere Reserve's attractions is Soroa, an "eco-retreat" set in a val-

THE CORK PALM

*T*his shaggy endemic palm, found only in Pinar del Río, is a souvenir of the Carboniferous era, when this valley was the ocean floor. Somehow the rare palms managed to stay above the waterline. The living fossil is a member of a family abundant 270 million years ago. It grows to six meters and sheds leaves every other year, leaving a ring around its fuzzy trunk that marks its age. It differs by sex: the masculine and feminine reproductive cells are emitted at different times, thus limiting the plant's propagation.

leyat about 250 meters elevation and perfect for nature hikes. Soroa is called the "the Rainbow of Cuba" for its natural beauty, although you need to get above the valley to appreciate the full scope of the setting.

The resort is named for Jean-Paul Soroa, a Frenchman who owned a coffee estate here two centuries ago and whose offspring still bear his name hereabouts. In the 1930s, it became fashionable as a spa with sulfur baths. Since the Revolution, it has gained a new lease on life, with a hotel and other facilities for tourists.

The road from the Autopista winds uphill until you see plastic signs by the highway pointing to individual attractions.

El Salto Cascades
This small waterfall is reached by a path with stairs that begin at the parking lot (on the opposite side of the road from the Orquideario) and descend 400 meters through fragrant woodlands of pine and wind-bent *coruba* trees to the bottom of the falls, which tumble 35 meters into pools good for bathing. The waters have medicinal properties and are good for treating respiratory and skin conditions. The cascades are at their most postcard-perfect in the early morning, when the sun shines full force on the glittering waters and you are held spellbound by the misty rainbow. There's a bar and restaurant overlooking the rippling Río Manantiales at the top of the cascades. Entrance is US$2.

The **Baños Romanos,** at the entrance to El Salto, is a dour spa facility.

Mirador de Venus
A rugged dirt track that will stump anything that doesn't have hooves leads uphill from the entrance to the El Salto car park to this hilltop lookout, overgrown with purple plumbergia. It's a stiff one km climb ending with a 100-step staircase that deposits you far above the valley with stupendous views over the valley and southern plains of Pinar del Río. Vultures swoop and slide overhead. You can hike or take a horseback ride.

Orquideario Soroa
Soroa's prize attraction is this orchid garden covering three hectares and claiming to be the world's second-largest orchid garden. It enjoys a fabulous hillside setting amid limestone formations, with views down the palm-tufted valley. The garden, nourished by the humid climate and maintained by the University of Pinar del Río, contains more than 20,000 plants representing over 700 species—250 of them indigenous to Cuba. Begonias flourish along with other ornamentals beneath the shade of tall palms and towering vine- and ephiphyte-clad trees, such as the peculiarly and aptly named elephant's feet.

The garden was created in 1943 by Spaniard Tomás Felipe Camacho, who built the hilltop house—now a beer garden and *mirador* with a souvenir store—and planted the craggy hillside with flowers on behalf of his daughter Pilila.

It's open 8 a.m.-4:45 p.m. daily except Friday, Oct.-April, and 9 a.m.-5:45 p.m. April-September. Entrance costs US$3 with an obligatory guide. Cameras cost US$2 and videos US$4.

Accommodations and Food
Virginia González Mendez offers a spacious and attractive cabin at **Hospedaje Virginia,** at La Flora Candeleria, Carretera Soroa Km. 4.5. The cabin has two beds, a/c, fans, a small TV, and private bathroom with hot water for US$20 s, US$25 d, US$30 three or four people. Meals are offered. "Don Pepe" has a *casa particular* half a kilometer farther up the road, with one large, well-lit, simply furnished room with a small TV and a fridge for US$20 (US$25 including breakfast).

There's also a *casa particular* in the hamlet north of Villas Turística Soroa.

La Caridad Campismo, one km uphill from Soroa, has basic cabins (US$12 d). Trails lead directly from the camp into the woods and hills.

Horizontes' **Villas Turística Soroa,** Carretera de Soroa Km 8, Candelaria, Pinar del Río, tel. (82) 2122 or 2041, is a delightful resort complex. Stone pathways lead through landscaped grounds to an Olympic-size swimming pool surrounded by 49 small cabanas on slopes backed by shade trees and forest. The small, recently renovated cabins offer pleasing ambience, with a/c, cable TV, and handsome tiled bathrooms with hot water. The resort also has 10 houses— **Casitas de Soroa**—with kitchenettes, TVs, VCRs, and cassette recorders. Eight have their own private pools! The restaurant is attractive and serves continental and *criollo* dishes. Try the Daiquirí Soroa, made of grenadine, rum, sugar, and lemon juice. Spa treatments are no longer offered. Rates were US$38 s, US$44 d low season, US$42 s, US$50 d high season.

The **Bar y Restaurante El Salto,** by the entrance to the cascade, is a handsome thatched eatery serving fish and meat dishes for US$4-7.

The restaurant at **Castillo de las Nubes,** two km above the orquideario, has been acclaimed for its "chicken Gordon blue." Since the Special Period, alas, the restaurant has lost its luster though the Spanish-style castle in the clouds still offers fine views and lunch (US$4-6).

You can dine with a local *campesino* family for about US$5—a good way to contribute to local welfare. Ask around locally, including the hotel staff.

Services

The hotel offers hiking, including a 20-km hike to the Canyon del Río Santa Cruz (US$4-10), plus horseback riding (US$3 per hour), bird-watching (US$15-25) including to Parque La Güira.

Transtur, at El Salto, has car rentals. It also rents mountain bikes (US$1 per hour; US$0.65 hourly after three hours) and scooters (US$10 first hour, US$13 two hours, US$15 three hours, US$29 daily).

Getting There

Soroa is seven km north of the Autopista. The turnoff is about 80 km west of Havana. You can also reach Soroa from the Circuito Norte, the north coast road. Trains from Havana and Pinar del Río stop at Candelaria, from where you can take a taxi to Soroa, nine km north.

Rumbos and **Tours & Travel** offer excursions from Havana. Soroa is also included in two one-week "ecotour" packages offered by **Horizontes.**

LAS TERRAZAS COMPLEJO TURÍSTICA

This unique "tourist entity" is centered on a one-of-a-kind model village and is touted as one of Cuba's prime ecotourism sites. It's highly recommend and offers a healthy calm and uplifting communal spirit that provides an example of one place where socialism works well, and there are many sights of interest hereabouts.

beasts of burden

Las Terrazas (pop. 1,200), website: www .lasterrazas.cu/indexns, is situated in a narrow valley above the shores of Lago San Juan and beneath palm-fringed, pinnacled mountains. It lies at the heart of a comprehensive rural development project that encompasses 12,355 acres. The village was founded in 1971. Its occupants are local *campesinos* and their offspring, some of whom work at La Moka, an ecologically principled hotel hidden from view on the forested hills behind the village.

French settlers who fled Haiti in 1792 planted coffee in these hills. After the coffee plantations failed, the local *campesinos,* isolated from education and health services and living amid mountain terrain ill suited for farming, continued to fell the trees for export and eke out a living as charcoal burners. Hillside by hillside, much of the region was turned to deforested wasteland. In 1967 the government initiated a 5,000-hectare reforestation project, employing the impoverished *campesinos* and providing them with housing in a prize model village designed by architect Osmani Cienfuegos, until recently Cuba's minister of tourism. Las Terrazas is named for the terraces of trees (teak, cedar, mahogany, pine) that were planted two at a time, side by side. Of each pair, only one will live. The other, destined to die in the struggle for life, will be used for charcoal.

The houses of whitewashed concrete with orange doors and blue shutters are aligned in terraces that cascade down the hillside to the lake, proving that communists can harmoniously blend man with nature. The village **community center,** facing a tiny *plazuela* with a fountain, houses a cinema, dentists' and doctors' offices, a small store, a post office, and a small **museum.** The museum shows pre-Columbian and plantation-era artifacts and tells the tale of Las Terrazas' development. A small *cafetería* sits over the lake, where boats are available for rent. There's even a rodeo ring where you can watch *guajiros* tussling with stallions and steers.

Looming over the community is **La Loma de Taburete,** a heavily forested, flat-topped mountain where Che Guevara trained his Bolivian guerrillas before his fatal departure for that country in 1965.

Day visits cost US$2 payable at the toll booths on the entrance roads.

Cafetal Buena Vista

Buena Vista preserves the ruins of a French coffee plantation constructed in 1801, the second-oldest coffee plantation in Cuba. At its peak in 1828, 125 slaves toiled these slopes.

The buildings have been lovingly restored and are exact reconstructions of the originals. The main building is now a handsome restaurant with lofty beamed ceilings and a steeply angled roof, a legacy of the European tradition of pitching roofs sharply to shed snow. Behind the restaurant are stone terraces where coffee beans were laid out to dry, the remains of the old slave quarters, and, on the uppermost terrace, an ox-powered coffee grinder where coffee beans would be placed in the circular trough, mixed with ashes, then ground to remove the husks. It is hoped that the land eventually will be restored to the point that this could again become a working coffee plantation.

It's very breezy up here at 250 meters, with spectacular views over the expansive plains. Guides (US$3 per hour) are available for local hikes. Stone cabins for rent are planned.

Centro Ecológico

This basic ecological center (locally called the Academy of Sciences) gathers scientific information for the reserve. Director Maritza García is in charge of studying and monitoring the different ecosystems. Visitors are welcome. You can rent guides for birding, nature hikes, and the like (US$5 per person per hour for up to four people, US$20 for more than four).

Hacienda Unión

This *finca,* two km west of Las Terrazas, is a conversion of the ruins of the old Unión coffee plantation. A *campesino* family raises chickens, geese, turkeys, and other fowl, and serves traditional meals at their rustic homestead sitting over a **botanical garden** where *Alpinia puparata,* colloquially called *espada de Santa Barbara* (Saint Barbara's sword), are grown.

Rancho Curijey

The administrative center for Las Terrazas and the biosphere reserve is here, about 400 meters east of the village. It offers a handsome thatched restaurant and bar over a lake with geese.

Ruinas de San Pedro y Santa Catalina

About eight km west of Las Terrazas, a dirt track—the **Cañada del Infierno Trail**—follows the Río Bayate south through dense forest to the ruins of San Pedro and the sulfur baths of Santa Catalina. (It's easy to miss the turnoff; look for the bridge over the Río Bayate. You may need a guide—several dirt roads confuse). The dirt road follows the river south two km to the ruins of the French coffee plantation. The crumbling remains are overgrown, and climbing figs clamber up the walls.

A faint hint of sulfur lures you downhill to the river, where natural pools encourage swimming. Locals favor the peaceful spot for picnics.

Baños de San Juan

These cascades and pools are about three km south of the rodeo ring in Las Terrazas. From the parking lot a paved path leads over a small bridge and along the river's edge past deep pools (good for swimming) and sunning platforms to a series of cascades. *¡Que linda!* Thatched ranchitas, including a small bar selling burgers and grilled meals, sit above the falls, and there are toilets.

The **Sendero San Juan River** trail follows the river valley to the San Juan Baths. En route, you'll pass the ruins of La Victoria coffee plantation and sulfide springs.

Trails

Several trails lead into the foothills of the surrounding mountains. Two that will appeal to nature lovers are the **Las Delicias Path** and the **La Serafina Path.** The former climbs Lomas Las Delicias, from where you have a fine view down the valley. The trip ends at the Buena Vista coffee plantation. La Serafina (four km) cuts through the Mango Rubio massif and is of particular appeal to birders. The Cuban trogon, the solitaire, woodpeckers, and the Cuban tody are common. The **Buenavista Trail** also leads two km to the coffee plantation.

Accommodations

A basic facility for Cubans—**Campismo el Taburete**—with 54 tiny cabanas spreads along the forest edge one km east of the community. Eastern bloc architecture prevails over good taste, with dour concrete structures (it's open daily, but only on weekends for Cubans), though they had been spruced up on my last visit. There's a bar and restaurant, TV room, and ponies for the kids. **Camping** is permitted (tents can be rented). Cabins cost US$5 (foreigners weren't accepted at press time, but plans were afoot to open it to tourists).

La Moka, Km 51, Autopista Habana-Pinar del Río, Candelaria, tel. (7) 78-600, (85) 2996, or (85) 2921, fax (7) 33-5516, is one of Cuba's showcase hotels—classy, romantic, intimate, and fully deserving of several nights' stay. The hotel is a contemporary interpretation of Spanish colonial architecture and features a splendid multi-tiered atrium lobby surrounding a lime tree with branches disappearing through the skylight. Breezes pour in through columned arches. The two-story accommodations block has magnificent red-barked trees growing up through the balconies and ceiling. The 26 rooms are designed to international standards and ecological vogue. Each room has a floor-to-ceiling glass window and French door leading onto a spacious terra-cotta-tiled balcony with tables, reclining chairs, and views through the trees to the lake. Take an upper-story room with high sloping wooden ceilings and antique ceiling fans. Facilities include a tennis court, small amoeba-shaped pool, sundeck, and lido café and bar reached by a path that winds uphill through lush, landscaped grounds. English-speaking guides are available for hire. You can rent bicycles, and steps lead directly to the lobby from the village. It gets cool here. Bring a sweater. Rates were US$58 s, US$96 d low season, US$80 s, US$118 d high season.

You can also rent the **Casa del Lago,** a two-bedroom house on the lakeshore, with its own pier, TV, bar, telephone, and kitchenette.

Food

An herb garden supplies the upscale **La Moka** restaurant whose menu option includes a buffet ($15). I recommend **Terraza de la Fondita,** a restaurant in Unit 9, in the heart of the village where Mercedes Dache cooks fabulous meals (my beef in a tangy sauce with rice and beans, plantain, and pimento, was one of the best I've had in Cuba; US$15, including beer and dessert) enjoyed on a terrace.

At **Cafetal Buena Vista** can have lunch on a tree-shaded terrace. Lunch costs US$13, including coffee, dessert, and a fabulous main dish of rice, lightly boiled potatoes, vegetables, fried bananas, and baked garlic chicken. The restaurant is open noon-4 p.m. Likewise, you can enjoy a hearty traditional meal at the *casa del campesino* at **Hacienda Unión** for US$11, including dessert and coffee.

A small bar and snack bar, **El Almacigo,** sits over a lily pond. And at **Café de María** María herself offers *cafecitos* for US$1.

Entertainment and Events

There's a **cinema** in the community center, plus the **El Almacigo** bar, and **Casa de Bota** bar down by the lake. There's sure to be someone playing guitar. Impromptu *canturías* featuring country music are often given. The **Dos Hermanos** bar in La Moka is named after one of Ernest Hemingway's favorite bars in Havana (the actual bar here is from the original).

Shopping

Local artisan Alberto González sells his beautiful kitchen implements handcrafted of local hardwoods at **Taller de Alberto.** Just up from the rodeo is **Taller de Fibras,** where a women's cooperative makes bargain-priced hats, baskets, and other items of banana leaves and straw. Whether you buy or not, call at **Lester's Art Studio,** in Unit 4. Lester Campa's fabulous works display staggering detail. Lester was born at Las Terrazas but studied at ENA (Escuela Nacional de Arte), in Havana. He says he needs brushes (especially fine ones) and other art supplies—take a gift. An artist named Duporté also has a studio. He specializes in paintings on Cuban flora, especially orchids. There's also a pottery workshop and a serigraphy workshop (**Taller de Serigrafo**), where items are on sale.

Services

The gas station—called EssTo—is hidden off the main road, 400 meters west of the turnoff into Las Terrazas. Gas costs US$1 per liter.

You can rent horses and mountain bikes (US$1 per hour) at La Moka, and rowboats are available on the lake at Casa de Bota for US$2 per hour (US$3 for pedal boats).

Getting There

Las Terrazas, 75 km west of Havana, is four km north of the Autopista, at Km 51 (there's a sign),

where a road runs into the mountains. You'll pass a barrier and guard post en route. You can also reach Las Terrazas north from Soroa. Turn right at the T-junction for Las Terrazas (17 km); if you continue straight at the junction, you'll drop down to Bahía Honda (29 km) on the north coast.

Tour agencies in Havana offer excursions to Las Terrazas. A taxi costs about US$40 each way.

SAN DIEGO DE LOS BAÑOS

Continuing west along the Autopista or Carretera Central, you'll pass the turnoff for San Diego de los Baños, a small but once-important spa town, 120 km west of Havana and 60 km east of Pinar del Río. This endearing village, about 10 km north of the Autopista, is centered on a tree-shaded plaza with a Greek Orthodox-style church erected in 1928 in on its north side.

The spa waters of the Templado springs were discovered in the 17th century and launched to fame when a leprous slave was supposedly miraculously cured after bathing here. German scholar and explorer Baron Alexander von Humboldt hyped the San Diego waters. Eminent people flocked. Subsequently, the resort was heavily promoted in the United States as the Saratoga of the Tropics.

The waters (a near constant 37° C to 40° C) brim with magnesium, sulfur, sulfates, and calcides and are an ideal soother for rheumatism, skin disorders, and other ailments. A modern facility with subterranean whirlpool baths was built after the Revolution. The **Balneario San Diego,** tel. (8) 3782, provides treatments from acupuncture (US$20) to massage (US$5 partial, US$25 full) and for everything from stress or obesity to "osteomyoarticulatory" (!) conditions. It's popular with Cubans, but gets few foreign visitors. Wheelchairs are provided for the physically impaired.

Accommodations and Food

The down-to-earth **Hotel Libertad,** tel. (8) 37820, and colonial-era **Hotel Saratoga,** tel. (8) 37821, were not accepting foreigners at press time.

Hotel El Mirador, tel. (7) 33-5410, is an attractive property with a beautiful setting above landscaped grounds, with a swimming pool and tiled courtyard. You'll find contemporary flourishes inside the colonial-style 1950s-era structures. The 30 large, a/c rooms feature attractive decor (rattan and pink floral prints), TVs, direct-dial telephones, and hot water in the showers. The classy restaurant lit by Tiffany lamps serves omelettes (US$2-4), spaghetti (from US$2), and fish and steak dishes. Book rooms through Servimed, Calle 18 #4304 e/ 43 y 47, Miramar, Havana, tel. (7) 33-2658, fax (7) 33-1630. It gets few visitors, however, and sometimes closes during off months. Rates were US$35 s, US$40 d.

Services
There's a post office opposite Hotel Libertad and a telephone office next door. The town also has a cinema and disco, and a **Cupet gas station.**

PARQUE NACIONAL LA GÜIRA

Parque Nacional La Güira protects 54,000 acres of sylvan wilderness that rise to pine forests on the higher slopes of the Sierra de los Organos, northwest of San Diego de los Baños. Timorous deer are found. And carp, trout, and a native fish called *viahaco* frequent the freshwater streams. The park occupies the former estate of Manuel Cortina, a wealthy landowner who traded in precious woods. Following the Revolution, the land was expropriated and made a preserve for the recreational use of all Cubans.

You enter the park through a mock fortress gate with turrets, beyond which the road rises to Cortina's former mansion—now in ruins—and a series of modest gardens, including a Japanese garden; a Cuban garden planted profusely with butterfly jasmine and flame trees; and a formal English garden with statuary and topiary that Mariano Verdecia, the gardener, keeps trim with his pruning shears. The Japanese house, alas, is derelict (robbers had stolen the museum's contents), and the zoo animals had all died with the exception of a lone vervet monkey during my last visit.

A road leads north through the park and continues to La Palma, on the north coast.

Cuevas de las Portales
This dramatic cave on the western edge of the park, about seven km from the entrance, should be on every tourist's list. The setting is stunning. Your first sight is of the Río Caiguanabo flowing beneath a fantastically sculpted natural arch that the river has carved through a great *mogote* (a freestanding limestone peak). The great cave, reaching 30 meters high, lies inside one wall of the arch. The massive chamber's curved walls and vaulted ceilings are stippled with giant stalagmites and stalactites.

Their remoteness and superb natural position made them a perfect spot for Che Guevara to establish his staff headquarters during the 1962 Cuban Missile Crisis, when he commanded the Western Army. The ever-smiling guide, Gilberto Cruz, will show you the table where Che and his men dined. Steps lead up to a cave within a cave where Che wrote his letters amid heaps of bat guano. The cave opens out to the rear, where stands Che's breeze-block office and dormitory, still containing the original table and chairs. Inside, a portal leads to another tiny cave with a floor of rough-hewn boards still supporting Che's narrow, iron bed.

Steps lead down to the fish-filled river through a "botanic garden" of wild philodendrons and strangler figs full of birdsong.

The road to the cave is much denuded; four-wheel drive is preferred.

Accommodations and Food
There's a bare-bones *campismo*—**Cajalbana**—at the entrance to Cuevas de las Portales, featuring spartan concrete bungalows. It also has **campsites** with barbecue pits beneath shade trees.

Cabañas de los Pinos, a cottage colony set loftily amid the cool pine-fresh forest a winding seven km uphill drive from the fortress gate, is closed. However, the guards may let you pitch a tent. There's a faucet for water. The air is as sharp as a needle, and it is marvelous to sleep with the wind whistling through the pines. You'll need to bring your own food.

Bar Maracas, about 400 m uphill from the fortress gate, is a down-to-earth eatery serving *criollo* dishes for pesos.

CLUB MASPOTÓN

Maspotón, 62 km east of the town of Pinar del Río, is a hunting and fishing club located near La

Cubana rice plantation, on the southern shores of Los Palacios Municipality. It has 134 square km of lowland marshes and woodlands dotted with lakes and canals bordered with mangroves. The lagoons teem with feisty tarpon ("silver bullets") which give fisher folk an unbeatable thrill. Since Maspotón lies directly beneath a migratory corridor between North and South America, the air is almost always full of birds settling and taking off. Blue-winged teal, shoveler ducks, pheasants, guinea fowl, snipes, and mourning doves abound.

Maspotón is popular with fishermen for its tarpon, bonefish, and snook in the Río Carragua estuary and for largemouth bass in nearby La Juventud reservoir. You negotiate the still lagoons of black water in flat-bottomed fiberglass boats.

Accommodations and Food

The lodge—described accurately by Carlo Gebler in *Driving through Cuba* as "like a dismal holiday camp"—has 34 a/c rooms in 16 soulless concrete cabanas built around a swimming pool and equipped with refrigerators, radios, and private baths. Don't trust the mosquito nets covering the tiny windows; you'll need to splash on the repellent liberally. There's a restaurant and bar, games room, and TV. I've not eaten here but am informed that the meals are grim—a good incentive to hook your own fish (take spices and condiments with you). Contact Horizontes Hotels, Calle 23 #156 e/ N y O, Vedado, tel. (7) 33-4042, fax (7) 33-3161, e-mail: crh@horizontes.ht.cma.net, website: www.horizontes.cu, or write the Club at Granja Arrocera la Cubana, Los Palacios, Pinar del Río (radio tel. COI-26). Rates were US$55 per person, including all meals.

Just before Los Palacios (see below) is **Restaurante Eltornado,** where I ate one of the best meals I've had in rural Cuba—a superb fish dish with heaps of boiled potatoes and a salted tomato salad. The fish was *tenca,* resembling pilchard. With a *refresco* of fresh-squeezed orange juice, my filling meal cost 11 pesos (US$0.50).

Getting There

Finding Maspotón is half the fun—or frustration. The turnoff from the Autopista is at the sign for **Los Palacios,** a neat agricultural town large enough to have its own small art gallery and bookstore yet described by Carlo Gebler as a "miserable town of wooden shacks, a few stucco-clad buildings in the center, and a rusting railway line running down the main street." Go to the east end of town, cross the railroad tracks to the right, bear immediately left, and take the first right for Maspotón. There are no signs. Follow the zigzagging, deeply gouged, muddy red track about 12 km until you reach a sign that reads *Club de caza y pesca* pointing to the right. Maspotón is about eight km farther. Just about when you're ready to pack it all in, you arrive.

PINAR DEL RÍO CITY

Pinar del Río, 178 km west of Havana, is the capital of its namesake province. The city (pop. 125,000) is named for the native pine trees that once flourished along the banks for the Río Guamá. Tobacco farmers established themselves nearby, in Viñales and Vuelta Abajo, and the city prospered on the tobacco trade (the first tobacco factory was founded nearby in 1761). During the 18th and 19th centuries when sugarcane came to dominate the Cuban economy, the city lost much of its early importance. Spanish authorities looked east, neglecting Pinar del Río, and the city became known as *Cenicienta* (Cinderella). Tourist literature stretches the truth in touting the city as the "Paradise in the West," but it is worth an overnight stay en route to Viñales or María la Gorda.

The town has a pleasant cosmopolitan feel, enhanced by neoclassical buildings, many with decorative art nouveau frontages, in fairly good state of repair. Many houses have recently received coats of fresh paint (albeit of Cuba's usual dowdy pastels) and there are several stores stocked with modern goods. Modern concrete apartment blocks and university buildings stand in ugly counterpoint around the city edges, and there are plenty of hovels hidden off the main roads on the city fringes.

Orientation

The Autopista slides into town from the east. It becomes Calle Martí, a wide boulevard that narrows to two lanes through the city center, dividing the town north and south.

The town is laid out in a rough grid. However, many streets are aligned or curve at odd angles, and it is easy to lose your direction. Martí is the main street, and most places of interest are here, or along adjacent Calle Máximo Gómez (one block south). The main cross street is Isabel Rubio, which leads north and south to the regions of Viñales and Vuelto Abajo. The city rises to the west, and at the "top" end of Calle Martí is a small triangular plaza where the most important historic buildings are found.

THINGS TO SEE AND DO

Museum of Natural Sciences

This small and mediocre museum displays the natural history of the province, both extant and extinct. The former includes stuffed mammals, birds, fish, and a collection of seashells. Concrete dinosaurs stand transfixed in the courtyard, including a plesiosaur (a giant marine reptile) and a *Megalocnus rodens* (an extinct oversized rodent once found in Cuba) surrounded by rare cork palms. The museum is housed in an ornately stuccoed building of Gaudiesque proportion, the Palacio Gausch, built in 1914 by a Spanish doctor to reflect elements from his travels around the world. Thus, the columned entrance is supported by Athenian columns bearing Egyptian motifs, while Gothic griffins and gargoyles adorn the façade. The museum is at Calle Martí #202 and Avenida Comandante Pinares. Open Tues.-Sat. 2-6 p.m., and Sunday 9 a.m.-1 p.m. Entrance costs US$1.

Museo Histórico Provincial

This small museum at Calle Martí #58 e/ Calles Isabel Rubio y Colón, traces the history of both the town and the province of Pinar from pre-Columbian days. Aboriginal artifacts (including in a mock cave dwelling) are displayed, along with antique furniture and weaponry. Concerts are sometimes held here. It's open Mon.-Sat. 8.30 a.m.-4 p.m. and Sunday 9 a.m.-1 p.m. Entrance costs US$1.

Fábrica de Tabacos

Sometimes referred to as the Tobacco Museum, the quaint little Francisco Donatién cigar factory is housed in the former Antigua Cárcel jail on Calle Antigua Carcel and Ajete. It's an intimate place, where five brands are made for national consumption. You can peer through glass windows to watch the 30 or so *tabaqueros,* who sit in two aisles, sorting their leaves and rolling, trimming, and gluing labels onto cigars. A guided tour costs US$5. You'll have a chance to listen to Segundo Pérez Carrillo reading from nov-

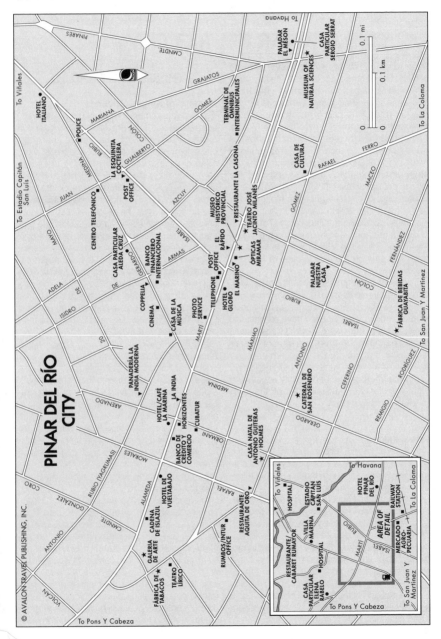

PINAR DEL RÍO CITY

To Viñales

To Havana

To Estadio Capitán San Luis

To Viñales

To La Coloma

To Havana

To Pons Y Cabeza

To Pons Y Cabeza

To San Juan Y Martinez

PINARES

CMDTE

GRAJATOS

GOMEZ

MARIANA

COLON

GUALBERTO

AZCUY

ISABEL

ARMAS

MARTI

DE 20

MEDINA

ORMANI

RAFAEL

MORALES

ARENADO

RUBIO (YAGRUMAS)

GONZALEZ

CORO

CMDTE

ANTONIO

VOLCAN

MEDINA

RUBIO

JUAN

MAYO

ADELA

ISIDRO

DE

GERARDO

RAFAEL

FERRO

MACEO

GOMEZ

FERNANDEZ

COLON

ISABEL

RODRIGUEZ

REMIGIO

CEFERINO

GERARDO

ANTONIO

MAXIMO

MAXIMO

HOTEL ITALIANO

POLICE

LA ESQUINITA COCTELERA

POST OFFICE

CENTRO TELEFÓNICO

CASA PARTICULAR ALEDA CRUZ

BANCO FINANCIERO INTERNACIONAL

COPPELIA

CINEMA

CASA DE LA MÚSICA

PHOTO SERVICE

TELEPHONE

POST OFFICE

EL RAPIDO

MUSEO HISTÓRICO PROVINCIAL

RESTAURANTE LA CASONA

TEATRO JOSÉ JACINTO MILANÉS

ÓPTICAS MIRAMAR

HOTEL GLOBO

EL MARINO

PALADAR NUESTRA CASA

FABRICA DE BEBIDAS GUAYABITA

CASA DE CULTURA

MUSEUM OF NATURAL SCIENCES

PALADAR EL MESÓN

CASA PARTICULAR SERGIO SERRAT

TERMINAL DE ÓMNIBUS INTERMUNICIPALES

PANADERÍA LA INDIA MODERNA

LA INDIA

HOTEL/CAFÉ LA MARINA

HORIZONTES

CUBATUR

BANCO DE CRÉDITO Y COMERCIO

CASA NATAL DE ANTONIO GUITERAS HOLMES

CATEDRAL DE SAN ROSENDRO

HOTEL DE VUELTABAJO

ALAMEDA

CADENA DE ISLAZUL

GALERIA DE ARTE

TEATRO LÍRICO

FABRICA DE TABACOS

RUMBOS/INTUR OFFICE

RESTAURANTE AQUITA DE ORO

0   0.1 mi

0   0.1 km

AREA OF DETAIL

To Havana

To Viñales

HOSPITAL

RESTAURANTE/ CABARET RUMAYOR

VILLA MARINA

HOTEL PINAR DEL RIO

RAILWAY STATION

To La Coloma

ESTADIO CAPITÁN SAN LUIS

HOSPITAL

CASA PARTICULAR ELENA RABELO

MERCADO AGRO PECUARIA

RUBIO

MARTI

ISABEL

To San Juan Y Martinez

To Pons Y Cabeza

© AVALON TRAVEL PUBLISHING, INC.

els or *Granma* to keep the rollers amused. Tom Miller describes his visits to the factory in his splendid book, *Trading with the Enemy.* It's open Mon.-Fri. 6:30 a.m.-4:30 p.m. and Saturday 7:30-11:30 a.m. You can buy cigars (including export brands) and souvenirs in a well-stocked shop.

Fábrica de Bebidas Guayabita

The blue building at Isabel Rubio #189, four blocks south of Calle Martí, is Casa Garay, where *guayabita,* a spicy, brandy-like alcoholic drink made from rum and guava, has been produced since 1892. This pleasant liquor is produced exclusively in Pinar del Río. It is made from the fruit of a wild bush—*Psidium guayabita*—that grows only on the sandy plains and pine woods of Pinar del Río. There are two kinds: a sweet *licor de Guayabita* and a dry *Guayabita seca* brandy. Tours are offered. In the tasting room, you can tipple various versions, including *guayabita* served with a shot of crème de menthe. You can buy small bottles for US$3.95. It's closed on weekends. Entrance costs US$1.

Other Sights

The **Teatro José Jacinto Milanés,** at the corner of Calle Martí and Calle Colón, boasts an ornate, circular, tiered interior made entirely of wood and capable of accommodating an audience of 520. The first theater here was dedicated in 1845, though the current theater dates to 1898, when it became a center for social life. A recent restoration has resurrected its fin-de-siècle splendor. Entrance costs US$1.

Worth a peek, too, is the **Casa Natal de Antonio Guiteras Holmes,** Avenida Maceo #52 e/ San Juan y Ormani Avenado, the former house of a local pharmacist and revolutionary hero brutally murdered in 1935 by the Machado regime. It is now an art gallery. Musical performances are offered in the back courtyard.

ACCOMMODATIONS

Casas Particulares

Guillermo Hernández and his mother, Marina, run **Villa Marina,** Calle Angeles #72 e/ A y Rafael Morales, tel. (82) 4303, with a self-contained upstairs apartment with a double and single bed, with a terrace, TV lounge, and hot water

for US$20 low season, US$25 high season. It also has a garage. Another excellent option is Elena Rabelo's *casa* at #286 Antonio Rubio, with three pleasantly furnished rooms that share a bathroom. She charges US$1 for the garage and US$3 for breakfast.

The other leading option is Aleda Cruz's *casa* at Gerardo Medina 67, tel. (82) 3133. This venerable colonial home (featured in two Cuban films, including *La Casa Colonial*) has three basically furnished rooms differing in size, but each with private bathrooms with hot water for US$20 with a/c, US$15 with fans. A patio to the rear has an exquisite little garden and secure parking.

Sergio Serrat Picart has a spacious *casa* on Calle Martí #255, tel. (82) 5893 (c/o a neighbor), with a/c, garage, and private bathroom with hot water, plus a garage. Nearby **Villa Odalys,** at Calle Martí #158, tel. (82) 5212, has two dark rooms with a/c, small TV, fridge, and private bathrooms with hot water for US$15. There are two other *casas* across the street.

A friend recommends the home of Magaly Suárez García, Calle Ormani Arenado #355 e/ Carmen y Emilito, Reparto Villamil, tel. (82) 2880, with one large room with a double and single bed (with adjustable partition between), private bathroom, a private entrance, and balcony for US$15.

A reader recommends the *casa particular* of Celeida Ramos Llano at Calle Pasajea #4 e/ País y Fernández, tel. (82) 3633. Also try Elena Rabelo's home at Antonio Rubio #284 e/ Méndez Capote y Coronel Pozo, tel. (82) 4295.

Hotels

The **Hotel Globo,** Calle Martí and Calle Isabel Rubio, tel. (82) 4268, is a moody place with a dark foyer lined with tiles and brightened by intriguing artwork and a stunning mosaic on the stairwell. The 42 rooms have lofty ceilings and are modest but adequate. Avoid rooms at the front, which pick up noise from the street. Rates were US$25 s/d. A similar option is the **Hotel Italiano** on Calle Isabel Rubio, tel. (82) 3049. Its 27 a/c rooms are small and modestly furnished. There's a pleasant restaurant downstairs. Rates were US$21/25 s, US$21/30 d low/high season.

Islazul's **Hotel Vueltabajo** on Calle Martí was being restored at press time.

TOBACCO

*g*t is generally acknowledged that the world's best tobacco comes from Cuba (the plant is indigenous to the island), and in particular from the 41,000-hectare Vuelta Abajo area of Pinar del Río province. The *vegas* (tobacco fields) of Vuelta Abajo are known to cigar connoisseurs the world over. The choicest leaves of all are grown in about 6,500 hectares around the towns of San Juan y Martinez and San Luís, where the premier *vegas* are El Corojo and Hoyo de Monterrey, each no bigger than a football field—650 acres given over exclusively to production of wrapper leaves for the world's preeminent cigars.

The climate and rich reddish-brown sandy loam of Vuelta Abajo are ideal for tobacco. Rainfall is about 165 cm per year, but, significantly, only 20 cm inches or so falls during the main growing months of November-February, when temperatures average a perfect 27° C and the area receives around eight hours of sunshine daily.

Most tobacco is grown on small holdings—many privately owned but selling tobacco to the government at a fixed rate. *Vegueros* (tobacco growers) can own up to 60 hectares, although most cultivate less than 4 hectares.

Raising Tobacco

Tobacco growing is labor-intensive, though, unlike sugarcane, it requires no brutal labor. Cultivation, picking, curing, handling, and rolling tobacco into cigars all require great delicacy.

The seeds are planted around the end of October in flat fields (maize is often grown on the same land outside the tobacco season). Straw is laid down for

shade, then removed as the seeds germinate. After one month the seeds are transplanted to the *vegas*. Buds have to be picked to prevent them from stunting growth. About 120 days after planting, they are ready for harvesting (the main harvest occurs in March and April).

There is a range of leaf choices, from *libra de pie*, at the base, to the *corona*, at the top. The art of making a good cigar is to blend these in such proportions as to give the eventual cigar a mild, medium, or full flavor and to ensure that it burns well.

The binder leaf that holds the cigar together is taken from the coarse, sun-grown leaves on the upper part of the plant, chosen for their tensile strength. Dark and oily, they have a very strong flavor and have to be matured for up to three years before they can be used. The finest leaves from the lower part of the plant are used as wrappers; these must be soft and pliable (making it easy for the roller to handle), and must also be free of protruding veins.

Plants designated to produce wrapper for the finest cigars are grown under fine muslin sheets *(tapados)* to prevent the leaves from becoming too oily in a protective response to sunlight. Wrapper leaves grown under cover ("shade tobacco") are classified by color. Those grown under the sun ("sun tobacco") have their own names. Generally the darker the color, the sweeter the taste.

Leaves are bundled in a *plancha*, or hand, of five leaves and taken to a barn where they are hung like smoked kippers and cured for about 40 days on poles or *cujes*. (Modern barns are temperature and humidity controlled. Traditional thatched barns face

If you don't mind staying out of town, I recommend the **Aguas Claras,** on the road to Viñales at Carretera de Viñales Km 7.5, Pinar del Río, tel. (82) 2722. It bills itself as an eco-resort and has 50 thatched and modestly furnished a/c bungalows spread amid landscaped grounds with bougainvillea and views through the trees and (down the river) decks where folkloric shows are performed. Facilities include a swimming pool, restaurant, snack bar, and tourism bureau. Guides are available for hikes, and horses can be rented (US$4 per hour). Rates were US$24 s/d, including breakfast. **Camping** is also allowed.

Hotel Pinar del Río, tel. (82) 5071, is on Calle Martí at the end of the Autopista on the eastern

fringe of town. The architecture is depressingly post-Stalinist, though mitigated by the warmth of the relaxed and friendly hotel personnel. The 149 large, a/c rooms are modestly furnished, with private baths, cable TVs, telephones, and radios. It has a boutique, and a nightclub where cabarets are offered. Other facilities include a restaurant, poolside grill, a café, and a lobby bar where mosquitoes will thank you for your visit. The swimming pool is a gathering spot for locals on weekends. Rates were US$23 s, US$32 d low season, US$29 s, US$38 d high season.

You can make reservations for Islazul hotels throughout the province at the **Cadena de Islazul** on Calle Martí #257, tel. (82) 3926.

west so that the sun heats one end in the morning and the other in the late afternoon, and temperature and humidity are controlled by opening and closing the doors.) Gradually the green chlorophyll in the leaves turns to brown carotene. After 45-60 days, they are taken down and stacked into bundles, then taken in wooden cases to the *escogida*—sorting house—where they are shaken to separate them, then dampened and aired before being flattened and tied in bunches of 50. These are then fermented in large piles like compost heaps for anywhere up to three months (the wrapper leaves are fermented

least). Ammonia and impurities are released. When the temperature reaches 44° C, the pile is "turned" so that fermentation takes place evenly.

The leaves are then graded for different use according to color, size, and quality. They are stripped of their mid-ribs and flattened, then sprayed with water to add moisture. Finally they are covered with burlap, fermented again, reclassified, and sent to the factories in *tercios*—square bales wrapped in palm bark to help keep the tobacco at a constant humidity. After maturing for up to two years, they are ready to be rolled into cigars.

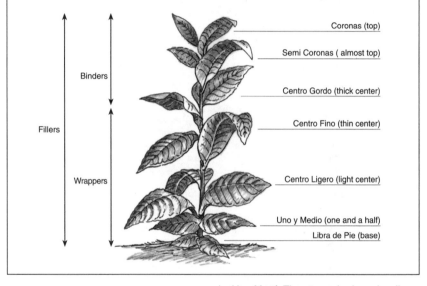

Coronas (top)

Semi Coronas (almost top)

Centro Gordo (thick center)

Centro Fino (thin center)

Centro Ligero (light center)

Uno y Medio (one and a half)

Libra de Pie (base)

Binders

Fillers

Wrappers

FOOD

My favorite restaurant is **Restaurante y Cabaret Rumayor,** tel. (82) 63007, one km north of town on Carretera Viñales. This fabulous Afro-Cuban restaurant features a huge thatch-and-log dining room decorated with African drums, shields, and religious icons. Service is keen. *Criollo* dishes include the famous house special, *pollo ahumado* (smoked chicken; US$5) and *chirna frita* (fish sautéed with garlic; US$7).

In town, the nicest place is *La India* on Calle Martí e/ Ormani Arenado and Gerardo Medina. You can dine on *criollo* food on a balcony over-

looking Martí. The atmospheric and well-run **Restaurante Aquita de Oro,** tel. (82) 4890, serves steaks from US$4.50. Tall doors offer views onto the street. It features dancing in a courtyard with an arbor of trumpet vine. You'll find chicken and rice (1.20 pesos), salads (40 centavos), and more at the **Café La Marina,** a jaded 1960s-style diner popular with locals for coffee and ice cream (open 7:30 a.m.-9:30 p.m.). The restaurant in the **Hotel Italiano** is also recommended for basic *criollo* food. **Restaurante La Casona,** opposite the Teatro Milanés, is a large, airy place also popular with locals. The basic pesos-only **El Marino** plays on a nautical theme with anchors and chains for rails outside.

Paladares are few. Try the **Paladar El Mesón,** Calle Martí, opposite the Museum of Natural Sciences, or **Paladar Nuestra Casa,** on Colón e/ Máximo Gómez y Antonio Maceo.

If all else fails, try **El Rápido** for fried chicken, on Martí e/ Colón y Isabel Rubio.

Seeking vegetarian food? Check out the **Eco-Restaurant Los Caneyes,** three km west of Pinar on the road to Cabeza. It serves natural health foods under thatch.

Coppelia, on Gerardo Medina, one block east of Martí, has excellent ice cream for 60 centavos (US$0.02) per scoop. There's a bakery—**Panadería La India Moderna**—at Antonio Rubio y 20 de Mayo. It's open 7 a.m.-noon and 5-7 p.m.

ENTERTAINMENT AND RECREATION

Don't leave town without checking out the **Cabaret Rumayor,** tel. (82) 63007. This excellent two-hour-long *cabaret espectáculo* is offered Thurs.-Sun. at 10 p.m. and features stiletto-to-heeled, befeathered mulatta dancers, comedians, and other performers. It's followed by a disco. The US$5 entrance includes one drink (locals pay 20 pesos). A folklore ensemble performs here on Monday and Tuesday.

Another favorite of locals is **Cabaret El Criollo,** also featuring an *espectáculo.* And the basic **Amelia Luz** nightclub in the Hotel Vueltabajo is also a favorite.

The **Casa de Cultura,** at Máximo Gómez #108, has an art gallery plus dances and live music, usually beginning at 9 p.m. The folkloric dances feature the *punta campesina,* in which *guajiros* recite poetry to each other in conversational fashion, each building on the work of the other in a form known as *controversias.* Children's programs are sometimes offered on weekends at 2 p.m. Kiddy films are also shown at **Sala de Video Satelite,** 50 yards up the hill. Live music is also featured at the **Centro Provincional Artes Plástico Galeria** and **Teatro Lirico,** and at the **Casa de la Música,** on Gerardo Medina y Antonio Rubio.

A good place to down a few beers with the locals is **La Esquinita Coctelera,** at Isabel Rubio esq. Juan Gualberto Gómez. It also serves *guayabita* and the house special, vermouth and rum, to help put the clientele in a singing mood with tunes on the jukebox. The younger crowd hangs out at the open-air **Cadena Servicio CS** at Calle Martí y Rafael Morales.

The Vegueros, the local **baseball team,** hosts visiting teams at the Estadio Capitán San Luís, on Calle Capitán San Luís, three blocks west of the Carretera Central for Viñales. There's a **go-kart** track just east of the stadium, where motorcycle races are also offered.

PRACTICALITIES

Shopping
The **Fábrica de Tabacos** has a well-stocked humidor where you can purchase export-quality cigars, plus a souvenir store selling cassettes and T-shirts. Pinar is known for quality ceramics; check out the workshops on Calle Antonio Maceo. And you can buy small bottles of *guayabita* at the factory on Isabel Rubio.

Caracol has stores selling Western clothing and other goods in the Hotel Pinar del Río and next to the cigar factory at the top of Antonio Maceo.

Information and Services
Cubatur, tel. (82) 7-8405, has a tour information office at Calle Martí #115 esq. Ormani Arenado. It rents cars and offers tours. It's open Mon.-Fri. 8 a.m.-5 p.m., and 8 a.m.-noon Saturday. **Horizontes** has an office next door. **Rumbos** has an office at Antonio Maceo #17.

There's a post office and DHL station in the Hotel Pinar del Río, tel. (82) 5070, ext. 251. The main post office is at Calle Martí esq. Isabel Rubio. You can make international calls from the **centro telefónico** on Gerardo Medina esq. Juan Gualberto Gómez.

There's a **Banco de Crédito y Comercio** on Martí e/ Rafael Morales y Ormani Arenado, and a **Banco Financiero Internacional** on Gerardo Medina y Isidro de Armas.

The local library—Biblioteca Ramón González Coro—has 90,000 books, including works by Alice Walker and William Faulker (and even Braille editions of Castro and Martí), a library of record albums, and a bookbinding room, reports Tom Miller in *Trading with the Enemy.*

The **hospital** is one km north of town, at the junction for Viñales. There's a 24-hour pharmacy next to the Hotel Globo, at the corner of Isabel Rubio, and another—Farmácia El Modernista—next to the Hotel La Marina.

Getting There

By Air: Aerotaxi, tel. (82) 6-3248; in Havana, Calle 27 #102 e/ M y N, Vedado, tel. (7) 33-4064, fax (7) 33-4063, flies to Pinar del Río from Havana.

By Bus: Víazul operates tourist bus service to Pinar del Río from Havana (see the Víazul Bus Schedule chart). For public bus service, see the Public Bus Service from Havana chart. The route follows the Autopista and takes about three hours (some public buses follow the Carretera Central, adding about one hour to the journey). They arrive at the **Terminal de Ómnibus,** tel. (82) 2572, on Calle Adela Azcuy, between Calle Colón and Comandante Pinares.

By Train: Trains depart Havana's Tulipán station daily (US$6.50). The journey ostensibly takes five hours but can take much longer (departure times are subject to change). The station in Pinar del Río is three blocks south of Calle Martí at Calle Comandante Pinares (see the Getting Away section in the Havana chapter).

Getting Around

Pinar is cozy enough to walk virtually everywhere. However, there are plenty of horse-drawn taxis, which gather on Máximo Gómez between Rafael Ferro and Ciprian Valdes. Tourist taxis are based at the Hotel Pinar del Río for trips farther afield.

Getting Away

Aerotaxi, tel. (82) 6-3248, offers flights by Antonov AN-2 biplane to Isla de la Juventud from Pinar's Aeropuerto Àlvaro Barba, two km northeast of town. Departures are Monday, Wednesday, Friday, and Saturday (US$20 one-way). No reservations are taken, so arrive early to sign up for the waiting list.

Bus no. 100 leaves for Havana from the **Terminal de Ómnibus Interprovinciales** at 3:30, 4:30, 5:30, 8:30, and 10 a.m., and 1, 2:30, and 4:35 p.m. Buses depart Pinar del Río from the **Terminal de Ómnibus Intermunicipales** (also at Calle Adela Azcuy e/ Calle Colón y Comandante Pinares) for destinations throughout the province, including Viñales and La Bajada.

Trains for Havana depart at 9:30 a.m. on Monday, Wednesday, Friday, and Sunday (US$6.50).

You can rent cars from Transauto and Havanautos, both in the Hotel Pinar del Río. **Micar** has an agency at Servicentro Oro Negro, tel. (82) 6-3317. **Transtur,** tel. (82) 7-8078, has taxi and rental car service.

There's a **Cupet gas station** at the bottom of Rafael Morales on the south side of town, and another station two km northeast of town, on the road to Entronque de Ovas, beyond the turnoff for Viñales.

Tours & Travel, tel. (82) 78254, fax (82) 78494, offers excursions throughout the province.

VIÑALES AND VICINITY

Viñales is a miniature Yosemite, with the most spectacular scenery in all Cuba. The valley (about 11 km long and five wide) is cut into the Sierra de los Organos and scattered with precipitous knolls the height of skyscrapers towering over a plain of impossibly deep green receding to distant mountains. The setting resembles a Vietnamese or Chinese painting, particularly in the early morning, when mists settle above the valley floor.

The great freestanding rocks are called *mogotes,* isolated, sheer-sloped, round-topped, cone-shaped mounds that are part of the oldest geological formation in Cuba. They are the remnants of a great limestone plateau—part of the Guaniguanico mountain range—that rose from the sea during the Jurassic era, about 160 million years ago. Over the ensuing eons, rain and rivers dissolved and eroded the limestone mass to form classic karst terrain, leaving hummocks as high as 1,000 feet.

Some *mogotes* are laced with holes—canyons, really—hundreds of feet wide, reached often by traipsing through natural tunnels to follow rivers that suddenly disappear down holes in their own valley floors. Pre-Columbian Indians inhabited the caves, and, during the colonial era, runaway slaves built villages amid these lonesome holes.

Between the *mogotes* are *hoyos,* small depressions, filled with deep deposits of rich red soil perfect for growing tobacco. One of the special memories you'll take home is the image of farmers in straw hats plowing their fields with oxdrawn plows. From January to April, a sweet aroma of tobacco hangs over the fields.

Many species of flora and fauna are found only atop the strange mesas, such as unique varieties of snails. Fauna is so highly endemic that certain mollusks are found only on one or a few *mogotes.* The formations are festooned with rough bush, ferns, and the rare and ancient cork palm *(Mycrocycas calocoma),* a botanical relic that has been declared a national treasure and grows only here. Below, on the valley floor, grow silk-cotton trees, royal palms, Palmita de Sierra, the *roble caimán* (a relative of the oak), and sweet-smelling mariposa, Cuba's national flower. Other rare endemic species include a pygmy boa constrictor, the *zunzún* (the world's smallest hummingbird), and the *tomeguín del pinar,* another tiny bird related to hummingbirds.

A good place to capture the valley on film is from the parking lot and *mirador* at Las Jasmines. You'll find a *ranchito* restaurant and gift stalls. If the heat is too much, you can buy a *pipa,* refreshing coconut milk in the husk (US$2).

VIÑALES

The town of Viñales (pop. 10,000), 26 km north of Pinar del Río and 212 km west of Havana, is a rural charmer, justifiably a national monument. In many ways it's still a cowboy town, and its wide main street—Calle Salvador Cisnero—is lined with turn-of-the-century, red-tile-roofed cottages and shaded by rows of stately pine trees. The handsome **main square** is shaded by palms and has a bust of José Martí at its center. To one side is a pretty 19th-century church. On the north side, a beautiful arcaded colonial building houses the **Casa de Cultura,** which posts a list of local activities on the door.

Calle Salvador Cisnero has a few other sights of note. The first is **Museo Municipal Adela Azcuy.** It has motley displays telling the history of the region, and, outside, a bronze bust of Adela Azcuy Labrador, a local heroine and captain in the War of Independence. The other local treasure is the **Casa de Don Tomás,** dating to 1822 and now an atmospheric restaurant where you can dine while looking out over the **Hogar Maternidad,** where pregnant women in nightgowns rock gently on the veranda.

Two widows, Carmen and Caridad Miranda, maintain the **Viñales Botanical Garden** full of fruits, orchids, begonias, and other ornamental and medicinal plants: Other villagers seeking herbal remedies consult the two sisters, who are happy to demonstrate for you how the pre-Columbian Indians extracted dyes from plants to paint their bodies.

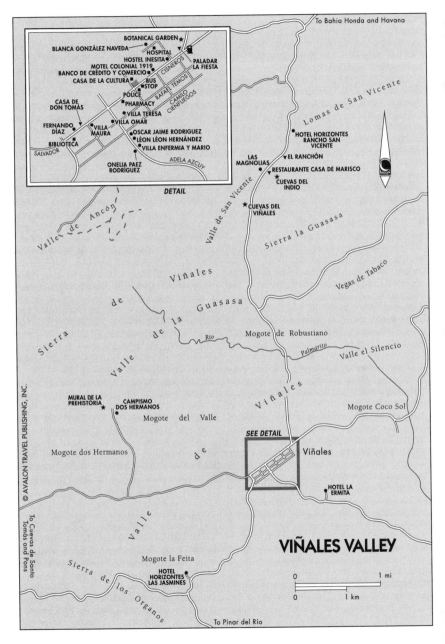

To Bahia Honda and Havana

DETAIL

BOTANICAL GARDEN ★
BLANCA GONZÁLEZ NAVEDA
HOSPITAL
HOSTEL INESITA
MOTEL COLONIAL 1919
BANCO DE CRÉDITO Y COMERCIO
CASA DE LA CULTURA
BUS STOP
POLICE
PHARMACY
CASA DE DON TOMÁS
VILLA TERESA
FERNANDO DÍAZ
VILLA OMAR
VILLA MAURA
OSCAR JAIME RODRIGUEZ
BIBLIOTECA
LÉON LEÓN HERNÁNDEZ
VILLA ENFERMIA Y MARIO
ONELIA PAEZ RODRÍGUEZ
PALADAR LA FIESTA
CISNEROS
RAFAEL TEMOS
CAMILO CIENFUEGOS
SALVADOR
ADELA AZCUY

Lomas de San Vicente

HOTEL HORIZONTES RANCHO SAN VICENTE
LAS MAGNOLIAS
EL RANCHÓN
RESTAURANTE CASA DE MARISCO
CUEVAS DEL INDIO ★
CUEVAS DEL VIÑALES ★

Valle de San Vicente

Sierra la Guasasa

Vegas de Tabaco

Viñales de la Guasasa

Río
Mogote de Robustiano
Palmarito
Valle el Silencio

Sierra de Valle

Viñales

Mogote Coco Sol

MURAL DE LA PREHISTORIA ★
CAMPISMO DOS HERMANOS
Mogote del Valle

SEE DETAIL
Viñales

Mogote dos Hermanos

de

HOTEL LA ERMITA

Valle

VIÑALES VALLEY

To Cuevas de Santo Tomás and Pons

Mogote la Feita

Sierra de los Organos

HOTEL HORIZONTES LAS JASMINES

To Pinar del Río

0   1 mi
0   1 km

© AVALON TRAVEL PUBLISHING, INC.

MOON

Accommodations

Casa Particulares: Private house rentals have blossomed in the past few years. All charge identical rates and offer meals (usually US$3 for breakfast, US$6-19 for dinner).

On the main street, **Villa Maura,** tel. (8) 9-3337, opposite Casa Don Tomás, has a large but gloomy room with lofty ceiling. The house has a TV lounge and a breezy patio facing the main street. Fernando Díaz, tel. (8) 93390, at #142 Salvado Cisnero, next to Casa Don Tomás, has two rooms furnished with antiques. They're pleasantly cool and spacious and have fans; one has a/c (US$20). East of the plaza, **Motel Colonial 1919,** tel. (8) 9-3110, has a large room for up to six people (US$20 for 3-6 people); and **Hostel Inesita,** Salvador Cisnero #40, tel. (8) 9-3297, with two somewhat dingy upstairs rooms with fans, a/c, and basic bathroom.

On Avenida Adela Azcuy, **Villa Omar,** tel. (8) 9-3183, has a simple room sleeping up to five people, with hot water in the private bathroom, and a TV lounge with a piano. Far nicer is **Villa Teresa,** Camilo Cienfuegos #10 e/ Adela Azcuy y Seferino Fernández, tel. (8) 9-3267 c/o a neighbor, with one well-lit, cross-ventilated room, although with cold water only for now (hot water is planned). Teresa and her husband are super hosts.

Oscar Jaime Rodriguez, tel. (8) 93381, has a room downstairs and a smaller, newer room upstairs with a nice bathroom, with meals served on a rustic patio. Oscar's mother-in-law, Rosa Artiaga, has a large, well-lit, but simply furnished room next door with hot water in a private bathroom. The other neighbor, León León Hernández, tel. (8) 9-3380, has an clean, attractive room for three people, with a/c, large closet, fans, and cross-ventilation, and a lounge with TV and CD music system. **Villa Enfermia y Mario,** tel. (8) 9-3380, next door, has a pleasant, well-lit room with a cramped bathroom with hot water. Across the street, Onelia Paez Rodríguez, tel. (8) 9-3381 c/o a friend, has a room with a large shower with hot water.

Others recommended by readers include Blanca González Naveda, at Edificio Colonial #2, Apto. #12, Calle Salvador Cisnero; and Tony Aracelys Fernández's house at Villa La Esquinita, Rafael Trejo #18 esq. Marian Grajales, for US$15 nightly, plus US$5 breakfast and US$10 dinner. Pigs, chickens, and ducks chase around the yard full of fruit trees.

At least five *casas particulares* are immediately south of town on the road to Pinar del Río.

Hotels: Visitors are blessed with two splendid options—and splendid bargains as well. The first is **Hotel Horizontes La Ermita,** Carretera de La Ermita Km 2, Viñales, Pinar del Río, tel. (8) 93-6071, fax (8) 93-6091, one km south of town and magnificently nestled atop the southern scarp of the valley. The gracious contemporary property on a classical theme—hints of ancient Crete blend with Spanish colonial design—wraps around a sundeck and swimming pool with poolside bar where you may settle beneath shady palms to drink in the heavenly views. The 62 a/c rooms are beautifully decorated. Make sure you get a room with a balcony (complete with Adirondack chairs) facing the valley. The restaurant serves reasonable cuisine and the local liqueur, *guayabita,* and the Group Valle Son entertains. There's also a well-stocked store. Rates were US$37 s, US$48 d low season, US$42 s, US$55 d high season.

Equally appealing is **Hotel Horizontes Las Jasmines,** Carretera de Viñales Km 25, Pinar del Río, tel. (8) 93-6205, fax (8) 93-6215, an older but recently restored Spanish hacienda-style hotel with fancy wrought-iron grillwork and a similar hilltop setting and fabulous vistas. The 16 a/c cabanas and 62 rooms have radios (but no telephones) and TVs. The rooms are clean and pleasantly furnished and have balconies facing an Olympic-length ice-blue swimming pool overhanging the cliff. Forty-eight newer rooms are in a separate block. An ornate wooden ceiling and French doors topped with beautiful stained glass lend elegance to the second-floor restaurant and bar. Rates were US$38 s, US$50 d low season; US$45 s, US$60 d high season.

Food

The restaurants at both Hotel La Ermita (US$5-9) and Las Jasmines are good bets. The grilled fish at La Ermita is excellent (US$7). *The* place to eat, however, is **Casa de Don Tomás,** an atmospheric wooden colonial charmer at 141 Calle Salvador Cisnero, tel. (8) 9-3114. I recommend the house special, *delicias de Don Tomás* (a rice dish with pork, sausage, and lobster; US$10), a beef dish called *tasajo a lo campe-*

a guajiro, *reminiscent of another time*

sino, or paella (US$10), washed down with a *coctel el trapiche* (US$2). The Trio Romántico serenades while you eat. It's open daily 10 a.m.- 4 p.m. and 6:30-9 p.m.

Most *paladares* had been forced to close by 2000, but one remaining option is **Paladar La Fiesta,** opposite the Cupet gas station at the east end of Salvador Cisnero. You dine in a rustic yet attractive patio, with three choices of buffets (US$10).

Entertainment and Recreation
Rumbos offers a cabaret at 10:30 p.m., Tue.-Sat., in the Cuevas del Viñales (see Viñales Valley National Monument, below), also known as **El Palenque,** tel. (8) 93-6290. The dance floor within the cave mouth is overhung with stalactites. It's open 8 p.m. until the disco closes in the wee hours. This is the in-spot for locals. The cabaret troupe, which travels up from Pinar del Río, is surprisingly good. It costs US$5, including a cocktail.

ARTEX on Avenida Salvador Cisnero, has occasional live music. Across the street, **Bar y Restaurante El Viñales** is a rustic bar with a patio for watching the street life.

Hotel La Ermita offers guided hiking excursions, plus horseback riding (US$5 pre hour).

Shopping
At the northwest corner of the plaza is a small **Galería de Arte,** where you may buy paintings of moderate quality. The block on Salvador Cisnero opposite the plaza has a few motley stores.

A Caracol store, 100 meters north of town on the road to Cuevo del Indio, sells cigars and music, as does the ARTEX souvenir store one block west of the plaza. Stalls along the block immediately west of the plaza sell baskets and straw goods.

Services
There's a 24-hour pharmacy, tel. (8) 9-3169, one block west of the plaza. The police station is opposite the plaza on Salvador Cisnero. The post office is one block south of the plaza, and there's an international telephone center about five km north of town at Rancho Horizontes San Vicente. There's a Banco Credito y Comercio one block east of the plaza; open Mon.-Fri. 8 a.m.-noon, and 1:30-3 p.m. The hospital is two blocks east of the plaza. The **Cupet gas station** is at the east end of town.

Getting There And Away
By Bus: Víazul operates tourist bus service to Viñales from Havana (see the Víazul Bus Schedule chart). For public bus service, see the Public Bus Service from Havana chart. The bus stop in Viñales is opposite the plaza. Buses also run along the north coast to San Vicente, where you can catch a bus south to Viñales. The bus for Havana leaves daily at 2:30 p.m. (US$8), tel. (8) 93119 (Omnibus) or tel. (8) 93195 (Astro).

By Car: From Pinar del Río, take the two-lane Carretera Viñales. Leaving town, take Isabel Rubio for one km and turn left at Hospital Quirúrgico. It's 27 km to Viñales. The road winds uphill through pine forest until you reach a billboard that reads Complejo Turística de Viñales, announcing your arrival above the valley at Hotel Las Jasmines, to the left. The road drops into Viñales town; at the T-junction, the road to the left leads to Los Murales; that to the right leads into town and continues to Las Cuevas and the north coast.

There's also a turnoff for Viñales from the Autopista, eight km east of Pinar del Río; it's a rough road with big potholes (after eight km you'll reach a T-junction, with Aguas Claras to the left and Viñales to the right).

Transtur, tel. (8) 93-6060, rents cars plus scooters (US$28.50 per day).

By Taxi: A licensed taxi from Havana will cost US$100 or more roundtrip. Better to negotiate a price for a private car and driver, which may be as low as US$40 (plus gasoline), depending on the car.

Organized Tours: Rumbos, Tours & Travel, and other tour agencies offer one-day excursions from Havana. (See Organized Excursions in the Getting Away section in the Havana chapter.)

Getting Around

Cubataxi offers service in Citroen minivans from the plaza (same telephones as the bus). **Transtur,** tel. (8) 93-6060, rents mountain bikes (US$1 per hour) from booth on the west side of the plaza.

VIÑALES VALLEY NATIONAL MONUMENT

Exploring the Valle de Viñales immerses you in an archetypal Cuban setting. Dominating the valley are the dramatic *mogotes* in whose shadow *guajiros* in straw hats and white linens (or faded military fatigues) lovingly tend their plots of tobacco and maize. Thanks to a very special microclimate of moist nights and cool mornings, tobacco grows well here, dominating the valley economy.

Farmers will be proud and delighted to take you out into their *vegas* and curing sheds to demonstrate the skill of raising tobacco, much of

which lies under acres of cheesecloth stretched over the plants to protect against insects and an excess of sun. Often you'll see pairs of oxen connected by a yoke pulling two great logs joined in a V and ridden ski-like by a *guajiro,* always with a faithful dog trotting alongside at his heels.

The valley contains several caves of interest, some of which are used for military purposes and are off-limits.

The Valle de Viñales deserves more than daylight perusal, and you should linger to savor the fabulous sunsets. It's a climactic moment viewed from the lofty Hotel La Ermita or Las Jasmines, from where you look down upon a thin haze of smoke settling in the valley floor from dinners being prepared in *bohios* (it dissipates shortly after sunup). Buzzards will be riding the last thermals, swooping and sliding like gliders. And the braying of donkeys and clip-clop of hooves far, far below can be heard clearly.

Cuevas del Viñales

This cave, four km north of Viñales, is mostly a curiosity. The cave entrance has been converted into a discotheque replete with laser lights. Bats and swallows nest in nooks and swoop in and out, disturbed by the flashing fandango of the lights and the discordant beat of the disco. Entrance costs US$1 with a guide (tip the guide).

Cuevas del Indio

Far more interesting is this cave, 1.5 km north of Cuevas del Viñales, named for the Indian remains found inside. The large grotto is entered via a slit at the foot of a *mogote.* You can explore the cave with or without a guide from either of its two entrances. The cave is four km long, although you only explore the first km by foot. A flight of steps leads to the main entrance, where you follow a well-lit path (slippery in parts) through the mesmerizing catacomb, which in places soars to a height of 135 meters. Eventually you reach an underground pier where a boatman waits to row you on a trip up the subterranean, milky green river that runs deep beneath the mountain and is a habitat for opaque fish and blind crustaceans. The cave is also inhabited by small bats. It is like a crossing of the

Valle de Viñales

Styx, setting your imagination racing in the Stygian gloom. It's open daily 9 a.m.-5 p.m.; entrance is US$3, including the boat ride.

You can ride a water buffalo outside the exit; US$1 for the photo-op.

Valle Ancón
Half a kilometer north of Cueva del Indio, a turnoff from the main road leads west through this dramatic, virtually uninhabited valley. It's six km to the village of Ancón along a steep and winding road lined with pine trees. The dirt road brings you to the valley head, in whose cusp lies a coffee and banana plantation. Don't attempt a complete circle or you may, as I did, find yourself bogged down in muddy pools.

Mural de la Prehistória
This much-touted mural is painted onto a long, exposed cliff face of **Mogote Dos Hermanos,** five km west of Viñales. Supposedly, the mural illustrates the process of evolution in the Sierra de los Organos, from mollusk and dinosaur to club-wielding Guanajay Indian, the first human inhabitants of the region. The mural, which measures 200 feet high and 300 feet long, was commissioned by Castro and painted by 25 *campesinos* in 1961 while the artist, Leovigilda González (a disciple of Mexican muralist Diego Rivera), directed from below with a megaphone. The cliff face has recently been repainted in gaudy colors—a red brontosaurus, a yellow tyrannosaurus, and a blood-red *Homo sapiens!* What was formerly a modestly appealing cu-

riosity is now a testament to bad taste splotched on the wall of what is otherwise a splendidly beautiful valley. Entrance costs US$1. The restaurant, however, is well worth the visit.

You can walk to the site via a footpath from Viñales village.

There's a small **Museum of Prehistory** in the Campismo Dos Hermanas (see below) with splendid murals and exhibits.

Accommodations
Cubamar Viajes operates **Campismo Dos Hermanas,** tel.(8) 9-3223; in Havana, Calle 15 #752 esq. Paseo, Vedado, tel. (7) 66-2523, fax (7) 33-3111, e-mail: cubamar@cubamar.mit.cma.net, a nicely renovated camp resort opposite the entrance to Mural de la Prehistória, with 54 basic cabins with private bathrooms (US$5), plus a swimming pool, game room, and restaurant. It's lively, and used primarily by Cubans . . . a good chance to mingle.

Hotel Horizontes Rancho San Vicente, Valle de San Vicente, Viñales, Pinar del Río, tel. (8) 93-6201, e-mail: crh@horizontes.hor.cma.net, www.horizontes.cu, 200 meters north of Cuevas del Indio, has traditionally specialized in therapeutic massage and spa treatments and offers a pleasing option following a sound restoration. There are 34 basic a/c cabanas spread among forested lawns, with modest furnishings, small cable TVs, phones, and private bathrooms with hot water. It's very peaceful, with many birds. The lukewarm, 30° C waters and algae-rich mud, enjoyed in rather mundane spa units, are good for alleviating rheumatism and other ailments (a massage costs US$15). Rates were US$31 s, US$40 d low season, US$33 s, US$42 d high season, including breakfast. The associated hotel was still closed and derelict at last visit.

Las Magnolias, tel. (8) 93-6062, opposite the entrance to Cuevas del Indio, has three a/c rooms for rent (US$35 s/d). Each is clean and adequate, with radio, two single beds, utility furniture, and private bathroom and hot water.

Food

Restaurante Casa de Marisco, outside the entrance to the cave, specializes in freshwater prawns. The touristy, glass-enclosed restaurant is nothing special. A better bet is *El Ranchón,* 200 meters farther north. It's famous for its *ajiaco* (meat and vegetable stew) and charcoal-grilled chicken, and serves mandarins from its citrus grove.

The rustic thatched restaurant at Mural de la Prehistória serves excellent *criollo* food (its specialty is grilled pork) and entertains you with musicians. A curiosity is the *organo pinareño,* an antique hand-driven organ fed, like a Jacquard loom, with a belt of cards punched with the musical score. It serves lunch only.

Services

There's a *correo telefónico* (post office and international telephone center) 100 meters west of Hotel San Vicente.

VIÑALES TO PONS

Continuing westward past the turnoff for the Murale de los Prehistórias, the road leads to Pons. It's a very beautiful drive for the first few miles, with serrated *mogotes* to the north. Farther west, tobacco gives way to coffee bushes as you rise to El Moncada and the saddle separating the Valle de Viñales and Valle de Santo Tomás, a scrub-covered, uncultivated valley. Don't be tempted to speed down the steep hill to Pons; there's a dangerous section at the bottom with huge potholes and a gravel surface.

At El Moncada, a turnoff leads to **Caverna de Santo Tomás,** which has more than 45 km of galleries, making it one of the largest underground systems in the New World.

At Pons, the road to the right leads via the copper mines of **Matahabre** to Santa Lucía, on the north coast. Or you can turn south for the drive through the **Valle de Quemado** and thence the stupendously beautiful Valle de San Carlos (see below).

WESTERN PINAR DEL RÍO

The region southwest of the town of Pinar del Río is predominantly flat. The climate becomes increasingly drier to the west, and the vegetation correspondingly stunted and harsh. Fish-filled lakes lure anglers. But there is nothing of visual appeal and only one beach worth the drive—María la Gorda, in the Bay of Corrientes to the south of the Peninsula de Guanahacabibes, Cuba's slender westernmost point. However, due west of Pinar del Río, the Cordillera de Guaniguanico are among the most dramatic mountains in Cuba and provide stunning scenery that begs for your camera.

PINAR DEL RÍO TO GUANES

Northwest of Pinar del Río, the **Valle Isabel María** rises into the heart of the Cordillera de

Guaniguanico. The road follows the valley of the Río El Cangre and rises to a crest where there's a staggering view down over the plains. Amid the low-pinnacled, pine-covered mountains, you'd swear you were in the northwestern U.S.

Midway to the sleepy community of **Cabezas** you'll pass **Finca La Guabina,** a 1,560-hectare ranch. It is surrounded by low mountains foraged by deer and is popular for horseback riding and nature hikes. Rustic accommodations are available. **Alcona S.A.,** Calle 42 #514 esq. Avenida 7, Playa, Habana, tel. (7) 24-9227, fax (7) 33-1532, offers trips to La Guabina, including an eight-day package combining a visit to the Cayos San Felipe (US$780).

At Cabezas, you can turn north for Pons or southwest for **Valle San Carlos,** hidden off the tourist beaten path yet offering perhaps the most superlative scenery in Western Cuba. The valley runs through the heart of the Cordillera de Guaniguanico, with mogotes soaring to each side, and the valley bottom intensely farmed in tobacco. All the elements of the Valle de Viñales are here, condensed into a long, tight-knit vale, that will have you stopping ever few minutes for yet one more photo. Alas, the road is badly deteriorated in parts. Drive with care.

Traveling via sleepy **Sumidero,** you'll arrive on the southwest plains at the town of **Guane.**

VUELTA ABAJO

About 15 km southwest of the city, you enter rich tobacco country around the communities of San Luís and San Juan y Martínez. The area has none of the dramatic beauty of Viñales, but due to a unique combination of climate and soil, the tobacco grown here is considered the finest in the world, better even than that of the Valle de Viñales.

In November, you can see farmers planting fresh tobacco seeds in well-irrigated and fertilized channels. It is planted in patches at different stages to allow for progressive harvesting when every tobacco plant is at its peak, a key to producing the best cigars. In Vuelta Abajo the traditional *bohio* shed has been replaced in recent years by ungainly wooden cubes on stilts, with tin roofs and chimneys, where humidity and temperature can be more strictly controlled so as to transmute what looks like old compost heaps into the world's finest cigars.

San Juan y Martínez, 23 km west of Pinar del Río, has a pretty main avenue lined with colorful columned streets.

A tobacco farmer, Alejandro Robaina, has been recommended for an intriguing visit. He has a kind of tobacco museum filled with eclectic cigar-related miscellany at his *vega* near San Luís.

CAYOS DE SAN FELIPE

This small group of 10 lonesome cays lies off the underbelly of Pinar del Río, about 15 km offshore and 30 km northwest of Isla de la Juventud. The cays are inhabited only by a few impoverished fishermen and several unique species of fauna, including a native woodpecker and three endemic species of lizards. There are 16 km of virginal white beaches, with pristine coral reefs. However, there are no facilities yet.

You can take a boat from La Coloma, with snorkeling and lunch, with a company called Flora y Fauna in Pinar del Río. Alternately, **Alcona S.A.** (see Pinar Del Río to Guanes, above) offers visits to Cayo de San Felipe by boat (including an option for scuba diving) as part of an eight-day package.

ISABEL RUBIO AND VICINITY

The landscape grows increasingly spartan as you move west from Vuelta Abajo to Isabel Rubio, a small yet relatively prosperous agricultural town that thrives on the harvest of citrus groves shaded from the wind by tall pines.

One km west of Isabel Rubio, beside the main road from Pinar del Río, is **Las Cuevas,** where you can explore a small cave system with stalactites and stalagmites. There's a bar inside, plus (outside the entrance) three little thatched wooden cabanas that cost five pesos for three hours. (Yes, it's a *posada,* a "love hotel" for paramours.)

North of town lies **Guane,** at the base of the Cordillera de Guaniguanico, popular with Cubans for hiking and exploring caves

Playa Bailén and Playa Boca de Galafre
At Sábalo, 12 km east of Isabel Rubio, separate turnoffs lead south to Playa Bailén, a miles-long golden sand beach, and, immediately east, Playa Boca de Galafre.

Villa Turista Bailén, tel. (8) 33401, is a basic *campismo* designed for Cubans but which accepts foreigners. It is still operating, though with very few guests. It has various standards of accommodation, all basic and slightly dilapidated. There's also a three-bedroom villa. The resort has meager facilities. Rates were US$12 s, US$22 d low season, US$15 s, US$27 d high season. There's a similar, though less substantial, facility at Playa Boca, also with tiny bungalows right on the sand, tel. (8) 33410. It, too, takes foreigners, despite its weatherworn decor and meager facilities. There's a crocodile farm to visit nearby.

cigar worker

The train from Pinar del Río to Guane stops at the road, five km from Playa Bailén and also two km from Playa Boca.

**Laguna Pesquero and
Embalse Laguna Grande**
The area southwest of Isabel Rubio is famous for its lagoons frequented by fishermen. The most popular are Pesquero Lagoon, 10 km south of Isabel Rubio, and Laguna Grande, 25 km west, reached via a turnoff leading north from the main highway. Both are stocked with tilapia and largemouth bass. Waterfowl flock here, but no hunting is allowed.

Izlazul offers simple cabins at **Laguna Grande** (no telephone) for US$15 s, US$18 d low season, US$19 s, US$22 d high season. At press time, all the boats were "broken" and no fishing was offered. It's rather drab.

PENINSULA DE GUANAHACABIBES

This willowy peninsula (90 km long and 30 km wide), juts out into the Straits of Yucatán, narrowing down to the tip at Cabo San Antonio. The geologically young peninsula is composed of limestone topped by mile after mile of scrubby woodland. The entire region is uninhabited, save for birds, wild pigs, iguanas, and land crabs that in springtime cross the road en masse, urged along by reproductive hormones.

The region became the final refuge for Cuba's aboriginal population as they were driven west by the more advanced and aggressive Taíno Indians. Several archaeological sites have been uncovered. The few people who live here today eke a meager living from fishing and farming.

There's a military check-point barrier about three km before you reach the shore at the hamlet of **La Bajada,** where's there's another checkpoint beside the huge bay—**Bahía de Corrientes**—lined with mangroves and mile upon mile of white sand beach washed by the coruscating Caribbean Sea. The road to the left swings around the bay and leads 14 km to Cabo de Corrientes and Villa María la Gorda, the area's only hotel; the semipaved road to the right leads along the shore of the bay to Cabo San Antonio, the tip of the peninsula, 54 km away.

The cape hooks around to **Punta Cajón,** where there's a small dock for local fishermen. Foreigners are not allowed beyond the lighthouse, though foreign boaters are welcome (you can stock up on fish and ice). The tarpon fishing is said to be good right off the dock. And scuba divers might take a look at the sunken wreck just north of the cape.

Buses operate from Pinar del Río to La Bajada.

María la Gorda
The deeply indented Bay of Corrientes sweeps east to a cape—**Cabo de Corrientes**—enclosing sparkling waters famed for their cut-glass transparency. Huge whale sharks are common-

ly seen, as are packs of dolphin and tuna. And the coral reefs are exquisite.

Experienced divers rave about the diving, ranging from vertical walls to coral canyons, tunnels, and caves, and even the remains of Spanish galleons, with cannons and other trinkets scattered about the coral-crusted seabed. Black Coral Valley has 100-meter-long coral walls. Many dive sites are just 200 meters from the María la Gorda International Dive Center, at **Playa María la Gorda.** Stay clear of the beach around sundown, when a zillion tiny no-see-ums emerge to feast on unsuspecting humans. There's no reason to visit unless you intend to dive.

The mediocre beach is named, according to legend, for a buxom Venezuelan barmaid, María la Gorda (Fat Mary), who was captured by pirates based in Bahía de Corrientes. María turned to leasing her body to passing sailors. She prospered on the proceeds of her ample flesh, and her venue became known as *Casa de las Tetas de María la Gorda* (House of Fat Mary's Breasts). The *tetas* in question may actually refer to the two protuberances jutting from the cliffs of nearby Punta Caimán.

María la Gorda International Dive Center, tel. (84) 3121, has its own compressor, two dedicated dive boats, and four dive masters. Resort course (initiation) dives cost US$55. Single dives cost US$40, night dives cost US$50, and a four-day certification course costs US$350-375. **Snorkeling** costs US$12.

Private yachters can moor alongside a wharf or in the shallows offshore. Contact **Marinas Puertosol,** tel. (84) 3121; in Havana dial (7) 24-5923 or fax (7) 24-5928. **Sportfishing** trips cost US$120-200 for up to four passengers.

Accommodations: Villa María la Gorda, tel. (82) 7-8131, has 40 a/c rooms with TVs, minibars, and private baths. There are two types of accommodations: older, simple cabins and newer, better, but still modest units. There's a restaurant, small bar, and gift store. The buffet meals are mediocre: breakfast costs US$5, and dinners are a steep US$20. Car rentals can be arranged with 24 hours' notice. Rates were US$29 s, US$34 d low season, US$37 s, US$40 d high season.

Parque Nacional Peninsula de Guanahacabibes

The entire low-lying peninsula (nowhere higher than 25 meters above sea level) is encompassed within the Parque Nacional Peninsula de Guanahacabibes, a 101,500-hectare reserve created by UNESCO in 1987 to protect the semi-deciduous woodland, mangroves, and wildlife that live here. At least 14 of the more than 600 woody species are found only on the peninsula. Endemic birds include the tiny *torcaza* and *zunzuncito* hummingbirds. Giant rodents called *jutías* are abundant, as are wild pigs, deer, iguanas, and various species of lizards.

The reserve is split into the El Veral and Cabo de Corrientes nature reserves.

There's an ecological station—**Centro Ecológico**—at the entrance, just before the military post at La Bajada. Contact Osmani Borrego Fernández, the main director, who is happy to act as a guide and speaks English.

There were no facilities at press time, but a bar and restaurant were to be built at the lighthouse.

Getting There: You must obtain a permit (US$6) from the Centro Ecológico before being granted access to the park. At press time, the first few kilometers of the road had been paved before giving out to rough *piste,* blazing white, underlain by coral, and covered in sand in place. Drive with care. For most of the way, the route is lined with thick scrub and palms. Stunning beaches lie hidden a stone's throw away. After 40 km or so, beyond Punta Hollandés, the road opens onto a cactus-studded coral platform, with fabulous views across the pellucid Caribbean.

Eventually you reach Cabo San Antonio, the westernmost point of Cuba, dominated by a lighthouse (Faro Roncali) and a military post.

ISLA DE LA JUVENTUD AND CAYO LARGO

INTRODUCTION

Slung below the underbelly of Havana Province in the Gulf of Batabanó, Isla de la Juventud is the westernmost and by far the largest and most important island in the Archipiélago de los Cannareos (Archipelago of the Canaries). Isla de la Juventud (Isle of Youth) is a special municipality, not a province. Barely 70,000 people live on the island, half of them in Nueva Gerona, the only town of significance.

It is hardly an island paradise. There are no striking physical features and no lush tropical vegetation (the island was once smothered with native pine and became known at an early stage as the Isle of Pines). The entire southern half comprises brush and marsh that harbor wild boar, deer, jutias, and *Crocodilus rhombifer,* the endemic Cuban crocodile that is aggressive from the moment it emerges from its egg. Turtles also come ashore to deposit the seeds of tomorrow's turtles.

The island appeals for some of the finest diving in the Caribbean, several historical sites of importance, untapped nature reserves, and a fascinating contemporary history as the setting

for the socialist experiment of International Youth Brigades (hence the island's name). The isle is dotted with boarding schools for foreign students from all over the world, though most are now closed, and the citrus groves they once tended are reverting to bush.

There is a fitting association between the island's history and the character of its people, who are called *pineros* and *pineras* and who refer to their island affectionately as *la islita.* (Even the local drink—a mix of grapefruit juice, white rum, and ice—is named a *pinerito*. It is consumed in the late afternoon as a remedy for the heat, but local lore says it's an aphrodisiac—all the more reason for a second one.) Isla de la Juventud has always had a bit of a Wild West feel, a legacy of its halcyon past as a pirate hangout and, in the mid-20th century, a haven for the riffraff, swindlers, and whores who frequented the free port at Neuva Gerona. It still revels in its reputation for going against the grain.

Isla de la Juventud can be explored fully in two days.

Land

Isla de la Juventud is shaped like an inverted comma. At 3,050 square km, it is about the same size as Trinidad or Greater London. Most of the island is flat, with a hilly central core that reaches 310 meters in elevation. Marmoreal hills—the **Sierra de Caballo** and **Sierra de Casa**—flank the city of Nueva Gerona and rise to 280 and 233 meters, respectively.

The north is predominantly flat or rolling lowland, perfect for raising cattle in the east and citrus (especially pink grapefruit) in the west, where the fertile flatlands are irrigated by streams dammed to create reservoirs. The sweet smell of jasmine floats over the island Jan.-March, when the citrus groves are in bloom. Most of the south is composed of limestone smothered in scrubland and the marshy **Lanier Swamp,** which extends the full width of the island and is a habitat for an endangered population of crocodiles, wild pigs, and flocks of ducks and other waterfowl. Beautiful white sand beaches rim the south shore.

Note: The entire southern half of the island is a military zone accessed by a single road. An official guide is compulsory.

History

The island was inhabited in pre-Columbian days by the Ciboney, whose legacy can be seen in cave paintings, most elaborately at Punta del Este, on the south coast. The early Indians knew the island as Sigueanea—the first of a dozen or so names given the island over the years. Columbus named it La Evangelista.

The island claims, unconvincingly, to be the setting for Robert Louis Stevenson's *Treasure Island,* though pirates *did* use the isle as a base from which to plunder Spanish treasure ships and raid mainland cities. The southwestern shore is known as the Pirate Coast—a four-mile strip between Point Francés (after the French pirate François Leclerc) and Point Pedernales. The English pirate Henry Morgan even gave his name to one of the island's small towns. The pirates named it the Isle of Parrots for the many endemic *cotorros.*

Although the Spanish established a fort to protect the passing treasure fleets, it remained a neglected backwater, and the first colony wasn't established until 1826, on the banks of the Río

---

SIGHTSEEING HIGHLIGHTS: ISLA DE LA JUVENTUD AND CAYO LARGO

Criadero de Cocodrilos: Cuba's ferocious endemic crocodile is reared here. Infants, juveniles, and adults offer toothy leers.

Playa Blanca, Cayo Largo: A stunning, miles-long white-sand beach. Iguanas roam the foreshore.

Playa Sirena, Cayo Largo: Perhaps Cuba's most beautiful beach shelving into jade-colored waters.

Presidio Modelo, Isla de la Juventud: Somber prison—now derelict—where Fidel Castro and other revolutionaries were imprisoned in 1953. The hospital and Fidel's solitary cell contain a museum.

Punta Francés, Isla de la Juventud: Superb diving off the island's southwestern tip, with fantastic coral formations, sponges, and wrecks dating back centuries.

Las Casas. The Spanish military billeted its new recruits on the isle to escape the tropical diseases that plagued them on the mainland, and those already ill were sent here to regain their health at the mineral springs in Santa Fé. After the Santa Rita hotel was built, in 1860, tourists from North America began to arrive.

Throughout the century, the Spanish used the island they had renamed Isla de los Pinos (Isle of Pines) as a prison for Cuban patriots, including national hero José Martí, who spent three months in exile here as part of a six-year sentence.

Following the War of Independence, the Treaty of Paris, signed in 1898, left the island in legal limbo. Its status was undefined. Although the Platt Amendment in 1902 recognized Cuba's claim on the island, only in 1925 did the island officially became part of the national territory. In consequence, Yankee real estate speculators bought much of the land and sold it for huge profits to gullible Midwestern farmers who arrived expecting to find an agricultural paradise. The 300 or so immigrants established small communities and planted the first citrus groves, from which they eked out a meager living. (Settlers of English and Scottish descent from the Cayman Islands also arrived in the 19th century and founded a turtle-hunting community called Jacksonville on the south coast. The island's intriguing meld also includes Chinese, Japanese, and African settlers.) Many U.S. citizens stayed; their legacy can still be seen in the cemetery and the ruins of their settlement at Columbia, near the Model Prison, which President Gerardo Machado built in 1931 and in which Fidel Castro and 25 followers were later imprisoned following their abortive attack on the Moncada barracks.

The U.S. Navy established a naval base here during World War II and turned the Model Prison into a prisoner-of-war camp for Axis captives. In the postwar years, wealthy Cubans sold land to another generation of U.S. citizens, who used it this time for vacation homes. By the 1950s, the island had become a favored vacation spot (at its peak, 10 flights a day touched down from Miami), and gambling and prostitution were staples.

On the eve of the Revolution, the island's population totaled around 10,000 people. The Castro government immediately launched a settlement campaign and planted citrus, which today extends over 25,000 hectares, fringed by tall pines and mango trees for windbreaks. (The Revolution, of course, killed the travel trade stone dead.) Thousands of young Cubans went to work as "voluntary laborers" in the citrus groves. In 1971, the first of over 60 schools was established for foreign students—primarily from Africa, Nicaragua, Yemen, and North Korea—who formed what were called International Work Brigades and came to learn the Cuban method of work-study. The Cuban government paid the bill (in exchange, the foreign students joined Cuban students in the citrus plantations for the September-December harvest). Together the young adults helped turn the island into a major producer of citrus. To honor them, in 1978 the Isle of Pines was formally renamed the Isle of Youth. At the height of Cuba's internationalist phase, more than 150,000 foreign students were studying on the island.

The Special Period dealt the international schools a deathblow. The number of foreign students rapidly dwindled, and most of the schools and citrus groves have been abandoned. At press time, the last foreign students were finishing their terms.

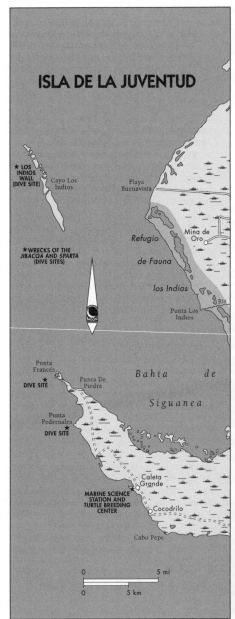

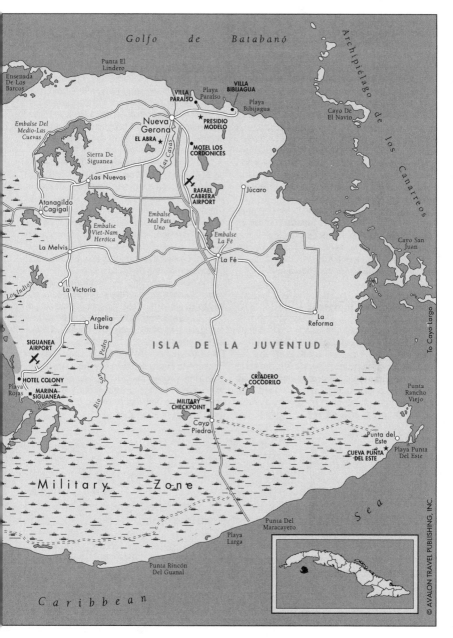

Golfo de Batabanó

Punta El Lindero

Ensenada De Los Barcos

VILLA PARAÍSO

Playa Paraíso

VILLA BIBIJAGUA

Playa Bibijagua

Cayo De El Navío

Embalse Del Medio-Las Cuevas

Nueva Gerona

EL ABRA ★

★ **PRESIDIO MODELO**

● **MOTEL LOS CORDONICES**

Sierra De Siguanea

Las Nuevas

Las Casas

★ **RAFAEL CABRERA AIRPORT**

Júcaro ●

Embalse Mal País Uno

Embalse La Fé

Atanagildo (Cagigal)

Embalse Viet-Nam Heróica

La Melvis

La Fé ●

Cayo San Juan

La Victoria ●

Los Indios

Argelia Libre

Río San Pedro

ISLA DE LA JUVENTUD

La Reforma ●

SIGUANEA AIRPORT

● **HOTEL COLONY**

Playa Rojas

MARINA SIGUANEA ●

★ **CRIADERO COCODRILO**

Punta Rancho Viejo

MILITARY CHECKPOINT

Cayo Piedra ●

Punta del Este ●

CUEVA PUNTA DEL ESTE ★

Playa Punta Del Este

Military Zone

Archipiélago de los Canarreos

To Cayo Largo

Punta Del Maracayero

Playa Larga

Punta Rincón Del Guanal

Caribbean

Sea

© AVALON TRAVEL PUBLISHING, INC.

NUEVA GERONA AND VICINITY

Nueva Gerona (pop. 30,000) lies a few km inland from the north coast along the west bank of the Río Las Casas. It's a port town and exports primarily marble and citrus. Several times daily, Russian-built hydrofoils come roaring up the mouth of the river, riding high on their thin foils like creations from a Flash Gordon movie. The hydrofoils and daily ferry slice past mangrove-covered cays, then rusting factories and a fistful of rickety hydrofoils raised on stilts in dry dock; others berth alongside a beat-up wharf.

The presence of foreign students lent the town a certain vitality. Despite the relative youth of its edifices, downtown Nueva Gerona is distinctly colonial. The historical core along Calle 39 (Calle Martí) was recently restored with fresh pink tile and pastel paints and is very beautiful.

SIGHTS

Nueva Gerona proper has no edifices that draw your attention, although Calle 39 (Calle Martí) is lined with attractive colonial buildings. It is pedestrians-only between Calles 20 and 30. The node is **Parque Guerrillero Heróico** (between Calles 28 and 30), a wide-open plaza facing a pretty, ocher-colored colonial church, **Nuestra Señora de los Dolores,** erected in 1929 in Mexican colonial style. The plaza was torn up at press time, awaiting restoration

El Pinero is the large ferry that carried Fidel and his fellow revolutionaries to freedom following their release from prison on the Isle of Pines. The vessel sits on stilts beside the riverbank, between Calles 26 and 28. It is steadily rotting away in the sun and rain.

Nearby is a life-size statue of **Ubre blanca,** a locally raised dairy cow that broke world milk-production records and has been immortalized in local marble next to the children's playground (Parque Diversiones) on Calles 28 and 37. Also of interest is the **Centro de Desarrollo de las Artes Visuales,** in a pretty colonial house on Calle 39. The tiny *plazuela* 50 meters south features a beautiful ceramic mural and intriguing ceramic seats of a pointillist design.

The rather grandly named **Academía de Ciéncias y Planetarium** is actually a small natural history museum, on Calle 41 about 0.8 km south of town. It has splendid little displays of endemic flora and fauna in re-creations of native habitats. There's even a small re-creation of the Cueva Punta del Este with crude renditions of humankind's evolution from ape to *Homo sapiens.* The adjoining planetarium hosts occasional demonstrations explaining the heavens. Both the museum and planetarium are open Tues.-Sat. 8 a.m.-5 p.m., and Sunday 9 a.m.-1 p.m. Entrance costs US$1.

Presidio Modelo

El Pinero

If you haven't had your fill of revolutionary history, check out the **Museo de los Clandestinos,** Calle 24 esq. Calle 45. It's open Tues.-Sun. 1-9 p.m. and costs US$1.

Sierra del Casa
The Sierra del Casa, immediately southwest of town, harbors its their low hills three caves—**Cueva el Agua, Cueva El Indio,** and **Cueva del Hondón.** They're worth a peek for their stalagmites and stalactites. The caves were used by pre-Columbian Indians and contain a few faded petroglyphs.

By following Calle 32 west, you'll loop around to the marble quarries, where gray *marmól* (marble) is quarried—the island has Cuba's largest reserves of marble and a long tradition of supplying most of the marble to the rest of Cuba. Visit the **marble factory** two km west of town, where huge gray marble blocks brought down from the nearby mountains are cut and polished.

El Abra
This farmstead, nestled in the lee of the Sierra Las Casa one km south of Nueva Gerona, is associated with José Martí, who lived here briefly in 1870 after being sentenced to six years' imprisonment for sedition at the age of 18. After a brief spell in prison on the mainland, Martí was released into the custody of José Sardá (a family friend and respected Catalonian landowner) at El Abra. Martí remained for only three months before departing for exile in Spain.

The museum is reached by a long driveway shaded by Cuban oak trees. At the end is the farmhouse, still a family home, with a large bronze bust of Martí outside. The exhibits are in the simple, thatched building to the right and include personal belongings, documents, and other artifacts of Martí's life. The museum is open Tues.-Sat. 9 a.m.-5 p.m. and Sunday 9 am.-1 p.m. Entrance costs US$1.

ACCOMMODATIONS

Casas Particulares
More than a score of *casas particulares* offer private room rentals.

One of the best is **Casa Particular Rafael Céspedes,** Calle 32 #4701-A e/ 47 y 49, tel. (61) 23167, with two modestly furnished, yet clean and adequate rooms that share a clean, modern bathroom with hot water (a second bathroom was to be added). There's a TV lounge, and an upstairs patio with rockers. The hosts are a delight. And Rafael might act as a guide in his 1949 Dodge.

Casa de la Alegria, Calle 43 #3602 e/ 36 y 38, run by Maribel Gaínza Sánchez, offers two modestly furnished a/c rooms (US$15-20). The first is large, has fans and a small but clean modern bathroom with hot water. The second is cross-ventilated, well lit, and more elegantly furnished, and has a fridge, larger modern bathroom with a bath/shower, and independent entrance. The home has a spacious lounge. Meals are offered.

Casa Particular Viviana Calle 2 #4110 e/ 41 y 43, is a handsome home with three a/c rooms, each with private bathroom with hot water (US$20). I've not seen inside.

Others to consider include **Casa Particular Elda Cespero,** Calle 43 #2004, tel. (61) 2774, a nice-looking home with a front garden; Roberto Figueredo Rodríguez's home at Calle 35 #1809 e/ 18 y 20, Apto. 1, tel. (61) 2-4892; Gerardo Ortega Abreu's home at Calle 20 #3508 e/ 35 y 37, tel. (61) 2-4147; Odalis Penia Fernández, at Calle 10 #3710, tel. (61) 22345; and Joel Díaz Prout's home at Calle 49 #2214 e/ 22 y 24, Apto. 4, with two rooms.

Budget

The slightly run-down **Motel Los Cordonices,** tel. (61) 24981 and 24925, near the airport, five km southeast of Nueva Gerona, is geared to Cubans. Its 43 a/c rooms are simple but acceptable, with double beds and telephones. There's a restaurant and bar, and cabaret by the pool, which was empty at last visit. Rates were US$17 s, US$25 d, US$31 t year-round.

The **Rancho del Tesoro,** near Motel Los Cordonices, was closed for renovation at press time.

Islazul's **Villa Isla de la Juventud,** Autopista Gerona-La Fé Km 1.5, tel. (61) 23256, two km southeast of town, is an attractive little property. The 20 a/c rooms are pleasingly furnished and look out upon a pool to which Cubans flock on weekends. Each room has marble floors, local TV, telephone, refrigerator, and clean, modern bathrooms with hot water. Rates were US$25 s, US$30 d, US$35 t year-round.

FOOD

You'll find a selection of atmospheric eateries along Calle 39. If you rent a *casa particular,* your host will usually feed you, which is generally a much better option than state restaurants.

Restaurante Dragon, on Calle 39 one block north of the church, has a chop suey special (US$6) and other quasi-Chinese dishes. The restaurant has romantic atmosphere with a strong Chinese flavor (the staff are Chinese-Cubans). Continuing south on Calle 39, you reach **Restaurante El Cochinito,** tel. (61)

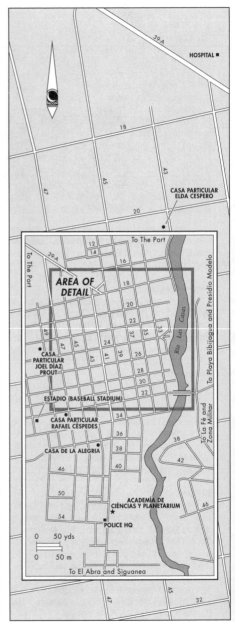

NUEVA GERONA

CUBANA AIRLINES OFFICE

MININT

BANCO DE CRÉDITO Y COMERCIO

POST OFFICE

CASA PARTICULAR ROBERTO FIGUEREDO

CADECA

CASA DEL VINO

PHOTO SERVICE

RESTAURANTE EL CORDERITO

CABARET LOS LUCEROS

HYDROFOIL TERMINAL

CASA DE LAS MIELES

CASA DE CULTURA

NUEVO CAFÉ VIRGINIA

RUMBOS DISCO

CABARET EL PATIO

FERRY TERMINAL

PHARMACY

RESTAURANTE EL COCHINITO

FONDA CUBANA DE BIENES CULTURALES

PARQUE DIVERSIONES

CENTRO DE DESAROLLO DE LAS ARTES VISUALES

EL PINERO FERRY

CALLE

JOSÉ

MARTI

NUESTRA SEÑORA DE LOS DOLORES

CENTRO TELEFÓNICO

CINE CARIBE

TELEPHONE

Parque

Guerrillero

Heróico

PIZZERIA ISOLA

COPPELIA

SHOPPING CENTER

PHOTO SERVICE

HAVANAUTOS

ASA PARTICULAR VIVIANA

Rio Las Casas

0   25 yds
0   25 m

© AVALON TRAVEL PUBLISHING, INC.

22809, which specializes in pork dishes, especially roast suckling pig; it's open 2-10 p.m. The **Restaurante El Corderito,** Calle 39 esq. Calle 22, tel. (61) 22400, includes lamb on its *criollo* menu.

On the eastern fringe of town, on the road to Playa Negrita, is **Parque Ahao,** an atmospheric thatched restaurant that serves *criollo* food and has nightly entertainment.

Basic pizzas cost five pesos per slice at **Pizzeria Isola,** Calle 30 esq. 35. Fried chicken and other fast foods are sold in the courtyard of Centro Comercial, on Calle 33. If you're wilting under the heat, head to **Coppelia,** Calle 32 esq. 37, for delicious ice cream. You can pay in pesos or dollars (inordinately more expensive).

Be sure to call in at the **Casa del Vino,** Calle 20 esq. 41. This rustic wooden home, painted bright blue, is festooned with fishermen's nets and has nautical windows. It sells bottles of locally brewed, flavored wines—Vino de Anis, Vino de Coco, Vino de Rosa—for 50-65 centavos per *trago* (shot), and 6.50-8.25 pesos per bottle. You can sup on a shady veranda. It's popular with locals.

You can buy fresh produce from the **mercado agropecuarias** at Calles 24 and 35, and on Calle 41 at the south end of town. Western packaged food items are available from the dollars-only supermarket on Calle 30, one block southeast of the main square.

ENTERTAINMENT AND EVENTS

The **Citrus Festival** (Festival de la Toronja), traditionally held at Christmas, is now held in mid-March and features a carnival atmosphere, with theatrical skits performed by foreign and Cuban students.

Watch for performances by Mongo Rivas and his relatives, who form **La Tumbita Crilla,** masters of the compelling dance rhythm *sucusuco,* born here early in the 19th century and deeply rooted in the island's culture. The word comes from the onomatopoeic sound of feet moving to its infectious rhythm (North American settlers at the beginning of the 19th century called it "shuck-shuck"). The group sometimes welcomes guests at Nuevo Gerona airport and travels the island. They and other exponents of traditional music perform at the **Casa de Cultura,** Calle 24 esq. 37.

Cabaret El Patio, Calle 24 e/ Martí y 37, offers a *cabaret espectáculo,* with a comedian, singers, and dance routines on a stage made up like a cave. The 11 p.m. show is followed by a disco. Entry costs US$3. Also try the **Cabaret Los Luceros,** on Calle 20, beside the river.

Of bars and discos, the two liveliest are **Rumbos** and **Cabaret El Patio,** facing each other on Calle 24 e/ Martí y 37. **Casa de las Mieles,** on Calle 39 e/ Calles 22 y 24, is a very pretty cocktail bar with a shady terra-cotta terrace; it serves *miel,* aguardente, and rum drinks. It adjoins the equally attractive **Nuevo Café Virginia,** on Martí esq. 24, which has live music plus a disco on Friday and weekends at 9 p.m.; US$1 cover.

Cine Caribe, on the east side of the main square, charges two pesos and shows mostly out-of-date Hollywood movies.

Baseball games are played at the stadium at Calle 32 e/ 49 y 51.

PRACTICALITIES

Shopping

The gallery of **Fonda Cubana de Bienes Culturales,** on Calle 39, sells leather shoes and beautiful ceramics, including the colorful ceramic tiles with relief decorations for which Nueva Gerona's potters are famous. The artisans also create African deities, diminutive parrots, crocodiles, and exquisite grapefruits in ceramic. Exquisite artists chisel precious majagua, acana, or oak into images of pirates hiding their booty. You can watch ceramics being made at the workshop at Calles 34 and 55. Another *artesanía,* at Calle 41 e/ Calles 18 y 20, specializes in woodcarvings and jewelry.

Photo Service has a store at José Martí #2010 selling a meager assortment of batteries and film.

Information and Services

There's a **Banco de Crédito y Comercio** at Calle 39 esq. 18. **Cadeca** has an exchange bureau at the corner of Calle 39 y 20. The main **post office** is on Calle 39 y Calle 18. **DHL** has an office in the Villa Isla de la Juventud. The

Centro Telefónico is on the corner of Calles 41 y 28.

The **Hospital Héroes de Baire** is at Calles 18 y 41. It offers no special service for foreigners. For minor ailments, you can seek treatment at the **policlínicos** at Calles 18 y 47 and Calles 24 y 33. There's a **pharmacy** in the hospital and another on the corner of Calles 39 and 24. The **police station** is one km south of town, on Calle 41.

There's a **Cupet gas station** on the southeast corner of the main square, at Calles 39 y 30.

Crime and Safety

Locals used to warn visitors not to walk the streets at night: *"Muy peligroso!"* (Very unsafe!). The presence of foreign students, many of them comparatively wealthy, drew *jiniteras* from the mainland. It seems that many of the wily women were prone to dispensing *miel* (a sweet honey wine that is a specialty of the island) laced with a knock-out drug. The poor Casanova woke up to find his valuables gone, along, of course, with the woman, who had slipped back to the mainland on the early-morning hydrofoil.

Today the problem (hopefully) no longer exists. Still, the usual precautions are called for.

Getting There

Take your passport. You'll need it to travel to the Isle of Youth.

By Air: Cubana operates two flights daily (US$22 one-way) from Havana using 44-seat Russian-built AN-24s. Additional flights depart on Monday and Friday. Flights take 40 minutes and land at Rafael Cabrera Airport, tel. (61) 2-2690, 15 km south of Neuva Gerona. Arrive early for check-in. Demand always outstrips supply, and if you're late, your seat will be given to someone else. For the same reason, it's best to book a round-trip ticket.

Aerocaribbean also operates charter flights from Havana and Varadero. And **Aerotaxi,** tel. (61) 2184; in Havana, Calle 27 #102 e/ M y N, Vedado, tel. (7) 33-4064, fax (7) 33-4063, operates flights in Russian biplanes from Havana and Pinar del Río ($20 one-way).

On the island, a bus marked *Servicio Aereo* connects flights with downtown Nueva Gerona, stopping at hotels en route (one peso or US$1, depending on your luck). A freelance taxi into town will cost US$4 (a licensed taxi will cost about US$6).

There's a small airstrip at Siguanea that serves the Hotel Colony. A flight departs daily from Nueva Gerona to Siguanea. **Aerogaviota** offers day excursions from Varadero.

By Ferry: A 500-passenger ferry *(barco)* departs Surgidero de Batabanó, on the mainland, 70 km south of Havana, on Thursday, Friday, and Saturday at 6 p.m. and arrives at noon at the ferry terminal on Calle 31 e/ Calles 22 y 24 (US$10 one-way). Your baggage is thoroughly searched before boarding. Horse-drawn taxis wait outside the ferry terminal. For reservations in Havana, telephone (7) 81-3642.

You can catch a connecting bus from Havana from the **Terminal de Omnibus.**

By Hydrofoil: Far quicker is the journey aboard the Russian-built *Kometa* hydrofoil from Surgidero de Batabanó, tel. (62) 8-3845. The sturdy, but time-worn, 106-passenger hydrofoils (called *lanchas cometas* locally and *hidrodeslizadores* officially) depart Batabanó at 10 a.m. and 4 p.m. and arrive at Nuevo Gerona two hours later. The fare was US$11 for foreigners.

Seats are aircraft-type recliners—appropriately, as the journey resembles a turbulent airplane ride. You're served a Spam *bocadito* (sandwich) and a *refresco.*

I strongly recommend buying return *(regreso)* tickets when you purchase your outbound journey *(ida)* tickets. You can buy tickets the same day at the ticket office at the end of the pier in Batabanó, or in advance in Havana, tel. (7) 78-1841. Five seats are reserved for foreigners on the *Kometa,* as are 20 seats on the ferry. However, these are quickly taken up by foreign students commuting to and from the island. If you're foreigner number six, tough luck. Thus you need to ensure you buy your ticket well ahead of time. The ticket office opens at 2:30 p.m. for the *Kometa* and 6 p.m. for the ferry. There's a waiting room and small bar selling *bocaditos.*

By Private Vessel: Private vessels can berth upstream of the hydrofoil terminal, in among the rusting tugboats. Few private boats arrive here (most dock at Siguanea), and arrival and departure proceedings are said to be less fluid than at other ports.

Taking a Vehicle: You can ship your car or motorbike aboard a flatbed barge towed by a tug (you, however, will have to take either the ferry or *Kometa* and meet the barge in Nueva Gerona). It departs daily at 11 a.m. The loading dock is next to the ferry terminal in Batabanó, tel. (62) 8-4455 (ask for Jorge or Pepo). You'll need to register your vehicle at least two hours in advance at the tiny office at the beginning of the pier in Batabanó. Cars cost US$20 each way, motorbikes US$4.40. The barge arrives in Nueva Gerona at 7 a.m. the following day, docking two km north of the ferry terminal. (The return barge departs Nueva Gerona at 11 p.m., arriving in Batabanó next day at noon.)

Getting Around
Nueva Gerona is small enough that you can walk most places comfortably. Bus service in town is limited, although buses operate to most areas of the island. There are no rail services.

The cheapest way of getting around is by **horse-drawn buggy.** Buggies congregate around the main square and by the ferry terminal when boats arrive. Two pesos (or US$2) will take you anywhere you want to go. **Licensed taxis** congregate at the corner of Calles 32 and 39, where a dispatcher controls things, often filling taxis to the brim.

Bicycle rentals are offered at Villa Isla de la Juventud (see Accommodations).

Sergio Morales Sosa, tel. (61) 2-2003, rents horses for US$5 per hour, plus a horse and cab (and driver) for US$1 per person per hour, or a volanta (a traditional horse-drawn hansom) for US$3 per hour for two people.

Havanautos has a rental car agency next to the Cupet station at the corner of Calles 39 y 32, tel. (61) 4432, and another at Villa Isla de la Juventud (see Accommodations, above). It rents sedans and jeeps. Be careful if the staff try to sell you a car with a partial tank of gasoline. This trick is a scam. Absolutely insist on being given a full tank of gas, otherwise you're going to be forced to pay for gas you don't consume. Don't accept the line told to me that the agency has no authority to rent a car with a full tank, nor that you can fill up the tank yourself at the Cupet gas station, both are attempts to get more dollars from you, as you're surely going to return with gas in the tank. No refunds are offered on unused gas.

Getting Away
By Air: Cubana has an office next to the Hotel La Cubanita on Calle 39, tel. (61) 2-4259. It's open Mon.-Thurs. 8 a.m.-noon and 1-4 p.m. and Friday 1-3 p.m. Book your flight as far in advance as possible, as flights fill up.

The bus to the airport departs from outside Cine Caribe (US$1).

By Ferry: The ferry departs Nueva Gerona on Friday, Saturday, and Sunday at 10 a.m. and arrives in Batabanó at 4 p.m. (US$8 one way). The ticket office is inside the ferry terminal, to the right of the entrance. Usually there are two *colas* (although "scrum" might be more correct); the

Russian-built Kometa *hydrofoils in dry dock*

right side is for advance tickets, the left is for same-day tickets.

By Hydrofoil: The *kometa* leaves Nueva Gerona at 7 a.m. and 1 p.m. Buy your ticket the day before. If you have to wait, there's a little snack bar that sells sandwiches of puréed ham (yummy!), plus *refrescos* and sweet mint tea.

Bus/Train Connections to Havana: You can buy advance tickets for the connecting bus or train from Batabanó to Havana (US$3) at the ferry terminal in Nueva Gerona. The booth is inside to the left as you enter the terminal. Reservations can be made up to five days in advance in Batabanó or up to two hours prior to departure in the Havana station.

AROUND THE ISLAND

EAST OF NUEVA GERONA

Presidio Modelo

The island's most interesting attraction—the Model Prison—is five km east of Nueva Gerona. It was built 1926-31 by President Machado and was designed—on the model of the penitentiary at Joliet, Illinois—on a "panopticon" plan that called for circular buildings that put prisoners under constant surveillance. The prison was designed to house 6,000 inmates in four five-story circular buildings, with 93 cells and two beds in each (considerably more prisoners were crammed in). At the center of each rondel was a watchtower, with slits for viewing prisoners. A fifth circular building, in the center, housed the mess hall, dubbed "The Place of 3,000 Silences" because talking was prohibited,. The last prisoner went home in 1967, and only the shells remain.

Prisoners followed a severe regimen, made worse by the wickedness of trusties, prisoners given preferential treatment and who were permitted all kinds of wanton excesses with fellow inmates. Prisoners were woken at 5 a.m.; lights out *(silencio)* was at 9 p.m.

The two oblong buildings that now house the museum were used during World War II to intern Japanese-Cubans and Germans captured in Cuban waters. In 1953 one of the buildings housed Fidel Castro and 25 other revolutionaries sentenced to imprisonment here following the attack on the Moncada barracks. They lived apart from the other prisoners and were privileged. Castro used his time here to good effect. Batista foolishly allowed him to set up a revolutionary school—the Abel Santamaría Academy—where the group studied economics, revolutionary theory, and guerrilla tactics. On 15 May

1955 the revolutionaries were released to much fanfare.

You approach an impressive neocolonial façade with a stairway of local marble that leads up to the old administrative building (now a hobby center and school for UJotaCe, the Young Communists). The rondels and museum are in back and are reached by following the perimeter road to the left. Follow it all the way around to the back.

The first wing of the museum contains black-and-white photos and memorabilia from the Machado era. Another wing was the hospital, where Fidel Castro and his 25 compatriots were imprisoned. Their beds are still in place, with a black-and-white photo of each prisoner on the wall. Fidel's bed is next to last, on the left, facing the door as you enter. The school run by Fidel—the Academía Ideológica Abel Santamaría—is cordoned off; it amounts to three long tables and a blackboard. Immediately to the left of the entrance is the pastel blue room where Fidel—prisoner RN3859—was later kept in solitary confinement. It's surprisingly large (about 400 square feet), with a lofty ceiling, marble seats, and a spacious marble bathroom with shower of gleaming white tiles. Fidel had it good! A glass case contains some of his favorite books.

The museum is open Mon.-Sat. 8 a.m.-4 p.m. and Sunday 8 a.m.-noon. Entrance costs US$3 (plus US$3 for cameras, US$25 for videos).

Playa Bibijagua and Playa Paraíso

Playa Paraíso, five km east of Nueva Gerona, has an attractive white sand beach—overgrown, alas, with sea grass. Another three km brings you to Playa Bibijagua, billed as a black sand beach. It's a narrow sliver of dirty gray sand fringed by a row of palms. The French pirate

Latrobe reportedly buried his treasure here, and a chest was, in fact, uncovered here this century—but it was empty. Buses serve the beaches from Nueva Gerona.

Accommodations

Villa Paraíso, tel. (61) 25246, at Playa Paraíso, is a basic Cuban *campismo.* The manager says it "might be possible" for foreigners to stay here. The small ranchitas are a bit gloomy, and have a/c, mini-fridge, local TV, and clean, simple bathrooms with cold water only. It has a small restaurant. Rates were US$20 s, US$31 d.

Villa Bibijagua is a basic holiday camp with concrete cabins at Playa Bibijagua. Supposedly it accepts tourists, but you may have to cater yourself. You can book through the **Carpeta de Reservaciones Campismo,** tel. (61) 24517, in Nueva Gerona. Rates were US$7 double.

SOUTH OF NUEVA GERONA

Calle 41 (Avenida Abraham Lincoln) exits Nueva Gerona and leads south past El Abra to Siguanea, 30 km away. En route you'll pass many international schools and modest agricultural communities surrounded by scrubland, poorly tended citrus orchards, and numerous man-made lakes stocked with bass. There are no sights on route.

BAY OF SIGUEANEA

This bay is the site of Columbus's landing on 13 June 1494. Later, it was a favored harbor for pirates. There are numerous beaches, but most are hemmed in by mangroves; only **Playa Rojas** is accessible by road. Playa Rojas is the setting for the island's premier resort hotel, the Hotel Colony. Day visitors pay US$1 to enter the Hotel Colony (you'll need your passport).

The shores of the bay are almost entirely uninhabited, except by rare wildlife and not-so-rare mosquitoes, which snooze during the day but are hungry and fierce by evening. Take repellent.

Refugio de Fauna los Indios

Much of the bayshore is a 4,000-hectare reserve protecting an extremely fragile environment that includes mangroves, savanna, and endemic pines and palms. There are at least 60 native floral species, 15 of them limited to this particular spot (14 are endangered, including a species of carnivorous plant). The 153 species of birds include the endemic Cuban sandbill crane *(Grus canadensis nesiotes),* called *la grulla,* and the lovable *cotorro*—the equally threatened Cuban parrot *(Amazona leucocephala),* which you may recognize from pirate movies, sitting on the shoulders of corsairs—which resides here in greater numbers than anywhere else in Cuba. A good time to visit is May and June, when you can see young parrots learning to fly. There are also at least six species of endemic reptiles, plus an endemic bullfrog and tiny frog species. *Jutía* (large guinea-pig-like rodents) are also abundant.

The reserve extends along the shore and inland north of the Hotel Colony and is centered on Punta Los Indios. Rough trails lead into the reserve from Siguanea, but the easiest access is by boat excursion from the hotel (US$25).

Scuba Diving

The bay is a renowned scuba-diving site and the setting for the annual Fotosub underwater photography competition. There are 56 dive sites concentrated along **La Costa de los Piratas** (the Pirate Coast), whose tranquil waters are protected from the Gulf Stream currents. The sites extend along a 10-mile axis just offshore between Punta Pedernales and Punta Francés. Off Punta Francés, the basin's wall begins at depths of 60 to 90 feet and plummets into the deeps of the Gulf of Mexico.

Huge coral parapets loom out over the cobalt abyss below. (Site 39 is renowned for the **Caribbean Cathedral,** said to be the tallest coral column in the world.) The wall is laced with canyons, caves, and grottoes. Two sites of particular interest are **Black Coral Wall,** and **Stingray Paradise,** where you may stroke and feed these friendly fish.

Galleons and Wrecks: A naval battle between Thomas Baskerville's pirate ships and a Spanish fleet resulted in many ships being sunk near Siguanea. And a cluster of partially submerged freighters was scuttled several decades ago to provide bombing and naval gunnery targets for the Cuban armed forces. Northeast of

Punta Francés, between the cape and Cayo Los Indios, are three well-preserved Spanish galleons close together.

International Scuba Diving Center: The Centro Internacional del Buceo is at Marina El Colony, tel. (61) 9-8181, 1.5 km south of the Hotel Colony. Puertosol offers dives for US$30 (US$60 for two; US$45 for a night dive). A full certification course costs US$300. It offers specialized courses for beginners, as well as night diving and underwater video courses for experienced divers. The facility has a large hyperbaric chamber, plus a scuba shop that sells and rents gear. If you arrive in your own vessel and have your own scuba gear, you must hire a dive guide, as the bay lies within the military zone (there's supposedly a submarine base).

Accommodations
The **Hotel Colony,** Carretera de Siguanea, tel. (61) 9-8181, fax (61) 2-6120, is a 1950s-style hotel surrounded by lush vegetation and surrounding an amoeba-shaped pool. It has 77 modestly decorated a/c rooms with, telephones, radios, and TVs, and private baths. Water sports include sea kayaks (US$4 per hour), aquatic bicycles (US$8 per hour), catamarans (US$10 per hour), and water-skiing (US$1.50 per minute). A narrow pier leads out to the Mojito Bar, a restaurant of modest appeal. Since you're a captive market, bar drinks are expensive. You can overcome this by buying a bottle of rum at the shop. Rental cars are available, as are bicycles (US$2.50 per hour) and scooters (US$7 first hour, US$3 each extra hour), but there's nothing for miles and miles. Excursions are offered. Rates were US$43 s, US$62 d, low season, US$46 s, US$70 d high season, including breakfast and dinner.

Yachting and Sportfishing
Marina El Colony, tel. (61) 9-8282, fax (7) 33-5212, has 15 berths with electricity, water, gas, and diesel. Berthing fees are about US$0.40 per foot. If this is your first port of arrival, you'll have a long wait for the officials to travel down from Nueva Gerona.

Deep-sea fishing trips are offered from the marina for US$150. You can also fish for bonefish and tarpon in inner waters from a *lancha* (small boat) for US$17.

Puertosol offers "seafaris" as far afield as Cayo Coco, plus excursions to Pinar del Río.

LA FÉ

A fast Autopista runs south from Nueva Gerona to La Fé, an agricultural town that was founded by U.S. citizens and originally called Santa Fé. Some of their plantation-style houses still stand around the main square. The overpowering presence today, however, is the modern concrete two-story apartment blocks of Soviet inspiration (or lack of it).

The road continues east to **La Reforma,** an agricultural center in the midst of dairy cattle country.

CRIADERO COCODRILO

This crocodile breeding farm has over 500 crocodiles of varying ages. Head honcho Oneldi Flores will happily lead you around, beginning with the pens for juveniles (they are separated by age, as older crocs are cannibalistic). A trail leads to natural lagoons where larger beasts swim freely amid the water hyacinths. You'll hear them plopping into the water as you approach. Others stick their ground and eye you leerily. Fortunately, the lagoons are rimmed with wire fences. Be cautious, however, as it's possible to chance upon stray crocodiles on the pathway, and they'll strike at anything that moves rather than turn tail. The juveniles feast upon the remains of sardines and lobster, while the full-grown monsters are fed hacked-up cattle. Feeding time is usually between 9 and 10 a.m.

The oldest and biggest male is a mean-looking sexagenarian giant who guards his harem jealously. Oneldi will probably prod the big beast with a branch to get him pissed off—have your camera ready to capture the crocodile's lunge.

There are no facilities. Bring your own sodas. It's open daily 8 a.m.-5 p.m. Entrance is US$3. Tip your guide.

The farm is 30 km south of Nueva Gerona, about five km north of Cayo Piedra. Look for a blindingly white alabaster road to the left just beyond Pino Alto. Follow the winding dirt road about five km past scrub and swamp. There are no signs.

THE MILITARY ZONE

The entire Isla de la Juventud south of Cayo Piedra along its east-west parallel is a military zone; there's a checkpoint just south of Cayo Piedra. You can visit, but only with an official guide (US$15 per day) arranged through Havanautos car rental agency or through the tourist bureau at Villa Isla de la Juventud.

The entire region is covered in scrawny bush and marshland long favored by hunters hoping to bag a wild pig or deer. Today the wildlife is protected. Deer are plentiful and often seen on the road.

The south coast is lined with glorious beaches whose sugar-white sands slope down to calm turquoise waters protected by an offshore reef. Alas, there's not even a crude *ranchita* restaurant or snack bar. Take lunch and sodas along.

Cueva Punta del Este

From Cayo Piedra, a dirt road leads east 20 km through the Cienaga de Lanier swamp to Punta del Este. The route isn't marked and there are various bifurcations. There's a beautiful beach here, but the main attraction is the group of caves containing important aboriginal petroglyphs on the roofs and walls. The caves are together considered Cuba's Sistine Chapel of rupestrian art—238 pictographs in perfect condition. The paintings date from about AD 800 and are among the most important aboriginal petroglyphs in the Antilles.

The petroglyphs, which display a high level of "geometric abstraction," seem to form a celestial plan thought to represent the passage of days and nights in the cult calendar. Among them are 28 concentric circles of red and black, pierced by a red arrow of two parallel lines and thought to represent the lunar month. Each day the sun's rays enter through the portal of the most important cave. As the sun follows its astral route, it illuminates different sections of the mural. On 22 March, when spring begins, the sun appears in the very center of the cave entrance, revealing a red phallus penetrating a group of concentric circles on the back wall, an obvious allusion to procreation.

Cayo Piedra to Punta Francés

The road south from Cayo Piedra leads directly to **Playa Larga,** a real stunner of a beach. Five km before the beach is a turnoff to the right that leads west 28 km to Punta Francés, at the tip of the peninsula that forms the claw of Isla de la Juventud. The badly deteriorated road runs inland of the shore the whole way, and there is no view of the beautiful shoreline until you reach the tiny seaside community of **Cocodrilo,** formerly known as Jacksonville, for Atkin Jackson, who founded the hamlet in 1904 and whose descendants still live here and where the English-language tradition remains strong. The isolated villagers eke a living from this austere land as fishermen or as workers in the eco-reserve. Many are descendants of immigrants who arrived from the Cayman Islands over a century ago; a lilting Caribbean English is still spoken.

One km beyond Cocodrilo, there's a **Marine Science Station and Turtle Breeding Center** at Caleta Grande; open 8 a.m.-noon and 1-5 p.m. The breeding center is making an effort to save the turtle populations and has about 6,000 green and hawksbill turtles in a series of pools (although Cuba has regulations against hunting and killing turtles, the laws are rarely honored or enforced; you'll see turtle carapaces and heads for sale all over Cuba).

Mid-way to Cocodrilo, you should stop off en route at the lighthouse *(faro)* at the very southernmost tip near Punta Rincón del Guanal.

Farther east you'll find perfectly lonesome beaches such as **Playa El Francés,** where Spanish galleons and coral formations await scuba divers a short distance from shore. However, you need to give 72 hours' notice to travel beyond Caleta Grande to Punta Francés.

Getting There: It's a full-day drive from Nueva Gerona and back. A taxi from Nueva Gerona will cost US$65 per day. Alternately you can rent a car from Villa Isla de la Juventud or Havanautos for about the same price (see Getting Around in the Neuva Gerona section, above). Excursions are offered at the Hotel Colony.

The journey is not worth the cost involved unless you are absolutely keen to see Cuevas del Este or the turtle farm, or to spend the day on a beach.

A bus leaves from the Cubana office in Nueva Gerona for Cocodrilo at 4 p.m. and returns at 6 a.m.

ARCHIPIÉLAGO DE LOS CANARREOS

To the east of Isla de la Juventud are several dozen tiny, uninhabited, low-lying islands sprinkled like diamonds across a sapphire sea. Most of the islands in this 160-km-long necklace are girt by beaches of purest white and haloed by barrier reefs guaranteeing bathtub-warm waters. For now, tourism development is limited to Cayo Largo, the easternmost island—and the only one accessible from the mainland. Cayo Rico, a tiny speckle just west of Cayo Largo, is slated for imminent development. To date, it has only a rustic restaurant serving lobster and seafood.

The cays are a scuba diver's delight. In addition to astounding coral formations, some 200 shipwrecks have been reported in the Canarreos. The Nueva España treasure fleet, for example, foundered in 1563 on the reefs between Cayo Rosarío and Cayo Largo. One of the best sites is Cabeza Sambo, 70 km west of Cayo Largo. The large shallow is strewn with cannons and nautical miscellany. Very little archaeological surveillance has been undertaken, and it is entirely feasible to find coral-encrusted Spanish doubloons.

WILDLIFE

The cays are rich in wildlife. The chief noises are a reptilian hiss and the caterwauling of birds. From a small population of monkeys on Cayo Cantiles (the only monkeys in Cuba) to the flamingos inhabiting the salty lagoons of Cayo

Pasaje, the Archipiélago de los Canarreos deserves a reputation for some of Cuba's best wildlife viewing.

Over 800 species of fish gambol among the exquisite coral. Where you find fish, you inevitably find birds. The cays shelter tens of thousands of seabirds, including crab-eating sparrow hawks perched in the branches; fishing orioles, cormorants, and pelicans that prey on the schools of *manjúas* and sardines; and egrets, majestic white and black herons, and other stilt-legged waders that patrol the shorelines, their heads tilted forward, long bills jabbing at the sand—pick, pick, pick. There are even mockingbirds and endangered parrots—*cotorros*—that flutter about freely on the larger islands.

Lizards, of course, are numerous, darting back and forth, seemingly inured to the sun. Marine turtles are always in the water, particularly during the nesting seasons, when big males hang off the edge of the reef, waiting for the females to return from laying their eggs in coral sand above the high-water mark. And Cayo Iguana, a nature reserve immediately north of Cayo Largo, is noted for its large population of endemic iguanas, as baked and lifeless as the ground they walk on.

CAYO LARGO

Cayo Largo, 177 km south of Havana and 120 km east of Isla de la Juventud, is a narrow (three-km-wide), 25-km-long, boomerang-shaped

IGUANAS

These dragons from the antediluvian dawn are found on many of the cays in the Archipiélago de los Canarreos, where they lie torpid, stewing in the sun, like prehistoric flotsam washed ashore.

It is thought that the reptiles came involuntarily, swept across the ocean on rafts of vegetation or logs. With their watertight skins and tolerance for heat and drought, the iguanas survived without water and food.

The iguanas are draped in Joseph's coats of black, orange-yellow, and ocher-red. They show little fear of man. The creatures are so seemingly tame and docile that they wait patiently for handouts while the sun beats heavily upon their backs. You can get eye-to-eye with them, but they can snap with toothy jaws if you're foolish enough to irritate them!

---

sliver of land fringed by the prettiest talcum-fine beaches on the planet—an unbroken 20-km stretch of beaches (Blanca, Lindamar, Los Cocos, Tortugas) with sand as blindingly white as Cuban sugar. For that reason, Cayo Largo is one of Cuba's premium resort destinations. If all you want to do is laze in the sun, this is the place to be. You won't learn a thing about Cuban life, however, as everything here is a tourist contrivance and you are totally cut off from the mainland and Cubans, other than service staff. (The only Cubans on the island are workers who live on their own plot on Isla del Sol, north of the airport.) Cayo Largo is favored by Canadians and Europeans, particularly French and, in the words of novelist Pico Iyer, "bronzed Teutons disporting themselves as if in some Aryan holiday camp."

Don't expect quality. The resort is badly managed, offers ho-hum accommodations, and resembles a Englsih working-class holiday camp with warm sea. Major enhancements are in the works, however. At press time, two new deluxe properties were being developed, to be run by Spain's Grupo Sol Meliá and possibly Jamaica's SuperClubs chain. And Leisure Canada had penned an agreement to develop three hotels linked by landscaped gardens, with one complex rising above the lagoon (each unit will have its own private jetty and sailboat), a second complex featuring two-story structures around a village with restaurants and shops, and a third in the far west corner of Cayo Largo with 14 luxury, one-story villas with private gardens and pools.

The English privateer Henry Morgan careened his ship here for repairs three centuries ago. Other pirates used Cayo Largo, and there are several galleons and corsairs on the seabed.

Orientation
A single road links the airport, at the northwest end of Cayo Largo, with the resort (three km away on the island's outer elbow, in an area referred to as Cocodrilo) and the marina and shopping complex immediately north of the airport at Isla del Sol (also called Combinado). The road continues east, unpaved, 14 km as far as Playa Los Cocos.

Beaches
Cayo Largo has 27 km of serene beaches, which run the entire length of the seaward side (the leeward side is composed of mangroves and salty lagoons). The sand's ultra-fine texture and unique crystalline structure prevent it from getting too hot in the midday sun. The beaches merge gently into waters that run from lightest green through turquoise and jade to deep cobalt far out. Topless bathing is tolerated. Playa Blanca has developed a name for nude sunbathing, and most people on the beach are in the buff.

The loveliest beach is 2.3-km-long **Playa Sirena,** on the west side of a narrow peninsula—Punta Sirena—that juts up at the western end of the island. The beach is reached by a 10-minute boat ride from the pier at Isla del Sol. Many people consider it Cuba's finest beach. It slopes steeply below the waterline (wading is not recommended for children). Jet skis can be rented, as can windsurfers and catamarans. Volleyball is popular. There are no hotels, but shady wood-and-thatch structures house a souvenir kiosk, toilets, game room, and the Rincón del Castillo Bar. And Cuban dishes are served at **La Parrillada** restaurant to the accompaniment of a music and dance troupe. A courtesy bus chauffeurs guests to the harbor, from where ferries run to Playa Sirena.

Red warning flags are sometimes posted when the seas get rough.

Playa Lindamar, setting for the Hotel Pelícano, is a scimitar-shaped beach encompassed by coral and extending east about two km, where a rocky point divides it from the longest beach, seven-km-long **Playa Blanca,** running the length of the foreshore where the villas are located. Immediately east—an unbroken extension of Playa Blanca—are **Playa Los Cocos** and then **Playa Tortuga,** where giant sea turtles come ashore to lay their eggs in the warm sands. The only beach on the north shore is **Playa Luna.**

Isla del Sol

This meager village with basic apartment housing for the hotel workers is located just north of the airport and marina, at the tip of Cayo Largo. It features a **Casa de Iso Orishas, El Galeón** jewelry store, ice-cream kiosk, souvenir shop, medical clinic, the **Taberna del Pirata** bar, and the **Granja de las Tortugas,** where you can see marine turtles in pools in a small turtle farm (US$1 entrance; 8 a.m.-noon and 1-6 p.m.).

Accommodations

The tourist complex comprises six hotels, each with its own personality and architectural style, from spartan bungalows to modestly upscale hotel rooms. All are operated on an all-inclusive basis as a single, integrated unit by Cuba's Gran Caribe chain. They share the same telephone and fax numbers for reservations, tel. (5) 79-4215 or 95-2104, fax (7) 33-2108 or (5) 95-2108. The main desk is at the Isla del Sur Hotel. You can book an all-inclusive package or room only (guests are given colored bracelets to indicate their entitlements). Bring your own toiletries. At last visit, rooms did not have shampoos, soap, etc.

Villa Capricho, the easternmost property, boasts thatched saddle-roof bungalows of wood and stone aligned along the shore, almost like a touch of Tahiti. They're rustic and somewhat jerry-built, yet cozy and full of ambience—perfect if you don't seek deluxe appointments. There are doubles and triples, all with shady porches with hammocks. Larger bungalows have lofty bedrooms and kitchenettes. The 60 a/c rooms even have satellite TVs, which seem out of place. The pool complex is the nicest on the island. Rates are US$70 s/d low season, US$100 s/d high season.

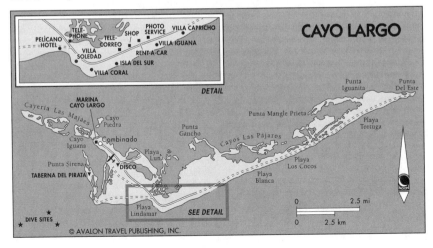

CAYO LARGO

DETAIL

© AVALON TRAVEL PUBLISHING, INC.

Villa Iguana has bungalows and 114 a/c rooms in two-story blocks. All have radios, telephones, satellite TVs, and safety deposit boxes. An attractive, timber-beamed dining hall serves buffet meals. Water sports are available through the Isla del Sur and Pelícano hotels. Rates were US$55 s/d low season, US$90 s/d high season.

Villa Coral has 60 rooms in bungalows amid scrubby lawns atop a coral ledge above the beach. Each cottage has two independent guest rooms on each level. Some rooms receive little light. They have simple decor and, at press time, bathrooms in need of restoration. A radio, telephone, satellite TV, king-size beds, and security box are standard. The rooms center on a half-moon pool with swim-up bar. Rates were US$60 s/d low season, US$95 s/d high season. The facility also includes the single-story bungalows of **Villa Soledad** and **Villa Lindamar,** to the west.

Climbing up the social scale, you may prefer **Isla del Sur,** tel. (5) 4-8111, fax (5) 4-8201, with 59 a/c rooms with satellite TVs and refrigerators in a twin-level hotel block fronting the beach. All rooms have terraces. At its heart is a circular swimming pool. The resort offers a panoply of evening entertainment and has a buffet restaurant, poolside bar, two grills, tourist bureau, and hairdresser. Rates were US$80 s/d low season, US$110 s/d high season.

Pelícano Hotel, tel. (5) 4-8333, is a low-rise hotel functioning as the main center of the island resort complex. It is built in Spanish colonial style and offers a full complement of services. . . but still manages only a two-star rating in my book. It has 324 rooms, including two suites and 110 bungalows, all with a/c and balconies overlooking the sea. Fifty deluxe rooms have satellite TVs and minibars and appealing moderne decor. There are four restaurants, a café, a piano bar, nightclub, small gym, and laundry. Recreation includes complete water sports, basketball, volleyball. Same prices as at Isla del Sur.

Food
Most guests arrive on an all-inclusive basis. If not, eating on Cayo Largo can seriously damage your budget. Even lobster, which is abundant locally, costs US$20 or more in most restaurants. The standard of cuisine is ho-hum.

Take your pick from buffet restaurants in the Villa Lindamar, Pelicano, and Isla del Sur, all serving mediocre fare. **La Pizzaoleta,** in Villa Coral, specializes in Italian dishes and has two sittings at 7 and 9:30 p.m., as does **El Universal,** serving international fare at the Club Pelicano. Despite its rustic appearance, **La Taberna del Pirata,** at the marina, serves seafood dishes, including lobster. The **Restaurant El Criollo** nearby serves the usual Cuban fare.

Entertainment and Events
Each September, Cayo Largo hosts two sport-fishing tournaments: the **International Fishing Tournament for the Blind and Visually Impaired,** at the beginning of the month, followed by the **International Marlin Tournament,** under IGFA rules.

The Hotel Isla del Sur hosts a poolside show nightly at 9:30. A *guateque,* or Cuban country hoe-down, is offered every Saturday at 3 p.m. in the **El Criollo** restaurant. A *Noche Caribeña* is sometimes held on Playa Sirena.

At night, the old airport terminal serves as a disco. A minibus service operates between the hotels and the discotheque, departing at 11:30 p.m. and returning at 1:30 a.m.

Water Sports
You can choose from every imaginable water sport: banana boats, windsurfing, jet-skiing, snorkeling, sea kayaks, and catamarans.

Sportfishing: The offshore waters teem with game fish, including white and blue marlin. Bonefish *(macabí)* and tarpon *(sábalo)* are abundant. Sportfishing excursions can be booked through the tour bureaus and at the marina (US$220 for four hours, US$250 six hours, US$290 eight hours, for two passengers).

Scuba Diving: A barrier reef lies about one km offshore, protecting Cayo Largo from rough seas. The reefs draw rave reviews from scuba divers jaded by the Cayman Islands and Cozumel. There's an absence of currents, and the water never falls below 25° C. Dives are available from the marina for US$35 (single dive) or US$60 (two dives). A 10-dive package costs US$127. Snorkeling costs US$14.

A Canadian company, **Hooked on Diving,** tel. (514) 843-8873, fax (514) 843-9439, offers weeklong dive packages on two live-aboard vessels, the MV *Caribbean King* and MV *Lindamar*. The latter sleeps 14 passengers in five a/c cabins; the former sleeps 14 in four a/c cabins. The boats, which are permanently based at Siguanea, are equipped with onboard compressors, aluminum cylinders, portable life-support oxygen, and an auxilary Zodiak. Weekly departures are offered from Montreal.

Shopping
There's a well-stocked store opposite the Isla del Sur Hotel, where you can buy everything from fashion wear, beachwear, and sandals to electronic items, music and video cassettes, film, duty-free items, and souvenirs. Don't buy black coral, stuffed turtles, or other endangered animal products, which are illegal to sell or purchase under international law.

Information and Services
There are medical posts at the Pelícano Hotel and at Villa Coral, plus a clinic at Isla del Sol. The small International Telecommunications Center, opposite the Isla del Sur Hotel, includes a post office, and a telephone and fax office. And there's an Etecsa phone booth outside the Pelicano. A meagerly-stocked Photo Service opposite the Isla del Sol sells underwater cameras and has a one-hour developing lab.

There are tourist bureaus in the Pelicano, Hotel Isla del Sur, and Villa Coral.

Getting There
Cayo Largo is a free port, and international travelers can arrive without visa or passport if they have no intention of visiting the Cuban mainland. This is true of sailors arriving by private yacht. Regardless, it's always wise to travel with your passport. You'll need it if you wish to visit the mainland. You can obtain a visa to visit the mainland upon arrival in Cayo Largo.

By Air: Charter flights operate directly from Canada, Europe, Mexico, and Grand Cayman. **Fiesta Sun, Magna Holidays,** and **Royal Air** are among the Canadian charter companies offering flights from Toronto. **Lauda Air** flies charters from Milan to Cayo Largo. (See By Air in the Getting There section in the On The Road chapter).

If you're already in Cuba, the only way to get to Cayo Largo is on a package through a Cuban tour agency. Cayo Largo is connected by air with Havana (285 km away), Varadero, Isla de la Juventud, Cienfuegos, and Santiago de Cuba. You can book your own flight and hotel reservations if you wish, but it is far more expensive than a package deal. Cubana serves Cayo Largo from Havana's Terminal Caribbean (and from Varadero). AeroGaviota's flights take off from the Baracoa airstrip, about 15 km west of Havana on the Mariel road. It's a 30-minute flight.

Aero Caribbean, Calle 23 #64, Vedado, tel. (7) 33-4543, fax (7) 33-5016, e-mail: aero-carvpcre@iacc3.get.cma.net, flies from Havana on Monday and Tuesday. **Aerotaxi,** Calle 27 #102 e/ M y N, Vedado, tel. (7) 33-4064, fax (7) 33-4063, also flies to Cayo Largo from Havana and Pinar del Río using Russian biplanes. And Horizontes operates a day excursion from Havana by Russian helicopter on Wednesday and Saturday (US$189), including lunch and snorkeling at Playa Baracoa.

The hotel complex is about five km away by courtesy bus or taxi.

Excursions: Most excursions from Havana begin with a hotel pick-up about 6 a.m. Charter flights usually depart at 8 a.m. On one-day excursions, upon arrival you are whisked to Isla del Sol for a 15-minute boat ride to Playa Sirena for sunning, water sports, and lunch at La Parrillada Restaurant. In midafternoon, excursion trippers take the boat back to Isla del Sol for shopping before their return flight. A typical one-day package costs US$150, including the flight.

Two-day excursions include an overnight at your choice of hotel. There are two price tiers depending on choice of accommodation. *Beware scams!* Many visitors who pay the premium for the Pelicano, for example, are sometimes told when they arrive that the hotel doesn't honor such packages. You may be sent to the Isla del Sur, which may book you into one of the cheaper villas. It happened to me. I was told that the booking agent in Havana would take care of a refund (a typical Cuban ploy), but when I returned to Havana, no documents relating to my trip could be found.

By Sea: Private yachters can berth at **Marina Puertosol Cayo Largo,** tel. (5) 4-8213, fax (5) 4-8212, e-mail: gcom@psolcls.get.cma.net, VHF channel 06. at Isla del Sol. It has 50 berths with 110- and 220-volt electricity, water hookups, and gas and diesel available. The berthing fee is US$0.45 per foot. There's a ship's chandler, laundry, and repair service.

Fifty bungalows were to be built to accommodate skippers.

Getting Around

Shuttle Bus: The **Trompo shuttle bus** runs between the hotels on a 30-minute cycle. A separate bus runs to Playa Sirena at 9 and 10:30 a.m. and 2 p.m. (returning at 11:30 a.m. and 1:30, 3, and 5 p.m.); and to Playa Paraíso at 9, 10:30, and 11:30 a.m. (returning at 1:30, 3:30, and 5 p.m.)

Car, Motorcycle, Bicycle: The best way to get around is by bicycle or scooter, available at the Paradiso and Isla del Sur hotels. One hour of bicycle rental is included in the room rate. Scooters cost US$10 one hour, US$13 two hours, US$24 per day. A bicycle tour to Punta Paraíso is offered. Car and jeep rental are offered through the Pelícano and Isla del Sur hotels, but what's the point? There's only 20 km of road. **Havanautos** charges US$33 for three hours for a dune buggy (US$40 for up to six hours, US$59 per day). **Transtur,** tel. (5) 4-8245, charges US$20 one hour, US$30 two hours, US$40 up to six hours, and US$57 per day for a Suzuki jeep.

Taxis: Transtur has taxi service.

Ferries: Ferries leave for Playa Sirena from the pier at Isla del Sol at 8:30 and 10:30 a.m. and 2:30 p.m. They return at 1:30, 3, and 5 p.m. A courtesy bus transports you to and from hotels.

Excursions: Cruise excursions are offered to **Cayo Iguana** aboard The Maximum motor launch, with snorkeling and lobster lunch on board (US$65), and aboard the Osprey catamaran (US$69). A full-day excursion to **Cayo Cantiles** costs US$79, including snorkeling and optional fishing. A sunset dinner cruise costs US$35.

Aerotaxi offers a panoramic sightseeing tour by Russian biplane, as well as one-day excursions to Trinidad, Zapata, Pinar del Río, Havana, Varadero, neighboring Grand Cayman, and even Cancún, in Mexico.

Yachts: Crewed yachts can be rented at the marina, and bare-boat yachts can be chartered from **Stardust Sun Yacht Charters,** tel. (5) 4-8320, fax (5) 4-8321, VHF16, e-mail: star2c@ip .etecsa.cu; in Havana, tel. (7) 33-1031, fax (7) 33-1032, e-mail: star2hav@ip.etecsa.cu; or, in France, 2 rue d'Athènes, 75009 Paris, tel. (01) 55-07-15-26, fax (01) 55-07-15-22. Weeklong charter rates range from US$1,540 in low season (US$2,660 during the Christmas and New Year's period) for an Oceanis 370 to US$3,500 (US$5,180 in high season) for a Kennex 445.

MATANZAS
INTRODUCTION

Matanzas Province has its fair share of attractions of note, including the namesake city of Matanzas, a once-wealthy sugar- and slave-trading port known as the "Athens of Cuba" for its literary and artistic vitality. Several structures attest to the cultural life of the city during its colonial heyday. The coast road linking the city of Matanzas to Havana follows the sharp slope that forms the northern wall of the **Valle de Yumurí**, a huge basin lushly cultivated with sugarcane. It is enfolded by a crescent of low mountains famed for their mineral springs, most notably at **San Miguel.** East of Matanzas, the broad, scrub-covered plain runs east to Villa Clara province.

The province's lodestone is **Varadero,** Cuba's trendiest beach town today as it was before the Revolution, when it was a playground for rich Habaneros and Yankees come to sun and sin. The resort, occupying the slender Peninsula de Hicacos, 45 km east of Matanzas, is a Cancún in the making and boasts a scintillating 20-km-long beach where almost three-quarters of the island's hotels are located. Immediately southeast of Varadero is the historic city of Cárdenas—a time-worn counterpoint to the resort's glitzy contemporary look and a popular, albeit disappointing, excursion destination for vacationers in Varadero.

Central Matanzas is smothered in a vast plain—the Llanura Roja—and its red soils support sugarcane fields (with yields unparalleled elsewhere on the isle) and citrus orchards. The area was Cuba's economic powerhouse in the 19th century. The city of Matanzas became a center of

---

SIGHTSEEING HIGHLIGHTS: MATANZAS

Criadero de Cocodrilos: Crocodile farm raising American and endemic Cuban crocodiles.

Delphinarium, Varadero: Watch Flipper flip at daily dolphin shows. You can even swim with the dolphins.

Museo de Playa Girón: Small but excellent museum celebrates the victory at the Bay of Pigs.

Parque Nacional de Zapata: Vast swampy region with superb fishing and birding.

Playa Mayor, Varadero: World-famous, miles-long beach lined with hotels. Offers a panoply of water sports, with scuba diving offshore.

the slave trade to satisfy the hunger of the labor-intensive sugar plantations, which generated huge wealth. Its proximity to Havana lent the region great importance and the area was vigorously contested and devastated in the wars of independence (in 1898, a U.S. general reported seeing nothing but "ruin and starvation").

The southern part of Matanzas province is taken up by the low-lying **Zapata Peninsula,** backing a mangrove shore on either side of the Bay of Pigs. This vast and virtually uninhabited marshland system is protected as Cuba's largest nature reserve, harboring fantastic bird life and a large population of Cuban crocodiles. **Laguna del Tesoro** and **Las Salinas** set a world standard for tarpon and bonefish angling.

In April 1961 the Zapata region was launched from obscurity to fame as the setting for the Bay of Pigs invasion, when Washington met its Waterloo. There are pleasant beaches at Playa Larga and Playa Girón, both major landing sites for the CIA-inspired invasion by Cuban exiles. Memories of the fiasco—and Cuba's proud moment (they refer to it not as the "invasion" but rather as *la victoria*) are kept alive at a splendid museum. Girón also offers good scuba diving.

Note for Boaters: Private skippers should note that the entire coastline from the Bay of Pigs (21° 45') to Cienfuegos harbor (21° 50') is strictly off-limits. If you're running east-west between Cayo Largo and Cienfuegos or Trinidad, beware a dangerous 36-square-mile submarine pedestal, the **Jagua Bank,** with a four-km radius from 21° 37'N, 080° 39'W.

Routes through the Province

The wide, fast **Vía Blanca,** or Circuito Norte, runs along the coast between Havana and Matanzas (102 km), and thence to Varadero, 34 km farther east. It's scenic for much of the way. So is a journey on the historic **Hershey Train,** a venerable electric train that passes through the Yumurí Valley.

The south-central plains are crossed by the **Autopista,** which skips all towns and runs through flat agricultural lands from Havana to Santa Clara. The winding **Carretera Central** parallels the Autopista farther north, linking the cities of Matanzas and Santa Clara and passing through dusty old country towns whose luster has faded since the freeway was opened.

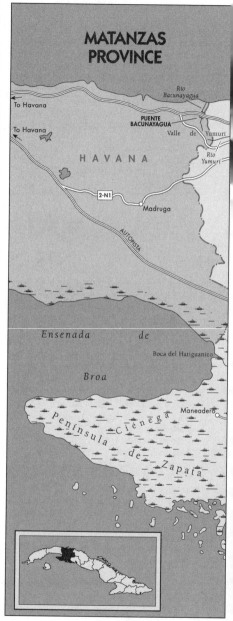

MATANZAS PROVINCE

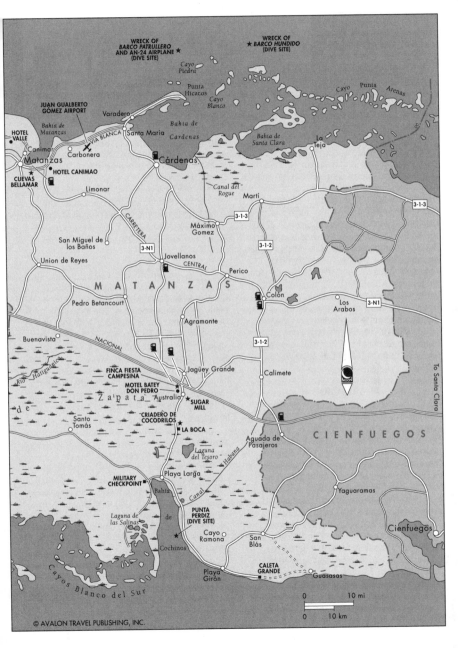

WRECK OF
BARCO PATRULLERO
AND AN-24 AIRPLANE ★
(DIVE SITE)

WRECK OF
★ BARCO HUNDIDO
(DIVE SITE)

Cayo
Piedra

Punta
Hicacos
Cayo
Blanco

Cayo   Punta   Arenas

JUAN GUALBERTO
GÓMEZ AIRPORT

Varadero

Bahía de
Matanzas

Santa María

Bahía de
Cardenas

Bahía de
Santa Clara

La
Teja

HOTEL
VALLE

Canimar

VIA BLANCA

Matanzas   Carbonera

Cárdenas

HOTEL CANIMAO

CUEVAS
BELLAMAR

Limonar

Canal del
Rogue

Martí

3-1-3

CARRETERA

3-1-3

San Miguel de
los Baños

Máximo
Gomez

3-1-2

Union de Reyes

3-N1

Jovellanos   CENTRAL   Perico

M A T A N Z A S

Pedro Betancourt

Colón

3-N1

Los
Arabos

Agramonte

Buenavista

NACIONAL

3-1-2

Río   Hatiguanico

Jagüey Grande

Calimete

MOON

FINCA FIESTA
CAMPESINA

Z a p a t a   Australia

MOTEL BATEY
DON PEDRO

★ SUGAR
MILL

C I E N F U E G O S

d e

Santo
Tomás

CRIADERO DE
COCODRILOS

■ LA BOCA

Laguna
del Tesoro

Habana

Aguada de
Pasajeros

MILITARY
CHECKPOINT

Playa Larga

Bahía

Canal

Yaguaramas

Laguna de
las Salinas

de

PUNTA
PERDIZ
(DIVE SITE)

Cayo
Ramona

San Blás

Cienfuegos

Cochinos

Playa
Girón

CALETA
GRANDE

Guasasas

To Santa Clara

Cayos   Blanco   del Sur

0   10 mi

© AVALON TRAVEL PUBLISHING, INC.

0   10 km

CITY OF MATANZAS AND VICINITY

The city of Matanzas (pop. 98,000) lies within a deep, 11-km-long, five-km-wide bay—the Bahía de Matanzas. The town itself is not particularly attractive and offers little appeal, although the setting is pleasing—Matanzas rises above the Yumurí and San Juan Rivers, which cut through the center of town, in the cusp of gently rising hills. More than 20 Spanish galleons lie at the bottom of Matanzas Bay (Cuba's deepest), sunk by Dutch Admiral Piet Heyn in 1628. Today the wide bay is filled with oil tankers and freighters waiting to be loaded with sugar. Tall chimney stacks rise to the north above the bayfront. They belong to a thermoelectricity plant fueled by hot underground waters, a chemical factory (pouring out insipid, sulfurous fumes), and the country's largest printing works.

Faded mansions and houses have neoclassical hints, with fluted columns inset into the walls and topped by faux pediments. There is hardly enough of note, however, to hold your attraction for more than half a day.

Los Muñiquitos, Cuba's best-known folkloric rumba group, hails from Matanzas, a potent center for santería and Afro-Cuban rhythms.

HISTORY

The city was founded at the end of the 17th century on the site of an Indian village, Yacayo. The Spanish wrought havoc on the Indians and renamed the site San Carlos y San Severino de Matanzas. In 1684 a castle—Castillo de San Severino—was built to guard the bay. A decade later the land between the Rivers Yumurí and San Juan was surveyed and lots distributed among settlers from the Canary Islands.

During the 18th century, Matanzas grew gradually as a port city exporting beef, salted pork, coffee, and, most important, locally grown tobacco. When a royal edict monopolized tobacco production, an exodus left Matanzas almost empty. Fortunately, the rising fortunes of sugar spawned an era of impending prosperity.

During the heyday of sugar in the mid-19th century, the region accounted for more than 50% of national sugar production. Black gold—slaves—came ashore, transported from Africa on ships that returned to Europe laden with the produce of the region.

Many citizens grew immensely wealthy on the sugar and slave trades, and a fashionable café society evolved. Matanzas sponsored the arts and sciences, attracting poets, artists, and the learned. In 1828 the citizens began printing Cuba's first newspaper. A philharmonic society and a library were formed, followed by three theaters, and the city quickly acquired its Athens of Cuba moniker.

Matanzas became a battleground during the wars of independence and was even bombarded by the USS *New York*.

ORIENTATION

Matanzas lies on the western and southern shore of the sausage-shaped bay. The town is divided by the Rivers Yumurí and San Juan into three distinct sections. To the north is **Reparto Versalles**, a late colonial addition climbing the gentle slopes. The predominantly 19th-century **Pueblo Nuevo** extends south of the Río San Juan along flatlands. The historic city center—**Reparto Matanzas**—lies between them and rises gradually to the west. **Reparto Playa** and its eastward extensions front the bay for several miles.

The Vía Blanca from Havana descends into town from the north and skirts the Reparto Playa bayshore en route to Varadero.

The town is laid out in a near-perfect grid. Odd-numbered streets run east-west, even-numbered streets north-south. Many streets have both a name *and* a number; most also have *two* names, one old and one post-Revolution. For example, Calle 79 is also called Calle Contreras, though locals still refer to it as Calle Bonifacio Byrne. Contreras and Calle 83 (Milanés) run west from the main square, Plaza de la Libertad. Calle Santa Teresita (Calle 290) runs perpendicular to the west, and Calle Ayuntamiento (Calle 288) to the east. Calle Medio, one block south of Milanés, is the main shopping street.

The first three digits of a house number refer to the nearest cross street.

SIGHTS

Plaza de la Libertad

The old parade ground (once known as Plaza de las Armas) is a pleasant place to sit under the shade trees and watch the world go by, especially in spring, when the trees are in bloom. At its heart is a granite edifice topped by a bronze statue of José Martí and of the Indian maiden breaking free of her chains. No buildings of architectural note stand out at first sight, but closer scrutiny reveals several historic gems, notably the **Casa de la Cultura** in the former Lyceum Club, and the **biblioteca** (library) in the former Casino Club, both on Bonifacio Byrne. Strolling down Byrne, pause at the private home at number 28203 to admire the ornate iron doors with bold lion door knockers. The former city hall on Calle Ayuntamiento today houses the **Poder Popular.** The **Hotel Louvre** and **La Viña** restaurant are also of historical note.

The most intriguing building by far is the **Pharmaceutical Museum** (Museo Farmacéutico), at the corner of Milanés and Santa Teresa, tel. (52) 3179. The wood-paneled pharmacy is housed in a beautifully restored building dating from 1882. The original pharmacy was opened here in that year by a French pharmacist, Trilet. It functioned as a family-owned pharmacy until 1964, when it metamorphosed into a museum preserving the store just as it was the day it closed—with salves, dried herbs, pharmaceutical instruments, and original porcelain jars neatly arranged on the exquisite carved hardwood shelves. Take a peek out back, where the laboratory contains a brick oven and copper distilleries and utensils. Note the bright red and orange *ventrales.* Originally they were red, white, and blue—the colors of France—but Spanish authorities insisted that they be replaced with Spain's national colors. Open Mon.-Sat. 10 a.m.-6 p.m., Sunday 9 a.m.-1 p.m. Entrance costs US$1.

Plaza de la Vigía

The city's other plaza of note is four blocks east of Plaza de la Libertad, at the junction of Mi-lanés and Calle 270, immediately north of the **Puente Calixto García** bridge over the Río San Juan. This, the original town plaza, has at its heart a marble statue of an unnamed freedom fighter during the wars of independence. It also boasts the **Teatro Sauto** (also known as Teatro El Antillano), considered one of Cuba's preeminent neoclassical buildings. It was built in 1863 in classical European-theater style at the height of the city's prosperity, and in its heyday it attracted the likes of Sarah Bernhardt. It is easy, staring up at the carved wood and delicate frescoes (representing the muses of comedy, dance, music, theater, and tragedy) to believe you hear the swish of crinoline ball gowns on the marble stairs. The auditorium boasts three tiers with circular balconies supported by thin bronze columns. The theater still hosts performances and is open for guided tours Wed.-Sun. 1-3 p.m. (US$1).

South of the theater is the tiny, neoclassical fire station, still functioning but also containing the **Museo de los Bomberos,** worth a visit to marvel at the antique fire engines on display (the oldest, from London, dates from 1864). It's open Mon.-Fri. 10 a.m.-5 p.m., and Saturday 1-5 p.m. Facing the fire station is the **Galería de Arte Provincial** (Mon.-Fri. 10 a.m.-5 p.m. and Saturday 1-5 p.m.; US$1) and, next door, the **Ediciones Vigía,** which produces exquisite handmade books in limited editions and open weekdays 9 a.m.-6 p.m.; US$1.

On the north side is the **Palacio Junco,** a sky-blue early-20th-century mansion housing the city's **Museo Histórico Provincial,** tel. (52) 3195, trace the city's development. Open Tues.-Sun. 10 a.m.-noon and 1-6 p.m. (US$1).

Catedral de San Carlos

The Catedral de San Carlos, built in 1878, is tucked on Milanés (Calle 282) one block east of the main square. A recent restoration was partly funded by a German tourist who developed an affection for the church. Today the opulently frescoed ceiling gleams. The church is usually open weekdays 8 a.m.-noon and 3-5 p.m. and Sunday 9 a.m.-noon. Masses are offered. You may need to rouse the curator, who has an office at the side of the church. She is usually available in the afternoons (except Monday).

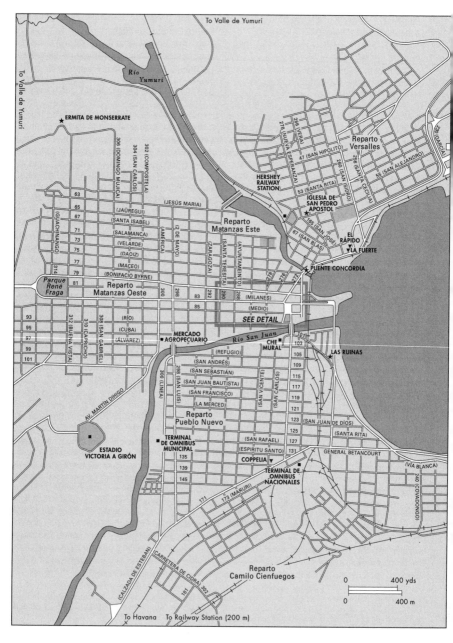

To Valle de Yumurí

Río Yumurí

To Valle de Yumurí

★ ERMITA DE MONSERRATE

306 (DOMINGO MUJICA)
304 (SAN CARLOS)
302 (COMPOSTELA)

(JESÚS MARIA)

63
65
67
71
73
75
77
79
81

(GUACHINANGO)

314

(JAÚREGUI)
(SANTA ISABEL)
(SALAMANCA)
(VELARDE)
(DAOIZ)
(MACEO)
(BONIFACIO BYRNE)

Parque René Fraga

Reparto Matanzas Oeste

AMÉRICA)
(2 DE MAYO)
ZARAGOZA)
(SANTA TERESITA)
(AYUNTAMIENTO)

Reparto Matanzas Este

Reparto Versalles

278 (VERA)
286 (NUEVA ESPERANZA)
47 (SAN HIPÓLITO)
55 (SANTA RITA)
380 (SAN ISIDRO)
256 (SANTA CECILIA)
55 (SAN ALEJANDRO)
290 (GARCÍA)

HERSHEY RAILWAY STATION

53 (SANTA RITA)

IGLESIA DE SAN PEDRO APÓSTOL

85 (SAN JOSÉ)
87 (SAN BLAS)

EL RÁPIDO
▼▲ LA FUERTE

▶ PUENTE CONCORDIA

93
95
97
99
101

312 BUENA VISTA
310 (CAPRICHO)
308 (SAN GABRIEL)

(RÍO)
(CUBA)
(ÁLVAREZ)

83
85

300
298
292
290
288

(MILANÉS)
(MEDIO)

SEE DETAIL

MERCADO AGROPECUARIO

Río San Juan

CHE MURAL

103
105
109
115
117
119
121
123
125
127
131

◀ LAS RUINAS

AV. MARTÍN DIHIGO

ESTADIO VICTORIA A GIRÓN

300 (LÍNEA)
298 (SAN LUIS)

(REFUGIO)
(SAN ANDRÉS)
(SAN SEBASTIÁN)
(SAN JUAN BAUTISTA)
(SAN FRANCISCO)
(LA MERCED)

(SAN VICENTE)
(SAN CARLOS)

(SAN JUAN DE DIOS)
(SANTA RITA)

Reparto Pueblo Nuevo

TERMINAL DE OMNIBUS MUNICIPAL

135
139
145

(SAN RAFAEL)
(ESPÍRITU SANTO)

COPPELIA ▼

GENERAL BETANCOURT

127

TERMINAL DE OMNIBUS NACIONALES

(VÍA BLANCA)

240 (COVADONGA)

171
173 (MARURI)

(CALZADA DE ESTEBAN)
(CARRETERA DE CIDRA)
302

181

Reparto Camilo Cienfuegos

0   400 yds

0   400 m

To Havana   To Railway Station (200 m)

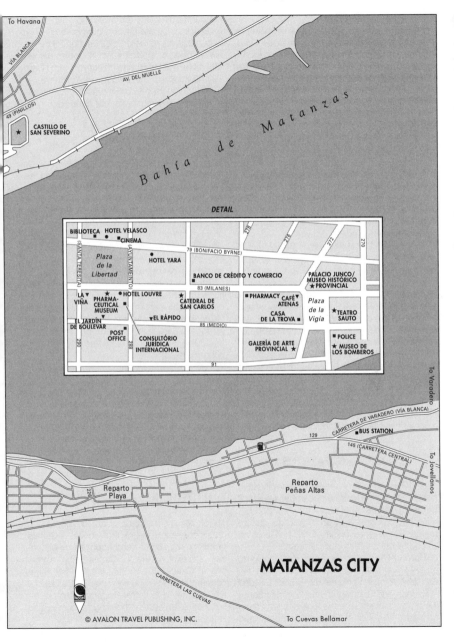

To Havana

VÍA BLANCA

49 (PINILLOS)

CASTILLO DE
SAN SEVERINO

AV. DEL MUELLE

B a h í a   d e   M a t a n z a s

DETAIL

BIBLIOTECA HOTEL VELASCO

CINEMA

(SANTA TERESITA)

Plaza
de la
Libertad

(AYUNTAMIENTO)

HOTEL YARA

79 (BONIFACIO BYRNE)

278

275

272

270

BANCO DE CRÉDITO Y COMERCIO

PALACIO JUNCO/
MUSEO HISTÓRICO
PROVINCIAL

83 (MILANES)

LA
VIÑA

PHARMA-
CEUTICAL
MUSEUM

HOTEL LOUVRE

CATEDRAL DE
SAN CARLOS

PHARMACY CAFÉ
ATENAS

Plaza
de la
Vigía

TEATRO
SAUTO

EL JARDÍN
DE BOULEVAR

EL RÁPIDO

CASA
DE LA TROVA

POST
OFFICE

CONSULTÓRIO
JURÍDICA
INTERNACIONAL

85 (MEDIO)

290

288

91

GALERÍA DE ARTE
PROVINCIAL

POLICE

MUSEO DE
LOS BOMBEROS

To Varadero

CARRETERA DE VARADERO (VÍA BLANCA)

129

BUS STATION

145 (CARRETERA CENTRAL)

To Jovellanos

230

Reparto
Playa

Reparto
Peñas Altas

MATANZAS CITY

MOON

CARRETERA LAS CUEVAS

© AVALON TRAVEL PUBLISHING, INC.

To Cuevas Bellamar

Other Sites of Interest

Note the decorative Babylonian-style columns at each end of **Puente Concordia,** built in 1878 over the Río Yumurí. Calle 272 crosses the bridge, where to the north is the old **Versalles district,** settled last century by French-Haitian refugees. Worth a peek are the **Iglesia de San Pedro Apóstol,** on the hillside at Calles 57 and 270, and, four blocks east, the **Cuartel Goicuría,** an imposing school—formerly an army barracks, which was assaulted on 29 April 1956 by a band of Castro's rebels.

With a restoration the **Castillito de San Severino**—northeast of Versalles, reached via the Centro Politécnico on Calles 57 and 230—could be a worthy attraction. Another tiny fortress, **Las Ruinas,** stands over the Vía Blanca, on the south side of the Río San Juan, and now functions as a bar and discotheque.

The **Tienda Ornotológica,** on Calle Medio e/ 288 y 286, is a curiosity for its rainbow assortment of songbirds, which sell for US$12 upwards.

Calle Contreras rises steadily westward from Plaza de la Libertad to **Parque René Fraga,** which compensates for its lack of beauty with views over the city. It contains a bronze bust of Bonifacio Byrne, National Poet (1861-1936). En route along Calle Contrera, turn right (north) onto Calle 306 (Domingo Mujica) and follow it uphill to **Ermita de Monserrate** (Monserrate Hermitage), a *mirador* offering spectacular views over both Matanzas and the Valle de Yumurí. Sadly, the hermitage itself is but a shell and has no inherent interest. It is fronted by four pedestals holding aloft very weathered statues of the Muses.

ACCOMMODATIONS

Casas Particulares: A reader recommends the home of Moel and Maria Elona at Calle General Betancourt #20615, e/ 206 y 208, tel. (52) 61-446. Another traveler from Colorado recommends a *casa particular* next to the Hotel Louvre whose owner charges US$5 a night.

Hotels: The slightly run-down **Hotel Louvre,** on the south side of Parque de la Libertad, tel. (52) 24-4074, is an antique gem brimful of jaded ambience and Spanish antiques. It could be a jewel with a facelift. Rooms face onto an atrium courtyard with palms. There's a basic bar and restaurant. The lofty rooms, some a bit musty, have rickety a/c and private bathrooms with cold water only. Rates were US$25 s, US$28 d. The **Hotel Yara,** one block east on Contreras, tel. (52) 4418, and the **Hotel Velasco,** at 28803 Calle 79 and Bonifacio Byrne on the main square, tel. (52) 4443, were pesos-only hotels for Cubans only but have taken foreigners in the past.

FOOD

Matanzas is a culinary disaster, pitifully served by eateries. **La Viña,** at Calles 290 and 83, on the southwest corner of the main square, boasts a colonial ambience but suffers from a lack of food. The restaurant next door in the Hotel Louvre is said to be adequate, with *arroz y morro* (rice and beans) for about US$1.50. Likewise, the counter bar of the **Hotel Velasco** is popular with locals for pizzas and snacks, and looks like something out of a 1940s Hitchcock movie.

The nicest place around is **Café Atenas,** opposite the theater on Plaza de la Vigía, with an outdoor patio with shady arbor, and a/c indoor dining. It serves pizzas, sandwiches, and snacks, as does **El Jardín de Boulevar** on Calle Medio, e/ 280 y 290, which also has a patio and bougainvilleas.

Two **El Rápido** fast-food cafés specialize in fried chicken and hamburgers. One is on Calle Medio behind the cathedral, and the other is on Vía Blanca and Calle 262. Adjoining the latter is another fast-food café, **La Fuerte,** open 24 hours and offering *bistec* and sandwiches. For US$2, you can fill up on fried chicken and fries.

Quasi-Chinese cuisine is served at **Pekin,** on Calle 83, tel. (52) 3902.

ENTERTAINMENT AND EVENTS

The place to hear Matanzas' famous Afro-Cuban musicians, such as Los Muñequitos—Cuba's premier rumba band—and AfroCuba de Matanzas, is at either of the two **Casas de la Trovas,** one at Calles 83 and 304, west of the main square, tel. (52) 2891, the other on Calles 272 and 121, tel. (52) 4129. Performances are offered on Saturday afternoons and evenings. **Las Ruinas** has a disco on weekends.

Classical concerts, jazz, and dance are offered nightly in the **Teatro Sal José White,** on the main square (one peso). On Friday and weekends, the sumptuous **Teatro Sauto,** on Plaza de la Vigía, tel. (52) 2721, also hosts classical and folkloric performances, plus comedy. The **provincial museum** also hosts classical concerts on Saturday evenings. And **UNEAC,** the writers' and artists' union, at Calle 83 between Matanzas and Magdalena, tel. (52) 4857, hosts poetry readings, discussions, and music events.

The **Centro Nocturno,** at Calles 83 and 268, tel. (52) 2969, offers **cabaret** featuring comedians, musicians, and a dance troupe. It's followed by a disco. The **Cine Velazco,** on the north side of the main square, shows camp classics and recently released English-language movies.

Matanzas' top-ranked baseball team—the Henequeneros (named for those who work with henequen fiber)—play at the 30,000-seat Estadio Victoria a Girón, west of town on Avenida Martín Dihigo. Cuba's first baseball stadium was supposedly built here, in 1874. Games usually take place Tues.-Thurs. 3:30-8 p.m. and Saturday afternoons (one peso).

SERVICES AND INFORMATION

The main **post office** is on Calle 85 and 290 one block south of the main square, between Santa Teresita and Ayunamiento. It's open Mon.-Sat. 7 a.m.-8 p.m. The **centro telefónico** is on Calle 83 and 288, open daily 6:30 a.m.-10 p.m. There's a **Banco de Crédito y Comercio** on Calle Medio one block east of the main square. If you need legal assistance, try the **Consultorio Jurídica Internacional,** on Calle 288 e/ Calle Milanes y Calle Medio.

The town **library** is on the northwest corner of Parque de la Libertad.

You'll find a **Cupet gas station** on the Vía Blanca, about two km east of town.

GETTING THERE AND AWAY

By Bus
The Víazul tourist bus will drop off in Matanzas en route to Varadero, three times daily (see the Víazul Bus Schedule chart in the On the Road

chapter). For public bus service, see the Public Bus Service From Havana chart, also in the On the Road chapter. Matanzas's chaotic main bus terminal, tel. (52) 7763, is at the junction of Calle 298 and 127. Local buses run from here to downtown and vice versa (take bus no. 16 from Calle 79, one block west of the main square).

Long-distance buses operate from the old rail station, now the Estación Ómnibus Nacional, at Calles 131 and 272. Buses leave from here for Havana and for Varadero (50 centavos) and Cárdenas. You must buy a ticket in advance, then wait for the bus. When the number is called, get ready to join the stampede.

By Train
The rail station is on the south side of town, at Calle 181, tel. (52) 9-2409. Morning trains depart regularly for Havana, and foreigners are given preferred seating (US$3.50 regular; US$4 express). Trains also depart from here for Camagüey (US$16), Cienfuegos (US$8), Santa Clara (US$7), and Sancti Spíritus, plus Bayamo and Manzanillo. The night express to Santiago (13 hours; US$32) stops at provincial capitals en route.

The "Hershey Train" leaves from the railway station three blocks northeast of the Río Yumurí bridge at Calle 67, tel. (52) 7254.

By Taxi
A licensed taxi will cost you about US$80 one-way from Havana. A taxi to Varadero from Matanzas will cost about US$40. An unlicensed driver will take you for about half the fare. *Colectivo* taxis operate; you should be able to find one at the rail and bus terminals.

Excursions and Tours
Tour agencies in Varadero offer day trips to Matanzas for about US$15. In the U.S., **Caribbean Music and Dance** offers study tours to Matanzas focusing on the region's Afro-Cuban music (see the Special Activities section in the On The Road chapter).

VALLE DE YUMURÍ

Humboldt called it "the loveliest valley in the world." The Cubans call it "the Valley of Delight."

The eight-km-wide Yumurí Valley is held in the cusp of 150-meter-high limestone cliffs—the Cuchilla de Habana-Matanzas—to the west of Matanzas. The hills form a natural amphitheater hidden from the modern world. Two rivers, the Yumurí and Bacunayagua, thread their silvered way to the sea through a landscape as archetypally Cuban as any you will find on the island.

Millions of years ago the valley was underwater, as demonstrated by marine shells and fossils embedded in the valley walls. The cliffs are pocked with caverns, many of them, like **Indian's Cave,** brimful of stalagmites and stalactites, high up on the southern cliff.

Accommodations

Hidden away in the valley bottom is the **Horizontes Casa del Valle Motel,** Km 2, Carretera de Chirno, Valle del Yumurí, Matanzas, tel. (52) 25-3300, a Spanish colonial-style villa dating from 1936 and surrounded by a newer, rather soulless block of rooms facing a swimming pool. The hotel is built atop a sulfurous mineral spring and specializes in treatments for stress, asthma, obesity, and high blood pressure. It has 42 modestly furnished but spacious and well-lit a/c rooms with private baths (some share), radios, TVs, telephones, and refrigerators. Two large bedrooms in the old villa have lofty beamed ceilings in Spanish colonial style. One bedroom has 18th-century fabrics and antique chairs; the other has a king-size bed and a huge bathroom. The restaurant is elegant and features quality artwork. The menu offers the usual Cuban fare: grilled chicken, *bistec,* pork, etc. Other facilities include a two-lane bowling alley and pool table, a poolside bar popular with Cubans, a sauna, and a small gym. Horseback riding and excursions are offered (including to a *campesino* home), and mopeds can be rented. Rates were US$29 s, US$38 d low season, US$38 s, US$46 d high season (US$10 more for rooms in the house).

Getting There

The Yumurí Valley is included in a one-week "Rainbow in the Horizon" tour offered by **Viajes Horizontes,** tel. (7) 33-4042, fax (7) 33-4361, e-mail: crh@s1.hor.cma.net, website: www.horizont.cu, The Hershey Train passes through the valley. (For the Hotel Valle de Yumurí, get off at Mena; it's a two-km walk from here.)

THE VÍA BLANCA

The Vía Blanca, also called the Matanzas-Varadero Expressway, hugs the coast, winds past spiky sisal plantations, and cuts inland through scrub-covered hills, with the turquoise sea teasingly appearing between the casuarina trees. Oil derricks by the water's edge nod lethargically, desperately sucking forth black gold atop coral platforms that separate intermittent beaches.

A tollbooth at Km 28 (28 km east of Matanzas) charges US$2 per vehicle.

Four km east of Matanzas, immediately beyond the bridge over the Río Canimar, a road to the left loops downhill into **Canimar Abajo,** where there's a tiny beach with fishing boats and a pleasant little restaurant. A small fort—**Castillo del Morrillo**—with cannons guards the rivermouth. The castle is now a museum dedicated to revolutionary leader Antonio Guiteras Holmes, who was gunned down in 1935 beneath the mahogany tree near the bridge. The valley is hemmed in by near-vertical limestone cliffs. Small, basic cabins are available for rent (they can be reserved through the *carpeta* of Campismo Popular in Matanzas). Cubamar, tel. (52) 615 or, in Havana, tel. (7) 66-2523, offers a 45-minute boat trip from the **Canimar Abajo Aquatic Center.** The journey takes you upriver to Cueva La Eloísa, a flooded cave where you may swim in the pellucid waters.

Continuing east, you'll pass **Playa El Mamey.** The little beach is a popular spot with Cubans from Matanzas. There are shade trees and a basic restaurant plus kiddies' swings. Camping is permitted, but there are no cabins.

There's a huge cave—**Cueva de Saturno**—whose lagoon and dramatic stalagmites and stalactites wait to be explored midway between Matanzas and Varadero, one km along the road to Varadero airport. It's popular with scuba divers. It's open daily 9 a.m.-5 p.m. Entrance costs US$3, plus US$5 for snorkeling. Excursions are offered from Varadero. The Casa del Valle Motel also offers an excursion, including lunch at a *campesino's* home (US$12).

Cuevas Bellamar

These little-visited caves form one of Cuba's largest cave systems, full of gurgling streams and shimmering flower-like crystal formations (many shaped like crystal goblets without stems) known as dahlias. There are more than 3,000 meters of galleries full of stalactites and stalagmites, including the 80-meter-long, 26-meter-high Gothic Temple. "It seemed the coolest, most magical place on the island," thought Lourdes, a character in Cristina García's novel *Dreaming in Cuban.*

The air is thin and temperate. Open Tues.-Sun. 9 a.m.-5 p.m. Entrance costs US$3 (plus US$2 for cameras, US$4 for video); English-speaking guides are provided. There's a basic restaurant serving mediocre food.

The caves are at Finca La Alcancía, in the hills above Matanzas, about five km southeast of town, reached by turning south from the Vía Blanca onto Calle 226, east of the town center. Bus no. 16 departs Calle 79 and will drop you about 1.5 km below the caves.

Accommodations

Hotel Canimao, tel. (52) 6-1014, west of the bridge over the Río Canimao, is one of Islazul's premier properties. It's an attractive 120-room hotel surrounding a pool amid landscaped grounds. Rooms are modestly furnished, but a reader reports "no water" and had to scoop water from the swimming pool to flush the toilet; apparently this is a regular problem. There's late-night cabaret (except Monday), and excursions are offered. Bus no. 16 stops at the Río Canimar bridge (it departs from Calle 300 and 83 in Matanzas). Rates were US$22 s, US$32 d low season, US$30 s, US$38 d high season.

A more basic option is **Campismo Faro de Maya,** a Cuban holiday camp beside the light-house on the eastern side of the Bahía de Matanzas. It has wooden cabins with private bath (cold water) for US$10.

VARADERO AND VICINITY

Varadero, 34 km east of Matanzas and 140 km east of Havana, is Cuba's tourist Mecca, the artificial Cuba of charter jet packages. A few years ago it developed a bit of a reputation for easy sex, in 1997 the Cuban girls were rounded up and herded out of town, taking much of Varadero's vitality with them. The Italian men went home, leaving the resort to mostly budget-minded Canadian and European charter groups. Topless blondes recline on equally blonde beaches reading novels in German. Varadero also offers snorkeling and scuba diving, although these are somewhat overrated. Water sports abound. And there are heaps of excursions for those who want to explore farther afield. If all you want is sun, sand, sea, and a meager nightlife, then Varadero could be for you.

The resort spans a Cuban village (pop. 15,000) that is fast losing any semblance of Cuban character. The Cuban government is hell-bent on developing Varadero as Cuba's Cancún. There are already more than 50 hotels, and the gaps are being filled in. According to the Cuban tourism development master-plan, Varadero alone has a potential capacity for 23,000 hotel rooms—almost as many as exist on the entire island of Jamaica.

Strictly speaking, Varadero is the name of the *beach* area. It lies on the north, ocean-facing side of a 18.6-km-long peninsula called Punta Hicacos (actually a slender island), which encloses Cárdenas Bay and is separated from the mainland by a hairline inlet, the Laguna de Paso Malo. The peninsula is only 1.2 km at its widest point. It slopes to the northeast, where its tip—Hicacos Point—is the northernmost point of Cuba. The scrub-covered eastern half is broken by a series of flat-topped mesas and low lying raised coral platforms pitted with sinkholes and caves full of marine fossils—evidence of uplifting over geological time.

At times, mosquitoes are a nuisance. And at night, when the breeze blows offshore, occasional fumes from the petrochemical works and oil rigs across Bahía de Calderas drift to town, bringing a stink of rotten eggs.

Beaches

"In all the beaches in Cuba the sand was made of grated silver," says a character in Robert Fernández's *Raining Backwards,* "though in Varadero it was also mixed with diamond dust." The main beach is a virtually unbroken 11.5-km-long swath that widens and improves east-ward (where facilities are more upscale), then

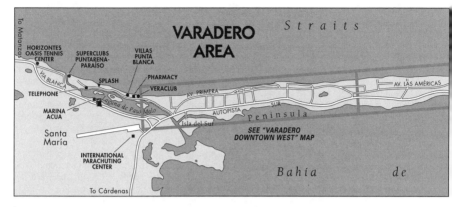

breaks up into smaller beaches divided by rocky headlands, where most of the deluxe hotels sit over their own "private" beaches. Topless bathing is common among European women. (As much as Cuban women love to flaunt their figures—skimpy *tangas* are the norm—I have yet to see a *Cubana* topless on the beach.)

Backed by sea grape, oleander, hibiscus, royal poincianas, and palms, the beaches shelve gently into waters the color of a Maxfield Parrish painting. A coral reef lies offshore. Red flags are often posted when seas are rough (there's often a dangerous undertow) or infested by schools of jellyfish. Occasionally, a four-wheel Honda ATV putters along selling soda pops and ice cream, and other hawkers sell papayas, coconuts, and other snacks. A few street vendors

of jewelry, carvings, and crafts have their wares laid out on towels on the beach. These include tortoiseshell and coral pieces, to be avoided.

HISTORY

For around 3,000 years before Christopher Columbus sailed by in 1492, Taíno Indians had lived on the Punta de Hicacos, which they named for the *hicacos* trees that grow here. The Spanish settled it as early as 1587, when Don Pedro Camacho developed charcoal and salt-pork enterprises on salt flats and began supplying Spanish fleets. A small community of fisher folk later sprouted on the south shore, in the village today known as Las Morals.

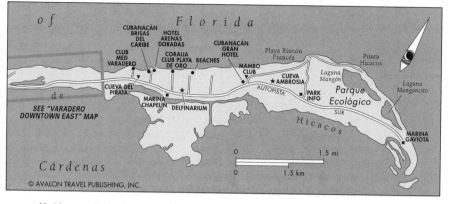

Nothing much else happened here until the 1870s, when families from Cárdenas built wooden summer homes and developed the beach for local tourism, with boardinghouses for summer vacationers. In 1883 the families formed a "council," purchased 26 hectares of local land, and four years later presented the town council of Cárdenas with a plan that divided the land into 40 blocks and included plans for the first outdoor baths and other facilities. Rowing regattas developed (the prize was the Cuban Cup), necessitating more lodging, and the first hotel—the Varadero Hotel—opened in 1915.

In 1926, U.S. industrialist Irenée Du Pont bought most of the peninsula beyond the town and built himself a large estate, complete with golf course. Other wealthy Norteamericanos followed, albeit in less grandiose style (Du Pont, of course, who had paid four centavos a square meter, sold them the land—for 120 pesos a square meter). Soon, Varadero was a budding Miami in miniature, with exclusive neighborhoods patrolled by private police. Al Capone bought a house here. So did the dictator Fulgencio Batista.

In the 1950s, U.S. hotels began to spring up, prompted by the building of the Hotel Internacional, which had a casino and was a favored hangout of Hollywood stars, high-class hookers, and mobsters. On the eve of the Revolution, virtually the entire peninsula was in private hands. (The Castro government likes to claim that Cubans were banned from the beach, but in reality this was only on privately owned sectors,

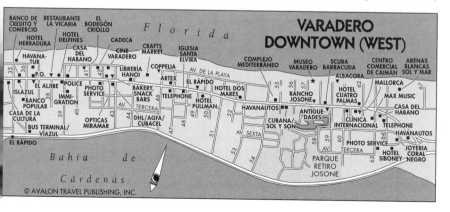

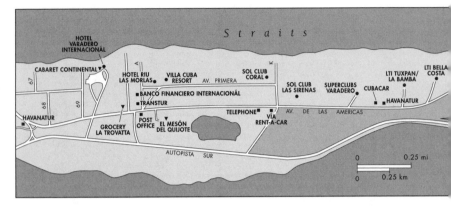

and villagers had access to the long swath in front of the village. Ironically, today only Cubans who live in the village are permitted access to Varadero, so things have come full circle.) Two years later, President Kennedy's "quarantine" put an end to the hotel trade. Varadero, however, remained Cuba's prime tourist asset: Russians quickly arrived to cavort, sun themselves, sip rum, and smoke Cuban cigars just 90 miles from Florida.

ORIENTATION

There is only one way onto the island-peninsula: the bridge over Laguna de Paso Malo, at the extreme west end of the Hicacos Peninsula (in the past foreigners have had to pay a US$2 toll at the police checkpoint, but this was not in effect at press time).

Two roads run east along the peninsula from there. The fast Autopista Sur runs along the bayfront all the way to the end. Avenida Primera (1ra)—the main street—runs along the ocean-front from Calle 8 in the west to Calle L and the Hotel Internacional in the east (west of Calle 8, Avenida 1ra becomes Avenida Kawama, which runs through the Kawama district to the west-ernmost tip of the island).

Cross streets begin at Calle 1, in the Kawama suburb, and run eastward consecutively to Calle 69, in the La Torre area. Farther east, they are lettered, from Calle A to L. The luxury hotel zone begins east of Calle 69, where Avenida 1ra becomes Avenida las Américas. The old village of

funky wooden houses occupies the central section of town, roughly between Calles 23 and 54.

The eastern tip of the peninsula—Punta Molas—harbors a military base that is strictly off-limits. Nearby is the former 26th of July International Pioneers Camp (now a hotel), where children from all over the world used to come to promote future friendship among the peoples.

SIGHTS

A castellated water tower next to the Mesón del Quijote restaurant, atop a rise on Avenida las Américas, looks like an old fortress tower but was, in fact, built in the 1930s. A quaint touch is added by a modernist sculpture of Don Quijote on his trusty steed, lance in hand, galloping across the hillcrest.

There's a small **Museo Varadero** in a turn-of-the-century house on Calle 57, 50 meters north of Avenida 1ra. Separate sections are dedicated to the local flora and fauna, aboriginal culture, Irenée Du Pont, and Fidel and his heroic achievements. Upstairs is the Salón de Deportes, dedicated to sports in Cuba. Open daily 9 a.m.-6 p.m. Entrance costs US$1.

The pocket-size cigar factory—**Casa Tabaqueros**—at Avenida 1ra and Calle 27 is worth a visit to see two rollers rolling for your pleasure. It's open daily 8 a.m.-8 p.m.

Las Américas

The most interesting attraction is Las Américas, munitions magnate Irenée Du Pont's colonial

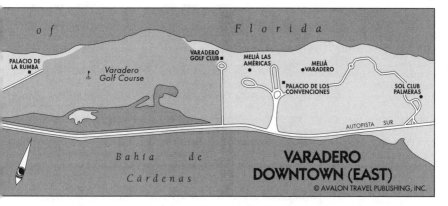

of   Florida

PALACIO DE LA RUMBA   Varadero Golf Course   VARADERO GOLF CLUB   MELIÁ LAS AMÉRICAS   MELIÁ VARADERO   SOL CLUB PALMERAS

PALACIO DE LOS CONVENCIONES

AUTOPISTA   SUR

Bahía   de

Cárdenas

VARADERO DOWNTOWN (EAST)

© AVALON TRAVEL PUBLISHING, INC.

Spanish-style mansion at the far eastern end of Avenida las Américas. The green-tile-roofed mansion, which Du Pont named Xanadu, was built in 1926 as a sumptuous winter hideaway (complete with nine-hole golf course) atop the rise on the small headland at the end of the main beach. The Du Pont family lived here until 1959. It has long been a tradition for Cuban girls to have their photographs taken here dressed in ball gowns of a bygone era on their 15th birthdays.

Du Pont fitted his house with a Carrara marble floor, great dark wooden eaves and precious timbers, original hardwood antiques, and an organ that could be operated hydraulically or electronically from a separate room. Du Pont built a massive wine cellar and wine bar beneath the house. Light pours into the library (where the vast array of volumes went unread). Another room resembles the interior of a captain's cabin, with porthole. On the top floor is a spectacular bar (once a ballroom) decorated in Italian rococo. The six marble-floored bedrooms can be rented (see Accommodation, below).

A faded tapestry in the dining room poignantly transcribes the lines of Samuel Coleridge's poem:

In Xanadu did Kubla Khan
A stately pleasure dome decree

Parque Retiro Josone

Varadero's well-kept municipal park, between Calles 54 and 59, is centered on an old mansion furnished with colonial-era antiques. Respected businessman José Fermin Iturrioz and

his wife Onelia lived here in the 1950s. After departing Cuba following the Revolution, Sr. Fermin had to give his property up to the Castro regime in exchange for safe passage from the country for the rest of his extended family. It was then used as a protocol house for foreign dignitaries such as Leonid Brezhnev and later rented out to wealthy visitors.

The landscaped park includes a lake with a few flamingos and geese, plus rowboats for rent. There are a swimming pool, two-lane bowling alley, several outdoor bars, three restaurants, and a guarapería. You can rent rowboats for US$0.50 per person hourly. Entrance costs US$1.

Parque Ecológico Varadero

This 450-hectare patch of scrub and woodland at the eastern tip of the peninsula is riddled with limestone caves, many of which contain important aboriginal pictographs. The most important of these is **Cueva Ambrosia,** in a cliff called Loma La Caseta, on the inner (south) side of the peninsula. The caves contain some 50 or so aboriginal drawings, many excellently preserved.

Offshore Cays

Cayos Blanco is a series of small beach-rimmed cays that lie about five miles due east of the peninsula and are a popular destination for boat excursions. Facilities for day-trippers include a panoply of water sports, plus thatched bars. Beach grills and entertainment is provided.

About eight miles northeast of Varadero is **Cayo Piedras del Norte Marine Park,** the only

fun on Varadero Beach

submarine park in Cuba and a popular scuba diving site, with several wrecks, including a plane, a 102-meter frigate complete with armor, and even a missile launcher (!) with four launch pads and artillery pieces, in addition to coral reefs. It is being developed by Gaviota, the military-tourism entity which donated the military hardware. A scuba center is on site, and excursions are offered from Varadero's marinas.

ACCOMMODATIONS

There are scores of accommodations to choose from (Varadero hotels collectively provide more than 15,000 rooms), with something for every budget. Many are conversions of dreary cement-block hotels that once catered to Cuban holiday-makers and workers making the most of rewards for high productivity. The older hotels are clustered at the west end of the peninsula. Accommodations tend, in general, to be more upscale as you move east, with the luxury resorts clustered east of Las Américas mansion and along Playa Los Taínos.

Most hotels have a swimming pool and their own restaurants and entertainment. Many offer water sports, including jet skis, waterskiing, and windsurfers. Upscale properties have tourist bureaus, boutiques, and car and bicycle rental facilities, plus poolside activities including evening "animations"—the Cuban phrase for audience-participation entertainment. Most hotels have a/c and TVs in rooms. Some people who book

packages are given apartment units with shared bathrooms and TV rooms; if you want a private bathroom, stress this at the time of booking.

Prices have skyrocketed in recent years and Varadero is no longer a bargain. Many properties are grossly overpriced. Hotels below are categorized according to high season rates for twin occupancy. Most deluxe hotels are managed by foreign hotel groups (but owned by Cuban entities) run on an all-inclusive basis, signifying that meals, alcoholic beverages, entertainment and, usually, water sports are included in the quoted room rate.

Casas Particulares
In the mid-1990s, dozens of locals took advantage of the tourism boom to rent rooms. Alas, in 1998 the government banned *casas particulares* in Varadero—it wants you to spend at the overpriced resorts. Still, you may be able to find illegal rooms for US$10-30.

If *casas particulares* are legalized again, I recommend an apartment on Calle 27 #207 run by "Tito" Hernández García, tel. (5) 6-3727. It's small but modern and has reliable plumbing and a kitchenette (US$30). A reader recommends the home of Lillet Castellanos at Calle 21 #303, e/ 3ra y 4ta, tel. (5) 61-2355. And Dr. Juan Barquet Farch is said to offer a legal room rental outside Varadero at Calle 13 #7 e/ 1ra y Mar, tel. (5) 29-1070, in Reparto Villa Solavento.

Inexpensive (US$35-60)
If you want an intimate place, try Horizontes' **Hotel Pullman,** on Avenida 1ra y Calle 49, tel.

(5) 66-7161. This down-to-earth hotel is in a colonial-style mansion. The 15 a/c rooms are clean, with satellite TVs, telephones, security box, colonial furniture, and recently renovated bathrooms. It has a small, airy restaurant and a patio bar. Rates were US$32 s, US$43 d low season, US$40 s, US$52 d high season. A better bet nearby is Horizontes' **Hotel Dos Mares,** Avenida 1ra and Calle 53, tel. (5) 61-2702, fax (5) 66-7499, a training hotel in an atmospheric old colonial-style house with bed-and-breakfast charm. It has 34 large, modestly furnished a/c rooms with cable TV and 24-hour room service. Its appealing restaurant offers a lobster enchilada for US$10, and there's a handsome bar. Rates were US$37 s, US$47 d low season, US$43 s, US$56 d high season, including breakfast.

Islazul runs **Villa La Mar,** Calle 3ra e/ 28 y 29, tel. (5) 61-3910, fax (5) 61-2508, with 260 simply furnished a/c rooms with private baths, satellite TV, video, and telephone, plus restaurant, grill, pool with thatched umbrellas, disco, and parking. Rates were about US$35 s, US$40 d low season, US$45 s, US$55 d high season.

The **Hotel Horizontes Club Internacional,** Avenida 1ra e/ Calles 21 y 22, tel. (5) 61-3915, fax (5) 61-4676, is an unempired property with 223 rooms. Rates were US$40 s, U$50 d year-round, including breakfast; US$55 s, US$100 d low season, US$67 s, U$110 d high season, all-inclusive.

Moderate (US$60-85)

Gran Caribe's self-contained **Villas Punta Blanca,** tel. (5) 66-7090, fax (5) 66-7004, e-mail: hotel@pblanca.gca.cma.net, dominates the Kawama peninsula. The prerevolutionary stone villas were recently upgraded and newer villas have been added in quasi-Spanish style. They are nicely albeit modestly furnished and include satellite TV and maid service. The resort has several bars and restaurants, plus water sports, Havanautos and Havanatur offices, and bike and scooter rentals. Rates were US$35 s, US$55 d, US$90 t low season; US$50 s, US$65 d, US$129 t high season.

The villa complex is part of the full-service **Hotel Kawama,** tel. (5) 66-7156, fax (5) 66-7004, closed for expansion at press time.

The rather gloomy and uninspired **Hotel Horizontes Aguazul,** Avenida 1ra y Calle 13, tel. (5)

60-3918, fax (5) 66-7229, is a three-star property with 240 a/c rooms with satellite TV and telephones. Rates were US$44 s, US$64 d low season, US$54 s, US$84 d high season. It adjoins **Apartotel Horizontes Varazul,** tel. (5) 66-7132, fax (5) 66-7229, part of the same complex. It has 69 one-bedroom a/c apartments with kitchens, bathrooms, living rooms, TVs, and telephones. Rates were US$41 s, US$58 d low season, US$48 s, US$72 d high season.

Gaviota's **Villa Caleta,** Calle 20 y Ave. 1ra, tel. (5) 66-7080, fax (5) 66-3291, has 46 a/c rooms with telephone, satellite TV, safety deposit box. Rates were US$42 s, US$60 d.

Horizontes Villa Caribe on Avenida de la Playa and Calle 30, tel. (5) 61-3310, has 124 modestly furnished two-room a/c apartments in need of refurbishment at press time. Rooms have TVs, mini-fridges, and security boxes but no telephones. The pizzeria is elegant. Other facilities include a swimming pool, hairdressers, four bars, disco, and a shop. Rates were US$31 s, US$63 d low season, US$38 s, $78 d high season.

The 64-room **Hotel Bellamar,** Avenida 1ra and Calle 10, tel. (5) 63-014, was closed for restoration at press time.

Hotel/Villas Horizontes Tortuga, Calle 7, e/ Camino del Mar y Bulevar, tel. (5) 62-243, is a modern, 280-room, two-story complex centered on a pool complex. The resort recently received a make-over. The rooms have heaps of light but no TV or telephone You can also rent villas. It has a tourist bureau and rents mopeds and proves popular with French Canadian and German package tourists. Rates were about US$55 s, US$65 d low season, US$65 s, US$75 d high season.

Another favorite of Germans is Horizontes' "three-star" **Hotel Herradura,** Avenida de la Playa e/ Calle 35 y 36, tel. (5) 61-3703, fax (5) 66-7496, a small, intimate option with 79 a/c rooms in apartments with TVs, telephones and refrigerators. There's a restaurant and two bars, plus a store and a tourism bureau. Rates were US$42 s, US$58 d low season, US$50 s, US$67 d high season, including breakfast.

Expensive (US$85-110)

One of Varadero's most popular hotels is the **Mercure Coralia Cuatro Palmas,** Avenida 1ra, e/ Calle 61 y 62, tel. (5) 66-7040, fax (5) 66-7583, in North America, tel. (800) 221-4542, boasting attractive contemporary colonial-era architecture. The hotel, which is run by the French Mercure chain, is built on the grounds of Fulgencio Batista's summer house and is centered on an attractive swimming pool. It has 170 rooms, all with a/c, satellite TV, hair driers, radios, and telephones (67 rooms are "standard," 100 have double- and king-size beds). Rates were US$90 s, US$120 d. The hotel was in midst of restoration at press time. Villa Cuatro Palmas, adjoining, has 130 a/c bungalows with living rooms, dining rooms, and kitchens. Rates were US$83 s, US$106 d. A full range of facilities is offered, including cabaret shows beside the pool.

The **Horizontes Oasis Tennis Centre,** Vía Blanca Km 130, tel. (5) 66-7380, fax (5) 66-7489, is out on a limb from the mainland. It has 147 a/c rooms with satellite TVs, phones, and mini-fridges. It has five tennis courts, a swimming pool, and other sports facilities, as wall as a disco three nights weekly. It's used by German tour operators, but offers little of appeal and is overpriced. Rates were US$80 s, US$93 d low season, US$88 s, US$104 d high season.

The once dowdy **Hotel Siboney,** on the bayside, was being totally refurbished at press time.

Very Expensive (US$110-150)
Gran Caribe' venerable **Hotel Varadero Internacional,** Carretera Las Américas, tel. (5) 66-7038, fax (5) 66-7246, is set in pleasing grounds and opens onto what is perhaps the most attractive segment of beach. The 1970s-era hotel has 163 double rooms and two suites. There are also 156 rooms in 66 one- and two-floor cabanas. All rooms have a/c, TVs, and attractive furnishings. Facilities include two swimming pools, four restaurants, four grills, a café, six bars, a boutique, bicycle and car rental, tour desk, sauna, hairdressers, and water sports. The Internacional is also venue for the Cabaret Continental. Rates were US$70 s, US$100 d low season; US$83 s, US$125 d high season; US$103 s, US$165 d peak season. Cabañas cost US$78 s, US$126 d, US$180 t low season; US$94 s, US$158 d, US$225 t high season; US$109 s, US$178 d, US$270 t peak season. A penthouse is available.

The Spanish-run, two-story **Hotel Arenas Doradas,** tel. (5) 66-8150, fax (5) 66-8158, e-mail: sistema@arenas.gca.cma.net; in Spain, tel. (095) 205-1308, fax (095) 205-0581, e-mail: hotelesc@vnet.es, in the Gran Caribe chain, offers 316 rooms set amid 20 acres of landscaped grounds surrounding a freeform pool with sunken pool bar, open-air jacuzzi. Interior decor is attractive. It has full water sports, activities, and entertainment. Rates were US$50 s, US$80 d low season, US$80 s, US$110 d high season, US$101 s, US$163 d peak season, plus US$10 for breakfast and US$20 for dinner.

Luxury (US$150 and above)
The twin-block, high-rise **SuperClubs Puntarena-Paraíso,** Avenida Kawama, Varadero, tel. (5) 66-7120, fax (5) 66-7074, e-mail: kees@rl-parad.gca.cma.net; in North America, tel. (800) 467-8737; in the U.K., tel. (01749) 677200, stands aloof at the westernmost tip of the peninsula, guaranteeing virtual privacy on its own section of svelte sands. The all-inclusive resort has been described in *Condé Nast Traveler* as "well-maintained, positively glistening with modernity." It is run to high standards by the award-winning Jamaican SuperClubs' chain, who at press time were in the midst of refurbishing and enlivening the previously ho-hum property in lively tropical colors. The twin towers span a huge sundeck and a freeform swimming pool. The a/c rooms are nicely furnished and were in the midst of a lively renovation at press time. Choose from seven bars, including swim-up bars, an ice cream parlor, and 14 restaurants, including an elegant Oriental and the a la carte Casablanca restaurant on a Mediterranean theme, plus a 24-hour cafeteria, with catering overseen by European chefs. It offers 14 different theme shows, plus special theme weeks such as October Bierfest and a Singles Week. No tipping is permitted. All-inclusive rates were US$196 s, US$248 d.

Gran Caribe also offers the **Club Kawama,** with 204-rooms in handsome two-story units in landscaped grounds for US$118 s, US$190 d all-inclusive, high season. I haven't inspected this property.

Another good option is the **Hotel Iberostar Barlovento,** Av. 1ra e/ 10 y 12, tel. (5) 66-7140, fax (5) 66-7218, at the west end of Varadero. This modern hotel (a contemporary interpretation of Spanish colonial style) has 276 double rooms, all attractively appointed and with satellite TV, balconies, telephones, and safe deposit boxes. The complex surrounds a large swimming pool and offers water sports and day and evening entertainment. All-inclusive rates were US$100 s, US$160 d low season; US$180 s, US$300 d high season, all-inclusive.

Hotel Delfines, Av. 1ra e/ 38 y 39, tel. (5) 66-7720, caters primarily to Italian package tourists but is open to all comers. It's modern Mediterranean-style decor appeals. All-inclusive rates were US$128 s, US$208 d high season; US$101 s, US$154 d, US$11-238 suite high season.

Gran Caribe's thoroughly modern, all-inclusive **Arenas Blancas Sol y Mar,** Calle 64 e/ Av. 1ra y Autopista, tel. (5) 61-4499, fax (5) 66-4490, e-mail: comer@arblcas.gca.cma.net, has 358 a/c rooms and 76 bungalows, all with cable TV, fridge, safe deposit box, and hair drier. The beautiful decor boasts contemporary art and exquisite marble-top bathrooms. The resort encusps a vast pool complex and offers upscale shops and a fine buffet restaurant. It has tennis courts and miniature golf. All-inclusive rates were US$134 s, US$228 d, US$298 t. It also offers two-story units **Bungalow Solymar,** with rates at US$113 s, US$176 d.

Gran Caribe's **Hotel Riu Las Morlas,** Avenida las Américas, tel. (5) 66-7230, fax (5) 66-7215, or, in Spain, tel. (0971) 74-3030, fax (0971) 74-4171, operated by Riu Hotels of Spain, is popular with Germans. Its elegant three-story units boast 143 attractively appointed a/c rooms, each with satellite TV, minibar, and terrace with ocean view. All-inclusive rates were US$121 s, US$195 d low season, US$174 s, US$274 d high season.

Next door, Gran Caribe's all-inclusive, 245-room **Villa Cuba Resort,** tel. (5) 66-8280, fax (5) 66-8282, offers a range of accommodations, including a/c hotel rooms with balconies and furnished in classy contemporary vogue. Two rooms cater to handicapped travelers. The complex, centered on a beautiful pool complex, offers 23 beachfront chalets with valet service (seven villas have their own pools). Facilities include a lobby bar suspended over the atrium lobby, a beauty salon, boutiques, and scuba-diving classes for beginners. Its entertainment includes cabaret. All-inclusive rates were US$108 s,

US$175 d, US$248 t low season; US$134 s, US$228 d, US$298 t high season for hotel rooms; US$224 low season, US$268 high season for cabanas.

Spain's Sol Meliá chain, website: www.solmelia.com, operates five luxury all-inclusive resort hotels under the Sol Club and Meliá trademark (they share similar decor and differ only in standard, with Meliá being a notch more deluxe).

Grupo Sol Meliá's 330-room **Sol Club Coral,** tel. (5) 66-7240, fax (5) 66-7194, due east of Villa Cuba, is an elegant all-inclusive complex centered on a mammoth pool complex. The 324 spacious and gracious a/c apartments and rooms in four-story blocks feature TVs, telephones, and liberal use of glass and a lively blend of tropical colors and ochers, adding up to some of the best rooms in Varadero. It has an arcade of salons and boutiques, two swimming pools, four restaurants, five bars (one open 24 hours), and facilities for children. All-inclusive rates for standard rooms were US$135 s, US$155 d low season, US$165 s, US$195 d high season, US$290 s, US$318 d peak season.

Immediately east is **Sol Club Las Sirenas,** Avenida de Las Américas y Calle K, tel. (5) 66-8070, fax (5) 66-8075, e-mail: sol.club.las.sirenas@solmelia.es, which has 248 elegantly appointed a/c rooms, all with satellite TV, direct dial telephone, security box, and patio. Two suites have jacuzzis. Facilities include a swim-up bar, piano bar, game room, kids' club, fitness center, sauna, two tennis courts, plus a soccer, handball, and basketball court, bocce ball and shuffleboard, and water sports, including a dive school. All-inclusive rates were US$215 s, US$235 d.

One of my favorites in this category is **Breezes Varadero,** Carretera Las Américas Km 3, tel. (5) 66-7030, fax (5) 66-7005, e-mail: clubvar@clubvar.var.cyt.cu; in North America, tel. (800) 467-8737; in the U.K., (01-749) 677200, a 270-suite property splendidly managed by Jamaica's SuperClubs chain. Spacious and handsome a/c rooms and suites feature king or twin beds, telephone, satellite TV, safety deposit box, lots of hardwoods, plus private terraces overlooking the ocean and 26 acres of grounds ablaze with plumbago and bougainvillea. Buffet meals are served in a hangar-sized dining room with French doors open to the breezes. There are also a pasta restaurant and a Cuban specialty restaurant. Facilities include an impressive aerobics room and gym, and every sport in, on, or under water. Rates—which include all meals, beverages, and activities—average US$200 s, US$260 d for rooms and US$225 s, US$300 for suites, depending on season.

Next, to the east, the **Hotel Tuxpán,** Avenida las Américas, tel. (5) 66-7560, fax (5) 66-7475, has been described as "a bewildering temple to the gods of generic pleasures," perhaps because the 233-room hotel, operated by the German LTI hotel chain, website: www.lti.de, has an atrium lobby loosely modeled on a Mayan pyramid. It's built around a huge, kidney-shaped swimming pool and features the La Bamba disco, tennis courts, and a mini-golf-course. All rooms have a/c and cable TVs and are tastefully furnished. All-inclusive rates were US$120 s, US$165 d low season, US$140 s, US$200 d high season.

A sister LTI property, the **Bella Costa,** tel. (5) 66-7210, fax (5) 66-7174, next door, features handsome Teutonically styled, three-story villas in addition to a hotel adjacent to the Tuxpán. It has 306 rooms, all with self-dial telephones, satellite TV, and refrigerators. Most have balconies with ocean views. There are also 76 suites and duplex suites with living rooms. The complex has a large pool with sunken swim-up bar, and three restaurants, including Mexican and Italian. It also shares restaurants, disco, water sports, and other facilities with the adjacent hotel. All-inclusive rates were US$180 s, US$200 d, US$285 t low season, US$280 s, US$320 d, US$456 t high season.

The most gracious rooms in town are at **Mansión Xanadu,** tel. (5) 66-7750, fax (5) 66-7388, at the Varadero Golf Club, where six rooms boasting names like Samarkand are perhaps the most gracious rooms in all Cuba. Imagine marble floors, wrought-iron beds, throw rugs, lofty ceilings with wainscoting, and all marble bathrooms with vast walk-in showers. The superb restaurants are at hand, as are both golf course and beach. Rates were US$130 s, US$160 d low season, US$190 s/d high season, and US$200 for the Du Pont Suite, including breakfast and green fees.

The following three are Meliá (website: www.solmelia.com) properties are adjacent to each other and together they take up a mile of beachfront.

The **Meliá Las Américas,** tel. (5) 66-7600, e-mail: melia.las.americas@solmelia.es, the glitziest of the trio, boasts a stunning lobby replete with artwork, stained glass, a fountain, and trickling streams. Elegant arched terraces support a beautiful pool and sundeck overlooking its own private beach. Its 225 rooms and 25 suites are in twin-level blocks and feature kitchenettes and small lounges below mezzanine bedrooms with pleasing bamboo and wicker furniture. Bathrooms are equally elegant. It has a wide range of room options, including luxury bungalows. Rates ranged from US$170 s, US$190 d in low season to US$360 s, US$380 d in peak season for standard rooms.

Separated from Las Américas by a shopping complex and convention center is the star-shaped **Meliá Varadero,** tel. (5) 66-7013, fax (5) 66-7012, e-mail: melia.varadero@solmelia. es. It has 483 rooms and seven suites in six arms that fan out from a lofty circular atrium with rooms spiraling upward and vines and ivy cascading down from the balconies. The effect is fabulous—made more so by the chattering of parrots. Rates ranged from US$120 s, US$140 d in low season to US$305 s, US$325 d in peak season.

Immediately east, the sprawling and gracious **Sol Club Palmeras** tel. (5) 66-7009, fax (5) 66-7008, e-mail: jefres@coral.solmelia.cma.net, is entered through a lobby with lush foliage, fountains, and caged birds adding a sense of the tropics. It has 375 rooms, 32 suites, and 200 bungalows. A huge pool with a thatched bar lies at its center. Rates ranged from US$97 s, US$129 d in low season and US$130 s, US$150 d in high season to US$182 s, US$242 d in peak season (Christmas and New Year's). Bungalows—set in lush grounds, with private terraces looking out over bougainvillea—began at US$104 s, US$139 d in low season, US$140 s, US$160 d high season.

Club Med Varadero, tel. (5) 66-8288, fax (5) 66-8340, or, in France, Club Med, 2 place de la Bourse, 75083 Paris, tel. (01) 42-96-10-00, fax (01) 40-20-91-44, or, in North America, tel. (800)

453-2582, fax (602) 443-2086, is billed as one of Club Med's finest villages, with complete water sports facilities, including scuba diving, deep-sea fishing, and even a trapeze in the sprawling, beautifully landscaped grounds. This superb 600-room property offers a modish and refined Mediterranean motif, with exquisite art in the sumptuous lounges. It has three restaurants, four bars, a nightclub, shops, cigar store, and the best gym in town. Most guests are French. All-inclusive per person rates were US$54 low season, US$142 high season, US$214 peak season, including breakfast; or US$658 low season, US$992 high season, US$1,495 peak season for one-week stays. *Recommended.*

The **Cubanacán Brisas del Caribe,** on Avenida de las Américas, tel. (5) 66-8030, fax (5) 66-8005, has 277 rooms in a spiffy new complex. All rooms have satellite TV, telephone, radio, safe deposit box, balcony, colorful floral fabrics, and spacious and elegant bathrooms with marble sink counters; suites have jacuzzis. The en-vogue resort has seven bars, a choice of restaurants, tennis, volleyball, gym, and a panoply of water sports, plus other tourism facilities and entertainment. Alas, the hotel has hints of shoddy construction. It is popular with British tour groups. All-inclusive rates were US$139 s, US$218 d high season, including massage and two excursions.

Gran Caribe's **Coralia Club Playa de Oro,** Carretera Las Morlas Km 17.2, tel. (5) 66-8566, fax (5) 66-8555, e-mail: comercial@poro. gca.cma.net; in North America, tel. (800) 221-4542, is an all-inclusive run by the French Mercure chain, tel. (01) 60-87-90-00, and opened in late 1999. It boasts a dramatic futuristic design and power colors: deep-sea blue and gold. It has 385 cavernous junior suites with green rattan furniture, king-size beds, terrace and minibar, and exquisite bathrooms. Eight suites have jacuzzis. Facilities include a bar, two restaurants, whirlpool, gym, water sports, tennis courts, volleyball and basketball courts, a bowling alley, and a disco with cabaret. Most guests are French. All-inclusive rates began at US$140 s, US$180 d low season, US$160 s, US$220 d high season.

Jamaica's award-winning Sandals chain operates **Beaches,** Carretera Las Morlas Km 14.5, tel. (5) 66-8470, fax (5) 66-8335, e-mail: varadero@beaches.var.cyt.cu; in Jamaica, tel. (876) 979-0721, fax (876) 952-4494; in Canada, tel. (416) 223-0028 or (800) 545-8283, fax (416) 223-3306; in U.K., tel. (0171) 581-9895, fax (0171) 823-8758, an all-suite deluxe all-inclusive for singles, couples, and families with children 16 and older. It offers 350 gorgeously decorated junior suites in five categories, all with king-size beds, sunken lounges with wrap-around sofas in fruit-colored fabrics and sea-green tile floors, and marble-counters in exquisite bathrooms. Fifth-floor Premium rooms have full bars. The neoclassical buildings arc around a natural lagoon with, at its heart, a large thatched entertainment complex and on a huge freeform pool with whirlpools. Grounds extend through natural woodland to the beach. Facilities include four restaurants (including a glamorous Italian restaurant), tennis, water sports, a sauna, gym, disco, and nightly entertainment. European chefs preside over international cuisine. All-inclusive rates began at US$101 s, US$180 d low season to US$196 s, US$326 d high season for garden view. *Recommended.*

The gracious **Cubanacán Gran Hotel,** Carretera Las Morlas Km 11.5, tel. (5) 66-8243, fax (5) 66-8202, is a 10-year-old (but recently remodeled) four-star hotel that uses aluminum and incorporates its bedrock of natural limestone into the lobby, with walls overgrown with ivy creepers. It has 331 rooms and 80 new bungalows, all with private bath, satellite TV, phone, minibar, and safe deposit box, plus marble floors and green-tinted windows. Facilities include four restaurants, a grill, four bars, a handsome swimming pool complex with kiddies' pool, water sports, boutique, car rental, tour desk, and entertainment, including cabaret and an adjacent disco. It's managed by an Italian company. All-inclusive rates were US$132 s, US$186 d low season, US$152 s, US$226 d high season.

The **Veraclub** is used exclusively by Italian tour groups of the Veratour.

SuperClub's five-star, 400-room **Grand Lido Varadero** was scheduled to open in 2002 as one of the most luxurious hotels in Cuba. This gracious hotel will boast luxury suites and junior suites, 24-hour room service, massages, and wedding services—all in the all-inclusive rates.

FOOD

Varadero has the largest choice of eateries outside Havana, including many nestled over the beach. *Criollo* cuisine predominates. International fare tends to be *criollo* with a hint of foreign lands. Don't set your standards too high, as standards in most state-run restaurants are mediocre. The upscale hotels managed by international hotel groups offer fare to international quality (some allow nonguests to eat in their restaurants and pool-side grills for a day-pass fee that permits use of other facilities). Alas, private restaurants—*paladares*—aren't permitted in Varadero, but some locals will prepare lobster and other meals for you on the sly. It's quite feasible to buy a meal for about US$4, although you should budget twice that for seafood. Lobster begins at about US$12.

No one seems to sell the once-famous Varadero punch (made of coconut milk, egg yolks, sugar, and frappé ice).

Fast Food and Snacks

El Rápido, Cuba's version of KFC, has two branches near each other on the Autopista Sur at Calle 30 and Calle 35, plus a branch on Avenida 1ra y 48, all serving fried chicken and fries for about US$2.

The **Restaurante/Café Mediterráneo,** tel. (5) 6-2460, is a down-to-earth place opening onto Avenida 1ra at Calles 54. It attracts local youth. To the rear is a more classical restaurant opening onto a shady courtyard; it charges Cubans in pesos (you pay in dollars). **Snack Bar Calle 13,** at Calle 13, catercorner to the Hotel Aguazul, is a bar serving *criollo* food. It's a popular hangout.

Criollo

Restaurante El Criollo, Av. 1ra y Calle 18, is a rustic colonial home-turned-restaurant serving lobster in pepper sauce (US$6), plus roast chicken with black beans and rice for US$3.50. It's open noon-midnight.

Restaurante La Vicaria, Av. 1ra y 38, offers alfresco dining under thatch, with the usual *pollo asado* (roast chicken) and fish dishes for US$5-8.

El Aljibe, Av. 1ra 7 y Calle 38, an outpost of the famous eatery in Havana, is recommended, although it falls short of its capital sibling. The filthy

table cloths hardly inspire. It offers an all-you-can-eat *pollo asado* for US$12. Lobster costs a ridiculously high US$24.

Another touristy favorite is **El Bodegón Criollo,** in a rustic old home at Avenida de la Playa y Calle 40, tel. (5) 66-7784. It attempts to replicate the famous Bodeguita de Medio in Havana, with classical music and signatures scrawled on the walls. You can dine outside on a shady veranda or inside in a rustic setting with eaves and ships' wheels-turned-lamps hanging from the ceiling. Typical dishes include roast leg of pork (US$7), creole mincemeat (US$6), or grilled pork steak (US$6). Open noon-10 p.m.

One of my favorite places is **El Mesón del Quijote,** tel. (5) 66-7796, on a hill above Avenida las Américas and boasting romantic rustic decor: beamed ceiling, metal lamps, brass plaques, and potted plants and climbing ivy on a solarium dining terrace. The menu features a wide range of wines to accompany soups, omelettes, salads, grilled fish, fried chicken, shrimp, and lobster (from US$2-24). Open noon to midnight. Try the *oferta especial* (special offer) of lobster with garlic sauce (US$14).

Restaurante Rancho Josone, tel. (5) 66-7224, opposite the entrance to Parque Josone, serves *criollo* food for under US$6 in a handsome thatched setting.

Mi Casita, on Camino del Mar e/ Calles 11 y 12, tel. (5) 6-3787, boasts a beautiful beachfront setting and an elegant a/c dining room with period antiques. A set meal of chicken (US$12), shrimp (US$18), or lobster (US$25) includes soup, salad, dessert, and coffee. It has vegetarian dishes. It's open 7 p.m.-1 a.m.

Continental

Al Capone would be shocked to see what has become of his former home, built in 1934 on the Kawama peninsula. His bootlegger's *bodega* is today the atmospheric **Casa de Al,** tel. (5) 76850, ext. 341, with indoor dining and a seafront terrace. The menu includes paella (US$10) and filet mignon "Lucky Luciano" (US$16). It has a large wine list.

The romantic **Restaurante Antiguedades,** Avenida 1ra outside the Parque Josone, tel. (5) 66-7329, is the most atmospheric place in town, with antiques, walls decorated with posters and photos of Hollywood stars, and genuine silverware and porcelain place settings. It offers set dinners, including filet mignon for US$15 and lobster for US$22. Wines cost US$10-20.

Almost as enchanting is the chic **Restaurante La Fondue,** opposite the Hotel Cuatro Palmas, tel. (5) 66-7747. Elegant place settings and decor combine with classical music for a romantic note. The menu lists a large range of fondues using Cuban cheeses (US$22-30 for two). Special cheeses such as Gruyere, Sbrinz, and Gouda cost extra, per gram. You can also order lobster and cheese (US$24), steak with cheese (US$14), and chicken with cheese (US$10). La Fondue has a good selection of wines. Open 1-11 p.m.

French: For ambience, consider the **Restaurante Las Américas,** on the ground floor of Mansión Xanadu, tel. (5) 66-7750, fax (5) 66-7388. The restaurant specializes in French-style seafood and meats, such as lobster (US$39), fish sautéed with capers (US$13), seafood casserole (US$19), Chateaubriand tenderloin (US$32). Open noon-10:30 p.m. Lunch and light snacks are served on the **Bar Terraza,** open 8 a.m.-midnight. You can enjoy an aperitif at **Bar Casablanca,** in the basement.

Italian: Kiki's Club, on Carretera Kawama at Calle 5, tel. (5) 61-4115, serves basic Cuban pizzas, pastas, and *criollo* dishes for US$2-5. And the **La Sangriá** snack bar, Avenida 1ra y Calle 8, tel. (5) 61-2025, offers an *oferta especial* of pizza, spaghetti, ice cream, and beer for US$5.

Restaurante Castelnuevo, Avenida 1ra y Calle 11, has an appropriately Italianate motif, and serves spaghettis, pastas, and pizzas for US$5-10. The elegant **Pizzeria La Trovalta Restaurant** is on Avenida Las Américas, next to the Resort Internacional.

Oriental: Chong Kwok on Avenida 1ra y 55, has a genuine oriental ambience plus a large menu priced below US$6. Also try **Lai-Lai,** on Avenida 1ra e/ 18 y 19, tel. (5) 66-7793. The menu includes spring rolls, fried rice with shrimp or lobster, lobster chop suey, and Tin Pan chicken, with entrées in the US$5-15 range. It tries hard for a Chinese ambience but falls short. It's open 7-11 p.m.

Spanish: The **Restaurant Mallorca,** opposite the Hotel Cuatro Palmas on Avenida 1ra at Calle 62, makes a poor pretense at being Spanish but can muster only paella in addition to the usual Cuban fare.

Seafood

Restaurante Arrecife, Calle 13 esq. Camino del Mar, tel. (5) 6-3918, is a pleasant place serving seafood specials, including excellent grilled fish and lobster (US$7-17). A complete special for US$10 includes soup, grilled fish, dessert, and beer. Its outside balcony catches the breezes.

The Villa Cuba, at Calle B, has the **Barracuda Grill,** a pleasant beachfront bar and restaurant playing Latin music. Here you can buy *mojitos,* screwdrivers, and daiquiris (US$2) to wash down seafood such as "Earth and Sea Brochet" (US$10) and grilled fish (US$7).

The **Mariscada Grill el Anzuelo,** tel. (5) 66-6265, a seafront restaurant in Parque Josone serves lobster, but also chicken, and beef dishes. Open 9 a.m.-6 p.m. Nearby **Restaurante Albacora,** on Calle 59, serves seafood on a terrace overlooking the breeze-swept beachfront.

Meats

The **Steak House Toro,** Av. 1ra y 25, is an atmospheric colonial house where you may dine alfresco on a shady terrace, or inside, where the modestly elegant decor attempts a steak-house ambience. The overpriced menu runs from veal chops (US$14) to a 20-oz. rib steak (US$29).

Also try *La Barbacoa,* on Calle 64 y Av. 1ra, tel. (5) 66-7795.

Supermarkets, Produce Markets

Varadero isn't geared to serve those catering for themselves. You'll find a bakery at Avenida 1ra y Calle 43. You can buy Western foodstuffs and a minimal amount of fresh produce in the **El Cacique Shopping Center,** on Avenida 1ra y Calle 62, and at **Grocery Caracol,** Calle 15 e/ Aves. 1ra y 3ra, and **Grocery La Trovatta** on Av. 1ra y Calle A.

Ice Cream and Desserts

Alas, **Coppelia,** Av. 1ra e/ Calles 44 y 46, tel. (5) 6-2866, no longer serves ice cream for pesos. It now caters to tourists and offers *helados* and sundaes for US$1-5, as does **BB,** at Av. 1ra e/ 24 y 25. Prices are lower at **Casa de la Miel La Colmena.**

Coffee shops are a rarity. Try the **Coffee Shop 25,** on Av. 1ra y Calle 25.

There's a bakery in Boulevard 43 on Av. 1ra esq. Calle 43.

ENTERTAINMENT AND EVENTS

Varadero is relatively dead at night. The majority of guests stay in the deluxe hotels, which feature their own bars, cabarets, and entertainment, so that few guests wander out. And the restriction on Cubans (especially females) entering Varadero that went into place in 1997 has taken the steam out of what could otherwise be a sensual scene.

Festivals and Events

Festival de Invierno is traditionally held each second week in December, sponsored by the Ministry of Culture, Av. 1ra y Calle 23, tel. (5) 6-2793. It attracts artists from throughout Latin America, with specific days dedicated to fashion shows, music, and classical autos.

Cubans are shipped in from far and wide to celebrate the **May Day Parade,** each May 1.

The **Varadero International Marathon** is held in November.

Varadero's homegrown street **Carnaval** is held in mid-July, with masquerades, music, and merrymaking.

Traditional Music and Dance

There's not much going on here, although many of the hotels provide Afro-Cuban shows. You can also check at the **Casa de la Cultura,** on Av. 1ra y Calle 34, tel. (5) 61-2562.

Bars and Discos

Most ritzy hotels have their own discos. Nonguests are usually welcome. Most are overly air-conditioned, all-tourist affairs. Discos don't get in the groove until 11 p.m. Most cost US$5 or less.

Habana Café, at the Hotel Sol Palmeras, is a snazzy disco with cabaret. It boasts a 1950s motif, with period movie posters and eclectic memorabilia on a Hard Rock Café theme. The US$10 entrance includes one drink.

La Bamba, in the Hotel Tuxpán, tel. (5) 66-7560, is popular. Entrance costs US$10 including all drinks, as it does at the **Palacio de la Rumba** disco, tel. (5) 66-8210, in the Hotel Bella Costa next door. And **Splash,** in the Kawama complex, is also popular, with both indoor and outdoor dancing (US$2 entrance). The other upscale spot is the **Mambo Club,** in the Gran Hotel at the east end of the peninsula. Entrance costs US$5.

The open-air **Discoteca La Patana,** behind the Anfiteatro Varadero on the west side of the bridge into Varadero, is a less touristy option. Farther west, near Marina Acua, is a fake pirate ship-cum-restaurant, **Discoteca El Galeón,** which doubles as a disco after 10 p.m.

A natural cave provides a unique backdrop to the cabaret espectáculos Cueva del Pirata.

There are very few bars, other than in the hotels, though you'll find several unremarkable open-air bars along Avenida 1ra. **Bar Beny,** on Camino del Mar e/ Calles 12 y 13, is open 24 hours. Another popular bar is **Bar Calle 13,** on Avenida 1ra, catercorner to Hotel Aguazul.

Cabarets *(Espectáculos)*
Several of the larger tourist hotels host floor shows featuring kaleidoscopes of stiletto-heeled mulattas teasingly swirling their boas and behinds while musicians beat out sambas and salsa.

Cabaret Continental, at the Hotel Varadero International, tel. (5) 66-7039, is the best show in town. The cabaret (US$25, or US$40 with lobster dinner) is offered at 10 p.m., Tues.-Sun, followed by a disco. I also recommend the **Cueva del Pirata,** tel. (5) 66-7751, an emporium of exotica where an Afro-Cuban cabaret show takes place in a natural cave at Km 11 on the Autopista Sur. It opens at 9 p.m. but the show begins at 11 p.m. Entrance costs US$10 including one drink. It's closed Sunday, and the show is often canceled on Monday for lack of guests. After midnight, a disco gets into full swing.

The **Mambo Club** also has a cabaret, nightly except Monday, as does the **Habana Café.** The **Cabaret Mediterráneo,** in the Complejo Mediterráneo on Av. 1ra e/ Calle 34 y 35, offers a basic *espectáculo* at 8:30 p.m. And **Cabaret Anfiteatro Varadero,** in the Varadero Ampitheater, tel. (5) 61-9938, on the Vía Blanca on the mainland side of the bridge, also serves locals with cabaret Wed.-Sun. at 9 p.m. Entrance for foreigners is US$5. It's followed by a disco.

Cinemas
The **Cine Varadero,** on Av. 1ra y Calle 42, and the Cine Hicacos often have films in English (US$3). The movies range from camp classics such as *King Kong* to more prosaic fare such as *Fresa y Chocolate.*

Dolphin Shows
Dolphins are the star performers at the **Delfinarium,** tel. (5) 66-8031, in a coral-rimmed lagoon 400 meters east of Marina Chapelín. It's open daily 9 a.m.-5 p.m. and shows are offered at 11 a.m. and 2:30 and 4 p.m. (US$25, plus US$4 if you wish to take photographs). You can even swim with the dolphins—for a rip-off US$50 extra. The dolphins swim in small circles between snacks, and you grab onto a dorsal fin for a three- or four-second spin.

SPORTS AND RECREATION

Golf
You can practice your swing at **Varadero Golf Club,** tel. (5) 66-7788 or 66-7750, fax (5) 66-8481 or 66-7388, e-mail: golf@atenas.inf.cu, website: www.golfvaradero.cu, at Las Américas. The once meager nine-hole course has metamorphosed as an engaging, Canadian-designed, 18-hole, par-72 course with complete services, including a well-stocked pro-shop (open 8 a.m.-5 p.m.), electric carts, and caddie house, plus restaurant and snack bar. Greens fees are US$60; club rental costs US$10; golf cart and caddy cost US$10. Golf classes (US$45) are offered. It's open 7 a.m.-7 p.m.

Parachuting
Varadero boasts the **International Parachuting Center,** or Centro Internacional de Paracaidismo, tel. (5) 66-7256, fax (5) 66-7260, at the airstrip at Km 15 Vía Blanca. It offers initiation courses, technical training, and jumps including a tandem jump in a two-harness parachute with a professional trainer. All you need is a smidgen of courage and a desire to see Varadero as the frigate birds see it. The center is at the aerodrome on Vía Blanca, just west of the bridge into Varadero, reached via the dirt road opposite Marina Acua. The 10-minute fall (actual free fall lasts less than one minute) is made from a World War II-vintage Russian biplane and costs US$150. You can book at the Aerotaxi office on Av. 1ra y 24, tel. (5) 66-7540.

Scuba Diving
Nature takes the starring role in the seas off Varadero, a mecca for divers, although the diving here is not as good as elsewhere in Cuba. The Varadero reef system extends from Matanzas Bay to the western extent of the Havana-Camagüey cay group. There are at least 25 acknowledged sites off Varadero, several with old

wrecks. One of the best sites is the famous Blue Hole—*Ojo de Mégano*—an underwater cave 70 meters deep in the reefs near Cádiz Bay, east of Varadero. Virgin forests of black coral are prevalent, especially at deeper levels. Hawksbill turtles are commonly seen. The calm sea has little current, so turbidity is minimal.

Most of the deluxe, and many of the upscale, hotels have scuba diving facilities staffed by qualified dive instructors.

S'Cuba Dive Club Alfredo at Villa Tortuga #208, tel. (5) 64-115 or tel./fax (5) 33-7054; in Canada, Alfredo Werosta, 10708 142 St., Edmonton, Alberta, offers daily dives, plus certification courses and resort courses for beginners. They have two Bauer compressors and an 18-passenger dive boat. Courses are also offered by **Scuba Barracuda,** Av. 1ra e/ Calle 58 y 59, tel. (5) 61-3481, fax (5) 66-7072, which also offers cave and night dives (US$40) and trips to Playa Girón, and charges US$105-240 for 4-10 dive packages.

Puertosol's **Acua Diving Center,** tel. (5) 66-8063, fax (5) 66-7456, at Marina Acua, charges US$40 for one dive, US$300 for a certification course. **Aquaworld** at Marina Chapelín, tel. (5) 66-7550, fax (5) 66-7093, charges US$35 per dive and has four- to 10-dive packages (US$105-215) and certification courses (US$365).

Snorkeling: All scuba outfitters rent fins, masks, and breathing tubes (US$5). Most also offer snorkeling trips to the reefs, as do the three marinas (typically US$25).

Sportfishing
Six-hour deep-sea sportfishing trips from Marina Acua cost US$300 for up to four people. Aquaworld, at Marina Chapelín, tel. (5) 66-7550, fax (5) 66-7093, also offers four-hour sportfishing trips (US$240 for four people, US$30 each additional person).

Tournaments: Varadero hosts the "Gregorio Fuentes White Marlin Fishing Tournament" in June, plus the "Friendship Fishing Tournament" in October. Telephone (5) 66-8060, fax (5) 66-7456, e-mail: marsol@marsol.mintur.tur.cu.

Water Sports
All the upscale hotels include water sports in their room rates. Several beach outlets rent water sports equipment: expect to pay US$4 per hour for rowboats, US$5 for snorkel gear, US$6 for double kayaks, US$15 for catamarans, US$10 for windsurfers, and US$15 for jet skis.

Other Activities
Restaurante Estrella, tel. (5) 66-2649, in Parque Josone, has pool tables and a bowling alley (US$2). Most of the deluxe hotels also have tennis courts (nonguests pay a court fee).

SHOPPING

Arts and Crafts
First stop should be the alfresco **crafts market** held daily on Avenida 1ra at Calle 44. For quality try the **Casa de la Artesanías Latinoamericano,** on Avenida 1ra y Calle 63. Its superb range of goods from Latin America includes jewelry, jackets, shawls, belts, satchels, and erotic carvings. It's open 9 a.m.-7 p.m. For truly world-class pottery and plates, ashtrays, and vases, head to **Taller de Cerámica Artística,** Av. 1ra y Calle 59, tel. (5) 6-2703, where you can watch local youths making pottery in a well-equipped modern workshop. Look for dining sets and individual plates by renowned artists such as Osmany Betancourt, Alfredo Sosabravo, and Sergio Roque. Each is unique, painted by hand, and a steal at only US$40 each. Next door is Varadero's **Galería de Arte,** tel. (5) 66-7554, with a range of wooden statues, paintings, and other artwork. Open 9 a.m.-7 p.m. Another good bet is **Barlovento,** a beachfront store on Calle 11, selling souvenirs, T-shirts, and postcards.

The **Arte Sol y Mar** gallery next to the Casa de la Cultura on Avenida 1ra y Calle 35 offers art.

The airport has an excellent duty-free store selling everything from cigars and cassettes to "special mint" gold and silver coins and peso bills. You can even buy bongo drums (about US$150) and handmade saddles (US$350).

Cigar Stores
Most hotels have humidors where you can buy cigars. Habanos S.A. employs cigar rollers in the lobbies of most hotels (the cigars they make are sold under a generic Habanos label). The **Casa de las Tabacos,** at Avenida 1ra y Calle 39,

tel. (5) 61-4719, is the best-stocked shop in town and has a bar and smokers' lounge. **La Casa del Habano,** on Avenida 1ra y Calle 63, tel. (5) 66-7843, also offers a large array and has a smokers' lounge upstairs.

Bookshops and Music

Most hotel stores sell music cassettes and CDs, plus a limited range of Western newspapers and magazines. The best selection is **Max Music,** Calle 63 y Av. 1ra, tel. (5) 61-4186, selling a wide range of CDs, cassette, etc. **ARTEX,** Av. 1ra y 12, and Av. 1ra y 46, also has a good music selection (open 9 a.m.-9 p.m.)

The only bookstore in town is **Librería Hanoi,** which offers a small range of social, historical, and political works on a leftist theme, plus a small selection of novels in English. Open Mon.-Sat. 9 a.m.-9 p.m.

Stores and Boutiques

Centro Comercial de Caimán, opposite the Hotel Cuatro Palmas on Av. 1ra e/ Calles 61 y 62, is a commercial center with a fistful of boutiques, cosmetic stores, and other dollar-only stores. **Joyería Coral Negro,** at Calle 64 y Av. 3ra, tel. (5) 61-4870, sells a wide range of duty-free name-brand watches (including watches with Che's visage by Swatch; US$50), plus perfumes and quality Cuban jewelry (mostly silver and black coral).

Other clothing boutiques are located two blocks farther east, and on Avenida 1ra at Calle 45. And several Caracol stores along Avenida Kawama sell Western clothing, swimwear, and touristy items.

Farther east, the **Centro Comercial Las Américas** shopping complex, between the Meliá Varadero and Meliá Los Américas hotels, offers a range of boutiques. And many of the newer deluxe hotels have high-fashion boutiques.

Photo Supplies

Photo Service has modestly stocked stores on Avenida Segunda y Calle 63, at Av. 1ra y Calle 42, and on Av. de la Playa e/ Calles 43 y 44. The stores have a limited stock of film and batteries but also sell cameras (Zeniths and Canon EOS), including a wide range of instant cameras. Open 9 a.m.-9 p.m.

SERVICES

Tourist Information

The **Centro de Información Turístico** (Tourist Information Center) is at Av. 1ra y Calle 23. It's open 8 a.m.-8 p.m. and sells maps of Varadero and other cities. An informal tourist information office is at **Casa de Isabel Martin,** Calle 33 #103 e/ Aves. 1ra y 3ra, tel. (5) 61-2257.

Asistur, Asistencia al Viajero, at Calle 23 #101, e/ Aves. 1ra y Tercera, tel. (5) 66-7277, tel./fax (7) 33-7277 in Havana, can provide medical assistance, insurance, cash advances, and legal advice, and help resolve other problems. It's open Mon.-Fri. 9 a.m.-noon and 1:30-4:30 p.m. and Saturday 9 a.m.-noon. Likewise, the **Consultório Jurídica Internacional,** Av. 1ra y Calle 21, tel. (5) 66-7082, offers legal services for foreigners. It's open 8 a.m.-noon and 1:30-5:30 p.m.

Most hotel lobbies have a tour information desk, and the leading Cuban tour agencies also have offices where you can arrange flights and excursions.

Banks and Moneychangers

Most hotels can cash traveler's checks or change small amounts of foreign currency. For larger sums, head for any of three banks, which all change money, give advances against credit cards, and cash traveler's checks including U.S.-issued American Express checks. The **Banco Financiero Internacional,** Avenida Playa y Calle 32, offers a special service for tourists Mon.-Fri. 2-6 p.m. and Sat. 8:30 a.m.-noon. It has a second branch next to Hotel Riu Las Morlas, at Calle A. The bank is upstairs and is open daily 8 a.m.-12:30 p.m. and 1:30-7 p.m. The **Banco de Crédito y Comercio,** Av. 1ra y Calle 36 (open 8 a.m.-3 p.m.), and the **Banco Popular,** across the road on Calle 36 (open 8 a.m.-noon and 1:30-4:30 p.m.).

There's also a **Cadeca** foreign exchange bureau on Av. de la Playa e/ 41 y 42, and another at Avenida las Américas y Calle C. Open Mon.-Fri. 9:30 a.m.-noon and 1-4 p.m. and Saturday 8:30 a.m.-noon. However, there is virtually nothing for which you'll need pesos.

Post and Telecommunications

The larger hotels sell stamps and have mailboxes. The main post office is on Avenida 1ra y 36. A smaller post office is in the gate house at Avenida las Américas y A, tel. (5) 61-4551, fax (5) 66-7330. It has a fax, telex, DHL Express Service, and telephone service (open 8 a.m.-8 p.m.). You can send packages and letters express delivery by DHL, Av. 1ra y 42, tel. (5) 66-7730.

The main Etecsa international telephone center—**centro telefónico**—is on Avenida 1ra and Calle 30. Etecsa also has telephone booths at the far west end of Avenida Kawama; along Avenida 1ra at Calle 15, at Calle 46, and at Calle 64; and on Avenida las Américas y K. You can rent cellular telephones for US$7 a day from **Cubacel,** Edificio Marbella, Av. 1ra e/ Calle 42 y 43, tel./fax (5) 80-9222, open Mon.-Fri. 8 a.m.-5 p.m. and Saturday 8 a.m.-noon.

Medical Services

Clínica Internacional, Av. 1ra y Calle 61, tel. (5) 66-7711, fax (5) 66-7226, is a modern facility serving tourists. A consultation costs US$25. A doctor and nurse are available 24 hours for hotel visits (US$40). The clinic has a pharmacy and can perform X-rays and laboratory tests. An ambulance is available. There are local pharmacies at Av. 1ra y Calle 28, tel. (5) 6-2772, and Av. Playa y Calle 44, tel. (5) 6-2636.

A **Sub-Aquatic Medical Center** (Centro Médico Sub Acuático), tel. (5) 2-2114, at Cárdenas, 10 km east of Varadero, has a decompression chamber.

The **Red Cross,** tel. (5) 61-2950, on Calle 27, north of Avenida 1ra, has ambulance service.

Other Services

The **police** station is at Avenida 1ra e/ Calles 38 y 39. MININT's **Immigration** office is around the corner on Calle 39, tel. (5) 61-3494. It's open Mon.-Fri. 1-5 p.m. and Saturday 8 a.m.-noon.

I'm not aware of any coin laundries in Varadero. It's easy, however, to find a local willing to wash your clothes for a few dollars. A large public locker facility is beneath Coppelia, on Av. 1ra y Calle 44. The **library** *(biblioteca)* is on Calle 33 e/ Av. 1ra y 3.

There are two **Cupet gas stations:** on the Autopista Sur y Calle 17, and next to Marina Aqua on the Vía Blanca west of town.

GETTING THERE

By Air

The **Juan Gualberto Gómez** airport, tel. (5) 66-3016, is 16 km west of Varadero. A taxi ride will cost about US$25.

Domestic: Aero Caribbean, Calle 23 #64, Vedado, tel. (7) 33-4543, fax (7) 33-5016, e-mail: aerocarvpcre@iacc3.get.cma.net, flies daily from Havana, and on Friday and Sunday from Santiago de Cuba. **Cubana,** tel. (5) 66-7593, tel. (7) 33-4949 in Havana, flies to Varadero thrice weekly from both Havana and Santiago de Cuba. It also connects Varadero with Baracoa, Cayo Coco, and Holguín. **Aerogaviota** also offers service to Varadero from Havana and other points in Cuba.

Inter Grupo Taca, in the Hotel Habana Libre, Havana, tel. (7) 66-2702, fax (7) 33-3728, introduced flights to Varadero from Cayo Coco, Cayo Largo, Havana, and Trinidad in 1999 but was promptly forced to cancel all service. Check to see if they've been resurrected. This Central American carrier is superior to all domestic carriers.

International: Cubana flies from Paris to Varadero on Saturday and from Montreal on Sunday. **Lauda Air** flies charters from Milan to Varadero on Saturday. **Martinair** (in Varadero, tel. 5-6-3624) operates flights from Amsterdam via Holguín on Saturday. Mexicana's regional carrier, **Aerocaribe,** flies nonstop from Cancún to Varadero on Tuesday and Wednesday. Several Canadian companies offer charter flights to Varadero.

Cubana charters operate from Jamaica to Varadero on Friday and Sunday (see the Caribbean section in the Getting There section, in the On The Road chapter). **Tropical Airlines,** tel. (876) 968-2473 in Kingston, tel. (876) 979-3565 in Montego Bay, flies twice weekly from Jamaica to Varadero. (See By Air in the Getting There section in the On The Road chapter for more details.)

By Sea

Marina Acua, tel. (5) 66-3133, (5) 66-7456; HF-2790 or VHF-1668, at 23° 10'N, 81° 17'W, is on the south side of Laguna Paso Malo, at the west end of the peninsula. It has berths for 60 vessels (US$0.45 per foot per day), plus electricity, water, diesel, and gas.

The smaller marina—**Marina Chapelín,** tel. (5) 66-7551, fax (5) 66-7093, channel 72 on VHF—is eight km east of downtown Varadero on Carretera las Morlas, but at press time was not accepting foreign yachts. Near the eastern top of the peninsula is **Marina Gaviota,** tel. (5) 66-7755, used mainly by the Cuban military and commercial concerns. It has dry-dock facilities, and pleasure craft can be rented, but foreign visitors are usually steered to the other marinas.

By Land
Víazul operates luxury bus service from Havana to Varadero, where it stops and departs from the Astro bus terminal (see the Víazul Bus Schedule chart, in the On the Road chapter). Its office in Varadero is at Calle 36 y Autopista, tel. (5) 61-4886. You can also transfer by **minibuses** operated by Cuba's tour agencies such as Havanatur for about US$25 each way. Hotel tour desks can make reservations.

Astro's public bus no. 323 operates twice daily from Havana's main bus terminal at 4:50 a.m. and 3 p.m. (2 hours 45 minutes; six pesos).

A **taxi** from Havana costs about US$90 one-way.

Tour agencies in Havana offer excursions to Varadero.

If driving, foreigners pay a US$2 toll at the toll booth on the Vía Blanca, about two km west of the entrance to Varadero. The fee applies in both directions.

GETTING AROUND

By Air
Gaviota operates **Aerotaxi,** tel. (5) 61-2929, using biplanes for excursions around Varadero (US$25 for 20 minutes; six passenger minimum) and to Cayo Largo (US$61 roundtrip), Trinidad (US$65), and as far afield as Pinar del Río (US$69). It also operates a DC-3 and modern L410 jets. You can book through major hotels or directly at the Aerotaxi office, Av. 1ra y 24, tel. (5) 66-7540. You can even take a ride in a tiny seaplane from the SuperClubs Puntarenas-Paradiso.

By Bus
A **Tur-Bus** minibus operated by Transtur runs up and down Avenida 1ra, as far west as Super-

Clubs Paradiso, 9 a.m.-midnight every 30 minutes. Bus stops are posted at regular intervals. Any journey costs US$1.

With pesos you can also hop aboard public buses no. 47 and 48, which ply the same route (10 centavos).

By Taxi
Tourist taxis hang around outside the major tourist hotels. No journey between Calle 1 and Calle 64 should cost more than US$5. Beware of being overcharged by taxi drivers, especially at night. Official rates are US$1 plus US$0.55 per km. You can call taxis from **Taxi OK,** tel. (5) 66-7092, **Transgaviota,** tel. (5) 66-7663, or **Turis-taxi,** tel. (5) 61-4444.

Coco-Taxis, hollow egg-shaped three-wheel motorcycles, rent for US$10 hourly, or US$4 to travel the length of Avenida 1ra.

Bicycles and Scooters
Two-wheel travel is a perfect way to get around Varadero. Scooters and mountain bikes can be rented at several locations along Avenida 1ra. Mountain bicycle rentals cost US$2 for one hour, US$6 for three hours, and US$10 per day. The beaten-up bikes can be rented from outside the SuperClubs Puntarenas and Parque Josone.

Horse-Drawn Cab
Horse-drawn *coches* trot along Avenida 1ra. They gather outside Parque Josone. A journey the length of Avenida 1ra You can ride the full length of Avenida 1ra for US$2.

Organized Excursions
Tour & Travel will help you get your bearings on a city tour (US$10). The main office is at Av. de la Playa #3606 e/ 36 y 37, tel. (5) 66-7279, fax (5) 66-7026. Offices are also at Calle 31 y Av. 1ra, tel. (5) 66-7154; in front of the Hotel Siboney on Avenida las Américas, tel. (5) 66-7203; in the Hotel Sol Palmeras, tel. (5) 66-7009; and in the Hotel Tuxpan, tel. (5) 66-7708. They're open 8 a.m.-8 p.m.

Puertosol, tel. (5) 66-8060, offers a range of boating excursions from Marina Acua, including a "seafari" to the Peninsula de Hicacos and Cayo Libertad and a "Caribbean Night" featuring dinner on Cayo Libertad, a santería ritual, and an Afro-Cuban *hechiceria* (US$49). Cubana's **Sol y Son**

Agencia Viajes, Avenida 1ra e/ 55 y 56, tel. (5) 66-7593, fax (5) 66-7385, offers day-long excursions to Cayo Piedra and Cayo Romero for US$35, including lunch.

A 90-minute underwater journey is offered by **Submarino Mundo Mágico,** Avenida Kawama #201 e/ 2ra y 3ra, tel. (5) 6-8455, a submarine that departs from in front of the SuperClubs Puntarenas and travels out to El Cayuelo, where you view the underwater world from large windows (I found the views disappointing), with a TV monitor for alternate viewing angles. Drinks (including rum cocktails) are included for US$35 (US$20 for children). A similar four-hour viewing experience is offered aboard the **Nautilo,** a glass-bottomed boat that sails from Marina Gaviota (US$25, including transfers).

The following operate from Marina Chapelín, tel. (5) 66-7550, fax (5) 66-7093. **Capitaine Duval Cruises** offers excursions around the peninsula aboard a motorized catamaran with underwater windows (US$30). **Aquaworld Varadero,** also offers a sailing safari—"Seafari Cayo Blanco"—to Cayo Blanco (US$65), as well as a nocturnal "Noche Marinera" with lobster dinner at the marina (US$45). **Jolly Roger** offers cruises by catamaran. The all-day cruise lasts 9 a.m.-4:30 p.m. and sails to the cays of the Bahía de Cárdenas (US$70, including lunch). A guided two-hour **jet ski** "Jungle Tour" is offered hourly, 9 a.m.-4 p.m. (US$35). And a **Challenge Tour** includes a trip up the Río Canimao by rubber Zodiacs plus a jeep trip to Campo Cubano for lunch and horseback riding (US$45).

Gaviotatours, tel. (05) 66-7864, offers excursions aboard the catamaran *Passiona,* plus glass-bottom boat tours aboard the *Nautilus* to Cayo Cangrejo with snorkeling and dolphin show (US$30), and Cayo Piedra (US$25). Gaviota Tours also offers a "seafari" aboard a sleek catamaran called *Tahiti,* plus a full-day snorkeling trips by yacht, and a separate trip to Cayo Blanco by motorboat. Excursions depart from Marina Gaviota, tel. (5) 66-7755.

GETTING AWAY

By Bus
The **Víazul** tourist bus departs for Havana twice daily, and daily for Santa Clara, Sancti Spíritus,

and Trinidad (see the Víazul Bus Schedule chart, in the On the Road chapter). Public buses also depart the Terminal de Ómnibus Interprovinciales at Autopista Sur and Calle 36, tel. (5) 61-6126, twice daily for Havana (two hours, 5.50 pesos) and for Santa Clara (three hours, eight pesos). Buses to Matanzas depart hourly (two pesos); no reservations are needed.

Cárdenas is served hourly by bus no. 236, which departs from the **Terminal Ómnibus de Cárdenas,** next to the main bus station, and from Avenida 1ra and Calle 13 (50 centavos).

By Car
Varadero has several rental agencies, all badly run. Beware scams (see the section on Car Rentals under By Car in the Getting Around section in the On The Road chapter).

Cubacar, tel. (5) 20-2188, and **Havanautos** have rental offices immediately east of Club Varadero. The main office of **Havanautos** is on Avenida 1ra y Calle 31, tel. (5) 66-4485. It also has an office in the Hotel Kawama and a third on Avenida 1ra, immediately north of Centro Comercial El Caiman. It charges a steep US$83 for small sedans, and US$25 per hour for dune buggies. **Cubanacán,** Calle 60 y 2da, tel. (5) 61-3317, also rents cars, as do **Transtur,** on Avenida 1ra y Calle 21, and Avenida las Américas y Calle A, tel. (5) 61-4444, and **Gaviota,** tel. (5) 61-9001. **Micar** has an office at Av. 1ra y Calle 20, tel. (5) 66-2218; in the Hotel Delfines, on Avenida 1ra e/ 38 y 39; and at Varadero airport, where Cubacar, Havanautos, Via, Gaviota, and Transtur all have outlets.

By Taxi
Tourist taxis cost US$0.55 per km. A slim bet is a *colectivo,* a communal taxi (usually an old Yankee clunker) that can usually be found outside the bus terminal. It's illegal, however, for drivers to take foreigners.

Hitching
If you want to try your luck hitching, stand by the traffic circle at the west end of Avenida 1ra, near Calle 11, or on the Vía Blanca (for Havana). The official hitching point is about 400 meters west of the bridge, on the Vía Blanca for Matanzas. The Vía Blanca is busy with tourist traffic heading to Havana, so you should have good luck.

Organized Excursions

In Varadero you are far removed from the "real" Cuba. I recommend exploring further afield. Typical excursions include Matanzas (US$15) and the Bellamar Caves (US$10); Havana (US$79, or US$115 including the Tropicana cabaret); the Bay of Pigs; Trinidad (US$60); and Cárdenas (which is a waste of time).

Several tour agencies compete, including: **Tours & Travel,** Av. de la Playa #3606 e/ 36 y 37, tel. (5) 66-3713, fax (5) 66-7036; Calle 31 y Av. 1ra, tel. (5) 66-7154; and in the Hotel Kawama, tel. (5) 66-7165—all open 8 a.m.-8 p.m.; **Gaviotatours,** Avenida 1ra y Calle 25, tel. (5) 66-7325, e-mail: vartour@gavvara.gav.cma.net; and **Cubatur,** Calle 33 esq. Avenida 1ra, tel. (5) 66-7217; and **Havanatur,** Avenida de la Playa y Calle 37, tel. (5) 66-7027, fax (5) 66-7026, plus offices on Avenida 1ra y Calle 31, tel. (5) 66-7154, and on Avenida las Américas, just east of Calle 64. **Rumbos** has a tourism office on Av. 1ra y 13, tel. (5) 61-2143, open 24 hours, and on Avenida 1ra y 23; **Cubanacán Agencia Viajes** is at Calle 24 y Playa, tel. (5) 33-7061, fax (5) 33-7062; and Cubana's **Sol y Son Agencia Viajes** is at Avenida 1ra e/ 55 y 56, tel. (5) 66-7593, fax (5) 66-7385.

CÁRDENAS

The Peninsula de Hicacos forms a natural breakwater protecting the large Bahía de Cárdenas, whose southern shore is fringed with oil derricks amid a desolate landscape covered with *marabú* scrub—stunted trees and henequen plantations. In their midst is the town of Cárdenas (pop. 75,000), a sleepy place a world away from the commercialism of Varadero, 10 km to the northwest.

The city was founded in 1828. Swampland was drained by canals and streets laid out like a chessboard. Many of the early population were refugees who fled Haiti following the Revolution. The town developed rapidly as a port serving the prosperous sugar-producing hinterland. Otherwise, Cárdenas has a lackluster history, punctuated by a singular event in 1850, when the Cuban flag was first flown here. That year, a Venezuelan adventurer called Narciso López came ashore with an invasion army to free the apathetic locals from Spanish rule and annex Cuba himself. Many of the 600 men that left New Orleans on 13 May 1850 were mercenaries from the state of Kentucky. Only six were Cubans. Although López's ragtag army captured the town, his meager force failed to rally local support and the invaders beat a hasty retreat. Cárdenas has forever since been called the "Flag City."

The town derives its meager income from sugar and fish processing, the Arrachebala rum factory, and the burgeoning oil industry. A full-scale oilrig stands in the waters offshore, pumping black gold from deep beneath the bay. Horse-drawn *coches* plod the streets, but cars— even 1950s-era American clunkers—are noticeably absent. In somnolent Cárdenas, the bicycle rules.

Cárdenas is hyped by several guidebooks for its architectural interest and, being close to Varadero, is favored for excursions. Alas, the town is dilapidated and can hardly make a good impression on day-trippers. Many tourists

Columbus statue, Parque Colón, Cárdenas

come to view the apartment building (in an area that looks like any American working-class neighborhood) where Elián González was born, the young Cuban boy rescued at sea in November 1999 after his mother and 10 others drowned at sea in a bid to escape Cuba for the U.S. The boy has become the town's cause célèbre, resulting in a feverish attempt to spruce up crumbling buildings for visiting news photographers.

Sightseeing

At press time, Elián's desk at the **Escuela Marcelo Salado,** Calle 13 #165, had been turned into a shrine, complete with a sign-in book for visitors to write their names. The first page, in large scrawl, reads: *"For the Freedom of Little Elián. Our Country, or Death. Fidel Castro."* In November 1999 the schoolhouse was as run-down as the other buildings on the block, but with the whole world watching it was painted a pretty shade of pink.

The town has a few examples of fine neo-classical architecture. An example is **Casa Natal de José Antonio Echevarría,** at Calle Genes #240, tel. (5) 4919. The two-story house—now a museum—was built in 1873 and features a beautiful, hand-carved spiral wooden staircase. The house is named for an anti-Batista student leader, born here in 1932 and assassinated in 1957. The museum's top floor honors Echevarría and other Cárdenians martyred for the Revolution. Open Tues.-Sat. 8 a.m.-4 p.m. and Sunday 8 a.m.-noon; free.

The train station, at the base of Calle Concha, is a sky-blue, Moorish-style edifice of note. Another oddity is **Plaza Molokoff,** a two-story plaza that houses the *mercado agropecuaria* (public market). The market, made of iron, is built in the shape of a cross with a lofty metallic domed roof in Islamic style. Its wrought-iron balustrades are held aloft by colonnades. Molokoff refers to the "dome-like" crinoline skirts fashionable in the mid-19th century, when the market plaza was built.

Tiny **Parque Colón** is dominated by the **Catedral de la Concepción Inmaculada,** a beautiful old cathedral fronted by an impressive patinated statue of Columbus with a globe at his feet. The monument dates from 1858. The church, built in 1846, has notable stained glass

windows. The former mayor's mansion, now the **Hotel Dominica,** is a national monument—it was here that Narciso López first raised the Cuban flag.

At the southwest end of Céspedes, a small fortress named for a revolutionary hero named Oscar María de Roja stands in the central median. It's now a popular café. There's a similar fortress at the west end of town, on Avenida 13 (Calzada) opposite the Cupet gas station.

Worth a browse in passing is the **Museo Oscar María de Roja,** in a beautiful restored colonial home at Calle Calzada #4. It's one of Cuba's oldest museums (founded in 1900) and contains an eclectic array of photographs and documents depicting the city's role in the wars of independence and the Revolution. It also houses a miscellany of butterflies and other bugs, including two fleas in dancing costumes, polished prehistoric axes, colonial weapons, and even a fountain-pen pistol that belonged to a Nazi spy who was captured in 1942. The *pièce majeure,* however, is an ornate 19th-century horse-drawn hearse, pure black baroque on wheels. Open Tues.-Sat. 1-6 p.m. and Sunday 9 a.m.-1 p.m. Entrance costs US$1.

Accommodations and Food

There were no hotels accepting foreigners at press time. You'll be equally hard-pressed to find anywhere exciting to eat. The best place seems to be the **Café La Cubanita,** a popular open-air eatery open 24 hours, on Avenida 5, one block southwest of Plaza Molokoff. Also check out the **Restaurante Las Palmas,** in an imposing mansion on Avenida Céspedes at Calle 16, tel. (5) 4762, or the **Pizzeria La Bolognese** on Céspedes and Calle 19. **El Rápido,** on the northwest side of Plaza Molokoff, and also at Calle 12 y Av. 3 Oeste, and **Los Almendros,** Avenida Céspedes and Calle 8, offers fried chicken, burgers, and pizzas.

The **Casa de las Infusiones,** on Parque Colón, serves tea and snacks.

Entertainment and Events

Cárdenas has traditionally held a **culture week** in early March to honor the founding of the city. Check out the **cabaret** held most nights at the Hotel Dominica (don't expect too much for your five pesos) or the one at the Restaurant Las

Palmas, which is followed by a disco. The **Bar Colonial,** Av. 3ra, e/ Calles 11 y 12, seems to be the liveliest bar around. You'll find a **cinema** on Céspedes at Calle 14.

Services

Amazingly, Cárdenas is blessed with a **coin laundry,** on Av. Céspedes y Calle 7 (five pesos per load). There's a **post office** on Parque Colón (Mon.-Sat. 8 a.m.-6 p.m.) and a **Centro Telefónico** on Av. Céspedes y Calle 13 (daily 7 a.m.-10:30 p.m.).

The **hospital** is on Calle 13, midway to Varadero. The Centro Médico Sub Acuática is here and has a decompression chamber.

There's a **Cupet gas station** at the west end of Calle 13 (Calzada), on the road to Varadero.

Getting There and Away

By Bus: Buses 376 and 236 run between Varadero and Cárdenas. The journey takes about 30 minutes and costs 50 centavos. You can catch the bus in Varadero on Avenida 1ra at Calle 12, or on Avenida de la Playa at Calle 35. Bus no. 376 for Varadero departs Cárdenas from Calle 14 and Avenida 8, no. 236 from the station at Calle 13 and Avenida 13 Oeste.

The main bus station in Cárdenas is at Avenida Céspedes and Calle 21, tel. (5) 52-1214. Cárdenas is also served by buses daily from Matanzas, Santa Clara, Jovellanos, Colón, and Jagüey Grande. (For service from Havana, see the Public Bus Service from Havana chart, in the On the Road chapter.)

By Taxi: You can reach Cárdenas by taxi from Varadero for about US$15. There are few taxis in Cárdenas, so if you plan on returning to Varadero, it is best to arrange a pick-up time with your driver.

By Train: A provincial rail line runs through town, connecting Cárdenas with Jovellanos and Colón (departures are in early morning). The station, tel. (5) 52-1362, is on Avenida 8 and Calle 5

Organized Excursion: Tours & Travel, Av. de la Playa #3606 e/ 36 y 37, Varadero, tel. (5) 66-7279, offers a city tour of Cárdenas for US$12.

Getting Around

A ride in a horse-drawn *coche* is the way to explore. They gather by Parque Colón.

CENTRAL MATANZAS

Travelers have a choice of two main routes across central Matanzas—the Carretera Central and the Autopista. From Havana the Autopista runs ruler-straight east to west through south-central Matanzas province. The entire route is lined with farmland. There are no diversions to distract you until you reach Km 142 and the turnoff for Jagüey Grande, Australia, and the Zapata Peninsula. Dozens of people hitch rides at this major crossroads. The Autopista continues east, skirting northern Cienfuegos province en route to Santa Clara province. There's a Cupet gas station is in Jagüey Grande. Alternately you can follow the slower Carretera Central through a string of dusty old towns.

SAN MIGUEL DE LOS BAÑOS

San Miguel de los Baños is a little spa town hidden deep amid rolling hills. It's reached via a turnoff from the Carretera Central (route 3-N-1) at Coliseo, 37 km east of Matanzas, at the junction with route 3-101 to Cárdenas. The town's lofty setting makes it cool and airy. This, combined with the healing properties of its mineral waters, fostered the town's growth last century as a popular health spa. The gentry built villas here in neoclassical style, others erected homes with a distinctly French provincial feel, with filigreed balconies and gingerbread woodwork. Though some houses are tumbledown, the town is in reasonably good condition. Bougainvillea abounds, and sunflowers are popular garden adornments.

As you enter town, you'll pass the ornate **Balneario San Miguel** on your left, topped by Islamic-style turrets. Sadly, it's in slightly derelict condition (Cubanacán has plans to restore the *balneario*). A *custodio* and Islamic tiles. The marble-topped bar downstairs still functions, but water is no longer for sale—having been replaced by rum.

Pathways lead down the garden to outdoor *baños,* now disused. In the center is the grand baths, resembling Roman or Turkish baths, with flint stones inset in the walls in a crude mosaic. Sulfurous-smelling water still runs into a small sink at which locals fill their pails.

There's one hotel in town, the **Rincón del Baño,** terribly run-down but with great potential for restoration. Downstairs, the columned restaurant retains its stuccowork. It serves *criollo* food for pesos, but the hygiene is questionable.

JOVELLANOS TO COLÓN

The Carretera Central continues east past great fields of cane silvered by the fierce wind. Sixteen km east of Coliseo, you reach the small agricultural town of Jovellanos. The town, which has a predominantly black population, is known

San Miguel de Los Baños

as a center of Afro-Cuban music and dance, influenced by the Arara tribe from Benin, who arrived in the late 18th century via Haiti. Jovellanos has a small museum dealing with local affairs, plus a couple of basic restaurants and the equally basic **Hotel Moderno,** Calle 11, e/ Aves. 16 y 18, tel. (5) 82837, rooms (some with a/c) for seven pesos s, 8.40 pesos d.

There's a **Cupet gas station** on the Carretera Central at the east end of town, with a dollars-only café. Bus no. 346 departs Havana's main bus terminal for Jovellanos at 2:10 p.m. (3.5 hours; 7 pesos).

South of Jovellanos, the 3-182 cuts southwest to **Pedro Betancourt,** a pleasant colonial town with a beautiful church at its core. Pedro Betancourt is the gateway to mile upon mile of citrus groves crisscrossed by ruler-straight roads and extending all the way south to the Autopista.

Colón

Colón, 33 km east of Jovellanos, is worth a quick browse. Its colonnaded streets are lined with tumbledown neoclassical structures, generating a sense that you've fallen into some sleepy 19th-century provincial setting.

Sightseeing: Colón is centered on **Parque de Liberated,** two blocks south of the main street, Máximo Gómez. The park is fronted by some attractive buildings and surrounded by shade trees and a wide promenade. At its heart is a life-size, patinated bronze statue of the town's namesake, Christopher Columbus (Cristóbal Colón), atop a pedestal with a lion at each diagonal.

Accommodations and Food: There are two options where you can lay your head, the **Hotel Gran Caridad** and the **Hotel Santiago Cuba.** Both are on Máximo Gómez and offer rooms with private bathrooms (cold water only) for about 15 pesos. Pickings are slim for the famished. **Restaurante Luzenye,** 50 yards southwest of the plaza, serves salads for one peso, pork steaks (15 pesos), snacks, and beer (US$1).

Getting There and Away: Colón lies on the main railway line from Havana to Santiago and is well served by trains. Local service runs between Colón and Cárdenas and Santa Clara. Buses also link Colón with Cárdenas, Jovellanos, and Matanzas (two hours; five pesos) several times daily, departing the bus terminal on Máximo Gómez.

There's a **Cupet gas station** on Gómez, one block west of Martí, and another outside town on the road (route 3-1-2) that leads south to Caliemete and the Autopista.

JAGÜEY GRANDE AND VICINITY

Jagüey Grande, is one km north of an important crossroads on the Autopista at Km 142. This agricultural town and railhead is encircled to the northwest by a vast citrus complex and to the northeast by sugarcane fields. Check out the **Centro de Desarrollo de Artes Plasticos,** where you can view works of art in the making.

Farther east along the Autopista, Route 3-1-2 links **Aguada del Pasajeros** with **Colón,** on the Carretera Central via Calimete. It's a 22 km bee-line past sugarcane and banana plantations shaded by thick stands of palms. The land is as flat as a billiard table. Agriculture is mechanized hereabouts, with few oxen in evidence. Tractors spread the red earth through the streets of **Calimete,** which has a 600-meter-long promenade lined by shade trees and lit at night by lanterns. Calimete is a neat country town.

Warning: five miles east of Jagüey Grande, an ungated railway track crosses the freeway. *Slow down!* You can be upon it before you know it if you're not alert.

Finca Fiesta Campesina

This contrived "peasant's farm," tel. (59) 3224, is an appealing tourist stop about 400 yards south of the junction at Km 142. Open 24 hours, the place offers cockfights and a small zoo inhabited by deer, agoutis, snakes, crocodiles, and birds. You can sample fruits, excellent Cuban coffee (served in earthenware cups), and *guarapo* (sugarcane juice) crushed in a traditional trapiche. There's also a cigar shop and souvenir shop, and a thatched restaurant serving *criollo* cuisine that includes *ajiaco,* a tasty *campesino* stew. There's no entrance fee. Horseback rides cost US$1 and you can even ride a bull!

Central Australia

One km south of the Km 142 on the Autopista, on the road to Playa Girón, a huge sugar factory—**Central Australia**—looms over the sugarcane fields. At a Y-fork, the road to the right leads to

Playa Girón, the one to the left leads to the sugar factory and museum (there are no signs). You see the factory first, then hear the distant tooting of whistles and clanking of engines and carriages, which goes on around the clock during the *zafra* (cane harvest). The *central* is home to an Alco-built Model 1515 steam train dating to 1914—one of the last working 4-6-0s in Cuba. During the *zafra* (sugar harvest) you can see it crossing the Autopista on an ungated crossing (the crossing-keeper stops traffic with a red flag).

Here on the afternoon of 15 April 1961, Fidel Castro set up his military headquarters during the Bay of Pigs invasion. Castro, who knew that the sugar factory had the only telephone for miles around, directed his troops from the *central* before dashing off to lead *"un barraje infernal"* (an infernal barrage) of howitzers against the invaders attempting to break out of Playa Larga. Remains of aircraft shot up in the fighting lie outside the administrative building, which is now a small **museum** open Mon.-Sat. 8 a.m.-5 p.m. and Sunday 8 a.m.-1 p.m.; entrance costs US$1.

Accommodations

In Jagüey Grande, there's a *casa particular* at Calle 15A #7211, e/ 72 y 74, with two small, dingy a/c rooms that share a clean and pleasing bathroom with hot water for US$20. The **Hotel 9 de Mayo,** Calle 13, e/ Calle 56 y 58, tel. (59) 2118, is a basic, modestly furnished pesos-only hotel in a colonial building. Rooms vary but are acceptable (12.05 pesos s, 12.56 pesos d).

The best place for miles around is **Motel Batey Don Pedro,** tel. (59) 2535, formerly Bohio de Don Pedro, which until recently was a traditional peasant house—*bohio*—and is named for Don Pedro, an amiable *campesino* who worked the small *finca* until his death in 1998. Shade trees enhance the splendid aesthetic. It has lost some of its enormous appeal since Don Pedro passed away, but retains a country calm. The pigs and horses are no longer a major presence, though chickens still bustle about the lawns. There are 10 rustic yet exquisite, roomy, thatched, all-log *bohio*-style cottages featuring terra-cotta tile floors, large bathrooms, TVs, ceiling fans, and small kitchenettes. Each has a veranda from where you can watch the chickens, horses, and other farm animals feasting and fornicating. Some cabins have loft bedrooms and sleep four people. A swimming pool and additional cabins are planned. Tasty and filling *criollo* meals are served in a thatched restaurant, but when there are few guests, Don Pedro's wife Hildelias might cook for you in her rustic but charming *bohio*. Rates were US$28 s, US$38 d. Reservations can be made through Rumbos offices islandwide.

Food

There's an atmospheric restaurant and bar, **Pío Cua,** about two km south of Australia, made of hardwoods with soaring thatched roof and stained-glass windows. *Criollo* dishes cost about US$5. The restaurant is open noon-11:45 p.m., the bar and café 8 a.m.-11 p.m.

In Jagüey Grande, the eateries of choice are the **El Chino Restaurant,** facing the south side of the plaza, and **Paladar La Roca,** at Calle 11 #5013 (four blocks north of Jagüey Grande). There's a farmers' market on Calle 15, e/ Calles 54 y 56.

Bar El Bosque, just before the entrance to the sugar mill, is a spit-and-sawdust place where you may sip *aguardente* with the field- and factory-hands.

Services

Rumbos has a **tourist information center** and snack bar on the Autopista at Km 142. You can buy a map of the Zapata area here (US$1), and arrange guides and excursions. It has a boat outside.

A **Cupet gas station** is at the junction of Calles 13 and 70, at the south end of Jagüey Grande on the one-way road that leads south to the Autopista.

THE ZAPATA PENINSULA AND BAY OF PIGS

South of Australia, the sugarcane fields and dark-soiled miles of agro-industry abruptly end and the sawgrass, reed, and *marabú* brush begins, swaying like wheat in the wind. This swampland (the **Cienega de Zapata**) sweeps south to the Caribbean Sea, smothering the Zapata Peninsula, a great shoe-shaped extension jutting west into the Golfo de Batabanó. The 4,230-square-km landmass is a region of limestone with flooded faults called *cenotes*. It is now a national park and wildlife reserve.

Zapata extends west of a deep, finger-like bay, the Bahía de Cochinos—**Bay of Pigs.** Zapata is considered a sensitive region for more than ecological reasons, and the Cuban government keeps a tight rein on foreign visitation to the swamps.

Route 3-1-18 runs like a plumb line from Australia to Playa Larga, a small fishing village tucked into the head of Bahía de Cochinos. The road branches west for Zapata and east for Playa Girón.

History

The region was inhabited by pre-Columbian Indians. The Spanish conquistadores managed to destroy the local Taíno Indian population before abandoning the region. It has remained a virtual no-man's-land ever since. Talk of draining the swamps was heard as early as 1854, but nothing was done until 1912, when the American-owned Zapata Land Company was formed. The survey report found the swamps as inaccessible "as Stanley's Tenebrosa Africa. . . a place of fogs and death where alligators are absolute masters." Eventually the company ran out of money. The sparse population (about 8,000 souls inhabited the area on the eve of the Revolution) remained cut off from the rest of Cuba in conditions similar to those reported by Columbus when he landed in the Bahía de Cochinos in June 1494. Columbus reported seeing naked Indians carrying "in their hand a burning coal, and certain weeds for inhaling their smoke." The burning coal was charcoal.

Before the Revolution (the *cenagueros*—swamp people—refer to the Revolution as a milestone, as if it separated B.C. from A.D.), there had been no roads, no schools, no electricity. Charcoal-making was the major occupation of the impoverished population (charcoal is prized as a fuel for cooking). The austere, hardworking *carboneros* axed *marabú* and mangrove branches to a length of two feet, then stacked them against a tepee-shaped *horno de carbón,* a charcoal oven made of straw and earth, hollow at the center. The branches were covered in grass and ash and left to burn slowly for a week or so. The wood smoldered and, at the critical moment, was drowned with water. The *carboneros,* forever blackened by soot, staggered to Cienfuegos with sacks on their backs where, reportedly, one day's labor might sell for as little as US$0.02.

The *cenagueros* were among the first beneficiaries of the Revolution. The youthful Castro government built highways of hard-packed limestone into the swamps. It also established schools, and more than 200 teachers from the national literacy campaign arrived. The indigent community of Cayo Ramón even got a hospital. Tourist bungalows went up at Girón. And an airport with a 4,100-foot runway was built. Today *carboneros* still build their pungent ovens, but their charcoal now goes to town on trucks.

ESTACIÓNES DE REPRODUCCIÓN DE FAUNA SILVESTRE Y ICTOFAUNA

These two farms are study and breeding centers for local wildlife. The first, set off the road about four km south of Australia, raises jutias and other mammal species. The second, on the right, about eight km south of Australia, breeds indigenous ichthyofauna (known as fish to you and me), including the endangered *manjuarí* (garfish), looking like a cross between a fish and a crocodile and tracing its ancestry back to the antediluvian dawn. Visitors are welcome.

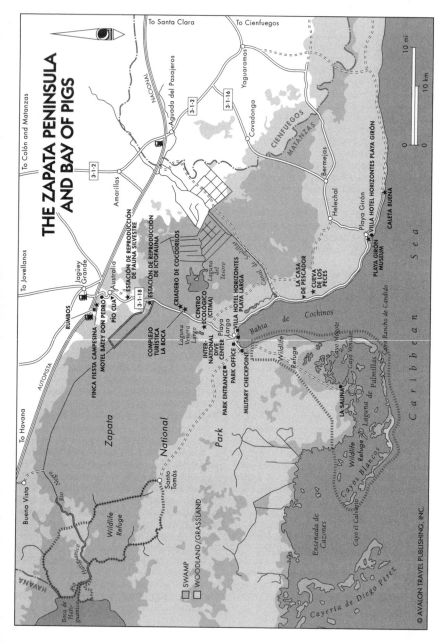

THE ZAPATA PENINSULA AND BAY OF PIGS

© AVALON TRAVEL PUBLISHING, INC.

LA BOCA DE GUAMA

La Boca, tel. (59) 2458, 16 km south of Australia, is an important roadside stop of thatched *bohios* with numerous attractions and services, including an atmospheric bar and equally attractive restaurant; a well-stocked souvenir shop that sells film as well as a wide range of crafts; a crocodile farm; and the **Guamá Ceramics Workshop,** where you can watch bowls, masks, teapots, and kitchenware being made in Arawak style before being baked in huge brick kilns (*ornos*).

A five-km-long canal leads from here to the Villa Guamá resort, in the middle of the Laguna de Tesoro. Rowboats can be hired during the day (US$2 per hour).

Crocodile Farm

The *criadero de cocodrilos* is Cuba's most important crocodile farm, with more than 10,000 crocodiles. Pathways lead past souvenir stalls and little bars to the large, circular pens surrounding natural lagoons where crocodiles laze in the sun. Raised wooden platforms provide vantage points to admire the awesome beasts lying still as death, jaws agape, hoping obviously for a careless visitor to stumble and fall into a pit. You can also see a "demonstration of crocodile capture" involving a docile two-meter-long youngster. Entrance costs US$3.

Food and Services

The atmospheric thatched **La Boca Restaurant** overlooks a lagoon full of water hyacinths. It serves *criollo* meals, including roast crocodile tail (US$7), a legendary aphrodisiac. It's open noon-4:30 p.m. The modestly elegant, a/c **Colibri Restaurant** also serves *criollo* fare, including lobster for US$11, plus pizza (US$4). You can dine inside or on a patio.

There's a gas station and several souvenir stores.

LAGUNA DEL TESORO

Laguna del Tesoro (Treasure Lagoon) is a 16-square-km lake stocked with whopping large-mouth bass, plus trout, haddock, carp, native biajacas, tarpon, tilapia, and meter-long *manjuarí*, an antediluvian fish with a crocodilian head. The lake is named for the priceless religious objects that the Taíno Indians supposedly threw into the water to hide them from the Spanish conquistadores. No gold has ever been recovered, but Indian artifacts have been raised from the lake and are now exhibited in the **Museo Guamá,** on an island in the middle of the lake.

The lake was one of Castro's favorite fishing spots. The Cuban leader spent many weekends in a bungalow that became known as "Fidel's Key." One day, lounging on his bed, he supposedly announced, "We're going to build a Tahitian village here!" And they did. The revolutionary government dredged a canal network and created a series of islands featuring a replica Taíno village, **Villa Guamá.** The 13 tiny islands are connected by hanging bridges and landscaped with hedgerows of fiery bottlebrush. One of the isles contains a mock Indian village and 32 life-size sculptures by Cuban sculptor Rita Longa, depicting Taíno Indians engaged in daily activities.

You can ascend the staircase in the restaurant and emerge atop a *mirador* to survey the scene. Tours of the lake are offered aboard a cruise boat—*Guamatur-2*—from Villa Guamá and La Boca. And three-hour fishing trips are offered.

Accommodations and Food

Villa Guamá, Laguna del Tesoro, Ciénaga de Zapata, Matanzas, tel. (59) 5551, has 59 adequate yet primitive thatched-roof octagonal *bohios* with private baths, telephones, a/c, and TVs. Most are built on stilts above the water, and each has a private boat mooring. Castro used to stay in hut #33. There's a restaurant whose specialty is grilled crocodile, a bar, *cafetería,* nightclub, and the usual tourism bureau. The tranquility is destroyed by excessively loud piped music by day and the disco by night. And if you forget your mosquito repellent, your stay may be misery. Rates were US$30 s, US$40 d, US$52 t, US$60 quad, low season; US$36 s, US$47 d, US$61 t, US$75 quad high season. Visitors can have lunch at the restaurant. Try the grilled crocodile, which has the texture and taste of chicken (US$6). Breakfasts are dismal.

Getting There

The facility is reached by an open-air tour boat that leaves La Boca for Villa Guamá at 10 a.m. and noon (US$10 per person). Speedboats are also available (US$10 per person).

Most Cuban tour companies in Havana and Varadero include a visit to Laguna del Tesoro in their packages to Playa Girón.

BAHÍA DE COCHINOS (BAY OF PIGS)

The fingerlike bay is 20 km long, with an average width of seven km. It is named for the local *cochinos cimarrones,* wild pigs, which once formed a staple diet for local Indians.

The name is known to every U.S. citizen for the Bay of Pigs invasion, when about 1,300 heavily armed, CIA-trained Cuban exiles came ashore fully equipped to establish a beachhead and provoke a counterrevolution to topple the Castro regime.

At its head is **Playa Larga,** which was one of the two main landing sites during the Bay of Pigs fiasco. A tourist haven has been salvaged from the bile. The village comprises a few fisherman's huts, military buildings, the International Bird-Watching Center, and a hotel facing a small cream-colored beach that stretches for half a mile. Shallow water provides for wading. The rectangular bay is shaped like a great swimming pool and has clear blue waters as warm and calm as bedtime milk. However, it's not as attractive as Playa Girón, and local lads often pester tourists with sales pitches for guides and other services.

A road leads west from Playa Larga two km to the ramshackle hamlet of **Buena Ventura.** There's a guard post here, at the entrance to the Zapata National Park. No one can proceed farther without a guide. Just beyond the guard post, a rough dirt road leads south to Laguna de las Salinas, and another leads west, to Santo Tomás and Maneadero (51 km). Aggressive mosquitoes replay the bombing runs by CIA B-26s. Take repellent!

The **International Dive Center,** tel. (59) 7294, at the Villas Horizontes Playa Larga, offers scuba diving daily at 10 a.m. and 2 p.m. (US$25 including equipment).

Accommodations and Food

The recently renovated **Villa Horizontes Playa Larga,** Playa Larga, Ciénega de Zapata, Matanzas, tel. (59) 7294, has 57 spacious, albeit modestly furnished, a/c rooms in *cabinas,* each with private bath, radio, small beds, tiny TV, and basic kitchenette. The cabins are widely spaced amid lawns and bougainvillea. There's a restaurant, bar, *cafetería,* and nightclub, beach volleyball, and water sports. It rents bicycles, scooters, and cars. Rates were US$30 s, US$38 d in low season, US$35 s, US$46 d in high season.

Casa Baby is a *casa particular* 100 meters west of the turn off for Zapata National Park. Alternately, try **Villa Nivaldo,** a quiet, nicely furnished home on the beach and also operated as a *paladar* specializing in crocodile dishes.

Getting There

Víazul operates tourist bus service to Playa Girón from Havana, stopping at Playa Larga (see the Víazul Bus Schedule chart, in the On the Road chapter). For public bus service, see the Public Bus Service From Havana chart, also in the On the Road chapter. Bus no. 818 operates local service between Playa Larga and Playa Girón.

ZAPATA NATIONAL PARK

Zapata, Cuba's most important wetland area, is enshrined as a national park. As yet, it is little utilized by ecotourists, though a handful of birders and fisher folk are savvy to its allure. Only two roads lead into the park, and they are patrolled to ensure no unauthorized access—even to locals.

The diverse and complex ecosystems include marsh grass, mangrove thickets, and thickly wooded swamp forest of dense *marabú* bushes, with their inch-long thorns. It is a biological mirror of the Everglades of Florida (there are even beautifully banded *liguus* snails, a kind of tree snail common in the Florida Everglades). And vegetation includes the button tree, so small that it looks like a bonsai.

Zapata harbors more than 900 species of flora (including poisonous *guao* plants), 171 species of birds, 31 of reptiles, and 12 of mammals, including the pygmy *jutía* native to the Zapata swamp. The Río Hatiguanico harbors Cuba's largest population of manatees. There are freshwater turtles, many of which end up as fricassee, a popular dish among the marsh people. Iguanas will come up to you, totally fearless. And the alligator gar *(manjuarí),* the most primitive of Cuban fish, is found in lagoons such as Laguna del Tesoro, as are crocodiles and caimans, a diminutive species of alligator. Crocodiles had been hunted to near-extinction during the past several centuries. Castro ordered them rounded up for breeding, saying, "When we have millions of them, we'll have an industry."

Birds

Of Cuba's 22 endemic bird species, 18 inhabit the marshes. Zapata protects the bee hummingbird (the world's smallest bird) as well as an endemic tanager and *gallinuela de Santo Tomás,* the Zapata sparrow, Zapata rail, and Zapata wren, all of which are limited to Santo Tomás lagoon. Cuba's national bird, the Cuban trogon or *tocororo,* is also found here, as is the long-tailed sparrow hawk, plus cormorants and a significant population of Cuban parrots.

Zapata is also a favorite stop for tens of thousands of migratory birds. The best time is October to April, when overwhelming numbers of birds flock in—sandhill cranes, great blue herons, tricolored herons, wood ibis (the only species of this family to be found in the Caribbean), and bitterns amid the muddy, pool-studded grasslands. Even flamingoes wade in the soupy lagoons.

The best spots for birding are La Salina and also around **Santo Tomás,** about 30 km west of Playa Larga (US$10 per person by boat), but there is splendid birding, too, just west of Playa Girón, where spoonbills, flamingoes, and ibis are easily seen by following trails of landfill (a guide is compulsory). The areas around Soplillar and Bermejes are splendid for upland birding, including the tocororo.

The two licensed guides, Orestes (El Chino) and Ángel Martínez, are said to be extremely knowledgeable and expert at guiding.

Fishing

Zapata has been isolated from fishing pressure since 1959, making this huge reserve as close to a virgin fishery as one can find in today's world. There are said to be places where you can catch the fish with your bare hands, the way the indigenous Indians did. Tarpon and bonefish are the species of choice. Bonefishing is most productive late fall through June; tarpon fishing peaks late February/early March through June.

There are two distinct areas for fishing—Laguna de las Salinas, and the 200-meter-wide Río Hatiguanico and its tributaries. **Laguna de las Salinas** is a vast expanse of flats, watercourses, and islets on the southern shores of Zapata, at the western entrance to Bahía de Cochinos. The dirt road is often flooded in places (then, you really get to see the crocodiles). Laguna de las Salinas is famous for bonefish. Several well-traveled anglers consider Las Salinas the standard by which all other locations should be judged worldwide. Being shallow and firm-bottomed, it is ideal for wading and spotting bonefish. Other species include *palometa* (also called permit), which can reach 20 pounds. Tarpon ("silver bullets") up to 40 pounds—ideal light-tackle adversaries—cruise the clear lagoons of the outer cays and will fight over a well-cast fly or plug as anglers drift the lagoons, sight

---

CRABS!

*Z*apata's roads receive little traffic, except for swarms of *cangrejos* (crabs) scurrying across in springtime. Mid-March through April, giant land crabs emerge from the vegetation and swarm, legion upon legion, to meeting grounds where they gather for vast orgies and egg-laying parties. They move in such numbers that the main coast road (and those along much of the southern and eastern coasts of Cuba) becomes a veritable carpet of crushed crabs—and the fetid smell draws vultures to feast on the banquet.

In *Driving through Cuba,* Carlo Gébler tells of driving around a corner and "suddenly the road ahead as far as we could see was strewn with the remains of crabs crushed flat onto the tarmac, thousands of them, a carpet of them, with hundreds of live ones crawling on top of the dead. . . . Through the open windows we heard the clacking of their claws on the tarmac as they ran across our path. Then came a noise like a Mib Mac styrofoam container exploding, and with horror we realised this was our first casualty. . . . From under the tyres came an almost continuous sound of their bodies exploding."

casting as the fish emerge from the mangroves or roll on the surface like trout in a stream in the midst of a heavy hatch.

The **Río Hatiguanico** and its mangrove-lined shores are also famous for tarpon. The river contains snook, too. Underpowered skiffs mean long periods getting to the best lagoons, but. . . wow! "My nerves were frazzled," recalls Gilberto Maxell, in *The Pan-Angler.* "Every cast was a strike, or so it seems, sometimes several tarpon hit the fly on the same retrieve."

A Swede called Erland von Sneidern ("Big Swede") has been issued an exclusive right to operate fishing trips in Zapata. **Rumbos S.A.,** locally at Central Australia #1, Jagüey Grande, tel. (59) 2535, fax (52) 5-3125, also offers hunting and fishing excursions for groups of up to five people. Per-person prices vary according to number of anglers: three days costs US$1,275 (eight people) to US$1,500 (two people) per person; six days costs US$2,250 to US$2,700 per person.

Centro Ecológica

This visitor's ecological center, five km south of La Boca, is run by the Ministerio de Ciencias Tecnológica y Mediomabiente (CITMA) and features a small but interesting museum and exhibition on the region, including a model map with illuminated highlights, such as archaeological sites. A live garfish *(manijuari)* swims in a fish tank. Leaf-cutter ants go about their business farming fungi in a glass case, and a separate exhibit details the Indian heritage locally. It's open daily 8 a.m.-4:30 p.m. Entrance costs US$3.

Permits and Guides

The entrance to the Zapata reserve is at Buena Ventura, two km west of Playa Larga, 32 km south of Australia. Access is by permit only, obtained from the **Oficina Parque Nacional** in Playa Larga, tel. (59) 7249. A permit costs US$10 per person, including an obligatory guide (you should tip the guide). You can also hire a guide and arrange nature hikes, jeep trips, birding, and crocodile tours through Rumbos at the visitors information center on the Autopista at Km 142, or at the Rumbos headquarters at Central Australia #1, Jagüey Grande, tel. (59) 2535, fax (52) 53125 (the official fee is US$53 for one person, less

per person for two or more people, but if you can find a guide yourself you can negotiate a much cheaper rate and directly—in secret, of course—and the guide will get to keep the money).

PLAYA LARGA TO PLAYA GIRÓN

East of Playa Larga, the coast road hugs the Bay of Pigs. Solemn concrete monuments rise from the bush, each one standing at the site where a Cuban soldier (161 in all) fell defending his republic during the three-day battle in April 1961.

There are views of white beaches extending around the bay, which here is prized by pelicans. At **Caleta del Rosarío,** about three km from Playa Larga, is a splendid little cove with a small beach and good swimming. It's popular with Cubans and has small cabins for rent, plus a café.

The route is also lined with *cenotes,* limestone sinkholes. Columbus discovered them and recorded that they contained subterranean streams with waters "so cold, and of such goodness and so sweet that no better could be found in the world." About eight km east of Playa Larga is **La Casa de Pescador,** a beautiful little ranchita restaurant overlooking a 20-meter-deep limestone sinkhole—**El Cenote**—filled with cool, pavonine waters. The place is exquisite. The grounds are landscaped, with hammocks slung between palms.

A short distance farther brings you to **Cueva de los Peces.** This is one of the largest *cenotes,* 15 km from Playa Larga. The huge cave, 70 meters deep and formed by a flooded fault, is a superb spot for scuba diving, with labyrinthine halls teeming with fish. It, too, has a bar and restaurant. Entrance costs US$1.

Rumbos has a beachside bar and restaurant—**La Casa del Mar**—in the shape of a ship about two km west of Playa Girón.

PLAYA GIRÓN

Finally you arrive at the spot where socialism and capitalism slugged it out. And what do you find? Vacationers from cool climates, lathered with suntan oil, splashing in the shallows where,

BAY OF PIGS

The Bay of Pigs invasion—Cubans call it the Battle of Girón or La Victoria (the victory)—was the brainchild of Richard Bissell, Deputy Director of the CIA. The plan was to infiltrate anti-Castro guerrillas onto the island so that they could link up with domestic opponents. The "Program of Covert Action Against the Castro Regime" called for creation of a Cuban government in exile, covert action in Cuba, and "a paramilitary force outside of Cuba for future guerrilla action." In August 1958 President Eisenhower approved a US$13 million budget with the proviso that "no U.S. military personnel were to be used in a combat status."

Under a flexible mandate, Bissell radically expanded the original concept. The CIA borrowed officers from the armed services and created an air force that eventually numbered 80 U.S. pilots. By the time President Kennedy was briefed, in November 1960, the plan had grown to include 1,500 men backed by a rebel air force of war-surplus B-26s and escorted by a U.S. naval task force. Bissell didn't tell the president the true scale of the planned invasion. The top brass were left in the dark about the CIA's expansion into the navy and amphibious-warfare business.

The U.S. Prepares to Invade

The CIA recruited Cuban exiles for the invasion force and used an abandoned naval base at Opa-Locka, outside Miami, to train the brigade. They were later moved to U.S. military locations in Guatemala (replete with brothels to keep the *brigadistas* on camp) and Puerto Rico (in violation of U.S. law). Meanwhile, a "government in exile" was chosen from within the *Frente,* a loose, feud-riven group of political exiles, many of them corrupt right-wing politicians nostalgic for Batista days. The group would be transformed into a provisional government once it had gained a military foothold in Cuba. Planes and ships circled Cuba, dropping off packages of small arms, ammunition, and demolition equipment to counterrevolutionaries in Cuba.

On 28 January 1960, Kennedy ordered the Joint Chief of Staffs to review the plans. The so-called "Trinidad Plan" called for an airborne assault and amphibious landing at Trinidad. Here the invasion force could link up with guerrillas operating out of the nearby Escambray Mountains. The chiefs concluded it had a 30% chance of success and "that ultimate success will depend upon. . . a sizable popular uprising or substantial follow-up forces." Kennedy rejected it as "too much like a World War II invasion."

Thus, Kennedy approved the second plan, for an invasion of the Bay of Pigs, more than 100 km west of the Escambray Mountains, where the brigade would land at three beaches 25 km apart and surrounded by swamps. The CIA assured Kennedy that the brigade could "melt" into the mountains. Moreover, "A great percentage of the [army] officers are believed ready to rebel against the government at a given moment, taking their troops with them," Bissell told Kennedy in an appallingly incorrect assessment.

In photos of Playa Girón taken by U-2 spy planes, the CIA's photo interpreter identified what he claimed was seaweed offshore. "They are coral heads," said Dr. Juan Sordo, a brigade member: "I know them. I have seen them." Another brigade member agreed. The water would be too shallow for the landing craft, he said. But the CIA wouldn't listen.

Nor did the CIA know that Castro knew the area intimately. In November 1960, Castro had inspected Girón, site of one of his pet projects: a new community that included a motel and recreation center. At one point he turned to a Cuban journalist and said, "You know, this is a great place for a landing. . . . We should place a .50-caliber heavy machine gun here, just in case." Two weeks later, that machine gun fired the first shots against the invaders.

Cuba Prepares to Defend

Castro knew an invasion was imminent. Cuban police began to round up people suspected of counterrevolutionary activities. Four days before the invasion began, Castro ordered a battalion moved to the Bay of Pigs (the order took too long to process, and the battalion never arrived).

The invasion plan relied on eliminating the Cuban air force. The CIA wanted U.S. air support; the State Department wanted it kept to a minimum so that the planes could later be claimed to have originated in Cuba (U.S. involvement was supposed to be deniable). On 15 April, two days before the invasion, B-26 bombers painted in Cuban air force colors struck Cuba's three military air bases.

So Castro was fully forewarned. Worse, only five aircraft were destroyed, and Cuba still had at least three T-33-jet fighters and four British-made Sea

continues on next page

BAY OF PIGS
(continued)

Fury light-attack bombers. Castro turned the funeral for the seven persons killed into a stirring call for revolutionary defiance: "What the imperialists cannot forgive us for. . . is that we have made a socialist revolution under the nose of the United States." It was his first public characterization of the Revolution as socialist. The debacle thus created the conditions by which socialism became acceptable to a nation on the brink of invasion during a period when Cubans felt about *la revolución* the way U.S. citizens would feel about the Declaration of Independence if it had been signed within recent memory.

The Invasion

The U.S. Navy aircraft carrier *Essex* and five destroyers were to escort six freighters carrying the Cuban fighters and their supplies. They moved in radio silence.

The landings began about 1:15 a.m. on 17 April at Playa Girón and Playa Larga. Landing craft (LCVPs) came roaring in. About 140 meters offshore, they hit the coral reefs the CIA had dismissed as seaweed. The brigade had to wade ashore. Meanwhile, the fiberglass boats used by the Second and Fifth Battalions capsized. The Cubans had installed tall, extremely bright lights right on the beach. "It looked like Coney Island," recalls Gray Lynch, the CIA point man who ended up directing the invasion. The

brigade has also been told that "no communications existed within 20 miles of the beach." In fact, there was a radio station only 100 meters inland. By the time the brigade stormed it, Castro had been alerted.

Kennedy had approved taking the Cubans to the beaches; beyond that, they were on their own. Worried about repercussions at the U.N., Kennedy ordered cancellation of a second strike designed to give the invasion force cover. With that decision, the operation was lost.

Castro set up headquarters in the Central Australia sugar mill and from there directed the Cuban defense. Castro, who displayed a remarkable control of events over the three days by telephone and handwritten messages, correctly guessed the enemy's plans.

He knew it was vital to deprive the invaders of their support ships before they could unload. As the exiles landed, Cuba's aircraft swooped down. Two supply ships containing ammunition and communications equipment, the *Houston* and *Río Escondido,* were sunk. Two other ammunition vessels (the *Atlántico* and *Caribe*) fled and had to be turned back by the USS *Eaton.* (The CIA had refused to outfit the ships with antiaircraft guns because it assumed no Cuban aircraft would survive the B-26 bombings.)

The brigade did, however, manage to unload World War II-era Sherman tanks. They fought the

30-odd years before, blood and bullets mingled with the sand on the surf. With the sun beating down on this idyllic spot, it is difficult to imagine the carnage and futility. You are welcomed by a huge billboard that reads, *"Playa Girón—The First Rout Of Imperialism In Latin America."*

Playa Girón is a small *pueblo* of a few hundred people. It was named in honor of Gilbert Girón, a French pirate captured here by a Spanish captain, who sliced off the corsair's head and pickled it so as to claim a reward.

The community lies inland of the tourist facility and beach, which has been off-limits to Cubans since 1998. The beautiful white sand beach is enclosed within a concrete barrier *(rompeola),* which protects against any future wave of CIA-backed anti-Castroites foolish enough to come ashore. Nonetheless, it's a carbuncle on the coast and made worse by the mil-

itary watchtower to the east end where soldiers with high-powered binoculars have nothing better to do these days than focus in on the topless bathers.

Playa Girón Museum

This superb museum gives an accurate portrayal of the drama of the revolutionary era. Black-and-white photographs confirm the appalling poverty of the local peasantry before the Revolution. Others profile the events preceding the invasion: the Agrarian Reform Law, the literacy campaign, and sabotage and other counterrevolutionary activity culminating in the act to which the museum is dedicated—the invasion of 15 April 1961 by 1,297 CIA-trained Cubans.

The whole story of the invasion—*la victoria*—is shown on maps that trace the evolution of the 72-hour battle. There are photographs, including

"battle of the rotunda" against Cuba's equally outdated Stalin tanks.

Despite the CIA's predictions, the local people ("armed only with M-52 Czech rifles," writes Peter Wyden in *Bay of Pigs*) defended their homeland until the first Cuban battalion of 900 student soldiers arrived in buses (half the cadet troops were killed when the convoy was strafed by the brigade's B-26s). Reinforcements poured in and encircled the invasion forces, and the fight became a simple matter of whittling away at the exiles.

A U.S. jet-fighter squadron flew reconnaissance over the invasion but was forbidden to engage in combat. As the situation deteriorated, Kennedy came under increasing pressure to order U.S. air strikes. He refused. By Tuesday, many of the *brigadista* pilots were "begging off" flying combat sorties. Hence, the CIA authorized its own U.S. pilots to fly combat missions. In the final hours of the battle, six U.S. pilots flew missions without President Kennedy's knowledge. Four were shot down and killed. The Cubans recovered the body of one of the pilots—Thomas Ray—and found his dog tags (his corpse remained in a Havana morgue unclaimed by the U.S. government; Ray's daughter brought his body home for burial in 1979).

Abandoning the *Brigadistas*

"The military," writes Wyden, "assumed the President would order U.S. intervention. The President assumed they knew he would refuse to escalate the miniature war." Instead, he ordered the Navy to remove the brigade from the beaches. The U.S. destroyers advanced on the shore. Castro instinctively knew they were sailing in for an evacuation and ordered Cuban artillery not to fire. If the Cubans had fired on the destroyers and the vessels had claimed that they were merely patrolling in international waters, there could have been "transcendent consequences." (The Soviet Union had guaranteed to come to Cuba's military aid in the event she was attacked.)

The destroyers picked up those *brigadistas* who had made it back to sea, then sailed away, leaving the survivors to fend for themselves. The brigade had lost 114 men (the Cubans lost 161), but a further 1,189 were captured. Eventually, 1,091 prisoners were returned to the United States in exchange for US$53 million in food and medical supplies.

"You didn't get any help from us," Kennedy remarked to Eduardo Ferrer, one of the brigade pilots at a ceremony at Miami's Orange Bowl, where each brigade member received US$300 in cash. "No, Mr. President, but I expect it the next time," Ferrer replied. "You better believe that there's going to be a next time," the president told him. A month later, brigade members received mimeographed letters advising that no further "compensation" would be paid. The U.S. government had washed its hands of the Cuban brigade, leaving the exile community feeling doubly betrayed.

---

gory pictures of civilians caught in the midst of explosions, and of all the martyrs—the "Heroes de Girón"—killed in the fighting (the youngest, Nelson Fernandez Estevez, was only 16 years old; the oldest, Juan Ruíz Serna, was 60). Note the photo of a young militiaman, Eduardo García Delgado, who wrote "Fidel" on a wall with his own blood before dying, facedown, with his hand on the L. And, of course, Fidel is there, leaping from his T-34 tank. A frieze in the museum portrays the invaders as rich reactionaries bent on seizing back what the poor had gained. Other displays include weapons, and a Sea Fury fighter-aircraft, complete with rockets, which sits on the forecourt outside.

There are guides on hand to give you a blow-by-blow account. It's open daily 9 a.m.-noon and 1-5 p.m. Entrance costs US$2. And you're charged US$1 per photo!

Scuba Diving

The waters off Playa Girón are noted for excellent diving, with abrupt ocean walls close to shore. There are many underwater caves. And gorgonians, sponges, and corals are abundant. **Playa Girón Scuba Diving Center** is located in the Villa Horizontes hotel. Initiation dives cost US$10. Single dives cost U$25, two dives US$42.

Accommodations

Villa Horizontes Playa Girón, tel. (59) 4110, is like a miniature Butlin's holiday camp of the 1960s. The hotel, which is popular with budget-minded Germans, has an attractive, amoeba-shaped pool. The 285 a/c rooms in 196 bungalows are soulless affairs, albeit adequate. They have private baths, radios, and TVs. Buffet meals are served. Nonguests can also eat here (break-

Playa Girón Museum

fast costs US$8, lunch and dinner cost US$14). Facilities include a disco, souvenir shop, and a tourist information desk that offers excursions to the crocodile farm at La Boca (US$27) and farther afield. Rates were US$32 s, US$40 d in low season, US$44 s, US$56 d high season, including breakfast.

Silvia Acosta Lima has a *casa particular*—**Hostal V. Silvia Acosta Lima**—400 meters along the road to Yaguaramas, tel. (59) 4370. The house is covered in seashells and offers one of the best places to stay outside Havana. He has four rooms, all appealing for their cleanliness and decor. They're well-lit, cross-ventilated, and have fans and private, tiled, newly-built bathrooms with large showers with hot water. A TV lounge boasts leather sofas. It's a bargain at US$20. Breakfast costs US$2-4; dining is on a shady patio.

There's another *casa particular* 100 meters farther north.

Entertainment and Services

The hotel offers meager entertainment, including cabaret. You can also try the **Club Nocturno Neptuno**, in the village and favored by locals.

There's a coin laundry, pharmacy, and dollars-only shop opposite the museum. The post office and telegraph office are 50 meters north of the museum. The hotel has medical services.

Getting There and Around

Víazul operates tourist bus service to Playa Girón from Havana, stopping at Playa Larga (see the Víazul Bus Schedule chart). For public bus service, see the Public Bus Service from Havana chart. Bus no. 818 operates local service between Playa Larga and Playa Girón.

Bus no. 818 operates from Jagüey Grande to Playa Girón via Playa Larga. Buses also operate from Cienfuegos daily at 4 a.m. (5 a.m. on Sunday) and 3:30 p.m., although service may be unreliable.

Most tour agencies in Havana and Varadero offer excursions.

Transauto tel. (59) 4144, opposite the Villa Horizontes, has taxi and rental car service office where you can also rent bicycles and mopeds. And **Havanautos** has an outlet in the hotel.

EAST OF PLAYA GIRÓN

The paved coastal highway (Route 3-1-16) turns inland at Playa Girón and runs north, then east, 39 km through scrubland to Yaguaramas (forsake the road from Covavango; it's terribly deteriorated). Here, it connects with Route 3-1-2, which runs north to Aguada de Pasajeros and the Autopista and east to Cienfuegos.

You can continue east along the coast from Playa Girón by a paved road that in springtime is littered with dead crabs, which cross the road in their thousands. The stench of rotten crabmeat attracts vultures, which lope about like sinister undertakers, making great hay of the carnage.

Caleta Buena, eight km east of Playa Girón and run by Horizontes, is worth every inch of the drive. This small, exquisite coral cove contains a natural pool good for swimming. There are pocket-size beaches atop the coral platform, with red-tiled *ranchitas* for shade and lounge chairs for sunning. The seabed is a multicolored garden of coral and sponges, ideal for snorkeling (US$5 for equipment rental) and diving (US$25). All-inclusive entrance costs US$12, with lunch served noon-3 p.m. (the bar is open until 5 p.m.). A multicolored extravaganza of fish can be hand-fed. Catamarans were to be added.

East of Caleta Buena, the road deteriorates rapidly and is of blindingly white, hard-packed coral and dirt. The area is uninhabited. Eventually you'll reach a sharp curve with a small cove to the right. The "main" route veers left and eventually leads to Yaguaramas. A narrow track straight ahead, however, will take you along virtually unexplored territory to Jaragua. This is adventure touring but is impassable to all but the most rugged 4WD vehicles.

CIENFUEGOS AND VILLA CLARA

INTRODUCTION

Villa Clara and Cienfuegos Provinces lie due east of Matanzas, with Villa Clara north of Cienfuegos. They are skipped by most tourists, who whiz by along the Autopista or Carretera Central, bound for Oriente or the colonial city of Trinidad, in Sancti Spíritus province. Such haste is a pity, for you are likely to miss another colonial gem, Remedios, a tiny charmer caught in its own time warp. Remedios and neighboring villages east of Santa Clara—the provincial capital of Villa Clara and an important industrial and university city—are renowned, too, for their *parrandas,* unique year-end carnival-style revelries that border on mayhem.

This eastern portion of the province is dominated by rolling uplands called the **Alturas de Santa Clara,** as photogenic and quintessentially Cuban in character as you'll find on the island—a medley of *bohios,* ox-drawn plows, and royal palms, with the rolling land given to tobacco and cattle, and hazy mountains forming a fabulous backdrop. Villa Clara is second only to Pinar del Río as a center of tobacco production, centered on the scenic **Vuelta Arriba** region, east of the provincial capital.

South of Santa Clara, the Alturas rise gradually to the steep, pine-clad **Sierra del Escambray,** whose reservoirs supply towns for miles around. In the mountains, *campesinos* raise coffee. During the Revolution, Che Guevara established a front in the Escambray and, on 28 December 1958, his rebel army swept down upon Santa Clara—the last battle of the Revolution before Batista fled Cuba. The Escambray were also a haven for counterrevolutionaries in the early years following the Revolution. Today cool forests tantalize birders and hikers, with man-made lakes good for fishing, a famous health spa, and a cool, invigorating climate—the wettest in Cuba—to lure you away from the coast.

The mountains extend south and west into Cienfuegos province, which, despite being Cuba's second smallest, surpasses even Havana in industrial output. **Cienfuegos** city is a major port town and industrial center with notable architectural sights, a fine botanical garden, and the curiosity of a ghostly nuclear reactor.

The coastlines have few pleasing beaches and resorts (an exception is Rancho Luna, south of the city of Cienfuegos).

ROUTES THROUGH THE REGION

Along the Autopista

The Autopista continues runs through northern Cienfuegos and southern Villa Clara Province. The turnoff for the city of Cienfuegos is at **Aguada del Pasajeros** (Passenger Watering Place), where there's a **Cupet gas station** alongside an appealing *ranchita* bar and restaurant, with an antique U.S. steam engine displayed on the forecourt. There's another **Cupet gas station** and **El Rápido** at Km 259, one km west of the turnoff for Santa Clara.

The road to Cienfuegos leads via Rojas, a few km northeast of which is **Ciego Montero Spring.** Much of the bottled mineral water sold in Cuba derives from this naturally carbonated spring, where there is a run-down spa-hotel and baths.

East of Santa Clara city, the scenery takes a dramatic turn as the Autopista cuts through the beautiful hills of the Alturas de Santa Clara and passes into Sancti Spíritus Province.

Warning: The Autopista is in superb condition the whole way. However, just east of Ranchuelo, an ungated railway track runs across the Autopista. Watch out for trains crossing: usually an attendant will stop traffic with a red flag.

Along the Carretera Central

A far more interesting route than the Autopista is the old Carretera Central through central Villa Clara. The route takes you through aged provincial towns, including **Santo Domingo.** Its venerable church displays an intriguing amalgam of styles: red brick frontage with thick limestone columns inset into the wall, and a clock in the pediment topped by an octagonal bell tower containing a patinated bell. The tower is incongruously capped by Moorish mosaics.

There are no gas stations or other facilities.

CIENFUEGOS

"This must be one of the quietest ports in the world," Wormold writes to his sister in Graham Greene's *Our Man in Havana.* "Just the pink and yellow street and a few cantinas and the big chimney of a sugar refinery. . . . The light here is wonderful just before the sun goes down: a long trickle of gold and the seabirds are dark patches on the pewter swell."

Cienfuegos (pop. 105,000) is a city of commerce. The city, 340 km east of Havana and 69 km southwest of Santa Clara, lies on the east side of the Bahía de Cienfuegos, a deep, 88-square-km bay with an umbilically narrow entrance and in which, as one 19th-century traveler remarked, "all the navies of the world could rendezvous and not crowd each other." It's Cuba's third-largest port and shelters a large fishing and shrimping fleet. International influences (especially French) have made themselves felt. Cienfuegos even had its own Chinatown (now long since devoid of Chinese people), west of Parque Martí on the edge of the port.

Cienfuegos means "100 fires" and is sometimes written "100 fuegos." Citizens call their town *La Perla del Sur* (the pearl of the south) or *La Linda Ciudad del Mar* (the beautiful city

by the sea). The city's appeal lies partly in the European flavor of its colonial hub, with a wide Parisian-style boulevard and elegant colonnades. Still, Cienfuegos has neither the grace of Trinidad nor the flair of Havana, and the contemporary restoration of Parque Martí and "El Bulevar" hide the slums in which the majority of citizens live. Still, there is a vital ambience that inspired Beny Moré, the celebrated Cuban *sonoro,* to sing, "Cienfuegos is the city I like best." The city has become popular with ex-pats, including Yankees, many of whom seem to live here on a part-time basis in union with their *chicas,* despite an abiding police presence that at press time had caused locals to shun conversations with tourists.

ORIENTATION

Approaching from the Autopista, the two-lane highway enters the city from the north and widens into a broad boulevard, the **Paseo del Prado** (Calle 37), the city's main thoroughfare. At Avenida 46, the Prado becomes the **Malecón,** a wide seafront boulevard stretching south one km along a narrow peninsula ending at Punta

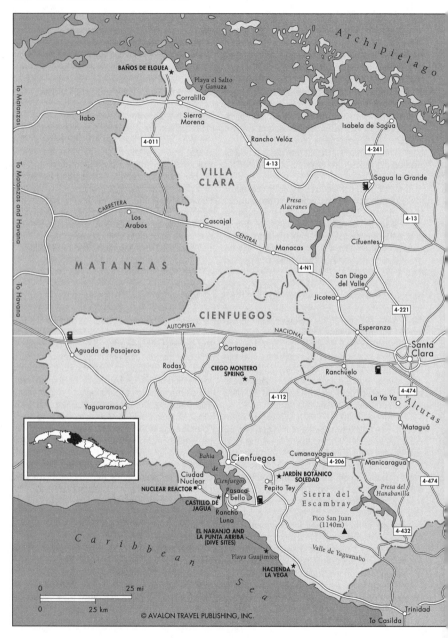

CIENFUEGOS AND VILLA CLARA PROVINCES

Gorda, a once-exclusive residential district that recalls 1950s North American suburbia, with Detroit classics still parked in the driveways of mid-20th-century homes. Beyond Punta Gorda, hidden behind and south of the Hotel Jagua, is a short, slender isthmus lined with old French-style plantation homes.

The city is laid out in a perfect grid, with even-numbered *calles* running north-south, crossing odd-numbered *avenidas* running east-west.

The historic core is called **Pueblo Nuevo.** It is centered on Parque Martí, the main plaza, four blocks west of the Prado, along Avenidas 54 and 56. Avenida 54 (El Bulevard), the principal shopping street, is for pedestrians only between Calles 31 and 37. Pueblo Nuevo occupies the La Majagua Peninsula. Surrounding it is a "ring," built this century with factories and Florida-style houses. The modern outskirts are composed of grim estates of *microbrigada*-built high-rise blocks.

A six-lane highway, the Circunvalación, by-passes the city to the north.

SIGHTSEEING HIGHLIGHTS: CIENFUEGOS AND VILLA CLARA PROVINCES

Cayo Santa María: Stunning white-sand beaches and jade waters on a remote cay accessed by a 45-km-long land bridge.

Jardín Botánico Soledad: Vast botanical garden on the outskirts of Cienfuegos, with separate sections for cactus, palm, etc.

Museo de Che Guevara, Santa Clara: Small but splendid museum beneath the imposing Che monument. A reverential mausoleum contains the revolutionary hero's remains.

Parque Martí, Cienfuegos: Restored colonial plaza surrounded by imposing buildings, including a cathedral.

Remedios: Beautiful colonial town, good for serendipitous discoveries. Time your visit for year's end to catch the **Parranda** . . . a fireworks battle like no other.

Sierra del Escambray: Scenic forested mountain range being developed for eco-tourism, with caves, and trails good for birding and horseback rides.

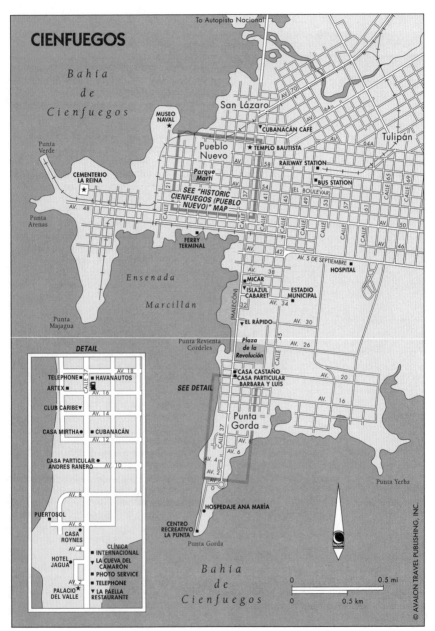

CIENFUEGOS

To Autopista Nacional

Bahía
de
Cienfuegos

Punta
Verde

MUSEO
NAVAL ★

San Lázaro

▼ CUBANACÁN CAFÉ

Tulipán

CEMENTERIO
LA REINA ★

Pueblo
Nuevo

★ TEMPLO BAUTISTA

AV. 70

CALLE 64A

RAILWAY STATION

*Parque
Martí*

SEE "HISTORIC
CIENFUEGOS (PUEBLO
NUEVO)" MAP

BUS STATION

EL BOULEVAR

AV. 48

Punta
Arenas

FERRY
TERMINAL

Ensenada

Marcillán

Punta
Majagua

Punta Revienta
Cordeles

AV. 42

AV. 5 DE SEPTIEMBRE

HOSPITAL

AV. 38

MICAR ■
ISLAZUL
CABARET

ESTADIO
MUNICIPAL

AV. 34

(MALECÓN)

AV. 32

■ EL RÁPIDO

AV. 30

*Plaza
de la
Revolución*

AV. 26

DETAIL

TELEPHONE ■
ARTEX ■

AV. 18

■ HAVANAUTOS

AV. 16

SEE DETAIL

CASA CASTAÑO ■
CASA PARTICULAR ■
BARBARA Y LUIS

AV. 20

CLUB CARIBE ▼

AV. 14

CASA MIRTHA ●

■ CUBANACÁN

AV. 12

CASA PARTICULAR ●
ANDRES RANERO

AV. 10

*Punta
Gorda*

AV. 16

AV. 8

PUERTOSOL ■

AV. 6

CASA
ROYNES ●

AV. 4

HOTEL
JAGUA ■

AV. 2

PALACIO ★
DEL VALLE

CLÍNICA
■ INTERNACIONAL
▼ LA CUEVA DEL
CAMARÓN
■ PHOTO SERVICE
■ TELEPHONE
▼ LA PAELLA
RESTAURANTE

AV. 8

AV. 6

AV. 4

AV. 2

AV. 0

● HOSPEDAJE ANA MARÍA

CENTRO
RECREATIVO
LA PUNTA

Punta Gorda

Punta Yerba

*Bahía
de
Cienfuegos*

0 ———— 0.5 mi
0 ———— 0.5 km

© AVALON TRAVEL PUBLISHING, INC.

HISTORY

Columbus supposedly discovered the bay in 1494. It was mapped a decade later by another explorer, Sebastián de Ocampo. Shortly after the Spanish settled Cuba and established their trade restrictions, the bay developed a thriving smuggling trade. Sir Francis Drake and Henry Morgan were among many cutthroat privateers who called for plunder.

Construction of a fortress—Castillo de Jagua—was begun in 1738 to protect the bay and to police smuggling through the straits, though no town had yet developed. It wasn't until 1817 that Louis D'Clouet, a French *émigré* from Louisiana, devised a settlement scheme that he presented to Don José Cienfuego, the Spanish captain-general. The Spanish government would pay for the transportation of white colonists from Europe, and every male would receive a *caballería,* a 13-hectare plot of land. The Spanish Parliament approved. By April 1819, the first 137 French settlers arrived. That hamlet was destroyed by a hurricane six years later but was rebuilt in 1831 and renamed Cienfuegos.

The city rapidly grew to wealth on the back of the deep-water harbor, a natural *entrepôt* for locally grown sugar, tobacco, and fruit. As the port trade prospered, nearby Trinidad's trade declined, adding to Cienfuegos' glory. Merchants and plantation owners graced the city with a surfeit of stucco. The French influence can be felt to this day.

The city continued to prosper during the early 20th century and had an unremarkable history—until 5 September 1957, when young naval officers and sailors (supported by the CIA) at the Cienfuegos Naval Base rebelled against the Batista regime and took control of the city's military and electrical installations (the electrical plant which they destroyed on the Prado and Avenida 48 is preserved as a monument). Members of Castro's revolutionary July 26th Movement—M-26—and students from the San Lorenzo School joined them. Batista's troops managed to recapture the city by nightfall.

Since the Revolution, the city's hinterland has grown significantly, mostly to the west in Reparto O'Bourke, where a new port and industrial and residential complex was initiated in the 1980s. The oil refinery (the country's biggest), wheat mills, fertilizer plants, a steel mill, and the Tricontinental Bulk Sugar Shipping Terminal are spread along the bay.

THINGS TO SEE

Parque Martí
Most of Cienfuegos' buildings of note surround Parque Martí, on the ground where the founding of the first settlement was proclaimed on 22 April 1819. The *majagua* tree that once stood at the center has long since died and been replaced by a bandstand and gazebo.

The city's most prominent and illustrious sons are commemorated in bronze or stone, including a statue to José Martí, guarded by two marble lions. Note the triumphal arch on the west side, unveiled in 1902 on the day the Cuban Republic was constituted. The plaza is worth visiting at night, when music and dance in the Casa de la Cultura occasionally spills into the square.

On the east side of the square is the **Catedral de la Purísima Concepción,** which dates from 1870. It has a splendid interior, at least by Cuban standards, with marble floors, and a pristine gilt Corinthian altar beneath a Gothic vaulted ceiling. The beautiful stained-glass windows of the 12 apostles were brought from France following the revolution of 1789. Try to visit for evening Mass, when the cathedral's beauty is more forcefully enhanced.

On the north side is the **Teatro Tomás Terry.** This impressive theater, now officially known as the Cienfuegos Theater, was completed in 1895. It was named for a local sugar baron, a Venezuelan who had arrived penniless in Cuba in the mid-1800s. Terry apparently rose to great wealth by buying sick slaves for a pittance, nursing them back to health, and selling them for a whopping profit. He invested his money in a sugar estate, then in railroads and other profitable ventures. His family built the theater using materials and craftsmen imported from Europe. The proscenium is sumptuously decorated with laurel wreaths, lyres, trumpets, and a bas-relief centerpiece of Dionysius. Allegorical figures cling to the arch over the stage, and naked nymphs cavort across the ceiling. The auditorium, with its three-tiered

HISTORIC CIENFUEGOS (PUEBLO NUEVO)

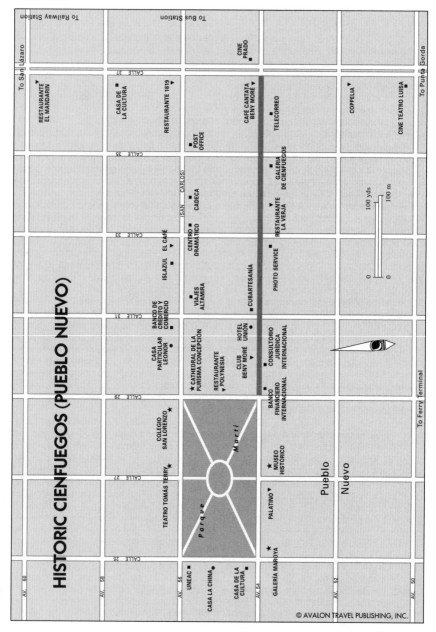

To Railway Station

To Bus Station

To San Lázaro

To Punta Gorda

CINE PRADO

CALLE 37

RESTAURANTE EL MANDARIN

CASA DE LA CULTURA

RESTAURANTE 1819

CAFÉ CANTATA BENY MORÉ

TELECORREO

COPPELIA

CINE TEATRO LUISA

POST OFFICE

CALLE 35

GALERIA DE CIENFUEGOS

SAN CARLOS

CADECA

100 yds

100 m

CENTRO DRAMÁTICO

EL CAFÉ

RESTAURANTE LA VERJA

CALLE 33

ISLAZUL

VIAJES ALTAMIRA

PHOTO SERVICE

0   0

CUBARTESANIA

CALLE 31

BANCO DE CRÉDITO Y COMERCIO

CASA PARTICULAR LEONOR

★ CATEDRAL DE LA PURISMA CONCEPCION

HOTEL UNION

CLUB BENY MORÉ

CONSULTORIO JURIDICA INTERNACIONAL

RESTAURANTE ▼ POLYNESIA

BANCO FINANCIERO INTERNACIONAL

To Ferry Terminal

CALLE 29

COLEGIO SAN LORENZO ★

Martí

MUSEO HISTÓRICO ★

Pueblo

CALLE 27

TEATRO TOMÁS TERRY ★

Parque

Nuevo

PALATINO ▼

CALLE 25

GALERIA MAROYA ★

AV. 60

AV. 58

UNEAC ■

CASA LA CHINA ●

AV. 56

CASA DE LA CULTURA ■

AV. 54

AV. 52

AV. 50

© AVALON TRAVEL PUBLISHING, INC.

balconies, is made entirely of Cuban hardwoods and can accommodate 900 people in old-fashioned, fold-down wooden seats. The theater floor can be raised to stage level to create a grand ballroom. Enrico Caruso, Sarah Bernhardt, and the Bolshoi Ballet have performed here. The Nacional Ballet and Opera de Cuba still perform, bringing the bats from their hiding places to swoop harmlessly over the heads of the audience. Entrance costs US$1. There are guides.

Adjoining the theater is **Colegio San Lorenzo,** a handsome neoclassical building fronted by thick columns.

Continuing your counterclockwise tour, you'll reach the **Casa de la Cultura,** on the west side, in the much-dilapidated former home of another wealthy sugar baron. It has a *mirador* tower with fine views across the bay (US$0.50 entrance). Be sure to pop into the **Galería Maroya** on the west side, with the city's finest collection of art. It's open Mon.-Sat. 8 a.m.-6 p.m.

Several intriguing buildings occupy the south side. First is the former Spanish Club (the initials CE, inset in the pavement, stand for Club Español), now housing the **Museo Histórico.** The museum commemorates local figures who fought in the War of Independence and offers a modest assortment of antiques, plus an archaeological room honoring the Indians of the Americas. It's open Tues.-Sat. 9 a.m.-4:30 p.m. Entrance costs US$1. Fifty meters east is the **Primero Palacio,** now the Poder Popular, the local government headquarters. It has a fine marble floor. Next to the Poder Popular is a fine bar and restaurant—the **Palatino**—whose shady terrace is supported by plump columns resembling milk bottles, affirming Cienfuegos' intriguing mix of architectural styles.

Paseo del Prado

Calle 37—the Prado—is lined its full length with plaques and busts honoring illustrious citizens, including a big white statue that Wormold in Graham Greene's *Our Man in Havana* thought looked in daylight like Queen Victoria. The Prado remains a social center and in the cool evenings bustles with gossipy life, when citizens still promenade as in colonial days and bootblacks still shine shoes beneath the pink colonnades.

At Avenida 62 note the **Templo Bautista,** a simple Baptist Temple in art nouveau style.

To the south, at Calle 42, the Prado becomes the **Malecón,** where lovers congregate to smooch on the seawall.

Palacio del Valle

Cienfuegos' architectural pride and joy is a palace at the tip of Punta Gorda. This architectural stunner—now a restaurant—originated as a modest home for a trader, Celestino Caceres. It passed out of his hands and was given as a wedding present to a member of the local Valle family, who added to it in virile Mogul style, with carved floral motifs, cupped arches, bulbous cupolas, and delicate arabesques.

The main dining room drips with ornate carvings in Venetian alabaster. Another room is a replica in miniature of Versailles. There are even Gothic flourishes. Note the mural of Magi on the Carrara marble staircase. A spiral cast-iron staircase deposits you at a rooftop bar and windy *mirador.* It's open daily 10 a.m.-midnight, tel. (432) 3021.

Cementerio La Reina

Other Sights

There is little to draw visitors to **Museo Naval,** situated on Cayo Loco on Calle 21 e/ Calles 60 y 62, tel. (432) 6617. The museum has a library containing important historical documents. It was here in 1957 that naval officers rebelled against the Batista regime. The museum exhibits naval vessels. Open Tue.-Fri. 9 a.m.-5 p.m. and Sat.-Sun. 9 a.m.-noon. Entrance costs US$1.

Tomás Acea Cemetery is worth a browse for its impressive neoclassical structures and tombs. It is entered via a gate that is a scaled-down replica of the Parthenon, supported by 64 columns. The cemetery overlooks the bay from atop a bluff on the road to Rancho Luna.

There's another evocative cemetery—**Cementerio La Reina**—at the west end of Avenida 50 (from downtown, take Avenida 48, then turn right), reached via the old and decrepit old Barrio Chino, or Chinatown, devoid of Chinese who fled en masse following the Revolution. The cemetery is entirely of Carrara marble. The walls contain tombs with the bodies of soldiers from the War of Independence. Much of the cemetery was destroyed by Hurricane Lily in 1996, and many of the tombs are caved in, with the skeletons open to view. The gates are usually locked; Teresa, the *custodio,* lives across the street and will open the gates and act as a guide.

ACCOMMODATIONS

Casas Particulares

Cienfuegos has plenty of *casas particulares,* notably in Punta Gorda along Calle 37. All the owners serve breakfast and meals.

Pueblo Nuevo: The best option is *Casa La China,* in a colonial home on Calle 25 #5407, tel. (432) 6527 (neighbor) on the west side of Parque Martí, and entered by a marble staircase that deposits you in a lofty lounge with antiques, opening to verandas to front and rear. The four modestly furnished rooms—US$20 apiece—are clean and spacious, with private bathrooms and hot water. The owner, Amparo Sánchez, is a delight. She'll prepare meals and wash your clothes on request.

Another excellent option is **Casa Particular Leonor,** on Avenida 56 #2927 e/ 29 y 31, tel. (432) 6143, one block east of Parque Martí, in a

much dilapidated colonial home. The three rooms are basic, as is the dour bathroom (US$15). However, the place is highly recommended by many past guests and I, too, enjoyed the hospitality of the hosts, dedicated socialists who make all-comers welcome with fine lively conversation. Pipe-smoking Armando Medina is an economist for the local government; Leonar welcomes you with her "Coctel Leonora" (made with *guayabito*) and gets rave reviews for her special chicken dish. The hosts allow girlfriends but not casual *chicas.*

Also try **Casa Marthica,** Avenida 50 #3908 e/ 39 y 41, tel. (432) 9389 (neighbor), with a large but uninspired, simply furnished room for US$15.

Punta Gorda: The nicest place is Andres Ranero's *casa* at Avenida 10 #3707 e/ 37 y 39, tel. (432) 7993, with three well-lit a/c rooms, all with fridges, pleasant furnishings, and clean, handsome bathrooms with hot water (the rooms share two bathrooms). Guests have their own small lounge. Meals are served on an outside patio. There's secure parking and you can rent a bicycle. Andres speaks English.

Casa Castaño, Calle 37 #1824 esq. 20, tel. (432) 5251, has two rooms furnished with antiques, fans, a/c, and a large shared bathroom with hot water for US$20 each. Meals are served in a cozy atrium patio, and there's a large lounge with TV and music system. It has secure parking. Next door, at #1822, Barbara and Luís, tel. (432) 7988, have two pleasing a/c rooms upstairs with private bathrooms with hot water for US$15 apiece. The TV lounge opens to a balcony, and there's parking.

A house at Calle 37 #603, tel. (432) 6188, has three modestly furnished a/c rooms with fans and large tiled bathrooms with hot water for US$20. Two are upstairs and open to a breeze-swept terrace with bay views. The hosts prepare huge breakfasts for US$2.50, and there's secure parking and a TV lounge.

Marialena y Tomás Álvarez have a *casa* around the corner, Av. 6 #3509A e/ 35 y 37, tel. (432) 6545, with three rooms, including a large self-contained apartment upstairs with a/c, hot water, and secure parking for US$20 per room, including breakfast. **Casa Roynes,** Calle 37 #403 e/ 4 y 6, tel. (432) 5854, nearby, has two a/c rooms with private entrance and bathroom and hot water, plus parking, for US$15. And **Casa Mirtha,** Calle 37 #1205 e/ 12 y 14, tel. (432) 5430 (neighbor), has three rooms in a slightly jaded 1950s house with secure parking.

Hospedaje Ana María, in a colonial home at Calle 35 #20, tel. (432) 3129, near the tip of Punta Gorda, has two rooms with private bathroom and hot water for US$20. A quiet courtyard to the rear opens to the bay. The owner speaks English.

Hotels
Moderate: The only designated tourist hotel in town is the **Hotel Jagua,** at the south end of Calle 37, e/ 0 y 2, tel. (432) 45-1003, fax (432) 45-1245, in North America, tel. (800) 221-4542. It was renowned prior to the Revolution as a ritzy hotel-cum-gambling joint run by Batista's brother. Today it is regained some of its former splendor after a total remake and is now marketed by the French Mercure group as part of the Gran Caribe chain. The 144 large, a/c rooms are pleasantly furnished and well lighted, with attractive black-tile bathrooms. They have safes and TVs. Ask for a fifth-floor room, which offers fine views over Palacio Valle and the bay. Facilities include a tour desk, restaurant, small pool, boutique, rental cars and scooters, and a nightly cabaret. Rates were US$49 s, US$68 d, US$97 t low season, US$56s, US$81 d, US$116 t high season.

The **Hotel Unión,** Av. 54 y Calle 31, one block east of Parque Martí, was being rebuilt at press time as a re-creation of a hotel that served Cienfuegos in the 19th century.

Islazul runs the **Hotel Puerta la Cueva,** tel. (432) 3956, about five km east of town on the road to Rancho Luna. This surprisingly appealing two-star option has 67 small, dark, modestly furnished, a/c rooms, most with views across the bay to Cienfuegos. Bathrooms are clean and feature marble tiles and hot water. There's a pleasant restaurant, bar, nurse station, small swimming pool, and boutique, and bougainvillea arbors provide shade and color. It's justifiably popular with Cubans. Rates were US$17 s, US$22 d low season, US$21 s, US$28 d high season.

FOOD

Cienfuegos has a larger roster of cafés and restaurants than most Cuban cities, though the fare is limited to the usual unremarkable *criollo* staples. Alas, *paladares* have virtually disappeared from the scene at last visit.

Punta Gorda
If you haven't seen it by day, plan on dining at **Palacio de Valle,** tel. (432) 45-1226. Its specialty is lobster prepared six different ways. The lobsters are huge—a half-order should suffice—albeit overpriced at US$25. Shrimp dishes cost US$15. The food is mediocre; you go for the ambience, assisted by Carmen Iznaga, a niece of acclaimed writer Nicolás Guillén, who plays an

Palacio del Valle

all-night medley of classical and modern pieces at a grand piano.

My favorite eatery is **Casa Garibeña,** Calle 35 #2004, e/ 20 y 24, tel. (432) 3893, in an old seafront wooden house with full-length windows and a shady veranda. Rattan furniture, beautiful artwork, and an old tiled floor add to the romantic ambience. The manager, Miguel Angel Chivandi, is fastidious and welcoming. The predominantly *criollo* dishes (fish runs US$6, fried chicken US$3) are prepared with more care than in many places. The menu also includes filet mignon (US$7). The accomplished Trio del Caribeño plays soothing music.

The elegant **Restaurante Escambray,** in the Hotel Jagua, serves the usual *criollo* fare (US$8-15). Tasty paella (US$6) is served at **La Paella Restaurante,** opposite the hotel. It has views over the bay toward the Escambray. Decor plays on a nautical theme, and a plaque notes that Fidel dined here. It's open daily noon to 2:30 p.m., and 7-10:30 p.m. Next door, **La Cueva del Camarón** specializes in seafood at twice the price of La Paella. Its art nouveau interior is a bit jaded and you might be the only diner. The menu includes a filling paella (US$10), lobster in spicy sauce (U$22), and grilled fish (US$9).

Pueblo Nuevo

Downtown options include **Restaurante 1819,** in a colonial mansion replete with antiques. It's open weekdays 6:30 a.m.-9:30 p.m. and weekends for lunch. It features "Cuban Night" entertainment on Saturday night. For quasi-Chinese food, try **Restaurante El Mandarin,** on the corner of Calle 37 and Avenida 60. It has suitably Chinese decor but a limited menu. Meals cost less than six pesos (open noon- 2:30 p.m. and 7-9:30 p.m.). **Café Cantanta Beny Moré,** at Prado y Av. 54, serves simple *criollo* fare, as does the **Cubanacán Café,** on Prado y Avenida 66.

My favorite place is **Palatino,** a handsome bar-cum-restaurant with an outside terrace overlooking Parque Martí. It offers grilled fish (US$10), pollo asado (US$5), and lobster enchilada (US$12), including salad, soup, and dessert. Also on Parque Martí, next to the cathedral, is the **Restaurante Polynesia,** with a Tahitian motif. The menu is *criollo* with hints of the South Seas (pineapple finds its way into chicken dishes, for example). It's open 6:30-11 p.m.

Several popular cafés are located on Avenida 54, plus the **Restaurante La Verja,** serving *criollo* staples in a colonial home full of antiques. The once notable menu still includes Hungarian goulash (US$8), but don't get your hopes up.

Outside town (on the road to Rancho Luna), you'll find **Finca Isabela,** a hacienda-turned-restaurant. You can watch a cockfight before savoring your roast suckling pig washed down with a house cocktail.

Coppelia, on the Prado, is always a good bet for ice cream. It's open 11 a.m.-11 p.m.

ENTERTAINMENT AND SHOPPING

Events

Cienfuegos hosts the week-long *Fiesta de los Amigos del Mar* (Party of Sea-Loving Friends) in mid-July, featuring a parade of fishermen, waters sports, rowing and sailing regattas, motorbike races, kayak races, beach volleyball competitions, swimming races, and even Formula T1 speedboat races, and more, with evening entertainment also.

Cienfuegos Bay was the setting in 1997 and 1998 for the **Grand Island Grand Prix,** part of the international T-1 speedboats championship (the boats are capable of speeds of 210 kph). It is expected to become an annual event.

The **Beny Moré International Festival of Popular Music** is held here each August.

Entertainment

Cienfuegos is a relatively dreary place with limited options for entertainment, despite its size. However, the **Palatino** bar, on Parque Martí is a pleasant spot to savor the mood of the plaza at night. To sup with locals, head to the lively and moody bar of the **Restaurant La Verja,** on Avenida 24. **Rumbos** operates several open-air bars with music on Punta Gorda, including **Club Caribe** at Calle 37 y Avenida 14.

The **Cine Prado,** Calle 37 y Av. 54, projects movies across the Prado onto an outdoor screen; viewing is free to one and all. **Cine Teatro Luisa,** Calle 37 y Av. 50, also shows movies.

The **Club Beny Moré**, Av. 54 e/ 29 y 31, tel. (432) 45-1105, is a modern cabaret theater with live music, comedians, and cabaret acts. Entrance costs US$3. It's open Thurs.-Sun. evenings. The laser-lit disco-cabaret—**Salón Guanaroca**—in the Hotel Jagua is the snazziest place in town. The in-vogue spot for locals at last visit, however, was the cramped, smoke-filled basement disco in the **Palacio del Valle**, playing hip Western sounds. Entrance costs US$1.

Locals also flock on weekends to an open-air pavilion next to El Rápido restaurant, midway down the Malecón, where a free disco is hosted. **Centro Cultural Artex**, on Calle 355 e/ 16 y 18, has outdoor music and dancing. And **Centro Recreativo La Punta**, at the very tip of the peninsula, is favored by young Cubans for its bar playing Western music. It's open 10 a.m.-6 p.m. and 8 p.m.-1 a.m.

Teatro Tomás Terry hosts performances ranging from classical symphony to live salsa music. Entrance costs US$1. The **Galería de Cienfuegos**, on Avenida 54, also has cultural shows, plus classical and traditional performances. The **Museo Histórico** also hosts classical music concerts. The **Casa de la Trova**, Av. 16 y Calle 35, and the **Casa de la Cultura**, Calle 37 y Av. 58, also host traditional performances.

For theater, try the **Centro Dramático**, on Avenida 56 e/ 3 y 35.

The **Galería Maroya** on the west side of Parque Martí, Avenida 54 #2506, tel. (432) 45-1208, hosts fashion shows and music on some Saturday nights.

Sports and Recreation

Puertosol, tel. (432) 8195, offers fishing trips (US$25) and scuba diving (US$37 including equipment) from Marina Puertosol, at Calle 35 e/ 6 y 8, tel. (432) 4-5124, fax (432) 4-51275, website: www.puertosol.cubaweb.cu, on Punta Gorda. Hobie Cats were to be rented at **Marina Marlin**, under construction at press time immediately north of the Hotel Jagua.

Baseball games (and athletic meets) are hosted in the **Estadio Municipal**, at Calle 45 and Avenida 34, four blocks east of the Malecón. On weekends you can watch young boxers sparring in an open-air ring on the Prado between Avenidas 46 and 48. Watch your purse.

Shopping

The **Galería Maroya** on the west side of Parque Martí, Av. 54 #2506, tel. (432) 45-1208, has a splendid collection of arts and crafts: leatherwork, batiks, carvings, and paintings. One room even features genuine antiques, although much is bric-a-brac.

Cubartesanía, at Avenida 54 and Calle 31, sells souvenirs, T-shirts, music cassettes and CDs. Likewise, the store in Hotel Jagua has a selection of crafts, music cassettes, and souvenirs.

For cigars and rum, check out **El Embajador: House of Cigars**, on Avenida 54 esq. 33.

PRACTICALITIES

Crime and Safety

The *jiniteros* that plagued visitors in recent years had disappeared at last visit, chased away by the omnipresent police. In early 2000 many locals were afraid to be seen talking with foreigners due to police harassment. Hence, you can walk anywhere by day unmolested. However, stick to the main streets by night. Cienfuegos has its fair share of poverty-stricken slums that are best avoided after dark.

Information and Services

Tourist Information: Cubanacán, Calle 37 #1208, tel. (432) 45-1680, has a tour agency offering excursions, open Mon.-Sat. 8 a.m.-6 p.m. **Islazul** also has tour agencies and hotel booking offices on the Prado #5022, tel. (432) 5294, and on Avenida 56 e/ 31 y 33. The Ministry of Tourism has an administrative office on Calle 37 but does *not* act as an information bureau.

If you need legal advice, cash advances, medical attention, hospitalization, or other emergency assistance, contact **Asistur**, in the Hotel Jagua, tel. (432) 6362 or (432) 66-6190.

Communications: There's a small **postal service** in the Hotel Jagua, where you'll also find an international telephone and fax office. Downtown, there's a **Centro Telefónico** (open 24 hours) at Avenida 54 e/ Calles 35 y 37, and Etecsa has telephone booths opposite the Hotel

Jagua; on Calle 37 e/ 16 y 18; and on the Prado e/ 48 y 50. **Cubacel,** Carretera Palmira Km 2, Cuatro Caminos, tel. (432) 45-8222, fax (432) 45-8037, rents cellular phones and will hook up your personal cellular. It's open Mon.-Fri. 8 a.m.-5 p.m. and Saturday, 8 a.m.-noon. (Also see the Communications section in the On The Road chapter for costs and conditions.)

A **post office** is one block west of the Prado, at Avenida 56 and Calle 35. **DHL,** in the Hotel Jagua, tel. (432) 6554, offers express domestic and international delivery. It's open weekdays 9 a.m.-6 p.m. and Saturday 8:30 a.m.-noon.

Money: Banco de Crédito y Comercio has a branch at Avenida 56 and Calle 31, and **Banco Financiero Internacional** is on the southeast corner of Parque Martí (open Mon.-Fri. 8 a.m.-3 p.m.). Both serve foreigners. **Cadeca** has an exchange bureau at Avenida 56 e/ 33 y 35.

Medical: Foreigners are served by the **Clínica Internacional,** Calle 37, e/ 2 y 4, tel. (432) 45-1622, opposite the Hotel Jagua. It has a doctor and nurse on 24-hour call, and a small pharmacy. Consultations cost US$25. **Ópticas Miramar** offers optical services for foreigners at Avenida 54 #3504, tel. (432) 45-1278, and sells contact lens solution and spectacles.

Need basic camera supplies? Try **Photo Service,** on Avenida 54 at Calle 33.

The **Cupet gas station** is on Calle 37 y Av. 18, four blocks north of Hotel Jagua. You'll find another about 10 km east of town just beyond the turnoff for Trinidad, on the road to Rancho Luna.

Getting There

By Air: Domestic service is offered to **Aeropuerto Internacional Jaime Gónzalez,** tel. (432) 5868, by Aerotaxi, Aerogaviota, and Aerocaribbean. Cubana does not fly to Cienfuegos. Royal Airlines has charter flights from Toronto. The airport is five km northeast of town.

By Bus: The **Víazul** tourist bus serves Cienfuegos from Havana on Tuesday and Friday (see the Víazul Bus Schedule chart in the On the Road chapter). For public bus service, see the Public Bus Service from Havana chart, also in the On the Road chapter. Most buses take five hours via the Autopista and Aguada de Pasajeros. There is also regular service from Santa Clara, Sancti Spíritus, and Camagüey.

The bus terminal is on Calle 49 e/ Avenida 56 y 58, six blocks east of the Prado, tel. (432) 5720.

By Train: Direct trains for Cienfuegos depart Havana's Estación La Coubre. Cienfuegos lies at the end of a branch line off the main Havana-Santiago railroad. You can catch an *especial* from Havana to Santa Clara and then connect to Cienfuegos. Trains also operate to Cienfuegos from Sancti Spíritus daily at 4:55 a.m., and from Santa Clara at 5:20 p.m. The train station is on Calle 49 e/ Av. 58 y 60, tel. (432) 5574.

By Private Yacht: Marina Puertosol, tel. (432) 45-1241, fax (432) 45-1275, has moorings for 30 yachts, with water, electricity, and diesel. Berthing costs US$0.40 per foot up to 55-feet (US$0.35 per foot for larger boats). Its facilities are meager. You must stop for clearance into the bay at the **Guárda Frontera** post, one km south of the Jagua fortress on the western shores of the entrance channel.

Getting Around

Most attractions are concentrated downtown, a 30-minute walk from the Hotel.

By Bus: Cienfuegos has a fairly good bus system. Journeys are a fixed 10 centavos. Bus no. 9 runs the length of the Prado and Malecón and stops outside the Hotel Jagua.

By Taxi: Horse-drawn taxis *(mulos)* are the main means of getting around for locals, plying the major thoroughfares. Foreigners are charged US$1 between the Hotel Jagua and downtown.

Taxi Turismo, tel. (432) 9145, charges US$2 between the Hotel Jagua and downtown. **Transtur,** Av. 52, e/ Calle 29 y 31, operates Transtaxi, tel. (432) 9-6256 or 9-6212.

By Car: You can rent a car from **Havanautos,** next to the Cupet station on Calle 37 y Avenida 18, tel. (432) 45-1154; **Transtur,** tel. (432) 9-6256, at the Hotel Jagua; and **Micar,** Calle 37 y Av. 28, tel. (432) 45-1353.

Getting Away

Hitchhiking: There's a designated hitching point north of the city, opposite the university (bus no. 6 will take you there from the Prado).

By Bus: There are five buses daily to Havana You can make reservations in advance at the **Oficina de Reservaciones de Ómnibus Nacional,** Calle 54 e/ Aves. 35 y 37, tel. (432) 6050 or 9358, which also has an information service. Buses also depart daily for Camagüey, Trinidad, Playa Girón, and Santiago de Cuba; for Santa Clara 10 times daily; and to Sancti Spíritus six times daily.

You can try for same-day service on local routes, but if you do, arrive first thing in the morning; you'll be given a ticket, then keep your fingers crossed that you can get on later that day. Long-distance routes are often booked solid days or even weeks in advance.

By Train: At press time, trains to Havana departed Cienfuegos daily at 1 p.m., and for Santa Clara and Sancti Spíritus daily at 4:30 a.m. and 2:40 p.m. The railway station is on Calle 58 and Avenida 49. Train schedules change almost daily: call the **Empresa Expreso por Ferrocarril** at tel. (432) 5574.

Organized Excursions: Sightseeing excursions are offered by Cubanacán (see Tourist Information, above); by **Rumbos,** Calle 20 #3905, e/ 39 y 41, Punta Gorda, tel. (432) 45-1121, fax (432) 45-1174; by **Tours & Travel,** on Calle 44, tel. (432) 45-1639, fax (432) 45-1370; and by **Viajes Altamira,** Av. 56 e/ 31 y 33, tel. (0432) 3171.

VICINITY OF CIENFUEGOS

JARDÍN BOTÁNICO SOLEDAD

This splendid garden is about 10 km east of Cienfuegos, on the main coast road to Trinidad, between the communities of San Antón and Guaos. It was begun in 1899 by a New Englander, Edward Atkins, who owned vast sugar estates in the area and brought in Harvard botanists to develop hardier and more productive sugarcane strains. Later, Harvard University assumed control under a 99-year lease, and a general collection making up one of the tropical world's finest botanical gardens—the Harvard Biological Laboratory—was amassed. Since the Revolution, the garden has been maintained by the Cuban Academy of Science's Institute of Botany.

Pathways leads through the 94-hectare garden, reached along an avenue of royal palms. It harbors a collection of some 2,000 species, 70% of which are exotics, including rare tropical plants with important medicinal uses. A rare bamboo collection has 23 species. Of rubber trees, there are 89 species; of cactus, 400. The prize collection is the 307 varieties of palms. My favorite feature is a cactus-strewn rock garden shaped like Cuba.

The garden maintains its connections with the international botanical gardens, including with Harvard University, but the gardens are run-down and weeds are taking over. The facility includes a laboratory (in Harvard House) and library. The garden is open daily 8 a.m.-5 p.m. Entrance costs US$2.50, including guided tour. The basic café serves drinks only.

The avenue of palms extends along the south side of the main road and leads to the Pepito Tey sugar factory, once owned by Atkins and today open for visits.

Getting There: The bus from Cienfuegos to Cumanayagua passes the garden. A taxi will cost about US$40 round-trip.

PLAYA RANCHO LUNA AND PASACABELLO

A turnoff at San Antón leads southwest to the coast and the entrance to the Bahía de Cienfuegos at Pasacabello. En route there's a pleasant beach: **Playa Rancho Luna,** with calm, shallow turquoise waters; it's popular with Cubans and features a basic café and bar. The beach has no-see-ums (called *jenjenes* locally) that emerge ravenous at dusk.

The road swings east past the **Faro Luna lighthouse** and follows the rocky coast eight km to Pasacabello, facing the Castillo de Jagua across the 400-meter-wide mouth of Cienfuegos bay, 22 km from Cienfuegos.

Water Sports
You can choose from a wide range of water sports on Playa Rancho Luna, including catamarans and windsurfers. Scuba diving is offered at the **Whale Shark Scuba Center,** tel. (432) 4-51287, fax (432) 45-1288, e-mail: whaleshark@ip.etecsa.cu, at the Rancho Luna Hotel. At least eight ships lie amid the coral reefs of Las Playitas and Barrera *ensenada*.

Accommodations

Casas Particulares: There are several private rentals to choose from near the Hotel Faro Luna, including **Villa Sol,** tel. (432) 4-53341, which has four modestly furnished rooms with fridges, and private bathrooms and hot water. Three have a/c. Rates are US$15 low season, US$20 high season. **Hospedaje La China** is next door, and 50 meters along is a *casa* of Braulio Delgado Hernández, tel. (343) 4-8146, with three small, meagerly furnished a/c rooms with fridges, TVs (local), and clean modern bathrooms for US$20.

The place to be, however, is **Finca las Colorados B&B,** Carretera de Pasacaballo Km 18, Playa Rancho Luna, tel. (432) 3808, a remarkable place enjoying a breeze-swept position on the cliffs 100 meters east of the lighthouse. This whitewashed contemporary charmer is the European-style home of English-speaking José Piñero and his wife Kety García, catering professionals who prepare classical Cuban cuisine in their kitchen boasting all modern facilities. Their home abounds in antiques and modern furnishings, with walls painted in Roman-style motifs. Four modestly furnished, cross-ventilated rooms have metal-frame antique beds, fans, and private bathrooms with hot water. You can dine on an outside patio beneath an arbor, with a Gaudiesque sculpture, barbecue pit, and outside bar. There's even a kiddies' playground. The couple are building a seafood restaurant adjacent. Dogs abound. Cuba? You'd hardly think so. All this costs a modest US$20. Breakfast costs US$4, dinner costs US$10. *A recommended bargain!*

Hotels: Islazul's **Hotel Rancho Luna,** Carretera de Rancho Luna, Cienfuegos, tel. (43) 4-48120, fax (43) 4-48131, is a staple of German and Canadian tour groups. It's modestly appealing, albeit uninspired, and centers on a huge pool and sundeck. Wide lawns fall to the golden sand beach with shade trees, a ranchita

A GLOW IN THE DARK

*T*o friend and foe alike, it is "the monster"—the Juragua nuclear power station, near Cienfuegos. Construction began in 1983, when Soviet aid flowed freely. The initial project called for four reactors, but that has since been downsized to two 417,000 kilowatt reactors, either of which could supply up to 15% of Cuba's energy needs and save around two million tons of oil a year.

Construction was mothballed in September 1992, after Cuba announced it could not meet the financial terms set by the new Russian government. When construction ceased, assembly on one of the reactors was about 90% complete (the second reactor was about 20% complete).

A multinational study in 1995 gave the green light for the resumption of construction. In October 1995 Cuba signed an agreement with Russia's Atomic Energy Ministry (Minbas) to complete the plant, despite threats to sever aid to U.S. Congress to Russia. Minbas (which has sunk over US$1 billion into Juragua) agreed to provide US$350 million of the US$800 million needed for completion. Meanwhile, about 1,200 workers are still employed as maintenance crews to keep the reactors rust-free while awaiting the day when construction resumes.

Cuba has suggested creating an international consortium to conclude construction and operate the plant (partners from France, Germany, and other countries would recover their investment from the sale to Cuba of the energy produced). Cuba has even invited the U.S. to participate. Instead of seizing the opportunity to become involved in securing the safety of Juragua, the U.S. seems determined to kill it.

Congress has held hearings dominated by anti-Cuba lobbyists, who claim that the plant will pose a serious threat to the safety of the United States (Juragua is 240 miles from Miami), although Florida has several nuclear reactors of its own. The U.S. government says the project is flawed by faulty design and construction; Congress has portrayed the plant as similar to the Chernobyl plant, which exploded in April 1986 in Ukraine. However, the International Atomic Energy Agency (IAEA) has approved the project as safe. The Pentagon commissioned its own study in 1993 and agreed that Juragua is an advanced VVER-440 model, pressurized water-cooled reactor, wholly different in design from Chernobyl's outdated graphite technology. The Geneva-based IAEA says it is similar to the world's most efficient reactor—the Russian-built VVER in Finland.

For now, the fields surrounding the plant are once more being plowed with oxen by farmers awaiting the day when the hum of energy surging from the reactors may keep the lights burning in Cuba.

bar and restaurant, and an array of water sports, including catamarans. The 255 a/c double rooms feature private bath, satellite TV, radio, and telephone. There are also 12 suites. Mopeds, bicycles, and cars can be rented, and Rumbos offers excursions. Other facilities include three restaurants, a small nightclub with cabaret, shop, and a scuba diving center. It appeals mostly to Cubans and is overpriced at US$34 s, US$45 d, US$59 t low season, US$49 s, US$53 d, US$69 t.

A more intimate option is Cubanacán's **Hotel Faro Luna,** Carretera de Pasacaballos Km 18, Playa Rancho Luna, tel. (432) 45-1340, fax (432) 45-1162, e-mail: dcfluna@perla.inf.cu, a stone's throw to the east of Hotel Rancho Luna. This recently upgraded hotel has 41 spacious, a/c, pleasantly decorated rooms with satellite TVs and balconies. The hotel has a small swimming pool, shop, and restaurant and offers scuba diving. Rates are US$39 s, US$45 d low season, US$47 s, US$56 d high season. It is frequented by with English, German, and French tourists, but nonetheless receives few guests.

Islazul's **Hotel Pasacaballos,** tel. (43) 4-8120, is popular mostly with Cubans. Its situation is appealing: on a hill at the entrance of the bay, facing Jagua Castle. Alas, the 188 a/c rooms face the other way—another example of communist design gone awry. The five-story hotel is described in its brochure as "the most beautiful hotel built since the Revolution and. . . probably the best hotel in all of Cuba." It looks like an enormous concrete block shipped in from Novosibirsk. Inside, things aren't too bad, but it wins no prizes. A flying staircase of black marble leads to the modestly furnished rooms. Facilities include a restaurant, post office, shops, and activities from billiard contests to cocktail lessons. Bicycles can be rented, but you're out on a limb. Rates are US$25 s, US$32 d high season.

Getting There

Buses depart daily from the Cienfuegos bus terminal three times daily (50 centavos; 45 minutes). A taxi will cost you about US$12. *Pesetero* ferries leave for Rancho Luna on a regular basis from the terminal on Avenida 46 and Calle 25. Ferries to and from Cienfuegos connect Pasacaballo with Jagua.

CASTILLO DE JAGUA

Across the bay from Pasacabello sits a 17th-century Spanish fort, Castillo de Jagua, guarding the entrance to the Bahía de Cienfuegos. The original fortress was expanded in the 18th century to defend against the English Royal Navy. A ghost—the Blue Lady—haunts the small fortress that overlooks a fishing village founded by immigrants from Mallorca and Valencia. It consists of delicate, whitewashed, red-tile-roofed houses perched above the water (some on stilts). Appropriately it is called **Perché.** Fishing boats bob at anchor (note, too, the Batman-style Russian speedboat).

A small museum is planned for the fortress, which today functions as a restaurant.

Getting There

Ferries depart the wharf on Avenida 46 and Calle 25 in Cienfuegos at 6, 8, and 11 a.m. and 1, 3, and 5 p.m. (US$0.50). It's a 30-minute journey. The ferry wharf in Jagua is immediately below the fortress. A ferry also operates between Pasacabello, across the bay.

You can also get there by road. Exit Cienfuegos on Calle 37 past the industrial complexes. Keep the bay on your left. Drive carefully: the road is deeply potholed.

CIUDAD NUCLEAR

Up on the hill behind Jagua is a modern city, Ciudad Nuclear (Nuclear City), built in the 1980s to house workers constructing Cuba's first nuclear power station nearby at Juragua, atop the westernmost tip of the entrance to the Bahía de Cienfuegos. The half-completed reactor stands idle about two km west of town, where it rises menacingly, like a bubble, attended by a coterie of rusting, courtesan cranes.

The dreary Soviet-built town consists of a dozen or so high-rise concrete apartment blocks with their mildewed façades. It's soulless and melancholic, despite the shopping centers and movie theater. Local inhabitants drown out the melancholy by setting up megawatt speakers in the streets for impromptu parties.

CIENFUEGOS TO TRINIDAD

THE COAST

Trinidad, Cuba's best-preserved colonial city, is 83 km east of Cienfuegos. The Circuito Sur coast road dips and rises as the saw-toothed Sierra del Escambray rise ahead and to the north, building ridge upon ridge. Below, in the rain shadow formed by the mountains, the road passes first through sugarcane fields, and the smell of molasses carries across the hummocky plains. The mountain foothills narrow down to the roadway, squeezing it against the coast. The heat builds gradually. The land becomes increasingly arid, the sugarcane is replaced with parched savanna grazed by hardy cattle. The *bohíos* become noticeably simpler and aged.

A series of beaches lie hidden in coves at the mouth of rivers that wash down from the hills, as at the mouth of the **Río La Jutía**, 42 km from Cienfuegos, and eight km farther east, at **Playa Ingles,** where you are deposited beside a beautiful and lonesome beach with fishing boats and a rustic hut that serves *refrescoes* and snacks to local fishermen.

Hacienda La Vega, about three km west of Playa Ingles, is a cattle farm—*vaquería*—where horseback riding is offered by Rumbos (US$4). A dirt road leads to a hilltop lookout with views over the mountains, coast, and lake; then continues to **Playa La Caleta de Castro,** a white-sand beach tucked inside a cove. A roadside restaurant at the entrance to La Vega serves snacks and *criollo* fare. Lather up with insect repellent—the *jenjenes* are fierce.

Three km east of the turnoff for Playa Ingles, you'll cross the **Río Yaguanabo** and pass into Sancti Spíritus Province.

Accommodations and Food

Cubamar runs **Villa Guajimico,** tel. (432) 45-1206 or (7) 66-2523, fax (7) 33-3111, e-mail: cubamar@cubamar.mit.cma.net, in Havana, at the mouth of the Río La Jutía. Some of the 51 a/c brick cabins line a pretty little white-sand beach in the river estuary. Others stair step a steep hill where a swimming pool and restaurant offers excellent views. All cabins are modestly yet pleasantly furnished, with satellite TV, private bathrooms, and hot water. Services include a medical facility, car rental, and scuba diving (US$35 including equipment) and catamarans (US$10 per hour). Rates were US$27 s, US$29 d, US$37 t low season, US$30 s, US$36 d, US$45 t high season.

Islazul operates **Villa Yaguanabo** at the mouth of the Río Yaguanabo, with 15 recently renovated, modestly furnished two-story cabins for US$18 s, US$21 d low season, US$21 s, US$26 d high season. The bar-restaurant is popular with Cubans.

VALLES DE MATAGUÁ AND YAGUANABO

At La Sierrita, about 30 km east of Cienfuegos, you can cut inland and ascend into the Sierra del Escambray via the valley of the Río Mataguá. It's a stupendously scenic route that rises past sheer-walled, cave-riddled limestone *mogotes,* at their most impressive near the town of **San Blas,** eight km east of La Sierrita. San Blas sits in the lee of great cliffs where huge stalactites and stalagmites are exposed in an open cave high atop the mountains. Bright red flame trees and bougainvillea in the valley add to the stunning effect.

The road winds and loops steeply until you are amid narrow valleys planted in coffee and bananas atop the *mogotes.* Look out for the gun slits in the cliffs at hairpin bends on the mountainside: they were used by Che Guevara's guerrillas to ambush Batista's troops.

Alternately, you can continue along the coast road and turn inland to follow the Río Yaguanabo through another stunningly scenic valley hemmed in to the north by the ragged southern slopes of the Escambray. The road rises to **Loma Palo Seco,** the Yaguanabo Valley's highest point. There are waterfalls with cool ponds at their bases to discover amid the pastures, thicket, and dense woodlands. The highlight is **Cueva Martín Infierno,** boasting Latin America's largest stalagmite—67 meters tall—as well as mineralogical rarities such as gypsum flowers *(flores de yeso).*

Rumbos offers excursions from Trinidad and Cienfuegos, including lunch at Hacienda La Vega (see The Coast Road, above; also see Cienfuegos and Trinidad sections).

SIERRA DEL ESCAMBRAY

The Sierra Escambray is Cuba's second-highest mountain range. The Escambray and adjacent ranges lie mostly within Cienfuegos Province, descending gradually into Villa Clara Province to the north, edging into Sancti Spíritus Province to the east, and dropping steeply to the southern coast, deeply indented by rivers. The Escambray's highest peaks and densest forests are protected in Topes de Collantes National Park, in the chain's southeast corner (see Topes de Collantes, in the Sancti Spíritus chapter). The mountains reach 1,140 meters atop Pico San Juan. It is remarkable how much cooler it is up here, even on a summer day. Dark nimbus clouds can freshen during the morning and cold rain may fall while the surrounding lowlands bake, even in the "dry season." The region is the rainiest in Cuba, especially during May-October.

The Escambray are a delight for birders and hikers. Guillermo Cabrera Infante wrote that "The ground is covered with a herbaceous green carpet; the trees, bushes, and jungle run the whole gamut of green. Tree trunks are covered with a lichen that is like green rust. . . Thousands of pearls of raindrops drip from the leaves, and as you step, the grass sinks with a crackling watery sound."

In the late 1950s, these mountains were the site of a revolutionary front against Fulgencio Batista, led by Che Guevara. After the revolutionaries triumphed in 1959, the Escambray hid another band of olive green-clad rebels, this time counterrevolutionaries who opposed Castro. The CIA helped finance and arm these resistance fighters, whom the Castro regime tagged "bandits." The resistance army had grown to at least 3,000 men by 1962, as many men as Fidel had in the Sierra Maestra at his peak. The groups, however, were split into various rival groups and had no philosophical program other than to resist Castro. Castro formed counterinsurgency units called Battalions of Struggle Against Bandits. He also forcibly evacuated local *campesinos* to deny the anti-Castroites local support. The "bandits" weren't eradicated until 1966. A museum in Trinidad tells the communist government's version of *la lucha contra los bandidos* (although the *bandidos* are portrayed by the Cuban governments as representatives of the corrupt Batista regime, many were simple, honest *campesinos*).

UNEAC, the Cuban Union of Writers and Artists, has a retreat—El Castillito—high in the Escambray.

PRESA DE HANABANILLA

This huge (32 square km) man-made lake fills what was once a deep valley on the northern slopes of the Escambray. The lake, which has an average depth of 35 meters and supplies water to Santa Clara and Cienfuegos, shimmers through every shade from pea-green to cobalt (depending on the mood of the weather) below its backdrop of pine-studded mountains. The lake is renowned for bass.

The folks in the hamlet of Hanabanilla make plastic recreation boats. The slopes are farmed by *campesinos* who grow malanga, tobacco, and coffee. The lakeshore curls like a jigsaw-puzzle piece, perfect for scenic boat trips from the dock of the Hotel Hanabanilla. A ferry (US$2) also takes passengers across the lake to the **Casa del Campesino,** where you can get a taste for the *campesino* lifestyle on this small working farm. You can also catch the boat that ferries *campesinos* and workers to and from remote hamlets on the steep slopes; it leaves from the tiny dock in Hanabanilla hamlet, reached by a side road just north of the dam and hydroelectric station below the hotel. Guides will lead you to local caves.

The turnoff for Presa de Hanabanilla is midway between Cumanayagua and Manicuraga, on the 4-206, at La Macagua, just west of Ciro Redondo.

Accommodations and Food

Sitting above the western lakeshore is Islazul's **Hotel Hanabanilla,** tel. (42) 4-9125, another Soviet complex, this one perched over the lake. It's pleasant and popular with Cubans, who gather by the swimming pool and sundeck. The hotel has 125 a/c, modestly furnished rooms, each with private bath, telephone, and radio. Facilities include a restaurant, bar, *cafetería,* nightclub, swimming pool, shop, and tourism bureau. I enjoyed a fresh-caught tilapia, superbly grilled and served with garlic, pickled cabbage, other condiments, and English-style chips (fries) in the hotel restaurant that, alas, has no views whatsoever. Rates were US$20 s, US$26 d low season, US$28 s, US$34 d high season.

Lunch is also served at the **Río Negro Restaurante,** on the Casa de Campesino (see above) on the southern shores of the lake and featuring *bohios* surrounded by bougainvillea. Here you're fed *criollo* cuisine such as roast pork (the house specialty is chicken with pineapple; *pollo saltón à la piña*) and entertained by Afro-Cuban rhythms. The restaurant is reached by a steep trail.

MANICARAGUA TO TOPES DE COLLANTES

The most beautiful vistas in the Escambray are on the north-facing slopes, as you rise from Santa Clara or drop through the valleys east and north of Presa de Hanabanilla (Lake Hanabanilla) to the agricultural town of **Manicaragua,** 30 km south of Santa Clara and 30 km north of Topes de Collantes, the main tourist center (see Topes de Collantes in the Sancti Spíritus chapter). The town is surrounded by rolling plains with hillocks resembling a basket of eggs. It's a classic Cuban landscape, with *bohios,* royal palms, and *guajiros* tending fields of tobacco with ox-drawn plows. There's nothing much to Manicaragua, though.

A road rises south of Manicuragua and climbs into the Escambray to Topes de Collantes. Midway between Manicaragua and Topes, you'll pass a T-junction at **Jibacoa,** where a road leads west to the southern end of Presa de Hanabanilla.

Accommodations and Food: The **Hotel Escambray,** on the western side of Manicaragua, on the road to Cienfuegos, tel. (42) 49-1548, has 20 basic, ill-lit rooms. It accepts foreigners and charges in pesos (seven pesos s, 10 d, 14 with a/c). It has a small restaurant and the El Rojito bar.

Manicaragua has several peso restaurants in the main square.

SANTA CLARA

Santa Clara (pop. 175,000), 300 km east of Havana, is the provincial capital of Villa Clara. Straddling the Carretera Central, it is strategically located on the southern fringe of fertile plains, in the northern lee of the Escambray, and is a gateway to the eastern provinces—a crucial strategic location at the center of Cuba.

The city was established within the confluence of the Ríos Bélico and Cubanicay in 1689 when residents of Remedios grew tired of con-stant pirate raids, pulled up stakes, and moved inland.

It functioned as a plum in Cuba's wars of independence and, again during the battle to topple Batista. On 31 December 1958, Che Guevara's Rebel Army attacked the town and derailed a troop train carrying reinforcements and U.S. armaments bound for Oriente. Two days later, the Rebel Army captured the city, which became known as *el último reducto de la*

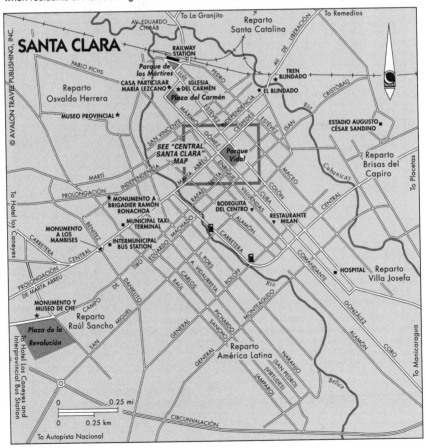

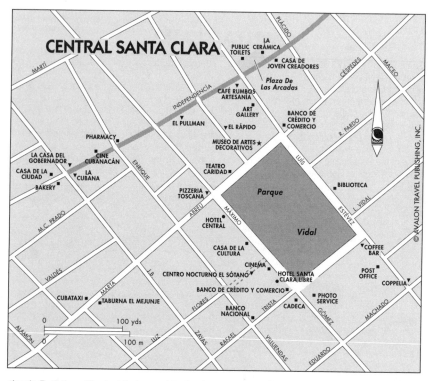

CENTRAL SANTA CLARA

tirania Batistiana (the last fortress of Batista's tyranny). Within 24 hours, the dictator fled the island.

Prior to 1959 there was only one factory of note: Coca-Cola's. As Minister of Industry, Che Guevara developed a soft spot for the city. Today Santa Clara is an important industrial town. The suburbs contain many factories, including the largest textile mill in the country and the Fábrica INPUD, which makes refrigerators, stoves, and other household appliances. It is also home to the University de las Villas, and the Ernesto "Che" Guevara Vocational School. A half-day's sightseeing will suffice.

ORIENTATION

Santa Clara is a large city, and although laid out roughly in a rectilinear grid, it's complicated to get around. The city is encircled by a ring road *(circunvalación);* use it to bypass the town.

The center is Parque Vidal. The Carretera Central enters town from the west and merges with Calle Marta Abreu, which runs to Parque Vidal (east of the square, Marta Abreu becomes Céspedes). Six blocks west of Parque Vidal (at the bridge over the Río Bélico), the Carretera swings south, then turns east again and exits town en route to Placetas. The main shopping street is Independencia, which runs parallel to Marta Abreu, one block north of Parque Vidal. Eastward, Independencia crosses the Río Cubanicay and (as Avenida de Liberación) leads to Remedios.

Máximo Gómez (also called Calle Cuba) and Luís Estévez (also called Calle Colón) run perpendicular to Abreu, on the west and east side of the park. Estévez leads north seven blocks to the railway station (beyond the tracks it becomes

Avenida Eduardo Chibás and leads to Sagua la Grande and the north coast).

THINGS TO SEE AND DO

Parque Vidal
This large paved square is named for the revolutionary hero Leoncio Vidal, who—according to a monument—was killed at this exact spot. A curiosity of the square is its double-wide sidewalk. In colonial days, this was divided by an iron fence, and whites perambulated on the inner half while blacks kept to the outside. In springtime, the park blazes with pink blossoms of *guasíma* trees and poinciana, full of sparrows and Cuban blackbirds caterwauling, honking, and chirping. The bandstand at its center is still used for concerts on weekends. Keeping her eye on things is a bronze effigy of Marta Abreu de Estévez (1845-1904), a local heroine and philanthropist who funded construction of the **Teatro la Caridad,** built in 1885 "for the poor of Santa Clara" but dedicated to the memory of Abreu's parents (her father was also a philanthropist, who funded the city's first free clinic and free primary school). Enrico Caruso considered it a fitting venue. Note the stunning muraled foyer.

Fifty meters east of the theater is the **Museo de Artes Decorativos,** tel. (422) 5368, featuring an eclectic array of stunning colonial antiques and furniture spanning styles from rococo and neoclassical to "imperial Cuban." Note the beautiful *ventrales* above the inner courtyard, and the so-called Empire Hall, with its delicate parquetry. Every room is sumptuously decorated with period pieces that would fetch princely sums at Sotheby's. It's open Monday, Wednesday, and Thursday 9 a.m.-6 p.m., Friday and Saturday 1-10 p.m., and Sunday 2- 6 p.m. Entrance costs US$2.

On the square's east side is the old **Palacio Provincial,** now housing the city *biblioteca* and with an imposing neoclassical frontage supported by Ionic columns. The building dates to 1922 and occupies the site of the original city hall. Opposite is the **Hotel Santa Clara Libre,** where many of Batista's troops ensconced themselves in December 1958 and where a fierce battle ensued to dislodge them. (In 1969, Black Panther leader Huey Newton and his wife sought exile in Cuba and, asking to "live like the people," were sent to Santa Clara. The couple, however, ended up in a suite in the Santa Clara Libre.)

The **Casa de la Cultura** is on the square.

El Bulevar (The Boulevard)
One block north of the square is a bustling pedestrian precinct—between Zayas to the west and Maceo to the east—on Independencia, with an intriguing blend of colonial and 20th-century buildings, lively bars and cafés in art deco and antique Spanish styles, and well-stocked stores selling Western goods. Midway along the boulevard, at Luís Estévez, is the tiny **Plaza de las Arcadas,** whose trees (intertwined with bougainvillea) are full of twittering birds.

Tren Blindado
The most interesting site is at the east end of Independencia, beyond the railway crossing, tel. (422) 2-2758. It was here on 29 December 1958 that rebel troops led by Che Guevara derailed one of Batista's troop trains. Four rust-colored carriages are preserved higgledy-piggledy in suspended animation as they came to rest after the train was run off the rails. There is an exhibit inside one of the carriages; open Tues.-Sun. 8 a.m.-noon and 3-7 p.m.; entry costs US$1. The carriages are fronted by an obelisk with a plaque telling the tale of the 90-minute battle.

Plaza de la Revolución
The battle is commemorated at this impressive plaza on the west side of the city, at the west end of Marta Abreu. Looming over the wide hilltop plaza is a massive bronze statue of Che Guevara bearing his rifle and, behind, a wall bearing a relief of the Sierra del Escambray and the Tren Blindado and revolutionary inscriptions. The panel to the rear has a relief map of Che's army route. The effect is dramatic, especially during a fiery red sunset with martial music playing. The evocative granite edifice is guarded by gun-toting soldiers.

The podium contains the fascinating **Museo de Che,** which worships the deeds of the revolutionary and has a detailed account of the capture of Santa Clara in December 1958. His history is traced from childhood, with many photos

Monumento Che Guevara overlooks the Plaza de la Revolución

from his youthful journey through Latin America. Exhibits include his pistol from the Sierra Maestra, letters to and from Fidel, his green PVC jacket with brown corduroy elasticized sides, and his black beret with the five-pointed star made memorable by the photo by Alberto Diaz Gutierrez (better known as "Korda"). The Korda photo forms a backdrop to the exhibit. Surveillance cameras watch your every move. It's open Mon.-Sat. 8 a.m.-5 p.m. and Sunday 8 a.m.-noon. Entrance is free. The entrance is on the north side. No cameras are allowed.

Che's remains (recently discovered in Bolivia) were laid to rest here in October 1997 in an adjacent mausoleum that has empty space for the 37 other guerrillas who lost their lives in Guevara's last campaign. The mausoleum is exquisite: stone floor, hardwood ceiling, walls of granite inset with the 3-D motifs of the revolutionaries, including Che's, with a small five-point star illumined top-right from a light beam inset in the ceiling. Upon entering you experience an overwhelming sensation of awe. Though held in awe by staunch loyalists, Che actually inspires indifference among ordinary Cubans and there is an eerie absence of Cuban pilgrims to this vast Stalinist shrine with, wrote Mark Ottaway, "its edgy staff and enough manouevering space outside for a regiment of tanks."

Other Sights
Walk two blocks east of Parque Vidal and you'll reach the **Iglesia Buen Viaje,** a beautiful church where black slaves once gathered on the patio to hear services (since they weren't permitted inside). Another church of note is the **Iglesia del Carmén,** on **Plaza del Carmén.** This national monument dates to 1748 and receives the sun at dusk, adding to its photogenic quality. It is fronted by a granite monument that arcs around a tree where the first Mass was held to celebrate the founding of Santa Clara in 1689. The church, which was used as a women's prison during the wars of independence, is riddled with bullet holes fired from the police station—now named El Vaquerito—across the street during the battle of 29 December 1958. Locals gather to fill their pails at an antique hand-pump adjacent. On the north side of the church is a life-size 3-D figure of revolutionary hero Roberto Rodríquez Fernandez—*el vaquerito*—of whom Che Guevara said, "They have killed one hundred men."

Museo Provincial, in the Escuela Abel Santamaría, at the north end of Calle Esquerra in the Reparto Osvaldo Herrera neighborhood, was formerly a military barracks (fulfilling Castro's dictum to turn all Batista's barracks into centers of learning). The museum is brimful of colonial furniture but is dedicated to the province's role in the wars of independence and the fight against Batista; it also features a large collection of weaponry, plus a natural history exhibit downstairs. Open Tues.-Sat. 1-6 p.m. and Sunday 9 a.m.-1 p.m. (US$1).

Migratory waterfowl flock to **Los Caneyes Game Reserve,** on the western outskirts of the city. Ducks and doves are favored species, although pheasant, quail, common snipe, fulvous tree duck, American coot, and guinea fowl are among the other beautiful species to be admired.

ACCOMMODATIONS

Casas Particulares

Eliar and Alina Cruz are friendly hosts at **Casa Particular María Lezcano,** facing Plaza de Carmén at Calle San Pablo #19 e/ Carolina y Máximo Gómez, tel. (422) 5175, with a spacious lounge with color TV, nicely decorated in 1950s style, and two spacious bedrooms that share a large, clean bathroom with beautiful tile work and intermittent hot water for US$20 apiece.

Bodeguita del Centro, Calle Villuendas #264, e/ San Miguel y Nazareno, tel. (422) 4356, is recommended by a reader; as are the rooms at **El Blindado,** Independencia #319, e/ San Isidro y La Cruz, tel. (422) 2-2901, for US$20. Another reader recommends the home of Marisela Rodríguez on Calle Bonifacio Martínez, Edif. 9, Apto. 4, e/ Sindico y Nazareno. A neighbor also rents a room at Apto. 8. And a third recommends the home of Jorge and María García Rodríguez on Calle Cuba #209 e/ Calle Serafin García y Morales, tel. (422) 2-2329, e-mail: garcrodz@ civc.inf.cu, with two rooms and private bath with hot water.

Hotels

Budget: Campismo Arcoiris, operated by Cubamar Viajes, Calle 15 #752 esq. Paseo, Vedado, Havana, tel. (7) 66-2523, fax (7) 33-3111, e-mail: cubamar@cubamar.mit.cma.net, offers 13 basic cabins in a simple holiday camp for Cubans. It's about three miles from town.

The **Hotel Central,** 50 meters north of the Santa Clara Libre on Parque Vidal, tel. (422) 2-2369, is operated by Islazul, which has a *carpeta* (booking office), tel. (422) 5959, here for reservations throughout the province.

Islazul's **Hotel Santa Clara Libre,** tel. (422) 2-7548, overlooks Parque Vidal. This high-rise has 160 rooms—most with a/c, each with TV and telephone, but dowdy and desperately in need of renovation at press time. There's a reasonable restaurant on the 10th floor and a rooftop bar above. You'll have to park your car on the square and should hire a local to guard it. Rates were US$20 s, US$26 d year-round, and US$1.50 additional for TV, and US$3 additional for TV, fridge, and a/c.

Inexpensive: The most appealing place is **Hotel Horizontes Los Caneyes,** Avenida de los Eucaliptos y Circunvalación de Santa Clara, tel. (422) 2-8140 and tel./fax (422) 4512, about two km west of town. It has 91 a/c rooms in thatched, wooden, octagonal cabanas spread amid lawns and bougainvillea. The recently refurbished bungalows have terra-cotta tile floors, large bathrooms, refrigerators, and small cable TVs. Facilities include an attractive restaurant, *cafetería,* snack bar, disco, small swimming pool, hairdresser, car rental, and a tourism bureau. Los Caneyes is popular with tour groups. You'll need a sweater for the near-frigid restaurant. Rates were US$38 s, US$50 d low season; US$45 s, US$58 high season.

A similar concept—thatched cabins in a landscaped setting—is offered at **La Granjita,** Carretera Malez Km 2.5, Santa Clara, tel. (422) 2-8190, fax (422) 2-8192, run by Cubanacán and built around a handsome pool and sundeck where a cabaret is hosted. The 24 rooms in bamboo, rattan, and thatch bungalows are pretty and feature a/c, cable TV, radio, and telephone, and marble bathrooms. New two-story octagonal cabins are furnished to international standards. There's a tennis court, restaurant, and shop, and horses can be hired. The facility is less utilized than Los Caneyes, with a more lonesome feel. Rates were US$42 s, US$55 d, US$62 t year-round.

FOOD

First choice (for quality) is the restaurant in the **Hotel Los Caneyes,** though standards can vary. The top-floor restaurant in the **Hotel Santa Clara Libre** is nothing special, but at least it has views over the square. Reasonable *criollo* fare is served at **Restaurante Milan** at Calle Villuendas #305, e/ Nazareno y Pastora, tel. (422) 4022; likewise at **Bodeguita del Centro,** Calle Villuendas #264, and at the **Pizzeria Toscana,** at the northwest corner of M. Abreu and M. Gómez, with a simple Cuban take on Italian fare.

There are few *paladares.* Try **Restaurante Renacer,** in a colonial home at Zayas #111 y Eduardo Machado y Tristá, tel. (422) 2-2272.

El Rápido, one block north of Parque Vidal e/ Independencia y Marta Abreu, is an if-all-else-fails standby.

There's a wide choice of bars and cafés for snacks and drinks. The "Boulevard" has several lively options, including **El Pullman,** a colonial-period setting with patio seating under awnings (make sure you sit in the dollar-only section). **Rumbos** has a similarly popular café overlooking the Plaza de las Arcadas—it's a favored hangout for tourists and *chicas.* My favorite is **La Casa del Gobernador,** at the corner of Zayas and Independencia. This colonial-era building, once the governor's house, is now a lofty-ceilinged bar. You can look down on life, so to speak, from the upstairs balcony. There's cabaret in the evening. Another favorite of locals is **La Cubana,** a café that also opens onto the "Boulevard."

For coffee, try the coffee bar on the southeast corner of the main square. **Coppelia,** one block south of the main square, on Calle Colón, sells ice cream. There's a bakery opposite the Casa de la Ciudad, on Independencia.

ENTERTAINMENT AND SHOPPING

Entertainment
Troubadors play most evenings (and weekend afternoons) at the **Casa de la Trova,** on Calle Colón, one block southeast of Parque Vidal. Classical and other performances are also hosted at **Teatro Caridad.** Look for the posters along the sides of Parque Vidal announcing upcoming events. Band concerts are occasionally held on weekends beneath the gazebo in Parque Vidal. And the **Casa de Joven Creadores,** Independencia e/ Luís Estéves, has art and theater programs for children.

The air-conditioned **Centro Nocturno Pullman,** on Independencia y Máximo Gómez, is a happening spot. It's open nightly 8 p.m.-2 a.m.; US$5 per couple *(pareja).* The most favored spot at press time was the **Centro Nocturno El Sótano,** on the west side of Parque Vidal. Also try **Taburna El Mejunje,** in brick ruins on Marta Abreu e/ Zaya and Alemán, with daytime programs for children and a variety of musical formats at night (closed Monday).

A **cabaret** at La Casa del Gobernador, on Independencia, features comedians and live musicians in the upstairs bar; Fri.-Sun. at 9 p.m.; US$5 including a *cuba libre.* Cabaret is also the forte of **Cabaret Cacique,** tel. (422) 4512, a dark and moody *bohio* with great ambience, on

Carretera Eucaliptos y Circunvalación. It's a five-minute walk west of Hotel Los Caneyes. Comedy (in Spanish) is big here, laden with typically Cuban transvestite humor. The crowd is all Cuban. Meals are served. Entrance is US$1.

There's a **cinema** on the west side of the main square, and another, **Cine Cubanacán,** on the "Boulevard." Entrance is one peso.

Shopping
Antique lovers may find some gems hidden behind the huge wooden doors of **Casa de la Ciudad,** at the corner of Zayas and Independencia. For ceramics, check out **La Cerámica** on Plaza de las Arcadas, or the art gallery at 11 Luís Estévez. There's also a souvenir store at the Hotel Los Caneyes.

PRACTICALITIES

Information and Services
There are small information desks at both the Hotels Los Caneyes and La Granjita. **Rumbos** has a tourist office at Independencia #167.

The **post office** is one block south of the square, on Colón. There's also a post office in the railway station. More reliable is the express delivery service offered by **DHL** at Colón #10, tel. (422) 4626. It's open weekdays 9 a.m.-6 p.m. and Saturday 8:30 a.m.-noon.

You can make international calls from the tourist hotels or from the **Centro Telefónico** one block west of Parque Vidal, e/ Calle Marta Abreu y Independencia.

There are **Banco de Crédito y Comercio** outlets on opposite sides of Parque Vidal, at Marta Abreu y Luís Estéves, and Máximo Gómez y Rafael Trista. You can change dollars for pesos at the **Cadeca** exchange bureau, also at Máximo Gómez esq. Rafael Trista.

Photo Service has a meagerly stocked branch at Gómez #1, one block south of Parque Vidal.

There are **public toilets** at Plaza de las Arcadas.

A Cupet **gas station** is on the Carretera Central at Calle General Roloff. There's an Oro Negro gas station two blocks north on the Carretera Central at Calle San Miguel.

Getting There
By Air: Santa Clara's **Abel Santamaría Airport,** tel. (422) 8-6183, was slated to be up-

TRAIN SCHEDULE (SANTA CLARA)

EASTBOUND

No.	Origin	Destination	Arrive Santa Clara	Depart Santa Clara
11	Havana	Santiago de Cuba (every three days)	11:19 p.m.	11:39 p.m.
13	Havana	Santiago de Cuba	8:32 p.m.	8:52 p.m.
15	Havana	Holguín (every two days)	6:18 p.m.	6:38 p.m.
17	Havana	Bayamo-Manzanillo	12:39 a.m.	12:59 a.m.

WESTBOUND

No.	Origin	Destination	Arrive Santa Clara	Depart Santa Clara
12	Santiago de Cuba	Havana (every three days)	6:57 a.m.	7:17 a.m.
14	Santiago de Cuba	Havana	2:57 a.m.	3:17 a.m.
16	Holguín	Havana (every two days)	12:55 p.m.	1:15 a.m.
18	Bayamo-Manzanillo	Havana	4:58 a.m.	5:18 a.m.
64	Santiago de Cuba	Morón (every two days)	9:50 a.m.	9:55 a.m.

graded to receive international jets for the year 2000.

By Bus: The **Víazul** tourist bus serves Santa Clara from Havana on Tuesday and Friday (see the Víazul Bus Schedule chart, in the On the Road chapter). For public bus service, see the Public Bus Service From Havana chart, also in the On the Road chapter. In Santa Clara, the **Terminal de Ómnibus Nacionales** is on the Carretera Central about 2.5 km west of the city center, tel. (422) 9-2114. Other bus service links Santa Clara with Cienfuegos, Sancti Spíritus, Remedios, Camagüey, Trinidad, and Santiago de Cuba.

By Train: Santa Clara is on the main line between Havana and the Oriente and is served by most trains traveling between these destinations. The railway station—Estación de Ferrocarriles—is at the northern end of Luís Estévez, seven blocks from Parque Vidal, tel. (422) 2-2895.

Getting Around

The municipal bus terminal is on Calle Marta Abreu, 10 blocks west of Parque Vidal. Licensed taxis and *colectivos* can usually be hailed from outside the stations.

Bus no. 11 runs between Parque Vidal and the Hotel Los Caneyes between 7 a.m. and 7 p.m. A taxi between the two points will cost about US$3. There are always taxis outside Los Caneyes. Otherwise call **Cubataxi** at tel. (422) 2-2691 or 2-6903.

Getting Away

By Bus: Buses depart Santa Clara's interprovincial terminal for Havana twice daily around midday. Buses also depart for Sancti Spíritus, Trinidad, Camagüey, Holguín, and Santiago de Cuba. Another leaves for Manicaragua, where you can catch a separate bus to Trinidad.

By Train: See the Train Schedules: Santa Clara chart for key departures. In addition, at press time a westbound Morón-Havana train departed Santa Clara at 11:35 a.m.; a Sancti Spíritus-Havana train departed at 1:17 p.m.; a Sancti Spíritus-Cienfuegos train departed at 7:50 a.m. A train for Cienfuegos departed at 5:20 p.m. Eastbound, a Havana-Morón train departed at 12:17 p.m.; a Havana-Sancti Spíritus train departed at 3 a.m., and a Cienfuegos-Sancti Spíritus departed at 5:25 p.m.

The railway station—**Estación de Ferrocarriles**—is on the north side of the tiny Plaza de los Mártires, at the northern end of Luís Estévez, tel. (422) 2-2895. You pay in dollars at the ticket office inside (the ticket office on the *south* side of the square is for locals paying in pesos). It's open 24 hours daily.

By Car: Transtur, tel. (422) 4512, has an outlet in the Hotel Santa Clara Libre. **Micar,** tel. (422) 4570, has an outlet at the Servicentro Oro Negro, on the Carretera Central y Calle San Miguel.

Organized Excursions: Cubanacán, Calle Maceo #453 e/ Carretera Central y Caridad, tel. (422) 5189, fax (422) 33-5071, offers excursions.

AROUND SANTA CLARA

ALTURAS DE SANTA CLARA

The Alturas de Santa Clara rise sensually to the south and east of the city. The hills and valleys are pocked with quaint timeworn villages and a quilt of tobacco fields tilled by oxen and tended by *guajiros* in straw hats and white linen field clothes. The region's mild climate and rich soils support some of the most productive *vegas* (tobacco fields) in Cuba.

Both the Autopista and Carretera Central pass through the region. The only place to eat along the Carretera is an attractive, thatch-roofed *paladar* on a hilltop about six km east of Santa Clara, midway to Manajanabo.

One of the most scenic drives in Cuba is the route directly south from Santa Clara to Manicaragua and into the foothills of the Sierra Escambray along route 4-474.

La Ya Ya

This self-contained "model village" (named for a flowering tree that grows locally), 20 km south of Santa Clara, was apparently conceived by Fidel Castro and created in 1972. Before the Revolution, the local population scraped by growing sugarcane on small plots ill suited to the crop. The *campesinos* were offered apartments in exchange for their land, from which the state formed a dairy-farming enterprise. Resistance from the peasantry was great—Castro's Agrarian Reform had given the peasants their own land only a decade before, and now the government wanted to take it back. Despite the plaudits that the government hands itself, there is nothing inspirational in the five-story, prefab apartment blocks (repeated all over the island). Still, the farmers now have electricity and hot water, which their old *bohíos* lacked, and the inhabitants have traditionally paid no rent. It is interesting as a sociological curiosity.

THE NORTH COAST

There is little to recommend along the north coast, as beaches are few and the scenery unimpressive. Still, a well-paved road (route 4-13) runs parallel to the shore, providing an easy, off-the-beaten-path route for travelers heading between Varadero and, say, Cayo Coco or other spots along the coast.

Playa el Salto y Ganuza, immediately east of the pretty little village of **Corralillo,** is a popular hangout for Cubans. It is served by a railway that connects it with Santa Clara. The **Baños de Elguea,** or Elguea Thermal Center, about three km northwest of Corralillo, are supplied by hyperthermal (up to 50° C) and hypermineralized springs containing bromine, sodium, radium, and sulfur. The waters, in shallow pools of varying temperature and potency, are good for treating rheumatism, skin ailments, and respiratory problems. It was renovated in 1998 with three swimming pools, a marching tank, mud baths, gym, solarium, massage rooms, and more.

Encrucijada, 25 km due north of Santa Clara, was the birthplace of revolutionary heroes Abel Santamaría and Jesús Menéndez. Their houses are now museums dedicated to their memory. East of Encrudijada, the 4-13 merges with route 4-321, which runs west to Santa Clara and east to Remedios and Caibarién.

Beach-fringed cays lie scattered like diamonds in the jade-colored waters offshore. The white sand beaches are untapped for tourism, and few snorkelers or scuba divers have as yet peered beneath the calm surface to discover a coral world more colorful than a casket of gems. The cays' landward shores are fringed by mangroves—havens for herons and other stilt-legged waders. And many of the cays are populated by iguanas and *jutías.* The largest cay is **Cayo Fragoso,** shaped like an arrowhead. A ship ran aground in the bight on the western side, and there it has rested and rusted since World War II —a perfect draw for scuba divers.

Accommodations

Horizontes Elguea Hotel & Spa, tel. (42) 68-6298 or 68-6367, is promoted as a spa resort but receives few guests. The spa has traditionally served Cubans, but the formerly spartan complex has been refurbished and is pleasant, albeit

AROUND SANTA CLARA 581

modest. It has 89 a/c rooms, four suites, plus a room for disabled, with bamboo furnishings, cable TVs, phones, security boxes, and refrigerators, and modern bathrooms. Facilities include volleyball, basketball, and tennis courts and a large swimming pool and sundeck. The hotel treatment includes a visit to Cayo Blanquizal, whose highly sulfurous sands are supposedly very effective for natural beauty masks. The modestly elegant restaurant is the only eatery for miles. Rates were US$29 s, US$38 d low season; US$37 s, US$45 d high season.

Services
There's a **Cupet gas station** in Sagua La Grande, at the junction of the roads for Varadero and Santa Clara.

SANTA CLARA TO ZULUETA

East of Santa Clara, the Carretera Central runs through **Placetas,** a small agricultural town lent a Wild West feel by wide dusty streets and arcades along the main street. Neither it nor the village of **Zulueta,** 10 km north of Placetas, holds any great appeal except during the period leading up to New Year's, when rockets whiz through the streets and hand-held fireworks and "mortars" explode with a military boom as the townsfolk divide into two historic camps and vie with each other to see who can produce the best parade float and the loudest din (see the special topic, Firework Fever, in the Cienfuegos chapter). In 1873, Julian Zulueta, one of Cuba's wealthiest sugar barons, laid a railroad to one of his mills. People in the hamlet of Guanijibes moved uphill and established a new settlement—La Loma—near the station. The *zulueteños* have ever since been divided into *guanijiberos* and *lomeros*. In 1894, they copied the citizenry of Remedios and held their first *parranda*. After the Revolution, the parade floats took on revolutionary themes. The Zulueta and Placetas *parranda* culminate on New Year's Eve.

Getting There
Bus no. 448 departs Havana's main bus terminal at 6:40 a.m., arriving Placetas around noon (16 pesos). The **Terminal de Ómnibus,** tel. (42) 8-2280, is on the main street.

Buses run to Zulueta from Santa Clara and Remedios. Bus no. 450 also departs Havana's main bus terminal daily at 11:40 a.m., arriving at around 5:15 p.m. (17 pesos). The terminal in Zulueta is at Avenida Eneida, tel. (42) 39-9188.

REMEDIOS

This time-warp town whisks you to a bygone era. Remedios, 45 km northeast of Santa Clara,

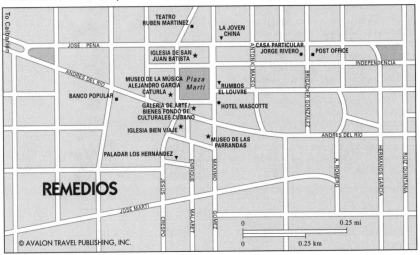

FIREWORKS FEVER

The villages and towns due east of Santa Clara are renowned islandwide for *parrandas*, the noisy year-end revels that date back more than a century. The festival apparently began in Remedios on Christmas Eve in 1822 when a zealous priest went through the streets making frightening noises meant to rouse the townspeople and scare them into attending midnight Mass. The villagers took the *fiesta*-like din to heart and gradually evolved a classic Mardi Gras-type carnival celebrated during the days around Christmas and New Year.

Eventually the *parrandas* spread to the neighboring villages of Zulueta, Placetas, and Camajuaní. Fireworks were introduced and the revels developed into a competition—really, massive fireworks battle—to see who could make the loudest noise. Each of the villages divides into two rival camps represented by mascots: the Carmelitas of Remedios, for example, are represented by a *gavilán*, (hawk), and the Sansacrices (from San Salvador), by a *gallo* (rooster).

The villagers invest ludicrous emotional value in their wars and spend months preparing in secret. Warehouses are stocked full of explosives and sawhorses studded with fireworks, and the final touches are put on the floats *(trabajos de plaza)* that will be pulled by field tractors around 3 a.m. Spies are infiltrated into the enemy camp. Even sabotage is not unknown.

The rivals take turns parading all through the night. Rum flows. The beating drums, singing and dancing gathers pace. Conga lines weave through town, accompanied by Polish polka music, a tradition that evolved in the 1880s and seems at odds with the spontaneity of the Cuban rumbas. Huge banners are waved, to be met by cheers or shouts of derision. *Viva La Loma! Viva Guanijibes!* The excitement builds as each neighborhood stages fireworks displays. The opposing sides alternately present their pyrotechnics. The streets are filled with deafening explosions from stovepipe mortars, rockets and whirling explosives whiz overhead and sometimes into the panicked crowd, and the smoke is so thick that you can barely see your way through the streets.

Din-making contraptions are exposed to add to the musical melée. The unique noise-making devices include a plow hit by an iron rod. Apparently, like fine wine, an antique plow matures with age. Villagers preserve its "vintage" by burying it in the earth between *parrandas*. The location is secret, and it is guarded jealously. Finally, the wildest fireworks are unleashed and the fiesta culminates in an orgy of insane firepower. Pretty fireworks don't earn points. The most relentless, voluminous bombast determines who wins.

When it is over, the triumphant neighborhood dances through the streets, accompanied by the losing team. Next day both sides fittingly proclaim victory. Thus sibling solidarity is overnight reaffirmed, proving once again in Cuba's exemplary fashion that what counts is the *spirit* of competition and conciliation.

Bottle rockets light up the night.

The annual parranda *features floats, fireworks, and nighttime revelry.*

is also one of the most beautiful little towns (pop. 18,000) in Cuba, full of Spanish colonial charm. Unlike Trinidad, Remedios is on the flat. Neither does it have cobbled streets. But it is in a good state of preservation, with a graceful symmetry and charisma. The entire city was justifiably named a national monument in 1979. It has been spruced up in recent years, and many residents have gained access to rare pots of paint, including a fluorescent turquoise.

Much of the pleasure is to be had in roaming the back streets, especially in late afternoon and early evening, when the low sun glows richly against the pastel walls and the church bells ring through town, tolling the hour. Bicycles and horse-drawn carriages wheel slowly through the narrow streets, where old men with cheroots and straw hats laze on rockers beneath red-tiled eaves.

History

Remedios is one of the oldest of Cuban cities, founded in 1514 when a land grant was given to a conquistador named Vasco Porcallo de Figueroa. A city hall wasn't built, however, and supposedly for that reason the town was never acknowledged as one of the first seven cities, despite its antiquity. It was originally situated closer to the shore. In 1544, it was moved a short distance inland to escape pirates. The town continued to come under constant attack and in 1578, the townsfolk uprooted again and founded

a new settlement, which they renamed San Juan de los Remedios del Cayo. (Later that century, a group of citizens moved inland and founded Santa Clara, which grew to become the provincial capital. Apparently the clique returned to Remedios to convince those that had remained to uproot and join them. They were rebuffed and ended up attacking and destroying the town.)

Sightseeing

The obvious place to begin is **Plaza Martí,** the main square. The city fans out from here. The square (formerly Plaza de Isabel) is shaded by tall royal palms beneath which you can sit on marble and wrought-iron benches.

Dominating the square is the venerable **Iglesia de San Juan Batista.** It dates from 1692, although extensions have since been added. Its pious exterior belies the splendor within, not least a carved cedar altar—the *altar mayor*—glimmering with 24-carat gold leaf, a statue of the Immaculate Virgin heavy with child, and—the *pièce de résistance*—a Moorish-style ceiling of carved mahogany, splendidly gabled and fluted, that had been sacrilegiously hidden behind plaster and was revealed only by a recent restoration. The church has an impressive bell tower with three stories (a bell in each). It was badly damaged by an earthquake in 1939 and restored over the ensuing 15 years at the behest of a local benefactor, who also donated European paintings.

The **Museo de la Música Alejandro García Caturla,** on the north side of Plaza Martí, recalls one of Cuba's foremost avant-garde composers. The house features beautiful green-tinted *mamparas,* period furniture, and many of Caturla's original manuscripts. The musical prodigy began writing music in 1920, when he was only 14. He was heavily influenced by the rhythms and sounds of Africa and fell under the sway of Stravinsky. The iconoclastic composer, born into a wealthy family, was moved by a concern for the poor and oppressed. His antiestablishment ways defied all conventions (for example, he married a black woman; when she died, he married her sister). The composer was a noted liberal and an incorruptible lawyer who rose to become judge for the city. Tragically he was assassinated in 1940 by a policeman who was due to come before him the next day for beating a woman to death.

One block west of the main square is the **Iglesia Bien Viaje,** a prim little church with a three-tiered bell-tower with a life-size figure of the Virgin Mary and Jesus in the "dove-hole." Between the church and the main square is a tiny plaza with a marble statue of the Liberty-like Indian maiden hewn from the rock and dedicated by the people of Remedios to *"los mártires de la patria."* Adjacent, check out the small **Galeria de Arte,** open Tue.-Sat. 1-9 p.m., and Sunday 8 a.m.- noon.

The **Museo de las Parrandas,** on Calle Máximo Gómez #71, celebrates the history of the famous festivals unique to the region and contains costumes, flags, and banners, examples of homemade fireworks, and floats. Open Tues.-Sat. 1-6 p.m. and Sunday 9 a.m.-1 p.m.

Haven't yet visited a cigar factory? Check out **Fábrica de Coronas** on Salado, tel. (42) 39-5340, where you'll be given a guided tour.

Calle Andres del Río and Calle Maceo both feature exquisite buildings. The **Museo Histórico** is at Antonio Maceo #56 e/ Calles Carilla y Ariosa, in a beautiful colonial home replete with period furnishings.

Remedios is linked to Santa Clara by Route 4-231, which dips and rises through photogenic tobacco country. Midway you pass through the unremarkable agricultural town of **Camajuani,** which, like Remedios and Zulueta, is famed for its year-end *parranda* (the rival sections of town are represented by a toad and a goat, depicted in roadside effigy at the entrance to town).

Accommodations

There are several *casas particulares.* During the end of year *parrandas,* when visitors flood town, restrictions on rentals are lifted and many non-registered households rent rooms—for a premium.

Casa Particular Jorge Rivero, Calle Brigadier González #29, tel. (42) 39-5331 (c/o a neighbor) two blocks west of the main plaza, is one of the most exquisite room rentals in Cuba. Jorge has two rooms in his well-furnished 1950s-style home with a gracious dining room and lounge (US$15-20). One well-lit room has a/c, neoclassical furnishings, large mirrors, and a beautiful tiled bathroom. The second, upstairs, has fans and a small, clean, modern bathroom and opens to a rooftop patio. A downstairs patio has pink flamingoes in a faux pool. There's secure parking.

Jorge Rodríguez was applying at press time for a license to rent his self-contained apartment at Calle Capitán Felipe Rodríguez del Río. His small home has a single bedroom, small kitchen, and a small bathroom. Jorge is a tremendous guy: very likable, gracious, and helpful. There's a secure garage two houses away.

The **Hotel Mascotte,** tel. (42) 39-5467 and 39-5144, is a small grande-dame hotel that was recently beautifully restored by Islazul. It has 14 pleasantly furnished rooms with lofty ceilings and modern amenities, including a/c, satellite TV, and marble and ceramics and hot water in bathrooms. A plaque on the outside wall records that here on 1 February 1899, Máximo Gómez met with Robert P. Porter, the special commissioner of U.S. President William McKinley. Here they negotiated the terms of the Mambí fighters' honorable discharge at the end of the Spanish-Cuban-American War. Rates were US$26 s, US$30 d low season, US$36 s, US$40 d high season.

Food

Private restaurants are thin on the ground. I enjoyed a fish dinner at **Paladar Los Hernández,** on Capitán Felipe Rodríguez.

The modern **Restaurante Las Arcadas,** in the Hotel Mascotte, serves undistinguished *criol-*

lo cuisine (US$1-5). Dine early during the *parranda*, as the place gets packed and it's an hour's-long scrum to get served.

The atmospheric **El Louvre**, one block south, is a touristy Rumbos café serving sandwiches and snacks, and coffee for 20 cents a cup. It serves an insipid mojito. Next door is the **Refresquera La Fe**, serving *refrescoes* of mango and, when available, anise. Don't be fooled by the name or by the Chinese dragon on the wall of **La Joven China**, on the west side of the main square. The former Chinese restaurant is now a café serving snacks and *refrescoes*.

Check out the local *vino dulce* called Brindis, a cheap port-style wine.

Entertainment and Events

Any time is a good time to visit, but if you are anywhere in Cuba during Christmas it should be here for the annual *parranda*, an awesome, one-of-a-kind experience. The time to visit is December, when the townsfolk feverishly begin preparing for their *parranda*, which culminates on the last Saturday of the year. Then the two sections of the city—El Carmen and San Salvador—compete with each other to make the most elaborate parade floats and the most deafening fireworks and mortars. Drunks abound, firing rockets out of their bare hands to show their bravery, while the crowd takes cover. Bring your earplugs and camera for a wild and racket-filled revelry you'll never forget. Be warned, it's a dangerous business, as rockets whiz into the crowd and every year several people are injured. Don't wear flammable nylon clothing. Be sure to check out the midnight Mass in the cathedral, a surreal experience, akin to attending Christmas Mass in St. Paul's Cathedral during the height of the Blitz! The crowd drinks through the night and into next day, when the streets on Christmas Day are littered with spent drunks and fireworks.

On 26 December those citizens still sober enough to participate celebrate the city's "liberation" by Che Guevara's Rebel Army.

You can savor traditional music performed by troubadours at the **Casa de la Cultura**, one block east of the main square, at the corner of Gómez and José de Pena. Also check out the **Bienes Fondo de Culturales Cubano**, on the west side of the main square. **Las Leyendas**, on south side of the main square, or the **Driver's Bar**, are popular hangouts for elderly citizens who gather to play dominoes and sip *aguardente*. And maybe there's a performance at the **Teatro Ruben Martinez**, at Camilo Cienfuegos #30, tel. (42) 39-5364.

Services

The post office is at José Peña #101. There's a *centro telefónico* at #20 Máximo Gómez, six blocks from the main square. You'll find a pharmacy on the southeast corner of the square, and a Cupet gas station on the west side of town, on the road to Santa Clara.

Getting There and Away

Buses for Remedios leave Havana's main bus terminal daily. The Remedios bus station is on the west side of town, on the road to Santa Clara, tel. (42) 39-5185. The railway station is eight blocks west of the main square, tel. (42) 39-5129.

Transtur Rent-a-Car has an outlet in the Hotel Mascotte.

CAIBARIÉN

The down-at-heels coastal town of **Caibarién**, eight km east of Remedios, is of no particular appeal, although it has some intriguing frontages downtown and a funky fishing fleet. Tiny **Cayo Conuco**, 600 meters offshore, is a popular holiday spot for Cubans and has a basic six-room hotel and a *campismo* with rustic wooden cabins overlooking the scintillating waters. Campers can set up tents (water, toilets, and showers are all present). A wooden dock grants boaters access, and you can drive across a small *pedraplen* (landfill bridge). Horses can be rented.

Accommodations

The **Villa Costa Blanca**, tel. (42) 3-3654, sits atop a breeze-swept promontory to the northwest of town and is utilized by Cubanacán functionaries, but accepts tourists when rooms are available. Rooms are nicely but modestly furnished in faux walnut decor and have a fridge, a/c, and small modern tiled bathrooms with cold water only. It has a small restaurant. It is difficult to find a room here Mon.-Wed. Rates were US$15-20 s/d depending on the room.

CAYO SANTA MARÍA

About five km east of Caibarién, a fabulously scenic, 50-km-long causeway departs the coast road and leaps from tiny cay to tiny cay, ending at Cayo Santa María. Eleven km of beaches run along its north shore, shelving into a coruscating lagoon with a coral reef beyond. The cay is slated for major development, with four hotels plus shops, a 30-berth marina, nightclub, and other ancillary services, all under the umbrella of Cubanacán. Hotels are also to be built on **Playa La Salina** on neighboring **Cayo Las Brujas,** which precedes Cayo Santa María and is 45 km from the mainland.

There's a military checkpoint three km along. You'll need your passport, plus a permit (US$5) from Cafetería Villa Blanca Rumbos, in central Caibarién.

Accommodations

The only property open at press time was the **Farallón Cayo Las Brujas** hotel run by Rumbos. It offers 24 modest bungalows (US$54 s/d).

Rumbos also offers accommodations on **Barco San Pasqual,** a 1920s-era boat moored near Punta Periquillo at Cayo Las Brujas. It has a bar, restaurant, and shop and specializes in nautical activities, including scuba diving. Rates were US$34 per cabin.

On Cayo Santa María, Cubanacán, tel. (42) 22-8264, has a *casa de negocios,* an elegant "businessman's house" for VIPs furnished in rattan, with kitchen, dining room, and three bedrooms (each with private bath).

The four-star **Club Santa María** was slated to open in 2000 with 300 rooms. A second deluxe 300-room property to be run by the Spanish Sol Meliá chain was due to open in 2001. Contact Cubanacán, Maceo #453 e/ Central y Caridad, Santa Clara, tel. (42) 22-6169, e-mail: delegado@centro.vcl.cyt.cu.

Getting There and Around

Domestic flights were scheduled to begin in 2000 to a new airstrip on Cayo Las Brujas.

Puertosol offers a series of six-hour **boat excursions** from **Marina Santa María.** An eight-hour **scuba diving** trip to Ojo del Mégano costs US$50.

SANCTI SPÍRITUS
INTRODUCTION

The relatively small southeast corner of Western Cuba is mighty big in tourist appeal. The province is physically diverse and encompasses the beautiful eastern portion of the Sierra Escambray, lush valleys, rolling plains, and a peninsula boasting the south coast's premier beach. Much of Sancti Spíritus Province is cattle country. To the north, rolling hills flow down towards the coastal plains, with beach-lined cays beckoning offshore.

The 16th-century city of Sancti Spíritus sits smack in the center of Cuba in the shadow of the eastern Escambray and Sancti Spíritus mountains. Trinidad, Cuba's best-preserved colonial city, nestles beneath the Escambray on the coastal plains of the Río Manatí. No visit to Cuba is complete without at least two days spent in this mellow charmer. It even has a great beach—Playa Ancón—close at hand.

Between Sancti Spíritus and Trinidad, you pass through the wide valley of the Río Manatí and Valle de los Indigenos (Valley of the Sugar Mills), full of reminders of the heyday of sugar.

The valley and Trinidad are both deservedly UNESCO World Heritage Sites.

Hunters, fisher folk, and nature lovers are served by a number of wetland reserves (the southeastern lowland plains are inhospitably marshy and humid, with few villages or roads). And hikers and birders are blessed with Topes de Collantes National Park, with hiking trails and cascades to visit in the high reaches of the Escambray mountains.

Sancti Spíritus Province is also littered with battle sites from the War of Independence, including **Arroyo Blanco,** east of Sancti Spíritus, where in 1895 a young British officer named Winston Churchill narrowly avoided being killed by a rebel bullet that whizzed past his head, spawning his famous statement that "There is nothing more exhilarating than to be shot at without result."

The Autopista, which runs 15 km north of the city of Sancti Spíritus, was in appalling condition in early 2000. It runs east for 20 km before ending abruptly at Tuausa, where signs point the way to the Carretera Central.

SANCTI SPÍRITUS AND VICINITY

Sancti Spíritus, 390 km east of Havana, is a modern city (pop. 100,000) laid out around a colonial core. It straddles the Carretera Central, which has helped boost the city's standing as the midway point between Havana and Santiago.

In 1895, Winston Churchill arrived in Sancti Spíritus. He loved the cigars but thought the city "a very second-rate place, and a most unhealthy place" (an epidemic of yellow fever and smallpox was raging). It hasn't improved vastly since Churchill passed through: most of the old town is forlorn and jaded despite a vigorous burst of improvements in the town center in the past few years.

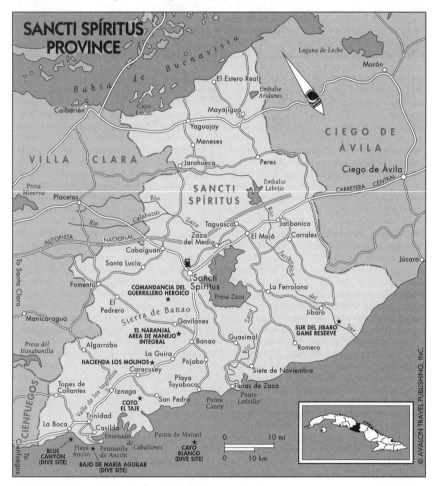

Still, it is worth at least a half-day visit. Quaint cobbled streets and venerable houses with iron filigree and wide doors for carriages attest to the city's antiquity. And the cathedral is worth the trip for its photogenic potential. The outskirts are rimmed with industry and nondescript modern buildings, including a large paper mill fueled by bagasse from the sugar fields serving the nearby *central* at Uruguay—the country's largest sugar mill.

Orientation

The city rises up the eastern bank of the Río Yayabo, centered on Plaza Serafín Sánchez (also called Plaza Central). The historic core lies immediately southwest of here, around the delightful Plaza de los Viejos at the heart of a tight little warren of narrow streets. Avenida Jesús Menéndez runs downhill two blocks to the river.

Newer sections north and east of Plaza Central form an uninspired assemblage of concrete and cement centered on the unremarkable **Plaza de la Revolución.** Streets are laid out in a grid, running northwest-southeast and northeast-southwest. The main street, Independencia, runs south to **Parque Honorato** and north to **Parque La Caridad.**

The most important east-west thoroughfare is **Avenida de los Mártires,** a broad boulevard that begins three blocks east of Parque Central. It crosses the equally wide **Bartolomé Masó,** which leads north through the modern city to the Autopista, and southward swings east and continues as the Carretera Central to Zaza and Ciego de Avila.

History

The settlement of Espíritú Santo was co-founded in 1514 by Diego Velázquez and Fernandez de Cordoba, who later rose to fame conquering the Yucatán. The city began life about six km from its current position. It was moved eight years later because the original site was plagued by biting ants. The city prospered from cattle ranching and sugar. Its prominence attracted pirates, and during the late 16th and early 17th centuries it was ransacked and razed twice in a short span of years.

Unlike Trinidad, Sancti Spíritus never evolved as a center of culture. After 400 years of Spanish rule, the city still lacked a library and museum (the university and other academic institutions arrived after the Revolution). Support for the in-

dependence cause was therefore strong, and the city contributed several leading military figures to the fight to end Spanish rule. A century later, Che Guevara established his headquarters nearby, in the Alturas de Sancti Spíritus.

SIGHTSEEING

Plaza Serafín Sánchez (Plaza Central)

Everything seems to happen around this modest square, laid out in 1522 and today named for Serafín Sánchez, a homegrown general in the War of Independence. The square—a bustling meeting place, busy with traffic—has none of the charm or grandeur of main plazas elsewhere in Cuba. It is surrounded by neoclassical buildings, including the impressive **biblioteca** (library) on the west side, and the **Teatro Principal** on the south side. The latter was once resplendent, and could be so again with restoration. Also check out the **Centro Provincial de Patrimonio Cultural,** a local cultural center next to the library and full of antiques.

To the northeast, the plaza extends one block along Independencia and opens into a tiny square with a statue of another local hero, Judas Mártinez Moles (1861-1915). South of the park, Independencia is pedestrians-only for two blocks and is lined with well-stocked shops plus the **Galería Oscar Moresa,** an art gallery with a precious treasure of modern and traditional art.

SIGHTSEEING HIGHLIGHTS: SANCTI SPÍRITUS PROVINCE

Alturas de Banao: Dramatic formations make for an adventurous drive with 4WD.

Playa Ancón: Superb, miles-long white-sand beach with scuba diving offshore. Hotel options, with Trinidad close at hand.

Trinidad: Cuba's most intimate colonial city set on a hill and preserved intact as a living museum. Charming plazas, cobbled streets, and architectural treasures, plus a wide choice of charming *casas particulares.*

Valle de los Ingenios: Beautiful valley blanketed in sugarcane, with several colonial sugar estates, including the **Torre de Managa-Iznaga.**

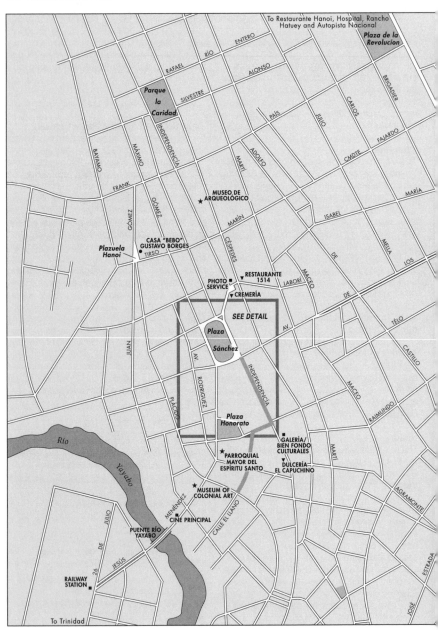

To Restaurante Hanoi, Hospital, Rancho
Hatuey and Autopista Nacional

Plaza de la
Revolucion

Parque
la
Caridad

RÍO
ENTERO
RAFAEL
ALONSO
SILVESTRE
BRIGADIER
CARLOS
JULIO
PAÍS
FAJARDO
MARTÍ
ADOLFO
CMDTE.
BAYAMO
MÁXIMO
FRANK
MARÍA
ISABEL

MUSEO DE
ARQUEOLÓGICO

MARÍN
MEJÍA
DE
LOS
GÓMEZ
GÓMEZ
CÉSPEDES

CASA "BEBO"
GUSTAVO BORGES

Plazuela
Hanoi

TIRSO
MACEO
LABORÍ
DE

PHOTO
SERVICE

RESTAURANTE
1514

CREMERÍA

TELO

SEE DETAIL

Plaza
Sánchez

AV.
CASTILLO

JUAN
AV.

INDEPENDENCIA
MACEO

RODRIGUEZ
RAIMUNDO

PLÁCIDO

Plaza
Honorato

GALERÍA/
BIEN FONDO
CULTURALES

MARTÍ
AGRAMONTE

PARROQUIAL
MAYOR DEL
ESPIRITU SANTO

DULCERÍA—
EL CAPUCHINO

Río
Yayabo

MUSEUM OF
COLONIAL ART

MENÉNDEZ
CALLE EL LLANO

CINE PRINCIPAL

JULIO

DE

PUENTE RÍO
YAYABO

26

JESÚS

RAILWAY
STATION

ESTRADA
JOSÉ

To Trinidad

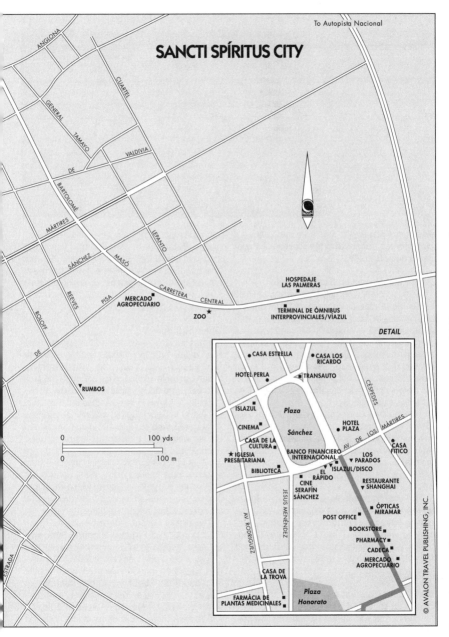

SANCTI SPÍRITUS CITY

To Autopista Nacional

ANGIONA
CUARTEL
GENERAL
TAMAYO
VALDIVIA
DE
BARTOLOMÉ
MÁRTIRES
SÁNCHEZ
LEPANTO
MASÓ
PISA
REEVES
ROLOFF
DE
ESTRADA

MOON

HOSPEDAJE
LAS PALMERAS

CARRETERA CENTRAL

MERCADO
AGROPECUARIO

ZOO

TERMINAL DE ÓMNIBUS
INTERPROVINCIALES/VÍAZUL

RUMBOS

0   100 yds
0   100 m

DETAIL

CASA ESTRELLA
CASA LOS
RICARDO
HOTEL PERLA
TRANSAUTO
CÉSPEDES
ISLAZUL
Plaza
HOTEL
PLAZA
CINEMA
Sánchez
MÁRTIRES
LOS
CASA DE LA
CULTURA
BANCO FINANCIERO
INTERNACIONAL
AV. DE LOS
CASA
FITICO
IGLESIA
PRESBITARIANA
LOS
PARADOS
BIBLIOTECA
ISLAZUL/DISCO
EL
RÁPIDO
RESTAURANTE
SHANGHAI
CINE
SERAFÍN
SÁNCHEZ
JESÚS MENÉNDEZ
ÓPTICAS
MIRAMAR
POST OFFICE
BOOKSTORE
AV. RODRÍGUEZ
PHARMACY
CADECA
MERCADO
AGROPECUARIO
CASA DE
LA TROVA
Plaza
Honorato
FARMÁCIA DE
PLANTAS MEDICINALES

© AVALON TRAVEL PUBLISHING, INC.

*the bell of the Parroquial
Mayor del Espíritú Santo*

And Jesús Menéndez runs from the southwest corner one block south to the Parroquial Mayor del Espíritu Santo.

Parroquial Mayor del Espíritu Santo

The small, Wedgwood blue cathedral, at Calle Jesús Menéndez e/ Honorato y Agramonte, is one of Cuba's oldest and best-preserved churches, maintained in near-pristine condition. The current church dates to 1680, when it replaced an earlier, wooden church built in 1612 but destroyed in a pirate raid. The triple-tiered tower wasn't completed until 1764, its cupola not until the middle of the 19th century. The bell still rings for Mass each Sunday.

The church is very simple inside, with minimal gilt work and an unimpressive altar. The ornately carved roof beams are splendid, however, with dropped gables carved and fitted in cross patterns and supporting a circular center. The crucifix looks like porcelain but is actually made of painted wood.

The church overlooks the diminutive **Plaza de los Viejos** to the west, and, to the north, the equally tiny **Plaza Honorato del Castillo,** honoring a local general in the War of Independence, yet highlighted by a statue of Rudesindo Antonio García Rojo, an eminent citizen in medicine and sciences.

Museum of Colonial Art

One block south of the cathedral, at Plácido 64 (on the corner with Jesús Menéndez) is a per-

fectly preserved time capsule—the ornately decorated **Palacio del Valle-Iznaga,** which belonged to one of the wealthiest families in Cuba. The beautiful home is now a delightful museum, amply furnished with period decor. It's open Tues.-Fri. 1-10 p.m., Saturday 1-5 p.m., and Sunday 10 a.m.-4 p.m. Entrance costs US$1.

Other Sights

Below Plácida, Jesús Menéndez crosses the Río Yayabo on a triple-arched bridge—**Puente Río Yayabo**—built of cut stone in medieval style. It was begun in 1817 and is said to be the only colonial stone bridge still extant in Cuba.

Calle El Llano is the quintessential colonial city street in Sancti Spíritu and one of very few that are still cobbled. This 100-meter-long street is lined with quaint houses painted pastel pink, canary, and blue, lent added grace by fancy wrought-iron balconies, hanging lanterns, and wooden *rejas* (turned grills). Alas, gone is the 1934-vintage Plymouth Deluxe with a white roof that for years parked here as if for a Hollywood movie, providing a touch of panache.

Two blocks west of Parque Central, on Plácido, is a quaint little **Iglesia Presbitariana,** built last century by a small Scottish community.

Also worth a brief peek is the **Casa Natal Serafín Sánchez,** on Céspedes between Frank País and Tirso Marín, where the patriot-hero was born. A house across the street now houses the threadbare **Museo de Arqueológico.**

Sancti Spíritus' most unusual site could be

the **Casa de los Refranes** (House of Sayings), opposite the entrance to Rancho Villa Hatuey. It's dedicated to aphorisms profound and strange. And during Christmas feel free to call at Juan Gilberto Gómez #116, where Lourdes Borges del Rey creates the most fabulous nativity scene you're ever likely to see in a domestic setting.

Last but not least there's a **zoo** on Bartolomé Masó, 100 meters south of Avenida de los Mártires, featuring lions, monkeys, hyenas, antelopes, and water buffalo. It's open Tue.-Sun. 9 a.m.-3 p.m. (US$0.30).

ACCOMMODATIONS

Casas Particulares

Dania León has **Hospedaje Las Palmeras,** at Bartolomé Maso #161 e/ Cuba y Cuartelo, tel. (41) 2-2169, on the Carretera Central about 200 meters east of the bus station. Her pleasant, modest home is fed by breezes. She has two a/c rooms (US$20 apiece) that share a bathroom with hot water. There's secure parking.

Casa Fitico, Céspedes #1 Altos, behind the Hotel Plaza and one block from the main square, is run by live-in owner, "Fitico" Jorge Rodriguéz, a likable if overly animated German-speaking Cuban who is a man-about-town. He has two cross-ventilated rooms with lots of light, sharing a clean but simple bathroom with hot water (US$15). They're basically furnished, but Fitico had just moved in at press time and promised to add furnishings.

Fitico's mother, Estrella González, has a nice house opposite the Hotel Colonial (Cubans only) at Máximo Gómez #25, e/ Antonio Viteras y Calderón, with two rooms and a clean, modern bathroom with hot water (US$10-15). The upstairs room to the rear is large, well lit, and has a fridge and rooftop terrace. Nearby, try **Casa "Bebo" Gustavo Borges** at Juan Gilberto Gómez #102 e/ Tirgo Marin y Frank País, tel. (41) 23352, e-mail: triana@cgmss.ssp.sld.cu, a colonial home on Plazoleta de Hanoi with three rooms with private bathrooms and hot water (US$15-20); two have a/c. You can watch TV in a stone-walled lounge.

I also like **Casa Los Ricardo,** in a centenarian house on the northeast corner of the main plaza, at Independencia #28 Altos, tel. (41) 2-

6805 (c/o Josefina) and entered via a marble staircase like a fortress dungeon. Ricardo Rodríguez ("el taxista") has three a/c rooms with balconies that open onto the plaza. They're clean and simply but adequately furnished, with private bathrooms with hot water for US$15.

Omaida Echemendía Echemendía has a *casa* at Maceo #4 e/ Av. de los Mártires y Doll, tel. (41) 2-4336. A reader recommends a room with Juan and Raul at Calle Independencia Sur #56, tel. (41) 2-3046.

Hotels

Budget: The **Hotel Plaza,** tel. (41) 2-7102 and 27-1068, is an Islazul property in a restored colonial building on the east side of Parque Central. Rooms are small but lofty and pleasantly furnished, with handsome dark tile floors, a/c, and attractive bathrooms. The small lobby bar has appeal, but the restaurant falls short and usually can muster little on the menu. Rates were US$20 s, US$26 d, US$33 t high season.

Islazul has a regional booking office *(carpeta)* next to the cinema on the west side of the plaza, for reservations throughout the province.

Moderate: Islazul's **Villa Los Laureles,** tel. (41) 2-7016, fax (41) 2-2562, on Bartolomé Masó, about five km north of town, offers 48 handsome and recently refurbished cabanas sprinkled throughout meagerly landscaped grounds. All have cable TV, a/c, refrigerators, and telephones. There's a large swimming pool and an elegant restaurant, and cabaret is offered in an amphitheater that attracts the locals on weekends. Rates were US$18 s, US$24 d low season, US$23 s, US$30 d high season. *A bargain!*

Nearby, Cubanacán operates the **Villa Rancho Hatuey,** Carretera Central Km 383, Sancti Spíritus, tel. (41) 2-8315, fax (41) 2-8350, e-mail: gerente@rhatuey.vcl.cyt.cu, by far the best place for miles. This charmer has 76 a/c rooms, all with satellite TVs and telephones in two-story bungalows in contemporary Mediterranean style. The small but elegant restaurant serves a house buffet. There's a squash court, a small swimming pool, and terra-cotta-tile sundeck surrounded by palms and bougainvillea. A nightly cabaret features disco and folkloric dances, and excursions include horseback riding (US$10). Rates were US$42 s, US$55 d year-round.

Cubanacán/s **Hotel Perla** was scheduled to open in late 2000 on the main square. This restored colonial structure will feature a rooftop swimming pool.

FOOD

Finding a good, wholesome meal is a withering experience. Your surest bet is to seek out one of the several locals who will prepare meals for tourists, or at the restaurants at **Villa Rancho Hatuey** and **Hotel Los Laureles.** The Hotel Plaza is a bomb, although there are a few simple restaurants nearby, including **Los Parados** one block south. **Restaurante 1514,** one block north at the corner of Lavorri and Céspedes, serves *criollo* dishes in a dowdy colonial building full of dusty antiques (average price, 10 pesos). You may end up, as I did, at **El Rápido,** on the south side of the main plaza.

For meat dishes try **Mesón de la Plaza,** on Plaza Honorato. Entrées cost less than 10 pesos (salads cost 80 centavos).

There are at least three quasi-Chinese restaurants: **Restaurante Shanghai,** on Independencia, one block south of Parque Central, and **Restaurante Yangset** *(sic)* and **Restaurante Hanoi,** both on Bartolomé Masó. All offer meals for about 10 pesos, but don't get your hopes up.

Snack stalls in front of Parque Diversiones on Avenida de los Mártires sell cold *guarapo,* the refreshing sugarcane drink. You can buy fresh produce at the **mercado agropecuario** on the corner of Independencia and Honorato, although hygiene standards are wanting. The charming little **Dulcería el Capuchino** one block south sells pastries, and there's a *panadería* (bakery) at Máximo Gómez and Frank País.

ENTERTAINMENT

The liveliest and most popular place in town for live music and dancing is **Disco Karaoke,** above the Banco Financiero Internacional on the main plaza. There's also a disco-cabaret at the **Cabaret Los Laureles** in the namesake hotel on Bartolomé Masó. It gets packed Fri.-Sun., when locals crowd in for an *espectáculo* beneath the stars. It offers karaoke Tue.-Thurs. The **Villa Rancho Hatuey** hosts a disco on weekends.

Another favorite is **Pensamiento,** next to the museum, on Plácido and Jesús Menéndez. Also check out **Rumbos,** on Carlos Roboff, three blocks south of Avenida de los Mártires. At the corner of Roboff and Los Mártires is the **Palacio de los Salsas,** which has dancing on Friday and weekends, as does a club in the colonial building on Independencia and Agramonte.

The **Casa de la Trova,** on Máximo Gómez one block north of the cathedral, features traditional performances Thurs.-Sun., including by *Coro de Clares* (Clear Choir), a local choral group. Likewise, **La Casa de la Cultura,** Calle Cervantes #11, tel. (410) 2-3772. Watch, too, for classical and other music performances in the now faded **Teatro Principal.**

Cine Serafín Sánchez, on the west side of Parque Central, and **Cine Principe,** 50 meters east of the old bridge on Jesús Menéndez, show movies. There's a **chess club** next to the cinema on the west side of the plaza. To keep kids amused, try the small children's park *(parque diversiones)* on Avenida de los Mártires or the small zoo three blocks south of the Avenida on Bartolomé Masó.

Baseball is played at **Estadio Victoria del Girón,** east of Plaza de la Revolución in Reparto Los Olivos.

PRACTICALITIES

Services

Banco Financiero Internacional has a branch on the southeast corner of Plaza Sánchez. You can change dollars for pesos at the **Cadeca** exchange bureau half a block south on Independencia.

The sparklingly modern **post office** is on Independencia one block south of the main plaza. Etecsa's main *telecorreo* is on Bartolomé Masó, 100 meters north of the Plaza de la Revolución.

The **hospital** is on Bartolomé Masó, opposite the Plaza de la Revolución. There are several **pharmacies** on Independencia south of the main plaza, and at Bartolomé Maso #57, plus a herbalist pharmacy next to the Casa de la Trova on Máximo Gómez and replete with antique apothecary jars.

Photo Service has a meagerly stocked outlet on Céspedes one block north of Parque Central. The *biblioteca* (library) is on the west side of Parque Central.

The only **Cupet gas station** is on Bartolomé Masó, about six km north of town.

Transportation

By Air: Aerotaxi, Calle 27 #102 e/ M y N, Vedado, Havana, tel. (7) 33-4064, fax (7) 33-4063; in Sancti Spíritus, tel. (41) 2-4316, offers service between Havana and Sancti Spíritus using aged AN-2 biplanes and modern jets (US$70).

By Bus: The **Víazul** tourist bus departs Havana for Sancti Spíritus on Tuesday and Friday (see the Víazul Bus Schedule chart, in the On the Road chapter). For public bus service, see the Public Bus Service from Havana chart, also in the On the Road chapter. The **Terminal Provincial de Ómnibus** in Sancti Spíritus is at the junction of Bartolomé Masó and the Circunvalación, east of town, tel. (41) 2-4142.

Buses depart Sancti Spíritus for Trinidad four times daily. Buses also serve Camagüey, Holguín, and Santiago de Cuba. Local buses serve nearby cities from the *Terminal Municipal,* at Calle Sánchez and Carlos Roloff, one block south of Avenida de los Mártires, tel. (41) 2-2162.

By Train: At press time, train #25 left from Havana for Sancti Spíritus daily at 9:25 a.m. (minimum six hours; US$13.50), and from Cienfuegos at 4:39 a.m. and 2:34 p.m. You can also catch the *especial* bound for Santiago; it stops at Guayos (15 km north of Sancti Spíritus), from where trains run to Sancti Spíritus (you may need to overnight in Guayos). Some *regular* trains take up to 15 hours to Sancti Spíritus.

At press time, trains departed Sancti Spíritus for Havana daily at 6:35 p.m. and for Cienfuegos at 10:05 a.m. and 4:55 a.m.

The **train station,** tel. (41) 2-4790 or 2-7914 (express trains), is at the bottom of Avenida Jesús Menéndez, at 26 de Julio, 400 yards south of the old arched bridge. Local commuter trains also operate from the **Salón de Ferromozas,** adjacent, Avenida, tel. (41) 2-3653.

By Car: Havanautos has a **car rental** office in the Villa Rancho Hatuey.

Hitchhiking: You can join the crowds of Cubans who gather at the official hitching points just east of the Terminal Provincial (eastbound) and along Bartolomé Masó (northbound).

Getting Around Town

Most people get around by **horse-drawn taxis,** which congregate around the main square and on Avenida de los Mártires, near the bus terminal. Ten pesos should get you anywhere you want to go, but you may be charged in dollars. Licensed tourist taxis also park here. **Cocotaxis,** tel. (41) 2-3758, (little egg-shaped, canopied three-wheelers) also operate from the main square. **Colectivos** (shared taxis) congregate outside the bus terminals.

Excursions are offered by Havanatur, tel. (41) 2-9309, and Islazul, tel. (41) 2-6390, which share an office next to the bank on the south side of the main square. Excursions are also available from the Rancho Villa Hatuey to the cigar factory in Cabaiguán, about 16 km north of Sancti Spíritus (US$5). You can also book an air tour by biplane (US$20).

PRESA ZAZA

This man-made lake, the largest in Cuba, immediately southeast of Sancti Spíritus, is studded with flooded forest and contains extraordinary numbers of trout and world-record-breaking bass. Marsh birds flock in from far and wide. Not surprising, Zaza is a favorite spot for birders, anglers, and hunters. Fishing costs from US$35 at the Hotel Zaza. The **Copa Internacional de Pesca** fishing tournament is held each September.

The lake is drained by the **Río Zaza,** which snakes south across the coastal plain to the Caribbean Sea, whose shores are choked by mangroves. At the river mouth is **Tunas de Zaza,** a ramshackle place with a large fishing fleet.

Accommodations

Islazul's **Hotel Zaza,** tel. (41) 2-8512, fax (41) 2-8359, is a hunting and fishing lodge, but accepts all comers. The faceless, two-story, all-concrete hotel has 128 a/c rooms with private baths, telephones, and TVs. Most rooms enjoy views over the lake and there's a rooftop mirador. Facilities include a pleasant lobby bar, a modest restaurant, nightclub, swimming pool, game room, and store. Amazingly, neither fish nor duck is on the restaurant menu. Horseback riding is offered. Rates were US$27 s, US$26 d low season, US$30 s, US$40 d high season.

SUR DEL JIBARO GAME RESERVE

This wildlife and hunting reserve lies in the middle of rice plantations and marshland on the banks of the Río Jatibónico. Migrant ducks, quail, white-crowned ringdove, mourning and white-winged doves, guinea fowl, and pheasant are sacrificed for hunters' enjoyment.

It is reached from the Carretera Central by turning south at Jatibónico, 29 km east of Sancti Spíritus. **Jatibónico** is an orderly town built around a huge sugar *central,* which pours a pall of black smoke over the town. Beyond Jatibónico, the Carretera Central continues east into Ciego de Ávila Province.

SANCTI SPÍRITUS TO TRINIDAD

The road southwest from Sancti Spíritus to Trinidad rises, dips, and swings magnificently along the foothills of the Alturas de Banao, whose sheer, barren crags remind me of the Scottish highlands. Coffee is grown on the upper slopes; lower slopes are covered mostly with rough pasture grazed by ashen, humpbacked stock attended by *vaqueros* (cowboys) in straw hats with machetes at their sides.

Che Guevara established his headquarters—**Comandancia del Guerrillero Heroico**—at El Pedrero, on the northern slopes (known as the Alturas de Sancti Spíritus), reached by a turnoff from the Trinidad road at the hamlet of **Las Brisas.** The route is fabulously scenic and offers good opportunities for birding and hiking.

Alturas de Banao

From the village of **Banao** you can follow the valley of the Río Banao north into the mountainous heights, where a virtually pristine and beautiful 3,050-hectare swath is protected in a reserve: **El Naranjal Area De Manejo Integral.** There are four separate ecosystems: semi-deciduous forest, tropical moist forest, rare cloud forest, and an endemic assembly associated with the freestanding limestone table-top formations called *mogotes.* The region is rich in flora, with more than 700 flowering plants (more than 100 of them endemic), including over 60 orchid species. Inevitably, the place is a paradise for birders—

parrots are numerous. El Naranjal also harbors cave systems, waterfalls, and mineral pools.

Alcona S.A., Calle 42 #514 esq. Av. 7, Playa, Havana, tel. (7) 24-9227, fax (7) 33-1532, a Cuban company specializing in nature tours, offers visits to El Naranjal with stays at **Casa del Guardabosques,** a rustic lodge in the Alto de la Sabina. It offers guided excursions. You can also rent horses to follow the Banao and Higuanojo Rivers to natural mineral springs.

VALLEY OF THE SUGAR MILLS (VALLE DE LOS INGENIOS)

West of Banao the Carretera de Sancti Spíritus drops spectacularly into the Valley of the Sugar Mills, also known as the Valle de los Ingenios and, more correctly, the Valle de San Luís and declared a UNESCO Cultural Heritage Site. It is named for the many sugar mills (43 at its peak) that sprang up over the centuries to grind the cane produced by the valley's remarkably fertile soil. The valley was the most important sugar-producing region in early colonial days—a predominance that lasted into the 19th century, when the development of the *centrale* plantation system elsewhere in Cuba and the collapse of world sugar prices in the 1880s sounded a death knell for the valley's relatively primitive sugar factories. Many of the mills and estate houses remain, albeit mostly in ruin. At press time several old *haciendas* were being restored. They are signed from the main highway.

Manaca-Iznaga Tower

No journey into the valley is complete without a visit to the quaint village of Iznaga, whose prim little railway station is a gem. The village, 14 km east of Trinidad, is most famous for the **Hacienda Iznaga** and its splendid tower, built 1835-45 by Alejo María del Carmen e Iznaga, once one of the wealthiest sugar planters in Cuba. According to legend, the tower was built as a wager. Alejo was to build a tower while his brother Pedro dug a well. The winner would be whoever went highest or deepest (no well has been found). The tower is 43.5 meters high. It has seven levels, each smaller than the one beneath. It was recently restored to its original grandeur as a colonial monument (entry US$1).

guajiro, *Valle
de Los Ingenios*

You can ascend the 136 steps with the *custodia,* who will tell you the history of the tower and estate (a tip is appreciated).

The owner's farmhouse has also been beautifully restored and turned into a fabulous restaurant (see below). A horse-drawn carriage sits on the wide front porch, where mammoth doorways open into a lofty lobby replete with artwork, glass cases containing a miscellany of period costume, and old maps.

Lacework is a local specialty sold at the base of the tower.

Horseback Riding
Want to play the Marlboro man? A working cattle ranch, **Hacienda Los Molinos,** welcomes guests seeking fun in the saddle. Guided horseback rides lead into the forested slopes of the Alturas de Sancti Spíritus. It's two km off the highway, a few km west of La Gúira, midway between Trinidad and Sancti Spíritus.

You can also go horseback riding at **Casa Guachinango,** 20 km east of Trinidad, a 200-year-old hacienda-turned-restaurant boasting a beautiful setting above the Río Ay.

Accommodations and Food
Hacienda Los Molinos has four rustic yet quaint rooms with ceiling fans in an old timber lodge. Meals are extra. Rates were US$15 s, US$20 d.

You may be able to camp at **Casa Guachinango.**

The restaurant at **Alejo del Carmen e Izna-**ga's farmhouse offers dining on an outside terrace overlooking the valley. It serves spaghettis (US$2.50) and *criollo* food, including a house special: grilled and spiced pork (US$4.50). A traditional *trapiche* at the rear serves fresh-squeezed cane juice.

Getting There
Sure, you can arrive by car. But I recommend you treat yourself to a journey aboard the local commuter train—a single diesel carriage, painted turquoise and white—that departs Trinidad daily for Condado via the Valle de los Ingenios at 5:26 and 9:21 a.m. and 1:41 and 5:26 p.m. (50 centavos).

A tourist steam train that formerly ran from Trinidad was under repair at press time.

COTO EL TAJE

About seven km east of Iznaga, a road leads south to the village of San Pedro. After four km you'll reach a turnoff for El Taje, a 15-square-km complex of lagoons and swamps favored by migratory birds. Blue-wing teal, shoveler, Bahamian pintail, and fulvous tree ducks are all present, as are other game birds. The area is popular with hunters.

Hacienda El Taje has seven a/c double rooms, all with private bathrooms and showers. There's a dining room, bar, recreation room with TV, and a souvenir and hunting store.

TRINIDAD

Trinidad (pop. 38,000) is tucked into the southwest corner of Sancti Spíritus Province, in the lee of the Sierra del Escambray. It was the fourth of the seven cities founded by Diego de Velázquez in 1514. Today, it is maintained as a living museum, just as the Spaniards left it in its period of greatest opulence. It is the crown jewel of Cuba's colonial cities and a must see on every traveler's list. After the dour melancholy of most other Cuban cities, it's fantastic. No other city in Cuba is so well preserved or so charming.

The town, 67 km southwest of Sancti Spíritus and 80 km east of Cienfuegos, reached its peak during the 19th-century sugar boom and seems to have been forsaken by history ever since. This time capsule is lent twin charms by its historical landmarks and its setting of great natural beauty, sitting astride a hill, where it catches the breezes and gazes out over the Caribbean against a backdrop of verdurous ring of mountains—the Topes de Collantes.

Its narrow, unmarked cobbled streets are paved with stones (chinas pelonas) shipped across the Atlantic as ballast or taken from the nearby river. The maze of streets is lined with terra-cotta-tile-roofed houses in soft pastel colors. Much of the architecture is neoclassical and baroque, with a Moorish flavor (there are no great palaces, however, as in Havana), reflecting the town's heritage of 16th-century conquistadores, 17th-century corsairs, 18th-century smuggler-traders, and 19th-century sugar lords. The exquisite buildings are fronted by mahogany balustrades, fancy rejas (grills) of wrought iron and turned wooden rods, and massive wooden doors with postigos (small windows) that open to let the breezes flow through cool, tile-floored rooms connected by double-swing half-doors (mamparas) topped by vitrales.

No tinkering is allowed, for the entire city is a national monument, protected by law. The city sparkles after a recent restoration and is virtually devoid of touristy superstructure—concessions, billboards, souvenir shops.

Life in Trinidad

Even the life of Trinidad has been preserved in aspic. By day, mule-drawn carts and vaqueros on

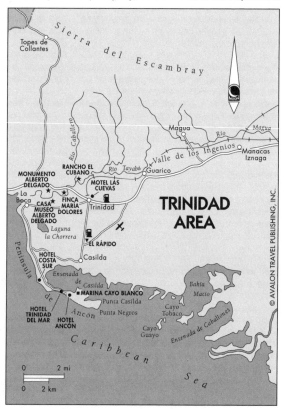

Plaza Mayor, Trinidad

horseback clip-clop through the cobbled streets. Laughing children chase hoops through the plazas. And old folks rock gently beneath shady verandas, serenaded by twittering songbirds in bamboo cages—a Trinidad tradition. In Trinidad, people seem content to let time pass them by.

Life in Trinidad is lived in full view. By day, perspiring tour groups crawl along the cobbled streets, glancing inside living rooms full of antiques and knickknacks. At night the town is eerily still—silent but for the barking of dogs, the slap of dominoes, and the staccato voice of television. Then the cool air flows downhill, the narrow alleys become refreshing channels, and it is a special joy to stroll the traffic-free cobbled streets that make the town feel even more adrift from the 20th century. By midnight the entire town has bedded down and is still as death, except for one or two local discos pounding out a contemporary beat.

Tourists are plenty . . . and so are petty thieves and *jiniteros* (hustlers) hoping to separate you from your dollars.

HISTORY

The initial settlement, named Villa de la Santísima Trinidad, was founded in 1514 by Diego de Velázquez on a site settled by the Taíno Indians. The Spanish conquistadores found the native Indians panning for gold in the nearby rivers. The gold-hungry Spanish had high hopes, and, indeed, established a lucrative (but short-lived) gold mine that lent vigor to the young township and the wharves of nearby Casilda. Hernán Cortéz set up base here in 1518 to provision his expedition to conquer the Aztec empire for Spain. Soon fleets bearing the spoils of Mexico gathered in Casilda, bringing new prosperity and eclipsing Trinidad's meager mines.

Trinidad was just far enough from the reach of Spanish authorities in Havana to develop a bustling commerce smuggling contraband to circumvent trade restrictions imposed by the Spanish Crown. Its position on Cuba's underbelly was also perfect for trade with Jamaica, the epicenter of the Caribbean slave trade. Trinidad grew prosperous importing slaves, many of whom were put to work locally, stimulating the sugar trade. A mild climate, fertile soil, and easy access to the Caribbean favored Trinidad's agricultural and commercial growth. Money poured in from the proceeds of sugar grown in the Valle de los Ingenios. When the English occupied Cuba, in 1762-3, Trinidad became a free port and prospered even further, entering its golden age.

Wealthy citizens built their sumptuous homes around the main square—Plaza Mayor—and along the adjoining streets (one owner petitioned the King of Spain for permission to embed coins in his floor; the king granted the wish on condition that the coins be laid sideways so that no one should walk on the monarch's face). Pianos from Berlin, sumptuous furniture from France, linens and lattices, and silverware from Colombia were

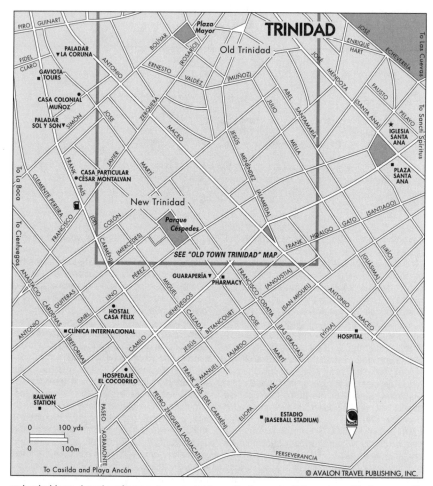

TRINIDAD

Old Trinidad

PIRO • GUINART • BOLÍVAR • Plaza Mayor • JOSÉ ECHEVERRÍA • To Las Cuevas • ENRIQUE HART • JOSÉ
FIDEL • CLARO • PALADAR ▼ LA CORUÑA • ANTONIO • ERNESTO • (ROSARIO) • VALDÉZ • (MUÑOZ) • JOSÉ MENDOZA • FAUSTO • PELAYO • To Sancti Spíritus
GAVIOTA ■ TOURS • JOSÉ • ZERQUERA • JULIO • ABEL • SANTAMARÍA • (SANTA ANA) • ★ IGLESIA SANTA ANA
CASA COLONIAL MUÑOZ • MACEO • JESÚS • MEILA • ■ PLAZA SANTA ANA
PALADAR SOL Y SON ▼ • SIMÓN • JAVIER • MARTÍ • MENÉNDEZ • (ALAMEDA) •
FRANK PAÍS • CASA PARTICULAR • CÉSAR MONTALVAN
CLEMENTE PEREYRA • COLÓN • New Trinidad • GATO • (SANTIAGO)
To La Boca • FRANCISCO • (DR. CARMEN) • (MERCEDES) • Parque Céspedes • FRANK • HIDALGO • (LIRIO) • (GUÁSIMA)
To Cienfuegos • SEE "OLD TOWN TRINIDAD" MAP
ANASTACIO • GUITERAS • PÉREZ • GUARAPERÍA ▼ • FRANCISCO CODAZA • (ANGUSTIA) • (SAN MIGUEL) • ANTONIO • MACEO
CÁRDENAS • LINO • MIGUEL • CIENFUEGOS • ▲ PHARMACY • JOSÉ • (VIGÍA)
ANTONIO • GNRL • ■ HOSTAL CASA FÉLIX • CALZADA • BETANCOURT • (LAS GRACIAS) • ■ HOSPITAL
■ CLÍNICA INTERNACIONAL • (REFORMA) • CAMILO • JESÚS • FAJARDO • MARTÍ
HOSPEDAJE EL COCODRILO • FRANK PAÍS (DEL CARMEN) • MANUEL • PAZ
RAILWAY STATION ■ • PASEO • PEDRO ZERQUERA (AGUACATE) • EULOPA • ■ ESTADIO (BASEBALL STADIUM) • MOON
AGRAMONTE • PERSEVERANCIA
To Casilda and Playa Ancón

0   100 yds
0   100 m

© AVALON TRAVEL PUBLISHING, INC.

unloaded here. Local craftsmen, too, reached their peak of perfection in the 19th century, and thriving industries developed in ceramics, gold, silver, and lace. Language schools and academies were even set up to prepare the children of the wealthy to complete their studies in Europe.

At first, the city created its own fleet to guard against pirates, but later decided to take the pirates to its bosom; many citizens prospered as victuallers to the sea-roving vagabonds, while some pirates bought property and settled.

By the early 19th century, Cienfuegos, with its vastly superior harbor, began to surpass Casilda, which had begun silting up. Trinidad began a steady decline, hastened by tumult in the slave trade and new competition from more advanced estates elsewhere in Cuba. Isolated from the Cuban mainstream, Trinidad foundered. By the turn of the 20th century, it was a down-at-heels little town. Only the faded beauty remained.

In the 1950s, Batista declared Trinidad a "jewel of colonial architecture." A preservation law was passed—a boon for latter-day tourism but regarded as a bane for the past 40 years, as development was prohibited, and the city continued to stagnate in its own beauty (the construction of the Carretera Central on the north side of the Sierra del Escambray had already stolen the through traffic, ensuring that Trinidad would be preserved in its past). The town was named a national monument in 1965. A Restoration Committee was established, and the historic core around Plaza Mayor has been completely restored. In 1988 UNESCO named Trinidad a World Heritage Site.

ORIENTATION

Old Trinidad
There are two Trinidads. The original enclave takes up the northeast quarter, on the higher slopes. This cobbled quarter is bounded to the south by Calle Antonio Maceo and to the east by Calle Lino Pérez. At its heart is Plaza Mayor, at the top of Calle Simón Bolívar. It's a warren—some streets end at T-junctions, while others curl or bifurcate, one leading uphill while another drops sharply to another Y-fork or right-angled bend. All this was meant to fool marauding pirates, but it does a pretty good job on visitors, too.

Many of the streets are known locally by older names—Calle Juan Manuel Márquez, for example, is better known as Amargura.

The streets are each sloped in a slight V, with gutters in the center. According to legend, the city's first governor had a right leg shorter than the other and could thereby be level when walking the streets by staying on the right-hand side.

New Trinidad
Below the original settlement, encircling it to the west, south, and east, is a newer, but still aged, nontouristy district laid out on a rough grid with Parque Céspedes at its center. The main street is Calle José Martí, which runs north-south and is lined with shops and bars. **Calle Bolívar** (also called Desengaño) is the most important of the streets leading east to the *ciudad antigua*. One block south of Parque Céspeda is Calle Camilo Cienfuegos, a major thoroughfare leading east, uphill, to the Motel Las Cuevas and Sancti Spíritus.

TRINIDAD STREET NAMES

COLONIAL NAME	NEW NAME
Angarilla	Fidel Claro
Alameda	Jesús Ménendez
Amargura	Juan Márquez
Boca	Piro Guinart
Carmen	Frank País
Colón	Colón
Cristo	Fernando H. Echerri
Desengaño	Simón Bolívar
Gutiérrez	Antonio Maceo
Gloria	Gustavo Izquierdo
Jesús María	José Martí
Media Luna	Ernesto Valdés Muñoz
Olvido	Santiago Escobar
Peña	Francisco Gómez Toro
Rosario	Francisco Javier Zerquera
Real	Rubén Martínez Villena
San Procopio	Lino Pérez
Santo Domingo	Camilo Cienfuegos

WALKING TOUR OF OLD TRINIDAD

The central streets are closed to traffic by stone pillars and cannons stuck nose-first in the ground (the cannons served in colonial days to protect pedestrians as carriages turned the corners). You should walk the cobbled streets, and let serendipity be your guide.

Plaza Mayor
Begin at Plaza Mayor, the heart of the original settlement. At its center is a pretty park ringed with silver trellises, with shiny white wrought-iron benches beneath the shade of palms and hibiscus bowers. The immaculately restored plaza is adorned with small neoclassical statues—including two bronze greyhounds that would be at home in a Landseer painting—and pedestals topped by ceramic urns. It is ringed by a cathedral and four museums, all once the mansions of wealthy colonialists.

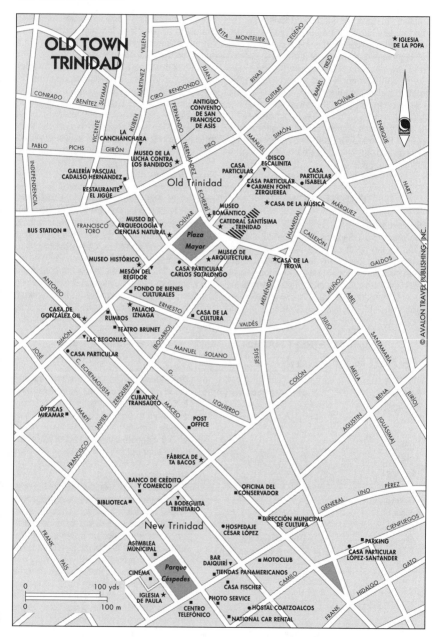

OLD TOWN TRINIDAD

★ IGLESIA DE LA POPA

CONRADO
BENÍTEZ
SUYAMA
VILLENA
MARTÍNEZ
CIRO RENDONDO
RITA
MONTELIER
CEDEÑO
JUAN
RIVAS
GUITART
TREJO
RAFAEL
BOLÍVAR
ENRIQUE

PABLO
PICHS
VICENTE
RUBEN
GIRÓN
LA CANCHÁNCHARA ★
FERNANDO
ANTIGUO CONVENTO DE SAN FRANCISCO DE ASÍS ■
PIRO
MANUEL
SIMÓN

INDEPENDENCIA

★ MUSEO DE LA LUCHA CONTRA LOS BANDIDOS
HERNÁNDEZ
ECHERRI
Old Trinidad
CASA PARTICULAR ▼
DISCO ESCALINITA ▼
CASA PARTICULAR ● CARMEN FONT ZERQUEREA
CASA PARTICULAR ● ISABELA

GALERÍA PASCUAL CADALSO HERNÁNDEZ ★
RESTAURANTE ▼ EL JIGÜE

MÁRQUEZ
HART

★ CASA DE LA MÚSICA

BUS STATION ■
FRANCISCO TORO
MUSEO DE ARQUEOLOGÍA Y CIENCIAS NATURAL
BOLÍVAR
★
MUSEO ROMÁNTICO ■
CATEDRAL SANTÍSIMA TRINIDAD

(ALAMEDA)
CALLEJÓN
GALDOS

Plaza Mayor

MUSEO HISTÓRICO ■
MESÓN DEL REGIDOR ▼
CASA PARTICULAR ● CARLOS SOTALONGO
MUSEO DE ARQUITECTURA ■
★ CASA DE LA TROVA

MENÉNDEZ
MUÑOZ
ABEL

ANTONIO

CASA DE GONZÁLEZ GIL ■
FONDO DE BIENES CULTURALES ■
★ PALACIO IZNAGA
RUMBOS ■
ERNESTO
CASA DE LA CULTURA ■
VALDÉS

JULIO
SANTAMARÍA

JOSÉ
SIMÓN
TEATRO BRUNET ■
▼ LAS BEGONIAS
(ROSARIO)
MANUEL SOLANO

MELIA
BENA
(LIRIO)

● CASA PARTICULAR
G.
JESÚS
COLÓN
IZQUIERDO

AGUSTIN
(GUASIMAL)

C. ECHENAGUSTA
ZERQUERA
JAVIER
MARTÍ

ÓPTICAS MIRAMAR ■
CUBATUR/ TRANSAUTO ■
MACEO
POST OFFICE ●

FRANCISCO

FÁBRICA DE TA BACOS ★

BANCO DE CRÉDITO Y COMERCIO ■
OFICINA DEL CONSERVADOR ■
GENERAL
LINO
PÉREZ
CIENFUEGOS

BIBLIOTECA ■
LA BODEGUITA TRINITARIO ●
DIRECCIÓN MUNICIPAL DE CULTURA ■

New Trinidad
HOSPEDAJE ● CÉSAR LÓPEZ
■ PARKING
CASA PARTICULAR ■ LÓPEZ-SANTANDER

FRANK PAÍS
ASEMBLEA MUNICIPAL ■
BAR DAIQUIRÍ ▼
● MOTOCLUB
GATO

CINEMA ■
Parque Céspedes
TIENDAS PANAMERICANOS ■
CAMILO
HIDALGO

IGLESIA ★ DE PAULA
CASA FISCHER ■
PHOTO SERVICE ●
CENTRO TELEFÓNICO ■
● HOSTAL COATZOALCOS
■ NATIONAL CAR RENTAL
FRANK

0   100 yds
0   100 m

© AVALON TRAVEL PUBLISHING, INC.

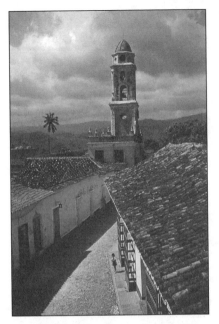

Calle Fernando Hernández Echerrí Trinidad

Begin your exploration on the plaza's northeast corner, at the modest, almost ascetic **Catedral Santísima Trinidad.** The cathedral, which was restored in 1996, is more English than Spanish inside, with a Victorian-Gothic vaulted ceiling and altar carved from mahogany and other hardwoods. The cathedral was rebuilt inside in 1894 on the spot where once stood the Parroquial Mayor, the original parish church. There's no baroque extravagance, although the carved statuary is intriguing.

One block away on the northwest corner is **Palacio Brunet,** a beautifully preserved, two-story, mansion dating from 1741 and housing the **Museo Romántico,** tel. (419) 4363. The dozen rooms are filled with intriguing artwork, fabulous antiques, and potted plants in profusion. Note the solid carved-cedar ceiling, dating from 1770, and the *mediopunto* arches, also carved from cedar. The main staircase leads upstairs, where you can step out onto the balcony to admire the view down over the square (traditionally, couples have their wedding pictures taken here). The stunning wrought-iron bed is the only heirloom of the Brunet family that originates from the house. Photographs are not allowed inside. It's open Tues.-Sun. 9 a.m.-6 p.m. Entrance costs US$.

Another impressive mansion, on the southwest corner of the plaza, at the corner of Bolívar and Mártinez, hosts the small **Museo de Arqueología y Ciencias Naturales,** the Museum of Archaeology and Natural Sciences, tel. (419) 3420, exhibiting mostly Cuban fauna and flora. Natural history displays include glass cases filled with stuffed birds and animals, including a manatee and a *guaican,* a suction fish used by Taíno Indians as a "hook" to catch other fish. There are also stuffed monkeys and representations of Stone Age man. A portion of the museum is devoted to the region's pre-Columbian peoples. The Indians called the region Guamuhaya, after which the museum is named. It's open daily except Sunday 9 a.m.-5 p.m. Entrance is US$1.

On the southeast side of the square, in the **Casa de los Sánchez Iznaga,** is the **Museo de Arquitectura,** the Museum of Architecture, tel. (419) 3208, which tells the tale of the history of Trinidad's development. Maps, model structures, and sections of houses in miniature demonstrate city planning, colonial construction techniques, and the fine craftsmanship of the period. Out back, as in so many buildings in Trinidad, is a courtyard full of flowers and blossoming fruit trees. Open Sat.-Thurs. 9 a.m.-5 p.m. (entrance costs US$1).

East of Plaza Mayor
Leaving Playa Mayor to the right of the cathedral, cobbled Calle Fernando Hernández (Cristo) leads past a wide staircase, which ascends to **Casa de la Música,** containing glass-case displays of old musical instruments. At the base of the steps is a handsome ocher-colored house—the **Mansión de los Conspiradores**—with an ornately woodworked balcony. On the other side of Cristo, opposite the mansion, is a home where Alexander Von Humboldt lived during his travels through Cuba in 1801.

One block east on Cristo brings you to the triangular **Plazuela de Segarta,** and Calle Jesús Menéndez, containing some of the oldest homes in the city, among them the **Casa de la Trova,** decorated with murals and dating to 1777.

North and West of Plaza Mayor

The **El Foturo District** northwest of the plaza was settled in the 18th century by foreign pirates, who were tolerated by Trinitarios (many of whom made a healthy living off the corsairs). At Ciro Redondo #261, for example, is a yellow house dating to 1754, built for Carlos Merlin, a French corsair. Nearby, on Calle Juan Márquez, are two houses with metal crosses on their exterior walls. They are two of 14 way-stops on the city's annual Easter religious procession.

A handsome tower one block west of the Museo Romántico guides you along Fernando Hernández Echarrí to Calle Pino Guinart and the **Antiguo Convento de San Francisco de Asís.** You can ascend to the top of the bell tower for a view over the city. The tower *(torre)* and church are all that remains of the original convent. A paucity of novices led to the convent's demise in the 19th century. The church was taken over by the government, and the convent was replaced by a baroque structure now housing the **Museo de la Lucha Contra Los Bandidos,** the Museum of the Fight Against Outlaws, tel. (419) 4121, which traces the campaign against the counter-revolutionary army in the Sierra del Escambray in the years following the Revolution. There are maps, black-and-white photographs, clothing and personal belongings of hero-soldiers, a CIA radio transmitter, and a small gunboat the agency donated to the counter-Castro cause. There is even a poster showing a boy shouldering a rifle. It reads, "My Mountains Will Never Be Taken!" The museum does *not* tell you that the guerrillas received considerable support from the local population. It's open Tues.-Sun. 9 a.m.-5 p.m. Entrance costs US$1.

Follow Calle Pino Guinart uphill through **La Varanca,** a suburb of packed-earth streets and tiny houses of wattle and daub. The **Iglesia de la Popa** stands atop the steep hill and has splendid views over the city. It was built in 1726. Three patinated bells hang over the door. The home next door is used for *santería* ceremonies. Visitors are welcome.

Walk back down Calle Piro Guinart and one block west of the convent you reach the **Plazuela Real del Jigüe,** a charming, tiny triangular plaza (one block west of Plaza Mayor) with a calabash tree in the center. The tree, planted in 1929, is the youngest in a succession of trees kept alive

since 1514, the year the Spanish celebrated their first Mass here. The colonial home (now Restaurante El Jigüe) fronting the plaza has a beautiful ceramic facia—a Trinitarian tradition.

Catercorner to El Jigúe, at Calle Piro Guinart #302, is the old town hall and jail, **Ayuntameinta y Carcel,** with a portion of the original stone-and-lime masonry exposed for view.

Southwest of Plaza Mayor

Calle Simón Bolívar leads downhill from Plaza Mayor. It is lined with former homes of once-important families, including the Palacio Cantero, whose Roman-style baths once amused 19th-century travelers, with a fountain that spouted *eau de cologne* for the ladies and gin for gents.

The Palacio, at the corner of Calle Francisco Toro, one block south of Plaza Mayor, today houses the **Museo Histórico,** tel. (419) 4460. The history of the city is revealed as you move through rooms furnished with rocking chairs, alabaster amphorae, marble-topped tables, and other antiques. Other intriguing exhibits include an antique bell, stocks for holding slaves, banknotes, and a magnificent scale model of the *Andrei Vishinsky,* which entered Trinidad harbor on 17 April 1960—the first Soviet ship to visit Cuba after the Revolution. Of course, the museum wouldn't be complete without exhibits honoring the 19th-century Cuban nationalist movement and the revolution that ousted Batista. Stairs lead up to a watchtower with a fine view over the city. It's open Sun.-Fri. 9 a.m.-5 p.m. Entrance costs US$1.

A few steps away is the **Museo de Artes Decorativos,** in the former home of Ortiz de Zúñiga, an outfitter of pirate ships who rose to become Trinidad's mayor. Hernán Cortéz supposedly lived here before his departure to conquer the Aztecs. Stroll downhill one block and you'll reach two other important colonial homes-turned-museums, **Palacio Iznaga,** and **Casa de González Gil,** both stuffed with antiques.

OTHER SIGHTS

The modest **Plaza Santa Ana,** at the top of Calle General Lino Pérez, is dominated by the ruins of **Iglesia Santa Ana.** On the east side is a beautifully restored ocher-colored colonial building containing a courtyard with a café, a bar, a specialty restaurant, and an artisans' gallery that includes a ceramic workshop.

The only site of major interest in the newer town is **Parque Céspedes,** on Calle José Martí and General Lino Pérez. It's a popular gathering spot for locals, who sit beneath an arbor of bougainvillea. On the southwest side is the **Iglesia de Paula,** containing some impressive carved wood and marble statuary. The main government buildings are here, too.

The **Fábrica de Tabacos,** tel. (419) 3282, a small cigar factory on the corner of Colón and Maceo, is one of Cuba's quaintest such *fábricas,* where 70 workers roll *brevas* for domestic consumption for five centavos apiece. Entry is free, although visitors are permitted entry only to a small room at the front where three rollers work for your camera.

ACCOMMODATIONS

Casa Particulares

Despite the town's popularity, hotel options are slim. Fortunately, Trinidad has as many as 300 *casas particulares* (this was the only city in the country where citizens were permitted to rent private rooms prior to the extension of the law throughout Cuba in 1996). Competition keeps prices low. It's best to compare several before making a choice—and don't forget to consider security (bars on the windows, for example, and locks on doors).

Outdoing all others for character is **Casa Colonial Muñoz,** Calle Martí #401 esq. Santiago Escobar, tel./fax (419) 3673, a venerable home built in 1800 and featured in *National Geographic* (October 1999, page 102). Imagine sleeping in a gilt antique bed. The house is replete with period furnishings, including swords. It offers two other rooms, each simply furnished with two double beds, a/c and fans, and modern, private bathroom with hot water ("You could cook a lobster in the sink," says the owner). The room with gilt bed is reserved for honeymooners and special guests. There's secure parking in the patio. The English-speaking owners Julio César Muñoz and Rosa Orbea Cerrillo are erudite and delightful hosts. Julio is a professional photographer and can act as a tour guide. Rates were US$20 low season, US$25 high season.

Likewise, the atmospheric *casa particular* of local art critic Carlos Sotalongo is a winner, not least for its position on the southeast corner of Plaza Mayor, at Calle Ruben Mártinez Villena #33, tel. (419) 4169. Vast front doors open to a cavernous lounge with antiques, modern art, and a colonial tile floor. Carlos rents two rooms to the rear; each has private bathroom with hot water (one room is colonial and has a terra-cotta floor and metal-frame bed; the other is modern and has a/c). Each costs US$20. Carlos' aunt, Carmen Font Zerquerea, also has a nice, historic *casa particular* immediately behind the cathedral at Calle Simón Bolívar #506, tel. (419) 2343. Her two rooms open to a charming patio and cost US$15 (US$20 with breakfast).

For the best bargain in town, try Isabela's large colonial home one block north of the main plaza, at Juan Manuel Márquez #32B, tel. (419) 3918. It has a lounge, two bedrooms (each with double bed), a large kitchen (poorly stocked with utensils), lofty ceilings, TV, telephone, and a small but modern bathroom—for only US$10 a day. A self-contained room to the rear has its own kitchen and bathroom with hot water, plus washing machine, fridge, and patio; it also costs only US$10. Isabela's sister, María Victoria, has a large colonial house nearby with two rooms sleeping up to five people for US$15 at Calle Juan Manuel Márquez #26.

For a self-contained apartment with kitchen, try **Hospedaje César López,** Calle Francisco Codahia #204 e/ Colón y General Lino Pérez, tel. (419) 3336. It is large, clean, open-plan, and has many modern facilities, including radio, TV and VCR, fans, modern lounge chairs, modern bathroom with scolding hot water, and a small, well-equipped modern kitchen. It sleeps up to five people, with three beds in the lounge and adjoining bedroom. César will make breakfast for you (US$5).

I also like Carlos Gil Lemes' home at Calle José Martí #263 e/ Colón y Francisco Zerquera, tel. (419) 3142, with two very nice rooms in a beautifully maintained colonial home with exquisite period furnishings for US$15 apiece. Each room has a private bathroom with hot water. There's a garden terrace, a safe for valuables, and secure parking. Carlos speaks fluent English.

Others that I've reviewed and like include Mayra González Cabrera's *casa* at Piro Guinart #36, tel. (419) 2351 (neighbor), with three rooms with private bath and hot water for US$15. It has a garage nearby, excursions are offered, and meals are served on a terrace.

Casa López-Santander, Camilo Cienfuegos #313 e/ Jesús Menendez y Camilo Cienfuegos, tel. (419) 3341, has three dark but adequately furnished rooms along a patio arcade with rockers for US$15 s, US$25 d. Two share a bathroom; the third has a private bathroom. The TV lounge is a pleasing spot to relax. It has secure parking.

Felix Matamoros' **Hostal Casa Félix,** Lino Pérez #158 e/ Frank País y Pedro Zerquera, tel. (419) 3166, is a clean and pleasing home with two simply furnished rooms that share a clean, modern bathroom with hot water and which open to a small courtyard where meals are served. Each has a/c, fans, and radio. Rates are U$15 low season, US$20 high season.

Hospedaje El Cocodrilo, Camilo Cienfuegos e/ Paseo Agramonte y Pedro Zerquera, tel. (419) 2108, has two pleasant, well-furnished rooms with a/c, fans, private bathroom and hot water. Meals are served in a patio to the rear, behind which the owner, "Pepe" Boggiano, raises fighting cocks—including Cuba's 1999 reigning champion.

Hostal Coatzoalcos, Camilo Cienfuegos #213, is run by a charming elderly lady, Delia Hernández, offering two spacious, basically furnished, cross-ventilated rooms with antique metal-frame beds for US$15 with shared bathrooms. Meals are served in a rear patio. A third room with a/c and a clean modern bathroom costs US$25.

Closer in to the center of the historic district, also recommended is **Hospedaje Estela,** Calle Simón Bolívar #557, tel. (419) 4329, a beautiful colonial home full of period furnishings and modern paintings run by Estela Velázquez. It has two rooms with fans, and private bathroom with hot water. A balcony overlooks a tree-shaded patio where *criollo* meals are served.

Lazaro and Lesvia Lorente have three rooms (one with a private bathroom; two share) at Calemente Percira #248, e/ Pablo Girón y Conrado Benitez, tel. (419) 3895. Rooms are spotless, have hot water, and cost US$13 d, including

breakfast. A veranda offers mountain views. Meals cost US$5.

Paladar Estela, Simón Bolívar #557, tel. (419) 4329, has two large rooms with private bathrooms for US$15 s (breakfasts costs US$1, dinner costs from US$6). You might try the **Hostal,** at Simón Bolívar #312, tel. (419) 4107, with three rooms, each for US$15, or the **Hospedaje,** with five rooms (also US$15) at Francisco Javier Zerquera #403, tel. (419) 3818. And a reader recommends the home of César Montalvan, at Frank País #366, tel. (419) 4269, for US$15 (plus US$2 breakfast, US$6 dinner; meals are described as "awesome"). Another recommends **Hospedaje de Yolanda,** Piro Guinart #227, tel. (419) 3051. A third recommends **Hostal Cristina,** Fernando Hernández Echerrí #31, tel. (419) 3054, with a private bedroom, sitting parlor, bathroom, and entrance; and another recommends a room with Tito at Calle Lino Pérez #472 e/ Jesus Menendez y Julio Antonio Mella, tel. (419) 3096.

You can also rent rooms in Casilda, but who would want to?

Few homes have parking. **Casa López-Santander,** charges US$2 per night for parking in a secure garden.

Hotels

Budget: Islazul's colonial-era **Hotel La Ronda,** on Calle #239 near Parque Céspedes, tel. (419) 2248, was recently renovated and is adequate though still meagerly furnished. It has 17 a/c rooms around an atrium courtyard, each with lofty ceiling, satellite TV, telephone, fridge, and safe deposit box. It has a restaurant, laundry, and other services. Rates were US$15 s, US$22 d low season, US$19 s, US$6 d high season.

Moderate: The **Motel Las Cuevas,** tel. (419) 4013, is favored by tour groups. It has 84 a/c rooms with private baths, phones, and radios in bungalows that crawl up the hillside above town. The rooms are modestly furnished though the setting is splendid. The restaurant and bar are in a huge thatched *bohio.* A swimming pool and shop are farther up the hill. The food is mediocre. It has car rentals, a tour desk, and nightly cabaret. Rates were US$38 s, US$45 d, US$55 t low season, US$45 s, US$58 d, US$75 t high season.

FOOD

Trinidad has a fistful of atmospheric restaurants, popular with tour groups though after dusk, most lie virtually fallow (being dollars-only they are beyond the means of Cubans).

You can brave the meager buffet breakfast at **Motel Las Cuevas** for US$4. Otherwise, breakfasts are hard to come by. An exception is **Paladar La Coruña**, on Calle Martí, tel. (419) 3838, which charges US$3 for breakfast and also serves *criollo* dinners under an arbor on a patio. It's open 7 a.m.-midnight.

Most other private restaurants had been forced to close at press time, and only three *paladares* existed at press time: the other two are **Paladar Estela**, tel. (419) 4329, where *criollo* meals are served on a tree-shaded patio, 6-11 p.m.; and **Paladar Sol y Son**, on Simón Bolívar e/ Frank País y José Martí. **El Cocodrilo** (at the bottom of Calle Cienfuegos), planned to reopen as a *paladar* (it does *not* serve crocodile, despite the stuffed beast outside).

The **Motel Las Cuevas** serves soulless meals in its restaurant, although it serves a delicious house drink—*cascos de naranja*—made from syrup and boiled orange peel.

My favorite restaurant is **Restaurante El Jigüe**, in a cool colonial home facing onto Plazuela Real del Jigüe. The wide menu features a filling *pollo el jigüe*, with spaghetti and cheese served in an earthenware dish (US$12). Most entrées cost less than US$10.

Another atmospheric option is **Mesón del Regidor**, on Simón Bolívar one block southwest of Plaza Mayor, tel. (419) 3756, which specializes in grilled meats and has an art gallery at the back. It has set meals for a bargain price: shrimp for US$9 and lobster for US$12, with salad, dessert, and white wine included. It serves until 10:30 p.m.

Likewise, **La Galería Restaurant** in the Plaza Santa Ana has a large *criollo* menu with the usual staples, plus caged songbirds adding to the splendid ambience. Meals cost US$4-23. And the equally atmospheric **Trinidad Colonial** at Maceo #55, tel. (419) 3873, also serves *criollo* cuisine and offers elegant indoor dining or a patio, and is bargain priced with grilled shrimp for US$5 and lobster in tomato sauce for US$7.

Alas, **Las Begonias**, an erstwhile elegant seafood restaurant at the corner of Antonio Maceo and Simón Bolívar, had been turned into a soulless snack bar at press time.

There are lots of peso snack stalls selling *batidos* and finger food along Calle Martí near Parque Céspedes. Need a pick-me-up? Check out the *guarapería,* selling fresh-squeezed sugarcane juice at the corner of Cienfuegos and Martí. If the heat gets to you, indulge in a delicious homemade lemonade at **Restaurante El Jigüe** (US$0.65).

You can buy groceries at the dollars-only stores sprinkled around town.

ENTERTAINMENT AND SHOPPING

Cultural Festivals

Trinidad has long had a tradition for *madrugadas,* early-morning performances of regional songs sung in the streets. Though rarely heard today, *madrugadas* highlight the town's weeklong **Fiesta de Cultura.**

Every Easter, a religious celebration—**El Recorrido del vía Cruces** (the way of the cross) —is held; the devout follow a route through the old city, stopping at 14 sites marked with crosses. And in 1999 the **Festival de Semana Santa** returned after being banned for forty years. This weeklong Catholic features Masses, plus street processions on Thursday and Friday.

Traditional Music and Dance

You'd expect a town such as Trinidad, pickled in time, to have heaps of traditional music. Visitors are not disappointed. Watch for performances by **Conjunto Folklórico de Trinidad,** which presents traditional Afro-Cuban dance routines. Genuine Afro-Cuban music is also a feature at the **Cabildo de San Antonio de los Congos Reales,** at Isidro Armenteros #168. This social club is strongly influenced by santería and is very colorful—the real McCoy!

Traditional music performances are hosted at the **Casa de la Trova,** at Calle Echerrí #29, one block east of Plaza Mayor, where musicians drift in to jam and locals whisk tourists onto the dance floor. It's open Tues.-Sun. 11 a.m.-2 p.m. and 10:30 p.m.-2 a.m. on weekends. Entrance costs US$1. Similarly, **Casa Fischer,** on General

Lino Pérez e/ Francisco Codatia y José Martí, hosts traditional music, including *boleros.* It's open Mon.-Sat. 10 a.m.-1 p.m.

The **Casa de la Cultura** on Francisco Izquierda and Martínez Villena, tel. (419) 4308, also hosts traditional music.

Check out the **Grupo Los Pinos Campesinos,** who play in the style of the Buena Vista Social Club, on Calle Francisco Toro one block south of Plaza Mayor. Fabulous!

Bars and Discos

Bars are few. **Bar Daiquirí,** at José Martí esq. Francisco Codatia, is an unofficial gathering spot of tourists, who sit in the shade watching the street life. One of the most atmospheric bars is **La Canchánchara,** on Calle Rubén Martínez, tel. (419) 4345. It features live music and is known for its house special, made of *aguardente* (raw rum), mineral water, honey, and lime (US$1.20). About 50 meters farther west is **La Luna,** another popular and charming bar with adult locals. Of the few local *cantinas,* one of the best is **La Bodeguita Trinitario,** good for joining locals for a beer and dance.

The happening dance spot is **Discoteca las Cuevas,** in the caves immediately west of the Motel Las Cuevas. Flashing lights amid the stalagmites and stalactites? Awesome! There are several rooms, including one hosting a *cabaret espectáculo.* It's popular with the locals and plays a mix of Cuban and European music. An electronic games rooms is planned. Entrance costs US$7 and includes all you can drink. Cigars are sold. It's open nightly 10:30 p.m.-3 a.m.

In town, three roofless ruins host live music and open-air discos playing world beat and modern pop music. Unfortunately the techno beat pulses through the surrounding streets, making a miserable time of things for neighbors who want to sleep. One such is **Disco Escalinita,** on Juan Manuel Márquez, behind the Casa de la Música. Entrance costs US$1.

Other Entertainment

The Motel Las Cuevas features cabaret entertainment nightly at 10 p.m. for the tour-group crowd (a magician performs on Saturday; Monday and Wednesday are "Noches Campesina"; and Tuesday is "Afro-Cuban" night). There's a **cinema** on Parque Céspedes.

Locals will take you hiking or on horseback to nearby waterfalls and natural swimming pools in the nearby mountains, with caves for exploring.

Shopping

All manner of arts and crafts are sold at the **artisan's market** held in the streets immediately east of Plaza Mayor. The widest option of arts and crafts under one roof is offered by **Fondo de Bienes Culturales,** one block south of Plaza Mayor, on Calle Simón Bolívar, selling a splendid array of handicrafts, including wickerwork. Paintings are also sold at the **Galería de Arte,** on the south side of Plaza Mayor. Its eclectic range runs the gamut of styles: contemporary work is displayed downstairs; more traditional works upstairs. Also try the **ARTEX store,** beside the entrance to Museo Romántico, and Pascual Cadalso Hernández's gallery at Ruben Martinez Villena #71, on Plazuela del Jigüe, tel. (419) 3788.

Much of the ceramic work is made at **El Alfarero Cerámica,** on the city's outskirts. There's also a **weaving factory** on Calle Bolívar, where straw hats and basketwork are produced. Pennywhistles made of bamboo are another local craft item.

The store in the **Casa de la Música,** tel. (419) 3414, has a wide selection of Cuban music on cassettes and CDs.

PRACTICALITIES

Information and Services

Tourist Information: There's no official tourist information office. However, various excursion agencies can assist (see Organized Excursions in the Getting Around section).

The **Banco de Crédito y Comercio** is on José Martí, 50 meters west of Colón.

There's a postal facility in the Motel Las Cuevas. The main **post office** is on the east side of Parque Céspedes. The **centro telefónico** is next door, open Mon.-Sat. 7:30 a.m.-noon and 1:30-5 p.m.).

The 24-hour **clínica internacional,** at the bottom of Lino Pérez #103, tel. (419) 3391, on the corner of Anastasio Cárdenas, has a small pharmacy as well as a doctor and nurse on hand. It charges US$25 per consultation (US$30 after

7 p.m.). There's also a local 24-hour pharmacy at Martí #332. **Ópticas Miramar** Martí #242, tel. (419) 3445, offers optical services and sells spectacles plus contact lens solutions. Consultations cost US$5.

The small **library** carries works almost exclusively on Cuba. It's open 8 a.m.-10 p.m. A minimally stocked **Photo Service,** Martí #222, has batteries, film, and small cameras.

The **Cupet gas station** is tucked into the corner of Frank País and Uzuerguera in the center of town. There's another at the junction for Trinidad three km southeast of Trinidad on the road to Casilda.

Getting There and Away
By Air: Aero Caribbean, Calle 23 #64, Vedado, tel. (7) 33-4543, fax (7) 33-5016, e-mail: aerocarvpcre@iacc3.get.cma.net, and **Aerotaxi,** Calle 27 #102 e/ M y N, Vedado, Havana, tel. (7) 33-4064, fax (7) 33-4063, both offer service between Havana and Trinidad. In 1999, **Inter Grupo Taca** introduced service to Trinidad from Havana, Varadero, and Cayo Largo, but service was suspended in early 2000 (see the By Air section in the Getting Around section in the On The Road chapter).

By Bus: Víazul operates tourist bus service to Trinidad from Havana (see the Víazul Bus Schedule chart, in the On the Road chapter). Its office in Trinidad is at Viro Guirnart e/ Antonio Maceo y Gustavo Izquierdo, tel. (419) 2404. For public bus service, see the Public Bus Service

From Havana chart, also in the On the Road chapter. The **Terminal de Omnibus** in Trinidad is at Calles Gustavo Izquierda and Piro Guinart, tel. (419) 2460. Buses also operate from Cienfuegos daily at noon (1.20 pesos; one hour and 50 minutes) and from Sancti Spíritus six times daily.

Paradiso, tel. (419) 2179 and 6308, charges US$25 for a transfer to Havana by minibus. A public bus to Havana leaves Trinidad daily at 2:30 p.m. Or take one of the six daily buses for to Sancti Spíritus, then catch a train or bus from there. There's a bus to Cienfuegos around 5 a.m. Buses to Topes de Collantes run thrice daily.

By Train: Train operates daily from Sancti Spíritus to Trinidad. If you're traveling from other cities, you'll have to connect in Sancti Spíritus. Trinidad's train station is at the bottom of Camilo Cienfuegos; the ticket booth is open 7:30 a.m.-noon for advance purchase.

By Car: Transauto tel. (419)-5314, offers a car-and-driver taxi service from the Motel Las Cuevas (four hours cost US$30, eight hours US$55, 12 hours US$85), where it has a car rental office. **Nacional Rent-a-Car,** tel. (419) 2577, has an office on Martí (between Cienfuegos and Perez). **Micar** has an agency at Calle Fausto Pelayo Alonson, tel. (419) 6192. **Gaviota,** tel. (419) 2282, also rents cars.

Organized Tours: Trinidad is a staple of excursions offered by tour agencies in Havana and other tourist centers.

Trinidad's streets are cobbled with stones once used for ship ballast, perhaps as early as the 16th century.

Getting Around

There is no public bus service in the old town. You must walk. Many streets are cobbled and uneven, the sidewalks are often high, the streets are poorly lit at night, and many are hilly.

Horse-drawn taxis operate through the new town. **Taxi Transtur**, tel. (419) 5314, provides the local taxi service, as does **Turistaxi**, tel. (419) 2479.

By Car: Gaviotatours, tel. (419) 2282, rents Suzuki Jeeps. Cubasol's **Motoclub,** on General Lino Pérez e/ Francisco Codatia y Antonio Maceo, rents scooters for US$7 the first hour, US$10 (two hours), US$24 all day, and US$144 per week, including one liter of gas per hour.

Organized Excursions: Cubatur, at the corner of Antonio Maceo y Francisco Javier Zerquera, tel. (419) 6314, offers excursions. It's open daily 9 a.m.-6 p.m. **Paradiso,** tel. (419) 2179 and 6308, which promotes cultural tourism, has an agency in the Casa Fischer, General Lino Pérez e/ Francisco Codatia y José Martí, and offers excursions to Topes de Collantes, Valle de los Ingenios, etc. **Gaviotatours,** Calle Frank País e/ Piro Guinart y Simón Bolívar, tel. (419) 2282, has excursions by minibus and by army truck.

When not laid low for repairs, a tourist train *(tren turístico)* runs to the town of Guachinango via the Valle de los Ingenios using old railway carriages pulled by a World War I-era steam engine. Contact **Rumbos,** Calle G. Izquierdo, tel. (419) 9-4204; Peninsula de Ancón, tel. (419) 9-4414; Calle M. Gómez #23, tel. (419) 9-2264. At press time the train was idle, awaiting repair. Rumbos also offers a hiking excursion in the Sierra del Escambray and a horseback ride to La Vega Rancho. You can book through the tour office at Motel Las Cuevas or in the Hotel Ancón. **Tour & Travel,** tel. (419) 6133, in the Hotel Las Cuevas, offers excursions locally.

Aerotaxi also offers air tours by rickety Russian biplane (US$25) from the airfield southeast of the city, tel. (419) 2547. You can book through Cubatur, Rumbos, and Gaviota tour agencies.

LA BOCA

La Boca is a quaint fishing village with traditional tile-roofed *bohíos,* five km west of Trinidad. It appeals for its pocket-scale beaches amid coral coves favored by Trinitarios on weekends. It has been described by another writer as the place "the inhabitants of the area meet to relax in a lively congregation of music, flirting, and fistfights. They're far more interesting," he continues, "than the dowdy crowd of pale visitors from the north along the Ancón Peninsula, and you'll be made more welcome, too."

There are numerous *casas particulares* to choose from, including the pleasant **Hostal Sol y Mar,** Avenida del Mar #87, a seafront option with two clean, cross-ventilated rooms, simply furnished and sharing a large, clean bathroom with hot water for US$15 (US$20 with a/c). Your host, Norma García Hernández, makes meals.

Rumbos runs the 24-hour **El Ranchón** by the beach.

PENINSULA DE ANCÓN

The coast extends south of La Boca to a small point, **Punta María Aguilar,** beyond which a long narrow peninsula curls east, limned by Playa Ancón (also called Playa María Aguilar), one of Cuba's premium beaches. Behind lies a mangrove-lined lagoon, the **Ensenada de Casilda.**

The four-km-long beach is fabulous, with sugary white sand and pavonine waters fringed with pines and palms. Topless bathing is tolerated. The sea is perfect for snorkeling: calm, crystal clear, with plenty of coral. Local youths stroll the beach selling polished seashells and jewelry carved from local hardwoods and endangered black coral.

Until recently, an army barracks was located here with a billboard reading: *Por Nuestra Frontera El Enemigo No Pasará!* (The Enemy Shall Not Pass Our Frontier). It was here with good reason. During planning for the invasion by Cuban exiles in spring 1961, Richard Bissel, the CIA director of operations, promoted Ancón as the preferred landing site. He advanced a combined airborne/amphibious assault. Kennedy rejected the idea as "too spectacular" and "too much like a World War II invasion." Instead, he settled for the Bay of Pigs—and a fiasco.

Accommodations and Food

Gran Caribe's **Hotel Ancón,** Playa Ancón, Trinidad, tel. (419) 6120, fax (419) 6147, at the far southern end of the beach, has 279 rooms, all with a/c, private baths, telephones, and radios. The Soviet-style structure has been nicely upgraded. Facilities include a game room, cabaret, a huge swimming pool, a tourism bureau, a Photo Service shop, an atmospheric restaurant, and seven bars. Excursions are offered. There's a car rental service, but demand far exceeds supply. And scuba diving is offered onsite. The lively hotel is a favorite of charter tour groups: Canadians, French, and Germans. Rates were US$41 s, US$58 d low season, US$58 s, US$65 d high season.

The smaller, low-profile **Hotel Costa Sur,** at Punta María Aguilar, tel. (419) 6174, has its own little white sand beach with volleyball. The waters are shallow, albeit rocky. The modestly appealing hotel is popular with German tour groups. The 131 a/c rooms and bungalows all have private baths, radios, and telephones. Facilities include a game room and volleyball and tennis courts, a pool, even a miniature rifle range. The hotel features scuba diving and excursions. Rates were US$35 s, US$45 d low season, US$41 s, US$52 d high season for standard rooms; US$38 s, US$54 d low season, US$47 s, US$62 d high season, including breakfast. It offers horse rentals (US$5) and has a full program of activities, service, and entertainment.

Ground had been broken at press time on Cubanacán's deluxe **Hotel Trinidad del Mar,** adjacent to the Hotel Ancón.

Water Sports and Excursions

Ancón's offshore coral reefs have more than 30 dive spots and the added attraction of sunken vessels, concentrated at Cayo Blanco de Casilda and along the peninsula all the way to the mouth of the Río Guarabo, at La Boca. **Cayo Blanco,** nine km southeast of Ancón, is famous for its kaleidoscopic variety of corals, sea fans, sponges, and gorgonians.

Scuba diving is offered by both the Hotel Ancón and the Hotel Costa Sur, and by Puertosol at the Marina Puertosol Trinidad. Puertosol charges US$9 for an initiation dive (resort course) and US$30 per dive for certified divers, plus US$35 for night dives. You can arrange a 10-dive package for US$230. Instructors, compressors, and tanks are included.

The Hotel Ancón offers jet skis, catamarans, and other water sports. You can go snorkeling for US$8 per hour on a catamaran, with snorkel gear included.

A six-hour "seafari" and a nocturnal "cabaret at sea" are available from Puertosol Marina Trinidad, as are excursions to Cayo Blanco (US$30) and nearby Cayo Macho (US$35). You can charter a sportfishing boat for four people (US$150 half-day, US$250 full day).

Getting There and Around

At press time a new shuttle bus service—**Trinibus**—was to be introduced from Trinidad to the beach. Public **buses** to La Boca leave Trinidad four times daily and continue to Playa Ancón. You may also be able to hop aboard the hotel workers' buses. A **taxi** between Trinidad and Ancón costs about US$11 one-way.

Transauto has a car rental office in the Hotel Ancón. You can also rent **bicycles** at the Hotel Ancón. The ride to Trinidad is flat all the way as you wind through the salt lagoons (it's a hot ride, however; take water).

Puertosol Marina Trinidad, tel. (419) 4011 or 4414, lies within a cove in the Ensenada de Casilda, adjacent to the Hotel Ancón. The marina has six moorings. Water, electricity, and diesel (US$0.90 per liter) are available. Before berthing, you must first call in to clear Customs and Immigration across the bay at the ramshackle wharf of Casilda, where the process is said to be a dreary chore.

A "seafari" to Cayo Blanco costs US$25 including cocktails, snorkeling, and fishing.

WEST OF TRINIDAD

The road west to Cienfuegos begins at the base of Calle Pino Guinart. It leads past a turn-off for **Rancho El Cubano,** reached by dirt road, run by Gaviota, and where horseback rides lead to cascades and natural pools good for swimming. You can rent boats and go fishing.

Nearby **Finca María Dolores,** tel. (419) 3581, is a rustic *finca* turned tourist attraction amid landscaped grounds on the banks of the Río Guaurabo, three km west of Trinidad. It's popular with tour groups. The representation of a traditional farm features an aviary, cockfights, milking, and other farm activities.

A turnoff from the coast road a stone's throw west of Finca María Dolores leads to a cave by the river where **Monumento Alberto Delgado** recalls a Castroite killed during the counterrevolutionary war. Delgado was hanged by *banditos* (counterrevolutionaries) after his identity as a spy for the Castro regime was discovered. His house, **Casa Museo Alberto Delgado,** serves as a museum and is two km east of La Boca, reached by a bumpy dirt road.

Accommodations and Food

The *finca* offers accommodations in 20 small brick cabanas, each with a/c, hot water, and showers. Rates were US$10 s, US$16 d, US$22 t.

The *criollo* meals are inexpensive (US$4-6 for pork and chicken dishes). You eat spit-roasted pig in a thatched restaurant, open to the sides, where folkloric shows featuring a *guateque* (a good ol' country hoedown) are offered nightly at 9 p.m. (US$15, including dinner).

TOPES DE COLLANTES NATIONAL PARK

Five km west of Trinidad, a turnoff from the coast road leads north and begins to climb precipitously into the southeastern Sierra Escambray, whose slopes swathed in Caribbean pines and an abundance of ancient tree ferns, bamboo, and eucalyptus are protected within Topes de Collantes National Park. The area is tremendous for hiking; there are plenty of trails, and the rich bird life includes an abundance of parrots. Bring raingear and waterproof footwear.

At its heart, at a refreshingly cool 790 meters, is a spa-hotel complex dominated by a massive concrete structure—the Kurhotel—designed in 1936, when it served as a sanatorium for victims of tuberculosis. Following the Revolution, the disease was finally eradicated in Cuba. The structure was then sanitized and turned into a teacher-training facility. The complex, which includes smaller hotels, was developed as a resort area in the late 1970s, with a view to nature and health tourism—the swimming pool stays heated year-round.

The complex is mostly used by Cubans, especially those seeking post-operative rehabilitation or specialized therapies. It also attracts spa vacationers from elsewhere in Latin America. It holds little appeal unless you're seriously seeking physical therapy, although you can take simpler treatments such as massages (general massage costs US$17, facial massage costs US$8). Medicinal plants are grown in the valley below.

Hiking

The two most important trails lead to two waterfalls—**Salto Vega Grande** and **Salto de Caburní,** (the latter, 75 meters high)—about four km northeast of the complex, and a stiff hike. The trail to Caburní begins beside the Aparthotel, east of the Kurhotel. It leads steeply downhill, zigzagging in places.

Another trail leads south seven km to **Finca Cordina,** an erstwhile coffee estate that now serves as a post for birders and hikers. Special luncheons are laid on for tour groups, with roast suckling pig and a house cocktail made from rum, honey, and ginger. After a couple of toddies, you may feel brave enough to wallow in a pool of medicinal mud. The surrounding hills contain an extensive cave system, much of which remains unexplored. The trail begins below Los Helechos.

Accommodations and Food

The massive **Kurhotel,** tel. (42) 4-0219 or 4-0180, has a Stalinist aesthetic, with hints of art deco outside. A monstrous TV and radio transmitter looms over the massive hotel. By contrast, the lobby—reached via a stone staircase on a Siberian scale—is pleasantly welcoming, with lofty columns and ferns, and the rooms are satisfactory, with rattan furniture, floral prints, and attractive bathrooms. A TV, refrigerator, security box, telephone, and a/c are standard in the 210 rooms and 16 suites. The hotel features its own TV station (Tele Caburni), a movie theater, cabaret acts (nightly except Monday at 10 p.m.), bowling alley, and a thermal swimming pool under a skylight in a separate building, where massage and therapeutic treatments are offered. It has a modestly elegant restaurant, five gyms, a beauty salon, and a small store. Most guests are Cubans; of the rest, Germans and Argentineans predominate. Each guest is issued a blood-red jogging suit. Rates were US$25 s, US$30 d low season, US$28 s, US$40 d high season for standard rooms.

The complex includes **Villa Caburni,** immediately next to the Kurhotel, with recently refurbished apartment bungalows for up to four people. Rates were US$32 s, US$38 d low season, US$52 high season.

You're alternative is **Hotel Los Helechos,** tel. (42) 4-0330 or 4-0180, fax (42) 4-0301, which hides in a cool valley below the Kurhotel. The grim exterior (shocking pink and green at last visit) belies a pleasing restoration inside, with nice bamboo decor in spacious a/c rooms with satellite TVs and telephones, and modern bathrooms. Take a room in the front, three-story blockhouse structure; the rest are poorly lit. There's a pleasant swimming pool and restaurant. Rates were US$23 s, US$28 d low season, US$31 s, US$38 d high season.

The **Hotel Serrano** and **Hotel Los Pinos** do not accept foreigners.

I can't vouch for the quality of meals in the Kurhotel or Los Helechos. The only other restaurant nearby is a pizzeria with *mirador* a few miles south of Topes, on the road to Trinidad.

Information

For information, contact the **Complejo Turístico Topes de Collantes,** tel. (42) 4-0117, fax (42) 4-0288, or **Gaviota,** Calle 16 #504, Miramar, Havana, tel. (7) 24-7670 or 24-5245, fax (7) 33-2780.

Getting There

By Bus: There's bus service (sometimes provided in an open-sided truck) to Topes from Trinidad, in Sancti Spíritus Province, with departures on Monday and Sunday at 4 p.m. and Thursday at 6 a.m. Tour buses leave from the Motel Las Cuevas, in Trinidad. You may be able to talk your way aboard, but expect to pay tour excursion prices. Buses also travel to Topes from Manicuragua and from Santa Clara.

By Car: There are three routes to Topes de Collante. The road from Trinidad, 21 km to the south (the turnoff from the coast road is five km west of Trinidad), rises in a steep, potholed switchback. Drive with utmost caution: the road has huge corrugations and hairpin bends, often in combination—extremely dangerous! A second road rises more gradually from Santa Clara via Manicaragua.

If coming from Cienfuegos, turn left at **La Sierrita** and follow the valley of the Río Mataguá (see above).

Organized Excursions: The **Gaviotatours** office at Topes de Collantes, tel. (42) 4-0228, fax (42) 4-0301, e-mail: toptour@gavtope.gav.cma .net, sells a splendid map of the area. Gaviotatours also offers guided hiking excursions to Salto Vega Grande and to Salto de Caburní (both US$5); by army truck to **Salto de Rocio** and **Hacienda Guanyara** for lunch, including swimming in a natural pool (US$25); and to **Hacienda Codena,** featuring an orchid garden and with interpretative trails that lead to waterfalls and caves (US$20 including lunch). The trips are offered from the Gaviotatours office in Trinidad (see Trinidad, above).

THE NORTH COAST

There is little of interest along the north coast, which has no beaches of note. The Circuito Norte coast road parallels the shore some miles inland. Heading east from Caibarién, in Villa Clara Province, the road skirts the scarp face of the **Sierra del Bamburanao,** a dramatic spur of steep, ruler-straight hills. At **Mayijagua,** you can turn north 20 km to **Punta de Judas,** where there's an extensive cave system to be explored behind the beach.

East of Mayijagua, the road rises onto the upper slopes of the Sierra, offering marvelous views down over the cane fields, with scores of tiny cays—those of Ciego de Ávila Province—floating in an azure sea to the north. About nine km east of Mayijagua, is **Sendero Ecoturístico Pelú de Mayijagua** with trails leading into the Sierra de Jatobónico. This recently opened reserve was still under development at press time.

Accommodations

Just east of Mayijagua, Islazul has the **Villa San José del Lago,** tel. (41) 2-6390, fax (41) 2-2562, a spa resort with cabins beneath palms surrounding a lagoon with rowboats, plus three swimming pools (one with thermal water). The 30

CIEGO DE ÁVILA AND CAMAGÜEY
INTRODUCTION

East of Sancti Spíritus lie Ciego de Ávila and Camagüey, geographically similar provinces which together form the central plains, dominated by rolling savannas.

Ciego de Ávila is Cuba's least-populous province (pop. 390,000), a dull, pancake-flat region that is the nation's leading pineapple producer, though almost three-fourths of the province is devoted to cattle. There are few sights of natural or historical interest here, even in the only two towns of importance, Ciego de Ávila and, due north, Morón, gateway to Ciego de Ávila's star attraction—Cayo Coco and the cays of Cayería del Norte, separated by lagoons in which flamingoes tip-toe around in hot pink.

The nation's largest province is Camagüey, though it too is sparsely populated. The grassy, honey-colored rolling plains are reminiscent of Montana, parched in summer by a scowling wind that bows down the long flaxen grasses. Sun-struck cattle gather beneath lonesome trees festooned with epiphytes. The numerous ranches—*ganaderías*—worked by *vaqueros* with lassoes and machetes lashed to the flanks of their

horses, making a poignant effect on the landscape. The city of Camagüey offers plenty of colonial charm despite its industry and modern pretensions. Camagüey is a staging area, too, for access to the cays of Cayería del Norte and Playa Santa Lucía.

Lay of the Land
Ciego de Ávila is a gentle plain; the average elevation of the land is less than 50 meters above sea level. There are few rivers and no distinguishing features. The wedge-shaped province (6,910 square km) is the narrowest point of Cuba—only 50 km from coast to coast. In Camagüey, the land broadens, bulging to the south like a pregnant cow. The land also rises along the central spine, forming an upland bounded to the north by a line of low mountains, the **Sierra de Cubitas,** beyond which lie coastal plains and the **Cayería del Norte,** low lying, sandy coral islands in a great line parallel to the coast, between 10 and 18 km from shore. Officially called the Archipiélago de Sabana-Camagüey, this sea-girt wilderness of coral reefs, cays, islands, and sheltered seas extends 470 km from the

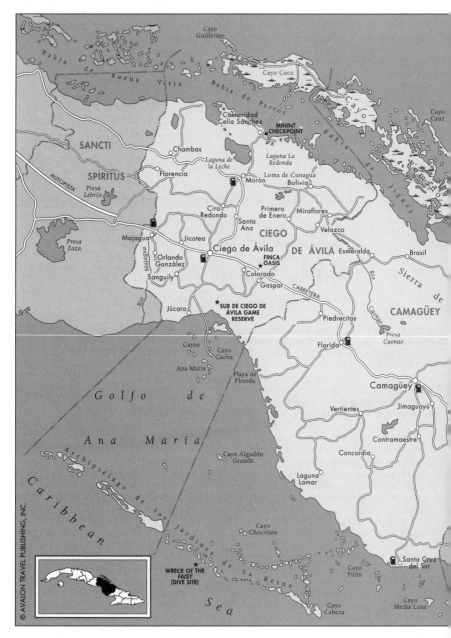

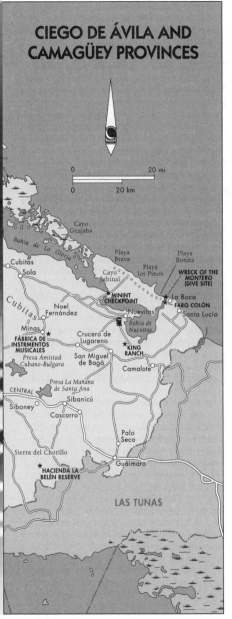

CIEGO DE ÁVILA AND CAMAGÜEY PROVINCES

N

| 0 | 20 mi |
| 0 | 20 km |

Cayo Guajaba

Bahía de La Gloria

Cubitas
Sola

Cayo Sabinal

Playa Brava

Playa Los Pinos

Playa Bonita

WRECK OF THE MONTERO (DIVE SITE)

Cubitas

Noel Fernández

MININT CHECKPOINT

La Boca

FARO COLÓN

Nuevitas

Santa Lucía

Minas

Bahía de Nuevitas

FÁBRICA DE INSTRUMENTOS MUSICALES

Crucero de Lugareno

San Miguel de Bagá

KING RANCH

Presa Amistad Cubano-Bulgara

Camalote

Presa La Mañana de Santa Ana

CENTRAL

Sibanicú

Siboney

Cascorro

Palo Seco

Sierra del Chorillo

HACIENDA LA BELÉN RESERVE

Guáimaro

LAS TUNAS

Peninsula de Hicaco (Varadero) in the west to Playa Santa Lucía in the east.

Ernest Hemingway actively pursued German submarines in these seas in the 1940s, immortalizing his adventures in his novel, *Islands in the Stream*. It is possible to follow the route of the novel's protagonists as they pursue the Nazis east-west along the cays, passing Confites, Paredón Grande, Coco, Guillermo, and on to Santa María. Papa was meticulous in his descriptions of landmarks, although he sometimes shifted their position.

The 400 or so cays are rimmed by stunning beaches, scintillatingly white as confectioner's sugar dissolving into crystalline waters. They are separated from one another by narrow channels and from the coast by shallow lagoons. And together they are among the least disturbed of all Cuba's terrain and a new frontier for resort development.

The otherwise uninhabited islands are mostly covered with low scrub (including mangroves), which forms a perfect habitat for wild pigs and iguanas and birds such as mockingbirds, nightingales, and woodpeckers. The briny lagoons are favored by pelicans, ibis, various duck species, and—the stars of the show—as many as 20,000 flamingoes, more by far than anywhere else in Cuba. They are all easily seen, especially on Cayos Coco, Guillermo, and Sabinal. Running along the northern edge of the cays are endless miles of coral reef teeming with tropical fish that thrive in waters that remain 26-30° C year-round. (Conch shells are tempting items, shining and glossy pink, and local Cubans will attempt to sell them to you for almost nothing. *It's illegal.* Taking conch shells out of the county ostensibly requires a permit. More important, the conch population is under pressure.)

A paved road runs along the coast, paralleling it at an average distance of five km inland. It is mostly in good condition. Feeder roads connect it with the Carretera Central and provincial capitals, and by land bridges with Cayo Coco, Cayo Romano, and Cayo Sabinal.

Much of the coastal plain is covered with barren deciduous scrubland grazed by cattle; swampy marshland, perfect for birding or hunting; and lagoons, perfect for fishing. Elsewhere, the flatlands are drowned by vast undulating seas of green sugarcane.

Camagüey

The sparsely populated southern plains are covered almost entirely by marshland and swamps. There are few beaches. A slender archipelago—the **Járdines de la Reina**—lies off the southern coast, sprinkled east-west in a straight line across the Gulf of Santa Ana María. This necklace of coral isles figures in Cuba's burgeoning tourism drive, with fabulous beaches and bird life, coral formations perfect for scuba diving, and shallow waters that offer angling delights.

CIEGO DE ÁVILA AND VICINITY

The provincial capital city (pop. 80,000), 460 km east of Havana, is sleepy and unremarkable—the least inspirational of Cuba's provincial capitals. There's no need to stop except for curiosity's sake. The city is also known as "The Pineapple Town" for the local fields of pineapple (now looking neglected).

The first land grants locally were given in the mid-16th century, when the region was almost entirely forested. Gradually cattle ranches were established. Local lore says that one of the earliest *hacienda*-owners was named Ávila. His property, established in 1538, occupied a large clearing, or *ciego,* and was used as a way-stop for travelers. A small settlement grew around it, known locally as Ciego de Ávila. The city gained commercial prominence this century as an agricultural center.

Ciego de Ávila was also the site of one of the 43 forts along La Trocha, the great barrier built from coast to coast across the province in the 1860s to forestall the rebel army's westward advance during the first War of Independence. The line was strengthened by the Spanish general Valeriano Weyler during the second War of Independence, with a dike paralleling the fence.

ORIENTATION AND SIGHTSEEING

The streets are laid out in a perfect grid. The Carretera Central (called Calle Chicho Valdés) runs east-west through the center of the city. The main street is Independencia, running east-west two blocks north of Chicho Valdés.

The heart of affairs is **Parque Martí,** a pretty little square on the north side of Independencia and the west side of Marcial Gómez. It has a bust of the hero at its center, plus Victorian-era lampposts and seating beneath shade trees. The most noteworthy structure is the **Poder Popular,** the old town hall, built in 1911. There are no other buildings of note.

The jewel of Ciego de Ávila is the **Teatro Principal,** one block south of Martí, on Joaquín Agüera and Honorario del Castillo. It is said to have been built at the whim of a local society figure. Its enormous hand-carved wooden doors

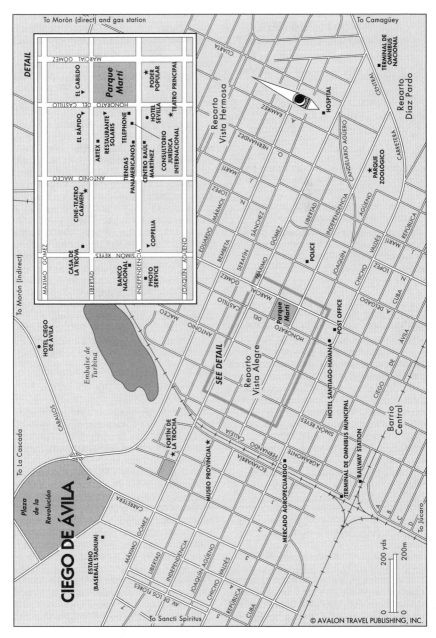

CIEGO DE ÁVILA

DETAIL

To Morón (direct) and gas station
To Camagüey

Detail area:
MARCIAL GÓMEZ
HONORATO DEL CASTILLO
ANTONIO MACEO
SIMÓN REYES
LIBERTAD
INDEPENDENCIA
JOAQUÍN AGÜENO
MÁXIMO GÓMEZ

EL CABILDO
Parque Martí
PODER POPULAR ★
TEATRO PRINCIPAL ★
EL RÁPIDO
ARTEX
RESTAURANTE SOLARIS ▼
TELEPHONE ■
HOTEL SEVILLA ■
TIENDAS PANAMERICANOS ■
CENTRO RAÚL MARTÍNEZ ■
CONSULTORIO JURÍDICA INTERNACIONAL ■
CINE-TEATRO CARMEN ★
COPPELIA ▼
CASA DE LA TROVA ■
BANCO NACIONAL ■
PHOTO SERVICE ■

Main map:
To Morón (indirect)
To La Cascada
To Sancti Spíritus
To Júcaro

CUARTA
TERMINAL DE ÓMNIBUS NACIONAL
CENTRAL
Reparto Díaz Pardo
HOSPITAL
Reparto Vista Hermosa
A. RÁMIREZ
HERNÁNDEZ
CANDELARIO AGÜERO
CARRETERA
PARQUE ZOOLÓGICO ★
MARTÍ
REPÚBLICA
VALDÉS
CUBA
ÁVILA
CIEGO DE
DELGADO
CHICHO
LÓPEZ
N
JOAQUÍN
INDEPENDENCIA
LIBERTAD
GÓMEZ
SÁNCHEZ
SERAFÍN
BEMBETA
EDUARDO
MÁRMOL
LÓPEZ
N
MARTÍ
O
POLICE ●
MÁXIMO GÓMEZ
MARCIAL GÓMEZ
DEL CASTILLO
HONORATO
Parque Martí
ANTONIO MACEO
SEE DETAIL
Reparto Vista Alegre
Embalse de Turbina
HOTEL CIEGO DE ÁVILA ■
CABALLOS
Plaza de la Revolución
CARRETERA
ESTADIO (BASEBALL STADIUM) ■
MÁXIMO GÓMEZ
LIBERTAD
INDEPENDENCIA
JOAQUÍN AGÜERO
CHICHO VALDÉS
REPÚBLICA
CUBA
AV DE LOS FLORES
FORTÍN DE LA TROCHA ★
MUSEO PROVINCIAL ★
ECHAVARRÍA
CALLEJA
FERNANDO
AGRAMONTE
MERCADO AGROPECUARIO ●
HOTEL SANTIAGO-HAVANA ●
POST OFFICE ●
SIMÓN REYES
Barrio Central
TERMINAL DE ÓMNIBUS MUNICIPAL ●
RAILWAY STATION ●
A
B
C
D

200 yds
200 m

© AVALON TRAVEL PUBLISHING, INC.

SIGHTSEEING HIGHLIGHTS: CIEGO DE ÁVILA AND CAMAGÜEY

Cayo Coco and Cayo Guillermo: Gorgeous white-sand beaches limn the shore of these contiguous isles. Deluxe hotels, plus water sports, horseback riding, and scuba diving. Flamingos flock to the inshore lagoons.

Cayo Sabinal: Lonesome pristine island boasting spectacular beaches and waters and rustic accommodations . . . Jimmy Buffet's *Margaritaville?*

Jardines de la Reina: Hard-to-reach string of coral cays offering some of the best fishing and diving in the hemisphere.

Laguna de los Flamencos: Stilt-legged flamingos parade around in hot pink.

Plaza San Juan de Díos, Camagüey: Beautifully restored cobbled plaza with distinctive architecture, including two atmospheric eateries.

---

open onto an elaborately decorated interior, a mix of imperial, baroque, and renaissance styles, with allegorical statuary, an oval grand marble staircase, and bronze chandeliers.

An old Spanish fort—**Fortín de la Trocha**—lies at the west end of Máximo Gómez, just beyond the railway tracks. It is the only one still standing of seven military towers built during the Ten Years' War of Independence. Today it houses a restaurant. Immediately west is the Instituto de Segunda Enseñanza, housing the modest **Museo Provincial,** tel. (33) 2-8431 or 2-8128, open Tues.-Sat 8 a.m.-5 p.m. and Sunday 8 a.m.-noon. Entrance costs US$1.

There's a small **Parque Zoológico** at the east end of Independencia that has a half dozen animals, including a zebra.

ACCOMMODATIONS

José García Quezada has a *casa particular* at Calle A #384 e/ 6 y 7, tel. (33) 2-4596. Also try Martha Corvea's home at José María Agramonte #19A e/ Independencia y Joaquín de Agüero.

Islazul operates the **Hotel Ciego de Ávila,** tel. (33) 2-8013, on the Carretera Ceballos, two

km northwest of downtown. It's a faceless Eastern bloc-style building but pleasantly furnished. The 144 a/c rooms all have telephones and private baths. There's a beauty parlor and barbershop, nightclub, and tourism bureau with rent-a-car service. Half of the city seems to flock to the swimming pool on weekends. Rates were US$22 s, US$29 d low season, US$27 s, US$36 d high season, including breakfast.

Islazul's **Hotel Santiago-Havana,** Independencia y Honorario del Castillo, tel. (33) 2-5703, dates back to 1957. The modest, newly renovated (but dourly furnished) hotel has 76 a/c rooms with TVs and hot water. There's a dark, moody bar (La Copa) and cabaret disco in La Cima nightclub. Rates were US$19 s, US$24 d low season, US$24 s, US$28 d high season.

A better bet is the **Hotel Sevilla,** Independencia e/ Honorario del Castillo y Antonio Maceo, tel. (33) 2-5603, a modest, two-star training hotel that plays on a Spanish theme and accepts both Cubans and tourists. It has 25 a/c rooms with no-frills decor, local TV, telephones, and meager but adequate bathrooms with cold water only. There's a pleasant lobby restaurant plus a lively breeze-swept bar upstairs that draws the locals during weekends and offers daily and nightly cabarets. Rates were US$24 s, US$28 d, US$31 t high season.

FOOD

Ciego de Ávila poses a challenge for gourmands (one writer advises travelers to "keep gastric juices firmly under control"). Your best option, though unremarkable, is to eat at any of the hotels. Otherwise the best bet is the **Restaurante Solaris,** atop the ugly red-brick building on the west side of Parque Martí, tel. (33) 2-3424. It's unmarked: the elevator is to the rear of the building. A dress code is in effect; no shorts are allowed.

For quasi-Chinese cuisine, try **Restaurante Yiesen,** far west end of Chicho Valdés, with suitably Chinese decor behind a circular door guarded by a huge "bronze" Buddha. There's even an authentic Oriental garden. The popular **La Cascada,** tel. (33) 8539, amid lakes and woodland about 1.5 miles west of town, is a seafood restaurant, but without views of the lake over which it sits—thanks to the frosted-glass windows.

Other options include **El Colonial,** on Independencia, and **El Fuerte,** in the Fortín de la Trocha, which serves homemade sausage and wines. Pizza slices (five pesos apiece) are sold at a shop opposite the Casa de la Trova on Libertad. **El Cabildo,** on the northwest corner of Parque Martí, specializes in chicken dishes. And **El Rápido,** at Libertad y Honorario del Castillo, is a fast-food last resort for fried chicken. And stalls outside the station sell pizzas and other snacks, *refrescoes,* and *batidos* (try a *piña fria,* an iced drink made of pineapple juice).

Coppelia, on Independencia, two blocks west of Parque Martí, sells ice cream.

You can buy fresh produce at the **farmers' market,** beneath the bridge at the junction of Chicho Valdés and Fernando Calleja.

ENTERTAINMENT, EVENTS, AND RECREATION

Visit **Artex,** at Libertad #162, to find out what's going on in town and around Ciego de Ávila province; it hosts live music on its patio. Also on Libertad, two blocks west of Parque Martí, is **Cine-Teatro Carmen,** which shows films and where the Festival Nacional de Humor is held each April; and **Casa de la Trova,** which hosts traditional music and dancing Wed.-Mon. 6 p.m.-midnight (till 2 a.m. Friday and Saturday). Entrance is US$1 for foreigners. The director, Luís Morales, is very friendly and helpful. The **Centro Raul Martínez,** on Independencia e/ Honorario del Castillo y Antonio Maceo, hosts exhibitions and cultural events.

Want to boogie? Try **Disco Marco,** on Chicho Valdés and Simón Reyes.

You can rent horses and boats (US$1 for as long as you want) at La Cascada, an area of lake and woodland two km west of town, tel. (33) 7731.

PRACTICALITIES

Information and Services
The **post office** is two blocks south of Parque Martí, at Marcial Gómez and Chico Valdés. **DHL** has an office in the Hotel Ciego de Ávila, tel. (33) 22573. It's open weekdays 9 a.m.-6 p.m. and Saturday 8:30 a.m.-noon. You can make international calls from the **Centro Telefónico,** in the ugly high-rise on the west side of Parque

TRAIN SCHEDULE (CAMAGÜEY)

EASTBOUND

No.	Origin	Destination	Arrive Camagüey	Depart Camagüey
11	Havana	Santiago de Cuba	[times unavailable]	
13	Havana	Santiago de Cuba	12:48 a.m.	1:08 a.m.
15	Havana	Holguín (every two days)	11:22 p.m.	11:42 p.m.
65	Morón	Santiago de Cuba (every two days)	8:29 a.m.	8:54 a.m.

WESTBOUND

No.	Origin	Destination	Arrive Camagüey	Depart Camagüey
12	Santiago de Cuba	Havana	[times unavailable]	
14	Santiago de Cuba	Havana	10:19 p.m.	10:39 p.m.
16	Holguín	Havana (every two days)	7:33 p.m.	7:53 p.m.
18	Bayamo-Manzanillo	Havana	12:30 a.m.	12:50 a.m.
64	Santiago de Cuba	Morón (every two days)	12:08 p.m.	12:33 p.m.

Fares are US$10 to Ciego de Ávila, US$13 to Santa Clara, US$23 to Matanzas, US$27 Havana, US$10 to Las Tunas and Holguín, and US$16 to Santiago de Cuba.

Martí. There's a **Banco de Crédito y Comercio** on Independencia at Simón Reyes, three blocks west of Parque Martí.

The **hospital** is at the east end of Máximo Gómez. If you need legal help, try the **Consultorio Jurídica Internacional,** on Independencia y Honorario del Castillo. The **police station** is one block east of the main square, on A. Delgado.

There's a **Photo Service** at Independencia, stocking batteries and film.

Getting There and Away

By Air: Weekly charter flights serve Ciego de Ávila from Montréal (Cubana) and Toronto (Canadian Airlines and Royal Airlines), bringing package tourists to Cayo Coco. Cubana flies twice weekly from Havana (US$35 one-way); it has an office at Calle Chicho Valdés #83 e/ Maceo y Honorario del Castillo, tel. (33) 2-5316. The Máximo Gómez airport, tel. (33) 2-5717, is 15 km north of town.

By Bus: The **Víazul** tourist bus departs Havana for Ciego de Ávila on Tuesday and Friday (see the Víazul Bus Schedule chart in the On the Road chapter). For public bus service, see the Public Bus Service from Havana chart, also in the On the Road chapter. There are also regular buses to and from Camagüey, Sancti Spíritus, and other cities. The **Terminal de Ómnibus Nacional,** tel. (33) 2-5109, is 1.5 km east of town, on the Carretera Central. The **Terminal de Ómnibus Municipal,** tel. (33) 2-3076, is next to the railway station (see below).

By Train: Ciego de Ávila is on the main east-west railroad between Havana and Santiago, and the *especial* between the two cities stops here, as do slower *regulares* between Havana and other cities (see the Train Schedule from Havana chart, in the On the Road chapter). Reservations can be made 8 a.m.-noon and 2-4:30 p.m. The station is at the west end of Calle Ciego de Ávila, three blocks south of Chicho Valdés, tel. (33) 2-3313.

By Car: **Havanautos** rents cars in the Hotel Ciego de Ávila. **Micar,** Carretera Central y Independencia, tel. (33) 2-2530. **Transauto,** tel. (33) 26-6228, also rents cars.

The **Cupet gas station** is on the northeast outskirts of town, at the junction of the *circun-* *valación* y Carretera Morón. The **Servicentro Oro Negro** is at the Carretera Central y Independencia.

For Morón, take Carretera A Caballo (Carretera de Morón), on the west side of town. For Júcaro, take Simón Reyes south to Calle D, then turn right to the railroad track; turn left and cross the railroad tracks after three blocks; immediately turn left onto Echevarria for Júcaro.

Getting Around

Horse-drawn cabs rule the roads. They line up outside the train station. No ride should cost more than two or three pesos, although as a foreigner you may be charged in dollars. For a real taxi, call **Cubataxi,** tel. (33) 2-7636 or **Transtur,** tel. (33) 2-2997.

SOUTH OF CIEGO DE ÁVILA

You can forego the South Coast without fear of skipping anything worth the drive. **Sur de Ciego de Ávila Game Reserve,** 40 km south of Ciego de Ávila, attracts migratory ducks, doves, snipes, quail, and guinea fowl. It serves hunters.

A road leads south 20 km to the funky fishing village of **Júcaro,** gateway to the Járdines de la Reina. The road, potholed farther south, is as straight as a billiard cue—and the fields of sugarcane are as flat and green as a billiard table.

A hurricane came ashore at Júcaro in 1932, killing many people. The dead-end village looks as if it has never recovered. There are no restaurants or other facilities, just fading wooden shacks and browbeaten fishing boats. The railway line extends out onto the wharf but is today little used, the trade having been stolen by Palo Alto. A sugar-loading facility there allows visitors to watch freighters loading from the huge wharf—Embarcadero Palo Alto—which extends one mile out to sea (the turnoff is three km north of Júcaro).

Marina Puertosol Júcaro, tel. (33) 9-8126, fax (33) 8-9104, is a rickety wharf with a gasoline pump, and six moorings with electricity and water. Diving and fishing excursions are offered to the cays of the Járdines de la Reina using live-aboard vessels.

CIEGO DE ÁVILA TO CAMAGÜEY

East of Ciego de Ávila, the Carretera Central continues almost ruler-straight to Camagüey. There are few towns of any significance. Dozens of Cubans wait for rides at the crossroads at **Gaspar,** where there's a café.

Entering Camagüey, you'll pass **Lake Porvenir,** renowned for its excellent bass fishing; and **Florida,** a relatively well-to-do town dominated by Central Argentina belching black smoke—a grotesque counterpoint to the pretty colonnaded streets with central medians and columned *portales.*

East of Florida, the landscape becomes more engaging as you begin a long, steady climb toward Camagüey. Sugarcane gives way to scrubland, then dairy country. Black-and-white cattle shelter under the wide, cool shade of spreading trees studding great cattle estates with names such as *Victoria de Girón.* There's a world-leading center for artificial insemination to the west of Camagüey city, which with its hinterland has traditionally had a thriving cattle industry. The Cuban government boasts about its accomplishments in the field, while local citizens mutter about how things were much better before the Revolution.

Farther east still, royal palms also stud the landscape in great, evenly spaced swatches—beautiful.

Accommodations and Food

Rumbos operates **Finca Oasis,** about 18 km east of Ciego de Ávila, three km before the turnoff for Gaspar. The facility, with its thatched *bohios,* attempts to re-create a traditional *campesino's* homestead. There are rabbits and guinea pigs in cages, and cattle, horses, and pigs in enclosures beneath the shade of mango trees. Accommodations in thatched cabins are planned for the future. There's an appealing restaurant and bar where you can down a shot of invigorating *guarapo* (sugarcane juice). Horseback rides are available for US$1. You can even watch a cockfight (the cocks' spurs are clipped).

About 1.5 km east of Florida is the **Motel Florida,** which has tiny brick bungalows with thatched roofs, plus more substantial cabins for only six pesos. Each cabin has one double and one single bed. The bathrooms are funky.

Hotel Florida, Carretera Central Oeste, Km 536, tel. (32) 5-3011, is a run-of-the-mill Soviet-style hotel operated by Islazul. The clientele is mostly Cuban. It has 72 a/c rooms with TVs, radios, and refrigerators. The staff provides good service. A very large and well-kept swimming pool is the center of activity, especially on weekends, when locals flock and the music blares. Come nightfall the **Nightclub El Valle** is the happenin' place. Rates were US$22 s, US$26 d.

CAMAGÜEY

Camagüey (pop. 270,000) sits in the center of the province on a bluff above the vast plains 570 km east of Havana and 110 km east of Ciego de Ávila. Cuba's third-largest city is often overlooked by foreign visitors, although it's full of beautifully restored plazas that lend the city its nicknames, "City of Squares" and "Corinth of the Caribbean." Much of the city has justifiably been declared a national monument.

Camagüey lacks the heavy baroque architecture of Havana. Its style is simpler, more discreet. Even the homes of the wealthiest Camagüeyans were built without palatial adornments: the bourgeoisie built their homes around a courtyard patio surrounded by arches and galleries, or, in more modest abodes, with eaves supported by unembellished wooden columns. Always there was a *tinajón,* the big earthenware

jars unique to the city and which lent it a third nickname: "City of the Tinajones."

It's a pleasure to walk the colonial streets, especially in late afternoon, when the sun gilds the façades like burnished copper; and at night, too, when light silvers the Spanish grills and façades of the poorly lit streets, full of impending intrigue. In the dark, full of shadows, it is easy to imagine yourself cast back 200 years.

Camagüey can be explored in one day but is fully deserving of two. At last visit there was no shortage of *jiniteros* waiting to part you from your dollar.

History

Camagüey was one of the original seven settlements founded by Diego Velázquez, though the first buildings were erected in 1515 miles to the

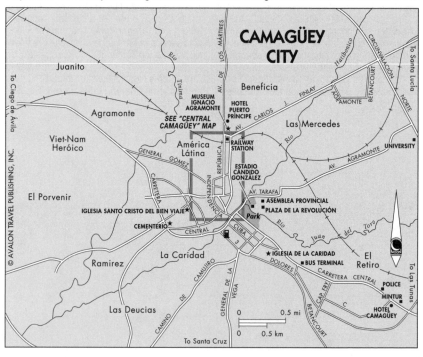

Lacking a source for fresh water, Camagüey was nicknamed the "City of the Tinajones" for the large earthenware jars or cisterns used to catch and save rainfall.

north, on the shores of Bahía de Nuevitas, when the city was known as Santa María del Puerto del Príncipe. The site was not well chosen. It lacked fresh water and came under constant attack from local Indians. It was finally moved to its present location, where it was built on the site of an Indian settlement; in 1903, the city was renamed for the local chieftain, Camaguei).

The early settlers were beset with water shortages. The town's Catalonian potters therefore made giant earthenware amphorae called *tinajones* to collect and store rainfall. Soon the large red jars (up to 2.5 meters tall and 1.5 meters wide) were a standard item outside every home, partly buried in the earth or standing in the shade to keep them cool, but always under the gutters that channeled the rain from the eaves. Citizens began to compete with each other to boast the most *tinajones,* and demonstrate their wealth. Today they are used for decoration, often containing a mariposa. Be careful—according to local legend, an outsider offered water from a *tinajón* by a local maiden will fall in love and never leave.

The city prospered from cattle raising and, later, sugar, which fostered a local slave-plantation economy. Descendants of the first Spanish settlers evolved into a modestly wealthy bourgeoisie that played a vital role in the national culture. The wealth attracted pirates, who often came ashore as small armies. The unfortunate city was sacked (and almost destroyed) twice during the 17th century—in 1688 and 1679.

Many Camagüeyans were themselves notorious smugglers who went against the grain of Spanish authority. "This town has always been looked upon with suspicion by the authorities on account of the strong proclivities its people had for insurrection," wrote Samuel Hazard in 1871, "and its sons have had a greater or smaller share in almost every revolution that has taken place on the island." (U.S. Marines even occupied the city 1917-23 to quell antigovernment unrest.)

The Camagüeyans' notoriety for insurrection did not translate to strong support for communism, however. True enough, its citizens vigorously opposed the Machado and Batista regimes, when student and worker strikes often crippled the city. It's also true that they supported the armies of Che Guevara and Camilo Cienfuegos when they entered the city in September 1958. But the province had been one of the most developed before the Revolution, and *fidelismo* apparently received little support from the independent-minded people of Camagüey.

Following the Revolution, the town and its hinterlands were administered by Huber Matos, the popular Camagüeyan military commander who challenged Castro's increasingly communist turn. He accused Castro of "burying the revolution." Situated as he was in the wealthy and conservative Cuban heartland, Matos posed a real threat. He was arrested for treason (Camilo Cienfuegos, whom Fidel sent to arrest Matos and reorganize the military command, mysteriously

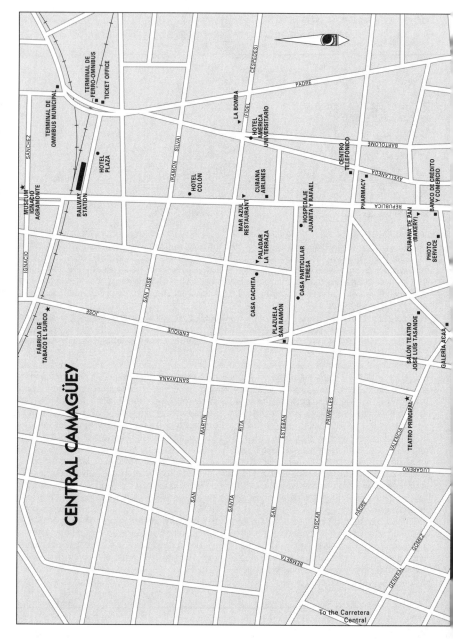

CENTRAL CAMAGÜEY

TERMINAL DE FERRO-OMNIBUS

TICKET OFFICE

TERMINAL DE OMNIBUS MUNICIPAL

SANCHEZ

HOTEL PLAZA

RAILWAY STATION

MUSEUM IGNACIO AGRAMONTE

IGNACIO

FÁBRICA DE TABACO EL SURCO

JOSE

ENRIQUE

SAN JOSE

SANTAVANA

MARTIN

RITA

ESTEBAN

SAN

SANTA

SAN

OSCAR

BEMBETA

GENERAL

GOMEZ

PADRE

LUGAREÑO

VALENCIA

TEATRO PRINCIPAL

PRIMELLES

SALON TEATRO JOSÉ LUIS TASANDE

GALERIA ACAA

CESPEDES

PADRE

EDEL

LA BOMBA

HOTEL AMÉRICA UNIVERSITARIO

RAMON SILVA

HOTEL COLÓN

CUBANA AIRLINES

MAR AZUL RESTAURANT

PALADAR LA TERRAZA

CASA CACHITA

PLAZUELA SAN RAMON

HOSPEDAJE JUANITA Y RAFAEL

CASA PARTICULAR TERESA

BARTOLOME

CENTRO TELEFONICO

AVELLANEDA

PHARMACY

REPUBLICA

BANCO DE CRÉDITO Y COMERCIO

CUBANA DE PAN (BAKERY)

PHOTO SERVICE

To the Carretera Central

© AVALON TRAVEL PUBLISHING, INC.

A bas-relief celebrates the Revolution with images of Che, Castro, and the workers.

died when his plane disappeared on the return trip to Havana). Matos was sentenced to 20 years in prison in a sedition trial in which other anti-Communists were sent to the firing squads, invoking a nationwide purge to consolidate Castro's iron-hand rule.

Hence it is claimed by some city residents that Fidel has been lukewarm to the city.

Orientation

The city spreads east-west along the Carretera Central for more than 10 km. It is encircled by a *circunvalación,* a concrete divided highway that carries virtually no traffic. The Carretera Central arcs south around the city center, then swings southeast as a broad boulevard called Avenida de la Libertad with, at the north end, a bridge—Puente La Caridad—over the Río Hatibonico, connecting the area of La Caridad to the old city (Puente Hatibonico is one block east).

Two plazas compete for status as the official center of town, but I use Parque Agramonte as the center. Calle Martí bisects the city east-west, passing the north side of Parque Agramonte and linking it to the Carretera Central to the west. Calle Cisneros runs north to south, connecting the square with Puente La Caridad and the Plaza de los Trabajadores, the city's other focal point. Ignacio Agramonte feeds the Plaza de los Trabajadores east to west. República runs parallel to Cisneros, three blocks to the east, and is the city's major north-south thoroughfare (farther north it becomes Avenida de los Mártires).

Maceo, the main shopping street, links Martí and República. Maceo is pedestrians-only.

The historical core lies between the Hatibonico and Tinima Rivers, south and west of Parque Agramonte. Fear of pirate attacks prompted the early founders to build the streets in a meandering labyrinth, with some bearing off at odd angles and others meeting at a single point where invaders could be ambushed.

Many streets have an official name and a colloquial name, the latter more commonly used among locals. For example, San Fernando is colloquially called Bartolomé Masó.

SIGHTSEEING

Parque Agramonte

A convenient starting point for a walking tour is this attractive plaza—a parade ground in colonial days—at Cisneros and Martí. The square has Victorian lamps, and its trees are ablaze with pink and yellow blossoms in spring. The tousled palms that stand at each corner, shading the square, are dedicated to local patriots—Joaquín de Aguero and Andres Manuel Sánchez—who were executed in the square in 1826. At its center is a life-size bronze statue of Ignacio Agramonte, mounted atop his steed and brandishing his machete, with the half-naked figure of an Indian maiden below.

The square is surrounded by venerable façades, including the beautifully preserved **Casa** de la Trova, on the west side, featuring stunning tile work and antiques and with a huge patio where musical recitals are given.

The **Catedral de Santa Iglesia** looms over the park on its south side. The cathedral was built in 1864 atop a predecessor, which had been established in 1530. In 1688, pirates led by the famous rogue Henry Morgan apparently locked the city fathers in the church and starved them until they coughed up the location of their treasures. It's worth a peek for its statuary and beamed roof in an otherwise simple interior.

Plaza de los Trabajadores

The Workers' Plaza is a triangular piazza with a venerable ceiba tree at its heart. In the 19th century, the square frequently served as a miniature Pamplona, where bullfights and circuses were held.

On the east side is the **Catedral Nuestra Señora de la Merced,** dating to 1748 but partly destroyed by fire in 1906. It has recently been restored to former grandeur and contains an elaborate altarpiece. Look in to the left at a separate chapel, where the devout gather to pay homage and request favors at a silver altar bearing the image of the Infant Jesús de Prague. And check out the catacombs, with skeletons in situ.

Casa Natal Ignacio Agramonte faces La Merced on the west side of the square, at Ignacio Agramonte 459, on the corner of Candelaria. Major General Ignacio Agramonte was born here on 23 September 1841. Agramonte, a sugarestate owner, led a brief yet intense life as head of the Camagüeyan rebel forces during the first War of Independence. He was killed in May 1873 at the Battle of Las Guasimas. The house was the Spanish consulate during the early Republic. The beautifully restored house is now a museum containing an important art collection, plus mementos and colonial furniture, including an original piano owned by the family. Open Monday and Wed.-Sat. 1-7 p.m., Sunday 8 am.-noon. Entrance costs US$1.

Plaza San Juan de Dios

The most impressive square—one of the most beautiful in all Cuba—is also known as the Plaza de Padre Olallo. It was here in 1873 that Ignacio Agramonte's corpse was brought by the Spanish and blown to pieces, and the remains burned as a public spectacle. On the west side is a beautiful blue-and-white house, still privately owned, where once lived poet and songwriter Antón Silvio Rodríguez. A bronze plaque on the wall has the words of his famous "El Mayor," which celebrates Agramonte in song.

The plaza is today a national monument. It has been magnificently restored. The bright pastel buildings have huge doorways, whitewashed steps, and beautifully turned *rejas* (wooden window grills). They date from the 18th century and reflect how the city must have looked at its prime, 200 years ago. Visit in late afternoon, when the glow of the fading sun gilds the square.

On the east side is the **Iglesia San Juan de Dios** (open Monday). Adjoining it is a fabulous building with a Moorish façade that was once a hospice and today houses the **Museo San Juan de Dios** and the headquarters of the Centro Provincial de Patrimonio, tel. (322) 9-3808, which is in charge of the city's restoration. It's open Mon.-Sat. 8 a.m.-5 p.m. (US$1)

The pink and yellow building on the north side is **Campaña de Toledo,** now a restaurant highlighted by a stunning modernist wall mural.

Schoolchildren gather for lessons in the plaza. I even saw children of eight or nine receiving fencing instruction alfresco.

Convento de Nuestra Señora del Carmen

This convent, built in 1825, could be beautiful if restored. The walls are intact and the tile work almost pristine, but the *ventrales* are shattered, the plaster much cracked, and the red-tile roof overgrown with ferns. It's on the north side of Martí, six blocks west of Parque Agramonte. Immediately east is a small plaza with cobbled streets and venerable houses in bright pastels.

Teatro Principal

Similarly begging for restoration is this once-exquisite theater on Padre Valendia, tel. (322) 9-3048. Camagüeyans (and tourist literature) claim that it is made entirely of marble, but it's not (not even *mostly*). A modest ocher exterior belies its fabulous interior, only hinted at by the lobby, with huge chandeliers reflected in faded full-length mirrors. Above, light filters through red and yellow *ventrales*. The theater was inaugurated in 1850, and such notables as Enrico Caruso have sung here. It is today the home of the Ballet of Camagüey.

Museum Ignacio Agramonte

This museum (also called the Museo Provincial) on Avenida de los Mártires, tel. (322) 9-7231, is in a huge colonial structure dating from 1884 and formerly a garrison for Spanish cavalry. It later became the Hotel Camagüey, a flashy place that served the rail traffic. Today it exhibits an impressive and eclectic array of Cubana, from artwork, archaeology exhibits, and stuffed flora and fauna to historical records up to the Revolution. It was closed for restoration at press time. Open Tues.-Sat. 9 a.m.-5 p.m. and Sunday 8 a.m.-noon. Entrance costs US$1.

Casa Natal de Nicolás Guillén

Cuban poet Nicolás Guillén was born in this modest house at Calle Hermano Agüro #57 e/ Cisneros y Principe, tel. (322) 9-3706, in 1902. A loyal nationalist and revolutionary and one of Latin America's foremost poets, Guillén was awarded the Lenin Peace Prize and also served as chairman of the National Union of Writers and Artists (UNEAC), which he helped found. Guillén died in 1989. The museum, opened in 1992, contains some of his personal possessions and a library of his works. It is now a cultural center and hosts the **Instituto Superior de Arte,** where music is taught.

Other Sights

One of the most overlooked places is **Iglesia Sagrado Corazón de Jesús,** on the Plaza de Pablo Trias, two blocks east of Parque Agramonte. Its exterior is dull, but it is very beautiful within, with much marble and gold. Another church—the tiny, neoclassical **Iglesia Santa Ana,** at the west end of Labrada, is closed (and badly in need of restoration). It dates from 1841. The red-brick **Iglesia Nuestra Señora de la Soledad,** at the corner of Agramonte and República and dating from 1755, is similarly dilapidated. The baroque structure has a thick bell tower, and the frescoed interior is said to have an elaborate wood-beamed ceiling held aloft on massive square columns.

Also worth viewing are the ornate marble tombs in the **Cementerio** on the west side of the old town, south of **Iglesia Santo Cristo del**

Bien Viaje at Crísto and the Carretera Central.

To see cigars being hand-rolled, check out the **Fábrica de Tabacos El Surco,** at the north end of Enrique José Norte. Workers sit at rows of desks in a warehouse-scale room lit by neon lights. Alas, it wasn't open to tourists at press time, but it has been in the past.

Several neoclassical buildings dominate the south side of the river, most impressively the **Instituto de Segunda Enseñanza** (Institute of Secondary Education), accessed via the stone-and-metal **Puente Hatibonico,** which dates from 1773. South from here, *portales* (colonnaded arcades) run the length of Avenida de la Libertad seven blocks to **Iglesia de la Caridad,** a simple red-tile-roofed, ocher-colored church dating to 1734. It guards an icon of Nuestra Señora de la Caridad (Our Lady of Charity), patroness of Camagüey.

The spacious park immediately to the east of the Instituto de Segunda Enseñanza is quiet and contemplative, with pathways leading past several prerevolutionary statues. It makes a pleasant respite from the bustling city streets. It features a **zoo** (free), with animals ranging from lions and monkeys to hyenas.

The **Estadio Cándido González** baseball stadium rises east of the park. Hidden behind it to the east is the rather dowdy **Plaza de la Revolución** with an impressive monument in marble and granite to Ignacio Agramonte inscribed with 3-D sculptures of Che and other revolutionaries, including Fidel, shown giving a speech. The pink-faced **Asemblea Provincial,** or town hall, occupies the north side.

ACCOMMODATIONS

Casas Particulares

At press time, local officials were not permitting *casa particulares* to offer meals or accept *chicas* (Cuban girls) with foreign guests. To get around the latter prohibition, several locals rent rooms by the hour illegally (US$15).

Teresa Santana Ortega has an appealing room in a nicely decorated and clean colonial home at Calle Santa Rita #37 e/ San Ramón y Santa Rosa, tel. (322) 9-5145. The spacious room has a private bathroom with hot water, plus a patio with poinsettias. There's a TV lounge.

Nearby, **Casa Cachita,** Calle Santa Rosa #7 e/ Santa Rita y San Martín, tel. (322) 9-7782, is a beautifully maintained colonial house with a spacious lounge and separate TV lounge. The cozy bedroom is roomy and well-lit with colonial tile floors, a clean, modern bathroom with hot water for US$20. There's a patio.

And **Hospedaje Juanita y Rafael,** Calle Santa Rita #13 e/ Santa Rosa y República, tel. (322) 8-1995, is also beautifully kept and offers a sunlit, breezy lounge filled with contemporary art. The owners rent four rooms, each spacious, modestly furnished, and with modern, private bathrooms with hot water for US$15-20.

Manuel "Manolo" Banegas Misa has a historic *casa* at Calle Indpendencia #251 (altos) e/ Hernanos Agüero y General Gómez, tel. (322) 9-4606, offering an ideal locale overlooking Plazuela Maceo. The cavernous upstairs home has a wrap-around veranda, and rockers in the cross-ventilated lounge. My lofty-ceiling bedroom had a comfy bed; another is huge, with two double beds and French doors that open to a balcony. The three rooms share two small bathrooms. Manolo's sister-in-law, Dargis, has an identical apartment next door.

Blanca Nieves has a room at Calle A #563 e/ Avenida 5ta y García, tel. (322) 9-1721 and 9-7442, with two rooms with color TV, fridge, gas stove, and private bathroom with hot water.

Estela Mugarra Carmona has a *casa* at Calle Cisneros #161 Apto. 2 e/ Cristo y San Isidro, tel. (322) 9-5053, one block from Parque Agramonte. Her two rooms with a/c share a clean, modern bathroom with hot water, and cost US$20 apiece. They are somewhat dark, but a breeze-swept patio over the street makes amends.

Lita Vaula rents two rooms at her colonial home, **El Hostal de Lita,** at Padre Olallo #524 e/ Ignacio Agramonte y Montera, tel. (322) 9-1065. It has a central patio and a garage, and Lita makes meals.

Luisa González Muñoz also rents a room at Calle Santa Rita #7, e/ Republica y Santa Rosa, as does **Hostal Julios Tabares,** at Calle Cisneros #211.

Hotels

Budget: The **Hotel América Universitario,** at Fidel Céspedes y Avellaneda, tel. (322) 8-2135, is a rather dismal place with a modest restaurant. It caters mostly to students attending the local university and offers minimally furnished rooms. Rates were US$10 s, US$15 d.

Islazul's basic **Hotel Isla de Cuba,** on Oscar Primelles, one block west of República, tel. (322) 9-1515, has meagerly furnished rooms plus a TV lounge and restaurant. Rates were US$17 s, US$14 d low season, US$21 s, US$27 d high season. Three blocks north on República is Islazul's **Hotel Colón,** tel. (322) 8-3368, with modest rooms with a/c, TV, mini-bar and telephone. It has an atmospheric lobby with a mahogany bar featuring gilt Corinthian columns and a fabulous picture in stained glass depicting Columbus' landing. Rates were US$13 s, US$18 d low season, US$17s, US$22 d high season.

Islazul also operates the **Hotel Puerto Príncipe,** tel. (322) 82403, next to the Museo Ignacio Agramonte. It's a 1960s-era structure with pleasant, recently refurbished, spacious, high-ceilinged rooms with TVs, a/c, and double beds. The restaurant is mediocre. Avoid the upper-floor rooms—the disco is above. A cabaret is hosted Tue.-Sun. Rates were US$22 s, US$28 d low season, US$28 s, US$33 d high season.

Your best bet is the **Hotel Plaza,** opposite the rail station at the top of República, tel. (322) 8-2413, another recently restored and atmospheric Islazul hotel. The 67 a/c rooms have nice fabrics and TVs. The atmospheric *cafetería* and restaurant are both popular with locals. It has a Transtur car rental office and shops. Rates were US$20 s, US$24 d low season, US$24 s, US$28 d high season.

Islazul has a reservation office on Agramonte at the tip of Independencia, tel. (322) 9-2550.

Inexpensive: If you're fond of Cuba's uninspired assembly-line hotels, try the **Hotel Horizontes Camagüey,** on the Carretera Central, about four km southeast of downtown, tel. (322) 8-7267. The 142 a/c rooms are adequate, but modestly furnished. It has a pleasant courtyard bar and restaurant, and a disco is held in an outside thatched bar. Three separate car rental agencies have offices. Rates were US$30 s, US$38 d low season, US$32 s, US$42 d high season.

If you don't mind being outside town, consider **Villa Tayabito,** off the Carretera, 8.5 km east of town, tel. (322) 7-1939. This hotel doubles as an alcohol- and drug-addiction treatment center, boasting pleasant grounds and a panoply of activities, from horseback riding to a sauna and even a bowling alley. Modestly furnished rooms cost US$18 s, US$20 d. Cabins cost US$20 s, US$30 d.

The **Gran Hotel,** on Maceo #67, tel. (322) 9-2314 and 9-2024, is a beautifully restored 18th-century building whose pleasing ambience is enhanced by dark antiques and centered on a soaring atrium patio. It has 72 lofty-ceilinged a/c rooms with modest yet handsome furnishings, telephone, cable TV, security box, and clean modern bathrooms. A lively café and snack bar faces onto the street, while the elegant rooftop restaurant provides buffet and a la carte options at a reasonable price. The small mezzanine courtyard features a swimming pool and a creative aesthetic, and proves popular on weekends with Cuban families. It has a moody piano bar with heaps of ambience. Rates were US$25 s, US$34 d low season, US$32 s, US$42 d high season.

Cubanacán operates the **Hotel Managuan,** tel. (322) 7-2016, surrounded by scrubland, about five km southeast of town on Camino de Guanabaquila, just off the Carretera Central. It has 48 rooms and suites in cabanas around a swimming pool surrounded by large *tinajones*. The restaurant is the high point—very elegant, with *ventrales* and chandeliers. It serves *criollo* food and has buffets when groups are in. It's very tranquil. It has a large children's playground, and a cabaret at night. Rates were US$47 s, US$55 d, year-round.

FOOD

Paladares
Camagüey has few private restaurants. Two *paladares* of note are **La Bomba,** Calle San Martín #408 e/ San Fernando y Padre Valencia, serving uninspired *criollo* dishes for US$7; and the more atmospheric **Paladar La Terraza,** on Calle Santa Rosa e/ San Estebán y San Martín, with a wood-paneled bar and, upstairs, a breeze kissed open-sided eatery serving *criollo* fare with a flourish, such as *bistec uruguyano* (stuffed beef).

The **Restaurante El Cardenal,** Calle Martí #309, is small and charming. It was being restored at press time.

Dollars Only
The best dollar eatery in town is the elegant rooftop restaurant of the **Gran Hotel,** where a lobster enchilada costs only US$6 and an adequate buffet dinner costs US$10. More historic albeit touristy options include **Campaña de Toledo,** tel. (322) 9-5888, overlooking the Plaza de Padre Olallo. It's full of ambience, with terra-cotta tile floors and rustic furniture. You can dine under shady eaves in the courtyard out back. *Criollo* meals cost less than US$7. The house specialty is a corn-based stew called *ajiaco*. Next door, Rumbos also operates the dollars-only **Parador de los Tres Reyes,** with a similar setting and mood. It specializes in chorizo but has a large menu of *criollo* dishes and snacks. Equally atmospheric is **El Overjito,** at Calle Hermano Aguero #280, tel. (322) 9-2540. The restaurant offers lamb (US$7.50) and pork dishes (US$7-15). The staff insisted that foreigners pay in pesos, but don't believe it.

El Rápido, Cuba's KFC-type fast-food café, is at the corner of Maceo and Gómez.

Peso Eateries
So where do the locals eat? Try **Nan King,** at República #222, tel. (322) 9-5455, with suitably Chinese decor—fans, porcelain, and Buddhas—and a few Chinese dishes (average US$4), but mostly pizzas and *criollo* food. A shrimp entrée costs US$7. **Mar Azul Restaurant,** at the corner of República and Fidel Céspedes, has set meals for 12 pesos, including salad, *congrí, papas fritas,* and *bistec*. And **La Piazza,** a basic eatery catercorner to the Iglesia Nuestra Señora de la Soldedad, is very popular for pizzas and spaghettis (US$2-6). You can dine below at the counter or more elegantly on the upstairs balcony. The fare changes daily.

The restaurant in the **Hotel Plaza** is another favorite of locals.

On Parque Agramonte, **La Volante** is housed in an old building with tall, wide-open windows offering views over the square. It serves basic *criollo* fare; nine pesos (US$0.50) will buy fried chicken, beans and rice, and salad.

There are also several eateries north of town on the road to Nuevitas, including **El Pavito,** specializing in turkey dishes.

Cafés and Ice Cream

There are lots of small *heladerías* and cubbyholes selling *refrescoes* and snacks along República. You can also buy mineral water for one peso at **Agua de Tinajón,** at the corner of Fidel Céspedes. **Coppelia** (with entrances on Maceo and at the southwest corner of Plaza de la Trabajadores) is usually packed when open (Tues.-Sun. 3-10 p.m.), as is the **Cremería la Palma,** on República, and the open-air, dollar-only **Café Ragazza,** midway up Maceo, next to **Donelia Dulceria Postreria,** selling baked confections for dollars.

A little coffee shop on the northeast corner of the main square sells *cafecitos* (espresso coffees) for 90 centavos. And **Cafetería Cubanitas** an open-air café facing the southeast corner of Plaza de los Trabajadores, is a good place to hang and watch the life flooding up and down Independencia.

Self-Catering

You can buy bread and confections at **La Espiga de Oro,** on Independencia, once block south of Plaza de los Trabajadores.

ENTERTAINMENT AND SHOPPING

In early February, the **Jornadas de la Cultura Camagüeyana** celebrates the city's founding. **Carnival,** traditionally held around 26 July, may soon be resurrected. A religious festival is held on 8 September to honor Nuestra Señora de la Caridad, the city's patron saint.

The world-acclaimed **Camagüey Ballet,** founded since the Revolution, performs works from classical to contemporary at the Teatro Principal, tel. (322) 9-3048, as does the city's symphony orchestra. Traditional theater is performed at the **Salón Teatro José Luís Tasande,** one block north of Plaza de los Trabadajores.

The **Casa de la Trova,** at Calle Cisneros #171, tel. (322) 9-1357, on the west side of Parque Agramonte, has a bar in the rear courtyard where you can enjoy traditional music Tues.-Fri. 5-8:30 p.m. and weekends 8:30-11 p.m. (US$1). The famous folkloric group *Caidije* often visits from its base in Nuevitas. You may be able to hear them perform in the **Casa de Promoción Cultural,** opposite the Palacio de Justicia on Calle Cisneros #258. The center even presents jazz concerts. A **puppet theater,** across the way at Cisneros #259, offers performances each Fri.-Sun. at 3 and 10 p.m.

Hotel Puerto Príncipe has a **cabaret** *espectáculo* and disco nightly at 9 p.m. (US$1). **Hotel Camagüey** also offers an "*espectáculo* under the stars" Thurs.-Sun 9 p.m. (US$2) and a fashion show and disco at 8:30 p.m. on Wednesday. You can make reservations in the Islazul office on Agramonte at the tip of Independencia, tel. (322) 9-2550. **Cabaret Caribe** also hosts a **cabaret** *espectáculo* and disco in the Casino Camagüey complex on the east side of the park. And the **Gran Hotel** hosts a *ballet aquático* nightly at 9 p.m. (entrance costs US$2)

The **Casa de la Cultura** on Plaza de los Trabajadores hosts a rooftop *(azoteca)* cabaret-disco nightly at 9:30 p.m. (US$1)

My favorite watering hole is the moodily dark piano bar in the **Gran Hotel,** where gracious contemporary art melds with a slightly salacious feel—you half expect the Rat Pack to show up and jive. Entrance costs US$1 (free to hotel guests). The music keeps going until 2 a.m. Likewise try **El Cambio,** on the northeast corner of the main square. The moody decor, old jukebox, popcorn machine, and lively music helps attract a young crowd late in the evening. It's the closest thing to a hangout you'll find. Beers cost US$1, but you can buy a bottle of rum for US$3, and a shot of cheap *aguardente* costs a mere US$0.35.

The in-spot for local youth at press time was Rumbos' open-air **Cafeteria Las Ruinas** on the west side of Plaza Maceo. **El Cinco Esquinas,** on Plaza de San Juan, and **La Tinajita,** five blocks west, are also good places to raise a glass with locals.

If you speak fluent Spanish, try the comedy and drama hosted at the **Sala Teatro José Luís Tasende,** 50 meters northeast of the Plaza de los Trabajadores.

The **Cine Casablanca** and **Cine Encanto,** both on Ignacio Agramonte west of República, show movies.

Shopping

Camagüey has few touristy shops. The best bet is **Galería del Asociación Cubana de Artesanos Artistas** on the north side of Plaza de los Trabajadores, with creative sculptures and art pieces. The **Galería de Arte** on the southwest corner of Plaza San Juan also sells naïve art. Also try the **Galería Julian M. Morales** on the southwest corner of Parque Agramonte, and **Galería de Arte Alejo Carpentier,** on Calle Cristo Luaces, 50 meters east of the plaza.

The *tinajones* are a bit hefty to take home as souvenirs, but you can buy miniatures, sometimes painted with Cuban landscapes. You can buy honey from the honey factory (nine pesos a bottle) on Enrique José Norte.

PRACTICALITIES

Information and Services

The main **post office** is on the south side of Plaza de las Trabajadores. There's another one and a **Centro Telefónico** next to each other on Avellaneda and Oscar Primelles; both are open 24 hours. You can also make calls from the Etecsa booth on Independencia and Ignacio Agramonte. You can send letters and packages by express service with **DHL** in the Hotel Camagüey, tel. (322) 7-1542. It's open weekdays 9 a.m.-6 p.m. and Saturday 8:30 a.m.-noon.

There are **Banco de Crédito y Comercio** branches on Plaza de los Trabajadores and on República one block north of Ignacio Agramonte, and a **Banco Financiero Internacional** two blocks south.

There are several **hospitals,** and you'll find a 24-hour **pharmacy** on Avellaneda and Primelles. Servimed operates a medical facility—**Tayabito**, tel./fax (322) 33-5548—for foreigners at Carretera Central Km 8.5. Tayabito specializes in rehabilitating alcoholics and drug addicts. Seven-day diagnostic programs are offered. Hospitalization programs last three months, including the first week with an accompanying person.

The **library** is Biblioteca Julio Mella, on Parque Agramonte. **Photo Service,** on Ignacio Agramonte west of República, sells instant cameras, plus film and batteries, as does **Agfafotovideo,** on Maceo. You'll find a travel agency—**Viajes Altamira,** in the Hotel Plaza, tel. (322) 8-3551.

There are two **Cupet gas stations** within 100 yards of each other on the Carretera Central, just west of Puente La Caridad.

Getting There and Away

By Air: **Cubana** and **Lauda Air** flies charters from Italy to Camagüey. Several charter companies offer flights from Canada and Europe.

Cubana flies from Havana four times weekly (US$60). Cubana also flies from Santiago. Other domestic carriers also serve Camagüey.

The Ignacio Agramonte airport, tel. (322) 6-1000, is 14 km northeast of the city, on the road to Morón. The Cubana office is at República #400 esq. Correa, Camagüey, tel. (322) 9-2156 or 9-1338, open Mon.-Fri. 8 a.m.-4 p.m. and Saturday 8:15-11 a.m.

Bus no. 6 runs to the airport from Parque Finlay, opposite the Terminal Ferro-Ómnibus.

By Bus: The **Víazul** tourist bus departs Havana for Camagüey on Tuesday and Friday (see the Víazul Bus Schedule chart in On the Road chapter). For public bus service, see the Public Bus Service From Havana chart, in the On the Road chapter. The journey takes seven hours. There is also daily service to and from Báyamo, Cienfuegos, Holguín, Las Tunas, Santa Clara, Sancti Spíritus, and Santiago. These buses are generally sold out days or weeks in advance, but your dollar bills may win you preference.

The **Terminal de Ómnibuses Intermunicipales,** tel. (322) 7-2302, is two km southeast of town, on the Carretera Central, and is served by local buses (no. 2, 14, and 72). Buses to provincial destinations depart from the **Terminal de Municipales,** tel. (322) 8-1525.

By Train: Camagüey is on the main railway between Havana and Santiago and is well served by trains. (See the Train Schedules from Havana in the On the Road chapter.)

You can also take trains from Santa Clara (#19, departing 3:12 p.m.) and Ciego de Ávila (#23, 6:10 a.m.). A train from Morón departs for Camagüey at 1:32 p.m.

The railway station is at the north end of Avellaneda, tel. (322) 9-2633, between República. The ticket office, tel. (322) 8-3214, is to the rear of the building on the east side of Avellaneda. Foreigners can buy tickets the same day. The following fares applied. Trains #12 and 20: Ciego de Ávila (US$10), Santa Clara (US$13), Matanzas (US$23), Havana (US$27). Trains #11 and 19: Las Tunas (US$10), Cacocum (US$10), Santiago (US$16).

The **Terminal de Ferro-Omnibus,** adjacent to the main station, on the east side of Avellanedas, serves local destinations. Commuter trains depart for Nuevitas, Santa Lucía, Gauimaro, Florida, Minas, and other places. Foreigners can pay in pesos.

Getting Around

The city's historical core is for walking. The streets are too narrow and labyrinthine for buses and taxis. Nonetheless, **bus no. 10** plies a route between the Terminal de Ómnibus Municipales, at Avellenadas and Avenida Carlos Finlay, and the historic quarter. You'll find **horse-drawn cabs** outside the rail station, and near the Iglesia de Nuestra Señora de la Soledad, on República.

Transtur, tel. (322) 7-1015, has taxi and rental car service. For **Cubataxi,** telephone (322) 9-1686. For **Turistaxi,** telephone (322) 8-1247 or 7-2428. *Colectivo* taxis (called *piqueros* locally) hang out outside the rail and bus stations.

You can rent cars from **Havanautos,** tel. (322) 7-3329, in the Hotel Camagüey, and **Transtur,** tel. (322) 7-1015, in the Hotel Plaza.

Tours & Travel, tel. (322) 9535, offers excursions locally.

VICINITY OF CAMAGÜEY

MINAS

This small town, 37 km northeast of Camagüey, is a worthy stop en route to Santa Lucía, or in its own right for its violin factory (the only one in Cuba), at the east end of town. The factory—**Fábrica de Instrumentos Musicales**—was opened in 1976 when a guitar-maker named Álvaro Súarez Ravinal applied his 50 years of experience to making violins. Súarez, who wanted to pass his skills on to the next generation, gained the support of the Cuban Ministry of Culture. Guided by Súarez's genius, workers turn native hardwoods into elegantly curved violins, violas, and cellos. Guitars are also made here. Visitors are welcome (US$2; closed Sunday).

Minas lies in the lee of **Sierra De Camajan,** dramatically backdropped by cliffs up to 200 meters tall in river-carved limestone gorges called *cangliones* and resembling the *mogotes* of Pinar del Río. The most famous ravine is **Pasaje de Paredones,** a popular excursion spot for Cubans. Others are concentrated near Solá, in the Sierra de Cubitas, 60 km north of Camagüey, and near Belén, southeast of Camagüey.

There's a **criadero de cocodrilos** (a crocodile farm) outside the village of **Senado,** northwest of Minas.

You may be able to stay at **Hotel Minas,** on Calle Cisneros #168, tel. (32) 9-6361.

SANTA CRUZ DEL SUR

South of Camagüey, the land flattens out, and first sugarcane, then marshland replace pasture. In the distance you can see beach-fringed coral cays floating offshore. The road dead-ends at Santa Cruz del Sur, a lifeless town 75 km of Camagüey, and trailing south for about three km to the Golfo de Guancanayabo. Santa Cruz is a staging post for trips to the Járdines de la Reina.

The shorefront faces dirty, brown-stained water. There's no beach. At the eastern end, a rusting fishing fleet harbors at a **fish processing plant,** Combinado Pesquero Argeríco Lara.

You'll find a couple of basic peso restaurants, a pizzeria, and a **Coppelia** south of the square. There's a **Cupet gas station** 400 meters north of the main square, and a **Banco de Crédito y Comercio** on the square's southwest corner.

A bus runs from Camagüey (two hours; 2.50 pesos).

HACIENDA LA BELÉN RESERVE

Southeast of Camagüey is an upland area—the **Sierra Guaicanama-Najasa**—marked by *cangliones,* dramatic, sheer-faced, free-standing hummocks. The formations lie within the 4,000-hectare Hacienda La Belén Reserve. The turnoff is at Sibanicú, 42 km east of Camagüey.

The reserve has two distinct regions—undulating plains with scrub and semi-deciduous woodland, and tropical montane forest. It protects 110 species of higher plants (six are endangered), a rare cactus called *mamilaria* (found only here), large numbers of *jutías,* and at least 80 bird species, including parrots. The hacienda pastures are nibbled by exotic species such as black and Indian antelope. Hiking trails leads to several mineral springs with cool pools.

Accommodations: The reserve has a modern chalet for eight people, and a traditional hacienda was being built at press time, to be furnished with rustic antiques.

Getting There: The road, via Najasa, was for 4WD only at press time, but the road was being improved. **Alcona S.A.,** Calle 42 #514, Miramar, Havana, tel. (7) 24-9227, fax (7) 33-1532, offers trips.

GUÁIMARO

Guáimaro, 65 km east of Camagüey, is a town of modest size (pop. 20,000) but historic importance. There's little of interest to see, except an intriguing statue in the town square—a round granite column with a carving of the Cuban flag wrapped around it and bronze plaques honoring local heroes of the War of Independence at its base. The monument commemorates the opening in April 1869 of the Constitutional Assembly, where the first Cuban constitution was drafted, Carlos Manuel de Céspedes elected President of the Free Republic of Cuba, and the abolition of slavery decreed. The building where the 1869 Assembly was held today houses the **Guáimaro History Museum.** Cuba's women's suffrage movement was initiated here, as a plaque on the monument depicts.

At the east end of town is a huge agricultural show ground used for cattle fairs, including the Feria Exposición Ganaderia, held in February.

Accommodations, Food, and Services
The town has a few basic restaurants, plus the **Hotel Guáimaro,** tel. (32) 8-2102, a 40-room Soviet-style motel with a pleasant restaurant a half mile east of town. Rooms have refrigerators and private baths (cold water only). It accepts foreigners. Rates were US$11 s, US$15 d, and US$14 s, US$18 d with TV.

East of Hotel Guáimaro, a dirt road leads uphill to **Centro Recreativo Las Colinas,** a large *ranchita* restaurant and bar dramatically perched atop the hill. It rents basic cabanas.

There's a **Cupet gas station** 400 meters west of the square.

JÁRDINES DE LA REINA

This chain of around 660 coral cays—arranged in three sub-groups and also known as the Labyrinth of the Twelve Leagues—forms a barrier to the Golfo de Ana María beneath Ciego de Ávila and Camagüey Provinces, extending east-west some 200 miles. Whoever named them the Járdines de la Reina (Garden of the Queens) had an eye for beauty. The archipelago, also called Cuba's "Last Paradise," contains literally hundreds of deserted cays, virtually all of them ringed by white sand beaches. An extensive coral reef runs along its southern shore, where marine turtles add to the attractions for scuba divers. Bright pink flamingoes can be seen wading in the briny shallows. Iguanas are common, and marine turtles consider these pristine beaches perfect for laying the seeds of tomorrow's turtles. Spanish treasure is abundant, too, sprinkled on the seabed and possibly hidden on the cays, which were frequented by pirates. Sir Francis Drake apparently died of dysentery here in January 1596.

So remote are the cays that in earlier days Cayo Piedra was "reserved for the *lider máximo's* most intimate and personal affairs," suggests Georgie Ann Geyer.

There's a **visitor center** on **Cayo Anclitas,** which also has a turtle farm, and there's a fishing lodge on **Cayo Bartolo.** Otherwise this is virginal terrain, though development for tourism is steamrolling ahead, overseen by the **Grupo de Desarrollo del Circuito Náutico Jardines de la Reina,** Céspedes y Carretera Central, Camagüey, tel. (322) 7-2162, fax (7) 33-5630, e-mail: delegado@dtcam.mintur.tur.cu, in the MINTUR office opposite the Hotel Camagüey. Development will be limited to fishing and scuba diving (the waters are fished by fleets, and skippers can buy more lobster than they can possibly eat).

Accommodations

At press time, a 20-room hotel was being built at **Algodón Grande,** and a 45-room hotel was under construction on **Cayo Caguamas** in association with French tour operator, Nouvelles Frontieres.

Puertosol, Av. 1ra #3001, Miramar, Havana, tel. (7) 24-5923, fax (7) 24-5928, e-mail: comerc@psol.mit.cma.net, website: www.puertosol.cubaweb.cu, offers scuba diving packages aboard **La Tortuga Lodge,** a former barge converted to a floating hotel that can accommodate 22 people in eight cabins. The per passenger cost of US$75 daily includes meals. Programs are seven or 14 days. One-day dives are also available. One dive costs US$27 (US$32 for night dives); two dives cost US$39. A full-day diving and fishing package is US$110 per person, including transfer from Júcaro. Transfers by launch cost US$5. International reservations can be booked through an Italian company, **Avalon Dive Center/Press Tours,** tel. (0335) 814-9111, fax (02) 714447, e-mail: avalon@avalons.net, website: www.avalons.net.

Avalon also operates two live-aboard dive boats that travel around the cays: the *Explorador,* with four double cabins; and the *Halcón,* with six double cabins. Both sail from Júcaro on six-night trips.

A Belgian company, **Havanatour Benelux,** Av. Louise 335, B-1000 Brussels, tel. (02) 627-4990, fax (02) 627-4998, offers scuba diving aboard the *Procyon,* a former Royal Marine vessel with beautifully appointed a/c cabins for 30 divers, and equipped with a decompression chamber.

Getting There

You can drive via a *pedraplen* to Cayo Caoca in Ciego de Ávila Province (the turnoff is about 10 km north of Jucaro), but there are no facilities.

There's an 800-meter airstrip on Cayo Caguamas serviced by Aerotaxi excursions from Santa Lucía (US$105 for a one-day excursion with lunch and snorkeling or scuba), plus Cayo Coco, Holguín, Ciego de Ávila, and Santiago de Cuba.

Boats serve the cays from Marina Júcaro, from where Puertosol offers eight-hour **excursions** to Cayo Cana (US$39) or Cayo Algodones, plus one-hour excursions to Cayo Chocolate (US$12). A marina was also planned for Santa Cruz to serve Cayo Caguamas, where there is a marina—**Base Náutica.** Marlin S.A. offers the "El Grand Descubrimiento excursion, departing from Cayo Caguamas for several cays, including Cayo Anclitas; and another snorkeling and diving excursion aboard the *Salvador.*

Simon Charles gives a good account of the passages in his book *Cruising Guide to Cuba.*

MORÓN AND VICINITY

Morón (pop. 50,000), 37 km due north of Ciego de Ávila and the gateway to Cayo Coco, is known as the City of the Rooster, a name bequeathed in the 18th century by settlers from Morón de la Frontera, in Andalusia, Spain. In the 1950s, Morón's city fathers erected a rooster at the entrance to town. Fulgencio Batista was present for the unveiling. After the Revolution, an officer in the rebel army ordered the monument's destruction. In 1981, the city government decided to erect another cockerel in bronze at the foot of a clock tower fitted with an amplifier so that citizens (called Moronians) could hear the rooster crowing daily at 6 a.m. and 6 p.m. It stands outside the entrance to the Hotel Morón.

The city is enclosed to north and east by a vast quagmire of sedges, reeds, and water in the path of major bird migration routes.

Sightseeing

The town has no distinguished sites, despite being full of colorful columns and colonnades. Much of the city is dilapidated, including the semi-derelict **Iglesia de Lourdes** at **Parque Agramonte**, at the north end of Martí. The park is surrounded by pretty houses, including the **Casa Parroquial.** Morón also has two museums, including the **Municipal Museum,** on Castillo one block west of Martí, displaying more than 1,600 pieces of pre-Columbian culture. The Teutonic-style **railway station,** built in 1923, is also interesting.

Outside the city are the remains of one of a series of

small forts known as **La Trocha de Júcaro.** The Spanish colonial army built the 50-km-long barrier from Morón to Júcaro, on the south coast, at the narrowest point in Cuba. La Trocha featured a thick wooden barricade and 43 forts meant to stop the east-west progress of the rebel army under General Máximo Gómez. The area around Morón was the scene of heavy fighting, and the

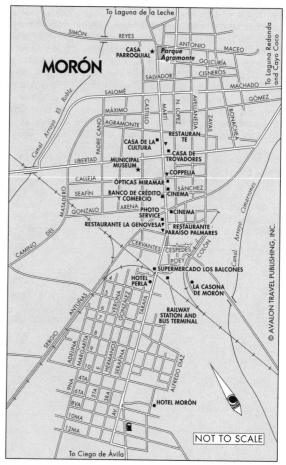

town itself was captured by rebel troops in 1876 (there's a memorial to the event outside the city).

Accommodations and Food

There are *casas particulares,* but I've not checked any.

Hotel Morón, Avenida Tarafa, tel. (335) 30-1347 or 33-3901, www.cubanacan.cu, operated by Cubanacán, is a modest concrete two-story hotel with 144 rooms, eight of which are junior suites, all with satellite TV. Suites in cabanas cost US$60. Facilities include a tourism desk, massage salon, barber shop, swimming pool, bar, coffee shop, and disco. Rates were US$32 s, US$40 d low season, US$39 s, US$45 d high season.

Far more atmospheric is Horizontes' **La Casona de Morón,** Cristóbal Colón #41, Ciego de Ávila, tel. (335) 33-4563, fax (335) 26-6268, also known as the International Hunting and Fishing Lodge La Rabiche (Centro Internacional de Caza y Pesca), the former home of the erstwhile owner of the railway station, 100 yards to the west. This colonial mansion has six a/c rooms reached by a marble staircase. Each of the mammoth but musty and dowdy rooms has a handsome tiled bathroom, ceiling fan, satellite TV, telephone, security box, minibar, and antique lamps. There's a meager bar, grill, elegant restaurant, and a swimming pool plus small disco. Rates were US$29 s, US$39 d, US$45 t high season.

The best eatery in town is **Restaurante Los Fuentes,** on Calle Martí e/ Libertad y Agramonte; its' clean and modern and has a *criollo* menu for US$2-6. Similar alternatives are the **Restaurante La Genovesa,** on Martí at the junction with Avenida Tarafa; and, nearby, **Restaurante Paraíso Palmares.** Also try the restaurants in the Hotel Morón and La Casona del Morón.

For ice-cream, head to **Coppelia,** on the corner of Martí y Calleja.

Entertainment and Events

The city hosts an annual "water carnival" that takes place in a canal leading to Laguna de la Leche. Musicians serenade the crowd while the city's prettiest young maidens row boats decorated with garlands of flowers.

The **Casa de Trovadores,** on Libertad, one block east of Martí, holds performances of traditional music, plus a *bolero* night and a children's *trova.* The **Casa de la Cultura,** on Calle Martí #224, tel. (335) 4309, also has traditional music. For hip-hopping nightlife, head to the **Discoteca Discoral,** in the Hotel Morón, or **La Cueva,** three km north of town on the road to Laguna de la Leche. There's a **cinema** at the junction of Martí y Tarafa, and another on Martí e/ Calleja y Serafin Sánchez.

Services

The **Banco de Crédito y Comercio** is on Martí e/ Serfain Sánchez y Gonzalo Arena. Etecsa has an international **telecorreo** outside the Hotel Morón. The **hospital,** tel. (335) 3530, is at the east end of Libertad. **Ópticas Miramar,** Martí #298, tel. (335) 5345, provides optical services. **Photo Service,** on Martí, three blocks south of Libertad, has a mediocre stock of batteries and camera supplies. The **Cupet gas station** is one block south of the Hotel Morón.

Getting There and Away

By Air: Cubana operates flights to Máximo Gómez airport, about 15 miles south of town, midway between Ciego de Ávila and Morón.

By Bus: See the Public Bus Service from Havana chart, in the On the Road chapter. The bus journey from Havana takes about seven hours. Buses also connect Morón with Ciego de Ávila, and other major cities. The bus and railway terminal is on Avenida Tarafa, tel. (335) 5398.

By Train: Train #21 departs Havana's Estación Central at 8:45 a.m., arriving Morón at 3:06 p.m. Morón is on the northern line that runs from Nuevitas to Santa Clara, with a branch line from Morón to Ciego de Ávila. Trains serve Morón from Ciego de Ávila at 8:32 a.m., and 1:30 and 5:50 p.m.; from Camagüey at 8:03 a.m. and 6:25 p.m.; from Júcaro at 5:50 p.m.; and from Esmeralda at 3:30 a.m.

Trains depart Morón for Havana at 8:40 a.m.; for Ciego de Ávila at 6:20 a.m. and 11:50 a.m. and 4:05 p.m.; for Camagüey at 3 a.m. and 1:08 p.m., for Júcaro via Ciego de Avila at 4:07 a.m., and for Esmeralda at 8 p.m.

Getting Around

Horse-drawn carriages congregate outside the railway station. You can also hire one outside the Hotel Morón for a ride around town. The hotel also rents cars and scooters.

Cubanacán has a tour excursion office at Calle Cristóbal #49, tel. (335) 3168, fax (335) 33-5026.

WEST OF MORÓN

Two km east of Chambas, a road leads north to the fishing village of **Punta Alegre,** where you can hire a boat to take you to Cayo Guillermo. The road ends at the village of **Máximo Gómez,** dominated by a large *central,* or sugar-processing factory. There's a modestly appealing beach, Playa Brisas del Mar.

Another road leads southwest from Chambas to **Florencia,** famous throughout Cuba as a center for horseback riding and rodeo. Rumbos offers a horseback excursion from here into the hills to a place called Boquerón, where you can swim in the cool river and enjoy a lunch of roast suckling pig.

NORTH OF MORÓN

Laguna De La Leche
This 66.5-square-km lake, five km due north of Morón, is named for its milky complexion, which derives when deposits of gypsum and calcium carbonate are stirred up from the lakebed by breezes. The lake is chock-full of tilapia, carp, snook, and tarpon. It is fringed by mangroves and woodlands. Bird life is abundant, including several thousand flamingos that occasionally fly in from the Bahía de Perros. You can rent **rowboats** on the southern shore at **La Boca,** where Rumbos operates **La Tarralloa** restaurant.

Aguachales de Falla Game Reserve, on the northwest shores of the lagoon, features seven small lakes surrounded by forest abounding in white-crowned pigeon, doves, ducks, quail, guinea fowl, and other game birds.

Horseback riding is available at **Rancho El Viejon de las Canteras,** about 10 km north of Morón.

Lago La Redonda
Fourteen km north of Morón, on the road to Cayo Coco, you'll pass a turnoff for **Centro de Pescadores La Redonda,** a basic angling center on the shores of this large lagoon and affiliated with Horizontes' La Casona in Moró. The lake claims the largest concentrations of bass in Cuba. Fishing programs are handled through the Hotel Morón and La Casona de Morón. I was quoted US$35 for four hours' fishing (US$70 all day), including launch and guide.

The lagoon is connected to the Bahía de Perros and open sea by a canal. Private boaters can berth here. There are eight moorings with electricity and water, and gas is available.

There's a restaurant and a bar, whose barman makes great *mojitos.*

Comunidad Celia Sánchez
This eye-catching "Dutch village," atop a hillock rising above Isla de Turiguanó, 28 km north of Morón, makes you do a double take. The clique of 59 gable-roofed houses supported by timber-beam façades transports you lyrically back to Holland. The village is named for Fidel Castro's secretary, lover, and revolutionary alter-ego, who apparently conceived the village, known locally as the Pueblo Holandés de Turiguanó.

Turiguanó was a U.S.-owned private cattle estate before the Revolution. It was cut off from Morón by swampy marshes. In 1960-61, the land was expropriated, the swamps drained, a paved highway built, and modern houses in Dutch style built for the 30 or so families who lived here. The community serves as a cattle-rearing center for the island's high-yield native beef breed, the Santa Gertrudis.

One km east of Comunidad Celia Sánchez is the turnoff, to the left, for Cayo Coco.

CAYO COCO

This 364-square-km cay is a stunner, and not simply on account of its 21 km of superlative beaches and limpid waters. For both scuba divers and birders, it is a destination par excellence. The island is separated from the mainland by Bahía de Perros (Bay of Dogs) and joined to it by a man-made *tombolo* (land bridge). Cayo Coco is named for a bird, the roseate ibis, or *coco*.

The whiter-than-white beaches are divided into five separate sections, most importantly **Playa Palma Real** (Royal Palm Beach). About a dozen properties are on the books, with a planned capacity of 13,000 hotel rooms under the existing tourism master plan. The island is off-

limits to Cubans and is often cited as a classic case of "tourism apartheid."

Cayo Coco was immortalized by Ernest Hemingway. The novelist gloried in waking up there early in the morning, to set sail with the sun at his back, advancing with an alert eye through a canal heading for a line of dark green keys rising out of the water till he was close enough to see their sandy beaches. In *Islands in the Stream,* his protagonist, Thomas Hudson, sets foot on the beach at Puerto Coco seeking traces of Nazi soldiers. Wandering farther inland, he discovers the lagoon where flamingos come to feed at high tide.

Cayo Coco has Cuba's largest flamingo

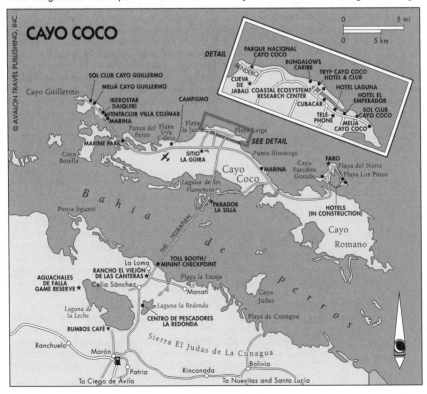

ERNEST HEMINGWAY, NAZI HUNTER

*In May 1942, Ernest Hemingway showed up at the U.S. embassy in Havana with a proposal to fit the Pilar out as a Q-boat, with .50-caliber machine guns, other armaments, and a trained crew with himself at the helm. The boat would navigate the cays off the north coast of Cuba, ostensibly collecting specimens on behalf of the American Museum of Natural History, but was in fact on the lookout for Nazi U-boats, which Hemingway intended to engage and disable. The writer was "quite prepared to sacrifice his beloved vessel in exchange for the capture or sinking of an enemy submarine."

Hemingway's friend, Col. John W. Thomason, Jr. was Chief of Naval Intelligence for Central America and pulled strings to get the plan approved. The vessel was "camouflaged" and duly set out for the cays. Gregorio Fuentes—who from 1938 until the writer's death was in charge of the Pilar—went along and served as the model for Antonio in *Islands in the Stream,* Hemingway's novel based on his real-life adventures.

They patrolled for two years. Several times they located and reported the presence of Nazi submarines that the U.S. naval or air force were later able to sink. Only once, off Cayo Mégano, did Hemingway come close to his dream: a U-boat suddenly surfaced while the Pilar was at anchor. Unfortunately, it dipped back below the surface and disappeared before Hemingway could get close.*

colony, at least 2,000 strong (estimates vary widely—up to 10,000), concentrated between Punta Almácigo and Punta del Perro. The rose-pink birds seem to float atop the water, like mirages. Every day during June and July, they fly over the north end of the *tombolo* shortly after sunrise and again at dusk. Flamingos are one of 158 bird species here, including the miniature hummingbird, Cuban cuckoo, ibis, herons, egrets, and sea-swallows. Migratory birds flock here, too, in vast numbers, and ducks and other waterfowl are common in the soupy shallows. The most prominent animals are *jabelí*—wild pigs—and endemic iguanas (if you don't see them in the wild, check 'em out in the iguana pit at Hotel Tryp). There are even deer. The island

(90% of which is covered by scrub vegetation) is a protected reserve; no hunting is allowed.

Parque Nacional Cayo Coco begins three km west of the Tryp complex, at **Playa Prohibida.** There are four nature trails.

PEDRAPLEN

Cayo Coco is connected by a 27-km land-bridge to the north coast of Cuba. The bridge, completed in 1988 and called the *Pedraplen,* is made of solid landfill and cuts the Bahía de Perros in two. There are only two sluices, preventing sufficient flow of currents (with who-knows-what-potential long-term effects for the ecology). Word is that the now-still waters are becoming nutrient-deficient and wildlife is already beginning to suffer.

MININT (Ministry of the Interior) has a security checkpoint at the entrance to the bridge, where there's a toll booth: US$2 each way.

It's a fabulous drive. On clear days, the transparent, mirror-calm waters reflect the clouds, mirages form, and the distant cays seem to float in midair, shimmering in the heat like a sort of dreamworld between hallucination and reality. At its northern end, the road snakes along the cays that precede Cayo Coco, winding and looping past briny shallows in shades of pea green and jade. Brine glistens in crusty patches picked over by herons and egrets. And gnarled trees add to the dramatic effect. Drive carefully. There are no barriers on the sides of the narrow road, which is deeply potholed in places, so one mistake and you'll be in the drink.

Eventually, you reach a traffic circle. The road to the right leads east to the marina and neighboring Cayo Romano and Cayo Paredon, where there are two lonely and beautiful beaches and a lighthouse. The road to the left leads west to the airport and Cayo Guillermo. The road straight ahead leads to the hotel complex and main beaches.

Coastal Ecosystems Research Center

The center, immediately east of the Tryp resort complex, is part of Cuba's Academy of Sciences and employs a staff of 26 specialists responsible for preserving the biodiversity on the Sabana-Camagüey archipelago, including its 1,000 km of beachfront. Visitors are welcome.

ACCOMMODATIONS

Campers may be able to pitch a tent at the simple *campismo* at Playa Uva Caleta, or at Playa Las Coloradas. Water is available.

The **Tryp Cayo Coco Hotel & Club,** Cayo Coco, Ciego de Ávila, tel. (33) 30-1311, fax (33) 30-1386, e-mail: htccc@club.tryp.cma.net; in Spain, Tryp Hoteles, Mauricio Legendre 16, 28046 Madrid, tel. (01) 315-3246, fax (01) 314-3156, is a world-class resort covering 6.7 hectares behind a four-km-long beach. A stunning contemporary lobby with shopping arcade opens to an elevated lobby bar with views down over a sprawling, serpentine swimming pool. The massive resort has 972 rooms in 85 two- and three-story Spanish villa-style units spread widely amid landscaped grounds that feature four large amoeba-shaped swimming pools. The rooms are nicely furnished, with cavernous bathrooms with large mirrors and heaps of marble. Each room has a/c, satellite TV, radio, minibar, and 24-hour room service. It's a popular and active hotel and has something that is missing in many Cuban resorts—vitality. The clientele is mostly Canadian, Argentinean, and French. You have a choice of an all-inclusive package or room-only. The former includes use of all facilities and water sports. It has a Transtur car rental agency, plus scooter rentals. All-inclusive rates ranged from US$84 s, US$103 d, US$141 t in low season to US$144 s, US$188 d, US$248 in high season, including breakfast.

Immediately west, a cobbled humpback bridge leads across an *estero* to the **Hotel Tryp Cayo Coco,** an eye-pleasing, make-believe, contemporary interpretation of a colonial village, a distinct entity sharing facilities with its sibling complex. Rates were the same as the Club.

Spain's Sol Meliá chain manages **Sol Club Cayo Coco,** tel. (33) 30-1280, fax (33) 30-1285, e-mail: solclub.cayococo@melia.solmelia.cma. net, a compact all-inclusive with 266 rooms and four suites in condo-style units around a long, sinuous swimming pool. The spacious, handsome rooms boast hardwood furniture with earth-tone fabrics, a/c, direct-dial telephones, satellite TVs, and security boxes. There's a Cubatur desk, and Havanatur rents

Suzuki Jeeps, and a full complement of water sports, bars, restaurants, and entertainment are at hand. All-inclusive rates were US$124 s, US$198 d low season, US$150 s, US$250 d high season.

Next door is the more gracious **Meliá Cayo Coco,** tel. (33) 30-1180, fax (30) 1195, e-mail: melia.cayococo@smcoco2.solmelia.cma.net, a beautiful, sprawling all-inclusive property nestled between the beach and a lagoon and built around a large swimming pool, with lush landscaping. The spacious rooms are done up in a subdued contemporary take on traditional Spain, and feature cable TV, security boxes, piping hot water. A specialty seafood restaurant is suspended over the lagoon, as are two-story villas. Two other restaurants (including a buffet restaurant serving Euro-style food catering to the mostly German and Canadian clientele), several bars, water sports, a beauty salon, boutique, and car and scooter rental round out the facilities. All-inclusive rates were US$95 per person low season, US$134 high season for a standard room (US$48/67 single supplement, respectively); US$106 low season, US$141 high season for a superior room (US$53/71 US$48/67 single supplement, respectively).

At press time Cubanacán's 262-room **Hotel El Empredador** and 470-room **Hotel Laguna** were being built west of Sol Club. Cubanacán was building the 256-room **Bungalows Caribe,** immediately west of the Tryp complex. A deluxe hotel was being built by Gran Caribe and a Spanish hotel company further east at Playa Las Colorados. And Jamaica's SuperClubs chain was building the four-star, 300-room **Breezes Coco Rojo;** in North America, tel. (800) 467-8737; in the U.K., tel. (01749) 67-7200.

FOOD

The hotels all have a choice of restaurants (nonguests can purchase a day pass or night pass that includes meals).

On one of the little cays that precede Cayo Coco is **Parador La Silla,** a thatched wayside café and restaurant with a *mirador* from which you can watch the flamingoes make their daily pilgrimage. A small bar and grill at Playa Prohibida sells basic *criollo* fare, but it's often unstaffed. Rumbos also has a snack bar Las Coloradas selling seafood and fried chicken dishes; and there's a *parillada* grill at Playa Flamingo.

The most atmospheric place is **Cueva del Jabalí**, five km west of the Hotel Tryp. The cave features a restaurant and bar, with tunnels leading to various rooms. It's open for dinner only. Bring insect repellent.

ENTERTAINMENT AND SPORTS

All the hotels offer theme parties, cabarets, and discos. A **cabaret** *espectáculo* is also offered on Tuesday to Saturday at 10 p.m. at the Cueva del Jabalí. Entrance is US$1. Excursions are available from the hotels. Bring repellent. By day the **Bar Los Trouzos** here has a *trova cubana*.

However, to jive with Cubans, head to the disco at *Villa Azul,* the hotel worker's complex located about one km west of the roundabout on the road to Cayo Guillermo.

The hotels all have **water sports.** Nonguests can pay for banana-boat rides and waterskiing (both US$5 for 15 minutes), snorkeling (US$15 for one hour), and catamaran and jet ski rental.

The offshore coral gardens teem with colorful fishes, offering fine **scuba diving.** There are 21 dive points between Caro Paredón in the east and Punta La Jaula to the west. Dolphins are frequently seen. The **Blue Diving** dive center is at Marina Cayo Coco, tel. (33) 80-6042 (cellular). A free introductory dive is offered. Scuba diving costs US$27 for one dive, US$49 for two, US$40 for night dives. You can rent equipment here. A resort course costs US$60; open-water certification costs US$288.

Horseback riding excursions are offered from **Sitio La Gúira,** a stable and nature facility that also has a thatched restaurant (US$7 per hour). Horses can also be rented at Playa Las Coloradas.

Sportfishing is also popular. Deep-sea fishing trips are offered from Marina Cayo Coco.

TRANSPORTATION

Getting There
Aero Caribbean, Calle 23 #64, Vedado, tel. (7) 33-4543, fax (7) 33-5016, e-mail: aerocarvpcre@iacc3.get.cma.net, flies daily from Havana via Varadero, and from Santiago de Cuba on Thursday and Sunday. **Cubana** operates service from Havana and Santiago direct to Cayo Coco. In 1999 **Inter Grupo Taca** introduced service to Cayo Coco from Havana and Varadero before suspending service in early 2000.

Several Canadian charter companies offer flights from Canada. **Lauda Air** flies charters from Milan to Cayo Coco/Ciego de Ávila on Saturday. (See the By Air section in the Getting There section in the On The Road chapter.)

Puertosol runs **Marina Cayo Coco,** east of Punta Almágico, at the eastern half of the cay. It has electricity, water, and gas, as well as a nautical store and restaurant. Servimar has a small supply vessel at hand to assist private yachters. You can call Servimar on VHF channel 16 for a boat to escort you through the shallows. Reportedly there is no Guardia Frontera here.

Getting Around
You can hire bicycles, mopeds, and cars at Hotel Tryp. You don't need a car if you're only interested in exploring the cays. A bicycle or moped is a fun and simple way to go. Drive carefully—some of the roads are covered with patches of sand and gravel.

All the hotels have tour desks offering excursions to Cayo Coco and farther afield. **Rumbos** offers a six-hour motorcycle excursion around Cayo Coco (known as "Cococross"). It also has horse-drawn buggy rides and an "ecotour" to Cayo Guillermo by jeep (US$21).

The Tryp resort offers a "seafari" that traces Hemingway's route aboard the *Pilar* as enumerated in *Islands in the Stream* and includes fishing and snorkeling (US$39). Sunset cruises (US$10) are offered from Parador La Silla. And snorkeling excursions to Cayo Paredón are offered from the marina (US$25 including cocktails and lunch).

CAYO GUILLERMO

This 18-square-km cay lies three km west of Cayo Coco, to which it is joined by an umbilical *pedraplen* elevated over the pavonine waters. The crossing is fabulous. The process of mangrove capture and cay development is wonderfully demonstrated along the drive from Cayo Coco. Snowy-white egrets and herons pick in the shallows, which are also favored by flamingoes.

The star attraction is chalky, five-km-long Playa El Paso. There are other beaches, including Playa del Medio and Playa Larga, at the far western end, where sand dunes pile up 15 meters high. At low tide, you can wade out for 400 meters or more on the sandbars. The inshore fishing is excellent: snapper, grouper, mackerel, and bonefish are the species of choice. Farther out, beaked marlin and swordfish run through the Old Bahama Channel—Hemingway's "great blue river." One of the first people to discover the charms of Cayo Guillermo was, in fact, the great fisherman and novelist. ("On the inner side, gentlemen, is Guillermo. See how green she is and full of promise?" says Hemingway's alter ego and main character, Thomas Hudson, in *Islands in the Stream,* inviting his partners to discover the beauty of the place.) Papa is still fondly remembered by elderly fishermen in the Bahía de Perros, who regale visitors with tales of his exploits. Another admirer of Guillermo's charms was dictator Fulgencio Batista, who had a hideaway on now-deserted **Cayo Media Luna,** off the western tip.

You can also reach Cayo Guillermo by boat from the fishing village of Punta Alegre, 68 km northwest of Morón.

Cayo Guillermo is in the throes of major resort development.

Accommodations

Ventaclub Villa Cojímar, Cayo Guillermo, Ciego de Ávila, tel. (33) 30-1012, fax (33) 33-5554, on Playa El Paso, is part of the Cuban Gran Caribe chain, jointly run by Venta Club of Italy, but open to all comers. Not surprisingly, the majority of guests are Italians. It's a beautiful low-rise property, with spacious lawns, 218 rooms, and two suites in small one- and two-story a/c cabanas each with satellite TV, international phone, hair drier, safe deposit box. Facilities include a tennis court and a soccer court, plus Transtur car rental. The Bodeguita del Guillermo restaurant beside the marina is smothered with graffiti in imitation of La Bodeguita de Medio, in Havana. The resort is being expanded to 750 rooms. All-inclusive rates were US$110 s, US$135 d, US$150 t high season, all-inclusive.

Iberostar Daiquiri, tel. (33) 33-6069, fax (33) 66-2822 (in Havana) is a ritzy new all-inclusive property build to international standards in contemporary Spanish vogue, with marble floors in the lobby centered on a sunken lobby bar that opens to a pool with a cascade. Its 312 a/c rooms in three-story buildings are pleasingly appointed with dark furniture in period style and feature telephone, satellite TV, fridge, safety deposit box, and balcony, plus beautiful bathrooms with colonial tile motifs. It has a full complement of facilities, including sauna, gym, a choice of restaurants (including Mexican), and a panoply of sports and water sports, including catamarans, windsurfing, and scuba diving. There's entertainment nightly. Separate facilities keep kids amused, so it's popular with families. All-inclusive rates were US$100 s, US$140 d low season, US$120 s, US$160 d high season, US$180 s, US$300 d peak season.

The **Sol Club Cayo Guillermo,** tel. (33) 30-1760, fax (33) 30-1748, e-mail: sol.club.cayo .guillermo@solmelia.es, is another beautiful 264-room property in a lively tropical motif. Accommodation is in two-story units and bungalows, all with a/c, satellite TVs, direct-dial telephone, mini-fridge, security box, and terrace. It has a thatched beach grill, a small specialty restaurant, and a handsome buffet restaurant, a mini-club for kids, plus disco, boutique, entertainment, car rental, and a full range of water sports. All-inclusive rates were US$106 s, US$154 d all-inclusive low season, US$174 s, US$232 d high season.

The adjoining **Meliá Cayo Guillermo** was under construction at press time.

Water Sports
Each of the hotels has water sports, and jet skis, catamarans, and **scuba diving** are offered at the scuba center at the Villa Cojimar. An initiation dive for beginners costs US$10. Certified divers can take guided dives for US$27. **Snorkeling** trips cost US$10. A full-day **deep-sea fishing** package costs US$250 including lunch (or US$150 for four hours without lunch) for up to four people.

"Seafari" boat excursions are also available from **Marina Cayo Guillermo,** tel. (33) 30-1738, fax (33) 30-1280, which consists of a lopsided wharf at the eastern tip of the cay. It has 10 moorings with water, electricity, diesel, and gasoline.

Services
There's a **Banco Financiero Internacional** outside the entrance to the Iberostar Daiquirí.

MORÓN TO NUEVITAS

The coast road continues east of Morón into Camagüey province through sugarcane country studded with huge *centrales* belching out inky black smoke.

East of Brasil, sugarcane gives way to poorly tended citrus orchards stretching mile upon mile. Between the groves are concrete, four-story housing blocks (each appointed with clinic and community center) about two km apart, offset from each other to either side of the ruler-straight road. East of **Cubitas,** the land is again farmed in sugarcane, the savanna grazed by gray cattle.

CAYO ROMANO

Cayo Romano is the largest of the cays in the Archipiélago de Camagüey. The cay actually comprises *two* huge cays (the westernmost abuts Cayo Coco, from which it can be accessed by road), and more than a score of sandbars and tiny cays sprinkled like stardust offshore. They are all deserted and virtually unexplored, despite translucent waters that provide some of the best snorkeling and diving in the hemisphere.

Like the other cays, Cayo Romano is all mangroves and brine pools and endless beaches. Hemingway writes in *Islands in the Stream,* "Now it was there at its barest and most barren, jutting out like a scrubby desert. There were wild horses and wild cattle and wild hogs on that great key.

"It was a wonderful key when the east wind blew. . . . It was country as unspoiled as when Columbus came to this coast. Then when the wind dropped, the mosquitoes came in clouds from the marshes. To say they came in clouds,

he thought, is not a metaphor. They truly came in clouds and they could bleed a man to death." Take repellent!

The turn-off for Cayo Romano is at **Brasil,** about 16 km east of Morón. The road reaches Cayo Romano via a 12-km-long land bridge and then leapfrogs to enchanting **Cayo Cruz,** a small, pencil-thin cay eight km north of Romano. Its north shore is an endless talc beach.

Tiny **Cayo Confite** lies farther offshore, marking the northerly tip of a long barrier reef that arcs to the southeast all the way to Holguín province. Today these cays are favored as a drop-off and pick-up point by international drug smugglers. The Cuban Coast Guard is ill-equipped to battle the trade by small plane and fast speedboat.

CASTRO AND CAYO CONFITES

*I*n 1947, a political adventurer and law student named Fidel Castro signed up for an expedition to overthrow President Trujillo of the Dominican Republic. Castro and about 1,200 other expeditionaries spent 57 days on Cayo Confites, a tiny and lonely cay a few km north of Cayo Romano. There the ragtag army underwent military training beneath a blistering sun and unrelenting assault by mosquitoes.

When the whole affair was called off, Castro's battalion sailed anyway, aboard a small freighter called *Caridad.* The vessel was boarded by a Cuban cutter and ordered to turn back. Castro, apparently fearing that he was going to be murdered by rival figures on board, leapt overboard and swam nine miles to Saetía, at the mouth of Nipe Bay.

lunch, Cayo Sabinal

At press time there were no facilities whatso-ever on either Cayo Romano or Cayo Cruz (other than a hunting facility). The government's tourism master plan, however, contemplates a maximum of 1,700 hotel rooms on Cayo Romano and 3,000 on Cayo Cruz. And Gaviota was planning to build a *delphinarium* in a natural lagoon on Cayo Cruz.

Cayo Guajaba, immediately east of Cayo Romano and west of Cayo Sabinal, is of no current interest to tourists, though there's a tiny hamlet on the western shore where adventuresome travelers may be able to find shelter in a humble shack. The cay is included in the government's master plan for tourism, but it will be many years before anything happens here.

Hemingway used Guajaba as his model for the fantasy Bahamian cay in which a Nazi submariner lies fatally wounded in *Islands in the Stream.*

CAYO SABINAL

Cayo Sabinal is the easternmost cay in the archipelago and one of my favorites. It is attached to the north coast of Camagüey by a hair's-breadth isthmus and encloses a great bay to the east, the Bahía de Nuevitas. It has 33 km of beaches protected by coral reefs. The offshore waters are prolific with game fish and lobster. The entire island is virgin marshland, brush, and small pines, dotted with saucer-like pools filled with an unappetizing broth.

In all your explorations, you will pass only a couple of military posts and no more than a half dozen humble *bohios* belonging to impoverished charcoal-burners and fishermen. There are plenty of birds and iguanas, however, small deer *(venado),* and wild pigs called *jabali,* a relative of the peccary. The *jabali* resembles a massive-necked razorback hog; it grows to the size of a midsize hound. The myopic animal is sharp-toothed, excitable, and quite vicious if cornered. It marks its territory with a pungent oil emitted by a musk gland located on the hindquarters. It is well adapted to arid conditions such as those of the cays, where it survives by shoveling up roots and bugs with its hardy snout.

The Cuban government reckons Sabinal has a potential capacity for 12,000 hotel rooms. *Ouch!*

Things to See
Crossing the isthmus, you'll see snowy white egrets, cranes, and flamingoes wading in the soupy shallows of **Laguna de las Flamencoes.** Don't be tempted to wander onto the mudflats in search of a close-up—you'll sink to your knees before your third stride.

At the far eastern end of Cayo Sabinal is a lighthouse—**Faro Colón**—built in the 19th century; and an even older fortress—**Fuerte San Hilario**—built to protect the entrance to Bahía de Nuevitas. Hotels in Playa Santa Lucía arrange excursions.

Beaches

There are three main beaches: **Playa Brava** to the west, **Playa Los Pinos** in the center, and **Playa Bonita** to the east (rugged going by 4WD). You can walk for two hours in either direction and leave your man-Friday footprints the whole way in white sand. The reef lies within one km of shore—within wading distance of the whitecaps that mark the boundary between the jade shallows and the aquamarine blues of the Old Bahama Channel beyond.

The best place to spend your time is fantastically lonesome Playa Los Pinos, with sand as white as Cuban sugar, and sea shading from the shore through an ever-deepening palette of greens. The shallows are as warm and calm as bedtime milk. The beach has rustic accommodations and a restaurant. You can even rent windsurfers here to go scudding across the limpid lagoon. Occasionally a small group of tourists may arrive for a day visit from Santa Lucía, but more likely you will have the place to yourself.

A breeze blows ashore by day. After dusk, all is still but for the muffled wash of the surf breaking on the distant reef and the drone of mosquitoes, absent by day but voracious at night.

Accommodations and Food

The only one place to stay is a series of five rustic yet handsome cabanas made of palm trunks and mangrove roots, with thatch for roof, set amid sand dunes on Playa Los Pinos. The simple and oh-so-endearing property includes a bucolic open-air restaurant and is run by a warm-hearted old Cuban, Francisco, and his son, Javier. Cabins have simple bathrooms with showers. When I was there, I ordered a lunch of fresh fish. As if by magic, a local fishing boat arrived within minutes and I was able to peruse the catch of red snapper *(pargo)* and lobster and choose my own lunch. Rates were US$25 per person, including breakfast and dinner.

Twenty more comfortable cabins are planned behind the beach.

Rumbos also operates a rustic restaurant and bar at Playa Brava (there's no accommodation).

Getting There

Cayo Sabinal is reached via a bridge over the Enseñada de Sabinal, where there's a military checkpoint (you'll need your passport). The road was unpaved at press time. After a few miles, you reach a crossroad. Playa Brava is straight ahead. Playa Los Pinos is signed to the right; after about six km, turn left (the beach is about five km farther). Keep going straight for the lighthouse but be aware that it's a challenging drive (4WD only). In places, the narrow tracks are smothered in sand and hemmed in by vegetation.

If coming from the east, your best route is through Nuevitas, linked to Sabinal via a road of hard-packed dirt and rock, blindingly white, that runs along the western shore of the bay, with fetid salt marshes on both sides. The great

a vintage Harley-Davidson,
Nuevitas

morass smells like vomit. There is no sign of life except for comical black *toti* birds and fawn doves dust-bathing in the road. From the west, the turnoff (about four km before the Nuevitas turnoff) is unmarked—look for the blindingly white road at a four-way junction, with Lugareno to your right.

Jeep safaris and boat excursions operate from Santa Lucía.

NUEVITAS

This major industrial town (pop. 35,000), seven km north of the coast road and 65 km northeast of Camagüey, sits astride a promontory that divides the vast Bahía de Nuevitas. Today the ramshackle town center looks every bit as if it has suffered through four decades of dissipation. An old wooden church in need of repair sits atop the hill that looms over the main square, where a huge cannon has cannonballs at its base. A baobab tree stands in the main square, where there's also a sturdy gold-domed church.

A fish processing plant, a fertilizer factory, a cement factory, and the second-largest thermoelectric plant in Cuba pour a horrible soup of pollutants into the bay. Palls of smoke rise from their stacks and are carried off by stiff breezes. A sugar-loading facility at the deep-water port (called Puerto Angola) handles the white gold produced in the province's 13 sugar mills.

The city is famous for **El Grupo de Caidije,** a folkloric group strongly influenced by Haitian music and dance, including a machete dance.

Practicalities

One wonders why you would visit, but just in case. . . . Islazul's **Hotel Caonaba,** tel. (32) 4-4265, has a view over the bay. Rates were US$16 s, US$20 d. For eats, try **Paladar Caribe Cuba,** one block west of the main street and two blocks south of the railway station at the end of the main street.

There's a **Banco Crédito y Comercio** on Máximo Gómez, and a **Cupet gas station** as you enter town from the coast highway.

Getting There

Bus no. 525 departs Havana daily at 7 p.m., arriving Nuevitas at 4:55 a.m. (31 pesos).

Nuevitas is the easterly terminus of the rail line along the north coast. Train #325 departs Morón for Nuevitas at 6:20 a.m., arriving 12:41 a.m.

NUEVITAS TO SANTA LUCÍA

East of Nuevitas the road is mostly in good condition. You pass through a spartan landscape of sagebrush savanna ranged by cattle. Bull rushes and water hyacinths thrive at waterholes, where flocks of egrets and herons gather.

At the huge traffic circle just north and west of **Camalote,** about 30 km east of Nuevitas, a turnoff leads north 26 km to the beach resort of Santa Lucía.

King Ranch

This working cattle ranch, between San Miguel de Bagá and Camalote, about seven km west of the turn for Santa Lucía, was once owned by the owners of the famous King Ranch in Texas. The Castro regime expropriated the property, which today receives tourists. You can watch the workaday *vaqueros* herding cattle and getting coated with dust and manure. A rodeo provides entertainment, and horseback riding is offered. It has a restaurant, and a guest quarters can be rented.

Excursions are offered through hotels in Santa Lucía.

SANTA LUCÍA

Just when you thought sand couldn't get any whiter or finer, or the sea a more brilliant blue, you arrive at Santa Lucía, 110 km east of Camagüey and 85 km north of Las Tunas. The beach (supposedly Cuba's third-longest) is virtually unbroken for an astounding 20 km, protected by an offshore coral reef. Sea grasses, however, have gained a foothold in places—rubber bathing shoes or sandals are a good idea.

The government's tourism master plan believes that Santa Lucía can support 7,000 hotel rooms. Santa Lucía was popular with Cuban vacationers until the onset of the Special Period put a serious dent in everyone's budget: most of the scores of basic bungalows remain unused. Today the resort is used primarily by German, Italian, and Canadian charter groups. Forget the promotional hype. Santa Lucía is embryonic, with minimal infrastructure. Facilities are spread out over several kilometers, with stretches of grassy nothingness between them. All in all, it's an ugly-duckling. Outside the hotels, the place is as dead as a dodo.

Flamingos occasionally flock to wallow by day in the lagoons behind the beach, then take off in a flash of bright pink at dusk.

West of Santa Lucía, at the end of the road, is a funky fishing hamlet—**La Boca**—with its own beach—**Playa Los Cocos** (also called Playa

Tararacos)—and atmospheric restaurants. Diving is said to be superb just offshore. The road continues west another km or so to the end of the peninsula, where Cayo Sabinal lies almost within shouting distance. There's no bridge; just a Guardia Frontera post.

ACCOMMODATIONS

In midwinter, charter tour companies reserve large blocks of rooms. At Christmas and New Year's, Santa Lucía often sells out; if you're going then, I recommend a reservation.

Cuban families live in modest villas and huts widely dispersed along the seafront. You may be able to rent one if you ask around. The impoverished locals in La Boca rent bare-bones rooms for US$15-20.

Cubanacán's **Villa Tararaco,** tel. (32) 3-6222 or 3-6410, fax (32) 36-5166, e-mail: aloja@tararaco.stl.cyt.cu, is a motel-style property recently brought back from the dead. It has 31 spacious a/c rooms modestly furnished with rattan and bamboo, and with telephones, radios, satellite TVs, security boxes, and small but modern bathrooms with heaps of forceful hot water. Facilities include a simple restaurant and bar, small store, plus water sports from the adjacent dive center. It in-

Playa Los Locos

tends to cater to divers. Rates were US$30 s, US$45 d, but due to rise to US$43 s, US$55 d.

Cubanacán's all-inclusive **Club Amigo Mayanabo,** tel. (32) 36-5168, fax (32) 36-5176, is a Soviet-style building dating from the 1970s but recently given a handsome facelift. It has 213 red-tile-roofed a/c rooms and 12 suites, all with balconies and king-size or twin beds, telephone, and satellite TV. There's a restaurant, a modern piano bar, tennis court, swimming pool with shady palm-leaf umbrellas, and water sports, plus tour desks. All-inclusive rates were US$60 s, US$98 d low season, US$65 s, US$110 d high season.

A more upscale and lively option is **Vita Club Caracol,** tel. (32) 36-5158, fax (32) 36-5307, e-mail: secre@vitaclub.stl.cyt.cu, an Italian-managed property catering to a mostly Italian clientele. It has 150 a/c junior suites, all with cable TV, large bedrooms and tiny lounges and that rarest find in Cuba—firm, comfy beds, plus balconies and ocean views over acres of palms. Bicycle and horseback excursions are offered, the resort has scuba diving, and the entertainment staff is mustard-keen. All-inclusive rates were US$55 s, US$90 d, US$120 t low season, US$80 s, US$120 d, US$162 t high season.

The **Hotel Cuatro Vientos,** tel. (32) 36-5120, fax (32) 36-5142; in Spain, tel. (095) 205-1308, fax (095) 205-0581, e-mail: hotelesec@vnet.es, is a modern, 214-room hotel operated jointly by Cubanacán and the Spanish Hotels C group. It has declined in standards in recent years, but still proves popular with budget-minded Canadians, Germans, and Argentineans. The low-rise property combines a contemporary design with traditional thatch and lots of hardwoods. All rooms have a satellite TV, radio, telephone, and minibar. At its heart is a magnificent swimming pool with swim-up bar. It offers entertainment nightly. High-season rates were US$50 s, US$60 d, US$84 t, including breakfast; US$80 s, US$120 d, US$168, all-inclusive.

Cubanacán's **Gran Club Santa Lucía,** tel. (32) 3-6429, fax (32) 36-5153, was due to open in 2001 with 400 rooms, including 150 in bungalows. It will be run in association with Italy's La Cascina group. The remade property, formerly the Villa Coral complex jointly operated by Golden Tulip (of the Netherlands) and Cubanacán, has had a troubled history.

FOOD

The hotels all have restaurants, and there are as yet few other options. Beachside restaurants include **Restaurante Las Brisas,** serving seafood and *criollo* dishes, and **Restaurante Bonsai,** for quasi-Chinese food. Budget about US$5-8 for meals—double that for lobster. The **Restaurante Las Bahamas,** near the gas station, also serves *criollo* food. **Oasis** is an outdoor bar and restaurant serving country cooking: try the grilled pork steaks with red beans and rice. **Restaurante La Concha,** immediately east of the Cupet gas station, is a simple thatched eatery.

The best eatery is the beachfront **Restaurante Luna Mar,** in the Centro Comercial, with an Italianate motif. You can dine on spaghettis and pizzas (US$4-9) or seafood, including lobster (US$12) in the a/c restaurant on alfresco on the terrace.

At Playa Los Cocos, the funky, privately owned seafood *paladares* have been forced to close. Your options are now Rumbos' **Restaurante La Cabaña,** festooned with fishing nets, and farther west, a modern bar and grill that sits right on the sand and serves seafood, burgers, and snacks.

The **Sodería Meñique,** in the Centro Comercial, sells ice-cream.

ENTERTAINMENT AND EVENTS

The **Santa Lucía Annual Festival** is hyped in mid-February, with beauty contest, beach games, music, and *espectáculos,* but it struggles hard to live up to the billing.

The major hotels have theme night *animaciones* (entertainment), some of it feeble, but some of it very good. You can buy a night pass for the Hotel Cuatro Vientos for US$25 deposit; you can partake of the resort in full, paying only for what you consume. It has an excellent little thatched disco by the beach with its own bar, but it's a purely tourist affair.

The locals gather at the **Disco Flamingo,** tel. (32) 3-6145, a modest open-air disco with pool tables. The police presence is heavy, and Cubans are wary of interactions with foreign tourists.

SPORTS AND RECREATION

Most of the hotels have water sports and beach volleyball. The Marlin Dive Center offers yacht, catamaran, and sailboat rentals, plus waterskiing (US$10 for 15 minutes), as does Base Naútico Taracora, which also offers sportfishing (US$177 for three hours).

Scuba diving is superb. The waters off Santa Lucía contain more than 15 dive sites. The warm waters support dozens of coral species and an infinity of gaudy fishes. Among the more exciting sites are Sponge Paradise, Coral Tower, and Gorgonian Garden, with their heaps of black coral and bright orange sponges hanging like garlands. There are also coral reefs in the shallow waters on the shore side of the drop, with plentiful queen conch, bright-colored starfish, and purple-lipped clams. Nurse sharks and barracudas occasionally pass by. And the mouth of the entrance to the Bahía de Nuevitas is a ships' graveyard of wrecks, including the steamship *Mortera,* which sank in 1898, its prow resting at a depth of 20 feet. The hull is now encrusted with coral, and sharks, turtles, and other marine species live within.

The dive center of the Cuatro Vientes offers specialized courses for beginners, and advanced courses, including night-diving and underwater video. Scuba diving is offered at the upscale hotels and from the **Shark's Friend Dive Center,** tel./fax (32) 36-5183.

Horseback rides cost about US$5, more with a guide.

PRACTICALITIES

Shopping and Services
Shopping opportunities are limited. Head to the small **Centro Comercial,** containing stores selling arts and crafts, cosmetics, clothes, and cigars and rum. You can also try the **MarVerde Centro Cultural** for arts and crafts.

There's an Etecsa international **telephone center** next to the **Cupet gas station** at the east end of Santa Lucia. A doctor and nurse are on 24-hour duty at the **Clínica Internacional,** next to door to Etecsa. Hotel visits cost US$40. Massages are offered at the **Club de Salud,** in the parking lot of Club Amigo Mayanabo.

Getting There and Away
By Air: Aerotaxi, Calle 27 #102 e/ M y N, Vedado, Havana, tel. (7) 33-4064, fax (7) 33-4063; in Santa Lucía, tel. (32) 6-1573 or 6-1986, flies to the local airstrip from Havana. It also offers local excursions. Charter flights arrive at the Camagüey and Las Tunas airports (see Las Tunas in the Las Tunas and Holguín chapter). A taxi from the airport will cost about US$50 one-way. You can hire a taxi for long-distance trips; expect to pay about US$80 roundtrip to Camagüey or Las Tunas.

By Bus: Public bus no. 125 departs Havana's main bus terminal at about 7:20 a.m., arriving Santa Lucía about 1 a.m. (10 pesos; foreigners may be charged US$10). The bus stop is near Villa Taracao. Buses also operate from Las Tunas and Camagüey.

By Car: Transtur, tel. (32) 3-6368, offers car rentals immediately west of the Cuantro Vientos. **Cubacar** rents cars, 200 m farther west, at the turnoff for Centro Comercial. And **Micar** has an outlet in the Villa Tararaco.

Organized Excursions: Rumbos and **Cubanacán,** tel. (32) 3-6212, have tour desks in the Cuatro Vientos and Club Amigo Mayanabo. They offer jeep safaris to Cayo Sabinal (US$25), and to King Ranch, as well as a sunset cruise (US$39), plus moped tour to a fish farm (US$25). Boat excursions to Playa Los Pinos, on Cayo Sabinal, are also offered, as well as an excursion aboard the *Mambo Cat* catamaran, with snorkeling and lunch at Playa Bonita (US$59). Excursions farther afield include to Cayo Largo (US$130), but why bother? Cubanacán also offers a trip to Camagüey; a nature excursion into the Cubitas Mountains; and two-day trips to Havana, Santiago de Cuba, and Trinidad.

Getting Around
Santa Lucía is too spread out to explore on foot. The resort has only one street, which parallels the shore. **Horse-drawn carriages** ply the route; rates are posted. **Taxis** charge about US$1 per km; call **Cubataxi,** tel. (32) 3-6496.

You can rent **bicycles and scooters** from CubaSol's MotoClub (a branch of Cubanacán) at the major hotels. Scooters cost US$7 one hour, US$13 three hours, US$30 per day.

Cubanacán offers excursions to La Boca by sea, with seafood lunch aboard. It also has a sunset cruise to La Boca, plus a snorkeling safari.

LAS TUNAS AND HOLGUÍN
INTRODUCTION

Las Tunas Province is a place to pass through en route to Holguín and elsewhere. The two namesake provincial capitals offer relatively little of tourist value. Las Tunas, or, more correctly, Victoria de las Tunas, is quaint and worth a quick browse. The larger city of Holguín offers three plazas of note, a natural history museum, some colonial structures of interest, and, outside town, the Finca Mayabe, where you can buy a beer for a suds-supping donkey.

Most sites of tourist interest lie along Holguín's coast, with scintillating white beaches (most notably the resort of Guardalavaca and nearby Playa Pesquero) and, inland, the dramatic formations of the Grupo de Maniabon, made more photogenic by working steam trains puffing through cane fields.

History buffs may be enticed to Bahía Bariay, where Christopher Columbus first set foot on Cuban soil in 1492, and to Banes, site of the most important pre-Columbian finds in Cuba (one-third of indigenous finds unearthed in Cuba to date have hailed from Holguín Province). And how about Fidel Castro's birthplace and childhood home at Birán?

A good online resource is Holguín Province's website at www.holguintravel.cu.

SIGHTSEEING HIGHLIGHTS: LAS TUNAS AND HOLGUÍN PROVINCES

Cayo Saetía: Wildlife refuge stocked with antelope, ostrich, water buffalo, and zebras. Lonesome beaches.

Finca Mayabe: Hilltop *finca* with fighting cocks and two donkeys, Pancho and Panchito, who entertain by guzzling beer.

Grupo de Maniabon: Upland region with quintessential Cuban scenery. Traditional *campesino* lifestyle.

Guardalavaca: Small resort region with good water sports, scuba diving, horseback riding, and a range of hotels lining Guardalavaca's **Playa Mayor** and **Playa Las Brisas,** and nearby **Playa Pesquero.**

Holguín: Provincial capital with three handsome colonial plazas and a vibrant cultural life, including the **Centro Nocturno** cabaret.

Rafael Freyre's steam trains: Antique puffing billies work the sugarcane fields and haul tourists on scenic tours through the Grupo de Maniabon.

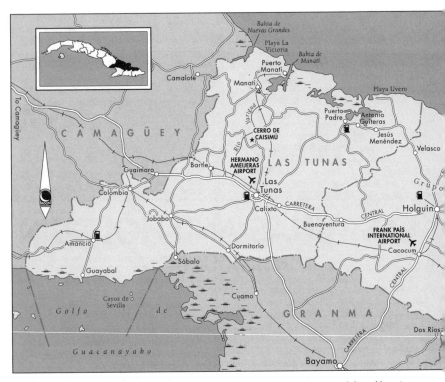

The Lay of the Land

Las Tunas Province forms a flat, narrow band across the island, broadening to the northeast. The capital city sits on a low-lying ridge (the Cuchilla Holguín) in the center of the province, on the eastern edge of the great plains that dominate central Cuba. It is dull, unvarying terrain, mostly farmed for sugar and cattle. The scenery begins to grow lusher and more interesting as you progress eastward toward Holguín, where stands of royal palms reappear. The swampy southern plains are of minimal tourist interest, although bonefish and tarpon provide challenging fishing in the coastal lagoons.

Holguín is far more diverse. The capital city lies in the midst of the bulky western half of the province, with the Bay of Nipes its eastern flank. The province extends east in a panhandle along the north coast almost to the tip of the island and is indented with neatly spaced, deep-pock-

et bays entered via narrow inlets. Here towns such as Puerto Padre and Manatí have grown up around chemical works or sugar-loading facilities. Much of the coast is covered with scrubby salt bushes atop raised coral shores.

Inland, tall palms rise proudly above lime-green cane fields and dun-colored cattle pastures, deep bottle-green woods far beyond, extending toward the sierras in the south. This is most splendidly seen in the mountain valleys that lie on the road from Banes to Guardalavaca.

Looming over eastern Holguín inland are mountains—the Sierra de Nipe, Sierra del Cristal, Cuchillas del Toa, and Alturas de Moa—that rise to 1,200 meters. The mountains are the color of heated chrome, betraying the presence of precious mineral ores. The area has been named a national park, a wilderness of pine forests laced by rugged mountain trails. And on

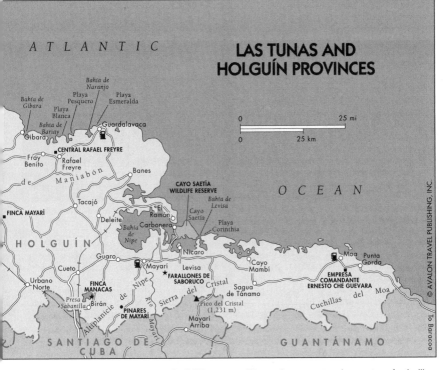

LAS TUNAS AND HOLGUÍN PROVINCES

Cayo Saetia, an island resort and wildlife reserve near the Bay of Nipes, exotic beasts imported from Africa leave hoofprints in sugar-white Cuban sand.

Holguín's roads are the worst in the country—dangerously potholed and eroded.

The Economy

Las Tunas relies on sugarcane and on cattle, raised in huge *ganaderias* named for revolutionary heroes. Tourism hasn't yet taken hold. Holguín Province also evolved an important economy based on cattle (in the west), tobacco (in the center), sugar (in the north and east), and fruit. Tourism, however, is booming, centered on Guardalavaca and today a rival in the Holguín economy to nickel, cobalt, and other mineral ores extracted from the Sierra Cristal and Sierra de Nipe and processed locally, most notably at the coastal town of Moa.

The region was a major center of rebellion during the wars of independence and suffered enormously. The vast sugarcane fields of Holguín gradually fell into the hands of U.S. corporations, especially the United Fruit Company, which bought the land for a pittance following the devastation wrought by the wars. United States companies came to dominate economic and political life in the region, and Cubans were under their sway. The U.S. workers and Cuban managers enjoyed a lifestyle of privilege that was denied Cuban field hands, the majority of whom faced a harsh and marginalized existence. Other U.S. companies established mining ventures. After the mining operations were nationalized in 1960, Soviet money financed future expansion. Today Canadian mining ventures have taken the lead.

One of the few Cubans who *did* benefit economically was Fidel Castro's father, Ángel Cas-

*Che Guevara
Nickel Plant, Moa*

tro, who leased lands from the United Fruit Company and grew to be relatively prosperous and powerful. The pitiful existence of many among the Cuban peasantry was not lost on the young Fidel, who, it is claimed, first agitated on workers' behalf as a boy—and on his father's estate!

The Carretera Central

The Carretera Central cuts through the center of Las Tunas Province. The road is in good condition. There are Cupet gas stations in Florida and the city of Las Tunas. There are no services along the road to Holguín. At Holguín, the Carretera it turns southwest for Granma Province and begins to deteriorate. Most other roads in Holguín Province are dangerously potholed and worn away.

If driving from Camagüey to Granma Province and Santiago, you can bypass the city of Holguín via a paved road that leads southeast from Las Tunas to Bayamo and cuts across the Río Cauto plains via the small agricultural town of Jobabo.

LAS TUNAS AND VICINITY

Las Tunas is a small-time capital of a small-time province, but it's a cozy town with a comfortable town center. The town is officially known as La Victoria de las Tunas, a name bequeathed by the Spanish governor in 1869 to celebrate a victory over Cuban patriot forces in the War of Independence. Needless to say, the name took on a different import after the patriots captured the town in 1895. Two years later, the town was put to the torch by rebel forces as Spanish forces attempted to retake Las Tunas. Alas, the fire destroyed many of the original buildings, and the town today lacks edifices of historical or architectural note.

Las Tunas is famed for its terra-cotta ceramics, expressed in contemporary art scattered all over the city. The town has thus earned the nickname "City of Sculptures." Look for works by some of Cuba's leading artists, such as *Fountain of the Antilles,* with a woman's body shaped like Cuba at its center, by Rita Longa; and the powerful *Liberation of the People,* by Manuel Chong, opposite the Provincial Assembly building.

Orientation

The town sits astride the Carretera Central, which enters from the west along Avenida 1ro de Enero, becomes Avenida Vicente García and slopes up to the central square—Parque Vicente García—where it turns 90° and runs southeast for Holguín as Calle Francisco Verona. A ring road *(circunvalación)* bypasses the town to the south.

The historic core is laid out in a grid, aligned northeast-southwest and centered on Parque García, at the top of Vicente García, between

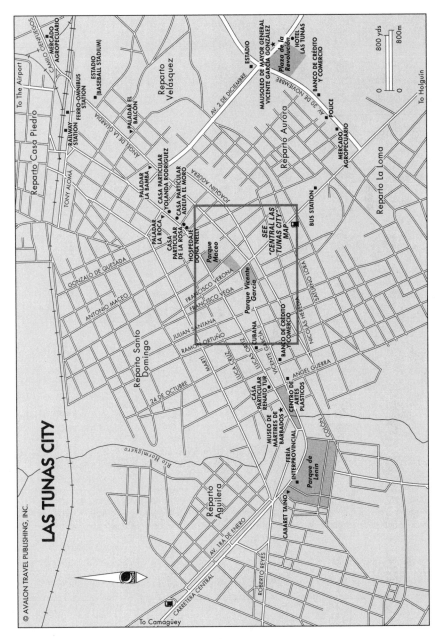

© AVALON TRAVEL PUBLISHING, INC.

LAS TUNAS CITY

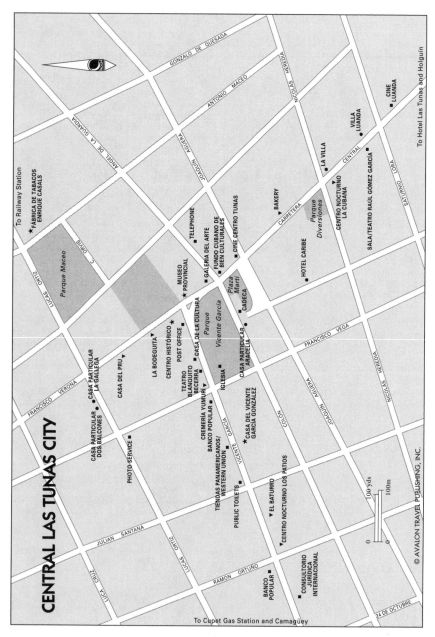

CENTRAL LAS TUNAS CITY

To Railway Station

★ FÁBRICA DE TABACOS
   ENRIQUE CASALS

GONZALO DE QUESADA

Parque Maceo

ANTONIO MACEO

NICOLÁS HEREDIA

To Hotel Las Tunas and Holguín

CINE
LUANDA

ANGEL DE LA GUARDIA

JOAQUÍN AGÜERA

VILLA
LUANDA ■

■ LA VILLA

■ TELEPHONE

CENTRAL

LORA

SATURNINO

LUCAS ORTIZ

C. ORVIS

■ GALERÍA DEL ARTE

FUNDO CUBANO DE
BIEN CULTURALES ●

■ BAKERY

CARRETERA

Parque
Diversiones

CENTRO NOCTURNO
LA CUBANA ▼

MUSEO
★ PROVINCIAL

● CINE CENTRO TUNAS

● HOTEL CARIBE

SALA/TEATRO RAÚL GÓMEZ GARCÍA ■

Plaza
Martí

CASA DE LA CULTURA ■

★ CENTRO HISTÓRICO

POST OFFICE ■

Parque
Vicente García

CADECA ●

FRANCISCO VEGA

CASA PARTICULAR
LA GALLEGA ●

FRANCISCO VERONA

▼ LA BODEGUITA

CASA DEL PRU ●

TEATRO
BLANQUITO ■
BECERRA

IGLESIA ■

CASA PARTICULAR
ARACELIA ●

NICOLÁS HEREDIA

JOAQUÍN AGÜERA

CASA PARTICULAR
DOS BALCONES ●

CREMERÍA YUMURÍ ▼

BANCO POPULAR ■

★ CASA DEL VICENTE
   GARCÍA GONZÁLEZ

COLÓN

PHOTO SERVICE ■

VICENTE
GARCÍA

TIENDAS PANAMERICANOS/
WESTERN UNION ■

PUBLIC TOILETS ■

▼ EL BATURRO

▼ CENTRO NOCTURNO LOS PATIOS

JULIÁN SANTANA

LUCAS ORTIZ

LUCA CRUZ

RAMÓN ORTUÑO

BANCO
POPULAR ■

CONSULTORÍA
JURÍDICA
INTERNACIONAL ■

24 DE OCTUBRE

0   100 yds
0   100m

© AVALON TRAVEL PUBLISHING, INC.

To Cupet Gas Station and Camagüey

Calles Francisco Varona and Francisco Vega. Ángel de la Guardia runs northeast to the railway station, where it forks for the airport and Puerto Padre, on the north coast.

SIGHTSEEING

Las Tunas's historic core can be explored on foot. The place to begin is the main square, **Parque Vicente García,** with its attractive marble statue of the local hero, Major General Vicente García González, who burned the city rather than let it fall into Spanish hands. It has granite seats beneath shady begonias. On the west side is an aged church, very small and simple yet in good condition.

Most buildings of interest lie along Avenida Vicente García, which is lined with columned colonnades. The houses west of Ramón Ortuño (two blocks west of the park) are in particularly good repair. Noteworthy among them is the **Casa del Vicente García González,** a restored colonial house where, on 26 September 1876, Vicente García González began the fire that burned the city. The building, which miraculously survived, is now a museum telling the tale of the city and the War of Independence, leading to the town's immolation.

At the base of Vicente García is the tiny **Monumento de Mártires de Barbados,** a dramatic piece of contemporary art—an arc of metal pipes and bronze remnants welded into an arm and clenched fist. The monument is to the side of the small wooden house where lived Carlos Leyva González, Cuba's champion *florete* (fencer). Leyva died, along with his brother and the entire Cuban fencing team, when Cubana flight CUT-1201 was destroyed by a bomb en route to Georgetown, Barbados, on 6 October 1976. In all, 73 people died, including 57 Cubans, five Koreans, and 11 Guyanese. Right-wing Cuban-American exiles have been implicated in the terrorist act. The house is now a **museum,** tel. (31) 4-7213, dedicated to the passengers who died. The museum showcases medals and diplomas won by Leyva and fellow *florete* Leonardo Mackenzie, as well as rapiers and a fencing suit. It's open daily 8 a.m.-7 p.m. Free. Lather up with mosquito repellent.

Other parks of interest include **Parque Maceo,** on Calle Lucas Ortíz, one block northeast of Parque García, and the petite and attractive little **Plaza Martí,** one block east of Parque García.

The **Museo Provincial,** tel. (31) 48201, at the top of Vicente García has changing exhibitions and a permanent exhibition of historical artifacts and photos on a local theme. It's open Tuesday, Wednesday, Friday and Saturday 1-9 p.m., Thursday 9 a.m.-5 p.m., and Sunday 8 a.m.-noon (US$1). There's also a **Museo Histórico** on General Menocal and Francisco Vega. And the **Centro Histórico,** tel. (31) 4-8201, on Francisco Verona 20 meters west of the main park, features meager exhibits on local

a monument to Major General Vicente García González, Parque Vicente García

history but is more noteworthy for the 3-D ceramic map of the historic city on its outside wall.

The **Mausoleo de Mayor General Vicente García González** honors the local hero of the wars of independence. This large-scale monument fronting the ugly **Plaza de la Revolución** is hewn in pink concrete with 3-D motifs showing the general with sword held high. The entrance hall features busts of other heroes of the wars of independence (there are no other exhibits despite the US$0.50 entrance fee).

The tiny **Fábrica de Tabacos Enrique Casals,** 50 meters north of Parque Martí on Lucas Ortíz, is a curiosity in passing. It produces for domestic consumption.

ACCOMMODATIONS

Casas Particulares

The best place by leagues is **Villa Luanda,** Francisco Verona #262 e/ Lora y Heredia, tel. (31) 4-3949, where Eduardo Arias and Sarai Carbonell López rent a single room in their modern, beautifully furnished home fitted to Western standards, including a modern kitchen. The a/c room has a small local TV, radio, and even fresh roses (US$25). It has secure parking. *Recommended.*

One block west, **La Villa** Francisco Verona #266, tel. (31) 4-2260 (c/o Richard) is a handsome and substantial house with four rooms (two up, two down), each nicely furnished and cross-ventilated, with a/c, fans, and 1950s furniture (US$20-25). The rooms share two bathrooms with hot water. There's a TV lounge with rockers, and an upstairs patio with swing chairs. Weekends get noisy, when an open-air disco is hosted across the street.

Hospedaje Doña Nelly, at Calle Lucas Ortíz #111, e/ Gonzalo de Quesada y Coronel Fonseca, tel. (31) 4-2526, is a large colonial home with a piano in the lounge, plus one a/c room with a private bathroom with hot water for rent for US$15-20. Laundry is offered, and there's a patio. Next door, **Casa Particular de la Rosa,** Calle Lucas Ortíz #109 Gonzalo de Quesada y Coronel Fonseca, tel. (31) 4-2657, offers three basically furnished, cross-ventilated rooms with a/c, fans, fridges, and private bathrooms with hot water for US$20-25. A breezy upstairs patio has rockers. The owner is aloof. Also with simply furnished

a/c rooms, but with shared bath (private bathrooms were to be built) is **Casa Particular Adelfa El Moro,** Calle Luca Ortíz #103 e/ Gonzalo de Quesada y Vilalon, tel. (31) 4-3684, with two rooms and a TV lounge and patio with rockers.

A better bet is **Casa Particular Yolanda Rodríguez,** next door at Calle Luca Ortíz #101, tel. (31) 4-3641, with a pleasant hostess and a admirable home furnished in 1950s style. Two rooms are rented in the breeze-kissed patio (with an arbor); each has a/c, fridge, and private bathroom with hot water (US$15, and US$20 for the room with kitchenette). Her daughter, Marianela, has additional rooms upstairs.

Ana Luisa González at **Casa Particular Dos Balcones,** Calle Luca Ortíz #210 (altos) e/ Francisco Vega y Francisco Varona, has three nicely furnished rooms upstairs (two with a/c) that share a bathroom with hot water for US$20. There's a TV lounge. Her neighbor, Angelo Couso, runs **Casa Particular La Gallega,** Calle Lucas Ortiz #208, tel. (31) 4-2677. The three modestly furnished rooms each have modern, tiled private bathrooms with hot water (US$15). Two rooms have a/c and fans; the third has fans. One room has its own kitchen, TV, and fridge (US$20). There's a TV lounge and a rooftop patio.

Casa Particular Renato Tur, Calle Lucas Ortíz #328, has one room with a/c, fridge, and a small private bathroom with hot water for US$15-20. It offers a small TV lounge and secure parking.

Aracelia Nuñoz, an aloof old main, has a *casa particular* at Calle Angel Guardia #141, with a spacious albeit gloomy room with faded 1950s decor and a private bathroom with hot water for US$15. A patio faces onto the main plaza. Aracelia makes breakfast.

Hotels

The **Hotel Caribe,** on Lorenzo Ortíz one block south of Francisco Varona, tel. (31) 4-4262, is run by Mercadu S.A. and caters mostly to students. This pleasing historic hotel was recently renovated with bright (but modest) furnishings and modern art, including glazed terra-cotta ceramics. Some of the 23 rooms have a/c, others have fans. Unfortunately bathrooms are small and some have cold water only. There's a bar and a pleasant little restaurant. It accepts both Cubans and foreigners. Rates were US$10 s,

US$15 d with fan, US$15 s, US$20 with a/c and fridge, US$25 with a "matrimonial" bed.

A more basic option is **El Cornito,** tel. (31) 4-5015, about 10 km east of town. It has 50 rustic, thatched, a/c cabanas amid palms and banyans on the banks of the Río Hormigo. Fishing and boating is offered, and the hotel hosts folk music concerts. Rates are about US$14 s, US$18 d. Avoid the musty motel rooms.

Most travelers stay at Islazul's **Hotel Las Tunas,** tel. (31) 4-5014, fax (31) 4-3336, one km east of town on Avenida de 2 Diciembre. The five-story neo-Stalinist prefab hotel sits atop a hillock a 20-minute walk east of town. The views aren't particularly appealing, but the hotel is quite adequate. The 142 rooms have a/c, TVs, telephones, and refrigerators. Rates were US$22 s, US$27 d low season, US$27 s, US$31 d high season.

FOOD

The town also several *paladares.* The best is **Paladar El Balcón,** popular with locals and serving huge portions. It sometimes has swordfish and snapper (US$9), served on a shaded patio. **Paladar La Bamba** is one block south on Ángel de la Guardia. The **Paladar La Roca,** at Calle Lucas Ortíz #108, is an also-ran, lacking in atmosphere and noisy, though the basic *criollo* fare is filling for US$3.

Times change, but when I stayed (twice) at the Hotel Las Tunas, the menu was a wish list. I felt like snatching the flies for protein! The restaurant in the **Hotel Caribe** is more attractive and serves lobster enchilada for US$4.50.

Of several restaurants on Francisco Varona, one block west of the main plaza, the best is **La Taberna,** a dark, vaulted, red-brick tavern that serves burgers and snacks. **La Bodeguita,** next door, is similarly moody and sells salads and *criollo* dishes, including fried chicken (US$4).

Los Patios, at Vicente García and Ramón Ortuno; it has a refectory-style dining area and serves burgers and snacks, plus beer for four pesos. Next to it is the basic but atmospheric **El Baturro,** where you can buy *refrescoes* served from a huge copper still.

Café Quique Marina, on the Carretera Central west of town, is renowned for its *caldosa,* a thick local stew combining chicken, banana, yucca, potato, and other vegetables.

You can buy ice cream for pesos at **Cremería Yumurí,** on the west side of Parque Vicente García. And the **Casa del Pru** on Francisco Verona, 50 meters west of Parque Vicente García, sells *pru,* a local nonalcoholic "infusion" of rice water.

Shopping for yourself? There's an *agropecuario* (farmer's market) on Camilo Cienfuegos, 200 meters north of the railway station. There's a bakery on Francisco Verona two blocks east of Parque Vicente García.

ENTERTAINMENT AND SHOPPING

Las Tunas is known for a festival called **Jornada Cucalambeana** (Cucalambé Folkloric Festival), when *trovadores* and songsters merge from all parts of Cuba to make merry in honor of Cristóbal Nápoles Fajardo (El Cucalambé), a native 19th-century poet known for his rhyming songs called *décimas.* It takes place at Motel El Cornito each June or July.

The *Carnaval Las Tunas* is hosted each September. And the **Fería Interprovincial** in mid-December features rodeos and horse and cattle fairs. It's held at Parque de Lenin, where the Carretera Central merges with Avenida Vicente García.

The **Galería del Arte** has special exhibitions, as well as permanent displays. You might also check out the **Casa de la Cultura,** tel. (31) 4-3508, on the west side of Parque Vicente García.

The happening spot is the **Disco Rumbos** on the Carretera Central at Saturno Lora. This Western-style disco features laser-lights and TV music videos. The US$4 entrance includes two drinks, but you can buy a bottle of rum at the bar for US$3 (US$4 with a can of coke)—a great place to meet a Cuban partner. Alternately, try **Discoteca Tropical** in the Hotel Las Tunas. **Cine Luanda,** on Francisco Varona four blocks east of Parque García, has a disco Wed.-Sat. at 9 p.m. Next door is **Centro Nocturno la Cubana,** a modest but popular night spot with live music and dancing. Another popular spot is **Centro Nocturno Los Patios,** at Vicente García and Ramón Ortuño. It has a bar and dance area.

Cabaret espectáculos are held at **Cabaret Taino,** tel. (31) 4-3823, on the Carretera Central outside Parque Lenin, at 9 p.m. (US$1).

For movies, take your pick from between the **Cine Centro Tunas** and **Cine Luanda.** Immediately west is the **Sala/Teatro Raúl Gómez García,** which hosts classical and contemporary performances.

You can catch a baseball game at the stadium on Avenida 2 de Diciembre, 300 meters west of the Hotel Las Tunas.

A wide array of ceramics, leather saddles (US$250), baskets, and art is sold at the **Fundo Cubano de Bienes Culturales** on the north side of Plaza Martí.

PRACTICALITIES

Services

You can buy postage stamps and make international calls at the Hotel Las Tunas. The main post office is at the top of Vicente García, on the west side of Parque García. The *centro telefónico* is one block northeast of Parque García, on Ángel de la Guardia.

The Banco de Crédito y Comercio has a branch 400 meters south and west of the Hotel Las Tunas, on Avenida 30 de Noviembre, and on Vicente García four blocks west of Parque Vicente García. The Banco Financiero Internacional has a branch one block east, on the corner of Vicente García y 24 de Octubre, and there's a Banco Popular across the street on the west side of Vicente García.

The post office is on the west side of Parque Vicente García. You can make international calls from the Hotel Las Tunas or from the Centro Telefónifco on Ángel de la Guardia one block north of Parque Vicente García.

The hospital is on Avenida 2 de Diciembre, tel. (31) 4-5012.

The immigration office is about one km north of the railway station on Avenida Camino Cienfuegos. Ostensibly you can get your visa renewed here. If you need legal assistance, contact the Consultorio Jurídica Internacional on Vicente García y 24 de Octubre.

You can buy batteries, film, and instant cameras at Photo Service, at the corner of Lucas Ortíz and Francisco Vega.

The Cupet gas station is on the Carretera Central on the west side of town, about 400 meters west of Parque Lenin. The Servicentro Oro Negro is on the Carretera Central, four blocks east of Parque Vicente García.

TRAIN SCHEDULE (LAS TUNAS)

EASTBOUND

No.	Origin	Destination	Arrive Las Tunas	Depart Las Tunas
11	Havana	Santiago de Cuba (every three days)	5:37 a.m.	5:39 a.m.
13	Havana	Santiago de Cuba	3:04 a.m.	3:08 a.m.
15	Havana	Holguín (every two days)	1:57 a.m.	2:02 a.m.
17	Havana	Bayamo-Manzanillo	[times unavailable]	
65	Morón	Santiago de Cuba (every two days)	11:19 a.m.	11:24 a.m.
77	Las Tunas	Holguín	-	12:40 p.m.

WESTBOUND

No.	Origin	Destination	Arrive Las Tunas	Depart Las Tunas
12	Santiago de Cuba	Havana (every three days)	12:42 a.m.	12:44 a.m.
14	Santiago de Cuba	Havana	[times unavailable]	
16	Holguín	Havana (every two days)	5:18 p.m.	5:23 p.m.
18	Bayamo-Manzanillo	Havana	[times unavailable]	
64	Santiago de Cuba	Morón (every two days)	9:50 a.m.	9:55 a.m.
76	Holguín	Las Tunas	11:10 a.m.	-

Getting There and Away

By Air: Cubana serves Las Tunas from Havana four times weekly. The **Hermano Ameijeras Airport,** tel. (31) 4-2484, is on the northern edge of town, on Carretera Rafael Martínez (a taxi will cost about US$5 to/from town; a horse-drawn *coche* should cost about US$2). Cubana has an office on Lucas Ortíz, tel. (31) 4-3060, open Mon.-Fri. 7 a.m.-noon and 1-3 p.m.

By Bus: The **Víazul** tourist bus departs Havana for Las Tunas on Tuesday and Friday. For public bus service, see the Public Bus Service from Havana chart in the On the Road chapter. The journey takes about 10 hours. Most buses traveling along the Carretera Central to whatever destination also stop in Las Tunas; they are always oversold, however. Buses arrive and depart from the **Terminal Intermunicipal,** tel. (31) 4-3801, on the Carretera Central, about 800 meters east of Parque Vicente García.

By Train: All trains between Havana and Santiago de Cuba stop in Las Tunas. (See the Train Schedules from Havana chart in the On the Road chapter and the Las Tunas Train Schedule.) The journey between Havana and Las Tunas takes about 12 hours on the *especial.* The train station, tel. (31) 4-8140, is on Calle Terry Alomá, at the top of Lucas Ortíz and Ángel de la Guardia

Major towns throughout the province are linked to Las Tunas by a two-car commuter train—*ferro-ómnibus* or rail-tram—which leaves from a separate station adjacent to the main rail station. Reservations are highly recommended; there's a specific time to make reservations for each train, usually the day before (check the schedule outside the station).

By Car: Havanautos, tel. (31) 4-6228, has a car and scooter rental outlet in the Hotel Las Tunas.

Getting Around

You can walk everywhere in Las Tunas with relative ease. The Hotel Las Tunas is a 30-minute downhill walk to the center.

Taxis are available outside the Hotel Las Tunas (US$2 to downtown). The locals get around by horse-drawn *coches,* which gather outside the railway station. You can hop aboard anywhere in the city (one peso for locals; US$1 or more for foreigners).

CERRO DE CAISIMÚ AND COTO DE CAZA YARIGUA

Cerro de Caisimú, 18 km due north of Las Tunas, is a pristine wilderness flush with guinea fowl, pigeons, and other game species. It is drained by the Río Yariguá, which flows north to the Bahía de Manatí through a second reserve, the **Coto De Caza Yariguá** This prize hunting preserve is set amid 255 square km of marshland and saltwater estuaries adjacent to a huge rice-producing area. Bass fishing is also offered.

Accommodations

A lodge at Coto de Caza Yariguá has 13 a/c double cabanas with private baths. There's a restaurant and bar. It's run by Horizontes de Pesca y Caza, tel. (7) 95-1072, in Havana.

THE NORTH COAST OF LAS TUNAS

Las Tunas' north coast is something of an ugly duckling. However, it has a few beaches of note —even if, as yet, no resorts.

Roads radiate north from the city of Las Tunas to the two coastal towns of importance—Manatí and Puerto Padre, which are also linked by a road that parallels the shore and connects westward with Camalote (gateway to Playa Santa Lucía, in Camagüey Province) and eastward with Gibara (in Holguín Province). The road between Camalote and Manatí is in lousy condition.

Manatí, 45 km northwest of Las Tunas, is a nondescript port town centered on a sugar *central.* Tourist maps show a road leading north from town to **Playa La Victoria** and **Puerto Manatí.** The road passes through miles of salty scrub and nothingness. Believe me, there's no reason to visit.

Puerto Padre (pop. 25,000), about 25 km east of Manatí, lies deep within a large pocket bay shaped like a flask. Again, there's no reason to visit other than the **Cupet gas station.** Puerto Padre has an enormous sugar terminal called Carupano, on Cayo Juan Claro, just inside the bay (private yachters must report here before berthing at the dock at Puerto Padre, where there's a bar frequented by seamen and females hoping to be captains' mates).

You'll find several beautiful white sand beaches nearby, including (to the northwest) **Playa Covarrubias,** a four-km-long strip of silky white sands with turquoise waters protected by a coral reef. At the beach's eastern end is a rocky cliff offering views over the beach and tidelands. Covarrubias has been earmarked for development, with a total potential capacity of 5,000 hotel rooms.

About 20 km east of Puerto Padre, you pass through Jesús Menéndez and Loma, where a road leads north to **Playa Uvero** and **Playa La Herradura,** which lie to the east of the mouth of the bay. Both are glorious. They're backed by salt-encrusted *esteros.* Two modest hotels for Cubans were being restored at press time.

HOLGUÍN AND VICINITY

Holguín, 775 km east of Havana and 200 km northwest of Santiago de Cuba, is the fourth-largest city in Cuba (pop. 195,000). When Columbus landed in 1492 at Gibara, believing he had arrived in Asia, he sent an expedition inland to carry salutations to the Japanese emperor's court. The explorers came across a large Indian village called *Cubanacán* (Center of Cuba), believed to have been the current location of Holguín. Three decades later, a land grant was made to Capitán García Holguín, who built a settlement on the site of the Indian village (which had, naturally, been razed) and immodestly named the site San Isidoro de Holguín.

The center of town contains many fine houses of Spanish origin. Still, Holguín's colonial charm has been virtually suffocated in recent decades. Today it is an industrial city that has expanded rapidly since the Revolution, when prefabricated concrete apartment blocks went up. It receives few tourists, though I have grown to like its stately provincial air. The city is surrounded by cattle *fincas* and steep hills, which offer fine views over the city.

ORIENTATION

Star-shaped Holguín is an unassuming town that conveys an impression of being smaller than it really is. The tight historic core is laid out in a grid. At its heart is Parque Calixto García, bounded by Calles Frexes, Martí, Libertad (also known as Manduley), and Maceo. Most sites of importance lie within a few blocks of Parque García.

Narrow, bustling Frexes leads west from the park to the Carretera Central, which skirts downtown and swings southwest, heading away from the city for Bayamo and Santiago. Frexes runs

east from the square and links up with the road to Guardalavaca. Martí parallels Frexes one block to the south and merges to the east with Avenida de los Libertadores (lined with statues and monuments to revolutionary heroes), which leads through the modern Plaza de la Revolución district and continues to Cueto and Baracoa.

Other roads radiate out, like the spokes of a wheel, to Gibara, Pinares de Mayarí, and Finca Mayabe. The city is bypassed to the south by a ring road *(circunvalación).*

SIGHTSEEING

Vicinity of Plaza Calixto García
The main square, Plaza Calixto García, known to locals as "el parque," has little visual appeal, but it is a pleasure to sit beneath the large shade trees and watch the activity. At its heart is a marble statue of General Calixto García, Holguín's most famous son, who was born in the simple house at Calle Miró #147, just off the square. Some of his personal effects are on view inside the museum.

The square also has the **Museo Provincial de História,** tel. (24) 46-3395, on the north side at Calle Frexes #198, with an eclectic range of historical artifacts and the usual photographs and displays recording the glories of the Revolution and the parts played by local inhabitants in Cuban contemporary history. It was formerly the Casino Español, where Spanish gentry caroused. One curiosity that locals enjoy telling is how the building (with its cage-like barred windows) became known as La Pariquera—the Parrot's Cage—supposedly after Spanish troops in their garish yellow, blue, and green uniforms barricaded themselves inside the building in 1868, when the

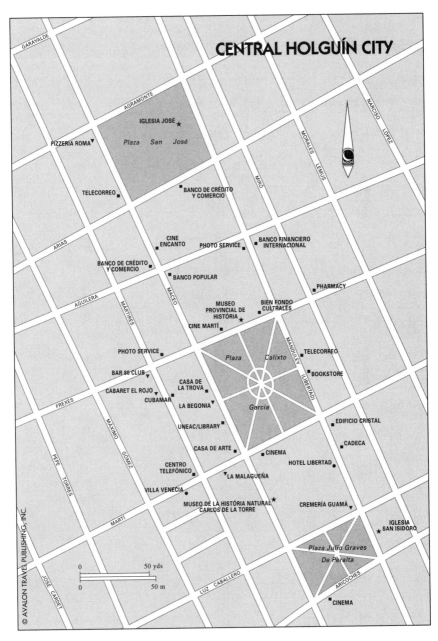

CENTRAL HOLGUÍN CITY

GARAVALDE

AGRAMONTE

IGLESIA JOSÉ ★

Plaza San José

PIZZERÍA ROMA ▼

TELECORREO ■

BANCO DE CRÉDITO
Y COMERCIO

MORALES

LEMUS

NARCISO LÓPEZ

MIRÓ

MOON

ARIAS

CINE
ENCANTO

PHOTO SERVICE ■

BANCO FINANCIERO
INTERNACIONAL

BANCO DE CRÉDITO
Y COMERCIO ■

BANCO POPULAR ■

AGUILERA

MARTIRES

MACEO

MUSEO
PROVINCIAL DE
HISTÓRIA ★

BIÈN FONDO
CULTRALES

■ PHARMACY

CINE MARTÍ ■

PHOTO SERVICE ■

Plaza   Calíxto

TELECORREO ■

BAR 80 CLUB ▼

CABARET EL ROJO ▼

CASA DE
LA TROVA ■

BOOKSTORE ■

(LIBERTAD)

MANDUJEY

CUBAMAR ▼

LA BEGONIA ▼

García

FREXES

MÁXIMO GÓMEZ

UNEAC/LIBRARY ■

CASA DE ARTE ■

EDIFICIO CRISTAL ■

CADECA ■

CENTRO
TELEFÓNICO ■

CINEMA ■

PEPE TORRES

▼ LA MALAGUEÑA

HOTEL LIBERTAD ●

VILLA VENECIA ●

MUSEO DE LA HISTÓRIA NATURAL ★
CARLOS DE LA TORRE

MARTÍ

CREMERÍA GUAMÁ ▼

IGLESIA
★ SAN ISIDORO

Plaza Julio Graves
De Peralta

JOSÉ CARDET

© AVALON TRAVEL PUBLISHING, INC.

0   50 yds
0   50 m

ARICOCHES

LUZ CABALLERO

CINEMA ■

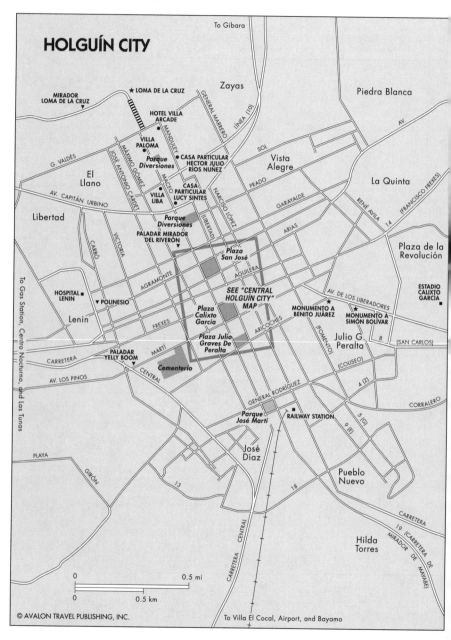

HOLGUÍN CITY

To Gibara

★ LOMA DE LA CRUZ

MIRADOR
LOMA DE LA CRUZ ▼

Zayas

Piedra Blanca

HOTEL VILLA
ARCADE

VILLA
PALOMA

*Parque
Diversiones*

● CASA PARTICULAR
HECTOR JULIO
RÍOS NUNEZ

Vista
Alegre

La Quinta

El
Llano

● CASA
PARTICULAR
LUCY SINTES

VILLA
LIBA

Libertad

*Parque
Diversiones*

PALADAR MIRADOR
DEL RIVERÓN ▼

*Plaza
San José*

Plaza de la
Revolución

ESTADIO
CALIXTO
GARCIA ■

HOSPITAL
LENIN ■

▼ POLINESIO

Lenin

*Plaza
Calixto
García*

SEE "CENTRAL
HOLGUÍN CITY"
MAP

MONUMENTO A
BENITO JUÁREZ ★

★ MONUMENTO A
SIMÓN BOLÍVAR

Julio G.
Peralta

[SAN CARLOS]

*Plaza Julio
Graves De
Peralta*

To Gas Station, Centro Nocturno, and Las Tunas

PALADAR
YELLY BOOM ▼

Cementerio

RAILWAY STATION ■

CORRALERO

*Parque
José Martí*

José
Díaz

Pueblo
Nuevo

PLAYA

Hilda
Torres

0   0.5 mi

0   0.5 km

© AVALON TRAVEL PUBLISHING, INC.

To Villa El Cocal, Airport, and Bayamo

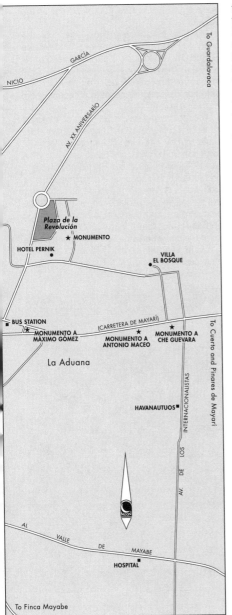

town was besieged by General Calixto García's troops. The museum's pride and joy is a 35-cm-long pre-Columbian axe carved in the figurine shape of a human. The axe has become the provincial symbol. Open Tue.-Sat. 9 a.m.-5 p.m. and Sunday 9 a.m.-1 p.m. Entrance costs US$1 (plus US$2 for a camera).

Other historic buildings on the square house the library and the **Bien Fondo Culturales** (next to the museum), the **Casa de la Trova** and Casa de Arte, and, on the south side, the art deco **Teatro Comandante Eddy Sunol.**

Follow Maceo or Manduley south one block and you pass the **Museo de la História Natural Carlos de la Torre,** tel. (24) 42-3935, in an impressive neoclassical building strongly influenced by Moorish design. Note the beautiful ceramic tile work. The museum houses an eclectic array of dead animals and birds, including a stuffed manatee and a leatherback turtle, plus a dazzling collection of over 4,000 colorful polymite (snail) shells. It's open Sun.-Thurs. 9 a.m.-5 p.m. and Saturday 1-5 p.m. Entrance costs US$1.

Plaza Julio Graves de Peralta

This small, attractive square, four blocks south of Parque Calixto García, is also known as Parque de San Isidoro. It is anchored by a marble statue of its namesake, looking remarkably like Karl Marx. At the northwest corner is a wall with a mural of a youthful Fidel holding a Soviet submachine-gun aloft, with other revolutionary heroes from the Americas to his right.

On the east side of Plaza Peralta is the **Iglesia San Isidoro,** dating from 1720 but restored in 1996. Its simple interior is entirely lacking in baroque or other typically Spanish colonial features, although the wooden ceiling is noteworthy.

Plaza San José

The most appealing and antique square is this quiet oasis two blocks north of Parque Calixto García and also known as Plaza Maceo. The reclusive cobbled square is surrounded by shade trees and simple colonial buildings. It is dominated on its east side by the beautiful **Iglesia José,** glowing incandescent in the Cuban light.

Loma de la Cruz

Looming over Holguín to the north is La Loma de la Cruz (Hill of the Cross), named for the cross that has stood here since 1790. The *mirador* (lookout) at the crest is dominated by a little castle-like structure. From here you can look across the dry, barren plains towards the strange mountain formations of the Grupo de Manabion.

You can climb the 450 or so steps that begin at the north end of Calle Maceo, 10 blocks north of Plaza San José. It's a stiff climb. A bar provides recuperative drinks, and there's an excellent thatched restaurant with views 200 yards to the west.

Fábrica de Órganos

This factory, also called Taller Polivalente, provides a fascinating peek at age-old Cuban craftsmanship as workers fashion organs and other musical instruments—a local tradition. A mile east of the base of La Loma, at Carretera de Gibara #301, it's the only organ factory in Cuba. Open weekdays 8 a.m.-4 p.m.

Plaza de la Revolución

The communists have built their own plaza, an ugly wide-open concrete parking lot dominated by a huge frieze depicting important events in Cuba's history. The plaza, in a new *reparto* (neighborhood) northeast of the city, can jam in 150,000-plus people. The plaza is dedicated to Calixto García, the homegrown hero of the War of Independence. His mausoleum is here. His mother (also a patriot) is buried behind the plaza beneath a copse of shade trees, where a bronze monument features a faux-Cuban flag draped in the shape of Holguín Province. By local custom, newlyweds deposit their bridal bouquets beneath the monument.

The huge Calixto García baseball and sports stadium, on Avenida XX Aniversario, 200 meters south of the plaza, can hold 30,000 spectators and is said to contain a **baseball museum.**

ACCOMMODATIONS

Casas Particulares

For a self-contained apartment, I recommend **Villa Venecia,** Calle Martí #137 e/ Mártires y Máximo Gómez, tel. (24) 46-1277, with a large bedroom and comfy bed, plus well-lit lounge with TV, VCR and sound system, and a kitchenette with fridge (US$20). It's one block from the main square; you can park your car at the square.

Most *casas particulares* on located on the north side of town where **Casa Particular Lucy Sintes,** Av. Cajigal #578, has one cool, modestly furnished a/c room with a small but clean modern bathroom (US$15-20). It has its own entrance plus secure parking. A second room was to be added.

The most appealing home—one of the finest *casas particulares* in all Cuba—is **Villa Liba,** Calle Maceo #46 esq. 18, tel. (24) 42-3823, owned by Jorge and Liba Mezerene. This beautiful 1950s home is replete with plump sofas and gracious furnishings in the spacious lounge. Light pours in through bay windows, and meals are served at a huge glass-topped table. Three a/c rooms are rented, all well lit, cross-ventilated and with period furnishings (US$25). One has a clean, tiled private bathroom with hot water; the two others share a second bathroom. The rear patio has a vine arbor. And there's secure parking. *Recommended.*

view of Holguín from Mirador de Holguín

Villa Paloma, Calle Maceo #8 esq. 12, tel. (24) 42-2579, two blocks north, is an equally beautiful and graciously furnished middle-class home owned by a Catholic family. It, too, has a vast lounge with circular windows, a large dining room, and two modestly furnished a/c bedrooms, each with fridge and a clean, tiled bathroom with hot water (US$20). There's a garage and a patio that opens to a fruit orchard.

Nearby, Hector Julio Ríos Nuñez rents one a/c room at his home at Calle Manduley #19. It's spacious and modestly but pleasantly furnished, with a beamed ceiling and handsome tiled bathroom with hot water (US$20). Meals are served at a rear patio.

Hotels

Budget: At the low end of the scale is the **Hotel Libertad,** Calle Manduley e/ Luz Caballero y Martí, tel. (24) 42-3469, one of the few basic hotels for Cubans that still accepts foreigners. The meagerly furnished rooms cost US$8 s/d.

Hotel Villa Arcade, Calle Manduley e/ 8 y 10, is run by Mercadu S.A. and offers rooms for both Cuban and international academics and students.

Islazul, tel. (24) 42-4718, has an office on the second floor of the Edificio Cristal where you can book rooms in Islazul hotels throughout the province. There's also an Islazul office on Manduley, one block south of Plaza San José. The booking office for **Cubamar's** *campismos populares* is on Mártires e/ Frexes y Martí.

Inexpensive: Islazul's Soviet-style **Hotel Pernik,** on Avenida Dimitrov, near the Plaza de la Revolución, tel. (24) 48-1011, is the principal tourist hotel in town. The hotel is named for the hometown of Georgei (Jorge) Dimitrov, the first leader of communist Bulgaria, which helped finance construction. The pleasantly decorated 202 a/c rooms have TVs and telephones. The hotel has a swimming pool, tennis court, and car rental. The restaurant is better than at most urban hotels of this type. Rates were US$29 s, US$38 d low season, US$35 s, US$48 d high season.

Islazul's **Villa El Bosque,** tel. (24) 48-1140, 400 meters farther east on Avenida Dimitrov, is a less appealing option, despite being refurbished. It has 69 a/c cabins—each with cable TV and refrigerator—set in uninspired grounds with a dowdy sundeck and pool. Facilities include a restaurant, car rental, shop, and a disco. Rates were the same as the Hotel Pernik.

Outside town, the place to be is either the Finca Mayabe (see below) or Cubanacán's **Villa el Cocal,** tel. (24) 46-8506, on the Carretera Central, about six km south of town. The latter is run by Servimed and offers health treatments. It has 40 rooms in two-story villas surrounding a pool and bar beside a huge spreading tree. The hotel boasts a large, atmospheric thatched restaurant.

FOOD

There is little to recommend. Try **Paladar Mirador de Riverón,** Calle Martínez #5-A e/ Cuba y Garajaldi, tel. (24) 42-4346, serving basic *criollo* fare (mostly pork) on an atmospheric rooftop with bamboo and thatch. Filling meals are prepared on an open grill. **Paladar Yelly Boom,** Calle Martí #180 e/ Carretera Central y Antonio Guiteras, serves *criollo* fare in a converted garage of this modern home.

The restaurant at Hotel El Bosque is a disappointment; somewhat better is the one at Hotel Pernik, with a full menu of Cuban dishes. The most popular spot in town is at the atmospheric **Mirador Loma de la Cruz,** tel. (24) 42-3868, with cowhide chairs and ox-carts for decoration, and which receives the breezes on hot days and offers open-air dining under thatch. Service is efficient, and the *criollo* food fairly priced.

If you have wheels, head out to **El Cocal,** or **Finca Mayabe,** where the restaurants are atmospheric and the food quality (and the prices) are higher; see the Finca Mayabe section, below.

Alternately, try the **Polinesio,** on the 13th floor of a high-rise unit at Avenida Lenin e/ Garayalde y Agramonte; and the **Pico Cristal,** on the third floor of the Edifico Cristal, at the corner of Calle Libertad and Martí. The **Islazul Café** on the ground floor is a clean modern snack bar. Likewise, Rumbos operates the 24-hour **La Begonia** snack bar with a pleasant little courtyard and an arbor for shade, on the west side of Parque Calixto García.

You can buy slices of pizza for five pesos apiece at **Pizzeria Roma,** at Calle Maceo and Agramonte.

Dozens of stalls sell snacks, *batidos*, and *refrescoes* is in the parking lot of the baseball stadium. Feeling the heat? Then head to **Cremería Guamá,** on Plaza Peralta for ice cream.

ENTERTAINMENT AND EVENTS

Festivals and Events: Mid-January is a good time to visit, during **Semana de Cultura Holguinera,** when the town is bursting with cultural events. Every 3 May, a religious procession—**Romería de Mayo**—ascends to the top of Loma de la Cruz, where a Mass is held. The **Festival Internacional de Ballet** is held in November every even-numbered year; and the **Fiesta Iberoamericana de la Cultura,** in October, celebrates music, dance, and theater.

Traditional Music and Dance: Traditional music and dance are performed at the **Casa de la Trova,** on the main square. Performances are also hosted in the **Teatro Comandante Eddy Suñol,** tel. (24) 46-3111, and the **Bien Fondo Culturales,** facing each other on the main square. The latter contains the **Galeria Bayado,** displaying experimental ceramics and art. Entertainment is offered on weekends. The **Casa de Arte** houses the **Centro de Artes Plasticos,** where jazz concerts are held each Saturday at 9 p.m. **UNEAC,** the Union of Writers and Artists, hosts musical and literary gatherings on the west side of Parque Calixto García.

On Saturday evenings, check out Parque Céspedes, where an organist plays at 8 p.m. Worth a peek, too, is the **Casino de la Playa,** at Manduley and Cuba, where a professional organ group practices.

Cabarets: The best cabaret show in town is Islazul's **Centro Nocturno,** tel. (24) 42-5185, two km west of town on the road to Las Tunas, and offering an excellent Tropicana-style open-air *cabaret espectáculo,* Tues.-Sun. at 9 p.m. (the show starts at 10 p.m.). Entrance costs US$10 including one drink. Meals are served. The crowd is almost exclusively Cuban.

The Hotel Pernik has a cabaret *espectáculo* featuring a magician, comedian, and singers. A lesser *espectáculo* is in the **El Pétalo** disco, in the Hotel El Bosque, tel. (24) 48-1012, US$5. **La Malagueña** is a local bar popular for dominos and which also has a cabaret Mon.-Sun. from 9 p.m.

Bars and Discos: The cabarets listed above all have discos following the shows. **Cabaret El Rojo,** Calle Mártires e/ Frexes y Martí, is a basic bar and dance hall next to the equally decayed **Bar 80 Club.**

Other: For movies, take your pick of the **Cine Martí,** on the north side of Parque Calixto García, or **Cine Encanto,** on Maceo one block south of Parque San José.

You can catch a baseball game at the huge Calixto García stadium, just west of the Hotel Pernik.

PRACTICALITIES

Services and Information

There are Banco de Crédito y Comercio branches on the south side of Plaza San José and one block south on Maceo; plus a Banco Financiero Internacional one block south on Manduley y Aguilera; and a Banco Popular one block west on Aguilera y Maceo.

The Hotel Pernik and El Bosque both have *telecorreos.* The main post office is at Calles Agramonte and Maceo. DHL, tel. (24) 46-8254, is in the Edificio Cristal at Libertad y Frexes; it's open weekdays 9 a.m.-6 p.m. and Saturday 8:30 a.m.-noon. An international *telecorreo* on the northeast side of Parque Calixto García offers postal and telephone and fax services. The main Etecsa building is two blocks west of the main square, on Martí e/ Mártires y Máximo Gómez. You can rent cellular phones at Cubacel, tel. (24) 46-8522, fax (22) 68-8022, in the Hotel Pernik.

Hospital Lenin, tel. (24) 42-5302, is on the west side of town. The Hotel Pernik and Motel El Bosque have nurses.

The library is on the west side of Plaza Calixto García. There's an Immigration office at Calle Frexes #76 if you need to extend your stay. Open Mon.-Sat. 8 a.m.-2 p.m.

The Photo Service shop on Plaza Calixto García sells a meager stock of batteries, film, and instant cameras.

Getting There and Away

By Air: Cubana flies between Havana and Holguín daily (US$79 one-way). **Aerotaxi,** Calle 27 #102 e/ M y N, Vedado, Havana, tel. (24) 33-

4064, fax (24) 33-4063, operates flights aboard Russian biplanes between Holguín and Havana. Cubana flies from Paris and Milan. Numerous charter flights also operate from Europe and Canada. **Cubana,** tel. (24) 46-8148, has an office on the second floor of the Pico Cristal building at Manduley y Martí. (Also see By Air in the Getting There section in the On The Road chapter.)

Flights arrive at the swank new **Frank País International Airport,** tel. (24) 46-2512, about 10 km of town. It has a Transtur car rental outlet in the international terminal, and a Havanautos outlet at the domestic terminal. A **Víazul** shuttle bus, tel. (24) 81-1413, operates between the airport and downtown Holguín. The domestic terminal is served by a bus from Calle Rodríguez, near the train station six blocks south of Parque Calixto García. A taxi costs about US$10.

By Bus: The **Víazul** tourist bus departs Havana for Holguín on Tuesday and Friday (see the Víazul Bus Schedule chart in the On the Road chapter). For public bus service, see the Public Bus Service from Havana chart. The journey takes about 12 hours. Buses also serve Holguín from Bayamo, Camagüey, Las Tunas, and Santiago, but getting a seat is extremely difficult due to overbooking. Buses arrive and depart at the **Terminal Interprovinciales,** tel. (24) 42-2111, west side of town on the Carretera Central at Calle 1 de Mayo. The **Terminal Municipales,** tel. (24) 42-2322, serving nearby towns, is eight blocks east. Buses to/from Guardalavaca, Moa, Baracoa, and other towns east of Holguín arrive and depart from a separate terminal on Avenida de los Libertadores, south of the baseball stadium.

By Train: Holguín is *not* on the main railway line, which serves Cacocum, 15 km south of town, and from where a branch line serves Holguín's **Estación de Ferrocarriles,** tel. (24) 42-2331, on Calle Pita. The ticket office for foreigners is opposite the station—you must pay for your tickets in dollars. The tiny station at Cacocum, 400 meters east of the Carretera Central, has no facilities.

At press time, train #15 left Havana for Holguín at 2:05 p.m. Other trains that operate between Havana and Santiago stop at Cacocum, which is also served from Las Tunas by train #431, departing at about 1:10 p.m. and arriving Holguín at 4 p.m., and from Santiago by train #410, departing at about 8:20 a.m. and arriving Cacocum at 11:35 a.m. (Also see the Train Schedules from Havana chart in the On the Road chapter.)

You can buy tickets at the Terminal Ferrocarril, on Calle Pita, eight blocks south of Plaza Calixto García.

By Car: Transtur Rent-a-Car has an outlet in the Rumbos Las Begonias café on the main square and another in the Hotel Pernik, tel. (24) 42-8196. **Havanautos,** tel. (24) 46-8017, has an office at Carretera de Mayarí, Km 5.5 y San Rafael; and in both the Hotel Pernik and Motel El Bosque.

Getting Around

Buses run through most areas of the city (10 centavos *regular,* 40 centavos *especial*). Bus no. 16 connects the Hotel Pernik with downtown. Bus no. 3 runs from the terminal to the foot of Loma de la Cruz.

The favored mode of transport in town is the horse-drawn cart or, failing that, a tricycle rickshaw. You should be able to get anywhere downtown for 10 pesos or US$1.

Call (24) 46-8294 for **Cubataxi.**

FINCA MAYABE

Finca Mayabe is a "typical" *campesino's* farmstead high above the Mayabe Valley, eight km southeast of town. The ersatz farm raises two dozen species of fruit trees. Enclosures hold turkeys, geese, and other farm animals. It even has a *yallah de gallos*—a cockpit—where you can watch cockfights. Horseback riding is also available. Just below the *bohio* is the **Mirador de Mayabe,** with a swimming pool and sundeck suspended over the cliff face, from where you can look down over the Valle de Mayabe, planted extensively with citrus groves.

The Finca's claim to fame, however, is a beer-loving burro called Pancho (born in 1960) and his equally thirsty sidekick, Panchito. Pancho has consumed over 45,000 bottles of beer—at an average of eight per day (on one occasion, he guzzled 46), and Panchito isn't far behind. They are given Monday off—presumably to sleep off their weekend hangovers. They live in a stall next to the bar, appropriately named Bar Burro. Entrance costs US$5, including a cocktail and use of the swimming pool. You'll need to buy the donkeys a beer (US$1.50) for photos.

Accommodations and Food

Villa Mayabe, tel. (24) 42-2160 or 47-3485 or c/o Islazul, Calle Manduley #126, Holguín, tel. (24) 42-4718, has 20 cabanas surrounded by palms and bougainvillea on the hilltop facing over the swimming pool and valley. The basic bungalows have radios and refrigerators. There's also a fully staffed house for rent—**Casa de Pancho.** This stunning house has four a/c double rooms decorated with pretty fabrics, modern furniture, and rattan wardrobes. Each room has a balcony, private bathroom, radio, color TV, and telephone. The facility includes a thatched restaurant and bar. The house specialty is sausage and pork cracklings. Seatings are supposedly at noon, 2, 6, and 8 p.m. A folkloric cabaret show is featured in the restaurant. Rates were US$55 per room.

HOLGUÍN TO GRANMA PROVINCE

South of **Cacocum,** the province is flat as a lake, with savanna and sugar sharing the landscape. Each of the little thatched *bohíos* is in its own little garden fenced by tightly packed cactus shaped like candelabras and neatly and lovingly trimmed. South of **Baches,** the topiary work takes on real form, with little bushes clipped into rondels and cones. In the distance the Sierra Maestra hovers luminously.

About 13 km south of Holguín is the basic

Motel Los Pinos, tel. (24) 27216, a self-contained resort surrounded by pine groves and with a shop, dark bar, and basic restaurant. It's a lively place, popular with Cubans. Foreigners may be accepted.

GIBARA

Gibara (pop. 20,000), 28 km north of Holguín, is a dusty, time-encrusted fishing port that curls around a coral nipple jutting into the Bahía de Gibara. It was a major port in colonial days, when it was known as Villa Blanca. Rising over the flatlands inland is a flat-topped mountain, the **Silla de Gibara** (Saddle of Gibara), considered to be the hill described by Christopher Columbus in his journal when he first landed in Cuba, on 28 October 1492. (Citizens of Baracoa, in Guantánamo Province, hotly defend their notion that Columbus landed *there* and that the mountain he described is their own El Yunque.)

There is very little to see, although you can gain a sense of Gibara's laid-back mood by walking the Malecón, a popular seafront promenade, where on weekends local couples still stroll arm in arm. Waves sweep in and break over the coral rocks. You may be surprised to find windsurfers and little sailboats in the breezy bay.

The streets rise steeply south and west of the pretty main plaza, which has a church with Byzantine-style cupolas and a stand of African oak trees. The church was recently restored. You might check out the **Museo de Arte Decorativo,**

Pancho, Finca Mayabe's claim to fame

tel. (24) 3-4407, in a neoclassical mansion at In-dependencia #27, a short distance away. This former home of a tobacco-trading family boasts a modest collection of period furniture (open Tues.-Sat. 8 a.m.-noon and 1-5 p.m. and Sunday 8 a.m.-noon; US$1). Gibara also has a small **Museo de História Natural,** at Independencio y Peralla (Tues.-Sat. 8 a.m.-noon and 1-5 p.m. and Sunday 8 a.m.-noon; US$1).

The coast road shown on maps as running west from Gibara to Playa Uvero and Playa La Herradura, in Las Tunas Province dead-ends midway amid mangroves.

A small bus runs once daily between Holguín and Gibara, where the bus stop is opposite the El Faro restaurant.

Accommodations
There are no tourist hotels here. However, you may be accepted, if grudgingly, at the pesos-only **Hotel Bella Mar,** tel. (24) 3-4206, on General Sartorio.

Cubamar Viajes, Calle 15 #752 esq. Paseo, Vedado, Havana, tel. (7) 66-2523, fax (7) 33-3111, e-mail: cubamar@cubamar.mit.cma.net, operates **Campismo Silla de Gibara,** a simple holiday camp with 42 basic cabins sleeping four (including a bunk), with fans and private bathrooms. It has a swimming pool, cafe, and medical services. It's about 15 km southeast of Gibara, off the awfully deteriorated road between Floro Pérez and Rafael Freyre (Santa Lucía).

GUARDALAVACA AND VICINITY

Guardalavaca (the name means "Watch the Cow") is a pocket-size resort about 70 km north-east of Holguín boasting a gorgeous beach. It has been hyped as Cuba's second-largest resort, but don't be misled. It's small-fry and may come as a disappointment to tourists who are expecting more (many buildings lay in ruins at last visit). Guardalavaca consisted at press time of five hotels, a fistful of small restaurants, a couple of artisans' shops, a disco, two car rental agencies, a grocery, and two fabulous beaches: the main beach—**Playa Mayor**—and, farther east, the narrower, 400-meter-long **Playa Las Brisas,** backed by a beautiful walkway. Between the two beaches is a series of smaller beaches separated by coral outcrops.

The resort is popular for scuba diving and snorkeling but is a tourists-only affair, virtually off-limits to Cubans.

Accommodations
All the hotels are run by Cubanacán.

If you're into self-catering, consider the **Villas Cabañas,** at the west end of Guardalavaca, inland of the beach. It offers modest bungalows with kitchenettes. A thatched restaurant serves meals. Rates were US$25 s/d.

Club Amigo Guardalavaca, tel. (24) 3-0121, fax (24) 30221, e-mail: booking@hguard.gvc.cyt.cu, of prefab concrete 100 yards inland from the beach, has 234 pleasantly appointed, re-cently refurbished a/c rooms with satellite TVs, and radios, telephone, safe deposit boxes, refrigerators, and 24-hour room service. Activity revolves around a huge swimming pool with a water slide and net ball, and there's tennis, volleyball, a game room, and entertainment. All-inclusive rates were US$68 s, US$110 d low season, US$78 s, US$130 d high season.

The **Club Amigo Atlántico,** tel. (24) 3-0180, fax (24) 3-0200, is similar, though a tad more upscale, with the advantage of a beachfront setting. Its 232 rooms and one suite all have a/c, TVs, telephones, and terraces. Not all have ocean views. The hotel features a game room beside the large swimming pool, car rental, a boutique, tourist bureau, and water sports. All-inclusive rates were US$78 s, US$136 d standard; US$80 s, US$80 s, US$140 d superior; US$82 s, US$142 d ocean view.

More impressive is **Villas Turnik,** tel. (24) 3-0195, fax (24) 3-0200, of striking contemporary design. It has 136 a/c rooms in gracious two-story villas around a swimming pool set in landscaped grounds. Each has a terrace, color TV, and telephone. There's a *ranchita* bar and an airy restaurant. All-inclusive rates were US$77 s, US$122 d low season, US$86 s, US$142 d high season.

The prize goes to the sleek **Las Brisas Club Resort & Villa,** tel. (24) 3-0218, fax (24) 3-0162, operated in conjunction with Canada's Transat Inc. This four-star resort, with 225 rooms, two

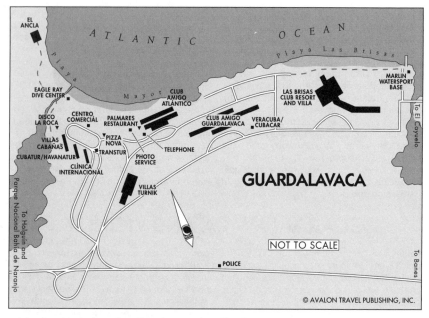

mini-suites, four junior suites, three bars, and a water sports center, is one of Cuba's more handsome hotels and is divided into the new villa complex and slightly older hotel complex, each with its own fabulous pool. The decor is marvelous. It also offers villas designed in tasteful neocolonial fashion, with the same facilities as rooms, plus minibars and hair driers and exquisite contemporary furnishings. It is fronted by its own virtually private section of beach and has two large pools, each with swim-up bar in the middle. It also has a poolside entertainment center plus a choice of restaurants—including an Italian restaurant, an open-air *ranchón* grill, and a cappuccino café. Windsurfing, kayaking, sailing, waterskiing, and beach and pool volleyball are offered, and there are two night-club tennis courts. The resort has a Kid's Kamp for children. All-inclusive per person rates were US$75 hotel, US$80 villa, low season; US$85 hotel, US$90 villa, high season. A single supplement costs US$25. Rates for mini-suites were US$170 d hotel low season, US$190 high season; US$190 villa low season, US$210 high season.

Food

The hotels serve overpriced, uninspired meals, although Las Brisas comes close to international standard.

El Cayuelo, on Carreteras de Banes, **El Patio,** and **El Ancla** specialize in seafood. The latter sits atop a coral outcrop at the west end of the main beach and serves fish dishes for US$6 and up (lobster costs US$17). **Pizza Nova** offers penne and fettuccine from US$6 and basic pizzas from US$5 (each extra item costs US$1, and shrimp adds US$4). The elegant bodega-style **Palmares Restaurant** serves pork, seafood, and *criollo* dishes from US$5. It's open noon-midnight.

You can buy **ice cream** from the *heladería* and snack bar opposite the Hotel Guardalavaca. You can buy groceries in the **Centro Comercial.**

Entertainment and Sports

The hotels all have nightly *animaciones* (cabarets) performed by the staff. You have to applaud the entertainers who put their all into getting the patrons in a dancing mood. All the hotel cabarets are followed by discos. *The* place to be, however, is **Disco La Roca,** tel. (24) 3-0167, at the west end of Guardalavaca. Its large dance floor is open on two sides, with seating beneath the stars and a terrace overlooking the beach. It gets full on weekends, when locals and tourists mingle. It has cabaret and karaoke (but no *espectáculo*). Entrance costs US$2.

The **Eros Nocturno** nightclub, atop the Centro Comercial, has an open-air disco-cabaret nightly except Wednesday, including a *cabaret espectáculo* (the "Lady Delmis Show"). Entrance costs US$2, including a beer.

A folkloric cabaret is hosted at the nearby aquarium at Bahía de Naranja (see below). **La Dolce Vita** disco, in the Las Brisas hotel, is ritzy but used mostly by the hotel guests. Tour agencies offer nocturnal excursions to the Cabaret Nocturno in Holguín.

Horseback riding is offered at stables at Playa Esmeralda (see below). You can book horseback rides at any of the hotels. The **Tennis Club Las Brisas** charges US$5 for use of its night-lit courts.

Marlin Watersport Base, on the jetty at the east end of Playa Las Brisas, offers banana boat rides (US$5 for 10 minutes), waterskiing (US$15 for 15 minutes), jet ski rental (US$15 for 15 minutes), snorkeling (US$8 for one hour), and deep-sea fishing (US$275 for five hours, up to three people). You can also rent small Hobie Cats (US$15 per hour).

Guardalavaca is renowned for its **scuba diving,** especially for its riot of colorful sponges (among the largest found anywhere in the Caribbean), deepwater gorgonians, and swordfish and barracudas slicing along an abrupt cliff known as "The Jump." Another exciting spot is Grouper Canyon, a fissure sheltering groupers. Marlin Watersport Base charges US$35 for one dive, US$45 per night dive, and US$365 for a certification course. Gear rental costs US$5 extra. **Eagle Ray Dive Center,** tel. (24) 33-6702, fax (24) 30-6323, at the west end of Playa Mayor, has similar prices.

Services
The post office and DHL Worldwide Express service are in the Las Brisas. You can make international calls from any hotel.

There's a Banco Financiero Internacional in the Centro Comercial, and a *Clínica Internacional,* tel. (24) 3-0312, fax (24) 3-0291, on the south side of the roundabout; the latter charges US$25 per consultation and has a doctor and nurse on 24-hour call.

Asistur, tel. (24) 3-0148, in the Centro Comercial, offers legal, financial, and other emergency assistance for tourists. It's open Mon.-Fri. 8:30 a.m.-5 p.m. and Saturday 8:30 a.m.-noon.

A Photo Service store next to the Palmares Restaurant sells batteries and film.

The Cupet gas station is one km west of town on the main road to Holguín.

Getting There and Away
Guardalavaca has no airport. Flights arrive at Holguín, where transfers are offered (see Getting There under Holguín, above). Buses operate from Holguín and Banes and drop off and depart opposite Villas Turnik. A taxi from Holguín will cost about US$40 one-way.

Private yachters can anchor at Marlin Base Naútica, (see Bahía de Naranjo, below).

Transtur, tel. (24) 3-0134, has a car rental office beside the traffic circle at the west end. **Cubacar** has an office between the Hotel Guardalavaca and Club Resort Las Brisas; it rents a range of Japanese sedans and jeeps.

All the hotels have tour agencies that offer excursions. Their offices are on the south side of the roundabout, at the west end of Guardalavaca, including **Cubatur,** tel. (24) 3-0170, and **Tours & Travel,** tel. (24) 46-8091. **Veracuba** has an office east of Club Amigo Guardalavaca. **Rumbos,** tel. (24) 3-0172, also offers tours.

Getting Around
You can walk everywhere, although horse-drawn buggies run up and down the beachfront road (US$2 maximum). **Bicycles** can be rented at the Las Brisas. You can rent Suzuki **scooters** at most hotels from **Cubasol** (US$7 one hour, US$12 two hours, US$25 per day, US$100 per week).

For **Taxi OK** call (24) 3-0124.

PARQUE NACIONAL BAHÍA DE NARANJO

This huge flask-shaped bay is about five km west of Guardalavaca. The entire 400-hectare *estero* is a national park fringed by mangroves. A fish hatchery is located here. Nonetheless, the bay and the beaches that extend to either side of its mouth are at the forefront of resort development locally, centered on sugar-fine **Playa Esmeralda,** extending east of the mouth of the bay, three km west of Guardalavaca and reached by a separate road from the main highway. The powdery white sand beach is spectacular. All the hotels are owned by Gaviota.

The road to Playa Esmeralda leads past a turnoff to the left pointing the way to **Rancho Mongo,** where the eclectic attractions include a small zoo, cactus garden, medicinal garden, collection of caged birds, and typical *campesino* buildings.

The bay's eastern headland is protected as **Reserva Ecológica Las Guanas,** an ecological preserve with trails that lead to archaeological sites and the **Cueva Ciboney,** a cave with petroglyphs. An interpretive center at the entrance offers excellent introductions to the flora and fauna. A 3-D model shows the various trails and *miradors* that provide a bird's-eye view.

Rancho Naranjo is an equestrian center opposite the entrance to the Sol Club Río de Luna.

Acuario Cayo Naranjo

This dolphinarium, tel. (24) 3-0132, fax (24) 3-0126, occupies a lagoon at the north end of the tiny island of **Cayo Naranjo.** Here sea lions and dolphins perform acrobatics at noon (US$12), including entrance and dolphin show; plus US$1 for cameras, US$3 for videos). Visitors can even swim with the dolphins (US$30). A restaurant serves seafood.

All the hotels in Guardalavaca offer excursions. Boats leave for the aquarium on a regular basis from both Rancho Mongo and Marlin Base Naútica.

Accommodations and Food

Marlin Base Naútica rents a two-room bungalow—**Villa Birancito**—on Cayo Naranjo, adjacent to the dolphinarium. It sleeps four people. Rates were US$65 including breakfast and a

swim with the dolphins. Rancho Mongo also offers a two-room villa, **Casa de Mongo Viña,** for US$20. You can book either through the marina: tel. (24) 3-0132, fax (24) 3-0126.

Spain's Sol Meliá hotel chain manages three all-inclusive Gaviota properties on Playa Esmeralda. The hotels adjoin one another and share certain facilities plus similarly lively tropical decor.

The four-star **Sol Rìo de Mares,** Playa Esmeralda, Carretera Guardalavaca, tel. (24) 3-0060, fax (24) 3-0035, e-mail: sol.riomares@ mares.solmelia.cma.net, website: www.solmelia. es, has 238 a/c rooms, including two for handicapped guests, all with satellite TV, direct-dial phone, minibar, and security box. A full complement of services includes an Italian restaurant, disco, gym, tennis court, and water sports, including a sailing school and scuba diving. All-inclusive rates were US$100 s, US$130 d.

Sharing the beach is a more upscale sister property, the **Sol Río del Luna,** tel. (24) 3-0030, fax (24) 3-0035, e-mail: solclub.riluna@luna. solmelia.cma.net, website: www.solmelia.es, with 204 a/c rooms and eight suites in four blocks set in beautifully landscaped grounds. The spacious rooms are nicely appointed, with satellite TV, telephones, and other modern conveniences, including gym, sauna, mini-golf, and the full array of resort activities and water sports. All-inclusive rates were US$165 s, US$220 d low season.

Better yet is the five-star **Meliá Río de Oro,** Playa Esmeralda, Carretera Guardalavaca, tel. (24) 3-0090, fax (24) 3-0095, e-mail:melia.rioro @oro.solmelia.cma.net, www.solmelia.es, an exquisite, modern all-inclusive property with 300 junior suites in two-story villa units. Decor is a blaze of tropical pastels. It also offers deluxe garden villas. All-inclusive rates were US$216 s, US$260 d low season, US$270 s, US$320 d high season; US$750 for garden villas.

The hotels sell a day pass (good for the evening, too) for US$50, which includes all you can drink or eat and use of all the facilities.

Rancho Mongo serves *criollo* meals in its thatched restaurant.

Getting There

The **Marline Base Naútica,** tel. (24) 3-0132, fax (24) 3-0126, is a small and basic marina on the south shore of the bay. A local Guarda Frontera provides clearance for private boaters (he or she can also call a taxi if you want to tour). Electricity and gasoline are available.

RAFAEL FREYRE AND VICINITY

This ungainly town, 23 km east of Gibara, is dominated by the Rafael Freyre sugar *central* (sugarcane processing factory). From Holguín, route 6-241 dips and rises through cattle country punctuated by steep-faced conical limestone formations called *mogotes.* The photogenic setting is made more so by the 1882 30-inch gauge Baldwin steam locomotive that works the Central Rafael Freyre and by larger antique steam trains that haul cane through this stupendous mountain terrain. Steam train enthusiasts flock from around the world to gawk and gasp at the puffing billies still doing the work they were built for a century ago.

The town, also known as Santa Lucía (not to be confused with the resort of that name in Camagüey), lies a few km inland of **Bahía de Bariay.** It is thought that the Genoese navigator first set foot in Cuba in the small bay, which is enshrined in **Parque Nacional Bahía Bariay,** encompassing over 30 beaches, numerous cays, and the low Grupo de Maniabon mountains (see below). If you zigzag through town and go past the *central,* the road north will take you to the bay and aptly named **Playa Blanca,** 600 yards beyond which a commemorative plaque to Columbus marks the site thought to be that of the explorer's first landing with his three caravels from Hispaniola. There are two monuments, one on each side of the bay. The first is near the end of the road to Playa Blanca and simply declares this the "site of the first landing of Christopher Columbus in Cuba." The second, more recent, is reached by turning north at Frey Benito, four km west of Rafael Freyre. The Rafael Freyre-Frey Benito road continues west in deplorably deteriorated state, but the quintessentially Cuban scenery is spectacular.

Another splendid beach, **Playa Pesquero,** extends east of Bahía de Bariay and is accessed from the Guardalavaca road, 10 km east of Rafael Freyre. The road leads north three km to this beautiful white sand beach with a wide cove at its westernmost end. Playa Pesquero is being developed for tourism. The first luxury hotel has already opened, and more are in the pipeline.

Steam Train Aventures

Gaviota Tours, tel. (24) 3-0139, fax (24) 3-0160, at Playa Esmeralda, and **Cubanacán,** tel. (24) 3-0114, fax (24) 3-0003, in Guardalavaca, offer one-hour steam-train excursions through the Grupo de Manabion (see below) using a restored 1920 Baldwin pulling renovated carriages for US$36 per person.

Far more fun is to rent your own train (US$100 per hour, two-hour minimum, including staff). Contact Rodolfo Betancourt, the Chief of Transport at Central Rafael Freyre, tel. (24) 2-0119 or 2-0300 ext. 275. You can either ride the train or—far more fun if your main purpose is to photograph the train—drive your own car, careening down rough-as-hell country lanes to get ahead of the train for more advantageous positions. Rodolfo will travel with you with a walkie-talkie to communicate with the train engineer so you can position the train as you wish. A 4WD is recommended. Allow at least two hours.

Accommodations

The impecunious can stay in Rafael Freyre at the basic **Motel Guabanajay,** which has rooms for 12 and 25 pesos. **Cabaret Guabanajay,** next door, provides entertainment and booze.

At Playa Blanca, the 36-room **Cubanacán Don Lino,** tel. (24) 3-0259, fax (24) 3-0427, looks over a small easterly extension of the main beach. Each a/c room has either one king-size or two double beds, a terrace, telephone, satellite TV, and ceiling fan. There's a freshwater pool and attractive *ranchón* restaurant, a gift shop, and recreational facilities. Rates were US$25 s, US$35 d, US$42 t low season.

MINAG (Ministerio de Agricultura) has a concrete cabana complex at Playa Blanca proper. Three six-person cabins are reserved for tourists: US$10 per person. There's a basic restaurant.

At Playa Pesquero, **LTI Costa Verde Beach,** LTI International Hotels, Parsevalstr. 79, D-40468 Düsseldorf, tel. (0211) 941707, fax (0211) 9417430, e-mail: sales@lti.de, website: www.lti.de, is a four-star all-inclusive property with 307 rooms and two suites, all with satellite TV, phone, security box, and patio or balcony. Facilities include three restaurants, four bars, three

STILL PUFFING AWAY

Cuba maintains about 200 operating steam trains, projecting yet another surreal image of an island lost in time—what railroad expert Adolf Hungry Wolf calls a "twilight zone in the world of railroading." Most of these puffing treasures date from the 1920s (the first Cuban railway was built by the British in 1837) and are still capable of thundering down the slim tracks with a full load of sugarcane. Almost all are of U.S. progeny—the largest and most varied collection of early-1900s U.S. motive power in the world—and operate on sugar estates, with a concentration around Guardalavaca. The oldest train in operation is a coal-burning Baldwin 0-4-2T at the Villena sugar mill built by Baldwin in 1878 (the oldest train in Cuba is La Junta, from 1843, displayed in the lobby of Havana's Estación Central); the largest are two Baldwin 2-8-2 Mikados—Dona Bella (1935) and Dona Flor (1925)—that haul cane at Central Ifrain Alfonso, south of Santa Clara. The trains are kept going because the sugar mills operate only four to five months a year, providing plenty of time to overhaul the engines and keep them in good repair so as to extract a few more thousand miles of hard labor.

Cuba is actively restoring many of its jaded jewels and sprucing them up for passenger and tourist endeavors. Rebuilding is centered on the Ferrocarriles de Cuba's workshop at Sagua la Grande. As many as 100 vintage U.S. steam locomotives may be introduced for passenger service in coming years. And the Cubans were planning to build *new* steam locomotives, with production planned to begin in 2001.

Railroading crews are exceptionally friendly and visitors are often welcomed aboard the engineer's cockpit.

Canadian Caboose Press, Box 844, Skookumchuck, BC V0B 2EO, Canada, cellular tel. (250) 342-1421, website: www.cal.shaw.wave.ca/~hfinklem/GoodMed, publishes the free *Cuba Travel & Steam Newsletter,* and sells videos of Cuban steam train plus *Trains of Cuba,* a thorough guidebook with

maps, rosters, and details on individual steam trains islandwide. I also recommend Adolf Hungry Wolf's *Letters From Cuba* regaling tales of his time chasing steam trains in Cuba, available from www.cubabooks.com.

In the U.S., the **Cuba Steam Center USA,** Bellaire Roundhouse, 5314 Bellaire Blvd. Bellaire, TX 77401, tel. (713) 667-7762, e-mail: RoundBell@aol.com, is a handy resource. Also check out the following website: www.ds.dial. pipex.com/steam/americas.htm.

tennis courts, and volleyball, gym, boutique, entertainment and water sports. All-inclusive rates were about US$120 s, US$140 d.

At press time, Jamaica's SuperClubs chain, in North America, tel. (800) 467-8737; in the U.K., tel. (01749) 677200, e-mail: info@superclubs .com, website; www.superclubs.com, was building the four-star, 480-room **Breezes Costa Verde,** an all-inclusive that will accept families, singles, and couples.

GRUPO DE MANIABON

This dramatic upland region lies between Guardalavaca and Banes. Route 6-241 cuts through the region, leading you through quintessentially Cuban scenery, with tobacco fields plowed by oxen in the lee of rolling hills. The landscape is dominated by great rounded outcrops, with tousled royal palms, girthy silk-cotton trees, and bright red flamboyants rising over the pastures. The *bohios* here are hedged by neatly trimmed rows of cactus.

In the midst of the valley, on a hilltop seven km east of Guardalavaca, is the **Museo Chorro de Maíta**, on the site of the largest aboriginal burial site thus far discovered in the Caribbean (almost 200 skeletons have been unearthed). It is thought that a large Indian village called Bani occupied the site. The site is a national monument. A gallery surrounds the burial ground within a building where the skeletons lie with arms crossed over chests in peaceful repose. A life-size model Indian village has been recreated. Open Tues.-Sat. 9 a.m.-5 p.m. and Sunday 9 a.m.-1 p.m.; US$2.

The valleys are farmed with sugarcane and form the setting for one of the finest steam train photography locales in the world. The **Barijay curve** is renowned spot to capture on film one of the trains that work the line to Central Rafael Freyre. You'll absolutely need a guide, as you're sure to get lost belting down the country lane system in your car in pursuit of the elusive railway line. The train normally arrives at the Barijay curve just after dusk, but you can rent your own steam train for your own photo shoot!

BANES

Banes, 20 km southeast of Guardalavaca, is a sleepy provincial town (pop. 95,000) with a colonial core of mostly wooden houses surrounded by modern, concrete apartment blocks.

For much of this century, the town was run by the United Fruit Company, which owned virtually all the land in the region and had a massive sugar mill called Boston (since renamed Nicaragua) five km south of town. Jamaicans were imported to work the fields, and there are still a few locals who speak English and attempt to maintain their ancestors' traditions.

Fulgencio Batista was born here in 1901. His future archenemies, Fidel and Raúl Castro, were born nearby at Birán. As youths, the brothers would come into town in a red convertible to party at the American Club. Here, on 12 October 1948, Fidel married Mirta Diaz-Balart, daughter of the wealthy mayor of Banes.

(Fidel gave little time to his wife, and the marriage dissolved five years later.) Mirta's brother, Rafael, headed Batista's youth organization and in 1950 arranged a meeting for the young Fidel—already a well-known political activist—with Batista at the latter's sumptuous estate outside Havana. Rafael would later be named Batista's Minister of the Interior, in charge of the secret police (he fled Cuba after the Revolution; his son keeps the right-wing flame burning as a U.S. congressman from Florida).

The U.S. spy-plane shot down during the Cuban Missile Crisis was felled near here.

The only noteworthy site in town is the **Museo Indocubano** (Museum of Indian Civilization), on Calle General Marrero #305, tel. (24) 8-2487. It exhibits a collection of shells, pottery, tools, carvings, statuary, and other artifacts and amazingly sophisticated jewelry, most important a small gold idol (thought to date from the 13th century and the first gold piece ever discovered in Cuba) wearing a feather headdress. There are also murals depicting the Indians and their ruin. Open Tues.-Sat. noon-6 p.m. and Sunday 2-6 p.m. Entrance costs US$1.

The oblong plaza one block east of the museum has an eclectic range of intriguing buildings, most notably the art deco church—**Iglesia de Nuestra Señora de la Caridad**—where Fidel Castro got married.

You can follow the main road east from Banes along a rolling plateau planted in sugar. At the end is a handsome beach—**Playa Puerto Rico**—reached by following the dirt road to the left along the ugly coral shore.

Accommodation and Food
The **Motel El Oasis**, tel. (24) 3447, at the entrance to Banes, has modest cabanas in nice grounds (18 pesos) and a restaurant and bar popular with locals.

Getting There
Buses operate between Holguín and Banes, where the bus terminal is at the east end of Calle Los Angeles. Bus no. 617 runs to Banes from Havana (40 pesos), and another afternoon bus goes to Holguín in time for the train to Havana.

HOLGUÍN TO GUANTÁNAMO PROVINCE

FINCA MANACAS

Fidel Castro's birthplace was at Finca Manacas, at **Birán,** below the western foothills of the Altiplanici de Nipe, 60 km southeast of Holguín. Fidel was born on 13 August 1926 in a two-story house on wooden pilings, with a cattle barn underneath. The property also contained a slaughterhouse, repair shop, store, bakery, and other facilities. Castro likes to claim that it was a simple property: "The house was made of wood. No mortar, cement or bricks," he told Brazilian theologian Frey Beto in *Fidel: My Early Years.* In truth it's a substantial house—clearly the home of a well-to-do man. The handsome ocher-and-blue *finca* is hidden amid a copse and looks out over a large lake to the west.

Castro's father, Ángel, began leasing land from the United Fruit Company in 1910, grew sugarcane to sell to the mills, and grew wealthy. His property grew to a 26,000-acre domain. Eventually, Fidel's father acquired forests and a sawmill in Pinares as well as a small nickel mine. He even owned the village store and was the most important man in the region. Fidel, however, has worked to downplay his social privilege and prefers to exaggerate the simplicity of his background. Perhaps for this reason, the house is not marked on tourist maps or otherwise promoted. It is surrounded by barbed-wire fencing, and the gates are padlocked.

To visit the *finca,* you must request a permit from the Communist Party headquarters, on the Plaza de la Revolución in Holguín, tel. (24) 42-2224. However, you can drive up and peer through the gate, where a guard will eye you warily. Note the graves of Castro's parents, Ángel and Lina, to the right.

From Holguín, take the Cueto road (6-123). Turn south five km west of Cueto to Marcané. Turn east just beyond the Central Loynaz Hechevarría. The community of Birán is seven km farther, and Finca Las Manacas is two km to the north. The roads hereabouts were abysmally potholed at last visit.

MAYARÍ ABAJO

This medium-size town is 80 km east of Holguín, on the banks of the Río Mayarí. It lies in the midst of a fertile region encompassing the Bay of Nipes, at 50 square miles the largest pocket bay

Fidel Castro's birthplace in Finca Manacas, 13 August 1926

in Cuba (it was here, according to legend, that in 1608 three fishermen found the wooden statue of the Virgin of Charity that now resides in the basilica at El Cobre, in Santiago Province.) The main coast road bypasses Mayarí, which has a **Cupet gas station.**

The town, six km inland from the bay, was the subject of José Yglesia's *In the Fist of the Revolution,* in which the author documents the changes wrought since the Revolution. At the time of Fidel Castro's birth at Birán, the town and surrounding region were in the hands of the United Fruit Company, which had carved out a "veritable private fiefdom." Says author Ted Szulc, "The Mayarí region. . . featured probably greater American presence and control than any other place in Cuba."

SIERRA CRISTAL

This mountain chain rises above the narrow coastal plain, climbing to the sharp-peaked **Pico de Cristal** (1,214 meters). The great mountainous bulk is deeply incised by rivers, the largest being the Río Mayarí. To the west of the valley is the soaring Altiplanice de Nipe, a flat-topped, steep-sided massif that was the playground for Fidel Castro as a youth.

About five km east from Mayarí, you'll pass a turnoff for the **Farallones de Seboruco,** a cavern system where indigenous Indian artifacts dating back 5,000 years have been found.

Integral Mountain Research Station
The Cuban Academy of Sciences has a scientific station at about 500 meters above sea level at Pinares de Mayarí. It was established in 1988 to research the mountain ecology and to evolve sustained development practices.

The mountain ecology is highly varied. Montane rainforest thrives adjacent to pine forest at these cool heights, where mists drift languidly through the branches. The mountains harbor endemic species, including orchids that have adapted to dry conditions by producing neither flower nor leaf in order to conserve life in their roots.

Accommodations and Food
In the heart of the majestic mountains, 20 km south of Mayarí, is **Pinares de Mayarí,** tel. (24)

5-3308, fax (24) 3-0126, an eco-resort operated by Gaviota. It has 10 rustic, wooden, red-tile-roofed one-, two- and three-bedroom cottages, plus 18 rooms of pinewood with private bathrooms (some with hot water). The recently renovated log cabins were originally built for Cuba's elite. There's an exercise room, steam baths, swimming pool, basketball, tennis, and even a baseball diamond. *Criollo* cuisine is served in the large open dining room. Rates were US$25 s, US$36 d low season, US$30 s, US$40 d high season.

Hiking and Horseback Rides
Horseback rides are available, and you can hire guides for hikes to El Gulyabo waterfall. You'll pass through four distinct ecological environments, from temperate forest to mountain rainforest. Signed stations point out features of the region.

Getting There
It's a scenic drive along a dirt road from Mayarí.

Tour companies in Guardalavaca offer day excursions to Pinares.

CAYO SAETÍA

This 42-square-km cay is an almost virgin island with white sand beaches as private as your innermost thoughts. It is separated from the mainland by a hair's-breadth waterway and forms the easternmost side of the entrance to the Bahía de Nipes. It is ecologically important, with a patchwork of ecosystems ranging from mangrove swamps to evergreen forests harboring many endangered species, including wild boar *(jabali),* plus exotic animals—ostrich, zebra, two types of antelope, and water buffalo—imported for the hunting pleasure of top communist officials, for whom Cayo Saetía was until recent years a private vacation spot. Fortunately it now caters to people with a greater respect for wildlife. Antelope are commonly seen as you drive the unpaved road to the hotel. Entrance costs US$15.

One-hour jeep safaris (US$9) and horseback riding (US$6 per hour) are available, as is a one-hour yacht excursion (US$5).

Accommodations

The **Villa Cayo Saetía,** tel. (24) 4-2350, fax (24) 3-0126, on the north side of the island, has seven handsome yet rustic cabanas amid lawns with bougainvillea and fruit trees. Rooms have telephones, TVs, and refrigerators. The hotel plays on the wildlife theme. The eyes of animals that wandered between crosshairs glower eerily as you pass by. There's a handsome bar and restaurant, where the meals are said to be good. Rates were US$35 s, US$45 standard, low season (US$10 more respectively for superior rooms, and US$30 for suites); US$40 s, US$50 d standard, US$55 s, US$75 d superior, US$75 s, US$90 d suite, high season.

Getting There and Away

If driving, note that many maps show a nonexistent road direct from the Carretera Costa Norte to Cayo Saetía. The real road leads to **Felton,** with a turnoff (unmarked) to the right for Cayo Saetía.

Cayo Saetía is 20 minutes by helicopter from Guardalavaca (90 minutes by jeep); contact Gaviota in Guardalavaca, tel. (24) 3-0139, fax (24) 3-0160. Tourist hotels in Santiago and elsewhere also offer excursions to Cayo Saetía, as does Havanatur.

Private boats can berth at the marina, on the southern side of the promontory at Saetía.

MAYARÍ TO MOA

Route 6-123 parallels the shore and leads past a series of port towns that rely on the nickel and mineral-ore industries. The first of these is the important ore-processing town of **Nicaro,** 12 km east of Mayarí. There's no reason to digress the four km from the coast road to visit this ugly place.

Well worth the visit, however, is **Playa Corinthia,** a seemingly endless beach of purest white sand shelving into turquoise shallows. There's nothing here—making it a perfect reclusive escape. The beach is backed by fir trees and perfect for camping. You can hear the muffled surf breaking on the reef 400 meters offshore. The beach is about eight km from the coast road, 25 km east of Mayarí.

Farther east the landscape takes an abrupt turn. The shore is lined with mangroves, and the beaches are, with rare exception, a grim disappointment. The climate becomes drier, and the farther east you go, the more scrub takes over until soon you are passing barren hills scarred by years of human abuse.

MOA

Tall chimneys belching out smoke—black, yellow, and white—announce your arrival at the coastal town of Moa, the center of Cuba's metal-ore industry. The town is smothered with red dust from the nearby nickel-ore processing plants that settles over the *repartos* (neighborhoods) of ugly prefab concrete housing. It has been claimed (probably in jest) that Cuban engineers would rather sacrifice their careers than work here.

The first mines were set up by U.S. companies before the Revolution. They were nationalized, of course, following the rancorous relations with Washington. The Soviets stepped in and hand-in-hand with the Cuban government hammered and sickled the dour landscape into a grotesque wasteland.

A few miles east of Moa, you'll pass a huge ore processing plant—**Empresa Comandante Ernesto Che Guevara** (whose statue stands outside the gates). The plant was financed by the Soviet Union. Today it is managed by the Sherritt Corporation of Canada, and most of the ore heads to Canada. Metallic dust floats over the road and has settled on everything. You can taste it in your mouth. You'll pass leaking pipes along the roadside hissing and bubbling who-knows-what noxious stews from every joint. The landscape looks like the Somme, and, like the Somme, seems to speak only of horror and suffering. Huge pestilential lagoons of industrial waste lie within a stone's throw of the road. Drowned trees rise from them like witches' crooked fingers. Blood-red rivers pour effluents into a sea of deepest blue. Ugh. Try not to notice the children swimming and fishing in the polluted bay.

This is the only place in Cuba where Photography Is Prohibited signs are posted, encompassing the entire region, suggesting that the Cuban government is embarrassed by this blight.

Accommodations and Services

If you must stay, Islazul's modern, Soviet-style hilltop **Hotel Miraflores,** tel. (24) 6-6103, fax (24) 6-6332, has 140 uninspired and modestly furnished rooms, plus a swimming pool, restaurant, and disco (Thurs.-Sun.), plus Havanautos car rental. Rates were US$20 s, US$27 d low season, US$23 s, US$30 d high season.

Cubacel, in the Hotel Miraflores, Suite 212, tel./fax (24) 8-8222, rents cellular phones and will hook up your own personal cellular. It's open Mon.-Fri. 8 a.m.-5 p.m. and Saturday 8 a.m.-noon. (See the Communications section in the On The Road chapter for costs and conditions.)

There's a **Cupet gas station** on the coast road, one km west of town, and a **Banco de Crédito y Comercio** in the town center.

Getting There

Bus no. 655 departs Havana's main bus terminal daily at about 5:10 p.m. You can also take the bus that departs Havana for Baracoa Fri.-Sun at 10:25 a.m.

Cubana flies from Havana twice weekly (US$80 one-way) to Moa's **Orestes Acosta Airport,** tel. (24) 6-4409, three km east of town.

GRANMA
INTRODUCTION

Granma takes up Cuba's southwest corner. Its economy is almost entirely based on sugar and rice production. The province has only two towns of size—Bayamo and Manzanillo—but abounds with sites of historical importance. Throughout Cuba's history, the region has been a hotbed of rebellion, beginning in 1512, when Hatuey, the local Indian chieftain, rebelled against Spain. The citizens of Bayamo were from the outset at the forefront of the drive for independence, and the city, which became the capital of the provisional republic, is brimful of sites associated with the heady days when Cuba's *criollo* population fought to oust Spain. At La Demajagua, Carlos Céspedes freed his slaves and proclaimed Cuba's independence. And Dos Ríos, in the northeast of the province, is the site where José Martí chose martyrdom in battle in 1895.

The region also became the first battleground in the revolutionary efforts to topple the Batista regime, initiated on 26 July 1953, when two dozen of Castro's rebels attacked the Bayamo garrison in concert with an attack on the Moncada barracks in Santiago. Las Colorados is the site where Castro, Che Guevara, and 80 fellow revolutionaries came ashore in 1956 to set up their rebel army. (The province is named for the vessel—the *Granma*—in which the revolution-

aries traveled from Mexico; prior to 1976, when the province was created, the region was part of Oriente).

Steep trails lead to sites of importance during the revolutionary war in the forested mountains, where an enormous swath is protected within Sierra Maestra Grand National Park. You can even ascend the trail to Pico Turquino, Cuba's highest peak (1,974 meters), where there are staggering views south over the coast and north across the plains. Here in Parque Nacional Pico Turquino is La Plata, headquarters of the rebel army.

The north side of the Sierra Maestra has a moist microclimate and is lushly foliated. The south side, however, lies in a rain shadow; the foothills and narrow coastal plain is semidesert favored only by thorny scrub and cactus. The southern shore provides a superb scenic drive past rocky bays and deserted beaches, with the mountains escalating to cloud-draped crescendos.

Granma Province receives less rain and is hotter than elsewhere in Cuba. Perhaps only one-third of the moist fronts that sweep down upon Cuba from the north and east reach this area, having spilled much of their rain in the mountains. Hence, the lowlands are relative-

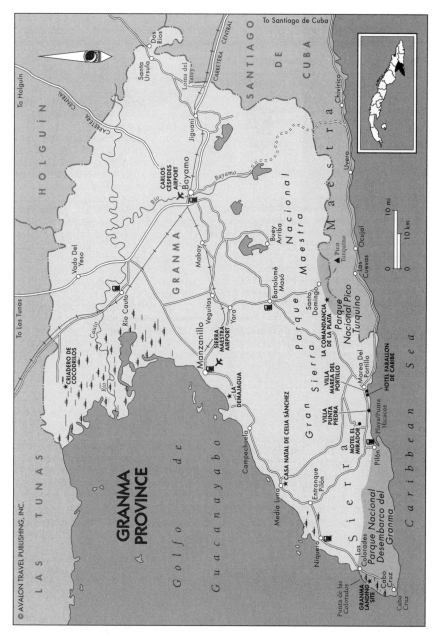

© AVALON TRAVEL PUBLISHING, INC.

GRANMA PROVINCE

SIGHTSEEING HIGHLIGHTS: GRANMA PROVINCE

Bayamo: Historically important town with a beautifully restored colonial plaza, and an exquisite church in the adjacent **Plaza de Himnos.**

La Comandancia de la Plata: Fidel Castro's headquarters in the Sierra Maestra are preserved. Reached via a dramatic drive and a hike along a forested mountain ridge. Off-limits at press time.

Niquero: Tumbledown coastal town with unique clapboard architecture.

Parque Nacional del Desambarcos del Granma: Rugged bush-covered terrain on the western slopes of the Sierra Maestra. Trails lead to caves, and to a *criadero de cocodrilos* (crocodile farm) amid the mangroves.

Pico Turquino: Cuba's highest peak, accessible by a steep, well-worn trail from the south coast (Santiago Province). Staggering views over Oriente. For the fit and hardy.

marshy floodplain that dominates the northern half of the province, feeding fields of rice and sugarcane.

The Lay of the Land

The province is neatly divided into plains (to the north) and mountains (to the south). Granma comprises the floodplain of the Río Cauto (Cuba's longest river), which empties into the Golfo de Guanacayabo.

The Sierra Maestra massif runs about 140 km west-east from the tip of the island (Cabo Cruz) to the city of Santiago de Cuba; at its widest, it has a girth of 48 km. The spine *(firme)* averages 1,500 meters elevation and rises to Pico Turquino (1,974 meters). It is forbidding terrain. From the north the mountains rise gradually, like a curve in a mathematical graph. From the south the steep scarp face edges right up along the coast, extending ruler-straight with only the narrowest littoral at its base. Cuba's highest peaks lie within five km of the shore.

The province tapers southwestward to an arrow-tipped point piercing the Caribbean Sea, with the Gulf of Guanacayabo to the north. In the extreme southwest, an intriguing feature is the series of wide marine terraces uplifted from the sea eons ago and rising like a giant's staircase up the eastern flank of the Sierra Maestra.

ly dry. Agriculture has the upper hand only because of irrigation from the many rivers flooding down from the mountains to form a

BAYAMO

Bayamo (pop. 130,000) lies at the center of the province, immediately east of the Río Bayamo, 130 km northwest of Santiago, and 95 km southwest of Holguín. The Carretera Central between Holguín and Santiago runs through Bayamo.

The town boasts a rich history. It was one of Cuba's first seven settlements (from here, Diego Velázquez set out to conquer the rest of Cuba) and the setting for remarkable events during the quest for independence from Spain. The city is called the "Birthplace of Cuban Nationality" and has earned the nickname "La Héroica." Much of the historic core is a national monument and is well worth a stop of a half-day or longer. The city was once famous for its troubadours and swains who composed songs to their Juliets: the women of Bayamo are said to be as pretty as any in Cuba, inspiring "La Bayamesa," the most famous Cuban love song.

The historic center has recently been spruced up and is appealing for its antique charm.

HISTORY

The first Spanish settlement (the second in Cuba) was founded in 1513 as Villa de San Salvador de Bayamo by Diego Velázquez on a site—near contemporary Yara—then known as Las Ovejas. It was later moved to its present site.

Almost immediately Diego Velázquez set to enslaving the aboriginal Indian population with cross and cutlass. Some Indians willingly subjugated themselves to Spanish rule. Others used guerrilla tactics to slay the strangers. The first Indian uprising occurred in 1528 and was ruthlessly suppressed. Soon barbaric treatment and

European epidemics had mowed the aborigines down like a scythe. Black slaves began to arrive from Africa, increasingly so as sugar was planted, giving rise to a flourishing slave trade through the port of Manzanillo.

Cradle of Independence

As early as 1528, local landowners were developing a nationalist spirit. That year they called for more local control over affairs. Spain's monopolistic restrictions on trade led to a flourishing illicit trade, and Bayameses from all walks of life were active in contraband. Manufactured goods were landed from Europe in exchange for hides, indigo, tobacco, and precious woods. The Río Cauto became the most active waterway for

smuggling in Cuba. When eight citizens were sentenced to death for smuggling in 1602, fellow citizens stormed the jail and freed them.

In 1604, a force led by French pirate Gilbert Girón raided Bayamo and took hostage the Bishop of Cuba, Fray Juan de las Cabezas Altimirano. Rather than pay the ransom, the citizen-army stormed the pirate camp, killing the bishop in the process. However, they also managed to kill Girón. His head was proudly displayed in the main square.

By the 19th century, the *criollo* whites sensed that their interests were no longer those of the Spanish colonialists. These were boom days for sugar in Cuba. The planters of southeastern Cuba, however, were isolated, relatively poor,

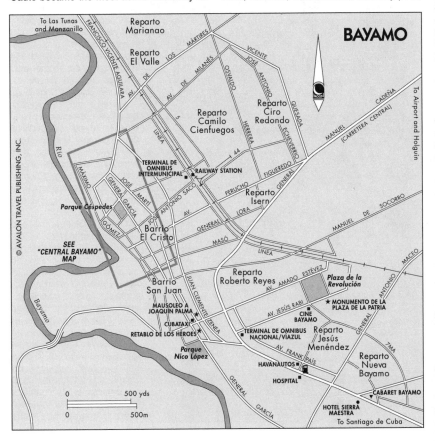

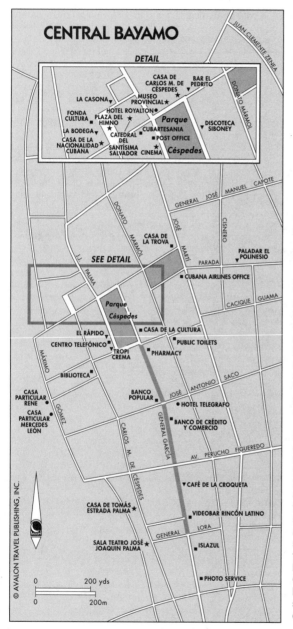

CENTRAL BAYAMO

and struggling, unable to compete with modern plantations inaugurated farther west. Bayamo's bourgeoisie were at the forefront of a swelling independence movement influenced by the American War of Independence and the revolutionary fervor then sweeping Europe.

The Cry of Yara

In 1867 Bayamo was a provincial town of perhaps 15,000 inhabitants, centered on Plaza Isabella II (today's Parque Céspedes). That year, following the coup that toppled Spain's Queen Isabella, the elite of Bayamo, led by Carlos Manuel Céspedes (1819-74), rose in revolt against the "motherland." As a young man, Céspedes, the owner of the La Demajagua sugar mill, south of Manzanillo, had been arrested several times for revolutionary activity. On 10 October 1868, he freed his slaves, enrolled them in an army, and, in an oration known as the *Grita de Yara* (Shout of Yara), declared an open revolt against Spain: independence or death.

Other nationalists rallied to his cause, formed a revolutionary junta, and in open defiance of Spanish authority, played in the parochial church the martial hymn that would eventually become the Cuban national anthem, "To the battle, Bayameses!" With a small force of about 150 men, Céspedes seized Bayamo from Spanish forces on October 20. The rebellion spread quickly. Soon Céspedes had 1,200 men in his command. The actions sparked the War of Independence that swept the Oriente and central Cuba, ravaging the region for 10 long years. When Spanish troops captured Céspedes' son Oscar and offered to spare his life in exchange for the father's surrender, the father claimed that all Cubans were his sons and that he could not trade their freedom for that of one person. His son was promptly shot.

In January 1869, as Céspedes' army of mulattos, freed slaves, and poor whites was attacking Holguín, Spanish troops were at Bayamo's doorstep. The rebellious citizens burned their beloved Bayamo to the ground rather than cede it to Spanish troops.

Alas, internal dissent arose among the revolutionary leadership. In 1873 Céspedes was removed from his position as President of the Republic in a meeting to which no one had bothered to invite him. He was cut down in a hail of bullets a year later—ambushed by the Spanish at San Lorenzo, where he had retreated to await a ship to take him to a life as a revolutionary in exile.

Spanish troops left Bayamo for a final time on 28 April 1898, when the city was captured by General Calixto García.

Modern Rebels

No more events of note occurred in Bayamo until 26 July 1953, when the army barracks were attacked by members of the 26th of July Movement. It was Castro's first open military challenge to Batista. At the time, there were no adequate communications between the military commands in Havana and Santiago, and the connecting highway from Holguín led through Bayamo. The attack on Bayamo was meant to secure the road and isolate the Oriente. However, the 21-man rebel unit, which attacked at 5:15 a.m., didn't realize that the gate in the fence, open during the day, was padlocked at night. They began firing on the barracks through the barbed-wire fence, and were cut down by machine-gun fire.

ORIENTATION

Bayamo is laid out atop the eastern bluff of the Río Bayamo, which flows in a deep ravine. The historic core sits immediately above the gorge.

The Carretera Central (Carretera Manuel Cadeña) from Holguín enters Bayamo from the northeast, skirts the town, then sweeps around to the southeast and becomes Avenida General Manuel Cedeño, a wide boulevard lined with azalea and oleander and which leads to Santiago. Avenida Perucho Figueredo leads off the Carretera Central and runs due west to Barrio El Cristo and Parque Céspedes, the historic heart of the city. Calle General Gárcia—the main commercial street and a pedestrian precinct—leads south from Parque Céspedes, paralleled by Calles José Martí and Juan Clemente Zeneo to the east. To the south they merge with the Carretera Central. To the north they merge into Avenida Francisco Vicente Aguilera, which begins one block north of Parque Céspedes and swings west over the ravine of the lily-choked Río Bayamo and leads to Manzanillo.

A grid-based modern neighborhood, built by microbrigades, extends east of the Carretera Central and centered on the Plaza de la Revolución, on Avenida Jesús Rabi.

SIGHTSEEING

Parque Céspedes

This beautiful square is where the townsfolk congregate to schmooze and flirt. The square is surrounded by important buildings with balconies festooned with black grillwork, and exterior walls made up of a limestone base with an upper level of tile work. Most of the buildings were recently restored and at last visit wore fresh coats of paint.

At its center is a granite column topped by a larger-than-life bronze statue of the "Father of Our Country," with motifs to each side. There's also a bust of the local patriot Perucho Figueredo, inscribed with the words of the *himno nacional* (national anthem) which he wrote:

Al combate corre Bayameses
Que la patria os contempla orgullosa
No temáis una muerte gloriosa
Que morir por la patria es vivir

To the battle, run, Bayamases
Let the fatherland proudly observe you
Do not fear a glorious death
To die for the fatherland is to live

Plaza del Himno, Parque Céspedes

Céspedes was born on 18 April 1819 in a handsome two-story dwelling on the north side of the square, at Calle Maceo #57, tel. (23) 42-3684. The house—**Casa de Carlos Manuel de Céspedes**—was one of only a fistful of houses to survive the fire of January 1869. Following independence in 1898, the building served as a post office. It was opened as a museum in 1968, on the anniversary of the Declaration of Independence. Downstairs are letters, photographs, and maps tracing the history of Bayamo and of Céspedes' life, plus his gleaming ceremonial sword. The ornately decorated upstairs bedrooms are full of his mahogany furniture, including a piano and a huge brass bed with headboard and footboard painted in Italianate and Moorish scenes. The law books that filled his study are still there, as is the printing press on which Céspedes published his *Cubana Libre,* the first independent newspaper in Cuba. Open Tues.-Fri. 9 a.m.-5 p.m., Saturday 9 a.m.-2 p.m. and 8-10 p.m., and Sunday 9 a.m.-1 p.m. Entrance costs US$1.

Next door is the **Museo Provincial,** on Calle Maceo #58, tel. (23) 42-4125, in a house where was born Manuel Muñoz Cedeño, composer of the *himno nacional,* "La Bayamesa." There are many exhibits from the colonial era, including the original score for the national anthem and eclectic miscellany. Open Tues.-Sat. 8 a.m.-6 p.m. and Sunday 9 a.m.-1 p.m.; US$1.

On the east side is the house (now the **Poder Popular**) where, as president of the newly founded republic, Céspedes announced the abolition of slavery. Next to it is the **Casa de la Cultura.**

Plaza del Himno

Parque Céspedes opens to the northwest onto this charming plaza, dominated by the small **Catedral del Santísima Salvador,** also known as the Parroquial Mayor. The revolutionary national anthem was sung for the first time in the cathedral (by a choir of 12 women) during Corpus Christi celebrations on 11 June 1868, with the dumbfounded colonial governor in attendance. Its most admirable feature is the beautiful mural of Céspedes and the Bayamesas above the altar. The ocher-colored church occupies the site of the original church, built in 1516, rebuilt in 1733, and rebuilt again following the fire of 1869. Its beautiful interior of stone and wood was lovingly restored in the 1970s, when it was declared a national monument. The entire structure was restored again in 1999, when a new roof was laid.

On the north side of the cathedral is a separate chapel—**Capilla de la Dolorosa**—which dates back to 1630 and miraculously survived the fire. It is small and simple but with a *mudéjar* ceiling, a figure of Christ (now in a glass case), and a baroque altarpiece of gilt and laminated wood. The original flag, sewn by Céspedes' wife, is preserved here.

The tiny square also contains the **Casa de la Nacionalidad Cubana,** a quaint colonial building now housing the town historian's office. It is not open to the public, but the staff is eager to answer questions.

At Christmas, check out the house at Calle #116, on the south side of the plaza, for its astonishing nativity scene taking up the entire front room. The doors are left open, and all comers are welcome.

Calle Céspedes
This narrow street leads south from Plaza del Himno. It has several buildings of note, including, on the block south of Avenida Figueredo, the house where in 1835 was born Tomás Estrada Palma, the first president of Cuba following independence. It's not marked (he is considered a puppet of Washington), and houses an art gallery—the **Casa de las Artistas.**

The ocher-colored **Sala Teatro José Joaquín Palma** is also here. It is classically Spanish, with an overhanging balcony.

Iglesia de San Juan Evangelista
This ruined church, at the foot of Calle Martí and Calle Amado Éstevez, was destroyed in the 1869 fire, though the bell tower (complete with bell) remains. Also here, immediately to the south, is the **Retablo de los Héroes,** portraying local patriots in stone. Carlos Manuel Céspedes is there in bas-relief. So, too, are revolutionary heroine Celia Sánchez and Frank País.

Immediately to the south is **Parque Ñico López** (also known as Plaza de la Patria), named for a revolutionary hero who, along with 24 other members of Fidel Castro's rebels, suicidally attacked Batista's troops here on 26 July 1953. López was one of the few survivors. The small **Museo Nico López,** tel. (23) 42-3742, is in the former officer's club on the west side of the square.

ACCOMMODATIONS

Casas Particulares
For a private room rental try **Casa Particular Mercedes León,** in a venerable home at Calle Máximo Gómez #44, tel. (23) 42-2644. The single upstairs room is simply furnished, cross-ventilated, and well lit (US$15). Next door at Calle Máximo Gómez #42, tel. (23) 42-4137, Rene ("El Gordo") rents three gloomy but nicely furnished rooms (two with a/c) with a shared bathroom with hot water (US$15). Take the more spacious front room, which is well lit and has its own bathroom with large walk-in shower.

Hotels
Budget: Islazul's **Hotel Sierra Maestra,** Carretera Central Km 7.5, tel. (23) 48-1013, fax (23) 48-1798, three km southeast of the city center, is a dour block-like structure built after the Revolution. Its 204 a/c rooms (18 in cabanas) all have private bathrooms, radios, phones, and TVs, but awaited refurbishment at press time (my room had a sagging mattress but neither hot water nor a toilet seat). The peace is regularly disturbed by the blaring piped music. Facilities include a clean swimming pool, nightclub, tourism bureau, car rental, post office, hairdresser, and an elegant but meagerly stocked restaurant. Rates were US$18 s, US$23 d low season, US$26 s, US$30 d high season.

Villa Bayamo, Carretera de Manzanillo, Bayamo, tel. (23) 42-3102, is six km outside Bayamo on the road to Manzanillo. It has 34 a/c rooms with phones, TVs, radios, and refrigerators. Twelve of the rooms are in *cabinas* spread throughout the grounds. It has a restaurant, swimming pool with bar, and a small nightclub. Rates were US$15 s/d, US$27 for cabins, and US$42 for a suite.

Islazul has reservations offices at General García #207 and Calle Mármol #120 e/ Aves. Francisco Vicente Aguilera y Antonio Maceo, tel. (23) 42-5321 or 42-5105.

Inexpensive: The old-fashioned **Royalton Hotel,** Calle Maceo #53, tel. (23) 42-2290, fax (0+23) 42-5831, on the west side of Céspedes Park, gleams after a recent restoration and is one of Islazul's showcase hotels, with plump leather sofas in the spacious lobby, with restaurant (offering a miserly menu) attached. An all-marble staircase leads to 33 small a/c rooms with telephone, firm mattresses, and small but modern private bathrooms, including a room for disabled persons. Rates were US$20 s, US$28 d low season, US$26 s, US$36 d high season.

Formatur's **Hotel Telegrafo,** Saco #108, one block east of García, tel. (23) 42-5510, fax (23) 42-7389, functions as a hotel school. It was recently refurbished and has a/c rooms with lofty ceilings, contemporary furnishings, patios, and thoroughly modern bathrooms. It has a diminutive bar and restaurant open to the street. It accepts both Cubans and tourists. Rates were US$18-25 s, US$35 d, US$45 junior suite.

FOOD

The best of the few *paladares* in town is **Paladar El Polinesio,** Calle Parada #125 e/ Cisnero y Pío Rosaro, with alfresco dining beneath the stars on an upstairs patio. A huge meal will cost about US$7 with beer.

Cafetería Oriente, on the northeast side of Parque Céspedes, serves simply but tasty *criollo* meals for less than US$1 in pesos. Otherwise your best bet is the restaurant in the **Hotel Royalton,** serving *criollo* dishes for US$3-10. The restaurant food in the Hotel Sierra Maestra is a third-rate disappointment.

Other options include **Café de Viajeros,** a popular outdoor café outside the bus station on General Manuel Cedeño; **Islazul Café,** on the north side of Parque Céspedes, and the tiny but atmospheric **La Casona,** on Plaza del Himno, selling *criollo* snacks and pastries. Craving Chinese food? Try **Chine Jai,** at Calle Zenea and Parada. If all else fails, there's **El Rápido,** on the west side of Parque Céspedes, for fried chicken.

For ice cream, try **Tropi Crema** on Parque Céspedes' southwest corner; you'll need pesos. Tropi Crema also sell snacks. A favorite *refresco* bar is the basic **Café de la Croqueta,** on García and Figueredo.

ENTERTAINMENT AND SHOPPING

Fireworks and candles are lit each 12 January on Parque Céspedes to commemorate the burning of the town in 1869, and a procession of horses symbolizes the abandonment of Bayamo by its residents. Another celebration is held on 20 October in Parque Céspedes to celebrate the composition of the national anthem.

Traditional musical performances are offered at the **Sala Teatro José Joaquín Palma;** at the **Casa de la Trova** at the corner of Martí y Maceo; and at the **Casa de la Cultura,** tel. (23) 42-5917, on the east side of Parque Céspedes.

You can get your kicks at **Cabaret Bayamo,** tel. (23) 42-5111, opposite the Hotel Sierra Maestra and acclaimed as the largest indoor *espectáculo* in Cuba, yet featuring only a small troupe of dancers. It's offered Fri.-Sun. at 10:30 p.m. Entry costs US$10, or US$30 including dinner and drinks. A cabaret is also offered in the Hotel Sierra Maestra. It includes comedy, music, and dance routines, but no *espectáculo.* Entrance is US$1.

The modest disco in the Hotel Sierra Maestra is the happening place in town. You can also try **Discoteca Siboney,** on the northeast corner of Parque Céspedes, or **Centro Nocturno El Cuco** on Donato Marmól, one block north of Saco. If you want to sup with locals, try **Bar El Pedrito,** on the northeast corner of Parque Céspedes, or the quaint **La Bodega,** next to the Casa de la Nacionalidad. The latter sells locally made wine.

The **cinema** is on the west side of the main square. On General García, you'll find the **Videobar Rincón Latino,** which shows movies Tues.-Sun. beginning at 7 p.m.

The **Casa de Bien Fonda Cultura,** on Plaza del Himno, sells beautiful artwork, including stunning ceramics, hardwood lampshades, Daliesque paintings, and leather furniture. **Cubartesania** also stocks quality art, including wooden miniature horse-drawn cabs. For camera batteries or film, try **Photo Service,** on General Gárcia.

PRACTICALITIES

Information and Services

There's a small tour desk in the Hotel Sierra Maestra, which also has a post office, fax, and telephone office. The main **post office** is on the west side of Parque Céspedes (open Mon.-Sat. 9 a.m.-6 p.m.). You can make international calls from the **Eteca office** on the west side of Parque Céspedes, or the **centro telefónico,** on Miguel Enrico Capote e/ Saco y Perucho Figueredo, open daily 7 a.m.-11 p.m.

There's a **Banco de Crédito y Comercio** on General García e/ Saco y Perucho Figueredo, and a **Banco Popular** one block north on the corner of Saco. You can change dollars for pesos at the **Cadeca** bureau on Saco e/ General García y Donato Marmól.

The **hospital,** tel. (23) 42-4225, is 400 meters north of the Hotel Sierra Maestra, on General Manuel Cedeño. There's a 24-hour **pharmacy** on the southeast corner of Parque Céspedes.

Caught short? There are public toilets *(baños)* on Donato Marmól, one block east of Parque Céspedes.

The **Cupet gas station** is on General Manuel Cedeño, one-half km west of the Hotel Sierra Maestra.

Getting There and Away
By Air: Cubana flies between Havana and Bayamo four times weekly (US$59 one-way). **Aerotaxi,** tel. (7) 33-4064, fax (7) 33-4063, also flies from Havana. Cubana has a booking office in Bayamo at the corner of José Martí and Parada, tel. (23) 42-3916. Aerotaxi, tel. (23) 42-2186, is based at the airport.

The **Carlos Céspedes Airport,** tel. (23) 42-4502, is four km north of town. A bus operates between the airport and the Terminal de Ómnibus.

By Bus: The **Víazul** tourist bus departs Havana for Bayamo on Tuesday and Friday. (For public bus service, see the Public Bus Service from Havana chart.) The journey takes about 14 hours. Buses arrive and depart the **Terminal de Ómnibus,** tel. (23) 4-3060, at the junction of General Manuel Cadeña y Augusta Márquez. Local buses leave from opposite the rail station. All the buses from Santiago to major cities throughout Cuba stop in Bayamo.

By Train: At press time, train #17 departed Havana for Bayamo daily at 8:25 p.m. (14 hours, US$28.50) and continues to Manzanillo. The Havana-Santiago trains also stop in Bayamo. The railway station, tel. (23) 42-4955, is one km east of Parque Céspedes, at the end of José Antonio Saco.

By Car: Havanautos, tel. (23) 42-7375, has an outlet behind the Cupet gas station on Avenida General Cadeña y José Menendez.

Organized Excursions: There's an excursion desk in the Hotel Sierra Maestra. The **Cadena de Islazul,** at Calle Marmos #120, tel. (23) 42-5105, takes bookings for excursions and hotels throughout Granma Province, as does the main Islazul office on Calle General García, tel. (23) 42-3273. However, the staff is indifferent, and there were no brochures or prices available at either office at last visit.

Getting Around
Horse-drawn *coches* are everywhere, especially in droves outside the rail and bus terminals. **Cubataxi,** tel. (23) 42-4313, has its outlet at Avenida Amado Estévez y José Martí.

Artex, Calle Saco #13 e/ Céspedes y Máximo Gómez, tel. (23) 42-6667, fax (23) 42-5302, offers guided historical sightseeing tours for US$3.

BAYAMO TO SANTIAGO PROVINCE

The Carretera Central runs east from Bayamo across the Río Cauto floodplain. The road parallels the railroad, skipping over it several times west and east of **Jiguaní.** Beyond Jiguaní, the road rises gradually along the foothills of the Sierra Maestra before dropping to Contramaestre, in Santiago Province.

JIGUANÍ TO DOS RÍOS

A minor road begins at the northeast corner of the town in Jiguaní and leads north to Dos Ríos, one of Cuba's most hallowed yet rarely visited historical sites. Following the route, you might think that you have entered a different country. The region is an alluvial plain of rolling hills, dominated by giant cattle ranches. The first impression is of Cuba at its least welcoming—a vast, barren pan of white earth, burning hot in dry season, when a smoldering wind tears across the tableland and everything that walks, crawls, or flies gathers in the shade beneath tattered trees. It's like riding across the drought-stricken Sahel of Africa, with the cactus and thorny scrub nibbled upon by rust-colored goats and herds of hardy cattle.

Twenty km north of Jiguaní, immediately south of the village of **Santa Ursula,** you pass a junction with a road to the left leading 10 km to **Monumento Nacional La Jatia,** a former homestead of national hero José Martí. Keep straight for Dos Ríos.

DOS RÍOS

Just beyond Santa Ursula, the road plummets into a steep valley bottom. Two hundred meters beyond the far rise is a turnoff to the right that leads one mile to Dos Ríos (Two Rivers), the holy site where José Martí, apostle of independence, national poet, indefatigable freedom fighter, and national hero, gave his life for the cause of independence.

On 11 April 1895, he had returned to Cuba from exile in the U.S. On 19 May, General Máximo Gómez's troops exchanged shots with a small Spanish column. Martí, as nationalist leader (he had founded the Cuban Revolutionary Party in 1892), was a civilian among soldiers. Gómez halted and ordered Martí and his bodyguard to place themselves to the rear. Martí, however, took off down the riverbank towards the Spanish column. His bodyguard took off after him—but too late. Martí was hit in the neck by a bullet and fell from his horse without ever having drawn his gun. Martí, "seeking romantic death on the battlefield," had hurried forward to meet it. Revolutionary literature describes Martí as a hero who died fighting the enemy on the battlefield. The truth is that he committed suicide for the sake of martyrdom.

Monumento Martí

Martí's memory is preserved by a simple 10-meter-tall obelisk of whitewashed concrete in a trim garden of lawns and royal palms. White roses surround the obelisk, an allusion to his famous poem: *"Cultiva una rosa blanca en julio como enero . . . "* A stone wall bears a 3-D bronze visage of Martí and the words, "When my fall comes, all the sorrow of life will seem like sun and honey." A plaque on the monument says simply, "He died in this place on 19 May 1895."

LOMA DEL YAREY

A far more scenic route to Dos Ríos takes you over the massif of Loma del Yarey via a road that leads north from the Carretera Central, seven km east of Jiguaní. This road snakes up over the great *loma* (massif) before dropping back down to the plains. The views are stunning—as splendid as anywhere in Cuba. The lofty road gives you 360° views across the rolling plains laid out far below. To the south, mesas rise above the parched plains, with the serrated Sierra Maestra beyond. Looking down upon this austere landscape, shimmering, phantasmagorical in its infinity, conjures images of the wanderings of the demented Don Quixote across stark La Mancha. Indeed, the beauty is such that it is easy to come under its quixotic spell.

Accommodations and Food

Villa el Yarey, Jiguaní, tel. (23) 6-6613, enjoys an enviable and breezy location atop Loma el Yarey. This Cubanacán property is well built of thatch and hardwood logs. There are 14 recently refurbished cabins in two categories. Each has soaring thatched ceilings, terra-cotta floors, wood-paneled walls, small single beds, local TV, and large modern bathrooms. Some have a refrigerator. The cabins, reached via stone walkways, are set amid cactus and bushes and trees full of old man's beard dangling like fishermen's nets. Birdsong is everywhere. The lobby hints of an African game lodge, and the swimming pool with swim-up bar is set amid a natural rock garden. The manager claims you can see for 80 km. The restaurant serves quality *criollo* food. It gets few guests. Rates were US$20 s, US$30 d.

WEST OF BAYAMO

Northwest of Bayamo, the Río Cauto and its tributaries have deposited vast acres of alluvial silt that are washed down to the Gulf of Guacanayabo. Near the river mouth is a swampy zone with innumerable lagoons and canals full of water hyacinths. Much of the region has been drained for large rice plantations. The rest is preserved as swamp that attracts a Noah's ark's worth of endemic and migratory birds and crocodiles. Stands of dwarf swamp palm add a note of attraction, as do cactus fences surrounding rustic *bohíos* that speak of the poverty of this region.

A straight road cuts through the region, linking Bayamo with Las Tunas.

VIRAMAS

The lagoons of Viramas, north of the Río Cauto, are a hunting and fishing preserve where the largemouth bass fishing is great and white-necked coots, guinea fowl, doves, and ducks flock. The fishing season is November through June. There's a **crocodile farm** *(criadero de cocodrilos)* at Viramas where you can see the pugnacious endemic Cuban crocodile, both juvenile and full-grown.

Accommodations
Viramas Hunting and Fishing Preserve, Carretera Vado del Yeso Km 32, Laguna, Viramas, tel. (23) 2-5301, has 20 rooms in a main building and eight in four wood-and-thatch cabins. All have terraces, telephones, and minibars. Facilities include cleaning and cold storage, restaurant, bar, swimming pool, and a game room. Fishing gear can be rented, and guides are available. It's reached via a rutted dirt road that runs for 32 km from the main highway. Contact Cubanacán, Av. 146 y Calle 11, Apdo. Postal 16036, Havana, tel. (7) 22-5511, fax (7) 22-8382.

BAYAMO TO MANZANILLO

The road west from Bayamo to Manzanillo is dramatically scenic. Fifteen km west of Bayamo you pass through **Mabay,** site of a victory for the rebel army during the War of Independence; a roadside monument honors the brilliant black general Antonio Maceo. Soon you are winding atop a deep gorge of the Río Yara, through pumpkin and banana fields, with the Sierra Maestra rising melodramatically to the south. Beyond **Veguitas,** whose entrance and exits are marked by busts of Martí, bananas are replaced with sugarcane, then scrubby pastureland grazed by cattle in the care of sombrero-wearing *vaqueros.* The rustic *bohíos* are here made of wattle-and-daub, with thatched roofs and squared-off gardens hedged with cactus fences as neatly trimmed as if by a barber's shears.

The only town of significance is **Yara,** where the rebellious Indian chief Hatuey was burned at the stake. There's no reason to stop here unless you need to cash money at the **Banco de Crédito y Comercio.**

South of Yara, rice paddies stretch toward the foothills of the Sierra Maestra and the town of **Bartolomé Masó,** dominated by a sugar *central* and gateway to Parque Nacional Turquino (see Sierra Maestra, below). You can skip Yara and take a faster, direct road from **Bueycito** direct to Bartolomé Masó, though few maps show it.

MANZANILLO

Manzanillo (pop. 105,000) is a fly-blown place of weatherworn façades and functions as a fishing port on the Gulf of Guanacayabo, where shrimp and lobster are landed. It also serves as a shipping port for sugar in the hinterland. The trade these days is legitimate, but not necessarily more enriching than in early colonial days, when Manzanillo was a smuggling port and a center of slave trading. Many buildings have been influenced by Moorish design. Elsewhere, as in Barrio de Oro, the cobbled streets are lined with rickety wooden houses where elders play dominoes or rock beneath sagging eaves with cactus growing between the faded roof tiles. Don't be surprised to chance upon a street organ being played—the tradition is strong here.

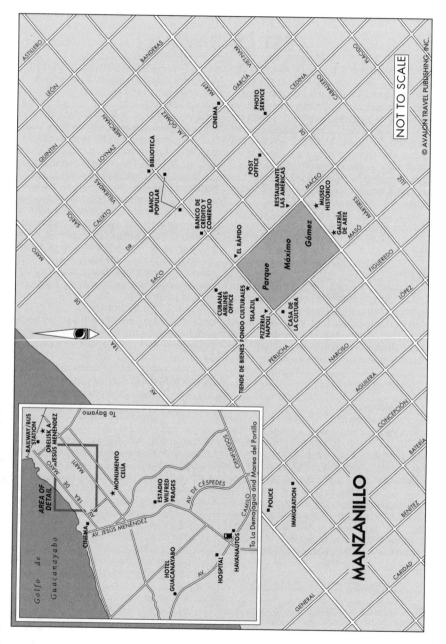

NOT TO SCALE

© AVALON TRAVEL PUBLISHING, INC.

MANZANILLO

The city was the main underground base for Castro's rebel army in the late 1950s, when locally born Celia Sánchez coordinated the secret supply routes and information network from here, under the noses of Batista's troops and spies.

Offshore are the Manzanillo cays, the easternmost cays of the Járdines de la Reina archipelago, floating on the horizon like flying carpets.

Orientation

Manzanillo extends along three km of shorefront on the Gulf of Guacanayabo. It is laid out in a grid and rises gradually from the shore to an escarpment, about on km inland.

The road from Bayamo enters Manzanillo from the east, becoming Avenida Rosales, which runs to the shore. The shoreline is fronted by Avenida 1 de Mayo. It is paralleled five blocks inland by Avenida Martí. Both roads run west to Avenida Jesús Menéndez. The old city lies within this quadrangle. Modern construction extends south of Jesús Menéndez along a seafront boulevard, the forlorn **Malecón.**

To the east the city is encircled by a ring road *(circunvalación)* that runs south from Avenida Rosales to the top of a hill before dropping down to the Malecón. Jesús Menéndez climbs inland (as Avenida de Céspedes) to meet the ring road at the junction for Las Coloradas, Cabo Cruz, and Marea del Portillo.

Parque Máximo Gómez

It all happens around this handsome square bounded by Martí, Maceo, Marchen, and Masó. Music is piped into the square, which has little stone sphinxes at each corner. It is ringed by

CELIA SÁNCHEZ

Celia Manduley Sánchez, an extremely intelligent woman and a dedicated revolutionary, was for many years the most important person in Fidel Castro's life.

Her father, Manuel Sánchez Silveira, was a doctor and an admirer of Martí; in 1953, father and daughter climbed to the top of Pico Turquino, where they erected a bust of the national hero. In time, she became dedicated to the ideals of Castro's 26th of July Movement, and was involved in propaganda and clandestine activities until she eventually joined Castro's guerrillas in the mountains. She set up the urban and peasant-based intelligence and supply networks based in Manzanillo, which she turned into a logistics center under the noses of Batista's spies.

Sánchez was 36 years old when she met Fidel for the first time, on 16 February 1957—the beginning of a 33-year association with the Cuban leader. She became his secretary, his "eyes and ears," and his lover. Celia was also his compass and kept Fidel in touch with the people; she helped balance and minimize Fidel's absolutist side. She was one of only a handful of people who could give him news and opinions he didn't want to hear. Her death from cancer in January 1980 profoundly shook him and removed from his life the only person with whom he could truly relax and be himself.

Monumento Celia

tall royal palms and Victorian-era lampposts. The most notable feature is an Islamic-style bandstand inlaid with cloisonné—very detailed, very pretty, and very out of place.

Of note are the Islamic-inspired building on the west side, now housing the **Tienda de Bienes Culturales,** and the **Casa de la Cultura,** on the south side, housed in an impressive Spanish-style colonial building with stunning tile work. Inside is a roofless courtyard with ceramic mosaics of Columbus' landing and Don Quixote tilting at windmills. The gallery displays faded prints.

On the east side is the meager **Museo Histórico** (open Tues.-Fri. 8 a.m.-10 p.m. and weekends 8 a.m.-noon and 7-10 p.m.; entrance, US$0.50) and, next to it, the **Galería de Arte.**

Calle Martí

Hoping for something serendipitous? Then follow Martí, watching for the splendid windows set high above the colonial building at the corner of Martí and Codina, and another building with a Moorish frontage at Martí #327.

At Calle Caridad (on Martí, seven blocks southeast of the central plaza), a terra-cotta tile staircase climbs uphill to Avenida Placido and the **Monumento Celia.** The houses to each side are graced with ceramic murals on the walls, and ceramic sunflowers are inset in the walkway. At the top is the striking ceramic monument to Celia Sánchez. Wreaths of cut flowers are kept at its base. It's moving. To one side is an **art gallery** dedicated to the memory of *"Lo mas hermosa y autóctona flor de la Revolución"* (the most beautiful native flower of the Revolution, who died in 1980.

At the southwestern end of Martí, beyond Avenida Jesús Menéndez, you enter Barrio de Oro, intriguing for a view of Manzanillo's parochial lifestyle.

Accommodations

The only *casa particular* in town isn't much to write home about. Cesar Espinosa's somewhat jaded house at Calle Sariol #245 e/ Saco y Dr. Codina, offers two spacious upstairs rooms with meager furnishings. They're entered via Cesar's bedroom and share a bathroom (with hot water) and are overpriced at US$18 and US$20.

The **Hotel Guacanayabo,** Avenida Camilo Cienfuegos, Manzanillo, tel. (23) 5-4012, fax (23) 62-34139, is a dreary-looking Soviet-style hotel on a hill on the south side of the city where it catches the breezes. Most of the simply furnished 112 a/c rooms face the ocean and have tiny balconies. Alas, when you fling open the curtains to take in the view, you discover only a peephole window—with frosted glass—that does nothing to stop the blaring music echoing up from the pool courtyard until the wee hours. Facilities include a solarium, video room, post office, rent-a-car, tour desk, and a restaurant. Rates were US$2 s, US$24 d low season, US$23 s, US$30 d high season.

Food

Manzanillo has few restaurants and *paladares.* The food in the restaurant of the Hotel Guacanayabo was better than average for an Islazul hotel at last visit, and is the best in town, offering well-prepared fish, shrimp, and pork dishes, washed down with Bayam, the local brew and aided by efficient and friendly service.

There's an open-air chicken joint on the northwest corner of the plaza. Also try the **Pizzeria Napoli,** on the southwest corner, or the **Restaurante Las Américas.** Good luck!

Entertainment and Events

There's a bar and a disco in the Hotel Guacanayabo. The **Casa de la Cultura,** on the main square, holds occasional live music performances; the city claims to be the birthplace of *son,* and you can hear it performed here.

If boredom sets in, you might join the *vuejos* (old boys) who play dominoes at the corner of Gómez and Benitez. They may look docile, but dominoes here is a fearfully strategic game (read Tom Miller's *Trading with the Enemy*).

Services

A **Banco Popular** occupies the neoclassical granite building at the corner of Marchan and Cordina (before the Revolution, it belonged to the National City Bank of New York), and there's a **Banco Crédito y Comercio** across the street.

The **hospital** is atop the hill, on the ring road, one-half km east of Hotel Guacanayabo. The **police station** is on Villimedas e/ Aguilera y Concepción. The **immigration** office is one block east on Saríol e/ Aguilera y Concepción.

There's a poorly stocked **Photo Service,** on Codina, east of Martí.

The **Cupet gas station** is immediately east, at the junction for Media Luna and Marea del Portillo. There's another Cupet station about two km east of town, on the road to Bayamo.

Getting There and Away

By Air: Cubana flies to Manzanillo from Havana four times weekly (US$59 one-way). Royal Airlines and Air Transat have charter flights to Manzanillo from Toronto, with transfers to Marea del Portillo (see Marea del Portillo, below). The **Sierra Maestra Airport** is 10 km south of town on the road to Cayo Espino. The Cubana office is at Calle Maceo #70, e/ Marchan y Villuenda, tel. (23) 5-2800.

By Bus: At press time, bus no. 626 departed Havana's main bus terminal daily at 8:15 p.m.

(US$32); it's an 11-hour journey. Buses leave regularly from Bayamo. For information call the bus terminal, tel. (23) 5-3404.

By Train: Train #17 departs Havana for Manzanillo at 8:25 p.m. (US$28), arriving at 11:40 a.m. Trains also operate to Manzanillo from Bayamo four times daily. Trains depart Manzanillo for Havana at about 9 p.m. Other trains serve Santiago (US$6) and Guantánamo (US$7). The railway station, tel. (23) 5-2195, is at the far north end of Avenida Marchan.

Getting Around

You can rent a car from **Havanautos,** tel. (23) 5-2056, next to the Cupet gas station, on the ring road one-half km east of the Hotel Guanacayabo.

THE SIERRA MAESTRA

The Sierra Maestra hangs against the sky along the entire southern coast of Oriente, from the western foothills near Cabo Cruz eastward 130 km to Santiago de Cuba. At its broadest, it is 50 km north-south. Its spine—*el firme*—averages 4,500 feet in elevation. The towering massif gathers in serried ranges that precede one another in an immense chain, churning dark sea green like the deepest water, and plumed with white clouds that conceal the highest peaks, including Pico Real del Turquino (1,974 meters), Cuba's tallest mountain and the node of the 17,450-hectare **Parque Nacional Pico Turquino,** in the very heart of the Sierra Maestra.

It is forbidding terrain creased with steep ravines and boulder-strewn valleys. Every fold and depression is veined with shadow. Ideal guerrilla territory.

The mountains remain sparsely inhabited. Cut off from civilization down on the plains, the hardy mountain folk continue to eke out a subsistence living, supplemented by a meager income from coffee, carried on mules laden with wicker baskets. Small schools, rural clinics, and farm cooperatives have been built over the past four decades, but the majority of local peasants remain so poor that they can't even afford to get married, so they simply live together in simple thatched huts without running water.

FLORA AND FAUNA

These mountains, especially the region encompassed by Parque Nacional Pico Turquino, are as important for their diversity of flora and fauna as for their historical importance. At least 100 species of plants are found nowhere else, and an additional 26 are peculiar to tiny enclaves within the park. Antediluvian tree ferns and wispy bamboo grow in patches. Fragile orchids cover the trunks of semi-deciduous montane forest and centenarian conifers. Higher up is cloud forest, festooned with old man's beard, bromeliads, ferns, and vines, fed by mists that swirl through the forest primeval. Pico Turquino is even tipped by sub-*páramo* above 1,900 meters, with wind-sculpted, contorted dwarf species on exposed ridges.

The calls of birds—including nightingales, woodpeckers, the *tocororo* (the national bird), and the tiny *passerine*—explode like gunshots in the green silence of the jungle. Hummingbirds are common. There are very few mammals, however, though wild pigs and *jutías* exist in small numbers. But there are especially large numbers of reptiles and amphibians, including three species of frog found only on Pico Turquino.

THE WAR IN THE MOUNTAINS

It is hard to imagine, as you watch groups of boys picking coffee beans, that amid the sweet peace of these green mountains war was waged. Between 1956 and 1959, this rugged terrain was the headquarters for Castro's rebel army. The mountains are replete with evidence of the struggle against Batista's troops. Many of the sites of importance can be reached by roads laid since the Revolution (en route, you'll pass billboards that announce where and under what circumstances columns of guerrillas crossed the road). However, rains regularly wash away sections of road, and you may need to negotiate boulders and deep crevices. Mules are the only reliable transportation past a certain point, where impassable streams stop your climb.

Fidel and Raúl Castro, Che Guevara, and a ragged band of survivors from the ill-fated *Granma* landing stumbled into the Sierra Maestra in December 1956. Here Fidel intended to establish and fashion a revolutionary army drawn from the peasantry and deal blows to the "army of tyranny"—a course of action that would eventually lead to the fall of the Batista regime. For the first six months, the famished, poorly armed band was constantly on the move. Its first goal was to stay alive and win the support of local peasants. "The story of how Castro was able to recover from a terrible initial defeat, regroup, fight, start winning against Batista units, and form an ultimately victorious rebel army is the story of the extraordinary support he received from Sierra Maestra peasants," writes Tad Szulc in *Fidel: A Critical Portrait.*

It wasn't difficult. Batista's troops tortured peasants, whose only hope out of destitution lay with a revolution that has as yet delivered only meager improvements. Peasants rallied to the cause, providing shelter and serving as conduits for supplies. As news of the revolutionary front spread, many peasants joined the rebel army. "When a Rural Guard trooper visited a mountain house," recalls Argeo González, a merchant who ran supplies to the rebels, "he would receive bread, eat a chicken. . . take away a daughter if there was one there—but the rebels were different: they respected everything, and this was the basis of the confidence that they gained."

Gaining Ground

The initial year in the mountains was difficult. The tiny rebel band won small skirmishes with Batista's troops, but gained their major coup on 16 February 1957, when Herbert L. Matthews of the *New York Times* was led into the mountains to meet the next day with Castro. The rebel leader arranged a charade to convince the reporter that his minuscule army, which was down to 18 men at the time, was large and had complete control of the Sierra Maestra. Matthews' report hit the newsstands on 24 February. It began, "Fidel Castro, the rebel leader of Cuba's youth, is alive and fighting hard and successfully in the rugged, almost impenetrable vastness of the Sierra Maestra." Batista had lifted censorship the week before, and Matthews' story ran as lead headlines in Cuba, creating a sensation that Castro milked by releasing his *Appeal to the People of Cuba,* a manifesto calling for violent uprising against the regime.

Castro had established a base at La Plata, on the northwest slope of Pico Turquino. The rebel army consolidated its control of the mountains throughout 1957. As the rebel force gathered strength, engagements became more intense. The first real battle occurred on 28 May, when Castro and a force of 80 men came down from the mountains and attacked a garrison at El Uvero, on the coast. They lost six men but gained two machine guns and 46 rifles.

On 12 July Castro issued *The Sierra Maestra Manifesto,* in which he committed himself to "free, democratic elections" within one year of defeating Batista (Castro would, of course, renege on his promise in the euphoria of victory).

In early 1958 the rebel army split into five separate units. Castro continued to lead from La Plata, Che Guevara held the northern slopes, Camilo Cienfuegos led a group on the plains near Bayamo, and Raúl Castro opened a new front in the mountains near Santiago (Raúl's army units were trained in Marxist theory). By spring the rebel army had control of most of the mountain regions of Oriente. The enemy was being denied more and more territory. And a radio station—Radio Rebelde—was set up to broadcast revolutionary messages, including Castro's *Total War* manifesto to the nation. All the while, Castro was kept abreast of rival groups in Havana and worked assiduously to maintain control of the opposition.

Many U.S. citizens contributed money for the cause. In a dramatic twist, the *CIA* even began channeling funds to Castro's movement—at least US$50,000 was delivered between November 1957 and mid-1958. The top-secret operation still remains classified by the U.S. government, which was re-arming the Batista regime in ignorance of the increasing strength of the anti-Batista movement. In 1958 it even re-armed Batista's warplanes at Guantánamo naval base; Castro would never forgive the U.S. for supplying arms—including napalm, which was used to bomb peasant villages. (Interestingly, Castro received into his army three U.S. citizens, all sons of servicemen at Guantánamo naval base.)

Victory

In May 1958 Batista launched an all-out attack—Operation FF *(Fin de Fidel)*—using air strikes, naval bombardments, and 10,000 troops. Batista's troops, however, were no match for Fidel's peasant-based rebel army, which knew "every path in the forest, every turn in the road, and every peasant's house in the immensely complicated terrain." To Fidel, "Every entrance to the Sierra Maestra is like the pass at Thermopylae, and every narrow passage becomes a death trap."

For three months they skirmished. By 19 June, Castro's troops were virtually surrounded atop their mountain retreat. The rebels rained mortars down into the valley, along with a psychological barrage of patriotic songs and exhortations blasted over loudspeakers to demoralize Batista's tired troops, many of whom switched sides (some were spies; when caught, they were summarily executed). Then at the battle of Jigue, which lasted 10 days, Castro's rebels defeated a battalion whose commander, Major José Quevedo, joined the rebels. Batista's army collapsed and began to retreat in disarray.

By the time Batista's offensive collapsed, Castro and his meager force of about 320 peasant soldiers had captured tanks, along with hundreds of modern weapons. Radio Rebelde broadcast details of the victories to anxious Cubans. Castro then launched his counteroffensive. In August 1958 Castro's troops came down out of the mountains to seize, in swift order, Baire, Jiguaní, Maffo, Contramaestre, and Palma Soriano. On 2 January 1959, the rebel army entered Santiago

de Cuba. Castro walked up the stairs of the Moncada barracks to accept the surrender of Batista's army in Oriente at the very site where he had initiated his armed insurrection six years before.

BARTOLOMÉ MASÓ TO SANTO DOMINGO

Numerous roads and trails lead into the mountains. The most important gateway, however, is the town of Bartolomé Masó, at the foothills of the mountains, 15 km south of Yara.

South of Masó, as the town is colloquially known, the road climbs steadily and the vegetation grows thicker. The cement road winds ever more steeply uphill to **Providencia**, a little village in the lee of a river valley. A road to the left at a T-junction here leads to Santo Domingo and Parque Nacional Pico Turquino (the village is to the right). There is only silence, but for the occasional braying of a mule, birdsong, and the buzz of insects. Little *bohios* cling to the precipitous slopes.

About eight km south of Providencia, the road dives sinuously to the Río Yara, where squats the tiny tumbledown village of **Santo Domingo** on a natural terrace on the east bank of the Río Yara and accessed via a rickety log bridge. The setting saw fierce fighting June-July 1958 during the war to oust Batista. Here there's the small **Museo Santo Domingo** in the former home of Lucas Castillo Mendoza, a collaborator of the Rebel Army killed in battle in 1958. It features a 3-D model of the Sierra Maestra with a plan of the various battles and movements of Castro's and Batista's forces. The guide gives a rambling blow-by- blow account. Small arms and mortars are displayed. Entrance costs US$1. The **Centro de Información de Flora y Fauna** exists only in name. A trail leads west along the river for five km to the site of the Second Battle of Santo Domingo.

In 1999 the park was closed to visitation and remained so at press time. Don't make the arduous drive without checking the latest situation beforehand with the Academia de Ciencias de Cuba (see Permits And Guides, below).

Accommodations and Food
Villa Santo Domingo, Santo Domingo, Bartolomé Masó, Granma, tel. LD 375 (via the op-

erator), or c/o Islazul, Calle Mármol #120, Bayamo, tel. (23) 42-5321, is a demure complex on the banks of the Río Yara at the base of Pico Turquino. The 20 attractive a/c cabanas are modestly decorated, each with two single beds and a refrigerator. There's a restaurant, bar, game room, video room, and tiny shop. The hotel is ideal for nature lovers and hikers, and you can go horseback riding along the banks of the river. Rates are US$22 s, US$28 d year-round.

Islazul also runs the basic **Villa Balcón de la Sierra**, 800 meters south of Bartolomé Masó, tel. (23) 059-5180, which serves mostly Cubans. It has 20 a/c meagerly appointed bungalows with jaded furniture but rockers on the patios. A restaurant, bar, and swimming pool are suspended above on a windswept hillock with all-around views. Cabins cost US$22 d.

PARQUE NACIONAL TURQUINO AND PICO TURQUINO

Pico Turquino, Cuba's highest mountain (1,974 meters) looms over Santo Domingo. Even here you cannot escape the Revolution. Pico Turquino is a revolutionary shrine. In 1952 Celia Sánchez and her liberal-minded father hiked up Turquino carrying a bust of José Martí, which they installed at the summit. In 1957 Sánchez made the same trek with the rebel army and a CBS news crew for an interview with Fidel beside the bust. It was Castro's first ascent of "El Pico." Che Guevara recorded how El Jefe checked his pocket altimeter to assure himself that Turquino was as high as the maps said it was (Castro never trusted anything or anybody).

At press time, the park was off-limits to all visitors and the road beyond Santo Domingo was closed. I've driven it before however, and things change. From Santo Domingo, for the next five km, the road climbs at an ever-increasing gradient until you are forced to drop into first gear. The last hundred meters is a breathtakingly steep climb, with hairpin bends to boot. Eventually you arrive at a parking lot (the end of the road), with views back down the mountains. You have arrived at **Alto del Naranjo,** the 950-meter-high gateway to Parque Nacional Pico Turquino. The drive is not for the fainthearted. *Check your brakes beforehand.*

It's 18 km to the summit from Santo Domingo, which is invariably swaddled in mulberry-colored clouds. It is reached from Alto de Naranjo via steep pathways that would stump anything without hooves. Hikers normally overnight at the humble little community of **La Mula,** the trailhead for the peak (hikers normally set off about 3 a.m. for the climb to the peak, or shortly after). It's possible to attain the peak and hike back in one day, but it is extremely arduous. Far better is to stay in the tent camp, four km below the peak. Hikers need to take their own food and water.

La Comandancia de la Plata

Fidel named his rebel army headquarters in the Sierra Maestra after the river whose headwaters were near his camp on a spur ridge west of Pico Turquino. The camp occupied a large forest clearing atop the crest, reached only by a single tortuous narrow track—a tough climb over rocks and mud. The wooden structures were well hidden at the edge of the clearing and covered with branches to conceal them from air attacks.

Castro's house was built against the side of a ravine, with an escape route into the creek. It consisted of a bedroom with double bed for Fidel and his secretary, lover, and confidante, Celia Sánchez, plus an office for Celia, a kitchen, and a deck, where Castro received visitors.

In time, a small hospital (run by Che Guevara, who was a qualified doctor), a guest house, and a dental office were added. La Plata was also linked by field telephone to outlying rebel units and by radio to the rest of Cuba (a transmitter for Radio Rebelde loomed above the clearing).

The headquarters is preserved today as a museum and was sadly off-limits to visitors at press time. It is reached by a trail to the right from the car park at Alto de Naranjo (it follows the ridge top for three km). A wooden billboard points the way. *You must be accompanied by a guide* (see below).

Permits and Guides

Now the bad news: The park is now under the purvey of the Academia de Ciencias, which closed it to visitors in mid-1999 except for limited access by permit only from Las Cuevas, on the coast road (see Hiking to Pico Turquino in the Santiago Province chapter).

As with everything in Cuba, the situation is fickle. In the past, tourists were allowed to visit La Comandancia and to hike to the peak's summit with a permit and a guide obtained at the Villa Turística (in early 1999, prior to the park's closure, a permit cost US$10 per person; guides cost US$5). Call the Villa for the latest information, or contact the Academia de Ciencias de Cuba, Capitolio, Industria y San José, Habana Vieja, Havana 10200, tel. (7) 57-0599, fax (7) 33- 8054, e-mail: museofin@infomed.sld.cu or acc@ceniai.inf.cu.

Alcona S.A., Calle 42 #514 esq. Av. 7, Playa, Havana, tel. (7) 24-9227, has previously offered a six-day package that includes a visit to La Comandancia with a hike to the top of Pico Turquino.

Basic camp cabins are available at *campamento de Joaquín,* on the flank of Pico Turquino (US$10 s/d). You can rent them at the Villa Turística or through Alcona S.A.

MANZANILLO TO CABO CRUZ

The coastal plains south of Manzanillo are awash in lime green sugarcane rippling in the breeze like sheets of green silk, with the turquoise sea in beautiful counterpoint. Rising over this swell are sugar *centrales,* whose industry is all-consuming. Great trolleys on wheels piled high with cut cane arrive through the night, when black smoke pours unseen from the *centrales.* The air is permeated by a thick, earthy scent of molasses. Smoke-smudged workers slashing at the burnt cane with glinting machetes make a wondrous sight, as do ox-carts trundling down the road, spilling pieces of cane as they go.

About five km south of Manzanillo you pass a turnoff for the **Criadero de Cocodrilos,** or crocodile farm, tel. (23) 42-4741, where you can see about 1,200 American crocodiles (the endemic Cuban species is absent) of varying ages wallowing in algae-filled ponds that lend the reptiles an eerie luminescent green hue. It's open Mon.-Fri. 7 a.m.-4 p.m., but is best visited in midafternoon when the beasts are fed. It's signed off the main road but is then easy to miss; turn left about 200 meters along the dirt road at a palm grove.

LA DEMAJAGUA

La Demajagua, 13 km south of Manzanillo, was the sugar estate owned by Carlos Manuel Céspedes, the nationalist revolutionary who, on 10 October 1868, unilaterally freed his slaves and called for rebellion against Spain. His house (of which only the original floor remains) is now a museum. The eclectic displays include the revolutionary Flag of Céspedes, proclamations from the period, a copy of the original *Himno la Bayamesa* (the national anthem), and period weaponry. It's open daily 8 a.m.-5 p.m. Entrance costs US$1.

A path leads to a monument of fieldstone in a walled amphitheater encircling two venerable trees and an old *trapiche.* Here a plaque bears inspirational words of Céspedes, José Martí, and Fidel Castro. On the right is the La Dema-

---

FOR WHOM THE BELL TOLLS

Since independence, the La Demajagua bell had been entrusted to Manzanillo as a national shrine. In November 1947, the leftist city fathers refused a request by the corrupt President Grau to transport the bell to Havana to be rung at the following year's anniversary celebrations.

A young law student named Fidel Castro (already a prominent political figure) thought the bell would toll well for him. He arranged for the venerable 300-pound bell to be brought to Havana to be pealed in an antigovernment demonstration. Castro accompanied the bell from Manzanillo to Havana, to great popular fanfare. The bell was placed in the Gallery of Martyrs in the university, but disappeared overnight, presumably at the hands of Grau's police. Castro, who some claim may have set up the theft himself, took to the airwaves denouncing the Grau government.

Several days later, the bell was delivered "anonymously" to President Grau and was immediately sent back to Manzanillo. The incident was over, but young Castro had achieved new fame as Cuba's most promising rising political star.

jagua bell, the Cuban equivalent of the American Liberty Bell, which Céspedes rang at his estate to mark the opening shot in the 1868 War of Independence. The antique bell is inset in the wall, beyond which sugarcane still undulates in the warm breeze.

LA DEMAJAGUA TO LAS COLORADAS

There are three towns of modest importance south of La Demajagua: Campechuela, dominated by stockyards, and Media Luna and Niquero, both dominated by *centrales*. On the main street in **Media Luna,** at Avenida Podio #11, tel. (23) 59-3466, is a simple green and white house—one of many gingerbread wooden houses in town—where Celia Sánchez, revolutionary heroine of Sierra Maestra, was born on 9 May 1920. Visitors are welcome (US$1). The mahogany tree in the backyard (full of fruit trees) was planted in 1980 by members of the Venceremos Brigade, U.S. citizens who make annual pilgrimages to Cuba to work in the fields and demonstrate their support for fidelismo.

Carlos Manuel Céspedes

Eight km south of Media Luna, at **Entronque Pilón,** a turnoff leads east to Marea del Portillo and Santiago. Continue straight, however, and you'll arrive at **Niquero,** unique for its ramshackle buildings in French-colonial style, lending it a similarity to parts of New Orleans and Key West.

Beyond Niquero, the road is in good condition all the way to **Playa Las Colorados** and Desembarco del Granma National Park, where it gives way to *piste* and the final few kilometers to Cabo Cruz. This is one of Cuba's poorest regions, attested to by simple mud *bohíos* and shoeless children, many in virtual rags.

Accommodations

Islazul's all-new **Hotel Niquero,** tel. (23) 59-2428, on the main street, opened in February 2000. It offers 26 rooms with colonial tile floors, elegant furnishings that include imitation walnut, and large, modern bathrooms. Facilities include an appealing restaurant, and a rooftop bar popular with locals for dancing. At its heart is an atrium courtyard with skylight. Rates were about US$24 s, US$35 d.

Services

Niquero has a **Cupet gas station,** and a **Banco de Crédito y Comercio** and **centro telefónico** on the main street, beyond the Hotel Niquero.

DESEMBARCO DEL GRANMA NATIONAL PARK

This park protects the southwesternmost tip of Cuba, from Cabo Cruz to Punta Hicacos, 40 km farther east. The park is named for the spot where Fidel and Raúl Castro, Che Guevara, and 79 other revolutionaries came ashore at the southern end of Playa las Coloradas on 2 December 1956. The narrow beach is named for its red-orange color. It's fringed by mangroves and has shallow waters good for wading. The site where Fidel fulfilled his promise to return from exile is marked by a monument. The area is more interesting visually, however, for its marvelous geomorphology and opportunities for nature lovers.

The land stair-steps 507 meters up toward the Sierra Maestra in an orderly series of marine terraces left high and dry over the eons by re-

THE *GRANMA* LANDING

Shortly after midnight on 25 November 1956, Castro and his revolutionaries set off from Tuxpán, Mexico, sailing without lights for Cuba. The 1,235-mile crossing was hellish. The *Granma* had been designed to carry 25 passengers. Battered by heavy seas and with a burden of 82 heavily armed men and supplies, the vessel lurched laboriously toward Cuba, which Castro had planned to reach in five days. Batista's army and navy were on alert. Castro figured they would not patrol far from shore, so he planned a route 170 miles offshore, beyond reach of Cuban surveillance.

In the violent seas the men, packed in like sardines, became seasick. The boat rose and dropped from beneath them. In the open, the drizzle began to turn into a cold, penetrating rain. Castro smelled victory, but to the men on the slippery decks the smell in the air was vomit. Then one engine failed and the boat slowed, falling two days behind schedule. Castro ordered rationing: for the last two days there was neither water nor food—which was probably just as well.

On 30 November, the scheduled date for landing, Celia Sánchez had gathered five trucks and several dozen supporters at the beach near Las Coloradas. They were to meet the rebels and transport them to Media Luna, where they would seize arms from Batista's troops and move into the Sierra Maestra, where sympathetic peasants were waiting to receive them.

At dawn on 2 December, the ship ran aground at low tide, two km south of the planned landing site at Playa Las Coloradas. Two hours later, just after dawn, Fidel Castro stood on *terra firma* alongside 81 men, with minimal equipment, no food, and no contact with the Movement ashore. "This wasn't a landing, it was a shipwreck," Che Guevara later recalled.

The motley group set out towards the safety of the Sierra Maestra none too soon. Within two hours of landing, *Granma* had been sighted and a bombardment of the mangroves began. Batista's military commander foolishly announced to the press that the rebels had been ambushed and captured or killed, "annihilating 40 members of the supreme command of the revolutionary 26th of July Movement—among them its chief, Fidel Castro." The United Press bureau sent the news around the world. Meanwhile, the exhausted, half-starved rebels moved unseen and unscathed.

On 5 December, however, the rebels were betrayed by their guide and ambushed by Batista's troops. Only 16 of the survivors eventually managed to meet up, including Fidel, Raúl, and Che.

Thinking that the danger was over, Batista canceled his search-and-destroy missions and withdrew his forces. On 13 December, Castro's meager force finally made contact with a peasant member of the 26th of July Movement, and with that, word was out that Fidel had survived. That day, 20 peasants joined the rebel army. Aided by an efficient communications network and intense loyalty from the Sierra peasants, the rebel unit was passed from homestead to homestead as they moved deeper into the mountains, and safety.

---

ceding sea levels. More than 80% of the park is covered by virgin woodland. The region lies in a rain shadow of the mountains. Floral and faunal species are distinct. Drier areas preserve cacti more than 400 years old. Two endemic species of note are the blue-headed quail dove and the Cuban amazon butterfly. Even endangered manatees are occasionally seen in the swampy coastal lagoons.

The park is well served by nature trails. Morlotte-Fustete Trail leads to the **Morlotte Hole,** a cavern that drops more than 70 meters. Nearby is the **Fustete Cave,** which extends for several miles, and the **Bojeo Cave,** the country's largest underwater system. The **Sendero Arqueológico Natural El Guafe,** about 10 km south of the monument, leads into the mangroves and scrub, where there's a crocodile farm, or **Criadero de Cocodrilos.** Inland the trail also features remains of Taíno Indian culture. I strongly recommend hiring a guide, which can be arranged at the motley **Interpretation Center** at Cabo Cruz, where an underwater tour of the coral reef is also available (the marine life supposedly includes massive colonies of conchs).

Entrance to the park costs US$3; you pay at a road checkpoint one km south of Las Coloradas. You need to show your passport.

Monumento de Desembarcadero

The exact spot where the *Granma* ran aground is one km south of the hamlet of Las Coloradas.

The site is a national monument consisting of a replica of the *Granma* and a bunker-like structure from where Fidel can address the crowd assembled in the dismal plaza.

Below the bunker is a small air-conditioned room, empty but for a large black-and-white photo of a young Fidel in the mangroves and, next to it (in a none-too-subtle piece of hero worship), a quote by Bertolt Brecht:

> *There are men who fight for a day, and they are good. There are others that fight a year, and they are better. There are some who fight many years, and they are very good. But there are those who fight all their life; those are the indispensable ones.*

A map shows the route of the *desembarcaderos* into the Sierra Maestras. Entrance costs an extra US$1, but it's not worth it. (Cameras cost US$2 extra, US$5 for videos.)

A cement pathway leads 1.8 km through the mangroves to the exact spot where the *Granma* bogged down. A pier extends partway into the crystal-clear, turquoise water and bears a Monumento Nacional marker. Otherwise there is nothing to indicate that this place was the pivotal point for the success of Castro's long-dreamed revolution.

A large café below the "pontification platform" raises your hopes for refreshment, but it is open only on the anniversary of the landing on 2 December or when tour groups are expected.

Accommodations
Cubamar's **Campismo Villas Las Colorados,** tel. LD-105 (long distance via the operator) at Playa Las Colorados, offers 13 simple cabins. Larger cabins have a/c, showers, and refrigerator. Facilities include a TV lounge, and a simple restaurant and bar. Rates were US$5 per person.

CABO CRUZ

The lonesome, badly potholed road south from Los Colorados dips and rises through dense scrubland. The road twists around a lagoon (Laguna Guafes), where wading birds jab for crustaceous food, and then you emerge atop a cliff overlooking a lagoon and the Caribbean Sea—miraculously blue and jade, with a reef where the waves break 100 meters offshore. You have arrived at the end of the road, at Cabo Cruz, the southwesterly tip of Cuba.

The ramshackle fishing village nestles on the rocky shoreline. It is inordinately pretty, albeit impoverished. The road is lined with conch shells. Bougainvillea adds a splash of color. And the mud-and-stone *bohios* are painted in pretty pastels. The road winds past the fishing cooperative to an old limestone lighthouse, built in 1877 and today containing a small museum. Pigs grub at the water's edge.

Simon Charles gives an excellent account of sailing conditions around Cabo Cruz in his book *Cruising Guide to Cuba.*

lighthouse at Cabo Cruz

THE SOUTH COAST

The south coast is a stunner. You won't regret it for scenic beauty and a sense of adventure. The journey begins in earnest east of Marea del Portillo, 40 km east of Entronque Pilón, where the road fades to rough dirt and stone. Landslides occasionally block the long, lonesome road, which periodically climbs over great headlands before sweeping back down to the coast. The teal blue sea is your constant companion, with mountains pushing up close on the other side. There are no villages or habitations for miles, and no services whatsoever, although the road (potholed and subject to landslides) is now paved the entire way. The bridge over the Río Macio marks the border with Santiago de Cuba Province.

You'll pass beaches of variegated colors. To cap it all, there are even several resorts tucked along the coast like pieces of pirate treasure.

In springtime, giant land crabs march up and down the cliffs in a paroxysm of egg laying. Amazingly, the battalions even scale vertical cliffs, often several hundred feet above the shore. The base of the steepest cliffs become graveyards that are a veritable potlatch of crabmeat for vultures. Drive with care, for the broken shells include sharp pincers that do everlasting damage to tires. This is no place for a puncture.

Getting There

There are only two ways to reach the south coast from Granma Province. The easiest is from Entronque Pilón, on the Golfo de Guacanaybo. A scenic road leads inland from here, rising slowly yet dramatically up the western foothills of the Sierra Maestra. Beyond the villages of **Sevilla** and **El Guaímaro**, the road drops sharply down through a narrow pass to emerge on the coastal plains above Pilón.

A second, infrequently traveled route, is via Bartolomé Masó, from where a road leads up over the western flank of the mountains via **San Lorenzo** and **La Habanita** before dropping down to Marea del Portillo. It's one of Cuba's most challenging and magnificent drives. You'll need a 4WD for the badly deteriorated road, which is dauntingly steep in places (be certain that your brakes are in good condition). But the scenery is awesome!

PILÓN

Pilón sits in a bowl ringed on three sides by mountains and on the fourth by the Caribbean Sea. The land west of Pilón is smothered in sugarcane and the town is eclipsed by a huge sugar *central.* This is the last greenery you'll see for a while; east of Pilón, the land lies in the rain shadow of the Sierra Maestra and is virtually desert. Tall cactus appear, and goats and white zebu cattle graze hungrily amid stony pastures in the lee of penurious hills.

The flyblown sugar and fishing town offers the tiny **Museo Celia Sánchez,** Calle Benitez #20, tel. (23) 59-4107, dealing with the area's aboriginal history and the revolutionary literacy campaign, as well as Celia Sánchez's life. The revolutionary heroine briefly lived in Pilón and utilized it as a secondary base for her underground supply network for the rebel army.

Offshore are reefs and countless little coral islets rimmed by tantalizing golden sand. Boaters are offered minimal facilities at a wharf inside the protective reefs, where fishing boats berth.

Services

There's a **Cupet gas station** at the entrance to town. It also offers car rentals. This is the last station before Santiago, about 200 km to the east.

MAREA DEL PORTILLO

Fifteen km east of Pilón the mountains shelve gently to a wide scimitar bay rimmed by a deep two-km-wide beach. The beach is of fine gray-brown sand and small pebbles, and when wet it resembles soil. Not the most appealing you'll ever see. A small down-at-heels fishing village is hidden within a cove at the northeast end of the bay, where mountains clamber down to the sea.

Four hotels are oases amid this barren landscape. Until 1993, when there was just one hotel, the tourist facilities were reserved for Cubans in summer and foreigners in winter. Now Marea del Portillo is a year-round favorite of Canadian and European charter groups. Private yachters can harbor in the cove.

There's an oyster farm at nearby **Cayo Portillito.** Bring insect repellent.

Accommodations

Villa Punta Piedra, tel. (23) 59-4421, is a Cubanacán hotel four miles east of Pilón. The modern Spanish-style complex has pretty villas in a landscaped setting looking down over the coast through the palms. Air-conditioned rooms are sizable and have full-length windows with views. There's a little beach below. The restaurant wasn't functioning when I called by, though it has a bar and café with a terrace, also with coastal views. It has a disco that draws Cubans plus guests from the other hotels hereabouts. Rates were US$20 s, US$25 d.

Villa Marea del Portillo, tel. (23) 59-7008, is another Cubanacán property, built to Western standards. The rooms are large, pleasantly furnished in contemporary vogue, with full-length glass doors opening onto the beach. There are 70 rooms and four suites in the main building, plus 56 bungalows, all with a/c, terraces, and ocean views. Suites and bungalows have TVs. Cuisine attains high standards in the a/c restaurant, where service is good. Cabaret is offered poolside for the predominantly Canadian and German clientele. Otherwise it's a bit stuffy. All-inclusive rates were US$55 s, US$90 d.

Better yet is the **Hotel Farallon del Caribe,** tel. (23) 59-7081, fax (23) 59-7080, an ultramodern, four-story, all-inclusive resort also run jointly by Cubanacán. It sits above the Villa Marea and is of eye-catching contemporary design. Hardwoods abound. There are low-slung leather chairs on airy, wide-open terraces, plentiful Spanish tiles, and huge glass frontages enfolding a curved swimming pool crossed by a footbridge and with a swim-up bar. At every turn there are splendid vistas over the bay. Each of the 140 double rooms has a TV. A full range of facilities and recreation is offered, including disco

and cabaret, plus car rental. All-inclusive Rates were US$35 s, US$70 d low season, US$60 s, US$100 d high season.

A fourth option, **Motel El Mirador,** tel. (23) 59-4365, sits on the mountainside, immediately north of Marea del Portillo. It has four simple cabins (US$10 d) and a thatch-roofed restaurant.

Services

The Villa Marea and Hotel Farallon share water sports at **Albacora Dive Center,** tel./fax (7) 33-5301 (in Havana). A doctor and nurse are available 24 hours at the Villa Marea del Portillo.

Getting Around and Away

You can rent cars and scooters at Villa Marea del Portillo and Farallon del Caribe. Scooters cost US$8 for the first hour, and US$3 for each extra hour, or US$22 all day.

Horse rentals cost US$5 for the first hour, and US$3 each additional hour.

Cubanacán Viaje Tours, tel. (23) 59-7024, offers excursions, including a day-tour to Bayamo and Manzanillo; one- and two-day excursions to Santiago de Cuba (from US$69 including sightseeing and the Tropicana cabaret); the *Granma* landing site at Las Colorados (US$35); to the Las Yaguas waterfall (US$39); and horseback riding into the mountains (US$35).

EAST OF MAREA DEL PORTILLO

East of Marea del Portillo, the mountains close in on the shore, beetling down to a sea the color of peacock feathers. Waves crash ashore. The paved but potholed road hugs the coast the whole way, climbing in places over steep headlands as far as the Río Macio, the border with Santiago de Cuba Province, 40 km miles from Marea. After rains, flash floods rip down through the foothills, washing great boulders onto the riverbeds that are normally dry as a bone. The road is often blocked. (See Santiago to Chivirico, in the Santiago chapter, for details on the rest of this superb drive.)

SANTIAGO DE CUBA
INTRODUCTION

Santiago de Cuba Province is one of the most interesting and beautiful regions in the country. Santiago de Cuba, the cosmopolitan capital city of irresistible charm, is well and truly on the tourist map, exceeded in popularity only by Havana and Varadero. Deservedly. It is the second-largest city in Cuba, distinctive in mood, and teeming with sites of historical and cultural interest.

Relatively few tourists travel far from Santiago de Cuba, however, despite the many attractions, including Parque Bacanao, a short drive east along the coast and featuring a cactus garden, an aquarium, the prehistoric world of Valle de la Prehistoria, and Gran Piedra National Park, reached by a circuitous road that leads through cool pine forest to a splendid garden perched atop a peak at over 1,200 meters. Another well-known haunt is the holy shrine of El Cobre. Diminutive beaches lie hidden in sheltered coves. There's even a crocodile farm.

The Sierra Maestra to the west and the remote Sierra de Cristal to the north lure hikers and birders, as well as anyone interested in revolutionary history. Santiago claims to be the Cradle of the Revolution. The first charge of machete-wielding *Mambís* was at Baire in 1868, and in 1953 Fidel Castro's attack on Batista's

barracks took place at Moncada, in the city of Santiago, initiating the Revolution that six years later brought him to power.

The province has a lighthearted side, too. The people carry themselves here with a certain lassitude and speak in a lilting tongue with a musical tone. The *c*s and *d*s are swallowed, and French and African words appear, a legacy of the many French and Haitian families that settled here in the late 18th century. Santiago (and adjacent Guantánamo Province) has the highest percentage of African blood in Cuba. Though the traditional architecture is mostly Spanish, the faces are mostly black—often with jade green eyes betraying hints of European blood. Santiagueros are lovers of music and dance—*muy festivante* in mood, as Santiago's lively annual *Carnaval* attests.

Lay of the Land
The greater part of the province is mountainous and sparsely populated. The majestic Sierra Maestra builds west of Santiago, rearing up like a great, crocodile-backed sea beast and extending along the coast as far as the westernmost tip of Granma Province. East of the city, an elevated plateau extends for miles, slanting gradually to the sea, with a great serrated whale-

SIGHTSEEING HIGHLIGHTS: SANTIAGO PROVINCE

Casa de la Trova, Santiago: Traditional music and dance at its best. The *Buena Vista Social Club* lives!

Cementerio de Santa Ifigenia: Cemetery chock-full of figures of historical import entombed in marble mausoleums and graves, including the all-important José Martí mausoleum.

El Cobre: This *basilica* (cathedral), tucked in the mountains, contains the shrine of the black Virgin de la Caridad, replete with votive offerings.

Gran Piedra National Park: Mountain reserve protecting flora and fauna, within Baconao Biosphere Reserve. Steep winding road leads to Gran Piedra. Dramatic views.

Moncada Barracks, Santiago: Old army barracks (today a school) attacked by Fidel Castro and followers in 1953. Contains the splendid **Museum de la Revolución.**

Morro Castle, Santiago: Great stone bulwark perched dramatically atop the cliffs at the entrance to Bahía de Santiago de Cuba.

Museo Bacardi, Santiago: Splendid collection of colonial artifacts and weaponry, plus art gallery and small ethnographic museum of the Americas.

Tropicana: Superb Las Vegas-style cabaret—a whirligig of sensual color.

Valle de Prehistória: Collection of kitschy, life-size concrete dinosaurs. Excellent little museum of natural history.

back of mountains—the tall *Cordillera de la Gran Piedra*—behind. Behind these rise the Sierra de Baracoa and Sierra Cristal, extending into Holguín and Guantánamo Provinces—wild and uncharted territory where Raúl Castro set up the Second Front of the rebel army in 1958.

Eastern Cuba is still rising from the sea, and temblors are common. Santiago and other cities in Oriente have survived several large earthquakes, most recently in 1942.

Climate

The climate of Santiago Province is much hotter than farther west. Relief may be found in the mountains and at beaches where breezes ease the heat. In general, temperature and rainfall vary according to altitude: cooling and wetter on higher slopes. Santiago de Cuba sits within a bowl surrounded by mountains that form windbreaks. Temperatures within the bowl can be withering in summer. The average temperature is 27° C. The average annual precipitation is one meter. The rainiest season is May to October.

SANTIAGO DE CUBA

INTRODUCTION

Santiago, home of rum and revolution, has an ongoing rivalry with Havana, its larger historical counterpoint. It can make one claim that Havana cannot: in 1994 Santiago de Cuba (pop. 375,000) was awarded the highest distinction conferred by the International Confederation of Tourism Journalists and Writers—the *Manzana de Oro* (Golden Apple), the Oscar of tourism, awarded once a year to cities or entities considered the most outstanding in tourist value. Santiago de Cuba is only the second city in the Americas to have won the distinction (the first was Cartagena, in Colombia). I think this is stretching things a bit far, but there is no doubt that Santiago has a unique, enigmatic appeal. Not least are its dozen or so museums, broad tree-lined boulevards, and intimate squares, its life syncopated with hoofbeats and the squeak of carriage wheels and trucks that bounce along the streets to the rhythm of the rumba on the radio.

Bucolic residential areas are replete with colonnaded houses lining tree-shaded boulevards. Closer in to the historic center are older, rustic, tile-roofed dwellings graced by fancy forged-iron railings, weathered timbers, shady hanging balconies, turned wooden *rejas,* Moorish balustrades, and façades painted in faded tropical pastels. Adding to the charm are the cacti growing profusely from red-tile roofs, fulfilling an Oriente superstition that a cactus will keep away the evil eye. If a Santiaguero lets his or her cactus die, a year of bad luck will follow.

Santiago's main shopping streets are still lit at night by neon signs of the capitalist era—adding, even in its modernity, another layer of *tiemps perdu.* Much remains as it was in the 1950s, when Graham Greene wrote that the night "was hot and humid, and the greenery hung dark and heavy in the pallid light of half-strength lamps." Greene noted how "abandoned the streets of Santiago were after dark," with the shutters closed behind iron grilles, and how his protagonist, Wormold, gets roughed up in the shadowy streets by two policemen. (Greene had arrived in Santiago in 1958 to research his book and agreed to carry a suitcase full of supplies to Castro, whom he was going to interview in the Sierra Maestra. Unfortunately, the interview fell through. He recalls his tension-filled times in Santiago in his autobiographical *Ways of Escape.*)

Santiago is the most Africanized of Cuba's cities. The city and surrounding region were a clearinghouse for nationalities: its east-facing position and proximity to Jamaica and Haiti fostered close links between the city and the two Caribbean islands. (It is sometimes referred to as "Cuba's most Caribbean city.") The majority of the 30,000 or so French planters and merchants who fled Haiti following the revolution in 1791 chose to settle in and around Santiago, stitching their habits and customs onto the cultural quilt of the city. Many French planters also established coffee estates in the surrounding mountains, adding to the city's importance for trade. (Santiago attracts many French tourists, drawn by the city's historical connections to France.) Eventually black Haitians came also, as workers. The rich racial mixture has produced some of the most exciting music, art and architecture in the Caribbean. The potpourri of influences can be felt to this day.

The proud Santiagueros never tire of telling you about their noble rebelliousness, their long history of revolt against authority. Santiago is the "Hero of the Republic of Cuba," the "Hero City," the *capital moral de la Revolución,* though this is belied by the extreme degree of *jiniterismo* (hustling), the worst in the nation.

The port city is also a major industrial center: the distilleries of the original Bacardi rum are here, as are a chemical factory, oil refinery, and electricity generating plant belting out smoke and pouring disgusting effluvia into the bay.

Plan at least a two-day stay, more if you want to explore all the museums and sites fully.

HISTORY

Diego Velázquez founded the city in 1514 and named it for the King of Spain's patron saint, St. Jago. The city was named the Cuban capital and grew rapidly on the strength of trade inspired by its splendid harbor. Its first *capitangeneral* was none other than Hernán Cortéz, soon to be conqueror of Mexico. Other famous conquistadores resided here, too, including Francisco Pizarro (conqueror of Peru), Don Pedro de Alvarado (founder of Guatemala), and Juan Ponce de León (colonizer of Puerto Rico). Many of the original buildings still stand, including Velázquez's own sturdy home, financed by wealth from nearby copper mines at El Cobre. Small quantities of gold were also discovered locally.

Santiago remained capital of Cuba only until February 1553, when the governor transferred his residence to Havana because "in the said town is the confluence of all the trade of the island." Santiago had lost its advantage. The El Cobre mines closed shortly thereafter, and the city diminished in size to only several hundred people. The city was subsequently damaged by earthquakes and razed by pirates, including the French buccaneer Jacques de Sores, who held a group of prominent Santiaguerans hostage for a ransom of 80,000 doubloons. The pirate Henry Morgan also captured the city, in 1662, after taking the Morro Castle.

Spanish settlers from Jamaica boosted Santiago's numbers when the island was seized by the English in 1655. And at the close of the century (when Santiago's population approached 10,000), a massive influx of French émigrés from Haiti doubled the city population and added new vitality. Another boost in fortunes came in 1793, when Spanish authorities granted Santiago an *asamiento* (unlimited license) to import slaves to be sold to sugar plantations elsewhere on the island. Countless West African slaves gained their first look at the New World as they stepped shackled and confused into the harsh light on Santiago's wharves.

The Heroes' City

Santiago has had a reputation as a liberal city dating to 1836, when city fathers proclaimed

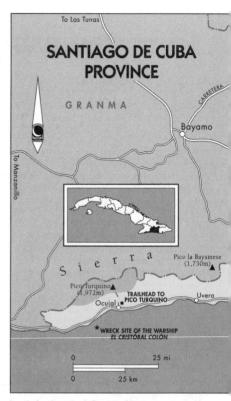

local elections in defiance of the governor in Havana. Governor Tacón won the battle, but Santiago had asserted an autonomy that propelled it to the forefront in the evolving quest for independence. Antonio Maceo (the Bronze Titan), a mulatto—mixed African and Spanish—who rose to become second-in-command of the patriot army during the two wars of independence, hailed from Santiago. Santiago, however, was never taken. Instead it became a concentration camp held by Spanish troops and enclosed by barbed wire.

Santiago was thrust into the military spotlight again in 1898, when the United States entered the fray. On 1 July U.S. troops reached the outskirts of Santiago and the defenses atop San Juan Hill that protected the city. Throughout the morning, the U.S. artillery softened up the Spanish defenders before about 3,000 U.S. and

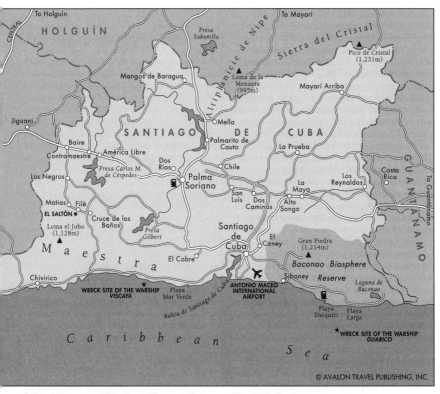

Cuban troops—one infantry and two cavalry regiments, including Teddy Roosevelt and the Rough Riders—stormed the hill under cover of punishing fire from Gatling guns.

In portraits, Roosevelt is portrayed leading the charge on a white horse, but it is thought that he himself was on foot. Though Roosevelt's part has been vastly overblown by U.S. history texts, the victory (at a cost of 223 U.S. soldiers and 102 Spanish troops) sealed the war. The Spanish navy, meanwhile, had gathered in Santiago harbor. On 3 July, it attempted to escape. A battle ensued. Several Spanish vessels were immediately sunk. Others grounded or were sunk as they raced west along the coast.

The Spanish surrender was signed on San Juan Hill on 17 July. The Spanish flag came down and up went the Stars and Stripes.

The 20th Century

To its credit, the U.S. military government initiated extensive construction projects, including hospitals, schools, and roads. Money talks louder than good intentions, however: U.S. forces came ashore in 1912 and again in 1917 (U.S. Marines were stationed in Oriente from 1917 to 1923) to protect U.S. sugar growers and mining interests from labor unrest and political insurgency. Hence, as a major industrial and intellectual center, Santiago became a hotbed of revolutionary activity during the decades prior to 1950.

The opening shots in Castro's revolution were fired here on 26 July 1953, when the hot-blooded 26-year-old lawyer and his followers attacked the Moncada Barracks at dawn in an attempt to seize arms and inspire a general uprising. Moncada was originally built as a fortress by the

Spanish, surrounded by crenellated walls. Castro had studied the barracks plans for months and concluded that the fort could be rushed through the southeastern gate. The commandos would then fan out through the barracks with newly seized weapons.

At 5 a.m. on Sunday, 26 July, the 123 young men sang the national anthem. Then, dressed in brown Cuban Army uniforms, they set out crammed inside 16 cars, with Castro in the fifth car—a brand-new 1953 Buick sedan. The third car, containing Raúl (leading a second unit), took a wrong turn and arrived at his target—the Palace of Justice—after the fighting had begun. Another car had a flat tire and yet another car took a wrong turn, which reduced the fighting force to 105 men, who attacked Mondada with a few .44-caliber sawed-off Winchester rifles, hunting shotguns, a single M-1 rifle, a single Browning submachine gun, and assorted sporting rifles.

At first, the attack went according to plan. The sentinels were taken by surprise and disarmed. As the commandos rushed into the barracks, an Army patrol appeared. Fidel gunned his car, but it hit the curb obliquely and stalled. Gunfire erupted. The alarm bells were sounded. Then a volley of machine-gun fire sprayed the rebels, who were forced to retreat. The battle lasted less than 30 minutes. Only eight rebels were killed in combat, but 61 others were caught and tortured to death.

Batista's army, which lost 19 soldiers, claimed that Moncada was attacked by "between 400 and 500 men, equipped with the most modern instruments of war," and that Castro's men had been gunned down at Moncada. A photographer, however, managed to get photos of the tortured *Fidelistas,* and Marta Rojas, then a young journalist for *Bohemia,* smuggled the film to Havana in her brassiere. The gruesome photos were printed five days later, exposing Batista's lie and unleashing a wave of disgust.

The failed and seemingly suicidal attack lent legitimacy to Castro's 26th of July Movement (M-26-7), the revolutionary group that evolved in subsequent years as the preeminent opposition body working to topple Batista. Santiago became a hotbed of underground rebellion. Assassinations and summary executions were common. It reached a crescendo on 30 November 1956, when a 22-year-old Santiago

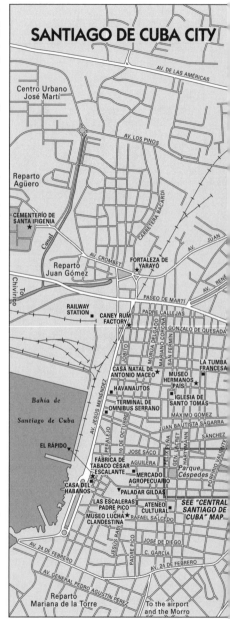

SANTIAGO DE CUBA CITY

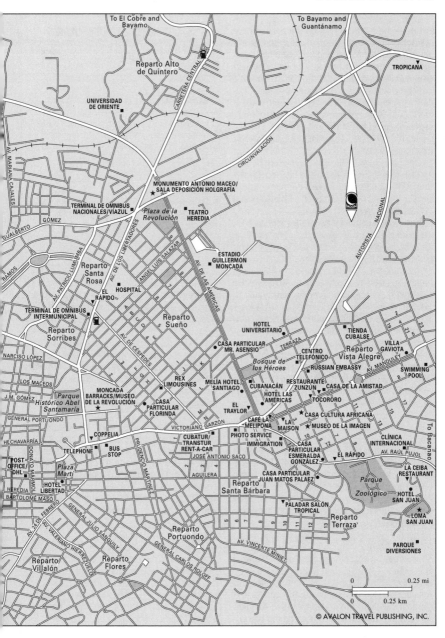

To El Cobre and Bayamo
To Bayamo and Guantánamo

Reparto Alto de Quintero

TROPICANA

UNIVERSIDAD DE ORIENTE

CARRETERA CENTRAL

CIRCUNVALACIÓN

AV. MARIANA CALAJES

MONUMENTO ANTONIO MACEO/
SALA DEPOSICIÓN HOLGRAFÍA

TERMINAL DE OMNIBUS
NACIONALES/VIAZUL

GÓMEZ

Plaza de la
Revolución

TEATRO
HEREDIA

AV. DE LOS LIBERTADORES

ANGEL LUIS SALAZAR

AUTOPISTA NACIONAL

GUALBERTO

RAMOS

Reparto
Santa Rosa

EL RÁPIDO

HOSPITAL

AV. PATRICIO LUMUMBA

ESTADIO
GUILLERMÓN
MONCADA

AV. DE LAS AMÉRICAS

TERMINAL DE OMNIBUS
INTERMUNICIPAL

Reparto
Sorribes

Reparto
Sueño

HOTEL
UNIVERSITARIO

TIENDA
CUBALSE

VILLA
GAVIOTA

NARCISO LÓPEZ

AV. DE CESPEDES

CASA PARTICULAR
MR. ASENSIO

TERRAZA

CENTRO
TELEFÓNICO

Reparto
Vista Alegre

SWIMMING
POOL

LOS MACEOS

Bosque de
los Héroes

RUSSIAN EMBASSY

AV. MANDULEY

J.M. GÓMEZ

REX
LIMOUSINES

MELIÁ HOTEL
SANTIAGO

CUBANACÁN

RESTAURANTE
ZUNZÚN

CASA DE LA AMISTAD

Parque
Histórico Abel
Santamaría

MONCADA
BARRACKS/MUSÉO
DE LA REVOLUCIÓN

CASA
PARTICULAR
FLORINDA

HOTEL LAS
AMÉRICAS

TOCORORO

GENERAL PORTUONDO

EL
TRAYLOR

VICTORIANO GARZÓN

CAFÉ LA
MELIPONA

LA
MAISON

CASA CULTURA AFRICANA

MUSEO DE LA IMAGEN

HECHAVARRÍA

COPPELIA

CUBATUR/
TRANSTUR
RENT-A-CAR

PHOTO SERVICE
IMMIGRATION

CASA
PARTICULAR
ESMERALDA
GONZÁLEZ

CLÍNICA
INTERNACIONAL

AV. RAÚL PUJOL

TELEPHONE

BUS
STOP

JOSÉ ANTONIO SACO

EL RÁPIDO

POST
OFFICE/
DHL

Plaza
Martí

PRUDENCIO MARTÍNEZ

AGUILERA

CASA PARTICULAR
JUAN MATOS PALAEZ

LA CEIBA
RESTAURANT

HOTEL
LIBERTAD

Reparto
Santa Bárbara

Parque
Zoológico

HOTEL
SAN JUAN

HEREDIA

BARTOLOMÉ MASÓ

PALADAR SALÓN
TROPICAL

Reparto
Terraza

LOMA
SAN JUAN

AV. 24 DE FEBRERO

GENERAL JULIO SANGUILY

AV. VALERIANO HIERREZUELO

Reparto
Portuondo

AV. VICENTE MINIÉ

PARQUE
DIVERSIONES

Reparto
Villalón

Reparto
Flores

GENERAL CARLOS ROLOFF

DONATO MÁRMOL

To Bacanao

0   0.25 mi

0   0.25 km

© AVALON TRAVEL PUBLISHING, INC.

teacher named Frank País led a group of M-26-7 rebels in a daring attack on the police headquarters in Santiago, timed to coincide with the landing of the *Granma* bringing Castro and other revolutionaries from exile in Mexico. País' attack was ill-fated, and after the fiasco, Batista's henchmen initiated a campaign of indiscriminate murders. Frank País was shot on the street on 30 July 1958. His funeral erupted into a massive protest led by Santiago's mothers. The city workers went on strike, inspiring similar protests throughout Cuba.

On 2 January 1959, two days after Batista fled the island, Fidel Castro and his Rebel Army arrived in Santiago to accept the surrender of Batista's general. Castro gave his victory speech in Céspedes Park.

The postrevolutionary years have seen a massive construction. An oil refinery was built north of the city, along with a power-generating plant, a huge textile mill, a cement factory, and port expansion. The suburbs grew rapidly, most notably in Reparto José Martí, northwest of the city (this giant housing complex was begun in 1965 to replace the San Pedro slums), where microbrigades built large apartment blocks, community centers, health clinics, and gardens. The complex is a staple of many tour excursions, most of which miss the contemporary slums, including the entire southwestern *repartos* of Van Van and Altamira, that are as squalid as the worst of Mexican shanties.

ORIENTATION

Santiago is built on hills on the east side of the Bahía de Santiago de Cuba. The old town falls gently toward the bay so that you can look down upon the red-tile roofs of the historic quarter. (Most streets have both modern and older names—Aguilera is also known as Marina; Sacó as Enramada.)

Historic Quarter
The narrow, bustling streets are roughly arranged in a grid. At its heart is Parque Céspedes, bounded by Félix Pena and Lacret (north-south) and Aguilera and Heredia (east-west). Aguilera and Heredia fall westward seven blocks to Avenida Jesús Menéndez, which runs along the harbor-

SANTIAGO STREET NAMES

NEW NAME	OLD NAME
24 de Febrero	Trocha
Aguilera	Marina
Antonio Saco	Enramada
Bartolomé Masó	San Basilio
Donato Marmol	San Agustin
Féliz Peña	Santo Tomás
General Lacret	San Pedro
General Portuondo	Trinidad
Jesús Menéndez	Alameda
Joaquín Castillo Duany	Santa Lucía
José Saco	Enramada
Hartmann	San Félix
Mariano	Corona
Mayia Rodríguez	Reloj
Padre Quiroga	Clarin
Pio Rosado	Carniceria
Porfirio Valiente	Calvario

front and broadens to the south into a wide boulevard with a grassy central median: Parque Alameda. The main shopping streets are Aguilera and Sacó, one block north.

Aguilera leads east from Parque Céspedes uphill to Plaza de Martí, a major hub on the eastern edge of the historic quarter. The wide Avenida Victoriano Garzón winds northeast from Plaza de Martí to an all-important traffic circle—**Parque Ferreiro**—at the junction with Avenida Las Américas. Five major spokes fan out from this hub.

A broad boulevard—Avenida de Libertadores—begins two blocks east of Plaza de Martí and leads north past the Moncada Barracks to Plaza de la Revolución. (It continues north as the Carretera Central to El Cobre, Bayamo, and Havana.) Avenida 12 de Agosto leads south from Plaza de Martí to the airport and Morro Castle.

Around Parque Ferreiro
Avenida las Américas runs northwest from Paque Ferreiro past the Hotel Las Américas and Hotel Santiago to Plaza de la Revolución. Avenida Manduley leads north from the traffic circle into the residential Reparto Vista Alegre district. Garón continues northeast from the traffic circle as Avenida Pujol (Carretera Siboney) to San

Juan Hill, the Hotel San Juan, and Baconao; and Avenida General Cabrera also leads north from the traffic circle through Vista Alega to the Autopista Nacional, which leads north from the city for only 22 km before petering out in the middle of nowhere. *Avoid the Autopista at night: it is unlit and unmarked and traveled by vehicles without lights. A very dangerous business!*

THE HISTORIC QUARTER

Parque Céspedes

Formerly known as Plaza de Armas, this compact square at the heart of Santiago de Cuba, is ringed with gas lamps, metal grills, and tall shade trees. It is crowded by important buildings and has at its center a stone statue of the square's namesake hero, who is buried in Santiago.

A lively flood of humanity ebbs and flows, lending Parque Céspedes a cosmopolitan air. The tour buses are thick around the main square, attracting *jiniteros* and *jiniteras* eagerly eyeing the foreigners entering and leaving the Hotel Casa Grande. At night it is awash with activity, when youth gather to smooch and converse. A tradition here is for small children to be given rides in little carts pulled by billy goats.

The beautiful white colonial building on the north side is the **Poder Popular** (also called the Ayuntamiento, or Town Hall), former headquarters of the Spanish colonial-governor. The original building to occupy the site was first occupied by Hernán Cortéz. The current structure dates from the 1950s and is based on a design from 1783 that inspired the prize-winning project for a municipal government house. Its antecedent, built in 1855, was toppled by an earthquake and had housed the U.S. military government during Cuba's occupation. It was from the overhanging balcony with deep sky-blue *rejas* that Fidel Castro gave the victory speech on 2 January 1959, after he entered town following Batista's flight from Cuba.

Dominating the plaza is the cathedral—**Santa Ifigenia Basílica Metropolitana**—raised on a pedestal on the southern side. The peach-colored cathedral is the fourth building to occupy the site. The original was begun in 1528. The current edifice dates to 1922, although its nave is held aloft by walls erected in 1810. Much of the interior decoration has been beautifully restored, including choir stalls hand-carved in precious hardwoods. Its ecclesiastical treasures and documents are displayed in a small museum. The remains of Diego Velázquez are entombed within. Between the church's twin towers is a statue of the Angel of the Annunciation holding a trumpet. The entrance is to the west side.

The east side of the cathedral contains the **Museo Arquidiocesano,** an art gallery with antique and contemporary religious art. It's open Mon.-Sat. 9:30 a.m.-5:30 p.m. Entrance costs US$1 (plus US$1 for cameras, US$3 for videos).

On the park's west side is **La Casa de Don Diego Velázquez,** the former home of Cuba's first colonizer. It dates from 1516 and is claimed to be the oldest house in Cuba. The somber Spanish mansion is fronted by dark wooden Moorish window grills and shutters. Cuba's oldest house is in remarkably good condition. Velázquez lived upstairs. A gold foundry was maintained downstairs (it is still there, in the rear). The house today contains the **Museo Colonial** (or Museo de Artes Decorativas), tel. (226) 52652, with separate rooms that concentrate on two periods—the 16th and 18th centuries. It is full of period furniture, tapestries, crystal ware, and artwork. It was previously open Mon.-Sat. 9 a.m.-5 p.m. and Sunday 9 a.m.-1 p.m. (US$2), but was closed for restoration at press time. The **Museo de Muñecas** (doll museum) is supposedly here, too, intending to display an impressive collection of dolls, most dressed in national costumes, from all over the world, arranged by region and country.

Calle Heredia

The cultural heart of the city is Calle Heredia, extending east three blocks from the southeast corner of Parque Céspedes. It is full of places of interest and resounds with the tap of clave and the beat of the drum. The street has traditionally been closed to traffic on weekend evenings, when it hosts a cultural fair drawing troubadours, clowns, mimes, and revelers from far and wide.

Your first stop should be the **Casa de la Trova** at Heredia #208, one block east of Parque Céspedes. What a tragedy befell this once-cozy institution in 1995, when a thoughtless remake stole much of the charm of this tremendously atmospheric place, dark and moody, the air thick

CENTRAL SANTIAGO DE CUBA

JOSÉ ANTONIO SACO   (ENRAMADA)

(SAN PEDRO)

(SAN FÉLIX)

(CARNICERÍA)

CASA PARTICULAR
MUJERES DE ARENAS

BANCO FINANCIERO
INTERNACIONAL

PODER
★ POPULAR

▼ CASA DE TÉ

CENTRO
TELEFÓNICO

MUSEO
COLONIAL/CASA ★
DE DON DIEGO
VELÁZQUEZ

BANCO DE CRÉDITO
Y COMERCIO

▼ DISCO
300

AGUILERA

(SANTO TOMÁS)

ISLAZUL

MUSEO ★
BACARDI

Parque

■ GALERÍA
ORIENTE

DHL

Céspedes

ROSADO

BANCO DE CRÉDITO
Y COMERCIO

■ ASISTUR/TRANSTAXI/
HAVANATUR

HOTEL
CASA GRANDE

POST
OFFICE ■

CASA PARTICULAR
■ EL HOLANDES

PIO

MUSEO EL
★ CARNAVAL

CALLE   HEREDIA

CENTRO
TELEFÓNICO

GALERÍA
SANTIAGO

▼ RUMBOS/
VÍA

■ CASA DE
LA TROVA

★ CASA JOSÉ
MARÍA HEREDIA

■ GALERÍA DE ARTE
UNEAC

CINE
RIALTO ■

CASA DEL
ESTUDIANTE

■ ÓPTICAS MIRAMAR

SANTA IFIGENIA BASÍLICA ★
METROPOLITANA

■ CASA CATEDRAL

PHOTO ■
SERVICE

CUBARTESANÍA ■

BARTOLOMÉ MASÓ   (SAN BASILIO)

▼ SANTIAGO
1900

FÉLIX PEÑA

GENERAL LACRET

HARTMANN

JOAQUÍN   CASTILLO   DUANY

© AVALON TRAVEL PUBLISHING, INC.

with smoke and charged with cheers from the audience. The dark wooden swing doors and paneling are gone, as is the nostalgic photo collection, replaced with the art of local musical heroes, such as the Trio Matamoros. At least the musicians, who perform for the love of it, the are still as good as ever, and their haunting melodies and plaintive *boleros* of the *trova* still reverberate down the street.

If thirsty, nip next door to the **Casa de Vino** to sample the locally made wines and cheeses.

One block east, between Hartmann and Pío Rosado, is **Casa José María Heredia,** the birth-place of the 19th-century poet José María Heredia (1803-39), the first Cuban poet to champion independence. The house is furnished in colonial fashion. Open Tues.-Sun. 9 a.m.-9 p.m. (US$1).

One block farther, on the north side of Heredia, is the **Museo el Carnaval,** tel. (226) 2-6955, which tells the history of Santiago's colorful carnival. Some of the outlandish costumes are on display. Folkloric shows are hosted daily at 4 p.m. (see the Entertainment section). It's open Tues.-Sun. 9 a.m.-5 p.m. (and possibly Monday by request). Entrance is US$1, plus US$1 for photos (US$5 for videos and professional cameras).

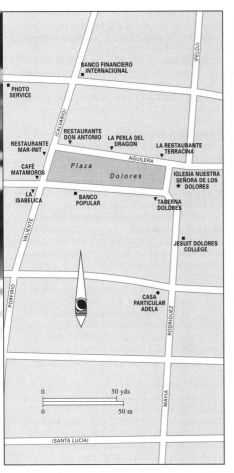

To the right of the church, extending to Calle Heredia, is the **Jesuit Dolores College,** where Fidel Castro was educated as a youth. It was one of the most profound intellectual influences in his life. (Fidel had earlier been enrolled in Santiago's Marist brother's La Salle school, a private establishment for boys from affluent families. There he established a reputation as a tempestuous tyke, according to teachers' reports.)

At night, the park is a hang-out for gays.

Plaza de Martí

This small plaza is laid out at the top of Aguilera, on the eastern fringe of the old city. At its center is a thick phallic column topped with a bulbous red cone. Large cannons sit at the base. A bust of Martí is at the southern end of the park, which has plenty of shade trees. The original plaza was built in 1860 as the Spanish parade ground and execution spot for Cuban patriots.

Museo Lucha Clandestina

The Museum of the Underground Fight, tel. (226) 2-4689, is dedicated to telling the tale of the 26th of July Movement. The museum is housed in the old police station that was attacked by revolutionaries led by Frank País on 30 November 1956. The building is one of Santiago's most splendidly restored colonial houses. Open Tues.-Sun. 9 a.m.-5 p.m. (entrance, US$1). To reach the museum, follow the road (Calle Rabi) lined by a crenellated wall that curves uphill from the top of Calle Padre Pico, in an area known as **Loma del Intendente,** settled in the late 18th century by French citizens fleeing Haiti. Its streets are lined with 16th-century houses.

Calle Padre Pico is a wide staircase that joins the upper and lower parts of the city. (Santiagueros gather beneath the shady eaves to play dominoes, gossip, or strum guitars.) Touristy hype urges you to climb the steps for a privileged view over Santiago. Females may receive a lift from unsolicited compliments—locals say that the steps make women undulate, and it has become a tradition for men to gather here to praise their movement with clever poetic phrases. Three members of the 26th of July Movement were killed on the steps of Padre Pico during the attack on police headquarters.

Plaza Dolores

The most enchanting of Santiago's squares is this delightful little plaza fringed by quaint colonial buildings. It was formerly a religious center and market (its name is taken from the church—**Iglesia Nuestra Señora de los Dolores**—that looms over the square). The teeny park is shaded by tamarind trees, bougainvillea, and hibiscus and has wrought-iron seats surrounding a marble column bearing a larger-than-life bronze statue of Francisco Vicente Aguilera, who was born in Bayamo in 1821 and died in New York in 1877.

You should return to Parque Céspedes via Calle Corona—one block east of Padre Pico—where, at Bartolomé Masó, you'll pass beneath arches that open to **Balcón de Velázquez,** a plaza offering splendid views over the city.

Museo Bacardi

This museum, at Calle Pío Rosado, e/ Aguilera and Heredia, tel. (226) 2-8402, was founded by Emilio Bacardi Moreau in 1928 and contains its astounding and eclectic collection. A member of the expatriate and anti-Castroite Bacardi rum family, Emilio, patriot writer and mayor of Santiago, is in good graces; he was imprisoned in the Morro Castle for his revolutionary activities last century. The museum is housed in a huge neoclassical edifice with Corinthian columns and statues in the heart of Santiago's oldest quarter, but it makes nonetheless for a dramatic effect.

The splendid museum has three floors. The first contains a superb array of colonial artifacts, including slave shackles and stocks, and eclectic miscellany from a printing press to a boomerang. Most impressive, however, is the huge array of antique daggers, blunderbusses, rifles, pistols, and the personal effects of leading 19th-century heroes.

The second floor is an art gallery, including 19th-century and contemporary works by leading figures. The basement, entered by a separate door off Aguilera, has a small but impressive display of pre-Columbian artifacts from throughout the Americas, including colorful feather headdresses, a shrunken head *(cabeza reducido),* pottery shards, and two Peruvian mummies folded up and squashed as if to fit in a box for mailing. There's even an Egyptian mummy and a mummified baby crocodile, both blackened as if pan-baked in engine oil.

The museum is open Mon.-Sat. 10 a.m.-8 p.m. Entrance costs US$2.

Casa Natal de Antonio Maceo

If you're interested in Cuban history, call in at the little house at Calle Maceo #207 e/ Corona y Rastro, tel. (226) 2-3550, the birthplace of Antonio Maceo, a mulatto who rose to become second in command of the Liberation Army during the wars of independence. Maceo was born here on 14 June 1845. The fearless leader and brilliant tactician refused to accept the treaty

ending the First War of Independence in 1878 (his act is known as the Protest of Baraguá). He fought on for several months until fleeing into exile. He returned with José Martí in April 1895 and led a rebel army all the way to Pinar del Río before being killed in battle on 7 December 1895. The house is now a museum containing a few personal effects (mostly letters). It's open Mon.-Sat. 9 a.m.-5 p.m. Entrance US$1.

Museo Abel Santamaría

This museum, at Calle Trinidad and Carretera Central, is in the former home of one of Cuba's most revered heroes. A confidante of Fidel Castro and his designated successor in the revolutionary movement, Santamaría helped organize the attack on the Moncada barracks. He led a contingent that captured the hospital across the street. Santamaría and his men continued to snipe at the barracks, unaware that the attack had failed. Batista's troops stormed the hospital, where Santamaría and his 23 men had taken to bed, pretending to be patients (his sister, Haydee, was one of the attackers and pretended to be a nurse). They were betrayed and ruthlessly tortured. Haydee's fiancé, Boris Luís, was beaten to death on the spot with rifle butts. Abel was brutally tortured and died later that day. Open Mon.-Sat. 8 a.m.-noon and 2-6 p.m. and Sunday 9 a.m.-8 p.m.

Museo Hermanos País

The house at Avenida General Banderas #266 e/ Trinidad y Habana, tel. (226) 5-2710, is where the revolutionary heroes Frank and José País were born. Frank, a teacher, was instrumental in running Castro's 26th of July Movement in Havana during the mid-1950s and became the movement's principal leader in Oriente, providing logistical support to the rebel army in the mountains. He led the ill-fated attack on the police headquarters in Santiago on 30 November 1956, timed to coincide with the *Granma* landing. José was shot and killed in June 1957, and Frank was assassinated by police agents one month later. It's open Mon.-Sat. 9 a.m.-5 p.m. (US$1).

Caney Rum Factory

This factory, at the north end of Avenida Jesús Menéndez, at Gonzalo de Quesada, is the oldest rum factory in Cuba. It was built in 1868 by the

Santiago's César Escalante cigar factory is worthy of a stop.

Bacardi family and nationalized in 1959, after which the Cuban government continued to make rum under the Bacardi title. Bacardi sued. The International Court of the Hague found in favor of Bacardi, which had set up shop in Puerto Rico. Today three rums are made here: Ron Matusalem, Ron Caney, and Ron Palmas Patricruzado. A warehouse across the railway tracks stores 42,000 casks, many of which have gathered dust for 15 years.

Guided tours have been offered in the past but were not longer at press time. There's a tasting room and a gift store selling rum: *tragos* (shots) cost US$0.85 to US$1.80 depending on rum. Supposedly, this is the only place in the country where you can buy Havana Club rum matured for 15 years (US$90), acclaimed as the finest rum in the country. Try the five-year-old Ron Paticruzados—"Crossed Legs Rum"— which Santiagueros swear is the best drink with which to keep cool in the sweltering heat. Open Mon.-Sat. 9 a.m.-6 p.m. and Sunday 9 a.m.- noon.

Fábrica de Tabaco César Escalante

Do visit the cigar factory on Avenida Jesús Menéndez and the foot of Bartolomé Masó, tel. (226) 23258. Here you can watch men and women rolling, snipping, and pressing fine Cuban cigars. There's a well-stocked cigar store attached. It's open Mon.-Fri. 8 a.m.-4 p.m. Entrance costs US$5 (a rip-off). No photos are permitted.

Far more interesting is to pop behind the factory to the *escuela de tabacos,* where trainees roll in a more earthy ambience. You'll be fobbed off and directed to the main factory, but a liberal dose of charm usually wins the day in your favor, and you may be permitted to earn a quick snapshot.

NORTH OF PLAZA MARTÍ

Moncada Barracks

A must-visit site, this former military barracks, on Calle Carlos Aponte, tel. (226) 2-0157, was a linchpin in Batista's control of the Oriente. The site is renowned for the fateful day on 26 July 1953, when Fidel Castro and 79 poorly armed cohorts dressed in Cuban Army uniforms stormed the barracks. It has a medieval countenance, with its castellated ocher-colored walls and its turrets with gun slits all around.

After the Revolution, Moncada was turned into a school, the Ciudad Escolar 26 de Julio. A portion of the main building near the entrance gate is riddled with bullet holes. They're not the originals however; Batista's troops filled those in. Castro apparently had the holes redone using photographs. This section today houses the superb **Museo de la Revolución,** which tells the tale of the attack (aided by an illuminated 3-D model), the Revolution, and subsequent history. One wall has the names of the 61 rebels and nine innocent civilians murdered to fulfill Batista's promise to kill 70 people in retaliation for the attack. There's a large-scale model of the barracks showing the attack. Prolific weaponry includes Castro's personal sharpshooter rifle. Blood-stained uniforms hang inside glass cabinets. A separate room is dedicated to José Martí.

Open Mon.-Sat. 9 a.m.-5 p.m. and Sunday 9 a.m.-1 p.m. Entrance costs US$2 (plus US$2 for cameras, US$5 for videos).

Parque Abel Santamaría

On the west side of Avenida de Libertadores, opposite Moncada, is a Mount Rushmore in miniature—a huge granite cube atop a column and carved with the faces of Abel Santamaría and José Martí. A fountain seems to hold the cube aloft magically.

The wide, tree-lined boulevard is lined with bronze busts of revolutionary heroes.

Bosque de los Héroes

This small park sits atop a rise opposite the Hotel Santiago on Avenida Las Américas. At first the monument looks totally uninspired: simple building blocks arranged higgledy-piggledy. However, on the east side are engravings of revolutionary heroes carved into the marble tableaux. Center place goes to Fidel, with José Martí, Celia Sánchez, and other to each side. The rest of the park is totally unkempt, and the bamboo bushes are used as toilets by Santiagueros. Watch where you step!

Plaza de la Revolución

This wide-open plaza at the junction of Avenida Las Américas and Avenida de los Libertadores is dominated by the massive **Monumento Antonio Maceo** dedicated to the hero-general of the War of Independence. Maceo was nicknamed the Bronze Titan, and the mammoth statue of the general on a rearing horse is appropriately cast in bronze. An eternal flame flickers in a marble-lined bowl cut into the base. Soaring, rust-colored, crystal-shaped metal sculptures are set obliquely into the ground like great pikes.

There's a museum—**Sala Deposición Holgrafía**—beneath the mound. It tells of Maceo's life and of the War of the Independence—using holograms, and featuring an illuminated 3-D model showing the route of his battles. The entrance is on the north side of the monument. It's open Mon.-Sat. 9 a.m.-5 p.m. and Sunday 9 a.m.-1 p.m. Entrance costs US$1.

REPARTO VISTA ALEGRE

This leafy residential district is bounded on the south by Avenida de las Américas and on the east by Avenida Pujol (Carretera Siboney). Avenida Manduley runs through the center of Vista Alegre and is lined with shade trees, bougainvillea, and once-upscale villas of varying ages and styles: venerable wooden Caribbean-style houses, grandiose neoclassical villas, and modern Miami-style homes. Many were confiscated by

Moncada Barracks

the government from their owners after the Revolution and turned into government offices, clinics, and schools. Note the grand three-story, pink, neo-baroque house with white columns that stands at the corner of Calle 9. This is the **Casa de Don Pepe Bosch.** It was once owned by a Mambí general. It is now a Young Pioneer's School and has a Soviet MiG fighter jet in the playground.

Museo de la Imagen
This museum, at the corner of Calle 5 and Calle 8, tel. (226) 4-2234, was established by famed cameraman Bernabá Muñiz (affectionately known as "Bebo"), who gained his first screen credit when he captured on film a man who decided to play Tarzan—naked—down Avenida de los Misiones in Havana. He went on to film Fulgencio Batista's coup d'etat in 1952, the surrender of the Moncada barracks to the revolutionaries in 1959, and the victory parade by tank with Fidel from Santiago to Havana.

His Museum of Images features almost 500 photographic, film, and TV cameras—everything from CIA espionage cameras to a stereoscopic viewfinder from 1872. The museum also contains a library of over 200 feature films, newsreels, and documentaries dating back to 1926. It's open Mon.-Sat. 9 a.m.-5 p.m. (US$1).

Casa Cultura Africana
Cuba's African legacy comes alive in this exquisite museum on Avenida Manduley e/ Calles 3 y 5. It is full of marvelous carvings and weavings. Entrance costs US$1.

San Juan Hill
Loma San Juan rises on the east side of Avenida Pujol to a pleasant park shaded by palms.

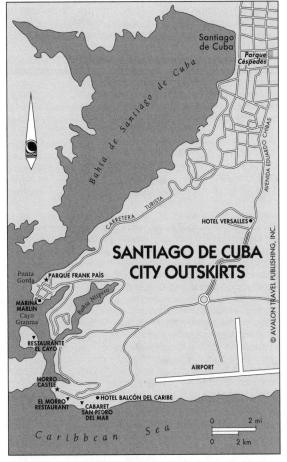

Every U.S. schoolchild knows that Teddy Roosevelt and his Rough Riders defeated the Spanish here. Today, the landscaped park contains various monuments and cannons. Plaques tell the tale of the War of Independence. There's a Tomb of the Unknown *Mambí*, the independence fighters (appropriately, the largest monument, erected in 1929, is also to the Mambí). One memorial is dedicated to Cuban revolutionaries and "the generous American soldiers who sealed a covenant of liberty and fraternity between the two nations." There are individual monuments to each U.S. battalion, and a replica fortified redoubt bears plaques naming all the U.S. soldiers killed and wounded. There is no monument, however, to Roosevelt and his Rough Riders because the Cuban liberationists who helped storm the hill weren't even invited to the surrender ceremony beneath the huge spreading ceiba tree on 16 July 1898. The tree still stands about 400 yards west of San Juan Hill in its own little park off Avenida Pujol. Alas, it had its branches torn off by a hurricane in 1999.

VICINITY OF MORRO CASTLE

Morro Castle

Santiago's most impressive structure is poised ominously atop the cliffs at the narrow entrance to Santiago Bay, about 14 km south of Santiago. This enormous piece of military architecture—a minotaur's maze of stairways and dungeons—was begun in 1638. The Morro was rebuilt and strengthened in 1664, after the English pirate Henry Morgan reduced it to rubble. It was recently restored using coral chunks and red brick alongside the much-worn original limestone blocks. The effect is not lost, however, and you still gain a full sense of the power of the Morro. There are cannons everywhere.

You enter via a narrow drawbridge over a deep moat glazed with colored colonial tiles. Guides will lead you through the passageways (don't forget to tip) the powder magazine (still full of cannonballs, and a tread for hauling them

to the batteries), and the chapel, which still has its original pews and a large wooden statue of Christ on the cross. One room has a marvelous exhibit of the naval battle off Santiago during the Spanish-Cuban War, including photographs and a splendid map of the engagements.

The castle houses the **Museo de Pirateria** (Museum of Piracy), with displays on piracy, colonialism, and slavery. There are old blunderbusses, muskets, cutlasses, and Toledo blades in glass cases. One room informs visitors of Operation Mongoose, the Kennedys' no-holds-barred efforts to destabilize the Castro regime. It was closed at press time for restoration.

The Morro is open Mon.-Fri. 9 a.m.-5 p.m. and weekends 8 a.m.-4 p.m. Entrance costs US$3.

Getting There: The Morro is signed from Santiago. Follow Avenida 12 de Agosto south from Plaza de Martí. This leads to Carretera del Morro divided highway and a traffic circle, about seven km south of Santiago. You'll reach a Y-junction. The road to the left leads to Morro Castle. Alternately, you can follow the bayfront Carretera Turística, which begins at the southern end of Avenida Jesús Menéndez. This serpentine road follows the bayshore to Punta Gorda and snakes in and out of inlets until you emerge atop the cliffs immediately east of the castle.

Punta Gorda

This slender peninsula lies between Morro Castle and town, with the Marina Marlin at the tip. It

Morro Castle, built in 1640, overlooks the entrance to Santiago Bay

was once fashionable with Santiago's upper class, who had their fine old wooden homes here. Most of the houses still stand, albeit in dilapidated condition. A large statue of the revolutionary hero Frank País looms over the point in **Parque Frank País.**

Cayo Granma
The Morro and Punta Gorda look out over a little island in the bay; less than one km offshore, it looks as if it has been magically transferred from the Mediterranean. Today it is a small fishermen's colony, and rowboats berth beneath the eaves of quaint red-tiled waterfront houses. No cars run through the narrow streets that lead up to a church atop the hill. There's a beach—**Playa Socapa**—and a tiny tree-shaded plaza, where locals gather to play dominoes.

The **Restaurante El Cayo,** tel. (226) 9-0109, sits over the bay and serves seafood and *criollo* dishes.

Getting There: A passenger ferry serves Cayo Granma from Marina Marlin and leaves on demand; US$3 round-trip. Another small ferry leaves from the Alameda wharf in Santiago (departure times are erratic).

OTHER SITES

The **Fortress De Yarayó** is located four hundred meters north of the rum factory on Avenida Jesús Menéndez, at the junction of Paseo de Martí. It's a little ocher-colored fortress (the first of 116 that the Spanish built around Santiago) with wooden turrets and gun slits.

The **Santa Ifigenia Cemetery,** on Calzada Crombet, tel. (226) 3-2723, is hallowed ground. Its inspired grand entrance is dominated by a gateway dedicated to Cuban soldiers who died fighting in Angola. Just beyond is the tomb of José Martí beneath a crenellated hexagonal tower (each side represents one of the six original provinces of Cuba). Marble steps lead down to a circular mausoleum suffused in soft light—designed so that the sun would always shine on his coffin. The casket is draped with the Cuban flag.

Narrow walkways lined with palms lead past scores of marble tombs, some simple, many grand, adorned with angels, cherubs, and other statues. The cemetery also contains the graves of Carlos Manuel Céspedes, Emilio Bacardi, Tomás Estrada Palma (Cuba's first president), and heroes of the attack on the Moncada barracks (look for the red and black flags on their graves). Heroes of the War of Independence are entombed in a tiny castle.

Before the Revolution, the cemetery was segregated by race and social position. The poor folks' section, as you may expect, is to the rear.

It's open daily 8 a.m.-6 p.m. Entrance costs US$1, including a guide.

Santiago's **Jardín Botánico**—botanic garden—is run by the Cuban Academy of Sciences and contains a library and laboratories in addition to its specimen trees and plants. The garden is about three km southeast of town, on the south side of Carretera Siboney.

Cuba's flora and fauna and aboriginal cultures are also displayed at the small **Museo Arqueológico,** in the University de Oriente, on the Carretera Central, north of town.

DANGERS AND ANNOYANCES

Jiniteros are more openly aggressive here than elsewhere on the island, and you may be regularly accosted by "professional" hustlers who see tourists as the best opportunity around. Many approach quite shamelessly and simply demand, "Give me one dollar!" Try getting rid of them with a civil, *"No moleste, por favor"* ("Don't bother me, please") before switching to something stronger.

ACCOMMODATIONS

Casas Particulares
By all accounts there are more than 400 *casas particulares* in Santiago de Cuba. The greatest concentration is in the Reparto Sueño district, with about 150 from which to choose. Every street has at least one. Most owners will be happy to cook for you for about US$6 a meal. At press time, Santiago was the most liberal place outside Havana for relationships between foreigners and Cubans, and *casas particulares* permit Cuban guests.

Downtown: Casa Particular Mujeres de Arenas Calle Santo Tomás #554 (altos) e/ Enramadas y Aguilera, tel. (226) 2-0076, is run by three women who rent one simply furnished a/c room with fan and a shared bathroom with hot water (US$15-20). The entrance, just 20 meters from Parque Céspedes, is dauntingly dilapidated, but don't be put off, as the old house is attractive and has heaps of light. One of the trio, Yadira, speaks English.

Casa Particular El Holandes, Calle Heredia #251 esq. San Félix, tel. (226) 2-4878, is a delightful old home with two spacious, simply furnished a/c rooms upstairs (US$20), plus an antique-filled lounge (there's even an antique dentist's chair). The rooms are clean and share a bathroom with hot water.

Casa Particular Adela, Calle Heredia #374 esq. Reloj, tel. (226) 5-4740, is a spacious old home with one simple but appealing and well-lit room with a/c, fan, a clean private bathroom with hot water, and its own private entrance (US$20). There are numerous other private room rentals along Calle Heredia, a noisy street. Ideally you'll want a room to the rear. Similarly, Calle Bartolomé Masó claims a sprinkling of *casas particulares.*

Calle Aguilera also has several **casas particulares.** Try Alejandro Tomás's home at Calle Aguilera #602 e/ Bernada y Paraíso, tel. (226) 2-0844, with two small, simply furnished upstairs rooms independent of Alejandro's house. Both have a/c, fridges, and modern private bathrooms with hot water, and share a kitchen and rooftop patio (US$15-20). Nardys Aguilera rents a room across the street at Calle Aguilera #565 e/ San Agustín y Barnada, tel. (226) 2-2409. It's pleasantly furnished in 1950s style, receives both breezes and heaps of light, and is sheltered from street noise. It has a/c and a clean, modern bathroom with hot water (US$20).

The venerable **Casa Catedral,** Calle San Pedro #703 (altos) e/ Heredia y San Basilio, tel. (226) 5-3169, has views over the plaza from a breeze-swept, marble-floored lounge with doors that open onto a balcony. The owners rent two rooms (US$25). One has a huge, tiled colonial bathroom that is a feature in itself. The room is simply furnished, and has a fan plus a separate sitting room with a balcony with views. The second room has a/c plus a small, modern bathroom, kitchenette, and private entrance.

Reparto Sueño: One of the nicest houses in is that of Florinda Chaviano Martínez at Calle I

#58 e/ 2da y 3ra, tel. (226) 5-3660, with a modern lounge and a single, well-lit, nicely furnished room with a/c, radio, fridge, and thoroughly modern bathroom with hot water (US$20). A handsome breeze-swept patio with grapevine arbor proves perfect for enjoying breakfast. The hosts are liberal and attentive.

Another good option is Caridad Oruña Hernandez' home at Calle I #210 e/ 4ta y 5ta, tel. (226) 2-8233, with an attractive lounge plus a large, well-furnished a/c room with its own voluminous and modern bathroom with hot water (US$20-25). It offers secure parking. Even better is **Casa Particular Gloria Boué Alonso,** Calle J #212 e/ 5ta y 4ta, tel. (226) 2-3837, with two a/c rooms (one up, one down) for US$20 apiece. Both are nicely furnished and offer a TV, radio, fridge, and large, clean modern bathrooms with hot water. A third, smaller, room to the rear is more simply furnished (US$15). The TV lounge boasts leather sofas.

I also recommend **Casa Particular Nancy Téllez,** Calle J #265 e/ 6ta y 5ta, tel. (226) 2-5109. This well-furnished, breeze-swept home has a large TV, plus two a/c rooms (US$20): one, though dark, has a large and handsome bathroom. The owner serves meals in a dining room that opens to a charming patio, and there's secure parking.

Ifrahim Alfonso has two rooms at Calle I #160 e/ Céspedes y 4ta, tel. (226) 5-1528, for US$20. They're nicely furnished and share a large bathroom with hot water (one room has an intriguing Chinese motif). And Daisy González has a two-room apartment at Calle Carlos Aponte #661, tel. (226) 2-6614, for US$35-40, plus three rooms in a small yet pleasantly furnished home on the east side of the Moncada barracks. Each room has a/c and fridge (US$20). They share a clean bathroom with hot water.

If you're seeking a self-contained option, head to **Casa Particular Mr. Asensio,** at Calle J #306 e/ Avenida Las Américas y 6ta, tel. (226) 2-4660, in Italy, tel. (019) 692-067. The upstairs a/c apartment is splendid, with lively 1950s decor, cross-ventilation, fans, and even an ironing board and burglar alarm (US$20). There's a small kitchen, plus a rooftop patio and private garage (free). Alternately, try **Casa Particular Ayde Haber Mendez,** Calle J #65 e/ 2da y 3ra, tel. (226) 2-5186, with a two-room apartment with a handsome TV lounge with rockers, simply furnished rooms, a dining room, kitchen, and a clean bathroom and small terrace (US$40 for up to four people).

Repartos Vista Alegre and Terraza: These contiguous leafy residential suburbs offers some of the nicest houses in town. **Casa Particular Esmeralda González** has a nice middle-class home at Avenida Pujol #107 esq. 5ta, tel. (226) 4-1783, with 1960s furnishings. Esmeralda rents a spacious, well-lit, cross-ventilated room with an independent entrance, a/c, fans, and a marvelous period bathroom with hot water (US$20). It has secure parking.

Nearby, in Reparto Terraza, is **Casa Particular Juan Matos Palaez,** a beautiful 1950s-style home with two nicely furnished downstairs rooms with a/c and ceiling fans. They share an exquisite tiled bathroom with hot water (US$20). Two rooms upstairs comprise a large rooftop apartment with spacious kitchen with four-ring gas stove, a handsome well-lit lounge, and a modern bathroom (US$50). There are huge patios to front and rear.

Hotels

Budget: The **Hotel Libertad,** on the east side of Plaza Martí, tel. (226) 2-3080, was being gutted at press time and was slated to reopen as an Islazul hotel. Likewise, the **Hotel Rex,** on Victoriano Garzon, one block east of Plaza de Martí, tel. (226) 2-6314, was being renovated to accept tourists. Also consider the modern **Hotel Deportivo,** tel. (226) 4-2146, behind the sports stadium on Avenida Las Américas. It has 84 rooms with TVs. Rates were about US$15 s, US$18 d.

Foreign students attending the University of the Oriente can consider the **Hotel Universario** on Calle L at Calle 7, tel. (226) 4-2398, in Reparto Vista Alegre, and operated by Mercadu S.A.; tel. (7) 33-5011 in Havana, as a hostel for students and teachers. The simply furnished rooms share bathrooms with cold water only. There's a modest restaurant and bar. Rates were US$7 single, US$9 with breakfast.

Islazul has a booking office on Hartmann, one block east of Parque Céspedes. And the **Oficina de Reservaciones de Turismo Parque Baconao,** at Sacó #455, makes reservations for Cuban *campismos* along the coast east of town.

Inexpensive: I recommend the **Hotel San Juan,** Avenida Siboney y Calle 13, tel. (226) 8-7200, fax (226) 8-7017, formerly Motel Leningrado, on the south side of San Juan Hill. The 112 recently refurbished rooms are in villa-style blocks (take an upstairs room with a lofty ceiling to help dissipate the heat). Each has a large satellite TV, modern (albeit modest) furniture, safety box, and large, newly renovated bathrooms. Facilities include a swimming pool, boutique, tour desk, and car rental. There's an elegant restaurant, a buffet restaurant, and a nightclub adjoining the hotel. It's popular with European tour groups. Rates were US$35 s, US$43 d low season, US$46 s, US$55 d high season.

On the southern outskirts of town is **Hotel Versalles,** Alturas de Versalles Km 1, Carretera del Morro, tel. (226) 8-6603 or 9-1504, fax (226) 8-6145, two km from the airport. It's a gracious property with a hilltop location with landscaped grounds offering fine views. The 46 spacious rooms, 14 *casitas,* and one villa have been beautifully refurbished with gracious furnishings and fabrics and all have a/c, balconies, telephones, refrigerators, cable TVs, and security boxes. The new *casitas* arc gracefully around a swimming pool. Excursions are offered. It's somewhat lonesome, especially since tour groups have decamped to more central hotels. Rates were US$53 s, US$60 d for rooms; US$25 s, US$35 d including breakfast for *casitas. Recommended.*

Izlazul's **Hotel Balcón del Caribe,** Carretera del Morro Km 7.5, tel. (226) 9-1011, atop the cliffs near the Morro Castle, has 92 refurbished albeit modestly appointed rooms with a/c, cable TV, telephones, and private bath. The cabins offer nicely furnished, spacious rooms with fridges, all-new bathrooms, and patios overlooking the deep blue, endless ocean. It has a restaurant and cabaret and accepts Cubans as well as tourists, but receives few of either. It's a great spot if you don't mind being far from town. Rates were US$27 s, US$34 d low season, US$34 s, US$42 d high season, including breakfast; and US$31 s, US$36 low season, US$38 s, US$48 d high season for cabanas.

Islazul's recently restored **Motel Rancho,** tel. (226) 3-3202 and 3-5280, beside the Carretera Central, on the hillside four km north of town, has 30 small, modestly but pleasantly furnished a/c cabanas with private bath, telephones, and cable TVs. An elegant restaurant offers views over Santiago. Rates were US$26 s, US$30 d low season, US$32 s, US$38 d high season, including breakfast.

Gaviota's **Hacienda El Caney,** Calle Marqueti #2, Reparto las Flores, Carretera de El Caney, tel. (226) 8-7134, has nine a/c rooms with satellite TVs and telephones. It has a pool and restaurant. Rates were US$39 s, US$47 d

Moderate: The recently refurbished **Hotel Horizontes Las Américas,** Avenida de las Américas y Avenida General Cebreco, tel. (226) 4-2011, fax (226) 8-7075, across from the Hotel Santiago, has 68 a/c rooms, all with satellite TVs, phones, radios, and in-room security boxes. The hotel has two restaurants and a bar, plus entertainment, a tour desk, and car rental. Rates were US$46 s, US$56 d low season, US$46 s, US$77 d high season, including breakfast.

Gaviota runs **Villa Gaviota** in Vista Alegre at Avenida Manduley #502 e/ Calles 19 y 21, tel. (266) 41368, fax (226) 87166. It features 13 three- to five-bedroom "deluxe" and "standard" a/c bungalows with modestly handsome furnishings, telephone and satellite TV. There's a swimming pool, store, and a restaurant and disco. I was told by the desk staff that *chicas* (Cuban girls) are permitted to stay with foreign guests, and I witnessed the same (if so, it's the only such tourist hotel in Cuba). Rates were US$42 s, US$50 d low season, US$47 s, US$55 d high season.

Very Expensive: Downtown, the place to be is the **Hotel Casa Grande,** Calle Heredia #201, e/ Lacret y San Felix, tel. (226) 86-600, fax (226) 86-035, in North America, tel. (800) 221-4542, splendidly situated on Parque Céspedes. Wormold stayed here in Graham Greene's *Our Man in Havana,* and he thought it "a hotel of real spies, real police-informers and real rebel agents." It lost its sheen following the Revolution and just a few years ago was described as "an establishment so magnificent in its squalor that it seems born out of an opium smoker's vision." All that has changed now that the hotel is in the process of being restored and is now run by the French Sofitel group. It has 58 rooms, including three junior suites (one for guests with disabilities), all with a/c, telephones, and satellite TV. Many rooms have splendid antique reproduc-

tions in walnut, including double beds with inlaid hardwood headboards. Suites even have gold silk fabrics. However, at press time only the fourth floor had been renovated, and older rooms retain dowdy furnishings. You can sit on its first-floor veranda (lent a Parisian feel by its red-and-white awnings) and sip a cuba libre, smoke a *puro,* and watch the flood of life through the colonial plaza. It's overpriced. Rates were US$73 s, US$96 d, US$88-115 suite, low season; US$83 s, US$112 d, US$100-135 suite, high season; US$103 s, US$152 d, US$120-175 suite, peak-season, including breakfast.

You'll either love or hate the architecture of the **Meliá Hotel Santiago,** Avenida de las Américas e/ Cuarta y Manduley, tel. (226) 4-2634 or 4-2612, fax (226) 8-6170, a 15-story modernist structure with an exterior that is all plate-glass and metal girders painted blood red and blue. The supposedly five-star hotel (owned by Cubanacán and managed by Spain's Grupo Sol Meliá) has 270 rooms plus three suites and 30 junior suites. The spacious rooms are done up in complimentary beige and mauve, with contemporary furniture (handmade in Cuba) of rose-colored tropical hardwoods, cable TVs and telephones, and bathrooms big enough for a house party and featuring piping-hot water. Facilities includes a jacuzzi, sauna and massage, a small gym, a vast swimming pool complex, cigar shop, solarium, beauty parlor, barber shop, and a business center. It was being refurbished at press time and a Habana Café was planned as a take on the Hard Rock Café. Rates were US$90 s, US$115 d high season.

FOOD

Creative dishes are as hard to find here as elsewhere in provincial Cuba. There are few local restaurants of note, and most *paladares* have been forced out of business. The water is barely potable. Stick to bottled water.

Paladares

The best *paladar* in town is **Paladar Salón Tropical,** Calle Fernández Marcané #310 e/ 9 y 10, Reparto Santa Bárbara, tel. (226) 4-1167, offering rooftop dining beneath an arbor. It offers a barbecue chicken special (US$8) and garbanzo stew (US$4), plus the usual *criollo* fare. Watch your bill.

Downtown, **Paladar Las Gallegas,** Calle San Básilio #305 (altos) e/ San Feliz y San Pedro, tel. (226) 2-4700, is a modest place serving goat fricassee, pork chops, and fried or roast chicken. Complete meals cost US$7. And **Paladar Gildas,** Calle Bartolomé Masó #116, tel. (226) 2-2725, offers similarly priced *criollo* fare in a charming albeit dark home with colonial furnishings.

Hotel Restaurants

The elegant restaurant in the Hotel Santiago, serves continental cuisine and Cuban staples. Expect to pay upwards of US$20 for a full meal. Some of the best cuisine in town is served at the **Restaurante Casa Grande,** in the hotel of that name on Parque Céspedes. The elegant setting is helped along by live classical music and a complimentary house special of rum, lemonade, and tamarind. Set meals cost US$15 and US$25. À la carte dishes, such as grilled fish, cost about US$10. Cuisine is *criollo* with a hint of the Continent.

The elegant **La Ceiba Restaurant** at Hotel San Juan, has an appealing aesthetic. It serves nouvelle Cuban cuisine such as snapper with fruit sauce, but the execution is lacking. All entrées cost US$10. It's open 11 a.m.-11 p.m. The **Leningrado** restaurant adjoining serves mediocre buffet meals (dinner costs US$12—about three times what it's worth).

El Toro, in the Hotel Horizontes Las Américas, specializes in surf 'n' turf.

Dollars Only

Plaza Dolores has several reasonable options, all run by Rumbos and with almost identical and uninspired menus offering *criollo* dishes for (US$3-8) and spaghettis and pizzas for US$2-5. On the northwest corner is **Restaurante Don Antonio,** tel. (226) 5-2205, in a beautifully restored colonial building. Next door is **La Perla del Dragon,** not surprisingly serving Chinese cuisine but closed for restoration at press time. **La Restaurante Terracina,** tel. (226) 5-2307, is a quasi-Italian restaurant with contemporary decor. On the south side, the elegant **Café Matamoros** serves burgers and spaghetti. **Restaurante Mar-Init** specializes in seafood.

In Reparto Vista Alegre, the **Restaurant Zunzún,** tel. (226) 4-1528, serves mixed grill of lobster, shrimp, and fish for a whopping US$25 in a garden setting to the rear of the Casa de la Amistad. The *pollo asado* is a better bargain at US$7. A touristy favorite nearby is **Tocororo,** housed in a colonial mansion on Avenida Manduley, tel. (226) 4-1410. Choose indoor or outdoor dining. Shrimp costs US$8 upward, and lobster double that. A similar option is **La Maison,** also on Manduley, with an elegant restaurant to the rear and a popular outdoor café-cum-bar to the front. I enjoyed a grilled fish with garlic (US$8). It serves the usual *criollo* fare, plus pizza and lobster (US$5-20). A US$15 package includes dinner and the fashion show and cabaret.

If you have a car, consider the **El Morro Restaurant,** tel. (226) 9-1576, out of town, immediately west of the Morro Castle and splendidly set atop the cliffs with fabulous views along the coast. You dine on a terra-cotta-tiled terrace shaded by a gazebo covered by trumpet vine. Dark colonial furniture, goat-hide chairs, and serenades by troubadours add to the ambience. A baked fish stuffed with shrimp costs US$15. Lighter fare includes bean soup (US$1.50). It's open noon-9 p.m.

Local Favorites

Taberna Dolores is a colorful old bar and restaurant on Plaza Dolores. It's very popular with locals and has an open courtyard out back serving *criollo* food.

Santiago 1900, San Basilico e/ Pio Rosado y Hartmann, also popular with Cubans, is in a mansion that once belonged to the Bacardi family. It has an outdoor patio beneath an arbor around a fountain where you may dine on overpriced *criollo* food (US$6 and up). Nearby is the **Casa del Vino** on Calle Heredia, serving wines and cheeses plus more substantial fare. Supposedly it operates in strict hourly shifts by reservation.

An intriguing excursion is to take the ferry from Marina Marlin to Cayo Granma for a meal at the simple seafood **Restaurante El Cayo,** on the eastern side of the island. It boasts a lovely view. Try the lobster or prawns.

Cafés and Snacks

Two atmospheric places to sip coffee are the little café on the corner of Calles Santo Tomás and Entramada and the atmospheric **La Isabelica,** a favorite of locals, in a 300-year-old house at the corner of Aguilera and Calvario, facing Plaza Dolores.

Another curious delight is the **Casa del Té,** on Aguilera, on the northeast corner of Parque Céspedes—"a small room with wobbling tables and a filthy floor. The tea was Russian, stewed black and drunk sweet," Carlos Gebler recorded in *Driving through Cuba.* The menu includes Asian

teas, mint teas, and *"plantas medicinales"* for 10 centavos a cup. You can have a rum made with honey at the **Casa de Miel,** nearby. Gaviota's **Café La Melipona,** sitting above the junction of Avenida de las Américas and Avenida Manduley, sells medicinal products made of honey, as well as the usual snack bar fare.

For ice cream, head to **Coppelia,** at the corner of Avenida de los Libertadores and Avenida Garzón, where ice cream is served in aluminum bowls delivered to your table. The bowl will be whisked away before the last spoonful touches your lips. Two big scoops costs 35 centavos. You pay first, then get your ticket and wait in line. Those ahead of you will probably be scattered all about, but everyone seems to know when their turn is due. It's closed on Monday.

Downtown, you can buy ice cream from the *heladería* below the cathedral on Félix Pena. For a refreshing *batido* (fruit milk shake), head to **El Batido,** Calle Heredia and Hartmann.

Self-Catering

Buying your own food is no easier here than elsewhere in Cuba. For produce and meats, try the farmers' market at Aguilera and Padres Pico. You can buy Western goods at any Tienda Panamericano, Cupet gas station, or in the stores of the Hotel Santiago.

ENTERTAINMENT AND EVENTS

Santiago is Cuba's second most dynamic city, with cultural activities and nightlife to keep you entertained for a month. The city is especially known for its musical traditions. A monthly tabloid called *Perfil de Santiago* lists forthcoming events.

Festivals and Events

The **Festival de Rumba** is hosted downtown in mid-January, with music and dance in the streets and centered on Calle Heredia.

If you can, time your visit for **Carnaval** (recently renamed the **"Festival of Fire" Fiesta del Caribe**), in late July, when everyone in town downs shots of *aguardente* and gets caught up in the street rumbas and conga lines. The center of carnival activities is the area of La Trocha, at the southern end of Avenida Jesús Menéndez, around Avenida 24 de Febrero. It traditionally

---

CARNIVAL!

*C*arnival in Santiago de Cuba has been performed since the 19th century, when it was an Easter celebration. Originally it was called the Fiesta de las Mamarrachos (Festival of the Nincompoops), when slaves were given time off and the opportunity to release their pent-up energies and frustrations in a celebration full of sinister and sexual content. The celebration was bound irrevocably to the secret societies of ancient Africa, transformed in Cuba into neighborhood societies called *carabalí* that vied with one another to produce the most colorful and elaborate processions *(comparsas)* led by a frenzied melee of fife, drum, and maracas. There are representations of the *orishas* (gods) in the *comparsas* and characters representing the various gods lead the way. Since each *comparsa* comes from a different neighborhood, each dance and tune varies.

The hourglass drums of the ancestors begin to pound out their *tun q'tu q'tu q'-tun* rhythm, which builds each day as the city becomes gripped by a collective frenzy. The wail of Chinese cornets *(corneta China)* adds to the racket. Young and old alike rush to join the conga lines full of clowns and celebrants in colonial period dress, finding a release from the melancholy of everyday life, culminating in a carefully choreographed orgy of dance.

The main procession takes place on Avenida Jesús Menéndez, where stands are erected for spectators. The conga lines are followed by floats (sponsored by various Cuban agencies) graced by girls (*luceros*—morning stars) in riotous feathers and sequined bikinis or outrageous dresses. Huge *papier-mâché* heads supported by dancing Cubans bash into each other. Every year there's a different theme, and contestants are judged on originality and popularity.

runs 22-28 July, focused on the 26 July public holiday that marks the attack on the Moncada barracks. Its roots, however, go much farther back. For information contact Roberto Fajardo, Cubanacán Viaje Tours, tel. (226) 2-3569, e-mail: upec@mail.infocom.etecsa.cu.

In August, people converge in Parque Céspedes for the **Festival of Pregón**, arriving in carriages smothered with flowers and dressed in traditional costume to compete in the improvisation of verse and song in the tradition of the old street vendors.

Traditional Music and Dance

Santiago's **Casa de la Trova,** on Calle Heredia, is the island's most famous. The *trova* tradition of romantic ballads was born here. The form mingles Spanish guitar, African percussion, and ballads that hauntingly tell of the struggles of traditional life. Many famous Cuban musicians perform here. Wednesday and Saturday evenings are traditionally the best times to go.

Similar music is performed in an atrium courtyard at the **Patio del Trova,** opposite the Museo del Carnaval on Calle Heredia. It packs in a younger crowd that the Casa de la Trova, and is a hip spot favored for boy-meets-girl.

Among the more exciting performances are those of **Ballet Folklórico Cutumba,** tel. (226) 22-5860, a world-famous Afro-Cuban dance group that has a workshop on Saco e/ Corona y Padre Pico. They give performances of *columbia, conga oriental, tumba francesa,* and other dance styles at Teatro Oriente, Calle Enramadas #115, tel. (226) 2-2441, each Saturday at 10 p.m. and Sunday at 11 a.m. (US$3), but you can call in to their workshop to see practice sessions held Tues.-Sun.

Also watch for performances by **La Tumba Francesa,** which has a traditional Afro-Cuban *rumba* nightly at 6 p.m. at the corner of Los Maceos y General Bandera. And the **Museo del Carnaval** hosts a "Domingo de la Rumba" on Sunday at 11 a.m., plus folkloric shows daily at 4 p.m. Another acclaimed troupe, **Conjunto Folklórico de Oriente,** is at Hartmann #407.

The **Alianza Francesa** (Alliance Française), tel. (226) 4-1503, the French-language school, at Calle 6 and Calle 11 in Vista Alegre, also hosts *tumba francesa* and cultural exhibitions playing on the town's French links. Free films are shown on Friday at 6 p.m. Also check out the **Casa de la Cultura,** at General Lacret #651 on weekends, when it hosts folkloric dancing (US$5).

Traditional music and dance performances are also offered at the **Teatro Guignol,** where a children's puppet theater *(Teatro Muñecos)* is also offered.

Cabarets and Discos

If you ever need convincing that Cubans know how to put on a show, head to the **Tropicana,** tel. (226) 4-1031, fax (226) 8-7090, beside the Autopista Nacional, four km northeast of town, and whose splendid theme show—"Around the Caribbean"—traces the history and culture from pre-Columbian days to contemporary Cuba. About 100 dancers appear in a never-ending parade of elaborate costumes, most prominently lanky females in high heels, fanciful frills, feathered costumes, and other accouterments befitting a Frederick's of Hollywood's catalog. Colored floodlights reveal feathered mulattas high amid the palm trees on the hills to each side, quivering and cooing like denizens of an exotic harem. There are three bars and a restaurant. The show is offered Wed.-Sun. at 10 p.m. (US$30, including drink). About half the guests are Cubans, who stay for the disco after the show. Excursions are offered through hotel tour desks.

The ritzy **Pico Real Bar** atop the Hotel Santiago hosts a minuscule Tropicana-style cabaret nightly at 10:30 p.m.(US$6, including one drink; hotel guests enter free), followed by a disco. And at press time an upscale **Habana Café** was being built at the Hotel Santiago to feature a cabaret and disco.

Cabaret San Pedro del Mar, tel. (226) 9-1287, outside town near Morro Castle, also offers an *espectáculo* on a much smaller scale, Wed.-Sun. at 8:30 p.m. (the show is at 10:30 p.m. (US$5). Dinner costs about US$5. The cabaret takes place on a Mediterranean-style white terrace high above the ocean. A disco follows.

La Maison, on Avenida Manduley (one block north of Parque Ferreiro), tel. (226) 4-1117 or 43965, fax (226) 3-35083, offers an alfresco fashion show nightly at 10 p.m., with male and female models displaying everything from swimwear to evening dress. The show is followed by a cabaret featuring a magician's act and a song-and-dance show. Entrance costs US$5, including one drink. Tell them you're having dinner and the entrance fee will usually be dropped.

Nearby on Manduley is **Cabaret Soroa,** a far less ritzy Tropicana for the local populace. It's popular with young Cuban couples and is followed by a disco. **Las Terrazas** also has a cabaret (disco, comedy, and magic act) and dancing to live music on weekends, as does the rooftop bar of the **Hotel Casa Grande,** on Parque Céspedes (US$10). And the **Hotel San Juan** hosts an open-air cabaret nightly at 9:30 p.m. except Tuesday (US$3).

A disco is also held each Saturday night at **Casa del Estudiante,** next to the Casa de la Trova on Calle Heredia. Entrance costs US$4. Live music and dance is also featured on Sunday night.

Classical Performances

The modernist **Teatro Heredia,** tel. (226) 4-1124, by the Plaza de la Revolución on Avenida de Las Américas, hosts classical performances and poetry readings on an infrequent basis. Its café has live music. **Poetry readings** are also given each Friday evening at UNEAC (Union of Writers and Artists of Cuba), in the Casa Heredia. And the Poder Popular purportedly puts on opera every Saturday night.

Bars

Disco 300 isn't a disco, but a dark and moody bar in a colonial home at Calle Aguilera, one block east of Parque Céspedes. It's a scrum to enter (US$2), but a tip usually does the trick. The clientele is mostly Cuban women and Italian males necking and engaging in promiscuous dancing. Rum drinks cost US$2.

Two good bars for vistas are the 15th-floor **Pico Real** bar of the Hotel Santiago, offering stunning views of the city, and the veranda bar at the **Hotel Casa Grande,** with views down over Parque Céspedes. The meager **El Traylor** sidewalk bar, outside the Hotel Santiago, draws the local youth, who spill onto the road. Watch your wallet.

Las Isabelita, on the southwest corner of Parque Dolores, is a venerable rum bar with an earthy ambience drawing withered locals and tourists alike. A violinist plays while a tobacco roller rolls. The **Bar Claqueta,** nearby at Félix Pena #654, has dancing and live music.

Other Entertainment

The **Ateneo Cultural** in the old Colegio de Abogados on Félix Peña e/ Castillo Duany y Diego Palacios, offers cultural activities by day and night (US$2), including videos.

The main movie-house is **Cine Rialto,** on Félix Pena, one block south of the main square. Also try **Cine Cuba,** at Saco #304, and **Cine Latinoamericano,** at Avenida Victoriano Garzón #390.

SPORTS AND RECREATION

There's a sports facility at the north end of Avenida de las Américas, opposite Plaza de la Revolución. The baseball stadium—**Estadio Guillermón Moncada**—is also on Avenida de las Américas, at Calle E. Games are usually held Tues.-Thurs. evening and Saturday and Sunday at 1:30 p.m., Nov.-March.

For Children

Kids will probably enjoy the **Parque Zoológico,** immediately west of the Hotel San Juan. Animals from most continents are represented, including mandrills, baboons, and other monkeys. It's open Tues.-Fri. 10 a.m.-5 p.m. and weekends 9 a.m.-5 p.m. Entrance costs US$1 (US$0.40 children). Nearby, at the foot of San Juan Hill, is the **Parque de Diversiones 26 de Julio** amusement park, a large fairground with rides.

Water Sports and Excursions

Marina Marlin, tel. (226) 9-1446, fax (226) 8-6108, at Punta Gorda, offers a range of recreational water sports, including sportfishing charters for US$130 for four passengers. It also offers excursions to Cayo Guamá. You can rent Hobi Cats for US$15 per hour. The marina was planning to rent yachts at press time.

SHOPPING

All the hotels have souvenir shops selling the usual range of T-shirts, music tapes, *muñecas* (dolls), and musical instruments. Santiago's stores close on Monday, with a few exceptions.

Arts and Crafts

Calle Heredia, east of Parque Céspedes, is lined with arts and crafts stalls. The **Galería de Art UNEAC,** on Heredia e/ Hartmann y Pio Rosada, tel. (226) 5-3465, has some superb art for sale. One of the most dynamic sculptures locally is Caridad Ramos Mosquera; she sells her work at Edificio C-7 Apto. 1, Centro Urbano Antonio Maceo, tel. (226) 9-2328, e-mail: tallercult@cult-stgo.cult.cu.

Cubartesania has a store at Bartolomé Masó and Félix Pena selling quality arts and crafts. You'll also find an **ARTEX** shop in the Casa de la Trova, on Calle Heredia, and **Galería Oriente,** on the east side of Parque Céspedes, has a wide range of quality art.

Check out **La Minerva,** a small antique shop on Heredia and Pío Rosado. Consider heading out to **El Oasis,** a small village dedicated to the production of arts and crafts (see the section on Baracoa below).

The rum shop in the Caney rum factory on Avenida Jesús Menéndez sells fine-quality silver and coral jewelry (see below).

Books

Santiago suffers the same paucity of reading matter as all Cuba. Hotel stores carry a motley array of English-language coffee-table books, novels, and pro-Revolution texts. For Spanish-language books hyping the glories of the Revolution, check out the bookstore at Sacó #356 or Librería Vietnam, at Aguilera #567. And **Librería La Escalera,** Calle Heredia #265 e/ San Félix y Carniceria, sells used books.

Boutiques

La Maison contains a series of boutiques selling import goods—clothing, jewelry, cosmetics, etc. Note the stunning paintings and bronze busts and statues in the lobby.

Rum and Cigars

Sure, you can buy these in the hotel stores, but I say go to the source. For rum, visit the rum factory on Avenida Jesús Menéndez e/ San Antonio y San Ricardo. The tasting room sells Havana Club, Ron Varadero, and Ron Matusalem (US$4.75-8.10 a liter). Here, too, is the only place in Cuba where you can buy 25-year-old rum in special porcelain bottles.

The best cigar selection is at the **Casa del Habano,** beside the cigar factory on Avenida Jesús Menéndez, at the foot of Masó. It has a small smokers' lounge and bar upstairs.

SERVICES AND INFORMATION

Tourist Information

Rumbos has a *buro de turismo* on the southeast corner of Parque Céspedes.

Maps: An accurate city map published by Ediciones Geo is sold at tourist outlets and post offices. Also look for the tourist guide *Guía Turística Santiago de Cuba.* This 250-page booklet has the most detailed maps available, as well as brief information on sites of tourist interest.

Travelers' Assistance: Asistur has an office beneath the Hotel Casa Grande, on Parque Céspedes, tel. (226) 8-6128. This agency can provide travelers with legal advice, help arrange a doctor's visit or other medical attention, and assist with cash advances and other matters.

Visa Extensions: If you need a 30-day extension *(prorroga),* go to the MININT **immigration** office at Av. Raúl Pujol #10, tel. (226) 41983, 200 meters east of the Hotel Santiago. You'll need your passport, tourist card, and airline ticket for departure from Cuba. First, however, you must go to the Banco de Crédito y Comercio on Parque Céspedes to get a *cello* (official stamp; US$25) that the Immigration official will affix to your visa. The immigration office is a madhouse in the morning; go in midafternoon, but expect a long wait. Be pushy, as the squeaky wheel gets the grease.

Money

You can cash traveler's checks and get advances against credit cards (except those issued by U.S. banks) at **Banco Financiero Internacional,** on Félix Pena, one block north of Parque Céspedes (open weekdays 8 a.m.-3 p.m.), and at **Banco Crédito y Comercio,** with branches on both east and west sides of Parque Céspedes. **Banco Popular** has an outlet on the south side of Plaza Dolores.

You can change dollars for pesos at the **Cadeca** bureau at Aguilera #508, tel. (226) 5-1383.

Post and Telecommunications

All the tourist hotels have postal and telephone facilities. The main **post office** is on Aguilera at Padre Quiroga. **DHL,** tel. (226) 7795, has its main office on Hartmann e/ Aguilera y Heredia, plus outlets in the main post office and in the Hotel San Juan for express letters and packages. You can make international calls from Etecsa's **Centro de Llamados Internacionales** in the arcade beneath the cathedral on the south side of Parque Céspedes, and at the Etecsa kiosk on Avenida Victoriana Garzón opposite Coppelia.

Cubacel, tel. (226) 8-7199, fax (226) 8-7122, in the Hotel Santiago, rents cellular phones and will hook up your own personal cellular. It's open Mon.-Fri., 8 a.m.-5 p.m. and Saturday, 8 a.m.-noon. (See the Communications section in the On The Road chapter for costs and conditions.)

Medical

The **Clínica Internacional,** on Calle 13 esq. 14, tel. (226) 4-2489, fax (226) 8-6801, caters to foreigners. It's one block north of Carretera Siboney. A doctor and nurse are on 24-hour duty (US$25 per consultation; US$30, between 4 p.m. and 7 a.m.) and will make hotel visits for US$30. The clinic has a modestly stocked pharmacy, an ambulance, and beds in the event that you need an overnight stay.

Ópticas Miramar, on Félix Pena, one block south of Parque Céspedes, provides optical services.

Other Services

The library, **Biblioteca Elvira Cape,** is at Heredia #259 e/ Pío Rosado and Hartmann.

There are **Cupet gas stations** at the junction of Avenida de Céspedes and Avenida de los Libertadores and, two km farther north, on the road to Bayamo.

GETTING THERE

By Air

Cubana has three flights daily from Havana to Santiago on Monday, Wednesday, and Friday, and two flights on other days (90 minutes; US$80 one-way). Cubana also offers thrice-weekly service between Santiago and Varadero, plus regular service from Camagüey, Baracoa, Moa, and other destinations. **Aero Caribbean** flies daily from Havana, and **Aerotaxi** flies to Santiago de Cuba from Havana and other Cuban cities using Russian biplanes. (See the By Air section under Getting Around in the On The Road chapter.) Also see the Getting There section in the On The Road chapter for details of flights from Europe, Canada, and the Caribbean.

Antonio Maceo International Airport, tel. (226) 9-1014, is eight km south of Santiago. Local bus service (no. 211 or 213) operates between downtown, opposite the hospital on Avenida de los Libertadores, and the airport. A taxi to downtown costs about US$12 one-way. A minibus transfer from the airport to downtown costs US$15 roundtrip, US$10 one-way, and can be arranged through Havanatur, in the Hotel Casa Grande, tel. (226) 8-6152, or by Rumbos, tel. (226) 8-6033, opposite the hotel entrance on Parque Céspedes.

The airport has car rental office and a Cubanacán tours office.

By Bus

The **Víazul** tourist bus departs Havana for Santiago de Cuba on Tuesday and Friday. (For public bus service, see the Public Bus Service from Havana chart.) The journey takes about 15 hours. Santiago is also served by bus from most major towns and cities.

Buses arrive at the **Terminal Omnibus Nacional,** tel. (226) 2-3050, on Avenida de los Liberadores y Avenida Juan Gualberto Gómez.

By Train

The #11 express *(especial)* train departs Havana for Santiago de Cuba every two days (but not the third) at 7:30 p.m., arriving at 9:10 a.m. Train #13 departs Havana daily at 4:40 p.m. arriving at 6:40 a.m., and #19 departs Havana daily at 10:40 a.m. arriving at 10:30 p.m.

Trains arrive at the new railway station opposite the old Bacardi rum factory on Avenida Jesús Menéndez, tel. (226) 2-2836.

By Sea

No cruise ships called into Santiago de Cuba at press time. However, they have in the past, and they surely will in the future.

Private yachters can arrive at **Marina Marlin** at Punta Gorda, tel. (226) 9-1446, fax (226) 8-

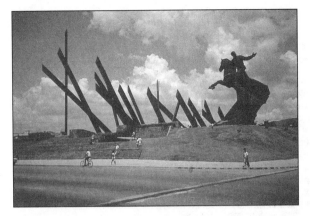

Monument to Antonio Maceo, Plaza de la Revolución, Santiago

6108. The all-new marina has moorings for 60 boats: US$0.40 per foot, including water and electricity plus 24-hour service. TV and telephone linkages are available. Facilities include a café, restaurant, and bar, and a mini-golf and game room were being built at press time.

The marina staff can call a taxi and arrange rental cars. A taxi ride into town will cost about US$12.

By Organized Tour

All the leading tour operators in Havana, Varadero, and other resort areas offer excursions to Santiago (see relevant chapters).

Caribbean Music & Dance Programs, 12545 Olive St. #241, St Louis, MO 63141, tel. (314) 542-3637 or toll free (877) 665-4321, fax (314) 469-2916, e-mail: caribmusic@igc.apc.org, website: www.caribmusic.com, offers weeklong study workshops in Santiago, including to the Festival del Caribe. Likewise, the **Center for Creative Education,** in Stone Ridge, NY, tel. (914) 687-8890, e-mail: CCEdrums@aol.com, offers study tours in conjunction with Artes Escenicas and UNEAC with classes in dance and percussion (US$1,895 for two weeks, including airfare).

The **Eleggua Project,** 7171 Torbram Rd., Suite 51, Mississauga, ON L4T 3WA, Canada, tel. (800) 818-8840, fax (905) 678-1421, e-mail: cancuba@pathcom.com, website: www.pathcom.com/~cancuba, also offers study tours music, culture, and dance in Santiago de Cuba.

(Also see Organized Tours in the Getting There section of the On The Road chapter for additional tour companies and organizations.)

GETTING AROUND

By Bus

Buses serve most of the city (fare is 20 centavos), but they are horrendously crowded. Bus no. 1 runs between Parque Céspedes and both the interprovincial and intermunicipal bus terminals. Most people get around on open-air trucks, penned in shoulder-to-shoulder like cattle!

Taxis

Taxis hang out below the cathedral on the south side of Parque Céspedes and outside the tourist hotels. A taxi between the Hotel Santiago or Hotel San Juan and Parque Céspedes should cost about US$3. Horse-drawn *coches* cost one peso or US$1. Call (226) 52323 for **Taxi OK. Transtaxi** has an office beneath the Hotel Casa Grande, on Parque Céspedes.

By Car

A car is fine for the outer suburbs but, in town, forget it. The streets in the center are too narrow and congestion too much to contemplate. A scooter, however, is a perfect mode of transport: **Transtur** rents scooters at the Hotel San Juan.

A Cuban named Jorge will drive your around town in his 112-hp 1930 Phaeton with the canvas top, which parks outside the entrance to the Hotel Casa Grande. His car (and other antique jalopies) has been lassoed by **Gran Caribe,** which charges US$15 for a city tour.

Excursions

Tours & Travel offers various city tours (from US$15) plus a wide range of excursions farther afield. It has offices beneath the Hotel Casa Grande, tel. (226) 8-6152; at the Hotel San Juan, tel. (226) 8-7185; at Calle 8 #54 e/ 1 y 3, Reparto Vista Alegre, tel. (226) 8-6281; and at Aeropuerto Antonio Maceo, tel. (226) 8-6380. **Rumbos,** Calle Lacret y Heredia, tel. (226) 8-6033, also has a city tour, as does **Cubanacán Agencia de Viajes,** at Avenida de la Independencia y M, tel. (226) 4-1517 (its main office wasn't much help when I last called in; they sent me to the tour desk in the Hotel Santiago).

Aerotaxi, tel. (23) 42-2186, offers flightseeing excursions by Russian biplane.

GETTING AWAY

By Air

The airport has a restaurant and bar above the departure lounge. You can also sip your Havana Club rum in an old Cubana DC-8 converted into a bar immediately east of the arrivals hall.

The Cubana office is beneath the Hotel Casa Grande on Parque Céspedes, tel. (226) 2-4156 or 2-2290.

By Bus

The **Víazul** tourist bus, tel. (226) 2-8484, departs from the Terminal Omnibus Nacional on the Avenida de los Liberadores y Avenida Juan Gualberto Gómez. Other long-distance buses also operate from here.

Local buses operate between Santiago and outlying destinations and as far as Guantánamo and Manzanillo from the **Terminal de Ómnibus Municipales,** at Avenida de los Libertadores y Calle 4, tel. (226) 2-4329.

Buses for El Cobre, Siboney, and other destinations within a one-hour striking distance leave from the **Terminal de Intermunicipales Serrano,** on Avenida Jesús Menéndez, e/ General Máximo Gómez y Juan Bautista Sagarra, tel. (226) 2-4325.

By Train

Trains depart the station on Avenida Jesús Menendez at the foot of Narciso López. You buy your tickets at the ticket office *(espendido de boletas)* outside, on the south side of the station: use the left-hand window only. There's no information listing train schedules or prices. You'll have to inquire at the information desk outside the entrance foyer.

The regular train to Havana departs daily at 5 p.m. (US$30.50). An *especial* (fast service; US$43) departs every first and second day, but not the third, on a rotating schedule. Reservations are required for the *especial.*

You can leave your bags in a locker (US$1 per bag).

By Car

There are rental car agencies in all the major hotels, including a **Havanautos** office at the Hotel Las Américas, tel. (226) 8-6160, and at the airport, tel. (226) 9-1773 or 8-6161, and on Avenida Jesús Menéndez at the foot of Calle Trinidad, where dune buggies are also rented. (Beware of scams: see the section on car rentals in the On The Road chapter for details.)

Vía has an outlet in the Rumbos office on the southeast corner of Parque Céspedes, tel. (226) 8-6033. And **Transtur,** tel. (226) 8-7000, fax (226) 3-3297, has an outlet in the Hotel San Juan that rents the Suzuki X-90, a sporty little 4WD two-seater that I love (US$60 daily with unlimited mileage, or US$55 daily for a week-long rental). **Gaviota,** tel. (226) 8-7278, also has an outlet.

Excursions

All the tourist hotels have tour desks offering excursions to the Tropicana nightclub, plus Baconao and Gran Piedra, Playa Daiquiri, El Cobre, Morro Castle, Baracoa, Cayo Saetía, and destinations further afield. Try **Cubanacán,** Avenida de las Américas y Calle M, tel./fax (226) 4-1517; **Cubatur,** on Avenida Victoriana Garzóny Céspedes, tel. (226) 8-6106 and 5-2560; **Rumbos,** at Lacret y Heredia, tel. (226) 8-6033; **Tours & Travel,** beneath the Hotel Casa Grande on Parque Céspedes, tel. (226) 8-6152; and **Viajes Horizontes,** at Avenida 1ra y M, Reparto Terrazas, tel. (226) 8-7095, fax (226) 8-7096.

NORTH OF SANTIAGO

EL COBRE

The small town of El Cobre, 20 km northwest of Santiago, takes its name from the large copper mine that the Spanish established in the mid-1500s, run by German engineers. By the end of the century the mine was providing Havana's artillery works' entire supply of copper. In 1630, it was abandoned, and the African slave-miners were unilaterally freed. A century later it was reopened by Colonel Don Pedro Jiménez, governor of Santiago, who put the slaves' descendants back to work. It is said that the Virgin de la Caridad del Cobre eventually interceded on their behalf. The slaves were officially declared free in 1782, a century before their brethren in the cane fields. The mine continued in operation throughout the 19th century.

The town sits in a valley surrounded by the Sierra de Cobre, the easternmost spur of the Sierra Maestra. Dominating the town from atop a small hillock is the ocher-colored, red-domed, triple-towered Basílica del Cobre.

Basílica del Cobre

The church—Cuba's only basilica—is imposing atop its lofty pedestal, although it can hardly compete with St. Paul's or Notre Dame. It is famed for its chapel full of propitiatory offerings, and as the shrine to La Virgen de la Caridad (Virgin of Charity), patron saint of Cuba, to whom miraculous powers are ascribed.

The church is called the "Cuban Lourdes." Once a year, thousands of devoted Cubans make their way along the winding road, many shuffling along on their knees, crawling painfully uphill to fulfill a promise made to the saint at some difficult moment in their lives. The unlucky fisherman in Ernest Hemingway's *Old Man and the Sea* promises to "make a pilgrimage to the Virgin de Cobre" if he wins his battle with the massive marlin. In 1952, Hemingway dedicated his Nobel Prize for Literature to the Virgin, placing it in her shrine, which also has a small gold figure presented by Fidel Castro's mother, Lina Ruz—the maid who married the boss—perhaps asking favor and protection for Fidel and his brother, Raúl. On 6 May 1988, two men stole Hemingway's Nobel medallion. It was found several days later, to much public fanfare. Today the medal is in the custody of the Archbishop of Santiago.

The main entrance is reached via a steep staircase lined with old lamps. More usual is to enter at the rear, from the car park. Touts will rush forward to sell you iron pyrite (fool's gold) culled from the residue of the nearby mine. *"¡Es reál!"* they say, attempting to put a small piece in

the road to the
Basílica del Cobre

THE LEGEND OF
THE BLACK VIRGIN

The 17th-century image of the black Madonna was supposedly found by two fishermen and their young slave, Juan Moreno, in the Bay of Nipe in 1608. According to legend, the three fishermen (the "three Juans") were caught in a tropical storm and doomed to die when the figurine appeared, floating atop a board that read *"Yo Soy la Virgen de la Caridad,"* "I am the Virgin of Charity." It was the very statue that, according to legend, had been given to an Indian chief by a conquistador, Alonso de Ojeda, in 1510, but had been set adrift on a raft when jealous chiefs tried to seize it.

The fishermen survived. Pope Benedicto XV declared her the Patron Saint of Cuba on 10 May 1916.

The Virgin is represented in effigy in churches all over the island, usually depicting her standing atop the waves, with the three fishermen gazing in awe from their little boat. In santería, the Afro-Cuban religion, she is *Ochún,* the powerful goddess of sensuality.

your hand. The church lobby—the Salon of Miracles—contains a small chapel with a silver altar crowded with votive candles and flowers. To left and right are tables with dolls, bottles, and a miscellany of objects you might find in your grandmother's parlor. The two centuries of exvotos ("all the heaped and abandoned hopes of Cuba laid before its patron saint," wrote Pico Iyer) include war mementos that narrate Cuba's history from the struggle for independence from Spain to the conflict in Angola (amazingly, the medals of men who fought *against* the Revolution lie side-by-side with those given by men who fought to defend it at the Bay of Pigs). On the walls hang scores of silver adornment and little *milagros* of limbs and other body parts.

The main church is plain except for its large marble altarpiece and the stained-glass windows in the upper reaches of the arched nave. Choral groups often perform here. The **Virgen de la Caridad del Cobre** resides in effigy in an a/c glass case in a separate altar above the main altar. You can view her up close by taking a staircase marked *Subida.* The virgin's figure, clad in a golden cloak and crown, is sur-

rounded by a sea of flowers, and the entire shrine is suffused with narcotic scents. On the saint's day, the church warden presses a button and, as if by magic, she turns to face the rapt audience.

The church is open daily 6:30 a.m.-6 p.m. Masses *(misas)* are offered Mon.-Sat. (except Wednesday) at 8 a.m., on the eighth day and the first Thursday of each month at 8 p.m., and Sunday at 8 and 10 a.m. and 4:30 p.m. The best time to view the church is during late afternoon, when its ocher exterior glows richly, like hammered gold, from the sunlight slanting in from the south.

In 1993, the church was briefly closed to foreigners after tourists forced their way inside to take photographs during a religious service. Common decency dictates that you honor any restrictions and local customs.

Accommodations and Food

The **Hospedaje El Cobre,** tel. (22) 3-6246, for pilgrims, in an old mansion behind the church, has 16 basic rooms where foreigners are welcome when space allows (seven pesos per person per night). You can also bunk in a dormitory (four pesos). Married couples must show ID with the same address. The place is appropriately ascetic. A refectory serves basic fare for seven pesos at 7:30 a.m., 11:30 a.m., and 6:30 p.m. For reservations, write Hermana Carmen Robles, Hospedaje El Cobre, Santiago de Cuba.

There are a couple of basic restaurants and snack stalls down the hill in town.

Getting There

Bus no. 2 operates four times daily to El Cobre from Santiago's Terminal Ómnibus Intermunicipales. A taxi from Santiago will cost about US$30 roundtrip. Tour operators in Santiago offer excursions to El Cobre. (See the Getting Away section in the section on Santiago, above.)

EL COBRE TO GRANMA PROVINCE

The Carretera Central continues northwest through **Palma Soriano,** an unappealing town with the virtue of possessing a **Cupet gas station.** A hotel and restaurant nearby called **Mirador Valle de Tallabe,** tel. (225) 2594, offers splendid views down the valley, in the Altos de los Coquitos.

This area is one of rolling hills and parched rangeland. Approaching **Contramaestra,** 72 km northwest of Santiago, the land is sweeping, with wide rolling plains (very scenic) planted in sugar and shaded by clumps of baobab trees. The town itself is attractive, with whitewashed curbstones and shady sidewalks. A curiosity (for its name) is the *central* called **Free America,** just outside town.

SIERRA MAESTRA

The easternmost spurs of the Sierra Maestra rise sharply west of Santiago de Cuba. The mountains are strongly associated with the actions of Che Guevara's Rebel Army.

SOUTH OF CONTRAMAESTRA

At the village of **Cruce de los Baños,** 25 km south of Contramaestra (and the highest point reached by paved roads), and three km south of Filé, you'll find one of the guerrilla headquarters—now a camp for Exploradores, revolutionary Cuba's version of the Boy Scouts. Beyond Cruce, the deeply rutted dirt roads are used only by adults on mules and by donkeys laden with coffee beans, making your arrival at **El Saltón** all the more breathtaking. Here, you'll find a natural pool and picture-perfect cascades nestled in a valley high in the mountains west of Cruce.

Accommodations
Club Vida Montaña Carretera a Filé, Contramaestra tel. (225) 6326, fax (225) 6492, at El Saltón, is an eco-lodge built in the 1970s as an anti-stress center for the Cuban elite. It is run by Servimed and still offers massage, sauna, and whirlpool, as well as hikes and horseback rides (US$2 per hour). Accommodations are in 22 attractive, modestly appointed double rooms in four separate buildings, with cable TV. There's an open-sided, thatched restaurant overlooking the river and where, after dinner, the band plays and locals gather to join in the dancing with guests. The menu includes spaghettis, tortillas, and canned tuna and sardine salads. Rates were US$29 s, US$36 d low season, US$36 s, US$43 d high season.

Getting There
Buses operate into the Sierras from Terminal de Transporte Serrano in Santiago.

If driving from Santiago, the road south from Contramaestra is best, as the road that leads west from Coco Palmas (and appearing more direct on maps) is badly deteriorated. With a 4WD vehicle, you can tackle the steep and rugged dirt road that crosses the Sierra Maestra from Río Seco, on the south coast. Allow several hours.

SANTIAGO TO CHIVIRICO

The drive west along the coast from Santiago is magnificent, with the sinuous road pushed right to the shoreline by the Sierra Maestra plummeting to a crashing sea. The road becomes gradually more lonesome as you pass rustic fishing villages tucked along paradisiacal bays. Several pleasing pocket-size beaches lie hidden in coves. And there are several evocations of history, including the ruins of a Spanish fort.

Playa Mar Verde, 17 km west of Santiago, is a beach popular with city dwellers. You might do a double-take as you pass through **Asseredero,** about 32 km west of Santiago—in the harbor is the wreck of the Spanish-American warship *Viscaya,* scuttled by the U.S. Navy on 3 July 1898, when the Spanish navy attempted to break out of Santiago harbor. The cruiser's forward guns point skyward above the water. (There are other wrecks in the shallow bay of Nima-Nima, 10 km west of Santiago.)

The only settlement of note is **Chivirico,** about 80 km west of Santiago. This small, dusty fishing village is protected within an enclosed cove in the lee of a steep peninsula. Here you'll find two splendid foreign-operated hotels with top-notch facilities and knockout views. To the west of town is a long brown sand beach that gets thronged by locals. One mile east of town is **Cayo Damas,** lying 200 meters offshore. It has a tiny beach where fishing boats lie at anchor. Nearby, too, are the Bat Caves, **Las Cuevas**

SANTIAGO DE CUBA

del Murciélagos, full of harmless bats. The main street has a cinema, two restaurants, and a shopping center where, with luck, you might find toiletries and other essentials.

West of Chivirico, the mountains *really* make their presence felt. The searing heat builds. Arable plots give way to parched pastures and cacti begin to appear. The small community of **Las Cuevas** is the start of a steep, arduous trail to Pico Turquino, which looms to the north (see Hiking to Pico Turquino, below).

Just east of **Ocujal** and the mouth of the Río Turquino, is a wartime wreck of the Spanish ironclad cruiser *Colón,* sunk in 1898 by the U.S. Navy. The wreck rests on a submarine shelf at a mere 20 meters, only 35 meters from shore. Its gun turrets are still in place. Ocujal lies directly beneath Pico Turquino, whose summit is less than five km from the shore.

Farther west you cross the mouth of the Río La Plata. It was here, on 28 May 1957, that Castro's rebel army first came down from the Sierra Maestra to attack a small garrison of Batista's Rural Guard. The small **Museo de La Plata** has an exhibit (open Tues.-Sat.; US$1). It's off the road, beside the river.

Accommodations

Campismo La Mula is a simple holiday camp where you can mingle with Cubans. It has 50 basically appointed cabins and a restaurant. Contact Cubamar, Calle 15 #752 esq. Paseo Vedado, Havana, tel. (7) 66-2523, fax (7) 33-3111, e-mail: cubamar@cubamar.mit.cma.net.

Budget: Motel Guamá, tel. (22) 2-6124, is an attractive little place frequented by Cubans and operated by the Empresa de Gastronomía to teach cooking to hotel staff. It sits atop a headland two km east of Chivirico, with small red-brick-and-stone villas on stilts on the hillside. Each has a wooden balcony with views over the bay. There's a basic restaurant and bar. Rates were US$15 s/d year-round.

Luxury: Cubanacán's **Sierra Mar,** Carretera de Chivirico Km 60, tel. (22) 2-9110, fax (22) 2-9116, e-mail: sierrmar@smar.scu.cyt.cu, is a beautiful 200-room oceanfront property on a hillside overlooking Playa Sevilla Guamá, 10 km east of Chivirico. First impressions are of the spacious and breezy lobby opening onto a wide terrace and swimming pool high above the beach, with views along the coast and mountains. *Ventrales* (stained-glass windows above alcoves) diffuse colors onto the white tiles. There are three blocks of rooms, which are furnished in upscale fabrics. Facilities include two restaurants, five bars, and a well-stocked upscale boutique. There's even an a/c fitness room down by the beach (ringed by a protective reef) and a sea-view jacuzzi aloft. The action takes place by the huge pool, which has a water slide and swim-up bar. Cycling, sailing, snorkeling, tennis, banana-boat rides, and windsurfing are offered; there's a volleyball and basketball court. Nice, but overpriced? All-inclusive rates were US$106 s, US$154 d low season, US$166 s, US$260 d high season.

Nearby is Cubanacán's smaller, more intimate **Hotel Los Galeones,** Carretera de Chivirico Km 72, tel. (22) 2-6160, fax (22) 2-9116, e-mail: sierrmar@smar.scu.cyt.cu, a 34-room all-inclusive property perched perfectly atop a headland with views along the entire coast and the village of Chivirico. It's a cozy little place with a contemporary Spanish feel, centered on a small swimming pool and sundeck. The charming restaurant overlooks the pool. Rooms are spacious, with king-size beds, hardwood ceilings, tile floors, and balconies. Facilities include a game room, basic fitness center, sauna, and dive shop, and the all-inclusive rates include a complimentary massage. A 296-step staircase leads to the private beach with bar. Guests can also use the facilities of the Sierra Mar, to which a shuttle operates. It's overpriced. All-inclusive rates were US$116 s, US$160 d low season, US$167 s, US$278 d peak season.

Food

Nonguests can buy day passes to the **Sierra Mar** and **Los Galeones** hotels for US$35 (8 a.m.-5 p.m., including all meals and drinks). A night pass (5 p.m.-11 p.m.) costs US$50.

There are two pesos-only restaurants in Chivirico, and stalls where you can buy a refreshing *batido* or fruit juice.

Excursions

Fishing and horseback riding are available at the upscale hotels, as are a jeep safari (US$35);

excursions to Santiago and the Tropicana night-club, and to Las Cuevas del Murcielagos (US$10); and helicopter trips to El Saltón, in the mountains (US$79).

Scuba Diving

The Hotel Sierra Mar offer scuba-diving to the off-shore coral reefs and to the submerged wreck of the *Colón,* near Ocujal (US$30, or US$60 for a wreck-dive; US$365 for a certification course).

HIKING TO PICO TURQUINO

Just as Edmund Hillary climbed Everest "because it was there," so Pico Turquino lures the intrepid who seek the satisfaction of reaching the summit of Cuba's highest peak. The trail begins at Las Cuevas, where the **Estación Biológica Las Cuevas del Turquino** claims to have a **Centro de Información,** which exists in name only. Wooden signs point the way to the summit, a 13-km hike that is normally done in one day. At press time, the only access to Parque Nacional Pico Turquino was here, although the park remained closed to visitors, as it has been since mid-1999. Hikers are being permitted to ascend to the summit with guides: you must request a permit (US$7.50) in advance from CITMA (Ciencias Tecnológia Medioambiente Nacional) in Santiago de Cuba, or in Havana and Holguín from the Academía de Ciencias, which oversees the park: Capitolio, Industria y San José, Habana Vieja, Havana 10200, tel. (7) 57-0599, fax (7) 33-8054, e-mail: museofin@infomed.sld .cu or acc@ceniai.inf.cu. You must also hire a guide (US$7.50)

A crude map posted beside the road and trail-head shows campsites at 600 meters from the shore at Gumajacua, at Pico Cuba, and elsewhere along the 6.7 km-long trail.

The weather is unpredictable. Dress accordingly. Cold winds often kick up near the summit; the humidity and windchill factor can drop temperatures to near freezing. Rain is always a possibility, and short downpours are common in mid-afternoon. Fog is almost a daily occurrence at higher elevations, often forming in mid-morning. You'd better have warm clothing for nighttime, when temperatures near the summit

plummet. With luck, you'll have fine weather the whole way.

Hikers normally ascend and return in one day, an eight- to 10-hour feat, although there are shelters at 1,650 meters on Pico Cuba and at 600 meters at La Esmajagua, midway between Pico Cuba and Las Cuevas. You may be able to camp: you'll need to be prepared with sufficient food and adequate clothing.

SIERRA DEL CRISTAL

This rugged, mineral-rich mountain region northeast of Santiago provides a spectacular drive. French coffee planters established estates here in the 19th century, though the region remained remote until the Revolution, when a paved road was built and community facilities arrived.

The only town of note is **Mayarí Arriba,** enfolded by peaks, 55 km northeast of Santiago. Céspedes established his revolutionary government here in the 1860s, and Raúl Castro established his military headquarters here when he opened the Second Front in 1958. A small **Museum of the Second Front** recalls those days. Open daily except Monday 9 a.m.-6 p.m. (US$1).

From Santiago, follow the Autopista Nacional north and exit at Boniato for El Cristo and **Alto Songo,** a crossroads town in the foothills of the mountains. From here, a road leads north to Mayarí Arriba.

SANTIAGO TO GUANTÁNAMO PROVINCE

The main road turns to Guantánamo leads via Alto Songo and rises along the northern foothills of the Gran Piedra Mountains. It's a scenic drive past rolling sugarcane fields. Beyond **La Maya,** the land becomes more lushly tropical. The area is pocked with poverty, with many hovels amid the fields of coffee and bananas and arable crops. Farther along, you pass rows of bottle-green coffee bushes beneath tall shade trees smothered in epiphytes.

The boundary with Guantánamo Province is about 25 km east of Alto Songo.

BACONAO BIOSPHERE RESERVE

The area immediately east of Santiago is replete with attractions and deserves at least a full day. The region is encompassed by the 32,400-hectare Baconao Biosphere Reserve, which officially begins at San Juan Hill, in the eastern suburbs of Santiago, and extends east 40 km to Laguna Baconao and the border with Guantánamo Province. The Sierra de la Gran Piedra forms a steep east-west backbone through the reserve, which includes parts of two other zones: the Santiago Reserve, extending along the coast; and the remote *altiplano* of Santa María de Loreto, north of Gran Piedra. The park contains many places of historical interest, including revolutionary shrines and coffee plantations established by the French settlers who came from Haiti in the 19th century. It features wildlife refuges, natural monuments, beaches, and museums.

It is reached via the Carretera Siboney, which is lined with 26 monuments to the heroes of the Moncada attack. Each has a plaque with a simple inscription that tells the hero's name, occupation, and how he died. They're signposted by blue markers and are numbered in order.

During the first half of this century, North American mining companies deforested much of the terrain. Extensive areas have also been felled for coffee and charcoal production—and, more recently, for cattle ranching. Still, there is incredible potential (as yet untapped) for hikers, birders, and other ecotourists.

The park was named a biosphere reserve by UNESCO for its biodiversity. Baconao harbors more than 6,000 species of higher plants. The north-sloping faces are more lushly forested due to higher rainfall. There are more than 800 insect species, 29 reptile species, 60 bird species, and 19 mammal species, many endemic to the region. This is a protected area. (Nonetheless, until recently Baconao contained a hunting reserve—**Caza El Indio**—for Cuba's political and military bigwigs.)

Services

There's a **Cupet gas station** at the entrance to the auto museum (see below). The Cupet facility also includes a **Havanautos** car rental office.

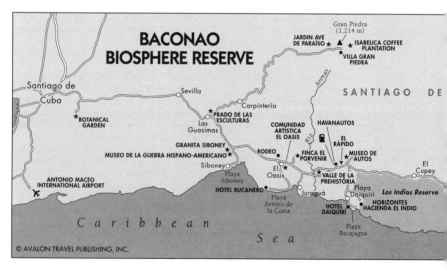

Getting There and Away

Bus no. 214 operates from Santiago's Terminal de Ómnibus Municipales on Avenida Pujol and travels via Playa Siboney to Playa Cazonal. A tourist bus departs Playa Cazonal for Santiago (US$10) at 9 a.m.; it returns at 4 p.m., departing from outside the Hotel Libertad on Plaza de Marte.

Tour agencies in Santiago offers excursions to Baconao from US$30. A taxi from Santiago will cost about US$35 roundtrip.

GRAN PIEDRA NATIONAL PARK

Prado de las Esculturas

Just beyond **Sevilla** (so named because it was settled by immigrants from Sevilla in Spain), you'll reach a T-junction at Las Guasimas, eight miles from Santiago. To the left, on a rise overlooking the road, is a sculpture garden amid a large park of wide-spreading trees and rocks. Most of the metal and rock pieces are ungainly contemporary works. It's open daily 7 a.m.-4:30 p.m. (entrance costs US$1).

Gran Piedra

The road past Prado de las Esculturas winds up through ravines, growing ever steeper and more

serpentine until it deposits you at the top of Gran Piedra (1,214 meters). The much deteriorated road winds and loops uphill for 14 km. You pass through several ecosystems. Below is lush and thick with forest. As you climb, the vegetation opens out, becoming more scrubby, and the views grow more dramatic. Suddenly you emerge on a ridge with a view down the mountains to the north. It's noticeably crisper and cooler up here, where clouds hover, swirling through the ancient tree ferns and tall pines and bamboo. The road follows the ridgeline, giving views of the Atlantic far off to the north and the Caribbean below to the right.

After about 14 km you arrive at a narrow bridge. Here a dirt road winds 400 meters downhill to Jardín Ave de Paraíso. A half-mile beyond the bridge is a restaurant and hotel at 1,150 meters elevation and from where a 454-step stairway leads up to the **Gran Piedra** (Great Rock), where you can climb a steel ladder onto the rock itself for a spectacular view down the mountainside. On a clear day you can see the Blue Mountains in Jamaica; and by night, the lights of Port-au-Spain, Haiti.

Fidel Castro and 18 other survivors of the Moncada barracks attack on 26 July 1953 fled into these mountains. On 1 August he was taken prisoner by a Rural Guard contingent. Castro was lucky. The troops wanted to kill him, but the squad commander, Lt. Pedro Manuel Sarría Tartabull, guaranteed Castro's life. (In 1957, Sarría was court-martialed and jailed. After the success of the Revolution he was named a Hero of the Revolution and later became a captain in the Revolutionary Army.)

Jardín Ave de Paraíso

What a surprise to discover this gem falling down the hillside in billowing waves. It's bloomin' lovely up here! This 45-hectare garden was created in 1960 on a former coffee plantation to raise flowers for hotels and for the celebration of the coming-of-age *Quince* of 15-year-old girls. The garden is a riot of color and scents (difficult to dampen in even the wettest of weather). The chief gardener, Nilsys Dominquez Mora, will gladly show you around her cherished garden, laid out as a series of interlocking, juxtaposed gardens, each with its own color scheme, surrounded by neatly clipped topiary hedges. Without extremes of conditions or temperature, the

*Jurassic Park?
No, it's the Valle de la
Prehistória, east of
El Rodeo.*

climate encourages an immense variety of plants: amaryllis grow with carnations, *salvia roja* spring up beside daisies, blood red dahlias thrive beside the garden's namesake "bird of paradise," almost overwhelming with their vivid oranges, blues, and purples. There are potting sheds, too, full of begonias and anthuriums, and a prim little courtyard with a small café and *floreria* (flower shop) where you can buy a huge floral display for US$25. Entrance costs US$1 (plus US$1 for cameras, US$5 for videos).

Isabelica Coffee Plantation
Two km east of Gran Piedra are the remains of a coffee plantation and manor built by Victor Constantin Couson, a French immigrant fleeing Haiti during the slave rebellion of 1792. The estate was named Isabelica, after his slave lover. In 1961 it was turned into a museum. The renovated two-story *finca* exhibits farming implements and furniture. The coffee-crushing wheel can still be seen. Trails lead through the now-overgrown estate and forests. It's open Tues.-Sun. 8 a.m.-4 p.m. (US$1). The road is badly deteriorated.

Accommodations
Horizontes' **Villa Gran Piedra,** Carretera de la Gran Piedra, Km 14, tel. (22) 8-6147, has 22 rustic red-brick cottages spread along the ridge crest—a spectacular setting! The recently refurbished cottages are pleasantly furnished. Each has a lounge, tiny kitchen, nice bathrooms, and mezzanine bedroom, plus satellite TV. An el-

egant new restaurant and bar sits atop the ridge. Rates were US$29 s, US$38 d low season, US$31 s, US$42 d high season.

SIBONEY

Playa Siboney
The little village of Siboney, replete with wooden French-style Caribbean homes, lies in a sheltered bay with a nice beach encusped by coral rocks. It's an away-from-it-all charmer. You can wade out at the eastern end, where the beach extends out to sea. It's a favorite with Cubans who flock from Santiago to relax, drawing Italian males in pursuit of a libertine lifestyle in the arms of mulatta lovers.

Granjita Siboney
About one km north of Playa Siboney, at the junction for Bacanao, this red-tile-roofed farmhouse from which Fidel and his loyal cohorts gathered in preparation for their attack on the Moncada Barracks. They sang the national anthem in whispers, and at five o'clock on the morning of Sunday, 26 July 1953, Castro and 123 fellow rebels set out.

A pathway lined with palms leads to the entrance, which is riddled with large bullet holes. Otherwise there is little to indicate that this site is of such historical import. Today it is a museum displaying weapons and blood-stained uniforms, along with a map of the Moncada attack. Newspaper clippings tell the tale of horrific torture. (Six of the attackers died in the attack; 64 others died in captivity, tortured in cold-blooded murder. Batista's henchmen then took the already-dead revolutionaries to Granjita Siboney, laid them on the porch and inside the house, then blasted them with gunfire to give the impression that they had been caught plotting and were shot in a battle.) Note the well to the side of the house where rifles were hidden in the weeks preceding the attack. The museum, tel. (22) 3-9168, is open daily, 9 a.m.-5 p.m.; entrance costs US$1.

Museo de la Guerra Hispano-Americano
This museum, 100 meters west of Granjita Siboney, is dedicated to telling the story of the Spanish-American War. It displays photos and original cannons and other weaponry, including shells and two Spanish torpedoes (one unexploded; the second the remains of a torpedo that struck the USS *Merrimac*), plus miscellaneous parts from both the U.S. and Spanish vessels. A 3-D model shows the various battles and routes of the combatants. It's open daily, 9 a.m.-5 p.m. (US$1).

Accommodations
You'll be hit up by *jiniteros* as soon as you hit town. Fob them off to save yourself hassles. About two dozen *casas particulares* cater to foreigners.

Ovidio González Sabaldo has a splendid *casa* above the store at the corner of Avenida Serrano and Calle del Barco, tel. (22) 3-9340. The attractive three-story wooden home has two modestly furnished rooms with private bathrooms with hot water (US$20). Upstairs there's a complete two-bedroom apartment, beautifully kept, cross-ventilated, with a cool tile floor and painted in tropical colors (US$40). Ovidio also has two rooms in another beautiful home at Avenida Serrano #1 (US$15), plus a third room with a/c (US$20). He offers meals for US$5 upwards. The home has a spacious veranda with Adirondack chairs.

Nearby, **Casa Particular Liliana,** on Calle Barco #17, tel. (22) 3-9413, is a 1950s-style home with three rooms with fans and small private bathrooms with hot water (US$20). It's simple but adequate and has a breeze-cooled patio with rockers and mountain views.

Casa Particular Fernando Bravo, tel. (22) 3-9115 (c/o a neighbor), is set back off the road behind the Rumbos restaurant, with two rooms with private bathroom with hot water (US$15), and a patio with rockers.

Many houses line Avenida Serrano. Try **Casa Particular Lucia Morán Zanbrano,** at Serrano #26, tel. (22) 3-9193, with two rooms (US$15) behind an old wooden home. One, albeit rather dark, has its own kitchen and dining salon, and an independent entrance. The second receives more light and has an ocean view plus a/c. There's secure parking.

Casa Particular Doña Yuyu, Calle Ovelico #12, has two rooms with private bathrooms with hot water (US$15) in a clean, handsome home with modern furnishings.

Some of the beaches of the Baconao Biosphere Reserve are reserved for another kind of wildlife.

Food

Rumbos's breeze-swept **Restaurante La Rueda** sits on the hill two blocks behind the beach, at the junction of the main street and Calle del Barco. It serves the usual *criollo* fare for less than US$5, enjoyed on a shaded open-air patio.

EL OASIS (EL CRUCERO)

From the T-junction immediately south of Granjita Siboney, the main road leads east to Laguna Baconao. About three km along you pass through El Oasis, a pretty little hamlet of fieldstone cottages that form the **Comunidad Artistas Oasis,** an artist's community where 10 families produce artwork of the highest quality—sculpture, ceramic masks, and paintings—and have open studios. Check out the beautiful masks made by Mariano Frometa, and the erotic ceramic sculptures of Eduardo Troche.

On the north side of the main road is a large rodeo ground that attracts *campesinas* from far and wide. The rodeo is overlooked by a large thatched restaurant and bar—**Finca Guajira Rodeo**—where you can dine on *criollo* cuisine (dollars only). Rodeos are given on Tuesday, Thursday, Saturday, and Sunday at 2:30 p.m. (US$5). Horseback rides are offered.

You may be able to rent a room from local artists.

PLAYA ARROYO DE LA COSTA AND PLAYA BUCANERO

A side road leads south from the rodeo to Playa Arroyo, another small, pretty cove popular with Cubans. The road continues two km west along the coral cliff to Playa Bucanero, a magnificent golden sand beach backed by limestone cliffs—the private reserve of the Hotel Bucanero.

About three km east of El Oasis, another road leads south to **Playa Jaragua,** a beige-colored beach popular with Cubans from Santiago.

Accommodations

You can rent basic cabanas on the tree-shaded hillside behind Playa Jaragua, tel. (22) 3-9161. The basic concrete cabins cost US$14. A three-room *casa* costs US$50. The basic **El Fortín**

Restaurant has a meager menu.

Coralia Club Bucanero, Carretera de Baconao Km 4, Arroyo La Costa, tel. (226) 8-6363, fax (226) 8-6073, in North America, tel. (800) 221-4542, is an attractive 200-room all-inclusive resort run by the French Mercure chain. The spacious rooms feature natural stone walls and are cool and atmospheric. Wide balconies overlook the ocean. The resort, which is popular with German and Canadian tour groups, also has *casas* for three and four people. There's a surf-and-turf restaurant, boutique, tour desk, and gym and an atmospheric restaurant and bar built on log stilts above the beach. The hotel stretches almost one km atop the coral terrace and is served by three swimming pools. Water sports, scuba diving, excursions, and car rental are available. It serves a mostly Canadian package clientele. It was being refurbished at press time. Rates were US$73 s, US$116 d, US$145 t low season, US$88 s, US$145 d, US$180 t high season, US$103 s, US$175 d, US$218 t peak season.

FINCA EL PORVENIR

Midway between El Oasis and the turnoff for Playa Juragua, a rutted dirt road to the left leads uphill one mile to the community of La Poseta, where a natural spring empties into a large bathing pool. It's very scenic and a popular spot on weekends for locals who come to cool off, sunbathe, and smooch and dance. *Criollo* dishes prepared on an outside grill are served at a handsome stone-and-bamboo restaurant.

VALLE DE LA PREHISTÓRIA

It's a shock to find a *Tyrannosaurus rex* prowling the valley of the Río Arenas, about six km east of El Rodeo. But there he is, in stalking pose, head down, tail up, eyes seeming to flick back and forth malevolently. The ferocious-looking dinosaur is one of dozens of life-size reptiles that lurk in a lush, natural setting. Apatosaurus (the erstwhile brontosaurus) is there, wallowing in a pool that dries out in the dry season. There are even woolly mammoths and a pterodactyl, wings outspread atop a nearby hillock. Real-life goats nibble contentedly amid the fearsome make-believe beasts made of metal rings and beams covered with cement.

No bones about it, the Valle de la Prehistoria is a must-visit. It's open daily 7 a.m.-6 p.m. (entry costs US$1; plus US$1 for cameras, (US$5 for videos).

Here, too, is the **Museo de Ciencias Naturales,** a natural-history museum full of butterflies, polymite snails, and impressive re-creations of mangrove and other marine environments replete with stuffed animals and birds. Guides give a lively presentation. Entrance costs US$1.

MUSEO DE AUTOS

Dowagers from the heyday of Detroit and Coventry are on view at this auto museum, run by Roberto Pérez Mirabent, tel. (22) 3-9197 or 4-1064, behind the Cupet gas station, 26 km east of Santiago. Roberto puts the spit and polish to about three dozen cars, from a 1912 Model-T Ford to a 1960 Lincoln Continental, a 1958 Thunderbird, a 1954 MG sports car, and singer Beny Moré's Cadillac. There's even a Jaguar 2.4 sedan from the 1960s. Most are in reasonably good condition. The cars are protected under galvanized tin roofs and can be viewed close-up from the pathway.

There's also a **Miniature Car Museum** *(auto miniatura)* containing more than 2,500 tiny toy cars, from the earliest models to modern-day productions. Separate cases are dedicated to fire trucks, ambulances, racing cars, etc. The collection once belonged to Fermín Fernández Hurtado, a Spanish Republican and Communist who fought in the Spanish Civil War and who donated his collection to Cuba in 1985.

Entrance costs US$1 (plus US$1 for cameras). There's a snack bar. For burgers or fried chicken, try the **El Rápido** fast-food café beside the Cupet gas station.

PLAYA DAIQUIRÍ

Playa Daiquirí lent its name to the famous drink. It was here that Teddy Roosevelt and his Rough Riders disembarked in 1898 during the Span-ish-American War and that U.S. Marines landed in 1912 and 1917 to quell a series of strikes in Santiago and Guantánamo.

The hamlet of Daiquirí consists of a half-dozen *bohios* that once housed workers at the old copper mine. Today it is dominated by a hotel overlooking the 400-meter-wide beach of unappealing gray sand overgrown with vegetation. The road continues east through the resort for one km to **Playa Bacajagua,** a beautiful golden sand beach within the deep cleft of a river mouth. There's an attractive *ranchita*-style bar and restaurant behind Playa Bacajagua, which has volleyball. Day visitors are charged US$2.

The turnoff for Daiquirí is 100 meters east of the Cupet gas station by the Museo de Autos.

Accommodations

Gran Caribe's **Hotel Daiquirí,** Carretera de Baconao Km 25, Daiquirí, tel. (22) 2-4849 or 2-4724, has 94 rooms and one suite, plus 62 bungalows that line the cliff top, all with a/c, terraces, radios, telephones, and refrigerators. Facilities include a restaurant, grill, bar, games and video rooms, a tennis court, and volleyball on the beach. Scuba diving is offered, and water sports include sailing and catamarans. Scooters and bicycles can be rented. Rates were US$120 s, US$160 d high season.

Nearby, in the heart of the scrubland inland of the beach is **Horizontes Hacienda El Indio,** tel./fax (22) 8-6213, a former hunting lodge that now functions as an eco-hotel offering hiking and horseback riding. It's a rustic facility, and an eco-lodge only in name. But it's peaceful, and the attractive all-wood rooms are attractive, though they get hot. Each has a/c, local TV, fridge, telephone, and radio. The hotels occupies a rock-strewn hillock, and has a swimming pool set in a man-made arena of faux rocks looking more fitting as a polar bear habitat in a zoo. Rates were US$30 s, US$40 d low season, US$36 s, US$47 d high season, including breakfast.

PLAYA DAIQUIRÍ TO VERRACO

About eight km east of the turnoff for Daiquirí, you'll come to a bend in the road with a huge, brightly colored mosaic of a *tocororo,* the national bird of Cuba, inlaid in the hillside. A few km beyond is the **Comunidad Artística Verraco,** where the entire community is engaged in arts and crafts in their individual stone cottages beneath shade trees. Signs point the way to individual studios, which you are welcome to visit.

Verraco lies one km inland of **Playa Larga,** a pebbly beach of little appeal.

Accommodations

Carlos Torres Franco and his wife have a *casa particular* in Nuevo Poblado #40, Playa Verraco, tel. (22) 2-3776, with two rooms in their stone house with a cement floor. The rooms are well-lit and cool, with a/c and fans, and share a bathroom (hot water was to be added) for US$15-20. The couple are a delight.

There are basic stone cabanas at **Villas Verraco,** utilized by Cuban workers on holiday at Playa Larga. Foreigners can't rent, but are welcome at the beachfront disco bar, where you can get your groove on with local lads and lasses.

You may be able to make reservations (essential) for the *campismos* at the **Oficina de Reservaciones de Turismo Parque Baconao,** at Sacó #455 in Santiago.

EAST OF VERRACO

Beyond Verraco, a massive limestone plateau shoulders up against the coast. The land is covered with scrubland and tall cacti, most spectacularly featured in the **Jardín de Cactos,** a small but impressive cactus garden set into the hillside just beyond the modestly appealing **Playa Sigua,** where there's a feeble take on Disneyworld called **El Mundo Fantasía.**

Expo Mesoamérica is another cactus garden containing Mesoamerican sculptures at the base of cliffs opposite the Hotel Los Corales.

The Carretera Baconao continues east to **Laguna Baconao,** a large lagoon encusped by mountains at the far east end of Bacanao reserve. At press time, there were eight dolphins in the lake, plus a few crocodiles. There's a meager floating restaurant in the middle of the lagoon. Boat excursions are offered (US$2). The small hamlet of **Baconao** lies on its eastern

side, at the end of the paved road, where there's a military barrier. The land farther east is off-limits.

There is good diving offshore, with three sunken ships as well as fabulous coral. Scuba diving is offered through the three hotels below.

Giant land crabs scuttle across the road in springtime to pursue their mating and egg-laying urges.

Acuario Bacanao

It's quite a surprise to come across this dolphinarium and aquatic park, tel. (22) 35-6156, in the middle of nowhere. By international standards, the exhibits are dismal and depressing, but the facility was being restored and enhanced at press time. Exhibits include moray eels, thresher sharks, and hawksbill turtles, and a walk-through glass tunnel enveloped by a tank containing sharks and large pelagians. The highlight is the 15-meter-wide dolphin pool into which you may plop to play tag with Floppy, Chalky, Jupey, and Flipper (US$25). A lone and venerable sea lion performs tricks alongside dolphins at 10 and 11.30 a.m. and 2:45 p.m. It's open daily except Thursday, 9 a.m.-5 p.m. Entrance costs US$3.

Criadero de Cocodrilos

This crocodile farm, on the southwestern shore of Laguna Baconao, has cages in which aggressive Cuban crocodiles are penned for your viewing pleasure. The crocs are bred here merely as a tourist attraction, according to the caretaker, who takes pleasure in irritating the beasts with a pole to get them thrashing. The lake itself contains only a few crocs. You can rent horses (US$3 per hour with guided). It's open daily 8 a.m.-5 p.m. (US$1).

Accommodations and Food

The **Horizontes Hotel Costa Marena,** on Playa Larga, Carretera de Baconao #350, Km 24, tel. (22) 35-6126, fax (22) 35-6155, formerly the Hotel Balneario del Sur, sprawls along the ungainly rocky shore. It has 125 rooms, most with private balconies and ocean views. Facilities include a thatched *bohio*-style entertainment center, three bars, a buffet dining room, game room, and dance hall, plus volleyball and tennis. Rocks prevent swimming directly in front of the hotel, but a sandy beach lies a short walk away. There's also a swimming pool and a natural saltwater tidal pool enclosed by a sea wall. The resort offers scuba diving and snorkeling excursions. Rates were US$25 s, US$35 d low season, US$35 s, $45 d high season, including breakfast; US$30 s, US$55 d low season, US$40 s, US$65 d high season, all-inclusive.

Cubanacán's **Club Carisol,** tel./fax (226) 35-6175, is an attractive beachfront property, and used exclusively by the French tour company. It backs a coral colored beach, Playa Cazonal. There are 166 a/c rooms in twin-level bungalows, all with terraces, satellite TV, and telephones. Some rooms have mountain views. The self-contained property has everything from scuba diving and water sports to a boutique, disco, and bicycle and car rental. All-inclusive rates were US$50 per person low season, US$55 high season.

Hotel Los Corales Carretera de Baconao, tel. (22) 35-6122, fax (22) 35-6116, two km east of Carisol, at Carretera de Bacanao Km 54, is managed by the German LTI-International Hotels. It, too, is a joint venture with Cubanacán and is popular with German and Italian tour groups. It's slightly more elegant than its sister property. It has 144 rooms in twin-level blocks and 28 rooms in seven villas. All have a/c, terraces, radios, and telephones. It has a wide range of facilities, including tennis, scuba diving, and other water sports. Excursions and car rentals are offered. Rates were the same as the Club LTI Carisol. **La Casa Rolando** is a thatched restaurant adjacent to the crocodile farm on the shores of Laguna Baconao, and offering fabulous views across the lake toward the dramatically ridged mountains. You can dine on *criollo* dishes for US$3 upward.

GUANTÁNAMO

Guantánamo. The name reverberates around the world. Everyone knows it as a U.S. naval base and a humiliating thorn in the side of Castro's Cuba. You will not find the base displayed on most Cuban maps of the province or the bay from which the contentious U.S. naval facility takes its name. With a little planning, yes, you *can* get to see the base from military *miradors*.

If Cuba has an untamed, undiscovered quarter, it is here. The wild eastern shore and secluded mountains of Guantánamo Province offer fantastic but as yet untapped opportunities for hiking, whitewater rafting, and ecotourism. The region retains a wild feel, so much so that the indigenous Indian population here managed to avoid total devastation by Spanish conquistadores. Runaway slaves—*cimarrones*—also managed to eke out a living in the remote fastness, safe from Spanish troops.

Traces of the indigenous culture linger. Baracoans—residents of the province's remote second city—wear it on their faces. The Oriente was peopled by the Taíno Indians on the eve of Columbus' arrival on this coast. There are many poorly excavated pre-Columbian sites, especially around Baracoa (a ball court similar to those of the Mayan culture has been discovered recently).

Baracoans attempt to boost their city's image (in fact, it is charming and needs no boosting) by claiming that Columbus first set foot in Cuba here and left a wooden cross (now on view in the town's cathedral) as a memento—the oldest Old World relic in the New World. Whatever the truth, it's undisputed that the first Spanish conquistadores who came on Columbus's heels established the first town in Cuba at Baracoa, and it retains its aged colonial feel in a setting that any other city would die for. It is one of the most endearing towns in Cuba.

The region has, however, long been one of Cuba's poorest provinces due to its remote location and relative lack of tillable land. Most of the province remained terra incognito until the late 18th century, when French settlers arrived from Sainte Domingue (Haiti) following the slave rebellion, bringing their coffee-growing skills to the mountains. The end of slavery in the late 19th century attracted migrant workers from Jamaica, Haiti, and other Caribbean islands, and their impact is felt to this day.

The Lay of the Land

Guantánamo Province tapers eastward to a rounded tip—Punta de Maisí—at the easternmost point of the island. The province is almost wholly mountainous. Except for a great scalloped bowl surrounding the town of Guantánamo, the lushly forested uplands push up against a thread-thin coastal plain. Much of the

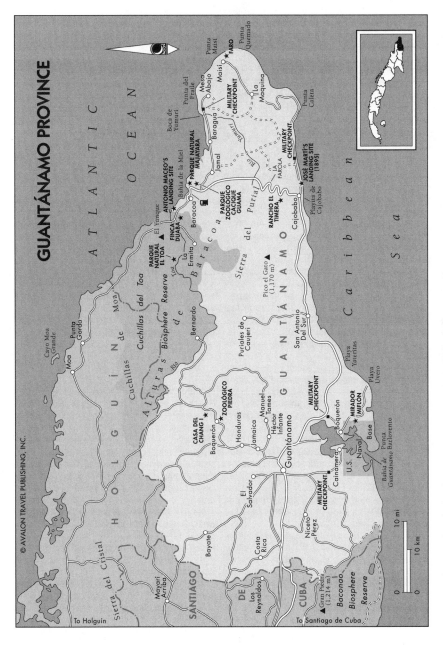

GUANTÁNAMO PROVINCE

© AVALON TRAVEL PUBLISHING, INC.

ATLANTIC OCEAN

Caribbean Sea

Cayo Moa Grande
Punta Gorda
Moa
Cuchillas del Toa
Alturas de Cuchillas del Toa Biosphere Reserve
HOLGUÍN
Bernardo
Sierra del Cristal
SANTIAGO DE CUBA
Mayarí Arriba
To Holguín
Los Reynaldos
Bayate
Costa Rica
Niceto Pérez
El Salvador
Gran Piedra (1,214 m)
Baconao Biosphere Reserve
To Santiago de Cuba

El Yunque
PARQUE NATURAL EL TOA
La Ermita
Río Toa
Sierra del Baracoa
FINCA DUABA
ANTONIO MACEO'S LANDING SITE
Baracoa
Bahía de Miel
Boca de Yumurí
PARQUE NATURAL MAJAYARA
Jamal
Baragua
Río Yumurí
MILITARY CHECKPOINT
Meso Abajo
Punta del Frale
Maisí
Punta Maisí
FARO
Punta Quemado
La Máquina
Punta Caleta
PARQUE ZOOLÓGICO CACIQUE GUAMA
La Farola
RANCHO EL TIMERA
JOSÉ MARTÍ'S LANDING SITE (1895)
Cojobabo
Playita de Cajobabo
MILITARY CHECKPOINT
Pico el Gato (1,170 m)
Sierra del Purial
Río Purial
GUANTÁNAMO
Puriales de Caujeri
San Antonio Del Sur
Playa Yateritas
Playa Uvero
ZOOLÓGICO PIEDRA
CASA DEL CHANG I
Boquerón
Honduras
Jamaica
Manuel Tames
Héctor Infante
Guantánamo
MILITARY CHECKPOINT
Boquerón
MIRADOR (MIFLÓN)
Base
U.S. Naval Base
Caimanera
MILITARY CHECKPOINT
Bahía de Guantánamo
Punta Barlovento
CUBA

0   10 mi
0   10 km

mountain terrain remains swathed in prime forest. Today a great part of the mountain region is protected within Cuchilla del Toa Biosphere Reserve. Few foreign travelers ever make the journey into these wildlife-rich mountains harboring rare plant and bird species and polymites—snails that haul fabulously colored shells on their backs. Portions remain virtually unexplored.

The northeast coast and north-facing mountains around Baracoa make up the rainiest region in Cuba, with precipitation ranging from 200 cm in the coastal zone to 360 cm in the upper Toa river valley and majestic heights of the Sierra Sagua-Baracoa. By contrast, valleys along the southern coast are pockets of aridity, and cacti grow in the lee of Cuba's wettest slopes.

GUANTÁNAMO AND VICINITY

Guantánamo, 82 km east of Santiago, is a large city (pop. 180,000) at the head of a deep bay of the same name and some 25 km north of the naval base (the base lies at the mouth of the bay, which opens up like the cloud of a nuclear explosion). The city is spread out on a broad plain surrounded by a meniscus of mountains. In *Driving through Cuba,* Carlo Gebler describes it as a "depressed city of miserable, low houses and railway marshalling yards filled with decrepit rolling stock." True, the city has grown rapidly in the past three decades, adding soulless concrete carbuncles and vast acreages of jerry-built brick-and-concret housing to the colonial core. There are many slum hovels, too, giving an impression of a city in Mexico or India.

But the colonial heart of the city has several buildings of interest. And the people are warm and lively. Much of the population is descended from Jamaican and Haitian immigrants who arrived in the 1920s to work in the sugar fields. Others arrived from Barbados, St. Kitts, and other islands. The connections are strong: a British West Indian Welfare Center (an association for English-speaking descendants, locally called *Ingleses*—Englishmen) and a Haitian cultural center, Tumba Francesa, work to keep alive the traditions and anomalous culture (Haitians are called *Franceses*—Frenchmen). Many Ingleses speak fluent English.

There's a local saying that the "sun rises in Guantánamo" (the island's easternmost city), meaning that things in Cuba happen first here. Baloney! It's a somnolent place, except when serious friction occurs between Cuba and the United States and the city gears up for a worst-case scenario. Given the proximity of the U.S. naval base, you'd expect a strong Cuban military

presence. Senior officers tote briefcases. The grunts are billeted on the outskirts of town in several military bases and a military school. I even saw an active platoon of women soldiers in full battle gear marching by, reminding me of something Tom Miller had written: "They all wore earrings, flowers in their hair, and wide smiles. Cuba has a lovely army."

Most locals seem to have nothing better to do than rock on their porches, waiting wistfully for something to happen. Local citizens even watch an armed-forces television station piped in from the U.S. naval base.

The salt industry is important locally (most of Cuba's salt originates here).

HISTORY

In 1494 Columbus anchored in Guantánamo Bay during his second voyage to the New World. He called it Puerto Grande (the exact site where he landed, Fisherman's Point, lies within the U.S. naval base). The area remained unsettled and undeveloped during the first centuries of colonial government, so much so that the English even attempted to settle the area in 1741. The city got its real start in the years following the rebellion in Haiti, when French exiles claimed a stake. The only event of note took place in 1871, when General Máximo Gómez and his troops stormed the city during the War of Independence. They were followed in June 1898 by U.S. marines during the Spanish-Cuban-American War—who haven't left yet!

The town developed a near-total economic dependency on the base, which employed hundreds of Cuban workers. It is claimed that prostitution was the major industry. Says an early guidebook, "The flourishing prostitution business passed from generation to generation like titles to land, and it was not unusual to find three generations of women in service to the base." Women flocked from all over Cuba to bed down with moneyed marines. During the 1950s, many of the prostitutes supported Castro's rebel army. "They would get rifles, bullets, grenades. The sailors had to pay twice, first with weapons, and then a lot of the prostitutes insisted on being paid in cash, too," author Tom Miller was told by Nydia Sarabia, who had helped run *red de mujeres,* the women's network during the Revolution.

In 1958 the Revolution closed in on Guantánamo. Raúl Castro set up base in the mountains. In June, Raúl's troops took 24 U.S. servicemen captive in an attempt to force Batista's air force to stop bombing his units and peasant communities in the mountain war zone. Fidel ordered the hostages released, and the air attacks resumed. The base was never attacked by Castro's rebel army.

ORIENTATION

Guantánamo is laid out in a near-perfect grid. It is approached from Santiago de Cuba by a four-lane highway that enters town from the northwest (note the regular exit ramps that dead-end into each side: the highway is intended to serve as a runway for military aircraft in the event that Cuba has to defend itself from a U.S. invasion; the side "roads" are meant to store warplanes).

The old Carretera Central enters town farther south and becomes Avenida Camilo Cienfuegos, a wide boulevard that runs east to the southern edge of the historic downtown. The center of town is Parque Martí, six blocks north of Camilo Cienfuegos, between Pedro Pérez and Calixto García (north-south) and Aguilera and Flor Crombet (east-west).

Paralleling Camilo Cienfuegos is Paseo (Avenida Estudiantes), a major shopping street 11 blocks north. Paseo leads west to the Reparto Caribe, where the Hotel Guantánamo, ministry buildings, and modern high-rise apartments are concentrated near Plaza de la Revolución, on Calle 6.

Calle 5 de Prado (four blocks south of Paseo) leads east across the River Bano for Baracoa. Calle Pinto runs south from the west end of Camilo Cienfuegos for Caimanera. A ring road *(circunvalación)* runs north of the city.

SIGHTSEEING

Parque Martí
Most of what little there is to see surrounds this attractive and cozy little square with its pretty, well-preserved, ocher-colored church—**Iglesia Parroquia de Santa Catalina**—on the north side. Where U.S. sailors once paraded with floozies, bench seats today offer a chance to sit and watch the ebb and flow of a more parochial life. In springtime, laburnum trees blaze with harmonious yellow and purple blossoms.

Museo Municipal
The streets immediately west of Parque Martí are lined with humble yet venerable houses, including the local museum at Martí #804, tel. (21) 32-5872. The building dates from 1862 and was once a prison. The museum contains artifacts and lithographs portraying life from the pre-Columbian through the revolutionary eras. It's open Mon.-Fri. 8 a.m.-noon and 2-6 p.m. Entrance costs US$1.

SIGHTSEEING HIGHLIGHTS: GUANTÁNAMO PROVINCE

Baracoa: Remote town with heaps of tumble-down charm. Places of note include a small cigar factory and **Catedral Nuestra Señora de la Asunción,** containing the **Cruz de la Parra,** supposedly left in Cuba by Christopher Columbus. Sensational views from El Castillito (today a pleasant hotel). Fascinating cultural life. Regional cuisine.

La Farola: Suspenseful road snaking up and over the Sierra del Purial. Incredible views.

El Yunque: Dramatic forest-draped formation good for hiking and birding.

Zoológica Piedra: Fascinating zoo of stone animals carved into the jungle-clad mountainside.

GUANTÁNAMO

Guantánamo (Gitmo) is the oldest U.S. overseas military base. It's also the only one located in a communist country—and a constant thorn in the side of Cuban-U.S. relations.

Since 1903 the U.S. has held an indefinite lease on the property, which it claimed as a prize at the end of the Cuban-Spanish-American War. Uncle Sam dictated the peace terms. The Platt Amendment stated that "to enable the United States to maintain the independence of Cuba, and to protect the people thereof. . . the Cuban Government will sell or lease to the United States the lands necessary for coaling or naval stations." The 45 square miles of land and water were formally handed over to the U.S. in ceremonies aboard the USS *Kearsarge,* anchored in the bay, on 10 December 1903.

In the original lease, the U.S. agreed to pay Cuba the sum of US$2,000 in gold per year. In 1934, when gold coins were discontinued, the rent was upped to US$4,085 (US$0.14 an acre), payable by U.S. Treasury check. The first rent check that Uncle Sam paid to Castro's regime, in 1959, was cashed. Since then, Fidel has kept the unclaimed checks in a drawer in his office desk.

The Platt Amendment was dropped in 1934, and a new treaty was signed. Although it confirmed Cuba's "ultimate sovereignty," the treaty stipulated that the lease would be indefinite and can be terminated only by agreement of both parties (or if the U.S. decides to pull out). "As a result," writes Tom Miller, "the United States is in the enviable position of an imperious tenant who establishes the rent, controls the lease, and ignores the landlord."

The gates between the base and Cuba were closed on 1 January 1959 and have not been reopened. It served as a detention center for refugees fleeing Haiti's political crisis in 1992. Two years later it housed more than 20,000 *balseros,* who were later returned to Cuba.

Life on the Base

The base occupies both sides of the entrance to the bay, which is inhabited by endangered manatees and marine turtles (iguanas roam on land; the iguana is the unofficial Gitmo mascot). The Naval Air Station (NAS) is located on the western side of the bay and separated by four km of water from the naval station, on the east side. Hence, the bay is crisscrossed by helicopters, boats, and an hourly ferry. The treaty guarantees free access to the waters to Cuban vessels and those of Cuba's trading partners heading in and out of the Cuban port of Boqueron. An Anti-Air Warfare Center monitors Cuban traffic.

Today, 7,000 U.S. servicemen and their dependents live here amid all the comforts of a small midwestern town. There are five swimming pools, four outdoor movie houses, 400 miles of paved road, and a golf course. McDonald's even has a concession (the only one in Cuba). Another 7,000 civilians also work here, including 800 Jamaican laborers and a small number of Cubans who chose to remain following the Revolution (they receive rent-free housing and have their own community center). A dwindling number of Cubans also "commute" to work daily through the base's North East Gate— "the last unfrozen trickle in our icy relations," wrote Tom Miller.

In 1964 the Cuban government cut off the base's water supply. It was replaced with a seawater desalinization plant that today provides 3,000,000 gallons of fresh water daily, along with electrical power.

The facility was until recently ringed by the largest U.S. minefield in the world, laid down during the Cuban Missile Crisis of 1962 (but dug up and disarmed in 1999). The Cuban mines remain and are clearly marked with red triangular warning signs in English and Spanish. Nonetheless, each year many young Cubans risk death to reach a "paradise" promised by radio and television stations broadcasting from the base. An average of 137 Cuban "fence-jumpers" made the crossing every year between 1964 (when records began) and 1992, when the figure leapt upward. The United States accuses Cuba of using weapons to stop people from swimming to the base. Cuba denies the charges and says that U.S. troops routinely provoke "clashes." One such incident, in the summer of 1986, led to the death of a private who snitched on a marine firing over the fence and died following a beating by 10 fellow marines (the episode was portrayed in the movie *A Few Good Men,* starring Demi Moore, Tom Cruise, and Jack Nicholson).

Castro asserts that "The naval base has only served to offend the honor of our nation." He has proposed to make it a regional medical center for all the Caribbean if Uncle Sam relinquishes his hold.

sign proclaiming "Socialism or Death" in front of the U.S. army base at Guantanámo

Plaza de la Revolución
Marian Grajales Coello

This huge, barren square faces the Hotel Guantánamo. Its two high notes are billboards touting the achievements of Karl Marx and Friedrich Engels and the **Monument to Heroes.** Steps lead up to a huge concrete structure with the faces of Martí, Maceo, and other heroes from the War of Independence, local hero Mariana Grajales Coello most prominent. The monument is illumined at night by dazzling arc lights. The bones of Los Mártires de Angola (Cuban military personnel who died fighting in Angola) are interred here. Military ceremonies are often held. And concerts and lectures are presented in the underground *salas.*

Other Sights

Check out the exquisite detail on the turn-of-the-century building at the corner of Prado and Pedro Pérez, built in Parisian fashion and topped by a cupola with a herald with trumpet.

Another intriguing structure is the **Plaza del Mercado,** on Antonio Maceo esq. Prado, built last century to house the original agricultural market and still used for that purpose. It's the city's most intriguing building: a pink neoclassical structure, with columns and pediments. Nearby, on Calixto García e/ Donato Marmol y Bernace Verona, is the **Taller de Escultura,** where sculptures and ceramics are made. The house across the street at #1068 is a classic example of Art Nouveau architecture.

Antonio Maceo leads south five blocks to the **Parque Zoológico,** at Ramón Pinto. The zoo's complement of wildlife includes a few geese, ducks, and other fowl, and—one of the saddest sights in all Cuba—two fully grown African lions kept in a diminutive cage. On the east side of the park is a wall bearing a 3-D mural of local Mambí general, Pedro Pérez.

There's a basic cigar factory, **Fábrica de Tabaco Lezara Peña,** two blocks east of the Hotel Guantánamo.

ACCOMMODATIONS

Casas Particulares

There are only five or six private room rentals in town.

Elisabeth Ramón runs **Villa Reve's,** Calle Pedro Pérez #670A e/ Paseo y Narcisco López, tel. (21) 32-2159, offering four rooms in a colonial home two blocks from the main square (US$10-20). The rooms vary. The two interior rooms downstairs are gloomy. The upstairs rooms are well lit and cross-ventilated, and share a clean, modern bathroom with hot water. Three rooms have a/c, and all have a fan and fridge. Meals are served in an airy patio to the rear.

Elyse Castillo Osoria rents two rooms at her *casa particular* at Calixto García #766 e/ Prado y Jesús del Sol, tel. (21) 32-3787, in a pleasant home with 1950s decor in the TV lounge (US$10-20). One room has wood-paneled walls, its own patio, a/c, and fridge, and shares a bathroom. The second room is smaller and darker, but has its own bathroom. Meals are served in a

GUANTÁNAMO CITY

To Santiago

To Villa María

CASA DE LOS ENSUEÑOS

RESTAURANTE CARIBE

HOTEL GUANTÁNAMO

Plaza de la Revolución

FÁBRICA DE TABACO LEZARA PEÑA

Río Bano

Río Guaso

To Baracoa

BUS STATION

HOSPITAL

PASEO (AV. ESTUDIANTES)

RAILWAY STATION

HAVANAUTOS

CENTRO GASTRONÓMICO RÁPIDO

CINEMA

BRITISH WEST INDIAN WELFARE CENTER

JESÚS DEL SOL

VILLA REVE'S

TUMBA FRANCESCA

5 DEL PRADO

SEE "CENTRAL GUANTÁNAMO CITY" MAP

FLOR CROMBET

Parque Martí

MÁXIMO GÓMEZ

PEDRO PÉREZ

ANTONIO MACEO

BARTOLOMÉ MASÓ

BERNACE VERONA

AV. CAMILO CIENFUEGOS

PEDRO PÉREZ

CENTRAL

CARRETERA

To Santiago

MININT

Río Guaso

CALLE PINTO

HOSPITAL

To Caimanera

0   0.5 mi
0   0.5 km

© AVALON TRAVEL PUBLISHING, INC.

handsome rear patio. The house is two-in-one, half being colonial, half being modern.

Liset Foster rents a single a/c room at her home at Lino Norte A #1011 e/ 2 y 3 Oeste, with fans and private bathroom with hot water (US$15).

Hotels

Islazul's **Hotel Guantánamo,** Calle 13 e/ Calles Ahogado y Oeste, tel. (21) 38-1015, is a standard Soviet-style two-block structure on with 124 mediocre but adequate rooms. The hotel is professionally run by Pedro (Peter) Hope, a gifted former professor who demonstrates a keen intel-

lect and sense of marketing. The restaurant serves the usual dismal (and overpriced) Islazul fare. Facilities include a tour desk, swimming pool, disco, and store. Rates were US$18 s, US$24 d low season, US$23 s, US$30 d high season.

What a disaster has befallen the **Casa de los Ensueños,** until recently a beautiful two-story rental villa in 1960s Miami style in Reparto Caribe. Alas, the exquisite decor has disappeared, replaced by mundane furnishings. It is now a poorly run hostel with three bedrooms that can sleep up to eight people. A bar café in the front yard blasts out music to wake the dead. Rates were US$19 s, US$22 d.

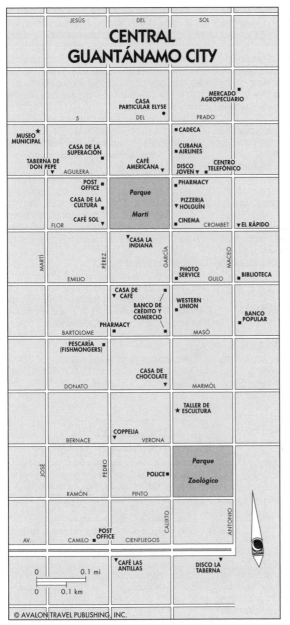

Villa Turística La Lupe, three miles north of town on the banks of the Río Bano, tel. (21) 38-2680, is a tranquil option but for the noise from the lively poolside bar that attracts Cubans on weekends. The hotel has 50 modestly appointed rooms with large bedrooms, most in two-story cabanas. Take an upstairs room with lofty ceilings. All have a/c, TVs, and refrigerators. Some have minibars. There are also two suites with connecting bedrooms overlooking the river. A small restaurant overhangs a weir and has a shady patio beneath a huge tree festooned with epiphytes. Rates were US$18 s, US$26 d low season, US$23 s, US$30 d high season.

Villa Santa María is a similar option northeast of the city, on the east bank of the Río Bano. Not inspected.

FOOD

Mother Hubbard would feel at home in Guantánamo. During my two recent visits, virtually every restaurant pantry was bare.

Paladar La Cubanita, Calle José Martí esq. Flor Crombey, serves the usual *criollo* fare for about US$6. The intriguing decor includes a bull's head on one wall.

Alas, the restaurant of the Hotel Guantánamo leaves much to be desired. An alternative option is the rooftop (9th floor) **Restaurante Caribe** atop a high- rise apartment complex immediately west of the Hotel Guantánamo.

Downtown, Islazul's modern a/c (but drab) **Café Oroazul,**

at the corner of Aguilera and Antonio Maceo, can manage only meager portions of *pollo frito,* pork steak, and ham sandwiches (US$1 apiece). Basic *criollo* meals are promised at the 24-hour **Café Sol,** next to the Casa de la Cultura on Parque Martí; at **Café Americana,** on the northeast corner; and at **Café Las Antillas,** on the corner of Camilo Cienfuegos and Pérez. Five pesos will buy you a slice of pizza at **Pizzeria Holguín** facing Parque Martí.

If all else fails, try the **Centro Gastronómico Rápido,** an open-air fast-food complex adjoining the railway station on Paseo.

Thirsting for coffee? Try **Casa La Indiana,** on the south side of Parque Martí; **Casa de Café,** on Pérez, two blocks south of the park; or **Casa de Chocolate,** one block southeast on Calixto García.

Coppelia serves excellent ice cream for 2.50 pesos a bowl at the corner of Pérez and Bernace Verona). And **Frozzen Arlequin** sells frozen yogurt; it's 50 meters north of Parque Martí on Pedro Pérez.

ENTERTAINMENT AND EVENTS

Festivals and Events
Every Saturday evening, Pedro Pérez is cordoned off and the locals bring their tables and chairs onto the street; roasted suckling pig, pizzas, and other food and drink are served; and musicians play on every block (often two or more bands perform on the same block, drowning each other out and vying against the radios or CD players that add to the general cacophony). The townsfolk pour in, and too much rum is downed. Beware aggressive drunks. You'll need your own container to buy rum drinks from the various street stalls.

Traditional Music and Dance
The **British West Indian Welfare Center,** Serafin Sánchez #663, e/ Paseo y Narciso López, tel. (21) 32-5297, founded in 1945 to give economic aid to Jamaicans and other English-speaking Caribbean residents leaving their homeland, hosts music and dance sessions featuring Caribbean forms such as *changuí* (an antecedent of *son*). One block south is **Tumba Francesa,** a similar association representing

the descendants of Haitian immigrants, and a great place to hear the music and dance styles evolved by Haitians (*tumba francesa* is a saloon dance where dancers imitate European rhythms such as the minuet with instruments and movements of African origin). By day, locals play dominoes and the women adorned in gaily colored traditional garb make for splendid photos (for a charge).

Also try the **Casa de la Cultura,** tel. (21) 32-6391, on the west side of Parque Martí.

Watch for performances by Elio Revé and his Orquestra Revé, a local (and world-famous) exponent of *son-changuí.*

The **Dirección Provincial de Cultura Guantánamo,** Calle Calixto García #806 e/ Aguilera y Prado, Guantánamo, tel. (21) 32-2296, fax (21) 32-4676, e-mail: chacon@gtmo.cult.cu, arranges excursions to Casa del Changuí to hear the **Estrellas Campesinos** perform traditional music.

Cabarets and Discos
A *cabaret espectáculo* is held on Friday night and weekends at the Villa Santa María at 11 p.m. (the doors open at 8 p.m.); US$3. **Club Nevada,** a rough-and-ready hangout for *Ingleses,* reportedly has cabaret followed by a disco. The Hotel Guantánamo has a disco, Tues.-Sunday.

The happening spot at last visit was the **Disco La Taberna,** at the junction of Camilo Cienfuegos and Antonio Maceo. It gets packed to the gills, and is gritty and sweaty. Entrance costs a steep US$5.

GUANTANAMERA . . . GUAJIRA GUANTANAMERA!

"Guajira Guantanamera" has become a kind of signature tune of Cuba. Everywhere you go, you'll hear it played by troubadours. It was written in 1928 by Joseío Fernández (1908-1979), who at the time was in love with a woman from Guantánamo. When the song was first played on the radio in 1934, it became an overnight hit. In 1962, Cuban musician Háctor Angulo went to New York to study and added the words of José Martí's *versos sencillos* (simple verses) to Fernández's melody. Popular folk-singer Pete Seeger performed Angulo's version at Carnegie Hall and launched it to international fame.

Be cautious. Guantánamo is a rough city, and discos are violent places. I've seen more than one bottle broken to be used in fights, which erupt frequently, especially on Saturday night, when drunks abound. And you should avoid the rooftop **Disco Joven,** above Etecsa on Aguilera.

Other Entertainment

La Taberna de Don Pepe, on Calle Aguilera esq. José Martí, is a lively local hole-in-the-wall bar that is an in-spot for males come to play dominoes.

The **Casa de la Superación,** on Pedro Pérez, one block north of the main square, is a music school that hosts classical performances.

There's a **cinema** on the southeast corner of Parque Martí. Entrance costs one peso.

PRACTICALITIES

Services

The **Banco de Crédito y Comercio** has a branch at Calixto García y Bartolomé Masó. **Banco Popular** is one block east. The **post office** is at Pérez y Aguilera. The **Etecsa** international telephone exchange is on Aguilera, one block east of Plaza Martí.

The **hospital,** tel. (21) 39-1013, is half a km south of town, on Carretera El Salvador. You'll find **pharmacies** on Pérez and Bartolomé Masó, on the northeast corner of Parque Martí, and on Paseo.

There's a **Photo Service** outlet one block south of Parque Martí, on Calixto García.

The **Cupet gas station** is 200 meters east of the bridge over the Río Bano, on the road to Baracoa.

Getting There and Away

By Air: The **Mariana Grajales Airport,** tel. (21) 32-3564, is 12 km east of town. **Cubana** flies between Havana and Guantánamo daily except Friday (US$60). You'll need to make reservations as far in advance as possible. Cubana has an office at Calle Calixto García #817, e/ Prado y Aguilera, tel. (21) 32-4533.

By Bus: Bus no. 640 leaves Havana daily for Guantánamo at 3:15 p.m., arriving about 7 a.m. next morning (US$38). The bus terminal, tel. (21) 32-3713, is about three km west of downtown, on

the road from Santiago. Buses depart from here for most major cities via Santiago. Reservations are booked solid for weeks in advance.

By Train: Trains #11, #13, and #19 depart Havana for Guantánamo via Santiago de Cuba. The fare between Santiago de Cuba and Guantánamo is US$4 (four hours).

A fast *especial* departs Guantánamo for Santiago and Havana at 4:30 p.m. (US$43) every two days but not on the third. A regular train departs Guantánamo for Santiago de Cuba and Havana daily at 1:30 p.m. (US$30.50). A separate *ferro-omnibus* commuter train departs daily for Santiago de Cuba at 1, 5, and 9 p.m. (four pesos).

The train station, tel. (21) 32-518, is on Pedro Pérez, one block east of Paseo.

By Organized Tours: Tour agencies in Santiago de Cuba offer excursions to Guantánamo.

Getting Around

There are plenty of horse-drawn carriages. With luck, you'll be charged in pesos (no more than 10 pesos anywhere in town; you should be able to go anywhere for US$2). Bus no. 9 runs past the Hotel Guantánamo.

Havanautos, tel. (21) 35-5405, has a car rental office on the east side of town, beside the Cupet gas station, and another outlet in the Hotel Guantánamo.

The Dirección Provincial de Cultura Guantánamo, Calle Calixto García #806 e/ Aguilera y Prado, Guantánamo, tel. (21) 32-2296, fax (21) 32-4676, e-mail: chacon@gtmo.cult.cu, arranges city tours and local excursions, including to the "Stone Zoo" and to Casa del Changüí (see below).

CAIMANERA

Caimanera is a small town 22 km south of Guantánamo, on a peninsula on the west shore of the bay. Surrounded by salt flats, it is a modern town, almost totally rebuilt since the Revolution, with soulless concrete apartment blocks abutting older wooden houses. Today its economy is based on salt and fishing and the Frontera Brigada military complex. Before the Revolution, many Caimaneros worked on the U.S. naval base, while Caimaneras worked in the strip joints and brothels that were the town's staple industry. Many of the former are due pensions, but Uncle Sam, the ol' skinflint, won't pay them their due—approximately US$5 million, according to author Tom Miller—unless they renounce their Cuban citizenship.

There's a **museum** that tells of the negative toll of the naval base. It is heavily slanted toward proving "enemy provocation" and contains photos of Cubans killed, others showing marines schmoozing with Cuban women at the fence, and even one of a marine sticking his naked butt at the camera.

From the Hotel Caimanera, with its three-story observation tower, you can look out past Cuban watchtowers and, farther back, the U.S. watchtowers clearly ringing the naval base that Castro has called "a dagger plunged in the heart of Cuban soil." The main *mirador*—Mirador Miflón—is on the *east* side of the bay, near Boquerón.

There's a police barrier just before Caimanera, a restricted military zone (residents hold special permits). At press time, you needed advance permission from the **Ministero del Interior** (MININT) to visit Caimanera or the Mirador Miflón. The MININT office is on Calle José Martí, three blocks south of Avenida Camilo Cienfuegos. Here I was told that visitors *must* obtain a permit in advance through MINREX (the Ministry of Foreign Relations), in Havana. If you follow this route, it can take forever. You can try to arrange a permit or excursion through the Villa Gaviota, tel. (226) 4-1368, fax (226) 8-7166, in Santiago.

Getting to the U.S. naval base itself is out of the question. The transit point from Caimanera to the base has been closed since 1961. Civilians must request permission from the U.S. Navy and, if granted, fly down on the charter flights from Norfolk, Virginia.

Accommodations and Food

The **Hotel Caimanera,** Loma Norte, Caimanera, tel. (21) 99-414, sits atop a low hillock in the center of town. It has 19 attractive a/c rooms with TVs and VCRs, and a restaurant, café, bar, and swimming pool with a water slide. You can order a *mojito*, put your feet up, and look out over the U.S. base, which blazes brightly at night like a miniature Las Vegas. The situation is fickle: both times I've called by, tourists weren't being allowed. Rates were US$24 s, US$30 d.

Getting There

By Train: Commuter trains depart Guantánamo for Caimanera four times daily (50 minutes). You can always try sneaking on board without a permit.

By Sea: Believe it or not, U.S. (and other) skippers can sail right past the U.S. naval base and into the Cuban-controlled harbor and port of Caimanera. Private yachters are not really made welcome (U.S. naval vessels may also board and search your vessel when you pass through the straits), and the hassle may not be worth it.

MIRADOR MIFLÓN

On the east side of Guantánamo Bay, opposite Caimanera, are several military bases and two Cuban naval facilities—Glorieta and Boquerón. The area is off-limits to foreigners without a permit. The area abounds in cacti planted in the 1960s to form a natural barrier (as much to stop Cubans from defecting as to stop U.S. troops from attacking); it's now called the Cactus Curtain.

The coastal plain rises to a north-south escarpment of the Sierra del Maquey with a crescent of tall hills at the southern end overlooking the U.S. installation. The Cuban military finds it a perfect vantage point and has a military command center buried deep beneath the mountain. The major lookout point—El Mirador Miflón (U.S. marines call it "Castro's Bunker")—is here, on the south side of a hill called Loma Malones. Few foreigners are granted access to this *mirador,* which is normally reserved for VIPs. Still, permits are sometimes granted: visitors are shown the bunker, which contains a diorama of the base. The camouflaged *mirador* has a restaurant from where you can look right down on the U.S. base. Cuban soldiers may even lend you their high-powered binoculars.

Getting There

Just east of Glorieta, at the turnoff for Boquerón, is a military post and barrier. You'll need a permit. It is 14 km from here through scrubland and cacti to Mirador Miflón. Excursions to Miflón are also offered by **Villa Gaviota,** in Santiago, which may be able to arrange an individual permit, with guide.

The **Vietnam Veterans of America Association** offers an annual trip to Cuba each November. Past trips have featured visits to Miflón. Trip members usually receive the VIP treatment (see the section on Organized Tours in the On The Road chapter for further information).

ZOOLÓGICO PIEDRA

The "stone zoo" features a menagerie of wild animals from around the world—lions, tapirs, hippopotamuses, elephants, and other species—hewn from huge calcareous rocks with hammer and chisel by a coffee farmer, Angel Iñigo. Iñigo has carved more than 385 animals that he had seen only in photographs in books, representing more than 20 years of work. Over a kilometer of stone pathways lead through the thick foliage, revealing such fabulous carved scenes as a buffalo being attacked by mountain lions (complete with intestines being ripped out), two monkeys picking fleas from each other, and Stone Age figures killing a wild boar. The zoo is a work in progress. Entrance costs US$1 (plus US$1 for cameras, US$5 for videos).

The zoo is near the village of Boquerón (not to be mistaken for the port on the east side of Guantánamo Bay), in the middle heights of the mountains of Yatueras, 25 km northeast of Guantánamo. To get there, follow the road for Jamaica from the traffic circle one km east of the Río Bano. Continue straight past Honduras (other villages north of Guantánamo are named for neighboring countries, including Costa Rica, El Salvador, and Paraguay). It's a beautiful drive, with exquisite views back down the mountain.

CASA DEL CHANGUÍ

The Tavera family keep alive the traditional culture of music and dance at this small *finca* in the hamlet of **Güirita,** about three km above the Zoológico Piedra. If you're seeking to hear and learn about *changuí,* the authentic music of Guantánamo, this is it, melding Afro, Jamaica, and Spanish influences. The Estrellas Campesinos (Country Stars), a group founded in 1952 and led by the indefatigable Pepe, perform the country music that evolved here last century and forms the basis of later Cuban sounds, such as *son* and *salsa,* and has its distinctive origins in *danzón.* The group performs *changuí* in its original form beneath thatch, where a rum drink is served, and you are encouraged to dance. Performances are on Tuesday and Saturday.

Impromptu visits are discouraged. The family prefers visitors by appointment only. Check with tour agencies in Santiago, or with Ernesto Chacón Domínquez of the Direción Provincial de Cultura Guantánamo, Calle Calixto García #806 e/ Aguilear y Prado, Guantánamo, tel. (21) 32-2296, fax (2) 32-4676, e-mail: chacon@ gtmo.cult.cu, or with the Hotel Guantánamo, in Guantánamo.

Zoológica Piedra (the Stone Zoo)

GUANTÁNAMO TO BARACOA

Immediately east of the turnoff for Mirador Miflón, the coast road rises up a two-km-long hill where you have your views back down over the milky bay towards Caimanera. The land for several miles is virtually uninhabited. Don't be tempted to part the barbed-wire fence and go hiking over the scrub-covered upland in search of a view of the base. Signs warn that you should not trespass; *Obey them! Much of the area is strewn with land mines.*

Beyond the crest, the road drops to the coast and you emerge at a beach—**Playa Yateritas**—in a wide bay. The golden beach is popular with Cuban schoolchildren and residents of Guantánamo on weekends, when the place can get lively. The calm turquoise waters are perfect for a refreshing dip. There are thatched *ranchitas* for shade, and a basic restaurant. Basic cabanas can be rented.

Just beyond Playa Yateritas is **Tortuguilla**, a truly rustic one-street village that fringes the coral cliff top. It would be a great place to rent a room with local fishermen for a few days of reclusive, offbeat escape. Bougainvillea and cactus add to the away-from-it-all charm.

For the next few miles, you'll pass little coves cut into the raised coral shore, with pellucid waters and tiny beaches as private as your innermost thoughts. The coast grows more dramatic, with mountains rising ahead. There are few villages. **San Antonio del Sur** is an exception. This small town has a tiny museum and a Casa de la Cultura on a main street lined with topiary and shrubs. Nearby, inland, is **Avre Mariana,** a mountain with a scarp face. Islazul was planning to offer hang-gliding packages from the Hotel Guantánamo.

Beyond the pleasant little village of **Imias**, the terrain turns to semi-desert, with scrub-covered hills and valley bottoms filled with orchards and oases of palms. Playa Imias is a broad, gray-sand beach fronted by shallow turquoise waters.

Accommodations

There are basic cabins at Playa Imias, with two beds and private bathrooms with cold water only for US$9 per cabin. The simple facility serves Cubans and has a restaurant and bar where no-frills fare is served.

CAJOBABO

Cajobabo, 45 km east of Guantánamo, is hallowed ground. Here, José Martí, Máximo Gómez, and four other prominent patriots put ashore in a small rowboat on 11 April 1895 after years of exile. There are two beaches. The first fronts Campismo Playita Cajobabo, at the end of the tiny hamlet, where there's a simple store and cantina. It's lonesome, except when schoolchildren are here on vacation. The shingle beach is unattractive. Hence, the preferred bathing spot is the river mouth. There's a tiny **museum** glorifying Martí's party and their respective deeds. **Campismo Playita Cajobabo,** which has simple concrete cabanas (six pesos d) and a café selling *refrescoes* and snacks, is open Fri.-Sun. only.

The beach where Martí and his troupe landed is two km farther east, past the museum, reached via a steep headland. There's nothing here, not even a plaque to mark the landing. It's a contemplative place where you can sit and listen to the hiss of the sea on the shingle.

The road continues east to Punta Maisí, one of the most dramatic drives in all Cuba. Unfortunately, in 1998 this southeast trip of the island was declared a military zone, and a military barrier now bars your way.

LA FAROLA

Immediately beyond Cajobabo, the road turns north and climbs into the **Sierra del Purial** along **La Farola** (the Beacon), built since the Revolution to link Baracoa with the rest of Cuba. This scenic highway spirals over precipitous peaks and through deep ravines and is sometimes called "Cuba's roller coaster." The road is a marvelous piece of engineering that includes 11 bridges suspended on the mountainside by columns.

La Farola hugs the mountainside, twisting and curling uphill through the valley of the Yumurí and Ojo Rivers, carpeted with palms like Moroccan oases. On the north side of the bridge over the Río Ojo, a sign points the way to **Rancho El Timera,** where Martí spent some time after his landing at Cajobabo. It's a rough five-km ride uphill along a dirt track to the farmstead.

Farther up, the scenery resembles the fir-clad canyons of Colorado. The road narrows with the ascent, the bends growing tighter, the views more dramatic and wide-ranging. Soon you are climbing through pine forests amid the most non-Cuban landscapes in Cuba.

Thoughtfully, near the summit is a *mirador* platform beside the road, then the summit ridge, smothered in pine and firs and with noticeably cooler air blowing up from the north, and a tiny café—**Alto de Coltillo**—with a *mirador,* where you can savor a *refresco* or coffee. Beyond Alto de Coltillo, the road drops through a moist valley brimful of banana trees until you emerge by the sea at Baracoa.

In rainy season, the road is subject to landslides. It's unlit at night.

BARACOA AND VICINITY

Isolation breeds individuality. Baracoa is both isolated and individual, so much so that the town has even been likened to Macondo in Gabriel García Márquez's surrealistic novel *One Hundred Years of Solitude.* Five centuries have passed, but the place has lost none of the exquisite beauty that so impressed Columbus. It is still "wonderfully beautiful countryside. . . not flat, but diversified by hill and vale, the most lovely scene in the world."

Baracoa is an Indian word meaning "highlands" (it is also sometimes translated as meaning "where the sea begins"). The somnolent town is nestled hard up against the ocean beneath rugged mountains, most notably the great hulking mass of El Yunque (the Anvil), a huge flat-topped mesa. This being Cuba's rainiest region, Baracoa is surrounded by fruitful countryside; the uplands are smothered in humid tropical forests festooned with epiphytes. Much of the mountainous region is protected within Cuchilla del Toa Biosphere Reserve—a last refuge of the ivory-billed woodpecker and the *amique,* an insectivorous mammal (both species are endangered). This area is as far off the beaten track as you can get in Cuba.

The fecund mountains are cut into deep valleys by rivers spilling onto the narrow coastal plain. Several of the rivers have precipitous lower courses that one day will surely be touted as classic whitewater runs. The Toa is the biggest. It was scouted in the 1970s by my friend Richard Bangs of Sobek Expeditions (California), with a view to operating commercial whitewater trips, but for years the tumbling waters were untapped. Finally, whitewater trips are now being offered.

There are miles of dark sand beaches east of Baracoa as far as the mouth of the Río Yumurí. Maritime terraces also rise along the east, most noticeably south of Punta Maisí, the remote easternmost tip of Cuba—a great adventure to reach.

Unlike the rest of Cuba, the region has no history of slave plantations or of African slaves. The Indians suffered greatly at the hands of the Spanish. But they were never killed off, as elsewhere in Cuba. Baracoans proudly point out those who have Indian blood, identified by their short stature, light, olive-brown skins, and squared-off faces.

BARACOA

On 27 October 1492, approaching Cuban shores for the first time, Christopher Columbus saw "a high, square-shaped mountain, which looked like an island." He called it Puerto Santo. For centuries, it was widely accepted that the mountain he saw was El Yunque. It is now thought, however, that Columbus was actually describing a similar flat-topped mountain near Gibara, many miles to the west (don't argue the case with a Baracoan, however; they're staunchly partisan on the subject). The town plays unashamedly on the Columbus tradition, most notably that it was here that the explorer planted a large wooden cross on the beach. The bar in the Hotel El

POLYMITES

*P*olymita pictas is a species of tiny snail unique to the Baracoa region. This diminutive critter is much sought by collectors for its Joseph's coat of many colors.

According to an Indian legend, the snails' shells were originally colorless. One snail, while sloooowly roaming the region, was taken by the area's lush beauty and asked the mountains for some of their green. Then he admired the sky and asked for some blue. When he saw the golden sands, he asked for a splash of yellow, and for jade and turquoise from the sea. And that's how the polymites get their colors, which are as unique to each individual polymite as fingerprints are to humans.

Castillo serves a rum-and-coconut-milk cocktail called El Yunque, and the name Puerto Santo now belongs to a modern luxury hotel at the spot where Columbus purportedly landed.

The city (pop. 65,000) lies 200 km east of Santiago and 120 km east of Guantánamo and is really miles from anywhere. The town has a greater simplicity, a less hurried pace, less of a revolutionary fervor than other parts of the island. It is altogether less sophisticated than Santiago de Cuba or Guantánamo, but it is full of delightful surprises. Baracoa looks and feels antique, with its little fortresses and its streets lined with venerable wooden edifices, rickety and humbled with age, with red-tiled eaves supported on ancient timber frames (the Cuban government has initiated a restoration project). The streets are virtually devoid of cars or other traffic. The fastest thing in town are the youngsters chasing hoops or flying kites, a local tradition. Watch for César Paumier Frómeta walking his pig along the Malecón.

Why, you may ask, do Baracoans place elephant statuettes with their rear ends facing the door? Supposedly it brings good luck

HISTORY

Baracoa was the first of the seven cities founded by Don Diego Velázquez de Cuellar. As such, it is the oldest colonial city in the Americas. The town retains the pioneering atmosphere of 1510, when Velázquez arrived fresh from Spain with 300 men and founded La Villa de Nuestra Señora de la Asunción. The indigenous Taíno population resisted the strange cutthroat proselytes who came dressed in leathers and metal helmets and breast-plates. A Dominican-born chief named Hatuey rallied the Taínos in a rebellion against Spanish enslavement. The city, the first capital of Cuba, was besieged and burned. The Spanish managed to hold out for three months before repelling the Indians and capturing Hatuey. The noble "savage" was burned at the stake. (Before putting flame to the pyre, the Spaniards offered Hatuey an option—redemption in Heaven by renouncing his pagan practices and accepting a Christian God, or a life in Hell. He replied that if all Christians were as wicked as Diego Velázquez's men, he would rather not go to Heaven. To hell with him!)

Alas, its inauspicious geographical circumstance did little to favor the settlement. Baracoa was remote and surrounded by mountains. After five years, Santiago de Cuba, with its vastly superior harbor, was proclaimed the new capital. Baracoa limped along based on a limited agricultural economy that produced yucca, coffee, cocoa, and maize.

Between 1739 and 1742, the Spanish authorities erected three fortresses to protect the city from invasion by English forces. The town languished in limbo for the next two centuries, without road or rail link to the rest of Cuba. Baracoa was briefly in the spotlight in the wars of independence: in 1877, the rebel army under General Antonio Maceo besieged the city (when Maceo returned from exile in 1895, he put ashore just west of town). The city produced its own legendary *Mambí* fighters, including Luz Palomares, a woman who went into battle with machete in hand.

The city remained underdeveloped during this century. A long-touted highway was supposed to connect Baracoa with Moa and, hence, the rest of Cuba. It was never built. When Panama disease blighted the local banana industry in the late 1940s, Baracoans called a general strike to protest the Cuban government's indifference. The town's status changed significantly with the Revolution. Health clinics and doctors arrived (up from four to 150), along with schools, cultural institutions, and sports centers. And a road—La Farola—was built over the mountains, linking Baracoa finally with Santiago and the rest of Cuba.

ORIENTATION

Baracoa curves around the wide Bahía de Miel (Honey Bay) within the cusp of high mountains, including a line of hills known as La Bella Dormiente (Sleeping Beauty), for reasons which are obvious when you look at them. The road from Santiago enters town from the east, via the modern section of Soviet-style apartment houses, fronted by the bay, which is fed at its eastern end by the Río Miel (it is claimed locally that if you bathe in its waters at midnight, you will fall in love and return to Baracoa). The bay is lined by a sweeping beach of shingly gray sand, **La Playita.**

The old city lies farther west, on a rocky terrace at the tip of which is the inlet of Porto Santo opening into a flask-shaped harbor. The town is only a few blocks wide, with roads (still laid out in its colonial guise) running parallel to the shore. The ugly shorefront boulevard is the windswept Malecón, lined to the west by hideous concrete housing blocks. The most important street is Calle José Martí, two blocks inland.

Both the Malecón and Martí run east-west from Fuerte Matachín, the tiny fortress at the east end of town, to Fortaleza de La Punta, at the west end. Avenida Primero de Abril curls south around the harbor and continues to the airport and, eventually, Holguín Province.

SIGHTSEEING

Fuerte Matachín

This tiny fortress, which dates to 1802, guards the eastern entrance to the old town. The fortress is in good condition and has low, thick walls topped with cannons in embrasures.

The storehouse in the fortress courtyard today houses the **Museo Matachín,** tel. (21) 4-2122, run by Alejandro Hartmann Matos, the city historian, whose passion for his subject is infectious. The glass cases are arranged in chronological order tracing the history of the region since pre-Columbian days. It tells of the barbar-

ities enacted on the indigenous population by the Spanish; the pirates' dastardly deeds (and those of the slave-and-sugar era); and the period when French coffee planters settled the surrounding hills. The museum also displays memorabilia from the War of Independence and in praise of the Revolution's achievements, plus polymites (the local polychromatic snails). It's open daily 8 a.m.-noon and 2-6 p.m. Entrance costs US$1.

On the fort's north side is a small plaza with shady cedars and a large **Statue of Columbus** (made of what looks like baked mud) with a large cross beside it. A bronze bust of **General Antonio Maceo** stands outside the fortress entrance.

The round tower—**Torreón de Toa**—immediately south of the fort served as a Spanish Customs checkpoint to quash the contraband trade. The house at Calle Juración #49 (opposite the tower) claims to be the oldest colonial home in the Americas. The home has been added to over ensuing centuries and there's nothing to distinguish it from any other.

Fábrica de Tabaco Manuel Fuentes

This intimate tobacco "factory" overlooks a triangular plaza at the corner of Roberto Reyes and José Martí, four blocks west of Fuerte Matachín. The *fábrica* is inside a colonial home on the south side. Visitors are welcome. Inside, two rows of men and women sit side by side, tenderly rolling and pressing fat cigars for local consumption. A blackboard shows production goals and achievements. It's open weekdays and alternate Saturdays, 7 a.m.-noon and 2-5 p.m. Entrance is free.

Plaza Martí

This little hive of activity, at José Martí and Ciro Frias, is where locals gather to gossip and flirt, have their shoes shined, or peruse the stalls selling cosmetics and domestic knicknacks. You *must* visit at night, when locals gather to watch the communal TV that by day is kept locked safely inside a box atop a pedestal.

Plaza Independencia

This triangular plaza is home to the most impressive buildings in town, most notably the **Catedral Nuestra Señora de la Asunción,** an ocher-colored edifice dating from 1805 on the

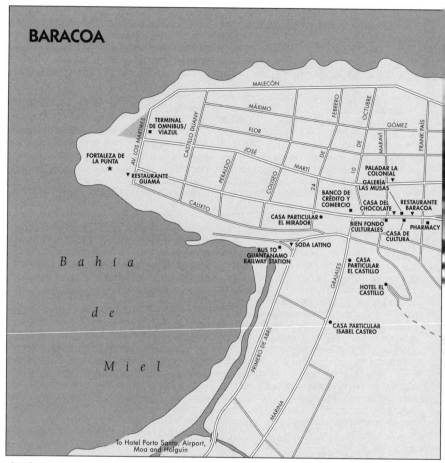

BARACOA

MALECÓN

MÁXIMO

FLOR

JOSÉ

MARTÍ

CALIXTO

TERMINAL
DE OMNIBUS/
VIAZUL

FORTALEZA DE
LA PUNTA ★

▼ RESTAURANTE
GUAMA

CASTILLO DUANY

AV. LOS MÁRTIRES

PERALEJO

COLISEO

24

DE

FEBRERO

OCTUBRE

MARAVÍ

FRANK PAÍS

GÓMEZ

10 DE

PALADAR LA
COLONIAL ▼

GALERÍA
LAS MUSAS ▼

BANCO DE
CRÉDITO Y
COMERCIO ■

CASA DEL
CHOCOLATE ■

RESTAURANTE
BARACOA ▼

CASA PARTICULAR ●
EL MIRADOR

BIEN FONDO
CULTURALES

CASA DE
CULTURA

PHARMACY ■

BUS TO
GUANTÁNAMO
RAILWAY STATION

▼ SODA LATINO

GRAJALES

CASA
PARTICULAR ●
EL CASTILLO

HOTEL EL ●
CASTILLO

B a h í a

d e

M i e l

PRIMERO DE ABRIL

MARINA

CASA PARTICULAR ●
ISABEL CASTRO

To Hotel Porto Santo, Airport,
Moa and Holguín

site of an earlier church, which was destroyed by
pirates in 1652. Masses are held here each
weekend by the young, bearded priest, Father
Valentín Sanz. The church is rarely open, and
you may need to search out the priest or caretaker in the beautifully restored house across
the street.

The church is famous not for its simple interi-
or, but for the **Cruz de la Parra**—supposedly
the oldest European relic in the Americas—on
display inside a glass case. With luck, you may
even be allowed to touch the relic (miraculous
powers are ascribed to it), which Columbus him-

self may have touched. Dr. Alejandro Hartman
Matos, Baracoa's official historian, loves to tell
the tale—possibly true, probably not—of how
Columbus supposedly left the cross upright amid
stones at the harbor entrance in 1492. Most
Baracoans believe the tale, including the detail
that Diego Velázquez's expeditionaries found
the cross in 1510 and used it to convert the aborigines. It has forever since been safeguarded
within the church. Carbon-dating analysis con-
firms that it is indeed about 500 years old.

The dark, well-worn, meter-tall cross has
been whittled away through the years by zeal-

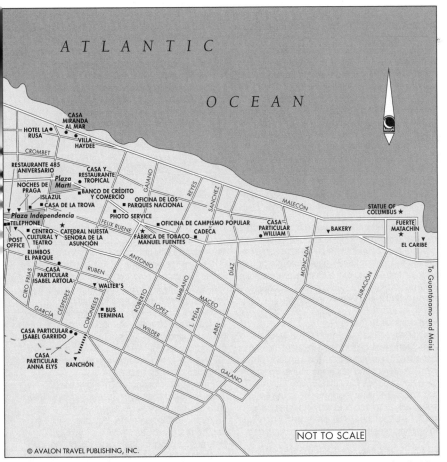

ous souvenir hunters and has acquired a deep, well-rubbed luster (along with ornamental silver surround added to stop worshippers pilfering splinters as souvenirs). In the mid-1980s, one sliver traveled back to Belgium for perusal by experts from the Royal Museum of Central Africa, who determined that the cross hadn't traveled from the Old World, but was instead made of *Coccoloba diversifolia,* a native hardwood of the sea grape family that grows abundantly around Baracoa. Even so, the legend endures. Perhaps Columbus whittled the cross himself in Cuba!

A **bust of Hatuey,** the Indian chief called the "first Cuba rebel," stands proudly in the center of Plaza Independencia.

El Castillo

Dominating Baracoa is this fortress built atop the rocky marine terrace that looms 40 meters above the city. It was constructed during the War of Jenkins' Ear (1739-41) between Spain and Britain, when the two nation's navies battled it out over the issue of trading rights in the new world. The war was named for an English captain, Robert Jenkins, whose ear was cut off by

street scene, Baracoa

the Spanish after they arrested him on charges of smuggling. The fort—known as Castillo Seboruco—subsequently became a prison. It recently metamorphosed again, emerging as an upscale hotel. Parts of the castle walls, including a turret, remain. It's a magnificent location offering a bird's-eye view of the city.

Fortaleza de la Punta

This small semicircular fort (at the west end of José Martí) was built in 1803 to guard the harbor entrance. It has gun slits all around but is of only modest interest and has no cannons. The courtyard now houses the Restaurante Guamá. To the left, a pathway leads down to the water's edge, with a "secret" boat slip where messengers could be dispatched. You half-expect Errol Flynn to appear, dressed in his swashbuckling best.

Parque Natural Majayara

This park is an archaeological park comprising the forest-covered headland about two km east of town. It features a stone pathway more than 500 years old, plus caves with dripstone formations and more than one km of tunnels featuring petroglyphs, and seawater pools for bathing. You need a guide to visit, arranged through the Parque Naturales de Baracoa office at Calle Martí #207, tel. (21) 4-3665 (US$10 with your own car, or US$14 with transport provided).

Other Sights

There's a **Fábrica de Cucurucho** near the Hotel Porto Santo; it makes a sweet sugar-and-co-conut candy called *cucurucho,* sold only here. And you can watch chocolate being made at the **Casa de Chocolate,** at Calle Antonio Maceo #121, two blocks north of El Castillo (open 7 a.m.-9:45 p.m.). Also check out the **Taller de Muñecitas,** Calle Martí #124, where you can watch women making traditional dolls.

There's even a small zoo—**Parque Zoológica Cacique Guama**—seven km east of Baracoa, containing monkeys, a hippo, a lion, birds, crocodiles, rodent-like *jutías,* and a near extinct relative, the *almiquí,* indigenous to eastern Cuba. Entrance costs 20 centavos.

For a souvenir snapshot of Fidel, head to the **Taller de Sarcófagos,** at Calle José Martí #300, where a coffin maker called Felipe is a dead ringer for *El Comandante.* You can even seek out the *real* Fidel Castro (well, *a* real Fidel Castro), a disarming mustachioed chap who lives on Calle Máximo Gómez (believe it or not, this Fidel also has a younger brother named Raúl).

ACCOMMODATIONS

Casas Particulares

There are scores of private rooms for rent for as low as US$10 including breakfast.

I like **Casa Particular William,** Calle Martí #287, tel. (21) 4-2798, a lofty-ceilinged colonial home with tile floors, a pleasant lounge, and three a/c rooms that share bathrooms with hot water (US$15). Meals are served in a pleasant dining room (US$7). It has secure parking.

Also highly recommended is **Casa Particular Isabel Garrido,** Calixto García #164-A, e/ Céspedes y Coroneles Gallano, tel. (21) 4-3515, with three upstairs a/c rooms, nicely furnished with clean, modern private bathrooms with hot water, plus entrance (US$15). There's a small TV lounge downstairs, plus secure parking. The hostess makes meals.

Likewise, Anna Elys Torres, a pleasant hostess, has two nicely furnished, medium-size a/c rooms with small but attractive bathrooms with hot water next door at Calixto García #162, tel. (21) 4-2754 (US$15). One room is inside; the second is on the terrace and has a private entrance.

Casa y Restaurant Tropical, Calle Martí #175, tel. (21) 4-3688, entered by tall wooden doors, abounds with hardwood features and rents four spacious whitewashed, albeit gloomy, a/c rooms with tile floors and clean private bathrooms with hot water (US$15). It offers indoor and patio dining (US$8).

Iliana Sotorongo Rodríguez's **Casa Particular El Mirador,** Calle Maceo #86 e/ 24 de Febrero y 10 de Octubre, tel. (21) 4-3592, is one of the best room rentals in town. Her attractive wooden colonial home is well kept and has two spacious upstairs rooms with a/c, fans, and lofty that open to a wide airy balcony with rockers and views (US$12-15). They share a clean, modern bathroom down the hall. Another veranda to the rear has views of El Yunque. Iliana makes meals.

I also like Isabel Artola Rosell's home at Calle Ruben López #39, tel. (21) 4-2136, an attractive 1950s-style home with two a/c rooms (US$15-20). One forms its own little *casita* and has its own rear patio plus a modern bathroom with hot water The second, less appealing room, in the house, is darker and has twin beds and has its own bathroom down the hall. The owner speaks English.

For a spacious self-contained apartment, first choice is **Casa Particular El Castillito,** Marian Grajales #9-A, e/ Calixto García y July a Mella, tel. (21) 4-3625, owned by César Arturo Martínez. Cesar's upstairs apartment has a large kitchen with open dining room attached, plus a modestly furnished bedroom and clean, modern bathroom with hot water (US$20). There's a laundry. It has its own entrance; Cesar lives next door.

Down the street is **Casa Particular Isabel Castro,** Marian Grajales #35, tel. (21) 4-2217, a colonial wooden home in fine repair, with 1950s decor. Isabel rents one room with a/c and a small, clean bathroom but with cold water only. The patio to the rear gets the sun and opens to a large garden with fruit trees. It has secure parking.

On the seafront, **Casa Miranda al Mar,** Malecón #42, has four meagerly furnished, cross-ventilated rooms (two with a/c, two without) sharing three bathrooms with cold water (hot water was to be added) for US$12-15. **Villa Haydee,** nearby at Malecón #43-A e/ Céspedes y Ciro Frías, tel. (21) 4-2756, has three simply but nicely furnished rooms sharing two bathrooms with hot water for US$15 (US$20 for a room with kitchenette and a/c).

Casa Atlantis, Calle Martí #393, tel. (21) 4-2571, on the right as you enter town from Guantánamo, is a seafront home 200 meters east of Fuerte Matachín. The number of rooms rented varies by season. All have fans, but no a/c, and modern private bathrooms with hot water (US$15). Meals are served at a *mesa china,* a revolving table (US$6-8). I stayed next door at **Casa Particular Daisy Camejo,** tel. (21) 4-2318, where Daisy and her husband Humberto, both delightful, offer the self-contained home for US$12 (plus US$4 per meal). It's modestly furnished and has a small lounge, basic kitchen, and a bathroom in need of repair. Fans kept the plentiful mosquitoes at bay.

Hotels

Budget: Islazul's **Hotel La Rusa,** Máximo Gómez #161, Baracoa, tel. (21) 4-3011, is an endearing little place facing the Malecón. It once belonged to a Russian woman, Mima Rubenskaya, who inspired the character Vera in Alejo Carpentier's novel *The Rite of Spring.* She fled the Soviet Union in 1917 and settled in Baracoa long before *it* turned communist. She is reputed to have belonged to Castro's M-26 (if you want to know more about her, check out the museum in the Fuerte Matachín). After her death in 1979, the property was converted into a hotel (Fidel Castro and Che Guevara both stayed here, apparently, as did Errol Flynn). It has 13 simple a/c rooms with louvered windows (overlooking the ocean) and small but nicely restored bathrooms. There's a small bar and open-air restaurant with seafront views. Rates were

US$17 s, US$22 d low season, US$21 s, US$28 d high season.

An alternative is the simple **Hotel Plaza,** tel. (21) 4-2252, hidden away up a flight of steps on the south side of Plaza Martí. At last report, rooms cost about US$20.

Inexpensive: Though twice the price of La Rusa, you get five times your money's worth at Gaviota's **Hotel El Castillo,** Calixto García, Loma del Paraíso, Baracoa, tel. (21) 4-2103, fax (21) 86704, in a contemporary structure built in Spanish-colonial style atop the foundations of El Castillo, overlooking the town and reached by a winding driveway or a steep 85-step staircase. It's one of my favorite Cuban hotels. The 35 exquisite a/c rooms are colonial style, with lofty ceilings, terra-cotta-tiled floors, private baths, telephones, and furniture carved from cedar by local craftsmen (the mattresses should be retired, however). There's a TV lounge. The swimming pool and sundeck offer stupendous views towards El Yunque. The bodega-style restaurant serves *criollo* dishes with a Baracoan flavor. Rates were US$29 s, US$40 d low season, US$33 s, US$44 d high season.

On the north side of the bay, a taxi ride or long walk from town, is Gaviota's **Hotel Porto Santo,** Carretera del Aeropuerto, Baracoa, tel. (21) 4-3590, fax (21) 8-6074, with 36 a/c rooms and 24 cabanas centered on an amoeba-shaped pool with views over the bay. It is neither as lively nor as appealing as the El Castillo. Facilities include a restaurant, two bars, a shop, tennis court, and car rental. Same rates as El Castillo.

FOOD

Despite its reputation for its regional cuisine, you'll be hard-pressed to find it. At last visit there were only three *paladares.* **Walter's,** Calle Ruber López #47 e/ Céspedes y Coroneles Galano, offers indoor dining upstairs in a soulless a/c room. It serves the usual *criollo* fare in huge portions for US$8-12, including beer or rum. More appealing by far is **Paladar La Colonial,** on Martí e/ Maraví y Frank País, with heaps of cozy colonial charm. It even serves swordfish and shark and dorado, in huge portions. And the service is ultra-efficient.

Your next best bet is the restaurant in the **Hotel El Castillo.** The menu is extensive and favors local dishes. The fish and shellfish dishes are prepared in coconut sauce that includes annato seeds, coriander, onion, hot pepper, oregano, and salt. The lobster is also splendid—as it should be for US$25. The *chicken casserole,* however, is really fried chicken.

Restaurante Baracoa, on Antonio Maceo one block west of Plaza Independencia, is a handsome colonial restaurant serving pizzas (US$1) and *criollo* fare in a patio to the rear. Also try **Restaurante 485 Aniversario,** a state-run entity on the north side of Plaza Independencia. Another popular option on clear days is **El Caribe,** overlooking the beach behind the Fuente Matachín, It serves a lobster enchilada.

Craving pizza? Three pesos will buy you a slice of *picadillo* pizza (ground beef with olives

---

THE LOCAL FLAVOR

*B*aracoa is acclaimed for its original cuisine—almost unknown in the rest of the country. Coconut is a staple of local menus. It finds its way into such local delicacies as *calalú,* a spinach-like vegetable simmered in coconut milk; *bacán,* a tortilla made of baked plantain paste mixed with coconut milk, wrapped in banana leaves, and filled with spiced pork; *cucurucho,* an ambrosial pudding made of shredded coconut mixed with papaya, orange, nuts, and sugar or honey and wrapped in palm leaves; and *frangollo,* a dish of green bananas toasted and mashed.

For drinks, try *chorote,* a tasty chocolate drink thickened with cornstarch (the region around Baracoa is also known for growing cacao, from which the townsfolk make chocolate). Also try the local drink called *sacoco,* a concoction of rum and coconut milk served in green coconuts; and the less appetizing *pru,* a drink made from pine needles and sugar syrup introduced from Haiti by French planters in the mid-19th century.

Local fishermen also net a local oddity, *tetí,* a tiny red fish that migrates like salmon up the Río Toa. The fish arrive at the mouth of the river enveloped in a gelatinous cocoon that splits apart on contact with freshwater. *Tetí* is eaten raw with cocktail sauce, like shrimp.

and raisins) *and* a shot of rum at **Pizzería Iser-nia,** at Calle Flor Crombet #175. Open 10 a.m.-9:40 p.m.

Refreshments

The **Soda Latino,** down near the port, sells *batidos* and *refrescoes* for 20 centavos—a perfect cure for impending heat stroke! You can buy ice cream and a drink of local chocolate or coffee at the **Casa del Chocolate** (open 7:20 a.m.-9:40 p.m.), which may have bars of chocolate for sale. If not, you can find "black market" chocolate (two bars for US$1).

The perfect thing on a hot day is a sno-cone or a zapote-flavored ice cream sold in a cone made with a waffle-iron (one peso). Try Luís Gamboa Borges at Calle José Martí #171.

Bakeries

There are several bakeries, including **Panadería La Mia** and **Panadería El Triunfo,** one and two blocks west of Fuerte Matachín, respectively. Try the delicious *pudin de boniato* (made from sugar, coconut milk, and sweet potato), the spongy biscuits called *panquecitos,* or the deep-fried pastry (made from the flour of the yucca root) called *buñuelo,* from **Arnaldo's,** at Calle José Martí #212. All cost one peso, which will also buy five *yemitas,* sweet balls made with chocolate, coconut, and sugar; or a delicious *turrón de coco,* a baked bar of grated coconut mixed with milk and sugar.

ENTERTAINMENT AND SHOPPING

Baracoa hosts a four-day **Carnival** in mid-September.

Half the town populace seems to gather in Plaza Martí at 7 p.m. every night to watch the TV that by day is locked inside its case atop a stand in the plaza (most residents of Baracoa have their own televisions; the public TV serves when power is cut in particular neighborhoods to conserve energy; at press time, each of the town's four sectors had a weekly four-hour blackout). Saturday nights are best, when the movie double bill lasts until 2 a.m.

Plaza Independencia is the nocturnal hang-out of choice for local youth.

On Sunday you can head to Plaza Independencia to take on one of the local kids at chess. Be wary if young Andrés Pierra challenges you—he's the local star and can often be seen completing against six opponents *at a time.*

Traditional Music and Dance

The **Casa de la Trova,** on Calle Antonio Maceo #149 e/ Ciro Frías y Pelayo Cuervo, is a great place to sample local music played by troubadours. Open daily 10 p.m.-2 a.m.; entrance costs US$1. Alternately, head to the **Casa de la Cultura,** on Calle Antonio Maceo e/ Frank País y Maravi, tel. (21) 4-2349, where locals perform adaptations of Cuban *són* known as *el nengen* and *el kiriba.* Live Afro-Cuban performances are also given at night at the **Galería Yara.**

Bars and Discos

The *mirador* bar at the **Hotel El Castillo** offers fine views but is rather dead. The most popular bar is **Rumbos El Parque,** on Plaza Independencia, where live music is offered and couples jive beneath the stars in the courtyard.

The happening hotspot is **Noches de Praga,** a Western-style disco on the north side of Plaza Independencia, where the young crowd gets in the groove to salsa and imported disco (entrance costs US$1; rum drinks cost US$2). The thatched hilltop disco called **Ranchón,** overlooking town 800 meters east of the Hotel El Castillo, ostensibly has a simple **cabaret espectáculo** on weekends at 11 p.m. (US$1), but there were so few guests when I called that the show was canceled.

Every Friday, Saturday, and Sunday night, an open-air disco—**Fiesta callejera**—is set up (the location varies weekly; bring your own drinks). The youngsters love it, but you have to pity everyone else. The designated street is cordoned off and lit with Christmas lights, the boombox music reverberates until well past midnight, and only the dead can sleep.

Other Entertainment

Still trying to catch up on 1950s camp classics? Check out what's showing at the **Centro Cultural y Teatro** cinema (one peso), on the south side of Plaza Independencia. Films show most evenings, cartoons on Saturday mornings.

The plaza is also the setting for an intriguing battle every Sunday morning, when the church choir tries to drown out the jazz riffs of the state-sponsored municipal band.

A **Semana de la Cultura**—culture week—is held the first week of April.

Shopping

Baracoa boasts several artists of note, including Pedro Sabo, a famous native painter who records life in Baracao in monochrome and riotous color. Noted painters Orlando Piedra and Roel Caboverde sell their works at their studio, **Galería Las Musas**, on Maceo e/ Maraví y Frank País. You'll pay US$20-200 for distinctive works of art. **Galería Yara**, in the **Bien Fonda Cultura**, on Antonio Maceo two blocks west of the cathedral, also has paintings, clothing, and simple carvings.

You might also check out the house of Pelay Alvarez López at Félix Ruenes #25. Alvarez makes furniture and carvings from precious hardwoods, often inlaid with mother-of-pearl.

SPORTS AND RECREATION

Baracoa is hardly a hive of activity, but you may be able to catch a **baseball game** in the large stadium east of town. **Whitewater rafting** trips were being planned on the Río Toa (see the Kayaking And Whitewater Rafting section under Baracoa To Holguín, below).

Computer nerds might head to the **Joven Club de Computación**, Calle José Martí #217, tel. (21) 4-3587, which offers free computer classes to all Baracoans, using IBM computers. Foreigners are welcome.

PRACTICALITIES

Services and Information

There are tour information desks in the Hotel El Castillo and Hotel Porto Santo. The **Parque Naturales de Baracoa** park office, Calle Martí #207, tel. (21) 4-3665, provides information on the four local nature parks: Parque Natural Duaba, Parque Natural Majayar, Parque Natural Taco Bay, and Parque Natural El Toa.

There's a **Banco de Crédito y Comercio** on Antonio Maceo, one block west of 10 de Oc-

tubre, and another on the north side of Plaza Martí.

You can make international telephone calls from the Hotel El Castillo or Hotel Porto Santo, where you can also buy stamps and mail postcards. The **post office** and main Etecsa **telephone exchange** are next to each other on the south side of Plaza Independencia (open daily 8 a.m.-10 p.m.).

The **hospital**, tel. (21) 4-3014, is two km east of town. There's a pharmacy on Antonio Maceo, one block west of the cathedral. If your teeth need attention, head to the Clínica Estomatológica, at Calle Antonio Maceo #82 (open Mon.-Sat. 24 hours).

The **library** (Biblioteca Raúl Gómez García) is at Calle José Martí #130.

The **Cupet gas station** is five km east of town, just before the turnoff for Punta Maisí. The police station is on Calle Antonio Maceo.

Getting There and Away

By Air: Cubana flies from Havana to Baracoa thrice weekly (US$78). There are also flights between Baracoa and Santiago de Cuba on Tuesday (US$20). **Aero Caribbean,** Calle 23 #64, Vedado, tel. (7) 33-4543, fax (7) 33-5016, e-mail: aerocarvpcre@iacc3.get.cma.net, flies from Havana on Thursday via Varadero.

Gustavo Rizo Airport, tel. (21) 4-2216, is on the west side of the bay. The Cubana office is at Calle José Martí #181, tel. (21) 4-2171; open Mon.-Fri. 8 a.m.-noon and 2-5 p.m.

By Bus: Bus no. 641 *especial* departs Havana for Baracoa on Friday and Sunday at 10:45 a.m. (US$43), depositing you 20 hours later at the **Terminal Interprovincial** in Baracoa at Los Mártires and José Martí, tel. (21) 4-2239. Buses for Havana depart Baracoa at about 7:30 p.m. (arriving 3 p.m. next day); at least 24 hours reservation usually required. Buses to Santiago depart daily at 1:50 p.m., but you'll normally need to book a week in advance.

Buses to and from Guantánamo, Santiago, and Moa arrive and depart the **Terminal Municipal** at the junction of Coroneles, Galano, and Rubio López.

An express bus service (Espresso Ferrocarríl) to the Guantánamo rail station leaves from down by the port. Buy your ticket early.

By Organized Excursions: Tour agencies in Santiago de Cuba offer excursions to Baracoa.

GETTING AROUND

Baracoa is small enough to walk everywhere. You'll need wheels, however, to visit Porto Santo or locations farther afield.

Horse-drawn carriages *(coches)* plod the main streets and follow fixed routes (one peso). You may be able to rent **bicycles** from the Hotel El Castillo, where **taxis** also hang out in the courtyard. For a **Cubataxi,** telephone (21) 5-1038 or 5-1039. You can rent an enclosed three-wheel **Cococtaxi,** tel. (21) 4-2307. You can hop aboard local communal taxis: look out for Nildo Ortíz Machado's super-long limo-Lada, which follows a fixed route through town. You might want to pass on Oscar Granada's offer, however; he's a renowned speedster and his Lada is called the "Death Car."

Rumbos S.A., Av. de los Mártires e/ Maceo y Calixto García, tel. (21) 4-3335, offers excursions locally.

BARACOA TO HOLGUÍN PROVINCE

The coast west of Baracoa is a lonesome region, hemmed in by the steep-faced **Alturas de Baracoa.** A road hugs the coast and leads to Holguín Province. Most is dirt (rocky in places), deeply rutted and potholed for the first 25 km, where a newly paved road begins.

Immediately west of Baracoa, you cross the wide, brown Río Macaguani, which runs into Bahía de Miel. At the mouth of the **Río Duaba,** five km west of Baracoa, is a long black sand beach where the mulatto general Antonio Maceo and 22 compatriots landed in April 1895 and, beyond, the site where he fought his first battle. He is honored by a roadside bust. There's a grove nearby where shards of pottery demonstrate the pre-Columbian presence of Indians. You can turn inland here and follow a dirt road one km to **Finca Duaba,** a fruit farm with a handsome though rustic thatched restaurant serving *criollo* meals beneath the shade of palms and plantains. Horseback riding is offered.

Five km farther west you cross the Río Toa, with banks smothered in virgin rainforest. Beyond, 37 km west of Baracoa, you'll pass the entrance to **Parque Natural Taco Bay,** protect-

ing mangroves, an offshore cay, and a white sand beach shelving to a coral reef. The park extends inland to waterfalls. Three trails were open at press time (more trails are planned). Boat trips are offered, and bicycle excursions are offered from Baracoa by the Parque Naturales de Baracoa office, at Calle Martí #207, tel. (21) 4-3665. A guide is compulsory (US$15 in your own car, US$22 with transport provided).

Cuchillas del Toa Biosphere Reserve

This 127,500-hectare reserve encompasses most of the ranges of the Alturas de Sagua-Baracoa, Cuchillas de Toa, and Cuchillas de Moa, and rises from sea level to 1,139 meters elevation. The region (one of the oldest geologically in Cuba) is composed mostly of igneous rocks, etched by rivers into countless knife-edged ridges *(cuchillas)* that rise like islands in a rainforest sea.

Two protected nature reserves—Jaguaní and Cupeyal del Norte—take up most of the region and owe their origin in part to a single bird species. Here the large ivory-billed woodpecker exists in isolation. The birds were once common throughout the American South, but logging has since devastated their habitat, and they have not been seen in the U.S. since the 1940s. The bird was considered extinct until the mid-1980s, when it was identified in these mountains. The sightings resulted in the Cuban government's establishing a 220-square-km protection area. Logging was banned, and a highway was rerouted. With luck (lots of it) you may see an ivory-billed woodpecker in the valley of the Ríos Yarey and Jiguaní, which feed the Río Toa. Whatever, the forests are filled with chirps and squawks.

The reserve has a great diversity of climate types and corresponding ecosystems. It protects the richest fauna in Cuba, including more endemic species of flora than anywhere else in Cuba—including several types of palms and the colorful *ocujé,* or Santa María tree. Much of the area is composed of rainforest bordered by brushwood and Cuban pine, a perfect habitat for the ivory-billed woodpecker and its cousin, the endemic and endangered royal woodpecker. These mountains are also known for the polymite, a rare and singularly beautiful snail species (well, at least the shell is beautiful).

The most dramatic formation is **El Yunque,** the spectacular table-top mountain (575 meters) that dominates the landscape southwest of Baracoa. It resembles the square-topped *tepuís* of Venezuela and seems to float above the surrounding hills. This sheer-sided giant is the remains of a mighty plateau that once extended across the entire area. Over time, the plateau was eroded, leaving El Yunque as a giant monument to its existence. It was a god-like presence for the Taíno Indians.

Mists flow down from the summit in the dawn hours, and it glows like hot coals at dusk, when the setting sun pours over the red rocky walls like molten lava. El Yunque is a lonely outpost of life with its unique flora and fauna—a result of isolation over millions of years. From its summit, waterfalls tumble down, washing away soil and mineral nutrients. The soils are thin, and the oases of orchids, lichen, mosses, and forest seem to survive on water and air alone. Little exploration has been done amid this "roofless Hades," and many new species await discovery atop the often-mist-shrouded plateau. Today it is protected within **Parque Natural Duaba,** administered independently of the biosphere reserve, which is under the aegis of the Academía de Ciencias, which extracts US$2 per visitor from the Parque Naturales.

Also within the reserve is **Parque Natural El Toa,** in the interior mountains. It offers nature trails and whitewater rafting was to be introduced in 2000.

Getting There: You can drive to El Yunque's summit: turn left—west—half a km south of the Río Duaba, then go left at the Y-fork and follow the road to La Ermita. The unpaved, potholed road climbs steeply to a lookout point where you can gaze down on the tumbling waters of the Río Duaba. A guide is compulsory. You can hire one at the park office four km beyond Finca Duaba, or at the Parque Naturales de Baracoa office in Baracoa, at Calle Martí #207, tel. (21) 4-3665 (US$13 with your own car; US$18 with transport provided).

Excursions can be arranged through Gaviotatours in the Hotel El Castillo, tel. (21) 4-2103, and Hotel Porto Santo, tel. (21) 4-3578.

Accommodations and Food

If you long for your own lonesome house miles from anywhere, check out Gaviota's **Villa Maguana,** about 28 km west of Baracoa, nestling in its own little cove with a scintillating white beach with shade trees. This reclusive charmer has four wood-paneled a/c rooms with terra-cotta floors, modestly furnished with double beds and TVs, and clean, modern bathrooms. Light pours in through wide windows. There's also a lounge with TV, and a shady veranda with rockers. The house comes with cook and maid. Reservations can be made through the Hotel El Castillo or Gaviota. Rates were US$35 s, US$45 d low season, US$55 s, US$75 d high season, including meals.

At El Yunque, you can **camp** at a basic *campismo,* which also has basic huts (US$5 d).

Rumbos has two simple thatched snack bars on the beach 400 yards beyond Villa Maguana.

Kayaking and Whitewater Rafting

The Río Tao and its tributaries have tempestuous rapids and a tremendous future for kayaking and whitewater rafting. Three-hour whitewater rafting trips were to be offered in 2000 through the Parque Naturales de Baracoa office, Calle Martí #207, tel. (21) 4-3665, using paddle boats.

BARACOA TO LA MAQUINA

If you want to visit the easternmost point of Cuba, you can take the coast road east from Baracoa. It begins five km south of town, at **Jobo Dulce,** and follows a winding course inland via the hamlet of Jamal up hill and down dale, touching the coast again 20 km east of Baracoa at **Baragua.** Baragua is famous for its long, ruler-straight silver sand beach backed by palms.

Beyond Baragua, the road passes through a cleft in the vertical cliffs spanned by a natural arch called **Túnel de los Alemanes** (Germans' Tunnel). A stone's throw beyond, you emerge at **Abra de Yumurí,** a ramshackle village where the road deposits you at the side of the river mouth, where the Río Yumurí cuts through a deep canyon and meets the hissing breakers of the Atlantic. Upriver the Yumurí narrows into a steep-faced gorge.

lighthouse, Punta Maisí

On the east bank of the river, the road continues along the coast, then rises sharply inland to **La Maquina,** 22 km beyond Abra de Yumurí. La Maquina, on the cooler eastern slope of the Meseta de Maisí, is the center of a coffee-growing region. Alas, the region has been declared a military zone, and a military checkpoint prevents you from reaching Punta Maisí.

PUNTA MAISÍ

La Maquina looks down over a vast circular plain spread out like a fan and overgrown with scrub and cacti. Far below, a lighthouse at Punta Maisí pins the easternmost tip of Cuba, where day breaks 40 minutes before it occurs in Havana. (Actually, Punta Quemado, five km south of Punta Maisí, is fractionally farther east, but it's accessible only by a stiff hike along the thorn-covered coral cliff top.) Maisí consists of no more than the *faro* (lighthouse) and a few miserable shacks.

Although I visited on my motorcycle in 1996, Punta Maisí is now off-limits. You can take a sightseeing trip by biplane from the Baracoa airstrip (US$16 roundtrip). If by some stroke of fortune you are permitted to drive, a rugged, much eroded track of red earth descends from La Maquina onto the plain. The distance is deceptive: the lighthouse looks close at hand but is actually 12 km away. Eventually you reach Land's End, 1,280 km from Havana.

CUBAN SPANISH

Learning the basics of Spanish will aid your travels considerably. In key tourist destinations, however, you should be able to get along fine without it. Most Cubans are well educated, and English is widely spoken in Havana, and the number of English-speakers is growing rapidly. (For example, English is now required of all university students and hotel staff. Most larger hotels have bilingual desk staffs, and English is widely spoken by the staff of car rental agencies and tour companies.) Cubans are exceedingly keen to practice their English and you will be approached often by such individuals. Many Cubans know at least the basics of one other European language (a surprising number are fluent in French and, of course, Russian). Away from the tourist path, far fewer people speak English.

Use that as an excuse to learn some Spanish. Cubans warm quickly to those who make an effort to speak their language. Don't be bashful. Use what Spanish you know and you'll be surprised how quickly you become familiar with the language.

Ediciones Universales, P.O. Box 450353, Miami, FL 33245, publishes books on Cubanismos, such as *Habla tradicional de Cuba: Refranero Familiar,* by Concepción Teresa Alzola, and *Diccionario de Cubanismos,* volumes I to VI, by José Sánchez Boudy. They have a free mail order catalog.

Pronunciation

Castilian Spanish, with its lisping "c"s and "z"s, is the Spanish of Spain, not Latin America (Cubans do not lisp their "c"s and "z"s; they pronounce the letters more like an "s," as do Andalusians and most other Latin Americans). In its literary form, Cuban Spanish is pure, classical Castilian. Alas, in its spoken form Cuban Spanish is the most difficult to understand in all of Latin America. Cubans have lent their own renditions to the Spanish sound: like a zebra that is not quite a horse, Cuban Spanish is white but with black stripes.

Cubans speak more briskly than other Latin Americans, blurring their rapid-fire words together. The diction of Cuba is lazy and unclear. Thought Richard Henry Dana, Jr., in 1859: "it strikes me that the tendency here is to enfeeble the language, and take from it the openness of the vowels and the strength of the consonants." The letter "s," for example, is usually swallowed altogether, especially in plurals.

The final consonants of words are also often deleted, as are diphthongs such as "d" and, often, the entire last syllable of words ("If they dropped any more syllables, they would be speechless," suggests author Tom Miller). Regional variants exist, too. I find the Spanish of the Oriente a bit slower and less confusing. Around Baracoa, the idiom of the Indians endures.

Cubanisms to Know

Cubans are long-winded and full of flowery, passionate, rhetorical flourishes. Fidel Castro didn't inherit his penchant for long speeches from dour taciturn Galicia—it's a purely Cuban characteristic. Cubans also spice up the language with little affectations and teasing endearment—*piropos*—given and taken among themselves without offense.

Many English (or "American") words have found their way into Cuban diction. Cubans go to *besbol* and today eat *hamburgesas.*

Formal courtesies are rarely used when greeting someone.

Since the Revolution, everyone is a *compañero* or *compañera* (*señor* and *señora* are considered too bourgeois).

The swallowed "s"s are apparently accumulated for use in restaurants, where they are released to get the server's attention—*"S-s-s-s-s-st!"* Because of this, a restaurant with bad service can sound like a pit full of snakes.

Confusingly, *ciao!* (used as a long-term goodbye) is also used as a greeting in casual passing—the equivalent of "Hi!" You will also be asked ¿*Como anda?* meaning "How goes it?"

A common courtesy when paying a call on someone, especially in the countryside, is to call out *"Upe!"* from outside the house to let him or her know you're there. As you enter, you should say *"Con permiso"* ("With your permission").

Language Study Programs

The Universities of Havana and Matanzas offer intensive Spanish language courses for foreigners. The courses (from beginner to advanced) include at least a modicum of workshops or lectures on Cuban culture. The norm is three to five hours of instruction daily, more in intensive courses.

See the special topic, Study Courses in Cuba.

SPANISH PHRASEBOOK

PRONUNCIATION GUIDE

Consonants

c   as c in cat, before a, o, or u; like s before e or i
d   as d in dog, except between vowels, then like th in that
g   before e or i, like the ch in Scottish loch; elsewhere like g in get
h   always silent
j   like the English h in hotel, but stronger
ll   like the y in yellow
ñ   like the ni in onion
r   always pronounced as strong r
rr   trilled r
v   similar to the b in boy (not as English v)
y   similar to English, but with a slight j sound. When y stands alone it is
    pronounced like the e in me.
z   like s in same
b, f, k, l, m, n, p, q, s, t, w, x, z as in English

Vowels

a   as in father, but shorter
e   as in hen
i   as in machine
o   as in phone
u   usually as in rule; when it follows a q the u is silent; when it follows an h or g
    its pronounced like w, except when it comes between g and e or i, when it's also
    silent

NUMBERS

0	*cero*	11	*once*	40	*cuarenta*
1 (masculine)	*uno*	12	*doce*	50	*cincuenta*
1 (feminine)	*una*	13	*trece*	60	*sesenta*
2	*dos*	14	*catorce*	70	*setenta*
3	*tres*	15	*quince*	80	*ochenta*
4	*cuatro*	16	*diez y seis*	90	*noventa*
5	*cinco*	17	*diez y siete*	100	*cien*
6	*seis*	18	*diez y ocho*	101	*ciento y uno*
7	*siete*	19	*diez y nueve*	200	*doscientos*
8	*ocho*	20	*veinte*	1,000	*mil*
9	*nueve*	21	*viente y uno*	10,000	*diez mil*
10	*diez*	30	*treinta*		

DAYS OF THE WEEK

Sunday — *domingo*
Monday — *lunes*
Tuesday — *martes*
Wednesday — *miércoles*

Thursday — *jueves*
Friday — *viernes*
Saturday — *sábado*

TIME

What time is it? — *¿Qué hora es?*
one o'clock — *la una*
two o'clock — *las dos*
at two o'clock — *a las dos*
ten past three — *las tres y diez*
six a.m. — *las seis a la mañana*
six p.m. — *las seis a la tarde*
today — *hoy*

tomorrow, morning
    — *mañana, la mañana*
yesterday — *ayer*
week — *semana*
month — *mes*
year — *año*
last night — *la noche pasada*
next day — *el próximo día*

USEFUL WORDS AND PHRASES

Hello. — *Hola.*
Good morning. — *Buenos dias.*
Good afternoon. — *Buenas tardes.*
Good evening. — *Buenas noches.*
How are you? — *¿Cómo está?*
Fine. — *Muy bien.*
And you? — *¿Y usted?*
So-so. — *Así así.*
Thank you. — *Gracias.*
Thank you very much. — *Muchas gracias.*
You're very kind.
    — *Usted es muy amable.*
You're welcome; literally, "It's nothing."
    — *De nada.*
yes — *sí*
no — *no*
I don't know. — *Yo no sé.*
it's fine; okay — *está bien*
good; okay — *bueno*
please — *por favor*
Pleased to meet you. — *Mucho gusto.*
excuse me (physical) — *perdóneme*
excuse me (speech) — *discúlpeme*
I'm sorry. — *Lo siento.*
goodbye — *adiós*

see you later; literally, "until later"
    — *hasta luego*
more — *más*
less — *menos*
better — *mejor*
much — *mucho*
a little — *un poco*
large — *grande*
small — *pequeño*
quick — *rápido*
slowly — *despacio*
bad — *malo*
difficult — *difícil*
easy — *fácil*
He/She/It is gone; as in "She left," "He's
    gone" — *Ya se fue.*
I don't speak Spanish well.
    — *No hablo bien español.*
I don't understand. — *No entiendo.*
How do you say . . . in Spanish?
    — *¿Cómo se dice . . . en español?*
Do you understand English?
    — *¿Entiende el inglés?*
Is English spoken here? (Does anyone
    here speak English?)
    — *¿Se habla inglés aquí?*

TERMS OF ADDRESS

I — *yo*
you (formal) — *usted*
you (familiar) — *tú*
he/him — *él*
she/her — *ella*
we/us — *nosotros*
you (plural) — *ustedes*
they/them (all males or mixed gender)
    — *ellos*
they/them (all females) — *ellas*

Mr., sir — *señor*
Mrs., madam — *señora*
Miss, young lady — *señorita*
wife — *esposa*
husband — *marido* or *esposo*
friend — *amigo* (male), *amiga* (female)
sweetheart — *novio* (male), *novia* (female)
son, daughter — *hijo, hija*
brother, sister — *hermano, hermana*
father, mother — *padre, madre*

GETTING AROUND

Where is . . . ? — *¿Dónde está . . . ?*
How far is it to . . .?
    — *¿Qué tan lejos está a . . . ?*
from . . . to . . . — *de . . . a . . .*
highway — *la carretera*
road — *el camino*
street — *la calle*
block — *la cuadra*
kilometer — *kilómetro*

mile (commonly used near the
    U.S. border) — *milla*
north — *el norte*
south — *el sur*
west — *el oeste*
east — *el este*
straight ahead — *al derecho* or *adelante*
to the right — *a la derecha*
to the left — *a la izquierda*

ACCOMMODATIONS

Can I (we) see a room?
    — *¿Puedo (podemos) ver un cuarto?*
What is the rate? — *¿Cuál es el precio?*
a single room — *un cuarto sencillo*
a double room — *un cuarto doble*
key — *llave*
bathroom — *retrete* or *lavabo*
bath — *baño*

hot water — *agua caliente*
cold water — *agua fría*
towel — *toalla*
soap — *jabón*
toilet paper — *papel higiénico*
air conditioning — *aire acondicionado*
fan — *abanico, ventilador*
blanket — *cubierta* or *manta*

PUBLIC TRANSPORT

bus stop — *la parada del autobús*
main bus terminal
    — *la central camionera*
railway station
    — *la estación de ferrocarril*
airport — *el aeropuerto*
ferry terminal
    — *la terminal del transbordador*

I want a ticket to . . .
    — *Quiero un boleto a . . .*
I want to get off at . . .
    — *Quiero bajar en . . .*
Here, please. — *Aquí, por favor.*
Where is this bus going?
    — *¿Dónde va este autobús?*
roundtrip — *ida y vuelta*
What do I owe? — *¿Cuánto le debo?*

FOOD

menu — *lista, menú*
glass — *taza*
fork — *tenedor*
knife — *cuchillo*
spoon — *cuchara, cucharita*
napkin — *servilleta*
soft drink — *refresco*
coffee, cream — *café, crema*
tea — *té*
sugar — *azúcar*
drinking water — *agua pura, agua potable*
bottled carbonated water — *agua mineral*
bottled uncarbonated water — *agua sin gas*
beer — *cerveza*
wine — *vino*
milk — *leche*
juice — *jugo*
eggs — *huevos*
bread — *pan*

watermelon — *sandía*
banana — *plátano*
apple — *manzana*
orange — *naranja*
meat (without) — *carne (sin)*
beef — *carne de res*
chicken — *pollo*
fish — *pescado*
shellfish — *camarones, mariscos*
fried — *frito*
roasted — *asada*
barbecue, barbecued
  — *barbacoa, al carbón*
breakfast — *desayuno*
lunch — *almuerzo*
dinner (often eaten in late afternoon)
  — *comida*
dinner, or a late night snack — *cena*
the check — *la cuenta*

MAKING PURCHASES

I need . . . — *Necesito . . .*
I want . . . — *Deseo . . .* or *Quiero . . .*
I would like . . . (more polite) — *Quisiera
  . . .*
How much does it cost? — *¿Cuánto cuesta?*
What's the exchange rate?
  — *¿Cuál es el tipo de cambio?*

Can I see . . . ? — *¿Puedo ver . . . ?*
this one — *ésta/ésto*
expensive — *caro*
cheap — *barato*
cheaper — *más barato*
too much — *demasiado*

HEALTH

Help me please. — *Ayúdeme por favor.*
I am ill. — *Estoy enfermo.*
pain — *dolor*
fever — *fiebre*
stomache ache — *dolor de estómago*
vomiting — *vomitar*

diarrhea — *diarrea*
drugstore — *farmacia*
medicine — *medicina*
pill, tablet — *pastilla*
birth control pills — *pastillas contraceptivos*
condoms — *contraceptivas*

BOOKLIST

The following books are available online at www.cubabooks.com, which offers hundreds of current titles at up to 40% discount.

ART AND CULTURE

Behar, Ruth, ed. *Bridges to Cuba/Puentes a Cuba*. Ann Arbor, MI: University of Michigan Press, 1995. An evocative and sometimes moving anthology in which Cuban and Cuban-American artists, writers, and scholars explore their identity, nationality and homeland.

Cabrera, Lydia. *El monte. . . notas sobre las religiones, la magia, las supersticiones, y el folklore de los negros criollos y el pueblo de Cuba*. Ediciones Universal. A compulsory work for understanding the identity and impact of African cultures on Cuba.

Camnitzer, Luís. *New Art of Cuba*. Austin, TX: University of Texas Press, 1994. Profiles the work of 40 young Cubans who formed part of the first generation of postrevolutionary artists.

Carmer, Mark. *Culture Shock! A Guide to Customs and Etiquette*. A brilliant, perceptive, and emotionally engaging all-round look at what makes Cuba and Cubans tick, told through anecdotal account.

Geldof, Lynn. *Cubans: Voices of Change*. New York: St. Martin's Press, 1991. Interviews with Cubans representing the spectrum of viewpoints and backgrounds.

Lewis, Oscar, Ruth M. Lewis, and Susan M. Rigdon. *Four Men: Living the Revolution, An Oral History of Contemporary Cuba*. Urbana, IL: University of Illinois Press, 1977.

Moore, Carlos. *Castro, the Blacks, and Africa*. Los Angeles: Center for Afro-American Studies, University of California, 1988.

Stubbs, Jean, and Pedro Pérez Sarduy, eds. *AfroCuba: An Anthology of Cuban Writing on Race, Politics and Culture*. New York: Ocean Press/Center for Cuban Studies, 1993. An anthology of black Cuban writing on aspects of "Afrocuba," including essays, poetry, and extracts from novels.

BIOGRAPHY

Anderson, Jon Lee. *Che Guevara: A Revolutionary Life*. New York: Grove Press, 1997. A tour de force, this definitive biography reveals heretofore-unknown details of Che's life and presents an astounding profile that shows the dark side of this revolutionary icon, severely tarnishing his image.

Castro, Fidel. *Che: A Memoir by Fidel Castro*, Melbourne, Australia: Ocean Press, 1983. Fidel's candid account of his relationship with Che Guevara documents the man, the revolutionary, the thinker, and the Argentine-born doctor's extraordinary bond with Cuba.

Castro, Fidel. *My Early Years*. New York: Ocean Press, 1998. In the twilight of his life, Fidel Castro reflects on his childhood, youth, and student activism, with a brilliant introduction by Gabriel García Márquez.

Deutschmann, David, ed. *Che: A Memoir by Fidel Castro*. New York: Ocean Press, 1999. For the first time, Fidel Castro writes with candor and affection of his relationship with Che Guevara.

Fernández, Alina. *Castro's Daughter: An Exile's Memoir of Cuba*. New York: St. Martin's Press, 1999. Castro's embittered daughter tells tattle on her despised father from exile in Miami. A scathing report on a man she calls "a mediocrity" and "a failure."

Franqui, Carlos. *Family Portrait with Fidel.* New York: Vintage Books, 1985. An insider's look at how the Sovietization of the Cuban Revolution occurred and precisely what goals Fidel Castro had in mind. The author debunks myths and provides startling revelations.

Gálvez, William. *Che in Africa.* New York: Ocean Press, 1999. Che Guevara disappeared from Cuba in 1965 to lead a guerrilla mission in the Congo. This book takes a sympathetic look at Che's failed mission, featuring Che's diary plus information from declassified CIA documents.

Geyer, Georgie Anne. *Guerrilla Prince: The Untold Story of Fidel Castro.* Boston: Little Brown, 1991. This sobering profile of the Cuban leader strips Castro bare, revealing his charisma and cunning, pride and paranoia, and megalomania and myth.

Gimbel, Wendy. *Havana Dreams: A Story of Cuba.* London, 1998. Virago. The moving story of Naty Revuelta's tormented love affair with Fidel Castro and the terrible consequences of a relationship as heady as the doomed romanticism of the revolution.

Gray, Richard Butler. *José Martí, Cuban Patriot.* Gainesville, FL: University of Florida Press, 1962.

Montejo, Estebán. *The Autobiography of a Runaway Slave.* Newark, NJ: Pantheon, 1968 (edited by Miguel Barnet). The moving real-life tale opens the doors to life and death in Spain's colonial slave system in Cuba in the late 19th century.

Quirk, Robert E. *Fidel Castro.* New York: W.W. Norton, 1993. A detailed, none-too-complimentary profile of the Cuban leader.

Szulc, Tad. *Fidel: A Critical Portrait.* New York: Morrow, 1986. A riveting profile of the astounding life of this larger-than-life figure. The book is full of never-before-revealed tidbits. A marvelous read.

Trento, Angelo. *Castro and Cuba.* Interlink Publishing, 2000. Part of the illustrated Histories Series.

CIGARS

Mara, William P. *Cubans: The Ultimate Cigars.* Lyons Press, 1998. A comprehensive, affordable companion to the world's greatest cigars. Color photographs.

Perelman, Richard B. *Perelman's Pocket Cyclopedia of Havana Cigars.* Perelman, Pioneer & Co, 1998. More than 160 pages with over 25 color photos providing a complete list of cigar brands and shapes. Handy 4" x 6" size makes it easy to carry in the coat pocket and invaluable as a reference source when shopping.

Shanken, Marvin R., ed. *Cigar Aficionado's Cigars.* Running Press, 1997. A practical yet inspiring tome of quotes from cigar aficionados is combined with helpful tips and information, plus a foldout ring gauge for measuring cigar diameters. Fully illustrated.

Shanken, Marvin R. ed. *Shanken's Cigar Handbook: A Connoisseur's Guide to Smoking Pleasure.* Running Press, 1997. Comprehensive reference text with colorful pictures and cigar brand data, plus a forward by Bill Cosby.

Todesco, Charles Del, and Patrick Jantet. *The Havana Cigar: Cuba's Finest.* Abbeville Press, 1997. A fascinating, behind-the-scenes look at Cuba's best-known export. Del Todesco details the processes of tobacco growing and treatment, plus the meticulous hand assembly of cigars. A catalog of Havana cigars and their characteristics caps the book. Lavishly illustrated.

COFFEE-TABLE

Aguilar Caballo, Juan Carlos. *Tropicana de Cuba.* Havana: Visual América, 1996. A Spanish-language review of Havana's famous cabaret from its inception to today, lavishly illustrated in a whirligig of erotic color.

Barclay, Juliet (photographs by Martin Charles). *Havana: Portrait of a City.* London: Cassell,

1993. A well-researched and abundantly illustrated coffee-table volume especially emphasizing the city's history. Written in a lively, readable style.

Beyrout, Olivier, and François Missen. *Memories of Cuba*. New York: Thunder's Mouth Press, 1997. This small-format book of photos covers the island and celebrates the spirit of the Cuban people, told in their own words.

Carley, Rachel. *Cuba: 400 Years of Architectural Legacy*. New York: Whitney Library of Design, 1997. Beautifully illustrated coffee-table book that spans the island in tracing the development of architectural styles from early colonial days to the communist aesthetic hiatus and post-Soviet renaissance.

Dawson, Barry. *Street Graphics Cuba*. London, Thames & Hudson, 2001. Cuba's eclectic street art portrayed in a lavishly illustrated coffee-table book by an Englishman with an eye for the fun, funky, and culturally cool.

Edinger, Claudio. *Old Havana*. New York: DAP, 1998. Powerful, evocative photography portraying life in Old Havana, with equally moving introductory text by Guillermo Cabrera Infante and Humberto Werneck.

Friedman, Marcia. *Cuba: The Special Period*. Madison: Samuel Book Publishers, 1998. A misleading title for this book of general imagery of contemporary Cuba, with text by Cuban exiles who "speak for the Cuban people who cannot."

García, Cristina, and Joshua Greene. *Cars of Cuba*. New York: Harry N. Abrams, 1995. A splendid book with color photographs of 53 lovingly maintained beauties from the heyday of Detroit. It also features a lively introduction.

Giovan, Tria. *Cuba: The Elusive Island*. New York: Harry Abrams, 1996. An evocative photography book that reflects the beauty and tragedies of contemporary Cuba; minimal text

Graetz, Rick. *Cuba: The Land, The People*. Helena, MT: American Geographic Publishing, 1990. A slender coffee-table book that shows Cuba's diverse beauty with stunning visual imagery. Meager text.

Graetz, Rick. *Havana: The City, The People*. Helena, MT: American Geographic Publishing, 1991. A tribute to Havana in full-color photography that captures the spirit of the 500-year-old city. Minimal text.

Harvey, David Alan, and Elizabeth Newhouse. *Cuba*. Washington, D.C.: National Geographic, 2000. An acclaimed photographer and *National Geographic* editor combine talents to brilliantly display their passion for Cuba in this poignant and stunningly illustrated book that puts a human face on the rich culture.

Kohly, Eddy. *Cuba*. New York: Rizzoli, 1998. This large-format coffee-table book ranges the island with surreal imagery and ethereal text.

Krantz, Jim. *Havana*. A fresh and poignant approach to photographing Havana that manages to capture the tender side of a city in lamentable decline. Krantz's mostly black-and-white imagery awakens our graphic sensibilities to the gentle beauty of a gritty place. Introduction and captions by Christopher P. Baker.

Kufeld, Adam. *Cuba*. New York: W. W. Norton, 1994. A stunning photographic portrait of Cuba depicting all aspects of life. The book is enhanced by Tom Miller's introduction: "Kufeld has achieved that rare perspective of looking at Cuba from the inside out, and in doing so he has given us a gentle look at a hard place."

Lewis, Barry, and Peter Marshall. *Into Cuba*. New York: Alfred Van Der Marck Editions, 1985. An evocative and richly illustrated coffee-table book widely available in Cuba.

Michener, James, and John Kings. *Six Days in Havana*. Austin, TX: University of Texas Press, 1989. A wonderful read regaling the noted novelist's brief but emotionally touching week in Havana. Beautifully illustrated.

Núñez Jiménez, Antonio. *The Journey of the Havana Cigar*. Havana: Empresa Cubana del

Tabaco, 1995. A large-volume treatise on the history of Cuban cigars lavishly illustrated with glossy photos.

Salas, Robert, and Osvaldo Salas. *Fidel's Cuba: A Revolution in Pictures.* Thunder's Mouth Press: New York, 1998. A powerful black-and-white study by Cuba's leading photographers (father and son) as they follow Castro from his clean-shaven days to the Sierra Maestra, the Bay of Pigs invasion, and through to the contemporary day.

Sapieha, Nicolas. *Old Havana, Cuba.* London: Tauris Parke Books, 1990. A beautifully illustrated coffee-table book accompanied by lively text.

Smith, Wayne (photographs by Michael Reagan). *Portrait of Cuba.* Atlanta, GA: Turner Publishing, 1991. A succinct, lucid, and entertaining profile on contemporary Cuba told by a noted expert. This splendid coffee-table book is superbly illustrated.

Stout, Nancy. *Habanos: The Story of the Havana Cigar.* New York: Rizzoli, 1997. Beautifully illustrated coffee-table book that tells you all you want to know about the growing and processing of tobacco and its metamorphosis into fine habanos cigars.

Stout, Nancy, and Jorge Rigau. *Havana.* Rizzoli, New York, 1994. A stunning coffee-table book that captures the mood of the city in color and black-and-white photography; superb text and essays add to the photographic perspectives on Havana's cultural and architectural history.

Walker, Evans. *Havana.* Pantheon, New York, 1989. A reissue of the classic collection of black-and-white photographs depicting life in Cuba in the 1930s, first published in 1933.

Williams, Stephen. *Cuba: The Land, The History, The People, The Culture.* Philadelphia, PA: Running Press Books, 1994. A richly evocative, lavishly illustrated coffee-table book with a concise and enlivened text.

COOKING

LaFray, Joyce. *¡Cuba Cocina!* New York: Hearst Books, 1994. A sweeping compilation of Cuban recipes, both classic and *nuevo cubano,* from both Floridian Cuban restaurants and such famous Havana restaurants as Bodeguita del Medio. Should be compulsory reading in Cuba.

GENERAL

Agee, Philip. *Inside the Company: CIA Diary.* New York: Bantam Books, 1975. This sobering work details the mission to discredit Cuba, including dirty tricks—disinformation campaigns, bombings, political assassinations, etc.—employed by the CIA against Latin America leftists. Told by a CIA "deep-cover" agent who eventually resigned because he "finally understood how much suffering [the CIA] was causing."

Benjamin, Medea, and Peter Rosset. *The Greening of the Revolution.* Melbourne: Ocean Press, 1994. A detailed account of Cuba's turn to a system of organic agriculture told by two noted authorities on the subject.

Benjamin, Medea, Joseph Collins, and Michael Scott. *No Free Lunch: Food and Revolution in Cuba.* San Francisco: Institute for Food and Development Policy, 1984.

Cabrera Infante, Guillermo. *¡Mea Cuba!* New York: Farrar Straus Giroux, 1994. An acerbic, indignant, raw, wistful, and brilliant set of essays in which the author pours out his bile at the Castro regime.

Calder, Simon, and Emily Hatchwell. *Cuba: A Guide to the People, Politics and Culture.* London: Latin America Bureau, 1995. A slender yet thoughtful and insightful overview of Cuban society.

Clark, Susannah and John Miller. *Chronicles Abroad: Havana.* San Francisco: Chronicle

Books, 1996. Short essays and extracts on Cuba (not just Havana), by such authors as Graham Greene, Ernest Hemingway, Mario Puzo, and Fidel Castro.

Cruz, Mary. *Cuba and Hemingway on the Great Blue River.* Havana: Editorial José Martí, 1994. A splendid critical study of Hemingway's writings in which the author presents the theory that Hemingway's works reflect core tenets of Cuban ideology.

Del Rio, Eduardo. *Cuba for Beginners: An Illustrated Guide for Americans.* New York: Pathfinder Press, 1970. The Mexican presents the internationalist view of Cuba-U.S. relations with comic inventiveness. Hilarious depictions of Uncle Sam's machinations and misadventures from a Marxist perspective.

Fuentes, Norberto. *Hemingway in Cuba.* Secaucus, NY: Lyle Stuart, 1984. The seminal, lavishly illustrated study of the Nobel Prize winner's years in Cuba.

Halperin, Maurice. *Return to Havana.* Nashville, TN: Vanderbilt University Press, 1994. An engaging and scathing personal essay on contemporary Cuba by a professor who taught in Havana and worked for Cuba's Ministry of Foreign Trade in the 1960s.

Hatchwell, Emily, and Simon Calder. *Cuba in Focus: A Guide to the Peoples, Politics, and Culture.* London: Latin American Bureau, 1995. A perceptive and savvy profile of the culture and political scene.

Hemingway, Gregory. *Papa, A Personal Memory.* New York: Pocket Books, 1976. A funny, serious, and touching account of the author's childhood, including a long period in Cuba with his father, Ernest Hemingway.

Howard, Christopher. *Living and Investing in the New Cuba.* San José, Costa Rica: Costa Rica Books, 1999. An invaluable and comprehensive guide for anyone considering future possibilities in Cuba, with a detailed look at existing regulations and investment climate.

Kutzinski, Vera M. *Sugar's Secrets: Race and the Erotics of Cuban Nationalism.* Charlottesville: University Press of Virginia, 1993. A thought-provoking book that focuses on images of the mulatta in Cuban poetry, fiction, and visual arts in the 19th and 20th centuries, and how the eroticism is a celebration of racial diversity that lies at the heart of Cuba's multiculturalism.

Matthews, Herbert L. *Cuba.* New York: Macmillan Publishing, 1964. Written during the McCarthy era, this book reveals Matthews as no Castro sympathizer (despite that reputation). On the whole, a balanced look at the young Revolution.

McManus, Jane. *Cuba's Island of Dreams: Voices from the Isle of Pines and Youth.* Gainesville: University Press of Florida, 2000. A history of the small island just off Cuba's southern coast from the turn of the 20th century—when American settlers and speculators moved to what was then the Isle of Pines—to the turn of the 21st—as the idealistic Cuban youth for whom it was renamed are retiring.

Murray, Mary. *Cruel and Unusual Punishment: The U.S. Blockade Against Cuba.* Melbourne: Ocean Press, 1992. Details the U.S. embargo from its inception in 1960 to today. Presents Cuba's perspectives.

Randall, Margaret. *Women in Cuba: Twenty Years Later.* New York: Smyrna Press, 1981. A sympathetic interpretation of what the Cuban Revolution has meant for women that demonstrates the remarkable and positive accomplishments in gender politics achieved under Castro.

Ripley, Peter C., and Bob Shacochis. *Conversations with Cuba.* University of Georgia, Press, 1999. A vivid, honest, insightful look at the confusion in modern Cuba by a longtime Cuba watcher who discusses his love affair with this proud, passionate, troubled nation, from his romanticized high school observances of Castro's revolution to his six illegal trips to the nation between 1991 and 1999.

Rudolf, James, ed. *Cuba: A Country Study.* Washington, D.C.: Government Printing Office (write to: Superintendent of Documents, Government Printing Office, Washington, DC 20402). Part of the U.S. Government Area Handbook Studies. A surprisingly balanced general study of Cuba, with detailed sections on history, economics, and politics.

Schwartz, Rosalie. *Pleasure Island: Tourism & Temptation in Cuba.* Lincoln: University of Nebraska Press, 1997. A vitalic study of the evolution of tourism in Cuba since the 1920s, the response of colonial-era Havana as it turned fleshpot and endless cabaret, and of mass tourism's influence on the behavior, attitudes, and cultures of two politically linked but diverse nations.

Segre, Roberto, Mario Coyula and Joseph L. Scarpaci. *Havana: Two Faces of the Antillean Metropolis.* New York: John Wiley & Sons, 1997. An engaging geographical text tracing the development of Havana from 1519 to the present post-Soviet era.

Shnookal, Deborah, and Mirta Muñiz, eds. *José Martí Reader.* New York: Ocean Press, 1999. An anthology of writings, poetry, and letters of one of the most brilliant and impassioned Latin American intellectuals of the 19th century.

Silva Lee, Alfonso. *Natural Cuba.* St Paul: Pangaea, 1996. An exquisitely illustrated and highly readable book celebrating the flora and fauna of Cuba by one of the island's best-known naturalists.

Smith, Lois, and Alfred Padula. *Sex and Revolution: Women in Socialist Cuba.* New York: Oxford University Press, 1996. An academic yet highly readable text on revolutionary Cuba's attempt to achieve sexual equality and "resolve the 'woman question' once and for all."

Timerman, Jacobo. *Cuba: A Journey.* New York: Knopf, 1990. A passionate, provocative, some-

times scathing, report of a recent journey through Cuba by a man who suffered torture at the hands of right-wing Argentinean extremists and who formerly idealized Cuba as a model socialist state.

Walker, Alice. *In Search of Our Mother's Gardens.* New York: Harcourt Books, 1983. This biography of experiences includes a chapter in which the noted novelist and activist explores her feelings about and recounts her experiences in Cuba.

Wolf, Adolf Hungry. *Trains of Cuba.* Skookumchuck, BC: Canadian Caboose Press, 1995. A steam-lover's guide to Cuba's vintage rolling stock.

HISTORY, ECONOMICS, AND POLITICS

Aguila, Juan M. del. *Cuba: Dilemmas of a Revolution.* Boulder, CO: Westview Press, 1994. An up-to-date, well-balanced review of the history and contemporary reality of Cuba.

Benjamin, Jules R. *The United States and the Origins of the Cuban Revolution.* Princeton, NJ: Princeton University Press, 1990. A superb study explaining how Cuba and the United States arrived at the traumatic rupture in their relations.

Bonachea, Rolando, and Nelson Valdés. *Cuba in Revolution.* New York: Anchor Books, 1972. A collection of essays by noted academics, providing a comprehensive, many-sided overview of the Cuban Revolution and the issues it raises.

Deutschmann, David, ed. *Che Guevara Reader: Writings on Guerrilla Strategy, Politics, and Revolution.* New York: Ocean Press, 1999. A wide-ranging anthology of Guevara's speeches and writings, including farewell letters to Castro and his family.

Eckstein, Susan. *Back from the Future: Cuba under Castro.* Princeton, NJ: Princeton University Press, 1994. A well-reasoned and balanced attempt to provide a broad overview of Castro's Cuba. Eckstein contends that Cuba is less rigidly Marxist than presented and that a revisionist view is needed.

Elliston, Jon. *Psy War on Cuba*. New York: Ocean Press, 1999. A comprehensive history of U.S. anti-Castro propaganda and covert operations using recently declassified documents.

Franklin, Jane. *Cuba and the United States: A Chronological History*. New York: Ocean Press, 1997. A chronological account of relations between the two nations from 1959 through 1995.

García, Julio Luís, ed. *Cuban Revolution Reader*. New York: Ocean Press, 1999. This anthology documents key moments from four decades from a revolutionary perspective, with works by Fidel Castro, Che Guevara, and others in the Cuban communist pantheon.

Halebsky, Sandor, and John Kirk, eds. *Cuba in Transition: Crisis and Transformation*. Westview Press, 1992.

Halperin, Maurice. *The Taming of Fidel Castro*. Berkeley, CA: University of California Press, 1981.

Johnson, Haynes. *The Bay of Pigs*. New York: Norton, 1964. Writing in collaboration with leaders of the Brigade, Haynes provides both perspectives in this masterful, encyclopedic work.

Kennedy, Robert F. *Thirteen Days: A Memoir of the Cuban Missile Crisis*. New York: Norton, 1969.

Kenner, Martin, and James Petras. *Fidel Castro Speaks*. New York: Penguin Books, 1969. A collection of 16 of Castro's most important speeches, made between his seizure of power in 1959 and 1968.

Lechuga, Carlos. *In the Eye of the Storm*. New York: Ocean Press, 1995. The inside story on the Missile Crisis from the Cuban perspective, by Cuba's former U.N. ambassador.

Lockwood, Lee. *Castro's Cuba, Cuba's Fidel*. Boulder, CO: Westview Press, 1990.

Martí, José. *Inside the Monster: Writings on the United States and American Imperialism*. 1975 (Phillip S. Fosner, ed.) New York: Monthly Review Press. Essential prose works of the late-19th-century activist, literary man, and national hero, who has exercised a lasting influence on the politics of 20th-century Cuba.

May, Ernest R., and Philip D. Zelikow. *The Kennedy Tapes: Inside the White House During the Cuban Missile Crisis*. New York: Belknap Press, 1998. A fascinating read that gives a minute-by-minute record of the tensions and emotions of men deliberating over the world's first nuclear confrontation, while displaying the naive thinking regarding Castro's role and intents.

Mesa-Lago, Carmelo, ed. *Cuba After the Cold War*. Pittsburgh, PA: University of Pittsburgh, 1993.

Meyer, Karl E., and Tad Szulc. *The Cuban Invasion*. New York: Praeger, 1962. A shrewd and fascinating interpretation of the Bay of Pigs.

Muñoz, Mirta, and Pedro Álvarez Tabio, eds. *Fidel Castro Reader: Forty Years of the Cuban Revolution*. New York: Ocean Press, 2000. A selection of the Cuban leader's speeches over the past four decades.

Oppenheimer, Andres. *Castro's Final Hour*. New York: Simon & Schuster, 1992. A sobering, in-depth expose of the uglier side of both Fidel Castro and the state system, including controversial topics such as drug trading. This book is anathema in Cuba.

Ortíz, Fernando. *Cuban Counterpoint: Tobacco and Sugar*. New York: Alfred A. Knopf, 1947. A seminal work on the decisiveness of tobacco and sugar in Cuban history.

Patterson, Thomas G. *Contesting Castro: The United States and the Triumph of the Cuban Revolution*. New York: Oxford University Press, 1994.

Pérez, Louis A. *Cuba: Between Reform and Revolution.* New York: Oxford University Press, 1988.

Pérez-Stable, Marifeli. *The Cuban Revolution: Origins, Course, and Legacy.* New York: Oxford University Press, 1993. A negative review of the past four decades that closes with a polemic offering a damning accusation of a revolution betrayed.

Ricardo, Roger. *Guantánamo: The Bay of Discord.* New York: Ocean Press, 1994. The story of the U.S. military base in Cuba.

Russo, Gus. *Live by the Sword: The Secret War Against Castro and the Death of JFK.* New York: Bancroft Press, 1998. A stunning, superbly documented new take on the JFK killing reveals how the Kennedy's relentless pursuit of Castro backfired, and the cover-up that followed.

Schulz, Donald, ed. *Cuba and the Future.* Westport, CT: Greenwood Press, 1994. A series of essays analyzing Cuba's contemporary economic and political dilemmas.

Smith, Wayne. *The Closest of Enemies.* New York: W.W. Norton, 1987.

Stubbs, Jean. *Cuba: The Test of Time.* London: Latin American Bureau, 1989. A comprehensive overview of Cuban economics, politics, religion, and social structure.

Thomas, Hugh. *Cuba: The Pursuit of Freedom, 1726-1969.* New York: Harper & Row, 1971. A seminal work—called a "magisterial conspectus of Cuban history"—tracing the evolution of conditions that eventually engendered the Revolution.

Thomas, Hugh. *The Cuban Revolution.* London: Weidenfeld and Nicolson, 1986. The definitive work on the Revolution offering a brilliant analysis of all aspects of the country's diverse and tragic history.

Wyden, Peter. *Bay of Pigs: The Untold Story.* New York: Simon and Schuster, 1979. An in-depth and riveting exposé of the CIA's ill-conceived mission to topple Castro.

LITERATURE

Cabrera Infante, Guillermo. *Three Trapped Tigers.* New York: Avon, 1985. A poignant and comic novel, described as "a vernacular, elegiac masterpiece," which captures the essence of life in Havana before the ascendance of Castro. Written by an "enemy of the state" who has lived in embittered exile since 1962.

Carpentier, Alejo. *Reasons of State.* Havana: Writers and Readers. A novelistic tour de force, alive with wit and erudition, about the despotic head of state of an unnamed Latin American country in the early days of the 20th century.

Coonts, Stephen. *Cuba.* New York: St. Martin's Press, 1999. Coonts mines the original Cuban missile crisis for source material in this military-techno thriller that has Castro on his deathbed.

García, Cristina. *Dreaming in Cuban.* New York: Ballantine Books, 1992. A brilliant, poignant, languid, and sensual tale of a family divided politically and geographically by the Cuban revolution and the generational fissures that open on each side: in Cuba, between an ardently pro-Castro grandmother and a daughter who retreats into santería; in America, between another, militantly anti-Castro daughter and her own rebellious punk-artist daughter, who mocks her obsession.

Greene, Graham. *Our Man in Havana.* New York: Penguin, 1971. The story of Wormold, a conservative British vacuum-cleaner salesman in prerevolutionary Havana. Recruited by British intelligence, Wormold finds little information to pass on, and so invents it. Full of the sensuality of Havana and the tensions of Batista's last days.

Hemingway, Ernest. *Islands in the Stream.* New York: Harper Collins, 1970. An exciting triptych. The second and third parts are set in Cuba during the war and draw heavily on the author's own experience hunting Nazi U-boats at sea.

Hemingway, Ernest. *The Old Man and the Sea.* New York: Scribner's, 1952. The simple yet profound story of an unlucky Cuban fisherman, the slim novel won the author the Nobel Prize for Literature.

Hemingway, Ernest. *To Have and Have Not.* New York: Macmillan Publishing, 1937. The dramatic, brutal tale of running contraband between Cuba and Key West.

Iyer, Pico. *Cuba in the Night.* New York: Alfred A. Knopf, 1995. A slow-moving story of a love affair between a globe-trotting photojournalist and a young Cuban woman. The spirit of José Martí hovers over the trysts and political musings. Set in Cuba during the Special Period, with the police presence weighing heavy.

Leonard, Elmore. *Cuba Libre.* New York: Delacorte Press, 1998. Set on the eve of the Spanish-American War, this electrifying novel is an explosive mix of high adventure, history, and romance.

Smith, Martin Cruz. *Havana Bay.* New York: Random House, 1999. Smith engages us in a best-selling murder mystery as Russian Cold War spy Renko returns, this time to the "faded, lovely, dangerous" Cuban capital.

TRAVEL GUIDES

Calder, Nigel. *Cuba: A Cruising Guide;* St. Ives, England; Imray Laurie Norie & Wilson, 1999. A superb navigational guide for yachters.

Charles, Simon. *The Cruising Guide to Cuba.* St. Petersburg, FL: Cruising Guide Publications, 1997. Invaluable reference guide for every sailor wishing to charter sailing or motorized craft. Charles gives it to you straight. His goal is "to seek only to ensure the safe passage of all who would use the seas to travel where they will."

Coe, Andrew. *Cuba.* Lincolnwood: NTC Publishing, 1995. Lavishly illustrated and evocatively written. Strong background and succinct regional overviews. Limited practical information. Avoids the political frame.

Perrottet, Tony, and Joann Biondi. *Insight Guides—Cuba.* Hong Kong: APA Publications, 1999. Lavishly illustrated. Detailed introductory material and succinct regional overviews.

Williams, Diana. *Diving and Snorkeling Guide to Cuba.* Oakland: Lonely Planet, 1999. A concise yet comprehensive and indispensable guide diving in Cuba.

TRAVEL LITERATURE

Baker, Christopher P. *Mi Moto Fidel: Motorcycling through Castro's Cuba.* Washington, D.C.: National Geographic's Adventure Press, 2001. Riveting and self-deprecating tales of the author's 11,000-km adventure by motorcycle through this captivating and perplexing island. Encounters with secret police and lascivious showgirls add excitement to a book full of eyebrow-raising insights.

Codrescu, Andrei, and David Graham. *Ay, Cuba!* New York: St Martin's Press, 1999. A trenchant and witty social criticism that takes a scything view of Castroism while reflecting the author's affection and sensitivity for the Cuban culture and people.

Gébler, Carlo. *Driving through Cuba.* New York: Simon & Schuster, 1988. The tale of a three-month sojourn through Cuba by car. Full of wry, often acerbic, commentary and a strong historical analysis.

Hazard, Samuel. *Cuba with Pen and Pencil.* Hartford, CT: Hartford Publishing, 1871. Lively historic account offers insights into life in Cuba last century.

Iyer, Pico. *Falling off the Map.* New York: Alfred A. Knopf, 1993. Includes a chapter on Cuba that presents a far rosier picture than the author's dour novel *Cuba in the Night.*

Miller, Tom. *Trading with the Enemy: A Yankee Travels through Castro's Cuba.* New York: Basic Books, 1996. A fabulous travelogue told by a famous author who lived in Cuba for almost a year. Thoughtful, engaging, insightful, compassionate, and told in rich narrative.

Ryan, Alan, ed. *The Reader's Companion to Cuba*. New York: Harcourt Brace & Co., 1997. A gathering of some of the best travel writing about Cuba dating from the mid-1800s, spanning an eclectic menu of authors from John Muir and Graham Greene to mob lawyer Frank Ragano and baseball's Tommy Lasorda. Indispensable!

Samuelson, Arnold. *With Hemingway: A Year in Key West and Cuba*. Maine: Thorndike Press, 1984. The true-life tale of a young Midwestern farm boy who wanted to become a writer and was hired to guard Hemingway's *Pilar*. For a year he accompanied "E.H." on fishing excursions around Key West and Cuba, recording this diary, in which he captures Hemingway "off-guard and all-too-human."

Smith, Stephen. *The Land of Miracles: A Journey through Modern Cuba*. London: Abacus. 1997. An Englishman's engaging tale of a journey through Cuba during the Special Period.

Symmes, Patrick. *Chasing Che: A Motorcycle Journey in Search of the Guevara Legend*. New York: Vintage Press, 2000. Symmes retraces the journey Che Guevara made across South America in 1952. His lyrical account captures the contradictions that endure in Latin America long after Che.

Wolf, Adolf Hungry. *Letters from Cuba*. Skookumchuck, BC: Canadian Caboose Press, 1995. An uplifting account of the author's passionate love for Cuba told in an anthology of letters written to family and friends, recounting his pursuit of his singular passion . . . a love affair for steam-trains.

VIDEOS

Arroz con Frijoles: The Budget Traveler's Guide to Cuba. A 60-minute review geared to the impecunious, no-frills traveler and profiling accommodation, transportation, and food issues. Copies cost US$39.95 from Fej Films, P.O. Box 24062, Lansing, MI 48909-4062, website: www.arrozconfrijoles.com (indicate PAL or NTSC).

Cuba. An 80-minute video that looks at the lives of Cubans. (US$25, plus US$2 shipping, from John Holod, 140 Mullan Road W, Superior, MI 59872).

Cuba 2000. This 35-minute video provides an overview of touristic interest, from the history to key sites, and scenes of everyday life in Cuba, from hospitals to housing conditions. Copies cost US$55.95 including shipping. Call (253) 265-2073 to order.

Cuba Va: The Challenge of the Next Generation. A fascinating 60-minute documentary released in 1993 captures the vigor and diversity of Cuban youth—the politically committed and the alienated—who express their divergent perspectives on the Revolution, the Special Period, and the future. Copies cost US$95 from Cuba Va Video Project, 12 Liberty St., San Francisco, CA 94110, tel. (415) 282-1812, fax (415) 282-1798.

Gay Cuba. This one-hour documentary takes a candid look at one of Cuba's most controversial human rights issues: the treatment of the gay and lesbian people in Cuba since the Revolution. Order from Frameline, 346 Ninth St., San Francisco, CA 94103, tel. (415) 703-8654, fax (415) 861-1404, e-mail: frameline@aol.com; website: www.frameline.org.

Havana Nagila: The Jews of Cuba. An hour-long look at the history of Jews in Cuba during five centuries. Copies can be ordered from Schnitzki & Stone, 819 W. Roseburg Ave. #240, Modesto, CA 95350, tel. (209) 575-1775, fax (209) 575-1404.

Trains of Cuba. This two-hour video is a delight for serious antique train buffs, with dozens of puffing billies shown at work. Copies cost US$39.95 plus shipping. Order from Canadian Caboose Press, Box 844, Skookumchuck, BC V0B 2EO, Canada; cellular tel. (250) 342-1421.

Workers Democracy in Cuba. A 30-minute video records the 17th National Congress of the Cuban Workers Federation, in April 1996; US$25, plus US$3 postage, from International Peace for Cuba Appeal, 2489 Mission St. #28, San Francisco, CA 94110, tel. (415) 821-7575, fax (415) 821-5782.

INTERNET DIRECTORY

INFORMATION ON MOON HANDBOOKS AND THE AUTHOR

Moon Handbooks: www.moon.com
Christopher P. Baker:
  www.travelguidebooks.com

INFORMATION SOURCES

AfroCuba Web: www.afrocubaweb.com
Cuba Books: www.cubabooks.com
Cuban government (official site):
  www.cubaweb.cu
Cubanet: www.cubanet.org
Cuban Studies Institute:
  www.cuba.tulane.edu/res
CubaWeb: www.cubaweb.com
(The) Cuban Experience:
  www.library.advanced.org/18355/
El Web de Cuba: www3.cuba.cu
Havana supersite: www.lahabana.com
La Casa del Habano: www.cubamall.com
Latin American Network Information Center:
  www.lanic.utexas.educ
Minsterio de Turismo: www.cubatravel.cu
Paginas Amarillas de Cuba (Yellow Pages):
  www.paginasamarillas.cu

AIRLINES

Domestic

Aero Caribbean:
  aerocarvpcre@iacc3.get.cma.net
Cubana de Aviación: www.cubana.cu

International

Aerocaribe: www.aerocaribe.com
Aeroflot: aeroflot@www.russia.net
  www.aeroflot.org
Air Canada: www.aircanada.ca
Air Europa: www.aireuropa-online.com
Air Europe : www.aireurope.it
Air France: www.airfrance.fr
Air Jamaica: www.airjamaica.com
Air Transat: www.airtransatholidays.com

Grupo Taca: www.grupotaca.com
Iberia: : infoib@iberia.com: www.iberia.com
KLM: www.klm.com
Lauda Air: office@laudaair.com:
  www.laudaair.com
LTU : service@ltu.de
  website: www.ltu.de
Martinair: www.martinair.com
Mexicana: www.mexicana.com.mx

CAR RENTAL COMPANIES

Cubacar: cubacar@cbcan.cyt.cu
  www.cubacar.cubanacan.cu
Havanautos: www.havanautos.cubaweb.cu
Rex Limousines: rex@ceniai.inf.cu
  www.rex-limousine.com
Transtur Rent-a-Car:
  webmaster@transtur.com.cu
  www.transtur.cubaweb.cu
Vía Rent-a-Car: dtor_rc@nwgaitov.gav.cm.net
  www.gaviota.cubaweb.cu

CRUISE COMPANIES

Club Med: www.clubmed.com
Cuba Cruise Corporation: cubacruising.com
Greta Line: italia.prima@flashnet.it
  www.4cubacruises.com/cruis
Nouvelle Frontieres:
  www.nouvelles-frontieres.fr
Sunquest Cruises: info@sunquest.ca:
  www.sunquest.ca

HOTEL GROUPS

Cuban

Cubamar: cubamar@cubamar.mit.cma.net
  www.cubamar.cubaweb.cu
Cubanacan: gerente.gen@viajes.cha.cyt.cu
  www.cubanacan.cu
Gran Caribe: www.grancaribe.cubaweb.cu
Horizontes: crh@horizontes.hor.cma.net
  www.horizontes.cu

Islazul: comazul@teleda.get.cma.net
    www.islazul.cubaweb.cu
Servimed: servimed@sermed.cha.cyt.cu

Foreign
LTI: www.lti.de
Sandals: www.sandals.com
Sol Meliá: www.solmelia.com
SuperClubs: www.superclubs.com

HOTELS

Havana
Hotel Bello Caribe :
    gcomerc@bcaribe.cha.cyt.cu
Hotel Comodoro:
    comercia@comodor.cha.cyt.cu
    www.cubanacan.cu
Hotel Copacabana:
    reserva@copa.gca.cma.net
Hotel Chateau Miramar:
    ventas@chateau.cha.cyt.cu
Hotel Qualton El Viejo y El Mar:
    comerc@oldman.cha.cyt.cu
Hotel Inglaterra:
    reserva@gcingla.gca.cma.net
Habana Libre: reserva@rllibre.tryp.cma.net
Hotel La Pradera: aloja@pradera.cha.cyt.cu
Hotel Mariposa:
    comercio@maripos.cha.cyt.cu
Hotel Meliá Habana:
    depres@habana.solmelia.cma.net
Hotel Nacional: reserva@gcnacio.gca.cma.net
Hotel Palco: info@hpalco.gov.cu
    www.cubaweb.cu/palco
Hotel Plaza: reserva@plaza.gca.cma.net
Hotel Riviera: reserva@gcrivie.gca.cma.net
Hotel Sevilla: reserva@sevilla.gca.cma.net
Hotel Victoria: reserva@gcvicto.gca.cma.net
    www.hotel-victoria.cubaweb.cu

Havana Province
Hotel Las Yagrumas: root@yagrum.hab.cyt.cu

Pinar del Río Province
Las Terrazas: : www.lasterrazas.cu/indexns
Villa Cayo Levisa: crh@horizontes.ht.cma.net
    www.horizontes.cu

Isla de la Juventud and Cayo Largo
Isla del Sur: reserva@isla.gca.cma.net

Matanzas Province
Arenas Blancas Sol y Mar:
    reserva@arblcas.gca.cma.net
Arenas Doradas:
    reserva@arenas.gca.cma.net
Beaches: varadero@beaches.var.cyt.cu
    www.sandals.com
Breezes Varadero:
    clubvar@clubvar.var.cyt.cu
    www.superclubs.com
Coralia Club Playa de Oro:
    comercial@poro.gca.cma.net
Gran Hotel: comercial@granhot.var.cyt.cu
Hotel Arenas Doradas:
    sistema@arenas.gca.cma.net
Hotel Atlántico: reserva@atlant.gca.cma.net
Hotel Brisas del Caribe:
    martell@bricar.var.cyt.cu
Hotel Cuatro Palmas:
    reserva@gcpalho.gca.cma.net
Hotel Internacional:
    reserva@gcinter.gca.cma.net
Hotel Kawama:
    reserva@kawama.gca.cma.net
Hotel Las Morlas:
    reserva@morlas.gca.cma.net
Hotel LTI Bellacosta:
    santos@bcosta.var.cyt.cu
Hotel Tuxpán: www.lti.de
Iberostar Barlovento:
    reserva@ibero.gca.cma.net
Meliá Las Américas:
    melia.las.americas@solmelia.es
    www.solmelia.com
Meliá Varadero: melia.varadero@solmelia.es
    www.solmelia.com
Sol Club Las Sirenas:
    sol.club.las.sirenas@solmelia.es
    www.solmelia.com
Sol Club Palmeras:
    jefres@coral.solmelia.cma.net
    www.solmelia.com
Superclub Varadero:
    reservas@clubvar.var.cyt.cu

Villas Punta Blanca:
   hotel@pblanca.gca.cma.net

Cienfuegos Province
Hotel Ancón: reserva@ancon.gca.cma.net
Hotel Faro Luna: dcfluna@perla.inf.cu

Villa Clara Province
Villa La Granjita: aloja@granita.vcl.cyt.cu

Sancti Spíritus Province
Villa Rancho Hatuey: aloja@rhatuey.vcl.cyt.cu

Ciego de Ávila Province
Hotel Tryp Cayo Coco:
   comerl@club.tryp.cma.cu
Meliá Cayo Coco:
   melia.cayococo@smcoco2.solmelia.cma.net
Sol Club Cayo Gullermo:
   reserva@cguille.solmelia.cma.net or
   sol.club.cayo.guillermo@solmelia.es
   www.grancaribe.cuba web.cu
Sol Club Cayo Coco:
   reserva@smcoco1.solmelia.cma.net or
   solclub.cayococo@melia.solmelia.cma.net

Camagüey Province
Club Caracol: aloja@carcol.stl.cyt.cu
Club Santa Lucía: aloja@clubst.stl.cyt.cu
Club Mayanabo: aloja@mayanabo.stl.cyt.cu
Hotel Cuatro Vientos:
   aloja@cvientos.stl.cyt.cu
Villa Tararaco: aloja@tararaco.stl.cyt.cu
Vita Club Caracol: secre@vitaclub.stl.cyt.cu

Holguín Province
Club Amigo Atlántico:
   recep@hatlant.gvc.cyt.cu
Club Amigo Guardalavaca:
   booking@hguard.gvc.cyt.cu
Hotel Guardalavaca:
   recep@hguard.gvc.cyt.cu
Hotel Las Brisas:
   reserva@deltabsa.gvc.cyt.cu
LTI Costa Verde Beach: sales@lti.de
   www.lti.de
Meliá Río de Oro:
   melia.rioro@oro.solmelia.cma.net:
   www.solmelia.es

Sol Río del Luna:
   solclub.riluna@luna.solmelia.cma.net:
   www.solmelia.es
Sol Rìo de Mares:
   sol.riomares@mares.solmelia.cma.net
   www.solmelia.es

Granma Province
Hotel Farallon del Caribe:
   pub@hfarcar.ma.grm.cyt.cu

Santiago Province
Hotel Bucanero: reserva@bucaner.scu.cyt.cu
Hotel Carisol and Hotel Corales:
   ventas@corales.scu.cyt.cu
Hotel Los Galeones:
   sierrmar@smar.scu.cyt.cu
Hotel Santiago: gercom@hotstgo.scu.cyt.cu
Hotel Sierra Mar: sierrmar@smar.scu.cyt.cu
Motel Versalles: comercial@versall.scu.cyt.cu

TOUR COMPANIES

Cuban
Amistur S.A.: www.igc.apc.org/cubasol/amistur
Cubatur: santo@cbtevent.cbt.cma.net
Gaviota Tours: gavitour@gaitur.gav.cma.net
Grupo Cubanacán: www.cubanacan.cu
Havanatur: www.havanatur.cubaweb.cu
Mercadu: mercadu@ceniai.cu
Paradiso: paradis@turcult.get.cma
   www.cult.cu\paradiso\index.html
Rumbos: director@rumvia.rumb.cma.net
Sol y Son: solyson@ceniai.inf.cu
Transtur: www.transtur.cubaweb.cu
Veracuba: vacgeren@cbcan.cyt.cu
Viajes Horizontes: crh@s1.hor.cma.net
   www.horizont.cu

U.S.
Caribbean Music and Dance Programs:
   caribmusic@igc.apc.org
   www.caribmusic.com
Cuba Connection: www.cuba.tc
Cuba Travel: info@cubatravel.com.mx
   www.cubatravel.com.mx
Last Frontier Expeditions: CopaBob@aol.com
   www.cubatravelexperts.com or

www.clubhavana.com
Marazul Tours: info@marazultours.com
www.marazultours.com
Tico Travel: tico@gate.net
www.destinationcuba.com

Foreign and International

Airtours : www.airtours.co.uk
Aerostar Viajes a Cuba: www.aero-star.com
Canada 3000 Holidays: www.c3holidays.com
Canadian Universities Travel Service:
www.travelcuts.com
Captivating Cuba : info@captivating-cuba.co.uk
www.captivating-cuba.co.uk
Caribic Vacations:
carhouse@caribiconline.com
www.caribiconline.com
Cubalinda.com: info@cubalinda.com:
www.cubalinda.com
Council on International Educational Exchange:
www.ciee.org or www.counciltravel.com
Explore Worldwide: www.explore.co.uk
Interchange: www.interchange.uk.com
Journey Latin America:
flights@journeylatinamerica.co.uk
www.journeylatinamerica.co. uk
MacQueen's Adventures Tours:
www.macqueens.com
Regent Holidays (Canada):
www.regentholidays.com
Regent Holidays (U.K.) :
www.cheapflights.co.uk
STA Travel:
www.statravel.co and www.statravel.co.uk
Taino Tours: taino@pceditores.com
www.pceditores.com/taino
Tour & Marketing: help@gocubaplus.com
www.gocubaplus.com
Trailfinders : www.trailfinders.com
Tropical Tours: tropical@cwjaimaica.com
www.marzouca.com

NEWS ORGANIZATIONS AND PUBLICATIONS

Cuban Daily News Digest: jhitchie@direct.ca
www.smallcapcenter.com

Cubanet: www.cubanet.org
Bohemia:
www.2.cuba.cu/cultura/revistas/bohemia
Granma: granmai@tinored.cu
www.granma.cu
Information Services Latin America (ISLA):
isla@datacenter.org
www.igc.org/isla
Juventud Rebelde: www.jreblede.cubaweb.cu
Latin American News Syndicate:
lans@txdirect.net: www.latam-news.com
Prensa Latina: www.prensa-latina.org
Radio Rebelde: www.2.cuba.cu/RRebelde

GENERIC

Caribbean Super Site:
www.caribbeansupersite.com/cuba
Consultoria Juridica Internacional:
www.cji.cubaweb.cu
Cuba (culture): www.2.cuba.cu/cultura
Cuba (education): www.2.cuba.cu/education
Cuba (general): www.city.net/countries/cuba/
Cuba (weather report): www.intellicast.com
Cuba (people): www.cubaweb.cu/pueblo
Cuba (medical sciences): www.infomed.sld.cu
Cuba (museums): www.cubaweb.cu/museos
Cuba (science): www.2.cuba.cu/cienciacuba
Cuba (sports): www.2.cuba.cu/deportes
Cuba (websites):
www.smallshop.com/cubawebsites.htm
Fidel Castro's speeches:
gopher://lanic.utexas.edu:70/00/
Havana weather report:
weather.yahoo.com/forecast/Havana

GOVERNMENT ORGANIZATIONS

Cuba

Academia de Ciencias de Cuba:
museofin@infomed.sld.cu or
acc@ceniai.inf.cu.
Grupo para el Desarrollo Integral de la Capital:
gdic@ceniai.inf.cu
Grupo de Desarrollo del Circuito Náutico
Jardines de la Reina:
delegado@dtcam.mintur.tur.c u

U.S.

U.S. Government health advisories:
www.cdc.gov
U.S. Government Cuba advisories:
www.travel.state.gov/cuba
U.S. State Department:
www.state.gov/www/regions/wha/cuba/index
U.S. Treasury Department:
www.treas.gov/ofac

NON-GOVERNMENTAL ORGANIZATIONS

Center for Cuban Studies: cubanctr@igc.org
www.cubaupdate.com
Cuban American Alliance Education Fund:
caaef@igc.org
www.cubamer.org
Food First: rosset@foodfirst.org
www.foodfirst.org/cuba
Global Exchange: globalexch@igc.org
www.globalexchange.com
Jewish Solidarity:
www.jewishcuba.org/solidarity
Pastors for Peace: ifco@igc.apc.org
www.ifconews.org
U.S.-Cuba Trade & Economic Council:
council@cubatrade.org
website www.cubatrade.org
USA*ENGAGE: www.usaengage.org
Witness For Peace:
witness@witnessforpeace.org
www.witnessforpeace.org

MISCELLANEOUS

Asistur: comercia@asistur.get.cma.net
www.asistur.cubaweb.cu.
Assist-Card: asistencia@assist-card.com
www.assist-card.com
Bodeguita del Medio:
reserva@bodem.gca.cma.net
Bluewater Books & Charts:
nautical-charts@bluewaterweb.com
www.bluewaterweb.com
Caribbean Hotel Association:
wpina@caribbeanhotels.org
www.caribbeanhotels.org
Caribbean Tourist Organization:
get2cto@dorsai.org: www.caribtourism.com
Consultoría Jurídica Internacional:
cji@imagenes.get.cma.net
www.cji.cubaweb.cu
Cuba AIDS Project: cubaaidspr@aol.com
www.cubaonline.org
Cubacel: www.cubacel.com
Cuba Medical Project: disarm@igc.apc.org
Cuban Solidarity Campaign:
cubasc@gn.apc.org
www.poptel.org.uk/cuba-solidarity
Eleggua Project: cancuba@pathcom.com
www.pathcom.com/~cancuba
El Floridita: reserva@flori.gca.cma.net
E-scriba: info@e-scriba.com:
www.e-scriba.com
International SOS Assistance:
individual@intsos.com: www.intsos.com
Holguín Province: www.holguintravel.cu
Madre: madre.org
Marina Hemingway:
comercial@comermh.cha.cyt.cu
Marinas Puertosol: comerc@psol.mit.cma.net
www.puertosol.cubaweb.cu
National Oceanic & Atmospheric Administration:
distribution@noaa.gov
www.chartmaker.ncd.noaa.gov
Palacio de los Convenciones:
info@hpalco.gov.cu
www.cubaweb.cu/palco
Stardust Sun Yacht Charters:
star@c@ip.etecsa.cu
Tropicana: reserva@tropicana.gca.cma.net
U.S.+Cuba Medical Project:
uscubamed@igc.apc.org
www.igc.org/cubasoli/infomed.html
U.S.-Latin American Medical Aid Foundation:
hornung@medaid.org
www.medaid.org
Varadero Golf Club: golf@atenas.inf.cu
www.golfvaradero.cu
Western Union: www.westernunion.com

INDEX

CONSERVATION/PRESERVATION

Cruz de la Parra: 766-767
Cuatro Caminos: 314
Cuba Exchange Program: 174
Cubana Airlines: 160-161, 181;
  see also specific place
Cubanacán: 332-334
Cuban American Alliance
  Education Fund: 214
Cuban American National
  Foundation: 214
Cuban-Americans: general
  discussion 102-103; Asociación
  del Patrimonio Nacional
  Cubano 282; travel permit
  regulations 164-165, 206, 208,
  233-234
Cuban Art Space: 129-130
Cuban Commission of Human
  Rights and National
  Reconciliation: 62
Cuban cuisine: 154-156
Cuban Institute of Friendship with
  the Peoples: 180
Cuban-Jewish Aid Society: 113,
  177
Cuban Liberty and Democratic
  Solidarity Act: 56-57
Cuban Missile Crisis: 46-48, 467
Cubans in the Struggle Against
  AIDS: 250
Cuban Solidarity Campaign: 180,
  214
Cuban Studies Institute: 174
Cuban Sugar Kings: 58-59
Cubartesanía: 565, 733
Cuchillas del Toa Biosphere
  Reserve: 21, 773-774
Cueva Ambrosia: 521
Cueva Ciboney: 676
Cueva del Hondón: 491
Cueva de los Peces: 548
Cueva de Saturno: 516
Cueva el Agua: 491
Cueva Martin Infierno: 571
Cueva Punta del Este: 500
Cuevas Bellamar: 516-517
Cuevas de las Portales: 467
Cuevas del Indio: 480-481
Cuevas del Viñales: 480
culture: see people/culture
Cupeyal del Norte: 21
currency/currency exchange:
  general discussion 61, 234-

235; Banco Nacional de Cuba
  290; Museo Numismático 265,
  291; street changers 235; see
  also banking/money matters;
  specific place
Currican Tournament, The: 140
customs: see conduct/customs;
  immigration/customs
CVD José Martí: 319

D

daiquiris: 280-281
dance: general discussion 124-
  129; aquatic dance 406;
  Camagüey 633; Festival
  Internacional de Ballet 670;
  Guantánamo 758-759; Havana
  and vicinity 310, 322, 332-333,
  346, 392, 404; Holguín 670;
  Isla de la Juventud 494; Museo
  de la Danza 265, 322; Santiago
  de Cuba 730-732; study
  programs 174-175, 177, 390;
  Trinidad 607-608; Varadero
  530; see also ballet; bars/
  discos/cabarets/nightclub;
  specific place
Danza Contemporánea de Cuba:
  404
Day of Children: 392
decompression chambers: 142,
  534
DEET: 224
deforestation: 20-21; see also
  conservation/preservation;
  specific place
dehydration: 223
Delfinarium: 531
Delgado, Alberto: 612
demographics: 91-92; see also
  specific place
dengue fever: 58, 224
departure tax: 210
Desamparados: 298-299
Desembarco del Granma National
  Park: 704-706
desserts: 156; see also specific
  place
diarrhea: 223
Diaz-Balart, Mirta: 58, 70
Diego, Eliseo: 134
Dimas: 460
dinosaurs: 746-747

Dirección Provincial de Cultura
  Guantánamo: 758
disabled persons: see
  handicapped/disabled
discos: see bars/discos/cabarets/
  nightclubs
discounts: 238
discrimination/social divisions: 92-
  96
dissidents: see Castro, Fidel;
  jails/prisons/labor camps
distances from Havana: 198
dive centers: see scuba
  diving/snorkeling
doll museums: 340, 717
dolphins: 18; see also
  aquariums/dolphin shows
Dominican Republic: Cubana
  Airlines office 161; travel from
  168
Dos Hermanos: 299
Dos Ríos: 693-694
Drake, Sir Francis: 26
drinking water: 154, 156-157,
  222-223, 289; see also specific
  place
driving/car rentals: general
  discussion 192-201, 443;
  accidents 197-198; Bayamo
  693; campervans 201;
  Cienfuegos 566; distances from
  Havana 198; drivers' licenses
  194-195; four-wheel drive
  vehicles 201; gasoline 198;
  Havanna 427-428, 436-437,
  443; Holguín 671; insurance
  198; Isla de la Juventud 495-
  496, 506; laws of the road 194-
  198; Pinar del Río 458; safety
  195-196, 426, 437; Sancti
  Spíritus 595; Santa Clara 579;
  Santa Lucía 652; Santiago de
  Cuba 735-736; scenic drives
  195; suggested itineraries 196;
  traffic police 197-199; Trinidad
  609-610; Varadero 536; vintage
  American cars 193; see also
  specific place
drugs/drug cartel: cocaine
  sale/use 57; execution of drug
  traffickers 58; laws regarding
  possession, sale, use 58, 209;
  Ochoa, Gen. Arnaldo Sánchez

ERNEST HEMINGWAY

MUSIC

Music Events/Museums

SCIENCE/NATURAL SCIENCE/TECHNOLOGY

ABOUT THE AUTHOR

Christopher P. Baker was born and raised in Yorkshire, England. After graduating with honors from University College, London, with a B.A. in Geography (including two Sahara research expeditions and an exchange program at Krakow University, Poland), he earned a Master's degree in both Latin American Studies from Liverpool University and in Education from the Institute of Education, London University. He began his writing career in 1978 as Contributing Editor on Latin America for *Land & Liberty*, a London-based political journal. In 1980 he received a Scripps-Howard Foundation Scholarship in Journalism to attend the University of California, Berkeley. Since 1983 he has made his living as a professional travel and natural science writer. His works have appeared in more than 150 publications worldwide, including *Newsweek*, BBC's *World Magazine*, *National Wildlife*, *Islands*, *Elle*, and the *The Los Angeles Times*. For seven years, Baker was president of British Pride Tours, which he founded. He has escorted group tours to New Zealand, Hong Kong, Korea, England, and Cuba. He appears frequently on radio and television talk shows, and as a guest-lecturer aboard cruise ships throughout the Caribbean and farther afield. His other books include Moon Travel Handbooks' *Havana Handbook* and *Costa Rica Handbook*, National Geographic Traveler's *Costa Rica*, Lonely Planet's *Jamaica* and *Bahamas and Turks & Caicos*, the *Passport Illustrated Guide to Jamaica*, plus *Mi Moto Fidel: Motorcycling through Castro's Cuba*, a literary travelogue published by National Geographic's Adventure Press. He also wrote the text for *Cuba: Within Sight, Beyond Reach*, a coffee-table book about Cuba by photographer Jim Krantz, and has contributed chapters to Tehabi Books' *Voyages:*

The Romance of Cruising, the Discovery Channel's *Rainforests*, Frommer's *America on Wheels: California & Nevada*, *Travelers' Tales: Food*, Nature Company's *World Travel: A Guide to International Ecoourneys*, *Writer's Digest Beginner's Guide to Getting Published*, and *I Should Have Stayed Home*. Baker is a member of the Society of American Travel Writers and National Writers Union and has been honored with several awards for outstanding writing, among them the prestigious Lowell Thomas Travel Journalism Award (four times, including "Best Travel News Investigative Reporter") and the 1995 Benjamin Franklin "Best Travel Guide" award for *Costa Rica Handbook*. In 1998 the Caribbean Tourism Organization named him "Travel Journalist of the Year." He lives in California. For a complete synopsis, visit the author's website: www.travelguidebooks.com.

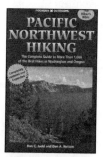

FOR TRAVELERS WITH
SPECIAL INTERESTS

GUIDES

The 100 Best Small Art Towns in America • Asia in New York City
The Big Book of Adventure Travel • Cities to Go
Cross-Country Ski Vacations • Gene Kilgore's Ranch Vacations
Great American Motorcycle Tours • Healing Centers and Retreats
Indian America • Into the Heart of Jerusalem
The People's Guide to Mexico • The Practical Nomad
Saddle Up! • Staying Healthy in Asia, Africa, and Latin America
Steppin' Out • Travel Unlimited • Understanding Europeans
Watch It Made in the U.S.A. • The Way of the Traveler
Work Worldwide • The World Awaits
The Top Retirement Havens • Yoga Vacations

SERIES

Adventures in Nature
The Dog Lover's Companion
Kidding Around
Live Well

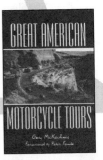

MOON HANDBOOKS

provide comprehensive coverage of a region's arts, history, land, people, and social issues in addition to detailed practical listings for accommodations, food, outdoor recreation, and entertainment. Moon Handbooks allow complete immersion in a region's culture—ideal for travelers who want to combine sightseeing with insight for an extraordinary travel experience.

USA

Alaska-Yukon • Arizona • Big Island of Hawaii • Boston
Coastal California • Colorado • Connecticut • Georgia
Grand Canyon • Hawaii • Honolulu-Waikiki • Idaho • Kauai
Los Angeles • Maine • Massachusetts • Maui • Michigan
Montana • Nevada • New Hampshire • New Mexico
New York City • New York State • North Carolina
Northern California • Ohio • Oregon • Pennsylvania
San Francisco • Santa Fe-Taos • Silicon Valley
South Carolina • Southern California • Tahoe • Tennessee
Texas • Utah • Virginia • Washington • Wisconsin
Wyoming • Yellowstone-Grand Teton

INTERNATIONAL

Alberta and the Northwest Territories • Archaeological Mexico
Atlantic Canada • Australia • Baja • Bangkok • Bali • Belize
British Columbia • Cabo • Canadian Rockies • Cancún
Caribbean Vacations • Colonial Mexico • Costa Rica • Cuba
Dominican Republic • Ecuador • Fiji • Havana • Honduras
Hong Kong • Indonesia • Jamaica • Mexico City • Mexico
Micronesia • The Moon • Nepal • New Zealand • Northern Mexico
Oaxaca • Pacific Mexico • Pakistan • Philippines • Puerto Vallarta
Singapore • South Korea • South Pacific • Southeast Asia • Tahiti
Thailand • Tonga-Samoa • Vancouver • Vietnam, Cambodia and Laos
Virgin Islands • Yucatán Peninsula

www.moon.com

Rick Steves

shows you where to travel and how to travel—all while getting the most value for your dollar. His Back Door travel philosophy is about making friends, having fun, and avoiding tourist rip-offs.

Rick's been traveling to Europe for more than 25 years and is the author of 22 guidebooks, which have sold more than a million copies. He also hosts the award-winning public television series Travels in Europe with Rick Steves.

RICK STEVES' COUNTRY & CITY GUIDES

Best of Europe
France, Belgium & the Netherlands
Germany, Austria & Switzerland
Great Britain & Ireland
Italy • London • Paris • Rome • Scandinavia • Spain & Portugal

RICK STEVES' PHRASE BOOKS

French • German • Italian • French, Italian & German
Spanish & Portuguese

MORE EUROPE FROM RICK STEVES

Europe 101
Europe Through the Back Door
Mona Winks
Postcards from Europe

WWW.RICKSTEVES.COM

ROAD TRIP USA

Getting there is half the fun, and Road Trip USA guides are your ticket to driving adventure. Taking you off the interstates and onto less-traveled, two-lane highways, each guide is filled with fascinating trivia, historical information, photographs, facts about regional writers, and details on where to sleep and eat—all contributing to your exploration of the American road.

*"Books so full of the pleasures of the American road,
you can smell the upholstery."*
~ BBC radio

THE ORIGINAL CLASSIC GUIDE
Road Trip USA

ROAD TRIP USA REGIONAL GUIDE
Road Trip USA: California and the Southwest

ROAD TRIP USA GETAWAYS
Road Trip USA Getaways: Chicago
Road Trip USA Getaways: New Orleans
Road Trip USA Getaways: San Francisco
Road Trip USA Getaways: Seattle

www.roadtripusa.com

TRAVEL ✦ SMART ®

guidebooks are accessible, route-based driving guides. Special interest tours provide the most practical routes for family fun, outdoor activities, or regional history for a trip of anywhere from two to 22 days. Travel Smarts take the guesswork out of planning a trip by recommending only the most interesting places to eat, stay, and visit.

"One of the few travel series that rates sightseeing attractions. That's a handy feature. It helps to have some guidance so that every minute counts."
~ San Diego Union-Tribune

TRAVEL SMART REGIONS

Alaska
American Southwest
Arizona
Carolinas
Colorado
Deep South
Eastern Canada
Florida Gulf Coast
Florida
Georgia
Hawaii
Illinois/Indiana
Iowa/Nebraska
Kentucky/Tennessee
Maryland/Delaware
Michigan
Minnesota/Wisconsin
Montana/Wyoming/Idaho
Nevada
New England
New Mexico
New York State

Northern California
Ohio
Oregon
Pacific Northwest
Pennsylvania/New Jersey
South Florida and the Keys
Southern California
Texas
Utah
Virginias
Western Canada

Foghorn Outdoors

guides are for campers, hikers, boaters, anglers, bikers, and golfers of all levels of daring and skill. Each guide contains site descriptions and ratings, driving directions, facilities and fees information, and easy-to-read maps that leave only the task of deciding where to go.

"Foghorn Outdoors has established an ecological conservation standard unmatched by any other publisher."
~ Sierra Club

CAMPING Arizona and New Mexico Camping
Baja Camping • California Camping
Camper's Companion • Colorado Camping
Easy Camping in Northern California
Easy Camping in Southern California
Florida Camping • New England Camping
Pacific Northwest Camping
Utah and Nevada Camping

HIKING 101 Great Hikes of the San Francisco Bay Area
California Hiking • Day-Hiking California's National Parks
Easy Hiking in Northern California
Easy Hiking in Southern California
New England Hiking
Pacific Northwest Hiking • Utah Hiking

FISHING Alaska Fishing • California Fishing
Washington Fishing

BOATING California Recreational Lakes and Rivers
Washington Boating and Water Sports

OTHER OUTDOOR RECREATION California Beaches
California Golf • California Waterfalls • California Wildlife
Easy Biking in Northern California • Florida Beaches
The Outdoor Getaway Guide For Southern California
Tom Stienstra's Outdoor Getaway Guide: Northern California

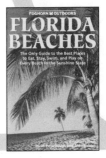

WWW.FOGHORN.COM

CiTY·SMaRT™

The best way to enjoy a city is to get advice from someone who lives there—and that's exactly what City Smart guidebooks offer. City Smarts are written by local authors with hometown perspectives who have personally selected the best places to eat, shop, sightsee, and simply hang out. The honest, lively, and opinionated advice is perfect for business travelers looking to relax with the locals or for longtime residents looking for something new to do Saturday night.

*A portion of sales from each title
benefits a non-profit literacy organization in that city.*

CITY SMART CITIES

Albuquerque	Anchorage
Austin	Baltimore
Berkeley/Oakland	Boston
Calgary	Charlotte
Chicago	Cincinnati
Cleveland	Dallas/Ft. Worth
Denver	Indianapolis
Kansas City	Memphis
Milwaukee	Minneapolis/St. Paul
Nashville	Pittsburgh
Portland	Richmond
San Francisco	Sacramento
St. Louis	Salt Lake City
San Antonio	San Diego
Tampa/St. Petersburg	Toronto
Tucson	Vancouver

www.travelmatters.com

User-friendly, informative, and fun:
Because travel *matters*.

Visit our newly launched web site and explore the variety of titles and travel information available online, featuring an interactive *Road Trip USA* exhibit.

www.ricksteves.com

The Rick Steves web site is bursting with information to boost your travel I.Q. and liven up your European adventure. Including:

- The latest from Rick on what's hot in Europe
- Excerpts from Rick's books
- Rick's comprehensive Guide to European Railpasses

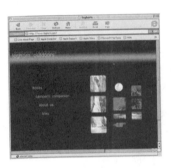

www.foghorn.com

Foghorn Outdoors guides are the premier source for United States outdoor recreation information. Visit the Foghorn Outdoors web site for more information on these activity-based travel guides, including the complete text of the handy *Foghorn Outdoors: Camper's Companion*.

www.moon.com

Moon Handbooks' goal is to give travelers all the background and practical information they'll need for an extraordinary travel experience. Visit the Moon Handbooks web site for interesting information and practical advice, including Q&A with the author of *The Practical Nomad*, Edward Hasbrouck.

U.S.~METRIC CONVERSION

1 inch = 2.54 centimeters (cm)
1 foot = .3048 meters (m)
1 yard = 0.914 meters
1 mile = 1.6093 kilometers (km)
1 km = .6214 miles
1 fathom = 1.8288 m
1 chain = 20.1168 m
1 furlong = 201.168 m
1 acre = .4047 hectares
1 sq km = 100 hectares
1 sq mile = 2.59 square km
1 ounce = 28.35 grams
1 pound = .4536 kilograms
1 short ton = .90718 metric ton
1 short ton = 2000 pounds
1 long ton = 1.016 metric tons
1 long ton = 2240 pounds
1 metric ton = 1000 kilograms
1 quart = .94635 liters
1 US gallon = 3.7854 liters
1 Imperial gallon = 4.5459 liters
1 nautical mile = 1.852 km

To compute celsius temperatures, subtract 32 from Fahrenheit and divide by 1.8. To go the other way, multiply celsius by 1.8 and add 32.

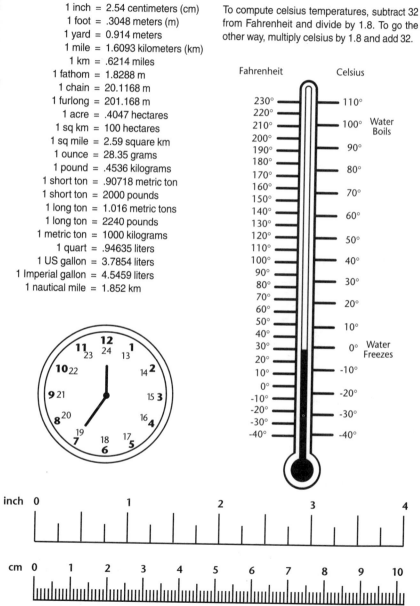

Next time, make your *own* hotel arrangements.

Yahoo! Travel

Do You
YAHOO!
?